BAROLO TERROIR

GRAPES
CRUS
PEOPLE
PLACES

ABOUT THE AUTHORS

IAN D'AGATA

Chief Scientific Officer, TasteSpirit

Editor-in-Chief, TS Wine Review

Co-editor of Hugh Johnson's Pocket Wine Book, Italy Section

Ian D'Agata is a multi-award-winning author who has been speaking and writing about wine for thirty years. His *Native Wine Grapes of Italy* and *Italy's Native Wine Grape Terroirs* (both published by the University of California Press in 2014 and 2019) are considered the bibles of Italian wine. The former was the Louis Roederer International Wine Awards Book of the Year in 2015 and one of the top wine books of the year for the LA Times, the Financial Times and the New York Times, while the latter was named one of the top wine books of the year by the NY Times and by Food&Wine magazine. His most recent book, *The Grapes and Wines of Italy: The definitive compendium region by region*, co-authored with Michele Longo, was the 2022 winner of the Gourmand Book awards, Wine Professionals category. Ian is also co-author of the Italy section and author of the Alsace section of Hugh Johnson's Pocket Book of Wine.
A trained medical doctor, Ian is a former staff writer at Stephen Tanzer's International Wine Cellar, Contributing Editor of Decanter, and Senior Editor of Vinous web wine magazine, and he is now the Chief Scientific Officer and president of the TerroirSense Wine Academy, and the Editor-in-Chief of the TerroirSense Wine Review.

www.iandagata.com
Instagram: @iandagata_vino
Bus. Emails: iandomenicodagata@outlook.it

MICHELE LONGO

Co-editor of Hugh Johnson's Pocket Wine Book, Italy Section

Contributor "Barolo&Co"

Contributor "Vinosity" of Academie du Vin Library

Associate Director "iandagata.com"

A graduate in Information Systems with a Master Degree in Engineering and Management, Michele is a certified Italian sommelier (AIS) who writes for "Barolo&Co" (curating the "Territori del Mito" column) and for "Vinosity" of Academie du Vin Library. He is currently the Associate-Director of iandagata.com and is co-curator, with Ian D'Agata, of the Italy section in Hugh Johnson's "Wine Pocket Book". His most recent book prior to Barolo Terroir was the award-winning "The Grapes and Wines of Italy: The definitive compendium region by region", co-written with Ian D'Agata.

Michele is also a former judge at the Decanter World Wine Awards, and is one of the past curators of the Wine Educational Board (W.E.B.), co-curator of the "W.E.B. Tasting Notes" section, and the co-curator, together with Massimo Comparini, of the "Best Italian Wines Guide" up to the 2017 edition.

Instagram: @michele_nebbiolo
Bus. Email: michelelongo@iandagata.com

BAROLO TERROIR

GRAPES
CRUS
PEOPLE
PLACES

Ian D'Agata

Michele Longo

Cover design by Ryta Barbero – www.purpleryta.it

Title of the artwork: "The Goddess of Barolo".

Technique: wine on paper

The artist: Ryta Barbero or Purpleryta is based in Barolo and she paints with wine. Painting has always been an important part of her life. Her last name, Barbero, reminds many of the most widely planted grape variety in the Langhe. She always worked in wine communication, was raised in the Roero wine region and now she lives in the Langhe. As you can see, her life is surrounded by wine. It was only natural that eventually these two aspects of her life collided and her technique was born! Her artistic identity coincides with her way of painting: She pours wine on paper. From a spot on the paper begins the creative process that produces the final work of art.

PREFACE

A word from Ian

I love Barolo, and it could not be otherwise. For if it were not for Barolo, it is highly unlikely I would have become a professional wine writer and educator. This is because while growing up, my father, a psychiatrist who liked wine but didn't think about it, preferred for us not to drink wine with meals at home. In his line of duty, he had seen too many families ruined by alcoholism and wanted us to grow up with a healthy respect for the beverage. Not that we were forced to live in the second coming of Prohibition: actually, both my parents liked wine, and we had a wine cellar replete with some truly great wines (I remember Pieropan Soave Calvarino, high-end Bordeaux, and more than a few top flight Barolos and Barbarescos, among others). Occasionally, during the festivities or parties at our house, I would taste wine: but at those large gatherings I never really drank anything that was either interesting or memorable (clearly, nobody's opening cases of Petrus, Bruno Giacosa red labels and Egon Muller TBAs at events packing fifty or sixty people). Then one day, everything changed.

On not just any given Sunday back during my high school days in Canada, but rather one that was to indelibly mark the rest of my life, a bunch of friends, who knew quite a bit about French wine already at that tender age (thanks to their parents working in or just liking wine), came over to swim at the family pool and asked to drink some "good Italian red wine". In retrospect, I now understand my future had already been written in the pages of the book of destiny: after all, how normal is it to have friends who at age eighteen want to drink wine not to get drunk but because they actually enjoy the stuff in a healthy manner? So off I went to the wine cellar to grab a bottle for them (note the "for them"). I admit I did not really know what I was doing; but as my father had always praised Barolo and Gattinara (the latter was his favorite wine), that's what I went searching for. As destiny would have it (there it is again: I am a huge believer in destiny) my hand fell on a 1971 Cantina Mascarello Barolo (what would later become Bartolo Mascarello). Fate must have been really smiling on me that day: the vintage was a stellar one, in fact one of the best Barolo vintages of all time (with a little homework and plenty of hard work, you and I could probably have made a good Barolo that year). But the producer was stellar too (still is, in fact), easily one of the five or so best Barolo minds of all. After just one sip, I understood immediately what being in the presence of greatness really means. More importantly, that wine opened up my eyes to the magic that great wine can deliver. I also realized that I had been missing out on something that was really pretty good; and given that my schoolfriends had families who loved wine and drank well, I decided to take them up on their offer to taste wines at their homes when I'd be next going over to their places. Now, my mother didn't raise any fools; and so, the very next day I went over to one friend's house where dinner featured a 1961 Chateau Latour (another memorable vintage) and the day after that, courtesy of another friend's family, I tasted a 1976 Mulheimer Helenkloster Riesling Eiswein (another spectacular vintage). With a similar trifecta, nobody can really be surprised if I started taking wine very seriously. Very.

Next up for me: the need to learn, to know, to understand. I bought a truly seminal wine book, André Simon's *Wines of the World* (the second edition, revised by Serena Sutcliffe) and found it beautifully written and beyond interesting. Still today I consider it the best wine book ever written, and not even by a small margin. After that, my fate was sealed: I have never stopped buying wine books and guides written in different ages and in different languages. I started attending wine courses; going to tastings and wine conferences; saving all my money to buy wines (how serious was I? Suffice it to say that though I love music and sports, for something like twelve or thirteen years I never bought a single ticket to any sporting event and only went to a concert once (Supertramp) in those years. About the only thing I spent money on was trout fishing and girlfriends, but otherwise everything I earned I basically sunk into wines and in so doing already had a noteworthy cellar by age twenty-six. And as I always enjoyed writing and drawing, the next logical step was to start writing about wine too. Once I arrived in good old Enotria to attend university, I began "moonlighting" on weekends and Monday nights at a wine magazine and in a wine shop. The rest, as they say, is history: but the point is that none of this would have happened had it not been for that one initial bottle of Barolo that kick started the whole process.

My lifelong journey in wine began with Barolo. It will not end with Barolo, because I now write about wines from all over the world, and especially about those made with Italy's many other native wine grapes, not just Nebbiolo. But Barolo provided the initial spark, and in some ways, this book wants to acknowledge that. Also important for me is that writing this book has also allowed me to work with Michele Longo, whom I first met roughly twenty years ago through my wine tastings. This text on Barolo follows closely on the heels of our first major written collaboration, *The Grapes and Wines of Italy: A Definitive Compendium Region by Region*, the award winner of the 2022 Gourmand World Book Awards (Wine Professionals category), and like this book, also published by Amazon Press. And it precedes the next book, entirely devoted to Barbaresco.) Michele is my best wine student ever: but since those Roman days now long gone, he has carved a very prominent career of his own in wine writing and wine education, such that he is really my student no longer. He's not just driven, passionate, extremely competent and gifted with impeccable ethics and honesty: he's just a good person too. And speaking of books, those who know me also know that that goes a long way in mine. I am happy to have met Michele, and hope this book will lead him to accomplishing even bigger and better things. Besides, without his help in writing a number of the book's chapters, it is unlikely I would have managed to complete this text anytime soon, such are my time constraints nowadays. But thanks to not having to worry about chapters he was brilliantly taking care of, I was able to sit down and re-read through, to decipher really, a Leaning Tower of Pisa-like stack of old notebooks accumulated over the years replete with anecdotes, interviews, facts, figures and the memories of those who have made Barolo over the last forty years and counting (yes, "to decipher": given the sorry state of my hand writing after a day's worth of non-stop tastings and winery visits, some parts of those notebooks remain unfortunately non-legible). Without the time to peruse over those books, I would have never accepted his offer to write a book on Barolo, for it is the stuff that is in those notebooks, those memories, those souvenirs, that lifetime really, that sets this book apart and makes it like nothing else on the subject.

A narration of Barolo as it was *yesterday*, much of which would have been conveniently forgotten without it being spelled out for posterity's sake.

But this book is also very much about what Barolo is *today*.

Yes, the book details a personal journey through a lifetime of Barolo beginning with my first wine tastings back in Toronto in the late 1970s and in Rome in the early 1980s. But *Barolo Terroir: Crus People Places* details not just all my meetings with the parents of many who are making Barolo today, it also commits to permanent memory my frequenting successive Barolo winemaking generations by living in Italy for twenty years straight (plus others off and on) such that I was able to visit Barolo and the Langhe every month or so for days and often weeks at a time. It is through all those visits over the years, something that would never have been possible (not with the same regularity and intensity, at least) had I spent my life living instead in Toronto, NYC, Boston, LA, Rio, London, Melbourne or Tokyo.

A few last words of thanks are in order. As usual, a BIG thank-you goes to all the Barolo producers who patiently put up with me over the years (no rest for the wicked: as if it wasn't bad enough, they had to see me, now they have the double whammy of having to put up with Michele as well). Those producers know who they are (more importantly, they know who they are not). Clearly, without their time, patience, generosity and passion, I would not have learned as much over the years as I have. But I also thank my mother, as always, without whose love, support and guidance I would have not been able to achieve much of anything in life, never mind writing this book. Simply put, without her and without them, this book would not have been possible: its content would never have seen the bright light of day, but have remained forever enshrouded in Nyx's dark embrace.

A word from Michele

I cannot even hazard a guess as to how many times I have told Ian over the years of our long friendship that he should write a book dedicated wholly to Nebbiolo – in all its expressions and denominations – and in the process, offering him my help in the research of eventual data and archival information. Over the years, I have seen and been allowed to leaf through the totem pole-like piles of fat notebooks crammed with handwritten information on Italy's many grapes and wines. Especially numerous were those partly or wholly devoted to Barbaresco and Barolo (containing never before published information on specific vineyards, crus, wines and producers, but also the likes of Nebbiolo Michet, Nebbiolo Rosé and Nebbiolo Bolla dating way back to the 1980s when basically everyone, and I mean everyone, talking and writing about Nebbiolo and its wines today save for a handful of Americans, British and Italians weren't even bothering with Italian wine.

I had always thought it an absolute shame Ian hadn't yet written a book on one of his absolutely favorite Italian wines. Then again, you understand just how hard it is to pin a guy down who gets up and is off at the drop of any hat just to go chase the latest wine grape unicorn. You think I'm exaggerating? Hardly. I remember when back in 2001 or 2002 he drove a little less than nine hours non-stop one day from Rome to the Valle d'Aosta just to taste the first wine ever made with the Broblanc, a rarer than rare biotype of the Cornalin variety nobody had ever made wine from before. At the time, I was involved in more than one tasting group, and a sommelier course too; and yet nobody I knew had ever heard of the Cornalin variety, never mind Broblanc. In essence, it is that outlook, drive, and passion that has made Ian not just the well-known and credible wine writer he is today, but also the rather unique figure he is in the field of wine writing. Nothing he does or writes is quite like anything else out there, but then again, how many wine writers do you know of who bother to, or even have the time or the interest, to sit down with old farmers, town priests, postmen and cops? And therein lies, I think, this book's truly immense value. For the stuff Ian uniquely knows about wine people and places (as in for example its grapes, vineyards, its people and wines) does not only come out of the mouths of those who make the wines. That's right: grapes, crus, people, places, not by chance the subtitle of our book.

But for every positive, there is a negative: like Two Face's famous coin, the flip side of this particular spinning disc is that getting Ian to find time to write a book on something as mundane as Barolo was quite the task. Given there was always some new producer of Arvesiniadu, Centesimino, Forgiarin, Greco Bianco (not the same thing as Greco), Mayolet, Pampanuto, Prëmetta, Semidano, Ucelut, Vuillermin, or the umpteenth Malvasia variety that seemingly always *just so needed* to be interviewed, you realize why this book has been an almost unbelievable eight (8!) years in the making. And that's just what it took to write; it does not take into account the twenty plus years of research data and interviews Ian compiled over that time period. At long last, one day Ian sat down to ask me just what it is I had in mind, and gave me the green light to start the process. For his part, he would finally set time aside to put some semblance of order in his many notebooks while continuing to compile new information on Barolo. Now I won't be ungenerous and point out that it took him four years longer than he said it would to do so (what are friends for, right Ian?), but I'm immensely grateful he finally put pen to paper, or rather finger to keyboard, and accepted my being a part of this wonderful project. I am extremely proud of this book and all the very long hours and very hard work that went into it: in fact, I consider this book my wine career's crowning achievement to date, because there is nothing else out there like it, on any Italian wine.

It really could hardly have been any different. During my lifetime, I have developed a dependence of sorts on Nebbiolo. This great wine grape's wines are my favorite of all, and I easily go into a sort of "Nebbiolo-abstinence syndrome" when not imbibing liquids made with it at a regular rate. Do not get me wrong: I love the world's many great wines, but it is the wines of Barbaresco and Barolo as well as other Nebbiolo wines that truly always make my heart sing. It is my belief that Nebbiolo is not just a grape but a state of mind nourished by the soul. Nebbiolo's wines should be drunk with mind, not just with heart. Why, you ask? Roses, violets, sour red cherries, spices…one descriptor on its own is not enough to really describe Nebbiolo's wines, rather it's their complex combination that brings about Nebbiolo's wines unique magic. There truly is an "ethereal" quality to Nebbiolo's best wines (a descriptive term often associated by many wine writers to Nebbiolo wines but not related to the perception of alcohol), though it remains a sensation difficult to define. I find it has more to do with the "spiritual realm" into which all great wines transport you into. Nebbiolo speaks directly to the person drinking it, to his/her soul and mind. I am aware that perhaps not everyone succeeds in understanding the language of Nebbiolo and its great wines, from Boca to Barolo to Lessona. Clearly, those individuals never grow fond of Nebbiolo's wines like they might of those made with Pinot Noir or Riesling. But those who do see the light, are then usually hooked for good.

In conclusion, allow me to thank those who have helped reach this stage of my life, all of whom have supported me in this enological "odyssey". In addition to my parents and my significant other, Rosanna, and of course Ian, I would like to thank (in order of appearance on my path in the world of wine, all who contributed to my becoming a wine writer): Saro, Daniele, Maria Rosa, Nicola I, Bruno, Sandro, Sergio, Ruggero, Mauro, Massimo, Giovanni R, Giovanni G, Gualtiero, Patrizia, Nicola II, Giancarlo, Terry, Guido, Andrea, and all those producers who, over the years, have welcomed me into their homes and wineries and patiently answered my questions. Without their important contribution, I wouldn't be passionate about wine in general (not just Barolo!) the way I am today.

A number of this books' chapters we always intended to write as such. Others were born from years of observation and all our time spent with the world's sommeliers, importers, educators and wine professionals in general, as well as the wine loving and buying public. Therefore, you might say that the way some chapters have been formulated and written was out of necessity. Not too long ago one evening, a wine educator had nothing better to say in public that Nebbiolo Michet and Nebbiolo Lampia don't matter as such, and that Barolos are more or less all the same, and that nobody should care much about them anyways, because differences in Barolo wines are related mostly to structure and different oaking regimens. An interesting viewpoint, given that over the last decade, Aubert de Villaine and his Burgundy associates have been busy spending time, money and energy in identifying over 500 different Burgundian biotypes of Pinot Noir and 300 of Chardonnay. Clearly, de Villaine and his colleagues seem to think that this might be a worthwhile endeavor and something worth knowing about. But when it comes to poor Italian wine, about which some "educators" seem to know very little, and care about even less, opinions such as the hilarious one mentioned previously are legion. For the good of Italian wine and for the good of all those who love wine in general, this needs to change. For this reason, as well as others we shall broach later on, you will find we have purposely written separate chapters on the historic three Nebbiolo biotypes of Barolo and Barbaresco: Lampia, Michet and Rosé. Furthermore, by listening to others in the wine business and by fielding their questions, it became apparent to us that outside of the four or five most famous Barolo vineyard districts, such as for example Bussia and Brunate, comfort levels with some of Barolo's even best vineyard sites is thin and does not go that far back. While most professional sommeliers are comfortable with Vosne-Romanée Les Suchots and Les Bruleées, and with Chablis Les Clos and Valmur, awareness about Fiasco, Lazzarito, and Sarmassa and other Barolo vineyard districts is not quite at the same level. This led us to write a very long and in-depth Section II of this book, entirely devoted to Barolo's official vineyard districts. It is our hope that through the memories, anecdotes, data and opinions we share that we will help our readers and all Barolo lovers gain a better understanding about, and a greater appreciation of, the specific vineyard sites where this wine is born. And why the Barolos from the different sites taste the way they do.

Our initial project was to write a book on Barolo and Barbaresco involving other wine writing friends and some other of Ian's wine class students, but it soon became apparent to us that it would have meant writing a tome of hernia-inducing weight and non-practical length. And so, rather than writing a book so large and so heavy that it would have been good only for those who own coffee tables made of titanium or in providing a means by which to save on gym fees (why go to a weight room when all you need to do for exercise is lift the book we intended to write?), we decided it was best to tackle our project in a different manner. Therefore, two books not one, each devoted to a major wine. We also changed our original writing schedule and plan and the result of our time spent visiting wineries together and in front of our respective computers is the book you hold in your hands. Devoting two separate books to Barolo and Barbaresco was also the best manner by which to include all the information we had compiled over the years. And in so doing, to give both Barolo and Barbaresco, the wines and their respective wine-production areas, not to mention the people who make them, all the attention they deserve.

Last but certainly not least, it bears underlining how this book would not have been possible, at least not in its present full scope, without the help of a few individuals and institutions we would like to thank specifically. To begin with, all or maps have been created by our good friend Raffaele Grillone who is a highly accomplished map/cartographer and designer who also created all the maps for our previous book, *The Grapes and Wines of Italy: The Definitive Compendium Region by Region* (Amazon Press) and winner of the 2022 World Gourmand Book Awards, Wine Professionals category. Maps that others besides us must think are just swell: for example, they have been chosen by New Wave Shanghai, the prestigious upscale bistro of one of the world's most famous restaurants (Italy's three Michelin star Da Vittorio ristorante) and located in the UCCA-Edge Museum in Shanghai to be used in their wonderful wine list.

Second, we would like to acknowledge the contribution of Matteo Calorio, geologist, who helped update and improve what Ian had already written on Barolo's geology, an extremely complex subject on which there is not yet full agreement. Calorio also runs guided tours in the Barolo area that we highly recommend should you be interested in visiting the Barolo production zone and gain a different perspective Barolo and its wines.

Third, we wish to acknowledge the kindness and availability of Dott. Moreno Soster (who sadly passed away last year) and Elena Piva (Agricultural Productions Dept. of the Piedmont Region), for their help with the Land Units and the Denominations Production Data. Also, Emanuele Coraglia of the "Consorzio di tutela Barolo Barbaresco Alba Langhe and Dogliani" who went above and beyond the call of duty in answering our questions and providing data we may have needed at one point or another during the (many) years it took us to write this book. Data that we either did not have or that we needed in order to verify and corroborate what we had found on our own. Clearly, we need to also thank Andrea Ferrero and the whole team at the Consorzio as well as Federico Scarzello, president of the Enoteca Regionale del Barolo, and his director Cristiana Grimaldi for their kindness, patience and insight they have blessed us with over the years. These two, the Consorzio and the Enoteca Regionale di Barolo, are two of the better run such institutions run in Italy.

All that admitted and recognized, what remains for us to state, unequivocally, is that this book is not, and has not been, sponsored or paid for in any part or any way by producers, producer associations, importers, restauranters, the "*Consorzio di tutela Barolo Barbaresco Alba Langhe and Dogliani*" or any government agency or institution. We do not get paid for and do not engage in creating blends for estates, to compile wine lists for restaurants, and for selecting wines for importers. All our travel to the area, accommodations, and meals have been paid for out of pocket by Ian. In ultimate analysis, this book is a true labor of love; a fool's errand perhaps, but a mission that we have tried hard to do our best with, and for.

Ian and Michele.

INTRODUCTION

Ian D'Agata and Michele Longo

For the last century or so, the most famous Nebbiolo wines have been those of Barbaresco and Barolo, but it was not always so. It might surprise the accidental wine tourist to learn that for a long time the wines of Gattinara and Lessona were more famous than those of Barolo. Times change however, and today it is Barolo that represents the pinnacle of Nebbiolo wines; for others, it is Barbaresco. But no matter which one of those two you pine for, the beauty of Nebbiolo is that it is a wine grape that expresses terroir like few others do (Riesling and Pinot Noir are example of other grapes that do terroir really well). It follows that all the many Nebbiolo wines, such as for example Carema, Donnas, Gattinara, Sfursat or Lessona, all have something beautiful, important even, to say. And different.

Barolo production areas and terroirs differ noticeably not just from those of all the other denominations, but within the ranks of the denomination too. Many physical and biochemical parameters set the area of Barolo apart from all the other places where Nebbiolo also grows: these include the unique presence of area-specific biotypes; the exposure and altitude at which vineyards lie; the slope gradient of generally gently rolling hills; the proximity (or not) of the Tanaro river; the temperate climate (and increasingly, climate change); the unique marly-clay, compacted sand and limestone soils; the alkaline soil pH (by contrast, the soil pH of other famous Nebbiolo-growing areas such as Carema, Donnas and Lessona hover in the acid range); and the skill set of the area's producers, arguably the most talented bunch in Italy. The beauty of it all is that thanks to Nebbiolo's penchant for telling it like it is, this multifaceted diversity is easy to recognize in the glass. With a little practice, identifying the communes and vineyard districts from which the Barolo you are drinking comes from is not all that hard (well... most of the time; and admittedly, it used to be a whole lot easier). But even without wanting to get into terroir-specifics, what matters most is that Barolo is one of the world's greatest wines: austere, slow to develop and very age-worthy, redolent of a truly mesmerizing perfume of red roses and sour red cherries, and real depth and complexity.

This book addresses all the relative points of interest that help define Barolo (Barbaresco is the subject of the next book in this series, and is meant to be the ideal accompaniment to this one). The book in your hands is an extremely detailed study and in-depth analysis of Barolo's history and present-day reality, and it helps set the record straight on at least a number of issues that have had at times varying and erroneous interpretations. And while enthusiasm for Barolo and its wines is at an all-time high, general knowledge levels about its terroir and producers are nowhere near those of the great crus of Burgundy, for example. In fact, there is considerable room for improvement in knowledge about Nebbiolo itself, along with Sangiovese Italy's most important and famous wine grape (See Chapter 1, NEBBIOLO LAMPIA; Chapter 2, NEBBIOLO MICHET; and Chapter 3, NEBBIOLO ROSÉ). By contrast, we have known, and know, a great deal more about Cabernet Sauvignon, Chardonnay, Merlot and Pinot Noir and other French grape varieties.

About the book ...

In this book, we discuss Barolo's grapes, history, territory, vineyard districts, and try to shine a spotlight on as many different, deserving, producers as possible. In other words, just as the title of the book reads: grapes, crus, people, places. Simply put, terroir.

Relative to Nebbiolo grapes, this book presents the latest scientific information on Nebbiolo and its many biotypes [Picotener, Chiavennasca and others, but also Nebbiolo Lampia, Nebbiolo Michet, and Nebbiolo Rosé (these last three have separate chapters devoted to each one)]. The latest research study results and how these have advanced our knowledge about the Nebbiolo grape variety and its origin are presented, and an in-depth analysis of Nebbiolo's biotypes and clones is documented. Relative to Nebbiolo Michet and Nebbiolo Rosé, this book presents never before published data on the distribution of each one in Barolo's vineyards. Nebbiolo Michet and especially Nebbiolo Rosé have been described to a degree never seen before anywhere in the literature, something that continues Ian's lifelong devotion to those two Nebbiolo grapes that he began researching back in the 1980s when he lived in Italy full-time, as numerous Barolo producers remember. The slow accumulation and piecing together of the information gathered since the 1980s on both Nebbiolo Michet and Nebbiolo Rosé during producer interviews and talks with researchers, as well as by way of vineyard walks and decades of wine tastings, has allowed us to compile what is the most complete, most in-depth and longest description of the Nebbiolo grape variety and its many biotypes ever written in any book.

Nebbiolo's grape-specific intricacies and complexities aside, it is the amazing ability it has to act as a translator of terroir that is one of its most endearing qualities and a never-ending source of fascination for wine lovers all over the world. Therefore, this book also broaches Barolo's vineyard districts extensively, with considerable amounts of energy spent in characterizing and qualifying them in their entirety. The Barolo denomination now has an official list of vineyard district names, the *Menzioni Geografiche Aggiuntive* (singular: *Menzione Geografica Aggiuntiva*) or MGA (sometimes also abbreviated as MeGA), which helps to identify specific vineyard areas within the Barolo production zone. These are not "crus" in the French sense of that word but rather large vineyard districts (see Chapter 8, BAROLO CLASSICO AND BAROLO SINGLE-DISTRICT WINES: THE IMPORTANCE OF SITE).

A "cru" identifies a viticultural site characterized by the production of quality wines over time, wines that express the same specific characteristics year after year in a recognizable manner linked to site and independently of vintage, to a degree at least. At the very least, Barolo's new official vineyard district names visible on the bottle labels manage to document the origin of the grapes (but only to a degree) that are used to make the Barolo you drink. Unfortunately, only these vineyard district names are found on the label: the communes to which the specific vineyard districts/MGAs belong are not. Clearly, this greatly limits their usefulness. It's a silly situation that would be analogous to Burgundy bottles being labeled with "Les Charmes" or "Les Amoureuses" only, while omitting the all-important Chambolle-Musigny.

In this book, we analyze and describe the MGA-named Barolo vineyard districts, whenever possible, not just in their present but also into their historic component parts. Even better, we shall try to determine and illustrate if Barolos made from each commune have commune-specific defining characteristics, much like the wines of, for example, Chambolle-Musigny do relative to Gevrey-Chambertin's. Even more specifically, if it is possible to distinguish between the Barolos produced with grapes sourced in different vineyard districts much like we can recognize between, for example, Gevrey-Chambertin Grand Cru wines of Griottes-, Mazis-, and Chapelle-Chambertin. We will provide, whenever possible, information regarding: soil, subsoil, and geology; climate; exposure; slope gradient; biotypes, rootstocks, vine age; producer anecdotes and opinions; history of the site and more. In other words, as detailed an analysis of the single Barolo vineyard districts as possible, based also on over thirty years of tasting the wines of Barolo, including those that are no longer being made.

Clearly, the people and places of Barolo are all-important in fashioning the wines of the area. Indeed, many of the anecdotes and recollections you will read in this book have been uttered not just by today's winery owners, but by their parents and grandparents as well, who were there to greet Ian in the wineries when he first began visiting the area back in the early 1980s. We will try to shine the spotlight on as many different producers and their wines as possible.

... and how to use it

Therefore, the book is divided into two sections.

- Section I is divided into eight chapters devoted to Nebbiolo Lampia; Nebbiolo Michet; Nebbiolo Rosé; the history of Barolo; its timeline; facts and figures; Barolo's terroir (climate, topography, altitude and geology, but also its communes); and the importance of site, in which the difference existing between vineyard district and *cru* is analyzed. We believe that Nebbiolo Michet and Nebbiolo Rosé each deserve to be analyzed at length, because they, like the more common Nebbiolo Lampia, characterize Barolo and its history as much as Barolo's people, soil geology and lay of the land. Perhaps even more so, in fact. Theirs is a story worth telling, and fascinating to listen to, because it is, in many respects, *the* history of Barolo. The most recently available information on Barolo's geology is also included.

- Section II is one big chapter entirely devoted to each of the officially-delimited and named vineyard districts of the Barolo denomination. You will find an entire file for each and every one of Barolo's vineyard districts, arranged in alphabetical order. Should you wish to know about one vineyard district that you may have heard of from friends, or because you drank a Barolo you liked from it, all you need to do is go directly to the file of that site. Given the alphabetical order they are presented in, the vineyard district of interest ought to be easy to find. As for the content of each vineyard district files, it is arranged always in the same manner. First, there is a table with facts and figures about the vineyard district, including the geologic time in which its soil was formed, the extension in hectares, its altitude, the lists of producers who own/farm land there and the names of the wines made from that vineyard district as of 2021. The introductory table is followed by an in-depth analysis of the vineyard district, including a general introduction to the site; whenever possible, or if of interest, why it has the name it does; its history; its present-day reality; producers making wine there; and benchmark/reference point wineries (those wineries that make the historically most relevant and famous (best?) wines from the site.

The book closes with the Appendices, filled with tables and data presented in easy-to-read format. Last but not least, you will find three different indices (devoted to general information, vineyard district names, and producers) at book's end.

CHAPTER OF CONTENTS

Barolo Terroir: Grapes, Crus, People, Places.

SECTION I

Chapter 1

NEBBIOLO LAMPIA

Ian D'Agata

By most expert and non-experts accounts, Nebbiolo is Italy's greatest grape variety, arguably meriting a place in a hypothetical list of the "world's ten best wine grapes". In fact, just like most things in life that are truly worthwhile and interesting (people included), Nebbiolo is stimulatingly complex, and not especially easy to make one's own. Getting it to behave and perform as well as it can is a challenge that many take up but who few outside of Barbaresco, Barolo and the rest of Italy really manage to win (though encouragingly, things are looking up in this respect, with many very fine Nebbiolo wines being now made all over the world).

Unfortunately, much of what has and is being said and written about Nebbiolo is inaccurate. Still today, you will hear and read that there exist three Nebbiolo clones called Lampia, Michet and Rosé, which is incorrect on a number of levels. First, they are not clones. Second, Nebbiolo Lampia is the original Nebbiolo, from which all other Nebbiolos descend, such as the Spanna of northeastern Piedmont (Alto Piemonte); therefore, Nebbiolo Lampia is neither a clone nor a biotype but is in fact the original Nebbiolo grapevine (and as we shall see shortly, of which there are many different biotypes). You may choose to call it Nebbiolo or Nebbiolo Lampia, but the fact remains that, at the present state of scientific knowledge, it is the original Nebbiolo we all know and love. Third, Nebbiolo Michet and Nebbiolo Rosé are different enough that, strictly speaking and depending on which current of scientific thought you adhere to, both could be considered to be distinct varieties; the current, prevailing, mode of thinking is to view them as Langhe biotypes of Nebbiolo Lampia (even though this is/may not be scientifically correct). To summarize, according to current scientific knowledge:

1. Piedmont, Valle d'Aosta, Lombardy and Sardinia are the only four Italian regions that Nebbiolo grows in relatively large numbers, though there are sporadic plantings in Veneto too

2. The original Nebbiolo is believed to be Nebbiolo Lampia.

3. Nebbiolo is in the *Registro Nazionale delle Varietà di Vite* (Italy's national grapevines registry) officially listed with code number 160 and is as such the only Nebbiolo-named grape variety in the list.

4. The only accepted, official, synonyms of Nebbiolo are three: Chiavennasca, Spanna, and Prünent. The last of those three synonyms can be used only for wines made in the DOC Valli Ossolane in the Province of Verbano-Cusio-Ossola (this is the northernmost Province in the region of Piedmont, created in 1992 through the fusion of three areas previously included in the Piedmontese Province of Novara).

5. There are numerous Nebbiolo Lampia biotypes. These live not just in the Langhe, but throughout Piedmont as well as outside of Piedmont in the other three Italian regions listed above at point n. 1. The two best-known non-Piedmont biotypes of Nebbiolo Lampia are Picotener and Chiavennasca, but they are not the only ones.

6. Picotener is a Nebbiolo Lampia biotype typical of the Valle d'Aosta and of the Carema area in northern Piedmont. It is not surprising that Picotener grows in both the Valle d'Aosta and Piedmont's Carema area, because Carema is located in northern Piedmont right at the border with the Valle d'Aosta.

7. The Chiavennasca of Lombardy is a biotype of Nebbiolo Lampia that is at home in, and typical of, Lombardy's Valtellina alpine area.

8. Picotener and Chiavennasca typify Nebbiolo Lampia biotypes outside of Piedmont, but there are other lesser-known, non-Piedmontese Nebbiolo biotypes, such as those of Lombardy's Franciacorta and those of the island of Sardinia.

9. Not surprisingly, the majority of Nebbiolo Lampia biotypes such as Spanna, Prünent, Cobianco, and Bolla exist in Piedmont (not just in the Langhe).

10. Though not everyone agrees, Nebbiolo Michet is currently viewed as a Langhe biotype of Nebbiolo Lampia that is virus-affected. Nebbiolo Rosé is Nebbiolo Lampia's closest relative, with only minimal genetic differences separating the two, but that are enough to make them distinct varieties. However, given how similar these three grapevines are, from a morphological, behavioral, and winemaking perspective, everyone tends to view them as biotypes of one and the same plant. Though this may not be strictly correct on a purely scientific basis, and something I shall broach in-depth in the specific chapters devoted to each one, it is a highly practical view that has many merits (see Chapter 2, NEBBIOLO MICHET; and Chapter 3, NEBBIOLO ROSÉ).

11. The genetic reality of grapevines is extremely complex, and its study is, if possible, even more complex. In this chapter I broach the genetics of Nebbiolo grapes as has never been done before in a non-academic mainstream wine publication in an effort to clear up confusion on this important subject. This chapter addresses all of the above statements by providing the latest research data and producer experience available, coupled with the historical documentation and the anecdotes pertinent to a full understanding of the Nebbiolo grape variety to the best of current available scientific and practical knowledge. To be crystal-clear, there is nothing presently available in the literature, books or websites, relative to Nebbiolo, Nebbiolo Michet and Nebbiolo Rosé even remotely similar to this chapter and the next two devoted respectively to Nebbiolo Michet and Nebbiolo Rosé.

THE GRAPE

Names both right and wrong

Nebbiolo's numerous complex charms begin with its name. Even though Nebbiolo is an ancient grape variety, the name it goes by today is only a very recent one. Up until the 1960s, the grape was routinely called Nebiolo (spelled with one "b" only), but in fact "Nebiolo" is not even close to being the only variation of this wine grape's name throughout history. This is because each viticultural area the grape was grown in, coined its own highly local name. A quick perusal of this extremely long list of names confirms that local farming circles were certainly not short on imagination: the most important of Nebbiolo's many names include (in alphabetical order): Brunenta, Prünent a and/or Prünent [typical of Piedmont's Val d'Ossola (or Ossola valley, in English) situated in the Verbano-Cusio-Ossola province]; Chiavennasca (in Lombardy's Valtellina area, in the Sondrio province); Melasca, Melaschetto and Melascone Nero (near the city of Biella, in Alto Piemonte); Marchesana (in Valtellina); Martesana (near Como in Lombardy, not far from the famous lake where George Clooney likes to hang out in his spare time); Nibieul Burghiri (on the left bank of the Tanaro river, around the commune of S. Stefano Roero); Picotener, Picoutener or Picotendro (in Valle d'Aosta and the Canavesano area of northern Piedmont, especially in the Carema denomination); Spanna, as well as the much rarer Spana and Span (in the provinces of Vercelli and Novara in the Alto Piemonte). At the end of the book, you will find the list of all the names by which Nebbiolo has been identified with over the years (see APPENDIX A. *Table 1.1: List of names Nebbiolo has historically been known by*).

Other names were, and are, less common, and always referred either to Nebbiolo's perceived geographic origin or to its variety-specific characteristics. The names recalling places of origin include: Nebbiolo Canavesano, but also Nebbiolo d'Asti, di Barbaresco, di Barolo, di Bricherasio, di Carema, d'Ivrea, di Lorenzi, di Masio, di Moncrivello, di Monsordo, di Nizza della Paglia, di Piemonte, and di Sciolze (all of which are helpful in confirming just how diffuse Nebbiolo cultivation was in prior centuries, as these towns are located all over Piedmont, and not just in the Langhe). Names that harken back to the Nebbiolo grape's specific characteristics and its sensory attributes (sight, smell or taste) as well as to viticultural/enological traits, in the best tradition of ancient Rome (D'Agata 2014), were just as numerous. For example, names related to Nebbiolo's color include: Nebbiolin Nero and Nebbiolo Rosato (which was most likely not Nebbiolo Rosé, but either a color variation of real Nebbiolo or a different variety altogether). Examples of the latter (mostly regarding the bunches and the berries, cultivation methods, productivity levels and wine characteristics) include: Nebbiolin Canavesano ("the small Nebbiolo of the Canavese area"), Nebbiolo Cobianco (or Còbianc or Cobianco only, where the "bianco" refers to the pale-colored stalk: this is a Nebbiolo typical of the Gattinara and Ghemme areas); Nebbiolo Corosso (or just Còruss or Corosso, where the "rosso" refers to the red-colored stalk: this Nebbiolo is also typical of the Gattinara and Ghemme areas, and is most likely the result of a viral infection of Cobianco); Nebbiolo Femmina (or Nebieul Fumela), Nebbieul Maschio, Nebbiolin, Nebbiolin Commune (with two "m"s, apparently). Also, Nebbiolin Lungo, Pignolo and Pugnent, Spana Grossa, and Spana Piccolo, all of which refer to the size of Nebbiolo's grape bunch.

Nevertheless, in the present day and age only three of Nebbiolo's many names are used much at all anymore: Chiavennasca, Picotener and Spanna. Even these three are now being used less and less (and this despite having very strong historical attachments to local viticultural areas): clearly, Nebbiolo's fame and fortune are such nowadays that most everyone in Italy prefers to call the variety with the instantly recognizable and universally well-known name of "Nebbiolo". Which may be just all fine and dandy, convenient even, but in so doing one loses the "somewhereness" each name implied, or at the very least, the association to a specific place that came embedded with the use of the previously common local names.

Along with the many different names that correctly referred to the real Nebbiolo variety, Nebbiolo also boasts a very long lineup of names that were/are erroneous. These other names are incorrect because they refer to other grape varieties altogether. Unfortunately, ampelographic recognition is difficult even for the experts, and so it is not surprising that many mistakes have been made over the years (and not just with Nebbiolo). As I have written before, DNA testing is of no help if the ampelographic data is all wrong to begin with: I refer you to my *Native Wine Grapes of Italy* for further reading on this important and interesting facet of our wine world (D'Agata 2014). The list of Nebbiolo erroneous attributions (names) includes: Barbesino (a name commonly used in the countryside around Casteggio in Lombardy; but the Barbesino grape was most likely Grignolino, not Nebbiolo, and some grape scientists believe it may have referred to yet another variety altogether); Nebbiolo Bianco (historically always used to describe a slew of different varieties, among them Arneis); Nebbiolo d'Antoni or Uva d'Antoni (most commonly used in the Piedmontese area of Saluzzo, this was not Nebbiolo but most probably the Nebbiolo di Monsumo variety, now extinct); Nebbiolo di Beltram (of Piedmont's Saluzzese area, and again, no relation to the real Nebbiolo); Nebbiolo di Dronero (known as Chatus today, this variety is typical of the Salluzzese area: you'll find many lovely wines made with it, but it's not Nebbiolo); Nebbiolo-Dolcetto (heaven help us…but rather than some weird Frankenstein-like living grape mosaic or *chimera*, the variety identified as such was most likely just Dolcetto, not Nebbiolo); Nebbiolo Pajrolé and Nebbiolo Pirulé (also of the Saluzzese, a dark-skinned variety that was not Nebbiolo at all but some not better identified local wine grape); Nebbiolo di Stroppo (honestly now, even I have no idea what this might have been); Nebbiolo Occellino (in the Rivoli area of Piedmont); Nebbiolo Pignolato (in the northern Piedmont area around Biella); Nebbiolo Polastro (around S. Stefano Roero); Nebbiolo Rosato (which was not Nebbiolo Rosé but Grignolino); Spanna-Nebbiolo or Spannibio (another Frankenstein-like sounding grape creature, this misnomer common to Lombardy's Oltrepò Pavese area identified Croatina, not Nebbiolo); Spannina and Spanni (commonly used in Ghemme, these two grapes were actually Freisa, not Nebbiolo).

And as far as mistakes go, a truly curious one is that of the grape called "Barolo" (reportedly the Gamay Blanc grape, whatever that one might have been), mentioned by various sources to being listed in the nineteenth century ampelography tome written by famous French ampelographer Odart. I write down "reportedly" because I have sat down and read through two different editions of Odart's *Ampelographie Universelle* in their entirety (not exactly a leisurely afternoon's read I may add, but a whole lot of fun nonetheless) and did not find any such mention, so I'm not sure what to think (in fairness and for accuracy's sake, there at least five major rewrites and updated editions of Odart's seminal work, so perhaps the Barolo-Gamay Blanc reference is in one of those three editions I have not yet been able to access). At the end of this book, in the Appendix, you will find a list of erroneous names Nebbiolo has been identified with over the years (see: APPENDIX A. *Table 1.2: List of erroneous Nebbiolo attributions*).

After all that, it is not without interest to realize that the name of the grape is much older than that of its wines. Documents show that some variation of the name "Nebbiolo" had been floating around many centuries before the wine name of "Barolo" ever came into the collective consciousness. The first official documentation of "Nebbiolo" appears as *nibiol* in a 1266 document: I caution my readers to make note of the fact that for the longest time that date was believed to be not 1266, but 1268. However, we now know that it was a mistake. Due to an unfortunate error in transcription, the date was originally reported as 1268 in many official documents (beware that currently numerous paper and internet sources routinely report that erroneous birthdate for grape's name), and I myself have done so on at least one occasion. However, there is now no doubt whatsoever that the word *nibiol* was first mentioned in 1266 (again: not 1268) as confirmed in the *Documenti per la Storia del Piemonte*, written by Stanisalo Cordero di Pamparato (1797-1863), a senator of the Kingdom of Sardinia who based his writings on a specific document that still exists, the "*Camerale Piemonte, Articolo 65, paragrafo 1, Conti della Castellania Di Rivoli, Mazzo 1, Rotolo 1*", currently in the custody of the State Archives of Turin. Instead, the word Nebbiolo is first mentioned in association with the Alba countryside in a 1292 rental contract of a piece of land located in the interestingly identified "*tra i due ponti*" locality (in English, "between two bridges": given how vague that reference seems, I guess there must not have been too many bridges in the area back then).

The contract stated that among the tenant's various obligations was the planting of "*filagnos de vitibus neblorii*" ("vines of Nebbiolo"). By contrast, Asti and Nebbiolo are first linked in 1295, when Tommaso Asinari's will includes "*... bottalli duos de nebiolo et duos de nostrali*" (two barrels of Nebbiolo and of two of wine made with local grapes"). This is interesting, given how much Nebbiolo is associated with Alba today; in fact, the variety has a long and distinguished history in the Astigiano as well. In the famous 1330 work *Ruralium Commodorum* written by Pier de' Crescenzi (perhaps not unimportantly, for many years a judge in Asti), the grape *Nubiola* is mentioned and described as giving excellent wines in the area of, you guessed it, Asti. In 1606, Giovan Battista Croce, in his landmark *Dell'eccellenza e diversità dei Vini che nelle montagne di Torino si fanno* mentions Nebbiolo as the "queen of the black grapes". But what about the wine, you ask? Barolo, or a word close to it, appears on the scene only much later: *Barol* (Barolo) is reported in the literature for the first time in 1751, in a document detailing the discussions between merchants and diplomats wishing to buy and import the wine to London (see Chapter 5, THE HISTORY OF BAROLO). In any case, we know that already in the early 1800s, locals believed the best Barolo wine to be made with 100% Nebbiolo. Only in some cases, when wanting for example to increase the wine's pale red color and/or diminish its sweetness, was up to 10% of Neiran added (Neiran was another local grape growing in the countryside at that time).

Nebbiolo's look

What Nebbiolo looks like depends on the specific clone or biotype (see below: Nebbiolo biotypes and clones) being examined. This is because Nebbiolo's well-recognized and noteworthy intra-varietal variability is strongly terroir-dependent. For this reason, ampelographic descriptions vary and comparisons might lead you to wonder if those doing the describing had perhaps been drinking way too much of their study matter. In general, Nebbiolo the wine grape is described as having a small to medium-large leaf with three to five lobes (very rarely seven); the bunch is most often described as medium-large, rarely medium-small (of an average weight close to 300 grams), medium-compact to fairly tightly-packed, and usually pyramidal in shape (but can at times be either conical or cylindrical) with one large wing (at times two). The grapes themselves are medium-small in size (with an average weight of 1.8 grams), and round to slightly oval in shape. The skin, though not thin, is not especially thick; however, it is very resistant. Be aware that the importance of Nebbiolo's skin cannot be overemphasized, as it helps to define its wines like no other of the grape's component parts.

First but not foremost, Nebbiolo's skin gives the variety its name: covered by plenty of bloom, the grapes have a slightly hazy, non-shiny appearance. In other words, Nebbiolo bunches look as if the they live perennially submerged in fog (which, given the Langhe's weather come fall and winter, is not at all that far from the truth). Therefore, it is not by chance that the word "nebbiolo" most likely derives from *nebula*, in Latin, and then *nebbia*, in Italian (both of which mean "fog"). Other highly unlikely derivations, such as the one that states "Nebbiolo" derives from the word "noble", are part of the many anecdotal memories and assumptions forwarded throughout the centuries with little or no factual basis (and unfortunately blissfully repeated in historical and modern writings that make the world of Italian wine so charming, but ultimately one in which it is very difficult to separate fact from fiction).

To be clear, I have never heard, and I do mean never, anyone even vaguely knowledgeable about Nebbiolo or anyone without vested interests say he or she believes that the grape's name derives from the word "noble". Given how important and remunerative Nebbiolo has become today, there may be an interest on the part of some people to give the wine grape a more polished origin, but really now. More importantly (much more importantly), Nebbiolo's skin determines the color of Nebbiolo's wines, which are not especially dark (the grapes aren't especially dark, either: in fact, when exposed to large amounts of sunlight, Nebbiolo grapes can show a pinkish tinge to their medium-dark hazy blue hue and actually tend to become pink-looking over time. This is why Nebbiolo Lampia, some biotypes of it at least, can be fairly easy to confuse with Nebbiolo Rosé; it is because of the similarity in their morphologies that our ancestors thought that all the various Nebbiolo grapes were clones of each other (See below; see also Chapter 3, NEBBIOLO ROSÉ). Color is the single most important characteristic of Nebbiolo wines, neatly separating them from those made with the likes of Syrah or Merlot. Just imagine that no less an expert than Bruno Giacosa used to tell me that he didn't even need to taste the Nebbiolo grapes coming into the winery to know if the year was going to be a stellar one or not: all he had to do was take one look at them, and he could immediately give a definitive judgement on the vintage's quality (no doubt easier for the *maestro* to do than you or I). In any case, while Nebbiolo boasts many different morphologic appearances, with some biotypes that can be darker than expected, Nebbiolo's color (of both grape and wine) is never too deep. This large variability in appearance (color, morphology), not to mention behaviors of Nebbiolo populations (something that farmers and scientists are well aware of), brings me now to launch into what is not just one of my absolutely favorite subjects in wine, but one of Nebbiolo's *raisons d'etre*, that of biotypes and clones. Fasten your seat belts…

BIOTYPES AND CLONES

Biotypes

As we have seen, Nebbiolo is a grape variety characterized by huge intra-varietal variability, leading to the existence of many Nebbiolo biotypes. Differences between biotypes are age-dependent and terroir-related, and so this explains why there are many populations of slightly different-looking and behaving Nebbiolos living not just in the different regions of Italy, but also within each individual region. Clearly, the ecological implications of biotypes are all-important, given that it is biotypes that have been living in a specific area for centuries, adapting to that area more or less perfectly over time. They consequently represent the most ecofriendly viticulture possible (as opposed to ripping everything up and planting new vines sourced from miles when not countries away). It is the specific interaction between grape variety and the different components of the local terroir, including: geology, climate, and water availability; human selection pressures and para-domestication efforts; and the individual grapevine's adaptive capacity to such specific habitats, that leads to the formation of biotypes (Myles et al., 2011; D'Agata 2019).

These terroir factors lead to mutations of the grapevine DNA that in turn lead to different protein coding, and ultimately, tissue and cell-modifications such that the grapevine no longer looks or behaves like the original plant. These genetic modifications accumulate over time: it follows that it is the world's oldest grape varieties that are invariably those that have incorporated the largest numbers of mutations, and that are therefore those with the largest number of biotypes. Clearly, as Nebbiolo is an ancient variety that has been documented on Italian soil since the thirteenth century at least, it is no slouch in the biotype numbers department. Obviously, Nebbiolo grapevines have had plenty of time in which to build up mutations. Furthermore, random mutations that occur during sexual reproduction and that are not directly terroir-related can also contribute to the appearance of even more different-looking Nebbiolo grapevines. If you like, you can think of biotypes as sub-varieties, although using that term is not scientifically exact.

The subject of Nebbiolo's biodiversity is not just an exercise in stimulating intellectual thinking and analysis, but bears a direct relationship to the wine made. If you don't understand that, then you don't understand wine. For industrialists it might certainly be more convenient to say grapes are all one and the same and conveniently lump them together or just do away with the less interesting/remunerative ones altogether, but that is neither correct nor intellectually acceptable (besides being an act of extreme ecological unfriendliness). What the existence of biotypes means is that not all Nebbiolo grapevines you will come across look and behave the same. What the existence of biotypes does *not* mean is that you can get them to make wines reminiscent of Tempranillo or Merlot.

With 100% Nebbiolo wine (and Barolo is a 100% Nebbiolo wine), that is just plain impossible. So even though Nebbiolo biotypes can lead to slightly differently nuanced Nebbiolo wines, their wines will (should) always remind you of a Nebbiolo wine. Many biotypes generated over time are still clearly recognizable as a Nebbiolo, and give a wine that is still recognizably Nebbiolo wine (if this weren't so, we'd be then talking about one or more new distinct varieties altogether). However, differences between biotypes are often relevant enough that the wines made with each one *do* differ to a recognizable degree (Santini, Mollo, Cascio, et al., 2012; Mannini, Santini, Mollo et al., 2015; D'Agata 2019). In other words, a Nebbiolo growing in the Carema area of Piedmont (which is an area that is different both geologically and climatically from the Langhe and where a different biotype of Nebbiolo grows compared to those that are typical of, and grow in, the Langhe) will produce a wine that though similar to the one made in the Langhe, will be noticeably different from it (see below: Understanding the many Nebbiolo biotypes). It should be so, after all, because such different tasting wines are, provided the viticultural and winemaking methods employed are more or less the same, the result of different terroirs. "Terroir" includes not just the soil, the climate and the topography of a specific place, but also the biotypes that grow there and are used to make the wines.

If you were to plant a Nebbiolo fresh out of the Langhe in the area of Carema, chances are high that the wine you make there with it will not be like the one already being made in Carema with the local Nebbiolo biotypes. That's because the local Nebbiolo grapevines have adapted to the Carema terroir over time and consequently give a slightly different wine than a Nebbiolo planted there straight out of the Langhe. This has been clearly demonstrated time and again, not the least example of which was planting Picotener in the Barolo area, which gave fairly poor if not disastrous results and is a subject I will broach shortly. In any case, it is important to understand that the relevance of grape variety biotypes, and distinguishing between them, has only recently become apparent to researchers and wine producers alike (awareness among the wine loving public lags further behind still). In fact, the ecological, genetic, biochemical and enological implications of biotypes and their random cultivation just anywhere have become increasingly clear, such that more and more study is being devoted to the subject in laboratories and universities all over the world (Filippetti, Intrieri, Centinari 1997; Silvestroni, Di Pietro, Intrieri et al 1997; Gonzàles-Techera 2004; Moncada, Pelsy, Merdinoglu et al 2006; Wegscheider, Benjak, Forneck 2009; Cabezas, Ibáñez, Lijavetzky, et al 2011; Emanuelli, Lorenzi, Grzekowiak, Catalano 2013).

In ultimate analysis, and this is important, it behooves me to repeat and make clear that though biotypes are invariably and unavoidably genetically different from the original plant they have derived from (they have to be: because if they weren't, even to the smallest of degrees, then the plants would be identical just like identical human twins are), all these biotypes belong to the same family. In this case, all the many Nebbiolo biotypes are all to be considered and viewed as being "Nebbiolo". Therefore, at the present state of scientific knowledge, there is one original Nebbiolo grapevine from which all others are derived. Granted, by strict scientific definition these genetically different plants should all be considered as being distinct varieties, but it is neither logical nor practical to do so. When all is said and done, the morphologic differences between the various Nebbiolos and the enological characteristics of their wines are not so different that we can speak of separate, distinct varieties. Wines from Gattinara in the Alto Piemonte and from Donnas in the Valle d'Aosta are clearly different from Barolos, but not to the extent that you cannot recognize them as being Nebbiolo wines. Clearly, if the Gattinara and/or Donnas wines tasted like something made with Cabernet Sauvignon or Syrah then that would be different, but it is not so. For example, we view Gattinara and Donnas as representing different expressions of the Nebbiolo grape, resulting from time spent living in and adapting to very different habitats, but we still consider them to be wines made with Nebbiolo. This is true of just about any other grape variety you can think of. Just imagine that in Burgundy a research team and group of producers headed by Aubert de Villaine of the Domaine de la Romanée-Conti have identified over 500 different variants of Pinot Noir and 300 of Chardonnay, so you understand that the possibilities that the many different biotypes offer relative to wines that all taste slightly different and that act as vectors of the diversity of terroir expression is almost infinite.

Clearly, there is no intention of renaming every single one of those Chardonnay and Pinot Noir subvarieties with a new name: they are still all Pinot Noir and Chardonnay. Indeed, it would be crazy if it were otherwise. Even if those 800 different biotypes look different and behave differently, and give wines that might differ somewhat in that some may be darker, paler, more perfumed, less perfumed, more structured, less structured, more acid and so forth, the 800 grapes give wines that are still recognizably as either Pinot Noir or Chardonnay. But make no mistake about it: even though the grapes are clearly Pinot Noir and Chardonnay and their wines relatively similar, the grapes all have structural and functional genetic differences to a degree. In fact, genetic differences in what were supposedly Chardonnay and Pinot Noir grapevine "clones" (which, by strict definition, should be genetically identical) were clearly demonstrated by Riaz and associates in 2002. By now, it should be clear to you that even if by definition genetic diversity implies different beings and different species, when genetic differences are minimal such that both the look of the plants and the taste of the wines (in the case of grapevines) are only minimally affected, then rather than different species we speak of biotypes.

Exactly the same line of reasoning applies to Nebbiolo and its many biotypes. For example, just like in the study mentioned earlier relative to Chardonnay and Pinot Noir, a recent study by Gambino, Dal Molin, Boccacci and associates (2017) based on short-reads genomic data clearly showed diagnostic single nucleotide variants among three Nebbiolo clones (CVT 71, CVT 185 and CVT 423) of three different Nebbiolo biotypes (respectively of Michet, Lampia and Picotener), which are associated to different cultivation areas. But as already mentioned at length, the genetic differences present, while they could be used to identify the three as distinct grapevine species, are so minor that we continue to consider all three as being "Nebbiolo". In any case, some Nebbiolo biotypes will give Barolos that are slightly darker in color, other biotypes will give wines that are paler, and other biotypes still will give wines of a color that falls somewhere in between that of all the others; some plants will give more structured wines, others less; some plants will give more acid wines, and so forth. The permutations are essentially endless depending on the degree of mutations that have taken place within the Nebbiolo DNA. So even in the case of the most different and most famous of all the Nebbiolos, Nebbiolo Michet and Nebbiolo Rosé, both are still very recognizably Nebbiolo grapevines and their wines recognizably Nebbiolo (see Chapter 2, NEBBIOLO MICHET; see also Chapter 3, NEBBIOLO ROSÉ). And this is why, even though they could be considered to be distinct varieties by strict genetic definition (as I myself have written in the past), I understand and accept that it is no doubt more practical and easier on everyone to view them all as biotypes of Nebbiolo Lampia. You know, when all is said and done, sometimes in life it really is best not to try and reinvent the wheel.

Clones

Clones are not at all the same thing as biotypes, though most everyone (producers included) confuse the two and use the names interchangeably. There is no kind way of saying it: to do so is completely wrong. Clones [from the Greek κλών (klōn, clonos) meaning "twig"] are, by definition, genetically identical individuals to the mother plant, which means their DNA has to be identical. It follows then that clones are clearly not the same thing as biotypes that as we have just seen, have DNAs that differ ever so slightly from each other and from that of the original plant from which they descend.

In 1903, plant physiologist Herbert J. Webber coined the term "clone" from the Greek *klon* (clonos) specifically to refer to the technique of propagating new plants using cuttings, bulbs or buds. From our viticultural and wine perspective, clones are developed in nurseries through asexual propagation by planting a twig (there's the *clonos*) or branch into the soil from which a new vine will develop. Clearly, no genetic recombination takes place and so the daughter plant will be genetically identical to the mother plant. What is born in this way is a true clone. In a brilliant and highly interesting 2022 study, Maestri and associates analyzed the presence of differentially occurring structure variations (see Chapter 3: NEBBIOLO ROSÉ) in the genome of two Nebbiolo clones, by comparing Nebbiolo clone CVT 71 (derived from a Nebbiolo Michet biotype) and Nebbiolo clone CVT 185 (derived instead from a Nebbiolo Lampia biotype). This study employed a multiple platform approach including optical mapping, long-reads and linked-reads to obtain long-range genomic data relative to the two clones under study. The stated goal was to study the incidence of structure variations across different organizational levels and analyze their role on genome function. Furthermore, to compare this role in not just the two clones, but also haplotypes and cultivars. Overall, the study showed that structure variations differentiating clones of the same cultivar are infrequent, and may not exist at all, though further research is required. This confirms what we have always believed to be true about the genetic identity of clones, as opposed to the differences existing between haplotypes of the same individual and between cultivars (where structure variations are instead present at higher rates).

In its essence, clonal propagation aims to preserve the phenotypic traits (what the grapevine looks like) that provide typicity to each cultivar (This, Lacombe, MR 2006; D'Agata 2014). Therefore, nursery personnel will scour the countryside seeking out those grapevines that have desirable qualities (or, more precisely, qualities that are perceived to be desirable at that particular moment in human history: be aware that today's desirable qualities of darker colored berries and wines, more loosely-packed bunches and lower productivity were not necessarily the cat's meow or the dog's bau a century ago). In other words, clones are created *ex-novo* "in vitro" (so to speak) by nurseries from selected biotypes living in the countryside and that are deemed to have good qualities. It is only after years spent studying that specific grapevine biotype's morphology and behavior in experimental vineyards and the wines made with it, that the nursery moves commercially to propagate those grapevine biotypes that made the grade (meaning those biotypes the viticultural and vinification results were deemed satisfactory enough to warrant moving ahead and creating clones to sell to eventual buyers). Clearly, the health status of all grapevines under examination is also studied (and specific curative actions instituted in the case of viral infections, including meristematic- and thermo-therapy).

The newly minted clones are identified by a combination of letters and numbers, such as for example Nebbiolo CVT 71. Compared to massal selections of biotypes, clones hold the supposed advantages of being more "standard" (or dependable, if you prefer) in the fruit they deliver as well as of being disease-free. Estates can then choose to buy the grapevines of specific clones that sport the viticultural and enological characteristics they are after. Most often estates choose (wisely) to plant a mix of clones so as to obtain a more complex wine: some clones give wines with higher acidities, and others wines with bigger structure, and so the thinking goes that making a wine from a blend of clones might lead to something more interesting, if not more complex. (I have been told over the years by various Barolo producers that to achieve a desirable degree of complexity with Nebbiolo you need to plant about fifteen to twenty-five different clones.) By planting many different clones, estates reap the added benefit of warding off the potential calamity of a disease arriving on the scene that targets one clone only. Clearly, in a similar scenario a monoclonal vineyard would certainly have proven to be a horrible idea.

What all of this also means is that once you plant the grapevine clones obtained from a nursery in your own back yard, both sexual reproduction (with its always possible random mutations) and the adaptation to the new terroirs begin (with its inevitable induction of mutations taking place too). It follows that the vineyard is soon, strictly speaking, no longer populated by clones but rather of descendants of that specific "clone lineage": in other words, individuals that descend from one clone but that are in fact no longer genetically identical to the mother clone plant (this is not a matter of mere semantics, but has very important practical implications, as we shall see shortly). In other words, the vineyard now harbors a new population of biotypes (descended from clones which, as we have seen, descended from biotypes themselves). Once again now: newly created biotypes that are the result of a combination of mutations arising from sexual reproduction and the adaptation to the new environment the grapevines have been planted in. The ability of clones to evolve over time, and in so doing to form new biotypes, leads to the vast range of grapevine diversity in vineyards (vineyards that over time are made up of an increasing number of different biotypes). It should be clear by now that clones and biotypes are not the same thing: so much so in fact that the Italian Ministry of Agriculture clearly refers to all grape varieties by distinguishing between clones and biotypes (for example: "Nebbiolo N. I–CVT C2: Clone belonging to the biotype *Cobianco'…*". See: http://catalogoviti.politicheagricole.it/scheda_clone.php?q=160-038).

In fact, knowledge relative to the differences between clones and biotypes is not as recent as might be thought: it is just the lack of awareness and knowledge on the part of basically everyone who speaks and writes about wine and grapes today that has led to the sorry present-day situation. For example, in Dalmasso's 1962 seminal description of the Nebbiolo variety (in fact still used today by Italy's National Registry of Grape Varieties) he wrote of biotypes, not clones. And as if all of this hasn't been fun enough, just continue reading on and see that it gets better, much much better. (I'm a medical doctor with a scientific/bench research background by studies and training, thus you know I'll just go on about this; and so, this is about as good a time as any to reach for the ibuprofen.)

KNOWING AND UNDERSTANDING THE MANY SPECIFIC BIOTYPES OF NEBBIOLO

As explained at length in *Native Wine Grapes of Italy* (D'Agata 2014) to which I refer you to now, academicians, farmers and wine producers alike have always been very aware of the huge biodiversity of Nebbiolo populations present in their vineyards. In fact, different Nebbiolo biotypes were first described in considerable detail already in 1799 by the Count Giuseppe Nuvolone-Pergamo (his name is usually shortened to Nuvolone), then the director of the *Società Agraria di Torino* (the Turin Agriculture society) and one of Italy's foremost historical grape luminaries. Already back then, people were aware of the many obvious differences in the appearance between Nebbiolo plants growing, for example, in the areas of Barbaresco, Carema, Fara,

Ghemme and Sizzano (all in Piedmont), the Donnas area of the Valle d'Aosta and Lombardy's Valtellina, but also between the Nebbiolo vines growing in vineyards within each one of those production zones. As we have seen, the differences between the various Nebbiolo biotypes are in relation both to the age of the vines and the characteristics of the specific terroirs.

Clearly, these differences increase with the increased difference between terroirs the vines grow in, as well as the number of centuries the grapevines have lived there (the longer by which to accumulate mutations in the DNA). As every terroir is defined by its very own set of specific physical, biological, geological, climatic and human conditions/parameters (for example, Boca's terroir could not be any more different from that of Gattinara or Barolo), it follows that the grapevines that grow in such different places will be unfailingly different, and their wines too, if and when similarly made. Similarly, the Spanna of northeastern Piedmont and the Prünent of Piedmont's Valli Ossolane area in the Province of Verbano-Cusio-Ossola look and behave differently from the original Nebbiolo Lampia too. At the very least, all these wines when similarly made, *should* be at least a little different: and when they're not, well…there's a problem (Seguin 2006; Wilson 2012; Gilbert, van der Lelie, and Zarraonaindia 2014; Foroni, Vignando, Aiello, *et al* 2017; D'Agata 2019).

It is only logical then that the Nebbiolo vines of three Italian regions that are as geographically, geologically, and climatically diverse as Lombardy, Piedmont and the Valle d'Aosta, look and behave slightly differently from each other (and from that of Sardinia's Nebbiolo too, though scientific knowledge about this specific but scarce Nebbiolo biotype population is still fairly thin). This is part of the reason why the Nebbiolo populations of the Valle d'Aosta and Lombardy have always each been identified with a name specific to each region: Picotener (and dialect/local language variations thereof) in the Valle d'Aosta, and Chiavennasca in Lombardy's alpine Valtellina area.

For the same reason, populations of Nebbiolo growing in different parts of Piedmont have also been called with different names over the centuries, such as for example the aforementioned Prünent and Spanna. All this came to be because locals believed the grape variety growing there to be specific to their land. In other words, to be theirs, and theirs only. You can hardly blame them: in fact, it's not at all hard to see -literally- why that would be. Picotener and Chiavennasca are, for example, Nebbiolo biotypes that are absolutely typical of the specific countryside each grows in and they do look and behave differently from the Nebbiolo you will observe in Piedmont and Sardinia. And not to make this anymore complex (but fascinating) than it already is, as we shall see very shortly, Nebbiolo's capacity to reflect the terroir it lives in is further showcased by the fact that there exist numerous secondary biotypes of these main biotypes within each region (Garner and Merritt 2000; Zoia 2004; Mannini, Mollo, Santini, *et al* 2013; D'Agata 2014).

Nebbiolo Lampia: the Biotypes of The Langhe and the Rest of Piedmont

The territory of Barolo and Barbaresco in the Langhe (a UNESCO World Heritage Site) is where the world's most famous Nebbiolo wines are made and where the grape variety has been growing since at least the thirteenth century. It is only logical, and therefore not surprising, that it is here that you will find the largest number of Nebbiolo biotypes. Just be aware that over the years, and even more so recently, much of what we know about the Langhe Nebbiolos has changed (practically everything you will find written on this subject in current books and websites is hopelessly outdated, when not downright inaccurate). The three main Langhe Nebbiolo biotypes are Nebbiolo Lampia, Nebbiolo Michet and Nebbiolo Rosé (again, strictly speaking, calling them biotypes may not be exact: See chapter 2, NEBBIOLO MICHET and chapter 3, NEBBIOLO ROSÉ), but are by no means the only ones. And as Nebbiolo Michet and Nebbiolo Rosé have been so strongly associated with Barolo production throughout the years, I will treat them in their own separate chapters, and focus here instead on Lampia's other many biotypes, the Nebbiolo from which, at least according to current scientific knowledge, all other Nebbiolo biotypes descend. Once again, to the best of my knowledge, practically everything you will read here has never before been written before to a similar degree, if at all, in any mainstream English-language (or Italian, for that matter) wine publication of any kind.

It bears repeating that whereas it was once held that there were three main, most common, "clones" of Nebbiolo named Lampia, Michet and Rosé, we know now, as previously stated, that this is not true. Current scientific thinking is that the Nebbiolo populations of Italy, of the Langhe and other areas, all descend from

Nebbiolo Lampia, which is the original, progenitor, Nebbiolo. All other Nebbiolos are, to a greater or lesser degree, biotypes of Lampia that have adapted over time to different terroirs and in response to human selection pressures and/or been hit by viruses. So not just the Nebbiolo Michet and Rosé of the Langhe, but also the Picotener of Valle d'Aosta and the Chiavennasca of Valtellina are apparently (at least at this point in time of scientific knowledge) all Nebbiolo Lampia that mutated over the centuries. In so doing, as we have seen, they gave rise to the Nebbiolo biotypes typical of their specific areas.

However, it is interesting to know that over the centuries, mutations have built up in the DNA of the Nebbiolo Lampia of the Langhe too, such that Nebbiolo Michet and Nebbiolo Rosé are but two of many different Nebbiolo Lampia biotypes that grow there. In other words, there are not just Nebbiolo Lampia biotypes typical of Carema (the Picotener of Carema), the Valle d'Aosta (the Picotener of Donnas and that of Arnad-Montjovet), of Lombardy (the Chiavennasca of the Valtellina and the Nebbiolo of the Franciacorta) and the little-known one of Sardinia (in the Colli del Limbara), but also different Nebbiolo Lampias of other parts of Piedmont, including the Langhe. Now what I am going to write next may come as a complete surprise to everyone who loves Nebbiolo and Barolo: believe it or not, there exist at least forty different Lampia biotypes in the Langhe alone, each identified with a separate name (see below). And so even though we talk of one Nebbiolo (or Nebbiolo Lampia) only, there are in fact many, many, many slightly different Nebbiolo Lampia grapevines out there, each of which can give a slightly different wine all of its own.

Nebbiolo Lampia's extreme terroir-sensitivity and its ability to mutate easily are such that any stroll in Barolo and Barbaresco vineyards reveals that there are many various intermediate forms of it that differ from the original in minor ways. Not all these vines have yet mutated sufficiently to warrant separating them distinctly from Lampia and adding to the forty or so Langhe biotypes we already know of. However, it is only a matter of time until these Nebbiolo Lampia grapevines accumulate enough mutations in their DNA to give noticeably different grapevines that will then be labeled as new biotypes of Nebbiolo (and eventually, new, distinct, varieties altogether). An example of one such Lampia grapevine that was previously a "pure" Lampia but that has built up enough mutations to start being reliably distinguished from the original Lampia is called Nebbiolo Lampia a Foglia Intera (in English: Nebbiolo Lampia "with a full leaf"). As its name implies, Nebbiolo Lampia a Foglia Intera differs from the regular Nebbiolo Lampia [the full name of which is actually Nebbiolo Lampia a Foglia Incisa (in English: Nebbiolo Lampia with "an indented leaf")] because of, as its name implies, the way its leaf looks. Nebbiolo Lampia a Foglia Intera is yet another biotype of Langhe Nebbiolo (along with the much better known Nebbiolo Michet and Nebbiolo Rosé).

With respect to the regular Lampia, Nebbiolo Lampia a Foglia Intera's leaf is much larger, with fewer indentations and has a tighter, closed, petiolar sinus (and do note that, at least to me, it is very interesting that all three of these morphologic characteristics are more typical of Nebbiolo Rosé than of Nebbiolo Lampia, which further shows how all these Nebbiolos represent different degrees of mutation of each other. See Chapter 3. NEBBIOLO ROSÉ). In any case, the two Lampias differentiated by the shape of their leaves give wines that, just like the grapes they are made with, also differ slightly, though the exact winemaking potential of this specific subpopulation of Nebbiolo Lampia vines is as yet unclear. For what it's worth, I have recently begun studying this aspect of Nebbiolo grapes and wines and am in the process of accumulating relevant data on the subject by identifying specific vineyards of Nebbiolo Lampia a Foglia Intera and the wines made from such plots and then getting wine micro-vinifications made from these grapes by admittedly very patient and very kind producers. For a variety of reasons, I am not at liberty to divulge exactly who is growing this biotype of Nebbiolo in potentially commercially relevant numbers. In any case, the vineyard and enological process is a difficult and time-consuming one and so it will be a few more years before any solid conclusions can be drawn (if there are any to draw, that is). Clearly, it would be impossible to do so for someone not living in Italy full-time, and with the Covid-plague in effect, it has become even harder.

Lampia is not just the original Nebbiolo from which all others descend, it is also by far the most common Nebbiolo of all; for example, in my estimation, it accounts for about 75-80% of all Nebbiolo plantings of the Langhe. Every Barolo producer grows it in his or her vineyards. All the ampelographic descriptions of Nebbiolo you read or hear of are all of Nebbiolo Lampia. It has always been a favorite of farmers because of its copious, steady production in the field and the high quality of its wines. Many of these vineyards and producers are some of Barolo's best known. The old section of the Francia vineyard is all Lampia, for example; and so are most of Giovanni Manzone's vineyards in Le Gramolere; most of Conterno Fantino's vineyards are also planted to

Lampia, large portions of Clerico's Ginestra Ciabot Mentin… the list goes on and on. In short, just about any Barolo you drink today will be almost always made with about 80-100% Nebbiolo Lampia of one form or another. Some Barolos may be made with 10-20% Nebbiolo Michet, and some may be made with anywhere from 1-20% Nebbiolo Rosé. However, though less common, there are Barolos that are made with up to as much as 100% Nebbiolo Michet and 100% Nebbiolo Rosé as well. And even if one day it is decided that they are in fact distinct varieties from Nebbiolo then the intelligent thing to do will be to amend the Barolo production guidelines so as to say that Barolo can be made from "Nebbiolo Lampia, Nebbiolo Michet and Nebbiolo Rosé", rather than insisting on the concept of one "pure" Nebbiolo, which as we have seen is neither realistic nor practical, besides being scientifically inaccurate. A pipedream, in fact. And besides, these grapevines have been living peacefully in the Barolo countryside for centuries, and are as much a part of the landscape as the people who have also lived in those same places for generations. Therefore, it behooves our sorry society to protect and safeguard all these old individual grapevines and their unique gene pools that represent an important local biodiversity. With all due respect, you might even go as far as to say that they are in fact much more Piedmontese than many of the "Piedmontese" people who live there, who have moved to Piedmont from other places.

Langhe Nebbiolo biotypes: Nebbiolo Bolla, Rossi and other anecdotal biotypes

Many Nebbiolo biotypes that used to be common are now only of historical or anecdotal significance. In fact, by the mid-twentieth century, besides Lampia, only five other Nebbiolos were still common in Langhe vineyards: Nebbiolo Bolla, Nebbiolo Lampia a Foglia Intera, Nebbiolo Michet, Nebbiolo Rosé, and Nebbiolo Rossi. Not all these Nebbiolo biotypes of the Langhe have fared as well.

Nebbiolo Bolla, fairly common up until the 1950s, was phased out in the second half of the twentieth century because of its copious yields, large berries and reportedly lesser quality wines (I refer you to *Italy's Native Wine Grape Terroirs* for the accurate history of Nebbiolo Bolla). As usual, one must always take anecdotal statements about the quality of wines and grape varieties from previous moments in the history of man and woman with a grain of salt, or at the very least situate them in the context of who is doing the talking and in what time period the talk is referred to. In other words, it is pointless to expect someone who likes to make and to drink big, dense, and as dark as possible wines to say anything good about Nebbiolo Bolla, a biotype characterized by big bunches and berries that to their way of thinking gave unfailingly dilute wines.

Really now, how could you ever expect someone with a similar taste in wine to appreciate Nebbiolo Bolla and its wines? Clearly, individuals fixated on reducing yields to push concentration to the fullest (and in their view at least, quality also) will not have much good to say about Nebbiolo Bolla. But then you taste older vintages of the amazing Corino Barolo Giachini that were made with a good deal of Nebbiolo Bolla and you realize immediately the grape could not really have been that bad. (As an aside, I will just mention here that in much a similar vein, had you spent the 1980s and 1990s listening to Chianti Classico producers like I did, you would have heard a never-ending litany of how bad it was to have white grapes allowed in the Chianti Classico blend only to realize today that the Chianti wines of the 1960s, that often had as much as 20% white grapes in the mix, were and are much better wines than some of the charmless and boring behemoths made in more "enlightened" modern times. But maybe I digress. Maybe.)

So perhaps Nebbiolo Bolla's reputation was at least partly undeserved, and I dare say it is not the first and probably not the last time a native grape gets saddled with an unfair assessment of its wine quality potential. That is exactly the same plight that befell Nebbiolo Rosé, a grape that many in Langhe are now scrambling to replant for many reasons (not the least of which is its drought- and heat-resistance, all the more valuable traits in these times of climate change. See Chapter 3, NEBBIOLO ROSÉ). And so, you realize the folly of people chasing or wanting to make wine following fads and fashions.

Nebbiolo Rossi, another Langhe Nebbiolo Lampia biotype, suffered a similar fate to Nebbiolo Bolla, but for different reasons. Unlike Bolla, its plantings dropped precipitously not because of (perceived) poor quality wines but as a result of its unreliable and low productivity. Consequently, the only Nebbiolo Lampia biotype that are still commonly found in the Langhe are Nebbiolo Michet and Nebbiolo Rosé (See Chapter 2, NEBBIOLO MICHET; and Chapter 3, NEBBIOLO ROSÉ).

Lampia biotypes have developed in other parts of Piedmont besides the Langhe. For example, the Nebbiolo of Gattinara, Ghemme, and other Alto Piemonte denominations is called Spanna: it too descends from Lampia, but over the centuries has morphed into something that looks and behaves differently, if ever so slightly, from the Nebbiolo Lampia most typical of the Langhe. People who wish to simplify things as much as possible for convenience's sake will tell you Spanna and Nebbiolo Lampia are one and the same and the two names should be viewed as synonyms, but as we have seen in this chapter and I have already discussed at length in my previous books, that is just not so. It is both simplistic and wrong. For practical purposes, we can and should most definitely consider Spanna as a non-Langhe biotype of Nebbiolo Lampia. This cannot surprise, if for no other reason that the Alto Piemonte habitat is wildly different from that of the Langhe, beginning with the acid pH of the soils compared to the alkaline soils of the Langhe, and so it does not take a degree in plant biology to figure out that Nebbiolo grapevines growing there will differ from those of the Langhe. However, from both a morphologic and winemaking standpoint, Spanna has not yet been sufficiently characterized, and so attempting to draw hard and fast conclusions about this biotype's (or rather, *these* biotypes, as there is more than one Spanna: see below) specific contributions to the Nebbiolo wine of the Alto Piemonte is perilous at best. Clearly though, given the very high quality of Alto Piemonte wines such as those of Boca, Bramaterra, Gattinara, Ghemme, Lessona, and Sizzano interest in these biotypes is very high. Some producers have tried planting Spanna grapevines in the Langhe, but what exactly Spanna might bring to Barolo's (and Barbaresco's) table, if anything, remains as yet unclear, and as we shall learn later in this section, such actions are not without risk.

Like any other card-carrying member of the extended Nebbiolo family, Spanna has shown a ready disposition to mutate, and we are aware of the existence of specific Spanna biotypes (in other words, biotypes of Spanna, itself a biotype; so, brace yourselves now, these are sub-biotypes of a Nebbiolo Lampia biotype) associated with different Alto Piemonte terroirs. One Spanna biotype that has gathered increasing attention over the last decade or so is the rare Nebbiolo Cobianco biotype (*còbianc*, in local dialect). This biotype's name is a reference to the pale hazelnut color of the grape bunch's stalk (*bianco* in Italian means "white"), as opposed to another local Alto Piemonte Nebbiolo biotype called Nebbiolo Corosso (or *còruss*, in local dialect) that is characterized by a red stalk (*rosso* in Italian means red). All the Corosso grapevines examined so far are affected by viruses (indeed, that might very well be the cause of the red coloration of the stalk, a feature commonly associated with virus-affected grapevines). It follows that, in this light, Nebbiolo Corosso can be classified as a virus-affected form of Nebbiolo Cobianco, much as Nebbiolo Michet is currently believed to be a virus-affected Lampia, though this viewpoint may not be correct (see Chapter 2, NEBBIOLO MICHET).

If we don't yet know much about the Cobianco and Corosso biotypes, we know even less about the Prünent biotype of the Val d'Ossola, not far removed from the border with Switzerland: in some respects, Prünent resembles Nebbiolo Michet, as both have more compact and smaller bunches and smaller grapes too. Given Nebbiolo's commercial importance and the extremely high quality of its wines, I am sure it is only a matter of time before someone studies it in some depth too. The fact that there are producers making wines with the Prünent biotype and who want to call their grape just so is very encouraging. It is an attitude and a way of thinking that underscores how aware wine producers are becoming of the importance of biotype when they set out to make a Nebbiolo wine that hopefully will transmit and express the characteristics of site and pride of place. It does not take a Cambridge or Harvard graduate in nuclear physics or medicine to realize that being able to boast about a Nebbiolo wine made with a local, specific Nebbiolo biotype that only they have is a good thing. Potentially, a very good thing, at least in terms of saving biodiversity, enotourism and financial windfalls. An old, now dated, study has hinted that Prünent is perhaps the oldest Nebbiolo of all, but without further ampelographic and genetic descriptions and more studies duplicating similar findings one cannot make broad statements about a grapevine's place of origin. In fact, we have some very good recent studies that do point out to where the original home of Nebbiolo was (see below), and it is not the Val d'Ossola.

Last but not least, the Canavese area (the home of Carema and Erbaluce wines) boasts a local Nebbiolo characterized by a small grape bunch that is cylindrical in shape (compared to the pyramidal shape that is more commonly associated with Lampia's and most Nebbiolo biotype grape bunches, save for Michet). As it resembles a small closed fist, locals had always identified this subvariety of Nebbiolo with the name Pugnet (*pugno* in Italian means fist). It had been planted in the Langhe too by a few estates, and I was able to taste the experimental wine made with these grapes (not at all bad, but there just wasn't much of it made, not surprisingly given the scrawny-looking plants), but the estates prefer not to have their names revealed. In any case, from what I know of Pugnet, it deserves to be studied some more.

Chiavennasca

Valtellina, a northernmost alpine outpost of Lombardy in the province of Sondrio, is the home of Chiavennasca. There the variety grows in terrifyingly steep vineyards (mostly terraced, of course) planted from 300 to 800 meters above sea level. The origin and exact meaning of Chiavennasca's name is a matter of some debate. It was Heinrich Lehmann who in 1797 first wrote that the name was in honour of the variety's original home, the Valle Chiavenna. However, this supposed origin has been proven wrong and so should not be reported anymore (according to an extremely interesting 2015 university thesis written by Antonioli, Lehmann also suggested that the grape came from Cleves, which is not just wrong but hilarious, to say the least). In fact, as is clearly documented in Carlo Gerini's 1833 *Monografia sulla Viticoltura Valtellinese* (Antonioli 2015), there wasn't even that much Nebbiolo Chiavennasca planted in the Val Chiavenna, which was rather the home of little-known varieties such as Bellola, Canina and Pezzè "… and other less qualitative grape varieties". It is the opinion of most of today's experts (and mine too) that it is most likely Chiavennasca's name derives from two very similar sounding and similarly written local dialect expressions (but that have slightly different meanings): either *ciu venasca* (meaning "a grape variety with more sap and vigor") or *ciu vinasca* (a grape variety that is most suited to winemaking).

In any case, while we know vineyards grew in the Valtellina already in 837 A.D. (Bongiolatti 1993), the first time Chiavennasca's presence as such is documented in the area dates to 1595 (D'Agata 2014). However, it is apparent that the grape made up for lost time quickly: it was recognized as the best of the roughly thirty different grape varieties growing in the Valtellina already in the 1600s, and there are numerous writings dating back to the 1700s attesting to the excellence of its wines, considered the region's best. I don't know about you, but I find it extremely interesting that when the local *Società Agraria Valtellinese* (Valtellina agriculture society), founded in 1856 by Pietro Torelli (the first president of the Valtellina community and governor of the province of Sondrio), decided to plant two botanical orchards in the towns of Sondrio and Tirano (a project begun in 1859 and finished by 1861) so as to study and propagate the different plant species growing in the area, it charmingly listed Chiavennasca as one of only three *viti di paese* (in English, "grapevines of the town/countryside", meaning local native grapes), but stuck *Nibiol* (Nebbiolo) in the *viti foresti* group (or "foreign grapes"), along with the likes of Barbera, Grignolino, Montepulciano and the so-called Bourgogne blanc and Bourgogne rouge varieties! More than anything else I could say or write, this story tells you a lot about the importance of biotypes right there! Of course, it also tells you about the intense local attachment the *Valtellinesi* (and Italians in general) have always had towards specific grape varieties and their biotypes (and especially towards those that grow in their back yard).

It follows that with well over 400 years of history in this one specific spot, you would expect an obliging chap like Nebbiolo to adapt to its mountain home; and that's exactly what it did. Gradually over time, the Nebbiolo living in the Valtellina morphed into what became locally called Chiavennasca, and then in turn developed numerous Chiavennasca biotypes, many of which still exist today. As documented by Pietro Ligari in his seminal *Ragionamenti di Agricoltura* (Ligari 1752) locals were aware of the Chiavennasca biodiversity in their vineyards already in the eighteenth century. At that time, at least three different Chiavennascas were known: Chiavennasca Comune, Chiavennasca Grossa and Chiavennasca Intagliata. By 1907, locals also believed there to be a difference between the Chiavennasca populations living in the countrysides of Sondrio and Castione, and proceeded, appropriately enough, to name them as such ("Chiavennasca di Sondio" and Chiavennasca di Castione"). Today, the three best-known Chiavennasca biotypes are called Chiavennasca Brioni, Chiavennasca Intagliata, and Chiavennascone (which is most likely the Chiavennasca Grossa of centuries past). By contrast, research performed in the early 2000s has shown that Chiavennaschino, long believed to be the fourth main Chiavennasca subtype, is actually not a Chiavennasca but Nebbiolo Rosé (D'Agata 2014). The Chiavennasca biotypes have not yet been studied enough and their numbers are still scarce, but the good news is that researchers are actively following them and that three brand new clones of Nebbiolo have been recently created from Chiavennasca (see below). We are sure to learn more on this topic in the (hopefully) near future.

One last thing: for precision's sake, I point out that when speaking or writing about the Nebbiolo of Lombardy, only the Valtellina is ever mentioned. In fact, it is not the only place where Nebbiolo lives in Lombardy. There exists another very small population of Lombardy Nebbiolo: as previously mentioned, it lives (survives would probably be the more apt term) in the Franciacorta, an area the fame of which rests on its sparkling wines and that is mostly planted to the international wine grapes Chardonnay, Pinot Blanc and Pinot Noir. The grapes culled from whatever few Nebbiolo grapevines are left standing are used in the Curtefranca Rosso blends. Clearly, little if anything is known about these Nebbiolos, and so the eventual existence of one or more Franciacorta Nebbiolo biotypes is really, for the time being, only a matter of conjecture.

Picotener

Picotener is the Nebbiolo biotype of Piedmont's Carema area and of the Valle d'Aosta, where it was born. It takes its name from the French words *picot tendre*, meaning "soft berry" (the Valle d'Aosta, located right on the border with France, is the most French part of Italy). A variation of the word "Picotener" first appears in an official document dating to the nineteenth century, when Gatta mentions it in his *Saggio sulle viti e sui vini della Valle d'Aosta* (1838), one of Italy's most important historical ampelographic reference texts. A little later, in 1877, Picotener was described at length in the *Bollettino Ampelografico del Ministero dell'Agricoltura, Industria e Commercio* and said to be cultivated extensively in vineyards planted from the towns of Pont St. Martin to Villeneuve (D'Agata 2014). Most likely, Picotener's wine has a much more ancient history. Citations referring to twelfth and thirteen century descriptions of the wine exist, but to the best of my knowledge, remain in need of further verification; however, it is certain that in 1635, Francesco Agostino della Chiesa (the bishop and Count of *Corvignasco*) in his correspondence with the Church in Rome mentions the excellence of the wines of Donasio (the ancient name of the Valle d'Aosta town known today as Donnas, which is also the name of Valle Picotener's main characteristics are its low yields and its high resistance to extreme winters and climates. Because of its cold weather hardiness, it is not surprising to find Picotener growing happily in the Valle d'Aosta (one of Italy's absolutely best alpine skiing destinations, so that tells you all you need to know about what its climate is like). Picotener also provides a shining example of why it is so absolutely necessary, I dare say downright fundamental, to be aware of the existence of biotypes and to understand what the implications are for both the grape variety and its wines. For one, Picotener produces wines of noteworthy color intensity, a deep (but not exaggeratedly so) red purple-tinged hue that is not a characteristic of Nebbiolo wines (however, as I shall discuss below, the dark intensity of color that Picotener is capable of is much more evident in wines made outside of the Valle d'Aosta rather than in the Valle d'Aosta itself). Clearly, though dark, such wines are never of a black/purple-like hue of Merlot and Syrah wines, so "dark" with Nebbiolo wine is a very relative term. But the capacity to give (relatively) darker-colored wines is not the only unique characteristic of this biotype: Picotener is also characterized by low vigor, another huge difference with non-Picotener Nebbiolos (and that of the Langhe's Nebbiolo in particular) which are instead very vigorous (much of the vineyard management efforts of Barolo and Barbaresco estates are especially geared to reining this vigor in).

I am not aware of any secondary biotypes of Picotener within the Valle d'Aosta, though if I had to bet, I would say there most certainly are (just take a walk in any of the vineyards there and you'll find yourself surrounded by different-looking Picotener populations). For example, the Nebbiolo/Picotener vines of the beautiful old and uncontaminated vineyards of the Arnad-Montjovet denomination ("uncontaminated" in the sense that this is a viticultural area that has been mostly forgotten and so people haven't been busy mucking up the genetic pool there by planting new clones and massal selections obtained from other parts of Piedmont, Lombardy or elsewhere) look different to my eyes than those of Donnas (and in some cases, very much so). However, if distinguishing between Valle d'Aosta populations of Nebbiolo is presently hard to do given the little experience we have with them and the even less amount of study done on the subject to date, there most certainly is a difference between the Picotener populations of the Valle d'Aosta and those of Carema. For the scientifically minded, I point out that these two Picotener populations differ recognizably on a number of morphologic and behavioral parameters, and so do the wines made with each (and in fact, Picotener clones descending from biotypes originating from the two different areas are identified with different numbers (for example, the Picotener 308 of Carema and the Picotener 400 series from the Valle d'Aosta). For this reason, I believe the two should probably be called with different names (for example, one possibility might be Picotener di Carema and Picotener Valdostano; another might be Picotener Canavese and Picotener Valdostano). Of course, this being Italy, it is unlikely anything so logical and helpful will ever be put into place. Picotener has also been planted in the Langhe, where it proved nothing short of a disaster and a showcase for why biotypes and their differences have to be taken seriously (see below).

KNOWING AND UNDERSTANDING THE MANY SPECIFIC NEBBIOLO CLONES

At time of writing, there are currently ninety-six different Nebbiolo clones available in Italy of which forty-three are currently registered in Italy's official national catalogue of grape varieties (see Appendix A. *Table 1.3*). Of these ninety-six clones, about twenty-five or so have proven the most popular. Roughly 75% of all Nebbiolo clones available today have been developed from progenitor Nebbiolos original to Piedmont, while 25% are from either from the Valle d'Aosta or Lombardy. Of course, farmers may decide against planting clonal selections and opt to plant their vineyards with massal selections (they do so by selecting the vines on their property they are happiest with and then propagating those exclusively). But when winery owners do decide upon clonal selections from a nursery, they will usually choose more than one nursery clone because polyclonal vineyards allow to mix and match different clone strengths. Such action is undertaken not just in the hope of making a more complex wine, but because it also allows the farmers to hedge their bets against diseases and other natural disasters (clearly, a vineyard planted entirely to just one clone is at risk of being wiped out either by a disease to which that clone is particularly susceptible to or by unexpected spring frosts in the case of early-budding clones). The complexity of the wine you make by using a limited number of clones is also an issue. Most producers will tell you that you need a mix of about fifteen to twenty-five different clones to ensure you will make as complex a wine as you can.

Not surprisingly, given how popular it is, Nebbiolo has been studied extensively from a clonal standpoint (Mannini, 1995; Mannini, Mollo, Santini 2013; Mannini, Santini, Mollo 2016). The goal has always been to create clones that might provide smaller bunches (smaller bunches are one way to tame Nebbiolo's proclivity to copious yields), better fertility (this has been successfully tackled with newer generation clones of Nebbiolo no longer plagued by sterility or partial fertility of the basal buds) and darker grape skins blessed with higher total anthocyanin concentrations (because of Nebbiolo wine's medium-red and at times garnet-tinged red color, presumed to be a disadvantage in terms of potential sales, kicking up Nebbiolo's wine color by a good notch or two has always been on the minds of every researcher and nursery scientist worthy of his graduated cylinders). The earliest available Nebbiolo clones date back to 1969: these were the R1, R3 and R6, derived from grapevines of Lampia, Nebbiolo Michet and Chiavennasca, respectively. It wasn't until 1980 when two more clones appeared on the scene: the CN 36 (Lampia biotype) and the CN 111 (the latter has always been known to be a clone of Nebbiolo Rosé, but current thinking now holds it to be too a Nebbiolo Lampia that looks and behaves like a Nebbiolo Rosé, though there is no consensus yet on the matter. See Chapter 3, NEBBIOLO ROSÉ). A problem with the older generations of Nebbiolo clones was that they were overly-productive and yields could easily get out of hand: that said, all those producers blessed with the right amount of elbow grease had no trouble making outstanding wines with these clones, turning out very elegant, excellent Barolos and Barbarescos that many among us miss (I know I do).

The most popular clones from the early 1990s are the CVT CN 142 and CVT CN 230 (both Lampia biotypes developed in 1990). The floodgates opened in 2001, with six new Nebbiolo clones unleashed on the market all at once: the CVT 63, CVT 66 and CVT 71 (all Nebbiolo Michet biotypes) and the CVT 308, CVT 415 and CVT 425 (all Picotener biotypes: the 308 from Carema, the other two from Valle d'Aosta). As I will discuss a little later in this chapter, while some of these new clones proved outstanding (for example the CVT 71, today one of the most frequently planted Nebbiolos in Langhe vineyards, but also the CVT 142, almost as common right up until the mid-90s), others were remarkably unsuccessful in the vineyards of Barolo and Barbaresco and had to be uprooted. In 2002, it was time for the Lampia biotype of Lombardy to have its time in the sun, with three Chiavennasca clones announced: the 12, 21 and 34. Other clone series developed subsequently include 2004's CVT 141, CVT 145 and CVT 185, and 2005's CVT 4 (all Nebbiolo Lampia biotypes); these were followed by VCR 430 (Lampia biotype, developed in 2007). The more the merrier, and so a boom year for Nebbiolo clones proved 2009, with ten different clones released, including the VCR 270 and

VCR 275 (both of the Chiavennasca biotype). Since then, more Nebbiolo clones have been registered, with an especially interesting one being 2012's CVT C2 (the first ever clone of the Cobianco biotype, sourced in an old vineyard in Gattinara). In Appendix 1, *Table 1.4*, I list an in-depth analysis of the viticultural and enological qualities of all the most important Nebbiolo clones available today. Over the years, it has not been all smooth sailing for Nebbiolo's clones, and not all have proved equally successful. For example, some of the Michet clones of the 1990s were prone to disease and needed to be replanted often, even every ten years, which is an economically unfeasible practice (see Chapter 2, NEBBIOLO MICHET).

Allow me to add a personal observation when it comes to nursery clones. I have a bone to pick. And no, it's not the usual mantra you hear that "massal selections are so much better than clonal selections". That may well be so, but it's not my point here. What I am getting at is that clones have become big business and I for one find it frankly tiresome to always hear of how the "new and improved" clones coming out every year at what seems to be breakneck speed are, wouldn't you know it, just always *so much* better than the old ones. Maybe so, but maybe not. All I know is that, time and again, if and when you visit nurseries or talk to producers, you get subjected to a long soliloquy about how great their latest range of clones are and how much better they are than the previously planted ones that were *just so* poor. Much better. Really? Really? At the very least, no, it's not always so.

There are excellent old clones that gave fantastic wines (see below), and to say they are poor nowadays just because you have something new to sell is unfair and historically inaccurate. Producers, wine writers and anyone else involved in wine, need not to swallow this spiel hook line and sinker. We have plenty of examples of history dictating decisions that we later regret: twenty years ago, the lust for black-colored red wines that were thicker than thick was rampant. Wines that nobody wants to drink anymore. And so, while twenty years ago any clone that gave such wines would have been deemed just swell, today its wines would gather dust on the shelves. So, uprooting everything in favor of the latest "clone-flavor of the month" hardly proves an enlightened idea. We need to be careful when we pay heed to people, usually with vested interests, telling us that the "new" is always *sooooo* much better than the "old". Sometimes it is. Sometimes it's not.

But for sure, when you uproot old vines, you lose the benefits provided by them in favor of new vines with shallow root systems. And you're not performing the most ecologically friendly of acts, either. At the back of the book, *Tables 1.3* furnishes the list of Nebbiolo clones officially recognized by the Ministry of Agriculture's National Registry of Grape Varieties and Clones. *Table 1.4* provides an abridged summary of the salient characteristics, as I see them at least, of Nebbiolo's most important and most commonly planted clones. *Table 1.5* provides more detailed viticultural and winemaking information about these clones. Last but not least, *Table 1.6* specifies the characteristics of Nebbiolo clones developed outside of Piedmont (see APPENDIX A).

Beware that haphazardly planting biotypes and clones just anywhere can be seriously problematic. For instance, that there are so many different biotypes of existing grape varieties is not an exercise of futility on nature's part: those biotypes exist for a reason, reflecting something in the environment that led to changes in their genetic makeup such that new biotypes were formed. Those genetic changes have consequences, but keep in mind they are changes born out of an adaption of the grape to its local environment and therefore is, from the grape variety's point of view, a good thing. Then along comes man or woman who decides that this grapevine is just swell (and its wines even more swell) and so why not select it and bring it back to where their estate is located (often miles if not continents away) as a massal selection. Or a nursery decides to do the same and create a clonal selection with that biotype. But why one would ever expect a grapevine that has adapted over centuries to a specific area to then perform just as well in another area that may (or may not) be altogether different is, to say the least, a strange expectation indeed. Nurseries develop their clones from grapevines of specific biotypes culled in their place of origin and that they then propagate in experimental vineyards. But for numerous reasons we do not fully understand yet, not all clones end up being as successful in their new homes as they are in their original ones. From a purely Darwinian perspective, it makes sense that a variety that has adapted over the centuries to live in one specific place may not perform as well in a totally new and different habitat.

Earlier in this chapter I mentioned that not all nursery Nebbiolo clones have performed well in the Langhe over the last twenty years. Very true. Barbaresco and Barolo producers decided to give Nebbiolo grapevines from other parts of Piedmont (as well as the Valle d'Aosta and Lombardy), a try, planting them along with their own local Langhe Nebbiolo biotypes. But what seemed to be a good idea at the time in some cases had disastrous results. Many of the new plantings gave wines that diverged sharply in the color, aroma and flavor profile of the Barolo (and Barbaresco) wines that growers and wine lovers had come to know, love and expect. As I have written before in *Native Wine Grapes of Italy* (D'Agata 2014), around the second half of the new century's first decade, I became systematically aware that some Barolos (especially) and Barbarescos (less so) made with the 400 series of Nebbiolo Picotener clones had basically no perfume and extremely deep colors (even more than the latter trait, it was the truly stunning absence of perfume that I remember being especially noteworthy, given that the magical perfume of Nebbiolo's wines is arguably their biggest selling point). Some producers will try to tell you today the problem was rather one of very small yields, but though that may too have been a part of the *debacle*, I know for a fact it was *not* the jist of the problem. Granted, there is so much money involved with Barolo these days that nobody ever wants to say anything less than good about the variety and its wines, so beware. (Unfortunately, you'll find revisionism is alive and well in the world of wine too.)

This happening had not been described or written up by anyone at the time and of course producers were slow to admit in public that there might be a problem. But there clearly was, because I knew full well that the 400 series of Nebbiolo Picotener clones gave delightful wines in the Valle d'Aosta (pale, perfumed wines of graceful disposition, nothing like ultra-dark perfume-less behemoths they were giving in the Langhe). And likewise, that the Nebbiolo Picotener 308 was responsible for many of the smashingly great wines of Carema. And so, it didn't really take a graduate in medicine with experience in bench research to realize that the problem did not reside in the Nebbiolo Picotener or even in the 400 series of clones.

For whatever reason, the problem must have been related (short of producer alchemy) to those clones (and massal selections too) having been planted in the Langhe. I admit that why this would be really fascinated me (and as you can tell by reading this chapter, and just about anything else I write, it still does today). In any case, many estates were left unimpressed by the results and so proceeded to uproot or graft over their Picotener series of clones (clearly, few are now keen to discuss this subject matter). I'm not saying every Picotener planting in the Langhe was a disaster, but for sure, the majority of wines I tried made with them were not especially interesting wines. And despite what some people might tell you today, my thoughts were theirs back then too. In ultimate analysis, this story provides a benchmark example of why just planting any grapevine anywhere is not an especially enlightened idea (though people do it all the time: how often during your winery visits have you heard something to the effect of "… I got my Cab Sauv vines from Château Latour" or "I sourced Pinot Noir from good friend XX in Musigny", despite the fact the vineyards they own and their winery might be located in Chianti, Maipo or Napa.

Besides that, just taking something from somewhere and replanting it miles away in a completely different environment and in the process uprooting what was already there is an act of extreme ecological unfriendliness, it is also an act fraught with peril (unless you're the admirably open-minded sort that thinks producers really enjoy going to the expense and effort of planting new vineyards, they then have to uproot only a few years later). In this respect, it has become clear that, over the centuries, Picotener Nebbiolos have adapted admirably to the habitats of Carema, northern Piedmont and the Valle d'Aosta and not so well to the Langhe; for example, studies have shown over time that Picotener performs better in northern Piedmont than in the Langhe (Mannini, Santini, Mollo *et al* 2016).

This is not at all surprising, given that the viticultural areas of the Valle d'Aosta and the Valtellina have very different weather patterns during the growth cycle, different soil mineral concentrations, different soil pH and water drainage characteristics, and different sunlight units than those of the Langhe. A whole lot of differences, as you can see. And so, does it really surprise anybody that when transplanted to a totally different environment these poor Nebbiolo grapevines apparently short-circuited and gave totally unexpected and less-than-desirable results? To be crystal-clear, to the best of my knowledge, the only successful Barolo made with the Picotener clone is Malvirà's Barolo Boiolo (see Section II, BOIOLO file). That a Langhe estate has recently taken to advertising its Picotener Nebbiolo wine can be taken on the one hand as a commendable effort at trying new things; on the other, it is an exercise that makes little intellectual or academic sense. On this note, an outstanding 2016 study by Mannini, Santini, Mollo and associates showcases how different Nebbiolo clones react in different environments, providing a scientific basis for my observations. In any case, at the very least, biotypes/clones ought to be planted in new habitats with the understanding that it might take many years before the grapevine feels "comfortable" in its new surroundings and starts to produce grapes (and ultimately wines) of the ilk one was hoping for all along. Relative to the Langhe-Picotener caper, there is most certainly a lesson buried somewhere in there for all those who wish to learn it.

NEBBIOLO RELATIVES

Much brilliant research (including ampelographic, ampelometric and nuclear microsatellite marker studies) has been conducted over the last twenty years with the effort to better understand Nebbiolo's parentage and complex familial relationships (Schneider, Mannini, and Culasso 1991; Schneider, Boccacci, and Botta 2003; Botta, Schneider, Akkak, *et al* 2000). Of the non-Nebbiolo Lampia grapes, Nebbiolo's closest relative is Freisa, a statement that won't surprise anyone experienced with Freisa's wines, as their perfume is remarkably similar to that of Nebbiolo. Furthermore, at about ten to fifteen years from the vintage, Freisa wines built to age are virtually indistinguishable (not just from an aromatic standpoint but taste-wise too) from Nebbiolo's: it is only Freisa's usually much tougher tannins (that soften only slowly and only partly with time) that give its identity away. Nebbiolo's other closest relatives are: Brugnola, Bubbierasco (a now extremely rare native of the Salluzese area of Piedmont), Negrera (a little known and rare variety from Valtellina in Lombardy), Neretto di S. Giorgio (also called Neretto di Bario), Pignola, Rossola, Rossolino Nero (another extremely rare variety typical of the Valtellina and distinct from the similarly-named Rossola), and Vespolina. All of these cultivars have a first-degree relationship with Nebbiolo, meaning they are either Nebbiolo's parents or offspring (in the case of Bubbierasco, we actually do know that it is an offspring of Nebbiolo and a rare, little-known variety called Bianchetto di Salluzzo).

These enormously interesting results were presented at a conference on Nebbiolo and written up in a seminal 2004 study that stoked curiosity but also caused some disappointment. Curiosity and disappointment were piqued because practically all the grapes on the aforementioned list imply that Nebbiolo's home is not the Langhe but the alpine foothills and higher slopes arching from northern Piedmont to northern Lombardy. In fact, all the grapes in this family tree share similar habitats. Vespolina's home is in Alto Piemonte; Neretto di S. Giorgio is mostly common in the Canavese, another northern Piedmont area; Bubbierasco is typical of the Salluzzese, still another cold Piedmont viticultural zone; and Brugnola, Negrera, Rossola and Rossolino Nero are not at all typical of Piedmont, but of Lombardy's Valtellina area. As you can tell, there is no Langhe present on that list. And so Nebbiolo, despite the fact it produces its greatest wines in the Langhe area of southern Piedmont and especially so in Barbaresco and Barolo, appears, based on these results at least, to be most likely born in alpine habitats, quite possibly those of Lombardy's Valtellina (where Nebbiolo Chiavennasca is the mainstay grape of local wines such as Sfursat, Grumello, Inferno, Sassella, and Valgella). Happily, for the Piedmontese (who would understandably prefer for Nebbiolo to be one of their own), more recent scientific data has come to the rescue suggesting that a Piedmontese birthplace for Nebbiolo may not be that unlikely after all.

Data presented by Gambino, Dal Molin, Boccacci, *et al* in 2017 shows the existence of seven different main Nebbiolo genotypes (in the study simply named genotypes A through G) that characterize all the Nebbiolo Lampia grapevines of Italy. In other words, on the basis of this study's results, it would appear that, at least at the present state of scientific knowledge (which unfortunately changes rather quickly), all of today's Nebbiolo Lampia grapevines descend from seven progenitors (and as we shall see, especially one in particular). Of these, the Nebbiolos of northern Piedmont and Lombardy (Valtellina) belong to the progenitor genotypes A and B, whereas those from southern Piedmont (Langhe and Roero) have the genetic profile of progenitor genotypes D, E, F, and G. Importantly, the study results also showed that there was a clear-cut geographical distribution of these Nebbiolo genotypes: some genotypes prevail in specific and at times very limited areas, and a few are altogether absent in some areas.

For example, genotype B was found to be most frequent in northern Piedmont: even more interestingly, it was the only genotype present in Valtellina (indicating that Valtellina has a very pure strain of Nebbiolo and quite possibly its very own). Genotype D was found in all areas under study (except Valtellina); genotypes G and E were associated mostly with southern Piedmont (the Langhe more so than the Roero). Northern Piedmont (Canavese and Alto Piemonte) and the lower Valle d'Aosta are apparently characterized by genotypes D, C and F (these last two genotypes are very closely related to genotype D). Therefore, this set of data, analyzing a likely network model of genotype relationships, suggests the ancestral genotype of Nebbiolo might be genotype D. Given it was determined to be the most widespread genetic profile in the cultivation areas of Nebbiolo (with the exception of Valtellina), it is likely (but not certain) that all other Nebbiolos descend from it, their genetic makeup morphing over time in response to the specific terroir factors at work in each specific area. As genotype D is of Piedmontese origin, and that written documentation of Nebbiolo's presence in Piedmont dates back to three centuries earlier than any known mention of Chiavennasca (Nebbiolo) in Lombardy, it stands to reason that Nebbiolo's Piedmontese origin makes some sense. It may not be the Langhe, but for some Barolo producers, at least it's Piedmont.

However, I caution readers that the volume of scientific data with respect to Nebbiolo's origin is still relatively small. For example, in order to confirm any one hypothesis relative to where exactly Nebbiolo hails from, a much larger number of genetic markers and old mother plants from all areas where Nebbiolo has been grown throughout the centuries must be investigated. Until this is done, there is simply no way of knowing for sure where Nebbiolo hails from exactly: what is certain for now is that it was probably not born in the Langhe, but in the alpine reaches of north-western Italy, probably in Piedmont, maybe not. Last but not least, I will also mention that Nebbiolo boasts a few other relatives, these slightly more distant than those mentioned previously, but still relatively close relatives nonetheless. These include Bressana, Ortrugo (a white grape from Emilia Romagna), and Chasselas (one of Switzerland's most typical white grapes, and not without interest in the context of this discussion, yet another alpine variety). Where there's smoke…

VITICULTURAL CHARACTERISTICS

A much-loved variety, Nebbiolo Lampia is actually a pain to work with. Perhaps not quite Sangiovese-like pain, but still. Its budbreak and flowering occur early (usually in the first ten days of April and the first ten days of June, respectively); *véraison* (the color change of the berries as they approach maturity) happens medium-early (usually in the second ten days of August) while the harvest takes place late in the year (Nebbiolo Lampia is rarely fully ripe before mid-October and it is usually picked in the last fifteen days of the month (and in days before climate change, November harvests were the norm). Those timelines clearly expose Nebbiolo Lampia to all sorts of weather-related problems (spring frosts, autumn rain and hail). Happily, it is a rather hardy variety: except for oidium (powdery mildew), Nebbiolo Lampia boasts very good to excellent resistance to most of the common grapevine diseases including peronospora (downy mildew) and grey rot. Its ability to stand up to *flavescence dorée*, one of the grapevine yellows diseases group (it's caused by *Candidatus Phytoplasma Vitis*, the vector of which is *Scaphoideus titanus*, a leafhopper) is far superior to that of Cabernet Sauvignon, Chardonnay, and Barbera. Such disease-resistance has a been proven to have a genetic basis, as recent scientific data has shown Nebbiolo Lampia's genome to have an over-representation of genes involved in disease resistance (Margaria, Ferrandino, Caciagli, *et al* 2014).

Biochemical data supported by transcript analysis showed that genes of the stem flavonoid pathway and of the anthocyanin and proanthocyanidin branches (this apparently a protective response to the disease) were expressed at greater concentrations in infected plants compared to healthy ones, and more so in Nebbiolo Lampia compared to Barbera. Compared to other wine grapes, for example Tannat and Corvina, Nebbiolo's DNA has a greater availability of disease resistance-associated genes (Margaria, Ferrandino, Caciagli, *et al* 2014; Roggia 2014; Gambino, Dal Molin, Boccacci, *et al* 2017) and consequently the grapevine benefits from greater disease-resistance. After that positive note, things become dicier for those who like to work with Nebbiolo Lampia.

As mentioned earlier in this chapter, Nebbiolo Lampia's early-budding and late-ripening makes it quite sensitive to both spring frosts and to autumn rains; but its early budding and late-ripening nature poses other problems too. Nebbiolo Lampia is a very vigorous variety and high canopies redolent of foliage are common in Nebbiolo vineyards (as compared to other Piedmontese varieties like Dolcetto that are trained low to the ground). With Nebbiolo Lampia, long pruning methods are necessary (the "long Guyot" technique, for example): however, while its fertility is good overall, Nebbiolo Lampia's first two-three basal buds are essentially sterile (or very poorly productive), and so planting vines within the same row closer than one meter apart is less than ideal. Farmers recuperate space by planting rows closer to each other (the sterility of Nebbiolo Lampia's basal buds is precisely one of the variety's aspects that nurseries have worked the most on in an attempt to develop clones unaffected by this problem). Limiting crop production is essential if a high quality Nebbiolo Lampia wine is the goal (yields have dropped from the three and a half kilograms of grapes per vine of the 1970s to the two kilograms of today), but excessively tight spacing of grapevine rows does not appear to be a great idea. Many producers have told me over the years that planting rows at greater than 5000-6000 plants per hectare does not work well with Nebbiolo Lampia (many still retain 4,000 as the ideal number of Nebbiolo plants per hectare) especially in view of the Langhe's rather rich, fertile soils which push an already vigorous variety to be even more vigorous. In general, excessively fertile soils characterized by high water-retention capacity push Nebbiolo Lampia's vigor to produces even more foliage than it normally would (so this is why soil drainage and slope gradient are very important when determining the quality of a Nebbiolo site: in this specific context, "quality" addresses more than just matters of lithological characteristics and mineral concentrations). Therefore, as Nebbiolo Lampia focuses its energy on vegetative growth, topping and deleafing are not options but absolutely necessary most years, even in these times of climate change (topping -also referred to as trimming- is the cutting off the ends of the shoots, a technique that ensures the grapevine no longer focuses on growing longer shoots, but redistributes its energy on the remaining branches and the grapes).

Of course, another manner by which to contain Nebbiolo Lampia's vigor is by matching it to an ideal rootstock, and this is why vigor-friendly rootstocks such as SO4 and Kober 5 BB are being phased out nowadays by most quality-oriented producers. However, the 5 BB rootstock is very common in many of the Langhe's older Nebbiolo Lampia vineyards, and the SO4 rootstock remains a darling of nurseries everywhere given its high rate of graft success. By contrast, note that a less vigorous Nebbiolo such as Nebbiolo Michet can get by on more vigor-inducing rootstocks and using them is probably a good idea in this case (see Chapter 2, NEBBIOLO MICHET). Nowadays, commonly used rootstocks for Nebbiolo Lampia include the 420A and the Paulsen 1103; by contrast, Nebbiolo Lampia does poorly when matched to the 3309 C and the 101.14 (in highly calcareous soils, at least). Many people feel that the Paulsen and the Kober prove better suited to Nebbiolo in more humid environments. Roberto Conterno also uses the 161/49, besides 420A and Kober rootstocks, but avoids the 41 B which he feels drives the production of big bunches with a less than ideal pulp to skin ratio and of too much vegetation (though much depends on what kind of soil type you deploy it in). Clerico's Ginestra Ciabot Mentin (ex-Ciabot Mentin Ginestra) was once all planted on 420A, a very good rootstock especially if there are larger quantities of active lime in the soil. At Giovanni Manzone they also like the 1103 Paulsen: it has the disadvantage of being very productive in fertile soils and if you fertilize too much (naturally or otherwise) it's even worse, but it does have the advantage of rooting deeply so it allows grapevines to resist droughty conditions well. And to show that opinions on the matter of rootstocks will vary considerably, Giovanni Corino says that the Kober rootstock is just fine especially in very dry years.

Despite Nebbiolo Lampia needing plenty of sunlight to ripen well, overly exposed, windy sites are best avoided, because excessively windy conditions are risky for Nebbiolo Lampia's buds and young shoots (characterized by rapid growth and considerable length). Still, the most prized Nebbiolo Lampia vineyard site in all of Barolo land has always been the *bricco* (in theory, the summit of the hill): beware that most everyone is under the mistaken impression that *bricco* refers to the "top of a hill", but in fact the term has a deeper meaning.

The exact translation of *bricco* is rather that of "well-protected summit of a hill", such as an amphitheatre. So, a *bricco* does not necessarily expose Nebbiolo Lampia to the windiest of situations. Nevertheless, Bruno Ceretto reiterates that well-exposed sites are always best for Nebbiolo Lampia. He once told me: "Ask anyone in Barolo where they'd ideally want their vineyards to be and the answer will always be the *bricco*, because those vines, despite being more exposed to the winds, are much better off when it hails and when it rains, neither one of which used to be rare events in this neck of the woods." And while Nebbiolo Lampia needs heat and sunlight to ripen fully (note that Nebbiolo Michet has a much lower requirement for heat units. See Chapter 2, NEBBIOLO MICHET), the heat has to be applied slowly and over a relatively long season in order for truly world class wines to be made. Otherwise, wines will be fleshy and thick, but without the magical perfume and overall complexity Nebbiolo's best wines are famous for (which is exactly what happens in those New World areas that are far too hot for Nebbiolo).

Nebbiolo Lampia's late ripening nature explains why historically it has been planted in mostly south-facing sites (*mezzogiorno*): also good are the *sorì della sera* (those vineyards exposed southwest in which grapes catch the afternoon sun), and even better nowadays given climate change, the *sorì del mattino* (those with southeastern exposures where the morning sun plays a bigger role). Differently from Nebbiolo Lampia, Nebbiolo Michet does not want too much sunlight and heat (its already small berries would only dehydrate and give even less juice), while Nebbiolo Rosé absolutely thrives in heat (see Chapter 2, NEBBIOLO MICHET. See also Chapter 3, NEBBIOLO ROSÉ). *Mezzanotte* exposures (or north-facing vineyards) have historically never been planted to Nebbiolo Lampia, though climate change may cause locals to rethink their options. Nebbiolo's need for enough heat and sun is why vineyard plots located at the top of hills (the aforementioned *bricchi*, the plural of *bricco*), where the exposure is 360 degrees and sunlight maximal, have always been especially prized (and this despite the risks posed by the potentially windy conditions).

In Barbaresco, examples of famous, high quality *bricco* vineyards are the Bricco di Treiso in the commune of Treiso and the Bricco di Neive in the commune of Neive; in Barolo, noteworthy *bricco* vineyards include the Bricco Fiasco vineyard (owned by the Azelia winery) and the Bricco Rocche (a Ceretto monopole), both of which are situated in the commune of Castiglione Falletto. In fact, some producers prefer a hillside *conca* position to the *bricco*: a *conca* is a small depression in the hill where wind is not a problem (though I suppose stagnating humidity might be). For example, a very famous, high quality *conca* vineyard in Barolo is the Conca of the Annunziata subregion of La Morra (as of 2011, the official name has been changed to just Conca), where wineries like Fratelli Revello and Mauro Molino have made some great wines over the years. Unfortunately, Barolo (and Barbaresco too) have become victims of their own success: as I have written before, the wines sell well and at high prices, and so Nebbiolo has been and still is being planted just about anywhere in the two denominations. In other words, even in those sites that had once been left for Dolcetto, Freisa and Barbera; and though producers are quick to point out that because of climate change what were once bad sites are now more than acceptable (of course they *would* say that, wouldn't they), but this is only true of some sites (D'Agata 2014). It is inescapable that, with a variety that is so site-sensitive, such decisions have repercussions; it follows then that not all Barolo wines are of the same quality level, even when made by the same talented producer, because the grapes do not really grow in what are first class sites for Nebbiolo Lampia. But while with Burgundy's wines (for example), the consumer is informed about the quality level of the various sites directly on the bottle's label (the *grand crus*, *premier crus*, *lieux-dits*, and *villages* levels), no such help is forthcoming with Barolo and Barbaresco (or any other Italian wine, for that matter). In Italy, when a producer is hot to trot and successful with one wine from one site, then all his or her wines are viewed, spoken of, and written up as being automatically wonderful, an attitude that defies logic but proves P.T. Barnum was right.

THE WINES

The importance of color

No discussion of Nebbiolo Lampia is complete, I dare say even acceptable, without at least mentioning this grape variety's unique pigment profile. Anthocyanidins are colored water-soluble pigments and belong to the phenolic biochemical group; they are responsible for the red, purple, and blue colors of fruits and vegetables (note that anthocyanidins appear red when placed in a low pH or acid conditions, but turn blue when the environment becomes alkaline). The anthocyanidins of *Vitis vinifera* grapevines are five: cyanidin, delphinidin, peonidin, petunidin, and malvidin, but are present in grapes and wines in only trace amounts; it is instead anthocyanins, or anthocyanidins bound to a sugar moiety (glucosides) that are common in wine grapes and responsible for their color. The five anthocyanins common to *Vitis vinifera* grapevines are called cyanine, delphinine, peonine, petunine, and malvine for short (their full, more accurate names are cyanidin-3-O-glucoside, peonidin-3-O-glucoside, and so forth).

These monomeric anthocyanins further experience acylation and/or polymerization to form conjugated grape anthocyanins derivatives; importantly, conjugated pigment concentrations vary greatly between different wine grapes and are a marker of wine grape identity (Escribano-Bailón, Guerra, Rivas-Gonzalo, *et al* 1995; Fossen, Cabrita, Andersen 1998; Castañeda-Ovando, de Lourdes Pacheco-Hernández, Páez-Hernández, *et al* 2009; Rolle, Torchio, Ferrandino 2012). In fact, the anthocyanins don't just help provide color, but are true phytochemicals that help maintain the plant's good health status. This is why anthocyanins are being increasingly studied as pharmacological agents, because they are potentially useful against human diseases too thanks to their anti-oxidant activity. At the time being, they are viewed by the scientific community as neutraceuticals that exert potential antidiabetic, anti-inflammatory, antimicrobial, antineoplastic, and anti-obesity effects, and may also prove helpful in the prevention of cardiovascular disease (Bors, Heller, Michel *et al* 1990; Tamura and Yamagami 1994; Wang, Cao, Prior 1997; Cho, Howard, Prior, *et al*. 2004; Ohguro, Ohguro, Katai, *et al* 2012; Pojer, Mattivi, Johnson, *et al* 2013). All these actions are related to their anti-oxidant and protective, defense activity.

Most importantly relative to wine grapes, is that individual anthocyanins are found not just in varying percentages in all wine grapes, but that each grape variety is characterized by its own specific pigment ratio. In other words, individual grape varieties are richer in some of the anthocyanins and less so in others, and this fact alone explains a great deal about the grape variety's characteristics (and consequently of their wines too). More important still is that the free forms and their derivatives (such as the acylated anthocyanins) differ greatly not just in terms of stability but in their concentration levels in wine grapes.

The anthocyanin derivates are much more stable than the free forms (the anthocyanin derivatives are conjugated or joined to another molecule, such as a sugar: this bond increases both the color and stability of the pigment molecule). The fact that free forms are relatively unstable is extremely meaningful, because all those grape varieties loaded with them are bound to make wines marked by less dark, less stable colors over time. Furthermore, some grape varieties have virtually no anthocyanin derivatives at all: examples include Nebbiolo Lampia, but also Pinot Noir and Sangiovese. It follows that 100% Nebbiolo Lampia wines (or 100% Pinot Noir or 100% Sangiovese wines) cannot have any large, or even small, presence of conjugated anthocyanins (in fact, relative to these three wine grapes, the anthocyanin derivatives make up less than 1% of the total pigment profile of the specific grape variety). Therefore, these molecules act much as fingerprints do in criminal law: if you were to find 4% or 6% or 10% or any other percentage of anthocyanin derivatives in a supposedly 100% Nebbiolo Lampia or Sangiovese or Pinot Noir wine, like it or not, the wine is not what it is said to be.

This finding is of extreme importance, *de facto* providing a means by which to tutor and verify the safety and authenticity of what we drink (or, more pointedly, of what we are *being told* we are drinking). It helps safeguard us all and succeeds where DNA analysis has not been especially successful up until now (the efficacy of the amplification technique on which DNA analysis is based is reduced in commercial wines given the presence of PCR inhibitors and the insufficient amounts of grapevine DNA), though a combination of new methodologies appears promising in this context too. (Nakamura, Haraguchi, Mitani, and Ohtsubo 2007; Pereira, Guedes-Pinto, and Martins-Lopes 2011; Bigliazzi, Scali, Paolucci *et al* 2012; Oganesyants, Vafin, Galstyan *et al* 2018; Boccacci, Chitarra, Schneider 2019).

Just as the red, brown, black or blonde hair of human beings is genetically determined, Nebbiolo Lampia's pigment profile is also gene-dependent, which means that Nebbiolo's variety-specific color is coded for by its DNA. And so, while viticultural and enological techniques might be able to kick up the wine's color by a notch or two, no amount of vineyard ingenuity or cellar alchemy will turn monovariety Nebbiolo Lampia wines into black-purple Merlot wine-wannabes. This is because monovariety Nebbiolo Lampia wines are specifically marked by a large proportion of peonine and cyanine, two relatively pale-colored and unstable pigments (they oxidize easily), and as mentioned previously (but it's worth repeating), by a virtual absence of conjugated anthocyanins (the latter represent less than 1% of the Nebbiolo total pigment profile).

This state of affairs determines not just the lighter hue of Nebbiolo Lampia wines relative to some other of the world's most famous red wines (say those made with Cabernet Sauvignon and Syrah), but also their relatively unstable coloration over time as well (wine lovers are well aware that for the most part, monovariety Nebbiolo Lampia wines, not just Barolos and Barbarescos, have a tendency to turn garnet sooner than wines made with say, Merlot or Syrah). Therefore, Barolos and Barbarescos are usually born medium- to dark red in color and often with a recognizable garnet tinge; none should ever look impenetrably deep ruby-blue, saturated purple or downright black.

A 100% Nebbiolo Lampia wine simply cannot be that color (although producers getting caught pouring you a purple wine – in fairness, a rare event nowadays compared to the late 90s - will look very distressed while giving you long-winded explanations as to why that might be so). As mentioned, there are methods by which Nebbiolo Lampia can be forced to give darker-colored (but not black or deep purple) wines than it would otherwise normally. All of the following contribute to making Nebbiolo Lampia wines with darker hues: judicious water deprivation and differentiated vineyard irrigation schedules; cluster exposure to direct sunlight; plant assimilate partitioning through leaf or cluster removal and stem girdling above or below bunches; pathogen infection; large reduction in yields; prolonged skin-contact of the must; and use of small oak barrels. Such decisions impact on the concentration of the total as well as the single pigment molecule levels in the grape skins (for that matter, not just of anthocyanins, but of other classes of flavonoids too).

Numerous studies have delved into the highly interesting world of Nebbiolo Lampia's pigments. For example, the anthocyanin profile of Nebbiolo Lampia skins and how it may be influenced by natural and human factors was investigated in an extremely cogent 2002 study conducted by Guidoni, Allara, and Schubert. The trio investigated the effects of cluster thinning (this term refers to removal of 50% of the cluster one month after bloom) for three consecutive years in a Barbaresco vineyard. Total anthocyanins and flavonoid concentrations were assessed by spectrophotometry (concentrations of individual anthocyanins were also determined by high-performance liquid chromatography). The data showed that, not unexpectedly, grape weight and grape skin weight increased slightly following thinning. Levels of soluble solids and berry skin anthocyanins and flavonoids were also higher in grapes from cluster-thinned plants. Very interestingly, cluster thinning increased the concentrations of cyanidin-3-glucoside, peonidin-3-glucoside, and, to a lesser extent, petunidin-3-glucoside, but concentrations of malvidin-3-glucoside and of acylated anthocyanins were not affected by cluster thinning. It is striking how in spite of viticultural management techniques aimed at increasing concentration of color in grapes (among other objectives), Nebbiolo Lampia remains faithful to its genetic disposition (as you would expect it to, frankly). Similar results and conclusions were drawn in a 2008 study by Ferrandino, Guidoni and Novello. Seasonal differences, 50% cluster thinning (CT) and 50% leaf removal (LR) were analyzed in Nebbiolo Lampia vines planted in the Barbaresco denomination.

Two different vintages were assessed: 2000 (generally hot and rainy) and 2001 (generally cooler than 2000 and at times downright droughty). Anthocyanin concentration increased only in the 2000 CT vines, but not significantly so (I caution my reader that I always use the term "significant", in all my wine writings with its scientific meaning only, otherwise I avoid using it), most likely because of overall reduction of anthocyanin concentration in the year's hot weather. By contrast, the 2001 wines boasted decreased total anthocyanin concentration (–20.7%) compared to the 2000 wines, most likely because of the year's droughty conditions. Individual anthocyanin concentrations varied as well: for example, the peonidin-3-glucoside/malvidin-3-glucoside ratio varied on average from 1.9 in 2000 to 1.2 in 2001 (clearly, it was higher in treated vines than in the control vines as well, but always remained in favor of the much lighter-colored peonine, which is typical of Nebbiolo Lampia and all Nebbiolos in general).

These observations confirm other study results showing that viticultural interventions cannot change the genetic imprint of Nebbiolo Lampia (or of all other grape varieties, for that matter): the fact that cluster thinning, a tactic that can make for darker looking and thicker-skinned berries is associated with increases of peonin and cyanin pigments (which are the paler colored ones) and not of the darker malvin pigment is telling. Even more important is the observation that conjugated anthocyanin concentrations remain unaffected (something that has been documented in studies of other grape varieties too), confirming that, independently of viticultural and winemaking methodologies, the conjugated anthocyanins in Nebbiolo Lampia wines remain unaffected and close to zero.

Therefore, monovariety Nebbiolo Lampia (or any Nebbiolo, for that matter) wines cannot have conjugated anthocyanins present in even small percentages (at most, around 1%). Such research data explains why proper Nebbiolo wines will never look impenetrably purplish-black *à la* Merlot. Nevertheless, and despite Nebbiolo's lack of deep hue, wines made with this grape variety age amazingly well, thanks to a combination of high dry extract, total acidity, tannins, and alcohol. And in ultimate analysis, I find the glowing red color of Nebbiolo wines, ranging from cherry red to crimson red to orange/garnet–tinged red to be just beautiful. I mean, who needs impenetrably dark colored wines anyways? You might even go as far as to say that unlike those steroid-enhanced bodybuilder-types who look great at a glance but then have trouble rising to the occasion, Nebbiolo's color and that of its wines always deliver.

Nebbiolo Winemaking in Barolo

Winemaking has changed considerably over the last fifty years in both Barbaresco and Barolo: greatly shortening the duration of maceration and fermentation and moving away from chestnut to oak barrels and/or barriques are just some of the modifications that have taken place in the Langhe. Initially, back in the nineteenth century, grapes were crushed mostly by foot, a messy but rather gentle manner by which to press grapes (certainly gentler than some of today's mechanical crushers). One of the last producers of Barolo and Barbaresco to engage in pressing his grapes by foot was Luigi Pira of the Barolo commune, who passed away in 1980; and while I don't know exactly how large a role pressing grapes by foot played in ensuring the high quality of his wines, clearly it didn't hurt the wines any (I have found Luigi Pira Barolos to be always amongst the best Barolos in all my tastings of old vintages such as those of, for example, Bartolo Mascarello and Vietti). Today, Luigi Pira's estate is owned by Chiara Boschis and is called E. Pira-Chiara Boschis (and though pressing grapes by foot is no longer done, the wines are still outstanding).

Another important technique of the time was the *ammostatura*, a technique in which uncrushed grapes were added back to the fermenting must that helped make for slightly fruitier and less tannic wines (in times when grapes were never destemmed and so stalks were left in the must all through maceration and fermentation). Fermentation was conducted in open-top fermenting vessels, the vertical wooden *tini* still visible in some of today's Barbaresco and Barolo cellars. The use of open-topped fermenting vats made sense, as it made breaking the cap (*cappello*, in Italian: those grape solids including pulp, skins and stalks rising to the top of the fermenting must thanks to the carbon dioxide produced by the yeasts) by using long poles a much easier endeavor. And at a time when temperature control was still nowhere in sight, having open-topped vats ensured that temperatures of the fermenting must wouldn't get out of hand and that the macero-fermentation process would be over in roughly two weeks.

These winemaking facts help explain why many older vintages of Barbaresco and Barolo, despite even excellent provenance (always a big problem with Italian wines) appear to have aged prematurely (clearly, premature and/or excessive oxidation is always a risk in wines left in contact with air), and why obvious nuances of volatile acidity are almost always present too (though a little volatile acidity adds a welcome note of freshness to wines, and unless it is present in copious amounts, I personally don't find a trace of it bothersome). It is also likely that this work methodology did nothing to enhance Barbaresco and Barolo's already palish red color any (remember that the color of a 100% Nebbiolo wine is never too dark to begin with, and if you allow the wine to have too much oxygen contact, well…).

Once the winemaking process was finished, wines were racked: before the arrival of pumps, this was done by hand (at least until the 1930s), with cellar staff carrying *brente* (wooden containers) strapped to their backs and so moved wine from one vat to another. The solids were pressed (and depending on the individual producer and vintage characteristics various amounts of press wine would have been added back to the liquid) and the wine aged for at least a year in large chestnut or Slavonian oak barrels (chestnut barrels were largely abandoned by the mid-twentieth century because of a variety of reasons: chestnut wood is too porous and tends to give off bitter flavors, and besides that, there's nobody left who still knows how to make barrels from chestnut wood anymore).

An important winemaking innovation became very important beginning with the 1930s. The *cappello sommerso* (literally "submerged cap" in English, from *sommerso*-submerged- and *cappello*-cap) technique was introduced and is still used to a degree by most producers of the area. It consists in not allowing the cap of solids to float freely atop the fermenting liquid as was done before, but rather in keeping the cap submerged (much as its name implies) by placing a wooden or stainless-steel disc a foot or two beneath the surface of the fermenting must. Therefore, the *cappello sommerso* technique allows the cellar staff greater freedom of movement (they do not have to worry about breaking up the cap at regular intervals) but also diminishes the likelihood of oxidation-and volatile acidity-related problems because neither is the fermenting must in contact with air nor do the cap solids run the risk of drying out.

However, in order to draw off sufficient color and tannin from the skins, and more so in those days of absent temperature control of the vats and the cellars, it was necessary to keep the must in contact with the skins for a relatively and dangerously long period of time (ranging from twenty to forty-five days on average). Clearly, such an extended duration meant running the risk of making tough, fruit-challenged wines as tannins would have plenty of time to leach out as alcohol levels began to rise. Wines made by the *cappello sommerso* method can be overly tannic for another reason too: it requires performing pump overs (or *rimontaggi*, in Italian) in order to help even the temperature and yeast populations within the vat. While less work-intensive and time-consuming than having to break up the cap manually, with pump overs liquid is moved from the bottom of the tank and sprayed into the top of the tank: in the old days this was done either by hand or more commonly with a pump (and neither method is particularly gentle on the skins). Even worse, some producers performed as many as four pump overs a day, further exacerbating the tannic content of the finished wine. There's no doubt that Barolo's and Barbaresco's reputation as being age-worthy wines of massive and at times brutal tannic power derived in large part from this method of winemaking.

Problems related to excessively long macerations/fermentations were greatly diminished with the development of temperature-controlled tanks. Such tanks come equipped either with refrigerant/cold water-filled belts (what in Italy are often referred to as *pance*, or "bellies"; I dare say not surprisingly, given that food is one of the two things Italians think most about) lining the tanks externally or with refrigerant-filled spiral tubes placed within the vats; all allow for temperature control of fermentation.

Generally speaking, most Barolo and Barbarescos of today are fermented at temperatures ranging between 26-30 degrees Celsius but it is safe to say that both lower and higher extremes have been reached and experimented with over the last three decades. I remember that temperature-controlled tanks became a common sight in Langhe cellars only in the late 1980s; prior to their advent, the only options winemakers had by which to quickly lower fermentation temperatures in years characterized by extreme heat were to either hose the wooden or cement tanks down with cold running water or to go as far as dropping (hopefully water-tight) packs of ice directly into the must. Umpteen producers including Bruno Giacosa told me that running cold water along the sides of the tanks was commonplace back in the 1970s and 1980s, and was still being done routinely in wineries without temperature control up until very recent times (in fact, right up until 2016 about 20% of Giacosa's vats didn't benefit from temperature control, although that clearly didn't stop the estate from making what are arguably Italy's best wines).

Producers have told me over the years this is exactly what they needed to do in the hottest years. At Luigi Oddero, they only had seven temperature-controlled tanks right up until 2008; in order to avoid temperatures going beyond 32 degrees Celsius, they used to perform a *délestage* in a temperature-controlled tank so as to cool off the must somewhat (then between 2009 and 2011 they increased their stock of temperature-controlled tanks so as to no longer have to do so).

Barbaresco and Barolo winemaking improved some more once a better understanding of the malolactic transformation process and its importance to fine wines was attained. For most of the twentieth century, the transformation of malic acid to lactic acid was left to run in an almost haphazard fashion; but in the 1980s producers became aware that greater control over this process and that carrying it out sooner rather than later (for example, immediately after the alcoholic fermentation) meant making much smoother wines endowed with a greater fruit presence. Finally, after the wine had finished its alcoholic fermentation and malolactic transformation, it was racked and aged for a minimum of two years in large 20-150 hectoliter round or oval Slavonian oak casks and another year in bottle or in cement tanks, then back into barrel. Prior to bottling (those estates that did estate-bottle rather than just sell bulk wine), producers would move their wine to large glass demijohns (*damigiane*, in Italian) so as to allow the wines further development in a wood- and oxygen-free environment.

Demijohns were everywhere in the Barolo (and Barbaresco) cellars as recently as the 1960s and 1970s: for example, in those years, at the Aldo Conterno estate roughly 80% of all the wine sat in demijohns before being bottled for sale. But the demijohns were done away with in the 1980s, as the transfer process from vat to demijohn is both energy- and time-consuming, not to mention rife with other potential problems too. The process of transferring wine from wood tanks to glass containers exposed the wine to the risks of oxidation, and wine quality was found to be too variable between bottled lots. Last but not least, the cumbersome glass vessels broke far too easily and often.

Up until the 1960s and 1970s, Barolo was mostly the home of the *negozianti* (the equivalent of the French *négociants*), as wine was not as popular as it is today and so didn't sell, forcing producers to bottle more because it was often just too difficult to sell all their grapes, and the economic return even when they did sell all their grapes was minimal. Producers remember that the less kind *negozianti* (a minority: for example, Borgogno and Ratti were considered true gentlemen) would purposely leave them with all the grapes on their cart in the middle of the town square until late in the day before buying. By doing so, the more unscrupulous *negozianti* would obtain a much more favorable price because the growers could not risk leaving their grapes to spoil in the midday heat and so were forced to sell. In this light, you understand why it is that estate bottling and labelling by *cru* was brought about more by necessity than conviction or desire.

These winemaking novelties introduced throughout the twentieth century had followed one another in fairly slow fashion, thereby making them easier to accept by the highly conservative Langhe producer fiefdom. All this changed in the early 1980s, when an onslaught of new winemaking theories and practical interventions took Barbaresco and Barolo by storm, and led to the creation of the local "modernist" and "traditionalist" schools of winemaking. In brief, the "modernist" school of thought believed that insisting on the winemaking ways of old meant continuing to make massively tough tannic, fruit-deficient wines that were unapproachable for as much as a decade after bottling and that were often marked by flaws.

Not unreasonably then, those who sponsored the "modernist" approach championed wines that were cleaner, more fruit-forward and much less marked by off-putting tannins, and that were readier to drink much sooner. In order to achieve such wines, the "modernists" expounded the virtues of a slew of winemaking interventions, such as greatly decreasing fermentation temperatures, with some modernist estates going as low as 22 degrees Celsius (lower fermentation temperatures help produce more approachable, fragrant wines); shortening the duration of fermentation (reducing it to as little to seven days but the better producers such as Conterno Fantino were careful to adapt to a vintage's characteristics, as opposed to blindly using a formulaic approach.

For example, in 1996, a slow ripening year, at Conterno Fantino they macerated for 10-12 days rather than the usual 7-8 days (typical back then) as there was more to extract; they used to go 20 days with cement tanks but were able to reduce this amount of time after 1994 when they got rid of them); introducing the use of roto-fermentors to shorten and speed up skin contact time; cultured yeasts; greatly increasing the frequency of racking (to as much as four times in the first year, and then twice a year in the following years); switching from large *botti* to *barriques*; moving away from Slavonian oak in favor of French oak (which is less porous and less aggressively tannic than its Slavonian counterpart); and using plenty of toasty new oak, at least in the early stages of their careers.

Clearly, all these actions were thought of and carried out with the goal of making higher pH, sweeter, gentler-textured wines generously endowed with notes of vanilla and other sweet spices (not by chance a flavor set much appreciated by the then burgeoning U.S. wine market and its wine critics, a population that unlike Europeans didn't drink much wine with their food -in those days, bottles of Perrier were a common sight on lunch tables, not bottles of wine- and so wines that had more in common with tropical fruit and butterscotch-loaded cocktails seemed just dandy in a wine tasting setting). Today, those producers that were once in the unabashedly modernist camp insist that large yield reductions were also part of their creed, though I for one don't recall that subject ever coming much up in discussions with any of them, discussions that were instead all too often bogged down by the I-can't-even-begin-to-tell-you-how-not-too-interesting were the pontifications about the many large gleaming roto-fermentors and endless stacks of brand new barriques crammed into the cellars. In fact, just as traditional winemaking needed to be woken up from the doldrums it had lulled itself into and had to change at least some of its ways, not all was good with the modernist winemaking approach.

For example, exaggeratedly decreasing skin-contact time was not a good idea, as it is now apparent that Nebbiolo Lampia wines made with minimal skin contact time have failed to develop the complexity they would have been capable of with more traditional winemaking approaches (witness many Barolos and Barbarescos from the stellar 1990 vintage which have aged less well than they should have, and without ever achieving the level of complexity one would have expected from a similarly memorable vintage).

The modernist mantra was in heavy contrast to the "traditional" way of making Barbaresco and Barolo, which relied on long skin contact, relatively high fermentation temperatures, use of natural yeasts, use of large Slavonian oak *botti* and aging the wines at glacial pace for at times extensive periods prior to going into bottle. Clearly, the modernists had more than a right to criticize this school of thought and action, because it meant making many wines that were literally undrinkable at a young age, and that never came around to being enjoyable, even if they did age (which I point out is altogether different from aging well).

Only those traditional producers who harvested perfectly healthy and optimally ripe grapes succeeded in producing wines that were yes, structured, but also blessed with velvety textures and noteworthy degrees of complexity, not to mention clean. In any case, differences between the two schools of thought were so marked that producers squarely divided into two camps, and the modernist-traditionalist confrontation took on the semblance of a holy war (back then, you were mostly either in one camp or the other). Mercifully, cooler heads and open minds prevailed, with both camps coming to realize that some of the stuff the other guys were prattling on about made sense after all.

For example, Bruna Giacosa, who comes from as traditionalist a winemaking family can be in either Barolo or Barbaresco has no trouble admitting that though she loved her father's wines she always found that having to wait fifteen years for them to come around was not exactly to her liking. She began to like them more when they became slightly more approachable early on (and not necessarily because of any major interventions in the vineyard or the cellar, but simply because the combination of older vines and climate change allowed for better physiologic ripening). Consequently, in a commendable sign of reciprocal open-mindedness, some of the innovations championed by members of one school were taken up by many of those belonging to the other.

As a result, very few truly purely "traditionalist" and "modernist" producers remain today (though there are a few). That fact recognized, wine lovers still routinely ask me in which of the two categories Barbaresco and Barolo producers fall into, but that division is best put aside once and for all, save for a handful of names where it might still be pertinent.

Aromas and flavors of Nebbiolo wines

In general, a good Nebbiolo wine will always smell and taste of rose petals, violet, red cherry (this in a large spectrum of possibilities: sour red cherry is the most common descriptor, but notes of candied red cherry and dehydrated red cherry are also common; black cherry is generally more common in warmer years), star anise, white pepper, minerals, tar, and sweet spices (cinnamon, nutmeg). By contrast, notes of coffee, cocoa, black pepper, bell pepper, sage (and other dried herbs), butter, vanilla, tobacco are not common at all in Nebbiolo's wines (unless the wine is especially old or strongly dominated by oak). I would encourage all wine lovers and experts alike to commit these descriptors to memory (this because a wine's aromas and flavors derive mostly, outside of oenological alchemy, from the specific variety's precursor molecules that thanks to alcoholic fermentation are turned into wine aroma and flavor descriptors we typically associate with each variety).

Be aware that the note of tar that is often described and written about in young Barolo and Barbaresco wines is really only found in wines with some age on them (in my experience, at five years or older); young Barolo and Barbarescos will exude a hint of camphor, not tar (though the two can be easily confused by less experienced tasters). By contrast, an obvious note of fresh apricot and/or peach is quite evident in young Barbarescos and Barolos, and even more so when whole bunch fermentation is carried-out (or when plenty of stems are left); such yellow stone fruit descriptors are never found in Barolos that are more than ten years old. For more information on the biochemistry of Nebbiolo's specific aroma and flavor molecules and terroir factors that make its wines smell and taste the way they do, I refer you to *Italy's Native Wine Grape Terroirs* (D'Agata 2019) where you'll find what remains to date the definitive dissertation and analysis of that fascinating subject.

Terroir or bust

It is not just the relatively pale color of its wines that characterizes all Nebbiolo biotypes and their wines. Another trademark of Nebbiolo Lampia and all the Nebbiolo biotypes is how well they translates even minute differences in terroir in the glass. In general, Nebbiolos prefer soils with good drainage, a subalkaline pH (though it fares very well in the acid soils of the Alto Piemonte too) and a wealth of micro-elements including magnesium, manganese, iron, copper, boron, zinc, potassium, copper and phosphorus. Limestone marls and compacted sands are most suitable to making great age-worthy wines. All of which describes the soils of the Langhe very well. For this reason, the Nebbiolo wines of Barolo and Barbaresco are absolutely unique and quite unlike

Nebbiolo wines made anywhere else. And the same can be said of monovariety Nebbiolo wines from areas as different as those of Boca, Donnas, Gattinara, Grumello and Lessona, for example.

Actually, Nebbiolo grows better than most people realize in a variety of soils and of altitudes; however, while perfectly fine wines can be made in a relatively large range of different weather and soil conditions, replicating the exact aroma and taste profile of a Nebbiolo wine that one might have liked from a specific "somewhere else" is inherently very difficult. This is because of the extreme site-specificity of Nebbiolo, a truly defining characteristic of the variety; site-specificity is the hallmark of great Barolo and Barbarescos, wines that are very different from all other Nebbiolo wines made outside of the immediate production zone.

In fact, Barolo and Barbaresco wines also vary greatly amongst themselves, mainly as a result of the site in which the grapes are grown (provided wines are made in a similar manner and all other parameters are more or less the same). There are undeniable differences in the soils that characterize each Barolo commune, a diversity that plays a huge role in what the finished wines will taste like; and in those cases where soil differences are minimal, then exposure and altitude become all important. I remember that Bruno Giacosa once told me (June 2005 interview) that there was literally no difference between Falletto and Vignarionda (back then spelled Vigna Rionda), a statement that seemed to border on the almost blasphemous to a Vigna Rionda lover such as myself. But Bruno's point was that the exposure changed so much in both vineyards that sections of one vineyard were better than some sections of the other, and viceversa.

And so it is that over the centuries farmers and grape brokers alike have been keenly aware of the highest quality sites for Nebbiolo: clearly, those were the grapes always sold at a premium. In reality, Barolo and Barbaresco producers were never much interested in making single vineyard wines, believing (not unreasonably) that a judicious blend of grapes grown in different parts of the production area would make the best, most balanced wines (documents from centuries past show how the French also shared this view –some, at least - despite that country's perceived *cru* first and foremost based mentality).

In Barolo and Barbaresco, the first wines labelled with a *cru* name began to appear in the 1960s (the 1961 Barolo Bussia was the first, courtesy of Beppe Colla, launched back when he owned Prunotto), and Alfredo Currado did the same with his Rocche di Castiglione (then called just Rocche). In more recent times, beginning with the 1980s, an increasingly large number of Barolo and Barbaresco vineyard areas/districts have been identified; with some sites that have always been prized more than others (Cannubi, for instance). The grapes grown in one specific vineyard district can potentially translate into the glass what that specific site is about (or perhaps more accurately, could be about). This is not at all dissimilar to the differences presented by wines made from Pinot Noir grapes grown in Chambolle-Musigny's famous Les Amoureuses *cru* or those made with grapes grown in Griotte-or Chapelle-Chambertin. Hence, just as it is, for example, with red and white Burgundy, Mosel Riesling and Alsace Gewurztraminer wines, the wines of Barolo and Barbaresco will differ noticeably from one another depending on where the grapes are grown (and in the case of those especially large (too large) vineyard districts, wines will also differ depending on where exactly the grapes are grown within that same cru).

I point this is true not just of some too large Barolo crus such as Bussia and San Pietro, but of many other viticulturally prized areas of the world too (for example, I can make a very strong case that Alsace's Brand grand cru should be broken down into one small grand cru and three premier crus, plus a bunch of *lieux-dits;* similarly, Burgundy's Clos de Vougeot and Charmes-Chambertin could also use going on a diet too, much as the Sonoma Coast AVA in California could also be much better defined and partitioned, with nobody being the worse for wear). All wine grapes can translate the nuances of site in the glass, but Nebbiolo, much like Riesling and Pinot Noir, seems to be better at it than most other wine grapes. Or at the very least, the key with monovariety Nebbiolo wines is that, as long as the wines being compared are made in fairly similar ways, their somewhereness in the glass, or their signature of place, will always be very recognizable.

In Italy, Nebbiolo Lampia and all the Nebbiolo biotypes only grow in Piedmont, Lombardy, Sardinia and the Valle d'Aosta, but it's in the first of those four regions where you'll find by far the largest expanses of Nebbiolo plantings. Sardinia's Nebbiolo plantings are smaller than initially believed because they were partially misidentified at the outset (some plots previously believed to be Nebbiolo are in fact of Dolcetto). However, it is neither accurate nor fair to write that all of Sardinia's Nebbiolo plantings are of Dolcetto, because Nebbiolo has long been grown in Sardinia, if in small quantities mostly in the island's northeastern Gallura area (it is more than likely the Sardinian Nebbiolo is all Nebbiolo Lampia, but until further studies are done on this little-known Nebbiolo population, we really cannot know for sure).

There locals still like to call it Nebiolo (with one "b" only, as was commonly done throughout Italy right up until the 1960s) to further underscore its local identity. In fact, documents exist that Nebbiolo was first brought to the island in the 1800s by General La Marmora who believed the hills around the town of Gallura to be ideally suited for this finicky variety. Nebbiolo has become such a fixture there that, in 1998, the *Confraternità del Nebiolo* (the Confraternity of Nebiolo, in English) was founded. Locals have nicknamed the Nebbiolo wine of the area as the "ruby prince of Luras", where it has been an integral part of the traditional lifestyles of local denizens.

Beyond Barolo: Nebbiolo and its wines elsewhere in the world

Wine lovers are well aware Nebbiolo undergoes a complete personality change once it leaves its homeland, and that Nebbiolo wines made outside of Barbaresco and Barolo, though not at all bad and in some cases downright excellent, bear very little resemblance to those two wines. Very site-sensitive, much like Pinot Noir and unlike Cabernet Sauvignon (the former, like Nebbiolo, is dominated by the terroir; the latter dominates it), it is hard to produce truly great Nebbiolo wines just anywhere (the fact that everyone keeps trying to, not just in Piedmont but all over the world, lends credence either to the saying of "no pain, no gain" or to the fact that Nebbiolo is a great grape everyone wants to, much like with Pinot Noir, try their hand at making great wines with).

But while getting Nebbiolo to deliver its magic in a large diversity of terroirs has long been the equivalent of a Sisyphean task, the good news is that it appears like it's no longer next to impossible to achieve. Just like it was with Pinot Noir, where as recently as the 1970s there were neither good nor large volumes of noteworthy Pinot Noir wines made outside of Burgundy (clearly no longer true today, with many wonderful Pinot Noir wines made in Oregon, New Zeland and Ontario's Niagara region, as well as in limited sections of California), worldwide quality of Nebbiolo wines is on the rise too.

Even more interesting is how some of these new wines not only are excellent wines in their own right, but how (probably to the chagrin of at least some Piedmontese) remarkably Piedmont Nebbiolo-like they are. Clearly, nobody will ever mistake wines from California, Chile or Australia for Barolo, but all you need to do is try the truly outstanding wines made by California's Giornata and Haarmeyer wineries to know exactly what I mean. Ad they are not the only names to come to my mind, because over the last five years, I have increasingly tasted good Nebbiolo wines from all over the world: all express a different aroma and flavor profile than the best Nebbiolo wines from Italy do, but each at least reminds you of the Nebbiolo variety while speaking of a specific place. And therein lies their charm and their importance.

Clearly, the unique magic that are the wines of Barbaresco and Barolo remains elusive, and most likely, given the large diversities in soil, exposures, climates, water regimens and other factors affecting the way wines look, smell and taste between the world's countries, it is neither possible nor reasonable to expect a New Zeland, South African or Oregon Nebbiolo wine to duplicate Barolo or Barbaresco in the glass (and viceversa, for that matter). But frankly, that shouldn't even be the point: striving for a similar result would be not only futile, but wrong, as wines should speak of the place they are from and the people who make them. I love Barbaresco and Barolo wines, but I also drink all the New World Nebbiolo wines I can get my hands on, finding it both fun and enlightening.

Italy boasts roughly 6,407 hectares planted to Nebbiolo of which roughly 5,499 hectares are in Piedmont, 811 hectares in Valtellina (Lombardy), and 45 hectares in the Valle d'Aosta; another 52 hectares are said to be grown in Sardinia but part of those grapevines are actually of Dolcetto, so Sardinia's actual total Nebbiolo hectarage is lower (what these numbers also tell us is that Piedmont boasts roughly 85% of all the Nebbiolo grown in Italy: it was only 75% ten years ago). Worldwide, there are plantings of Nebbiolo in many different countries: roughly 191 hectares in Mexico, 115 hectares in Australia (and roughly a hundred growers/producers!), 66 hectares in the USA, and 10 hectares in Chile (OIV data, 2015).

Chapter 2

NEBBIOLO MICHET

Ian D'Agata

Nebbiolo Michet (just so you know, the purists in the Langhe prefer to write this biotype's name as Michét) is a biotype of Nebbiolo Lampia resulting from an infection with the grape fanleaf virus (GFLV) and/or the grapevine fleck *virus* (GFkV). That is what we have all believed to be true of Nebbiolo Michet for the last fifteen years or so. Therefore, under this light, I could have very well just included the discussion of Nebbiolo Michet in a generic "Nebbiolo" chapter, but given how important this type of Nebbiolo has been throughout the last century or so in Barolo, and how it has always been considered one of the three main types of Nebbiolo (along with Nebbiolo Rosé: see Chapter 3), I believe Nebbiolo Michet deserves its own chapter. In fact, both Nebbiolo Michet and Nebbiolo Rosé present enough distinguishing features from Nebbiolo Lampia that it is worth highlighting each on its own. It's not just the grapes that show differences, but their wines too: you need to recognize as much, because otherwise you just don't know Nebbiolo and its wines. In ultimate analysis, Nebbiolo Michet (and Nebbiolo Rosé) have been an integral part of Barolo and its wines throughout history, and their contributions to the wine and the area need to be known, highlighted, and remembered. After all, without studying the past and learning from it, we are forever condemned to repeating our mistakes, and we will always be invariably and inevitably poorer. As I have written before, there is no future, without a past.

AMPELOGRAPHY AND WINES OF NEBBIOLO MICHET

Nebbiolo Michet: a Lampia biotype or maybe not?

Everything we know (or rather, that *we think* we know) about Nebbiolo Michet is based on the premise that virus-induced mutations in Lampia's DNA led to the birth of Michet, a Nebbiolo biotype with a very different morphology and vineyard behavior. A morphology and a behavior that really do seem like they are the result of an infection that stunts growth and life expectancy to a degree. Michet grows more slowly and less effectively than Lampia: and so not surprisingly, Michet's bunch looks scrawnier, smaller, and cylindrical (by contrast, Lampia's bunch is much fuller and typically pyramidal in shape: it just looks healthier). Nebbiolo Michet's bunch is also much more tightly-packed; it's also a smaller bunch, its grapes are smaller than Lampia's too and with usually have a slightly darker coloration. Importantly, Michet is characterized by short internodes (which leads to more foliage than with Lampia), highly indented leaves, and reduced fertility and vigor (the highly indented leaves are almost always a sign of viral infection). With a little experience, it is impossible to confuse Michet with Lampia when walking in the vineyards. After all, it is Michet's appearance that gives it its name: *michet* derives from the Piedmontese dialect word *micca*, or a *baguette*-shaped loaf of bread.

Therefore, there are plenty of clues by which becomes only logical to infer that Nebbiolo Michet is a virus-affected grapevine, not the least of which are enzyme-linked immunosorbent assay (ELISA) test results proving the presence of the virus in Nebbiolo Michet populations. And so it was that we all have come to believe that because of its disease what was originally a Nebbiolo Lampia mutated over time into Nebbiolo Michet. In so doing, the grapevine became another of Lampia's many biotypes (and for a while, given the quality of its wines, the most famous biotype of all). However, that belief may not be as solidly grounded as we all think. In fact, it may well be wrong (and it wouldn't be the first time that what we think we know about wine grapes has been proven to be incorrect). For example, it has long been known that some Nebbiolo Michet plants show no evidence of the virus whatsoever. Why this is so has never been clearly understood, but was always attributed to either to our technology's inability to pick up the virus presence or to some error in experimental procedure. But can we be sure that is really the case? More than one producer has told me over the years that, though rare, Barolo's vineyards harbor Nebbiolo Michet vines that do not appear to have ever been touched by any virus. Gaja, for example, has found non-virused Nebbiolo Michet grapevines in the Silio-Santa Maria area.

Furthermore, many Nebbiolo Michets behave unexpectedly and completely differently from other Nebbiolo Michets (see below, "What the producers say"). For example, there exist Nebbiolo Michet vines the productivity and life expectancy of which isn't really that stunted at all.

The question arises: could it be that what we think we know about Nebbiolo Michet is at least partly mistaken? Current scientific wisdom has led us all to accept that Nebbiolo Michet is nothing but a virus-affected biotype of Nebbiolo Lampia. But is that really true? I wonder. It could also be that there exist different populations of similar-looking Nebbiolo grapevines that we have all conveniently lumped together under the "Nebbiolo Michet" banner, but that are different grapevines. Some of these Michet-looking grapevines may actually not be virus-affected at all, and are instead a distinct variety/ies from Nebbiolo Lampia much as been shown to be the case with Nebbiolo Rosé. Or maybe they are just Nebbiolo Lampia biotypes that through habitat- and/or sexual reproduction-induced mutations look and behave something like Nebbiolo Michet, but are *not* Nebbiolo Michet as we know it. To be clear, there is no doubt whatsoever that there exists a very large population of fanleaf virus-affected Nebbiolo Lampias that morphed into what we describe as Nebbiolo Michet. But this does not mean that all Nebbiolo grapevines in the Barolo vineyards out there that look and behave like Nebbiolo Michet are in fact virus-affected Nebbiolos or that they are all what we consider to be "Nebbiolo Michet". This would go a long way in explaining why some Nebbiolo Michets seem to live relatively long healthy lives and produce more than enough grapes. Yes, they live less long and produce less grapes than does Nebbiolo Lampia, but that might be normal behavior for this "other" Nebbiolo variety or biotype that we yet don't know much about, the behavior and morphology of which have nothing to do with a virus being present or not. Clearly, it is not lost on me that it may well be that these healthier looking and behaving "Nebbiolo Michets" that show no sign of viral presence do carry it because it is such a minimal viral load that we are unable to pick its presence up 100% of the time. However, I trust you will agree with me when I say that there is, at the very least, something to think about here.

On this subject, the totally brilliant 2017 work by Gambino, Dal Molin, Boccacci and associates (see chapter 1, NEBBIOLO LAMPIA) provides further food for thought. In their study, short-reads genomic data clearly showed single nucleotide variants among three Nebbiolo clones (CVT 71, CVT 185 and CVT 423) that were diagnostic of three different Nebbiolo biotypes, respectively of Michet, Lampia and Picotener. Now we assume that the DNA differences presented by the Michet and the Picotener relative to the Lampia are the consequence of a virus in the case of the Michet and to a different habitat for the Picotener, but it may not be so simple. Just as the Picotener might have genetic differences induced by the environment it lives in, it may be that not all of Michet's genetic differences are only and all the result of a viral disease. Perhaps some of differences in morphology and behaviors it expresses are not due to a virus at all; and perhaps it's not even a Nebbiolo Michet at all. At the present state of our scientific knowledge, all that I have just written is only a matter of conjecture, and whether there is any truth or consequence to that line of reasoning remains to be seen. But that's the way science works: you make an observation; it dawns on you that it's a little strange or novel and you wonder why it is; you think about the potential mechanisms that might make it happen; you reason about what the potential outcomes might be; and how ultimately those outcomes may help, hinder or just simply what they might mean for humanity. In the case of Nebbiolo Michet, I think there is still much we need to learn, and just conveniently lumping all of Nebbiolo Michet into the "virus-affected Nebbiolo Lampia" cauldron may neither be correct nor the right thing to do. As we have seen countless times before with many other grape varieties growing in countries all over the world, what we believe and what we think we know about wine grapes are often very different things from what is actually going on and is true.

What Nebbiolo Michet brings to the table

The morphologic and viticultural characteristics of Nebbiolo Michet (or what we have identified up to this point in time as being "Nebbiolo Michet") are such that recognizing its presence (or absence) in any Barolo you drink is really not that hard. In truth, that comment applies especially to Barolos from the 1970s and 1980s made by competent producers: in that case, Barolos top-heavy with Michet were fairly easy to recognize, because Barolos made with Michet really were more concentrated and structured. Characterized as it is by a smaller bunch and berries (hence a higher skin to pulp ratio), Michet wines always tend to be even more concentrated and structured than Barolos made with Lampia. Of course, you could find yourself thinking that given just how big and structured any Barolo made with Nebbiolo Lampia normally is already, how much more structure do you really need? But back then, yields were much higher, and so Barolos were less concentrated than they are today; therefore, Michet's contribution was not just recognizable, but much appreciated. Actually, (true) Michet is about much more than just structure: its capacity to give wines that are at once powerful and velvety, exuding noteworthy amounts of charm and refinement despite their sheer power, is this biotype's trump card.

In fairness, such characteristics are hardly lacking in wines made with Lampia, which is a great Nebbiolo in its own right and has the advantage of being a much more dependable and reliable producer of grapes than Michet (which is, after all, at least at the present level of scientific knowledge, a diseased grape). Unfortunately, outside of the well-documented clonal selections they might have planted over the years, most producers don't really know what biotypes are planted in their older vineyards, and so trying to discuss the merits of your favorite current Barolo (or Barbaresco) in terms of "Michet to be or not to be" is difficult (actually, as I have found out the hard way in over thirty years of talking to Barolo's producers, when it comes to old vineyards even simple stuff like rootstock data is unavailable, never mind the biotype planted there).

In any case, because Nebbiolo Michet had always been favorably viewed in the past (an opinion that has somewhat changed recently, as I shall address shortly), there was a strong push to rid Nebbiolo Michet of the virus and create disease-free clones to plant. Which is exactly what happened: today, many modern-day Nebbiolo clones are derived from the Nebbiolo Michet biotype (see APPENDIX A, *Table 1.3*; *Table 1.4*; *Table 1.5*; and *Table 1.6*). Therefore, when it comes to Nebbiolo Michet, today's Barolo vineyards are partly planted to old vine authentic Michet as well as newer Michet clones that, as I shall address shortly, may or may not *really* be as Michet-like as people were hoping they would be.

Where to find it

It follows that unless you drink Barolos and Barbarescos made from young vines for which there exists a traceable clonal selection documentation (but whether the new clones really replicate the greatness of old Michet is the subject of much debate, as we shall see), the exact contribution of each Nebbiolo biotype to the wine in your glass is admittedly hard to come by. An extremely interesting summary (Soster and Cellino 1998) of the proceedings at a conference devoted to Barolo zonation comes to our rescue. It presented data relative to twenty-four Barolo estates and thirty different vineyards showing that Nebbiolo Lampia was present in twenty-eight of the thirty vineyards studied; Nebbiolo Rosé was found to be growing in five of the thirty vineyards (confirming my impression that this cultivar is much more present in Barolo vineyards than even the producers themselves realize); by contrast, Nebbiolo Michet was found in only two vineyards. But differently from Nebbiolo Rosé, which was never found to be the dominant variety in any of the thirty vineyards, Michet was the most planted Nebbiolo in those two vineyards.

My own experience, based on roughly thirty years of visiting Barbaresco and Barolo wineries, interviews with the owners, their vineyard and cellar hands, as well as poring over the specific, very long, questionnaires I have had producers respond to over the years, is that you can extrapolate these findings to hundreds of Barolo wineries. Simply put, back in the 1970s and 1980s, there were entire vineyards planted to Nebbiolo Michet, because it was felt to be, no ifs, ands, or buts, the superior Nebbiolo variety.

Make no mistake about it: that is precisely what you heard, time and again, every single time you visited a Barolo producer. Every. Single. Time. Today producers sing a different tune, but it does not change the fact that entire generations of Barolo producers felt that Nebbiolo Michet was the best of the best of all possible Nebbiolo worlds. And no, they weren't all drunk. So, when you hear Barolo producers tell you just how swell everything is today and so much better than the past, it has to give you, me, and everyone else at least some pause for thought as to exactly *why* that is. In any case, though Nebbiolo Michet's plantings never reached the *numero uno* position, this biotype did have entire vineyards devoted to it. By contrast, Lampia (I include both Lampia a Foglia Intera and Foglia Incisa in this count is found in practically every single Barolo (and Barbaresco) vineyard.

And so, while the exact percentages of Michet planted in Barolo (and Barbaresco) vineyards is unknown, based on my data, a reasonable guess is that the Nebbiolo of the Langhe is so divided: 75-80% Nebbiolo Lampia,

20-25% Nebbiolo Michet and 5-10% Nebbiolo Rosé (but the total Langhe Nebbiolo Rosé hectarage is likely more than is commonly believed/known. See Chapter 3, NEBBIOLO ROSÉ). Relative to the wines, a rough but fairly accurate estimate is that 75% of all Barbaresco and Barolos made are 100% Nebbiolo Lampia, and the rest are blends of the three main biotypes. For the most part, 100% Nebbiolo Michet Barolos were more common up until the mid-1990s, but such wines are now rare. They were also always much more common in Barolo than they are in Barbaresco; and while that statement may not seem intuitively logical at first, for reasons I shall illustrate shortly it is actually easy enough to understand why things would have been so (see below).

If all this talk has brought out the Indiana Jones in you and you are now set on embarking on a Michet viti-archeological quest, where do you go looking for old vine true Michet? Well, let's see: for one, over the years, at some estates they have told me that Nebbiolo Michet performs best in Barolo's Monforte commune, especially in those areas characterized by sandier soils, such as those of Bussia Soprana and Pianpolvere Soprana.

The reference to the presence of "sandier soil" and the Bussia cru is not the throwaway line or comment it might appear to be at first glance: quite the contrary, it is highly relevant in this context. Given that Michet contributes even more power to the finished wine, it makes sense that there would not be much need for it in parts of Monforte and of Serralunga, the wines of which are already more than well-equipped in the power department thanks to the abundance of clay and limestone in the soils. By contrast, it is only logical to assume that sandy-rich sites that are not known for especially powerful Barolos may indeed benefit from the planting of Nebbiolo Michet, and this explains why Nebbiolo Michet was always planted more in some parts of the Barolo denomination than in others. But as any five years old expert in the building of sand castles will tell you, there is sand and there is sand.

For example, my own experience over the years is that Michet does not perform especially well in La Morra, doing well only in very specific parts of that township. From those sections of La Morra's territory that are very sandy (think of, for example, the Santa Maria fraction: see Chapter 7, BAROLO TERROIR, The Barolo Communes subchapter), the Michet wines have always struck me as certainly more structured (even massive, by La Morra standards) but lacking in the nuance and fleshy fruit of La Morra's best Barolos. Understandably enough, in the past some La Morra producers did look to plant Michet almost exclusively there, in an attempt to make up for the lack of structure of typical sandier soil-derived Nebbiolo wines with Michet's power; but in practice, I don't think things really worked out that way. Or rather, the power might have been there, but at the expense of everything else. So, you might say that, depending on where you plant it, what power giveth, it also taketh away.

A very good Barolo that was 100% Nebbiolo Michet, if you can still find it, is Gianni Voerzio's 1982 Barolo La Serra, which, besides being a very good if somewhat rigid and monolithic (a lack of nuance that Barolos made wholly with Michet are at times saddled with) Barolo, proudly stated on the back label that it was made with "100% Michet" (go ahead, just take a look). The perception of Nebbiolo Michet's superiority was so strong that producers also planted it in less sandy sites too. For example, another Barolo made with 100% Nebbiolo Michet was the Cordero di Montezemolo/Monfalletto estate's Barolo Enrico VI, made from the Villero vineyard district of Castiglione Falletto. That was one of the most famous Nebbiolo Michet Barolos of all time (and remained a 100% Nebbiolo Michet wine until the end of the 1970s).

One might think that Michet would have also been planted prevalently in the Verduno commune, given that Barolos from there tend to be earlier-maturing and lighter-bodied than those of other communes. After all, Verduno's Barolos have plenty to boast when it comes to perfume but much less so in the way of architectural framework. It would seem logical for Verduno's producers to like having some extra backbone in their wines as provided by Michet's presence, but my research doesn't really point to a preponderance of Michet planted there (see below in *What the producers say*). Conversely, one would also expect places such as Serralunga to be less planted to Michet (given that Serralunga's wines have no shortage of power and structure and so do not need Michet) but again, I am not sure that is the case either.

There are other reasons that help explain why Nebbiolo Michet might have been more or less planted in specific viticultural areas. In fact, besides soil, the microclimate of the vineyard in which Michet is or is going to be planted in is just as important. Given Michet's morphologic characteristics I illustrated earlier, and its penchant to give more powerful, concentrated wines, it follows that very warm sites are, in theory at least, more prone to giving Nebbiolo Michet wines dangerously teetering on the brink of overipeness and of being almost too massive for their own good. This is why the more competent producers always planted Michet in vineyards situated at slightly higher altitudes, or in the highest reaches of any vineyard (this has changed a bit with the onslaught of global warming). However, the end result also depended very much on what the individual producer liked, and what she or he were after.

For example, the vineyard owned by the Mauro Molino estate located in what used to be the Gallinotto vineyard area (now a part of the larger Berri vineyard district) was once mostly planted with Michet. Not at all surprisingly, there the Michet was planted in the highest reaches of the vineyard area only (in the *parte alta*), but not in the much warmer lower part of the slope (the *parte bassa*) where Lampia rules undisturbed. I cannot stress to you enough just how very interesting this observation is, because Gallinotto (and the larger Berri vineyard district it is located within: see Section II, Chapter 9, BERRI file) is not in and of itself an especially warm site. And still, already back in the 1990s, Molino felt that Michet was best suited to cooler parts of the vineyard (so just imagine nowadays, with climate change). For this reason, unlike other producers like the Fratelli Revello (see below), Molino never planted any Michet in his Conca vineyard, a much hotter site than Gallinotto.

In my experience, at the best estates at least, such things never happen by chance: Michet is found in a specific spot and not elsewhere for a good reason. Most likely, the original owner of the vineyard that had originally planted the site that Molino later bought did not want to grow even smaller berries than Michet normally has. Which is exactly what would have happened had he planted the lower reaches of his vineyard in Gallinotto with Michet. (Are you beginning to understand why saying that it doesn't matter if it's Nebbiolo Lampia, Michet or Rosé in the vineyard and the wine, is wrong at best and ridiculous at worse?) Why do I say smaller grapes? Smaller because of the unavoidable dehydration resulting from growing Michet in the vineyard's warmer lower section. Remember, in those days nobody was trying to make quality wines, but rather were looking to just sell grapes and/or wine, and lots of them; therefore, it is only logical to assume that raisin-like grapes didn't bring much money home and were at a competitive disadvantage.

Of course, in more modern times the prevalent taste preferences were such that a little grape dehydration was not looked upon as being such a bad thing. And besides, people have different tastes, and like different things: some of us like chocolate, others vanilla. And so it is that at the Fratelli Revello estate (that formally split up in 2013, see Section II, Chapter 9, GIACHINI file; see also CONCA file), differently from the Mauro Molino estate, they once grew very old Nebbiolo vines (planted in 1954) in their holdings in the Conca *cru* that were all Michet (differently from their holdings in the Giachini *cru*, also dating back to 1954 but entirely planted to Lampia). As mentioned previously, Conca is a warm site, and much warmer than Giachini. But because the Revello brothers were blessed at the time with so many different vineyards they could farm and made Barolos from many individual vineyard districts (as many as five different single-site Barolos in one year) a little variation in the aromas, flavors and textures of their wines was not disdained. It follows that they purposely looked for that extra fleshiness delivered by Michet grown in a hot site. A case of different strokes for different folks, I guess.

The state of the (Nebbiolo Michet) art

Without doubt, Nebbiolo Michet's standing in Barolo producer circles has somewhat fallen today. In some respects, its growth and popularity curves are diametrically opposite those of Nebbiolo Rosé, that began life never much considered but has now surged to an increasingly important status and ever-increasing popularity. By contrast, Nebbiolo Michet, that started out at the top of the popularity heap, has endured a slight fall from grace. Its popularity has taken a beating for a variety of reasons.

Michet's initial popularity and sky-high quality reputation was in many ways a consequence of the times. The fact is Nebbiolo Michet was extremely popular at a time when the climate and Barolo's vineyard reality and production methods were much different from those of today. Back in the 1950s and 1960s, even the 1970s, there was still a lot of Nebbiolo Bolla and Nebbiolo Rosé in the vineyards, both of which were felt at the time (right or wrong that those opinions may have been) to give generally more dilute wine, and even the Nebbiolo Lampia of the time had been selected on the basis of very big bunches and berries. Plus yields were much, much larger than today's. These were all vineyard choices that were a sign of the times, in that back then Barolo didn't sell much, and so the last thing on anybody's mind was to make less wine, no matter how qualitative it may have been (or been perceived) to be (for there was no way, back then, of making less wine and selling it for a higher price). Italy in the 1950s was just coming out of two almost successive World Wars, the vineyards were in generally horrible shape and one had to survive with what had been planted. Nobody had any money with which to uproot and replant even if they had wanted to (and they did not want to, as we have seen). That mindset began to change in the 1970s, when wine quality became more of an objective. Clearly, at that new point in time, selecting grapevines that would give better wine became the thing to do, and so producers began selecting Michet grapevines, looked upon as ideal because of their smaller bunches, berries, and leaves, not to mention reduced vigor.

A number of wineries led the way in Michet research and plantings: for example, the Mascarello family of the Giuseppe Mascarello estate where Maurizio Mascarello had always believed in Michet, and the Cordero di Montezemolo family of the Monfalletto estate in La Morra. The latter family worked closely with the Ministry of Agriculture, the University of Turin's Agrarian faculty and the Centro Nazionale Ricerche (the CNR) or Italy's national research institute to select and plant Nebbiolo Michet vines of the best possible quality. In fact, such was the Cordero di Montezemolo family's interest in new clones that it planted an experimental vineyard with eighty different Nebbiolo clones (the vineyard was near their famous cedar of Lebanon tree), something that was essentially unheard of at the time.

This was done in 1976 or 1978 (the exact year is unclear because my handwritten notes taken back in the mid-1980s during a winery visit are unintelligible and when I more recently asked a confirmation of which year it was, Alberto Cordero di Montezemolo himself was unsure of the exact date.) As mentioned previously, their plot in the Villero vineyard district of Castiglione Falletto was entirely planted to Nebbiolo Michet; from there they made the estate's best, most highly reputed Barolo called Enrico VI (from a vineyard in Castiglione Falletto's Villero vineyard district). The Enrico VI Barolo was all Nebbiolo Michet until the end of the 1970s, and was still about 85% Nebbiolo Michet well into the mid-1980s. In any case, as I shall detail shortly, the Cordero di Montezemolo family gained a big reputation as Nebbiolo Michet experts, and their winery became the destination of many a Barolo producer pilgrimage, all of whom were looking to learn more about Nebbiolo Michet and to obtain the highest possible quality cuttings of it.

Nowadays, Nebbiolo Michet faces the problem of its disease. Many producers are leery of growing a diseased plant that could spread the virus to their other, healthy, grapevines. Nurseries are even more leery of doing so, and don't really want to select, grow and propagate Nebbiolo Michet because it is too much of a risk for them to do so. Clearly, things were different back in the 1970s when, as explained previously, there was effectively a huge need for Nebbiolo Michet, given the dearth of other feasible/desirable Nebbiolo options (and actively reducing yields was not yet accepted by all). Thanks to there being a clear-cut business opportunity, nurseries back then were more inclined to take up the Nebbiolo Michet challenge. This is why a number of new, treated Nebbiolo Michet clones were developed between 1993 through 1997: the CVT 63, CVT 66 and the extremely successful and much planted CVT 71 (they were all propagated as of 2001). Before that, nurseries did the best they could with the scientific armamentarium and treatment options they had at their disposal, and came up with and admittedly high-quality Nebbiolo Clones CVT CN 141 and CVT CN 142, two Nebbiolo Lampia a Foglia Incisa clones (careful: these two are not Nebbiolo Michet clones, as many producers mistakenly believe and will tell you) that behaved somewhat like Nebbiolo Michet (and to a degree, looked like it too). Clones 141 and 142 gave only seven to nine bunches per plant and were not too vigorous and were just what producers were looking for; in the absence of real Nebbiolo Michet clones, they were the next best thing (in fact, a really very good alternative).

In time, with advances in scientific knowledge making it possible to treat grapevines and therefore to eliminate the virus from Nebbiolo Michet (either by thermotherapy or by meristematic therapy: the end-result with each is slightly different, so getting rid of the virus is neither quite as easy, nor the results as uniform, as you might think; if you are a producer, knowing which method was used is not so trivial), the goal of nurseries everywhere became to clear the grapevines of the virus and offer for sale new Nebbiolo Michet finally devoid of the virus. Not surprisingly, once the treated Nebbiolo Michet clones became available, they took the countryside by storm, getting planted just about by everyone and everywhere. Unfortunately, over time two things became apparent, neither one of them especially great.

First, save for CVT 71, the "new and improved" Michet clones failed to deliver: in other words, the treatment the vines were subjected to seemed to strip the Nebbiolo Michet not just of the virus, but of its qualities too. As many producers have told me over the years (see below), the wine made with these new clones was nowhere as good as the one made with the old, diseased clones (this is by no means the only instance in which a diseased grapevine is found to give much better wine than treated ones: for example, every Chianti Classico producer will tell you that the wine made with the virused Sangiovese clone T-19 clone is far superior to that of many healthy clones). In fact, as we have already discussed, a good deal of the discrepancies in Nebbiolo Michet morphology, behavior and wine quality may be due to the fact that there is not just one Nebbiolo Michet, but rather that there exist different Nebbiolo Michet populations, some of which may not be of Nebbiolo Michet at all but of an altogether different biotype or even a distinct Nebbiolo variety (see above, "Nebbiolo Michet: a Lampia biotype or maybe not?"). Perhaps some of the old Nebbiolo Michet vines growing in the field were not of the same "Michet" that ended up getting treated, but admittedly, I'm just taking an educated guess here. In truth, despite its generally lofty and excellent reputation, the jury is still out on Nebbiolo clone CVT 71, though it remains by far one of the best Nebbiolo clones ever developed (it has only small problem, but it's one every producer I have talked with over the years seems to find acceptable; and that is that it has slightly bigger bunches than one might like, but not excessively so).

And so it was that thanks to treated clones that turned out to be not as good as expected, Nebbiolo Michet's popularity took its first hit. The second hit came when it began to be apparent that the health status of the treated Nebbiolo Michet clones is not stable: more than one producer has told me that after a few years the plants begin to behave as if they were once again virus-affected, which unfortunately also appears might be the case with the CVT 71. All that being true, I need to point out that at least some producers don't have a problem with Michet being virus-affected: they will tell you that it really doesn't matter, because outside of a slightly higher mortality, Nebbiolo Michet seems to be very sturdy and produces quite well (though in irregular fashion) so it doesn't seem like its disease is such a detriment to its natural abilities and capacity for survival.

Besides its virus-affected state (apparently only partly resolved with the current methods of treatment, if it has been in fact resolved at all), Nebbiolo Michet presents another problem, a "new" weakness that, rather paradoxically, used to be instead one of its strengths. For the Michet biotype is characterized not just by smaller bunches and berries, but also by smaller leaves. And fewer of them. But whereas in this more quality-oriented day and age it is good for a grapevine to have less vigor, smaller bunches and smaller grapes, it absolutely needs to have leaves, because canopy thickness and shading of the grape bunches is all-important in times of climate change. Consequently, Nebbiolo Michet is at a real disadvantage now.

For this and other reasons, Nebbiolo Lampia has completely taken over at winery vineyards everywhere, and is now the Nebbiolo that is planted almost exclusively; and for the same reason, producers everywhere are starting to look very long and very hard at Nebbiolo Rosé, that not only is the most drought-resistant and heat-resistant of all the Nebbiolo biotypes, but it is also the one endowed with the biggest leaves of all (see Chapter 3, NEBBIOLO ROSÉ). Suffice it to say that even at Cordero di Montezemolo/Monfalletto, one of the recognized experts of Nebbiolo Michet and one of the leading proponents of its qualities only twenty-thirty years ago, they now plant mostly Nebbiolo Lampia (about sixteen different clones at a time).

After all that, where does Nebbiolo Michet stand today (literally, you might say)? It's complicated. Notwithstanding the fact that there might exist diverse Nebbiolo Michet populations in the vineyards that behave differently and give different wines because they aren't Nebbiolo Michet at all, even what we know about the classically virus-affected Nebbiolo Michet grapevines is tainted by a number of factors. As always, you need to take what people tell you, then and now, in its proper temporal, historical and social context. In wine (and not just wine), best not to just accept anything and everything people tell you. Doing your homework so as to have at least a little knowledge by which to make informed decisions when you go visit wineries and talk to people, allows for a measure of logic and of accuracy in the conclusions you draw. Keep this in mind, when you read the next subchapter.

What the producers say

As it turns out, plenty. Over at the beautiful Cogno estate in Novello, Valter Fissore is a believer of Nebbiolo Michet's charms, and roughly 40% of his Nebbiolo vineyards are planted to this biotype. His Nebbiolo

Michet is of the old, original, Nebbiolo Michet clone R3 as well as of massal selections that are now seventy years old. Very importantly, Fissore points out that Nebbiolo Michet, despite its diseased status, is actually more resistant to many of today's common diseases, including *flavescence dorée* and *esca*, not to mention grey rot (this is another example of how what we believe to be true of Nebbiolo Michet neither holds up under further scrutiny nor does it apply to all Nebbiolo Michet populations, given that the variety is generally thought to be more sickly and less resistant). According to Fissore, Nebbiolo Michet also does very well in cooler years and in less hot vineyard sites. For this reason, Fissore believes it is best to plant Nebbiolo Michet at mid-slope or at lower altitudes that have less sunlight hours, as opposed to the *bricco* or the hill's usually sunny summit. As for negatives, Fissore cites a certain irregularity in production volumes, as these can present noteworthy variations from year to year. Fissore also finds that compared to Barolos made with Nebbiolo Lampia, Michet's wines are even more structured and concentrated on the palate, while on the nose they tend to be somewhat simpler, even monotonal. Consequently, he is not a big fan of 100% Nebbiolo Michet wines, while he is very much a fan of including it as a component of wines made with blends of other Nebbiolo biotypes. In Fissore's opinion, such blends are always improved by Michet's presence.

Chiara Boschis of the E. Pira-Chiara Boschis estate in the middle of the town of Barolo is one producer who is in the Nebbiolo Michet camp. In fact, she estimates that about 30-40% of all her Nebbiolo planted is of the Michet biotype. Chiara states that the secret to success with Michet is to make sure that a variety of different Nebbiolo Michet clones are planted and each specifically matched to different parts of the vineyard that are more suited to them; in other words, not every vineyard position is equally suited to all Nebbiolo Michet clones (this observation echoes others I have already mentioned). Furthermore, she also believes that a percentage of old massal selections are necessary to make the best possible Barolo. According to her, in very humid years Michet holds many advantages over Lampia, that tends to take on too much water and develop huge bunches; by contrast, in extremely droughty years it is Michet that is at a disadvantage because its yields are reduced drastically. In this light, and differently from Nebbiolo Lampia, it is important not to use rootstocks that reduce vigor too much with Nebbiolo Michet, a normally low-yielding Nebbiolo.

Fabio Alessandria of the G.B. Burlotto estate in Verduno says they are very happy with Michet in some respects, while in others they have cause for worry. On the positive side, the structure and quality of the wines produced with their Nebbiolo Michet is noteworthy. The negatives are that their older Nebbiolo Michet clone R3 vines, planted in the 1980s, have shown a progressively decreasing productivity with age, not to mention increased mortality. They are also still in the process of evaluating their Nebbiolo Michet CVT 71, but are slightly concerned that it appears to be acting as if it were once again virus-affected, even though it is a clonal selection that had undergone thermotherapy (and was therefore deemed healthy (sanitized) and fit to be planted.

Enrico Rivetto of the Rivetto estate in Serralunga finds that Nebbiolo Michet's advantages are the same as those mentioned by Alessandria and Fissore: wines of wonderful depth and structure, especially when planted in richer, slightly more fertile soils that retain humidity better (while in their experience, such advantages are lost when Nebbiolo Michet is planted on poorer, drier, and sandier soils). About 32% of the estate's total Nebbiolo plantings are Nebbiolo clones: Nebbiolo Michet CVT 71 (29%) and Nebbiolo Michet CVT 4 (3%). This is actually a much higher percentage than it at first appears, because only 75% of the estate's vineyards are planted with clonal selections (25% of the estate is planted to massal selections). This means that the Michet presence at Rivetto is actually 32% of 75%, or in other words 43% of the Nebbiolo clones on the property are of Nebbiolo Michet (and it may well be that some of the massal selections are of Nebbiolo Michet as well -though Enrico does not know for sure- but this could then mean that about half if not much more of the estate's vineyards are actually planted to Nebbiolo Michet, a noteworthy amount by any measure).

Over at Vietti, Luca Currado told me that a little less than 10% of his vineyard holdings are planted to Nebbiolo Michet, and that it is almost all clonal selections nowadays (like at Rivetto, the preferred clones are Nebbiolo Michet CVT 71 and Nebbiolo Michet CVT 4). Based on his experience, Luca Currado believes that while clonal selections of Nebbiolo Michet behave in a more homogenous manner and give the wine they are expected too (deeper in color and richer in structure, massal selections (at least the ones he used to have) were less uniform in the wines they delivered. For example, wine colors that varied considerably in their depth of hue. This cannot really surprise, given that massal selections are by definition selections of plants that are not genetically identical; therefore, a certain amount of diversity in their behavior and the wines they produce is not just to be expected, but wholly logical. While that is true, also keep in mind that part of what was observed might be because not all those massal selections were really of Nebbiolo Michet in the first place, because as we have seen there may exist different populations of Nebbiolo Michet, some of which may not be of Nebbiolo Michet at all. Interestingly, Currado mentioned that in his experience, the wine's qualities and characteristics were not ultimately defined by the clone or biotype used, but had more to do with the combination of biotype, soil type, rootstock, altitude, exposure and viticultural decisions taken. In other words, according to Currado, depending on what one chooses to do, a Barolo that is deeply colored and concentrated is just as possible with Nebbiolo Lampia as it is with Michet.

At Clerico, winemaker and general manager Oscar Arrivabene tells me that, though he has never had any specific genetic testing done, he believes that all the Nebbiolo from which he makes his Percristina bottling to be Michet, while his Ciabot Mentin is probably all Lampia (only one of the two plots, the one named Gepe Alto: see Section II: GINESTRA file) used to make the Ginestra Ciabot Mentin might have some Nebbiolo Michet (the rest is Nebbiolo Lampia). Arrivabene finds that the Nebbiolo Michet is characterized by less vigor and more loosely-packed bunches and that while the wine is richer, bigger and deeper, it is also less elegant. He is quick to point out though not to take his considerations as gospel because as he has never had the vines tested: his impressions may in fact relate to different soils and/or vine age, and not biotype.

At Cavallotto, Alfio Cavallotto raises an interesting point, one that he makes when discussing Nebbiolo Rosé clones too. And that is the existence of "intermediate forms" of Nebbiolo Lampia-Michet-Rosé (see Chapter 3, NEBBIOLO ROSÉ), so in other words, vineyards aren't always planted to what people think they were planted to. They might believe they have Rosé or Michet growing in their vineyards, but it might well be a Lampia that over time busily mutates into one of the other varieties (as we have seen, Nebbiolo mutates at the drop of a hat, or of a gene: see Chapter 1, NEBBIOLO LAMPIA). Cavalotto believes that about 30-35% of Nebbiolo vines in his Bricco Boschis holdings are of the "true" old Michet, but that percentage rises to about 60% if he includes within that percentage the newer Lampia clones that look somewhat and behave like Nebbiolo Michet. That said, the majority of the Nebbiolo Michet he owns are of clone CVT 71, that as already mentioned has long been accepted to be one of the most successful Nebbiolo clones ever developed. In Alfio's words, "… clone 71 is hard to beat because as far as Michet goes, it is the one that gives not just the most regular but also the less extreme results".

His take on the advantages and disadvantages of Nebbiolo Michet are the same as those mentioned by just about all his colleagues: the positives include deeper color and greater structure, the negatives include less aromatic complexity and depth, excessively prominent tannins, and irregular yields. It is absolutely fascinating to listen to producers over the course of many years, decades even. The advantage of my having lived in Italy at length and essentially growing up with many of those making Barolo today is that my learning curve has grown along with theirs, and it really is enlightening to realize just how experience and age form and modify previously held judgements and opinions. For example, back in the early 2000s, Cavallotto found that wines made with many of the newer Nebbiolo Michet clones he had planted seemed less adept at giving complex wines; the problem appeared to resolve to a degree as a result of increased vine age, but now he believes that with some Nebbiolo Michet clones, it is a problem that is never completely overcome. For this reason, Cavalotto is among those producers who, not unreasonably, stress the importance of planting vineyards to mixes of clones and massal selections; this not just to hedge one's bets but to also make the most complex wine possible, as there is no one nursery clone that is markedly better than any other.

However, not everybody is convinced by the newer clones of Nebbiolo Michet. Over at the Giovanni Manzone estate in Monforte, they planted their holdings in the Castelletto vineyard district entirely with new generation Michet clones in 1999, but concluded it really wasn't worth the effort, as they did not find that the finished wines to be all that different from those made with older Michets or even from wines they made with Lampia, for that matter. Elisa Scavino of Paolo Scavino once went as far to say that "…I have the utmost respect for everyone's job, but really, with some of these new clones you really have to wonder. For example, we planted the Nebbiolo Michet clone CVT 71, but I can tell you that it looks nothing like the old Michets that Cordero di Montezemolo has in his vineyards, so even though I have planted Michet in my vineyards, or what I have been told is healthy Nebbiolo Michet, it looks and behaves completely differently from other Michets planted elsewhere. So, I ask you, what am I supposed to think? I don't know whether it's a matter of soil, sunlight, water, or of genetic material. What I do know is the grapevines look and behave completely differently. Are they even the same grape?". I dare say, my point exactly.

Giacomo Conterno of Aldo Conterno also confirms that polyclonal vineyards are the only way to go if wine complexity is the goal. Like many of his colleagues, he planted a lot of Nebbiolo Michet CVT 71 over the years but didn't find it was superior to the Nebbiolo clone CVT 142. Today, Nebbiolo Michet represents an infinitesimally small portion of his vineyard plantings and he really does not seem too impressed by it. At Conterno Fantino, they chose to plant ten different Nebbiolo clones in their Vigna del Gris portion of the Ginestra *cru* in 1998 (some of Nebbiolo Michet too), expecting to make wines showcasing lovely noteworthy complexity from that specific portion of the vineyard when the vines reach twenty-five years of age or so, but the jury is still out currently.

Even though they know of colleagues who swear by Nebbiolo Michet's capacity to give stellar wines, many Barolo producers avoid it like the plague. Marco and Paola Oberto of the outstanding (and underrated) Ciabot Berton estate in La Morra are amongst those who really aren't in Michet's camp: "The really old plants are so loaded with virus that you cannot get much in the way either of color or alcohol degree from them; and we have found wines made from the virus-free, treated vines not that interesting". Other producers agree with the Oberto siblings, and also say that the new Michet clones don't especially excite them (because they either do not differ all that much from Lampia or do not replicate the qualities of the Michet vines of yesteryear). Pietro Ratti of the Renato Ratti estate put a slightly different spin on it, and this already back in 2008: "It's just not worth the risk: Michet is a diseased plant, it's less hardy, less resistant, and produces less; and besides, we have Lampia that is excellent, so why bother with Michet?". Claudio Conterno of Conterno Fantino agrees and echoes what Ratti said. "The reason for Michet's fall from grace and diminished presence in the Langhe vineyards is simple: Michet produces so little it becomes almost anti-economical to plant and farm; and besides, we are all aware just how spectacular Lampia's wines can be, so why bother with Michet?". (Note that, as previously stated, producer experiences with Michet differ: for example, at Cogno they find Michet to be more resistant then Lampia.)

According to some producers, it's not even clear if the new Michet clones are cost-effective, because yields are so low with them that one has to prune carefully or risk not making much wine at all. Marco Marengo (of the excellent Mario Marengo estate) points out that while it is true the original virus-affected Michets didn't produce much, at least they lived long lives and were fairly resistant despite their sickly condition. By contrast, he found that some of the new Michet clones get sick right away (Marco told me that after ten years he had to replant, which besides being an incredibly expensive proposition, isn't exactly normal: whether that was related to soil or rootstock choice is not entirely clear). In fact, Michet's morphologic characteristics made it so the biotype would not have enjoyed much popularity even had people back in the 1970s been interested in quality first and foremost (and at the time they weren't, not the majority at least).

A few years back, Pio Boffa of the Pio Cesare estate clearly explained to me that "… Ian, you have to remember that up until the 1980s most if not all of the Nebbiolo grapes were sold at the Alba market in piazza Savona. There the grapes would be weighed: you were in fact paid on the basis of the total weight of your grapes. It follows that Michet was at a huge disadvantage relative to Lampia because as small as its bunches are, they don't weigh much; hence, all those growing Michet were left holding the short end of the stick. And back then, in what were much poorer times in which grapes weren't paid that much, nobody cared about wine quality, since they all needed to sell as many grapes as possible just to survive! You understand that producers could get Lampia to produce so many grapes that each bunch weighed as much as two kilograms. So clearly, Lampia was always going to be the farmer's favorite!!!". I truly loved listening to Pio Boffa, and was immensely sorry to hear of his passing away.

In fact, his statement was echoed closely by Nicola Oberto, the ultra-talented young winemaker and co-owner of Trediberri. In his view, the presence or absence from Barolo vineyards of Nebbiolo Michet was not always linked in a straightforward manner to the advantages and disadvantages posed by the grape but rather to the financial possibilities an estate had (or had not). When asked about whether he had any Michet in his vineyards, his answer was disarmingly simple: "No, Ian, unfortunately not: my grandparents were poor, and they could not afford Michet". Asked to elaborate, he made a pretty convincing statement that harkens back to what was the economic reality of those darker times, so different from today's "Golden Age" of Barolo: "I honestly believe that having Michet in your vineyards or not having it was in function of how wealthy the single estate was. If you had money, you were willing to put up with Michet because of the higher quality that Michet gave you; but if you were poor, you wanted to grow Lampia, which gives larger productions of larger bunches.

Therefore, if you were amongst the poor who had to sell their grapes at the Alba market, by weight, you wanted Lampia. This is why my grandparents uprooted all their Michet back in 1951 and 1961".

Actually, Pio Boffa also pointed out that there's not much of the original Nebbiolo Michet left anyways, something that many other producers have told me over the years too. Some, like Renato Corino, go as far as saying that the original Michet is extinct. So that's the other issue with Michet: does any of the original grapevine even really exist anymore out there in the vineyards? And once again, is what we are calling Michet today another Nebbiolo variety or biotype altogether? While there's no doubt plenty of clonal Michet planted in today's vineyards (the one freed from viruses), it appears there's really not much left of the original "true" Michet. Or as we have discussed already, that there might have been different Michets living in vineyards once and that some have since gone the way of the dodo and the saber-toothed tiger.

Claudio Rosso, still of the Gigi Rosso winery in the early 2000s (the estate that used to own part of the Arione vineyard district in Serralunga but sold their nine hectares to the Giacomo Conterno winery in 2015) is also not a huge Michet fan, confirming that the "true" Michet of yesteryear is now rare: according to him, "The really old Michet vines, despite what some people will tell you, are few and far between…Cappellano and Cordero di Montezemolo have some for sure, but otherwise it always was, and is, rare". While some producers have been left unimpressed by Nebbiolo Michet, the biotype still has many fans among winery personnel: massal selections of old vines continue to be planted even despite their virused condition because Michet, by their account at least, gives an outstanding wine. These individuals are of the opinion that the modern-day clones of Michet available, treated so as to eliminate the virus, do not behave similarly to and do not deliver the same quality of wines like the old massally selected Michets do. These individuals steadfastly maintain that old Michet vines were the ingredient by which to make the best Barolo of all.

For example, at the Giuseppe Mascarello winery, Nebbiolo Michet has always been extremely important and in fact the winery is strongly associated with it. Mauro Mascarello uses his own massally selected old Michet biotype in order to make his top of the line, ultra-expensive Ca' d'Morissio Barolo. The Cà d'Morissio Michets were derived from a previous massal selection carried out by Mauro's father Giuseppe at the end of the 1950s on Michet grapevines planted by Maurizio Mascarello (Mauro's grandfather) in the early 1920s. So at least with this one particular wine and vineyard, we are sure to be dealing with a Michet that has lived and adapted to a terroir of a specific Barolo vineyard district (the Monprivato: see chapter 9, MONPRIVATO file). Unfortunately, to make room for the new Michet plantings with which to make what is now the estate's top Barolo, Mascarello uprooted two plots of old Nebbiolo Rosé vines. Of course, whether it was a good idea or not to rip out the old Nebbiolo Rosé biotypes is another kettle of fish altogether. And whether they might regret that choice nowadays, also.

In ultimate analysis, opinions about Nebbiolo Michet vary considerably, but for the most part people seem to agree that the original Nebbiolo Michet may have had qualities that the newer clones do not seem to possess. Whether it is a matter of different populations of Nebbiolo Michet or newer clones just not being up to snuff, we don't know yet. Many producers have uprooted their Michet, while others hang on to their old vines of Michet jealously; still others have replanted with clonal selections of Nebbiolo Michet that no longer show signs of disease, but the exact merits of such clones, and whether they manage to remain disease-free over time, are still the subject of debate. Still other Barolo producers consider Nebbiolo Michet a vestigium of the past, one that was necessary at one point in time but is no longer needed in today's day and age. Undoubtedly, Nebbiolo Michet's world is a complex one, but as always, the truth lies somewhere in the middle. *Table 1.7* lists all the Nebbiolo Michet holdings as we know of them today based on Michele's and my research conducted over the years (see APPENDIX A, *Table 1.7: Documented presence/absence of Nebbiolo Michet clones and biotypes in holdings of Barolo wineries*).

Chapter 3

NEBBIOLO ROSÉ

Ian D'Agata

Nebbiolo Rosé is one of Italy's greatest but least-known wine grape varieties (it has also always been one of my absolute favorite grape varieties, but I imagine that's probably beside the point). Unfortunately, for the longest time very little was known about this specific grape variety; and what was known, has turned out to have been mostly wrong. For example, Nebbiolo Rosé is not a clone of Nebbiolo. By today's level of scientific knowledge it is more exact to consider it a distinct variety from Nebbiolo Lampia (though extremely closely related to), as I have outlined in both *Native Wine Grapes of Italy* (2014) and in *Italy's Native Wine Grape Terroirs* (2019). That much admitted, the fact is that Nebbiolo Rosé is essentially similar to Nebbiolo Lampia in both its vineyard behavior and its winemaking requirements. It follows that for practical purposes, both Nebbiolo Rosé and Nebbiolo Michet can be considered to be biotypes of Nebbiolo Lampia (even though it may not be scientifically accurate to do so) that present slightly different characteristics (and so do their wines). Furthermore, recent thinking (however accurate it may or may not be) has also postulated that the lone Nebbiolo Rosé clone we know of, Nebbiolo clone CN 111, may in reality be a Nebbiolo Lampia that looks and behaves as a Nebbiolo Rosé (but most knowledgeable people I have talked to don't agree with this revisionist view).

It is apparent now that our learning curve about this important wine grape has been a steep one, and as we shall see in this chapter, it remains so, by and large. Then again, exactly the same thing can be said of Nebbiolo Michet (see chapter 2, NEBBIOLO MICHET). Nebbiolo Rosé's existence was further hampered by those sorry two decades (beginning in the late seventies and lasting until the end of the nineties) in which ultra-dark, high pH and needlessly thick wines were all the rage (a style of wine that couldn't have been farther removed from the type of wine Nebbiolo Rosé delivers; or even Nebbiolo Lampia, for that matter). A real "situation" if you will, that led to poor Nebbiolo Rosé getting (very misguidedly) uprooted almost everywhere. Not Barolo's finest hour, frankly.

Mercifully, fads and fashions change, and most human beings (the successful ones, at least) learn from their mistakes; consequently, things are looking up for those grape varieties like Nebbiolo Rosé that give wines long on elegance and perfume, if shy on color and size. With the arrival of the twenty-first century, Nebbiolo Rosé has begun, albeit slowly, to rise from its ashes, a phoenix-like transition from inconsequential grape variety to the potentially front-lining wine grape it can and should in fact be. Trending positively, its fortune has undergone a complete about-turn, in contrast to Nebbiolo Michet, the popularity of which is currently on a downward spiral. It really never ceases to amaze me just how quickly times and opinions change.

In the 1980s, I began to systematically compile information on Nebbiolo Rosé, drawing up files on what admittedly very kind and very patient Barolo (and Barbaresco) producers had to tell me about it. Not many of them had much Nebbiolo Rosé in their vineyards (see Chapter 1, NEBBIOLO LAMPIA. See also Chapter 2, NEBBIOLO MICHET); in the 1980s and 1990s, it was Nebbiolo Michet that was all the rage and the grape everyone wanted to tell you about. With a few important exceptions, Nebbiolo Rosé was viewed, at best, as a mostly small component of their Barolos that helped add perfume; but at worse, Nebbiolo Rosé was a nuisance, something that only diluted their wine and was best uprooted. And they did uproot it. And so, I am grateful to all those producers and their families who over the years spent time with me narrating what they knew about the variety. Clearly, you understand why I am grateful, because despite their having very little to gain by devoting time talking about something they had little interest in and even less to gain by in doing so, they *did* do so. Out of nothing else but passion, there they sat with me (a young man who was at the time in no way famous or influential, so their kindness and dedication are that much more commendable), in kitchens, in studies, in living rooms, gifting me with their knowledge on the subject (such as for example Chiara Boschis, who once brought out, in response to my questions on the subject, three small bunches to the table: one of Lampia, one of Michet and one of Rosé).

I therefore use the word "gift" with intent, because I consider those moments spent together a real gift. I have combined that large body of interviews with other recollections, anecdotes, research results, facts and figures I gleaned from more recent interviews, scientific papers and nursery data together into a compendium on Nebbiolo Rosé like has never been written before. You will find those producer memories, impressions and anecdotes peppered throughout this chapter, and my hope is you will enjoy reading them as much as I had fun in listening to them, and then writing them up. As much as I had *living* them, in fact.

Last but not least, I have been able to draw up the most up-to-date list (in fact, the only list) available anywhere on the individual Barolo estate vineyard holdings of Nebbiolo Rosé and Nebbiolo Clone CN 111 (see Appendix A, Table 1.8 *Documented vineyard holdings of Nebbiolo Rosé/Nebbiolo Clone CN 111 in Barolo*). By the way, I have compiled the same table for Barbaresco and it will be included in the upcoming book entirely devoted to that wine. Clearly, as I have only limited time and resources at my disposal, I am certain the breadth and precision of such lists can be improved upon; my hope is that its appearance will finally spur the powers to be (who by contrast, *do* have the means and resources to do so) to document in detail the exact presence of Nebbiolo Rosé and Nebbiolo Clone CN 111 in the vineyards of Barolo (and Barbaresco). Given that is apparent to everyone nowadays that Nebbiolo Rosé and its specific clone have many positive viticultural selling points that actually make it/them an especially suitable for this day and age of climate change, it only would seem logical that this should happen. Just like Nebbiolo Michet and its clones have many positives too.

Nebbiolo Rosé, then and now

The first official mention of Nebbiolo Rosé dates back to 1798, when Count Nuvolone wrote of a "Nebieul Rosé", the description of which was consistent with the Nebbiolo Rosé we know today. But despite people knowing about Nebbiolo Rosé for centuries, the body of written work devoted to this cultivar is thin, limited mostly to one or two lines here and there in chapters and books about Barolo, Barbaresco and Italian wine (if even that). In fact, I know of only two other books that have chapters devoted entirely to Nebbiolo Rosé: and it just so happens I wrote both of them [see *Native Wine Grapes of Italy* (D'Agata 2014); and *Italy's Native Wine Grape Terroirs* (D'Agata 2019)]. Apart from those chapters, there is very little written on this grape variety in any mainstream wine media source meant for the general public, and close to nothing in the scientific literature.

This state of affairs is hardly surprising, given that there was never much known about Nebbiolo Rosé: not its parentage, not its exact relationship to Nebbiolo, and neither its viticultural characteristics nor its enological needs. Much of what people know about the variety today (or *think* they know) essentially derives from the accumulated experiences of Valter Fissore at the outstanding Cogno estate who was, for the longest time, the only one making a Barolo with 100% Nebbiolo Rosé. In fact, as I shall broach shortly, after analyzing and reviewing the data and my records at length, I find his experience with the variety differs somewhat from what the majority has told me over the years. Given that Cogno's was the only Nebbiolo Rosé wine available, it is only logical that the estate's experiences would be taken to be the benchmark by which to evaluate the grape; but that's only if you don't have a body of experience dating back decades to draw upon. It is only through decades of comparison of comments, memories, experiences, and knowledge that a fuller, probably more accurate, and ultimately more helpful picture emerges. I myself was starting to get confused, and had to think long and hard at why there are so many divergent commentaries made about this grape and how it behaves in the vineyard, and after twenty years of thinking it over, reading what little scientific studies there are, and speaking to those who know more than anyone else about wine grapes and Nebbiolo Rosé specifically, I think I have come up with a reasonable understanding of this wine grape's reality.

In fact, the sorry state of affairs Nebbiolo Rosé long languished in was not unique to it. Its story is in fact that of many other poor Italian native wine grapes too, all long forgotten and cast aside, only to be rediscovered in recent friendlier, more forward-thinking, and aware times. For the longest time in Italy and elsewhere, most people failed to grasp just how important wine grapes are relative to the wines we drink. And even more pertinently, how useful and meaningful native grapes are, and how unbelievably lucky the country is to have them. In this respect, Nebbiolo Rosé suffered the exact same fate of many Italian native grapes that are viewed today as being of major importance; but were not too long ago completely forgotten and disparaged; believe it or not, only twenty years ago absolutely nothing (or close to nothing) was written about, and even known about,

Carricante, Cornalin, Fumin, Malvasia Bianca di Basilicata, Mayolet, Minutolo, Nerello Mascalese, Pecorino, Uva di Troia, and a litany of other now famous Italian wine grapes. Can you imagine that hardly anyone outside of local drinking circles had ever tasted a wine made with Carricante or Nerello Mascalese as recently as 2000? In other words, that Etna Bianco and Etna Rosso wines as we know them today literally did not exist only a few decades ago? Is that crazy or what? And yet it was exactly so. Much the same is true of poor Nebbiolo Rosé. Forgotten. Pushed to the roadside. Trampled. Insulted. Removed. If a grape variety could ever sue for mobbing, Nebbiolo Rosé would stand to get rich. And it's not the only grape that could apply for a day in court.

The best example of just how little was known about Nebbiolo Rosé is that throughout the entire twentieth century, the variety was believed to be, along with Michet and Lampia, one of the three major Nebbiolo "clones". As discussed at length previously (see Chapter 1, NEBBIOLO LAMPIA) and in my previous books on the subject of wine grapes, use of the term 'clone' in this context is not just improper but downright wrong. In fact, the clonal origin was not the only erroneous hypothesis out there. Some were of the notion that Nebbiolo Rosé was not a clone after all, but rather a virus-affected Lampia just like Nebbiolo Michet was; another view was that Nebbiolo Rosé was not virus-affected itself, but was a progeny of a virus-affected Lampia; still others believed that it was just color variant of Lampia (much like black panthers are color variants of jaguars and leopards, two big cats that usually have spotted yellow coats). I could go on: you have no idea the stuff relative to this subject that my ears have heard over the years. Its identity unknown, some of the hypotheses regarding Nebbiolo Rosé were so far out to be truly hilarious (and before you ask, no, nobody ever went as far as telling me that Nebbiolo Rosé donned a cape and a mask at night and went around fighting crime). Given what they did to it, maybe it should have.

Barolos have always been made mostly with Nebbiolo Lampia (or only with Nebbiolo Lampia) and a little, or a lot, of Nebbiolo Michet; by contrast, in most Barolos, Nebbiolo Rosé made up only about 5-20% of the blend, though its presence could range anywhere from zero to 100% (but both those extremes were rare). Still, I find it rather amazing that for a grape hanging around (literally) the Piedmontese countryside from at least the eighteenth century onwards, it was only thanks to the seminal work done by Botta, Schneider, Akkak, and associates in 1998 (and published in 2000), that everyone learned Nebbiolo Rosé is, at least at the present stage of scientific knowledge, a variety distinct from Nebbiolo. The two are each other's closest relative, related by first-degree parentage as demonstrated by analysis of microsatellite markers (Schneider, Boccacci, Torello Marinoni, et al 2004).

Interestingly, the next closest relative of both is Freisa, a wine grape that not surprisingly shares many viticultural and winemaking characteristics with the Nebbiolos. But although we know that Nebbiolo Rosé is directly related to Nebbiolo, we still don't know which is the parent and which the child. Is Nebbiolo Rosé the result of a natural crossing between Nebbiolo Lampia with an as yet unidentified other variety, or is Nebbiolo Rosé itself one of the two parents of Nebbiolo? The latter hypothesis seems less likely given that mention of Nebbiolo in the literature precedes that of Nebbiolo Rosé [but that may be due to Nebbiolo Rosé, long believed to be a color variant of Nebbiolo, being lumped together in generic descriptions of the "Nebbiolo" grape (see Chapter 1. NEBBIOLO LAMPIA)]. Part of the problem is that in the past Nebbiolo Rosé was often mistaken for unripe Nebbiolo Lampia: so it may very well be that it was in fact present in the countryside many centuries before we believe it first appeared. I'm not sure we'll ever be able to find out one way or another.

In any case, this "situation" led to erroneous data collection on Nebbiolo Rosé, but also fatefully limited its study and research (because all the attention and efforts were directed, and relevant funds awarded, to what was believed to be the one and only "Nebbiolo"). By genetic definitions of today, Nebbiolo Rosé ought to be classified as a distinct variety from Nebbiolo; however, for all intents and purposes it is more useful to view it as a biotype of Nebbiolo. For in ultimate analysis, when all is said and done, what we consider today by strict but perhaps not very practical genetic-based thinking to be a "distinct variety" and what to be a "biotype" needs at least some degree of interpretation, an important subject I will tell you about next.

Biotype or distinct variety: a HIGHLY practical viewpoint on Nebbiolo Rosé, Nebbiolo Michet and Nebbiolo Lampia

According to recent research results obtained by Raimondi and associates (2020), Nebbiolo Rosé, Pignola and Rossola Nera are Nebbiolo Lampia's full-siblings, in agreement with identical by descent (IBD) coefficients.

If you have ever seen them, then you know how much these varieties look like each other (especially Rossola, Nebbiolo Lampia, and Nebbiolo Rosé, which can be truly hard to tell apart). And while Pignola and Rossola Nera are both typical of Valtellina (Pignola was also propagated to northeast Piedmont, under the name of Pignolo Spano), Nebbiolo Rosé lives not just in the Valtellina but basically everywhere Nebbiolo Lampia grows. The two literally go (or grow) hand in hand.

As already mentioned, by strict genetic definition, given that Nebbiolo Rosé's DNA is ever so slightly different from that of Nebbiolo Lampia, the two should be viewed as distinct varieties. But after all these years of talking to people, reading all the scientific articles, attending and/or speaking at university conferences on the subject and just plain thinking about it, I ask myself (and you): honestly, just how practical is that? I mean, even if we take into account a few small differences in the way these two grapes look and behave, and how their wines taste, the two grapevines really do look almost exactly alike and the wines are really very similar too. Whatever differences there are can easily be included in, and accepted as being, a part of a "variety/subvariety spectrum" that characterizes Nebbiolo Lampia.

For strict genetic definitions aside, it all ends up being "Nebbiolo" in the end. After all, the vinegrowers and wine producers of the Langhe of centuries past always viewed Nebbiolo Rosé as one of the three Nebbiolo "clones", and that's because they all three really do look and behave more or less the same. And as wrong as that might have been, it was born out of the fact that while clearly presenting some differences, the three - Lampia, Michet and Rosé- really weren't *that* different after all. As mentioned previously (see Chapter 1, NEBBIOLO LAMPIA), and this is important, even "clones" of Chardonnay and Pinot Noir have been proven to have very minor genetic differences (Riaz, Garrison, Dangl *et al* 2002): and yet, despite those plants presenting scientifically demonstrated genetic differences, nobody is running around saying the things are not Chardonnay and that they are not Pinot Noir. In France at least, nobody's really *that* stupid. Furthermore, it is now well-known that different Nebbiolo grapevines, just like Chardonnay and Pinot Noir, have different genetic patrimonies. For example, a recent study by Gambino, Dal Molin, Boccacci and associates (2017) based on short-reads genomic data demonstrated the presence of diagnostic single nucleotide variants among three Nebbiolo clones (CVT 71, CVT 185 and CVT 423) of three different Nebbiolo biotypes (respectively of Michet, Lampia and Picotener), which are associated to different cultivation areas. To be clear, the genetic differences present could be used to identify the three as distinct grapevine species: but they are so minor that we continue to consider all three as being "Nebbiolo".

Nebbiolo Rosé might be a more extreme form of Nebbiolo Lampia, but it is still very much a Nebbiolo in looks, behavior, where it lives and the wines it gives. More perfumed and paler-colored wines, but recognizably Nebbiolo. In fact, when Nebbiolo Rosé is hit by fan leaf virus, it morphs into a grape that looks very much like Nebbiolo Michet, or like a cross of Nebbiolo Lampia and Michet would look like. There are in fact populations of these 'Nebbiolo Michet-Rosé' grapevines in numerous vineyards of the Langhe area, something that I am documenting and will be writing about more in a future publication. Once again, this is but an example of how large the Nebbiolo morphology and behavior spectrum really is. Like it or not, there simply isn't just "one" "Nebbiolo": just like Aubert de Villaine and his Burgundian associates have shown the existence of over 500 different Pinot Noir and 300 Chardonnay grapevines, so no, there is not just "one" Pinot Noir and "one" Chardonnay, but many variants thereof. And no, they don't all give exactly the same wine either, so much so that de Villaine &Co. insert, for example, each of the 500 Pinot Noir plants they have identified thus far into three different quality levels (*supérieur, fin* and *très fin*). If they bother to categorize these different biotypes so, that probably means they aren't all quite one and the same, correct? So the Nebbiolos are not all one and the same either, though just like all those Pinot Noir and Chardonnay grapes can be taken to be variants (biotypes) of the same grapevine that have come to express themsleves differently over time, the same line of thinking can be applied to the many Nebbiolo grapes out there.

In recent years the consensus that has developed in grape scientist, academician, producer and legislative circles is that science is all fine and good but, in ultimate analysis, some pragmatism is necessary in these matters. It follows that even if by strict definition genetic diversity implies different beings and different species, when the genetic differences are minimal such that (in the case of grapevines) both the look of the plants and the taste of the wines are only minimally different, then rather than different species we can speak of subvarieties or biotypes. By contrast, if differences in morphology, behaviors and in the wines produced are markedly different, then the grape varieties under exam must be considered to be distinct even if genetic testing at the present state of scientific knowledge tells us that the two grape varieties are "identical".

While it is true that Nebbiolo and Nebbiolo Rosé differ genetically, they do so ever so slightly; and while strictly speaking they really ought to be considered as different seedlings, the truth of the matter is that the differences in both grapes and wines are so small that it is more practical, reasonable even, to consider Nebbiolo Rosé as a biotype or subvariety of Nebbiolo. Again, a subvariety that gives a slightly different wine and that adds a little something different to a wine made mostly with Nebbiolo Lampia; but ultimately, not that different and still very recognizably "Nebbiolo". Clearly, if the grape looked and behaved more like Syrah or Merlot than Nebbiolo, or gave wines reminiscent of Syrah or Merlot and not Nebbiolo, then it would be a very different matter. In that case, Nebbiolo Lampia and Nebbiolo Rosé would have to be viewed as wholly separate varieties. But that is not the case, because Nebbiolo Lampia and Nebbiolo Rosé are far more alike than they are different. In fact, it turns out that even what has long been thought to be one of the defining characteristics of Nebbiolo Rosé is actually not so defining at all: the supposed lighter color of its berries.

In what is one of the many scoops of this book, for to the best of my knowledge it has never been written as clearly anywhere before in the mainstream wine book literature, Nebbiolo Lampia's berries tend to become much paler, pinkish even, when exposed to large amounts of sunlight. In other words, they look very much like those of Nebbiolo Rosé, that are somewhat lighter-colored (pinkish-blue rather than deep blue) by definition. That is one of the reasons why it can be very hard to distinguish between these two grapes in vineyards, unless he or she who is doing the observing has quite a bit of grapevine-viewing experience. I can honestly tell you that I have been hunting relentlessly for Nebbiolo Rosé in Barolo's and Barbaresco's vineyards for thirty years now and I still have trouble telling them apart with 100% certainty, so imagine just how hard it is for someone living in New York, London, Pretoria, Melbourne, or Tokyo all year long and who might get to Italy only once in a while (if that) throughout the year. You want to know just how hard it is to distinguish between Nebbiolo Lampia and Nebbiolo Rosé? Well, even producers standing right there in their vineyards and looking at the grapes with me, even though they know for a fact they have both Lampia and Rosé growing there, often can't tell me which is which. *That's* how hard.

Furthermore, the current understanding of grape genetics is still evolving, and so what we know today might well be proven wrong tomorrow. Looking to the future and taking into consideration the incredible speed at which our scientific knowledge base changes, not to mention the complexity that is the grapevine DNA, there are some other helpful notions to be aware of. For example, grapevines are well-known to have very heterozygous genomes, in which there can be found a great number of genomic rearrangements including deletions, insertions, duplications, and translocations (Kosugi, Momozawa, Liu *et al.* 2019). Those rearrangements that are larger than 50 bp are called "structural variations". Presently, structural variations represent a not completely understood source of genetic variation mainly because of a lack of study and as a result of detection limitations of the currently available scientific research methodologies. However, it has become apparent that characterizing structural variations in grapevines is of fundamental importance, given that these have great impact on a variety of grapevine characteristics, including phenotypic traits of productive interest. Such as, for example, color (Carbonell-Bejerano, Royo, Torres-Pérez *et al* 2017); resistance to pathogens (Roach, Johnson, Bohlmann, *et al* 2018); and features associated with the determination of sex type (Massonnet, Cochetel, Minio *et al* 2020).

However, we cannot run out and change our ampelographic platform data every year, if for no other reason that denominations are at least partly based on specific ampelographic guidelines that cannot be realistically changed at every turn of test tube, graduated cylinder, PCR or Western blot. Until only recently, basic scientific understanding was that there exists only one genome for one species, with minor variations accounting for the existence of biotypes. But as mentioned above, as long as genetic differences are minor, the individuals can all be considered to be part of the same species (a spotted yellow jaguar or leopard is still the same animal as a black panther even though the two have very different coats, because everything else is essentially the same). By contrast, when the variations become substantial, then we can speak of different varieties altogether (so for example, a jaguar is not the same thing as a leopard, even though the two are big cats and have spotted coats; in fact, they live in completely different parts of the world, and present many differences save for a similarly looking spotted coat, but in fact even the spots of these two big cats are in fact very different). Therefore, modern research and scientific advances have made increasingly clear that there exists the need to study the entire genome assemblies of multiple individuals of the same species. In other words, single references are not sufficient in identifying the genetic complexity of a species. This new way of thinking has led to the introduction of a new concept in genetic science, that of "pan-genomes". Pan-genomes is a term that refers to the reality of a species in its entirety, whereby species are characterized not just by the core genomic template common to all individuals of that species, but also by a "disposable" genome composed of genomic features not shared by all individuals (Morgante, De Paoli, Radovic 2007). The pan-genome of many different plant species have been identified: for example, of cabbage (Golicz, Bayer, Barker *et al* 2016) and of the sunflower (Hübner, Bercovich, Todesco *et al* 2019). Grapevines are now being increasingly studied in this light too. The concept of pangenomes further allows us to view Nebbiolo Rosé and Nebbiolo Lampia as biotypes or subvarieties; at least until the day in which one of the two will have mutated to a degree such that taking it to be a distinct variety will be unavoidable. This based not just on genetic grounds but on practical ones too (because of eventual obvious morphological, viticultural and enological differences that are however not present currently).

For sure, the grapevine DNA is far more complex than we first imagined, and if some leeway is not accepted, then we will likely be forced in the near future into distinguishing between hundreds and hundreds of grapes that are now considered to be one and the same. Where would it end? This situation has come about because modern science is giving us tools by which to further refine our identification of grape varieties, but in so doing we risk getting to the point where it becomes almost too much of a good thing. As Emanuelli and associates stated clearly (2013), if and when the grapes and their wines present noteworthy differences, then they ought to be considered as distinct varieties, but in all other cases it is perhaps more practical to consider them as biotypes or subvarieties of each other. Clearly, it would be just so easy to state that Barolo can be made not just with "Nebbiolo" but with "Nebbiolo and Nebbiolo Rosé", but in the bureaucratic world we all live in, that really is too much to ask.

Personal observations, memories and anecdotes

Twenty or thirty years ago when I went around asking about Nebbiolo Rosé, while everybody I talked to was kind, patient and generous with their time and knowledge, most told me that Nebbiolo Rosé was not worth wasting much time on. (Others elsewhere in Italy were telling me the same thing about Bellone, Bombino Nero, Centesimino, Malvasia del Lazio, Nerello Mascalese, Pecorino, Trebbiano Abruzzese, Uva di Troia and the likes, so Nebbiolo Rosé was unfortunately in very good company.)

Despite this, I began to realize it really couldn't be so, and that the variety was not just a real good wine grape, but quite capable in the right hands of giving fantastic wines. No, I'm not a genius: as mentioned, it's just I had seen the same thing happen before, for example with a bunch of other forgotten grape varieties that hinted they might potentially be excellent wine grapes after all, and so I was well aware of the importance of wine grapes relative to wine. It was apparent to me that with Nebbiolo Rosé along the way something had been lost in translation. So why was it that I started thinking things might not be exactly the way everyone seemed to think? I believed in Nebbiolo Rosé's outstanding wine grape potential for at least three very good reasons.

First and foremost, some of the best Barolos and Barbarescos I have ever tasted were reportedly (supposedly?) 100% Nebbiolo Rosé. I have learned from experience that when this happens it is never by chance, and that a great deal of the merit must go to the wine grape, not just to the producer (which is instead where all the credit usually goes, unless it's automatically assigned to the type of oak or of natural yeast used or some other thing). Years ago, everyone believed Trebbiano Abruzzese to be a garbage wine grape: and yet, Valentini made, and makes, one of Italy's five best white wines with it (for many people, Italy's best white wine, period). Still, that very obvious fact got poor Trebbiano Abruzzese no traction whatsoever.

Valentini being a remarkably talented genius, everyone believed his wine to be a fluke that existed in a vacuum: to them, such a great wine was possible thanks *only* to Valentini being a supremely gifted winemaker. I heard this over and over again from countless people and "experts" throughout my early years. To their way of thinking, this happened *despite* the grape variety he was using. Not so: we have now learned that Valentini (actually, Valentinis: both father and son boasted/boast crystalline talent), grew the real, authentic, Trebbiano Abruzzese variety, that was instead basically non-existent in the rest of Abruzzo's vineyards (for the longest time, Trebbiano Abruzzese was confused with Bombino Bianco, Mostosa and even Trebbiano Toscano: most

Abruzzo vineyards are planted with those grapes, not Trebbiano Abruzzese, which is an exceedingly rare variety). We have since seen that those talented producers who, like Valentini, *do* own vines of the real Trebbiano Abruzzese (Tiberio, Valle Reale) also happen to make outstanding wines with the variety. Consequently, it's not the grape that is or was the problem; and though producer talent is clearly all important, it is not the only factor accounting for the greatness of a wine. I mean, let's face it: if they give you lemons, I don't care how talented you are, but you are still only going to make lemonade. Maybe good lemonade, even very good lemonade: but it's still lemonade. Analogously to the plight of Trebbiano Abruzzese and many other grapes, when in the 1990s it became apparent that Italy was making some truly noteworthy Müller-Thurgau wines (such as those of Tiefenbrunner and Pojer & Sandri), pundits everywhere refused to take the wines too seriously and were saying and writing Italy should be planting Riesling instead. You can hardly blame them: given the oceans of mediocre, flat, sweet and cheap German wines of no pedigree made with it, few wine grapes had a reputation worse than that of Müller-Thurgau. It was suggested in writing that Riesling planted in the same sites would have made a much better wine, so why waste them on Müller-Thurgau? Maybe so, though it's not a given that Riesling planted in the same sites would give great results: but anyways, who cares? The Müller-Thurgau wines in question happened to be excellent and delicious made from beautiful old vines that had adapted perfectly to a finite production zone. And you have to give up on the grape just because it's not famous so that you can plant Riesling there because it's the cool one? *Puh-leeze.* With all due respect, I trust you realize this is a wrong mindset and framework to be working out of. You can't just label a grape variety negatively even in the face of clear-cut evidence (right there in your glass) that it can in fact make very good wine, if only it is given a chance to do so. Practically the whole Franken is planted to Silvaner, so unless they're all drunk there, it's likely that Silvaner isn't a lowly grape variety either; in Niagara, they make lovely wines from Gamay, hardly anybody's idea of a noble grape. But if those people grow it (and an increasing number at that), there's probably a reason. And the wines made there with it are delicious.

And so it was, and is, with Nebbiolo Rosé. People were uprooting it left and right because it either gave wines lacking in body (or so they thought) and lacking in color (that much is partly true, but not always. See below). Nobody was giving it much of a chance. And yet, there were plenty of hints that the variety wasn't quite the also-ran that most people made it out to be. For example, though sporadic, there were plenty of great wines made entirely with Nebbiolo Rosé. Still today, one of the four or five best Barolos I have ever tasted is the Vietti 1971 Barolo Briacca (100% Nebbiolo Rosé), a wine I have been fortunate enough to taste on a number of different occasions, from North America to Italy to Asia. As talented as Alfredo Currado was, a similar result cannot be due to his talent alone, given that I like the Briacca even better than his other excellent 1971 wines. Other reportedly 100% Nebbiolo Rosé Barolos and Barbarescos were almost as spectacular as the Briacca; they too were, quite literally, unforgettable wines. For example, even though it's not a Barolo, the Giovannini Moresco Barbaresco Podere del Pajoré is in my opinion the best Barbaresco of its era, a wine the quality of which has rarely been reached since in Barbaresco. Besides the old-timer wines, we also have the outstanding 100% Nebbiolo Rosé Barolo made in modern times by Cogno (the Barolo Ravera Riserva Vigna Elena), plus a bunch of Barolos in which Nebbiolo Rosé is front and center (as well as an increasing number of wines from Barbaresco I will detail at length in the upcoming book on Barbaresco) that showcase just how fantastic Barolos (and Barbarescos) made with the supposedly "lowly" Nebbiolo Rosé can be. And more and more producers are using Nebbiolo Rosé to make, perhaps appropriately enough given its name, a Nebbiolo Rosato wine.

Second, every Barolo and Barbaresco I tasted over the years that boasted a large percentage of Nebbiolo Rosé was almost always (and is) a more interesting, if not better wine than many Barolos and Barbarescos without any Nebbiolo Rosé. In general, I have found that including 20% Nebbiolo Rosé clearly marks that wine, which will often (but not always) have a slightly lighter color and more of a garnet hue, but at the same time a very specific, highly recognizable perfume (see below) and texture that borders on the sexy and sultry. And at 40-50% of the blend, the Barolo is for all intents and purposes a Nebbiolo Rosé wine, as the variety completely takes over from Nebbiolo Lampia and Michet. The presence of Nebbiolo Rosé in a wine really is very recognizable: at a recent tasting in a winery the producer gave me a mystery red wine to taste. After sniffing and tasting, I told him that it seemed to me like it had been made with Nebbiolo Rosé. And it was in fact 100% Nebbiolo Rosé (my friend I was visiting the winery with almost fell off his chair, while the producer smiled knowingly). More or less at the same time, a visit at the Poderi Oddero winery had the same outcome. Upon tasting one of the new vintages of a Barolo the estate is reputed for, I remarked it struck me as being made with at least some Nebbiolo Rosé. Mariacristina Oddero looked at me squinting her eyes and asked: "Why do you say that, Ian? I'd really like to know". I answered that it was mostly because of the wine's very particular olfactory profile (but not just): the combination of sultry sour red cherry, violet, cinnamon stick and nutmeg just made me think there was at least a little Nebbiolo Rosé in the blend. And there was.

Clearly, Nebbiolo Lampia needs no help from Nebbiolo Rosé or any other grape in giving world class wines that are often unforgettable. But it always struck me as downright singular that when tasting from cask and bottle, more often than not, my favorite Barolos were always those made with a percentage of Nebbiolo Rosé. Granted, some of this may be nothing more than just a matter of personal preference (you like Syrah, I like Cabernet Franc, he likes Durif, she likes Marselan), but over the years I have found others feel the same as I do. I mean, given that most everybody (but admittedly not everybody, and that too was important in forming my thought process) was saying the variety was worthless or close to it, I was left scratching my head. How could it be? Those Barolo producers who didn't mind a little Nebbiolo Rosé in their wines (actually, it was more like they tolerated it) always mentioned that such wines were more perfumed and elegant than their wines where when Nebbiolo Rosé was absent. And so it was that I slowly began to think that there was more to Nebbiolo Rosé than everyone seemed to think. But just *how much more* was driven home to me one specific day.

In fact, to be precise, not one day, but two days. And about two years apart. Two Eureka-like moments that enlightened me for good on just how great a wine top-heavy with Nebbiolo Rosé could be. The first moment occurred in 2005, the second in 2007 (time flies, doesn't it?), and in both occasions, I was visiting the Ruggeri Corsini estate in Monforte d'Alba (which is important, because it helps diminish confounding variables).

This little-known, high-quality estate is owned by Nicola Argamante, one of Italy's foremost grape scientists and researchers, not to mention an individual who knows a great deal about Nebbiolo Rosé. Still today, I consider that very first interview I recorded with Nicola Argamante to be amongst the most interesting three or so hours I have ever spent in the company of a wine producer. And so it was that in 2005 I was visiting the winery and tasting through Argamante's lineup of wines and also learning about Nicola's Russian heritage (Argamante is a name adapted from Agamentow: his great-grandfather was a general in the Russian Army). Argamante is not just a nice man, he's a brilliant one who excels not just at wine research but at winemaking too. His estate (and of his wife Loredana: he makes the wines, she tends the vines, helped out now by older daughter Francesca) is really a gem. On that occasion, I tasted his 2004 Langhe Nebbiolo, an utterly amazing wine (and as you see by my writing about it eighteen years later, I still remember it). That wine was an incredibly pure concentrate of sour red cherry, sweet spices, cinnamon, nutmeg, minerals and red rose perfume blessed with an utterly refined, penetrating perfume and mouthfeel. It literally blew me away and was, and still is, easily the best Langhe Nebbiolo I have ever tasted. The. Best. Ever. Tasted.

I mean the thing was even better than many Barolos I had tasted all week long: granted, it didn't have the power of a Barolo, but it wasn't really supposed to, being a Langhe Nebbiolo. The wine's secret? To my way of thinking that it had been made, by Argamante's own admission, with 40% Nebbiolo Rosé. Forty. As far as I was and am concerned, there was no other way by which to explain that wine's exceptional goodness, uniqueness and remarkable purity of fruit and perfume. This because the vineyard's age wasn't especially old; the pedigree of the vineyard area was in no way comparable to Roero's Valmaggiore or Occhetti vineyard districts (all Roero *grand crus* for Nebbiolo, rather than Barolo, wines); and Argamante, though talented, likeable, and a very good winemaker in his own right the wines of whom I personally really like, was not accredited by anyone with Bruno Giacosa- or Roberto Conterno-like levels of *bravura* (in fairness, few wine people anywhere are).

Therefore, the reason for the wine's magnificence had to lie elsewhere, and it was the wine's amazing perfumed purity that truly opened my eyes to the importance of Nebbiolo Rosé in any Nebbiolo wine. By adding this revelation to what I already knew about the goodness of some old Barolos made with large percentages of and even 100% Nebbiolo Rosé, it was all too easy for me to see the light. Never before a truth in wine became so apparent to me, never before had this point been driven home so well and so deep. Suffice it to say, there weren't that many Nebbiolo wines or Barolos being made with 40% Nebbiolo Rosé back then, so believe you me, that revelation stuck a chord. A revelatory chord, you might say.

That first eureka-like moment was followed up by a second one, roughly two years or so later when I was back at Ruggeri Corsini to taste the estate's new vintages. On that occasion, I drank the 2006 Langhe Nebbiolo (I don't know why but I can't find any of my notes on the Ruggeri Corsini 2005 Langhe Nebbiolo, though I am sure I tasted it at one time or another). Having never forgotten the 2004 Langhe Nebbiolo, I was really looking forward to my visit at the winery and tasting the 2006 version. (As an aside, it tells you exactly how good that 2004 Langhe Nebbiolo must have been inasmuch I was so looking forward to, in visiting a Barolo producer, to tasting not one of his various very fine Barolos but his Langhe Nebbiolo.) But I was left dumbfounded. Though good, the 2006 Langhe Nebbiolo completely unmoved me: so much so, that even Argamante noticed my lack of enthusiasm, and it's something that I usually hide well in front of producers.

Honestly: it's hard for me to effectively put into words, but I was really shocked by how different the 2006 Ruggeri Corsini Langhe Nebbiolo was compared to the 2004 that I remembered so well. The 2006 was a perfectly fine Langhe Nebbiolo, but so different from the 2004 that I just had to ask Argamante why it was so; given that both the 2004 and 2006 were stellar vintages (though admittedly very different vintages), and that the estate's viticulture and winemaking had not changed, I couldn't understand what had happened. The 2006 Langhe Nebbiolo was much deeper in color, bigger, and fleshier than I remembered the wine being back in 2004; furthermore, it was fairly shut down on the nose. By contrast, the 2004 was magically perfumed (and keep in mind that in the Langhe, the 2004 growing season was hotter than 2006: if anything, it should have been the 2006 wine showcasing more perfume and grace, not the other way around).

Argamante told me the only difference he could think of was that over that short time span his new Nebbiolo vineyards had started producing grapes, and so, given the vines were too young to be used to make Barolo, in they went to make more Langhe Nebbiolo. But in so doing, the percentage of the Nebbiolo Rosé in the Ruggeri Corsini Langhe Nebbiolo fell from the 40% of 2004 to the roughly 10%-15% of the 2006 wine (the new vineyards had been planted not with the "lowly" Nebbiolo Rosé CN 111 clone but with an array of new generation Nebbiolo clones that everyone in the Langhe, nurseries included, raved about at the time).

Which was all fine and dandy, but for me the result was nothing short of a disaster: and again, I want to stress that it was not because the bigger, fleshier 2006 wine was a poor wine (quite the contrary). But it completely lacked the unique perfume, vibrancy and magical balance of the 2004 I remembered so vividly. I can safely say that in all my lifetime dedicated to wine, I have rarely had a better demonstration of just how important grape varieties can be in the making of a wine. You know, people ask me all the time why I became interested in native grapes; what it is I like about them; and why I continue to write about them. Well, here you have a crystal-clear example of *why*. To this day, I rate this one cellar visit as one of the ten most important and formative of my entire wine career. For I didn't have just a good time: I learned. In fact, a life-altering moment of learning.

Clearly, it is not lost on me that my Ruggeri Corsini Langhe Nebbiolo example won't be of much use to any of you in helping to reach an understanding of the potential greatness of Nebbiolo Rosé (those two 2004 and 2006 wines are long gone and not available for anyone to taste and compare anymore). No problem: happily, there are some other outstanding Barolos (Barbarescos too, and even table wines) that showcase the potential greatness of Nebbiolo Rosé in the Langhe and what it may add to a Nebbiolo wine. For example, Sylla Sebaste's Barolo Bussia and Bricco delle Viole bottlings provide an affordable and illuminating taste test that is easy to do. While the Bricco delle Viole bottling has little or no Nebbiolo Rosé in it and is a very average quality Barolo at best, the Barolo Bussia, which boasts instead as much as 40% Nebbiolo Rosé in its blend, is simply a fantastic wine, a real standout. The difference between the two is striking, to say the least.

Need more intel? Well, at the Giovanni Canonica estate, two different Barolos are also made: the Barolo Paiagallo and the Barolo Grinzane Cavour (or more accurately, the Barolo del Comune di Grinzane Cavour). The more famous Barolo of the two is the former (it's more famous only because it boasts the name of a vineyard district/MGA on its label, while the other wine does not): but though an excellent wine, Canonica's Paiagallo Barolo is not so different from many other big and fleshy Barolos made everywhere in the denomination.

By contrast, Canonica's Barolo Grinzane Cavour, which isn't even made from one specific reputable *cru* (the grapes come from just outside the Borzoni vineyard district), is a much more interesting, perfumed, elegant wine. The most important difference between the two? Simple: the Grinzane Cavour bottling includes up to 30-40% Nebbiolo Rosé (at least), compared to a big fat *el zilcho* in the Paiagallo (though in fairness, I am sure the relatively older vines of the Grinzane Cavour bottling also play a role in delivering a wine of much greater depth and complexity). And though I am not discussing Nebbiolo Rosé relative to Barbaresco in this book (I will do so in the next soon to come book on Barbaresco), I will briefly mention the Sottimano estate. As good as Sottimano's Barbaresco wines are (I love them all), there is no doubt that it is the Barbaresco Pajorè bottling that is almost always the estate's best wine in every vintage. The secret to that wine, besides the magic of the Pajorè (by all accounts one of Barbaresco's five best vineyard districts) and the old vines planted there, is the up to 40% Nebbiolo Rosé in the blend (an amount lacking in the other Sottimano Barbaresco single-site Barbarescos).

By the way, the plight of Ruggeri Corsini's Langhe Nebbiolo is not, in my experience, an isolated incident. Nebbiolo Rosé's Rodney Dangerfield-like "can't get no respect" reality caused infinite harm. Any chance producers had to get rid of it in favor of something else, they did. Giuseppe Mascarello's fantastic Barolo Monprivato, one of the truly historical and great wines of all Barolo, tells a similar tale to that of Argamante's Langhe Nebbiolo. Rather unfortunately, when the ultra-talented Mauro Mascarello decided to make his super-expensive, top of the line Ca' d' Morissio Barolo beginning with the 1993 vintage, he ripped out two plots in the Monprivato cru planted to Nebbiolo Rosé to make way for the supposedly higher quality and better performing old Nebbiolo Michet massal selections. I don't know about you, but to be perfectly candid, I think that neither the Barolo Monprivato nor the Ca' d' Morissio benefited greatly from the move. I could very well be wrong in my assessment, but I don't think so at all.

The third reason why I believed Nebbiolo Rosé was a grape variety of potential greatness was thanks to Bruno Giacosa, the recognized *maestro* of Barolo and Barbaresco. Though it's not common knowledge because he never much talked about this aspect of his winemaking (or perhaps more precisely, nobody knew to ask), I can tell you that Giacosa purposely looked for and sourced Nebbiolo Rosé, and was very aware of which vineyards it grew in. Given that Giacosa was Italy's single greatest winemaker (I'm in good company in believing this), that in and of itself should tell you something right there. I know it tells me something.

Clearly, Giacosa's intent was always to look for the best Nebbiolo grapes possible, and not to buy Nebbiolo Rosé *per se*, as he wasn't convinced that the variety could make a truly stellar wine on its own (mind you, it helps put things in perspective to know that Giacosa didn't think La Morra could give truly great Barolos either). And yet, he was convinced that Nebbiolo Rosé's presence could be useful in making much better Barolos and Barbarescos overall ("it helps me fix my Barolo", he used to tell not just me but some of the producers he bought Nebbiolo Rosé grapes from: the use of the word *aggiustare* or "fix" in this context is highly telling of the improvement he thought an addition of Nebbiolo Rosé could bring). I trust you will catch the immense irony of the fact that Italy's best winemaker searched for and wanted to have Nebbiolo Rosé in his wines (in some years and in some cases, at least), while the vast majority of far less talented Barolo and Barbaresco producers were ripping it up and doing away with the variety altogether. If you think back at what I told you about Valentini and Trebbiano Abruzzese, you realize you don't need to listen to Shirley Bassey and the Propellerheads to realize there really is such a thing as "history repeating".

A quick word about biodiversity

One more observation about my early years in the company of Nebbiolo Rosé bears highlighting, and it has nothing to do with me, you, or Barolo (at least, not on a merely and oh-so lowly individual scale). Shining the spotlight on Nebbiolo Rosé by asking questions when visiting producers and then talking and writing about it was a means by which I could show producers that some people out there were in fact paying attention and believed in the grape. Producers are very cognizant of what sells and what does not: wine is, after all, their livelihood.

If nobody ever asks about a specific wine grape, or asks to drink the wine made with it, while clamoring instead for stuff made with a more fashionably popular grape, producers start thinking that they might be better off doing away with the former and planting more of the latter. It's inevitable. It follows that by showing interest in a specific grape and wine, you are doing something for that grape and for wine (besides looking like you know a little something and that you care). So, you are actually doing something highly positive. In the grander scheme of things, every time you inquire at a winery, or in a wine shop or a restaurant, about a little-known grape variety and its wines, you are doing something on behalf of the Earth's biodiversity. Now I don't know just *how* true that last statement may or may not be. To what extent, I mean. But what I do know is that every time I visit a winery in Barolo and Barbaresco nowadays producers everywhere are quick to tell me about their Nebbiolo Rosé vines and wines, and they pull out experimental samples for me to try. This was almost never the case before; but now they do, and to the point where it's becoming a stampede. Nowadays, I get Nebbiolo Rosé and its wines shoved into my face even without opening my mouth. (Of course, they do so because they know I'm interested and will write about it, but I'm honestly surprised by how much things have changed over the years.) For in ultimate analysis, I'm just happy they either still have, or have thought of replanting, Nebbiolo Rosé in their vineyards. In the long run, they, me, and everyone else will be better for it. Clearly, all of us who love grapes and pine for the biodiversity of our sickly planet still need to remain vigilant and engaged. For if the sun also rises, it also sets.

Where to find it

Nebbiolo Rosé has always been most common in the Langhe, well represented in both Barolo and Barbaresco. Though Nebbiolo Rosé was grown everywhere in the Barolo denomination, it appears to have been more abundant in the townships of Barolo, Castiglione Falletto, Diano d'Alba, La Morra, and Serralunga d'Alba. Apparently, there was never too much Nebbiolo Rosé planted in Monforte, an impression confirmed to me by Claudio Conterno. It was also fairly scarce in Verduno, because as Fabio Alessandria of G.B. Burlotto points out, Verduno's Barolos are already so relatively light in structure, perfumed and forward that there was no need to gentrify the wines any further with Nebbiolo Rosé's gentler charms.

For all its relative scarcity, Nebbiolo Rosé was and is also present in the Roero and Lombardy's Valtellina, while it seems to have not been all that common in Alto Piemonte and the Valle d'Aosta. Why this may be is absolutely fascinating and closely linked to how little we still know about Nebbiolo Rosé (a subject that I will broach below). In any case, surveys of historical importance have documented that in Valtellina, Nebbiolo Rosé was identical to the local Chiavennaschino variety (previously believed to be Grignolino, which as I mentioned before was often confused with Nebbiolo Rosé). As Nebbiolo Rosé can tolerate higher ambient temperatures than does Nebbiolo Lampia, it has always been well-liked in the Valtellina and its potentially hot (in the summertime, at least) viticultural areas such as Inferno (this name tells you all you need to know) and Sassella. An added plus that Nebbiolo Rosé is that it is more drought-resistant than Nebbiolo Lampia (something that is of increasing importance in the Langhe, and Barolo producers are now keenly aware of this advantage Nebbiolo Rosé brings to the table).

Tellingly, documents such as those of the Ampelography Commission of the province of Sondrio (Gerini 1884) mention a Chiavenasca Piccola or Chiavennaschino (Nebbiolo Rosé) cultivated over a not small surface of five hundred hectares, compared to the only one thousand hectares grown of the Chiavenasca Comune (Nebbiolo), and the two hundred hectares of Chiavenasca Intagliata (very likely Nebbiolo Michet, as *intagliata* refers to the subvariety's heavily indented leaf, typical of Michet). Yes, I have written *chiavenasca*, with one "n": this is not a typo, for that was in fact the spelling (with only one *n*) used back then and so it is written in the old records I have sourced (by contrast, it's called and written *chiavennasca* today).

What the producers say: then and now

In fact, it is not completely true that everyone thought poorly of Nebbiolo Rosé: it just seems that way, but if you actually take time to dig a little further, a slightly different tale emerges. It is a tale that tells of two centuries worth of Italian viticultural and enological difficulty, and the forlorn White Queen-Black Queen scenario that is the human mind.

Clearly, in the late 1980s and 1990s when winemaking became a dog race in which the participants were all bent on coming ahead in making the biggest blackest and meanest wine possible, Nebbiolo Rosé stood no chance. But it was not always so. In centuries past, when wine was mostly a matter of survival and not the object of what were believed to be high-quality productions (and Italy being a fundamentally poor country, survival was very much an everyday reality for numerous families), Nebbiolo Rosé was reportedly appreciated by farmers because of its capacity to accumulate sugar, generally copious productivity, and outstanding resistance to drought and diseases (all of which are superior to Nebbiolo Lampia's).

Though there appears to have always been more Nebbiolo Lampia growing in the Piedmontese countryside than Nebbiolo Rosé, the latter variety was tended to with care. In fact, Claudio Rosso (of the Gigi Rosso estate at the time of the interview in which he told me as follows) told me that in the late nineteenth and early twentieth century it was common for growers to use their Nebbiolo Rosé vines to make wine for personal use, often interrupting fermentation to leave it slightly sweet (Nebbiolo Lampia also has a long history of being used to make sweet wines). Given the haphazard winemaking conditions of those days and Nebbiolo Rosé's penchant for easy accumulation of sugar, the wine ended up being slightly sweet more often than not (because come the cold weather, fermentations would stop, leaving some residual sugar behind). Rosso told me that people were generally fond of Nebbiolo Rosé and its wines: this much is apparent from the fact that it was regularly offered to important guests and relatives, a sure-fire sign that they didn't think Nebbiolo Rosé's wines to be so poor after all, or they wouldn't have chosen to serve such wines (unless of course they neither liked the relatives nor the guests). Furthermore, knowledgeable producers appreciated that including a small portion of Nebbiolo Rosé in their Nebbiolo wines led to more perfumed and refined wines that, though not necessarily better than those made with Nebbiolo Lampia alone, scored points due to their being so different. As a matter of fact, back in the eighteenth and nineteenth centuries, the Italian nobility and those with the means to buy wines in large volumes preferred elegant, lighter-styled wines because those stood out from the pack of the more common (literally) bigger, thicker and ultimately coarser wines that were then the norm. This same preference also accounts for the eighteenth and nineteenth centuries popularity of Grignolino (a variety often confused with Nebbiolo Rosé) the wines of which were held in much higher esteem than those of Barbera, for example (D'Agata 2019).

Nebbiolo Rosé's fortunes began to plummet in the 1980s when Barolo was beginning to be made as an "important" red wine that was slowly starting to attract more and more foreign importers. Clearly, there wasn't much interest in a grape that had most people thinking would bring a dilutional component to the finished wine. A situation made that much worse by the tendency in some quarters to give high scores only to those wines, or so it seemed at least, that had more in common with bodybuilders than they did fine wine.

In fairness, people preferring darker-colored and increasingly thicker-textured wines was not the only reason why Nebbiolo Rosé grapes were harder to sell at the time. Nebbiolo Rosé's pale-colored grapes had *negozianti* and mediators shunning them, in the belief that what they were looking at was really unripe Nebbiolo. In other words, not a Nebbiolo the grapes of which were naturally pale pinkish-reddish-blue in color, but a Nebbiolo that had been picked before reaching full ripeness. So those trying to sell their Nebbiolo Rosé grapes at the Alba market and elsewhere were often left holding the bag (of grapes). In time, a greater awareness of the complexity that is the world of Nebbiolo grapes led people to realize that Nebbiolo Rosé had its own traits that differ slightly from those of Nebbiolo Lampia. And as these things tend to go, fads finally fade (alliteration intended) and so, early in the twenty-first century, the pendulum swung again: perfumed, refined red wines of a less extreme color were suddenly back in vogue. The problem being of course that by the time Nebbiolo Rosé and its wines were finally beginning to garner new admirers, there wasn't really much Nebbiolo Rosé left in the vineyards (unfortunately, in viticulture you can't just flip a switch and undo decades of neglect). This is why it is vital to intervene before the damage done is too great. This is also one of the reasons why I write about the things I write about: because I hope such observations will get people to stop and think, if even for just a split second: then they are free to disagree of course, but at least I have done my small part.

Among today's producers, opinions on Nebbiolo Rosé fall squarely into two camps: those who don't care for it, and those who do, though the pendulum has recently been shifting more and more in favour of the latter view. However, there are discordant opinions about the variety's characteristic traits between producers. A minority of producers believe the variety not to be so early-ripening after all, and finds its wines can be rather full-bodied, but after reviewing the data and my interviews accumulated over the years, it is clear that that this is not the view of the majority. For the most part, the preponderant opinion about Nebbiolo Rosé, its viticultural behavior and its wines, is that Nebbiolo Rosé is a relatively early-ripening variety (relative to Nebbiolo Lampia that is, but both are actually late ripening varieties, and therein lies part of the confusion); that it is characterized by big bunches and grapes not to mention copious productivity; and that it will produce relatively pale red wines blessed with outstanding perfume.

There are more Barolo producers who think highly of Nebbiolo Rosé than is commonly imagined. Back in July 2008, Cordero di Montezemolo pointed out to me that he thought Cogno's Barolo Riserva Vigna Elena was an outstanding wine. In another 2008 interview, Claudio Rosso, then of the Gigi Rosso estate confirmed that he actually quite liked Nebbiolo Rosé and that over the years he had followed three specific Nebbiolo Rosé grapevines very closely and was planning to have his favorite local nursery proceed with a massal selection. Osvaldo Viberti of the eponymous winery in the Serra dei Turchi fraction of La Morra also liked Nebbiolo Rosé and owned 0.5 hectares of 45 years old Nebbiolo Rosé vines he believed gave great wines; at the Giovanni Viberti estate they believe Nebbiolo Rosé to be a big part of the secret of their wine's easy drinkability and perfumed, refined charm. So much so that they use Nebbiolo Rosé to make their Nebbiolo Rosato wine. Get it? A Nebbiolo Rosato wine, or a Rosé wine (pink wines are commonly referred to all over the world with the French word), that is made with Nebbiolo Rosé! A Rosé of Rosé, if you will. What can I tell you, I get my thrills where I can.

Luciano Sandrone of the Sandrone winery has had a ton of experience with Nebbiolo biotypes of all kinds: count him among those convinced that Nebbiolo Rosé's biggest asset is the perfume it endows wines with. Already back in 1993, when we were chatting on this and other subjects during a visit to his estate (back then the Sandrone winery was not where it is today, but housed in a much less grandiose but functional building located at the top of hill way above where the modern-day winery is located). In the company of my good friend Brad, a wine loving gourmet and doctor from Chicago with whom I studied with, Sandrone told us that Nebbiolo Rosé added another dimension to Barolo, but that there wasn't that much left of it in the vineyards anymore (again, that was the reality already in 1993). Though he did not think there was any in his vineyards in Cannubi Boschis, he did have some amongst the older vines that made up his Le Vigne bottling at the time (the vineyard grape sources for Le Vigne have since changed).

Like Sandrone, Roberto Conterno of Giacomo Conterno does not mind Nebbiolo Rosé, but does not believe it can give a truly great wine on its own, as for him, the wine's color is just too light. That said, he likes the wine's perfume, and believes he owns anywhere from 10-15% Nebbiolo Rosé in his Francia vineyards (to the best of his knowledge there isn't any in his new Cerretta holdings, though there might be a little in the Arione vineyard he bought from Gigi Rosso). At the small but high-quality Giovanni Canonica estate located in Barolo's town center, owner Gianni (Giovanni was his father) admits to being a fan of Nebbiolo Rosé, though he recalls that his first time working with the grape he was left initially shocked. "The first time I vinified Nebbiolo grapes from my vineyard plots in Grinzane Cavour (the first vintage of his Barolo del Comune di Grinzane Cavour was the 2012), I couldn't believe what my eyes were seeing: I pressed the grapes, but despite the usual amount of skin contact, the must was pink, almost clear in fact, rather than red. I thought I had done something wrong!" he laughs. No, he had not: it was just that he didn't realize he had as much Nebbiolo Rosé in the vineyard as he did (which tells you just how difficult it can be, in some cases at least, to distinguish Nebbiolo Rosé from Nebbiolo Lampia, an important matter I shall tackle in some depth shortly).

Claudio Conterno of the Conterno Fantino estate believes that Nebbiolo Rosé expresses aromas unlike those of any Nebbiolo he has ever worked with, and speaks of a delicate but piercing wild red rose smell that is immediately recognizable and unmistakable. In merit to the intensity of the penetrating perfume of Nebbiolo Rosé wines, I find very interesting what Roberto Vezza of the Josetta Saffirio estate told me back in 2001. Vezza, a friend of Luciano Sandrone (the two worked together for a long time before each had their own estate to work in: Sandrone at his own eponymous estate and Vezza, husband of Josetta Saffirio, at that estate) told me that he and Sandrone had tasted together countless Barolos over the years. He complained that differently from the 1980s, when they could clearly tell from which township the various Barolos they blind tasted came from, for a variety of reasons this was much harder to do by the 1990s. In contrast, he emphasized that it was always still possible to recognize when a Barolo had at least 10% Nebbiolo Rosé in it, as the wines really stood out thanks to their perfume and gracefulness.

Virna Borgogno of the Virna estate in Barolo (Virna was the first woman to graduate from enology school in Italy) says that about 10% of her vineyards in Cerviano Merli (Novello) and Sarmassa (Barolo) are planted to Nebbiolo Rosé. Rather acutely, she states that Nebbiolo Rosé is not just extremely interesting because of its heat- and drought-resistance (always a topic of interest in these times of climate change) but because practically all the Nebbiolo Rosé vines left in the vineyards are very old. Therefore, sourcing any small plot of Nebbiolo Rosé vines would amount to, logically enough, a welcome stroke of luck and be a real plus, in her eyes. You can hardly fault her logic.

In the early 2000s, Mauro Manzone of the Giovanni Manzone winery in Monforte was a big believer in Nebbiolo Rosé. He made the point that in his opinion at least, the relative paucity of Nebbiolo Rosé-dedicated vineyards was oftentimes not so much a consequence of producers not wanting to plant Nebbiolo Rosé because of its perceived defects, but because it was just very hard to find and plant vineyards with (and that's still true today). According to him, Nebbiolo Rosé was neither easy to source in vineyards so as to obtain massal selections, nor did nurseries ever have much of it on hand. Therefore, even if a Barolo estate wished to plant Nebbiolo Rosé, it was just not available for them to do so. In this light, the Viberti estate has told me that getting the Nebbiolo clone CN 111 from the nursery, even though the nursery describes it in its catalogue, is easier said than done and that everyone now just has to rely on massal selections. Given that Nebbiolo Rosé is more resistant to heat and drought and that it gives very good to downright great wines, maybe the nursery will think things through and figure out that maybe having Nebbiolo clone CN 111 to sell might be a very good idea after all. I will broach this very interesting aspect of the Nebbiolo Rosé discussion a bit more in-depth at the end of this chapter.

Just how much Manzone liked Nebbiolo Rosé is well exemplified by the following story. In the late 1990s and early 2000s, Manzone was happily renting a very steep vineyard loaded with old vines in Monforte's extremely high-quality Santo Stefano di Perno *cru* (this plot of vines was adjacent to the one owned by Rocche dei Manzoni. See Section II, Chapter 9, BUSSIA file) from which he made roughly seven to eight vintages of a Barolo. Manzone was very happy with this arrangement not just because he had always wanted to make a wine from what he believes to be one of Monforte's best vineyard districts, but also because this specific plot was planted to 50% Nebbiolo Rosé. But then one day the plot's owner decided to replant the vineyard and get rid of the old vines (replacing them with younger vines that would produce more grapes thereby allowing him to make more money). Manzone's efforts to knock some sense into the vineyard's owner having gone fruitless, he stopped renting the vineyard altogether. (Now I don't know about you, but I get downright emotional when I meet someone like Manzone who has his or her priorities so admirably straight.) Manzone's Barolo Bricat included up to 10-15% Nebbiolo Rosé: it was Manzone's opinion that, rather paradoxically (in the sense of what most people believed to be true about Nebbiolo Rosé wines), the Bricat tended to be a much bigger wine than his Barolo Castelletto, which didn't have any Nebbiolo Rosé in it. In Manzone's estimation (and I agree), this was due to the much higher clay content of the soil of the Bricat, compared to the sandier soil of the Castelletto vineyard. Manzone's keen observation was that even more so than with Nebbiolo Lampia, itself one of the most sensitive translators of terroir in the wine grape world, soil type overrode any innate tendency Nebbiolo Rosé had to give lighter-styled wines. So, in Manzone's opinion, the fact that Nebbiolo Rosé gives lighter wines than Nebbiolo is not necessarily true, but is rather at least in part a soil-dependent phenomenon.

As already mentioned, not everyone in Barolo was enthusiastic about Nebbiolo Rosé. Pio Boffa of the Pio Cesare estate, when asked back in 2005 "…and so, did you have Nebbiolo Rosé in your vineyards?", answered "Unfortunately yes! I hated it, and uprooted every plant I found". (You do realize that, for someone who loves Nebbiolo Rosé as much as I do, it's a real miracle I was still talking to the guy after that!). In 2008, Paola Oberto of Ciabot Berton was just as negative, telling me she really didn't care for Nebbiolo Rosé because its wines were just too orange in hue for her liking. In that light, one can fully place Paola Oberto's comment in context, given that part of her vines grow in the Santa Maria fraction of La Morra, hands down one of the sandiest parts of that commune and where even Lampia has a tough time making a deeply hued and full-bodied wine (so much so that the large estate to which the Obertos used to sell wine to before striking out on their own -or deciding to bottle even more of their wine- always complained that their wines were much too light in shade).

The high quality Fratelli Revello estate made a slew of delicious Barolos from some of La Morra's best sites in the 1990s and 2000s, including Rocche dell'Annunziata, Gattera and Giachini (the family split up in 2013, so the estate has now been carved up in two parts). And although Carlo Revello told me he also did not particularly care for the light, garnet-tinged color of Nebbiolo Rosé wines, they did have some growing in their Gattera vineyard holdings, readily admitting that for all its lack of color, the wine, when tasted blind, was immediately recognizable from all their other Nebbiolo wines because of its intensely perfumed and very appealing floral nose. Interestingly, the high part of Revello's vineyard holdings in Gattera were planted back in 1954 and that is where some Nebbiolo Rosé was growing. And though Carlo Revello did not believe there to be any Nebbiolo Rosé in the lower part of their Gattera holding (characterized by much younger vines planted in 1988, and that were supposedly all of Dolcetto), he told me he was often left wondering when tasting that

Gattera section's wine if there wasn't some Nebbiolo Rosé that had snuck in anyways at time of planting; he wondered because he often found the Dolcetto wine from that specific part of his vineyard exuded a highly atypical note of pomegranate (which would be the Nebbiolo Rosé talking, given that pomegranate is a very common descriptor of Nebbiolo Rosé wines while not at all common of Dolcetto's wines). Interesting, right? By contrast, and rather differently from these producers who criticized Nebbiolo Rosé's wine color, Pietro Ratti of the Renato Ratti estate was mostly unhappy with Nebbiolo Rosé's large bunch, which according to him meant the need for more vineyard work, or otherwise risk making more dilute wine.

Over time, opinions about a grape variety's qualities can slowly change. What might have once been hard and fast convictions, morph into somewhat more open and hopeful views. For example, when I first asked Mariacristina Oddero of the famous Poderi Oddero estate about Nebbiolo Rosé back in the early 2000s, she made it clear she wasn't too convinced by it. In both late 2003 and then again on 2008 (July 14), during two long chats at the winery, Mariacristina confirmed what many others were also saying: that Nebbiolo Rosé's wine is characterized by simply amazing perfume, but for her "…its color is really at the limit of what I can accept for a great red wine". Briefly put, for her, Nebbiolo Rosé's color was just too pale and garnet-tinged. And though she remains somewhat on the fence about it, her views have become somewhat more kind to Nebbiolo Rosé over the years. During my most recent visit at the estate, in July 2020, her curiosity was visibly piqued when I picked out the presence of Nebbiolo Rosé in her Barolo Vignarionda bottling, and as mentioned previously in this chapter, asked me what it was about the wine that made me say that there was Nebbiolo Rosé in this wine.

When I explained to her that of all her Barolos, I detected the telltale presence, only in her Vignarionda, of penetrating red roses coupled with a strong whiff of pomegranate, brown spices (nutmeg mostly, but also cinnamon and cumin) and a touch of herbs that was characterized by a special mouthfeel, she shook her head smiling and admitted that in fact, yes, they had become aware only recently that the upper part of their Vignarionda vineyard was planted to rows of Nebbiolo Rosé. As her Vignarionda Barolo is clearly the star of her portfolio (of course, one could make the claim that a wine from that magical *cru* would be the star of any portfolio, with or without any Nebbiolo Rosé) she was not surprised by the fact that I preferred it to the other excellent wines in her stable.

But what intrigued her most was that for me it stood so apart from her other Barolos, and that this difference was clearly attributable to a specific grape variety rather than just to specific geology of site or meso/microclimate. Mariacristina had begun to realize, she said, how the Nebbiolo Rosé was adding something extra that wasn't there in her other wines. Furthermore, she pointed out that the variety is becoming "increasingly interesting" (her very words) because it is much more heat- and drought-resistant than Nebbiolo, something that in times of climate change carries considerable weight. She concluded this part of our discussion saying that she was looking into planting perhaps more Nebbiolo Rosé in the future, possibly from a massal selection obtained from the Vignarionda plot. Isn't it wild and interesting the way a person's opinion can change with the passage of time?

My reflections on differences in Nebbiolo Rosé morphology and behaviors, and in its wines

Ampelographic descriptions of Nebbiolo Rosé, as well as the descriptions of its wines, don't exactly match. Apparently, many producers throughout the Barolo denomination are convinced that Nebbiolo Rosé has a large bunch, and a bigger one at that than Nebbiolo Lampia. However, this is in complete contrast with some modern ampelographic descriptions, all of which speak of a small bunch for Nebbiolo Rosé. On this specific matter, over at Castello di Verduno, Marcella Bianco and her father have a very interesting tale to tell. They own vineyards in both Barolo and Barbaresco, and back in 1987 planted a small vineyard in Barolo with the Nebbiolo Rosé clone CN 111. However, they don't speak of it as a "true" Nebbiolo Rosé, because according to them, the grapes were of a much smaller size than what they felt the grapes of the real Nebbiolo Rosé should have been. The fact that Nebbiolo clone CN 111 is described as having a small bunch also flies in the face of it really being a Nebbiolo Rosé, given that the latter wine grape is generally thought to have big bunches. Some producers find that the grapes of their Nebbiolo Rosé vines have a slightly oval appearance, something that in my experience I have never see with true Nebbiolo Rosé. Instead, what I have invariably found over the years is that grapes of clone CN 111 also have skins of a slightly dark blue color, rather than a pinkish-red-blue one. The slightly deeper color tonality of these grapes is consistent with the Nebbiolo clone CN 111, the grapes of which appear to sport a deeper color than what might be that of "true" Nebbiolo Rosé.

This difference in color is an extremely important observation, because it really flies in the face of the conventional wisdom about Nebbiolo Rosé; at the same time, it is very consistent with what we know about biotypes and clones, in that their morphological aspect and viticultural behaviors, not to mention their wines are heavily influenced by where they are planted (just think of Pinot Noir and all its clones and related wines, and how different those of New Zeland are from those of Oregon and Burgundy). Everything you will hear about the Nebbiolo Rosé variety is that it gives pale red wines of light body, of a perfume so intense that is almost inebriating, and that it is early-ripening. But Giovanni Manzone, and as we have seen he is not the only one, is of the notion that while all that is true, it can however be subverted to a degree if and when Nebbiolo Rosé is planted in clay-rich soils. That helps us understand why a minority of producers will also tell you that their Nebbiolo Rosé wine is darker, richer and later-ripening than one would normally expect. Furthermore, wines differ too. The 1971 Barolo Briacca by Vietti tastes very different from any older wine made by Scarpa out of the Pajorè vineyard in Barbaresco, and the differences go far beyond those you'd expect to find between a Barolo and Barbaresco. Besides, in the case of Scarpa at least, it's the Barbaresco that is the bigger wine.

Another possibility that I have already alluded to that might help us understand things a little more. It has to do with the recent realization that perhaps the Nebbiolo Rosé clone CN 111 may in fact not be a true clone of Nebbiolo Rosé but rather of a Nebbiolo Lampia that looks and behaves like Nebbiolo Rosé. To be clear, the majority of people I have talked to do not believe this to be true, but it would help explain at least in part why, as we have seen, some grapevines thought to be of Nebbiolo Rosé and their wines don't really remind one of what one would expect a Nebbiolo Rosé grapevine and wine to respectively look and taste like. While it might be that in some instances it is clay-rich soils that are the cause for such differences, in others it might be that Nebbiolo Rosé clone CN 111 behaves a little more like a Nebbiolo Lampia than expected and this helps explain why its wine isn't quite what we would have expected it to smell and taste like. If we take Nebbiolo Rosé to be a Nebbiolo Lampia that mutated into a new, distinct (even if very similar) variety over the centuries of ongoing adaptation to its specific environments, then it makes perfect sense that Nebbiolo Lampia and Nebbiolo Rosé would share a majority of features in common. And therefore, that Nebbiolo Rosé CN 111 can behave more like a Nebbiolo Lampia than we might expect.

A good example of this is Elvio Cogno's Vigna Elena, made by Valter Fissore and Nadia Cogno who run the Cogno estate together. The Vigna Elena is a Barolo Riserva that is both very slow to develop and rather massive: therefore, based on what we know or think we know about Nebbiolo Rosé, it has to give one pause for thought. Made with Nebbiolo Rosé clone CN 111, the wine is not especially light in color either, though it certainly is a less intense shade of red than Cogno's other Barolos. It is also very full-bodied and textured, so much so that Fissore makes it as a Riserva (in fact, his only Barolo Riserva), which would be really the opposite of what one would expect with Nebbiolo Rosé (that should in theory not be giving wines ideal for Barolo Riserva production). Furthermore, the Nebbiolo Rosé clone CN 111 is almost always the grape Fissore harvests last, when by most accounts we know that Nebbiolo Rosé is an early ripening grapevine.

So why is it that at Cogno Nebbiolo Rosé behaves rather differently from what might normally be expected? Is it the marly-clay rich soil of Novello (or perhaps more precisely, that specific portion of Novello) that greatly modifies the more typical expression of Nebbiolo Rosé in the finished wines? Could be, but Fissore has always told me that the vineyard soil in which his Nebbiolo Rosé clone CN 111 is planted in contains quite a bit of sand. So, might it really be, as some people believe, that Nebbiolo Rosé clone CN 111 might present at least some behaviors and traits typical of Nebbiolo Lampia, after all? It might be. It might also be that that they are two different expressions of the Nebbiolo Rosé grape variety: after all, if Nebbiolo Lampia can have something like forty different biotypes (and those are the ones we know of), it is very likely that, logical even, Nebbiolo Rosé has its own series of biotypes too. Last but not least, the existence of Nebbiolo Rosé-Michet grapevines in the vineyards (those are Nebbiolo Rosé vines affected by fanleaf virus much as the Nebbiolo Lampia turns into Nebbiolo Michet when it is hit by fanleaf virus) further adds to the potentially large spectrum of Nebbiolo Rosé morphologies and vineyard behaviors. For sure, any Nebbiolo Rosé-Michet grapevine is bound to have much smaller grapes than a "true" Nebbiolo Rosé, which has by most accounts very large berries, that has not been hit by the virus (one of the distinguishing features of Nebbiolo Lampia when it is hit by fanleaf virus is smaller berries). This can account for the fact that some producers tell you that their Nebbiolo Rosé has small grapes.

Clearly, it has become apparent (at least to me) that the presence of strong amounts of clay in the soil plays an important role relative to modifying what we know about Nebbiolo Rosé, both viticulturally and enologically. I say this because of the modification that the presence of clay-rich soils brings to the variety's ripening curve. Given its relationship to Nebbiolo, Nebbiolo Rosé is clearly enough also a late-ripening variety; however, most everyone will tell you it ripens much earlier than does Nebbiolo Lampia. That much admitted, a few producers will tell you that, in their locations characterized by heavy clay soils, Nebbiolo Rosé tends to ripen later than expected. But wait: then these fine folks, who must obviously enjoy making the life of a poor wine writer just that much harder, also add that exactly when their Nebbiolo Rosé grapes reach physiological ripeness may not be dependent only on the soil-clay content.

For example, Claudio Conterno of Conterno Fantino believes that whether Nebbiolo Rosé reaches full physiologic ripeness depends mostly on where it is planted, but at the same time, he also believes that there are other important factors besides the soil type in affecting the maturation curve of Nebbiolo Rosé. He points to the altitude and the exposure of the site Nebbiolo Rosé is planted in. He tells me that at his estate, he always picks the Nebbiolo Michet earliest, while Nebbiolo Rosé is ready to be picked sometime in between Michet and Lampia (in other words, after the Nebbiolo Michet, which is in and of itself strange, but perhaps it has to do with climate change). He cautions however that this is not always so, and there are many vintages in which he picks his Nebbiolo Rosé well before his other Nebbiolos; and in still other vintages, he does so last, well after all his Nebbiolo Lampia vines. You know sometimes, more than a glass of wine, I think it's an aspirin I need.

By contrast, Chiara Boschis of the Chiara Boschis-E. Pira estate in Barolo is among those who believes Nebbiolo Rosé ripens much earlier than both Nebbiolo Lampia and Michet in just about every condition known; and she's in very good company there, given that about 90-95% of all the other producers you will talk to about Nebbiolo Rosé will tell you exactly the same thing. Chiara, who is one of the most driven people and among the sharpest minds in all of Barolo, has long made a few bottles of 100% Nebbiolo Rosé wine from a couple of rows she owns, both for experimental purposes and for her own learning curve. She recalls that in the past her dad also made a few attempts at making a 100% Nebbiolo Rosé after finding the variety's vines in a small vineyard area near the winery. Like many of his colleagues, he found that Nebbiolo Rosé accumulates sugar with greater ease than Nebbiolo Lampia and that it ripens on average about ten days faster. Today, about fifteen years after I first broached this topic of discussion with her, she states, like many others in Barolo do today, that she has been told by a well-known ampelographer that what she and her father were probably dealing with at the time was not true Nebbiolo Rosé but perhaps a Nebbiolo Lampia that behaves like a Nebbiolo Rosé. Frankly, I wonder. Bruno Giacosa once grew about 10-15% Nebbiolo Rosé in his Falletto vineyard (his daughter Bruna tells me there is less Nebbiolo Rosé in Falletto than there once was), and generally speaking, believed that there was more Nebbiolo Rosé in Barolo's vineyards than people commonly realized. Giacosa told me in no uncertain terms that it was his belief that because most of the locals making Barolo lacked first-hand experience with the Nebbiolo Rosé variety, they just failed to recognize it as such and were probably vinifying it without being aware. This may very well be, because as we have seen, thanks to ampelographic variability, Nebbiolo Rosé can be hard to distinguish from Nebbiolo Lampia (furthermore, as mentioned previously, when exposed to large degrees of sunlight, Nebbiolo Lampia's grapes tend to become much paler and really look a lot like Nebbiolo Rosé).

At Luigi Oddero, current consultant and chief winemaker Francesco Versio tells me that roughly 5% of their total Nebbiolo holdings are of Nebbiolo Rosé and that they are very happy with it. At the Cavallotto/Bricco Boschis winery in Castiglione Falletto's, Alfio Cavallotto, one of Barolo's brightest and most precise minds, told me that there was quite a bit of Nebbiolo Rosé growing in the Punta Marcello portion of his Bricco Boschis (see Chapter 9, BRICCO BOSCHIS file). Until the 2000s, the Punta Marcello was bottled separately and sold as a Barolo under that vineyard section's name; today, it is a wine that is no longer made, with all the best grapes blended into the Barolo Riserva San Giuseppe and the remaining ones used to make the classic Barolo Bricco Boschis). For example, the 2005 Cavallotto Barolo Punta Marcello (a great wine, in my opinion) was at least 20% Nebbiolo Rosé; but in fact, all three Bricco Boschis Barolos had Nebbiolo Rosé in their midst (the Barolo San Giuseppe and the Barolo Colle Sud-Ovest too). In a sign of just how much Nebbiolo Rosé will change the makeup of a Barolo, the Barolo Punta Marcello always struck Alfio as being the most different of all his Barolos. And it was the same for me. At Cavallotto, they liked the grape so much that they ended up planting more Nebbiolo clone CN 111 in 1992, in both the Colle Sud-Ovest portion as well as the Punta Marcello section of the same vineyard (a telling move, as there had never been much Nebbiolo Rosé in the former before-hand, just a little Favorita, so that tells you how impressed they were at Cavallotto with Nebbiolo Rosé). But interestingly, while fifteen years ago, or so, Alfio Cavallotto told me that they had replanted with Nebbiolo Rosé clone CN 111, today he adopts the more commonly held view that rather than a true Nebbiolo Rosé, Nebbiolo Rosé clone CN 111 is actually a subvariety of Nebbiolo Lampia that behaves very strongly like a Nebbiolo Rosé.

Nomenclature issues and the sorry state of the human condition aside, Alfio Cavallotto has also told me over the years that he is of the inclination that Nebbiolo Rosé/Nebbiolo clone CN 111 is an exceptional variety that was, and is, unfortunately besotted mostly by two problems. First, because the variety's strength is that it gives mostly floral, not fruity, wines: back in the 1990s (when everyone wanted to drink fruit bombs) this was a virtual kiss of death. Second, and this is super-interesting, because in the 1970s and 1980s it was being planted on the wrong rootstock, mostly the Kober 5BB that really pushes vigor; pushing vigor is just about the last thing that an already vigorous variety such as Nebbiolo Rosé needs. "Planting Nebbiolo Rosé on the Kober rootstock was akin to asking it to really, and I mean really, produce pink or rosé wines" muses Cavallotto. Which the poor thing then did, of course. Cavallotto is also among those producers who believe that planting Nebbiolo Rosé in lighter soils with a high sand content (such as those of La Morra) meant making very light-bodied wines, something which also contributed to the loss of interest in this variety at a time when size was being paid at a premium.

In a 2006 interview, Mario Gagliasso of the Gagliasso estate in La Morra confirmed as much to me: the color of Nebbiolo Rosé's wines posed just too much of a problem for La Morra's wineries, because in that township's highly sandy soils, not just Nebbiolo Rosé but even Lampia itself had trouble giving much color to the wines. He joked that to "… go plant Nebbiolo Rosé in La Morra really meant you must have had secret masochist tendencies!".

Putting the pieces together: viticultural and enological aspects of Nebbiolo Rosé

There is only a limited amount of information available on the viticultural and enological characteristics of Nebbiolo Rosé; as I have documented before (D'Agata 2014; D'Agata 2019) and as we have just read from what producers say and have said over the years, some of what we know (or rather, *think* we know) is contradictory. After what we have seen thus far, all matters relative to Nebbiolo Rosé seem to be up to debate: what it looks like, when it ripens, and what kind of wines it can give. I have rarely seen so much confusion among producers talking about the same subject, that I ended up getting confused myself! But for reasons I have already broached and shall discuss further shortly, this may be partly explained. In any case, just why these discrepancies regarding the variety's morphological, viticultural and enological aspects existed in the past and to a certain extent still do today has always fascinated me, but I think that I can now give a more definitive and accurate description of this cultivar. It is, to the best of my knowledge, the definitive description of Nebbiolo Rosé available to date in the literature.

For the most part, everyone agrees (more or less: this is Italy, after all) on the variety's appearance. Nebbiolo Rosé's leaf and grapes are larger than those of Nebbiolo Lampia, and so is the bunch (although there are a few producers who steadfastly maintain Nebbiolo Rosé's bunch to be actually smaller than Nebbiolo Lampia's, I don't think that's so: to me their view is tainted by the fact that they might be growing the variety in heavy clay soils, or that it is a biotype of clone CN 111 they planted that may be a Nebbiolo Lampia that looks and behaves like Nebbiolo Rosé, or that they are dealing with a fanleaf virus affected Nebbiolo Rosé, what we can refer to as Nebbiolo Rosé-Michet). Nebbiolo Rosé's bunch is more compact than that of Lampia (but never as compact as that of the Nebbiolo Michet biotype, the ultimately tightly-packed Nebbiolo). Nebbiolo Rosé's bunch is usually characterized by a conical and only very rarely cylindrical shape (by contrast, Michet's is almost always cylindrical) with just one wing.

The Nebbiolo clone CN 111 is usually shorter than that of other Nebbiolo Lampia clones (which may be why some producers believe that Nebbiolo Rosé's bunch looks smaller than that of Nebbiolo Lampia). Just imagine that Claudio Conterno states that old massal selections of Nebbiolo Rosé's bunches can be so huge "…that five bunches can easily weigh two kilograms". So, it hardly has a small bunch. In my experience (though it is admittedly not full-proof), one easy way to tell Nebbiolo Rosé from Nebbiolo Lampia is simply by looking at the leaves of the plants in the vineyards. Nebbiolo Rosé's is immediately recognizable: it is thicker than Nebbiolo's; it has a typically bullous upper surface (and larger bullae on average than Nebbiolo Lampia's); a less intensely bright green color (Nebbiolo Rosé's leaf is more of a silvery-green-grey color); a petiolar sinus that is more closed than Nebbiolo's; Nebbiolo Rosé's leaf has three large lobes compared to Nebbiolo Lampia's more common five or even seven-lobed leaf; in a Nebbiolo Rosé leaf, the superior lateral sinuses are wider than the inferior ones, while Nebbiolo Lampia's leaf has medium-deep to deep but very narrow lateral sinuses. All Nebbiolo leaves may showcase deeper or shallower indentations (or in other words, a more or less jagged appearance), but the degree of these and their amount depends on which Nebbiolo biotype is under observation (whether it is Rosé, the two Lampias or Michet) and their degree of viral contamination (more on this below).

Relative to the bunch and grapes, the Nebbiolo Rosé grapes have a lighter dusty-silvery pale red-pink-blue hue (the telltale bloom characterizing Nebbiolo is very much present in Nebbiolo Rosé too), with an obvious pale gray-violet tinge to its berries. Nebbiolo Rosé's grapes are always much less blue and dark than those of Nebbiolo (unless, as we have seen, the latter's bunches are placed in full sunlight). Nebbiolo Rosé's grapes are round and to the best of my knowledge practically never oval like those of some other Nebbiolo biotypes, and they are also usually much larger, with an obviously bigger pulp to skin ratio. In fact, Nebbiolo Rosé's grapes are so filled with juice, and the skin stretched so thin, that they look almost translucent when held up to the light. Again, if the Nebbiolo Rosé is affected by fanleaf virus, or if it is planted on heavy clay or if it is clone CN 111 rather than a massal selection of an old Nebbiolo Rosé grapevine, things aren't quite so.

From a viticulture behavior perspective, according to the majority of producers, Nebbiolo Rosé buds in the first week of April, and flowers in the latter part of the first half of June. It flowers slightly later than Nebbiolo, making it more resistant to late spring frosts; therefore, it is also not surprising-that Nebbiolo Rosé presents fewer cold and rainy spring-associated flowering issues: berry shatter and millerandage are less problematic with Nebbiolo Rosé. It will change color (*véraison*) in mid-August and can be harvested as late as mid- to late October, but most producers I've talked to over the years point out that in general it ripens about fifteen to twenty days earlier than Nebbiolo (as mentioned earlier, not everyone agrees, but again, I think this discrepancy is in relation to producers having planted their apparently later-ripening Nebbiolo Rosé in clay-heavy soils and/or that they have the Nebbiolo clone CN 111). In this light, it is not without interest that Claudio Rosso points out that Anna Schneider, the scientist whose research team has done the most work on Nebbiolo and Nebbiolo Rosé, referred to it in slang colloquial terms as Nebbiolo Precoce ("precocious" Nebbiolo, as in the sense of early-ripening Nebbiolo) for this very reason. In fact, producers are so convinced that Nebbiolo Rosé ripens earlier in the season than does Nebbiolo that another name for the variety is Nebbiolo Matiné (*matiné* as in the *mattino,* or morning), also a reference to its early ripening personality. According to the Bianco family, Nebbiolo Rosé fares better in well-ventilated areas, because the compact bunch (of their vines at least) is prone to rot in rainy years.

Nebbiolo Rosé grapes are usually very sweet (and in fact Nebbiolo Rosé wines have no problem clocking in with high alcohol levels) but are less rich in anthocyanins and other polyphenols. Just like Nebbiolo Lampia, Nebbiolo Rosé is also characterized by long internodes, poor fertility of the basal buds and a requirement for long pruning techniques. More vigorous and fertile than Nebbiolo, Nebbiolo Rosé likes the same training methods, though most experts I have talked to over the years believe it does best when trained slightly higher up from the ground than Nebbiolo Lampia. Outside of the Langhe, many other training systems are used for it as well: for example, the pergola (canopy) in the Lower Valle d'Aosta, Carema and the Val Ossola; and the classic *meggiorina* and similar training techniques of the Vercelli and Novara provinces where wines such as Boca and Gattinara are produced (but keep in mind that Nebbiolo Rosé is fairly rare in all these viticultural areas).

Nebbiolo Rosé has excellent affinity to the 420A rootstock, while it fares very poorly with the members of the Riparia x Rupestris group of rootstocks such as the 3309C and the 101.14, especially when employed on highly calcareous soils. In general, matching Nebbiolo Rosé to behavior a vigorous rootstock (both vigorous varieties, this is neither a good idea with Nebbiolo Lampia nor is it with Nebbiolo Rosé) will unfailingly lead it to make even lighter wines than it would normally. Winemaking with Nebbiolo Rosé is essentially the same as that used for Nebbiolo Lampia (or at least it is at the present state of knowledge, which as we have seen is somewhat limited). That said, Nebbiolo Rosé does present peculiarities that need for it to be dealt with somewhat differently than Nebbiolo Lampia. For one, Nebbiolo Rosé's technological curve of maturation is much less synchronized with its polyphenol maturation curve compared to Nebbiolo Lampia's. What this means is that while Nebbiolo Rosé has no problem accumulating sugar, its tannins ripen much more slowly, so harvesting too early (always a possibility given Nebbiolo Rosé's capacity to pack in the sugar) means risking making wines marred by green streaks.

Some producers believe that getting Nebbiolo Rosé to ripen fully is the biggest challenge the grape poses, and this is especially true when Nebbiolo Rosé is grown at high altitudes (though it hardly seems to present this problem in the Valtellina's alpine reaches). Deleafing therefore has to be done judiciously, but airing out of the rot-prone compact bunches is all-important too. Protecting the wine from oxidation is of paramount importance, to avoid further burning off of what little anthocyanin presence there is. In this light, Bruno Giacosa first, and Natale Simonetta (of the Cascina Baricchi estate in Neviglie, and estate that makes Barbaresco) later told me that traditional winemaking methods are best for Nebbiolo Rosé.

According to them, using the *cappello sommerso* technique is the best manner by which to protect the grape skin's low concentration of anthocyanins, and prolonged oak aging helps smoothen out the variety's at times edgy tannins. And while that is most certainly true for some Nebbiolo Rosé out there, once again, much depends on exactly which Nebbiolo Rosé one is farming and making wine from, because old massal selections of (true?) Nebbiolo Rosé, both those unaffected and those affected by fanleaf virus, and the CN 111 clone all behave somewhat differently. To give you an example, data from one producer shows the anthocyans concentration of his Nebbiolo Rosé and Nebbiolo Lampia grapes (grown in the same way and in the same vineyard area, which is important to know for it reduced confounding variables) clearly differed (459 mg/L in the Nebbiolo Rosé grapes and 632 mg/L in the Lampia grapes), while differences in the finished wines were practically negligible (221 mg/L versus 225 mg/L). Interestingly the total polyphenol content in the finished wines wasn't all that different either, though it was marginally higher for the Nebbiolo Lampia wine (2250 mg/L versus 2350 mg/L). I will elaborate on this further once I have finished collection and elaborating data relative to this subject which I will present in future articles written for the TerroirSense Wine Review (terroirsense.com/en/) I am the Editor-in-Chief of, and in another future book too.

Nebbiolo Rosé clones: to be or not to be

As we have seen, there is only one official clone of Nebbiolo Rosé available today, the Nebbiolo CN 111 (where the CN stands for Cuneo, an important city in Piedmont and a provincial capital), though the more knowledgeable producers I have talked to over the years suggest and believe that Nebbiolo CN 36, CN 142 and CN 230 all present some viticultural characteristics intermediate between those of Nebbiolo Lampia and Nebbiolo Rosé. As we have already discussed, this much might also apply to some populations of Nebbiolo CN 111. For sure, this would account for some of the morphological features and viticultural behaviors of this clone that do not quite jell with what we know of Nebbiolo Rosé (but once again, I stress that the majority of people I have talked to do not believe CN 111 to be a Nebbiolo Lampia, despite what the grape scientists, who have been often wrong in the past, are busy saying). Another confounding factor may be the presence or not of fanleaf virus, given that clone CN 111 grapevines hit by this virus will inevitably lead to a different morphology and behavior. Furthermore, it is extremely interesting to me that more than one producer has told me that over time Nebbiolo Lampia begins to take on more and more of Nebbiolo Rosé's traits.

The CN 111 is one of the five oldest Nebbiolo clones to have ever been created (developed in the 1970s, it was officially certified and recognized in 1980), and is to my mind one of the best wine grape clones ever developed. The CN 111's vigor, fertility and productivity are all very high. From a phenological perspective, much like CN 36 (one of the Lampia clones I mentioned earlier that presents characteristics intermediate between those of Nebbiolo Rosé and a Lampia), CN 111 is an early-budding and late ripening clone, while flowering and *véraison* occur at the same times of the year as most other Nebbiolo clones. And once again like CN 36, it has high and average resistance to grey rot and oidium, respectively. Its bunch can be conical or more rarely cylindrical in shape, generally long, and tightly packed, often but not necessarily winged. The grapes are medium-small in size and round to at times slightly oval in shape. Some producers still believe CN 111 to be able to give wines only of noteworthy perfume (true) but little or no color (not so true, or true only up to a point) and structure (not true at all: as we have seen, it depends on where you plant it, and besides, at Cogno they make a Barolo Riserva from it, so clearly structure is not at all a problem with this clone). I have summarized the characteristics of Nebbiolo Rosé clone CN 111 in Appendix A, Tables 1.4 and 1.5.

For these reasons (fears?), clone CN 111 has always been planted in Langhe vineyards in parsimonious amounts, making up from 5-20% or so of the various field blends. But over time, the quality of its wines has been reviewed increasingly favorably. (I have documentation from the 1990s in which the quality of CN 111 wines was deemed "poor", only to be later changed to "average" when the desire to make black and big wines had fallen by the wayside). The problem is whether the CN 111 clone is still available or not, because producers have voiced to me the concern that though it is listed as available by nursery information material, in fact it is never made available. Hopefully it is all a misunderstanding. In ultimate analysis, make no mistake about it, clone CN 111 is a magnificent clone: whether it really is a Nebbiolo Rosé or a Nebbiolo Lampia that behaves very much like a Nebbiolo Rosé, it doesn't matter in the least, given that its wine is clearly and recognizably a Nebbiolo wine.

Last but not least, at least one prominent researcher I have talked to over the years maintains that back in the 1970s a number of other clones were developed from Nebbiolo Rosé but that for a variety of reasons were never certified and have since gone lost. However, as they had been planted in experimental vineyards, producers who liked what they saw and tasted, went ahead and propagated the plants anyways despite their not being officially approved and legal to plant (visiting vineyards in the darkest moments of the night has long been a fun pastime of many a viticultural zone). I point out that a "mixed population" as pertaining to Nebbiolo grapevines has already been described before in at least one scientific research study I am aware of; as the paper was written at a time when Nebbiolo Rosé was still thought of as a "clone" of Nebbiolo, it is likely that the mixed population of Nebbiolos under observation included grapevines with Nebbiolo Rosé-like characteristics too.

My conclusions: the state of the art of Nebbiolo Rosé

In my experience, Barolos made wholly or with strong percentages (in my view, 30-40% or more) of true Nebbiolo Rosé are characterized by an absolutely enchanting, mesmerizing perfume of wild red roses, rosehip tea, candied rose petals, pomegranate, red cherries and redcurrants; notes of nutmeg, cumin and cinnamon are always evident even in young wines, along with vibrant violet and mineral nuances; the brown spice notes, along with a hint of herbaceous tobacco, increase as the wines age but are not usually found in young wines. In fact, I find some of these descriptors to be more common in some Nebbiolo Rosé than they are in others: another example of how there are likely different biotypes/populations of Nebbiolo Rosé growing in the vineyards today. This is because while all Nebbiolo Rosé or Nebbiolo Rosé-containing Barolos exude aromas and flavours reminiscent of brown spices, some express sweeter cinnamon and nutmeg nuances compared to other Nebbiolo Rosé or Nebbiolo Rosé-containing Barolos more marked instead by notes of cumin, curry and coriander. The wines of the latter group also exude less of the very penetrating, sultry red cherry presence of those in the former group. When Nebbiolo Rosé is less than 20% of the blend its contribution is somewhat lost in the mix, with it influencing mostly the color only (more garnet-tinged) than aroma and flavor profiles (but again, that may be in part due to the type of soil the Nebbiolo vines are planted in). Some Nebbiolo Rosé Barolos do boast a great deal more power than expected, and in my experience, those are all wines made with the Nebbiolo CN 111 clone an/or planted on very marly-clay rich soils. This same clone does not behave at all in the same way in sandier soils, in which case the wines resemble those said to be typical of the variety. So, it is my belief that just what the Nebbiolo CN 111 clone delivers depends either on *where* it is planted or on *which* biotype of the CN 111 clone you have planted. What impression of power and structure there might be with Nebbiolo Rosé wines is no doubt also related to the higher acidity levels this clone is known for (but that can drop very quickly) and less obvious fruity fleshiness, all of which make the grape's tannins (that can be gritty in wines derived from grapes grown in heavy clay soils and/if harvested too early) stand out. Lesser Nebbiolo Rosé wines present slightly drying tannins either because the grapes did not reach optimal physiologic ripeness or because there is too much tannin for the lightness of fruit present.

In summary, it should be apparent by now that Nebbiolo Rosé has been burdened with an unfair reputation and is more than capable, in the right hands, of giving world class wines, either on its own or when judiciously blended in with Nebbiolo Lampia and Michet. It should also be apparent that if you don't know exactly about this variety and where it is grown, you will have a hard time understanding and steering around the noteworthy discrepancies between what producers will tell you relative to Nebbiolo Rosé's look and behavior. In ultimate analysis these different views on the variety may be linked to the type of soil, the altitude, the rootstock and the actual grape variety used. I have seen enough Nebbiolo Rosé vines and vineyards, heard enough about the variety from so many different people, and tasted so many of the wines to be able to draw conclusions I am completely comfortable with.

First, much like there exist many different Nebbiolo biotypes (Lampia, Bolla, Michet…all of which may be modifications of Lampia), I believe there are also different Nebbiolo Rosé biotypes Some of these diverse populations of Nebbiolo Rosé biotypes in the field might be virus-affected just like Nebbiolo Michet, while some are unaffected, all sporting viticultural and enological behaviors that differ between populations. So much like there exist many different biotypes of Lampia and most likely of Michet too (see chapter 1, NEBBIOLO LAMPIA. See also chapter 2, NEBBIOLO MICHET), and even sub-biotypes of the biotypes of each one, there are obviously biotypes of Nebbiolo Rosé too that have developed by adapting to their terroirs over the centuries. Whether they all descend from Nebbiolo Lampia or not (see Chapter 1, NEBBIOLO LAMPIA) is still not clear, but it is more than likely that what we have in the field is grapevine populations made up of various "grades" of Nebbiolo Rosé as well as potentially of a Nebbiolo Rosé/Nebbiolo Lampia, some of which behave more like Lampia and some of which behave more like Nebbiolo Rosé. Consider this as a spectrum of "Nebbioloness", where Michet sits at one extreme and Nebbiolo Rosé at the other, with Lampia somewhere in the middle (the Lampia a Foglia Intagliata closer to Michet and the Lampia a Foglia Intera closer to Rosé). Perhaps some of the differences in these Nebbiolo Rosé populations are due to virus-affected plants; some of them are almost certainly to be virus-affected, and just looking at the leaves of many different Nebbiolo Rosé populations has led me to feel pretty comfortable with that assertion. Also, as mentioned before in the "Nebbiolo Rosé clones" subchapter section above, although there is reportedly only one clone of Nebbiolo Rosé described and available for sale (the aforementioned CN 111), there exists the possibility that other clones were developed from Nebbiolo Rosé but that for a variety of reasons were never certified, but that planted in experimental vineyards were propagated anyways by producers who liked what they saw and tasted. This "mixed population" as pertaining to Nebbiolo grapevines has already been described before. It is not unreasonable to assume that the family of Nebbiolo Rosé, most of which is made up of very old plants, is also likely to contain intermediate forms of the original grape variety that look and behave differently from the progenitor species thanks to the inevitable mutations that have accumulated over time. In the hope I haven't given you an incredible headache, I am happy to inform you that I will address this fascinating subject further in the upcoming Barbaresco book. So just when you thought it was safe to go back in the books…

In conclusion, when analyzing the diversity of opinions on Nebbiolo Rosé and the different wines made with it, it is important to be aware of its link and relationship with specific terroir parameters such as grape biotypes and variety, soil geology, exposure, altitude, climate and rootstocks. There is no doubt in my mind that Nebbiolo Rosé (massal selections and clone CN 111) behaves very differently in the soils and mesoclimate for example of Novello, those of Monforte and Diano d'Alba, not to mention the altogether different viticultural reality that is Barbaresco. A high presence of sand in the soil allows the magical perfume of massal/clonal selection Nebbiolo Rosé Barolos to explode in all their glory, at the price of making a more graceful but less structured wine. When planted on soils rich in marls, loam and especially clay, some Nebbiolo Rosé grapevines give wines that boast surprising tannic heft even by Nebbiolo standards and that are much more closed on the nose (these may be wines simply showcasing their "Lampianess" as opposed to their "Roséness". Altitude and average day/night temperatures are also very important in helping determine the type of Nebbiolo Rosé Barolo produced; in some soil types and at high altitudes, Nebbiolo Rosé may not ripen as well as it should (but in alpine Valtellina it seems to do just fine, where the Growth Degree Days and the angle of inclination of sunlight to slope is different there than the Langhe). While Nebbiolo Rosé never has any trouble accumulating sugars, its polyphenol maturity curve lags farther behind (farther than Nebbiolo's). In the past, people were forced to harvest Nebbiolo Rosé early just so as to not let the potential alcohol in the wines creep too far out ahead (something that no doubt contributed to Nebbiolo Rosé's early-ripening reputation, but in fact it may not be that early-ripening at all, as it also depends in part on where and how the variety planted and how fast the grape sugar is allowed to rise).

In the end, all these factors (biotype, soil type, rootstock, altitude, climate and exposure) may account in part for the at times marked differences between some modern-day Nebbiolo Rosé wines and those of yesteryear. Clearly, when it comes to older bottles, bottle storage, cork seal, producer vineyard management and winemaking decisions, as well as still other factors, also likely play a role. And while things are much clearer to me now, the identity of Nebbiolo Rosé remains a bit of a mystery. You know what? Give Nebbiolo Rosé some time and we may yet find out that it *does* go out at night and fight crime while donning a mask and cape.

Chapter 4

BAROLO: FACTS, FIGURES

Michele Longo

According to 2021 data, the Barolo wine production area is 2,214 hectares and it has fairly steadily increased over the last twenty thirty years:

1993	2002	2007	2010	2013	2016	2018	2019	2020	2021
1,178	1,573	1,804	1,886	2,054	2,091	2,149	2,184	2,208	2,214

plantings in hectares

Of the hectares under vine to Nebbiolo in Barolo, roughly 18% of the territory is devoted to organic farming, (see Appendix B, *Table 2.4: Number of organically farmed hectares in Barolo*). In Appendix B, *Table 2.1* shows the number of hectares under vine in Barolo, Roero and other Langhe denominations (Other grape varieties besides Nebbiolo that are also planted in the Barolo denomination are shown in Appendix B, *Table 2.2: Hectares under vine in Barolo of Nebbiolo and other grape varieties*)

The eleven communes of the Barolo denomination do not show the same planting density: table 2.3 shows the number of hectares of Nebbiolo planted in the territory of each commune (see Appendix B. *Table 2.3: Hectares of Nebbiolo planted in the Barolo denomination by commune*).

At the same time, plantings of Nebbiolo by which to make Langhe Nebbiolo or Nebbiolo d'Alba wine have also increased steadily: for example, from 2011-2021, hectares jumped from 818 hectares (149.57 Langhe Nebbiolo and 668.83 Nebbiolo d'Alba) in 2011 to 2,075 hectares in 2021, so it appears the world's thirst for Nebbiolo wine rages on unchecked.

	2011	2012	2013	2014	2015	2016	2017	2018	2019	2020	2021
Langhe Nebbiolo	149.57	171.79	194.05	228.56	281.76	384.40	487.78	606.93	734.85	844.65	939.52
Nebbiolo d'Alba	668.83	679.86	688.79	705.73	735.15	808.62	887.70	959.85	1,030.16	1,096.22	1,135.48

plantings in hectares

Similar to Barolo's hectarage devoted to Nebbiolo, the denomination's annual bottle production numbers have also increased steadily. There were 6.480.600 bottles of Barolo produced in 1993, and 14,916,396 in 2021.

1993	2003	2007	2010	2013	2016	2018	2019	2020	2021
6,480,600	8,711,200	10,964,027	12,147,200	13,902,404	14,039,461	14,377,634	14,362,496	14,495,619	14,916,396

bottles produced/year

The average value/sales price of a hectare of Barolo has also increased dramatically over that time span, and especially so over the last five years with new moneyed foreigners setting their sights on the area. While the sales price of a hectare of Barolo averages 1.5 million euros (source: CREA, formerly INEA - National Institute of Agricultural Economics), that figure easily reaches 2.2-2.5 million for the most important vineyard districts (and that number is destined to increase further in the near future). Both Ian and I have been told by very reliable sources that if the right vineyard parcel were to come up for sale, there are mediators that have been given the green light to buy at 4-5 Million euros/hectare.

How quickly things change: just remember that as recently as 1991, grapes used to make Dolcetto d'Alba fetched a price that was only about 10% less than Barolo's Nebbiolo grapes. Go further back, say to the 1970s, and you'll hear from countless locals that in those days Dolcetto grapes were more expensive than Nebbiolo's; in fact, producers were in the habit of generously throwing in a case of Barolo (then a very hard sell, as very few people wanted it) when people sent for big orders of Dolcetto wine.

Chapter 5

THE HISTORY OF BAROLO

Ian D'Agata and Michele Longo

THE EARLY DAYS

Considering just how important Barolo is today, it is at least a little surprising to learn that its history is not an exactly ancient one. In fact, it is the Nebbiolo grape variety (or rather Nebiolo, with one "b", as it was called and written right up until the 1960s) and not its wines that has the much more distinguished and far-reaching history (see: chapter 1. NEBBIOLO LAMPIA). The word "Barolo" is also a relatively recent addition to Italy's lexicon: as previously mentioned in this book, the first documentation of it by which to identify a wine is dated 1730 in a deed detailing the goods traded between the royal court of Savoys, wine merchants, and the English ambassador in London.

However, both Nebbiolo and Barolo made up for lost time rather quickly after that. Already in 1751, Barolo wines sent to London were deemed as being better than the best French wines, though not all Barolo wines sent to London were a success (apparently mostly due to transport issues). That the English were interested in Piedmontese wine is shown by the fact that two négociants, Voodmas and Clies, were sent in 1766 to speak with the Piedmontese king about the possibility of importing the wines of twenty-four different Piedmontese areas into England. Interestingly, the Barolo areas of interest at the time were *"Barol, Serralongae, Verdun"*. In 1797, Thomas Jefferson, future President of the United States of America, drank Nebbiolo wines during his stay at the Hotel d'Angleterre in Turin and described the experience as "… off-dry and like smooth Madeira, at once structured like the wine of Bordeaux and fizzy like Champagne". Clearly, back then Barolo as we know it today was very much a work in progress; it was still, more often than not, a slightly bubbly and sweet wine given that the process of alcoholic fermentation had not yet been explained by Pasteur (and hence stuck fermentations were common).

In 1820, Count Giorgio Gallesio, a famous Italian ampelographer of the time, stated that the "Barolo" wines were better than those from "Nizza" (another famous wine production area of those times). However, it is unclear whether this statement actually referred to Barolo wines made exclusively with Nebbiolo, or to wines made in the general vicinity of Barolo (the town), and perhaps with other grape varieties altogether. Other authors have subsequently argued in favor of the latter hypothesis, but doubts remain (Casalis, 1834; De Bartolomeis, 1847). In any case, the best Nebbiolo wines of those times were most often made outside of the Barbaresco and Barolo areas as we know them today. At the 1849 Paris and 1862 London International Exhibitions Nebbiolo's wines were praised, winning medals. By contrast, it appears the wines did not meet the favor of the experts at the 1865 Dublin International Exhibition, though it appears likely that the poor showing was the consequence of less-than-ideal travel and storage conditions. Ever since, the successes of Nebbiolo wines have far outweighed the disappointments, and numerous other authors have since attested to the quality of Nebbiolo's wines time and again throughout the last four centuries. Undoubtedly, ever since the nineteenth century at least, Nebbiolo and its wines have been on a roll.

THE ORIGINS: CAVOUR, COLBERT, OUDART, AND STAGLIENO.

The problem with Barolo's story is it has been repeated so many times, wrongly, that in the end trying to figure out what is true and what isn't becomes an almost Sisyphean task. Why so many mistakes have been made in detailing Barolo's exact history would make a very good treatise on human nature, but here in this space we'll limit ourselves to giving as accurate a rendition of Barolo's history as possible. And clearly, we'll likely make our share of mistakes too, though to the best of our knowledge the description in this chapter is as documented and as accurate as current knowledge allows it to be. Just beware that when it comes to Barolo's history, ballpark generic statements ("beginning of...", "early 1800s...") abound while specific dates are hard to come by. And what precise dates are reported are not always correct.

In any case, the story of modern-day Barolo essentially dates back to the first half of the 19th century thanks to the energy, intuition and passion of a number of different individuals. It is thanks to their pioneering efforts that the production processes needed to turn Barolo into a classically dry, age-worthy, and structured red wine were implemented. Four people who played the biggest role in turning Barolo into the wine we know today were (in alphabetical order): Camillo Benso, the Count of Cavour; Julia Colbert de Maulèvrier; Louis Oudart; and Francesco Paolo Staglieno.

Before the nineteenth century, when winemaking knowledge in the Barolo area finally moved up to speed, Nebbiolo wines were more often than not rather Lambrusco-like, bubbly and with a hint of residual sweetness. If anything, such wines sporting carbon dioxide, high acidity, and a touch of residual sugar proved a well-suited match to the local hearty cuisine, in which pork, butter, numerous cheeses, *salumi* and wild game had and have always featured prominently. In fact, it appears that back then late harvesting and air-drying of Nebbiolo grapes was a fairly common practice (just as it, still today, in colder northern Italian lands such as the Valle d'Aosta and the Valtellina). Apparently, some producers reportedly went as far as to bake grapes in ovens in order to raisin them as much as possible.

How many of these sweet and fizzy wines was by design, and how much the result of chance, remains open to question. Undoubtedly, being a late ripening variety, Nebbiolo's fermentation would often take place in cold weather conditions late in the year (remember that before climate change, Nebbiolo was regularly harvested in middle to late November). Clearly, as there was no artificial heating of cellars in the nineteenth century (or most of the twentieth, for that matter), stuck fermentations were commonplace. In fact, cellars weren't even used at all by some producers (or at least, not for the entire winemaking process). Until more functional winemaking decisions became routine at the various Piedmont wine estates, it was common to leave the fermenting vats of Nebbiolo wine outside, barely protected under makeshift roofs or arched colonnades (underground cellars were then not common; for example, there were none at the Marchesi Falletti estate before Julia Colbert's arrival). The cold weather in which alcoholic fermentation took place (not to mention old and dirty barrels) likely were responsible for the aforementioned stuck fermentations; it follows that Barolo wines then easily refermented in the bottle. Clearly, if Barolo was ever to become a world class red wine, things needed to change.

It appears that Barolo wine slowly transitioned to the modern classically dry wine we know today between 1830-1850: apparently, the first Barolo vintage to have been bottled in a classically dry style and so labeled was of the 1844 vintage, the famous "Dry Nebiolo Wine of Polenza of 1844". Though the documentation available is porous at best, it is likely that classically dry "Nebiolo" wines were being made before that date. And dry "Nebiolo" wines were finally being made thanks to two men: a French winemaker-*négociant*, Louis Oudart, and an Italian Army General but also a serious winemaker, Francesco Paolo Staglieno. We realize we are digressing now, but really now: isn't it just deliciously Italian how an army general could also be a famous winemaker?

The contributions of Louis Oudart (1802-1881), a French winemaker and *négociant,* to the creation of modern-day Barolo were of immense importance and value and cannot be underestimated (he has often been referred to as the "father of Barolo", though we fear this diminishes the important role also played by Staglieno in the creation of the wine as we know it today). Unfortunately, descriptions of Oudart's exact role in the genesis of modern-day, classically dry Barolo are peppered with mistakes, beginning with the way his name has been spelled (for example, you'll often find it written as Oudar, when his family name was instead quite clearly Oudart). It has been written that Oudart played a major role in improving the wines of both the Marchesi di Falletto and Castello di Grinzane Cavour, but a recent excellent book by Riccardi Candiani (2012) has helped set the record straight, clearing away long held misconceptions and beliefs.

Apparently, most if not all of the confusion relative to the birth of Barolo wine stems from *Storia della Vite e del Vino*, an important work written by Manescalchi and Dalmasso in the 1930s (between 1931 and 1937, published for example in 1939 by Milan's Gualdoni Editore), from which apparently all other subsequent written accounts relative to Oudart's involvement with the wines of Barolo were derived or copied. Apparently, Manescalchi and Dalmasso mentioned that Oudart had been summoned by Juliette Colbert to help improve the wines at her estate, but we now know this not to be true. In what was originally an archival inquiry performed during her PhD research, Riccardi Candiani went on to author a truly brilliant and engaging book about Oudart, highlighting his numerous accomplishments but also underscoring the lack of any documentation or bibliographical citations confirming the existence of services rendered by him to the Marchesa Falletti di Barolo. Or, for that matter, of a specific link of any nature between Oudart and the town of Barolo. In fact, Oudart's relations with the world of Piedmont enology were described in his 1874 letter of presentation to the Count Rovasenda (one of Italy's most famous ampelographers): "…at the Ministry they know very well that for 48 years I have never ceased to work for the progress of viticulture and enology in Piedmont -- at the beginning in Pollenzo for the King, then in Grinzane for Count Camillo di Cavour…". Clearly, it is only logical to assume that had there been any collaboration with the Marchesi di Barolo, Oudart would have mentioned it in the letter, but he did not do so. This letter is also helpful because it tells us that Oudart, according to his own computations, arrived in Italy, or was at least working there, already in 1826. In 1833, he and his cousin Jacques Philippe Bruché founded the Maison Oudart et Bruché in Genoa to produce, sell and export quality wines from bought grapes (the company owned no vineyards: it was especially famous for its sparkling wines similar to "Champagne" that were very sought after).

It appears that Oudart was quite the businessman and was always looking to improve his wine sales. Not surprisingly then, in 1842 he wrote to Cesare Giambattista Trabucco, Count of Castagnetto, at the time acting director of the Royal Estate of Pollenzo. By so doing, Oudart was hoping to have King Carlo Alberto of the Kingdom of Piedmont-Sardinia try his wines, with the objective of possibly obtaining a Royal Warrant of Appointment. Apparently, Oudart knew the Royal Estate well, as he had previously made wines with grapes he bought from there. This connection led to Oudart's debut as a winemaking consultant at the Royal Estate of Pollenzo in 1842, a post that lasted until 1845. It was here he first met and collaborated with General Staglieno, then the technical director (cellar master and chief winemaker) of the Agenzia di Pollenzo, with whom Oudart developed what appears to have been a strong professional relationship. The two must have been on good terms: we know that, for example, Oudart sent Staglieno a copy of his manuscript on viticulture and winemaking, *Le buone pratiche per la vinificazione e la conservazione dei vini giustificate dalla scienza moderna*, in 1849 (a manuscript that was finally published as a book in 1879). Subsequently, Oudart acted as a winemaking consultant at the Castello di Grinzane too, where he made the wines but also bought the estate's grapes for his own personal use and that of his company in Genoa. Oudart was certainly an extremely competent winemaker and his presence was a definite plus for Piedmont and it's rather archaic winemaking of the times. It is unanimously recognized that it was he introduced many important improvements to the region's vineyards and wines (for example, a more correct approach to the use of selected yeasts by which to gain a better control of fermentation).

There appears to be no doubt that the wines made at estates under Oudart's stewardship improved noticeably after his arrival on the scene, with many garnering medals and trophies. Such as for example, the very famous "Dry Nebiolo Wine of Polenza of 1844", a wine borne out of the collaboration between Oudart and the Tenuta di Pollenzo presented for the first time in London to much acclaim in 1862. The 1847 is another famous, classically dry Nebbiolo wine made by Oudart. Simply put, the man had a long and glorious career in Italian wine circles. Oudart's wines won numerous medals at fairs in Italy and abroad, but his legacy also includes the incessant promotion of the image of Piemontese wines in export markets; being named to many government ampelographic committees; and to judging panels and wine boards. He greatly helped propel not just Piedmont's wines, but all of Italy's, to a whole new, much higher, quality level. And so, still today, he is remembered with gratitude by Italian wine professionals (and not surprisingly, especially so by the Piedmontese).

However, some confusion regarding Oudart's exact, very important, role in the genesis of modern-day Barolo has resulted from Oudart's family name being very similar to another last name, that of Odart. This similarity and the resulting misinterpretation helped cast, if however briefly, Oudart's importance as a Barolo benefactor in doubt, something the man and his memory, and we dare say Barolo the wine, do not deserve. Differently from Oudart, Odart was a French ampelographer who to the best of our knowledge never had anything to do with Barolo and is yet cited in internet sites, magazine and newspaper articles as having had instead just that. Alexandre Pierre Odart (1778-1866), was born in Parçay-sur-Vienne at the Chateau de Prézault (and not Prévault, as has also been erroneously written) in the French Indre et Loire department. He is considered by many to be if not the father, then one of the founding fathers of the science of ampelography (his is the world-famous 1845 *Traité d'Ampélographie*, republished as the *Ampélographie Universelle: ou traité des cépages les plus estimés dans tous les vignobles de quelque remom* in 1849).

Three more editions followed, published in 1854, 1859 and 1862 (plus a posthumous edition dating to 1874, which included notes that had been left unfinished by Odart at the time of his death). Interestingly, more than one source documents that Odart, plagued by bad eyesight, travelled very little in his lifetime; and when he did, it was mostly in France, and then only to international wine conferences such as those held in Dijon, Bordeaux and Angers. One foreign trip he did undertake was to Hungary, when in 1839, at 61 years old, the French Agriculture Ministry put him in charge of a mission devoted to the study of the grape varieties and vineyards of the Tokay region. But there is no mention in the literature, none that we can find at least, even that written by people who knew him well, of a trip to Barolo or of an even minimal involvement with the making of a new, drier style of Barolo. In fact, as far as we can tell his only tie to Piedmont was related to hemp: Odart began his agricultural career at his Domaine de Beauregard in Chcillé (one of the family's five estates, including the Chateau de Prézeault where he was born) in the Bréhémont (Regine-Ussy), an agricultural zone famous in France for the production of hemp. Hemp was much used at the time in the making of boat sails and ropes, but the local French species was very low-yielding. And so it was that, after Piedmont's annexation to France in 1802 by the Consulate, France had access to, and began importing, the much more generously yielding Piedmont hemp, also called Giant hemp (as its name implies, a much larger and productive tree). This species was common in Piedmont's Carmagnola Valley south of Turin (Desbons 2013). Among his other achievements, Odart served as Mayor of Esvres from 1818-1826 and the city has gone on to name a street after him, the Allée du Comte Odart. Odart died in his son-in-law's house in Tours in 1866, a member of the Chevaliers of the Legion d'Honneur. He is buried in the La Salle cemetery in Tours, where his tomb is still visible (block 118, number 116). Odart is no doubt a very successful man and a prominent figure in the history of wine, but to the best of our knowledge, unlike Oudart, never had anything to do with Barolo.

One individual who did have plenty to do with Barolo and whose contributions to the birth of modern Barolo wines cannot be underestimated was major general (essentially a two-star general) Paolo Francesco Staglieno (1773-1850), heir to a famous patrician family of Genoa. Staglieno was not just an accomplished military figure, but an erudite scholar of enology as well. Upon his retirement from military career, he was appointed by King Carlo Alberto to manage wine production at the royal estates (the Tenute Reali of Verduno, Roddi, Santa Vittoria and Pollenzo) under the banner of the Agenzia di Pollenzo, a post he held from 1836 to 1846. According to Berta and Mainardi (1997) in their *Piemonte-Storia regionale della vite e del vino*, in reference to the cellars of the castle of Grinzane Cavour "… in the year 1847, the cellar contained both the wines in the Staglieno style and the French style" (the French style being that wine made in the manner of Louis Oudart).

In 1835 (so ahead of Oudart), just a year before beginning his tenure at Pollenzo, Staglieno wrote the book *Istruzione intorno al miglior metodo di fare e conservare i vini in Piemonte ("Instructions on how to best make and conserve the wines of Piedmont")*. Considered already at the time a milestone in the history of Italian wine writing, the book sold out immediately. Many of Staglieno's contributions to wine quality really stand out, such as for example that finished wines require patience (meaning cellar time) in order to develop fully and show best. Consequently, he was the first enologist in Piedmont to insist on a minimum aging period for what he believed were the noble Nebbiolo wines of Alba, famously saying "… Wines made from Nebbiolo are not perfectly good if they have not yet reached four years of age."

Apparently, it was Staglieno who first introduced winemaking practices such as destemming, punching down the cap, fining, and adding small amounts of sulfur dioxide prior to bottling, while also insisting on better overall cellar hygiene. In an age where wines were made in open vats side by side oftentimes with animals also milling around in the barn, he was strict about enforcing cleanliness in the cellar. He believed in controlling wine fermentation temperatures, and was a major proponent of the French Gervais method, named after French winemaker Elisabeth Gervais who in 1820 fermented her wines in partially covered vats. Staglieno did so too and noted the improved quality of the wines he made.

Not everyone supported Staglieno when he insisted on using her vats: for example, the historian Fantini (1885) wrote that many stopped following Staglieno's recommendations believing that fermenting Barolo in contact with air was the right thing to do because such a practice "enhanced its bouquet". But in the long run, Staglieno's theories took hold: after all, his wines met with so much success that his was ultimately taken to be the way. Perhaps most important to this retired soldier's legacy was something we hear repeatedly from producers everywhere in the world today: that the quality of the wine starts with the grapes. In fact, Staglieno even went as far as to divided harvests by wine grape quality, an unheard-of practice at the time. Staglieno loved wine, and he was especially partial to the grapes of Roddi and Santa Vittoria (as was his king), from which he made Nebbiolo, "Dussetto," and Barbera. Because of Staglieno's many merits, it is fair to say that, at the very least, there were two "fathers" of Barolo, Oudart and Staglieno.

While the technical advances in Barolo's viticulture and winemaking were the domain and merit of Louis Oudart and Italian Francesco Paolo Staglieno, it is only fair to recognize that their work was supported and made possible by the passion and intelligence of an enlightened noble, Camillo Benso, the Count of Cavour. Cavour (1810-1861) is still remembered today as one of Italy's all-time most accomplished statesmen and key political figures in the movement toward Italian unification. He was Prime Minister of the Kingdom of Piedmont–Sardinia from 1852 to 1861 (except for a brief six-month period in which he had resigned) and was later named the first Prime Minister of Italy, a position he held onto until his death. Crazy as it may seem, given all those accomplishments that would last not one but three or four lesser men a lifetime, Cavour's legacy is almost as important relative to wine.

Cavour was not just an astute politician, but also a keen businessman, an acute observer, and a real sybarite (there's more than one famous Piedmontese cuisine dish named after him); for instance, it has been documented that he was very aware of who grew the best grapes in his native area. Fully realizing just how important agriculture would be in the future of the Italian economy, he lost no opportunity to encourage his noble friends to take viticulture and winemaking more seriously. Named the Mayor of the town of Grinzane when still only in his twenties, his Castello di Grinzane winery quickly became one of the best estates of the area (there are numerous documents attesting to Cavour's first-hand involvement in following his estate's affairs). Cavour's legacy in wine, and specifically relative to Barolo, was sealed for posterity when, in 1916, the town of Grinzane was renamed Grinzane Cavour by the municipality in honor of its most illustrious mayor (Grinzane Cavour is one of the eleven wines producing communes of the Barolo denomination). And it is Cavour who worked with both Staglieno and Oudart and contributing to their turning Barolo into the world class wine it is today.

Last but certainly not least, Juliette Victorine Colbert (1785-1864), the wife of the Marchese (Marquis, in English) Carlo Tancredi Falletti of Barolo was a noblewoman also associated with the birth of modern Barolo. She too undoubtedly helped Barolo's wine become not just better known but improved its reputation. Born into a very prestigious French family, Juliette was the great-granddaughter of Jean-Baptiste Colbert (1619-1683), who served as the Minister of Finances from 1661 to 1683 during the reign of Louis XIV, the famous "Sun King". If not quite at the same level, her husband Tancredi Falletti was no slouch in the prestige and fame department himself: he was born into a family of wealthy bankers that had bought numerous large and important properties in and around Alba ever since 1250. Colbert is famous for having promoted Barolo actively throughout her lifetime, and is famous for, legend or not, having sent one *brenta* of Barolo wine from her estate for every day of the year to the King when he happened to mention that he liked the wine. This is no doubt one of the first examples of a major-league marketing and pr move in the history of Italian wine! There is however no clear-cut evidence of her having ever been involved with Oudart or Staglieno directly.

There is a brief and generic reference ("beginning of the 1800s") that is not more precisely dated in regards to the Marchesi di Barolo estate believing and investing in Barolo wine in Canon Domenico Massè's oft-cited *Il Paese del Barolo*. But we cannot know if the wine made there at that time was still of the sweet kind that was then the norm. In fact, when Gallesio visited the town of Barolo in September 1834, he spoke admiringly of the beautiful underground cellars of the castle, mentioning that the 1833 wine he tasted was "harsh and ungiving" while the 1832 was "soft and succulent". But it has been pointed out that the e translation from Italian into English and then back is not quite precise: the Italian author's word used was not "succulent" but *amabile*, which in Italian means "off-dry" and is a term routinely used to describe levels of wine sweetness in Italy (Orlandi 2011). Furthermore, Orlandi states clearly that "… Juliette, for her part, was personally motivated to provide her wine with a lasting prestige, to which end she asked her friend the Count of Cavour…, to allow her to consult with his French enologist…". It only seems logical to infer that had her wine been of the ilk she would have liked it to be, she wouldn't have needed to ask Cavour permission to take matters up with his winemaker (clearly, the Frenchman in question would have been Oudart).

Colbert and Cavour certainly knew each other, and so it is possible that Falletti did ask him about the possibility of having Oudart join her or help her team's winemaking practices at the castle, but as we have seen from Riccardi Candiani's well-researched and documented book, there is no evidence of this having happened.

Not that we have as yet found, at least. In any case, upon Falletti's death in 1864, with no heirs to the family fortune, her will led to the creation of the Opera Pia Barolo, a charitable institution that administered the family's fortune and whose mandate was to perform good acts, and so was born the Collegio Barolo, that between 1875 and 1958, was one of the few places were the area's youngsters could learn and go to school thanks to bursaries set up for this purpose. Giulia was also devoted to improving the lives of women in jail and created a school for the poor female inhabitants of the Borgo Dora in Turin as well as the Ospedaletto di Santa Filomena for disabled children, and much more. No doubt, Julia Colbert was a gentlewoman far ahead of her time: she played a seminal role in the genesis of modern-day Barolo and there is much to admire about her and to remember her for, especially in an age when it was anything but easy for women to emerge and to lead (and we are well aware that some would argue it is unfortunately so still today, to a degree).

Chapter 6

A TIMELINE OF BAROLO

Michele Longo

The following timeline of important dates in the birth of Barolo from its origins to today have been put together by interviewing wine producers, historian and scouring through old texts. Much work on this subject has been performed by historian and winemaker Lorenzo Tablino (Tablino, 2015).

FROM 1800 TO 1940:

1858: "*Atto di comando del regio delegato* ("Act of purchase of the royal delegate") in the commune of Serralunga d'Alba. It is a document attesting to a purchase made on behalf of Vittorio Emanuele II (who at that time had not yet become the King of Italy) of a piece of land owned by a Giacomo Roggeri (roughly 52 hectares large) located in the locality of Fontanafredda (interestingly, registry data from 1860 shows that this plot of land was passed on to Maria Vittoria and Emanuele Alberto Mirafiori, the children of King Vittorio Emanuele II and of Rosa Vercellana, as part of the King's private assets handed down to his children).

1861: During the celebrations for the unification of Italy after the Independence War and the Risorgimento, the wine of Giacomo Borgogno's winery has the honor of being served at the official celebratory lunch (most possibly this was a Barolo, though we cannot be sure).

1867: A document in the Turin's State Archives regarding the royal estate of La Mandria makes a clear reference to a wine, a "Nebbiolo di Barolo 1868", and even to a "Barolo 1865". It is believed that they were made from grapes grown in the vineyards of Serralunga and Barolo but vinified in the royal cellars of Pollenzo. This is apparently the first mention of Barolo as such (Barolo, not Barol), but above all, it is the first document in which a clear-cut differentiation is present between "Barolo" and "Nebbiolo". Among the wines listed, there were: 'vino di Barolo 1865", "nebiolo di Fontanafredda 1865", "nebiolo di Barolo 1865-66-67".

1869: The pastor of Barolo don Bona pushed for an official document that would reserve the name Barolo only for those wines produced with grapes grown within the town's walls (and four years later, a communal advisor named Ghisolfi -a fairly common name amongst Barolo producing families still today- proposed the establishment of an annual register of grape buyers who bought the grapes grown within the territory of the commune of Barolo only.

1869: At the Turin Exhibition, the Barolos of Matteo Cav. Fissore and of Debenedetti, producers in Bra, are awarded bronze medals.

1873: At the royal estate of Fontana Fredda (apparently spelled so at the time, with two separate words) in Serralunga d'Alba, a "Barolo 1871" is documented. At the time, the estate was the property of the Fondo Real Casa, privately owned by then King Vittorio Emanuele II.

1873: At the International Exposition of Vienna, the Barolo by Fissore wins the gold medal. At the time, the city of Bra was the major production center of Barolo wine.

1874: The Austrian journal *Die Weinlaube* lauds Barolo for "*… its richness of flavors and pleasant aromas; it can, without fail, compete with more prestigious French wines*". The wine was probably made in the cellars of Pilone estate in Barolo and in the wine agency of Serralunga d'Alba. Also, entries in the registry of the Opera Pia Barolo's cellars clearly write either of "Nebbiolo" or "Barolo".

1878: The winery "E. di Mirafiore" is founded in Serralunga d'Alba. Hence Fontana Fredda is no longer managed as the King's private assets. The estate becomes an important one, making a name for itself with high quality Barolo wines.

1881: The Enology School of Alba is founded, enabling young locals who want to work in wine to be able to study and train close to where they live. Soon the school forms all or close to all the winemakers who will one day manage wine estates in Alba. The first director is Domizio Cavazza, one of the greatest all-time Nebbiolo experts and the recognized father of Barbaresco.

1885: A scholar, Lorenzo Fantini, publishes an important work called *"Monografia sulla viticoltura ed enologia nella provincia di Cuneo"*. It is he who names Barolo "...the King of Wines".

1887-1894: Commercial success of Barolo wine on the Italian market and overseas with special thanks to "valorous count Emanuele di Mirafiore". He was the owner of the estate and cellars of Fontanafredda. He succeeds in, as reported by Lorenzo Fantini *"... to make headway with his wine into an overseas market earning the highest recognition"*.

1890-1895: In Alba, two pharmacists, Giuseppe Cappellano (with shops in Serralunga d'Alba and Torino), and Mario Zabaldano (of Monforte d'Alba) carry out a long and patient series of tests, experiments and trials, adding *Chincona Calisaya* and other herbs and spices to Barolo, to produce the now world-famous Barolo Chinato wine (at the 1899 Franco-Italian exposition of Nizza the *"delicious Barolo chinato"* made by Zabaldano won a gold medal).

1896: The first cement vinification tanks are installed in the zone of Alba. They are produced by Swiss firm Borsari Zollikon. Some of these are still used today in the cellar of Fontanafredda. Also, the Barolo of the E. di Mirafiore winery won its first gold medal in Cologne, Germany.

1896: The Ministry of Agriculture delimits the Barolo zone.

1899: The Barolo wines of the commander Giovan Battista Burlotto (G.B. Burlotto) in Verduno accompany the Italian expedition of the Duca degli Abruzzi to the North Pole.

19th century to the beginning of 20th century: Important estates in Alba for the production and sale of Barolo are created and consolidated: Calissano, Cav. Luigi Pira, Comm. Giovan Battista Burlotto, Cav. Arnulfo, Coppa, Cordero di Montezemolo, Enrico Serafino, Felice Abbona, Francesco Costamagna, Giovanni Cappellano, Giuseppe Tarditi, Giovanni Genesio, Napoleone Ravinale, Pio Cesare, Prunotto, Rinaldi-Barale, and Virginia Perrero.

1903: The Ufficio Agrario Provinciale di Cuneo (the "Provincial Agricultural Office of Cuneo", in English), published in the *Guida vinicola della provincia di Cuneo* ("A viticultural guide to the Province of Cuneo"), one of the first documented maps of the Barolo production zones. Apparently, maps and Barolo have gone hand in hand for quite some time.

1908: The "Associazione per la tutela del Barolo contro le frodi e false indicazioni" (or Association for the protection of Barolo against frauds and false indications") was created in Alba (while the Consorzio was founded nineteen years later, in 1927).

1909: A new delimitation of the Barolo production zone was drawn by the Comizio Agrario di Alba at the request of the Barolo commune.

1919: Acquisition of the lands and the cellars of the Opera Pia Barolo by Count Gastone di Mirafiore. *"In the administration of Opera Pia Barolo represented by the vice president ing. Melchiorre Pulciano ... and Gastone Guerrieri Mirafiori deputy of the Parliament... One agrees to sell the wineries in Barolo and Serralunga...at the price of 3.650.000 lire (3 millions...) and in the condition of specifications of May 15th 1911..."*. The act was stipulated in Turin on June 25th, 1919 (notary deed by Vittorio Torretta). And so, at the time Fontanafredda owned the cellars and vineyards of Opera Pia Barolo as well. In retrospect, it was a remarkably important acquisition, with which Count Gastone di Mirafiore came to possess some of the best Nebbiolo vineyards of all (54 hectares in Barolo, 58 in Serralunga, 31 in La Morra).

1927: A *consorzio* (producer association) is established to protect Barolo and Barbaresco wines.

1933: The official decree that identifies the Barolo production area is published: *La zona di origine delle uve atte a produrre il «Barolo»*, that had already been identified as of August 31, 1933.

1958: The social cooperative "Terre del Barolo" was founded in Castiglione Falletto (forty original members). The coop's members are producers from Castiglione Falletto, Serralunga, Monforte, Barolo, and La Morra.

1961: The first single vineyard Barolo wines are made, leading to the future official recognition of Barolo subzones. The first to do so were Beppe Colla, who bottled a Barolo Bussia cru, and Alfredo Currado with his Rocche (today's Rocche di Castiglione).

1966: The Barolo Denominazione di Origine Controllata (DOC), one of the first four in Italy, is created following numerous meetings with the Ministry's representatives in Rome. It was formed under the initiatives of Alba's mayor Paganelli; the DOC Committee included the producers Beppe Colla, Renato Ratti, Giuseppe Crestodina, and Felice Cavallotto.

1970: The Administration of the commune of Barolo acquires the castle of Barolo. After important restoration works were carried out, the "Enoteca Regionale del Barolo" (1981) was established within the castle of Barolo grounds. It is still today one of the best places to visit in Barolo for information and great wines.

1972: A bottle of 1886 Barolo Borgogno, at auction of historical wines held in Turin, was sold for 530.000 lire (roughly $200), which was, at that time, an absolute record auction price never before attained by any Italian wine.

1976: The place names of important historical and qualitative interest are noted on a map of the Barolo production zone made famous by Renato Ratti.

1980: The DOCG is awarded to Barolo.

1994: Numerous entities and organizations, coordinated by the Regione Piemonte, kick off the project for the so-called "Zonation of Barolo". The area of study coincides with that of Barolo DOCG production zone and is the reference used in this book for the classification of every vineyard district by the use of "Land Units".

2009: The Regional Wine Committee of Piedmont passes a law allowing the use on the labels, starting from vintage 2010, of the individual source of grapes (in theory vineyards, in practice much too large and so best thought of as vineyard districts), or in Italian, the *Menzioni Geografiche Aggiuntive* ("Additional Geographical Mentions" or MGAs, also sometimes referred to as MeGAs). The zone of Barolo is composed of 181 vineyard districts or "MGAs" including 11 townships approved in 2010. It should be noted that the MGAs are not to be confused with single vineyard wines, for these are born from single vineyards located within the newly delimited and officially named vineyard districts. In this case the name of the vineyard district is used along with the word *vigna* ("vineyard"). In this book we use either the word vineyard district, as it conveys immediately that it is not usually a small vineyard area that is being talked about we commend Barolo producers for their ability and dedication to working together in reaching this important milestone, something that has escaped the almost totality of other important Italian wines and denominations (Barbaresco and Dolcetto di Diano d'Alba excluded, as they also have officially zonated their territories) that have not yet been able to reach a consensus (happily, many are working on this at time of writing). Congratulations are therefore in order to all Barolo (and Barbaresco) producers.

Chapter 7

BAROLO TERROIR

Ian D'Agata

The Barolo denomination extends (in whole or in part) over the territories of eleven townships (or communes, both words can be used interchangeably): it is from the territories of these eleven towns, and only these, that a wine called Barolo can be made. In alphabetical order, these communes are: Barolo, Castiglione Falletto, Cherasco, Diano d'Alba, Grinzane Cavour, La Morra, Monforte d'Alba (or Monforte for short), Novello, Roddi, Serralunga d'Alba (or Serralunga for short), and Verduno. Of the eleven, it is the territories of Barolo, Castiglione Falletto and Serralunga d'Alba that fall entirely within the Barolo denomination; by contrast, only parts of the territories of the other eight communes fall within the Barolo denomination's boundaries. Broadly speaking, these eleven communes are associated with the two major types of Barolo, the earlier-maturing and relatively lighter-bodied (I write "relatively light-bodied" because these are still Barolos, after all) wines of the communes of Barolo, Cherasco, Diano d'Alba, Grinzane Cavour, La Morra, Novello, Roddi and Verduno, and the much more structured, slowly-maturing wines of Castiglione Falletto, Monforte, and Serralunga. And while that distinction always remains true, a fair bit of overlap exists. All the communes are associated with Barolos of both lighter and bigger structure, for subtle changes in soil, exposure and altitude can make for much rounder or tougher wines throughout the denomination. However, no matter how "politely-styled" a Barolo of Monforte and Serralunga might be, they remain the toughest and most structured of all Barolos in their youth (and always recognizably so), not to mention the slowest to evolve. In my experience, even relative beginners to wine can identify with reasonably accurate approximation the Barolos of those two communes when tasting blind (say something like anywhere from half to two thirds of the time) just by focusing on what is their telltale tannic structure.

As I have written before, much as it is with the wines of Burgundy, Bordeaux, the Mosel, and the world's other great terroir-based wines are made, knowing the styles of wine associated with each Barolo commune makes drinking the wines even more enjoyable and stimulating. And perhaps more importantly, also much easier to understand. And just like it isn't very difficult, with a little practice, to figure out if the wine in your glass (when tasting blind) is from Margaux or Pauillac, or from Chambertin or Volnay, or from Forst or Piesport, identifying where each Barolo comes from is not impossible either with a little practice (D'Agata 2019). Furthermore, just as there are differences between, for example, Margaux's many wines and between the many wines made within the Chambolle-Musigny commune (a Chambolle-Musigny wine from the *premier cru* Les Baudes is recognizably different from one of the *premier cru* Les Amoureuses), there are also clear-cut differences between the wines made within vineyard districts of each of the Barolo communes. Not necessarily easy to do, but finding a sense of place in each glass of Barolo put before you is very possible. Of course, you might think that identifying a sense of place in your glass of Barolo really isn't that important, and all you want to do is sit back and enjoy your glass of wine. Fair enough, that's a valid viewpoint that I can totally subscribe to. But in the subchapters that follow, I hope to help you learn how to interpret, to understand, and to remember the characteristics of the Barolos of each commune. Even more specifically, wherever possible, of the Barolos of each vineyard district. Cheers!

THE GEOGRAPHY OF BAROLO: TOPOGRAPHY, ALTITUDE, CLIMATE, AND GEOLOGY

Geography is about a lot more than just looking at maps. It's actually a far-reaching subject that involves many different study areas, and its old definition as "the study of the physical features of the Earth's surface and atmosphere" has long been surpassed (Unstead, 1907; Rosenberg, 2020). Today, it is more precise to view geography as the study of places and the relationships between people and their environments. Therefore, geography also involves the evaluation of how human interaction affects those physical features, and in turn how they affect humans; in other words, how people and places are connected to the world. To help you grasp

Barolo Terroir: Grapes, Crus, People, Places.

how complex a subject geography really is, and that it is hardly limited to drawing up and looking at maps, keep in mind that there are six essential elements to geography. These are: the world in spatial terms; places and regions (including climate and topography); physical systems; human systems; environment and society; and uses of geography (Boehm and Bednar, 1994).

However, in order to make such a complex subject matter much easier to grasp, geography can be broken down into two large subgroups: physical geography and human geography (Haines-Young and Petch, 1986; Gregory 2000). Clearly, the study of rocks and minerals, landforms, water regimens, rivers and other bodies of water, climate and weather are all part of physical geography; while agricultural systems, populations, and social traditions are some of the study areas of human geography. Both the physical and human geography elements play a role in the genesis of a specific wine's terroir. To keep this discussion as simple as possible in a way that you will be better served in understanding how the specific geography of the different sections of the Barolo denomination affects the wines made there, I will focus on the four physical elements I personally believe (and not just I, actually) to be most important relative to wine.

These four physical elements are: topography, altitude, climate and geology. Knowing the details of these four elements relative to the site you are drinking the Barolo of will help you not just know what to expect from the wine even before you drink it, but to also understand that specific wine better when you do drink it. Clearly, because the human factors are a part of the geography of wine and greatly influence terroir, in order for my line of reasoning to work and be somewhat useful, we need to eliminate from the equation the human elements of geography relative to the wine. In other words, we need to compare wines made in a similar way (including how the grapes were grown and the winemaking involved).

To really grasp the differences in terroir expressed in each Barolo, you need to taste wines from the different sites made by the same producer, or at the very least from the same site by different producers who work more or less in the same way (in both the vineyard and in the cellar). Luckily, that is not easier said than done nowadays. Clearly, comparing wines from the same site that were made in completely different manners will not allow you to understand what role the various physical factors have in fashioning the Barolo you are drinking, for there would then be just too many confounding variables at work. In that case, drawing any useful inferences from what it is we have just tasted is not just wishful thinking, but downright non-sensical. So, when in this book I write "the Barolo of site X tastes like this compared to wine Y…" and "… by contrast, the Barolo of site Y tastes different from that of site Z because of…" it is with the understanding that we are not comparing apples and oranges, but rather similarly made wines (in other words, wines X, Y and Z are similarly made). This is possible because Barolo winemaking, after a brief moment of strongly divergent methodologies and styles (the so-called modernists versus traditionalists) has now found a common ground, and for the most part, differences in how wines are made are not so marked. But you still need to be aware of how each wine is made: for example, to know if the winemaker believes in using whole bunches or not, or believes in cement vats or not. Happily, in today's Barolo scenario, it is possible to find (for the most part) relatively similarly made wines, and therefore one in which the roles of altitude, climate, geology, and topography become all the more relevant.

The Barolo denomination is located immediately southeast of Alba, a small prosperous town which is to the Langhe (that specific area of Piedmont in which both Barolo and Barbaresco are found) what Beaune is to the Côte d'Or. Though both Barolo and Barbaresco make sublime Nebbiolo wines that rank with the world's greatest red wines, the topography, climate and geology of these two denominations could not be any more different (and as already mentioned, the respective wines reflect this in spades, and then some). For this reason, in this book, we deal with Barolo only, while Barbaresco is the subject of its own, upcoming book.

Barolo's topography

According to the Collins English dictionary (2020), topography (as an uncountable noun) is defined as the study and description of the physical features of an area (for example its hills, valleys, or rivers), or the representation of these features on maps. So, let's check out Barolo's.

The Barolo production zone is a horseshoe-shaped basin that, broadly speaking, can be divided by a ridge that starts at Castiglione Falletto and proceeds in the direction of Monforte. Thanks to this ridge, the Barolo denomination is split into two valleys: a larger western valley that runs from Gallo D'Alba to Barolo and includes the town and territory of La Morra and of Barolo (the town); and a smaller eastern valley (called the Serralunga valley) where Castiglione Falletto, Monforte and Serralunga are located. This entire area is closed off to the east and west by two other hilly ridges, both of which run in a generally north-south direction. The ridge to the west runs from Verduno in the north, passes through La Morra's territory and reaches Novello. The ridge to the east divides the Serralunga territory in two halves.

What this means is that the whole Barolo denomination can be loosely subdivided into six contiguous sections, each associated with its own specific vineyard districts, with a seventh and separate section being the lower-lying area of the Grinzane Cavour commune, off on its own in the northeastern corner. The six contiguous areas of Barolo are:

1. The section that spreads west of the Verduno-Novello ridge (for example, the vineyard districts of Brandini, Bricco Cogni, and Neirane are all located in this subsection)

2. The section to the east of the same ridge (with Bricco Luciani, Bricco Manescotto and Cannubi Boschis examples of vineyard districts located there)

3. The section to the west of the Castiglione Falletto-Monforte ridge (with vineyard districts such as Castellero and Pugnane)

4. The section of this ridge to the east that looks towards Serralunga (the Ginestra and Mosconi districts are found here)

5. The fifth section is made up of the Serralunga's ridge western flank (this is where you will find the districts of Briccolina, Margheria, Vignarionda)

6. Last but not least, the sixth section is the eastern flank of the Serralunga ridge (Badarina and Brea are examples of two vineyard districts of this subsection).

Map created by Raffaele Grillone

As stated previously, the seventh area is that of the Grinzane Cavour commune. All the vineyard districts associated with each one of these-seven sections all have different topographies, altitudes, geologies and meso- and microclimates. And different wines.

Note that Barolo's vineyard districts are found not just on the six slopes of the three main ridges just described, but also on the slopes of smaller crests that jut out perpendicularly from the aforementioned three long ridges. So, while the three main ridges run from north to south, the shorter crests run instead in an east-west direction. Therefore, many of Barolo's vineyard districts are also situated on the two flanks of these transversally-running hillside crests, that are all more or less parallel to each other. Clearly, as these shorter hilly crests extend in an east-west direction, they will have one slope that is north-facing, and another that is south-facing. Given that Barolo is in Piedmont, a northern and relatively cool-climate region of Italy, it follows that practically all of the vineyard districts found on the hilly crests are located on the more sunlit and warmer south-facing slopes of these crests. Simply put, even in this day and age of climate change, north-facing slopes are still too cold for Nebbiolo to ripen properly: historically, such slopes were in fact never much planted to any grapevines. If they were or are, it was/is mostly white grape varieties that grow there. And even if and when Nebbiolo is planted there, those are Nebbiolo grapes that are mostly used to make Langhe Nebbiolo or Nebbiolo d'Alba wines. Clearly, climate change may end up modifying this state of affairs. Examples of very famous Barolo vineyard districts located on the southern-facing flanks of the transversal crests are Castiglione Falletto's Monprivato and Villero and Serralunga's Parafada.

Last but not least, the morphology of the hills is also important relative to Barolo's wines. In fact, the non-stop undulating nature of the Barolo production zone is a very important parameter in determining a vineyard district's suitability for Nebbiolo grapevines, besides the intrinsic quality of the site itself. For the most part, the hilly crests have one side that is gently sloping while the other is steeper (such as in the case of Rocche di Castiglione, one side of which drops precipitously down in almost cliff-like fashion). And while in Barolo slopes are generally soft (Barbaresco's are even gentler), there are exceptions. The gentleness (or not) of the hill's rise upwards from the plain is what is referred to as the slope gradient (by definition, this is a measurement in degrees or a percentage of the change in vertical direction from a horizontal plane). Slope gradient is important for several reasons: it affects the potential for soil and slope erosion; it influences air flow through the vineyard canopies; has a bearing on the relative ease or not of working in the vineyards (slopes of more than 30% usually need to be terraced) and of harvesting; and even on soil drainage.

As always, too much or too little of something can become a negative (just try eating too much chocolate ice cream one day and see what happens): so while a slope gradient of 5-10% is generally speaking a favorable topographical feature as it facilitates the dispersion of cold air towards the bottom of the hill (cold air is denser and heavier than warm air), a slope gradient of 30% or more is not, for it makes just standing in the vineyard safely a very hard thing to do, never mind picking grapes (hence the need to build terraces at 30% or more gradients). In any case, Barolo's hills allow for the presence of anabatic and katabatic breezes (those breezes that blow up and down the hills, respectively) that provide relief from extreme temperatures. Therefore, this hilly landscape contributes to a warmer macro-, meso- and microclimates than might be expected given the denomination's northern location. This is but one of the many examples why the slope gradient is an important factor when evaluating Barolo vineyards.

Barolo's altitude

The vineyards of Barolo lie mostly between 200-400 meters above sea level, but can be found higher up, such as in La Morra's Serradenari vineyard district, where Nebbiolo can bask in cool sunshine up at 500 meters above sea level. For comparison's sake, be aware that Barolo is very different from beautiful Montalcino and its territory: whereas in the latter the higher you go the usually better off you are, that's not the case with Barolo. Because of Barolo's latitude, Nebbiolo has real trouble ripening at higher altitudes (the farther the latitude from the equator, the steeper the slope needs to be to ensure adequate sunlight and grape ripening). According to Pietro Ratti, as recently as 2008, Nebbiolo in the area reached full physiologic ripeness above 400 meters in altitude only in five or six years out of ten.

All you need to understand this is to think of, or just take a look at, where all of Barolo's farmhouses (*cascine*) are built: always down low, in lower-lying, sunlit, open amphitheaters where it is much warmer. In the words of Bruno Ceretto, nobody in his or her right mind would have ever thought of building a *cascina* on a *bricco* (the summit of a hill), no matter how protected. In any case, research clearly shows statistically significant differences in terms of growth, technologic and polyphenol indices of maturation and productivity between Nebbiolo vines grown on the top of a slope and vines cultivated at the foot of the slope.

An important corollary to altitude is the new role of exposure in Barolo nowadays. For the longest time, it was the Barolo vineyard's exposure that was the rate-limiting step, so to speak, in the making of fine Barolos. As recently as twenty years ago, it used to be that the best exposure (actually the only exposure), that was felt to be good enough for Nebbiolo to make Barolo (as opposed to Langhe Nebbiolo or Nebbiolo d'Alba wine) was full-south, or at most, southwest (vineyards with the latter exposure were dubbed *sorì della sera*). As I have written previously in the Nebbiolo chapter, this is why those vineyards where the snow melted first have always been the most prized in Barolo. Even southeastern exposures (*sorì del mattino*) were looked at with suspicion: honestly, if over the last forty years someone had given me one hundred dollars (or Euros) every time a producer told me that one of his vineyards was less ideally suited to the making of great Barolo because of its southeastern-facing aspect, I'd really be a rich man today. Clearly, nobody's saying so anymore: currently, most everybody pines for those very southeast-facing vineyards they sneered at before, because that way grapes do not bask all day in the sun (like they do with the southwestern exposures) and are less likely to end up giving Barolos marred by overripe aromas and flavors and pushing 15% alcohol by volume.

What all this really means is that the Barolo vineyard districts that were most prized once (because of their warmer microclimates resulting -for the most part- from their combination of altitude and exposure) are not necessarily as good or quite as prized in today's increasingly hot climate, short of completely revamping their viticulture. This is an obvious reality of the world we live in today, but it's a reality very few individuals are willing to accept or even talk about.

A majority still evaluate the relative quality level of Barolo vineyard areas based on their exposure (just listen to most producers or read any recently written book on Barolo), but this not the correct way to go about things nowadays. Yes, with attentive viticulture and vineyard work and management, much can be done to decrease a microclimate's "degree of warmth", but the simple truth of the matter is there is only so much you can do. Which is precisely why everybody today, not just in Barolo but in viticultural areas all over the world, are increasingly looking to plant vines higher up and avoid full south-facing locations like the plague. To believe that "…this site is less good/interesting because it faces east or southeast" is non-sensical. However, there is one caveat. Where exposure is still all-important is at the higher elevations. In Barolo vineyards planted at 400-420 meters or higher, it is undoubtedly harder to get Nebbiolo to reach full physiologic ripeness every year, especially where exposures look east or even to the north. In such areas the old southwest and full south exposures are still a *vignaiolo's* best friend. But as we have seen, it is not as cut and dried as it once used to be. This is also why I adamantly and steadfastly believe that soil and subsoil (geology, if you will), not exposure, are the single most important factors in determining the quality of the Barolos of today (see subchapter: *Barolo's geology*, below). Or to put it somewhat differently, in ultimate analysis, when you want to know if a site is a top quality one for Barolo or not, don't look up to the sky: look down to the ground.

Barolo's climate

By definition, Barolo's climate falls in the continental category, but that characterization is dangerous, in that the temperature extremes typical of other viticultural areas with continental climates never materialize in Barolo. This is mostly because of the tempering effect provided by the many small streams that flow through the Barolo production zone (such as the Bussia stream, the Talloria dell'Annunziata stream and others). The range of Barolo's average daily temperatures is 12.5-14.5 degrees Celsius (data referred to the years 1981-1996); 1987 was the year in which the average temperature was lowest (11.3 degrees Celsius), while 1981 is the year in which the highest average temperature (13.6 degrees Celsius) was recorded. Diurnal temperature variations can be noteworthy (as much as 18.5 degrees Celsius). It is also helpful to know that Barolo's Winkler index range is 1750-2180, while its Huglin index range is 2000-2450 (ERSA data).

As I have documented before, Barolo's annual precipitation average ranges between 800-900 mm/year (with slight differences present between communes) but drought is potentially scary only in July and August. At about 150 millimeters, October has the highest mean monthly precipitation (including rain, snow, and hail), but interestingly, October is not necessarily the most humid month of the year. Do note that in some years, rainfall can be much higher (or lower) than the average: for example, at 1489 mm/year, the 1959 vintage is correctly remembered as one of the rainiest ever. By contrast, the 366 mm/year of 1989 have locals remembering that year as one of the driest ever. Torrential downpours are rare in Barolo and especially so nowadays (but you would have never have guessed that in the 2002 then again, with climate change, weather patterns of today and the future are anybody's guess and there is an obvious generalized worsening of climate conditions). In general, it is the southern sectors of the Barolo denomination that locals consider to be the rainiest. In fact, this impression is confirmed by the numbers: for example, over a sixty-eight years span (from 1929-1996), the average annual rainfall in Verduno and La Morra was 745 and 829 mm/year respectively (La Morra is the more southernly of the two). For more information on this subject, I refer you to *Italy's Native Wine Grape Terroirs* (D'Agata 2019) where the subject is treated in-depth.

But, once again, we are forced to reckon with climate change, because those numbers are misleading. For example, while La Morra's average annual rainfall in those sixty-eight years I just referred to was reported to be 829 mm/year, it was a much, much, much lower 693 mm/year over the last sixteen years (from 1981-1996) of the same sixty-eight years period. Interestingly, that precipitation figure tells us that there hasn't been much difference between La Morra's annual rainfall over those sixteen years and that of Castiglione Falletto's (707 mm/year). But without question it rains much less lately than it used to. And the 2022 vintage will long be remembered as one of the most despairingly driest yet.

Barolo's geology

Geology is an amazingly fascinating subject but one that is also extremely complicated. While I firmly believe it is the key to understanding the wines you drink (not just Barolo), I also am very much aware that unless it is explained in a logical and easy to comprehend manner, then it is a totally pointless exercise in which to engage. And though Barolo geology is not easy to grasp and even harder to remember, I do think it can be simplified to a degree that the wines you drink will make at least some sense to you. I have already written on this subject at length in my *Italy's Native Wine Grape Terroirs* book (D'Agata 2019), but in here I update some of the information of the area's soils. In so doing, I will try to avoid to give you a headache with complicated sounding names, and will attempt to break down Barolo's soil and subsoil to a degree by which you will gain enough of a basic knowledge about the subject so as to understand and appreciate the Barolo you are drinking even more than you already might.

When comparing Barolos of similar viticulture, winemaking and vintage, I believe that geology is the single most important physical geographic factor in determining the type of Barolo you are drinking (I say this fully realizing that soil microbiology is all important too, but we do not as yet have soil bacteria characterized for each Barolo commune or vineyard district, as these studies have not yet been systematically carried out by anyone). Not that exposure isn't important, for it is: but the continued reiteration on south-facing vineyards as the best possible ones for Barolo is, to be politely blunt, not looking at modern reality in the face. A reality that says we live in a world of climate change. In Barolo today, southeast exposures are probably far better than full south or southwestern ones; but that means subverting the *status quo* of accepted wisdom relative to what and to which Barolo's best vineyards are (and which have been bought and sold over the years, often at very high prices, with that reputation in mind). Consequently, you understand why there is resistance in many quarters to accept and say that, for example, maybe Brunate and Cerequio (two increasingly warm-weather sites) aren't quite the great vineyards they once were (not every year, at least). There are however a couple of caveats.

As previously discussed, higher altitude vineyards represent a case apart (see Barolo altitude subchapter). Also, I firmly believe there are geologies that are superior to others when it comes to the making of fine wine. Ask any Frenchman worthy of his/her tastebuds and he or she will tell you there is no great wine possible without limestone (of course, I could point out that France has a great deal of its vineyards planted on limestone, but I'm sure that's a coincidence and beside the point). And no Mosel winemaker will ever tell you it's possible to make the greatest of Riesling wines without slate soils. It is most likely not an unfortunate accident that practically none of the world's greatest wines are made with grapes planted on fertile flatland alluvial soils.

So, it follows that relative to fine wine there is something to not just geology, but rather the kind of geology your vines happen to grow in association with. It's a reality that plays an immense role in determining what the wine will be like and has an influence in determining the quality levels of sites in many of the wine site classifications of France. This is true of Barolo as well: individual taste preferences aside, there is no doubt that the denomination's greatest Barolos have never been much associated with, for example, some of the sandier sites of the farthest western reaches of the denomination. And if nobody ever talked much about the grapes or wines of Roddi decades ago it probably wasn't all due just to colder weather. Nebbiolo may finally ripen nowadays where it never used to ripen before, but just reaching more or less optimal physiologic ripeness does not mean the Barolo made from that spot will be as great as the best of those of Serralunga, for example. Without doubt, like it is elsewhere, soil differences are at the core of the intrinsic quality level of Barolo's vineyards: some of the best vineyards of, for example, Serralunga, Monforte and Castiglione Falletto may have the same altitude, exposure, topography and vine age of vineyards in Novello and other communes, but you will find that the complexity and depth of the Barolos from one commune are often superior to the others. Provided you are comparing wines made in a fairly similar manner and by equally hard working and talented producers, what's left that will help determine the quality of the end-result is the soil and subsoil diversity of the areas in question.

Geology provides a key by which to unlock the world's key vineyard areas. Hence, of Barolo too. Even better, if you know the geology of the individual Barolo communes and of their vineyard districts (the most famous ones at least) chances are good that you will be able to distinguish between a Barolo from Novello, from Roddi and Serralunga. This is also true of other world wine areas: for example, if you know where the Oxfordian and the Portlandian soils are located in the Chablis Appellation, you can take a pretty good guess at why the Chablis wine you are drinking tastes like it does, and where it might come from. If you know that you have been given an Alsace Riesling from the Brand and one from the Rangen, it really shouldn't be that difficult to tell the two apart when tasting blind (given that the former is most likely -but not necessarily, given the Brand's size- made from granite soils and the latter from volcanic ones). Clearly, it's not always easy, but you'd be surprised how good and oftentimes accurate a guess you will be able to make, once you have a little experience and knowledge about the specific area's geology under your belts. With soils, we always speak in terms of geology, but in fact we should really talk of both pedology and geology. Soil is essentially studied by the field of pedology (defined as that branch of soil science that integrates and quantifies the formation, morphology, and classification of soils as natural landscape bodies), while subsoil is the domain of geology (the study of the rocks and similar structures such as soil layers that make up the earth's surface in order to know more about the earth's history and life on it).

Barolo is generally thought of as having soils and subsoils that are rich in loam, clay, sand and limestone; gravel and/or large stones are not a big part of Barolo, save in a few vineyard districts such as Sarmassa. In a broad sense, that is undoubtedly true: but there are huge variations in soil and subsoil throughout the Barolo production area. These differences have a huge impact on the wines made. The soil is derived from disgregation of the subsoil beneath and the action (weathering) of the external elements (such as wind, rain, heat) on top of it. It can therefore be divided in younger and older soils not just in terms of when it was formed, but also on how much it has evolved over time. In Barolo you will hear, for more than one person might tell you, that the more evolved soils have a darker red-brown color compared to the younger bluish-gray ones. However, I'm not sure that knowing as much, or even recognizing if a soil is older or younger, will really help you much in understanding what the Barolo you drink is all about or where it comes from. That key is provided by other information.

In order to study rocks, geologists have created the term of "formation". A formation is the basic unit of rock measurement in geology (or more precisely, it's the fundamental unit of stratigraphy, the branch of geology the studies sedimentary sequences) and is made up of similar rock types resulting from a series of depositional events over time (such as rock granules depositing at the bottom of a slow-moving river). A specific formation is characterized by its composition and how it looks, and so can be easily distinguished from other formations. As we shall see and many reading these pages already know, there are many different formations typically associated with the Barolo terroir.

These formations are intimately linked to the geologic time moment in which they were formed and to the way a Barolo will taste. How and when was the soil/subsoil complex of the Barolo denomination (and the Langhe in general) formed? The geological formations of the Langhe are mostly (not just) the result of sea sediments deposited during the Miocene Epoch, which lasted 17.7 million years, from 23.03–5.33 million years ago. According to the International Commission on Stratigraphy (ICS), the Miocene Epoch can be subdivided into six stages: the Aquitanian (23.03–20.43 million years ago), the Burdigalian (20.43–15.97 million years ago), the Langhian (15.97–13.82 million years ago), the Serravallian (13.82–11.63 million years ago), the Tortonian (11.63–7.25 million years ago), and the Messinian (7.25–5.33 million years ago). As I have written previously at length in *Italy's Native Wine Grape Terroirs* (D'Agata 2019), the most relevant for us Barolo-lovers are the last three.

In the beginning, there were no Langhe as we know them today, and no Barolo hills. The whole area was in fact under water, part of the Gulf of the Po Valley, then an inlet of the Tethys Ocean. The Tethys Ocean was a large body of water that divided Europe from Africa during the Jurassic (201-145 million years ago) and Cretaceous (145-66 million years ago) periods, respectively the second and third periods of the Mesozoic Era. (Remember that words such as "era", "epoch", and "period" refer to specific geologic moments of time and should not be used interchangeably because they mean and refer to totally different things.) That ocean dried up when the land masses collided, and the only bodies of water surviving resulted in today's Aral, Black, Caspian and Mediterranean Seas. What would one day become the Langhe was a wedge-top-basin, known as the Tertiary Piedmont Basin, a Late Eocene-Miocene succession composed by continental, shallow and deep marine deposits that covered the entire area connecting the southern part of the western Alps and the western part of the northern Apennines (Mutti, Papiani, DiBiase, Davoli 1995; Mutti, Di Biase, Mavilla, Sgavetti 2002). Its monocline structure caused the present-day characteristic "cuestas" morphology of the Langhe hills (Calorio, Giardino, Lozar, Perotti and Vigna 2017). For those who are interested, in 1968 Gelati published an excellent, easy-to-read stratigraphic chart of the deposits occurring in during the Oligo-Miocene in the Langhe (see below for further details and to see the chart).

It is generally agreed that the Tertiary Piedmont Basin evolved in response to a changing tectonic setting, becoming the site of ongoing deposits in sedimentary fashion (note that the sediments deposited in different fashion and thickness in relation to turbidity currents of different force and from the erosion of the surrounding land masses) such that new deposits layered over the old ones creating a very complex soil/subsoil structure. However, while the complex evolution of the basin is well documented, conclusions about its evolution are often contradictory (its origin and development can be explained in either compressional or extensional tectonics terms, and there appears to be on this and other related matters a measure of disagreement amongst scientists). For this reason, Maino, Decarlis, Felletti, and Seno (2013) have labeled the Tertiary Piedmont Basin as "enigmatic" (which is an elegant way of saying that while we think we know something about something, in fact it's not so cut and dried) and state clearly that "Despite this abundant information, chronological constraints of the tectonic stages experienced by the basin, in particular of the early phases, need to be strengthened". In any case, as the early phases of the genesis of the Tertiary Piedmont Basin are less important to Barolo and its wines (because the sedimentary succession began in the late Oligocene and early Miocene when Barolo's land masses were not yet formed as we know them today), I will focus on those moments in time that have a more direct bearing on our specific liquid of interest.

However, even so, the exact geology and formation of the Barolo area remain unclear and reportedly suffer from a lack of documentation. According to Calorio, the geologic database regarding Barolo is incomplete (unlike that of Barbaresco), and hence a complete description of the complex geology of the Barolo production zone is at the current state of scientific knowledge simply not possible (private communication, 2022). This is why a true geologic map of the Barolo denomination does not exist presently; in fact, this is why you will have no doubt noticed that the latest map available to date has been defined as a "geo-viticultural map", and not as a "geological map". This is in fact only reasonable, given that according to Calorio, geologic data relative to about 25% of the Barolo production area is very ancient, dating back to the 1800s and early 1900s and has not been updated, which would be a very expensive and time-consuming proposition to do. In particular, it appears that the area of the territories of Verduno and La Morra remains extremely complex and relative to the succession of the sedimentation stratifications, still the subject of discussion and debate.

All this notwithstanding, in an effort to further knowledge about the Langhe's geology and geodiversity, Calorio and associates have focused with their work on studying and promoting existing geosites in the Langhe. They have described the specific geological, geomorphological and paleontological characteristics of the Langhe and searched for new geosites through field activities on geological mapping. They also focused on the production of geothematic maps, and because the Langhe area clearly shows noteworthy links between geology and wine, they also started analyses on geological components of terroir that are currently ongoing (studies not limited to the Barolo area, in fact; more to come on this subject in the years ahead).

Barolo geology: facts from 1929 to the end of the twentieth century

The Barolo landscape was essentially formed during the last three stages of the Miocene epoch. From oldest to youngest, these are: the Serravalian, the Tortonian and the Messinian. It was Fernando Vignolo Lutati, university researcher, author, and great expert on all things Barolo (the Vignolo vineyard district of Castiglione Falletto is named after him), who in 1929 wrote that the Barolo region could be subdivided into three main areas distinguishable by when in the Miocene Epoch their geology was formed. He believed that the oldest of the three areas, formed during the Serravalian (once called Helvetian), gave rise to the south-eastern area of today's Barolo denomination. It included the territories of Serralunga, Monforte, Castiglione Falletto and partially, Barolo. The middle of the three temporal stages, known as the Tortonian, is when the soils of the rest of the Barolo territory, of Novello and most of La Morra were formed. The third and most recent of these stages, known as Messinian, is when the soil/subsoil complex of the north-westernmost part of La Morra and of the Verduno territory were formed.

Each of these three stages is associated with a specific soil/subsoil complex. As mentioned, Serravalian stage soils are the oldest of all (they were formed roughly twelve to eleven million years ago): they are sandstone-based, ranging from whitish-beige to pale yellow-reddish in color, characterized by loosely-packed arenaceous and sandy layers alternating with calcareous marl and limestone, rich in iron and phosphorous. Note that these are Barolo's soils with the highest limestone content, and you can generally tell as much when tasting Serralunga Barolos. Next oldest are soils of Tortonian origin (formed roughly eleven to eight million years ago), blueish-grey marls with some sand, rich in magnesium and manganese. They not only have a different mineral composition, but are also more fertile than those of Serravalian origin. Barolo's youngest soils are those of Messinian origin (formed roughly six and a half to almost five million years ago) characterized by gypsiferous-sulfur formations that are relatively light in texture, as are the wines made from them. These are Barolos of great perfume and vibrant lift, but that do not have the structure of those born off Serravalian soils, or even Tortonian soils. It is the Barolos made from grapes grown on Messinian soils that are the most approachable early in life, while Serravalian soils will give life to the most tannic, slowly developing Barolos of all (that are often hard as nails when young), with Tortonian soil Barolos falling in between these two extremes. Though partly outdated, as we shall see shortly, this breakdown of Barolo soils is extremely easy to understand and to remember, and even better, there really is a noteworthy correspondence (though far from fullproof) between the Barolos you drink, the Nebbiolo grapes that were used to make them, and the temporal stage in which the soils on which those grapes are planted on were formed. Within very clearcut limitations, it really does make sense to speak of Barolos from the Messinian stage, Tortonian stage, and Serravalian stage soils, because more often than not the wines really are recognizable as belonging to one of those three categories.

Barolo geology: the twenty-first century

Vignolo-Lutati's work is extremely helpful and remarkably accurate from a scientific perspective given that he wrote his treatise way back in 1929 without any of the modern technology available nowadays by which to gain information and data. However, in time it became clear that Barolo's geology was a little more complex than initially believed. For example, based on Vignolo-Lutati's stellar work, the soils of Castiglione Falletto and Monforte are "only" of Serravalian origin, while those of Cherasco are of Messinian origin. However, the situation appears to be more complex than that, with a different viewpoint emerging at the beginning of the twenty-first century. Thanks to modern technology, further studies broaching Barolo's geology have led to a greater breakdown of the geologic time events which in turn has led to a more finite characterization of Barolo's soils and their attribution to the different communes.

A number of extremely interesting and useful research papers published in the 1990s and early 2000s shone the spotlight on the geological complexity of the Barolo denomination to full effect. Studies carried out by the

Istituto per le Piante da Legno e per l'Ambiente (I.P.L.A.) in Torino classified Barolo's soils by lithological parameters, showing there were four basic soil types in the Barolo denomination (Soster and Cellino, 2002). Clearly, there are many more than just four soil types, but those that interest Barolo (and Barbaresco) most closely are specifically four. These four soil types were named on the basis of their lithology and not of the geologic time period of origin (lithology is the macroscopic and microscopic study, description, and classification of rocks and rock formations). Proceeding from the eastern to the west half of the denomination (which as we have seen is also moving from the oldest to the youngest soils) the four lithological soil types are the: *Formazione di Lequio* (Lequio Formation); *Arenarie di Diano* (Diano Sandstone); *Marne di Sant'Agata Fossili* (Saint Agatha Fossil Marls or more simply, just Saint Agatha Marls); and *Formazioni gessoso-solfifere* (Gypsum-Sulfurous Formation) renamed as the *Vena del Gesso* (Chalk Vein Formation) in more modern times. Each of these four lithological types is associated mostly with one geologic time stage.

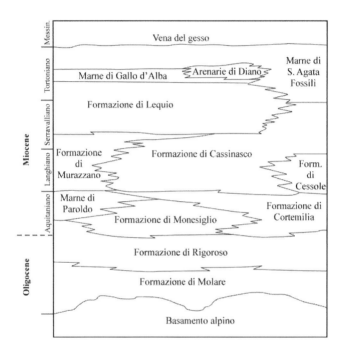

Stratigraphic Column from "Gelati R. (1968) - *Stratigrafia de l'Oligo-Miocene delle Langhe tra le valli dei fiumi Tanaro e Bormida di Spigno, «Riv. It. Pal. Strat.»,* 74, 865-967, 34 ff"

Lequio Formation (*Formazione di Lequio*)

Mostly present in parts of the communes of Monforte and of Serralunga d'Alba, this formation originated in the Serravalian stage; based on that knowledge alone, it shouldn't surprise you that it is made of layers of reddish- and yellow-tinged whitish-beige marls and compacted sands, cemented together by carbonate salts. Soils of the Lequio Formation are generally characterized by excellent water capacity due to a mix of sand and loam, and are rich in calcium, phosphorus, potassium and iron. This is the soil formation that has the highest concentration of limestone of the whole Barolo denomination, and this is why Lequio's soils are usually much paler in color than the others. The Barolos made from grapes grown in areas characterized by this formation are the most powerful yet refined Barolos of all, quite tannic when young and very slowly developing. not to mention blessed by crisp, citrussy, lip-smacking acidity that contributes to the wines an impression of steeliness that is quite unlike that of any other Barolo. They are the longest-lived of all Barolos, lasting fifty years plus in a good cellar without problems. It is because of what the Lequio Formation brings to its wines that wine lovers speak of "Serravalian Barolos" each time they come across young Barolos that are really tough, high acid and powerful, and in need of plenty of cellaring prior to reaching their optimal drinking stages.

Diano Sandstone (*Arenarie di Diano*)

Generally speaking, soils of this type characterize the townships of Castiglione Falletto, Monforte and Barolo. Originally believed to have been formed in the heart of the Serravalian stage thanks to underwater turbidity currents, it is now commonly held that the Diano Sandstone originated during the Tortonian stage. It is a grey-brown to yellowish more or less compacted sand and grey sandstone soil that gives structure to wines but may confer less balance (especially when the vines are still young). These Barolos are very full-bodied and recognizably fleshier, sweeter even, than those born off the Lequio Formation, with less of the high-acid, almost citrussy, steely mouthfeel of the latter wines; however, they also require rather long aging to approach their optimal drinking stage. Interestingly, the Lequio Formation and the Diano Sandstone are both present in the territories of Serralunga and of Monforte, but as they are quite different in their mineral and textural aspects consequently so are the wines made with grapes grown on each. This is a good example of why classifying Barolos based on their geologic stage origin alone is insufficient and ultimately inaccurate, because not all of Serralunga's Barolos have, for example, that same steely profile the commune's Barolos are famous for. Based on what I have told you so far, it should be apparent that those Serralunga Barolos born off Diano Sandstone soils are going to be more fleshy/thicker and less steely/citrussy acidic from the Serralunga Barolos made with grapes grown on Lequio Formation soils.

Saint Agatha Marls (*Marne di Sant'Agata*)

Also known as Saint Agatha Fossil Marls (Marne di Sant'Agata Fossili), these are mostly present in the communes of Barolo, La Morra and parts of Verduno. These lithological formations developed in the Tortonian stage from sedimentation of debris in the open sea. Thanks to their wealth of manganese and magnesium carbonate salts, these are very typically grey-blue in color (but soils rich in Saint Agatha Fossil Marls are typically lighter in color on the surface and darker below). Saint Agatha Fossil Marls are essentially marly-clays with fine sand, characterized by higher fertility than the Serravalian soils. Saint Agatha Fossil Marls have a high-water retention capacity: this means that great wines can be produced here especially in drier years, because the vines usually suffer less water stress. Drainage can be a problem in some of the lesser sites where clay dominates, but slope gradients are generally such that adequate water runoff is ensured; here choosing the right rootstock is of key importance, as these soils can have surprising concentrations of active lime. Thanks to the variable presence of sand, these Barolos are elegant and boast intense and precise aromas, fine tannins and slightly shorter aging potentials (but this is very relative with Barolo: in fact, any La Morra Barolo from an excellent vintage kept in a good cellar will have no trouble lasting forty years).

Vena del Gesso Formation (*Formazione della Vena del Gesso*)

Previously known as Gypsum-Sulfurous Formation (*Formazioni gessoso-solfifere*), the term *gessoso-solfifero* (gypsum-sulfurous) was first used in 1960 by Selli, but has been replaced by the newer term of Vena del Gesso Formation (which translates to Chalk Vein Formation, in English). These soils characterize the north-western side of La Morra and Verduno, mostly, and at the time of these studies, believed to be typical of the Cherasco township as well. The gypsum-sulfurous formation originated in the Messinian stage, and is mostly made of sandy deposits with chalk and soft sulphate (gypsum). Today we know that these soils, that originated in a chronological sequence associated with the Messinian Salinity Crisis, actually contain a large variety of rocks and are not as simple as initially believed. The diversity of rocks ranges from marls and mudstones derived from deep sea sediments; sandstones deposited in low salinity waters rich in vertebrates and mollusks (fossils); calcareous marls; and gypsum selenite and laminate (formed instead in waters of high salinity). These are the most approachable of all Barolos at an early age, offering relatively gentle textures and very bright perfume. However, some of the lesser sites characterized by these soils do not allow for extremely age-worthy wines and that can lack a little power.

In summary, thanks to the work Cellino and Soster and of others, we learned that Serralunga's territory does not all have the same soil/subsoil type; and for that matter neither does Monforte's nor do the other communes. For example, Serralunga's territory, though it is mostly characterized by the Lequio Formation, also has areas of Diano Sandstone and the same is true of Monforte. So, unlike what we initially thought, Serralunga and Monforte, for example, do not have soils only of Serravalian origin. This is why the Barolos within the territory of Serralunga and of Monforte, though they remain faithful to the "Barolo type" of each commune (muscular, structured, ageworthy), can differ by truly noteworthy degrees from other Barolos made within that commune. For example, the Barolos of the Monforte vineyard districts of Bussia and Mosconi differ greatly in terms of their texture and palate weight, even though they are Barolos of the same Monforte commune. While both have the tannic oomph of Barolos from the Monforte commune, there is no denying that many Bussia Barolos are far lighter in mouthfeel and more refined than Mosconi's chunkier, fleshier, mouthcoating Barolos (clearly, they are still far more structured than the Barolos of Verduno, Barolo or La Morra, for example). And it's not just that the Barolos of Bussia are different from those of Mosconi: in fact, given that the soils change throughout Bussia and also throughout Mosconi (neither one of these vineyard districts has just one type of soil), there are different Barolos emerging from within each of these vineyard districts as well. In other words, there is more than one type of Mosconi Barolo and more than one type of Bussia Barolo; and though the Barolos from each vineyard district do share some sort of "family" resemblance to each other, they can be at times markedly different too. This is the problem with having created vineyard districts that are very large and often much too large (at close to 300 hectares, there's no denying that Bussia is one large site, and at close to eighty hectares, Mosconi is another big one: for comparison's sake, the Chapelle-Chambertin *grand cru* is about 5.5 hectares large and the Chambertin *grand cru* is just a little more than thirteen hectares). In fact, old-timers have long distinguished between subareas of today's Bussia and Mosconi, and I do too. I shall discuss this at length in the next subchapter and in all the single Barolo vineyard district files of Section II, chapter 9, in this book (so see, for example see chapter 9, BUSSIA file. See also the MOSCONI file).

Last but not least, the twenty-first century's second decade has brought us even more information on the subject of Barolo's geology such that what used to be a relatively easy scenario to grasp has suddenly become much more complex. Today we have an even larger subdivision of soil formations in Barolo and the temporal moments in which they came to be. During his time spent brilliantly mapping the Barolo area, Masnaghetti looked at the geology of Barolo in association with Edmondo Bonelli (geology), Gian Piero Romana (viticulture), and Francesco Dellisanti (laboratory analysis). Their work has led to the identification and naming of different Barolo soil types and their attribution to different stages:

Serravalian

Lequio Formation (remember that though mostly associated with the Serravalian, this formation was partly formeded during the very Earty Tortonian too).

Localized to the central-south part of Serralunga and in the eastern half of Monforte.

Tortonian

1. Diano Sandstone

    Found in the areas around Monforte, Castiglione Falletto, Barolo, and Diano d'Alba. These were initially thought to have been formed during the Serravalian stage, but scientific analysis dating fossils found in the sandstone has allowed attribution of this soil lithology to the Tortonian, just like the Saint Agatha Fossil Marls.

2. Saint Agatha Fossil Marls

    According to Masnaghetti and associates (2018), these were formed not just during the Tortonian, but in both the Tortonian and the Messinian stages. They also repute it to be the most common formation in the Langhe. This soil type can be further subdivided into:

    a. Typical Saint Agatha Fossil Marls or Saint Agatha Fossil Marls of the typical form: common in Grinzane Cavour, Verduno, Santa Maria di La Morra, the lower part of Castiglione Falletto and Serralunga d'Alba. These are characterized by repeating layers of fairly uniform and thick silt and clay. These authors believe them to be identical to the Gallo d'Alba Marls Formation, but there is disagreement on this matter, with other geologists, scientists and authors believing the two to be distinct.

    b.   **Saint Agatha Fossil Marls** of the sandy form: these are found in the more southern sections of Monforte and Castiglione Falletto, as well as in Annunziata di La Morra. This formation represents a transitional form between the Diano Sandstone and the typical Saint Agatha Fossil Marls and is characterized by repeating layers of sand and marl in which the sandy layers are especially thick.

    c.   **Saint Agatha Fossil Marls** of the laminated form: found in Novello, La Morra and Verduno.

Messinian

1.   La Morra Conglomerates

Found in La Morra only, around the ridge that joins its territory to that of Verduno, these are rare Barolo gravel-rich soils. Here again, not everyone agrees with their classification as such, considering them instead to be just a variant of Diano Sandstone.

2.   Vena del Gesso Formation

As already mentioned, this was previously called gypsiferous-sulfur formation, and is similar to the Saint Agatha Marls but enriched with chalk. It is found on the western hills of La Morra e Verduno and vineyard districts such as Pisapola, Neirane, Campasso and Brandini are characterized by it.

3.   Cassano Spinola Formation

Of which there are two different kinds in the territories of La Morra and Verduno:

    a.   *Cassano Spinola Formation of the sandy type*: mostly present in the southern part of the western slope of La Morra, such as for example in the Berri and Serradenari vineyard districts. This is the soil type that originated from fresh water such as fluvial and lagunar deposits I mentioned earlier; in fact, other than the soils that are of mostly terrigenous origin such as the Diano Sandstone, this is the only soil of Barolo not of marine origin.

    b.   *Cassano Spinola Formation of the marly type*: this is similar to the Saint Agatha Marls of the laminated form and characterizes for example the San Giacomo, Ascheri, and Castagni vineyard districts in the township of La Morra; and the Neirane vineyard district in the township of Verduno (it is also present in the eastern half of Sant'Anna, in the La Morra township).

Zanclean

The Zanclean is the first stage of the Pliocene epoch, a more recent epoch that follows immediately after the Miocene epoch. Therefore, the Pliocene's Zanclean stage is immediately subsequent to the Miocene's Messinian stage. Therefore, it is characterized by even younger soils (formed from 5.3 to 3.6 million years ago) than those of the Messinian. Relative to Barolo, it is typically associated with the lithological formation of Pliocene Marls (those soils that were formed during the Zanclean stage and are limited to the commune of Cherasco). They are characterized by a balanced presence of sand, silt, clay and not so much limestone.

Though it makes matters a great more difficult, this new information is helpful in making us think in different but also in more precise terms about the Barolos we drink. Whereas before we knew of these further geologic specifics we talked of "one" Saint Agatha Fossil Marls only which basically meant that we were operating under the assumption that most of La Morra's territory had one soil type only, the Saint Agatha Fossil Marls, we now know thanks to Masnaghetti and associates that there are three different types of the Saint Agatha Fossil Marls (typical, sandy and laminated) and that are in fact most typically associated with that commune's territory. This in turn helps us greatly in understanding and explaining the different Barolos coming from La Morra but from other communes of the Barolo denomination that may have different areas characterized by different types of Saint Agatha Marls. This knowledge helps us understand why these Barolos might all taste rather different even when the grapes are similarly grown and the wines similarly made. The different lithologies are all associated with varying percentages of sand, clay, loam, and silt, not to mention minerals. This in turn means different percentages of soil limestone, but also varying degrees of soil texture and drainage. For example, our own soil composition data show sand percentages varying between 10-40% within the La Morra township vineyard areas. And you'll agree, that ain't hazelnuts (er, peanuts). But the importance of these different lithological types goes far beyond a mere difference in mineral concentrations and of soil composition (meaning by that varying percentages of sand, clay, loam/silt, limestone and more still). Very importantly, the phenological behavior of the Nebbiolo grapevine forcibly changes depending on the soil lithology the grapes grow on. For example, budbreak generally occurs earliest in those Nebbiolo vineyards planted on Diano Sandstone, followed closely by those planted on Saint Agatha Fossil Marls of the sandy type [though clearly all the many other factors of terroir (Nebbiolo biotype, climate, exposure, altitude) will have a say in just when budbreak might occur]. By contrast, Nebbiolo planted on soils of the Saint Agatha Fossil Marls of the laminated type lithology tend to budbreak and flower much later, but because of better water retention due to a higher soil clay content, also accumulate sugars much faster than the Nebbiolo grown on all the other lithological soil types (except the typical Saint Agatha Fossil Marls). Therefore, provided the phenolic maturation (of the grape polyphenols) is also in step with the technological one (the grape sugar concentration), these are the Nebbiolo grapes that might more often than not be harvested before Nebbiolo grapes growing on other soil lithology types. It follows that the exact lithology of the soils grapes are planted in is extremely important and influences and defines the Barolo you will drink by way of much more than just soil mineral concentrations (for example, of potassium, boron, phosphorus, magnesium, manganese, iron) and varied soil compositions and textures. Therefore, it becomes clear how soil lithological type also helps define the quality of a Barolo vineyard district: because in those vineyard districts where the lithology pushes the grapes to budbreak sooner, but the climate is less than ideal, those Nebbiolo grapevines will be at risk and at the mercy of unexpected spring frosts and hail episodes. By definition, the world's best vineyard sites, the best *crus* if you will, are not those where the budding grapevines get routinely slammed. Sites with microclimates and mesoclimates where spring frosts occur may not necessarily be as bad as one would automatically assume provided the soil lithology doesn't push the vines to bud early. Clearly, soil geology is a truly rate-limiting step in this regard.

The existence of different types of Saint Agatha Fossil Marls means that the differences in the soils will ultimately translate to the wines. And so, the wines are "different" because even though they are, say, Barolos of La Morra, the grapes grow on different soils within the commune, effectively coming from "different" places. In the past, we were told they were all born off essentially the same soil called "Saint Agatha Fossil Marls", but we know now that that was too simplistic an approach. Because such knowledge did not previously exist and people were not aware of these soil type differences in the nineteenth and for most of the twentieth century, this helps explain in part why exposure and other physical parameters of terroir were considered to be so important (and they are of course, but perhaps not quite to the same degree as was previously thought).

In effect, it didn't make much sense that the many Barolos made in a commune's territory (made in similar manner) were so remarkably different, if the soils were really all one and the same; and so that meant looking for other reasons as to why that might be. Now that we understand that there is not just one Saint Agatha Fossil Marl soil type but many, all of which have different compositions (in reference to percentages of loam, clay and sand, not to mention differences in individual mineral concentrations), it follows that this reality certainly contributes in no small measure to the diversity of Barolos made all over the denomination.

Making it easy: how to understand the Barolos you drink based on the soil their grapes grow in

Messinian, Tortonian and Serravalian: this is perhaps not the most accurate way by which to qualify Barolo's soils and its wines, but it's the easiest. And, don't say this out loud lest some way too serious geologist person hears you, but it is also fairly accurate and helpful, at least for all those individuals out there who do not have a degree in geology. Helpful also in terms of guessing where the Barolo you are drinking is from, because referring to a Barolo as being "Tortonian" or "Serravalian" tells you immediately some information about that wine's characteristics. Clearly, the Barolo denomination's soils are not Tortonian or Serravalian soils *per se*: those names refer to the moment in time in which they originated (so you should really say "Tortonian stage" and "Serravalian stage", as there is no such thing, for example, as a "Tortonian" soil, but rather a soil formed during the Tortonian stage in time).

Remembering that the soils formed in the three main geologic periods are mostly located in three different, specific sectors of the Barolo denomination and with specific Barolo communes is of great help too. A wine from Rocche dell'Annunziata (a vineyard district of La Morra) really does taste like you'd expect a wine from La Morra to taste like, while a wine from the Lazzarito vineyard district of Serralunga could never be mistaken for one from the Verduno or Cherasco communes (just as it is difficult to confuse a red Burgundy from Chambolle-Musigny with one from Pommard or Gevrey-Chambertin, or a Bordeaux from Pauillac with one from Moulis or Margaux). Therefore, it follows that it becomes relatively easy to pinpoint from which commune the Barolo you are tasting might come from, even before you taste it: and this just by knowing in which commune or section of the Barolo denomination the grapes used to make that Barolo were grown in. This is the first step in understanding the Barolos you drink: pinpointing the commune they are from. Is it a Barolo from Verduno? Or Novello? Or Roddi? This is something that wine lovers all over the world do all the time when they are drinking Burgundies, for example: part of the fun is in figuring out if the wine is really a Puligny or a Chassagne, a Chambolle or a Gevrey. And it's exactly the same with, for example, wines from Bordeaux (is it a Pauillac or a Margaux?), the Mosel (is this a wine of Graach or of Piesport?), of New Zeland (is this Pinot Noir wine from Central Otago or Marlborough?) or from Niagara (is this Riesling wine from St. Catharines or Jordan?). Then of course, for all our knowledge and hard study, we still all routinely get the identification of wine sites wrong during blind tastings, but that's part of the fun (masochism?) of being a wine lover or wine geek.

The next step in further wine appreciation is of course to be able to pinpoint single vineyard districts: is it a Barolo from Brunate or Santa Maria? From Fiasco or Monprivato? Much as people do all the time in trying to identify if the wine they are drinking is typical, for example, of Meursault Charmes, Perrières or Genevrières; is this an Alsatian Riesling wine from the Brand, the Rangen or the Schlossberg?; or in the case of Ontario's Niagara region, the Twenty Mile Bench or the Short Hills Bench? Unfortunately, identifying even the commune from where a wine is made is not quite so easy, and not just with Barolo (never mind the vineyard districts and the single vineyard sites within their boundaries). There are many times we think a wine is from Margaux only to find it is a Saint-Julien or even a Pauillac. And telling wines of Nuits-Saint-Georges apart from Gevrey or even Corton isn't exactly a walk in the park either. It's much the same with Barolo. But for the most part, with Barolo, the "three soil stage" characterization is quite helpful.

I can hear you asking: how to know and remember where each of the three soils is mostly located within the Barolo production zone? It's easy. Get a map of the Barolo denomination. Then draw an imaginary diagonal line that runs from the north-east downwards in a south-west direction, passing more or less immediately west of the town of Castiglione Falletto. In so doing, you have separated the Barolo production zone very neatly into two sections. Generalizing greatly, the western half (the one to the left of the diagonal line) is the Barolo area characterized by soil of Tortonian origin, while the area on the right side of our diagonal line (the eastern half of the Barolo denomination), is characterized by Serravalian soil. In order to figure out where the third soil type is found (the soil of Messinian origin) all you need to do is look at the left section of your map (the western half of the denomination) and further subdivide it into two sub-sections, a smaller northern one (draw your boundary just a little south of the Verduno commune and you won't be too far of the mark) and a much larger southern one. The northern subsection is where most of Barolo's Messinian soils are found, while the southern part is characterized mostly by soils of Tortonian origin.

The next step for you to become a full-fledged Barolo wine expert, or at least one more or less able to take educated guesses at where the Barolos you are drinking come from even before being told (and become the focal talking point at parties), is to know where the eleven towns of the Barolo denomination are located. If you know more or less their position within the denomination, then you will also have a rough idea of the origin of the soil they are on. The townships of Castiglione Falletto, Monforte, and Serralunga, are located in the eastern half of the denomination; and the communes of Barolo, Cherasco, Diano d'Alba, Grinzane Cavour, La Morra, Novello, Roddi and Verduno, lie in the western half. Of these five last communes, it is Verduno and Cherasco that are situated in the northern subsection of the western half and are therefore those communes characterized by mostly Messinian soil.

And so there you have it. Recapitulating, and putting it in the easiest possible way, look at the following charts we have drawn up for you and hopefully it all come singing home:

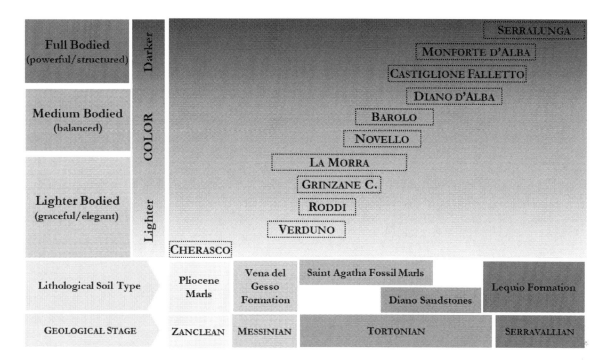

Lithological Soil Type	Geological Stage	Soil Composition	Communes	Wine Style
Lequio Formation	Serravalian / very Early Tortonian	Silty marls (yellow to whitish), compacted sands, sandstone, clay, limestone	Serralunga d'Alba Monforte d'Alba	The most powerful, structured and refined. Quite tannic when young. The longest-lived of all.
Diano Sandstones	Tortonian	Rich in sand (grey-brown to yellowish) and grey sandstone	Monforte d'Alba; Castiglione Falletto; Barolo; Diano d'Alba; La Morra	Very full-bodied and recognizably fleshier (than those from Lequio Formation). Both structure and elegance
Saint Agatha Fossil Marls	Tortonian	Limestone, clay and blue-gray marls	Barolo; La Morra Verduno; Novello; Grinzane Cavour Castiglione Falletto Monforte d'Alba	Elegant and boast intense and precise aromas, fine tannins and slightly shorter aging potentials.
Vena del Gesso Formation	Messinian	Sandy deposits with chalk and soft sulphate	La Morra Verduno	The most approachable of all Barolos at an early age. Relatively gentle textures and very bright perfume.

As mentioned, the soil/subsoil complexes formed during these three different stages of geologic development differ in age, mineral concentration and type, texture, lithology, water availability and much more. It follows that Nebbiolo grapes grown on each type of soil will also differ. When tasting Barolos blind, you can assign each one in your glass to one of the communes with a reasonable degree of confidence (you' still get it wrong more often than not, but as mentioned a little bit of masochism typifies all us wine geeks; all kidding aside, by following this line of thinking and analysis you are making slightly more educated guesses than you might otherwise). And if you also know the vineyard districts of each commune (at least the most important ones you are most likely to taste the wines of) then it becomes somewhat easier to say "This Barolo tastes like it might come from Bussia" rather than saying it comes from Monvigliero or Cannubi, and be completely wrong.

The reason why you might guess the thicker, mouthcoating Barolo in your glass comes from Bussia in Monforte rather than a similarly tannic one from Serralunga is that the former has a fleshier disposition and the latter usually has higher acidity levels and a steelier personality. As we have discussed, these traits are directly linked to the Bussia being characterized by Saint Agatha Fossil Marls and the Serralunga territory characterized by the Lequio Formation, each of which is associated with a specific Barolo type. Clearly, it helps if you remember the communes, the geologic stage and the soil type of each of the most important or commonly found vineyard districts of Barolo. A complete description and list of which geologic stage and soil type the individual Barolo vineyard districts belong to is included at the beginning of each Barolo vineyard district description in the Barolo files chapter (see the Section II, chapter 9, Barolo Vineyard Districts). Unfortunately, as we have also discussed previously, there is not just one geology that characterizes each vineyard district, but there is in fact considerable overlap between communes in their soil formations, which makes all this much more complicated. And so, there are vineyards in each commune that are located on soils that are a mix of Tortonian and Serravalian origins; furthermore, there are vineyard districts the soils of which differ considerably from each other despite they were all formed during the same geologic stage. A good example of this is the famous Mosconi vineyard district of Monforte. It boasts soils formed both during the Serravalian and the Tortonian stages; but Mosconi's soils formed during the Tortonian are also not all the same. Based on these soil-related differences alone (never mind other important factors such as altitude, exposure, and Nebbiolo biotype percentages) you would expect there to be many different Mosconi Barolos made (see Section II, chapter 9, MOSCONI file). And you'd be right.

Similarly, Monforte's just as famous Bussia vineyard district also boasts different soils all of Tortonian origin, and so its wines are also going to be different one from the other. Yet another example is the Coste di Rose vineyard district of Barolo: given its location in the western valley (it's a vineyard district of the township of Barolo) it has soils of Tortonian origin only, but while some of its soils are of Saint Agatha Fossil Marls lithology, other sections of Coste di Rose are characterized by Diano Sandstone and the two give very different Barolos despite their being both of Tortonian origin. This doesn't really surprise me and shouldn't surprise you either, for the mouthfeels of some Coste di Rose Barolos are surprisingly tannic and downright steely for wines made in the Barolo township; in fact, to my taste and to my way of thinking, Coste di Rose Barolos have a lot more in common with the Barolos of Monforte or Serralunga despite their birth in the Barolo commune. Similarly, a large portion of Novello's soils are also just as complex. Even though the commune is situated in the western part of the denomination (just like the town of Barolo which is immediately north of Novello), some of Novello's Barolos seem to have more in common with those of Serralunga and Monforte than those of La Morra and Barolo. Some Novello Barolos taste approachable already when young, while others are much tougher and need extended cellaring. But even knowing the geological stage of origin and soil lithology might not be enough to shed light on the "why's" of the Barolo in your glass. For example, the Novello vineyard districts of Corini-Pallaretta and Bergera-Pezzolle are both characterized by Tortonian origin soils and both by Saint Agatha Fossil Marls lithology (specifically, of the laminated type in both vineyard districts). And yet, despite all that being the same, and that you might be comparing two wines that are similarly made by the same winery (for example, Le Strette), the wines are different because of individual mineral element concentrations or textures. Even if other parameters of terroir are all the same (and they rarely are) such as Nebbiolo biotype, altitude and exposure, the Corini-Pallaretta vineyard district has less sand in its soil than does Bergera-Pezzole (the breakdown for Corini-Pallaretta is tilted in favor of the loam/silt content). It is easy to understand then why the wines of those two vineyard districts are different. And this despite the vineyard districts are both in Novello, both have soils formed in the Tortonian stage and both have the same type of Saint Agatha Fossil Marls. Not surprisingly, the wines from Corini-Pallaretta are generally the fresher wines (the wines generally have a lower pH) and less deep and powerful of the two vineyards.

Looking ahead at section II of this book, devoted to the individual vineyard districts/MGAs of the denomination, I will try to tell you, whenever it's clear and/or possible to do so, which MGAs/vineyard districts have which soil formations, and which have more than one type. Whenever possible, I will tell you also where within the vineyard district's boundaries the soils are located, so if you know where the producer's vineyards are located within the district, you will be able to know, or at least better understand, the Barolo that it is likely he or she makes (see Section II, chapter 9, Barolo vineyard districts: facts, figures and analysis) even without tasting it. Then you taste the wine and can determine if the wine corresponds to your assumptions. If it doesn't, then things really get interesting.

As stated previously, I think knowing the geology of Barolo is the single most important and helpful thing to know in understanding Barolo's wines, but it's by no means the only factor worth knowing. And besides, it is rare that you get to compare wines that are made with similar Nebbiolo percentages, grown at similar altitudes and exposures and so on. But the Messinian-Tortonian-Serravalian classification of soils is extremely helpful, and knowing about the individual lithologies of each vineyard district further helps. By combining this information with what you know about the other physical parameters of terroir of that site (such as for example climate (vintage effect), slope gradient and topography, not to mention Nebbiolo biotype), it becomes much easier to understand the Barolo you are drinking and to grasp its nuances. So there clearly is a need to unite the information on geology with the other physical geography parameters mentioned earlier. Enter the study of landscapes and of Land Units.

The Land Unit is a fundamental concept of landscape ecology, and it expresses landscape as a system. Specifically, it refers to an ecologically homogeneous tract of land and provides a means by which topologic and chronologic landscape ecology relationships can be studied. The previously mentioned I.P.L.A. studies helped characterize Barolo's terroir even further by developing a map demonstrating that there are nine different Land Units in the Barolo denomination. These Land Units were identified on the basis of the following parameters: land use, geomorphology, lithology, photo-interpretation, chemical analysis and soil physical properties (Soster and Cellino, 1998; Soster and Cellino, 2002). In other words, the Land Units give us more information than just soil lithology (say Lequio Formation or Diano Sandstone) or just geologic time origin (Serravalian versus Tortonian), but combine information together in such a way as to paint a more complete picture of the place where the Barolos we drink are made from. Remember that the Land Units carry names that may be the same as some of the Barolo communes, but this does not mean the Land Unit is associated only with that commune's territory. Much like the geology of Barolo is varied throughout the denomination, so too the Land Unit distribution is a bit of a jigsaw puzzle: for example, the Land Unit of Castiglione is not found just within the borders of Castiglione Falletto's territory, but is found in the Serralunga township as well.

Some vineyard districts sit on more than one Land Unit (a good example is the little-known vineyard district of Castagni, that belongs to the La Morra commune and is characterized by three different Land Units: it has the Land Unit of Verduno in its north-west section bordering the San Giacomo and Neirane vineyard districts; its north-east/east section bordering the Rocche dell'Olmo and Roncaglie vineyard districts belong to the Land Unit of La Morra; while Castagni's remaining central-southern sections are of the Berri Land Unit. Clearly, given that nobody has much tasted any Barolos from Castagni and that the Castagni reality is obviously pretty complex, you understand why so little is known about Castagni Barolos. Mercifully, things are much easier with better-known vineyard districts such as Vignarionda or Brunate.

In ultimate analysis, the Land Units provide you with even more information than just geologic time period and soil lithology regarding the place where that producer's Barolo vineyards grow, and hence what the Barolo might be or should be like. Though undoubtedly complicated to use for lay people, the classification of Barolo by Land Units is the most complete way by which to understand and describe the Barolo you drink. More than any other geologic classification or physical geographic factor on its own, they make clear why, for example, some areas of Castiglione Falletto give Barolos that taste more like those of Monforte, or why some Barolos of La Morra taste more like those of Verduno. Clearly, just like it is for the soil types, for these Land Units to be useful in identifying Barolos by place of birth, you also need to remember exactly where the Land Units fall within the denomination. So much as it is with the lithology of each vineyard district, in order to better appreciate the nuances of the Barolo you are drinking, it would help to both know where the specific producer's vineyards lie within the vineyard district and then extrapolate that knowledge to identifying which specific Land Unit they belong to.

The Land Unit approach to terroir is remarkably useful and furnishes a scientific basis for what at times seem to be head-scratching inducing decisions relative to the establishment of the modern vineyard district boundaries. For example, with the official naming and establishment of the boundaries of the vineyard districts, Monforte's Castelletto vineyard district became much larger because of the inclusion within its confines of the area previously known as Pressenda. But in this case the inclusion has a basis that is easy to understand, which is not always the case. Many of the newer, enlarged officially delimited and named vineyard districts of today have done a disservice to both Barolo producers and wine lovers because many of these now include other vineyard districts the wines of which were different from the area they were annexed to (Bussia and Mosconi are good examples of vineyard districts that have become hodgepodges of different subregions, many of which very different one from the other and so are the wines made in each). In the case of Pressenda and Castelletto the differences between vineyard areas and their wines are not so marked; and so, uniting the two into one larger district is reasonable and acceptable. And the accuracy of the Land Unit classification is well exemplified by the fact that both Castelletto and Pressenda are classified as having the same Land Unit (the Serralunga Land Unit). However, even though the Land Unit classification offers a further aid in understanding the Barolo terroir, it is far from fullproof too. A case in point are the Serralunga vineyard districts of Cerretta and San Rocco, both of which are classified as Land Unit of Castiglione; this helps explain why the wines of these two vineyard districts might resemble each other to a degree. However, as Cerretta has soil lithologies of both the typical Saint Agatha Fossil Marls and of the Lequio Formation, you realize that Cerretta Barolos made with grapes grown on the parts of Cerretta with Lequio Formation lithology will taste very different from those wines made with grapes grown on the typical Saint Agatha Fossil Marls. And given that San Rocco has typical Saint Agatha Fossil Marls lithology only, it follows that it is likely that it will be the Cerretta wines made with Nebbiolo grown in that vineyard district's sections where the soils are also of typical Saint Agatha Fossil Marls lithology that will resemble stylistically those of San Rocco, and not the others. Even without tasting the wines, based on this knowledge alone, you can be fairly sure that Cerretta's wines made from Lequio Formation lithology will be anything but like the wines of San Rocco.

Another example are the Barolos of La Morra's Conca and Roddi's Bricco Ambrogio vineyard districts, two vineyard districts that are quite different from each other. Not surprisingly, the two vineyard districts belong to different Land Units: Bricco Ambrogio's Land Unit is the Land Unit of Barolo, while Conca is divided between the Land Unit of La Morra and the Land Unit of Barolo. If we were to taste similarly made Bricco Ambrogio and Conca Barolos that are both made with grapes grown in areas of the Barolo Land Unit only, they might/ought to find they taste similar; but if the Conca Barolo is made with grapes grown in both Land Units (that Bricco Ambrogio does not have), or from the Land Unit of La Morra only, then we ought to expect slightly to very different wines. Continuing with other examples, Novello's vineyard districts of Corini-Pallaretta and Bergera-Pezzolle both belong to the Vergne Land Unit, so we'd expect the wines to be very similar. And while surely not identical, the wines from those two vineyard districts do share a great deal in common. For sure, the wines of each resemble each other a great deal more than they do the wines of Lazzarito (Serralunga Land Unit) or Villero (Land Unit of Barolo).

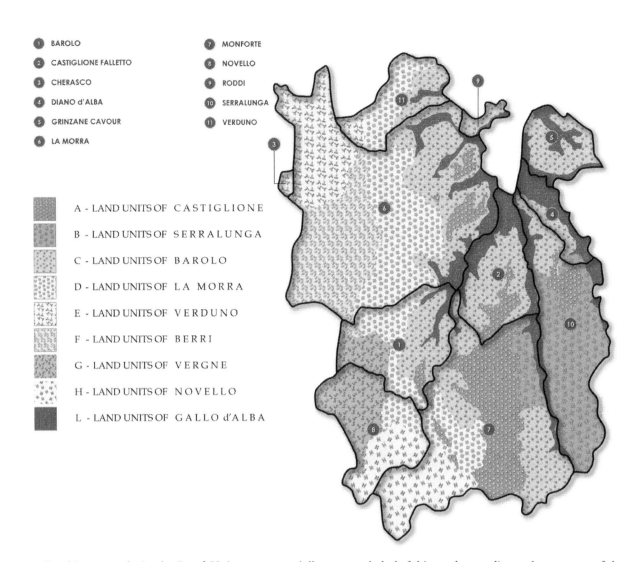

Legend (map markers):

1. BAROLO
2. CASTIGLIONE FALLETTO
3. CHERASCO
4. DIANO d'ALBA
5. GRINZANE CAVOUR
6. LA MORRA
7. MONFORTE
8. NOVELLO
9. RODDI
10. SERRALUNGA
11. VERDUNO

A - LAND UNITS OF CASTIGLIONE
B - LAND UNITS OF SERRALUNGA
C - LAND UNITS OF BAROLO
D - LAND UNITS OF LA MORRA
E - LAND UNITS OF VERDUNO
F - LAND UNITS OF BERRI
G - LAND UNITS OF VERGNE
H - LAND UNITS OF NOVELLO
L - LAND UNITS OF GALLO d'ALBA

In ultimate analysis, the Land Units are potentially extremely helpful in understanding at least some of the characteristics of the Barolo one is drinking. Clearly, the Land Units cannot help us predict exactly what the Barolo you taste will be like 100% of the time (if for no other reason because they do not take into account if the wines are made only with one or more biotypes of Nebbiolo); but for the most part, they help. In Section II, chapter 10, BAROLO VINEYARD DISTRICTS: MAPS AND LAND UNITS, you will find a list of all the vineyard districts listed with the Land Units they belong to, as well as maps, which makes it very easy to understand how it is that wines made from vineyard districts that have the same lithology and geologic origin taste so different. Another mnemonic aid for you is provided by the map below which illustrates the Barolo denomination broken down by Land Unit. The color-coded areas are very easy to see and distinguish. A description follows of each Land Unit updated from my *Italy's Native Wine Grape Terroirs* book (D'Agata, 2019), to which I refer you for further information on this subject. The capital letters after each Land Unit refer to the previously mentioned map above.

LAND UNIT OF CASTIGLIONE (A)

Surface extension: 764 hectares. Geographical Localization: this Land Unit is found in eight distinct areas of the denomination. The largest extension (547 ha) of this Land Unit covers the area of the upper part of the ridge that joins Monforte d'Alba to Castiglione Falletto. Other areas in which this Land Unit is found are east of La Morra; north, east and southeast of Barolo; and south of the Fontanafredda MGA in Serralunga. Altitude: from 219 to 533 meters asl. Dominant exposure: northwest (31%), northeast (19%) and southwest (17%). Mean slope gradient: 22%. Lithology: Diano Sandstone. Pedologic features: these are soils that have seen little evolution, constantly renewed by vineyard-soils treatment and by erosion; prevalence of loam soil texture; relatively low permeability; often presence of artificial drainage. <u>Maximum water capacity</u>: high (225-300mm). <u>Soil pH</u>: From subalkaline to alkaline. <u>Topography</u>: generally speaking, the Castiglione Land Unit is found in areas of Barolo that are mostly characterized by a series of moderately steep slopes. <u>Land use</u>: Specialized viticulture alternated with hazelnut cultivation. Presence of *Robinia pseudoacacia* is more common here than on most other Land Units. <u>Barolo MGAs</u>: Castiglione Falletto: Bricco Boschis, Fiasco, Mariondino, Monprivato (part of), Rocche di Castiglione, and Villero); La Morra: Conca (a part of), Gattera (part of); Barolo: Coste di Rose; Serralunga: Fontanafredda (part of), Prapò (part of), Cerretta and San Rocco; Monforte: Gramolere.

LAND UNIT OF SERRALUNGA D'ALBA (B)

<u>Surface extension</u>: 701 hectares. <u>Geographical location</u>: the major part of this Land Unit (586 ha) extends from the Sierra of Serralunga d'Alba to the residential area of Baudana that constitutes the northern boundary. The remaining hectares of this Land Unit are located on the left bank of the valley of the Talloria di Castiglione stream. <u>Altitude</u>: 216 to 441 meters asl. <u>Dominant exposure</u>: northwest (24%), northeast (20%), southwest (19). <u>Mean slope gradient</u>: 22%. <u>Lithology</u>: Lequio Formation. <u>Pedologic features</u>: this soil has seen little development and is constantly rejuvenated by agriculture and erosion. The texture is prevalently that of loam and silty-loam; moderately low permeability; presence of artificial drainage. <u>Maximum ground water capacity</u>: high (225-300mm). <u>Soil pH</u>: from subalkaline to alkaline. <u>Topography</u>: basically, one massive asymmetrical ridge with a complex sinuous dislocation (in the shape of an amphitheater, actually) with rounded corners. Structurally the immersion of the layers determines an inclination of asymmetrical, generally concave slopes. <u>Land use</u>: Mostly specialized viticulture. <u>Barolo MGAs</u>: Monforte: Castelletto (part of); Serralunga: Cerratti, Collaretto, Colombaro, Falletto, Francia, Lazzarito, Marenca, Margheria, Meriame (part of), Ornato.

LAND UNIT OF BAROLO (C)

<u>Surface extension</u>: 1696 hectares. <u>Geographical location</u>: the most extensive of all the Land Units, it is essentially subdivided into four territorial areas: 1. to the southeast of Verduno (no major vineyard districts correspond to this area though); 2. from Barolo to Castiglione Falletto; 3. from the northeast of Castiglione Falletto to Grinzane Cavour; 4. and to the east of Monforte d'Alba. <u>Altitude</u>: from 185 to 462 meters a.s.l. <u>Dominant exposure</u>: northwest (23), northeast (21%), southeast (19%). <u>Mean slope gradient</u>: 16%. <u>Lithology</u>: Saint Agatha Fossil Marls. <u>Pedologic features</u>: a soil that has seen little evolution, constantly rejuvenated by agriculture and erosion; prevalence of clay-loam soil texture, low permeability with presence of artificial drainage. <u>Maximum ground water capacity</u>: >300mm. <u>Soil pH</u>: from subalkaline to alkaline. <u>Topography</u>: a hilly landscape formed by symmetric, narrow and long ridges, simple or composite, with sharp corners and generally linear directions but with rapid changes of exposure. <u>Land use</u>: mostly specialised viticulture. Where conditions are unfavorable for viticulture, cultivation of oak trees, poplars and *Robinia pseudoacacia* is frequent. <u>Barolo MGAs</u>: Barolo: Ciocchini, Le Coste; Castiglione Falletto: Altenasso, Codana, Fiasco, Monprivato (part of), Pugnane; Monforte: Ginestra (part of), Monrobiolo di Bussia, Mosconi (part of); Grinzane Cavour: Castello, Garretti; La Morra: Gattera (part of), Giachini (part of); Monforte: Le Coste di Monforte (part of), Ravera di Monforte; Serralunga: Costabella; Serralunga/Diano d'Alba: Riva (part of), La Rosa (part of); Verduno: Massara (part of).

LAND UNIT OF LA MORRA (D)

<u>Surface extension</u>: 1154 hectares. <u>Geographical location</u>: that strip of land to the east of the Verduno-La Morra-Novello watershed. It's actually one of the easiest of all Land Units to locate geographically, as it corresponds roughly to a long vertical band that runs immediately east of Verduno in the north, Barolo in the center and Novello to the south (which to be practical, means that this is one of the Land Units where it is easiest to remember the MGAs associated with it). <u>Altitude</u>: 220-554m a.s.l. <u>Dominant exposure</u>: northeast (42%), southeast (29%). <u>Mean slope gradient</u>: 18%. <u>Lithology</u>: Predominately set on Saint Agatha Fossil Marls, but note that the upper part of the slope in the area south of La Morra sits on Chalk Vein Formation (gypsum—sulfurous)

deposits from the Messinian stage. <u>Pedologic features</u>: soil that has evolved only slightly, constantly renewed by agriculture and erosion; silty-clay-loam soil prevails; low permeability, presence of artificial drainage. <u>Maximum ground water capacity</u>: very high (>300mm). <u>Soil pH</u>: from subalkaline to alkaline. <u>Topography</u>: mostly concave slopes. <u>Land Use</u>: specialised viticulture is prevalent. Presence of *Robinia* where conditions are unfavorable to vines. <u>Barolo MGAs</u>: Barolo: Boschetti, Liste, Paiagallo, Rivassi, Rué; La Morra: Arborina, Brunate, Cerequio, Fossati (part of), Giachini (part of), La Serra, Rocche dell'Annunziata, Rocchettevino; Castiglione Falletto: Riva Rocche; Novello: Ravera (part of); Verduno: Boscatto, Massara (part of), Monvigliero, Pisapola, Rocche dell'Olmo.

LAND UNIT OF VERDUNO (E)

<u>Surface extension</u>: 390 hectares. <u>Geographical location</u>: west and southwest of Verduno. <u>Altitude</u>: 190 – 406 m a.s.l. <u>Dominant exposure</u>: northwest (52%), southwest (16%). <u>Mean slope gradient</u>: 10%. <u>Lithology</u>: Chalk Vein Formation (Gypsiferous-sulfurous formation) of the Messinian stage. <u>Pedologic features</u>: soil not much evolved, constantly renewed by agriculture and erosion. <u>Soil pH</u>: subalkaline to alkaline. <u>Topography</u>: wavy and linear slopes with gentle gradients. <u>Land Use</u>: Prevalently hazelnut farming, then viticulture and grassland farming. <u>Barolo MGAs</u>: Cherasco: Mantoetto; La Morra: Brandini (part of), Bricco Cogni, Castagni (part of); Verduno: Neirane, San Giacomo, Sant'Anna (part of).

LAND UNIT OF BERRI (F)

<u>Surface extension</u>: 555 hectares. <u>Geographical location</u>: to the west of La Morra. <u>Altitude</u>: 285 – 486 meters a.s.l. <u>Dominant exposure</u>: northwest (38%), southwest (27%). <u>Mean slope gradient</u>: 22%. <u>Lithology</u>: marine deposits of the Messinian stage. <u>Pedologic features</u>: soil that is minimally or moderately evolved, constantly renewed by agriculture and erosion in the vineyard zones; silty-clay-loam soil prevails, with the mineral portion rich in chalk; low permeability; presence of artificial drainage. <u>Maximum ground water capacity</u>: very high (>300mm). <u>Soil pH</u>: from subalkaline to alkaline. <u>Topography</u>: slopes that are slightly wavy or flat, in a linear profile, separated by deep splits. <u>Land Use</u>: predominately viticulture and cereals, followed by hazelnut growing and forest management. <u>Barolo MGAs</u>: La Morra: Ascheri, Berri, Brandini (part of): Barolo: Bricco delle Viole (part of), Castagni (part of), Coste di Vergne (part of), Serradenari.

LAND UNIT OF VERGNE (G)

<u>Surface extension</u>: 360 hectares. <u>Geographical location</u>: north of Novello and west of Barolo. <u>Altitude</u>: 310-476 meters a.s.l. <u>Dominant exposure</u>: northwest (34%), southwest (20%). <u>Mean slope gradient</u>: 12%. <u>Lithology</u>: Saint Agatha Fossil Marls. <u>Pedologic features</u>: the soil is minimally or moderately evolved, constantly renewed by soil work and erosion in the vines-growing zones; silty-clay soil prevails; low permeability; presence of artificial drainage. <u>Maximum ground water capacity</u>: very high (>300mm). <u>Soil pH</u>: from subalkaline to alkaline. <u>Topography</u>: wavy slopes with linear profiles. <u>Land Use</u>: viticulture and cereals. <u>Barolo MGAs</u>: Barolo: Bricco delle Viole, La Volta; La Morra: Coste di Vergne (part of); Novello: Ciocchini-Loschetto, Corini-Pallaretta.

LAND UNIT OF NOVELLO (H)

<u>Surface extension</u>: 482 hectares. <u>Geographic location</u>: between Novello and Monforte d'Alba. <u>Altitude</u>: 243 – 481 meters a.s.l. <u>Dominant exposure</u>: southeast (28%), southwest (27%). <u>Mean slope gradient</u>: 20%. <u>Lithology</u>: in the sections at the higher altitudes, Sant 'Agathe's Fossil marls dominate; while the Lequio Formation dominates in the lower-lying parts. <u>Pedologic features</u>: minimally evolved soil, constantly renewed by soil work and erosion; mostly loose-textured; moderately low permeability; presence of artificial drainage. <u>Maximum ground water capacity</u>: high (225-300mm). <u>Soil pH</u>: from subalkaline to alkaline. <u>Topography</u>: similar shape to

Land Unit of Barolo. Slopes have generally linear profiles but present sudden changes of exposure. <u>Land Use</u>: viticulture with cereal growing farming and forest management near the river beds. <u>Barolo MGAs</u>: Novello: Cerviano-Merli, Ravera, Sottocastello di Novello.

LAND UNIT OF GALLO D'ALBA (L)

<u>Surface extension</u>: 727 hectares. <u>Geographical location</u>: the valley floor of Talloria stream, typically found outside of Serralunga d'Alba and below Grinzane Cavour. <u>Altitude</u>: 183–210 meters a.s.l. <u>Dominant exposure</u>: northeast (27%), northwest (20%). <u>Mean slope gradient</u>: 6%. <u>Lithology</u>: recent alluvial deposits. <u>Soil ph</u>: subalkaline to alkaline. <u>Topography</u>: generally flat alluvial plain. <u>Land Use</u>: cereals and poplar tree farming, not to mention Piedmont's famous and very high-quality hazelnut trees. Nebbiolo can give decent to good results on this Land Unit provided that soil fertility is curbed, good water drainage in ensured and short pruning techniques are avoided. <u>Barolo MGAs</u>: Grinzane Cavour: La Corte (part of); La Morra: Rive (part of); Verduno: Breri (part of).

THE BAROLO COMMUNES

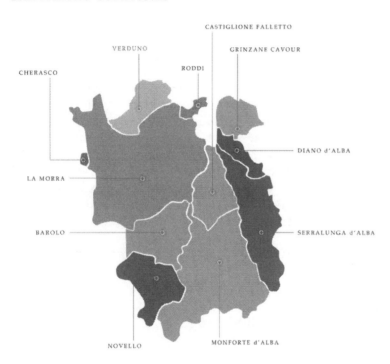

For those curious to know a little more about each Barolo commune beyond the characteristics of the wines they make, here is some information on their population, population density, hectares under vine and sights worth seeing (population data and vineyard data: 2017, Regione Piemonte). For an in-depth analysis of the communes and the vineyard districts/MGAs each is associated with, I refer you to my book *Italy's Native Wine Grape Terroirs* (D'Agata 2019) that has a truly extensive coverage of this subject.

<u>Barolo</u>

Population: 683. Population density/km²: 120.04. Altitude: 301 meters a.s.l. Hectares under vine/Nebbiolo hectares: 343.20 hectares/261.49 hectares. Number of MGAs: 30 (two are shared with La Morra). Sights worth seeing: Barolo Castle (10th Century), Enoteca Regionale del Barolo (Barolo Regional Wine Promotion Centre, inside the Barolo Castle), WiMu (Wine Museum, inside the Barolo Castle), Corkscrew Museum, Castle della Volta (12th Century), San Donato Church (18th Century). Major vineyard districts/MGAs: Brunate (part of), Cannubi (Centrale), Cannubi Boschis, Cannubi Muscatel, Cannubi San Lorenzo, Cannubi Valletta, Cerequio (part of), Sarmassa.

<u>Castiglione Falletto</u>

Population: 698. Population density/km²: 147.88. Altitude: 350 meters a.s.l. Hectares under vine/Nebbiolo hectares: 220.62 hectares/144.99 hectares. Number of MGAs: 22. Sights worth seeing: Castiglione Falletto

Castle (13th Century), San Lorenzo Church (19th Century). Major vineyard districts/MGAs: Fiasco, Monprivato, Rocche di Castiglione, Villero.

Cherasco

Population: 9,366. Population density/km²: 114.86. Altitude: 288 meters a.s.l. Hectares under vine/Nebbiolo hectares: 24.68 hectares/2.2 hectares. Number of MGAs: 1. Sights worth seeing: Visconti Family Castle (14th Century), Salmatoris Palace (or Peace Palace, 17th Century), San Peter Church (13th Century). Major vineyard districts/MGAs: Mantoetto.

Diano d'Alba

Population: 3,603. Population density/km²: 205.42; Altitude: 496 meters a.s.l. Hectares under vine/Nebbiolo hectares: 517.95 hectares/19.79 hectares. Number of MGAs: 3 (one shared with Serralunga). Sights worth seeing: Ruffino Palace (City Hall, 17th Century), "The Red Door Palace" (17 Century); S. Giovanni Church (18th Century). Major vineyard districts/MGAs: Sorano (part of).

Grinzane Cavour

Population: 1,966. Population density/km²: 516. Altitude: 195 meters a.s.l. Hectares under vine/Nebbiolo hectares: 91.41 hectares/58.88 hectares. Number of MGAs: 8. Sights worth seeing: Grinzane Cavour Castle (11th Century, owned by Camillo Benso Count of Cavour) within which are located: Piedmont Region Wine Promotion Centre, where the World Alba Truffle Auction takes place annually. Major vineyard districts/MGAs: Castello, Garretti.

La Morra

Population: 2,715. Population density/km²: 112.33. Altitude: 513 meters a.s.l. Hectares under vine/Nebbiolo hectares: 828.59 hectares/532.22 hectares. Number of MGAs: 39. Sights worth seeing: San Rocco Church (18th Century); Monument to Langa's Winemaker (1972), Bell Tower (18th Century), Falletti Palace (16th Century, hosting the La Morra Wine Promotion Centre); and in the Annunziata hamlet, the San Martino Benedictine Monastery and cellars (15th Century), where the Ratti's Alba Wines Museum is located. Major vineyard districts/MGAs: Brunate (part of), Cerequio (part of), Conca, Giachini, Rocche dell'Annunziata.

Monforte d'Alba

Population: 1,949. Population density/km²: 77.13. Altitude: 480 meters a.s.l. Hectares under vine/Nebbiolo hectares: 1031.12 hectares/441.55 hectares. Number of MGAs: 10. Sights worth seeing: Horszowski Auditorium (1986, a natural auditorium); Saint Agostino Oratory (17th Century); Scarampi Palace (13th Century); Bell Tower (17th Century). Major vineyard districts/MGAs: Bussia, Ginestra, Gramolere, Mosconi.

Novello

Population: 967. Population density/km²: 82.58. Altitude: 471 meters a.s.l. Hectares under vine/Nebbiolo hectares: 221.68 hectares/182.10 hectares. Number of MGAs: 7. History/sights worth seeing: Novello castle, Medieval tower, Chapel of the Little Madonna of the Small Cross (17th century); Novello town Enoteca/wine shop (where you can taste not just the Barolos but also the lovely Nascetta wines of all the producers). Major vineyard districts/MGAs: Bergera Pezzolle, Ravera, Sottocastello di Novello.

Roddi

Population: 1,585. Population density/km²: 169.52. Altitude: 285 meters a.s.l. Hectares under vine/Nebbiolo hectares: 118.72 hectares/24.21 hectares. Number of MGAs: 1. History/sights worth seeing: Roddi castle (11th century); open-air truffle museum, Bell tower (13th century). Major vineyard districts/MGAs: Bricco Ambrogio.

Serralunga d'Alba

Population: 545. Population density/km²: 65 Altitude: 414 meters a.s.l. Hectares under vine/Nebbiolo hectares: 500.10 hectares/346.19 hectares. Number of MGAs: 39. History/sights worth seeing: Serralunga castle, San Sebastiano church. Major vineyard districts/MGAs: Arione, Ceretta, Falletto, Francia, Lazzarito, Vignarionda.

Verduno

Population: 538. Population density/km^2: 75.14. Altitude: 380 meters a.s.l. Hectares under vine/Nebbiolo hectares: 198.16 hectares/109.80 hectares. Number of MGAs: 11. History/sights worth seeing: Verduno castle (10th century); San Michele church (18th century). Major vineyard districts/MGAs: Boscatto, Monvigliero, Neirane.

Chapter 8

BAROLO "CLASSICO" AND BAROLO SINGLE-DISTRICT WINES: THE IMPORTANCE OF SITE

Ian D'Agata

Throughout the better part of its history, Barolo has always been made by blending grapes from different sites, and not the product of single vineyards. This practice was favored for a number of reasons. Surely the most important was that picking and choosing grapes from sites peppered throughout the Barolo production zone allowed producers to make the best possible wine in their usual house style, and to do so in every vintage. This is not unlike Champagne and Franciacorta houses that do much the same with their signature cuvée blends; those too define the specific house's style. Keep in mind that in centuries past the majority of Barolos available for commercial sale were made by large firms; most of the (poor) individual farmers made only a little wine for home use (estate-bottling in Barolo became a reality only in the late 1960s and 1970s, and really took off only in the early 1980s).

Grapes brought to the town squares on market day were bought by the *negozianti* (the Italian equivalent of the French *négociants*) and by mediators; it was they who would then make the wines (or in the case of the mediators, sell the grapes to the larger firms that trusted their ability to source the best possible grapes in each vintage). The large firms were happy with this arrangement as they could easily buy low and sell (relatively) high, and because they could make more or less the same type of wine they were known for year in and year out. Depending on the style of Barolo one wished to make, producers would choose grapes from Serralunga and Monforte for structure; from La Morra or Barolo for perfume; and from Castiglione Falletto for balance. (Other communes as a source of Nebbiolo grapes really didn't exist as such -meaning there was little or no interest in them- until the 1990s and later.)

Clearly, sourcing grapes from multiple sites instead of using grapes from just one vineyard or one commune was an insurance policy against poor weather during the growing season and come harvest time. In years in which, for example, La Morra was hit by hail or Serralunga was drenched in rain, producers would just increase their blend's percentage of grapes from other communes where the weather had cooperated more. Clearly the mediators and the *negozianti* had their favorite sites, as well as their favorite grape farmers, and so looked for grapes from those specific sources whenever possible. But they all believed it was best to choose and mix grapes from multiple sites. Bartolo Mascarello said it best already in the 1980s when he simply enunciated that "…Barolo single vineyard wines are an exercise in theory and nothing short of an historical falsehood. It should be obvious to everyone that no single vineyard performs well every year; by contrast, it is the blending of grapes from different vineyard areas that allows the competent winemaker to produce a Barolo of the best aroma, flavor, complexity and balance". Not everyone shares that view, but spoken like the true statesman of Barolo that Bartolo was.

Single vineyard wines and wines named after larger specific sites recognized for the high quality of their grapes were never much a thing in Barolo. They are in fact an only very recent development, in large part a copy of Burgundy's wines made from many diverse vineyards of different quality levels. Single vineyard district wines began emerging in large numbers from Barolo only in the 1980s when they fast became an obsession of sorts in the area. But it is historically true and easily demonstrated that for the better part of three centuries, nobody thought to bottle Barolos as single vineyard wines.

Even though there are now 170 specific Barolo vineyard district sites officially recognized, of these only Cannubi was famous enough to have its name placed on a wine's label as early as 1752. And note that it was just Cannubi on that label, without any mention of Nebbiolo or Barolo (as written earlier in this book, Barolo's name rose to prominence even later than did Nebbiolo's). No other Barolo vineyard name ever appeared on a Barolo label until Beppe Colla took the plunge in 1961 with his Barolo Bussia (and Alfredo Currado did the same with his Rocche di Castiglione, at the time called Rocche only). After that, vineyard names began slowly making an appearance on labels of the 1960s and 1970s, a movement that turned into a veritable stampede by the early 1980s.

However, there can be too much of a good thing and it was so with Barolo's vineyard jamboree. One problem was that many of the named vineyards gracing labels in the 1980s were nothing to write home about; it hardly seemed like many deserved such pride of place. That is not to mean that locals were unaware that some vineyard areas gave better wines than others: they were. For back in a time when climate change was on nobody's mind, and the weather was generally much colder than it is today, one of the crucial aspects people looked for in grapes was ripeness. For this reason, grapes from those vineyards in which snow melted first in the spring (implying that the vineyards had warmer microclimates) were especially sought after and sold at a premium. In fact, the names of Barolo's better sites were known already centuries ago. Lorenzo Fantini's 1883 seminal *Monografia sulla Viticoltura ed Enologia nella Provincia di Cuneo* was the first published work in which specific communes were graded and a quality scale determined (in fact, his map and assessments of the Barolo production zone did not differ too much from what many people believe is true of the modern Barolo production zone). He was of the inclination that the best wines of Barolo were made in the territories of Barolo, Castiglione Falletto, Perno and Castelletto Monforte, and that small portions of Verduno, Novello, La Morra, Grinzane, Serralunga and Monforte were of the same level.

The merits of specific sites were also recognized and documented by Ferdinando Vignolo Lutati in his 1929 *Sulla delimitazione delle zone a vini tipici*. As written in the geology subchapter that precedes the one you are reading now, Vignolo-Lutati believed soil to be the key factor in determining wine quality. Hence, he conducted the first ever geologic survey of the Barolo production area.

In the late 1970s and early 1980s, a new generation of young, forward-thinking Barolo winery owners and winemakers began taking over the helm of their family wineries, and they pushed their parents to stop selling grapes or bulk wines and to estate-bottle, often for the first time in their family's history. Clearly, many of these new estates owned only small plots of vines and were therefore obligated to bottle wines from one vineyard or one vineyard district only, *de facto* making single-vineyard/single vineyard district Barolos an immediate reality. But I have no doubt that other factors played an important role in the genesis of single vineyard Barolos.

One was that this younger, hipper set was much more knowing and aware of the world's great wines; while their parents had never tasted the great wines of, for example, Burgundy, Bordeaux, the Mosel and Napa, the youngsters did have the opportunity to do so. Furthermore, also unlike their parents who had had limited opportunity to study, these youngsters were well-travelled and well-studied, and were keen to follow the example of Burgundy and other wine regions they had visited. Still another factor contributing to the rise of single vineyard and single vineyard district Barolos was the demand of US and UK importers who believed (correctly) that associating Barolo to single vineyards or prized sites would mean higher sales prices and better sales volumes. That course of action had certainly not hurt Burgundy or Alsace any. [Clearly, whether all of Burgundy's, Alsace's and Barolo's vineyard-designated areas (*grand crus, premier crus, lieux-dits*, MGAs) or whatever you want to call them are really that good and worthy of being singled out so is another matter altogether.]

Importantly, by the 1980s and especially the 1990s Barolo producers began to understand and appreciate the "importance of site". Bruno Ceretto once told me: "By travelling around the world and coming into contact with other winemakers and wine lovers, we began to realize just how important the vineyard site is. The vineyard area, that specific site, stays with you forever: a winery owner can change, but the importance of site is there forever. There is a sense of permanence to vineyards and specific places that is all important". I really don't think I could have said it better myself.

Yet another factor leading to Barolo wines being bottled vineyard site by vineyard site was linked to financial and lifestyle reasons. With the 1980s, running a winery became less of the chore it had always been: fine wine was fast becoming popular all over, as was the "wine country lifestyle". In short, winery owners and winemakers suddenly morphed out of the lowly farmer status they had always been saddled with to a much cooler, almost star-like personality, and were wined, dined and treated royally everywhere they went. That younger, better-schooled and much travelled generation I mentioned previously rapidly took notice of the changing times, and needless to say this brave new world was much to their liking.

Add also that wine prices were inexorably on the rise, year after year; and so, there was finally real money to be made in owning a winery and in bottling one's own wines. Many of those in line to take over the family winery who might have previously thought to work at a local bank branch or at car company (the norm for the previous decades), began to think that making wine wasn't such a bad idea after all. Clearly, this meant that many new small wineries bottling their own wines from many small vineyard plots began sprouting all over the place in Barolo much like mushrooms after a forest rain shower.

However, with all the good that came from that exhilarating run of events, some negative events tagged along for the ride too. The emergence of single site wines, what everyone in Barolo called "crus" in deference to the Burgundian system of *crus* (and you will find that the older generations in Barolo still routinely refer to specific vineyards as *crus*) was that these single-site wines fatefully reduced the standing of classic Barolo ("classic" Barolo being the wine made by blending grapes from different sites) to also-ran status.

This was an unfortunate turn of events that producers like Pio Cesare's Pio Boffa bemoaned at length (every chance he got to do so, in fact). "I always get hot under the collar when my colleagues refer to their classic Barolo as an 'entry-level Barolo'. You're an idiot, I tell them: clearly, I do so as kindly as possible and smiling nicely. But I insist, and explain that we are all so incredibly lucky to be making one of the world's most famous wines and what do they do? They willfully demean their own wine by referring to it as an entry-level wine?". Boffa's words still linger in my mind to this day. After all, his point was a very valid one, and you can hardly find fault in his logic. If for no other reason that many classic Barolos are far better than many Barolo wines made from single sites. For example, there isn't anyone I know who is even mildly knowledgeable about Barolo who wouldn't say that Bartolo Mascarello's Barolo (a blend of grapes from different sites) isn't one of the five or six best Barolos of all, so the superiority of single-site Barolo over classic Barolo is hardly a given. Like everything else in life, it depends.

That much recognized, the plight of classic Barolo was not the only problem brought about by the massive influx of Barolo single-site wines: another problem that soon became obvious to everyone was the seemingly endless proliferation of site and vineyard names on labels. This was inevitable, because unlike Burgundy where a quality classification and a rigorous delimitation of vineyard boundaries (official and not) had been in place for centuries, no such things were anywhere to be seen in Barolo. Back then, Barolo was a Wild West sort of place where in terms of vineyard names just about anything was allowed, and everyone got happily into the act.

So the locals talked about his "cru" and that "cru'", completely oblivious to the fact that the only people who might have thought the vineyard they were speaking about was really "cru-worthy" were them and practically nobody else (this is a huge problem in Italian wine still today, where every producer you talk to, from Veneto to Abruzzo, from Friuli to Sicily, will talk to you about their "cru" wines with no factual basis to support that judgement on, outside of the fact they like to think the wine is better than, or different from, the others they make). Anyways, the proliferation of random "vineyard" names not only engendered confusion, but ultimately began to cheapen the whole movement, because many of the vineyard sites appearing on labels were neither especially good nor famous. Some weren't even clearly related to a specific vineyard.

While the problem posed by a lack of quality hierarchy to the area's vineyards remains unaddressed to this day, Barolo producers and government officials were sensible enough to realize that allowing the misrepresentation of vineyard names (and potentially the source of grapes) to fester unchecked would spell disaster in the long run. And so it was that Barolo producers, under the aegis of the Barolo Consorzio, commendably devoted themselves to identifying the sites most suitable for Barolo production in each commune, a body of work culminating in 2010's official list of MGA vineyard district names (Barbaresco did as well too: in fact, before Barolo did, presenting their list of MGA vineyard district names in 2007).

As already mentioned in this book, this Italian term, MGA, is not the equivalent of the French word "cru" but is rather more like "vineyard district", and translates in English to "additional geographic characterizations or mentions". While a *cru* is a specific vineyard area associated over a long period of time with a very fine wine production that distinguishes itself from that of other lesser sites and produces similar wines independently of vintage variability, an MGA is nothing more than an administrative subdivision of a specific territory (vineyard district) based on historical and modern-day data. In other words, a piece or section of that territory's zonation, but one that provides no indication of quality of site. And as an MGA is usually quite large and made up of multiple different vineyard plots/blocks, "vineyard district" is the best possible translation and way to think about what it is.

It is also worth repeating that the MGA vineyard districts are not single vineyards either (but producers can choose to bottle single vineyard wines from a Barolo vineyard district if they so wish, as long as they follow the official production guidelines; in such cases, the label carries the vineyard district name (for example, Bussia, Falletto, Fiasco, Ginestra) followed by the specific *vigna* name, such as Vigna Elena or Vigna Bric). As many vineyard districts are very large (up to 300 hectares!), they are clearly not single vineyard areas and this is why they are thus best thought of as districts, with different sections within each district giving different wines (if anything, it is these different sections within each vineyard district that might be *crus* in the French sense).

As mentioned, there are 181 officially designated and delimited vineyard districts, of which one hundred and seventy are specific, named, vineyard districts, and eleven are village designations (for example, Barolo del Comune di La Morra and Barolo del Comune di Novello). Clearly, while the largest vineyard districts as they have been drawn up are really too large to express much sense of place, it is also true that by so doing, Barolo avoided having hundreds and hundreds of small crus (as they have in Burgundy) which are very hard to remember for anyone but diehard Burgundy fans. Consider there are a whopping 585 *premier crus* in Burgundy's Côte d'Or and Côte Chalonnaise, which isn't exactly peanuts, or perhaps hazelnuts, given we're in Piedmont, after all.

In that light, you can understand what the Barolo producers and legislators were thinking when they came up with some vineyard districts that seem to be the size of small countries. It is also true that in some cases the powers that be had their hands tied: over the decades, in the absence of a law or of official guidelines dictating what producers could or could not do with regards to naming wines, everyone and their sister had begun calling their wines with the more prestigious place names around. So, when the time came to have to tell people they could no longer use that place name they had been using for a while, things got a little testy, as you can well imagine. If for no other reason that people had built up a reputation of sorts and a brand image associated with their wine's name. Furthermore, vineyard land and wineries had been bought and sold based on the premise of what had been on record up until then, and its perceived value resulting from that brand and public awareness of it. Clearly, to want to remove all of that in one fell swoop was, understandably enough, unacceptable to many. For example, it appears that attempting to reduce use of the word "Bussia" alone was cause for a number of lawsuits to be threatened: and so, for lack of a better solution, some communes decided to allow a rather broad use of place names.

The list of Barolo's vineyard districts identifies a series of specific places guaranteeing in theory that wines bearing an vineyard district's name on the label are made with grapes from that specific vineyard site, but little more than that. And so unlike in Burgundy, where labels provide not just the Appellation and the village name, but also further specifications such as *grand cru* and *premier cru*, there is no such indication of quality level associated with the MGA vineyard districts. The usefulness of vineyard district names is further limited because the names of the Barolo communes to which the vineyard district belongs to are not clearly indicated on the front labels: and so, unless you remember to which of the eleven communes all 170 different names belong to (a tall task indeed) you really have no way of knowing if the wine you are drinking is from, for example, La Morra or Serralunga. And as I explained at length in chapter 7, BAROLO TERROIR, though not full-proof, knowing which township the Nebbiolo grapes were sourced in goes a long way in helping one understand the Barolo he or she is drinking. But the lack of a quality hierarchy also means that Barolos from sites never highly prized could and can often sell for a premium just because the estate making the wine is a famous one. Today, we have the ridiculous situation in Barolo that there is no way of knowing if a Barolo from the Serralunga commune labeled with the vineyard district name of Carpegna is better or worse than one labeled Vignarionda or Francia. If you know, you know. If you don't, well...good luck.

Of quality of site, cru systems, and maps

While it is true that Barolo lacks a classification of wine sites based on perceived quality, or a *cru classé* system, it is also true that, as we have seen it is one of the very few places in Italy with a history of having looked into this. A number of individuals over the years have done amazing work to forward our knowledge about Barolo's terroir and attempted to establish a hierarchy of quality.

I have already mentioned the forerunners in this field, Fantini and Vignolo-Lutati, to whom all Barolo lovers owe a huge collective "thanks". In more recent times, everything that has been written up on Barolo's vineyard sites (my over thirty years body of work included), owes at least something to the writings of Luigi Veronelli, Italy's first and to my mind best wine writer of all time. Every Italian wine writer today, bar none, owes Veronelli something. Maybe not everything he wrote was exact (can that be said of anyone?) but much of what he wrote about Barolo's best *crus* (he called them so too) in the 1960s, 1970s and very early 1980s is still true today. I for one became aware of the importance of site in Italy's vineyards only thanks to his teachings and writings; and if already in the early 1980s I knew to go looking and asking for a Barolo Vigna Rionda (so it was spelled at the time) or Villero, it was only thanks to Veronelli, who penned many large and small books and guides detailing wines with place names in full view.

As an adjunct to Veronelli's amazingly fun prose, the first graphic representation of the Barolo area's *crus* was delivered by the late, esteemed, Renato Ratti, a real gentleman and one of the recognized fathers of Barolo. He was the first to draw up a map of Barolo's *crus* (and of Barbaresco): the idea for the Barolo map, or *Carta del Barolo* as it is known and remembered in Italy, came to Ratti from his observations of the Burgundian reality and so he set out to do the same. I remember Ratti coming to my favorite wine shop in Rome during what were my university years to present and talk about it (he gifted everyone in attendance with a copy).

It's a wonderful body of work, rightly much used and admired, though criticism on some of his evaluations emerged already at the time. For example, some locals are of the idea that in his map Ratti gave high value to Serralunga while Castiglione Falletto and Monforte were somewhat penalized. But in fairness to Ratti's outstanding vision and effort, even La Morra at the time boasted only three, maybe four or five, vineyards most people knew anything about: Rocche (now called Rocche dell'Annunziata), Brunate, and Cerequio (the other two possibly Conca and La Serra). Ratti's map provides an important snapshot of the Barolo reality as it was known in the 1980s. A third work that described Barolo's production area in terms of sites was Slowfood's *Atlante delle Vigne di Langhe*; a large book, it is enjoyable for its wealth of anecdotes and memories, while being hampered by truly poor graphics (the maps are practically unusable).

To this day, one of the best book ever written on Barolo (and Barbaresco) remains, and not by a small margin, Garner and Merrit's *Barolo: Tar and Roses* (Garner and Merrit, 1990), the first time that the prose of truly competent-and knowledgeable wine experts was combined with highly simplified but very well drawn maps of Barolo's (and Barbaresco's) *crus* that are still today the easiest to read and to use. It is also the first book written on Barolo to offer truly useful information on Barolo's wines, production sites and estates of the time. The other truly seminal work, and the first to look at individual Barolo *crus* in detail, was Sheldon and Pauline Wasserman's *Italy's Noble Red Wines: An Annotated Guide to the Eminent Red Wines of Italy* (1985), later updated (and published with a shorter title in 1991). In it we have a long list of tasting notes going abck to the 1800s but most importantly, fairly detailed descriptions of the vineyard holdings of the more important Barolo wineries. Last but not least, Alessandro Masnaghetti (Italy's version of Burgundy's Sylvain Pitiot), penned two MGA-titled books (one for Barolo and one for Barbaresco) that map out the vineyards of those denominations exceptionally well, and that have to be viewed as the benchmarks on the subject. Nowhere else will you find similar painstakingly detailed mapwork showing not just where each of Barolo's MGA vineyard districts lie but where each producer owns vineyard plots too. It is a truly amazing body of work.

Given that the MGA system of classification carries no qualitative assessment of the site or of its wines, that many of these vineyard districts are far too large to be viewed as a single and even useful entity (because in such cases, the wines from one section of the vineyard district are often completely different from those of another, even when similar viticultural and winemaking methods are employed), and that many vineyard districts and their names are little-known with very few people anywhere (outside of the immediate locals) having much, if any, experience with their wines, it is objectively hard to draw hard and fast conclusions about each one. Even harder is to describe in all-encompassing fashion what their Barolos are like.

A truly great site for wine grapes, one that gives magnificent, really memorable wines year after year and does so over the years, decades and centuries, is one characterized by superior geology, exposure, climate, excellent soil water regimen, ideal altitude and talented, hard-working, passionate men and women who are able to express that potential in their wines. In the case of Nebbiolo, site is especially important because it is a late-ripening variety and achieving optimal physiologic maturity can be tricky. Terroir is important, and knowing which are the best *crus* even more so, because it is the top sites that yield the perfectly ripe fruit in most vintages. But Nebbiolo struggles to ripen fully in lesser situated sites and that is even more true in vintages characterized by poor weather. For a specific vineyard area to be of *grand cru* quality it is absolutely necessary that all these conditions come together.

When Nebbiolo is planted on the best soil type for it, in a relatively cool climate environment (where cool September nights extend the growing season into October, though thirty years ago I would have written cool October nights extending the growing season into early November) allowing for technological and polyphenol ripeness to converge seamlessly, the right producers can make the right wine. The right stuff, if you will. When such conditions are met year after year (and truly great sites, those of *grand cru*-worthiness, are in fact characterized by good meso- and microclimates), a slew of great wines are normally made by competent producers year after year, and for decades after decades. It is for such sites that there exists a body of proof, both in the bottle (the wines) and in the literature (historical documentation) attesting to the greatness of the site and its wines.

To the greatness that can be Barolo.

Classifying Barolo vineyard district/MGA quality

Clearly, everyone loves a classification and sooner or later we all want to try our hand at devising our own classification of say Bordeaux's growths, Burgundy's *crus*, and why not, Barolo vineyard sites. But it is an immensely difficult undertaking, if it is not done with logic and at least a minimum of scientific basis (and even then, a good deal of subjectivity is still involved). Unless wines are compared over many different vintages, wines that have been made more or less in the same way (meaning not just soil type and exposure and altitude, but biotype, clone, rootstock, training and pruning system, vine age, date of harvest, and a whole lot more, not to mention winemaking methods) then said undertaking is nothing more than whimsical amusement at best, and an exercise in futility at worst. And a highly damaging exercise at that, given we are talking and writing about people's livelihoods. You need look no further at the recent problems had with the Saint-Emilion *cru* classification to see just how hard it is nowadays to come up with a classificaton that is perceived as being devoid of vested interests. Those fears notwithstanding, (right or wrong that they may be), it remains that to create a quality classification of any vineyard area in this day and age is admittedly hard to do.

Consider two high-quality Barolo producers such as Silvio Grasso in La Morra and Guido Porro in Serralunga. The former makes wines in an area known to give lighter-styled, earlier-maturing wines, while the latter does so in another known for wines famous for their power and slow development. And yet it is Silvio Grasso's wines that are far more powerful (and oaky) than anything Porro has ever produced. It's not that one's wines are better than the other, just that these two estates make wines along their own stylistic preferences, so who's to argue? Both estates offer very fine Barolos indeed: but they are Barolos that are completely the opposite of what you would expect them to be, given the communes from where Grasso and Porro source their grapes from.

Furthermore, important winemaking differences affecting your perception of what each Barolo cru can give exist not just between the wines of different estates, but within those of the same winery too. If a producer farms two different Barolo vineyard districts in more or less the same way (and that's not always the case either), but then goes and vinifies the Barolos from each in two completely different manners (and I point out that even minor changes in the vinification process will impact heavily on the wine's final outcome) then trying to characterize each wine with a specific vineyard district-somewhereness is really moot. It follows that speaking of wines in terms of "grand cru" and "premier cru", or simply assigning definitive, characterizing, traits to each vineyard district based on the wines made in each becomes next to impossible.

In fact, this has always been a problem with Barolo (and Barbaresco). For example, back in the 1980s I remember asking producers what the differences were between say their Rocchettevino and Cerequio wine (I want to make clear I choose these two vineyards as examples and haphazardly: their use in this instance in no way implies a specific wine estate), I would routinely receive this response: "It's simple, Ian: I age my Rocchettevino in large oak barrels and my Cerequio in barriques". Clearly, being steeped in Burgundy and Mosel sensibility as I was when it came to discussing vineyard characteristics in wines, what kind of oak and size barrel people were using was the last thing I was thinking or even cared about, but such was the level of terroir-knowledge (or lack thereof) in Italy back in the 1980s. And even admitting that there might have been some perverse logic to that answer (you could argue that wines from Rocchettevino, being lighter and less concentrated, cannot stand up to prolonged barrique-aging, while the fleshier, rounder wines from Cerequio might stand a chance, in the hands of a competent winemaker), but that wasn't, and isn't, the point at all. And it really wasn't what the producers were thinking: but then, they really didn't know any better at the time.

When analyzing terroir, and the potential of a site to make fine wine, it is necessary to focus on the terroir-specific factors characterizing each site: the prevalent grape variety (in this case, Nebbiolo), but also the biotypes of it (comparing a Barolo made with 50% Nebbiolo Rosé and one made with 100% Michet is akin to comparing trouts, tunas and sharks: yes, I get it that all three are fish, that they all swim, and that they all live in the water, but, really …); physical factors (geology, exposure, topography, water regimen, altitude); biologic factors (soil microbiology); climate; and human intervention. Clearly, in these times of climate change a great deal of what we thought true about specific vineyards and their fine wine potential has to be reassessed, for vineyards that were once too cold for Nebbiolo to ripen fully are now more than warm enough for that to happen every year. But a positive change in climatic conditions alone does not allow that site to suddenly pole-vault into the upper echelons of the quality hierarchy, as people will often tell you (wouldn't you know it, it's always those who own vineyards there and make wine with those grapes). In fact, all the other factors need to be taken into consideration too.

Clearly, in viticulturally challenging times the role played by humans becomes even more important than before, and cannot be underestimated. There are producers who vinify their vineyards all in the same manner, which allows insight into the vineyard district's traits. A good example are the wines of the Giovanni Corino estate, where Giuliano Corino treats his wines made from three different vineyard districts all in the same manner. For his Barolo Giachini, Barolo Bricco Manescotto and Barolo Arborina, vinification is one and the same, consisting in the use of rotomacerofermentators for four to five days; fermentation finishing without skin contact; malolactic transformation carried out in stainless steel; and aging in Allier oak barriques (30-35% new) for about twenty-four months, with all three Barolos spending another six months in stainless steel before bottling, and going on sale after another six months in bottle. Clearly, in this case it becomes much easier to attribute, to a degree at least, vineyard district specific traits to the Barolos and to distinguish between the wines made in each site.

Furthermore, some individuals are just more talented than others and will always succeed where others fail. And if talent isn't the rate-limiting step, then the amount of elbow grease the winery owners are willing to employ in order to make the best wines possible also goes a long way in determining who will be making the best wines year after year. It follows that it is much easier to determine a site's quality when there are a plethora of quality-minded estates all making wine from a specific area. As an example of the importance that men and women can play in producing quality wines (or not), we shall cast our gaze on Barolo's most recent vintages.

The 2019 vintage will undoubtedly be remembered as a good one, if for no other reason that there was as much as a 20-25% reduction of yields with respect to 2018 as a consequence of the abundant rainfall during flowering that fatally reduced fruit set. By contrast, the 2018 vintage will be remembered as a very generous one and those estates that did not intervene drastically in order to reduce yields were unpleasantly surprised when the finished wines went into bottle (and in fact I found many of the 2018 Barolos tasted from cask to be dilute already at that stage of development). By contrast, the 2019 vintage's nature-enforced yield reduction helped wineries produce generally better wines across the board, even at those estates where owners aren't especially yield-reduction inclined. Climate is also important in evaluating the quality of a site, but again, limiting oneself to saying "this was a hot year and last year was a cool one" or "that site is a hot one and the other a cool one" buys you only so much mileage in the "identification of site" motor-sweepstakes. For instance, hot vintages always get written and talked up as being "great" vintages: nothing could be further from the truth, as the vastly overrated wines of 1997 and 2007 show clearly (and from a quality of tannins standpoint, you can throw 1998 and 2000, with the wines of only a few estates excepted, into that cauldron too). And so it is that you will hear and read that 2019 is one of three hottest Barolo vintages of all time, and therefore, specific sites performed much better than others because of their being better suited to producing great wines in hot years.

But in 2019 it really wasn't that hot during the entire growing season, and the vintage's wines are absolutely nothing like those of 1997, 2003 and 2007. The song remains the same relative to two of the best Barolo vintages in recent memory, 2015 and 2016. For example, 2015 was a great (and quite warm) vintage, but unlike the potentially even better (certainly more classic) 2016 vintage, it required a great deal more vineyard work to make wines as good as those of 2016. In mid-October 2015, grapes tasted throughout many vineyards were extremely sweet, but as Barolo producers are in the business of making wine and not the sale of table grapes, similarly sweet grapes may actually not be as great as it sounds.

For this reason, those quality producers who had not employed enough judicious deleafing and topping measures during the growing season had no option but to resort to not using the grapes of the *bricchi* (the highest and best-exposed parts of the crus, where grapes usually ripen best), which is practically unheard of. Those producers who couldn't stand the thought of not cashing in on their ripest grapes and used them anyways ran two risks: either making high alcohol, round wines with little nuance, grace and expression of site, or wines that might be lusciously fruity on the nose and palate entry but then reveal tough, green, gritty tannins (especially true of those grapes that had begun to dehydrate directly on the vine before full phenolic maturity had been reached). Even in 2016, a year that was slightly cooler than 2015 in its seasonal profile but still a relatively warm year, you will find many producers made wines with 15.5% alcohol. Stuff like that tells you a lot about a specific site's terroir relative to the role played by the estates that farm them.

All that aside, with some MGA vineyard districts it is extremely difficult, and not even fair or realistic, to accurately determine their precise fine wine potential; this is because either not enough producers make wine from them or there just hasn't been enough wine made from that vineyard district-over the years. Relative to the former caveat, drawing hard and fast conclusions about anything when you only hear one voice on the subject is a perilous exercise at best, and unfair at worst.

SECTION II

Chapter 9

BAROLO VINEYARD DISTRICTS: FACTS, FIGURES AND ANALYSIS

Ian D'Agata and Michele Longo

THE MGA FILES: FACTS AND FIGURES

Michele Longo

In this chapter, we list and describe the 170 Barolo officially named and delimited vineyard districts that refer to specific vineyard sites (so we do not broach the eleven communes and the characteristics of their terroir and wines that have already been discussed previously; see chapter 8, BAROLO TERROIR. Subchapter. The Barolo Communes). We also assess the wines that most characterize, for various reasons, each specific vineyard district. Wish to understand how the kind of soil (soils) a specific vineyard area is characterized by and how the altitude at which its vineyards lie might play into the finished wines? And why a Barolo Cannubi or a Barolo Bussia tastes the way it does? And perhaps more importantly, what each should really smell and taste of? To be enabled to hopefully distinguish between (and even recognize, when tasting blind) a Barolo Ginestra from a Barolo Mosconi, much as you might do when enjoying at dinner and/or blind tasting a Chambolle-Musigny Les Amoureuses, a Les Feusselottes and Les Sentiers? Even better, in this chapter you will learn about the different subregions within the various vineyard districts and their respective wines, because many of the Barolo denomination's vineyard districts are too large, such that very different Barolos are born from within their boundaries. And anyways, many of the Barolo denomination's official vineyard districts of today are made up of what used to be historically relevant, different, and finite vineyard areas that have been lumped together for a variety of reasons. Those specific subregions gave (and still give, in fact) very different wines. For example, Barolos now being labeled as "Cannubi" or "Bussia" are made with grapes sourced from two vineyard districts that range in size from large to very large; and despite what some might tell you, there really is no such thing as "a" Barolo Bussia or Barolo Cannubi, but rather many different wines made with grapes from Bussia and from Cannubi, just like there are Barolos made the many other various subregions of those vineyard districts. Similarly, knowledgeable wine lovers know that to speak of "one" Echezeaux (a Burgundy grand cru) and "one" Brand (an Alsace grand cru) is just as ineffective, and avoid doing so. It follows that just like with Burgundy, Alsace, and all the other world production areas of great terroir wines, it would be nice to be able to do so with Barolo too, that is to have the same level of knowledge about these matters when speaking and writing about Barolo.

Barolo's official vineyard district are presented in this chapter, one after the other, in alphabetical order; and each with its own all-inclusive file. The information used to compile these files has been arrived at by studying and verifying numerous data sources, including: distilling the information gleaned in over thirty years of visiting wineries and walking Barolo's vineyards; producer interviews at the wineries; their answers to specific questionnaires; information obtained thanks to the auspices of the Enoteca Regionale del Barolo, the Consorzio and the Regione Piemonte; the analysis and the study of university research papers and other scientific data; and well over twenty thousand Barolos tasted over the course of thirty years. These files represent first-hand, reference-quality information that has never been, and is (at least in part and to the best of our knowledge) simply not available anywhere else.

HOW TO READ AND USE THE BAROLO MGA/VINEYARD DISTRICT FILES

To make reading, following, understanding, and learning from each Barolo cru file as easy as possible, each vineyard district area file follows the same format, with exactly the same subheadings. For each of Barolo's vineyard district, we provide fundamental data included under the following headings and subheadings:

General facts and figures

a- *Township*	The township/commune the vineyard district belongs to (For example, La Morra, Novello or Diano d'Alba) and its relative position inside the map
b - *Reference map*	Reference Map: see in Chapter 10, BAROLO MGA VINEYARD DISTRICTS: MAPS AND LAND UNITS
c- *Size (ha) (Tot / Barolo MGA)*	The vineyard district's size in hectares/The number of those hectares specifically claimed to that MGA-named vineyard district (related to the 2021 vintage)
d - *Production 2021 (hl)*	The total production specifically claimed to that vineyard district in hectoliters (hl) related to the 2021 vintage (and if claimed, also the production of Barolo MGA vineyard district "Riserva" or "Vigna")
e - *Altitude*	The altitude range at which the vineyard district's vineyards lie in meters above sea level (abbreviated as a.s.l.) *
f - *Exposure*	The vineyard district's exposures
g - *N. Claimants MGA*	Number of producers who own/rent plots of vines in that vineyard district claiming the official MGA name at the time of the 2021 vintage (this does not necessarily imply that they will then bottle as a single-MGA vineyard district Barolo and use that name on their label). See below: Producers claiming the MGA vineyard districts.
h - *Other grape varieties planted:*	Other wine grapes (other grape varieties also planted in that specific vineyard district besides Nebbiolo)
i - *Land Units*	Soil type described by Land Units and lithological formations (see chapter 8. BAROLO TERROIR; Subchapter, Land Units)
l - *Soil (stage):*	Serravalian / Tortonian / Messinian

*: Please note and be aware that the exact altitudes at which vineyards lie are more often than not reported erroneously in websites and publications. There are a number of reasons that help understand why this is.

First, we have verified on military maps and other recently available official topographical data the altitude of each vineyard district; and in comparing these values with generally reported data, the differences are at times noteworthy. We may have made mistakes of our own in determining the precise altitude values of each district, but the figures reported here have been double-checked prior to publication and represent, to the best of our knowledge, the latest and most precise altitude figures of Barolo vineyard districts today. Secondly, when producers are asked by scribes "… at what altitude do the vineyards in Brunate or Fiasco lie…", the producers naturally respond with the altitude of their own vineyards within that vineyard district; unfortunately, those values are then reported/written as the generalized altitude figures for the whole vineyard district, which conveys wrong information about the site's reality. Third, if you have enough experience visiting wineries all over the world, you will have realized by now that over the years, perhaps because of climate change, some vineyard altitude figures that were mentioned to you years ago seem to have gained, in people's assessments and memories, an average of fifty-sixty meters in height in the interim. Curious.

Producers claiming the MGAs

A list of the names of all the producers who rent or own plots in the vineyard district–and claimed use of the MGA vineyard district name for the 2021 vintage.

Wines

A list of all the producers who make wines from the official vineyard district and the complete names of their wines.

In other words, those estates producing a Barolo that carries that specific MGA vineyard district's name on the label at the time of publication. Depending on their individual needs and/or the vintage, some producers might decide to not use their vineyard district's grapes to make a site-specific Barolo, preferring instead to blend the grapes together with those picked in other vineyard areas to make a classic estate Barolo (traditionally, blends of Nebbiolo grapes from different vineyard sources). For example, in some weather-challenged vintages grape production might be so low to warrant making more of a regular Barolo rather than very small volumes of myriad different single-site wines, which might be instead that estate's norm in good vintages when grapes are plentiful or the wines distinguished and different enough to deserve being bottled singly. Therefore, it is in this section that you will find every Barolo made from the specific vineyard districts, including those Barolos also carrying specific single vineyard names (and so: Producer name/Barolo/MGA vineyard district name/plus eventual single vineyard name if one is present. For example: Bruno Giacosa Barolo Falletto and Barolo Falletto Vigna Le Rocche).

What the producers say

This section refers to pertinent commentary made over the years by those producers who make wines from that specific vineyard district and whom we have visited at the wineries, met at tastings and in other occasions, and gleaned from myriad (and we mean myriad) email exchanges and questionnaires said producers were kind and patient enough to answer. Please note that when the names of the estate is similar to that of many other estates or there is more than one family member involved at the estate, we write both the name of the estate and of whom exactly it is we are quoting. In other words, the first name listed is that of the specific owner's name who gave us his/her insight; follows in brackets the name of the wine estate, as present on the wine label [for example: Claudio Viberti (Viberti)]. In some cases, we may have two contributions from different members of the same family, hence the need to clarify who said what. So, for example: Alessandro Ceretto (Ceretto); Federico Ceretto (Ceretto).

Sample Barolo vineyard district file

In this case of the Albarella vineyard district:

ALBARELLA

Township	Barolo (a)
Reference Map	See Map of Barolo MGAs (Ch. 10) (e)
Size (ha) (Tot / Barolo MGA)	9.96 (a) (b) / 1.41 (b) see note below
Production 2021 (hl)	76.8 (a) (b)
Altitude	240 – 280 meters. a.s.l. roughly (a)
Exposure	Predominantly northwest (a)
N. Claimants MGA	3 (a)
Other grape varieties planted:	Barbera; Dolcetto (b)
Land Units	Land Units of Barolo (c)
Soil (stage):	Tortonian

Producers claiming the MGA (d)

Andrea Oberto; Viberti; F.lli Serio e Battista Borgogno.

Wines (d)

Andrea Oberto - Barolo Albarella; **Viberti** - Barolo Albarella (*).

(*): The (*) indicates that the producer has claimed use of the MGA vineyard district's name but not necessarily that he or she has then bottled the wine as an wine labeled with that specific vineyard district's name after all (as previously noted, given the vintage's weather and what the finished wine tasted like from tank or barrel, they may have decided to declassify the wine and sold off as bulk wine (a rare event) or to use it to make the estate's "classic" Barolo, made from a blend of grapes from different vineyards).

Key/legend to reading the files (names and sources that helped compile some of the factual and numerical data):

(a)	Data provided by the "Consortium of Barolo Barbaresco Alba Langhe and Dogliani"
(b)	Data provided by "Department of Agriculture of the Region Piemonte" on the basis of the producer claims for each MGA vineyard district in 2021
(c)	Data obtained by the authors studying the Official Map of the MGA vineyard districts provided by the Consortium of Barolo Barbaresco Alba Langhe and Dogliani, the Barolo Land Units Map and producer interviews
(d)	Data obtained by the authors, cross-checked with data provided by the "Consortium of Barolo Barbaresco Alba Langhe and Dogliani" (vintage 2021) and by producers. This list is updated at the best of our knowledge considering data from Consortium (vintage 2021) and wine released in 2022.
(e)	MGA vineyard district maps: extracted from "Barolo – The Official Map" of the "Consortium of Barolo Barbaresco Alba Langhe and Dogliani"

ANALYSIS OF THE MGAS, THEIR WINES, AND BENCHMARK WINERIES

Ian D'Agata

In this subchapter, you will find:

Ian's assessment of the vineyard district, its wines and its potential

Under the heading, you will find my detailed analysis of each vineyard district in terms of, where pertinent, its: history; extension; topography; soil type; exposure; altitude; Nebbiolo biotypes; Nebbiolo clones; rootstocks; and human factors as related to the characteristics of the Barolos made there and the "cru" potential of each site.

(Vineyard district's name) producers and the wines

In which the most important estates (relative to the vineyard district being discussed), their holdings, and their specific wines, are described.

Benchmark wineries / Reference point producers of Barolo

Under this heading, you will find a very short list of wineries that have historically made excellent to outstanding wines from the site. The list is irrespective of how famous or big the name of the estates may or may not be and the wineries are listed in alphabetical order. This is because the list is intended to provide the names of the wineries making the most representative wines from that specific vineyard district: wineries that have more often than not been associated with that specific vineyard district, and excellent wines from it, for a very long time.

Keep in mind that when a famous or big-name estate moves into any vineyard district and starts making wines there, it is almost always automatically assumed, said and/or written, that the Barolos are just dandy; but things may not be necessarily so. In fact, it is intuitive that it could well be otherwise: moving into a site only recently following the vineyard district's rise in prominence thanks to somebody else's wines of skyrocketing fame, almost always places the newcomer at a disadvantage. This is because the best vineyard sites within a vineyard district have either long been bought up by locals who live there (Ravera in Novello is a good example of this: Cogno was the first to move in there and gobbled up the choicest plots of the vineyard district that were still available) or are held on to by their owners because that land has been in the family for generations and locals are usually fiercely attached to it. It follows that even though the newcomer may be an extremely talented and hard-working individual, he or she may not have the best sites to work with and so the fine wine potential of his/her vineyards is fatefully limited. Furthermore, the newcomer does not have the first-hand experience built up over many vintages to truly know or understand that site which is new to him or her. What works for the Nebbiolo grapevines of Lazzarito or Ginestra may in fact not work quite as well for the Nebbiolo vines growing in Serradenari or Bricco Ambrogio, as both grapevines and habitats are completely different. To put this another way, do you really believe that a world-famous orthopedic surgeon who has always operated on the hands and who suddenly begins to also operate on the feet is going to be as good at it as an equally competent but much less famous surgeon who, despite being less famous, has been operating on feet all his life? You think about it, and you decide. I know what I think, and who I'd want my feet to be operated on by. Clearly, any person's energy, drive, passion and talent may help make up, to a degree, for their inherent lack of experience and, going back to wine, the quality of the vineyard site they bought or rent. This is why the wines of star-quality producers such as Vietti and Vajra from Ravera or Giacomo Conterno in Cerretta and Arione are often spectacular wines: but that is not the norm, nor is it logical to expect or believe that it would be so, and even when good results arrive, it takes time. Producers will honestly tell you that in some instance they had to change the way they were first making wine in a vineyard district that was new to them in order to achieve better results, because their usual techniques weren't as suited to the new vineyard district's reality (for example, see RAVERA file).

SPECIAL ADDENDUMS

Typical organoleptic descriptors of the Barolos of the vineyard districts

Over the decades, I have attempted to classify the aromas and flavors associated with the Barolos of each specific vineyard district. Just as when we discuss the wines of specific *crus* of Burgundy, Alsace, the Mosel, and the wines of Bordeaux's communes with specific descriptors (for example, the telltale smokiness of the wines of Pessac-Léognan, and of Pessac especially), much the same can be done for Barolo. In my experience this was much easier to do with the wines of the 1980s, for a variety of reasons (the absence of climate change, for one, but it's not the only reason). And not just in my experience, in fact: numerous producers have told me as much over the years, including for example Sandrone, Enrico Scavino, and Roberto Vezza. However, general aroma and flavor descriptors are still cogent and apply to today's wines as well (a certain mintiness to many of Monforte's wines, for example). For this book, I have carefully combed over all the information I have gathered in old notebooks during interviews with Barolo producers dating back to 1981; but also through the use of questionnaires and the analysis of well-designed and well-conducted sensory analysis scientific research papers that have been published over the years. By analyzing and compiling all the organoleptic data for the wines of each vineyard district I have accumulated over these years, I have been able to assign specific descriptors to the wines of each Barolo vineyard district. These descriptors are listed in *Appendix D, Table 4.5: Ian D'Agata's typical organoleptic descriptors of the Barolos of the vineyard district*. For example, the Barolos of the Conca vineyard district of La Morra are very clearly associated with a specific mintiness that is not typical -at all- of the Barolos of nearby La Morra vineyard districts like Giachini and Arborina. Furthermore, it is a mintiness that is very recognizably different from the mintiness of the Barolos of La Morra's Berri vineyard district. I have provided a list of such descriptors for all the vineyard districts where it is reasonable to do so (meaning there have been enough wines made from each over the years, decades even, and by more than one producer). Clearly, my list of vineyard district-specific wine descriptors cannot be all-encompassing, for the are many Barolo vineyard districts of which there really aren't too many or at times even any wines with which to form an opinion on. And though I have tried hard to include and summarize the impressions and beliefs on this matter of those producers who have farmed the specific sites for a long time, the list remains subjective to a degree. There will no doubt be a descriptor that you might associate with a specific Barolo vineyard district that I have failed to mention. It's inevitable.

.

ALBARELLA

Township	Barolo	
Reference Map	See Map of Barolo MGAs (Ch. 10)	
Size (ha) (Tot / Barolo MGA)	9.96 / 1.41	
Production 2021 (hl)	76.81	
Altitude	240 – 280 meters a.s.l. roughly	
Exposure	Predominantly northwest	
N. Claimants MGA	3	
Other grape varieties planted:	Barbera; Dolcetto; Favorita; other white varieties	
Land Units	Land Unit of Barolo	
Soil (stage):	Tortonian	

Producers claiming the MGA

Andrea Oberto; Viberti; F.lli Serio e Battista Borgogno.

Wines

Andrea Oberto - Barolo Albarella.

What the producers say

Andrea Oberto: "The Albarella vineyard gives a Barolo that is fleshy on the nose with pronounced notes of quinine, tobacco and dried flowers. The palate offers structure and power, softened and sweetened by an acid backbone that gives a Barolo that is very pleasurable to drink".

Enrica Scavino (Paolo Scavino): "Albarella is a site of undiscovered beauty and that confirms the character of a Barolo from the Barolo commune: great aromatics combined with a classic texture and elegant tannins. We planted our holding in this site with a selection of the best vines, chosen by Enrico Scavino, from the Paolo Scavino estate".

Ian's assessment of the vineyard district, its wines and its potential

Albarella's name derives neither from Alba, the city, nor *alba*, the dawn (the latter always being a nicely poetic possibility with vineyard names). Rather it stems most likely either from *albarello* (a pharmacist's jar in which herbs and medical remedies were kept) or *albarella/albanella* (a jar used to conserve foodstuffs). In fact, it was Emanuela Bolla of the Serio e Battista Borgogno estate in Barolo (known for its Barolo Cannubi but that recently has also begun bottling a Barolo Albarella), who alerted me to the fact that the term is an ancient one, possibly descending from *arbarela*, as defined in the *Vocabolario Piemontese-Italiano e Italiano-Piemontese del Sacerdote Michele Ponza* (Ponza, 1846).

Relative to the quality level of Albarella (or its exact potential) as a source of Barolo, it is tough to judge because outside of the talented Andrea Oberto of the eponymous estate there have never been any producers making single-Albarella site Barolos (not to the best of my knowledge, at least). That said, I know Andrea Oberto's wines extremely well as they were excellent and much sought after already back in the mid-1980s when I used to be a wine-crazed university student in Rome. The number of evenings I spent in the company with my wine-loving university friends and of Andrea Oberto's wines (his Dolcetto d'Alba too, a beauty) at such legendary Rome watering holes like the Enoteca Roffi Isabelli, Semidivino and Cul de Sac are too numerous to count. So yes, I have a history with this estate's wines. But clearly, memories of halcyon bygone days, friends and wineshops/bars aside, it is hard to gauge quality or characteristics of site based on the wines of what was long a one-man show only, and this independently of how good the wines may be or have been. This is one of the reasons why in Alsace they do not include *monopole* wines, even those of famous *clos*, in the regional list of "Grand Crus": for example, right or wrong that it maybe, you won't find the words "Grand Cru" anywhere on the label of Trimbach's world-famous Clos Ste.Hune (Zind Humbrecht's just as famous Clos Saint-Urbain bottling does carry the words *grand cru* but there they are referred to the Rangen vineyard, listed at the top of the label as Alsace Grand Cru Rangen, not to the *clos*, which is located within the Rangen; by contrast, Trimbach does not mention the name of the Rosacker *grand cru* on the label, because in this case the Clos Ste.Hune is actually more famous than the *grand cru*).

So just how good is the Albarella site and what are its Barolos like? Certainly, the fact that other producers who also own vineyards in Albarella choose not to make a Barolo with this vineyard district's grapes, but have up until recently used said grapes to make "just" a Nebbiolo d'Alba or Langhe Nebbiolo wine, or have used them in their classic Barolo estate blends gives one pause. This may be due to an individual's lack of faith in the specific site: but it may also be a result dictated by more mundane considerations. For example, the extremely small size of the plot owned in the vineyard district by said estate: in such cases, there is often the need to make more of the classic, non-vineyard designated Barolo, an important source of income for the winery as it is often sold at a more user-friendly price and serves as the ideal "business card" by which the estate gets to be known initially. Or it may be that the estate believes that the small volume of grapes coming from a high-quality site will help improve the quality of their classic Barolo, which is traditionally neither a single vineyard nor a vineyard district-designated Barolo. Still another reason not to produce a vineyard district-designated Barolo from a specific site such as Albarella might be the very young age of the vines planted there; but once that site's vines are old enough to give a wine deemed to be sufficiently complex, deep, and rich to be worthy of the name Barolo or of a single-site Barolo, then the producer may well decide to go ahead and bottle the wine as a Barolo (as opposed to a Langhe Nebbiolo wine), and even as a Barolo sporting the vineyard district's name. All these considerations notwithstanding, based on my tastings of Andrea Oberto's Barolos over the years (like I wrote earlier, I began doing so with the 1982 vintage, a bottle or two of which are still lying around somewhere in my cellar in Rome), I think all of Andrea Oberto's wines have always been recognizable (save for a brief parenthesis at the beginning of the 2000s when they became unexplainably chunky) for their purity of fruit and refinement. That much is also true of the estate's very fine Barolo Albarella, a pleasant Barolo of early appeal and easy drinkability.

The Albarella vineyard district, situated on a ridge to the northwest of the town of Barolo just across from the Cannubi centrale (the historic, central portion of Cannubi, or Cannubi proper) on the western aspect of the same hill, is sandwiched in between the Crosia and Sarmassa vineyard districts (a small section of Albarella borders the San Lorenzo vineyard district). At 240-280 meters above sea level, Albarella vines are not especially high up; furthermore, the vines receive plenty of solar irradiation, and so Albarella is a relatively warm site, in fact one of the earliest to be harvested in the area (done in order to avoid overripeness). The soil was formed during the Tortonian stage of the Miocene epoch, and is about as typical a soil of the Barolo commune as is possible to find (boasting the magnesium- and manganese-rich blue-grey marls of the typical form of the Saint Agatha Fossil Marls that is associated with perfumed, earlier-maturing wines of relative palate weight, texture and drag).

Albarella producers and the wines

For the most part, what I have just written applies fully to Albarella's wines (at least in the Andrea Oberto rendition): these are approachable and expressive Barolos already in their youth, with an easy to drink quality that I personally find enchanting. However, the wines also boast a noteworthy freshness that is no doubt related to the site's exposure and to its clay-rich soils that hold on to water relatively well (an important point, given to the district's relatively warm mesoclimate). For all its ripeness, I point out that Andrea Oberto's Barolo Albarella has an obvious underlying tannic backbone (as any self-respecting Barolo should have), but it's a tannin that stays, for the most part, rather "politely" in the background. This is not always the case: especially in droughty years, despite its soil clay content, I find that the Albarella Barolo can fall just over this side of gritty.

A different take on Albarella is given us by the excellent, underrated, Serio e Battista Borgogno estate. In 2016, they began renting 2,900 square meters (0.29 hectares) of vines in Albarella planted between 2015-2016 at about 260 meters above sea level; the plot is divided in two by a headland (*capezzagna*) such that only about 1250 square meters are destined for production of a Barolo Albarella [grapes from the remaining less favorably exposed vines (east-facing) are used to produce a Nebbiolo Langhe: but note that unlike the Barolo Albarella which is 100% Albarella grapes, the Langhe Nebbiolo is a blend of grapes from Albarella and vineyards in the Diano d'Alba commune]. The estate's first vintage of the latter wine was the lovely 2018 (if I'm not mistaken, with about 5% Diano d'Alba Nebbiolo grapes) matured in stainless steel only. It's a very pretty, juicy, Nebbiolo wine boasting plenty of verve and focus, one that bodes well for what the future may hold, with increased vine age. Unfortunately, there were only 700 bottles of the truly lovely Barolo Albarella made, packaged as a four-bottle box, with each bottle bearing a different label depicting a different season.

Another producer who farms Albarella is Viberti (which, just like Oberto, is a very common family name in this neck of the Barolo denomination's woods: here I am referring to the Viberti estate in Vergne, the family that also owns that town's bastion of very good and very traditional Langhe cooking known as the Il Buon Padre trattoria). Viberti owns 1.2 hectares in Albarella, planted between 220-250 meters above sea level on a highly loamy portion of the vineyard district, with little clay in the soil and even less sand present. His is a vineyard with very good drainage and the Nebbiolo grapes grown there deliver wines of good perfume and suaveness of texture, but with good tannic backbone, such that the wines have a delicately austere quality. At Viberti, they choose to blend part of their Albarella grapes into their classic estate Barolo "Buon Padre" (decades ago made only with grapes from the La Volta and Bricco delle Viole vineyard districts, but today this Barolo is a blend of grapes from three different townships and eight different vineyard districts, including Albarella) and the rest to make a Langhe Nebbiolo. Over at Paolo Scavino in Castiglione Falletto, Albarella grapes are used to make the winery's classic Barolo (made with Nebbiolo grown in many different vineyard districts, up to seven different ones at once, from different communes). Enrica Scavino believes that their Albarella vines (the estate owns about 0.5 hectares planted at about 280 meters above sea level), planted in 1999, deliver noteworthy aromatics to the finished wine. On a more curious note, the Bricco Rocca estate also farms Albarella; however, it's not Nebbiolo they grow there, but Favorita, a white grape that is the Piedmontese biotype of Liguria's (and Sardinia's) Vermentino.

Benchmark wineries/Reference point producers of Barolo Albarella: Andrea Oberto.

ALTENASSO/GARBLET SUÈ/GARBELLETTO SUPERIORE

Township	Castiglione Falletto
Reference Map	See Map of Castiglione MGAs (Ch. 10)
Size (ha) (Tot / Barolo MGA)	4.27 / 2.34
Production 2021 (hl)	96.73 (of which 81.50 hl of Barolo Riserva *MGA*)
Altitude	225 – 250 meters a.s.l. roughly
Exposure	From west to northwest
N. Claimants MGA	2
Other grape varieties planted:	Barbera; Dolcetto
Land Units	Land Unit of Barolo
Soil (stage):	Tortonian

Producers claiming the MGA

Brovia; Cavalier Bartolomeo.

Wines

Brovia - Barolo Capezzana Garblet Suè; **Cavalier Bartolomeo** - Barolo Altenasso.

What the producers say

Alex Sanchez (Brovia): "The Brovia family owns this vineyard since 1943. Our philosophy is to maintain in our wines the identity of our grapes and our diverse terroirs which we believe to be one of the principal assets of the zone, capable of establishing Barolo as one of the world's truly unique, terroir-driven wines. As a result, our *crus* are vinified and aged in a way that their diverse characteristics are shown to their fullest. This is a very interesting Barolo of real longevity—which I dare say is typical of the Barolo from the Castiglione Falletto commune. Pleasant perfumes of plums, berry fruit and minerals. On the palate, it enters smooth and sweet, then emerges opulent with decisive but fine tannins and a long finish".

Ian's assessment of the vineyard district, its wines and its potential

Altenasso, or Garblet Suè (I have never heard or seen anyone use the moniker of Garbelletto Superiore for their wine, though it's the name of a fraction of Castiglione Falletto, as you can easily see by the road signs there), makes classic Barolos, at once elegant and powerful, and that age remarkably well. Most interestingly, the wines are always characterized, in each vintage, by a ripe red fruit quality and especially by an easily recognizable citrussy acidity that speaks of the strong limestone content of the soil. This vineyard district is the northwesternmost, lower-lying, and less steep continuation of a ridge that is in the western part of the Castiglione Falletto commune's territory. The ridge runs from the town itself in a southwest to northeast direction almost to the border with the territory of the Barolo commune. In fact, it's but one of a series of ridges in the area, all of which are of varying lengths and that run more or less parallel to each other. For example, the one immediately to the north is where you'll find the Monprivato vineyard area, made famous by the Giuseppe Mascarello estate. Altenasso's ridge starts out just south and to the west of the town of Castiglione Falletto: the more central section of this ridge is occupied by the well-known Fiasco vineyard district, one from which there are many more Barolos produced each year, in comparison to the paltry number of wines from Altenasso (or one of its other name-permutations).

In my view, the Fiasco name should be reserved only for the central sections of the aforementioned ridge (specifically that section with a south/southwestern exposure). However, the official Fiasco vineyard district was extended to include also north-facing and northwest-facing parts of the hill overlooking the Altenasso. This is not precise, in my opinion: those sections of the ridge are really still Altenasso, comprising its upper section, and should therefore not be identified with/as Fiasco (and neither should the wines). This is relevant, for it can be argued that the higher and central sections of Altenasso are of potential *premier cru* quality, while the lower-lying ones (where in fact Barbera and Dolcetto have been historically and are still mostly planted, rather than Nebbiolo) are only of *lieu-dit* quality. For example, Vietti owns holdings in Fiasco but the vines are located in what is really the highest part of Altenasso (admittedly, one of the better portions of Altenasso). Fact is, the name Fiasco carries more *gravitas*, and helps sales; but still, it's a pity that Altenasso has been so reduced and handcuffed. In my view, Altenasso is one of Barolo's most underrated vineyard areas and its potential to make very good to great wines is noteworthy, as has been demonstrated time and again over the years by the excellent and underrated wines of Cavalier Bartolomeo. But because of the paucity of producers who have made or make a vineyard district designated Barolo from Altenasso, this vineyard district has lacked the visibility of others, and thus its wines have remained somewhat in the shadows. And you cannot blame estates that paid a premium for vineyard land thinking it belonged to an all-important vineyard district like Fiasco, to then understandably balking at having the name of the vineyard district changed to a much less famous one such as Altenasso.

Altenasso producers and the wines

The two producers who make a Barolo Altenasso (and that I have tasted enough wines of to express a reliable judgement on the site) are Brovia and Cavalier Bartolomeo.

Brovia's vines were planted back in 1970 and 1979 and that sort of vine age is evident in the depth and complexity their Barolo Garblet Suè boasts in practically all vintages; it is also a wine where the limestone presence in the soil is evident at every sip. This Brovia Barolo is a beauty, always rather lusciously textured and ripe, not to mention loaded with sweet red cherry fruit. But at the same time, it boasts noteworthy refinement too. In my experience, it's one of the surest bets in all Barolo, and one that won't break the bank when you decide to buy a bottle.

While less famous than Brovia, I have always found the wines of Cavalier Bartolomeo to be excellent. This is but one of the many very fine but little-known Barolo estates, and that's a pity, for the wines can be remarkably good and cost a fraction of those from more famous wineries. Cavalier Bartolomeo's Altenasso Nebbiolo vines are planted at about 220-240 meters above sea level with a south/southwest exposure. Most of them are forty-five years old, but about 500 plants are over sixty-five years of age. This Barolo was previously called Solanotto-Altenasso, as it included grapes from the nearby Solanotto vineyard district, but with the 2010 official naming of the vineyard districts with an MGAs, listing two separate vineyard districts on the label is no longer allowed (unless that happens to be the vineyard district's official name: this is the case with many of the commune of Novello, such as for example the vineyard districts of Bergera-Pezzolle and Corini-Pallaretta). The small percentage of Solanotto grapes notwithstanding (you can legally include up to 15% of grapes from another vineyard district and still call the wine with the name of the vineyard district from where 85% of the grapes were picked), Cavalier Bartolomeo's Barolo Altenasso improves markedly with two to three years in the bottle (it starts life out slightly tough and rustic), so this is one Barolo that really should not be opened too soon in life.

To my taste, comparing Cavalier Bartolomeo's Barolo Altenasso with Brovia's Barolo Garblet Suè (at the same age) shows that the former is fleshier, sweeter and rounder than the latter, which is marked by greater freshness and lift. Both showcase the ripe red cherry, mid-palate fruity flesh, and overall suave texture that so typifies the Barolos not just of the Altenasso but of Castiglione Falletto; and both are excellent, underrated Barolos that fly under the radar. In just a few words, Barolos that really speak of the Barolo Land Unit and its typical form of the Saint Agatha Fossil Marls Formation in that they are very easy to drink and to like, but with sneaky levels of concentration and reasonably good aging potential.

Benchmark wineries/Reference point producers of Barolo Altenasso: Brovia, Cavalier Bartolomeo.

ANNUNZIATA

Township	La Morra
Reference Map	See Map of La Morra MGAs (Ch. 10)
Size (ha) (Tot / Barolo MGA)	109.42 / 5.29
Production 2021 (hl)	256.15 (of which 57.45 hl of Barolo Riserva *MGA* and 26.47 hl of Barolo *MGA* Vigna)
Altitude	220 – 380 meters a.s.l. roughly
Exposure	Predominantly from north to northwest. East in the remaining parts.
N. Claimants MGA	7
Other grape varieties planted:	Barbera; Dolcetto; white varieties
Land Units	Land Unit of Barolo; Land Unit of La Morra; Land Unit of Castiglione
Soil (stage):	Tortonian

Producers claiming the MGA

Lorenzo Accomasso; Borgogno; Paola Capra; Cascina del Monastero; Silvio Grasso; Groppone; Mario Olivero.

Wines

Lorenzo Accomasso - Barolo Annunziata; **Brandini** – Barolo Annunziata; **Cascina del Monastero** - Barolo Annunziata (Bricco Riund); **Silvio Grasso** - Barolo Annunziata Vigna Plicotti;

What the producers say

Paolo Grasso (Silvio Grasso): "Our Barolo made from grapes grown in this vineyard district are used to make a specific wine called Barolo Annunziata Vigna Plicotti. We believe that the Vigna Plicotti is known for being a classically-styled Barolo; this specific vineyard, Plicotti, belongs to our family since 2000".

Ian's assessment of the vineyard district, its wines and its potential

The first thing to make sure is that you do not confuse this vineyard district with another that carries a similar name, Rocche dell'Annunziata. While the latter vineyard district is arguably one of Barolo's six-seven best, Annunziata is nowhere near that level: to help you understand, think of the name "Annunziata" in the same terms you would Puligny-Montrachet or Chassagne-Montrachet Villages: so not a *premier cru* and certainly not a *grand cru*, but at the same time, no doubt a source of very good, even excellent wines (I don't know about you, but to my way of thinking and to my taste, a good Puligny or Chassagne is still one of the world's greatest

Chardonnay wines). In fact, parts of the Annunziata vineyard district are quite a bit better (relative to making fine Barolo wines) than many other La Morra vineyard districts, or sections thereof. Broadly speaking (an apt choice of words, given its size), the Annunziata vineyard district is characterized by very different soil lithologies (various types of Saint Agatha Fossil Marls and even Diano Sandstone Formation in the Castiglione Land Unit) and mineral concentrations throughout its extension (therefore, there exists in Annunziata a range of soil composition from sections with a higher limestone content to those where sand dominates). It follows that wines made from grapes grown in this vineyard district can boast varying degrees of power or grace, depending on where exactly the grapes are sourced from. And while for the most part Barolo Annunziata wines are on the light and perfumed side, in fact there is a large spectrum of potentially different types of Barolo that can be made from Annunziata.

Annunziata producers and the wines

Silvio Grasso's Barolo Annunziata Vigna Plicotti is by far the most famous wine from this vineyard district and it is more tannic than the majority of Barolos I have tried that were/are said to be made with grapes from the Annunziata vineyard district; however, I cannot help but wonder if my impression is just a function of Grasso's winemaking style, more so than of any defining trait of the Plicotti vineyard. The estate owns a really beautiful stretch of vines, about one hectare of Nebbiolo in the famous Vigna Plicotti site (careful now, don't confuse it with the similarly-sounding Vigna Plucotti: see below) that are roughly forty to fifty years old, face southeast and are planted at 250 meters above sea level. The wine is full-bodied, but pliant and silky, with very succulent and pure rose petal, violet and red cherry aromas and flavors. There is an underlying steely tannic backbone to this Barolo that is hardly typical of La Morra, and that will have you thinking of Serralunga (which is, by the way, exactly how they refer to this Barolo in the family, jokingly calling it their "Serralunga" wine).

Another fine estate making an excellent Barolo Annunziata is Cascina Monastero. Owned by the Grasso family (don't confuse the umpteen Grasso families all making wine in Barolo and Barbaresco!), this estate was founded in 1990 when Giuseppe Grasso decided to part ways with his brother and set up shop, so to speak, on his own. In 1993 he began to produce his first Barolos, and when vintage conditions allowed, single-vineyard district Barolos too from Bricco Luciani and Bricco Rocca. In the 2000's, it was Annunziata's turn to have a Barolo made from its grapes. And speaking of avoiding confusion, beware that Cascina Monastero's Barolo Annunziata is made from the Vigna Plucotti (Plucotti, not Plicotti, which is instead the one that Silvio Grasso bottles); in fact, the two are located on opposite flanks of the same hillside. Cascina Monastero's vineyard is divided in two parts, one in which the Nebbiolo vines were planted in 1964, while the other dates back to 2010. Perhaps not the last word in complexity or mouthcoating richness, this is a nonetheless lovely and easy to drink Barolo. Given how little prestige this vineyard district has, it's hard not to think that these two wines actually make it (or more accurately, specific sections of it) come out looking pretty darn good.

The Fratelli Revello estate of La Morra also farms vineyards in Annunziata. Brothers Enzo and Carlo split up in 2013, dividing up their holdings between them; the first vintage they vinified in separate wine cellars is the 2016. Enzo kept the original estate name of Fratelli Revello, and among the vineyards he ended up with from the split were also those of the Annunziata. The grapes from this site have always been blended with those of the Bricco Manescotto and used to make the estate's classic Barolo blend (the Annunziata is where they also have Barbera vines, with which they produce their Barbera d'Alba Ciabot du Re).

Beginning with the 2018 vintage, the Mario Oliviero estate will begin making a Barolo del Comune di La Morra, that takes the place of their Barolo previously called Vigne Unite. This is because this Barolo will now be made with grapes from three La Morra vineyard districts, two of which have recently come into the estate's fold (thanks to a ten-year rental agreement): Annunziata and Boiolo. The grapes from these two vineyard districts will be blended with those of the Bricco Rocca (from where the Mario Oliviero estate made a single-vineyard district Barolo from the 2009 to the 2015 vintages included). Oliviero's holdings in Annunziata are planted on Saint Agatha Fossil Marls soils of the sandy type at about 300 meters above sea level. Clearly, it is too early to tell what those grapes may give, but their old age (their Annunziata Nebbiolo vines were planted way back in 1968) is cause for excitement.

Benchmark wineries/Reference point producers of Barolo Annunziata: Cascina del Monastero, Silvio Grasso.

ARBORINA

Township	La Morra
Reference Map	See Map of La Morra MGAs (Ch. 10)
Size (ha) (Tot / Barolo MGA)	10.81 / 5.41
Production 2021 (hl)	266.36
Altitude	250 – 320 meters a.s.l. roughly
Exposure	From south to southeast in the central part, east on the lateral position
N. Claimants MGA	7
Other grape varieties planted:	Barbera; Dolcetto
Land Units	Land Unit of La Morra
Soil (stage):	Tortonian

Producers claiming the MGA

Elio Altare; Gianfranco Bovio; Giovanni Corino; Renato Corino; Marco Curto (Nadia); Erbaluna; Mauro Veglio.

Wines

Elio Altare - Barolo Arborina; **Gianfranco Bovio** - Barolo Arborina; **Giovanni Corino** - Barolo Arborina; **Renato Corino** - Barolo Arborina; **Marco Curto** - Barolo Arborina, Barolo La Foia; **Mauro Veglio** - Barolo Arborina.

What the producers say

Renato Corino: "At the old Govanni Corino estate, we started cultivating our Arborina plot already in 1968; in 1995 we decided to no longer blend its grapes with those of our other vineyards, and began bottling it apart, as a Barolo Arborina. Arborina is always more exposed to winds and susceptible to hail than other surrounding vineyard districts, but gives a Barolo that is more refined, more feminine if you will allow me, with respect to those other nearby crus. For me, that's where its charm lies".

Nadia Curto (Marco Curto): "We were farming this vineyard already in 1950. The Barolo from this vineyard is known for its elegance, drinkability, and aromatic richness with a lovely note of rose petals and a hint of mint. If I really had to criticize something about it, then I would say that its wines are not blessed with a powerful structure".

Mauro Veglio: "Arborina is a Barolo that is characterized by its elegance and freshness. Fresh notes of small red fruits, raspberry, redcurrants, wild roses, which will evolve into licorice and spices in time. Complex, but extremely delicate, Arborina wines are similar to the others from La Morra vineyard districts with their freshness and elegance. When young, one can appreciate more the freshness of Arborina's wines. It's a freshness with an edge, but harmony and balance are also perceptible early on. With time, the wine softens a little but maintains nonetheless its original personality for still a few years in good cellars".

Giuliano Corino (Corino): "I think it is important to underline that Arborina's soil is mostly clay and loam, with a little sand that runs throughout the site. Its clay component is important, a much darker clay than that for example of the nearby Giachini vineyard district, but with sandy veins making it more or less friable in sections. Generally speaking, Arborina is a more south-facing site too, and for me it is always characterized by a more expressive nose but also tougher tannins than some other La Morra vineyard districts".

Ian's assessment of the vineyard district, its wines and its potential

At roughly eleven hectares (10.81 hectares, to be exact), Arborina is one of the smaller vineyard districts (see Chapter 10: BAROLO MGA VINEYARD DISTRICTS: MAPS AND LAND UNITS) located in the Annunziata fraction of the La Morra commune (just northwest of Annunziata itself). Roughly circular in its extension, Arborina is completely surrounded by the La Morra vineyard districts of Rocchettevino and Annunziata; its vineyard area is on the side of a hill that slopes up in the direction of the Cascina Nuova, towards the village of Ciotto. From a topographical standpoint, thanks to its small size, Arborina is a fairly homogenous vineyard district; however, it is the central portion, with its south/southeast exposure, that is held to be the best as far as quality Barolo is concerned (the two extremities of the vineyard district curve somewhat, and thereby have less favorable exposures for Nebbiolo). I have always found that Arborina's typically fruit-forward, politely-styled Barolos speak of its La Morra Land Unit, characterized by a predominance of Saint Agatha Marls

Formation of the sandy type (my data shows that Arborina has a bit more sand than other vineyard districts with a similar soil formation, but as we shall see shortly, soil-wise that is not the only relevant difference: parts of this vineyard district are characterized by pockets of Diano Sandstone, meaning a completely different lithology and so wines too).

Arborina is an excellent site from where to make Barolo, though my view has always been that it is not at the level of Barolo's very best vineyard districts. I'm actually in good company there. It is one of the many Barolo vineyard districts that has risen to fame over the years mostly because of one producer's talent: if it had not been for Elio Altare Arborina might not have reached the (deserved) fame it has. In fact, the vineyard district's name itself (*arbor/arboretum*, meaning trees or forest), tells you that a long time ago nobody ever thought of planting vines there. Furthermore, the vineyard is climatically challenged, with adverse weather effects such as hail not exactly rare, which by definition excludes it from the discussion of Barolos top sites (for example, hail hit Arborina hard in 2006, but in that outstanding if difficult vintage many other vineyard districts were not). As one famous La Morra producer told me flatly and perhaps somewhat crudely, "… Arborina didn't even exist as such once: it is a recent creation, a *cru* that has become famous on the strength of the talent level of the people who farm it, much as we have seen happen with some very overrated Burgundy *premier crus*". Over the years some other producers have voiced more or less the same opinion.

A very good way by which to gain an understanding of the site's reality was (and still is, if you can find the wines) to taste, side by side, three different Elio Altare Barolos from the same vintage (unfortunately he is no longer making them, and that's why I wrote "was"): the Barolo Arborina, the Barolo Brunate (made from grapes Altare used to trade for with Marco Marengo of the excellent Mario Marengo estate) and Barolo Cannubi. While all three were (and still are) absolutely magnificent wines (Altare's talent is peerless and not many have ever gotten as much out of Arborina as he has), it's almost embarrassing how much deeper, complex and just plainly better the Barolo Brunate was (and is) compared to Arborina, with the Barolo Cannubi floating around somewhere in its own unique "Cannubiness" (but still clearly a much deeper and more complex Barolo than the Arborina). That said, I want to make clear that the Altare Barolo Arborina was and is a really excellent wine, so I do not wish to imply that it is a wine unworthy of attention, praise, high scores and all the rest of it; quite the contrary. But much like it is with the Barolo Arborina wines also made by other outstanding La Morra producers, when compared to the Barolos from other famous vineyard districts made by those same producers, the Arborina wine is rarely the best of the bunch.

There are parts to Arborina that are undoubtedly of very good *Premier Cru*-level status. In fact, few people are aware that locals have always talked about two different Barolos made from Arborina: the so-called *Arborina di testa* (*testa* or head, mostly south-facing but that also turns slightly to the east) and an *Arborina di coda* (*coda* or tail, from southeastern-facing vines, but situated at the other end of this specific section of the vineyard district, after it has arched in a fully southern direction). It's hard to say if one of the two extremities is better than the other; but if I had to decide based upon my experience tasting these wines, I'd point out that there are fewer better Arborina wines than Giuliano Corino's (of the Corino estate), and that his vines are located in the coda section of the vineyard district. Perhaps not unrelated to this observation, and notwithstanding Giuliano's amazing level of talent, this is the section of Arborina that boasts a higher soil sand content (a relative statement in and of itself, because sand content is low throughout Arborina, a mostly loamy-clay site).

Arborina producers and the wines

Undoubtedly, the two Corino estates, Corino (run by Giuliano Corino) and Renato Corino (run by, appropriately enough, Renato Corino), have had a great deal of experience with Arborina over the years. I find that Giuliano's wines from Arborina express greater florality on the nose and more refinement (of its tannins too). By contrast, the soils of the central and the *testa* portions of Arborina have more clay, and wines made from grapes grown there invariably speak more of red fruits than flowers, and generally have bigger and more assertive but generally round tannins (none of which is a bad thing, clearly). Kicking this level of knowledge up a notch (or two), it is also worth knowing that some sections of the clay-rich portions of the cru boast the presence of ferrous inclusions, and these slightly reddish-hued spots give wines that boast a hint of spice and thicker mouthfeels than the majority of Arborina's wines. Clearly, those who appreciate a little tannic oomph prefer Arborina wines made with grapes sourced from such spots. According to Renato Corino, Arborina wines made with grapes grown on the red clay-rich soils also usually have a slightly higher total acidity level and lower pH, making their tannins stand out even more. He finds that Arborina is much better overall than are large parts of the Annunziata vineyard district, for example (he's certainly not wrong there). You know, given how very good to excellent all the wines from Arborina usually are, when it is all said and done, whether you think very highly of the vineyard site or just highly, may well just boil down to a case of different strokes for different folks.

Mauro Veglio (Veglio is yet another common family name in Barolo) is another producer of an excellent Barolo Arborina. This estate's vines face south/southeast and were planted in Arborina in the early 1970s and in 1988 at about 280 meters above sea level (from 250-300 meters in altitude range). Without doubt, I believe the barolo Arborina is not just the freshest, but also the most elegant of all of Mauro Veglio Barolos. It really is a very pretty wine.

Last but not least, I wish to point out that Lorenzo Accomasso (of the Accomasso winery in La Morra), someone who really knows what he's talking about, repeatedly told me over the years that he always liked Arborina wines. Honestly, that's got to count for something. According to his recollections, back in the 1950s he used to drink excellent Barolos that were made by blending grapes from Arborina and Conca (another well-known La Morra vineyard district). Clearly, those wines are all gone now, but I for one would have loved to taste them and see just what it was about them that Accomasso so liked. I have nothing but admiration for Accomasso, and as he knows a lot more about La Morra's wines than I ever will, and so I take his viewpoints seriously.

Benchmark wineries/Reference point producers of Barolo Arborina: Altare, Corino. Also good: Bovio, Renato Corino, Veglio.

ARIONE

Township	Serralunga d'Alba
Reference Map	See Map of Serralunga d'Alba MGAs (Ch. 10)
Size (ha) (Tot / Barolo MGA)	5.72 / 3.1
Production 2021 (hl)	167.96 (of which 142.12 hl of Barolo Riserva *MGA*)
Altitude	330 – 435 meters a.s.l. roughly
Exposure	From south to southwest
N. Claimants MGA	2
Other grape varieties planted:	
Land Units	Land Unit of Serralunga d'Alba
Soil (stage):	Serravallian

Producers claiming the MGA

Enzo Boglietti; Giacomo Conterno.

Wines Enzo Boglietti - Barolo Arione; **Giacomo Conterno** - Barolo Arione

What the producers say

Enzo Boglietti: "We acquired this vineyard in 1999 and we have vinified it on its own since 2003. We believe Arione gives generally fine, elegant and complex wines. In the more difficult years, its wines are too delicate and probably best used in blends. Among the last fifteen vintages or so, in our view the site performed best in 2004 and 2010".

Maurizio Rosso (Gigi Rosso): Owner of the vineyard until 2015 when the Rosso family sold it to the Giacomo Conterno estate, Maurizio recalls that "… We acquired this vineyard in the '60s and began bottling its wine as Barolo Arione in the '70s. In 1982, we launched the Barolo Arione Riserva dell'Ulivo, a reserve wine. In my experience, the Barolo Arione often offers very rich aromas of faded flowers, ripe fruits with typical balsamic notes that can, in some years, be reminiscent of mint leaves. It is a full-bodied wine, warm and intense, dry and tannic, with mineral notes. Its aromatic plenitude and powerful structure make it a Barolo that ages well. Arione has a very unique microclimate, as is attested by the fact that in the center of the Cascina Arione, in the heart of our Arione estate, there stands an olive tree that has survived cold

Piedmontese winters for more than 100 years. It is the best testimony to the exceptional microclimate of that unique spot within the Arione vineyard district, and it is why we chose the tree to be the name of our Barolo Riserva. We just find that in the best vintages, grapes from the Ulivo vineyard (approximately 0.8 hectares large) reach a degree of ripeness and intensity of perfume that are uncommon for Serralunga. A powerful wine, it could stand up to extended oak aging, and so we used to age it for more than four years in the barrel and then in bottle (only in the fifth year could the wine legally become a Riserva back then) and we made approximately 3,900 bottles/year (only in the best vintages). Complex, ethereal and earthy, with aromas of licorice, black cherry, dried figs and plums, complicated by hints of clove, smoke and slate, it's just a very powerful Barolo, as only those of from Serralunga can be".

Roberto Conterno (Giacomo Conterno): "Long before I bought Gigi Rosso's holdings in Arione, I had always thought it to be an excellent site that made very lovely Barolos, and so I wanted a shot at vinifying its grapes. I believe Arione gives extremely refined wines characterized by lateral, slippery tannins, and an almost ethereal light-bodied personality. It never became famous as a Barolo *cru* because it was owned by small farmers, mostly ex-sharecroppers, who needed to survive and in order to do so planted Barbera there, not Nebbiolo. Back then, the wines of the former were much easier to sell. And so, Arione never became famous as it probably might have deserved".

Ian's assessment of the vineyard district, its wines and its potential

Arione is the southernmost vineyard district of the Serralunga commune, closed off to the northwest and northeast by the Boscareto and Francia vineyard districts, respectively. It is the first Serralunga vineyard district you come to as you drive northwards when entering into Serralunga's territory (Arione's vineyards are on your left, facing to the south and southwest). It is relatively high-altitude site though actually it is lower down than the other Serralunga vineyard districts to the north. It is characterized by the Land Unit of Serralunga, hence has a Lequio Formation lithology with soils that are compacted sands alternating with marls, plus limestone. It is the typical soil of Serralunga, and it really defines its wines: high in acidity, steely, very tannic, not immediately and obviously fruity, with a vibrancy quite unlike the Barolos of any other commune. Perhaps not for everyone, but to know Serralunga Barolo is to love it.

Like with many other Barolo vineyard districts, gauging the exact quality potential of Arione and its wines has always been hard because up until recently there weren't that many producers making wine from there. Clearly, the fact that Bruno Giacosa made wines from this vineyard district in the 1970s (to be precise, in the 1971, 1976 and 1978 vintages) certainly speaks well for the site. Given what I know of Bruno, and even taking into account his love for Serralunga Barolos and his huge lifelong friendship with Gigi Rosso (who owned vines and sold Arione grapes), he would not have bought grapes from the site if he didn't think it was at least a very good one. Certainly, when it comes to Arione, I find there are things to like and others not so much. Among the former, Arione is a fairly calcareous site (though percentage-wise, the limestone is not as present as it is in Serralunga's best and most famous vineyard districts) and therefore delivers wines of pleasant citrussy, refreshing acidity. The acid presence is such that Arione's wines have noteworthy lift in most vintages and are lighter on the palate than might be expected from a Serralunga vineyard district, leaving in the best vintages a really enchanting, unique impression of lifted steeliness on the palate (and in your memory cells). And thanks to a slightly higher percentage of sand (but see below), Arione's wines are also characterized by a rigid but refined tannic framework (for a site in Serralunga, Arione's are generally lighter-styled wines, characterized by, to use Roberto Conterno's very apt words, "*lateral*" tannins as opposed to for example Francia's more assertive "*frontal*" tannins). Among the latter factors, those that make me like Arione less, is its mesoclimate: the site is prone to inclement weather, as opposed to truly blue chip Serralunga grapevine real estate (for example, Vignarionda, or even Francia, just slightly further up the road). Arione is one of the most open and luminous valleys in all of Serralunga, but this also means vines are fully exposed to the vagaries of fickle weather patterns (i.e., hail), to a greater extent as such than more "upstream" vineyard districts (for example, Francia and Ornato, where hail strikes less frequently, for the simple reason that the meteorological turbulence conditions that might lead to hail formation lose power and thrust by the time they reach the Serralunga vineyard districts further upstream).

Though not especially large (in fact Arione is one of the smaller vineyard districts in the Serralunga denomination: see Chapter 10, BAROLO MGA VINEYARD DISTRICT: MAPS AND LAND UNITS), I can still, easily, make a case that not all of Arione is of the same quality level; for example, there are parts of the vineyard district that strikes me as having a lot more in common with that of the Roddino township rather than that of Serralunga. I could be wrong of course, and after all, I do wear glasses. That much admitted, I believe there is also a difference between the central section of Arione and its western section, meaning by that the ridge close to the border with the Boscareto vineyard district. If you go looking there, you will find that while the soil is still calcareous-clay in nature and poorly fertile, there is an uptick in the loam content and consequently of its fertility. In my estimation, it's an area that while good for Nebbiolo, is probably more suited to making very fine Barbera d'Alba and/or Langhe Nebbiolo wines.

Arione producers and the wines

It almost goes without saying that the individual (and estate) who did the most to showcase what Arione wines were about over the years was Gigi Rosso who owned almost the entire vineyard (ever since 1974, though they owned vines in Arione already back in the 1960s), but unfortunately there were no other Gigi Rosso Barolos made from other vineyard districts (and from the same vintage) to compare with those they made from Arione. In my experience, Gigi Rosso's Arione wines were slowly maturing and of potentially noteworthy tannic refinement, but with a lovely aromatic presence and a tendency to develop notes of tar rather quickly (much more so than the wines of other producers making wines from the nearby Francia or Boscareto vineyard districts, for example). As already mentioned, the Gigi Rosso estate sold its stake in Arione to the Giacomo Conterno estate in order to expand their winery in Castiglione Falletto and develop new vineyard sites, so we have no longer any Gigi Rosso Barolo Arione wines to compare with those of other producers. (The Rosso family continued to sell its remaining stock of Barolos from the Arione vineyard district from 2011, 2012, 2013 and 2014 vintages after the sale until their stock was all sold.)

As always, in order to come to a (more or less) informed and hopefully objective decision of any site's potential, a good tactic is to look at how the wines from the site compare in the same vintage with other Barolos from the same producer (provided vine age is comparable and the producer uses the same farming practices and winemaking techniques to make all his or her wines). This is easy enough to do with the Boglietti estate's many excellent single vineyard district wines. Boglietti owns 0.7 hectares in Arione, planted in 1999 with four different Nebbiolo clones (but beware that the winery website has not been updated and still says two only, when in fact it should be: clone 230 (40%), clone 142 (35%), clone 36 (15%), and clone CN 111 (10%), facing south/southwest at 450 meters above sea level on mostly silty-sandy soil with high content of marine fossils. Thanks to the relatively high sand content present here (but I believe the presence of clone CN 111, a clone of Nebbiolo Rosé that plays a very noteworthy role, even at only 10%: see chapter 3, NEBBIOLO ROSÉ). Boglietti's Arione Barolo is always very elegant, rather floral, ethereal even, characterized by fine tannins (the employment of a long post-fermentation time on the skins is aimed at further increasing elegance). In many ways, I find that Boglietti's Barolo Arione is the most elegant of all their Barolos, a real iron fist in velvet glove but a remarkably lithe one. It shares the perfumed nature of the estate's Barolo Fossati (both wines have Nebbiolo Rosé to thank), but it also boasts a Serralunga austerity and steeliness that Boglietti's Barolo from Fossati does not have. For sure, all Barolos from Arione need to be tasted carefully, since the site does not deliver wines that impress because of huge amounts of flesh and power; they are Barolos that play instead the cards of refined, lifted austerity and purity of red fruit. Unfortunately, those last two qualities are not always a winning hand with less experienced wine lovers and professionals.

The refinement of Arione's Barolo is very evident when tasting from barrel and bottle at Giacomo Conterno with Roberto Conterno, who runs the show brilliantly. Tasting the Barolos from Francia, Cerretta and Arione side by side is revelatory, because while all have their selling points and are truly remarkable wines, the Arione jumps out for its sheer elegance and harmonious mouthfeel. In fact, if the amazingly good Arione wines made by Roberto Conterno are any indication, the exact potential of Arione may yet surprise us all. After all, it has to mean something that in the 2015 vintage Conterno thought his best Barolo overall to be the Francia, but that he also believed that the single best barrel of Barolo he made in that vintage was from Arione. Suffice it to say that the 2015 Monfortino was the first to include some Arione grapes, so that tells you all you need to know about Arione's fine wine potential. A potential that perhaps has not yet been yet fully brought to the surface. I don't know about you, but my wine glass is ready and waiting.

Benchmark wineries/Reference point producers of Barolo Arione: Boglietti, Giacomo Conterno.

ASCHERI

Township	La Morra
Reference Map	See Map of La Morra MGAs (Ch. 10)
Size (ha) (Tot / Barolo MGA)	83.96 / 4,69
Production 2021 (hl)	255.29
Altitude	270 – 400 meters a.s.l. roughly
Exposure	Predominantly west
N. Claimants MGA	4
Other grape varieties planted:	Barbera; Dolcetto; white varieties
Land Units	Land Unit of Berri
Soil (stage):	Messinian

Producers claiming the MGA

Ascheri; Ellena (Giuseppe Ellena); Giancarlo Marengo; Reverdito.

Wines

Ellena (Giuseppe Ellena) - Barolo Ascheri (and Riserva); **Reverdito** - Barolo Ascheri

What the producers say

Michele Reverdito (Reverdito): "We have owned plots in this vineyard since 1985 and we thought so highly of the site that we immediately started bottling it separately from our other holdings, putting its name on the label. In our opinion, the vineyard district Ascheri offers wines that have an intense nose that is at once floral and spicy, often deploying a rich note of caramel and of balsamic oils that in our opinion are not due to the oak. It delicately enters the palate with a real sweetness but is always a wine of massive structure that will go a long way".

Ian's assessment of the vineyard district, its wines and its potential

A gently sloping hill at the far north of the La Morra township's territory that looks towards Verduno, Ascheri the site has the same name of a Barolo producer. In the Langhe it is not at all uncommon for sites to carry names derived from those of ancient local landowners (for example, Cannubi Boschis, a name derived most likely from the local Boschis family). Location-wise, Ascheri the vineyard district is situated next to La Morra's Castagni vineyard district and immediately to the south of Verduno's San Giacomo vineyard district with which it shares all of its northeastern border. The Sant'Anna vineyard district is to its southwest. This placement within the La Morra commune's territory is important because it tells us a good deal (or should tell us) about what to expect from wines made with grapes grown there. While Ascheri's soil has some pockets of iron-rich clay, being located close to the Tanaro River it is not surprising to learn that its soils are mostly alluvial silt in origin (Ascheri's lithology is that of the Cassano-Spinola Formation of the marly type, which is not an unexpected finding: it is the most typical lithology of the northwestern La Morra area and of the lower portion of the Verduno commune's territory, such that other nearby vineyard districts like Neirane in Verduno and Castagni in La Morra are also characterized by it (see Chapter 7, BAROLO TERROIR. Subchapter, Barolo geology). Given its proximity to the river, Ascheri is a relatively warm site (though not quite as warm as you might infer given the river's nearby presence). Though no monsters of concentration and palate weight (this is La Morra, after all), this vineyard district's wines tend to be generous straightshooters, with an earthy nuance and notes of red cherry (more often than not of cherries macerated in alcohol rather than fresh cherries). In short, medium-bodied wines that have a degree of opulence, with less of the lightness of being typical of the Barolos of La Morra (and of Verduno, for that matter) and that you'd expect from this section of La Morra.

Ascheri producers and the wines

In fact, only rarely does one find Ascheri-named Barolos, either from well-known or little-known estates. One little-known but good wine that carries the "Ascheri" vineyard district name is made by the Giuseppe Ellena estate (now run mostly by Giuseppe's son Matteo). It's a medium-weight Barolo (Ellena owns a small plot just about one hectare large planted to fifty or more years old vines); and though I have limited experience with the wine as Ellena started estate-bottling again only in 2009, it strikes me as one of the freshest and livelier Barolos made from the Ascheri vineyard district (but keep in mind I've tasted only four vintages of it thus far, so it's hard to arrive at far-reaching conclusions). Interestingly, Ellena was able to make a Riserva wine in 2009 (a hot year) and that the 2017 (another much too hot year) is actually also a very pretty wine, not that far off the quality level of the 2016 (a much better vintage) provides food for thought.

Michele Reverdito is another producer that also makes a good Barolo Ascheri (their first vintage dates back to 2000), in the estate's typically richer, fleshier, almost chocolaty-accented style. The wine used to be called Moncucco, but was later changed over to that of the vineyard district when these names became the official coin in 2010 (the same happened to his Barolo previously named Codane: after 2010, it was renamed Castagni, like the name of the vineyard district where the grapes used to make it are sourced from).

And last, I guess it couldn't really be that Ascheri, the producer, would not produce a Barolo Ascheri; and in fact, he does (the family once lived in the area). Beginning in 1999, Ascheri the estate launched a number of single-vineyard district designated Barolo wines, but their Ascheri from the vineyard district in La Morra was released for the first time only in 2010. In Ascheri the site, Ascheri the producer owns roughly 1.5 west-facing hectares planted at about 330 meters above sea level (roughly at mid-slope, a good spot to be). The wine is large-shouldered yet lifted, and it provides an interesting contrast, not to mention learning opportunity, with the same producer's Barolo Pisapola from the Verduno township; while the Ascheri is more horizontal, the Pisapola is more vertical, and both are fairly saline. As it often happens in Barolo (and not just Barolo), differences between two are not related to the quality of the wines but to individual wine traits, and so which you prefer will boil down to a case of different strokes for different folks.

Benchmark wineries/Reference point producers of Barolo Ascheri: Ascheri, Giuseppe Ellena.

BABLINO

Township	Grinzane Cavour
Reference Map	See Map of Grinzane MGAs (Ch. 10)
Size (ha) (Tot / Barolo MGA)	4.00 / 0.0
Production 2021 (hl)	0
Altitude	230 – 265 meters a.s.l. roughly
Exposure	From west to northwest and a small part facing northeast
N. Claimants MGA	-
Other grape varieties planted:	Barbera; Dolcetto
Land Units	Land Unit of Barolo
Soil (stage):	Tortonian

Ian's assessment of the vineyard district, its wines and its potential

Bablino is one of the Barolo's denominations smallest vineyard districts of all: at all of four hectares, it finds itself in the bottom-feeding positions of the vineyard districts listed by size in hectares (see chapter 10, BAROLO MGA VINEYARD DISTRICTS: MAPS AND LAND UNITS). Located in the Grinzane Cavour commune at in the northeastern reaches of the denomination, Bablino is situated south and east of the town of Gallo d'Alba's most developed area and next to Raviole, a slightly better-known and much larger vineyard district. Bablino's altitude is not especially noteworthy, while it's mostly northern exposure certainly is and explains the dearth of Barolo Bablino wines made to date. Also noteworthy is that Bablino's landscape can be classified as that of the Land Unit of Barolo, even though this vineyard districts located in the commune of Grinzane Cavour which is generally characterized by the Land Units of Serralunga and that of Gallo d'Alba. What this means is that Bablino's soil lithology is consistent with that of the Saint Agatha Fossil Marls of the classic or typical form (that some believe to be synonymous with the Gallo d'Alba Marls Formation, but not every geology luminary agrees with this view) and therefore you'd expect its Barolos to be somewhat similar to those made in parts of the communes of Barolo and parts of La Morra.

At the time of writing, there are no Barolo Bablino wines made, and so it follows that it is hard to say much that's useful about the vineyard district's wines and its exact fine Barolo-making potential. More often than not, the grapes from Bablino are used to make an estate's classic Barolo wines as was typical of the past, when Barolos were the result of blends of grapes from many different vineyard sites. One example of this is the Barolo of the Bricco Carlina estate (founded in 2014, their first Barolo vintage was the 2015) that fashions its classic Barolo by blending grapes from the vineyard districts of Bablino, Castello and Raviole, all in the Grinzane Cavour commune. All of these vineyard districts are characterized by calcareous-clay soils and the vines basically have south/southwest exposures, but my experience with the wine is very limited. Normally, with many vineyard areas all over Italy, I have accumulated specific tasting experience over the years by tasting individual microvinifications or by tastings from individual tanks, prior to the wines all being blended into a final estate bottling. Unfortunately, I haven't been able to do so with the Nebbiolo wines from Bablino, and as such I really cannot venture much of an informed and truly believable guess as to what the wines might be all about, or this vineyard district's exact fine Barolo potential, and so I'll pass.

Benchmark wineries/Reference point producers of Barolo Bablino: None currently available.

BADARINA

Township	Serralunga d'Alba
Reference Map	See Map of Serralunga MGAs (Ch. 10)
Size (ha) (Tot / Barolo MGA)	21.02 / 11.4
Production 2021 (hl)	617.87 (of which 18.60 hl of Barolo Riserva *MGA*)
Altitude	340 – 440 meters a.s.l. roughly
Exposure	Southeast in the better exposed parcels; northeast in the remaining parts
N. Claimants MGA	4
Other grape varieties planted:	Dolcetto
Land Units	Land Unit of Serralunga d'Alba
Soil (stage):	Serravallian

Producers claiming the MGA

Bersano; Bruna Grimaldi; Poderi Gagliassi; Reverdito.

Wines

Bersano - Barolo Badarina, Barolo Badarina Riserva; **Bruna Grimaldi** - Barolo Badarina; Barolo Badarina Riserva (Vigna Regnola); **Reverdito** - Barolo Badarina.

What the producers say

Bruna Grimaldi: "It's a vineyard that gives grapes with thick skins, rich in both tannins and color. Over the years we have learned to vinify our plots separately and then assemble them into a finished wine, as each sub-section of the vineyard has a different maturation curve and the grapes aren't all exactly the same. No matter, these are grapes that offer plenty of extract and structure in most vintages and so are ideally suited to long macerations".

Michele Reverdito (Reverdito): "We own this vineyard since 1999. Badarina sets itself apart with an intense nose, fresh with hints of berries (blackberry and raspberry), accompanied by a floral note. Delicate note of oak with hints of licorice. In the mouth, it is rich, structured and finishes long with tannic mouthfeel".

Ian's assessment of the vineyard district, its wines and its potential

Badarina is a vineyard district that gives very solid if not especially sexy Barolos but insiders who love Barolo know to look for wines from this site. For example, Bruna Grimaldi's Barolo Badarina is excellent, if little-known. Domenico Clerico's Barolo Aeroplanservaj, of which I have tasted every vintage of beginning with the first one directly with Clerico himself at the winery when it had not yet been released for sale and he was still deciding upon what to call it (I still have trouble bringing myself to thinking that Domenico is no longer with us), is also a lovely Barolo. Over the years, the overall quality level of Barolo Badarina wines has been such that the vineyard's potential has always struck me as being at the very least very good to excellent. I would venture to say that my estimation of Badarina's fine wine potential, say akin to that of a good *premier cru* level, is probably not lost out in left field somewhere, given the site's calcareous whitish soil (streaked with red throughout parts of the vineyard) and its high elevation (from 350-450 meters), never a bad thing in days of climate change. One of the steeper vineyard districts (when you lean from it you feel like you're falling off a precipice), Badarina's location close-by other well-known Serralunga vineyard districts such as Arione, Francia, Boscareto and Falletto (it's basically across the road from Francia and Boscareto, with the small northernmost sliver of Badarina across the road separating it from the bottom part of Falletto) also attests to the type of Barolo that can be made in this vineyard district.

Badarina's Barolo is a typical expression of the eastern flank of the southern reaches of the Serralunga commune (which is essentially divided in two by a long north-south running hillside ridge: Badarina is the eastern- and southernmost prolongation of the Serralunga ridge's eastern flank). These are Barolos that are quite different (slightly richer, rounder, fleshier) from those of the cooler, wilder, northern reaches of Serralunga but that thanks to the generally cooler eastern-facing flank still boast the typical Serralunga vibrancy and "iron fist" qualities (crunchy red fruit, high acidity, steely core). With Badarina, there is a little bit of the velvet glove too (though less so than in wines from Francia, for example, that is situated on the western flank of the ridge), a hint of velvet gloss not always present in this township's Barolos. In other words, despite its Lequio formation soil (which should translate to potentially quite tannic wines especially when young), I find that Badarina Barolos, though certainly tannic, are rarely mind-numbingly and palate-coating so. Perhaps not the most concentrated and complex Barolos you'll ever drink, but as far as Serralunga's potentially very tannic and tough when young Barolos go, Badarina's seem to have an innate balance to them, one that personally I quite like. They are also almost always fairly pale to medium red in color, which is very typical of Serralunga's nutrient-poor, sparse, limestony soils. Besides wines of noteworthy lift and linearity, I find Badarina's Barolos to share a musky-balsamic edge (that I have found over the years in the wines of both Bruna Grimaldi and Bersano, for example).

Badarina producers and the wines

Should you try Bruna Grimaldi's Barolo Badarina and try to make inferences as to what the site can deliver, beware the winemaking there has changed somewhat over the years, for example in relation to the oak regimen used. While the 2016 was aged only in large barrels (30 hectoliters) and was vinified for roughly 30 days on 50% submerged skins, the 2015 is an altogether different animal, aged half in new tonneaux and another half in 20-21 hectoliter barrels, the same regimen that had been adopted for the vintages preceding it. Clearly, the presence of newer and smaller oak slightly obfuscates the delivery of the site's message, though it's a wonderful wine. The Bruna Grimaldi estate also makes a Barolo Badarina Riserva from a special plot of relatively old vines (on average over 20 years of age) called Vigna Regnola (that usually ages 36 months in oak), located in the central and upper reaches of her holdings in the vineyard district (roughly at about 400 meters above sea level, and Badarina only goes as high up as about 440 meters.

Bersano is the largest landowner of Badarina, and its Barolo is somewhat underrated, always offering a fine, well-balanced drink that has the typical steely core, lift and perfume of Serralunga's wines. It is wines such as those of Bruna Grimaldi and Bersano that illustrate Badarina's potential capacity to give wines of complexity and sweetness that leads me to believe Badarina is not just an excellent site for Barolo production, but an underrated one at that.

Last but not least, you should know that Clerico's excellent Barolo Aeroplanservaj was made with Nebbiolo grapes from Badarina up until the 2008 vintage included. Then in 2009 a landslide took place in the rented vineyard and so the wine was not made. For this reason, beginning with the 2010 vintage, the Clerico winery has made the Barolo Aeroplanservaj with grapes from a rented vineyard in another Serralunga vineyard district, Baudana (the wine is labeled as Barolo del Comune di Serralunga d'Alba). This is extremely useful information to have because you can compare the Aeroplanservaj wines made before 2009 and those after that year: comparing between them allows you to grasp the different characteristics and nuances that the Badarina and the Baudana vineyard districts confer to the wines (see BAUDANA file).

Benchmark wineries/Reference point producers of Barolo Badarina: Bersano, Bruna Grimaldi. (Clerico up to the 2008 vintage).

BAUDANA

Township	Serralunga d'Alba
Reference Map	See Map of Serralunga d'Alba MGAs (Ch. 10)
Size (ha) (Tot / Barolo MGA)	19.00 / 8.05
Production 2021 (hl)	411.31 (of which 85.86 hl of Barolo Riserva *MGA*)
Altitude	230 – 360 meters a.s.l. roughly
Exposure	Southeast in the better exposed parcels; northeast in the remaining parts
N. Claimants MGA	6
Other grape varieties planted:	Barbera; Dolcetto; white varieties
Land Units	Land Unit of Castiglione in the higher parcels; Land Unit of Serralunga d'Alba in the remaining parts
Soil (stage):	Serravallian

Producers claiming the MGA

Flavio Baudana; Marco Gallo; G.D. Vajra; Poderi Sorì; Sandrone (Luciano Sandrone); Zunino.

Wines

Domenico Clerico - Barolo Aeroplanservaj; **G.D. Vajra** - **Baudana Luigi** - Barolo Baudana; **Cascina Adelaide** - Barolo Baudana; **Poderi Sorì** - Barolo Baudana; **Tenuta Rocca** - Barolo del Comune di Serralunga d'Alba.

What the producers say

Cascina Adelaide: "We acquired our parcel in Baudana back in 2011. We find this Barolo sets itself apart from others because of its notes of white peach and red cherry, ending on a long and flavorful finish – a symphony!".

Andrea Ciravegna (Tenuta Rocca): "The Barolo made from this *cru* is produced since 2012 and we choose to label it simply as "Barolo del Comune di Serralunga", rather than Baudana. The soil of this parcel gives rise to a more elegant Barolo with sweeter tannins and a paler color than our Barolo coming from Bussia. It's perhaps a slightly less flattering wine at first, certainly bolder and direct, but extremely elegant".

Aldo Vaira (G.D. Vajra): "We have rented this parcel of vines since 2009. Baudana is a rich Barolo of structure and minerality, and rather traditional, almost austere, in style. I think the clay soil confers to the wines the distinctive taste of Barolo di Serralunga, but the tannins are supple. The sweet fruit flavor intensifies on the long finish, making for a Barolo that is at once powerful, round and elegant".

Luca Sandrone (Sandrone): "I find Baudana is rather similar to Cerretta di Perno (another parcel we own since a few years ago now). This *cru* gives darker colored Barolo, richer and more concentrated than most, and with a remarkable tannic structure. The olfactory impact is more towards dried and stone fruits such as prunes and cherries. But with respect to Ceretta di Perno, Baudana's Barolo is almost always more concentrated, hinting at notes of fruit jam. Its concentration is apparent already on the nose but also in the mouth, while the acidity is less pronounced".

Ian's assessment of the vineyard district, its wines and its potential

Too many Baudanas: readers need to avoid getting confused between the vineyard district called Baudana, the village Baudana (*borgata* Baudana) from which it takes its name, and the wines of the producer Luigi Baudana (an estate now run by the Vajra family). Also, beware that the Luigi Baudana estate, among its various Barolo wines, also happens to make one from the Baudana vineyard district. And so it is that one day you might be able to say that you have tasted a Baudana Baudana! All kidding aside, Baudana is one of the northern vineyard districts of the Serralunga commune, from where you are just a hop, skip and jump away from the territories of Diano d'Alba and further on, Grinzane Cavour (two more of the Barolo's denomination eleven communes). And it's not just that there are too many Baudanas, because at only nineteen hectares and a whopping forty-five estates (at last count) claiming the vineyard district's name with which to potentially make a Baudana vineyard district specific Barolo, that's a whole mess of people tending to Baudanas's vines.

Perhaps such modern-day popularity shouldn't surprise, though it comes on the heels of a relatively undistinguished period for the site and its wines. In fact, until its recent surge in popularity, Barolos from

Baudana were a relatively rare sighting and no producer or winemaker I ever talked to in the 1980s and 1990s ever mentioned Baudana among Barolo's better or famous Nebbiolo sites. By contrast, a long time ago Baudana was well-regarded as a very fine source of Nebbiolo grapes. Old timers (really old) will tell you that in the early to mid-1900s local farmers could sell all their Baudana grapes without problems whatsoever. By their accounts, it appears that the *negozianti* clamored after Baudana's grapes and sold them to the area's big winemaking firms. It follows that because Baudana's grapes were easy to sell, there was no push for anyone who owned vines there to make their own wines. This was true as recently as the 1970s, when bottled Barolo was neither the big nor the remunerative thing it is today. By contrast and by comparison, the grapes from what is today's vineyard district Cerretta were less sought after; this might come as a surprise to many a reader and Barolo enthusiast, given that, of the two, Ceretta is the much better-known vineyard district today. However, it really should not be so: taken globally, Cerretta is undoubtedly a lesser-quality site compared to Baudana (if for no other reason because Cerretta vineyard district is much too large in its present-day extension, such that the lesser sections drag down the value of the whole vineyard district). Cerretta is more famous than Baudana today only because many famous producers have recently bought land in the former and are now making Barolos with that vineyard district's name on the label. Perhaps not unexpectedly, everybody's kneejerk reaction is to naturally talk up the quality of wines made by famous producers. Contributing to Cerretta's greater notoriety (at least compared to Baudana's) is the fact that it had a more fragmented property ownership, leading some of Cerretta's owners (those who owned small vineyard plots only or those who had a slightly harder time convincing *negozianti* to buy their grapes) to bottle small lot wines on their own (and in so doing, ended up making Cerretta's vineyards better known than Baudana's, the grapes of which were instead ending up mostly in estate blends).

Baudana the vineyard district straddles Serralunga ridge draping over the upper parts of both its flanks surrounding the *borgata* of same name (you can admire its vineyards very easily while driving -or much better, as a passenger in said car- along the provincial road SP 125, that runs atop the ridge and cuts through the *borgata*). From an aerial perspective, the vineyard district of Cappallotto is lower down on the same slope and to the west (don't confuse Cappallotto with La Morra's similarly-sounding Capalot vineyard district); to the south it is close to a small section of Meriame; the Cerretta vineyard district lies to its southeast and east; with the San Rocco and Costabella vineyard districts to the north. Masnaghetti (2018) believes Baudana's vines situated around the Cascina Belvedere and those close to Meriame to be particularly noteworthy: I remember Francesco Versio of Luigi Oddero telling me the same thing, and going as far as saying as that particular patch of Baudana vines should really go by the name of Belvedere. By contrast, I don't know much about Baudana's vines closer to Meriame and the kind of Baudana Barolo they can give: but if Masnaghetti says it's a good spot, then I'm happy taking his word for it (and given his level of knowledge of Barolo maps and geology, so should you). For sure, Baudana, though small, has a complex landscape, one that features elements of both the Land Unit of Castiglione and that of Serralunga, which imply the presence of lithologies mostly of the Diano Sandstone Formation and of the Lequio Formation, the two most typical of the Serralunga commune.

That said, Masnaghetti cites for Baudana a preponderance of Gallo d'Alba Marl Formation (which he prefers to call Saint Agatha Fossil Marls of the typical form) and only a secondary presence of Lequio Formation. This is not a moot point, given that those two (three?) soils, as we know (see Chapter 7, BAROLO TERROIR) are associated with very different Barolos. For Luciano Sandrone and a number of other local producers have always characterized Baudana's wines to me as being a mix of "*concentration and power*", which makes them seem less likely to be born off Saint Agatha Fossil Marls, but pinpointing exact geological realities is never easy. Clearly, Michele and I might be mistaken but this is what our research has established and so we will stick with our view and discuss the wines of Baudana accordingly.

Baudana producers and the wines

In my experience, Baudana gives powerful wines that when young are on average quite tough, austere and mineral. In short, they are very typical of the Barolos of the northern half of Serralunga commune. An excellent way by which to understand, or just simply get to know, the wines of the Baudana vineyard district is to compare different Barolos made by the G.D. Vajra winery in the same vintage. Their Barolo Bricco delle Viole (from the commune of Barolo) is dramatically different from the Barolo made from Baudana at the Luigi Baudana estate (as well as that of Ceretta, which the winery also farms and makes a Barolo from). When the two (or three) Barolos are compared at the same stage of development, Bricco delle Viole is a much "lighter" Barolo – lighter is a relative term with Barolo- than the more austere, tauter, tougher wine from Baudana. And this despite the employment of similar winemaking techniques (i.e., long macerations of 30-45 days and long aging in large oak casks). And even if such a tasting exercise might not help you pinpoint the exact characteristics of the Baudana vineyard district, it will certainly drive home the difference between a Barolo from the commune of Serralunga and one from the commune of Barolo.

Another well-regarded producer, Luigi Oddero, makes his classic Barolo with a good dollop of grapes from Baudana (Baudana the site, not the producer): last time I was able to visit the winery and meet with consultant winemaker Francesco Versio, just after the Covid pandemic broke out in a moment of respite (summer 2020) we had a chance to talk about Baudana. According to Versio, their vineyards in Baudana are about fifty years old and lie at about 280 meters above sea level, facing southwest. The winery does not make a Barolo Baudana as such, preferring to blend the grapes along with those in other sites to make their classic estate Barolo. That blend will change from vintage to vintage: recently, it has Nebbiolo grapes from La Morra's Rive (30%), Castiglione Falletto's Scarrone (or what the estate has always called Rocche dei Rivera; another 30%), and Serralunga d'Alba's Baudana and Broglio vineyard districts (about 40%). Please note that this mix is true of both the Luigi Oddero 2016 and 2015 Barolos (in which the grape provenance percentages from each *cru* are the same), while both their 2014 and 2013 Barolos had more grapes from La Morra (these two wines were made with 40% La Morra, 30% Castiglione Falletto and 30% Serralunga grapes; the wines in these two vintages differ also because of partly different vineyard districts from which the grapes were sourced, including Bettolotti in La Morra and Belvedere in Serralunga). All this makes it hard to understand the exact contribution of the Baudana vineyard district to Luigi Oddero's finished wine, but you can certainly tell that the '13 and '14 Barolos are much lighter on their feet than the '15 and '16 (and this independently of the fact the last two vintages gave bigger, fleshier wines). If nothing else, this does tell you just how big a difference an extra 10% Serralunga grapes can make in a finished wine. For sure, Versio believes that Baudana's wines are of the powerful and structured type.

As mentioned previously, so does Luciano Sandrone. According to Luciano, compared to Perno, another vineyard district he farms, the Barolo of Baudana is almost always more concentrated, hinting at notes of fruit jam. Sandrone believes the vineyard's concentration is apparent already on the nose but also in the mouth, while the acidity is less pronounced. He believes Baudana's grapes to be just what the doctor ordered to make his famous Barolo Le Vigne, in which he blends together the grapes of Baudana (concentration), Villero (power and elegance), Merli (fruitiness) and Vignane (balance). It's a great wine that combines the strength of each of its vineyard districts and the communes they belong to, and Baudana does its part.

Benchmark wineries/Reference point producers of Barolo Baudana: Luigi Baudana (G.D. Vajra).

BERGEISA

Township	Barolo
Reference Map	See Map of Barolo MGAs (Ch. 10)
Size (ha) (Tot / Barolo MGA)	7 .00/ 0.38
Production 2021 (hl)	20.01
Altitude	235 – 290 mt. a.s.l. roughly
Exposure	From southeast to northeast
N. Claimants MGA	1
Other grape varieties planted:	Barbera; Dolcetto; white varieties
Land Units	Land Unit of La Morra
Soil (stage):	Tortonian

Producers claiming the MGA

Le Strette.

Wines

Le Strette - Barolo Bergeisa.

What the producers say

Daniele Savio (Le Strette): "We bought our portion of this cru in 1998. This Barolo is characterized by elegance and its fine-grained tannins".

Ian's assessment of the vineyard district, its wines and its potential

Another of the Barolo's denomination's smaller-sized vineyard districts, Bergeisa isn't very well-known because of the paucity of producers bottling wines from it but it has always struck me as being a very fine site with the potential to give just as fine Barolo. Situated in the midst of the Barolo commune's vineyard districts of Cerequio, Albarealla, Zonchetta and Sarmassa, it drapes over the lower slope of a wedge-like conformation of the hilly ridge right next to Sarmassa. Bergeisa is characterized by a mostly marly-calcareous soil, a very steep gradient, and a not especially high altitude, all of which have direct bearing on the Barolos that are made from there. Its landscape is classified as Land Unit of La Morra, and its lithology of Gallo d'Alba Marls (that some researchers identify with one of the three Saint Agatha Fossil Marls Formations, precisely of the typical type) ensures the wines are nicely balanced, juicy, fruity, and smoothly tannic, in short very much like you'd expect a Barolo from the commune of Barolo or even La Morra to taste like. In fact, very similar to those of the portion of Sarmassa that lies next to it (the northeastern corner of the Sarmassa vineyard district) given that Bergeisa and that section of Sarmassa share the same lithology (beware that this piece of the Sarmassa vineyard district is very different from the rest of Sarmassa –especially compared to the southeastern part of Sarmassa that is closer to the town of Barolo and the San Lorenzo vineyard district; as a result of its geologic and topographical complexity, the wines from Sarmassa can differ greatly one from the other, though in general they are far more powerful and structured than wines from Bergeisa and that piece of Sarmassa next to it. See SARMASSA file).

Bergeisa producers and the wines

Le Strette's Barolo Bergeisa has always been my benchmark for this vineyard district. It is the only Barolo made by Le Strette that features grapes from the Barolo commune and not Novello (the latter is the commune the winery is located in and most associated with). The Le Strette Barolo Bergeisa is a very characteristic Barolo from the namesake commune, made from grapes growing at about 280 meters above sea level and facing southeast. The Nebbiolo vines were planted in 1982, and they tend to give Barolos that are very typical of that commune's wines; in other words, no blockbusters or ultra-tannic behemoths as you'd find from Monforte or Serralunga, but slightly bigger than many Barolos of La Morra (without their perfume, however) and more elegant and complex than the majority from Novello. With their Bergeisa, the Savio brothers (owners of Le Strette, but sadly Mauro passed away in 2021 after a long battle with a bad disease) offer all wine lovers a great opportunity to get to better know and understand the wines of this specific vineyard district. While not the most powerful or most complex Barolo you will ever drink (or even in the Le Strette portfolio, for that matter), I find it to be almost always the most balanced already at a young age, which is probably how I, you and everybody else should expect things to be. Over the years, it has struck me that Bergeisa is a site that gives Barolos that are more about fruit rather than herbs and spices (such as licorice, rhubarb, and nutmeg, though cinnamon does appear repeatedly in my tasting notes over the years) that more often than not seem to take a back seat. In any case, he Le Strette Barolo Bergeisa provides not just a delicious drinking experience but also a learning, and I dare say didactic, opportunity.

Benchmark wineries/Reference point producers of Barolo Bergeisa: Le Strette.

BERGERA-PEZZOLE

Township	Novello
Reference Map	See Map of Novello MGAs (Ch. 10)
Size (ha) (Tot / Barolo MGA)	48.69 / 15.06
Production 2021 (hl)	818.48
Altitude	350 – 420 meters a.s.l. roughly
Exposure	From east to southeast around Pezzole; predominantly southeast around Bergera
N. Claimants MGA	6
Other grape varieties planted:	Barbera; Dolcetto
Land Units	Land Unit of Vergne
Soil (stage):	Tortonian

Producers claiming the MGA

La Spinona; Le Strette; Luca Marenco; Angelo Rapalino; Roberto Sarotto; Viberti

Wines

La Spinona - Barolo Bergera; **Le Strette** - Barolo Bergera Pezzole; **Roberto Sarotto** - Barolo Bricco Bergera and Riserva Audace.

What the producers say

Daniele Savio (Le Strette): "We began farming and making wine from this cru in 1997. Bergera-Pezzole is a Barolo presenting an optimal amalgam of power and elegance, of spicy character, complexity and color".

Ian's assessment of the vineyard district, its wines and its potential

Located in the Novello commune, Bergera-Pezzolle is one of the many Novello vineyard districts that has a double name because it carries the names of the hamlets overlooking the vineyards, Bergera and Pezzolle (a collection of just a few houses: blink, and you'll miss them).

This vineyard district's landscape is characterized as a Land Unit of Vergne with a mostly Saint Agatha Fossils Marls of the laminated type lithology, with a little sand present among the clay, loam and limestone. This accounts at east in large measure for wines of a slightly gentler disposition than those of some other more clay-rich Novello vineyard districts such as for example large swaths of the Ravera vineyard district (which are instead characterized by the Land Unit of Novello, such that soils there are not just of the Saint Agatha Fossils Marls of the laminated type lithology, but also of the sandy type and of Diano Sandstone Formation. The large lithological diversity of the Ravera vineyard district helps explain the large spectrum of different Barolos that can be made there. See RAVERA file). In fact, though Bergera-Pezzole is named as if it were one entity, the reality is that the Bergera and the Pezzolle sections of the vineyard district are rather different, and so are, potentially at least, the wines that can be made from each. I write potentially because to date there aren't enough

Barolos made with Nebbiolo grapes from just one of the two subdivisions to gain a clear-cut understanding of what each can give (and sometimes getting the producers to tell you precisely which subdivision the grapes come from can be a chore). My observations about what Bergera might give compared to Pezzolle are based on microvinifications tasted before a final blend was made and/or on producer impressions, but clearly there isn't much opportunity to do so (at least not in a repeatable way year after year so has to give some semblance of validity to any conclusions one might want to derive from the exercise). The greater presence of sand in the Bergera portion of Bergera-Pezzolle (overall, the percentages of sand, loam and clay are about equal throughout the vineyard district, but it's worth knowing that Bergera has more sand while Pezzole has more clay (Pezzolle has about 38-40% soil clay, compared to the 27-30% soil clay content of Bergera) accounts for the more floral organoleptic profiles and the lighter-styled texture of Bergera's wines. The exposures are also slightly different: east and southeast for Pezzolle and southeast for Bergera, and that too has a bearing on the wines made from each. Bergera-Pezzolle wines develop well but slowly, leading many to wonder, when tasting the wines young, whether they will ever develop much complexity, at least compared to those of other famous vineyard districts. I think this may just be a function of vineyard age. For example, the Le Strette vines in this site were planted only in 1997 and 2009 (plus a small 0.3 hectares section set down in 2016) and so these are really not very old vines. With increased vine age, it is likely the Barolos of Bergera-Pezzolle are likely to show greater complexity than they do nowadays.

Bergera-Pezzolle producers and the wines

I would say the wines from Bergera-Pezzolle are excellent Barolos that often showcase an obvious note of ripe red fruit complemented by sweet spices; and if you're amongst those who likes their Barolo with an impactful and mouth-filling but juicy-fruity backbone, and I dare add a gentle soul too, then you too will agree with that assessment. However, I wish to point out that there is an inherent, and perhaps only potential, complexity to the Barolos from this site: trust me, the complete picture of the Bergera-Pezzolle Barolos is not one that is fully into focus yet. Whether it ever gets brought into focus is another matter, and much will depend on how popular wines from this vineyard district will become in time. Were they to encounter Monvigliero or Ravera degrees of success, you can rest assured that a lot more will become common knowledge about what Bergera-Pezzolle is really all about. Read on to get a taste of just what I mean.

The benchmark Bergera-Pezzolle Barolo is the one of the Le Strette estate (one of the wonderful things of a life devoted to wine is the memories you end up with: still today, I remember how easy it is to miss the winery, the search for which the first time I visited there something like twelve years ago, probably more, caused me more than a headache). Le Strette's vines in Bergera-Pezzolle are relatively high-altitude (400-420 meters above sea level) for the Barolo denomination; the grapes are blessed with plenty of sunlight, and so consequently Le Strette's Barolo from this vineyard district does showcase a ripe and fleshy side. However, it is also very Novello (or more precisely, of one part of Novello) in its austere, monolithic side (especially in its youth), and "tannically challenging" personality (if you allow me the term). It's a structured but fine-grained Barolo that offers a tactile, mouth-filling sensation: it also strikes me that Bergera-Pezzolle's wines are, at least in Le Strette's expression, somewhat more perfumed and lighter on their feet than the general average offered by Novello Barolos. The "expression" word there is key.

Another estate farming Nebbiolo in Bergera-Pezzole is the Viberti winery of Vergne (a fraction of the Barolo commune). Their vineyard holding is located in the Bergera side of the vineyard district at about 350 meters in altitude just below the Church of the Nativity. It faces south and looks towards the town of Novello. The soil there is loamy but with a very good proportion of both clay and sand: it all adds up to a Nebbiolo wine that is fruity and structured, but not at all austere. Given the limited vineyard extension of these rented vines, Viberti chooses to add the wine into the estate's classic Barolo Buon Padre blend made with grapes from as many as eight different vineyard district sources, depending on the vintage.

Not many people are aware that the Serio e Battista Borgogno estate in Barolo also produces a wine with Bergera-Pezzole grapes simply labeled "Barolo" (though depending on the vintage characteristics, grapes from other vineyard districts can be blended in). Though the vineyard district is the same, this estate farms vines at a much lower altitude than Le Strette (Serio e Battista Borgogno's are at about 350 meters above sea level: not 380 meters as has been written and re-written elsewhere) and I believe this shows through in the finished wines. The Bergera-Pezzolle grapes used by Serio e Battista Borgogno estate are farmed by the Rapalino family of

Novello (the family shares Serio e Battista Borgogno's viticultural and winemaking philosophy) with whom they have along working relationship. Interestingly, these vines face south-east and are located squarely in the middle of the Pezzole half of the Bergera-Pezzolle vineyard district, between the Nativity Church and Tarditi-Pezzole farmsteads (so removed from the Bergera-Saccati side). It's an area characterized by a mostly greyish-coloured marly soil that guarantees freshness as well as structure to the finished wines. Over the years, this sort of intel greatly helps when tasting the wines in arriving to some semblance of a conclusion on what characters the Barolos from the Pezzolle side of Bergera-Pezzole might have. This is especially useful when you taste Bergera-Pezzolle Barolos from the next estate I am going to tell you about.

And so, let me tell you about an outsider, one who is far removed from the Novello reality, and yet makes absolutely delightful wines from Bergera-Pezzolle. Did you know an estate in Barbaresco makes an excellent Barolo Bergera-Pezzolle? And so it is: the La Spinona estate in Barbaresco, owned by the Berutti family. Gualtiero and Pietropaolo Berutti own 4.16 hectares of fully south-facing vines that they have subdivided into two parts: an upper part that is one hectare large planted between 430-470 meters above sea level and from where (beginning with the 2017 vintage) it makes its Barolo Bergera-Pezzolle Sorì Gepin; and a lower portion, three hectares large, planted 360-430 meters above sea level and from where they make the Barolo Bergera-Pezzole (clearly distinguishable from the other thanks to its bright red label). Interestingly, these two were originally named Barolo Bergera and Barolo Bergera Sorì Gepin, but because of the official vineyard district nomenclature, they are now labeled as Bergera-Pezzolle rather than Bergera only; the Gepin is named after the grandfather that brought up owner Gualtiero Berruti). The two wines are different in that the grapes for the Sorì Gepin are harvested seven to ten days later and bordering on superipeness (the wine also undergoes a longer maceration/fermentation and is aged in small oak barrels compared to the larger 50 hectoliter barrels used for the Barolo Bergera-Pezzolle). La Spinona bought its holdings in Bergera-Pezzolle in 1994; the roughly forty years old vines are located in the Bergera rather than the Pezzolle portion of the vineyard district and I guarantee you that much will be evident upon the first taste of either one of their two Barolos: theirs are much bigger, thicker Bergera-Pezzolle wines than those made with grapes picked on the Pezzolle side. The differences are independent of winemaking variables, as La Spinona's wines are fairly traditionally made; in Gualtiero's view, Bergera offers better exposures and a higher soil limestone content than Pezzolle (clearly, if you talk to someone whose Nebbiolo vines are only in Pezzolle you'll get a similarly rosy picture painted: and so all you can do really learn and know is visit, visit, visit; listen, listen, listen; and taste, taste taste). Interestingly, and a sign of how much times have changed in the Barolo denomination over the last forty years, La Spinona's vineyard had been planted to Nebbiolo originally, but its previous owner uprooted it and planted Dolcetto instead. So when Berutti took over, they had to start all over again, proceeding to graft Nebbiolo onto the pre-existing vines.

In ultimate analysis, the full scope and potential of Bergera-Pezzolle as a prime site for very fine Barolo remains somewhat unknown at the present time; more importantly, it appears that the two different souls of the vineyard district can give very different wines. However, the degree to which that may be true is also unclear given the paltry wine information we have presently at our disposal. While more wines and more time will needed to arrive at meaningful conclusions relative to those two quandaries, there is no lack of satisfaction in the realization that preliminary evidence hints that in Bergera-Pezzolle, there does appear to be very much a there, there.

Benchmark wineries/Reference point producers of Barolo Bergera-Pezzolle: La Spinona, Le Strette.

BERRI

Township	La Morra
Reference Map	See Map of La Morra MGAs (Ch. 10)
Size (ha) (Tot / Barolo MGA)	87.89 / 9.84
Production 2021 (hl)	535.36
Altitude	350 – 500 meters a.s.l. roughly
Exposure	From south to southeast
N. Claimants MGA	4
Other grape varieties planted:	Barbera; Dolcetto
Land Units	Land Unit of Berri
Soil (stage):	Messinian

Producers claiming the MGA

Ferdinando Borgogno; Gheddo; Mauro Molino; Trediberri;

Wines

Mauro Molino - Barolo Gallinotto; **Trediberri** di Nicola Oberto - Barolo Trediberri.

What the producers say

Nicola Oberto (Trediberri): "We became proprietors of our vineyard in this vineyard district in 2007; from 2009, it is vinified by itself but then assembled into our classic estate Barolo. The duration of the maceration varies from 15 to 18 days – for they are still young vines and their skins are not ideal for longer maceration times".

Ian's assessment of the vineyard district, its wines and its potential

Berri is a small collection of houses that gives the vineyard district in the Barolo denomination its name. Only 1.5 kilometers removed from the Tanaro river, it's the westernmost vineyard district of the La Morra commune (and one of the furthest west of all the Barolo denomination). It is bordered by the Serradenari vineyard district to the east, but otherwise is removed from all other vineyard districts (Brandini and Sant'Anna, two other La Morra vineyard districts to the north of Berri, are the other nearest ones to it, but are actually located quite a bit away). In the past, the Berri area was never one much sought after as a source of grapes for Barolo: but thanks to climate change, it's wines of generally low pH are consequently marked by freshness and very good lift, and are garnering increased attention and praise nowadays (so I write "thanks to climate change" in this context only, because otherwise...). Berri's soil was formed during the Messinian stage of the Miocene epoch: this fact, coupled with its lithology (corresponding to the Cassano Spinola Formation of the sandy type typical of the Land Unit of Berri and that is very common in this section of the La Morra commune's territory), as well as with its generally cool mesoclimate tells us right away much that we need to know in order to understand, even expect, the wines that can (should?) be made there. Put into simpler terms, the soil composition is that you'd expect to find in a site so close to a river basin, with pebbles, limestone and some sandstone outcrops, with big rocks overhanging the river. That soil origin and type, plus the cool climate, accounts for Berri's wines, typified by oodles of freshness, nervous tension and plenty of energy, if not mind-blowing complexity.

Berri producers and the wines

Even though Berri is not one of the historic, more famous vineyard districts of the Barolo denomination, there are some very talented producers making Barolos from grapes grown there (Mauro Molino and Trediberri immediately spring to mind), leading to predictably good results in our wine glasses. For all us terroir-lovers out there, this is just grand, because besides getting to drink more good Barolos, anytime you have wines made from capable producers, it becomes much easier to identify the characteristics of a specific vineyard site. Historically, Berri was the dominion of farmers who sold all their grapes to *negozianti*, and so who had little interest in making and bottling their own wines.

Then in the 1960s, just like in other parts of Italy, the vineyards were abandoned while individuals went searching for more remunerative factory or office jobs (in the case of Berri, I am told that inhabitants either left for the big cities or took jobs in the light metal-working factory next to the hamlet). In the early 2000's, wineries like Mauro Molino, Renato Ratti, Elvio Cogno, and Marcarini decided to replant the area with grapevines, but I think it's only fair to recognize that it was Mauro Molino who was the first to do the most for Berri's gaining of more visibility and fame.

In the 90s, Mauro Molino took an interest in the area because he was curious about what a Barolo would taste like when made from Nebbiolo grapes grown at much higher altitudes than those he had worked with beforehand. From 1992 to 1995, he rented vines in Berri, buying them outright in 1995 because he liked both the Nebbiolo and the Barbera wines he had made from there during that time. Then from 1995 to 2000, he experimented with new viticultural and winemaking techniques, such as heavy deleafing (no surprise, given the cool climate of the high-altitude district), planting cover crops, and using different barrels made with different oak tree species. Over the years, when visiting at the winery, Molino and his kids (Matteo and Martina, who now run the winery) have told me they believe Berri gives lighter-structured but fruitier wines than are those they make from Conca (see: CONCA) and Gancia (see: BRICCO LUCIANI), both of which have more classic Barolo tannins and structure. Trust me: one taste of their three wines and you'll immediately understand why they believe that.

That said, don't go looking for any Mauro Molino Barolo Berri wines, because the estate has always bottled their Berri wine with the name of Gallinotto. This is because Molino's 1.5 hectares of Berri are divided into two sections: an upper plot (indeed, at close to 500 meters or roughly between 450-500 meters above sea level in altitude, this is one of Barolo's vineyards located highest up) that is planted with much older vines (over forty years old), and a lower section where the vines are about half as old (these were initially rented in 2008 from an 88 years old man, for whom, in the words of Matteo Molino, "… to let go of the vines was probably the single worst thing he had to do in his life"). The wines made from each portion are very different: it is the grapes of the upper section (the soil of which is 45% loam, 32% clay and 25% sand) only that are used to make the Barolo called Gallinotto (the first vintage of which was the 2001), while those from the lower piece are blended into Molino's Barolo "classico". The Barolo Gallinotto is beautifully steely and perfumed, boasting a combination of La Morra perfume and cool climate personality that is enchanting.

Another high-quality estate associated with the Berri vineyard district, and not just because it harbors the word "*berri*" in its own, is La Morra's Trediberri. Trediberri owns about five hectares of vines there, facing south and southwest, planted in 2007 and 2008. The name "Trediberri" refers to the three individuals who founded the winery: Federico Oberto (who follows the vineyards and actually had the same role for decades at the Renato Ratti winery), his son Nicola (who makes the wines), and longtime supporter, fan, and financial backer Vladimiro Rambaldi. Three musketeers who have taken the Barolo denomination by storm and who I was the first English language wine writer to bring into the spotlight now many years ago.

Federico Oberto believes the Berri vineyard district to have unique qualities: of course, you *would* expect him to believe that given he owns vines there, but in fact he makes two reasonable observations. First, that Berri is located very close to the Tanaro river and second, that it is characterized by very white calcareous-rich soils. In this light, Berri is therefore not unlike the Monvigliero *cru* in Verduno, another site close to the river and some parts of which are blessed with extremely calcareous soils (though with noteworthy differences, the wines of the two sites do resemble each other somewhat). Trediberri has planted five different Nebbiolo nursery clones in Berri, on three different rootstocks, so as to study its best possible expression [interestingly, they owned a few rows planted to nursery clones of the Picotener Nebbiolo biotype (it was commonly planted at one point in the Langhe. See Chapter 1, NEBBIOLO LAMPIA. Subchapter, Nebbiolo biotypes] that they too confirm gave wines of very deep dark colour but of little or no perfume, as I have documented in the aforementioned NEBBIOLO LAMPIA chapter in this book and numerous other times before (for example: D'Agata 2014; D'Agata 2019).

While Federico believes the fruit of Berri to be of similar quality, or very close, to that from their holdings in the Rocche dell'Annunziata (a much more famous, historically important, vineyard district than Berri), Nicola does not share the same opinion. However, Nicola, a bright young man who is one of the most talented, up and coming, "new" names in Barolo today, emphasizes that given the young age of their vines, it is still too early to judge and to define the characteristics of the wines from Berri. It his, not unreasonable, view that at the present time the biggest impact on Berri wines is given by the clones that are used to make the wines, and that more time is needed to discern what the vineyard district can actually give, or not. For this reason, during the years they were also renting a vineyard in the Capalot vineyard district, they chose to blend together the grapes from the two sites (the Capalot vineyard was much older and had an eastern exposure, so the two sites complemented each other nicely allowing Trediberri to make a more complex, deeper Barolo).

While it is true there isn't much information to go on by to come away with hard and fast conclusions about the characteristics of Barolos from the Berri vineyard district, it is also true that thanks to Mauro Molino's Gallinotto bottling and Trediberri's own classic Barolo (at least relative to the wines made in the years they weren't blending Capalot in it) we can actually broach the subject without looking or sounding silly.

In my view, the first thing to keep in mind when discussing Berri is that it's the same hill on which the vineyard districts Case Nere and La Serra are found. Partly because (but not just) it is located higher up, Berri is generally a more ventilated site than many others in this part of the Barolo area (something that becomes immediately obvious to anyone standing among the vines there without a jacket in the evening), and as such has greater diurnal temperature variations. Its soil is very poor in organic matter and has generally low concentrations of potassium, magnesium and phosphorus relative to other sites in La Morra and other communes of the Barolo denomination. In fact, the soil is not just poor in nutrients but also very pebbly, and has a greater proportion of clay than neighboring sites. All of which makes for an interesting combination that helps explain the wines, generally among the sleeker ones of the commune, with higher acidity levels (or they taste like they have a lower pH) and hence more assertive tannins (certainly more so than the Barolos made in the more eastern sections of the La Morra commune). In general, I find Berri's wines to be blessed with noteworthy perfume. Certainly, the fruity, lively, expressive wines of Berri are noticeably different than the generally more chunky, even thick ones made with grapes from the Case Nere and La Serra vineyard districts to the east (clearly, I use "chunky" and "thick" by La Morra standards, which are nothing like those of Monforte, for example). If you taste an old Gallinotto wine by Molino next to one from La Serra, the differences between the two *crus* are immediately obvious (at least in their general aspects) even to the non-initiated. This is even more obvious when comparing Molino's Barolo wines from Gallinotto and Conca (the latter a much lower-lying, warmer La Morra vineyard district that at 60% loam, 25% clay, and 15% sand also has a completely different soil texture: given the differences in climate and soil between the two, the wines cannot help but be very different, and they are).

Benchmark wineries/Reference point producers of Berri: Mauro Molino (Barolo Gallinotto). Also good: Trediberri.

BETTOLOTTI

Township	La Morra
Reference Map	See Map of La Morra MGAs (Ch. 10)
Size (ha) (Tot / Barolo MGA)	58.76 / 0.56
Production 2021 (hl)	27.20
Altitude	200 – 270 meters a.s.l. roughly
Exposure	From northwest to northeast passing to north
N. Claimants MGA	1
Other grape varieties planted:	Barbera; Dolcetto; white varieties
Land Units	Land Unit of Barolo
Soil (stage):	Tortonian

Producers claiming the MGA

Silvio Alessandria.

Wines

Silvio Alessandria - Barolo Bettolotti (Only vintage 2020 and 2021).

Ian's assessment of the vineyard district, its wines and its potential

Bettolotti is one of the northernmost La Morra vineyard districts, essentially on one flank of the hill of which the other, better-exposed, flank is occupied by the Rive vineyard district. Up until very recently, there were no Barolo Bettolotti made: the few producers who own vines there use grapes grown in Bettolotti for their classic Barolo made by blending grapes from different sites, as tradition would have it and is in fact in the DNA of Barolo (and Barbaresco). Part of the reason is Bettolotti's exposure, as written in the facts and figures introduction above: a lot of north-facing all around, meaning that the late-ripening Nebbiolo historically had a tough time reaching optimal ripeness there in most years. For this reason, total plantings of Barbera and Dolcetto have historically outnumbered Nebbiolo in Bettolotti, though that may change with the onslaught of climate change (and to an extent, it has already happened, as we shall see).

While Bettolotti's exposure has long been the bane of farmers, its soil is actually of interest and potentially noteworthy. Bettolotti belongs to the landscape category of the Land Unit of Barolo, meaning that the soil lithology is mostly that of the typical Saint Agatha Fossil Marls formation that characterize so much of the territory of La Morra and Barolo. In my experience, Bettolotti is characterized by a fairly high percentage of sand in a great part of its extension, otherwise it is mostly loamy in nature (or more precisely, it's loamy-marl with pockets of light red-clay and sand), not to mention a solid sprinkling of stones/pebbles throughout. I therefore classify Bettolotti as a mostly sandy-loamy site (soil analysis shows low amounts of clay: samples average out to 60-65% loam, 20-25% sand and 15-17% clay). This means that Bettolotti's wines are very different from other nearby La Morra vineyard districts such as for example Bricco San Biagio, that broadly speaking is marked by its sand presence, and Roggeri, which is in parts very clay-dominated. And the little clay that there is in Bettolotti is mostly a light clay (very different from Roggeri's heavy clay: so yes, there is clay, and then there is clay). That fact, combined with the preponderance of sand, tells you immediately what the wines from such sections of Bettolotti are going to be like. The wines are bright, floral, perfumed and politely-styled, but not without depth or size; as we saw earlier, the impression that Bettolotti Barolos are not especially massive is borne out by laboratory analysis.

Bettolotti producers and the wines

An excellent estate that owns vines in Bettolotti is Crissante Alessandria. This winery's Barolo del Comune di La Morra, first made with the 2014 vintage, is a blend of Roggeri (60%), Bricco San Biagio (20%) and Bettolotti (20%). The Bettolotti vines face east. The winemaking involves about two weeks skin contact, fermentation in stainless steel at a maximum temperature of 26-28 degrees Celsius and aging is for twenty-four months in large Slavonian oak barrels. Crissante Alessandria owns two plots in Bettolotti. One is entirely devoted to the production of Nebbiolo, while the second is divided into an upper and a lower section; the grapes of the former are also used to make Barolo, while the Nebbiolo grapes of the latter section, which give a fresh, less structured wine, are used to make a Langhe Nebbiolo. And while Crissante Alessandria's Barolo del Comune di La Morra is made with a blend of grapes from different vineyard districts, his Nebbiolo wine is 100% Bettolotti, which allows us real into insight into what the vineyard district can deliver. The estate's 2017 Langhe Nebbiolo was aged in large 30 hectoliter oak barrels as opposed to small ones and the wine is light and lively, fresh and fruity, with pretty Nebbiolo characteristics (more fruity than floral) and a note of incense and aromatic herbs that appear to be Bettolotti-specific. The tannins are gentle, and the wine has a silky mouthfeel: it's a very pretty wine that is very likely due in large part to the low clay content of the soil.

Another estate in La Morra, also called Alessandria, farms Bettolotti: Silvio Alessandria (now run by Enzo), who has made a Barolo labeled as a single- vineyard district Barolo from this vineyard district for the first time in the 2021 vintage (previously, they sold the wine in bulk as a generic Barolo, even though they had claimed the possibility to use the vineyard district name on the label also for the 2020 vintage). Is their decision to start bottling a Bettolotti Barolo a sign of climate change? Or is it just that single-vineyard district Barolos apparently sell well? Or is it because of real belief in the site's intrinsic quality level? Perhaps a combination of all those realities. The plot is 0.59 hectares large (the estate owns only 2.5 hectares in total) and is planted to very young vines at an altitude of 250 meters above sea level and that face west. The wine is light and lively, lifted and perfumed with balsamic and aromatic herb nuances mixed in with small berries. I'd say it's really quite good and promising.

Another estate farming Bettolotti grapes is Luigi Oddero, the winery that owns the Cascina (farmhouse) Bettolotti. Their 2013 and 2014 classic Barolos included a percentage of grapes from this vineyard district, but given the inclusion of grapes from myriad other crus (Scarrone, Baudana, Broglio, Rive and others still), it is impossible to know just what, and how much, Bettolotti contributes to the mix. Negretti makes a Barolo called Mirau that is a blend of Nebbiolo grown in Bettolotti and in the Rive vineyard district (of La Morra). The Bettolotti Nebbiolo vines were planted back in 1990 at about 230-270 meters above sea level, south-east facing. Interestingly, Negretti has also made Barbera and Chardonnay wines from within Bettolotti.

Over the years I have found that almost all the Barolos I have tried that were made with at least some Bettolotti grapes had a strong presence of botanicals and spices in their organoleptic profile: bay leaf, mint, incense, and even curry come to mind. I have probably not had enough wines made with Bettolotti grapes, and certainly not enough 100% micro-vinifications of the site, to suggest or to be sure that these nuances are in fact signatures of the Bettolotti vineyard district, though a certain spicy-herbal note does appear to be part of what the site can deliver.

Benchmark wineries/Reference point producers of Barolo Bettolotti: Silvio Alessandria.

BOIOLO

Township	La Morra
Reference Map	See Map of La Morra MGAs (Ch. 10)
Size (ha) (Tot / Barolo MGA)	87.79 / 10.72
Production 2021 (hl)	568.04 (of which 33.36 hl of Barolo Riserva *MGA*)
Altitude	230 – 450 meters a.s.l. roughly
Exposure	Southeast in the part bordering on Rocche dell'Annunziata, and east in the central part, from north to northeast in the remaining part
N. Claimants MGA	12
Other grape varieties planted:	Barbera; Dolcetto; white varieties
Land Units	Land Unit of La Morra
Soil (stage):	Tortonian

Producers claiming the MGA

Enzo Boglietti; Pierangelo Bosco; Camparo; Gillardi; Malvirà; Mauro Oberto; Carlo Revello; Massimo Rivata; Enrico Sanino; Fratelli Savigliano; Spirito Agricolo; Giorgio Viberti.

Wines

Enzo Boglietti - Barolo Boiolo; **Camparo** - Barolo Boiolo; **Pierangelo Bosco** - Barolo Boiolo; **Gillardi**- Barolo Boiolo (*); **Malvirà** - Barolo Boiolo; **Fratelli Savigliano** - Barolo Boiolo (*); **Arnaldo Rivera** - Barolo Boiolo.

What the producers say

Enzo Boglietti: "Since 1993, we began to acquire plots in this vineyard in several steps, finally leading to its solo vinification as of the 2009 vintage. In my opinion, Boiolo's wines are aromatically rich and ready early in offering absolute drinking pleasure".

Stefano Pesci (Arnaldo Rivera): "Our Boiolo Nebbiolo vines were planted back in 2002. It's a Barolo marked by notes of sweet spices and ripe fruit. Silky and not especially structured, I don't believe Boiolo's are the longest-lived Barolos, but the wines from this site tend to offer plenty of early accessibility and charm".

Ian's assessment of the vineyard district, its wines and its potential

Little-known, Boiolo is fascinating, and this for many reasons. For starters, it is my experience that the Barolos of this *cru* can be rather good: never amongst the most ageworthy or complex, but the wines have a certain recognizable fruit-forward charm and better than average complexity. However, in the light of Boiolo's sheer size, and its range of altitudes and exposures, its wines can be extremely varied, though it all depends on what you consider the "true" Boiolo to be: the "real", historic, Boiolo is actually small in size. Hence, wines from that historic core are (with one noteworthy exception, at least in the past), not so varied after all. But Boiolo *is* large, and so its situation is not unlike that of, for example, Alsace's Brand and Burgundy's Echezeaux, two *grand crus* that in modern times have been enlarged to the point where neither one corresponds anymore with the historic, best vineyard cores of each. It's the same with Boiolo, the wines of which range from the elegantly dense (when made with grapes from the section called Fontanazza) to the somewhat lighter but politely-styled ones made from the Boiolo proper (see below). As an aside, there are many who believe that the area of Fontanazza deserved its own MGA official vineyard district status, because of its history and the quality of its wines (but do note that agreement amongst producers on exactly just how good, or not, Fontanazza really is relative to its Barolos is practically non-existent).

Boiolo's landscape is that of the Land Unit of La Morra: it's characterized by clay-calcareous soil of Saint Agatha Marls formation lithology (in its three different permutations); and so, that in and of itself tells us the wines won't have the tannic power of wines from Serralunga or Monforte, which cannot surprise given that Boiolo is located in the La Morra township. I find that the Barolos from Boiolo generally show a lightness in texture partly resulting from the elevation at which the vines lie, but there can be also sneaky levels of density. I have also found a very typical minty-balsamic note, tea even, to the Barolos of Boiolo over the years and across producers. This herb/spice component veers towards, in some vintages, to juniper (in my experience an uncommon finding in Barolo wines, but not so in Boiolo's). It is also accurate to say that Boiolo's are early-maturing Barolos, approachable sooner than not just the Barolos of other communes, but of also other La Morra vineyard districts as well (for example, wines from Brunate and Cerequio are more austere from the outset, will develop slower, and age longer).

However, the Boiolo vineyard district is so large that variations in grape biotype, altitude, lithology and mesoclimate abound, and can potentially generate wines of noteworthy diversity. At 88 hectares (87.79 hectares, to be exact), Boiolo is the second largest of the vineyard districts on the eastern slope of La Morra, sandwiched between the Rocchettevino and Rocche dell'Annunziata vineyard districts to the northeast, Torriglione to the east, and the vineyard districts Brunate and La Serra to the south. As mentioned in previously in this book (see chapter 8: BAROLO "CLASSICO" AND BAROLO SINGLE-DISTRICT WINES; THE IMPORTANCE OF SITE), in the interest of simplicity and in an effort to make the official vineyard district delimitations easier to accept and to understand, many smaller sites that had previously gone by very specific, even historic names were incorporated together to make one large vineyard district. This approach is best exemplified by the undertakings of the Monforte commune (the officially-named vineyard districts of which are very few and very large), but it is an approach that was used elsewhere too, such as for example when the boundaries of La Morra's Boiolo were drawn up. And so it was that the vineyard area of Fontanazza, once fairly well-known and highly-thought of, was included within Boiolo.

Today's Boiolo vineyard district can be divided into two main segments differentiated by exposures and geology (the lower half is characterized by Saint Agatha fossil marls of the sandy type, while Saint Agatha marls of the laminated type characterize the upper half of the vineyard district). Of the two, it is the larger upper portion (about two thirds of the extension of the Boiolo vineyard district) that is best for Barolo production (because of a combination of more suitable exposures and soil), and is from where the almost totality of Barolo Boiolo wines you will taste come from. In turn, this higher situated portion can be further subdivided into two subsections of its own: one close to the Rocche dell'Annunziata vineyard district, and the other closer to the Brunate vineyard district. The part that extends from close to the Rocche dell'Annunziata vineyard district to the collection of buildings that is the Boiolo village is believed by some to be the "real" Boiolo, or Boiolo proper; the section spreading out towards Brunate is Fontanazza (the name, clearly derived from *fontana* or fountain, refers to an area with large quantities of water, present even in the droughtiest summers such that land erosion is always a risk in this section of the Boiolo hill).

In my opinion, such a subdivision is not wholly correct. While the Boiolo proper is higher up than Fontanazza (which ought to be identified with the that portion of the central part of today's Boiolo that is closest to the border with Brunate), the true Boiolo, or Boiolo proper, is actually that part of the slope immediately below the Borgata Boiolo and spreading out towards the central part of the slope and towards Fontanazza. In other words, the Boiolo proper extends between 330 to 400 meters above sea level, just up to the hamlet of Boiolo (a collection of houses situated at about 400 meters above sea level). The extension of vines found further up and reaching out towards Rocche dell'Annunziata are now also part of the Boiolo vineyard district, but the true Boiolo is the section immediately below the hamlet. To make a long story short, the best part of today's Boiolo is the central part of the slope, which includes the Boiolo proper and Fontanazza. Interestingly, while today not everyone you will talk to is as sold on Fontanazza's exact merits, with different producers giving me over the years wildly divergent opinions on its merits at least relative to Barolo production, it behooves me to tell you that this was not always so. I remember very well that back in the early 1980s Fontanazza was highly thought of by various producers and one Italian wine expert in particular (Veronelli). Clearly, relative to Barolo-making potential, Fontanazza's proximity to Brunate didn't hurt its reputation any; in fact, still today some producers refer to the sections of Fontanazza closest to Brunate with the latter's name, though I'm not so sure just how correct, or even accurate, that habit really was, and is.

Boiolo producers and the wines

An outstanding, if briefly very atypical, Barolo Boiolo is made by the talented Damonte brothers of the Roero estate Malvirà (also not so arguably one of the three best Roero Arneis wine producers). Why atypical, you ask? Here goes. The Malvirà 2011 and 2012 Barolo Boiolos were some of the weirdest-looking Barolos I ever gazed upon: I remember remaining literally dumbfounded when, now many years ago, Roberto Damonte first poured his 2011 Barolo Boiolo in my glass. Granted, it was a weird enough already because this had taken place not in his cellar back in Piedmont but at a trade show in Hong Kong, we were both at; but in fact it was even weirder because of that Barolo's colour, that left me absolutely speechless. Never before had I seen (and in fact, never have again) as darkly tinted a Barolo (which being a 100% Nebbiolo wine by law can never be impenetrably inky-coloured, because Nebbiolo wines cannot be of that hue. See chapter 1, NEBBIOLO LAMPIA). But Malvirà's Barolo Boiolo really was 100% Nebbiolo, and its dark hue was easily explained. The wine was a downright benchmark example of what happened to producers who planted the Picotener series of nursery Nebbiolo clones in the Langhe, that as I discussed extensively in an earlier chapter of this book (see chapter 1, NEBBIOLO LAMPIA), not to mention elsewhere (D'Agata, 2014; D'Agata, 2019), gave/give very disappointing wines in Barolo and Barbaresco. Wines that were uncharacteristically dark in colour and had virtually no perfume (the most damning aspect of all, given perfume is arguably the single greatest feature of Barolo). And I repeat, not because Picotener is in and of itself a "bad" Nebbiolo biotype; after all, it does just swell in the Valle d'Aosta and in Carema. But it isn't the right biotype for the Langhe, or at least hasn't proven to be up until now, given that Picotener has adapted over the centuries to the alpine and cold-climate Valle d'Aosta and that northern part of Piedmont that borders it (two areas that have a climate and geology that could not anymore different than that of the Langhe). In fact, the first year Damonte made his Barolo, the wine was so different from what Roberto was expecting that he told me he was beside himself with worry that the nursery had sent him the wrong grapevine by mistake! That said, those initial vintages of Malvirà's Barolo Boiolo (the 2011 and the 2012, namely) were by far the best Picotener Barolos I have ever tasted: for one, they did have at least some perfume (though not much), very good density, suave tannins, and pure Nebbiolo fruit offered in a forward style typical of La Morra and Boiolo [this wine has since become more normal in colour, meaning lighter red, over the years, as the percentage of Picotener used to make the wine has been steadily decreased (no surprise there)]. The Malvirà 2015 and 2016 Barolo Boiolo are really lovely wines. Damonte owns 0.88 hectares in Boiolo [Damonte's older sister Gianna married Giovanni Oberto, a commercial agent who owned vines in Boiolo: Damonte bought the plot in 2006 (the estate website says 2007, but Damonte has told me it was actually in 2006)], later adding another nearby 2000 square meters of vines so as to reach the present-day total of 0.88 hectares. He then proceeded to replant the site (and that's when his problems started) and made his first Barolo

Boiolo with the 2009 vintage. In fact, they chose not to use the Boiolo name in the first two vintages (2009 and 2010), beginning to do so only with the 2011 (in 2018, they bought two other small plots of Nebbiolo, one in Boiolo and one in the Serradenari vineyard district, and blended both into the wine, a tactic allowed by the vineyard district rules and regulations that allow up to 15% of another vineyard district to be blended in a wine carrying the name of the vineyard district from which at least 85% of the grapes come from).

Whereas it was once rare to find any Barolos carrying the Boiolo name (I don't believe I ever saw or tasted any Barolo Boiolo in all the 1980s and 1990s), there are now many other producers making noteworthy Barolos from Boiolo. For example, Boglietti, Camparo and the Terre del Barolo cooperative (in their top of the line, premium Arnaldo Rivera portfolio of excellent single-vineyard district Barolos). The Arnaldo Rivera Barolo Boiolo is made from a vineyard the coop owns since 1999; the Nebbiolo vines were planted in 2002 at about 420 meters above sea level, facing southeast. This Barolo is typically soft and forward already at an early age, with ripe red fruit tinged by balsamic nuances and not much in the way of steely tannin. It's a charming, ripely fruity wine that is best drunk up early (say within ten to fifteen years from the vintage date) while your Barolos from Monforte and Serralunga mature in the cellar. Boglietti's holdings in Boiolo are not small (1.95 hectares in total), part of the inheritance left by Matteo Boglietti (class of 1889 and grandfather of the current owners: lucky guys, he also gifted them with 0.52 hectares of vines in Brunate). The Boiolo is the softest and most immediate of Boglietti's many Barolos (the east/south-east facing vines were planted with a massal selection in 2002 at 300-350 meters above sea level), but the winemaking has changed considerably over the years. While the wine was once aged in used barriques for twenty-four months (and it used to be as much as 30% new oak), most recently (for example the 2018 vintage), all the Boglietti Barolos were aged in used barrels mostly ranging in size from 15 to 40 hectoliters. The wine is usually marked by notes of tea (a descriptor I have found in Malvirà's Boiolo wines as well), earth tones, and very noticeable blue and red fruit. By contrast, Camparo's version is made from twenty to fifty years old south/south-east facing vines planted at around 250 meters above sea level, or in the lowest reaches of the vineyard district (so much lower-down from those of Boglietti and Malvirà), aged in 25 hectoliter oak casks for twenty-four months. That altitude and the different lithology plays a role in the way wines taste, as is immediately obvious when you taste these three Barolo Boiolo wines together. Usually, the Camparo version is fleshier than the Arnaldo Rivera, with the Malvirà and Boglietti's falling somewhere in the middle. Given that, all range from at least very good to excellent to outstanding, and which you prefer depends mostly on the type of wine you like best.

Recently, the Mario Oliviero estate has signed a ten-year rental agreement that will provide the winery with grapes from the Boiolo vineyard district. Beginning with the 2018 vintage, they will begin making a Barolo del Comune di La Morra, that takes the place of their previous Barolo Vigne Unite. This is because that wine will now be made with grapes from two other La Morra vineyard districts (Annunziata and Boiolo) that have recently come into the estate's fold (thanks to a ten-year rental agreement), that will be blended with those of the Bricco Rocca. Oliviero's vines in Boiolo were planted in 1999 on Saint Agatha Fossil Marls soils of the sandy type at about 380 meters above sea level. Being squarely in the camp of Boiolo-believers (though I enjoy just about every type of wine made, I happen to think there's plenty to like in balanced, pretty wines that do not need cellaring forever to be enjoyed), I for one am excited and curious to learn what those grapes might give.

Benchmark wineries/Reference point producers of Barolo Boiolo: Arnaldo Rivera (Terre del Barolo), Boglietti, Malvirà.

BORZONE

Township	Grinzane Cavour
Reference Map	See Map of Grinzane MGAs (Ch. 10)
Size (ha) (Tot / Barolo MGA)	7.08 / 0.22
Production 2021 (hl)	11.80
Altitude	200 – 245 meters a.s.l. roughly
Exposure	From south to southwest.
N. Claimants MGA	1
Other grape varieties planted:	Barbera; Dolcetto
Land Units	Land Unit of Barolo
Soil (stage):	Tortonian

Producers claiming the MGA

Le Cecche;

Wines

Le Cecche - Barolo Borzone.

What the producers say

Canonica Giovanni: "We own vines just outside the Borzone vineyard district's border, but the soil is essentially the same. We started to vinify our holdings only since 2012. Borzone is a Barolo noted for its spicy notes, and our grapes give us wines that share those characteristics".

Montaribaldi: "The perfect exposure of the Borzoni vineyard (Montaribaldi refers to it so, Borzoni, though the majority of individuals call the vineyard district Borzone, with a final "e"), along with the features of the area's climate and the soil, lead to an extremely elegant and long-lived wine, ample and rich in its perfume in the way that only Nebbiolo grape is capable of giving. Hints of spices and flowers marry well with notes of prune, tobacco, clove and black pepper. Tannins are austere, but neither bitter nor setting your mouth on edge. The finish is pleasantly long with flavors reminiscent of fruit jam".

Ian's assessment of the vineyard district, its wines and its potential

Borzone, in the territory of the commune of Grinzane Cavour, is close to that commune's Canova vineyard district-but is otherwise fairly removed from all the other Grinzane Cavour vineyard districts. It is one of those little-known vineyard district s from which wines have emerged only recently. That said, it is easy to understand that Borzone is a good and potentially excellent viticultural site: at 7.08 hectares, it is one of the smallest of all of the Barolo denomination's vineyard districts, but it is practically completely covered in vines (something like 95-97% of its total surface is planted to vines) and virtually all of that is Nebbiolo. So clearly, somebody's impressed.

Borzone's landscape is categorized as a Land Unit of Barolo and its soil is mostly a mix of deep clay, loam and sandstone. Remember that despite belonging to the Tortonian stage, having a Saint Agatha Marls lithology and what the word "Barolo" in the Land Unit name might lead you to believe, the Land Unit of Barolo is usually associated with slightly bigger wines than other vineyard districts that are also characterized by Tortonian stage soils. Not by chance, the famous Monforte vineyard districts of Ginestra and Mosconi (two vineyard districts associated with wines that are anything but wimpy), are also characterized by the Land Unit of Barolo landscape so that tells you plenty about the Barolos that can be potentially made in Borzone.

Borzone producers and the wines

An outstanding producer of Barolo who owns vines just outside the Borzone boundaries is Giovanni Canonica, whose lilliputian Barolo production is of truly Brobdingnagian quality and quite rightly sought out by wine lovers and collectors the world over. Let me be crystal-clear: he is one of the best at his craft, in the same league as the famous Conternos and Mascarellos you can think of. Canonica makes two Barolos, one from the

Paiagallo vineyard district and the other from vines planted in the territory of the commune of Grinzane Cavour (hence the wine is called Barolo del Comune di Grinzane Cavour). In the early 2010's, Gianni (Giovanni was his father) inherited a small amount of vines in the sector of Grinzane Cavour that are over 50 years old and contain a high percentage of Nebbiolo Rosé (other vines planted more recently are only ten years old). Gianni Canonica's first vintage of this wine was the 2012, and make no mistake about it, it has proven to be, time and again, a simply fantastic Barolo. And while practically everyone you'll talk to will gush on about his Barolo Paiagallo [no surprise there, because it's his Barolo carrying a single vineyard district's name that everyone automatically believes is (or more accurately, that *has to be*) the estate's best wine], the fact is that the real star in the Canonica galaxy is this Barolo, the "lowlier" Barolo del Comune di Grinzane Cavour. The Barolo Paiagallo is certainly a solid wine, but at the same time I find it to be a little lacking in nuance and very similar to many other super-fleshy ripe Barolos made in Barolo's "modern age"; by contrast, Canonica's Barolo del Comune di Grinzane Cavour is refined, elegant, better balanced and extremely perfumed. It's an outstanding wine and it speaks in part of the greatness that might be Borzone, given that part of the grapes used to make it grow right next to the vineyard district on very similar soil.

Wine estates that are bottling a Barolo Borzone include Le Cecche and Montaribaldi (once again, the latter prefers to use the name "Borzoni" for it, rather than Borzone). Other estates such as La Biòca bottled a Barolo Borzone in the past but apparently no longer do so; other estates, such as Bruna Grimaldi, own vines in the vineyard district but choose to use these grapes to make their classic Barolos, consisting in blends of grapes from different vineyard districts, as was always the area's tradition. Le Cecche is owned by a Belgian MD and his Italian wife since 2001. The estate is located in the hamlet of Le Cecche, a fraction of Diano d'Alba, one of the Barolo's denomination eleven communes. The estate boasts eight hectares under vine and holdings in three Barolo vineyard districts: Borzone is the second they bought, in 2014 (before that, they had bought vines in the Sorano vineyard district in 2010, and then in Monforte's Bricco San Pietro in 2015). Their vines in Borzone are south-facing and located at 220 to 230 meters above sea level. The technical staff is topnotch, the fermentation takes place in temperature-controlled steel tanks and aging is carried out for twenty-four months in 30% new French oak barriques and tonneaux. Montaribaldi's Barolo Borzoni is made from south-facing vines grown at about 230 meters above sea level that were planted back in 1980. The vinification involves destemming the grapes and one week-long fermentations in stainless steel tanks at 28-32 degrees Celsius. The wine is aged a longish thirty-eight months in both new and once used barriques. As that description might lead you to infer, theirs is usually a very austere wine in youth (see my discussion on this vineyard district's wines below).

By contrast, Bruna Grimaldi (the name of a very fine and to my way of thinking, underrated, Barolo estate in Serralunga d'Alba) owns vines in Borzone (planted in 2007 and 2012 at about 220 meters above sea level), but chooses to blend the grapes with those from other vineyard sources into the estate Barolo called Camilla (along with grapes from Raviole, another Grinzane Cavour vineyard district, and from Roere di Santa Maria, a vineyard district in La Morra). The Bruna Grimaldi winery knows this vineyard well as it calls Grinzane Cavour is home to the winery (and was also the birthplace of Bruna's father Giovanni). The estate owns two plots in Borzone, one with older vines, and the other planted in 2007. Both have a south-facing aspect and an altitude range of 220-250 meters.

Benchmark wineries/Reference point producers of Barolo Borzone: Montaribaldi. Also outstanding: Giovanni Canonica (though his Barolo del Comune di Grinzane Cavour is not all Borzone, it stands in my opinion as a very good example of this vineyard district's wines).

BOSCARETO

Township	Serralunga d'Alba
Reference Map	See Map of Serralunga d'Alba MGAs (Ch. 10)
Size (ha) (Tot / Barolo MGA)	53.15 / 6.47
Production 2021 (hl)	331.09 (of which 100 hl of Barolo Riserva *MGA*)
Altitude	300 – 440 meters a.s.l. roughly
Exposure	From west to southwest in the better exposed parcels, from north to northwest in the remaining parts
N. Claimants MGA	4
Other grape varieties planted:	Barbera; Dolcetto; Moscato Bianco
Land Units	Land Unit of Serralunga d'Alba
Soil (stage):	Serravallian

Producers claiming the MGA

Batasiolo; Ferdinando Principiano; Francesco e Giuseppe Principiano; Regis.

Wines

Batasiolo - Barolo Boscareto; **Ferdinando Principiano** - Barolo Boscareto and Barolo del Comune di Serralunga; **Francesco e Giuseppe Principiano** - Barolo Boscareto; **Regis** - Barolo Boscareto (*).

What the producers say

Batasiolo: "Boscareto is characterized by an intense and persistent perfume, offering notes of fruit and dry flowers (such as rose and violet), as well as pronounced aromas of sweet spices, and leather. Though full-bodied and austere, the remarkable tannic structure remains soft and the wine easy-going and pleasant on the palate".

Ian's assessment of the vineyard district, its wines and its potential

Boscareto is one of the southern Serralunga vineyard districts. It encapsulates the Francia vineyard district and reaches Badarina to the east, touches Arione to the south, and borders Falletto and Ornato to the north; west of Boscareto, there is the territory of Monforte. The soil is mostly clay-calcareous and its landscape category is that of the Land Unit of Serralunga (which is typical of most of the southern Serralunga vineyard districts, including Arione, Francia and Ornato).

Hence, the lithology is the classic Lequio Formation that so characterizes the commune of Serralunga and accounts in large part for its steely, mouthcoating, citrus-accented wines. Boscareto's are perfectly fine, serviceable Barolos. At fifty-three hectares, it's a relatively large vineyard district with varying exposures, and so not surprisingly, some sections of it are better than others (a large part of Boscareto isn't even planted to Nebbiolo, though this may change with the advent of climate-change).

Boscareto producers and the wines

Of the various Barolo Boscareto wines made, the Giuseppe and Francesco Principiano estate ages theirs two years in 25 hectoliter Slavonian oak barrels and then another in stainless steel tanks. Ferdinando Principiano's vines are farmed naturally (no pesticides, no herbicides, all sorts of cover crops between rows and fruit trees everywhere) and his wines are remarkably pure and clean, never funky or downright flawed. The estate owns six hectares, 2.5 of which were planted by Ferdinando's grandfather and another 3.5 hectares in the 1990s (so their Boscareto vines range from about 25-60 years of age). They face southeast and are planted at about 400 meters above sea level on whitish limestone-rich soil (also containing clay and sand) in the southern reaches of the Boscareto vineyard district near where the Francia vineyard district is situated. I have always found his Barolo Boscareto (and his wines in general) to boast a penetrating perfume and a real tangy personality. In order to understand why his wines are the way they are, it is important to know that Ferdinando Principiano uses 100% whole bunches, and ferments for 25-30 days at about 25-30 degrees Celsius. His classic estate Barolo is also made mostly with Boscareto fruit, either from young vines or declassified stuff, with a smattering of grapes from the Lirano vineyard district. While its fermentation is the same as the Boscareto, it is aged only 20-24 months in oak. I admire the purity these wines exude, with lovely Serralunga-typical mineral and sour red cherry aromas and flavors, with a slightly rounder mouthfeel than say the wines of Francia (which, as mentioned earlier, is characterized by the same Land Unit lithology). As good as the wines of Ferdinando Principiano are (excellent Barolos all), it is my view that even the best Boscareto wines, though smooth and well-balanced, almost always lack the depth and complexity of those from Barolo's greatest sites. But I may well be proven wrong in the years to come as more Boscareto Barolos emerge and reach the market: nothing would make me happier.

Benchmark wineries/Reference point producers of Barolo Boscareto: Ferdinando Principiano.

BOSCATTO

Township	Verduno	
Reference Map	See Map of Verduno MGAs (Ch. 10)	
Size (ha) (Tot / Barolo MGA)	27.96 / 0.89	
Production 2021 (hl)	44.54	
Altitude	250 – 370 meters a.s.l. roughly	
Exposure	Predominantly east	
N. Claimants MGA	2	
Other grape varieties planted:	Barbera; Dolcetto; Pelaverga Piccolo; white varieties	
Land Units	Land Unit of La Morra	
Soil (stage):	Messinian	

Producers claiming the MGA

Comm G.B. Burlotto; Diego Morra.

Ian's assessment of the vineyard district, its wines and its potential

Boscatto is situated in the southern part of the Verduno Township's territory, just south of the two itself. The vineyard districts of Riva Rocca are to its north, Rocche dell'Olmo to its south, Neirane to the west, while it is the La Morra communes of Silio and Roere di Santa Maria that are immediately to its east. Its landscape category is that of the Land Unit of La Morra, and like all the vineyard districts of Verduno's southern reaches, its lithology is very different from that of the northern part of the commune's territory. According to Fabio Alessandria of G.B. Burlotto, Boscatto is dominated by a soil of younger geologic age compared to others found around Verduno: the Cassano Spinola formation of the marly type (see: Chapter 7, BAROLO TERROIR). Though less sandy than soils of the Cassano-Spinola Formation of the sandy type, Boscatto's main lithological entity still has more sand and less limestone than the Saint Agatha Fossil Marls of the laminated type that are typical of Verduno's northern reaches (where the famous Monvigliero vineyard district is located, for example), no doubt contributing to very different wines made in each section of the Verduno commune and each of its vineyard districts. Other factors that play a role in the makeup of Boscatto's Barolos are its location in the commune (close to town, which translates to a warmer mesoclimate) and its topography.

Boscatto producers and the wines

I don't know of any present-day Barolo Boscatto bottlings. Michele Reverdito and Bel Colle both used to make one but do not do so anymore. The G.B. Burlotto and I Brè wineries also farm Boscatto and use its grapes to make estate Barolo blends. G.B. Burlotto owns 1.13 hectares in Boscatto, and uses those grapes in the blend that makes up the estate's Barolo Acclivi (Acclivi is a fantasy name: it is the winery's Barolo meant to best showcase the Verduno terroir and the type of Barolo wine that Verduno can give: so for this reason, it is made with a blend of grapes from different Verduno vineyard district s). In my experience from past bottlings (Bel

Colle's 2009 Barolo Boscatto springs to mind) and from what those who regularly perform microvinifications prior to blending the resulting wine into their estate's classic Barolo blend, Boscatto's wine is very pure and lively, but less complex than that of Monvigliero. Aroma and flavor-wise, it reminds of licorice and darker red fruit than some of the other Verduno vineyard districts (possibly because of more soil marl and less sand); according to Fabio Alessandria of G.B. Burlotto, the wines of Boscatto represent an ideal crossing of those of Neirane and Rocche dell'Olmo, two other Verduno vineyard districts. He also believes this to be one of Verduno's vineyard districts to give more tannic wines than those of most of the township's vineyard districts (once again, this is most likely a consequence of the site's greater soil marl content). The I Brè winery owns 2.5 hectares in Boscatto, mostly planted to Nebbiolo for Barolo production (they have a little Barbera planted there too); the vines grow at an elevation of 270 meters, but I don't have much experience with the wines (yet).

Benchmark wineries/Reference point producers of Barolo Boscatto: None currently available.

BOSCHETTI

Township	Barolo
Reference Map	See Map of Barolo MGAs (Ch. 10)
Size (ha) (Tot / Barolo MGA)	23.87 / 10.31
Production 2021 (hl)	560.53 (of which 54.76 hl of Barolo Riserva *MGA*)
Altitude	300 – 360 meters a.s.l. roughly
Exposure	Predominantly west for the parcels facing Barolo, and east on the opposite side
N. Claimants MGA	3
Other grape varieties planted:	Barbera; Dolcetto
Land Units	Land Unit of La Morra
Soil (stage):	Tortonian

Producers claiming the MGA

Lodovico Cabutto; Gomba; G.D. Vajra.

Wines

Gomba - Barolo Boschetti Sernìe, Barolo Boschetti (Riserva as well); **Lodovico Cabutto** – Barolo; **Scarzello** (Scarzello Giorgio e Figli) Barolo Boschetti.

What the producers say

Gomba Cascina Boschetti: "The Boschetti Sernìe is made from our best grapes (the word *sernìe* means "*scelte*" in Italian, which translates to "choice" or "best"), picked from the vines right at the summit of the Boschetti hill that overlooks the town of Barolo. These vines are planted facing south/southwest at 320 meters above sea level. Fermentation and maceration take place over 21 days in temperature-controlled tanks and the wine is aged in mix of small and large French oak barrels, plus for another 18 months in bottle prior to going on sale. We find it to be a spicy-floral Barolo, but that also shows good ripe red fruit notes. Differently from the Boschetti Sernìe, the Barolo del Comune di Barolo is made with grapes picked from lower-lying vines in Boschetti, at about 285-310 meters above sea level, but are also south/southwest facing. Vinification is essentially the same as for the Sorí Boschetti, but we keep it in bottle for only twelve months before releasing it for sale. It's an altogether different Barolo, lighter-styled, more elegant and floral, but with a strong nuance of licorice".

Ian's assessment of the vineyard district, its wines and its potential

Boschetti is one of the most easternmost vineyard districts of the Barolo commune: the Preda vineyard district is situated immediately to its north, while the Zoccolaio vineyard district is directly south and the Bricco San Giovanni vineyard district lies to its southeast. To the northwest, it overlooks the town of Barolo (in itself low-lying), while to the west it looks at the slope where the Le Coste di Barolo, Rivassi and Ravera di Barolo vineyard districts, and Terlo higher up. To the east of Boschetti there is the Coste di Rose vineyard district and the Monforte commune's territory.

Walking the Boschetti site numerous times over the years (when I lived in Italy I spent about sixty days a year in the town of Barolo, and it was easy to either take early morning walks or jogs there), I was able to admire this vineyard district's soil blueish-gray tint, and that it is rich in clay. There is also a yellowish marl and limestone streaked by sandy veins more commonly associated with soils of Serravalian stage soils. It follows that Boschetti, which is a vineyard district close to the border with Monforte territory, is characterized by wide-ranging lithological realities. In fact, Boschetti is characterized both by the Saint Agatha Marls Formation and of the Diano Sandstone; but it is my view that Boschetti's dominant lithology is the former, not the latter. Given that the Boschetti vineyard area also presents noteworthy differences in altitude and exposure too within its boundaries, it strikes me that the vineyard district has the potential to give rather different wines.

Boschetti producers and the wines

Clearly, the problem with going out and proving what I just wrote is that there just aren't that many Barolos Boschetti made. The winery that has been perhaps most associated with the Boschetti vineyard district is Gomba [the estate is usually called with the longer moniker of Cascina Boschetti Gomba by locals and just about everyone else (the estate's website uses this terminology as well)]. Sergio Gomba bought his estate in 1991 and hit the ground running given that the winery came with a vineyard that was already then about fifty years old. At Gomba they make more than one Barolo from the site which helps showcase the range of Barolo expressions Boschetti can deliver. The estate makes a Barolo del Comune di Barolo with its lower-lying vines, and the Barolo Boschetti Serne from the best grapes that grow about forty to fifty meters higher up. In exceptional years, they will make a Barolo Boschetti Riserva from vines that are now seventy years old (and possible more).

Recently, a fine young producer, Federico Scarzello of the Scarzello estate (formerly Giorgio Scarzello) has also started making a small number of bottles of Barolo Boschetti. In 2015, he reappropriated himself of vineyards he had previously rented out, attracted to the extremely sandy soil (according to Federico, a mix of typical Saint Agatha Fossil Marls down low and Diano Sandstone higher up) but also the extremely old age of the vines (close to one hundred years old!); although the wine he made was certainly interesting, production was so low (only 1440 bottles made of the 2017 vintage, for example) that it was economically unsustainable to continue using the old vines only. Massal selections of the old vines were performed, the vineyard uprooted and the site replanted in 2022. A traditional winemaker, Scarzello likes long macerations, delicate extractions, and ages his wines in big oak barrels for roughly eighteen months -depending on the vintage- followed by prolonged bottle aging. His wines strike me as being a little fleshier and more balsamic than those of Gomba, but on the whole, differences are minimal.

Another name to watch in Boschetti is that of Francone, the very fine producer based in Neive, of the Barbaresco denomination, but that in fact has been also making Barolo since 1958. With the 2019 vintage, the winery has begun working also with Boschetti's grapes, from a west-facing vineyard holding planted between 320-360 meters above sea level. Fabrizio Francone told me that, despite Boschetti being neither very famous nor even well-known as a source of high-quality Barolo, he's especially excited by this vineyard district and looks forward to producing their first Barolo Boschetti soon enough. This is not just because its altitude and cooler mesoclimate imply good things in times of burgeoning climate change, but because the first vinifications have shown that grapes ripen with great regularity every year, giving balanced wines of noteworthy freshness and fine-grained tannins. Given that I believe Francone makes excellent wines that are fairly priced, they are most certainly not the only ones looking forward to their first Barolo Boschetti.

Why has there been such a dearth of Barolos made from Boschetti over the years? Most likely because, given its location and altitude, Boschetti was likely too cool a site for Nebbiolo to ripen fully there in most vintages. In that light, it can't surprise then that the locals I have talked to over the years all told me that historically, this specific area of the Barolo production area was never much planted to Nebbiolo (something that is still true today, given that less than half the site is growing Nebbiolo). For the most part, Boschetti strikes me as allowing for elegant Barolos, in which I find nuances of balsamic oils, licorice and flowers (in all of Gomba's and Scarzello's wines); but more than in their descriptors, the difference between the various wines lied in their texture and levels of concentration.

BRANDINI

Township	La Morra
Reference Map	See Map of La Morra MGAs (Ch. 10)
Size (ha) (Tot / Barolo MGA)	87.14 / 1.23
Production 2021 (hl)	66.03
Altitude	400 – 445 meters a.s.l. roughly
Exposure	From south to southeast on the better exposed slopes; northwest on the opposite side
N. Claimants MGA	2
Other grape varieties planted:	Barbera; Dolcetto
Land Units	Land Unit of Berri for the most; Land Unit of Verduno for the parcels bordering Sant' Anna
Soil (stage):	Messinian

Producers claiming the MGA

Brandini; Boglietti Enzo.

Wines

Brandini - Barolo R56.

Ian's assessment of the vineyard district, its wines and its potential

Brandini offers early drinking Barolos of early accessibility, in line with where the vineyard district is located in the denomination, its topography and soil lithology. It is the westernmost La Morra vineyard district, on the border with the township of Cherasco (another of Barolo's eleven communes) and situated immediately below the Sant'Anna vineyard district, that like Brandini is not a household name in Barolo circles. Brandini and that whole westernmost part of the Barolo denomination is an area that was long better thought of for its hazelnut production possibilities: in fact, of the 87 total hectares, to date only 1.23 hectares are planted to Nebbiolo for Barolo Brandini production and that tells you just about all you need to know. I don't mean to be unkind, but those numbers are such for a reason, mostly in relation to less than favorable exposures and a soil-type that gives nicely accessible Barolos but that can lack a little stuffing (and before climate change, even that was a challenge). That said, the Barolos made from the Brandini vineyard district are perfectly fine, much as are many Burgundies from fine producers made with grapes from *Villages*-level sites. The advantage of course is that such sites provide wines of early appeal that usually don't cost an arm and a leg, and there's plenty to like in that.

Brandini producers and the wines

There is one winery especially linked to the Brandini vineyard district, and in fact shares the same name as the site: the Brandini estate. A young estate, founded in 2007, Brandini is now run by the sister duo of Serena and Giovanna Bagnasco, who also make a Barolo from the Annunziata vineyard district (also in La Morra), plus two from the Serralunga commune's Meriame and Cerretta vineyard districts. Their Barolo Brandini is a politely-styled, easygoing Barolo that offers early accessibility, in keeping with what the area can give. It is to this estate's credit if we now know something about the Brandini site, because prior to this winery setting up shop in the area we had little if any information to go by. In 2021, the excellent Boglietti estate has also declared the intention to use Nebbiolo grapes grown in the Brandini vineyard district to produce their first Barolo bearing that vineyard district's name (whether they do in the end still needs to be seen). That too is a feather in the Brandini winery's cap, because if it had not been for their good Barolos, neither Boglietti nor anyone else would have thought of making Barolo there. There is infinite merit in being a trailblazer: just look at Cogno and what he did for the Novello township.

Benchmark wineries/Reference point producers of Barolo Brandini: Brandini.

BREA

Township	Serralunga d'Alba
Reference Map	See Map of Serralunga d'Alba MGAs (Ch. 10)
Size (ha) (Tot / Barolo MGA)	10.99 / 5.06
Production 2021 (hl)	208.95 (of which 74.28 hl of Barolo *MGA* "Vigna")
Altitude	300 – 370 meters a.s.l. roughly
Exposure	From south to southeast on the better exposed slopes; east in the remaining parts
N. Claimants MGA	1
Other grape varieties planted:	Barbera; Dolcetto; Moscato Bianco
Land Units	Land Unit of Serralunga d'Alba
Soil (stage):	Serravalian

Producers claiming the MGA

Brovia.

Wines

Brovia - Barolo Brea - Ca' Mia.

What producers say

Alex Sanchez (Brovia): "The Brovia family is the proprietor of this holding since 1995. Until the 2009 vintage, it was simply labelled as Ca' Mia. The maceration lasts approximately 3 weeks in cement. For our *crus*, we use 30-42 hectoliter French and Slavonian oak cask. The Nebbiolo grapes coming from this *cru* give a Barolo complete and of an impressive structure and longevity. The nose is intense, balanced, pleasantly spicy with hints of prune, cedar, tobacco, liquorice and flowers. It proves to be classic, full-bodied, concentrated and rich on the palate with a good tannic structure that guarantee its great aging capacity".

Ian's assessment of the vineyard district, its wines and its potential

Brea is a Serralunga-vineyard district of small size (less than eleven hectares) but big repute, mostly on the strength of the excellent Barolo Ca' Mia produced over the years by the very fine Brovia estate. Located to the northeast of the town, Brea lies on the other side of the road from the Bricco Voghera vineyard district (and partly Gianetto). But while Bricco Voghera is a more or less flat, sunlit hilltop (after all, that's what the word *bricco* refers to), Brea drops off the side featuring a steep gradient. Part of the vineyard district Giannetto lies next to Brea on this same slope (while up at the summit it snuggles right next to Bricco Voghera).

Brea is a very typical Serralunga vineyard area, especially those of the Serralunga ridge's eastern flank, generally characterized by less luminosity, steeper slopes and cooler meso- and microclimates. Its landscape belongs to the Land Unit of Serralunga and its main soil lithology is the classic Lequio Formation, both of which typify the majority of this commune's vineyard districts. It follows that Barolos from Brea will be what you'd expect from a Barolo made with Serralunga grapes: steely, vibrant, loaded with sour red fruit and a strong acid and tannic spine, with plenty of minerality (whatever "minerality" is due to, but the sensation of sucking on wet stones is certainly found in Brea's wines).

Brea producers and the wines (monopole)

So why aren't more estates making Barolo wines from what is undoubtedly an excellent site? That's because Brea is in fact a monopole of Brovia's. Therefore, only Brovia has ever made any Barolos from Brea in modern times (the site was well-thought of in the early part of the last previous century but had been essentially abandoned until Brovia bought it). In fact, Brea wasn't really the name most associated with this wine, given that for the longest time, the Brovia family's preference was to call its Barolo from Brea "Ca' Mia" (at least until the official vineyard district names came into being

While the site is not planted only to Nebbiolo (Brea is also planted to Barbera, Dolcetto and Moscato Bianco) which is understandable given the site's topography and diversity of vineyard microclimates, the Barolos from Brea are delicious. Even more, they are recognizably different from many others made in the Serralunga commune. This is partly because Brea is situated on the eastern side of the hilly ridge that runs up and down the Serralunga territory. This southeastern to eastern-facing vineyard means grapes bask in a gentler morning sun and that ripen neither as fast nor as intensely as those from Serralunga vineyard districts located on the western slope of the Serralunga ridge (or for that matter, grapes of those Serralunga vineyard districts on the same eastern slope as Brea but that are full south-facing, such as Cerrati). This explains the cooler-climate descriptors and fresher texture/mouthfeel of Barolos from Brea (Barolos that I find are generally marked by crisper red fruit aromas and flavors, and in cooler vintages, by hints of chlorophyll and underbrush as well). To be clear, those tasting notes you might read that are replete with references to tobacco, ripe black fruit and the likes tell you more about the level of knowledge and tasting ability of who's tasting the wine than the wine or the site themselves. In fairness, in hot years Brea's cool-climate personality does get thrown out of the window: witness the surprisingly jammy and exotic wines (showing dark fruit instead of Brea's more typical red fruit, plus hints of cardamom and cumin) made there in less than stellar vintages such as 1997 and 2017. In all vintages, a Barolo Brea is always characterized by incisive, etched, tannins that stick out: but it wouldn't be a Barolo from Serralunga then, would it?

Benchmark wineries/Reference point producers of Barolo Brea: Brovia.

BRERI

Township	Verduno
Reference Map	See Map of Verduno MGAs (Ch. 10)
Size (ha) (Tot / Barolo MGA)	53.94 / 0.99
Production 2021 (hl)	53.62
Altitude	220 – 250 meters a.s.l. roughly
Exposure	From west to southwest on the better exposed slopes; east and north in the remaining parts
N. Claimants MGA	3
Other grape varieties planted:	Barbera; Dolcetto; white varieties
Land Units	Land Unit of La Morra; Land Unit of Barolo
Soil (stage):	Tortonian

Producers claiming the MGA

Cadia; I Brè; Fabio Oberto.

Wines

I Brè - Barolo Corona Teresina;

Ian's assessment of the vineyard district, its wines and its potential

Mark my words: Breri is a Barolo vineyard name you ought to be hearing more from in the near future. And not because of some hot shot estate moving in making hyped wines of average quality, but because there is something about Breri's Barolos that is well above average. Think Monvigliero, but with a little less oomph and complexity. So the painting you're inheriting might not be a Monet: no sweat, I think you would be very happy with "just" a Sisley or a Pissarro too. And if you aren't, please then just give it to me, OK? I'd be evry happy to take it off your hands.

Sisley- and Pissarro-like, there is a beauty to Breri and what it can deliver. Breri is a vineyard district lies opposite the more famous one of Monvigliero, and is therefore a **vineyard district** of the northern part of the Verduno township (this automatically tells you something: the wines of Verduno's northern reaches are very different from those made in the southern half of the commune, for example where other **vineyard districts** such as Boscatto and Neirane are found). Of note, Breri boasts the full range of exposures, from southeast through southwest, including full south, and this undoubtedly plays a role in the wines made by different estates from vines there. The landscape is also an extremely diversified one, meaning potentially different wines could be made from grapes within Breri's boundaries, but the dominant lithology is the same as Monvigliero's (Saint Agatha Fossil Marls of the laminated type), further bringing fuel to my "it's Monvigliero-like" fire.

Breri producers and the wines

You learn about Breri and you realize just how apt this book's subtitle, "Grapes Crus People Places" is. Grapes: Nebbiolo, in its various types. Crus? Easy, Breri. People and places: amazing just how intertwined they can be. In the 1970s, Luciano and Teresina Brero set up a winery in the *borgata* (hamlet) of Breri, located in the territory of the commune of Verduno. It is also where you will find the Barolo vineyard district Breri. So, let's see now: here we have a Brero family that sets up shop in the Borgata Breri, makes wines from the Breri vineyard site, and is potentially able to make a Barolo Breri: could I fit anymore Brero-Breri words into one sentence? Corrado Brero (who took over running the estate from his parents in 2001) started out small and has turned that very small outfit into a winery that makes noteworthy wines from a not exactly small twenty hectares of vines (of which almost half of are planted to Nebbiolo for Barolo production). He deserves further credit for it is thanks to him if we know a little about, and have a chance to taste, the Barolos made from the Breri vineyard district (he has also planted Pelaverga Comune and Barbera).

Besides the I Brè estate, G.B. Burlotto also owns vines in the Breri vineyard district (interestingly, these two wineries each own plots of Nebbiolo in the Boscatto vineyard district as well, allowing you to taste and compare wines from each, provided you get there when the individually vinified lots have not yet been blended together). G.B. Burlotto's plots are full south-facing: super-talented technical director Fabio Alessandria blends the grapes grown on the estate's 0.77 hectares of Breri with some of those of Monvigliero to make the estate's classic Barolo (which is not the Barolo Acclivi: Acclivi is made with a blend of grapes from their Boscatto, Neirane and Rocche dell'Olmo vineyard districts, while the classic Barolo is a blend of Breri grapes with some from Monvigliero). As mentioned previously, from a geological perspective Breri is not too dissimilar from Monvigliero, and guess what, their Barolos are somewhat similar too. The Barolo made from Breri is generally open/develops sooner than Monvigliero's, and is less deep than that one (independently of vine age). Its wines always seem to have an extremely intense note of rose, and are floral to the utmost degree. Like I said at the start, Breri is probably a vineyard district that deserves more attention: in my view, it's a site with outstanding Barolo winemaking potential. And so it is that I believe it likely that more Barolo Breri wines will be available soon enough.

Benchmark wineries/Reference point producers of Barolo Breri: I Brè.

BRICCO AMBROGIO

Township	Roddi
Reference Map	See Map of Roddi MGAs (Ch. 10)
Size (ha) (Tot / Barolo MGA)	48.24 / 19.07
Production 2021 (hl)	1035.95
Altitude	220 – 275 meters a.s.l. roughly
Exposure	From south to southeast passing through south and a small part facing north
N. Claimants MGA	9
Other grape varieties planted:	Barbera; Dolcetto
Land Units	Land Unit of Barolo for the most
Soil (stage):	Tortonian

Producers claiming the MGA

Michele Alessandria; Bruna Grimaldi; Groppone; Lodali; Negretti; Mario Olivero; Paolo Scavino; Piero Mario Ravinale; Salvetti.

Wines

Bruna Grimaldi - Barolo Bricco Ambrogio; **Eredi Lodali** - Barolo Bric Sant'Ambrogio and Barolo Lorens; **Negretti** - Barolo Bricco Ambrogio; **Mario Olivero** - Barolo Bricco Ambrogio; **Paolo Scavino** - Barolo Bricco Ambrogio.

What the producers say

Enrica Scavino (Paolo Scavino): "Recognizing the potential of this *cru*, my father decided to acquire holdings in Bricco Ambrogio in 2001 when it was not yet very well-known. Importantly, this was our only vineyard spared by the horrific hail of 2002, the year we bottled it for the first time as a single *cru* (carrying the name Bricco Ambrogio on the label), which testifies to the site's noteworthy quality potential considering the difficulties we encountered that year with all our other more famous, sites. In our opinion, the Bricco Ambrogio is a Barolo that has an intense aromatic spectrum, with elegant nuances of fresh flowers and ripe red fruits. We find it the vineyard district gives wines characterized by round textures and well-balanced acidity and tannins".

Ian's assessment of the vineyard district, its wines and its potential

The only vineyard district of the Roddi commune, Bricco Ambrogio is located next the Ciocchini vineyard district of La Morra. Only about half the vineyard district is under vine, but of that almost 100% is Nebbiolo. Slopes are steep and the soil is mostly a Saint Agatha Fossil Marls lithology. It follows the wines should have plenty in common with those of the commune of Barolo and some of those of La Morra, and for the most part, that would seem to be so.

Bricco Ambrogio producers and the wines

The previous statement is based on the Barolos I have tasted blind from Bricco Ambrogio over the years, wines that never seem like they might come from Monforte or Serralunga. A number of producers own vines in Bricco Ambrogio, such as for example (in alphabetical order) Bruna Grimaldi, Lodali, Negretti and Paolo Scavino: most use the grapes in their classic Barolos made by blending together grapes from different sites. For the longest time, there was nobody producing a Barolo from this vineyard district, that was really not well known at all. So, in this light, there can be no doubt that Bricco Ambrogio's rise to prominence, or at least to the attention of wine lovers everywhere, is due to the Scavino family of the Paolo Scavino estate in Castiglione Falletto. It is only fair to recognize as much: after all, Enrico Scavino (of the Paolo Scavino estate) was the first to produce a wine wholly from this vineyard district (the rather remarkable 2002, I would like to add). His Bricco Ambrogio is really the benchmark for this site: Scavino's vines are planted on soils with a good proportion of limestone scattered amongst the nutrient-poor blue-grey marl, but benefit also Savino's plenty of ventilation so as to cool down a generally warm mesoclimate, and many old vines. Given how well the vineyard performed for Scavino in the rainy, hail-plagued 2002 vintage, it seems logical to infer that the site does well in rainy years.

Since 2006, Bruna Grimaldi owns two plots in the heart of the Bricco Ambrogio vineyard. It is with the Nebbiolo grapes of the larger (0.7 hectares) of the two, south-facing and with older vines (up to forty years of age) with which they make their Barolo Bricco Ambrogio. The smaller east-facing plot (0.2 hectares), has younger vines (twelve years old), and its grapes are usually blended in the estate's classic Barolo). The first Bruna Grimaldi Barolo Bricco Ambrogio is the 2007 vintage. There are other estates making a Bricco Ambrogio wine, but at least I haven't yet tried anything that is even remotely memorable. The very fine but little-known Mario Oliviero estate has also been making a Barolo Bricco Ambrogio beginning with the 2015 vintage, from vines planted in 2002 at about 250 meters above sea level. In my experience, it's a Barolo that is characterized by smooth tannins and a ready to drink personality already at a young age. It always seems to boast a strongly floral nose, something that Lorenzo Oliviero of the winery also believes.

Bricco Ambrogio tends to give very slowly evolving, somewhat one-dimensional wines when young but that develop into something more interesting with five to eight years in bottle depending on the vintage. In due course, notes of peach, even of passion fruit, sandalwood and pine needles complement violet, rose and red cherry nuances, though Bricco Ambrogio's wines are rarely loaded with oodles or gobs of flesh and fruit. Never the last word in complexity, and not devoid of a certain tannic spine that can leave behind a slightly one-dimensional impression because of that lack of deep and diverse fruit nuances, this vineyard district's easily accessible wines offer plenty of easygoing drinking pleasure.

Benchmark wineries/Reference point producers of Barolo Bricco Ambrogio: Paolo Scavino. Also good: Bruna Grimaldi, Mario Oliviero.

BRICCO BOSCHIS

Township	Castiglione Falletto
Reference Map	See Map of Castiglione MGAs (Ch. 10)
Size (ha) (Tot / Barolo MGA)	17.65 / 11,42
Production 2021 (hl)	432.60 (of which 100 hl of Barolo Riserva *MGA* Vigna)
Altitude	230 – 337 meters a.s.l. roughly
Exposure	From south to southwest in the central part; east on the top of the hill which turns to Serralunga d'Alba; from west to northwest the remaining parts
N. Claimants MGA	2
Other grape varieties planted:	Barbera; Dolcetto; Freisa; Grignolino
Land Units	Land Unit of Barolo in the west side; Land Unit of Castiglione in the east side.
Soil (stage):	Tortonian

Producers claiming the MGA

Cavallotto Tenuta Bricco Boschis; Roccheviberti.

Wines

Cavallotto Tenuta Bricco Boschis - Barolo Bricco Boschis, Barolo Riserva Bricco Boschis Vigna San Giuseppe; **Roccheviberti** - Barolo Bricco Boschis.

What the producers say

Alfio Cavallotto: "From 1928 to 1947, the wine made from the Bricco Boschis cru was bottled in demijohns without labels. From 1948 to 1959 it was bottled as Barolo only, and from 1960 to 1964 as Barolo, Barolo Riserva and Barolo Riserva Speciale. Later, from 1965 to 1969, we changed the wine names so as to have: Barolo, Barolo Bricco Boschis, Barolo Riserva Bricco Boschis, Barolo Riserva Speciale Bricco Boschis. Then, from 1970 to 1993, we bottled a Barolo Riserva Bricco Boschis Vigna San Giuseppe (still in production), Barolo Riserva Bricco Boschis Vigna Colle Sudovest, and a Barolo Riserva Bricco Boschis Vigna Punta Marcello; finally, from 1995 onwards, a Barolo Bricco Boschis and a Barolo Riserva Bricco Boschis Vigna San Giuseppe only and that is where we stand today. We use grapes from all the parts of the hill (higher, lower, central; south, southwest, southeast) so as to give this Barolo better balance, aroma complexity and elegance even in youth, with always sweet tannins and a medium to long aging potential".

Ian's assessment of the vineyard district, its wines and its potential

Essentially a Cavallotto *monopole* (but not quite: see below), Bricco Boschis is an excellent site, one from where many outstanding wines have come from over the last fifty years or so. Curiously, Renato Ratti left it out of his seminal 1980s map on Barolo's crus, something I never had a chance to ask him about; for sure, the *crus* of Castiglione Falletto were somewhat penalized in that otherwise splendid work. A really beautiful place, Bricco Boschis is characterized by an amphitheater of vines situated on its own ridge, just north of the town of Castiglione Falletto, that runs parallel to and in between another ridge to the north (where the Montanello vineyard district is found) and one to the south, where the famous Monprivato vineyard district is located.

Bricco Boschis is an excellent site known for its very balanced Barolos. It is commonly held that the balance of its wines is in large part the result of Bricco Boschis being situated at a meeting point of soils formed during the Tortonian and Serravalian Stages (such that this vineyard district's soils are characterized by both Diano Sandstone Formation and Saint Agatha Fossil Marls lithologies). Though that is partially true, it is hardly so cut and dried. Its landscape classified as a Land Unit of Castiglione; therefore, we know the Bricco Boschis will have a dominant Diano Sandstone presence. However, from a geologic perspective, the Bricco Boschis is a rather unique site in that the summit is sandier than its lower parts, a rare situation indeed, as it's usually the exact opposite. The presence of sand is especially noteworthy, because parts of the Bricco Boschis are really the only sand-dominated of the entire Castiglione Falletto commune.

Bricco Boschis was a fifteen hectares *monopole* of the Cavallotto family until 2010, but at the time of the restructuring of the Barolo vineyard area and the launch of the official MGA vineyard district names for Barolo's vineyard district, it was enlarged with the addition of the Melera area, such that Cavallotto now owns "only" sixteen of the total 17.5 hectares of Bricco Boschis. Over the many years Cavallotto has farmed this site and made Barolo, the family became aware that different parts of the vineyard gave different wines. Eventually, they subdivided the Bricco Boschis into three different sections that they vinified separately beginning with the 1970 vintage, producing three very different Barolos (of Riserva and even Riserva Speciale quality level): the Vigna Colle Sud-Ovest (the name means "southwest hill", but in fact that was a misnomer: the slope faces due south); the Vigna San Giuseppe (currently 2.38 hectares large, which is the central part of the hill, extending out in front and to the left of the Cavallotto winery); and last but not least, the Vigna Punta Marcello (situated immediately to the right of the main winery and houses complex, it's the highest part of the Bricco Boschis). The Punta Marcello's vineyard soil is mainly characterized by the presence of Diano Sandstone and is therefore the sandiest part of the Bricco Boschis (my data shows a composition of 30% loam, 50% sand, 20% clay). By contrast, the soils of the San Giuseppe and the Colle Sud-Ovest vineyards have both the Diano Sandstone and the Saint Agatha Fossil Marls of the sandy type in varying proportions (the composition there is 40% loam, 30% sand, 30% clay). I essentially grew up in Italy drinking these wines throughout my teenage and early adulthood years and I can vouch not just for their difference but also their excellence. For example, I think that in my lifetime I have sat through the complete verticals of the Vigna Colle Sudovest and Vigna Punta Marcello at least on two different occasions, if not three. Plus, as I liked them, I collected these wines too, and so am very well versed in what this specific piece of Nebbiolo real estate offers. Which is plenty.

Of the three Barolos made between 1970 and 1993, the family members always felt the most different and best was the southwest-facing, sunlit San Giuseppe, a function not just of its mesoclimate and soil, but also of vine age (planted in 1961, it was the oldest vineyard of the three: however, not all its vines were that old: only those closest to the Colle Sud-Ovest section were especially old). The San Giuseppe vineyard was special also because of the presence of about 10% Nebbiolo Rosé amongst its old Nebbiolo vines but in fact, there was even more Nebbiolo Rosé (30% or more) in the Punta Marcello vineyard, in the southeastern section of the Bricco Boschis. Sadly, in 1992 those old biotype (or perhaps biotypes?) of Nebbiolo Rosé was/were uprooted in favor of the Nebbiolo clone CN 111, which is an excellent clone of Nebbiolo Rosé (Cavallotto now refers to this clone as a variant of Lampia as some have recently begun postulating that it may actually be a Nebbiolo Lampia clone that looks and behaves very much like Nebbiolo Rosé, though most people I have talked to, despite what the supposed experts are saying now, don't believe it is a Lampia at all. See chapter 3, NEBBIOLO ROSÉ).

In 1993, the family decided to simplify its range of Barolos and beginning with the 1995 vintage, have made only two Barolos from the Bricco Boschis: a Barolo Bricco Boschis and a Barolo Riserva San Giuseppe (in 1994, a miserable year, the whole production was declassified to Langhe Nebbiolo, which tells you a little something about how seriously and passionately the Cavallotto family takes its job: good show!). The Barolo Riserva San Giuseppe is made with grapes from the central part of the Bricco Boschis, which, as it's felt to be the best part of the vineyard, ought to give grapes of Barolo Riserva quality. For sure, it's the section of Bricco Boschis that gives the most powerful and the most balanced wines. This is in no small measure due to San Giuseppe's soil water availability (independently of whether the growing season is dry or rainy, the vines of San Giuseppe always suffer drought less than those of other parts of the Bricco Boschis). By contrast, the Barolo Bricco Boschis is made from the remaining grapes grown in the amphitheater, and especially from what used to be the other two named areas. Those two wines were phased out for reasons that are easy enough to understand. Given the very sandy nature of Punta Marcello's soil, the wines from this section of the Bricco Boschis were always less structured and so it made little sense to use them to make a Riserva wine; and the Colle Sud-Ovest, being the direct prolongation (or continuation, if you will) of the Vigna San Giuseppe, gave a wine that mostly duplicated what the San Giuseppe was already offering and therefore the family felt there was need to complicate its portfolio offerings so. That much recognized, call me a Barolo geek all you want, but I loved the three different permutations of the Bricco Boschis vineyard and was sorry to see those three wines disappear (two of them, at least), because I for one did think there were differences between their three vineyard-designated Barolos (and I'm not the only one). However, such differences might have escaped most casual wine drinkers; given the need to simplify one's range of wines, I see the Cavallotto family's point in doing so.

Bricco Boschis producers and the wines

For sure, the two wines made by the Cavallotto family nowadays from the Bricco Boschis are better defined and very different one from the other. I have always viewed their Barolo Bricco Boschis as an archetype of the Barolo of the Castiglione Falletto commune: never the most powerful or perfumed Barolo, but always amongst the most balanced. It delivers its classic mix of power and grace (in most vintages) with perfect charm and equilibrium. (In fact, their Barolo Bricco Boschis has no shortage of power.) By contrast, the Barolo Riserva San Giuseppe is a bit of a monster, an almost un-Castiglione Falletto wine because of its brooding and surprising toughness when young (it ages four to five years in oak). While both wines age remarkably well, I find the Bricco Boschis Barolo is best within its first fifteen-twenty years of life, while the Riserva Vigna San Giuseppe has much longer staying power (forty years and counting are not a stretch, in good vintages, though I doubt very many bottles are ever allowed to reach that ripe old age).

On an unrelated note (unrelated to Nebbiolo and Barolo wines, that is), I wish to make everyone aware that Cavallotto still farms vines of Grignolino and Freisa planted within the boundaries of the Bricco Boschis. These two native grapes (once very common in the Langhe but that have lost much ground to Nebbiolo over the last few decades) make absolutely lovely wines and they deserve your attention and support. Clearly, it would make a lot more financial sense for the Cavallotto family to just uproot everything and plant the much more remunerative Nebbiolo. But that would be a real pity and clearly not the best way to help preserve our planet's biodiversity: the Grignolino vines were planted in 1974 and make just a lovely wine that can be really spectacular in some vintages, while the Freisa, of which there are thrice as many plants, was planted in 1991 and the resulting wine is also a knockout. Listen, as good as the Cavallotto Barolos are, and they are, their Grignolino and Freisa wines are absolutely noteworthy too, so don't miss out on them.

The Roccheviberti estate owns a small piece of vines in the Bricco Boschis but started producing a Barolo Bricco Boschis only recently (prior to that it sold the grapes to another famous Barolo winery, but not Cavallotto as has been previously reported). His Bricco Boschis holdings amount to two plots, a larger one that was recently replanted (so the vines are about ten years old) and a smaller plot with much older vines (about 35 years old). The wine is not that distant in aroma and flavor profile from the Cavallotto Bricco Boschis bottling, as it should be.

Benchmark wineries/Reference point producers of Barolo Bricco Boschis: Cavallotto. Also good: Roccheviberti.

BRICCO CHIESA

Township	La Morra
Reference Map	See Map of La Morra MGAs (Ch. 10)
Size (ha) (Tot / Barolo MGA)	14.00 / 3,86
Production 2021 (hl)	161.34
Altitude	210 – 290 meters a.s.l. roughly
Exposure	Southeast
N. Claimants MGA	2
Other grape varieties planted:	Barbera; Dolcetto
Land Units	Land Unit of Barolo
Soil (stage):	Tortonian

Producers claiming the MGA

Silvio Alessandria; Poderi Oddero.

Wines

Silvio Alessandria - Barolo Bricco Chiesa; **Poderi Oddero** - Barolo Bricco Chiesa (*).

What the producers say

Mariacristina Oddero (Poderi Oddero): "This vineyard has been always part of our family. These heterogenous four hectares were acquired in different times. It's biologically certified since 2008 and at the time it was almost an experiment for us to try go down this path. This vineyard district boasts a soil rich in clay, but I find Barolos from this *cru* are very perfumed, round and endowed with good color, characterized by a very floral note and a lighter, fresher fruit nuance than say Barolos from Brunate (especially so on the nose). Most importantly, they are perfect in blend with grapes from Fiasco and Capalot. For this vineyard area we choose a very traditional vinification with maceration and fermentation lasting roughly 25 – 30 days or more".

Ian's assessment of the vineyard district, its wines and its potential

Bricco Chiesa is a little-known Barolo production area that makes elegant wines that nonetheless are of sneaky structure and mettle. The vineyard district is located in the Santa Maria section of La Morra (and that bit of knowledge immediately tells you, or should tell you, a lot about what Bricco Chiesa Barolos will taste like), sharing mostly small extensions of its borders with the vineyard districts of Bettolotti to the north, Rive to the northeast, Capalot roughly to the west, Galina to the southwest, and Santa Maria to the south and east. The *strada provinciale* SP 236 that passes through the village or fraction of Santa Maria on the way to Alba also cuts more or less through the middle of the Bricco Chiesa vineyard district and its vines (isn't progress just so wonderful?). In fact, the real Bricco Chiesa, or Bricco Chiesa proper, is the expanse of vineyards found on your right side (higher up) as you drive downhill towards Alba; while those on the left, on the other side of the road and lower down than those on the right, really belong to the area historically known as La Sarmassa (careful, don't confuse this Sarmassa with the very famous Sarmassa vineyard district of the Barolo commune).

Bricco Chiesa producers and the wines

To wit, the only estate producing a Barolo Bricco Chiesa today, Silvio Alessandria, is located in the *borgata* (hamlet) Sarmassa of the *frazione* (fraction) Santa Maria of the La Morra commune. The estate's history dates back to at least 1883, when the great-grandfather of current owner Enzo Alessandria (the Alessandria Silvio estate is named after Enzo's father Silvio) used to own vines and made wine for home consumption. The winery's Bricco Chiesa vineyard was planted in 1958, and it is the first Barolo the estate ever produced; but it is not the only Barolo made from old vines you will find from this address. Beginning with the 2018 vintage, Alessandria Silvia also launched a Barolo Capalot from the vineyard district of same name (Alessandria actually owns very old vines in the Rive vineyard district as well, that like those of Capalot, were planted in 1950). Alessandria's Bricco Chiesa holding is 0.486 hectares large, south/southeast-facing, and the wine traditionally made, aged two years in 25 hectoliter Slavonian oak barrels. It's a floral, softer Barolo that can be drunk even at a young age, and therein lies part of its charm. Unfortunately, there's not much of this lovely nectar to go around: for example, in the 2018 vintage, only 1620 bottles and 254 magnums were made (plus forty double magnums, all reserved for the Danish market).

Other very fine estates own vineyards in the Bricco Chiesa and use its grapes to make their classic estate Barolo wines. Poderi Oddero's vineyard is an historic one for the family, in fact it's the vineyard that surrounds the main winery building and cellar (just imagine that documents filed away in the old records of the La Morra Parish attest to the Oddero family owing houses and fields/vineyards in the Santa Maria fraction of La Morra already in the seventeenth century, which is when their winery building and cellar dates back to). It is also an historic vineyard in that up until the 1960s the Barolo of Poderi Oddero was entirely made only with La Morra grapes, and not too many wine lovers are aware that the vineyard area known as Bricco Chiesa today always contributed to a greater or lesser amount to Poderi Oddero's Barolo of the time, depending on the vintage.

Poderi Oddero's Bricco Chiesa holdings are 2.56 hectares with south/southeast-facing vines planted at about 275 meters above sea level. Vine age there varies. The oldest section is the one closest to, and just above, the Santa Maria delle Neve church: those Nebbiolo vines are over seventy years old. Other sections of the vineyard were planted in the 1970s, and others still in 1997. Up until now, the estate has always used the grapes for their classic estate Barolo, and has not thought of making a single-vineyard district wine from Bricco Chiesa (I grant you, it's not as if Poderi Oddero doesn't already have enough single vineyard district bottlings to offer). The soil is a classic mix of very fine clays, loam, and sand. Over the years, Mariacristina Oddero has always told me that though Bricco Chiesa's wines never have much color it's an easygoing Barolo that offers plenty of charm and early accessibility, but has plenty of body to stand up to all the usual fare Barolos are routinely paired with. In fact, these characteristics may be due to more than just the site's geological and topographical characteristics. For one, Poderi Oddero's Bricco Chiesa parcels are planted with the Nebbiolo 142 clone, which tends to give wines that are more perfumed and lighter in texture.

To be clear, I think that the 142 clone is an excellent one that makes for lovely, balanced Barolos, wines that are always so much more elegant and easier to drink, a signature of the Bricco Chiesa vineyard district. Unfortunately, as it commonly happens to older clones, nowadays they get bypassed in favour of newer clones that are always said to be so much better and improved with respect to the older pre-existing clones: this may well be the case, but it is not always so, and clone 142 was and is a real good one, despite it being developed a long time ago (See Appendix A, Table 1.4: *Abridged characteristics of the most important Nebbiolo clones*. See also: Table 1.5: *Viticultural and winemaking characteristics of Nebbiolo's most common clones* and chapter 1, NEBBIOLO LAMPIA). Very interestingly, in better vintages Poderi Oddero plans to tweak its winemaking with Bricco Chiesa's grapes, utilizing the *cappello sommerso* technique after the alcoholic fermentation process has just about terminated. In such cases, skin contact is prolonged in excess of thirty days, so that the resulting wine is always more structured than it usually is. I point this out because if you have had any experience at all with Poderi Oddero's classic Barolo, you know it can seem different vintage to vintage, and that difference is therefore due to more than just the grapes source. Clearly though, the Poderi Oddero signature house style is always the dominant factor at play in all vintages.

Another estate that owns Nebbiolo vines in the Bricco Chiesa is Francone. Francone may not be one of the better-known producers of Barolo (if for no other reason because they are a Barbaresco estate based in Neive, but have in fact producing a Barolo since 1958), theirs is a very solid Barolo indeed (in fact, their Barbaresco is excellent too). Francone's holding in Bricco Chiesa is a southeast-facing plot planted at 220 meters above sea level characterized by the typical Saint Agatha Fossil Marls lithology. The soil composition there is 60% loam, 25% clay and 15% sand. It is Fabrizio Francone's belief that the Bricco Chiesa grapes give a fruitier, more forward type of Barolo that is not especially structured. In fact, he picks the grapes at practically a "late-harvest" stage, or slightly later than he might otherwise (which no doubt accentuates his Bricco Chiesa Barolo's profile of superripe sultry fruit). This happens because Francone's vineyard holdings in Barolo are small: between the grapes grown in Bricco Chiesa and those they grow in their Ravera di Monforte vineyard district holding, they can only make about 4000 bottles of Barolo a year. As such, they prefer to blend the grapes from the two vineyard districts together in order to make a classic estate Barolo. A traditionally bent producer, Francone ferments for roughly twenty-two days (on the skins for the first sixteen) in stainless steel vats at controlled temperatures ranging between 24-28 degrees Celsius and is aged in French oak 700-1200-liters barrels for about thirty months. Given the blend with grapes from a very different site such as Ravera di Monforte, it's impossible to discern what Bricco Chiesa is about by tasting this specific finished wine; suffice it to say that uniting grapes from La Morra and Monforte achieves that balanced blend of power and grace that the best Barolos always showcase to very good effect.

Based on my experience, I'd say that the typical descriptors of a Bricco Chiesa Barolo are violet, redcurrant and red cherry. Darker notes (black cherry, plum, blackberry), that are generally rare in Barolo, are more typical of Francone's blend and most likely derived from the presence of Ravera di Monforte grapes (at least based on my experience tasting the wines of the latter vineyard district). For the same reason, the freshness and tannic framework of Francone' Barolo is Ravera di Monforte-derived, while the Bricco Chiesa contributes a warm and suave red cherry and floral fruit sensations. Truth be told, the latter's contribution of warmth and softness is partly due to the grapes being harvested at a slightly superripe stage, bordering on the late harvest, while the estate waits for the Nebbiolo in the cooler Ravera di Monforte habitat to reach optimal ripeness. It's a delicate balancing act to get just right, but at Francone, they do so brilliantly. Well done.

Benchmark wineries/Reference point producers of Barolo Bricco Chiesa: Silvio Alessandria.

BRICCO COGNI

Township	La Morra
Reference Map	See Map of La Morra MGAs (Ch. 10)
Size (ha) (Tot / Barolo MGA)	43.91 / 1.78
Production 2021 (hl)	97.02
Altitude	250 – 330 meters a.s.l. roughly
Exposure	West
N. Claimants MGA	3
Other grape varieties planted:	Barbera; Dolcetto; white varieties
Land Units	Land Unit of Verduno
Soil (stage):	Messinian

Producers claiming the MGA

Reverdito; Prandi; Cantina Stroppiana.

Wines

Reverdito - Barolo Bricco Cogni.

What the producers say

Michele Reverdito (Reverdito): "My family acquired a holding in this cru in 1967. Our Bricco Cogni Barolo is characterized by intensely rich perfume with an impressive combination of notes of herbs, toast, flowers and spices, and we believe it offers very good sweetness of fruit. Deep, complex and fleshy, it has, in our estimation, great aging potential".

Ian's assessment of the vineyard district, its wines and its potential

At forty-four hectares, Bricco Cogni is a relatively large vineyard district located in the northwestern corner of La Morra commune's territory. Close by are the La Morra vineyard districts of San Giacomo and Castagni, and the Neirane of Verduno. It's not surprising then that Bricco Cogni shares a similar geology to all these sites (save for Neirane, which differs somewhat): that of the Cassano-Spinola Formation of the marly type, created during the Messinian Stage of the Miocene epoch. It is a soil formation associated with lighter-styled Barolos that are more floral than fruity: their trump cards are levity and grace, rather than brute power and size. But given that only about 20% of Bricco Cogni is under vine, which in and of itself tells us something, it's not as if there are many Barolos from here one gets to try (however, it is encouraging that three quarters of the wine grapes that are planted are of Nebbiolo).

Although others own or farm vineyards in Bricco Cogni such as for example the Terre del Barolo cooperative, to the best of my knowledge the only one currently producing a Barolo Bricco Cogni is Michele Reverdito, who is lucky enough to own very old vines, planted by his father Silvano back in 1967 at about 300 meters above sea level. Reverdito's first vintage of Barolo Bricco Cogni actually dates back to 2000. A delightful Barolo, Reverdito's Barolo from Bricco Cogni highlights the benefits brought on by the altitude of the vines as it is rarely marred by jammy or overly fleshy tones. Fairly traditionally made from organically grown grapes, the wine is a politely-styled Barolo in keeping with this part of the La Morra terroir (and the Land Unit of Verduno, which is associated with rather politely-styled Barolos) and often boasts a strong note of licorice. A good site, Bricco Cogni is most likely undervalued.

Benchmark wineries/Reference point producers of Barolo Bricco Chiesa: Reverdito.

BRICCO DELLE VIOLE

Township	Barolo
Reference Map	See Map of Barolo MGAs (Ch. 10)
Size (ha) (Tot / Barolo MGA)	45.74 / 19.38
Production 2021 (hl)	1,078.79 (of which 627.15 hl of Barolo Riserva *MGA*)
Altitude	390 – 480 meters a.s.l. roughly
Exposure	From east to southeast in the part below the road and from south to southeast on the Bricco Estate side.
N. Claimants MGA	7
Other grape varieties planted:	Barbera; Dolcetto; white varieties
Land Units	Land Unit of Vergne; Land Unit of La Morra; Land Unit of Berri
Soil (stage):	Tortonian

Producers claiming the MGA

460 Casina Bric; Carlo Dogliani; Domenico Franco; G.D. Vajra; Mario Marengo; Cabutto - Tenuta La Volta; Viberti.

Wines

460 Casina Bric - Barolo Bricco delle Viole; **G.D. Vajra** - Barolo Bricco delle Viole; **Mario Marengo** - Barolo Bricco delle Viole; **Viberti** - Barolo Riserva Bricco delle Viole; **Sylla Sebaste** - Barolo Bricco delle Viole.

What the producers say

Aldo Vaira (G.D.Vajra): "Bricco delle Viole has been in the family for generations. We started to vinify and bottle it separately in 1985. The fine and silky texture of tannins is the element that characterizes the best Barolo Bricco Delle Viole wines. It's a Barolo from the Barolo township, meaning that the characteristic notes of Nebbiolo are delineated in their most delicate and elegant way. Notes of cherries, dark berries, withered violet and rose that run through nuances of citrus fruit, and sometimes mint. It's always very balanced, and with a long finish of fresh delicate spices. Bricco delle Viole is a synonym of elegance; it's also a wine that with its nature has guided the style of the estate and has taught us about patience".

Marco Marengo (Mario Marengo): "Barolo Bricco delle Viole has been part of the estate since about 60-70 years ago. I believe this cru is noted for its floral notes".

Claudio Viberti (Viberti): "Bricco delle Viole is one of the major *crus* falling within the township of Barolo and also one of the highest in terms of altitude. For example, our vineyard sits at 400-500 meters above sea level, with south and southeast exposures and a clay-limestone soil. The wines produced here are undoubtedly elegant with fine and feminine characteristics; the site's high altitude can be identified with the lovely freshness and minerality of its wines, supported by a noteworthy acidic backbone".

Bricco delle Viole takes its pretty name from the fact that, when they are in season it is truly full of wild violets. Neighboring vineyard districts are Coste di Vergne to the west; San Ponzio to the southwest and to the south; La Volta to the southeast, but mostly to east; San Pietro to the northeast; and Fossati to the north. It is one of the larger vineyard districts of the municipality of Barolo and is also one of the highest, since the altitude of its vineyards ranges roughly between 380 and 500 meters above sea level. This is especially true of the section of Bricco delle Viole that is to your right as you drive on the road going from the town of Barolo to that of Vergne; the stretch of vines to your right is the historic portion of Bricco dell Viole (the side with the Cascina Bricco), ranging in altitude from about 420 to 500 meters above sea level compared to the roughly 360-420 meters of the section of the vineyard district on your left. Given Bricco delle Viole's high altitude, Nebbiolo had trouble ripening here as recently as the 1970s, but in today's hotter times, the 400+ meters above sea level at which the Nebbiolo is planted at (on average) throughout the vineyard district are just what the doctor ordered. In this light, and like many other modern-day vineyard districts that were once not especially renowned for the quality of their Nebbiolo grapes and their potential for producing extra-fine Barolo, Bricco delle Viole is a site that has undoubtedly benefited from climate change. Soil-wise, Bricco delle Viole is very complex (made up of not one, not two, but three different landscape land units) but it is visibly clay-rich (and deep clay at that) and lithologically speaking, mostly consistent with the Saint Agatha Marls Formation of the laminated type. Every time I walk the Bricco delle Viole, I find that in some spots its soil reminds me of parts of Brunate (the soils of both tend to be rich in white calcareous-clay: though of the two, Bricco delle Viole is undoubtedly the one that has more clay). This is something that local producers such as Marco Marengo (of the Mario Marengo estate), who obviously are all more expert in the matter than I, agree with.

Bricco delle Viole producers and the wines

That Bricco delle Viole is a great site in which to make Barolo today is easily attested to by the noteworthy wines made by estates like G.D. Vajra and Mario Marengo; Sylla Sebaste and Giovanni Viberti (or Viberti, as the label writes clearly) have made good wines from this site over the years as well, though it behooves me to say that the former estate's Barolo Bussia is a wildly better wine than the Barolo they make from Bricco delle Viole (for reasons I shall outline clearly: see BUSSIA file). Casina Bric 460, owned by Gianluca Viberti is one of the at least two different Viberti estates making wines from Bricco delle Viole (careful now, don't get your Vibertis all mixed up: Viberti is a very common family name in Barolo, and there's a slew of them making wines at different estates). The name "Casina Bric 460" combines Piedmontese dialect words meaning "*cascina bricco*" (or "house on top of the hill") and the 460 meters that is the average elevation of the estate's vineyards. Besides standing out for the original shape of its bottle (but perhaps not so original: after all, it is the "*poirinotta*", a very old bottle design made in the town of Poirino on the outskirts of Turin back in the 1700s), Casina Bric 460's wines are also remarkable for their organically farmed grapes, traditional winemaking and accessible prices.

However, there is no doubt whatsoever that over the years, the estate that has done the most to bring to the fore the intrinsic qualities of Bricco delle Viole and its wines is G.D. Vajra. The estate owns eleven blocks in the vineyard district but usually only five are used to make the Barolo that bears the vineyard district name (these are vines that average about 50-80 years of age). Like most of the producers in the area, they own vines in both sections (sides) of the Bricco delle Viole. Their Barolo from this site is a wine of remarkable grace and refinement: it's the benchmark by which all other Bricco delle Viole Barolos must be measured against. At G.D. Vajra, in an effort to understand and showcase all that the Bricco delle Viole terroir can express, they have planted there all the different known Nebbiolo biotypes, and on different rootstocks as well. As mentioned previously, not all the Nebbiolo plots within the Bricco delle Viole are used every year by the Vaira Family (just in case you didn't know, the estate name is spelled with a "j", but the family name is actually Vaira, with an "i") to make the Barolo Bricco delle Viole (those grapes not selected for the Barolo Bricco delle Viole go into the estate's classic Barolo). Very interestingly, this means that the Nebbiolo biotype makeup of the wine changes from vintage to vintage. For example, only three biotypes made it into the 2009 Barolo Bricco delle Viole; it was two in 2008; four in 2010; and all five were used in the 2011, 2012 and 2013 bottlings. In 2013, they vinified a trial single plot Bricco delle Viole with the Picotener biotype only and made a Barolo Riserva that has not (yet?) been put on sale. Otherwise, I point out that the 2013 Bricco delle Viole is an especially interesting wine made mostly from Nebbiolo Michet with small percentages of both Nebbiolo Lampia and Rosé. Independently of how good the wines are (and they are) and how nice the Vaira family is, such desire and quest for knowledge and research, well…you just can't help but love these people.

Marco Marengo, who runs the Mario Marengo estate, owns 0.45 hectares in Bricco delle Viole that were originally the property of Marco Bianco, his wife's grandfather, who had always sold the grapes. With the 1997 vintage, the grandfather finally let go (given just how attached to their grapes the older generation in Piedmont are, believe me, you cannot even begin to imagine just how apt my specific and intended choice of words really is in this context), and Marengo was at last able to bottle the wine (at the time, it spent two years in oak barriques, 25-40% of which new oak). Marengo's plots in the Bricco delle Viole are even higher up than those of G.D. Vajra, and this reality will be very apparent to you if and when you taste the two wines side by side in the same vintage. Of these two different wines, Marengo's is always, the fresher and lighter-bodied wine of the two (though both are almost always, in most vintages at least, vibrant Barolos): which you'll prefer is really a matter of different strokes for different folks. Claudio Viberti of the Giovanni Viberti (not just a wine producer but also a restauranteur of some repute, with the traditional Trattoria del Buon Padre in Vergne a source of excellent *piatti langaroli*), owns four vineyard plots inside the vineyard district. The vines face mainly south and southeast, and the soil has that vineyard district's classic clay-calcareous composition. The resulting wines are decidedly elegant, with very fine, nuanced primary aromas that build towards licorice, tar and tobacco with age. The altitude at which the grapevines grow is recognizable in this estate's wines too, characterized by wonderful freshness thanks to a noteworthy acid spine. One plot is almost always used to make the estate's Barolo Riserva Bricco Delle Viole (it extends for 0.5 hectares), while grapes from the other three vineyard plots are mostly blended in the winery's classic Barolo Buon Padre. I want to point out that in the heart of this vineyard district grows a roughly 80 years old Barbera vineyard (used to make Viberti's Barbera Bricco Airoli).

Claudio Viberti is the talented, passionate young man that is now at the helm of the Viberti estate (also known as Viberti Giovanni in Italy, or Giovanni Viberti) in Vergne. He is lucky man in that his family, besides owning and running the excellent Trattoria Buon Padre in Vergne [located just a stone's throw away from the G.D. Vajra winery (the restaurant is a good spot for truly traditional, authentic, Langhe home cooking)], also owns a large collection of vineyards in some of the most famous vineyard districts of the Barolo denomination. Viberti has five vineyard plots in the Bricco delle Viole divided in two holdings, one below the road at 400-420 meters and the other above the road at roughly 450 meters in altitude. The soils are typically loamy-clay with very little sand. From the oldest vines in Bricco delle Viole, planted at 420 meters above sea level in 1967, Viberti makes in the best years a Barolo Bricco delle Viole Riserva. I find it is always immediately recognizable even in blind tastings for its strong notes of mint, eucalyptus and balsamic oils (which of the three prevails will depend on how hot, or not, the vintage was). Like the wines of almost every other producer making a Barolo from the Bricco delle Viole, the acidity levels are high and the perfumed red fruit aromas and flavors are typically crisp and vibrant.

In ultimate analysis, all the Bricco delle Viole wines I have tasted over the years were characterized by freshness and refinement, with a sleek, vibrant mouthfeel. That much admitted, I wish to point out that differently from some other vineyard districts, in warmer vintages not all the Bricco delle Viole wines have struck me as being really as cool-climate in their profile as one might expect. Witness for example the G.D. Vajra 2000 Bricco delle Viole, in which, though a wonderful Barolo, its superripe, borderline jammy fruit makes it taste nothing like a wine made so higher up. It may just be a matter of "the degree of heat", given that the G.D. Vajra's 2001 Barolo Bricco delle Viole is instead one of the best wines of that great vintage, and that, as I wrote earlier in this subchapter, Vajra's Bricco delle Viole is almost always a Barolo marked by noteworthy lift and vibrancy. The 2001 vintage was also characterized by a warm growing season (so that is why I write of "degrees of heat"), but it wasn't quite as hot as the 2000, and that really seems to have made a big difference in the finished wines (all other things being equal, but at G.D. Vajra, ever the passionate students and the talented tinkerers, I am not sure they were).

Benchmark wineries/ Reference point producers of Barolo Bricco delle Viole: G.D. Vajra. Also good: Mario Marengo, Viberti.

BRICCO LUCIANI

Township	La Morra
Reference Map	See Map of La Morra MGAs (Ch. 10)
Size (ha) (Tot / Barolo MGA)	16.09 / 2.82
Production 2021 (hl)	153.16
Altitude	220 – 255 meters a.s.l. roughly
Exposure	From southeast to southwest in the better exposed parcels, from north to northeast in the remaining parts.
N. Claimants MGA	3
Other grape varieties planted:	Barbera; Dolcetto; white varieties
Land Units	Land Unit of Barolo
Soil (stage):	Tortonian

Producers claiming the MGA

Cascina del Monastero; Silvio Grasso; Mauro Molino.

Wines

Cascina del Monastero - Barolo Bricco Luciani; **Silvio Grasso** - Barolo Bricco Luciani; **Mauro Molino** - Barolo Bricco Luciani.

What the producers say

Paolo Grasso (Silvio Grasso): "Bricco Luciani belongs to our family since 1927, and we feel like it has been part if it since always. Bricco Luciani is a Barolo of structure and elegance".

Matteo Molino (Mauro Molino): "In our view, this wine typifies the elegance of La Morra. The Bricco Luciani, located in Annunziata of La Morra, is named after the farmhouse which in the past used to be a monastery of nuns. The vineyard is at about 270 meters in altitude and presents a fairly compact soil of clay and limestone. The winery owns an area of 0.8 hectares, with a southeastern exposure. We feel it's an extraordinarily elegant and pleasant Barolo, with an intense floral aroma".

Loris Grasso (Cascina del Monastero): "The pride and joy of Cascina del Monastero, Barolo Bricco Luciani is made from selected grapes grown on a vineyard facing due south on a thin strip of land between Annunziata and Cascina Luciani. The calcareous-clayey soil is quite compact, and the grapes harvested here have always produced big wines packed with aromas. There is a curious story behind the name of this small hill: towards the end of the 1700s, when the farm was still owned by Benedictine monks, it was visited by a priest who was to become famous several years later as Pope Pius VII. He tasted the precious nectar made from the grapes grown there and was so enchanted by the beauty of the place and the wine it produced that he is said to have exclaimed with delight: "Ah! Morra! Beautiful skies and good wine!". In memory of this event, the hill has been known ever since as "Bricco Luciani" (*luciani* from "luce", the Italian word for light), and it has to be said that the brightness of the garnet red wine seems to conjure up a long-standing tradition of country-style genuineness and sincerity. Barolo Bricco Luciani is still produced according to the traditional style of days gone by".

Ian's assessment of the vineyard district, its wines and its potential

Bricco Luciani is one in a series of four Bricco-something vineyard districts of La Morra located roughly northeast of the Annunziata fraction; moving roughly diagonally from northeast to southwest the four are in order Bricco Manescotto, Bricco Manzoni, Bricco Luciani and Bricco Rocca (the last three occupy independent and roughly parallel wedge-like ridges). If you are into your geography then you realize that from an aerial perspective and using the four cardinal points of the compass to direct yourself by, this also means that Bricco Luciani has to its east Bricco Manzoni; to its north Gattera; and to the northwest/west Conca, all La Morra vineyard districts.

Bricco Luciani's landscape is classified as a Land Unit of Barolo, which essentially means the vineyard district has soils formed during the Tortonian stage of the Miocene epoch. It follows that the lithology is of the Saint Agatha Fossil Marls, that in Bricco Luciani are mostly of the sandy type. In fact, studying the soil composition throughout the vineyard district demonstrates remarkable consistency in percentages of soil loam, sand, and clay: my own data bank of Bricco Luciani soil analysis compiled over twenty years shows remarkable similarity between samples sourced in different sections of the vineyard district (essentially 45% loam, 30% sand, and 25% clay). This is especially interesting given that Bricco Luciani is a newly formed vineyard district (resulting from the restructuring of the Barolo denomination's vineyards and the launch of the official MGA-named vineyard district names that took place in 2010) annexing the area previously known as Gancia (therefore, if you have tasted Barolo Gancia wines in the past, those would be named Barolo Bricco Luciani today).

Bricco Luciani producers and the wines

It's probably fair to say that of the previously mentioned four "Bricco" vineyard districts, it is Bricco Luciani that is best known, most likely on the strength and visibility of the Barolo Bricco Luciani of the Silvio Grasso estate. I always thought that the Nebbiolo vines in this area gave perfectly serviceable, even good wines, but I never really thought of this as a top-tier source of Barolo. That is, until one fateful day now many, many years ago (early 2000s or so) when I tasted Silvio Grasso's 1996 Barolo Bricco Luciani once again but with some bottle age on it. A wine or site that had never struck me as being exceptional before that one time, I changed my mind after the first sip (and many many sips after that, just so I could be sure: for the purposes of study, you understand). Had I written this book before that fateful day, I would have placed Bricco Luciani at the *lieu-dit*, or excellent, level; but after that wine, I started paying increased attention to the wines from this vineyard district and have to admit I understand its terroir and its wines much better today than I ever did before. Sometimes, a little more time really is a necessity to the writing of a better book on any given subject.

Silvio Grasso is by far the name most associated with the site, thought there are many fine estates making wine from this vineyard district. At Silvio Grasso they have been making wine since 1927, but it was Federico Grasso who started estate-bottling in 1980. At first, the wines were almost always characterized (some might say marred, but I never thought so: they were just wines that needed time) by use of very toasty oak, as was fashionable at the time (admittedly, a copious use at that: two years of aging in new barriques was typical) but the wines are handled more gingerly today, much to the benefit of the expression of signature of site. Grasso's Bricco Luciani holdings span about 1.5 hectares and are located just above the section of the vineyard district that was previously known as Gancia (and that is now part of the roughly sixteen hectares that makes up the modern-day Bricco Luciani). The vines are about forty years old, face full south and are planted at 250 meters above sea level. It's a very complete wine that offers notes of violet and rose, plus an underlying current of licorice and sweet spices.

On that note, let me add that prior to the official naming of the Barolo vineyard districts in 2010, "Gancia" is the name that the Mauro Molino winery used for its Barolo (and they weren't the only ones) made from their 0.8 hectares of Nebbiolo vines grown in what is today's Bricco Luciani. Why Gancia? Well, "Gancia" was a very common family name in the area: basically, everyone who owned land there was called Gancia. I'm not exaggerating, or kidding: Molino himself bought his piece of the vineyard district from a Mr. Gancia too (in fact, "Gancia" is also the name of a *borgata*, or hamlet, located on the summit there). Molino's piece of Bricco Luciani is right behind the house, southeast-facing vines planted on very calcareous soil (meaning a very basic pH) but that also has quite a bit of sand in it (for those scientifically-inclined like me, the actual soil composition is 45% loam, 30% sand and 25% clay), accounting for an element of grace and steeliness in the finished wines that is really never missing. Their plot is an amphitheater and has a fairly warm mesoclimate, something the relatively low-lying location also contributes too. No matter: these are always wines that speak of La Morra very clearly, and with a little experience, it's very hard to confuse them with those of any other Barolo commune. Molino first made a wine from this site with the 1995 vintage: he believes this is his most classic Barolo, more structured and astringent when young than his Conca and Gallinotto bottlings (which makes total sense, given what we know of the three sites) with very good age-worthiness (and based on my experience, I'd agree with that too). This is another wine that began life aged for up to two years in barriques (again, that was the new normal back then), about 30% of which were new; but you need to be aware that Molino experimented often and didn't mind trying different things. And so, for example, the 2006 Barolo Gancia was aged in large oak barrels, but Molino remained unconvinced and so in 2007 went back to all barriques again. Interestingly, back then Molino used only six to nine days maceration for this wine, and for reasons I don't remember now, used to macerate the classic Barolo more (about twelve days). Even more interesting to me is that Molino's Gancia was planted all to the Nebbiolo Michet biotype (but Matteo Molino told me already ten years ago or so: "… or close to it; but I'm not sure we'll keep it that way, as you learn almost immediately, it doesn't produce much at all"). I have good memories of Molino's 2008 Gancia, really very good (and at the time, the vineyard was only about twenty-five years old), and the 2001 and 2006 were even better.

Bricco Luciani is a very important vineyard district for the Cascina del Monastero winery too. Founded in 1990 when Giuseppe Grasso separated from his brother, the estate bottled its first wines in 1993. Over the years, the estate has made either single Barolo wines from the Bricco Luciani and the Bricco Rocca (and later from the Annunziata vineyard district as well), or in less favorable vintages blended the grapes from the two into one Barolo. Its excellent Bricco Luciani Barolo is made from fully south-facing vines planted on clay-calcareous soil. There are essentially two plots: the older vineyard, up at the summit of the *bricco*, was planted in 1952, but the lower-lying vineyard that stretches out almost to the Conca vineyard district is no slouch in the "old vines" department either, given that it was planted in 1970. Fermentation lasts for roughly 25-40 days in stainless steel tanks and the wine is aged in a mix of barriques and larger oak barrels for a minimum of thirty-six months up to a whopping sixty, depending on the vintage and what the wine tastes like. It is a sturdy but perfumed wine that ages well, though I think it's best drunk within the first ten years of its life.

Another Bricco Luciani wine that was once also called by the Gancia moniker was Angelo Veglio's Barolo Bricco dei Gancia. I liked the 2006 and even the 2007; part of that statement surprises even me, given that I believe 2007 to be one of the worst and most overrated Barolo vintages of all time. And yet this wine was balanced and juicy and not marred by gritty tannins and high unbalanced alcohol levels like many were from that sorry vintage. The Angelo Veglio estate traces its roots back to 1886 or so, when Francesco Veglio founded the company. Today the Angelo Veglio estate does not make a Bricco Luciani wine (and they couldn't call it Gancia even if they wanted to), but do make a Barolo from another La Morra vineyard district, Gattera.

Fratelli Ferrero also own vines in Bricco Luciani, but make Barolos from the Gattera and Bricco Manzoni vineyard districts only, blending their grapes from Bricco Luciani into their classic Barolo Pinin (first made in 2013, it's essentially all Bricco Luciani grapes and 30% bought Nebbiolo grapes from other sites). Their Bricco Luciani vines were planted in 1987 at about 220-250 meters above sea level.

Benchmark wineries/Reference point producers of Barolo Bricco Luciani: Cascina del Monastero, Mauro Molino, Silvio Grasso.

BRICCO MANESCOTTO

Township	La Morra
Reference Map	See Map of La Morra MGAs (Ch. 10)
Size (ha) (Tot / Barolo MGA)	27.01 / 0,46
Production 2021 (hl)	25.00
Altitude	210 – 265 meters a.s.l. roughly
Exposure	From east to southeast for the parcels facing Castiglione Falletto, and from west to northwest on the opposite side
N. Claimants MGA	1
Other grape varieties planted:	Barbera; Dolcetto; white varieties
Land Units	Land Unit of Barolo and Land Unit of Castiglione in the central part
Soil (stage):	Tortonian

Producers claiming the MGA

Giovanni Corino.

Wines

Giovanni Corino - Barolo Bricco Manescotto

First off, do not confuse Bricco Manescotto with the Cascina Maniscotto in the Monforte Bussia territory (besides, the names are also spelled slightly differently). Bricco Manescotto is a vineyard district located in the northeasternmost section of the La Morra commune's territory. It's a low-lying, broad, open hillside slope that is very easy to admire as you drive down from Alba to Barolo (it's on your right). Very close to La Morra's border with the territory of the Castiglione Falletto commune (of which Bricco Manescotto offers an unimpeded view given there is nothing but flat plain stretching out in front of it), the soil presents elements of those formed during both the early and late Tortonian stage of the Miocene epoch (or in other words, of the soils of La Morra and Castiglione Falletto, which boast mostly differing lithologies). Therefore, the wines of Bricco Manescotto, though mostly light and floral like you'd expect from wines born off Tortonian soils, can also showcase interesting levels of noteworthy power, especially in those wines made with grapes grown on soils characterized by the presence of Diano Sandstone, which though not commonly known, I have been told to be present in the vineyard district. In fact, the soil lithology of Bricco Manescotto is mostly Saint Agatha Fossil Marls Formation (of both the sandy and typical forms), but surprising amounts of soil clay in sections of it (see below).

Bricco Manescotto producers and the wines

Relative to the wine, Bricco Manescotto's is an interesting story, at least in my particular case, as it is one of those vineyard districts that over the years has led me to do a real double take. I never thought of it as anything more than an average site (at best), and in fact no Barolo Bricco Manescotto wines were made from there until recently. Furthermore, quality producers like the Fratelli Revello estate long owned vineyards in Bricco Manescotto; but while the brothers (when they were still working together before their split) chose to make many single-site Barolo wines from other vineyard districts they never did so with their holdings in the Bricco Manescotto. Just from that, you might infer something. But you could also be wrong.

The Paolo Scavino and Batasiolo estates also own vines in Bricco Manescotto, as does Borgogno, but again, none have ever used the grapes from Bricco Manescotto to make a vineyard district-designate Barolo. The only producer who does, and has, is Corino (of Giuliano Corino) and though this is one of the most talented estates in all of Barolo, even their Barolos from the Bricco Manescotto failed to light a fire in my pants, so to speak. However, that all changed with the Barolo that the Corino winery made from the Bricco Manescotto in the 2017 vintage. A generally poor vintage (too droughty and too hot) the wines of which that I generally did not care for much (I believe there were few truly great Barolos made in 2017: clearly, viticulture, winemaking and technology have reached such a level of sophistication nowadays that making good wines is possible in almost every vintage, but even in this day and age many 2017 Barolos are average at best, most being marked by gritty tannins and overripe aromas and flavors. Then enter the 2017 Corino Barolo Bricco Manescotto, a truly amazing wine. What Giuliano Corino (of the Corino or Corino Giovanni estate) achieved in this vintage sent from the opposite of Paradise is nothing short of admirable and remarkable. The wine is deep, layered, fresh, and extremely complex, while remaining very pure and impeccably balanced. It is, without any fear of exaggeration whatsoever, a work of art; it is vastly better than the also majority of 2017 Barolos made from much more famous vineyard districts (for example, Brunate, Rocche dell'Annunziata, the various Cannubis and Bussia portions, and others still) and ultra-famous producers. Granted, Giuliano Corino is one of Barolo's best producers, one who is flying somewhat under the radar, and that level of skill undoubtedly contributes to the 2017 Bricco Manescotto's superb showing.

I have been tasting and drinking Barolo long enough to know that when I come across a wine of similar quality it is never the result of just one cause: producer talent and/or the grape variety and/or the site, there are always other contributing factors, often a combination thereof, of immense importance. And so, it dawned on me that Bricco Manescotto is a far better site than I had ever imagined. This wine's showing led me to review and retaste the other wines Corino has made from this vineyard district throughout the years, and it has become apparent to me that, even accounting for the differences in winemaking techniques used to make the various wines, this vineyard district is likely suited to hot years. I feel comfortable making this statement, because it actually makes sense: although the elevation at which Corino's vines grow is not especially noteworthy (his lie at 240-260 meters above sea level), and the west-facing orientation of the vines the very low percentage of sand (unlike Arborina, for example) in the mostly clay-rich soil makes for a site that will weather (literally) reasonably hot and droughty conditions well. You might argue that there haven't been too many vintages yet of this wine for me to be so adamant about its hot/drought resistance, and that's fair, so I guess it is also fair to say the jury's still out on this one. The Bricco Manescotto is the last vineyard district-designate Barolo that Corino Giovanni has launched. Though he would have liked to make it already in 2013, two different hail episodes that year prevented him from doing so. For this reason, Corino's first wine from this site was the 2014, but as that was, to be kind, a less than stellar vintage (too cold, too rainy), Giuliano understandably decided it wasn't the right vintage in which to launch his new wine (even though the 2014 Bricco Manescotto had turned out quite well, Corino feared the negative backlash of the vintage's bad reputation and thus the wine was never released as such, ending up incorporated in other wines). Therefore, the first official vintage of Bricco Manescotto available to all is the 2015, an excellent vintage by which to showcase the vineyard district's potential.

The Fratelli Revello estate (see ANNUNZIATA file) owns about one hectare of Bricco Manescotto, vines planted at 230-265 meters above sea level, west-facing, that look out towards the Gattera and its famous Cedar of Lebanon tree. There is an interesting plot in that it's sandier up high and richer in marly clay down below, which is not the way that geology usually works out (it's actually the contrary). To the best of my knowledge, the estate never released a Barolo Bricco Manescotto as such.

Bricco Manescotto's Barolo is usually characterized by notes of dark red fruit (quite dark, actually), licorice, menthol (rather than sweeter balsamic oils) and forest floor. With that in mind, I am guessing that those more experienced in tasting Barolo will find a Castiglione Falletto-like nuance in Bricco Manescotto's wines. The organoleptic profile, but also the texture and tannic framework of its Barolos, not to mention the overall sense of balance they convey, do bring the wines of Castiglione Falletto to mind. A resemblance that isn't really so uncanny after all: Bricco Manescotto is a vineyard district located close to the La Morra-Castiglione Falletto border and its wines take on nuances of the wines made in the latter commune (and in this respect, Bricco Manescotto's landscape classification of Barolo and Castiglione Land Units further bears this out: Castiglione Falletto vineyard districts Bricco Boschis, Fiasco, Monprivato, Rocche and Villero are all characterized by the Castiglione Land Unit too and that can't help but tell you plenty).

Benchmark wineries/Reference point producers of Barolo Bricco Manescotto: Giovanni Corino.

BRICCO MANZONI

Township	La Morra
Reference Map	See Map of La Morra MGAs (Ch. 10)
Size (ha) (Tot / Barolo MGA)	11.98 / 1.08
Production 2021 (hl)	58.96
Altitude	210 – 230 meters a.s.l. roughly
Exposure	From east to southeast in the better exposed parcels, and from east to north in the remaining parts.
N. Claimants MGA	3
Other grape varieties planted:	Barbera; Dolcetto; white varieties
Land Units	Land Unit of Barolo
Soil (stage):	Tortonian

Producers claiming the MGA
Claudio Alario; Fratelli Ferrero; Silvio Grasso.
Wines
Fratelli Ferrero - Barolo Bricco Manzoni; **Silvio Grasso** - Barolo Bricco Manzoni (Barolo Ciabot Manzoni)

What the producers say
Silvio Grasso: "Bricco Manzoni has been part of the family estate since 1984. Among those that we vinify, Bricco Manzoni is a Barolo of substantial structure".

In between Bricco Manescotto to its north and Bricco Luciani to the southwest, Bricco Manzoni is a low-lying vineyard district of La Morra draped over a short ridge that juts out below and in front of the Gattera amphitheater, pointing towards the Castiglione Falletto border close by. Just like the Bricco Manescotto and the Bricco Luciani, its landscape is classified as a Land Unit of Barolo: it's not surprising then that the soil lithology of Bricco Manzoni (Saint Agatha Fossil Marls of the sandy type) is similar to that of Bricco Luciani and partly to that of the Bricco Manescotto (see file: BRICCO LUCIANI. See also: BRICCO MANESCOTTO).

Bricco Manzoni producers and the wines

The key to making good to great wines from the Bricco Manzoni is to lower yields, that's all there is to it. It's one of those Barolo sites that flies a little under the radar because there aren't that many people bottling a wine from it, but I think it's fine Barolo potential is quite good, as demonstrated by some excellent wines made from there over the years. More structured, more austere, and less flamboyant than say the wines of Bricco Luciani, Bricco Manzoni delivers a classic Barolo of polished tannic heft but with more than enough flesh. Furthermore, it ages well and in noble fashion. Silvio Grasso's Barolo Bricco Manzoni is downright excellent, a wine that I find always punches well above its weight (and price) class. At fifty years of age and counting, these are probably the estate's oldest Nebbiolo vines; they are planted facing southeast at 250 meters above sea level. The wines of Silvio Grasso from this vineyard district have been really quite good over the years and I urge you to search out not just the new vintages but older vintages too.

Fratelli Ferrero is another quality estate that farms the Bricco Manzoni. Their vines, situated between 220 and 260 meters above sea level, are quite old (they were planted in 1960 and 1971). They first made their Barolo from this vineyard district in 1990, and over the years have developed a slightly curious vinification protocol for the Nebbiolo of this site, which features some carbonic maceration. It's a very pretty wine, less textured and mouthcoating than Silvio Grasso's, but just as delicious and enjoyable.

Benchmark wineries/Reference point producers of Barolo Bricco Manzoni: Silvio Grasso. Also good: Fratelli Ferrero.

BRICCO ROCCA

Township	La Morra
Reference Map	See Map of La Morra MGAs (Ch. 10)
Size (ha) (Tot / Barolo MGA)	10.94 / 3,66
Production 2021 (hl)	195.53 (of which 195.53 hl of Barolo Riserva *MGA*)
Altitude	220 – 255 meters a.s.l. roughly
Exposure	From east to southeast, with some parcels facing from south to west, and from north to northeast in the remaining parts.
N. Claimants MGA	3
Other grape varieties planted:	Barbera; Dolcetto; white varieties
Land Units	Land Unit of Barolo
Soil (stage):	Tortonian

Producers claiming the MGA

Cascina Ballarin; Cascina del Monastero; E. Molino (Sergio Molino).

Wines

Angelo Germano - Barolo Bricco Rocca; **Cascina Ballarin** - Barolo Bricco Rocca and Barolo Riserva Bricco Rocca Tistot; **Cascina del Monastero** – Barolo Riserva Bricco Rocca Riund; **E. Molino** - Barolo Bricco Rocca and Barolo Riserva del Fico.

Cascina Ballarin: "The vineyard area takes its name from the word "*bricco*", meaning the highest part of a hill, and "*rocca*", which is the name of the neighborhood located at the foot of the hill. Bricco Rocca offers a rich, slightly herbal, nose with scents of fruit peels, rose and violet. On the palate it's intense, rich, sweet, soft, and persistent. The portion of the vineyard Bricco Rocca that we use to produce this wine comes from a 60-years old vineyard, owned by our uncle Giovanni Battista, better known as "*Tistot*". So, we decided to name a wine after him. The 1997 vintage was the first one made of Tistot, by carefully selecting bunches which we late harvested in October. It was the best of beginnings, thanks to the high amount of sugar and polyphenols and the right amount of air-drying of the Nebbiolo grapes. Tistot was vinified according to the traditional method, with long maceration on the skins. It's a perfumed, structured wine that presents, however, good balance and great elegance".

Ian's assessment of the vineyard district, its wines and its potential

Like the nearby Bricco Luciani and Bricco Manzoni vineyard districts, Bricco Rocca is yet another La Morra vineyard district in this specific northeastern corner of the commune's territory the vineyards of which are draped over a ridge stretching out towards the territory of Castiglione Falletto. But unlike other La Morra vineyard districts such as Rocche dell'Annunziata or Conca that have an amphitheater-like disposition, Bricco Rocca is located on the lower half of a hill shaped like a muffin. It sticks out as such immediately behind the excellent if perhaps underrated Cascina Ballarin winery.

Not an especially high-altitude vineyard district (the vines are all at less than 250 meters above sea level) which puts Bricco Rocca at risk for late spring frosts, it is instead extremely steep (it climbs up to 250 meters rather fast and should you wish to try to walk it, I guarantee you'll be huffing and puffing in no time – been there, done that). Personal painful memories aside, this conformation allows for an ideal degree of solar irradiation and luminosity leading to ultimately good grape ripeness in most vintages and in most sections (but not all) of the vineyard district. As Bricco Rocca is close to the territory of Castiglione Falletto, it's not surprising that its wines show (some of them at least) elements in common with Castiglione Falletto Barolos (just like those of Bricco Manescotto do too. See BRICCO MANESCOTTO file). Bricco Rocca's landscape category is that of the Land Unit of Barolo, such that its soil is characterized by a high percentage of loam, but in Bricco Rocca's specific case there is also a good amount of sand. Its lithology is therefore mostly that of the Saint Agatha Fossil Marls of the sandy type, exactly like it is wholly or in part with the other Bricco-something vineyard districts of this section of La Morra (see BRICCO LUCIANI file. See also: BRICCO MANESCOTTO file) but unlike more inland La Morra vineyard districts such as Arborina. This soil reality, in addition to the steep slope and muffin-like topography, means Bricco Rocca has, for the most part, excellent drainage. In fact, I believe that Bricco Rocca's best results are achieved, Cannubi Centrale-like, in cool, wet, but clearly not excessively cold, years.

Bricco Rocca producers and the wines

Estates that own vines in this vineyard district include Cascina Ballarin, Cascina del Monastero, E. Molino, Mario Oliviero, and Angelo Germano.

One estate that obviously believes in the potential of Bricco Rocca and the high quality of its wines is Cascina del Monastero: this much is clear, given that they choose to bottle their lone Barolo Riserva from this vineyard district. And I am sure you will agree with my assessment that wineries are not usually in the habit of bottling their Riserva wines from what they believe to be lesser sites. As mentioned earlier on in this book (see: BRICCO MANZONI file), the Cascina del Monastero estate was founded in 1990 when Giuseppe Grasso separated from his brother and started up his own estate. From then on, Cascina del Monastero has bottled a Barolo Bricco Rocca save in vintages that were less than ideal (in such years they proceeded to blend together the Bricco Rocca grapes with those of Bricco Manzoni to make one estate Barolo).

The old name of the estate's vineyard in Bricco Rocca was always that of Bricco Riund, but the estate can no longer use it given that terms such as "bricco" have been disallowed since 2007 (unless they are part of a fantasy wine name, but cannot be used to indicate a favored geographical position such as the *bricco* part of the hill is). The reason why Cascina del Monastero opted to make a Riserva wine from the Bricco Rocca and not from another of their vineyard district holdings is because the locals had always spoken highly of their specific vineyard plot in that it gave bigger, more ageworthy wines than the surrounding vineyard areas. Therefore, it seemed like the ideal spot from which to produce a Riserva. Accordingly, the soil composition there has a slightly higher limestone content and the resulting wine is always darker in color (relatively darker: this is Barolo, after all, and so the wine should never be pitch-black or even close to that hue); higher in acidity; and blessed with a solid tannic backbone. Interestingly, a tannic structure that Grasso finds to be especially noble and different from that of his other Barolos, further making this vineyard site, in his eyes at least, ideal for the production of a Barolo Riserva. But it is noteworthy that local old-timers always pointed to the limestone vein that characterizes this specific vineyard spot and that it was the common opinion the site really gave better wines than the immediately surrounding areas: you know, I don't know what your thoughts might be on the matter, but I've always listened very closely, and paid attention, to local farmer wisdom. Another reason that helps understand why this specific site makes an ideal Barolo Riserva is that the vines are very old: a large part of the vineyard was planted in 1970 (so we're talking already fifty years old), but the section located highest up boasts a noteworthy number of vines that were planted entirely by hand way back in 1947 by Loris Grasso's great-grandfather (can you believe that? Talk about back-breaking work: I think I'll stop complaining about how strenuous my long days are just sitting at the computer writing away!). In any case, I have always liked the Barolo from this site for its balance; and like all the Barolos from Bricco Rocca, I find it is also usually marked by strong floral notes (violet, rose).

The Angelo Germano estate (as I have mentioned numerous times in other files of this book, remember that there are many family names that are very common in the Barolo denomination, and Germano is one such name) is currently run by Davide Germano. The estate takes its name from its founder, who launched the winery in 1908 (in fact, members of this Germano family had long been active in local wine circles: Angelo's grandfather Teobaldo was the founder and first president of the local Barolo cooperative, the Cantina Sociale, founded in 1902). This is an excellent, under the radar winery that I urge you to get to know better. They have made a Barolo Bricco Rocca since 2015, but make it only in the best years. Otherwise, they like to use their Bricco Rocca grapes as the major component of their classic estate Barolo Trevigneti, where *trevigneti* means "three vineyards" (the three vineyards are in three different communes: Barolo, La Morra and Monforte). Germano's Bricco Rocca vines grow in two different sections of the vineyard district: an upper part that is characterized by a drier microclimate and good drainage, and a lower section that is more humid but has very good water retention. It follows that blending the grapes from the two sections makes for a potentially more balanced wine. Some of the vines, planted at about 280 meters above sea level, are quite old, planted back in 1952, though other vines are much younger, planted as recently as 2005. The must is kept on the skins and fermented for about fifteen days; and ageing takes place for two years in 500 liters tonneaux, 20% new (what to do with the remaining 80% is decided upon on the basis of the vintage characteristics).

At the Mario Oliviero estate in Roddi, Lorenzo and his father Mario Oliviero have until recently blended their Bricco Rocca grapes with those from Serralunga's Teodoro vineyard district so as to make their Barolo Vigne Unite bottling. Their small (0.25 hectares) Bricco Rocca holding was planted in 1951 and 2002 with a southwest orientation at about 220-240 meters above sea level. The wine was made by macero-fermentations of about two weeks carried out at 27-28 degrees Celsius and the wine is aged for about 26-28 months in French oak barrels (for an initial period in barriques, then in 500 liter and 600-liter tonneaux). I write "was" because beginning with the 2018 vintage, the winery will begin making a Barolo del Comune di La Morra, that will take the place of the Barolo Vigne Unite. This is because this Barolo will now be made with grapes from two other La Morra vineyard districts that have recently come into the estate's fold (thanks to a ten-year rental agreement), Annunziata and Boiolo, that will be blended with those of the Bricco Rocca (in fact, the estate made a single-MGA vineyard district Barolo from Bricco Rocca from the 2009 to the 2015 vintages included).

Sergio Molino of E. Molino (where the "E" in that name stands for Ernesto, Sergio's father) makes a very small quantity of Barolo Bricco Rocca (depending on the vintage, a little less than 2000 bottles a year; this is a true micro-winery, given that the total annual production from the 2.5 total hectares of vines owned is only of about 6000 bottles a year…in total) from his small holding (0.75 hectares) of rather old vines (almost entirely planted in 1951, with a few vines added in 1975 and 2000). Though a little bottle variation is unavoidable given the artisanal working environment, the wines are usually impeccably made, which cannot surprise, given that Sergio is a very well-regarded consultant winemaker. Just be careful not to confuse this Molino with the myriad other Molino families making wine all over the Langhe and Piedmont!

Benchmark wineries/Reference point producers of Barolo Bricco Rocca: Cascina Ballarin, Cascina del Monastero, E. Molino. Also good: Angelo Germano, Mario Oliviero (from 2009-2015).

BRICCO ROCCHE

Township	Castiglione Falletto
Reference Map	See Map of Castiglione MGAs (Ch. 10)
Size (ha) (Tot / Barolo MGA)	1.46 / 0.94
Production 2021 (hl)	50.80
Altitude	350 – 365 meters a.s.l. roughly
Exposure	From southeast to southwest
N. Claimants MGA	1
Other grape varieties planted:	
Land Units	Land Unit of Castiglione
Soil (stage):	Tortonian

Producers claiming the MGA

Ceretto.

Wines

Ceretto - Barolo Bricco Rocche.

What the producers say

Alessandro Ceretto (Ceretto): "From 1982, we have vinified separately grapes coming from this vineyard. The Barolos from this vineyard are blessed with complexity, elegance and austerity".

Ian's assessment of the vineyard district, its wines and its potential

Now this one's a piece of cake, or of Barolo if you will: simply put, the Bricco Rocche has given me some of the finest Barolo tasting experiences and memories of my life. As such, it never ceases to amaze me how wine collectors and wine lovers rarely talk about Ceretto's Barolo Bricco Rocche, which is for my money, at least in most vintages, a wine good enough to rank with the top ten Barolos of the year. This may be in part a function of the Bricco Rocche being a *monopole* (there just aren't any other wines to try other than those of Ceretto, the site's owner) and the small number of bottles made every year, such that some wine professionals just don't get to try the wine. At 1.46 hectares, Bricco Rocche is, after all, the smallest vineyard district of all Barolo.

In Italy they say *"il buongiorno si vede dal mattino"* (loosely translated, that means "you see it's a good day by how the morning goes") and this was most certainly the case with the first Barolo Bricco Rocche wine ever made. That would be the glorious 1982 vintage. Make no mistake about it: a truly monumental wine and still to this day one of the best Barolos I have ever tasted, it was masterpiece featuring power, flesh, refinement, and unforgettable balance. Even more impressive is that the 1982 was made from extremely young vines: Ceretto had bought its holding in Bricco Rocche in 1977 and planted in 1978. So that wine, which I remember vividly and am lucky enough to have tasted at the time of release and presentation to the Italian wine press and professionals, has always been a rather unbelievable feat in my books. Planted with south-facing vines between 312 to 340 meters above sea level, Bricco Rocche's landscape category is that of the Land Unit of Castiglione, which tells us the lithology should be at least partly that of Diano Sandstone, but there's also Saint Agatha Fossil Marls of the sandy type. In fact, the soil composition is 20.5% loam, 20,50% sand and 59% clay. Interestingly, despite its name references the Rocche di Castiglione close by, and hence conjures up images of sand blowing everywhere (Rocche di Castiglione is a vineyard district famous for its sandy nature), the Bricco Rocche is in fact characterized by a healthy presence of clay. Rather than Rocche (and despite the vineyard district's official name), the high soil clay content of Bricco Rocche is more typical of Villero, the other great vineyard district of Castiglione Falletto that is located close by. The clay component of Bricco Rocche's soil contributes the power, the sand the elegance, the *bricco* summit position plenty of sunlight, and so…*ecco fatto, un grande vino*.

Fact is, Bricco Rocche is just a blessed site: as part of its name implies, *bricco*, the vineyard area lies at the very top of the hill above the Rocche di Castiglione-vineyard district (not so arguably one of Barolo's five best vineyard districts). In fact, the Bricco Rocche was once a part (the best part, in fact) of the vineyard area known as Serra, but Ceretto renamed their holding Bricco Rocche (in other words, the "well-exposed summit of the Rocche"), in consideration of the fact that Bricco Rocche is the direct continuation, higher up, of the Rocche di Castiglione vineyard area. Furthermore, despite the differences alluded to previously, the two areas have at least partly very similar soils (the aforementioned Saint Agatha Fossil Marls of the sandy type). Given that the Rocche di Castiglione (once simply known as Rocche) is a much more famous and valued vineyard than Serra ever was (with the official naming of the vineyard districts, Serra has disappeared altogether, its territory divided up between the vineyard districts of Mariondino, Villero and Bricco Rocche).

In fact, there was a time in which the "to be or not to be Serra" conundrum was not the only quandary posed by the site's name, and by extension, of the wine. A less than ideal situation was inadvertently created because, since the beginning, the real, full, name of this Barolo was actually Barolo Bricco Rocche Bricco Rocche: the repetition of the words "Bricco Rocche" in the name was necessary, because at the time Ceretto boasted a line of estate wines called "Bricco Rocche" [that's right: exactly the same name of their specific Barolo and the vineyard district it belonged to (at the time, it was not yet an official vineyard district name)]. Consequently, all the Barolos included in this part of the Ceretto portfolio were identified with the words Bricco Rocche written at the top of the label); and so in the lineup of Ceretto Barolos there were also a Barolo Bricco Rocche Brunate and a Barolo Bricco Rocche Prapò, besides the Barolo Bricco Rocche Bricco Rocche. This last, clearly unfortunate, name led to much confusion and inaccurate reporting, given that practically nobody ever wrote the wine's name correctly, limiting it to a simplified "Barolo Bricco Rocche". But that meant nothing in and of itself, for there were at the time many other "Barolo Bricco Rocche"-named wines at the time. I well remember one day back around in the late 2000s when Federico Ceretto surprised me with a phone call asking if I had any suggestions on what they should do, given that someone at a famous English-language wine publication at the time had gotten the name wrong yet again and the family had had enough, and realized they needed to do something. Anyways, the problem was solved and happily, it no longer exists: today all the Ceretto Barolo vineyard district-designate wines just go by the name of their–vineyard district only. And so, Barolo Bricco Rocche it is.

Bricco Rocche producers and the wines (monopole)

Nomenclature issues aside, to repeat myself and be crystal-clear, it is my opinion that Bricco Rocche is one of the ten or so best vineyard districts of all Barolo: that should be fairly easy to imagine given the site's location right between Rocche di Castiglione and Villero. The wines that Ceretto has made, and makes, from this site are mostly spectacular, and I mean spectacular. Outstanding Barolo Bricco Rocche wines over the years that immediately spring to mind include (besides the wondrous 1982) the 1996 and 2001. Smooth, deep, complex, penetrating, precise, offering a panoply of small red berries, red cherries, sweet spices, marzipan, cinnamon, sweet pipe tobacco, black pepper and, later in life, also tar, licorice and faded flowers, the Bricco Rocche is a quintessential Barolo from Castiglione Falletto. It is therefore very well-balanced, walking the tightrope between grace and power like very few other Barolos manage. Get one from a good vintage and you will have no trouble viewing it in the same light as you would a truly great wine from Richebourg or Chambertin (from a very great producer).

Benchmark wineries/Reference point producers of Barolo Bricco Rocche: Ceretto (monopole).

BRICCO SAN BIAGIO

Township	La Morra
Reference Map	See Map of La Morra MGAs (Ch. 10)
Size (ha) (Tot / Barolo MGA)	28.84 / 4.81
Production 2021 (hl)	261.85 (of which 40 hl of Barolo Riserva *MGA*)
Altitude	220 – 290 meters a.s.l. roughly
Exposure	From southeast to southwest passing through south on the better exposed parcels, and north in the remaining parts
N. Claimants MGA	2
Other grape varieties planted:	Barbera; Dolcetto; Riesling; other white varieties
Land Units	Land Unit of Barolo for the most, and Land Unit of Castiglione in the central and higher parts
Soil (stage):	Tortonian

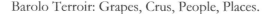

Producers claiming the MGA

San Biagio; Osvaldo Viberti.

Wines

San Biagio - Barolo Bricco San Biagio

What the producers say

Marco Oberto (Ciabot Berton): "We have been following our holding of Bricco San Biagio for more than 50 years. The rather light soil of this cru confers floral and aromatic nuances".

Gianluca Roggero (San Biagio): "Bricco San Biagio is produced from a historic Nebbiolo vineyard lying at the heart of one of the finest Barolo crus, the San Biagio hill in the village of La Morra. The particular hollow-shaped conformation of the slope enables the warmth captured during the day to be retained and then be released during the night. The nose is expansive, featuring notes of berries, dog rose, lime, jam, and cooked plums. Appealingly spicy and balsamic overtones stand out in the older wines, especially star anise, licorice, mushrooms and dried figs, as well as hints of tobacco and leather".

Ian's assessment of the vineyard district, its wines and its potential

The Bricco San Biagio vineyard district may not feature any historic buildings amidst its beautiful expanse of vineyards anymore, but it does offer some of the Barolo denomination's most uniquely characteristic wines. It is located in the Santa Maria sector of the La Morra commune, a relatively sandy area that gives some of the lightest-bodied, most graceful Barolos of all. In some respects, Barolos made in the general vicinity of the Santa Maria hamlet share some similarities with those of the southern portion of the Verduno commune's territory (mostly because both areas share a wealth of sand in the soil). I think that Bricco San Biagio is one of Barolo's underrated Nebbiolo sites, something that is probably very much in relation to the high sand content of its soils making for pale-colored red wines of a steely if very perfumed disposition but without much in the way of flesh and body. But the gracefulness of Bricco San Biagio Barolos is something to be marveled at, as are the almost magical aromas of wild strawberry, redcurrant, violet, lavender, orange peel, lemon jelly, white pepper and minerals. That perfume is way of life with Bricco San Biagio is also shown by the fact that the peaches from this site were always much sought after because of their intense perfume and sweet juiciness; for these very reasons, they fetched much higher prices.

Viewed from above, the Bricco San Biagio vineyard district is roughly the shape of a bowl, surrounded to the north and northwest by the Santa Maria vineyard district; to the northeast by Serra dei Turchi; to the west by Roggeri vineyard district; and to the south by Rocchettevino. Bricco San Biagio's landscape category is complex, in that it presents features of the Land Unit of Barolo but of the Land Unit of Castiglione too. Therefore, the soil lithology varies from the dominant Saint Agatha Fossil Marls of the sandy type you'd expect given the site's fame for lighter styled, more perfumed Barolos, but there are also pockets of Diano Sandstone that make for slightly bigger wines. In fact, while some parts of the Bricco San Biagio have soil compositions that are marked by the sand component and light clay, others are more loamy, with sand and clay present in about equal amounts (or 43 % loam, 27 % sand, and 30% clay).

Relative to soil composition, it's amazing how just a few meters in distance can change things. Compared to the much bigger and fleshier wines of the nearby Roggeri vineyard district (Roggeri is very clay-dominated site, and heavy clay at that), those of Bricco San Biagio are much more graceful and lighter in palate weight. My comparison has always been that Bricco San Biagio's wines are art school drawings compared to the more obvious, flashier and simpler kindergarten drawings that are Roggeri's. True, some Bricco San Biagio wines push the gracefulness envelope almost to the point where it teeters on the brink of becoming a fault (i.e., the lesser wines from this site lack stuffing). It is a matter of record that big *negozianti* who used to buy grapes from all over the Barolo denomination often bought those of Bricco San Biagio reluctantly, unhappy with the pale color and the light mouthfeel of the wines. Furthermore, the high sand content of some sections of the vineyard district is a drawback in hot and droughty years: for example, in the hellaciously hot 2003 vintage, the Ciabot Berton estate had to harvest its Bricco San Biagio vines fifteen days before normal, a less than ideal scenario. That said, the better Barolos from Bricco San Biagio are very perfumed and stylish wines that age better than their light structure might imply, especially in magnums. And I am not the only one who thinks that Bricco San Biagio is a potentially a very good site: over the years, when I have asked producers to name one La Morra vineyard site they would like to own, it was Bricco San Biagio that many mentioned. Renato Corino went as far as saying that in his estimation it is, along with Roncaglie, the most beautiful spot in which to make Nebbiolo in the Santa Maria fraction of La Morra.

Bricco San Biagio producers and the wines

While numerous producers own Nebbiolo vineyards in the Bricco San Biagio, not all of them make a vineyard district-designated Barolo with the grapes. Perhaps not surprisingly, the San Biagio estate, that carries the same name as the vineyard district, does. Run by Giovanni Roggero (given that name and the way things go in Barolo, you'd almost expect the winery to also make a Barolo Roggeri, but no, it does not) who hails from a winemaking family now generations old, San Biagio makes an excellent Barolo San Biagio aged up to thirty months in large Slavonian oak barrels. The wine is just how you'd expect a Barolo from San Biagio to be like: pale red in color, lots of aromas and flavors of strawberry jelly, orange peel and mint, and noteworthy lightness of being. No blockbuster, but smashingly fun and easy to drink, and there's lots to say for that.

Poderi Oddero is one of Barolo's better-known estates, the wines of which are exported all over the world. It owns a large section of the Bricco San Biagio: about 6.85 hectares planted at mostly about 200 meters above sea level, but the vines reach as high as 250 meters in the part of the district known as "Briccaccio". It is only fair to recognize that the "Briccaccio" is probably the best piece of the whole Bricco San Biagio vineyard district. (This is something that numerous other producers have told me over the years.) Poderi Oddero's large expanse of vines in Bricco San Biagio has many different exposures (south, southwest, northwest). Given all those exposures (some of which are not ideal for Nebbiolo), only the Briccaccio, which is not just the highest but also the oldest 2.5 hectares of Nebbiolo vines Poderi Oddero owns in the Bricco San Biagio, is used for Barolo production (another two hectares are used to make the estate's Langhe Nebbiolo; for Riesling lovers, I will point out that Poderi Oddero's Riesling vines are here in the Bricco San Biagio too, 1.45 hectares looking northwest). The estate does not bottle a Barolo Bricco San Biago, but uses the grapes to add a measure of elegance to their classic estate Barolo, made with grapes from many different vineyard districts.

Crissante Alessandria is another estate that owns vineyards in the Bricco San Biagio. They own 2.9 hectares of fully south-facing vines in there that were planted in 1982 at about 230-240 meters above sea level on a mostly light clay and sandy soil. Vinification is carried out in stainless steel tanks at 26-28 degrees Celsius with punching down and *remontage* for up to four times a day from the fifth day until the end of fermentation. Malo is done in the steel tanks while aging is in large Slavonian oak barrels for twenty-four months. Alberto Alessandria of Crissante Alessandria has told me over the years that the grapes of the Bricco San Biagio help increase the sense of refinement and gracefulness, not to mention fruitiness, of their Barolo del Comune di La Morra wine.

Another estate long associated with the Bricco San Biagio is Ciabot Berton; it takes its name from the union of the words *ciabot* (the tool shed that is a typical site in many Langhe vineyards) and *berton,* from the name of the twenty hectares large parcel where once stood a *ciabot*. The *ciabot* was just below the road where they used to make fireworks, and so, one day, BUUUMMM. In fact, the name Ciabot Berton was born only in 1988: prior to that date, wines were sold (in the USA, at least) under the estate name of Luigi Oberto. I have always liked Ciabot Berton's wines and believe this to be one of Barolo's more underrated estates: their wines are sure bets and don't cost an arm and a leg. The estate was founded by Giovenale, the grandfather of current owners, siblings Marco and Paola Oberto (Giovenale owned vines only in Bricco San Biagio, but by marrying Maria Beatrice Roggero, plots of vines in the Roggeri and Rive vineyard districts also came into the family fold; today the estate also owns land in the Rocchettevino vineyard district. See ROGGERI file; see also ROCCHETTEVINO file). Among many other reasons, Giovenale is fondly remembered by the family because he loved it when foreigners visited the estate: he used to fill up their wine glasses repeatedly, all night long, right to the rim. Numerous refills later, the no doubt happy visitors were always left completely tipsy!

His son, Luigi, was among the founders of the Terre del Barolo cooperative, because in the mid-twentieth century it was tough to sell grapes and as farmers, a cooperative was the best way to survive. In 1961, he bottled his first wine, under the label of Oberto Giovenale and Figlio. With the arrival of Marco and Paola at the helm, the estate has slowly but surely moved up the quality ranks and is now at or close to the top of the Barolo quality heap (as recently as 1991 they were still selling a large part of their wine to big Barolo firms, or *negozianti*). Paola worked briefly as a vineyard inspector of the Regione Piemonte, so she knows the potential of the area's many vineyard sites extremely well; add that she did stages with Barolo super-experts like Claudio Vezza and Luciano Sandrone (just imagine that the Oberto siblings bottled their first ever Barbera d'Alba wine in 1991 at Sandrone's insistence, who thought it was great: I don't know about you, but I'd say that having Luciano tell you your wine is great is a pretty nice feather in the old cap) and so her formation/background is top-rate. Marco is a very talented winemaker, and always wished to showcase what each one of their vineyard sites was capable of expressing.

And so, the two began single-site vinifications in 1993-94; their father thought the pair was completely crazy, but they persevered, and this allowed the siblings to learn exactly what each one of their vineyards could (and could not) give. In fact, that was not the only thing good old Luigi had to object about: like many people of his (older) generation, he didn't believe in, or like, green harvesting (to his generation that grew up in much poorer times, throwing grapes to the ground was a horrible act). I remember Paola laughing during an interview at the winery back in 2003 or 2004 when she told me how one day in those early years her father nailed her while she was busy throwing down grapes in the vineyard. He didn't say anything, and she went home and just pretended to watch TV nonchalantly, thinking that was the end of that. But the next day, her father surprised her with the news that she wouldn't be needed in the vineyards, and she could just go to the market with her mother instead! Those were really different times (in many respects).

Ciabot Berton does not make a Barolo solely with Bricco San Biagio grapes, though their Barolo Ciabot Berton 1961 (the name is in honor of that first bottled wine) is a blend of grapes from the Roggeri, Bricco San Biagio and Rive vineyard districts (and in fact, it is made mostly with Bricco San Biagio grapes). The wine undergoes macero-fermentations in concrete tanks and is aged in Slavonian oak barrels and concrete tanks, but the siblings have experimented over the years. For example, in the early 2000s they were macerating and fermenting for roughly eighteen days but in the 1993, 1994 and 1995 vintages they reduced both the temperature and the duration of the fermentation (down to ten days only). The siblings vinify the Bricco San Biagio on its own and they hold on to a few bottles from each vintage for study purposes. I am very grateful to them for having generously allowed me to taste those rare wines over numerous vintages so that I could fixate very clearly in my memory and my palate what Bricco San Biagio's Barolos are like. In turn, I was very happy to show students of my various wine courses and younger wine writers who wished to learn about Barolo in-depth, what a sandy site could give in the way of La Morra Barolo. When all is said and done, over the years I have had many wonderful Barolos from this Oberto family (once again, *caveat emptor*: don't get your Obertos confused, as this is another extremely common family name in the Langhe, with many different Obertos producing Barolo), but it all started with Giovenale, and I wish to remember him here and now. He loved his vineyards and spent as much time there as he could: and in fact, that's where he died. One day when the family didn't see Giovenale coming home at the usual time, they all went off to look for him: they found Giovenale peacefully propped up against one of the vineyard poles, the victim of an ischemic attack. That too is very much part of the history and reality of the Bricco San Biagio vineyard district. Allow me: of Barolo.

BRICCO SAN GIOVANNI

Township	Barolo
Reference Map	See Map of Barolo MGAs (Ch. 10)
Size (ha) (Tot / Barolo MGA)	3.84 / 1.64
Production 2021 (hl)	89.08
Altitude	370 – 400 meters a.s.l. roughly
Exposure	Predominantly from west to south, and a small part facing east and northwest
N. Claimants MGA	1
Other grape varieties planted:	Barbera; Dolcetto
Land Units	Land Unit of Castiglione
Soil (stage):	Tortonian

Producers claiming the MGA

Villa Lanata.

Ian's assessment of the vineyard district, its wines and its potential

A vineyard district that ranks with the smallest (at 3.84 hectares, it is tied with the Prabon vineyard district for tenth smallest), Bricco San Giovanni is located in the territory of the Barolo commune. It is surrounded by the vineyard districts of Boschetti to the north, Zoccolaio to the west and south, with San Giovanni is to its east. Boschetti and Zoccolaio are on the same west-facing ridge as is the Bricco San Giovanni, that occupies a small portion of the summit; on the other, east-facing, flank of the same ridge begins the Monforte territory (so careful now, don't get confused: differently from the Bricco San Giovanni, the aforementioned and similarly-named San Giovanni is a vineyard district not of Barolo but of the Monforte commune). The proximity to the Monforte commune explains Bricco San Giovanni's lithology of mostly Diano Sandstone, rather than the Saint Agatha Fossil Marls that tend to dominate within the Barolo commune. I have really no knowledge about this vineyard district's wines, as I don't believe I have ever tasted one. If I have, even of a microvinification in some winery cellar somewhere sometime, I do not have any recollection or tasting notes of it. However, the site must have some viticultural/winemaking merits, because it is almost completely under vine: and of those vines, over 90% of those vines are of Nebbiolo. That tells you something right there. Hopefully, someone sooner or later will decide to take the plunge and make a Barolo bearing this vineyard district's name.

Benchmark wineries/Reference point producers of Barolo Bricco San Giovanni: None currently available.

BRICCO SAN PIETRO

Township	Monforte d'Alba
Reference Map	See Map of Monforte d'Alba MGAs (Ch. 10)
Size (ha) (Tot / Barolo MGA)	380.09 / 39.83
Production 2021 (hl)	2,145.74 (of which 94.76 hl of Barolo Riserva *MGA*, 137.03 hl of Barolo *MGA* Vigna and 34.18 hl Barolo Riserva *MGA* Vigna)
Altitude	300 – 520 meters a.s.l. roughly
Exposure	From southeast to southwest, passing through south, in the better exposed parcels; from west to northwest and from east to northeast in the remaining parts
N. Claimants MGA	26
Other grape varieties planted:	Barbera; Dolcetto; white varieties
Land Units Barbera; Dolcetto	Land Unit of La Morra and Land Unit of Castiglione in the north/north-east side; Land Unit of Novello in remaining parts
Soil (stage):	Tortonian

Producers claiming the MGA

Anna Maria Abbona; Broccardo; Ca' Brusà; Cascina Canavere (Flli. Giacosa); Cascina Cappellano; Cascina Sot; Aldo Clerico; Diego Pressenda; Famiglia Anselma; Cristian Ferrero; Gigi Rosso; Gomba; Le Cecche; Fratelli Manzone; Monti; Podere Ruggeri Corsini; Raineri; Reverdito; Rocche Dei Manzoni; Simone Scaletta; Franco Schellino; Luigina Schellino; Sordo (Giovanni Sordo); Tenuta Rocca; Vietto; Vinory.

Wines

Anna Maria Abbona - Barolo Bricco San Pietro; **Broccardo** - Barolo Bricco San Pietro (and Riserva); **Ca' Brusà** - Barolo Bricco San Pietro Vigna d'Vaj (and Riserva 10 years); **Cascina Sot** – Barolo Bricco San Pietro (and Riserva); **Aldo Clerico** - Barolo (Bricco San Pietro); **Diego Pressenda** - Barolo Bricco San Pietro; **Le Cecche** - Barolo Bricco San Pietro; **F.lli Manzone**– Barolo Bricco San Pietro Fraschin; **Monti** - Barolo Bricco San Pietro; **Podere Ruggeri Corsini** - Barolo Bricco San Pietro; **Reverdito** - Barolo Bricco San Pietro (from 2016); **Rocche dei Manzoni** - Barolo Vigna - Bricco San Pietro (Barolo d'La Roul); **Simone Scaletta** - Barolo Bricco San Pietro and Riserva (Barolo Chirlet); **Vietto** - Barolo Bricco San Pietro; **Vinory** - Barolo Bricco San Pietro (from 2019).

What the producers say

Simone Scaletta: "In 2002, we claimed ownership of this vineyard. The wine has power and tannic structure, rich and complex but with elegance too. In our view, its balanced character respects the characteristics of the territory of the Monforte township".

Vietto Davide (Vietto Luigi): "Since 2003, we have vinified and bottled separately our vines in San Pietro to make a Barolo Bricco San Pietro. Bricco San Pietro is a Barolo of character and harmony that we find to be more suitable for early drinking. The nose is clean and generous with notes of cherry, violet, clove, licorice and leather, which open up harmoniously in the mouth with a slightly tannic pleasantly spicy finish".

Michele Reverdito (Reverdito): "Unfortunately, we only had the opportunity to vinify the 2013 and 2014 vintages. Yet this *cru* impressed me. The soil has a good structure, almost perfect, for the Nebbiolo grape. Sweetly tannic, the wine we made is round and supple with an impressive structure and deep color".

Rodolfo Migliorini (Rocche dei Manzoni): "Our plots in Manzoni Soprani with a full south exposure are the source of grapes for the Barolo Vigna d'la Roul (or *Vigna della Rovere*, in Italian: the vineyard takes its name after the huge oak tree in the middle of the estate), which is one of our principal sites for the production of Barolo. The clay-limestone soil guarantees impressive structure and noteworthy longevity. One of the most masculine Barolo in the production zone".

Ian's assessment of the vineyard district, its wines and its potential

Like Bussia, Bricco San Pietro is a very large Monforte vineyard district: in fact, the two are the largest of all of Barolo's vineyard districts, with Bricco San Pietro holding the honour (?) of being the single largest vineyard district of the entire Barolo denomination (see Chapter 10, BAROLO MGA VINEYARD

DISTRICTS: MAPS AND LAND UNITS). But unlike Bussia, Bricco San Pietro is not an especially famous Barolo vineyard district.

Located in the southernmost part of the Monforte territory, Bricco San Pietro covers an area immediately to the south of the vineyard districts of Sottocastello di Novello, Cerviano-Merli and Panerole in the Novello Commune; the Monforte vineyard districts of San Giovanni and Bussia are to its north and east, respectively. Given its vast expanse of vines, pinpointing the characteristics of Bricco San Pietro Barolos is objectively hard to do: this vineyard district is so large that it can be described with three different landscape categories. Topography, geology, altitudes, and exposures of Bricco San Pietro are all so variable that to quote Gertrude Stein, there is seemingly "no there, there". For example, some areas within Bricco San Pietro have a soil lithology consistent with that of the Saint Agatha Fossil marls (mostly of the sandy type, while those of the laminated type less common and limited to the easternmost portion of the vineyard district), others are characterized by the presence of Diano Sandstone (in general, limited to the higher parts of the Bricco San Pietro ridge) and still others.

Therefore, the best approach in trying to understand what the Bricco San Pietro Barolo you are drinking is or should be about, is to know exactly in which part of the vineyard district's territorial extension the grapes used to make that Barolo grow in. This is no different than knowing if a Burgundy producer's vineyards are located in Mazis-du-Haut or Mazis-du-Bas (or Mazis-Hauts and Mazis-Bas, the latter having deeper, richer, more fertile soils), or if in any generic portion of Échézeaux as compared to being in the highly desirable section of Échézeaux du Dessus. In fact, the Bricco San Pietro vineyard district can be effectively broken down into different sections that for the most part correspond to old vineyard areas the names of which were obliterated and swallowed up at the time of the declaration of the official vineyard district names so as to make one big vineyard district. In my view, the best known of the subregions of today's Bricco San Pietro were Corsini and Manzoni; others like Vignoni, Cucchi and Tantesi were less well-known and sought after but were also associated, at one time or another, with wines that were more or less noteworthy. Perhaps in the years to come we will all gain a better understanding of this large vineyard district and come to learn that it can give really spectacular Barolos, but for now, I don't think anyone really knows what its potential is really all about.

Bricco San Pietro producers and the wines

There is probably no more famous producer of Bricco San Pietro wines today than the Rocche dei Manzoni estate. Its Bricco San Pietro Barolo can be taken to be an example of Bricco San Pietro's Manzoni subregion (though it might be argued that, at least in the past, Rocche dei Manzoni's wines were for a long time more about the Rocche dei Manzoni house style than of the Manzoni subregion itself). The Barolo Bricco San Pietro Vigna d'La Roul is a big, fleshy wine redolent of eucalyptus and ripe red cherry that marries power and refinement exceptionally well. First made in 1974 from south-facing, roughly forty years old vines planted around the Manzoni Soprani section of Manzoni, this has long been the most famous wine of the vineyard district.

Another very fine producer of Barolo Bricco San Pietro is Ruggeri Corsini, the estate owned by Nicola Argamante, one of Italy's greatest grape scientists and who played a major role in getting the Monforte producers to finally agree on the commune's official MGA vineyard district delimitations and names (admittedly, no easy task, so good for him). The estate was founded in 1995, after Nicola and his wife bought a small property and vineyards in the Ruggeri area of Monforte (that was one day to become part of the Bricco San Pietro vineyard district). The estate's name is therefore derived from the union of the words Ruggeri (the surname of Nicola's mother who helped him out financially in enabling him to buy and launch the estate) and Corsini (the name of the small hamlet and of the specific Monforte subregion where the winery is located). Corsini has a slightly cooler, less sunny mesoclimate than Manzoni, so its wines, though very Monforte-like in their minty-eucalyptus notes and fleshy charm, are sleeker and more lifted. Ruggeri Corsini's vines are planted high up, between 420-470 meters above sea level and the wine is aged for about thirty months in large Slavonian oak barrels.

There are many other fine producers who own vines in the Bricco San Pietro and who either bottle a single-vineyard district wine or include its grapes in a classic Barolo estate blended from more than one vineyard district. The Diego Conterno Barolo is an example of the latter: grapes culled from Bricco San Pietro are blended with those of other Monforte d'Alba-vineyard districts (San Giovanni, Ginestra). The 2016 was aged for twenty-four months in 50 hectoliter Stockinger casks, followed by eight to nine more months in cement tanks prior to bottling. They believe that the grapes from Bricco San Pietro add freshness, Ginestra's the tannic spine and San Giovanni's a welcome softer element. Unfortunately, without tasting the wines from each site separately prior to the blend, there really is no way to make up one's mind about what Bricco San Pietro delivers, or not. I hope to get to do so soon. The 2015 Barolo, though very good, is even less helpful in this regard, given that grapes from even more vineyard sources were included (along with the three previously mentioned vineyard districts, there were also grapes from the Pajana portion of Ginestra). At seven hectares, the Monti estate is one of the largest if not the largest land owner there and the winery's Barolos are solidly made, if perhaps not always exciting. There are also other Bricco San Pietro Barolos worth looking for. For example, Simone Scaletta (their vines are in the subregion previously known as Viglioni), Gagliasso's and Aldo Clerico (their vineyards are in the subregion called Cucchi). But I haven't accumulated enough tasting experience with any and all these wines over enough vintages to venture what would amount to nothing more than a guess as to what the Barolos from each of these subregions are really like (or even what they are *supposed* to be like, which given how things go, is actually even more important).

In ultimate analysis, there is no doubt that some subregions within the much larger Bricco San Pietro vineyard district are of noteworthy Barolo quality potential; unfortunately, the rest of the vast expanse of vineyards lacks the star power to emerge above its current also-ran status. It may be that in the future, with both land and bottle prices of Barolo seemingly going nowhere but up, that Bricco San Pietro will gain in fame, with its wines and different terroirs better characterized. Who knows, perhaps a big-name estate buys vineyards in Bricco San Pietro and starts making wine bringing hype and attention to the area. It's happened before, after all. No matter: nothing would make me happier (and producers there even happier, I'm sure). But for now, Bricco San Pietro showcases the perils of creating appellations, denominations, *cru*s, vineyard districts and any other type of vineyard designated area that are much too large, without a clear-cut sense of history and/or of somewhereness.

Benchmark wineries/Reference point producers of Barolo Bricco San Pietro: Rocche dei Manzoni, Ruggeri Corsini.

BRICCO VOGHERA

Township	Serralunga d'Alba
Reference Map	See Map of Serralunga d'Alba MGAs (Ch. 10)
Size (ha) (Tot / Barolo MGA)	7.15 / 1.88
Production 2021 (hl)	75.02 (of which 50 hl of Barolo Riserva *MGA*)
Altitude	370 – 405 meters a.s.l. roughly
Exposure	From south to southwest in the better exposed parcels, and east and northwest in the remaining parts
N. Claimants MGA	2
Other grape varieties planted:	Dolcetto
Land Units	Land Unit of Serralunga
Soil (stage):	Serravallian

Producers claiming the MGA

Azelia; Tenuta Cucco.

Wines

Azelia - Barolo Riserva Bricco Voghera; **Tenuta Cucco** - Barolo Riserva Bricco Voghera.

What the producers say

Scavino Luigi (Azelia): "We selected the Bricco Voghera specifically for the production of a Barolo Riserva. Here the vines are among the oldest in this town. The bunches are extremely small, the yield extremely low and the grapes reach at maturation an extraordinary concentration, from which we select those for making the Riserva. Despite the fact that the yield is already low naturally thanks to the age of the vines, we still perform green harvests that allows further maturation. The hill is incredibly steep, receiving in the summer enough sunlight and heat guaranteeing the defining characteristics of the grapes and wines. Bricco Voghera gives a Barolo of incredible concentration: dry flowers, dry fruits with great freshness and intensity of aroma. Black cherry, prune, blackberry with rose, violet and black chocolate are the typical notes on the nose. Tannins are round and generous with an incredible length on the mouth".

Ian's assessment of the vineyard district, its wines and its potential

The site is located on the eastern flank of the Serralunga ridge and is sandwiched between the following Serralunga vineyard districts: Lazzarito to the north and northwest; Gianetto to the northeast and east; and Brea to the south, southeast and east. In fact, Bricco Voghera shares the same hill with Brea: the whole area was actually once known as Voghera Brea, but with the reorganization of the Barolo denomination's vineyard districts and the launch of the official Barolo vineyard district names, it was decided to separate the two into different vineyard districts with different official names. Brea is therefore the lower half of the slope, Bricco Voghera the top part. Bricco Voghera is not just a small site, but also a very steep one, fairly open to the elements and so wind and sunlight here are plenty. It is also a high-altitude site for Barolo, with most of the vines planted between 370 and 400 meters above sea level. Its landscape category is that of the Land Unit of Serralunga; geologically, it's soil lithology is that of the Lequio formation, highly characteristic of the Serralunga commune. These are soils that are clay-calcareous in nature with plenty of limestone and compacted sands, rich in iron, phosphorus and potassium elements; but at Bricco Voghera they are especially rich in clay, which is, soil-wise at least, the site's defining feature.

Bricco Voghera producers and the wines

The benchmark Barolo from Bricco Voghera is the Barolo Riserva made by Azelia: the estate farms 0.85 hectares of full south-facing extremely old vines planted at about 360 meters above sea level. The wine was initially called with the vineyard area's original name, Voghera Brea (so if you go looking for older vintages of it, and you should, remember you need to look for this name on the label, not the new one of "Bricco Voghera" only). The last vintage of Azelia Barolo Riserva Voghera Brea was the 2004, then beginning with the 2006 vintage it changed name to Barolo Riserva Bricco Voghera. The extremely old vines (roughly 75 to 100 years old on average, but some reach as much as 120 years of age) give only about three bunches per vine; furthermore, the bunches are about half the size of "normal" Nebbiolo bunches, with grapes that have much thicker skins. For all these reasons, Luigi Scavino understandably decided to make his Barolo Riserva from the Bricco Voghera. Vinification is with indigenous yeasts, for approximately 55 - 60 days using the submerged cap technique at a maximum of 31 degrees Celsius; ageing has changed over the years, ranging anywhere from 30 months/three years to five years in large wooden casks and another three to five years in bottle. Today the wine is aged for five years in large wooden casks and another five in bottle, such that the Azelia Barolo Riserva Bricco Voghera is released only ten years after the vintage. As of the 2017 vintage, Tenuta Cucco (owned by the Rossi Cairo family who also run the La Raia estate in Liguria) has also begun making a Barolo Bricco Voghera: organic farming, natural yeasts (selected by the University of Turin from grapes in the estate's Cerrati vineyard) are used for fermentation, a submerged cap maceration follows (the length of time is decided upon from year to year depending on the vintage's and wine's characteristics) and ageing takes place in 25 hectoliter oak casks for twenty-four to thirty months. Not all Tenuta Cucco's grapes from Bricco Voghera (it owns about half the vineyard district's expanse of vines) are used to make this wine: the grapes of less favorably exposed vines (the estate owns vines in Bricco Voghera that face south, west and a small plateau that veers towards the north) are used to make the estate's Barolo del Comune di Serralunga d'Alba (blended with those from the lower portion of their holdings in Cerrati).

Benchmark wineries/Reference point producers of Barolo Bricco Voghera: Azelia.

BRICCOLINA

Township	Serralunga d'Alba
Reference Map	See Map of Serralunga d'Alba MGAs (Ch. 10)
Size (ha) (Tot / Barolo MGA)	17.93 / 10.04
Production 2021 (hl)	504.80 (of which 73.80 hl of Barolo Riserva *MGA*)
Altitude	300 – 370 meters a.s.l. roughly
Exposure	From southeast to southwest in the amphitheater below the Briccolina estate; from west to south in the remaining parts
N. Claimants MGA	5
Other grape varieties planted:	Barbera; Dolcetto
Land Units	Land Unit of Serralunga
Soil (stage):	Serravallian

Producers claiming the MGA

Batasiolo, La Briccolina, Pio Cesare; Rivetto; Vietti.

Wines

Batasiolo - Barolo Briccolina (Barolo Vigneto Corda della Briccolina); **Enrico Serafino** – Barolo Riserva Briccolina; **La Briccolina** - Barolo Briccolina; **Rivetto** - Barolo Briccolina.

What the producers say

Enrico Rivetto: "We have holding in this *cru* since 2004 and we have started to vinify it singly since 2007. With a southwestern exposure and the soil composition marked by alternating strata of marl, limestone and sand, Briccolina gives birth to wines of excellent finesse, structure and elegance. We opt for minimal intervention in the cellar and a long maceration to fully express the elegance and minerality of this *cru*".

Batasiolo: "Briccolina has intense and persistent aromas of ripe fruit, flowers and spices with delicate flavors of the wood. Its power, elegance and charm, give fullness to the palate and great intensity".

Ian's assessment of the vineyard district, its wines and its potential

Briccolina is a vineyard district on the western flank of the crest of hills that runs north to south in the Serralunga commune. Other vineyard district close by include: to its north there is Collaretto, to the east Ornato and to the southeast Boscareto. Briccolina's landscape category is that of the Land Unit of Serralunga. Its soil lithology is of the Lequio Formation, so clay-calcareous in nature but with plenty of silt and loam; the strong presence of limestone generates the typical whitish color that is visible to the naked eye. Briccolina's mesoclimate is a rather dry and windy one, in fact one of the driest and windiest in Serralunga territory (a good thing given the typical Langhe autumnal weather).

Briccolina producers and the wines

A small site, only seven estates or so farm vines in Briccolina. There have been some much awarded and hyped wines from Briccolina in the past, but frankly I have never understood why. If I had to go by what I've tasted from this vineyard district ten-twenty years ago, I'd have to say Briccolina is a very average-quality Barolo site at best. Happily, the Rivetto estate has come along with its Barolo Briccolina to help me understand how wrong I was in my evaluation of the Briccolina as a site for top-quality Barolo production. Owner Enrico Rivetto is an extremely bright and passionate young man that has turned his estate into a jewel of biodynamically farmed organic wines (the estate also produces truly delicious corn cakes and fruit juice from organically grown corn, pears and grapes). Though the Barolo Riserva Leon is the most famous Rivetto wine, in my view it is the Barolo Briccolina that is the qualitative apex of Enrico Rivetto's production. A result that is all the more impressive given that his Nebbiolo vines in Briccolina were planted only in 2005. A walk among Rivetto's vines will confirm that he really has turned the vineyard into a garden, as he is fond of saying: planted between the rows of vines are numerous trees, flowers and medicinal plants. The Nebbiolo grows there at about 335 meters above sea

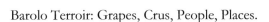

level and faces west/southwest. The clay-calcareous soil has very strong percentages of silt and loam (55% loam, 25% sand, 20% clay). Vinification involves long maceration, up to three months with a submerged cap (*cappello sommerso*) and aging lasts twenty-four to thirty months in fifteen hectoliter casks made of Slavonian oak. The wine boasts a wonderful equilibrium between luxurious ripeness and sheer steeliness: in short, it is a wine of impressive balance.

The highest and perhaps most beautiful part of the Briccolina vineyard district belongs to the aptly named La Briccolina estate owned by the Grasso family (related to Elio Grasso family of Monforte). It first made a Barolo carrying the Briccolina designation with the 2012 vintage (so the wine came out for sale in 2015). The family has had ties to the area since at least 1922, but sold off grapes for most of its history; with Barolo not selling well for most of the twentieth century, and family members holding down different jobs (for example, Tiziano Grasso worked at Fontanafredda), this was unavoidable. It was Tiziano's son Daniele (who like his father, also had a day-job, working at another winery, Batasiolo) who pushed his family to start estate-bottling a small part of their production, choosing to make their own wine from the best 0.4 hectares (of the total 5.5 hectares they own). While the winery looks west, the fifty years old vines face southwest; vinification involves roughly twenty days of maceration and fermentation and ageing is in large Garbellotto oak casks (with a stay in cement tank prior to bottling).

Since about forty-five years, the famous Pio Cesare winery (the only one still with a cellar facility, and a beautiful one at that, within the town of Alba) also farms the Briccolina vineyard district, though it blends the grapes into its classic Barolo blend. Their Briccolina vines (of Nebbiolo clones 180, 141, 185, 71, 63, 423, 415) were planted in 2003, face southwest and grow at about 380 meters above sea level on soils that are 45% clay, 40% loam and 15% sand. Do note that those percentages are wildly different from those of the portion of Briccolina estate farmed by the Rivetto estate: they furnish a good example of how soil variations are noteworthy within the same vineyard district, contributing to the great diversity of wines made within each site. Given those percentages, it is accurate to say that Pio Cesare's portion of the Briccolina is clay-calcareous in nature, while Rivetto's is loamy-sandy, with a strong calcareous presence (to an extent, these differences help characterize the respective Briccolina wines). Microvinifications (Pio Cesare has always vinified all its Barolo plots separately, so it's easy to gain insight on what each vineyard district can deliver) show clearly that the Briccolina site gives wines of deep color and structure, as would be expected from the majority of Serralunga sites. Batasiolo is another estate that has also long been associated with the Briccolina vineyard district.

Benchmark wineries/Reference point producers of Barolo Briccolina: Rivetto.

BROGLIO

Township	Serralunga d'Alba
Reference Map	See Map of Serralunga d'Alba MGAs (Ch. 10)
Size (ha) (Tot / Barolo MGA)	12.15 / 3.80
Production 2021 (hl)	203.27
Altitude	340 – 385 meters a.s.l. roughly
Exposure	From east to southeast in the better exposed parcels, and northeast in the remaining parts
N. Claimants MGA	3
Other grape varieties planted:	Barbera; Dolcetto
Land Units	Land Unit of Serralunga
Soil (stage):	Serravallian

Producers claiming the MGA

Sergio Giudice; Schiavenza; Luigi Oddero e Figli.

Wines
Schiavenza - Barolo Broglio and Barolo Riserva Broglio.

What the producers say
Schiavenza: "Fermentation occurs in cement tanks for 15-20 days; aging in 20-40 hectoliter Slavonian oak casks for three years. Broglio is an elegant and delicate Barolo; on the nose, the perfume of faded rose prevails".

Ian's assessment of the vineyard district, its wines and its potential

The Broglio vineyard district is close by the houses of the town of Serralunga itself: it's a small vineyard district situated between the Cerratti and Colombaro vineyard districts (respectively to the north and south of Broglio) all of which are on Serralunga's cooler eastern flank. It's a very typical Serralunga vineyard district in that it boasts a lithology of Lequio Formation, meaning the wines will be typical of the commune in their steeliness and sour red cherry charm. However, compared to other Serralunga vineyard districts such as Baudana, Broglio's is a rather more compact soil (so even among sites characterized by the Lequio Formation, there are soil differences, and hence differences in the wines made from each). Very few producers are currently making Barolo from Broglio: but be aware that the limit to Broglio becoming better known is not a lack of intrinsic quality relative to Barolo production, but it's a small size. In my estimation, Broglio is a site of noteworthy fine Barolo potential, one that we ought to hear more of in the near future. You read it here first.

Broglio producers and the wines

To the best of my knowledge, the only producer who bottles a Barolo Broglio as such is Schiavenza, though other fine estates farm or own small plots vines in this vineyard district (Bruno Giacosa, Luigi Oddero, Massolino Vigna Rionda), and who usually choose to use the Broglio grapes to make their classic estate Barolos. Schiavenza's southeast-facing vines are located at about 360 meters above sea level on clay-calcareous limestone, loam and sand rich soil. In the past, Schiavenza has also made a Barolo Riserva from Broglio, so you know he thinks highly of the site.

Gaja owns 1.2 hectares of twenty-five years old Nebbiolo vines planted facing east/southeast on what is a mostly sandy soil. Their vineyards are located in the portion of the Serralunga commune's territory that is close to the border with that of the Sinio commune, in the Val Talloria. The Talloria being a small stream that separates the two territories, it is not surprising that the soils there are more alluvial (sandy) in nature. In Gaia Gaja's experience, the Barolos made from this site are, perhaps not unexpectedly, very delicate and fruity.

Luigi Oddero's owns 2.6 hectares in Broglio: part of the vineyard is forty-five years old and another part was planted in 2001. Broglio vines contribute in large part to the estate's Barolo [the 2015 Barolo is a case in point; whereas there is more or less always a 30% of Serralunga grapes in this blend (Broglio and some Baudana), in the 2015 the presence of Broglio is especially noticeable]. The winery's Broglio holdings consist in three southeast-facing hectares planted on limestone whitish-colored soil.

Based on my tasting of Schiavenza's wines over the years and based on what I know from microvinifications of Broglio Nebbiolo grapes at other wineries, the Barolos of Broglio can be intensely colored and structured, though not quite as powerful as the wines from other Serralunga sites. Nevertheless, it seems to me like Broglio is a perfectly good source of refined, delicate Barolo and probably deserves to be better known.

Benchmark wineries/Reference point producers of Barolo Broglio: Schiavenza.

BRUNATE

Township	La Morra and Barolo
Reference Map	See Maps of La Morra MGAs and Barolo MGAs (Ch. 10)
Size (ha) (Tot / Barolo MGA)	9.16 (Barolo)+19.19 (La Morra) / 20.24
Production 2021 (hl)	1,015.65 (of which 11 hl of Barolo MGA Riserva)
Altitude	Barolo: 230 – 280 meters a.s.l. roughly; La Morra: 260 – 405 meters a.s.l. roughly
Exposure	From south to southeast.
N. Claimants MGA	14
Other grape varieties planted:	Barbera; Dolcetto
Land Units	In the lower parcels of Brunate, Land Unit of La Morra is combined with Land Unit of Barolo; Land Unit of La Morra in the remaining parts
Soil (stage):	Tortonian

Producers claiming the MGA

Batasiolo; Claudio Boggione; Claudio Boglietti; Enzo Boglietti; Francesco Borgogno; Ceretto; Mario Marengo; Marcarini; Poderi Oddero; Francesco Rinaldi; Giuseppe Rinaldi; Flavio Saglietti; Vietti; Roberto Voerzio.

Wines

Batasiolo - Barolo Vigneto Brunate; **Claudio Boggione** - Barolo Brunate; **Enzo Boglietti** - Barolo Brunate; **Francesco Borgogno** - Barolo Vigneti Brunate; **Ceretto** - Barolo Brunate; **Damilano** - Barolo Brunate (*); **Fabio Oberto** - Barolo Brunate (*); **Marcarini** - Barolo Brunate; **Mario Marengo** - Barolo Brunate and Riserva; **Poderi Oddero** - Barolo Brunate and Riserva; **Francesco Rinaldi** - Barolo Brunate; **Giuseppe Rinaldi** - Barolo Brunate; **Flavio Saglietti** - Barolo Brunate; **Vietti** - Barolo Brunate; **Roberto Voerzio** - Barolo Brunate.

What the producers say

Marta Rinaldi (Giuseppe Rinaldi): "We have owned vines in this *cru* since the birth of our estate in 1915. All the parcels that we possess are vinified separately. Until 2009, we produced a blend of Brunate and Le Coste, and of Cannubi San Lorenzo and Ravera. Since the 2010 vintage (the production rules concerning the MGAs came into effect) we produce just a Barolo Brunate and a Barolo Tre Tine (a blend of Cannubi San Lorenzo, Ravera, Le Coste). Brunate enjoys a good sun exposure (south-facing) and is a cru characterized by a fantastic balance of vegetative growth and the capacity for water and nutrient transfer, making for Barolos of great richness".

Enzo Boglietti: "Brunate has been in our family for three generations, but we vinify it singly only as of 1991. The biggest strength of this Barolo is its great structure infused with supple and elegant tannins, while a small defect is its tendency to accumulate a high level of sugar in hot years".

Alessandro Ceretto (Ceretto): "We vinify separately this vineyard since 1978. Barolo Brunate is a velvety Barolo, delicately perfumed and is characterized by its distinctive elegance".

Mariacristina Oddero (Poderi Oddero): "This vineyard is in the family since 1968. Traditional vinification. Brunate has a bouquet of rose and violet, accompanied by a hint of wet earth and of ripe red fruit. It finishes long on a sweet tannic note, which reminds one of a perfectly aged wine".

Mauro Sebaste: "Brunate is a Barolo that is delicately perfumed with nuances of rose and violet, of a great aromatic complexity. On the palate, it's velvety, austere, powerful, and persistent, with a good tannic structure."

Luca Currado (Vietti): "We have this vineyard since always and recently we have made a few more acquisitions. Long maceration from three to five weeks. The wine of Brunate is the typical expression of the terroir of La Morra: harmoniously generous body, balanced and with a velvety texture. Classic, very perfumed, with notes ripe red fruit, spice, violet, prune and tar are also very typical of Brunate. Tannins are round already in youth, finishing long and savory".

Paola Rinaldi (Francesco Rinaldi): "The vineyard of two hectares is on the border between the villages of Barolo and La Morra, facing south-east. Here you can find the old farmhouse 'La Brunate' that has been part of the winery since the early days. Our Barolo Brunate has great body, excellent fragrance and is full of elegance and softness. A captivating and full taste thanks in part to well-balanced tannins".

Marco Marengo (Mario Marengo): "This vineyard has been part of the estate for 100 years. The Barolo Brunate is characterized by elegance and finesse on the nose. Oftentimes, nuances of spices are also found".

Davide Voerzio (Roberto Voerzio): "We vinify this *cru* separately since 1987. This vineyard is located below the town of La Morra and the soil is calcareous, poor, with a dominance of bluish-gray marl. Brunate is a Barolo that is more masculine, of remarkable power and structure, with intense flavors and important tannic structure. One often recognizes hints of small dark fruits (blueberry and blackberry) enriched by notes of spices and tobacco. A classic Barolo that knows how to combine freshness and power".

Marcarini: "For several generations, our family has owned a considerable part of the Brunate vineyards; and we have indicated this origin on our bottles since 1958. As far as wine production methods are concerned, we are proud to call ourselves "traditionalists". The nose is composite, rich, full and persistent, with hints of vanilla, sweet spices, tobacco, mountain hay and underbrush. Impressive taste sensations reveal the wine's imperious, noble, warm and velvety character, and the flavor is long and intense".

Ian's assessment of the vineyard district, its wines and its potential

One of Barolo's most famous vineyard areas, Brunate is a vineyard district mostly located in the territory of the La Morra commune but a small piece falls into the Barolo's commune territory as well. And so, while generally viewed as a vineyard district of La Morra (because the majority of its extension falls within the boundaries of that commune), Brunate actually belongs to two different communes and is therefore an inter-communal vineyard district (like Cerequio, for example). And that is something well worth knowing about, as we shall see shortly. Taken as a whole, the Brunate vineyard district is one long slope surrounded by a bunch of La Morra vineyard districts: Boiolo is to the north, La Serra to the west, and Cerequio to the southwest; Zonchetta is to Brunate's southeast and Crosia is to the east, but these last two vineyard districts are vineyard districts of the Barolo township.

Brunate's name most likely derives from the Latin word *brinatam*, meaning early morning frost or fog. While the reference to frost isn't really that encouraging relative to fine winemaking, we can all breathe easier thinking that fog is a very typical sight in Langhe vineyards come autumn. Just like its ancient name, the site as a vineyard area goes a long way back too. Famous for its grapes already in the 1300s, Brunate has always been viewed as one of the Barolo denomination's five or so best sites, and more than one knowledgeable colleague I know considers it the best one of them all. Fair enough: there can be little doubt as to Brunate being one of the very best places to grow Nebbiolo in the world, and as I pointed out earlier in this book, that much is immediately obvious when you compare Barolos from different sites but made by the same producer in the same vintage (see ARBORINA file). But there are many other examples I could give attesting to the high esteem Brunate is held in. For example, almost every producer I have talked to or corresponded with over the years has told me they would love to own vines in and make wines from Brunate: Altare, Renato Corino, Ratti, Revello…the list could go on and on (see Appendix D, *Table 4.3: The Top Barolo Vineyard Districts according to Barolo's producers*. See also: Appendix D, *Table 4.4: The Top Barolo Vineyard Districts Barolo's producers would love to own/ be gifted*.) Yet another example is provided by the anecdote once told me by Marco Marengo of the outstanding Mario Marengo estate: at least until a few years ago, Brunate is the one vineyard his family had never taken out any hail insurance on, because the site's mesoclimate was so good that hail never posed much of a threat there (clearly, with the advent of climate change that may well change, unfortunately). Remember that micro- and meso-climate are defining features, of truly cardinal importance, in determining what amounts to a *grand cru* and what are just *premier crus* or *lieux-dits*.

However, much like Burgundy's Echezeaux and Clos de Vougeot *grand crus*, Brunate is not all of the same exciting quality level: it's a complex site the full understanding and appreciation of which (and of its wines) requires a bit more in-depth analysis. Actually, much more analysis than is commonly done. For one, Brunate is a relatively hot site that has always had the tendency to give ripe grapes packed with sugar: a highly desirable quality fifty years ago or so, but in times of climate change this is hardly the case anymore. There are vintages nowadays in which other less famous Barolo vineyard districts fare much better than does Brunate and the Barolo wines of which are simply better balanced, more enjoyable to drink, and with better aging potential (witness the best Barolos of difficult years like 1997, 2003, and 2007, almost none of which came from Brunate). This analysis is not an illogical one, and applies to other great Barolo sites too (and not just in the Barolo denomination or even Italy, for that matter); in fairness, for the time being, this observation is true only of extremely hot vintages such as those I listed. For the most part, Brunate has a unique *grand cru* capacity to give Barolos that very rich and powerful wines (clearly, "powerful and rich" by La Morra standards) but also fresh.

Though everyone tends to speak and write in terms of "one" Brunate, that is not how things really are. As mentioned, the vineyard district is a rare intercommunal one, unequally divided between La Morra (the territory of which is where the largest part of Brunate is situated: to put a figure to it, a little less than 70% of the vineyard district's total extension) and Barolo (a little more than 30% of the vineyard district falls within the latter commune's territory). This is knowledge worth having, because while nobody talks about it much (producers included) and despite what you might be told, the two sections of Brunate are remarkably different, and so are the wines. In fact, not all Brunate is created equal: differences between the two subsections of Brunate in terms of soil, exposure, topography and altitude may be more or less visible, but they are very real. And even if you were willing to accept the statement that the soils between the two subsections are more or less the same (they are not), just opening your eyes for a moment will demonstrate clearly that the altitude and the topography of the two sections are obviously not the same.

For example, Brunate starts out low, on the lower section of a gentle slope (as low as 230 meters above sea level), and slopes upward sharply upwards to just slightly more than 400 meters, before giving way to the La Serra vineyard district. Clearly, growing Nebbiolo grapes at 250 meters above sea level and growing them at almost 400 meters are two very different things; and as if that weren't enough, there is noteworthy slope gradient diversity too (which translates to different angles of solar irradiation). It follows that the Brunate piece in Barolo is lower-lying and gentler in slope than the one in La Morra. Unlike the altitude, differences are less marked in Brunate when it comes to exposure: most of the vines throughout the vineyard district-face south and/or south east, and sunlight availability is excellent everywhere. Brunate's soils are also interesting to analyze. They are classic Tortonian stage soils, a mix of blue-grey marls with sand, limestone and clay, rich in manganese and magnesium. While most producers you'll talk with like to say the soil is essentially the same on both sides of the communal fence, that is not exact. The soil of Brunate is important: more than one producer has told me over the years that they think it's the real secret to Brunate's wines. For example, Paola Rinaldi of Francesco Rinaldi says that "I like to think that there is a very strict relation between the sediments in the soil and the fine and dense tannins that characterize the Barolos from Brunate".

Yes, it's true when they tell you that Brunate is mostly characterized by a Saint Agatha Fossil Marls lithology; but these are different between the La Morra section of Brunate and that of Barolo. Generalizing somewhat, the sand component is slightly higher in the La Morra section of Brunate (because there you have mainly Saint Agatha Fossil Marls of the laminated type with only a little of the typical type, compared to the mostly typical type of the Brunate section that falls within Barolo). That the two sections of Brunate differ in terms of topography, altitude, slope gradient and soil lithology is well demonstrated by the fact that the two are placed in different landscape categories: a mix of the Land Unit of Barolo and of the Land Unit of La Morra for the Brunate section within the Barolo commune, and the Land Unit of La Morra only for that portion of Brunate that belongs to the La Morra territory.

Clearly, all of the above has repercussions on the wines. Generally speaking, Brunate, a relatively hot site, gives richer, deeper, more dark red fruit-accented Barolos than most other vineyard districts of La Morra. But do not accept the throwaway line that Brunate's Barolos are also darker-coloured than most Barolos from La Morra. True, Brunate's Barolos can be somewhat darker, but that depends on where the Nebbiolo grapes grow within Brunate. Those sections of Brunate with more sand tend to give lighter-hued wines (as are the Barolos of the Santa Maria fraction of La Morra, for example: in this context, Brunate's wines are very much Barolos of La Morra). However, keep in mind that sites higher up tend to give darker hued wines (because their ventilation and the diurnal temperature variations are less damaging to the grape anthocyanins), and so even the sandier areas, depending on the vintage, can give wines that are a little darker than expected (clearly, never even close to purple-ruby or pitch black, because it is still Nebbiolo we are talking about, after all). Though Brunate's wines are never as textured and broad as those of Cerequio, they are relatively big Barolos ("big" by La Morra Barolo standards). Reduced to simplest possible terms, the Barolos made from the La Morra section are generally more floral and perfumed, while those from the Barolo side have less intense aromas and more obvious notes of fruit and sweet spices, and a generally broader mouthfeel. The sweet spice note of Brunate is different than that of many other Barolos from other vineyard districts (some soil minerals, like manganese, are believed to leave an impression of spiciness in wines, as well of increased tannicity). In any case, in Brunate's Barolos I find a singular brown spice note (which is different from the one you'll pick up in Barolos with more than 10% of Nebbiolo Rosé. See Chapter 3, NEBBIOLO ROSÉ). I think this finding applies to all of Brunate and its wines: over the years, I haven't been able to pinpoint it with absolute certainty to the Barolos of one of the two sections (believe me, I have tried: but I find it in Barolos from both sides of Brunate). All of the above is not meant to imply that the Barolos of one section of Brunate are better than the other's; rather, the two Brunate sections give slightly different wines, and therein lies an added measure of their charm and interest. You might say that if Piedmont were Burgundy, Brunate would surely have been divided into a Brunate-*dessus* and a Brunate-*dessous*, or a Brunate-*du haut* and a Brunate-*du bas*. Again, the wines of one are not necessarily better than the other, but interestingly different. To help readers gain a better understanding of the Barolos of Brunate here is a list of the "who's who" and the "where" relative to the different sections of Brunate:

Estates with plots in Brunate (Barolo section): Cavalier Bergadano, Claudio Boggione, Giuseppe Rinaldi.

Estates with plots in Brunate (La Morra section): Batasiolo, Damilano, Enzo Boglietti, Flavio Saglietti, Francesco Borgogno, Mario Marengo, Poderi Oddero, Roberto Voerzio, Vietti.

Estates with plots in Brunate (in both the Barolo and La Morra sections): Ceretto, Francesco Rinaldi, Marcarini.

In ultimate analysis, the Barolos of Brunate are some of the best wines of the entire denomination. Independently of the section of Brunate in which the Nebbiolo grapes grow, it's just an amazing site in which to grow Nebbiolo, period. Its Barolos stand out for their unique combination of refinement and power, that is generally lacking in the vast majority of La Morra Barolos, but above all the rather amazing silkiness of tannins (in most vintages), something that only the greatest vineyards in the world (not just of Barolo) are capable of delivering. And climate change be damned.

Brunate producers and the wines

As you can tell from the list immediately above, many outstanding estates own vines in Brunate and have made many memorable Barolos from there over the years. The Mario Marengo estate (run by Marco Marengo) owns some of the best-situated plots in the whole vineyard district, and his Barolo Brunate Vecchie Vigne is potentially one of Barolo's greatest wines in almost every vintage. Marengo's Brunate wine provides us with an interesting lesson in terroir. He owns two plots of vines in Brunate: one is located next to plots owned by Marcarini and Boglietti, while the other plot is next to the one farmed by Roberto Voerzio. Interestingly, the two plots are only fifty meters and a five-minute walk apart, and yet there's a huge difference in the quality of grapes each one provides. The first plot (the one near Marcarini and Vietti) has very homogenous soil; it's planted with 60 years old vines that ripen four to five days before those of the other plot. This other plot is also characterized by old vines (fifty years old vines) but the soil is variable throughout the holding and the wine is never as profound as that of the first plot. Not surprisingly, Marengo makes his Brunate *vecchie vigne* bottling from the first plot of vines only. As good as Marengo's regular Barolo from Brunate is, and it is, the Brunate *vecchie vigne* is just at a whole other level of complexity and depth. Remarkably so, actually.

Another very high-quality estate farming Brunate is Enzo Boglietti: they own south to southeast facing Nebbiolo vines planted in 2005 with Nebbiolo clones CVT 71 and CVT 142, plus clone 423 (a Picotener) at 300-350 meters above sea level. Of the many single-vineyard district Barolos Boglietti bottles every year, their Brunate is perhaps the most austere and complex of all. Which Boglietti Barolo you prefer however will depend mostly on the style of Barolo you like: for example, I am often left enthralled by their Barolo Arione's levity and purity (see ARIONE file), but those who prefer a little oomph in the fermented grape juice will take a bigger shine to the Brunate. Which is perfectly fine: different strokes for different folks, after all.

Poderi Oddero owns 0.43 hectares of Brunate in the highest portion of the vineyard district at roughly 380-400 meters above sea level. The small plot is located on the road that takes you from Brunate to Cerequio, and though it's fully south-facing, it's in the coldest part of the Brunate vineyard district (the altitude certainly has something to do with it), which as I have written above is actually a fairly warm, and in some years, downright hot site. And especially so now that climate change has reared its ugly head. In fact, I can guarantee that when walking around in that specific plot in August, especially towards evening, you are better off wearing a light sweater. The reality of this situation means that whereas the top part of Brunate did not allow grapes to ripen fully there in a recent past (exposure to cooler, lively winds, steep gradient, higher altitude: all of which in turn mean a cooler mesoclimate), today this is no longer the case. It follows that owning vines there that are so high up is actually may well be a blessing nowadays. To be clear, the difficulties posed by the climate is but one of the reasons why Poderi Oddero, despite owning vines in Brunate since 1967, never bottled a Barolo Brunate until the 2004 vintage (prior to this date the Brunate grapes were blended in the estate's Barolo classico). The other reason was that back in the 1960s and 1970s barriques were practically nowhere to be seen in Barolo, and clearly, the amount of wine you can make from a 0.43-hectare site is not exactly conducive to getting aged in a twenty or even larger hectoliter oak barrel. Hence the Barolo from the Brunate plot went into the classic estate Barolo. Where Poderi Oddero's Nebbiolo vines are is a very specific part of Brunate, the highest part of the vineyard district close to the Fontanazza Soprana collection of rundown houses (you will see that name on one of the houses there the name "Cascina Fontanazza" is still visible). The name Fontanazza, which was once much better-known than it is today and actually identified what some thought was a high-quality site (I remember Veronelli always speaking highly of Fontanazza's wines, and did so in terms of outstanding Dolcetto wines too, not just Nebbiolo) is progressively being lost. In fact, it is now included in the Boiolo vineyard district (a shame: in my view, they could have created two separate vineyard districts: Fontanazza, and Boiolo. See BOIOLO file). By the way, for those of you who are foodies at heart as well as wine lovers, Mattia Martinelli and his wife run the Locanda Fontanazza, an easygoing restaurant where the service sometimes borders on the unacceptable but the simple food is good and the ambience charmingly Italian (meaning everybody's packed together closely, loud, and happy).

Francesco Rinaldi has long bottled a wine from Brunate that for the longest time they called Brunata in honour of the Cascina (farmhouse) 'La Brunata' (or 'La Brunate') that is located near the vines and has been a part of the winery since forever. Their vineyard had already been planted when they bought it, and save for some sick old vines they have had to substitute from time to time, the vines are more than sixty years old overall. The wine is thicker, denser, and ripely fruitier than some of the Barolos made from the higher reaches of Brunate (Francesco Rinaldi owns vines in both sections of Brunate, but in general, they are all situated lower down the slope) and it provides not just an excellent wine but also a clear-cut demonstration of how different Brunate Barolos can be.

The similarly named Giuseppe Rinaldi estate makes its most famous wine from Brunate, and it remains their only vineyard district-designate Barolo remaining after the official launch of the Barolo's vineyard district names. Prior to that the estate also bottled a Cannubi-Le Coste Barolo, but the use of two vineyard district names for one wine is no longer allowed (unless of course that is the official name of the vineyard district, such as is the case with a number of Novello vineyard districts). And so, at the time they opted to make one Barolo Brunate and one Barolo called "Tre Tine", a blend of their remaining vineyards (Rinaldi has since bought vines in Bussia vineyard district of Monforte). Their Barolo Brunate, always a wonderful example of fairly traditional Barolo, is at once elegant and powerful, with lovely perfume and silky tannins. I wish to point out that this estate makes one of the best Freisa wines of Piedmont, and that if you love Barolo, you really shouldn't miss out on a wine made with its closest relative.

Last but not least, Ceretto is another estate that owns vines in both sections of Brunate and has been making a Barolo Brunate for a very long time. The Nebbiolo vines are planted over two large plots facing southeast, between 276 to 342 meters above sea level, and close by the colorful and pretty chapel, an example of modern art as applied to an old building by Sol Lewitt and David Tremlett. The soil composition in Ceretto's section of Brunate is 32% loam, 16% sand, and 52% clay. A portion of Ceretto's 5.3 hectares is planted to Nebbiolo vines that are now close to fifty years old (planted in 1978, 1984 and 2008); unfortunately, a 1.5-hectare piece replanted in 2008 with a massal selection has turned out to have problems related to viruses and so is not producing currently. Ceretto's CEO, Giacolino Gillardi, has fond memories of Brunate, having been involved in the winemaking since the early 1990s, and he says the greatest challenge was to come up with a wine that truly showcased the unicity of Brunate. I want to alert you to the fact that I believe Ceretto made their best Barolo Brunate ever in the 2016 vintage: I am not sure why, and Federico Ceretto as well was unsure as to why this might have been, but he too was extremely pleased with the result. For sure, it's an absolutely knockout Barolo.

BRUNELLA

Township	Castiglione Falletto
Reference Map	See Map of Castiglione MGAs (Ch. 10)
Size (ha) (Tot / Barolo MGA)	5.01 / 2.83
Production 2021 (hl)	126.48
Altitude	280 – 314 meters a.s.l. roughly
Exposure	Southwest in the better exposed parcels, and from northwest to northeast in the remaining parts.
N. Claimants MGA	1
Other grape varieties planted:	Dolcetto; white varieties
Land Units	Land Unit of Barolo in the north-east side bordering Fiasco; Land Unit of Castiglione in the remaining parts
Soil (stage):	Tortonian

Producers claiming the MGA

Boroli.

Wines

Boroli - Barolo Brunella.

What the producers say

Boroli: "Brunella is nestled in between La Morra and Barolo on one side and Monforte and Serralunga on the other; it gives a full and complete wine, combining the softness and elegance of the first two zones and the structure and austerity of the latter. The vines enjoy a south, southeast exposure and are planted on soil composed mainly of clay and limestone, with traces of sand. The bouquet is elegant with hints of red ripe fruits, leather, tobacco and sensations of oak, while on the palate the powerful structure emerges with a long persistent finish".

Ian's assessment of the vineyard district, its wines and its potential

Brunella is one of the more beautiful spots in all of Castiglione Falletto. I have had the pleasure (Michele too) to be there on numerous occasions visiting the winery and tasting all the new vintages with owner Achille Boroli, and as much fun as that is, just catching the amazing view from the winery is reason enough to visit. The winery is located at the top of the ridge from where Brunella dominates its surroundings: just by walking the circumference of the winery building, you can see standout vineyard districts nearby such as Villero (of which Brunella is essentially a prolongation of), Fiasco, Monprivato and even Bricco Rocche. The names of those vineyard districts, all of which are associated with some of Barolos greatest wines, tells you the kind of Barolo real estate company Brunella keeps: in other words, this is a prime area of Nebbiolo vineyards if there ever was. The existence of a *cascina* (farmhouse) La Brunella was documented already in official records dating back to 1666; today it is associated with the Brunella vineyard district, a vineyard district of Castiglione Falletto that is *monopole* of the Boroli estate. Brunella was given official vineyard district status after Achile Boroli found an old map from the 1960s that demonstrated the existence of an historic vineyard entirely located within the property of the Cascina, that Achille's father Silvano had bought back in 1997 (just a few months after having bought the Cascina Bompè over in Madonna di Como and adding to it a hotel and Michelin star restaurant. In 2017, the Boroli family kept the restaurant and hotel but sold the Cascina Bompè and part of its vineyards to Poderi Colla so as to concentrate on their Brunella winery).

The Brunella landscape is classified as a Land Unit of Castiglione, the Unit that so characterizes the vast majority of the Castiglione Falletto territory. Its soil lithology is mostly Saint Agatha Fossil Marls of the sandy type (at Brunella, there is a thin to thick layer of sand beneath the clay, about fifty centimeters below the surface) but with pockets of Diano Sandstone formation.

Brunella producers and the wines (monopole)

Initially, Boroli was blending most of Brunella's Barolo into its estate Barolo blend; a small percentage of the grapes also went into the Barolo they made from their holdings in Villero (not at all an unreasonable move, given that Brunella is the western continuation of Villero and the two vineyard areas more or less smoothly segue into each other). In fact, Boroli told me that he has never found a mention (yet?) of the wine from Brunella being bottled on its own or sold as such in the Cascina's past; but clearly, once it became obvious that the site had the potential to qualify for single vineyard district status, well, that was just too good an opportunity to pass up. And so it was that Boroli released its first Barolo Brunella with the 2013 vintage; it could have done so already in 2012 but Boroli preferred to wait until the announcement of Brunella being included in the Barolo denomination's official list of vineyard districts became official.

Like I said, er wrote, previously, I was at the estate tasting regularly every three to six months or so from barrel in those years and got to see first-hand the genesis of the Barolo Brunella, and for sure, the wine stood out then just as it stands out today. From day one, the Brunella Barolo always stood out for its conspicuous Castiglione Falletto-somewhereness: it really does resemble the Barolos of Fiasco, Monprivato, Bricco Rocche and parts of Villero. I specify "parts of Villero" because wines from some sections of that vineyard are much more "of Villero" than they are "of Castiglione Falletto", even though the vineyard district is in the Castiglione Falletto commune (see VILLERO file). The pockets of Diano Sandstone formation contribute to the wine's rich, textured, suave mouthfeel, while the sand accounts for the penetrating floral perfume that is the single biggest descriptive trait of Brunella's wine. Generally speaking, Barolos from Brunella are more lifted and less massive than the wine Boroli makes from Villero. But while the Brunella Barolos released to date are characterized by noteworthy balance and a seemingly gentle disposition, they are not at all wimpy wines, their mouthfeel, size and levels of tannin being truly noteworthy (though it behooves me to point out that the strongly tannic personality is in at least large part a result of Boroli's winemaking style: in fact, all of the estate's wines have real tannic bite, and especially so in their youth).

For sure, the quality of the Brunella Barolo is evident not just when tasting it on its own, but in reviewing what its presence (and absence) did for the winery's classic Barolo blend. While Boroli's 2012 estate Barolo was a lovely wine (and especially so when viewed through the lens of what was a hot vintage many wines of which are often marred by gritty tannins), pleasantly floral and compellingly sweet, the 2013 estate Barolo, which lacked the Brunella (that had gone off into its own wine), was slightly disappointing (especially so given that 2013 was a much, much, better vintage than the 2012). Boroli recognized this and went out and bought other Barolo vineyards to make up for the loss of the Brunella component in his estate wine (which I am happy to report is now firmly back on track and a very good Barolo indeed).

A fact that is not much known about the Barolo Brunella is that, depending on characteristics of each vintage, Achille Boroli uses different parts of the vineyard to make his Brunella-designated Barolo. And so it was that in 2013, only the grapes grown on the eastern and southern sections of the Brunella hill were used. In 2014, it was only the south-facing vines that made it (no surprise there, given what the 2014 vintage's growing season was like); and in 2015, a great vintage, the Nebbiolo grapes from all three sides of the hill were included in the final blend (again, hardly surprising). Undoubtedly, Achille Boroli has worked very hard, with uncommon passion and energy, to improve his winery and wines over the years and bring their quality to the attention of wine lovers and collectors everywhere. *Bravo davvero, e tanto di cappello, Signor Boroli.*

Benchmark wineries/Reference point producers of Barolo Brunella: Boroli (monopole).

BUSSIA

Township	Monforte d'Alba and Barolo
Reference Map	See Map of Monforte d'Alba MGAs (Ch. 10)
Size (ha) (Tot / Barolo MGA)	292.31 (Monforte)+6.58 (Barolo) / 122.12
Production 2021 (hl)	6,203.89 (of which 574.24 hl of Barolo Riserva *MGA*, 655.43 hl Of Barolo *MGA* Vigna and 167.48 hl of Barolo Riserva *MGA* Vigna)
Altitude	220 – 460 meters a.s.l. roughly
Exposure	From south to southwest in the better exposed parcels; from west to east passing through north in the remaining parts
N. Claimants MGA	57
Other grape varieties planted:	Barbera; Dolcetto; Freisa; white varieties
Land Units	Land Unit of La Morra near Monforte (Bussia Corsini); Land Unit of Castiglione for the higher parcels; Land Unit of Barolo for the remaining parts.
Soil (stage):	Tortonian

Producers claiming the MGA

Adriano F.lli; Francesco Borgogno; Ceretto; Cantina Tre Pile; Barale Fratelli; Batasiolo; Giancarlo Boasso; Bussia Soprana; Stroppiana; Cascina Ballarin; Cascina Pugnane; Antonella Chiado' Caponet; Chionetti; Conterno Fantino; Franco Conterno - Cascina Sciulun; Costa di Bussia Tenuta Arnulfo; Domenico Clerico; Dosio; Enoteca Caffè Rocca; Ettore Fontana Livia Fontana); Famiglia Anselma; Alessandro e Gian Natale Fantino; Alberto Fenocchio; Elio Fenocchio; Giacomo Fenocchio; Sara Fenocchio; Domenico Franco; Angelo Germano; Federico Ghilino; Attilio Ghisolfi; Aldo Giachino; Fratelli Giacosa (Cascina Canavere); Korwin Krukowski Alessandro; La Bioca; Mascarello; Monti; Mariano Moscone; Paolo Scavino; Armando Parusso; Pecchenino; Pian Polvere Soprano; Podere Ruggeri Corsini; Poderi Aldo Conterno; Poderi Colla; Poderi Poderi Oddero; Poderi Fogliati; Poderi Luigi Einaudi; Margherita Pressenda; Prunotto; Giuseppe Rinaldi; Ribote; Monia Rullo; Silvano Bolmida; Cascina Amalia; Tenuta Rocca; Vinory.

Wines

Baccà - Federico Ghilino - Barolo Bussia; **Fratelli Barale** - Barolo Bussia, Bussia Riserva; **Batasiolo** - Barolo Vigneto Bofani; **Silvano Bolmida** - Barolo Bussia, Bussia Riserva and Barolo Vigne dei Fantini; **Bussia Soprana** - Barolo Bussia, Barolo Vigna Colonnello and Barolo Riserva Gabutti della Bussia; **Cantina Tre Pile** - Barolo Bussia; **Cascina Amalia** – Barolo Bussia; **Cascina Ballarin** - Barolo Bussia; **Cascina Pugnane** - Barolo Bussia; **Ceretto** – Barolo Bussia; **Chionetti** – Barolo Primo and Barolo Bussia Vigna Pian Polvere; **Franco Conterno** - Barolo Bussia Riserva; **Costa di Bussia** – **Tenuta Arnulfo** - Barolo Bussia; Barolo Bussia Vigna Campo dei Buoi; Barolo Bussia Luigi Arnulfo and Barolo Bussia Riserva; **Famiglia Anselma** - Barolo Bussia and Barolo Bussia Vigna Pian Polvere; **Alessandro e GianNatale Fantino** - Barolo Bussia; **Alberto Fenocchio** - Barolo Bussia; **Giacomo Fenocchio** - Barolo Bussia; Bussia Riserva; Barolo Bussia 90 Dì; **Livia Fontana** - Barolo Bussia Riserva; **Angelo Germano** - Barolo Bussia; **Fratelli Adriano** - Barolo Tenuta Pian Polvere; **Attilio Ghisolfi** - Barolo Bussia, Barolo Riserva Ciabot Minat Nuova, Barolo Bricco Visette; **Fratelli Giacosa** - Barolo Bussia; **La Bioca** – Barolo Bussia; **Marrone** – Barolo Bussia; **Fratelli Massucco** - Barolo Bussia; **Monti** - Barolo Bussia; Bussia Riserva; **Fratelli Moscone** - Barolo Bussia; **Armando Parusso** - Barolo Bussia; Bussia Riserva Oro; **Pecchenino** - Barolo Bussia; **Pianpolvere Soprano** - Barolo Riserva Bussia Pianpolvere Soprano; **Podere Ruggeri Corsini** - Barolo Bussia Corsini; **Poderi Aldo Conterno** - Barolo Bussia, Barolo Riserva Granbussia, Barolo Bussia Cicala, Barolo Bussia Colonnello, Barolo Bussia Romirasco; **Poderi Colla** - Barolo Dardi Le Rose Bussia; **Poderi Fogliati** - Barolo Bussia; **Poderi Luigi Einaudi** - Barolo Bussia (from 2016); **Poderi Oddero** - Barolo Bussia Vigna Mondoca; **Prunotto** - Barolo Bussia and Barolo Riserva Bussia Vigna Colonnello; **Ribote** – Barolo Bussia; **Giuseppe Rinaldi** - Barolo Bussia (from 2019); **Sylla Sebaste** - Barolo Bussia; **Dario Stroppiana** - Barolo Bussia and Bussia Riserva; **Tenuta Rocca** - Barolo Bussia; **Arnaldo Rivera** - Barolo Bussia; **Cascina Amalia** – Barolo Bussia; **Vinory** - Barolo Bussia Vigna Fantini (from 2018).

What the producers say

Bolmida Silvano: "Bussia and Bussia Vigna dei Fantini have been in the family since always but it wasn't until 2000 that they were vinified separately from the others. Vigna dei Fantini boasts a steep slope and a looser soil, factors that complicate work in the vineyard but at the same time make the site less problematic relative to fungal diseases. Bussia on the other hand boasts a more complete and balanced soil composition".

Maurizio Giacosa (Fratelli Giacosa): "We came to acquire this parcel in 1991 and we have always vinified and bottled it separately. The balance between the clay and limestone soil, the high presence of magnesium and micronutrients, the diurnal difference thanks to the high altitude and its location at the entry of the valley, give rise to the production of wines characterized by a fresh fruitiness and velvety, suave tannins".

Mariacristina Oddero (Poderi Oddero): "Our family possesses the Bussia Vigna Mondoca parcel since 1979. Traditional vinification. Bussia Vigna Mondoca is a wine of fine texture and elegant perfumes reminiscent of small berries, balsamic vinegar, Mediterranean herbs, dried rose petals and with age, tar. Barolo of absolute balance, long and complex, with fine and firm tannins".

Marco Parusso (Armando Parusso): "In Bussia, we are owners of Vigna Rocche since 1925 and of Vigna Munie since 1988. From 1986, we started to do individual site vinification and bottling. Bussia always give us an elegant yet powerful Barolo in which structure is built into freshness strengthened by silky tannins. Typical perfumes are flowers, red and black fruits with a hint of tobacco, mint and plenty of balsamic nuances".

Orlando Pecchenino (Pecchenino): "We own our vineyard parcel in Bussia since 2007. Bussia is a Barolo that is more powerful than say Le Coste di Monforte, and offers hints of small red fruits, licorice and spices".

Giacomo Conterno (Poderi Aldo Conterno): "Our parcels in Bussia became part of the estate at the end of the 1960s. In the Bussia, our estate produces three crus: Colonnello, vinified and bottled singly since 1969, Cicala since 1969, and Romirasco since 1978. The average age of vines in Cicala and Cicala vineyard is around 65 years old, and 75 years old for those in Romirasco. Long maceration for 4 to 5 weeks is our standard".

Tino Colla (Poderi Colla) "From 1961 to 1993, with my brother Beppe, we vinified this parcel as a Prunotto *cru* Bussia. Since 1994 as Poderi Colla, we call it Bussia Dardi Le Rose. This is a parcel selected by Beppe Colla in the 50s as he believed that, within the Barolo area, this *cru* had, and still has, characteristics of complexity, elegance, balance and great longevity".

Andrea Ciravegna (Tenuta Rocca): "We own this parcel since 1996 and since then it has been vinified separately. The *cru* gives wines that are intense and persistent with notes of violet, cherry, spices (cinnamon, clove), vanilla and leather. It's a well-structured Barolo, powerful yet smooth, tannic yet not too austere, balanced with a persistent and intense aftertaste".

Rodolfo Migliorini (Pianpolvere Soprano): "Sitting right below our property, the parcel is vinified since 1998 as the Barolo Pianpolvere Soprano Bussia Riserva 7 Anni. This cru is noted for keeping a good balance between power and elegance."

Ian's assessment of the vineyard district, its wines and its potential

A totally magical name, Bussia is also the source of some pretty magical Barolos. But as I have said and written many times before, at 300 hectares (give or take), the modern-day incarnation of Bussia is just too big. Imagine that it extends from the hill in Pugnane to the hamlet of Sant'Eligio and that's over four kilometers long, with a variance in altitude of a whopping 250 meters. Proponents and backers point out that the area shares similarities of geology and soil, but that's really wanting to look at this situation through very rose-colored glasses. And so, rather than evoking Gertrude Stein's just as magical quote "There is no there, there" I think the correct way to look at Bussia today is by paraphrasing that saying into: "There are many theres, there". In fact, there was most certainly a "there, there" once: Bussia is the first Barolo vineyard district name to appear on any wine label in association with the name Barolo, as labeled by Beppe Colla in the 1961 vintage. [The Currado family of Vietti fame bottled a 1961 Barolo Rocche (today Rocche di Castiglione); but the first Italian vineyard name ever to grace an Italian wine bottle is in fact that of another Barolo vineyard, Cannubi, but that 1752 label did not also carry the word 'Barolo'. See CANNUBI file.]

Three hundred hectares: again, no reasonable person will, or can, say that Bussia is just the right size. That is, not if its wine-somewhereness and wine-specificity of site we are talking about. As I have written many times before, take Chambolle-Musigny in Burgundy as an example. The *grand cru* Musigny is about eleven hectares large; and all of the Chambolle-Musigny *premier crus* together amount to about sixty hectares, and so… in a brilliant piece written a few years ago, Michele Longo goes one better, pointing out that given the entire Barolo denomination is 1800 hectares large, this means that the Bussia vineyard district that was officially delimited and named in 2010 covers, all on its own, 17% of the entire Barolo production area (Longo, 2021). Clearly, a vineyard area that large (any vineyard area that large in fact, not just Bussia), can neither deliver wines that are really similar to each other nor that are of the same quality level. The large expanse of vines that is the Bussia production area of today boasts: many different exposures (full south, southwest, southeast, east, west, and I'm probably forgetting some); altitudes (more or less from 220 to 460 meters above sea level); lithologies (Saint Agatha Fossil Marls formation of at least two different types, sandy and typical, plus Diano Sandstone); micro- and mesoclimates; and slope gradients. Not surprisingly then, the total Bussia area landscape is classified as belonging to three different Land Unit categories: of Barolo, of La Morra, and of Novello. And so you realize just how diverse the terroir of Bussia really is. It follows this vineyard district's wines are pretty diverse too.

Granted, there are some stylistic similarities to be found in all Barolos from Bussia: namely a silkiness of tannins that are really, recognizably, powerful in nature. It is a mouthfeel unlike that of any other Barolo from anywhere, but it is only a vague *trait d'union* between the vineyard district's wines that are, for the most part, recognizably different. It follows that when you drink a Bussia wine nowadays, it behooves you to know exactly from what part of the Bussia vineyard district the grapes were sourced from, as that will go a long way in helping you understand the Bussia Barolo you are drinking (and why it is so different than another Bussia Barolo you might have tried in another place and at another time). Just as it is in the case of other famous world wine appellations that are in fact too large, witness for example Burgundy's Clos de Vougeot and Échézeaux or Alsace's Brand, it's not necessarily that one Barolo Bussia is better than another, but they are (can be) different, just as the areas within Bussia from where the grapes were sourced are very different too. Honestly now: it would really be very strange if it were otherwise. And everybody in Barolo knows this.

Somewhat unfortunately, in order to get the official names passed in a timely matter (and for other reaons), Bussia was turned into one large (too large, in fact) vineyard district by incorporating many other previously distinct vineyard areas into it. This is why once relatively famous Monforte vineyard areas (the names of which are well-known and remembered by all Barolo lovers, given they were plastered on Barolo bottles everywhere as recently as the 1990s and 2000s) such as Arnulfo, Brovi, Bussia Soprana, Crocini (Corsini), Dardi, Fantini, Mondoca, Munie, Pianpolvere, Pianpolvere Soprano, Rocche (Rocche di Bussia), Visette and others exist no longer (officially, at least). As discussed previously in this book, such a course of action was necessary because otherwise the Monforte commune would have been unable to reach an agreement on the new names and boundaries of their vineyard districts (given that there were many who wanted to be part of "Bussia"). But a Barolo made in the Munie section of the Bussia is different from one with grapes from Rocche di Bussia and Corsini (if and when made in the same manner, clearly). Again, it's not that one area is necessarily better than the other, but for sure, some are more famous than others, and just as surely, they are going to give different wines. And so there exists today a wide spectrum of Bussia wines (some undoubtedly made from what are lesser vineyard areas than others). You don't have to take my word for it: just taste the old vintages of many different Barolos (Munie, Rocche...) made by the excellent Parusso estate and the differences between the various subregions of today's Bussia will become all too apparent. Heck, never mind all of Bussia: just tasting the Barolos Cicala, Colonnello and Romirasco from the world-famous Aldo Conterno estate will clearly highlight how there are noteworthy differences even within one single Bussia subregion (in this case, that of Bussia Soprana). In Appendix C, *Table 3.3: Barolo vineyard district subregions* lists all the Bussia subregions.

For all the reasons mentioned, it should be apparent by now that the various subregions of Bussia are bound to give different wines. It is unavoidable, in fact. For the same reasons, the many different vineyard sites within Bussia will give wines of varying quality levels. That too is unavoidable. And so, while many wines made within the various Bussia subregions are more or less similar quality-wise, there are some that stand out more than others. That some vineyard areas of Bussia give better wines than others has long been apparent to wine lovers and wine experts alike. Clearly, this is true not just of Barolo, but of all wine world areas: that is precisely why a country such as France has identified *premier crus*, *grand crus* and *lieux-dits*. The same line of reasoning applies to Barolo, and any other world wine production zone, as it does to those world-famous French wine *crus*: independently of producer talent (that certainly factors in to a very large degree but as we all know very well is by no means the only determinant of wine quality), there is no doubt that the Échézeaux wines made in the Échézeaux du Dessus portion of that large vineyard area outshine most of the others, just as the wine from Clos Saint Hune does when compared to other Riesling wines from the Rosacker *grand cru* within which that venerable Clos is located. Again, you don't have to take my word for it (but you should): for example, taking Renato Ratti's first map as a reference (that you should also do), very few of the many vineyard area subregions included in today's Bussia were listed by him as 'historic wine-growing sub-areas of traditional vocation' that offered 'particular qualitative characteristics'. As listed by Ratti, these were: Bussia Soprana, Bussia Sottana, Fontanile (Munie), Pian della Polvere (Pianpolvere) and Pugnane. He also listed Arnulfo, Dardi and Granbussia, without attributing a specific quality level to them. Even when similar vineyard management methods and winemaking techniques are used, wines from these subregions will give deliciously different wines in the same vintage: this was true at the time of publication of Ratti's map and it is still so today. And the Barolos of some sites within Bussia are clearly always better than others, year in and year out.

In alphabetic order, the Bussia subregions that I think it is important to be aware of, not just on historic grounds but mostly because of the wines that were long made there, are: Arnulfo, Bussia Soprana, Bussia Sottana, Corsini, Dardi, Fantini, Mondoca, Pianpolvere, Pianpolvere Soprano, Rocche (also called Rocche di Bussia in the past, but a better name would be Rocche di Monforte, similarly to the Rocche di Castiglione vineyard district, and so that is the one I use), and Visette. Some of these can be lumped together, but keep in mind I actually distinguish between the Bussia subregions and their wines to a greater degree than most people tend to today (of those who know to, that is).

Bussia subregions

To help you situate where within Bussia each of these subregions is located, remember that they are, from north to south (or in other words, moving from the town of Castiglione Falletto down towards the town of Monforte):

1. Pugnane: Wedge-like shaped, it is the most northern subregion of Bussia. It used to be a vineyard area shared between the communes of Castiglione Falletto and Monforte, the totality of which was called Pugnane. Today, it is only the portion falling within the territory of the Castiglione Falletto that is the official Pugnane vineyard district, while the Pugnane of the Monforte territory has been made a subregion of Bussia (logically enough, this section of Bussia borders the modern-day Pugnane vineyard district). Though the two Pugnane sections are similar in various aspects, there are differences; for example, the soil mineral concentration in at least parts of the Pugnane Bussia subregion are less high than those of the section that is now the Pugnane Castiglione Falletto vineyard district. See PUGNANE file). Relative to the Pugnane subregion of Bussia, its slightly lower-lying vineyards and a warm microclimate translates to wines that are large, fleshy and ripe, with the typically suave, compellingly sweet mouthfeel of the wines of Castiglione Falletto, but with a Monforte texture and oomph. I have always thought Pugnane to be an outstanding, somewhat underrated section of today's Bussia.

2. Bussia Sottana: Named after the hamlet of same name, this Rubenesque, round-shaped area falls in between the Pugnane and the Bussia Soprana subregions of the 'new' Bussia. As its name of '*sottana*' indicates, it is situated lower down than Bussia Soprana. The vineyard districts of Castellero, Vignane and Zuncai are to the west; Mariondino to the east, and a small piece of Rocche di Castiglione is to its south. Generally speaking, the wines of Bussia Sottana are lighter in texture, more nervous, and seem less concentrated than those of the Bussia Soprana (beware that I, unlike others, do not consider Munie to be part of Bussia Sottana, believing these two areas and their wines to be distinct: see below at point n.3). However, there are locals I have talked to over the years who do not believe there is really much difference between these two Bussia areas, elevation of the vineyards aside (see more on this below when I discuss individual producers). So perhaps I'm looking too hard to find differences in the wines that aren't really there; but you know, I don't think so. In any case, it is also true that Bussia Sottana delivers some really mighty fine Barolos.

3. Munie: For some producers, the Munie ought to be considered as a part of the Bussia Sottana. Honestly, I'm not so sure.

    First, because of a bunch, and I do mean a bunch, of historical reasons: back in the 80s, everybody I spoke to about Bussia Sottana always discussed it as a distinct entity, and never in the same breath as of Munie. Furthermore, Renato Ratti referred to Munie as Fontanile (see his map) and Ratti knew full well of Bussia Sottana, so the fact he felt compelled to differentiate between the two tells me plenty. And last but not least, because I know for a fact, having lived those golden years of Italian wine in Italy, that for the locals the Munie area had its own dignity of place, even of nomenclature (Munie was so-called in honour of the nuns that lived in the Cascina Lanza: so '*munie*' from *monache*, or nuns.

    Second, for oenological reasons: thanks to the Parusso estate and the Barolo they have made from there over the years, the Munie are well-characterized as a well-defined Barolo type that was and is different from their other Barolos made with grapes sourced from other parts of today's Bussia. In fact, Munie can be further subdivided into two portions. Parusso's vineyards are located in the higher of the two sections; in the lower section, Batasiolo makes what has always been, at least to my taste, that winery's best Barolo, calling it Bofani after the *cascina* of the same name.

And then there are, pure and simple, the realities of the terroirs. In my experience, Munie, an open and sunlit, warm, area (for example, the harvest usually takes place there about a week before it does in the much cooler Visette subregion of the Bussia), gives fairly big, broad, nicely meaty Barolos that may not always be the most nuanced. So that tells me Munie is a special site: because while it is not my favored style of Barolo, I know full well that I really quite liked the wines made from there. So, there must have been something to them.

4. Rocche di Monforte (previously Rocche or Rocche di Bussia): Located further south from Munie, in a far western section of the Bussia, close to that very small piece of the Rocche di Castiglione vineyard district that falls within the territory of Monforte (see ROCCHE DI CASTIGLIONE file). Past vintages of wines made with grapes from this subregion were some of the most luscious and suave wines of all the Bussia, and in fact I always found they shared elements with the better wines of the Castiglione Falletto territory. Others feel the same way, and take this sensation a bit further, stating outright that the Rocche di Monforte don't exist, and that this area should have been made a part of the official Rocche di Castiglione vineyard district outright (a vineyard district of the commune of Castiglione Falletto), rather than of the Bussia vineyard district.

5. Bussia Soprana: This subregion follows Bussia Sottana to the south, just above Dardi to its southwest, and Pianopolvere/Pianpolvere Soprano to its southeast. It has Monrobiolo di Bussia to the west, while to its east there are the vineyard districts of Perno and Gramolere. It is within the boundaries of Bussia Soprana that you find the famous Barolo vineyards of Colonnello, Cicala and Romirasco (made famous by the legendary Aldo Conterno estate), as well as Gabutti (don't confuse this with the Gabutti vineyard district of Serralunga: the small Gabutti vineyard area of Monforte is sort of a westwards prolongation of the Romirasco slope, and therefore looks southwest just like Romirasco). When standing in the Bussia Soprana hamlet with your back to the town of Barolo, Colonello is to your left, Cicala further above it near the woods, Romirasco to your right and Gabutti farther out. Colonello gives the lightest, most perfumed wine of them all, Cicala gives Barolos of greater body, Romirasco's wine is the ideal blend of the two and by far the most complex. The wines of Gabutti (Gabutti is where Rocche dei Manzoni's famous Vigna Mesdi' is located) are potentially very good too and it's only a matter of time before an estate decides to bottle wines referencing this specific portion of the Bussia Soprana, though altitude and climate change may prove rate-limiting steps, so to speak.

6. Mondoca: Immediately south of the Bussia Soprana, some consider Mondoca and Dardi to be part of the Bussia Soprana subregion, but I think their wines are much too different for the two to be considered a part of Bussia Soprana. By contrast, Mondoca and Dardi are part of the same hill, so if anything, it is these two that could be lumped together in the same subregion (Mondoca is the part higher up, Dardi is the lower part of the same hill). However, here too, I disagree with this viewpoint, because once again, the wines of these two subareas (Dardi and Mondoca) of the subregion (Dardi-Mondoca) are just too different. I might be wrong, but to my taste Mondoca Barolos are especially structured and tough when young (in fact, some of the toughest Barolos of the entire Monforte commune, never mind Bussia), and greatly benefit from extended cellaring. Dardi's Barolos are much more perfumed and lighter in texture ("lighter" used as a comparative, but I mean it in terms of a Monforte-lightness, which means hardly light at all, of course).

7. Dardi: As mentioned, differently from the Barolos of Mondoca, the wines of Dardi are much more elegant and creamier. In fact, I think Dardi's wines have more in common with those of the Pianpolvere areas than with Mondoca and Bussia Soprana.

8. Pianpolvere and Pianpolvere Soprano: Again, some producers and experts believe that Dardi Mondoca and Pianpolvere are nothing less than an extension of the Bussia Soprana. But as I have already stated in the Mondoca section, I believe all these subregions should be kept separate. If one really wants to look at these specific areas in a more holistic manner, then we can say that Dardi and the Pianpolveres form a band-like subregion where the western half is Dardi, while the eastern half corresponds to the area of

Pianpolvere and Pianpolvere Soprano. As the latter's name implies, it is the higher up of the two Pianpolveres areas: Pianpolvere is the one closest to Dardi. Barolos from Dardi and the Pianpolveres are not just some of the greatest wines of today's Bussia, but of all Barolo, boasting superlative depth, complexity and balance (to my taste, those of Pianpolvere Soprano have perhaps just a touch more depth and complexity than those of Dardi and Pianpolvere, but I'm probably splitting hairs here. All are excellent).

9. Visette, Arnulfo and Fantini: In a band-like shape, these follow one another from west to east. While some producers I have talked to over the years consider these three to be one common, extended, area, I have never thought so. And I know for a fact that anyone tasting (in the past at least) in blinded fashion a similarly made Barolo from Visette and one from Fantini, could tell them apart about 90% of the time, so it's not just a case of me imagining things. While all three give relatively fresh, vibrant wines, Visette's are the most mineral, Arnulfo's perhaps the most vibrant and lighter in weight, Fantini's the broadest and most textured of the three ("broadest and most full-bodied" relative to the wines of Visette and Arnulfo, given that Fantini's vines are located high up in altitude and its Barolos are also fairly mineral-etched and steely). In fact, if we really wanted to be more precise about this (and no, we are not getting needlessly granular), the Fantini area can further be subdivided into a Fantini-proper and a Sant'Eligio (or Fonte Sant'Eligio). These two are essentially southwest-facing amphitheaters separated only by a forested, hilly crest; and though not quite the same, the altitudes of these two Fantini subareas (at roughly 380-390 meters and 430-440 meters above sea level respectively) are more or less the same too. For this reason, given also similar soil lithologies, for the time being the two can be considered as belonging to one Fantini subregion only. In the future, if and when wines start being made specifically with grapes from only one of these two areas, and so-labeled, then we might/will be able to break down the already too large Bussia subregion of Visette-Arnulfo-Fantini further into its logical individual component parts. But we are not at that stage of the game yet: at the present time, in viewing Fantini as one subarea of the Visette-Arnulfo-Fantini subregion of Bussia, it is important to know that it is an area heavily characterized not just by its altitude (Fantini's Barolos are very vibrant and lifted) but by the presence of sand pockets that create better water drainage and also contribute to very different Barolos than those say of Pugnane, Bussia Soprana or Munie. Just like Visette, Arnulfo, Dardi, Pugnane, Bussia Sottana, Munie and others still, all excellent sites from where to make potentially world-class Barolos, I think it would have been good to keep Fantini (and Arnulfo, and Visette) separate from the others and give it its own vineyard district designation. But what can you do, it is what it is. At least now you have a little more information by which to base and make your own tasting decisions upon.

10. Corsini: The southernmost portion of Bussia, it lies west of the Bricco San Pietro vineyard district. This is one of the coolers, less sunlit part of the Bussia and the wines taste accordingly, freshly vibrant and nervous.

There may well be other subregions I should/ought to include, but I neither know much about them nor have I tasted many if any of their wines. However, after decades of serious Barolo tastings (beginning with the 1982 vintage, every year upon release) I can make a pretty good case as to what the individual characteristics of the Bussia subregions of today and their wines are like, or more importantly *ought* and *should* be like. Once again, even though I do not believe all the above-mentioned subregions should have been included under the "Bussia" name umbrella, they all are remarkably good sites for Barolo production (at least, these that I am listing here). Over the years, these vineyard areas have given wine lovers everywhere some of the greatest Barolos of all. How much of that is due to a generally very high level of producer talent (it is undoubtedly true that some of Barolo's best estates farm vines in the extended Bussia area of today) and how much is due to individual site characteristics is not so clear, but the point is that the wines are (mostly) truly something else. For example, in using a classification system similar to that of Burgundy's *cru*s, all these Bussia subregions are of at least a *premier cru* quality level (some better than others: after all, though they are all *Premier Crus*, I think most wine lovers would prefer having a Chablis from Montée de Tonnerre as opposed to one from Vau de Vey or Côte de Léchet) with a few of clear-cut *grand cru* status (Bussia Soprana, Pianpolvere Soprano).

As far as the different sections of Bussia go, it is only honest to recognize that there were initially two Bussia-named areas only, the Bussia Sottana and the Bussia Soprana. What always has made the wines of the "true" Bussia so highly prized (in truth, only of the Bussia Soprana part), is that they were typically characterized by real brooding power and noteworthy tannic spine but also an amazing silky elegance, a combination the level of which is not easily found in the wines of any other of Barolo's vineyard districts. Already decades ago, it was this quality that made it so that just about anybody you'd talk to would say Bussia (Bussia Soprana) was one of Barolo's five or so best vineyard sites (and for some local experts, the best one of them all, period). By contrast, the Nebbiolo grapes of the Bussia Sottana, an area that differently from the Bussia Soprana is more at the mercy of cold wind currents (as it's less protected by natural barriers), were less sought after. Today, such candid statements are much harder to come by, and given the value of vineyard land and prices fetched by Barolo's wines today, it is perhaps not surprising and one can certainly sympathize. The differences between the two areas are mostly related to climate, because the soils of the two Bussias are fairly similar: a mix of Saint Agatha marls of the sandy type and Diano sandstones, though the marly component clearly prevails. However, while it is in the minority, Bussia's sandstone component is important because it has a lower calcium carbonate content than that of other Monforte vineyard areas and vineyard districts, thereby allowing for good nutrient uptake in what are generally poor, slightly barren soils where the vine has to work for its sustenance. So that leaves us with differences related to climate, in a world slapped around like a punching bag by climate change. Admittedly, back in the 50s, 60s and 70s, before the advent of climate change, it was climate that was the single most important factor in determining Barolo site quality, and so that is a big part of the reason why Bussia Sottana was less highly considered than Bussia Soprana. Furthermore, what also contributed to the Bussia Sottana and its wines being less famous was that back then there were fewer producers and wines made there: Bussia Soprana had the benefit of a world-class wine estate such as that of Aldo Conterno acting as its flagbearer, but Bussia Sottana had no such luck. Clearly, this kept the area out of the limelight somewhat. But in ultimate analysis, even though climate change has favored the Sottana zone somewhat, and more valid producers are looking to make Barolos with grapes from it these days, it remains that I have never had any wine from the Bussia Sottana that has-measured up to the best from Bussia Soprana. Being a die-hard Barolo lover, I would only be delighted to find out otherwise, in the near or distant future.

Bussia producers and the wines

As already mentioned, the winery most associated with the Bussia vineyard district is that of the venerable Aldo Conterno, who made the Bussia Soprana famous. Aldo Conterno created his estate in 1969 and immediately began highlighting the qualities of his Bussia vineyard area. Over the years, he and his sons (Stefano, Giacomo and Franco) have done so by producing a long lineup of one great wine after another, as well as by showcasing the different aspects of the Bussia Soprana through four wines that rank amongst Italy's best red wines. These famous wines are the Barolo Bussia Colonnello, Bussia Cicala, Bussia Romirasco and a superblend of grapes from the three vineyards, the Barolo Riserva Granbussia. The three vineyards, though located very close to each other, are very different, and so are the wines made from each. The Colonnello vineyard, the soil lithology of which is Saint Agatha Fossil Marls and Diano Sandstone, is planted with east- and west-facing 45 years old vines at 350 meters above sea level. It is an amazingly sandy site (a stroll through it is like walking on a beach); it's that high content of sand, a sand rich in magnesium and manganese, that allows for wines characterized by a noteworthy sweetness of tannins (perhaps not quite so in the droughtiest of years) associated with a very delicate perfume. By contrast, the Cicala vineyard (its Italian name, *cicala*, means "cricket": you will hear the little critters singing away, loudly, in the woods near the vineyard) is located at 370-375 meters above sea level and planted to 50-55 years old vines. It boasts a soil that contains a higher percentage of clay and limestone than the Colonnello, plus it has a strong iron component. It follows that the wines have an imposingly tannic structure that persists on the palate with earthy, even leathery, nuances and hints of balsamic oils that are practically always absent in the more floral wines of Colonnello. Really, with even minimal experience, it's impossible to confuse the two wines: for those who do not yet quite fully grasp the huge differences that wines can express because of their respective terroirs, there are fewer better learning opportunities available anywhere than tasting these two Aldo Conterno Barolos side by side. Last but definitely not least (most definitely not least), the Romirasco vineyard's soil is rich in tufa and limestone characterized by a small but noteworthy percentage of magnesium. Differently from the Barolos of the other two vineyards, Romirasco (planted to sixty years old vines at about 390-395 meters above sea level), gives wines that are densely fruity and quite spicy (the spiciness of Romirasco's wines renders these Barolos immediately recognizable, but I'd say their very pure and very rich fruitiness does too). Though all three vineyards have to be considered *grand crus*, there is no doubt whatsoever that Romirasco is the grandest *cru* of these *grand crus*, if you will: it's a site that used to belong to the Countess Faustina Demagistris, who already back in the nineteenth century had it mapped out and drawings made of it. Clearly, this speaks volumes about the high esteem Romirasco was held in already at that time:

mapping out a vineyard was a very rare occurrence in Italy back in those days. Therefore, it's not surprising then that Aldo Conterno has always used Romirasco's grapes as the backbone of the winery's most important product, the Barolo Riserva Granbussia. The Granbussia is usually a blend of 75% Romirasco, 15% Colonnello and 15% Cicala grapes (save for the 1982 and 2001 wines, when there was respectively less Romirasco and Cicala in the blend). And so, while the Barolo Colonnello and Barolo Cicala were both first made in 1969, the Barolo Romirasco was launched as such only in 1978 (no doubt part of the reason was also that the Conternos did not own their Romirasco holding initially, but were just renting it: understandably enough, they waited to release an important Barolo from Romirasco until the vineyard came into the family fold). Initially, a Barolo Romirasco was not made as such every year; but with the success of the 1993 and the 2004 Barolo Romirasco bottlings (the former being strikingly reminiscent of a great tannic version of a Burgundian Pinot Noir wine) the Conternos decided to bottle the wine every year like they were already doing with the two other vineyards. In the end, they also did so because they reasoned it was a pity not to showcase what one of Barolo's greatest sites could give every year. Differently from these three individual vineyard Barolo bottlings, the Aldo Conterno Granbussia Riserva Barolo was created as a means by which to shine the spotlight on the greatness of the Bussia (the Bussia Soprana, that is), as a source of fantastic Barolo. Granbussia was officially born in 1974, and for a while (at least until Romirasco came along at a more regular clip) represented the summit of Aldo Conterno's production; and it still does for many collectors, who are quite happy to swing for the fences anytime they can latch on to the difficult to obtain cases of it.

Another ultra-famous Barolo producer who has made a Bussia Barolo of note was Domenico Clerico (not just a talented producer but a super nice man too who sadly passed away a few years ago). At first, he made a Bussia Barolo he called Briccotto Bussia (until 1979, the last vintage) then started making it again with the 2008 vintage, but selling it only in magnums and double magnums. He was able to do so because he had bought 4000 square meters in the Bussia Soprana back in 1977 located right below Aldo Conterno's Cicala. Very interestingly, despite Clerico making his wine in slightly different fashion than Aldo Conterno, the two wines do bear a resemblance to each other, ultimately speaking of the Bussia, and more specifically of Cicala, in slightly diverse but also similar ways.

The venerable, world-famous Alba wine estate of Ceretto has long believed in the concept of "cru" and has long made Barolos highlighting specific high quality vineyard districts. Their portfolio includes Barolos from Brunate, Bricco Rocche and Prapò, and that's just in Barolo (see BRICCO ROCCHE file. See also BRUNATE, CANNUBI SAN LORENZO, ROCCHE DI CASTIGLIONE and PRAPÒ files). But differently from the famous Barolo Bussia wines of Aldo Conterno and Clerico that have seemingly been around forever, Ceretto's has only recently appeared on the scene (only Ceretto's Barolo Rocche di Castiglione is a more recent addition to the winery portfolio of wines). However, just like the wines by Conterno and Clerico, Ceretto's Barolo Bussia is also outstanding; in fact, there are vintages when Ceretto's Barolo Bussia is either the best or second-best wine in their entire lineup of wines (witness the 2015 and 2016, two absolutely superb wines). Like the wines from Aldo Conterno and Clerico, it is also made with grapes from the Bussia Soprana. Ceretto own 0.71 hectares there, in a real sweet spot located between Romirasco and Cicala, right above the Colonnello. Federico and Roberta Ceretto told me the vines were planted in 1984 and 2013. The southwest-facing vines lie at about 350 meters above sea level and grow on a soil that is 45% loam, 25% sand, and 30% clay. It is a beautifully austere wine, yet fleshy in the typical way of Monforte (a flesh that Serralunga Barolos usually lack). We do not have too many vintages to go by, but for the time being at least, call me impressed. Very impressed.

Marco and Tiziana Parusso of the Parusso estate have long made many different outstanding Barolos from subregions of today's Bussia, such as for example Munie and Rocche, (clearly, names you will find only on the labels of older vintages). The many different sections of today's Bussia that Parusso farmed (and still farms) gave very different wines, and those differences were easy to pinpoint even when tasting blind. Their holding in what was called Rocche di Bussia has southeast to southern-facing vines that range between 20-25 to 60 years old. These two hectares gave very deep wines that were quite mineral in their flavour profile. The Barolo Munie was made from a one-hectare large plot with a mostly south and southwest-facing vines (back in 2010, three quarters of the vineyard was planted with 50-year-old vines and a third with twenty-year-old vines, which explains in part why the wine was so deep, long and complex). Munie's topography is fairly undulating, and it probably gave the wines that differed the most from all the others Parusso made. I always found them to exude a truly amazing note of ripe yellow peach, perhaps the result of Munie being a broad, well-illuminated site; its wines were also broader, fleshier and less tannic than some other Monforte Barolos. Tobacco and cherry jelly were also common findings. Parusso also used to make a Barolo Fiurin from the lowest-lying 1.5 hectares (vines that now all face south but once also faced southwest). A much colder microclimate than the one of Munie and the Rocche, the wines were tannic and tough when young, requiring extended cellaring. Interestingly, the soil of the three Bussia subregions that Parusso made those Barolos from are characterized by a noteworthy and fairly similar presence of sand, so it has always been Marco Parusso's opinion that the factors that counted most in determining differences among his three Barolos were light and heat units, rather than soil per se. Today he blends the grapes from all three vineyards into his Barolo called, simply enough, Bussia. (If it hadn't already become apparent to you that "Bussia" as such is really neither that accurate nor that helpful, what I've just finished telling you about Parusso's wines should make it even more obvious than it already is. In the best vintages, the estate releases after prolonged cellaring (ten years after the vintage) Silver and Gold label Riserva Barolos from Munie and Rocche di Bussia grapes; nowadays he labels those wines as Barolo Bussia Riserva Vigna Rocche and Barolo Bussia Riserva Vigna Munie. Clearly, using the names of these two Bussia subregions as vineyard names is an intelligent way by which the problem posed by Bussia's large extension is circumvented to a degree.

Aldo Conterno aside, there may be no bigger expert on all matters pertaining to Bussia than the Colla family. In fact, the first Barolo bearing a vineyard name was the Barolo Bussia that Beppe Colla made in 1961 while working for Prunotto (at the same time, Vietti also bottled his Barolo bearing the name of Rocche -now Rocche di Castiglione-on the label). Sadly, Beppe Colla passed away a few years ago, but his family continues to farm and make Barolo from the Dardi part of Bussia, vineyard land he clearly knew well and which he moved to buy after branching out on his own. The name of the vineyard area from where Colla makes his Barolo Bussia is Dardi-Le Rose: Dardi is a small hamlet where basically all the inhabitants had family names of Dardo (it was a Giovanni Dardo, born in 1909, who sold Colla his piece of the vineyard). For this reason, the area was known as "ai Dardi" (or "at the Dardis", in English). The "Le Rose" portion of the name comes from the old practice, common in many other vineyards, to plant bushes of roses at the head of the vine rows to increase not just the beauty of the surroundings but also to have a natural alarm system in place relative to the health status of the vineyard (roses being more delicate than grapevines, they start showing effects of disease and pests sooner, giving the *vignaiolo* hopefully enough time to intervene should it become necessary to do so). Giovanni Dardo began selling his grapes to Colla in the 1950s and Colla used them uninterruptedly from that famous 1961 bottling right up until 1993 when he went on to create his own estate, Poderi Colla, after having sold Prunotto to the Antinori family. Colla's vines in Dardi were planted facing south/southwest in 1970 and 1985, at about 300 to 350 meters above sea level. Colla's Barolo Dardi-Le Rose is a wine that require plenty of patience, starting life out very closed and shut down but develops beautiful floral nuances in time while maintaining an elegant austerity throughout its lifetime. Dardi is actually a famous site, mentioned already in Lorenzo's Fantini standout 1880s treatise *"Monografia sulla Viticoltura ed Enologia nella Provincia di Cuneo"* in which he detailed what the best sites of Barolo were. Fantini's work has to be considered a benchmark text, so Dardi getting named as much is no small feat. And while some locals nowadays have taken to including Dardi within an extended Bussia Soprana, it differs noticeably from Colonnello, Cicala and Romirasco, if for no other reason because those three occupy a different slope (as mentioned previously, the one with Gabutti). Dardi is actually situated much closer to the Mondoca subregion of the Bussia. It also differs in its soil composition from Bussia Soprana, in that Dardi has more clay: for example, average soil sample values show 42% loam, 20% sand, 28% clay in Dardi compared to the Bussia Soprana's Colonnello soil composition of 17% loam, 63% sand, 20% clay.

Speaking of Mondoca, Poderi Oddero's Barolo Bussia is made from just that Bussia subregion, and so their wine is called Barolo Bussia Vigna Mondoca (like with Parusso, use of the words "Vigna Mondoca" in the wine's name is the stratagem by which to highlight the exact subregion within Bussia from where the Nebbiolo grapes are sourced from). Maria Cristina Oddero has been scouring the cadastral archive of the Monforte commune (*l'Archivio Catastale del Comune di Monforte*) to learn what the name Mondoca derives from, but to no avail thus far. What I have been told is that it might derive from members of the Catharism sect (a twelve-thirteen century dualist heretical religious Christian or Gnostic movement) that had settled in the area from Languedoc and Occitanie and called the area *Mont d'oc*, two words that later became the Italian 'Mondoca'. But who knows: for sure, I'll be much more comfortable with Maria Cristina's findings on the matter (and so should you). The estate's 1.13 hectares of Mondoca grapes grow at 340 meters above sea level on a soil that is loam (65,4%), sand (21,8%) and clay (12,8%), rich in iron, zinc, copper and manganese. They age their wine for thirty months in 32 hectoliter barrels and then three more years in bottle before being released for sale. That long amount of time before release is not at all surprising given this one of the toughest, most tannic Barolos from Bussia in its youth and extended cellaring is only beneficial to it. Poderi Oddero's highly traditional winemaking style tends not to make for easy-drinking forward Barolos right out of the gate, and never is this more apparent than with their Barolo from Mondoca. That much said, it's a wine that like all Poderi Oddero Barolos develops splendidly, if you just cellar it for the appropriate amount of time.

You know, when it comes to wine, it's often hard to get two people to see eye to eye on numerous topics: asking people to identify the best vineyards in any given area is an example of how results can be all over the board. But I have found over the years that when it comes to the perceived quality of the Pianpolvere subregion of Bussia just about everyone agrees: it's one of the best areas not just in Bussia, but of all Barolo. In fact, the Pianpolvere area has always been subdivided into two subsections: Pianpolvere and Pianpolvere Soprano (obviously, the latter is the part that is located higher up). The two Pianpolvere sections of Bussia carry this name because Napoleon had built a deposit of gunpowder there (*polvere*, or powder in English, referred to the presence of gunpowder, and not the powdery consistency of the area's very sandy-rich soil). According to most people I have talked with over the years, the area is really quite homogenous and the differences between Pianpolvere and Pianpolvere Soprano are not so marked. This is relevant, because when you ask similar questions nowadays, given the huge economic interests involved in Barolo land ownership, the standard answer you get is that all areas are more or less of equal value (see what's happening for example with Bussia Sottana and Bussia Soprana), but in fact that is very hardly ever the case. However, in the case of the Pianpolveres, already three decades ago most people were of the inclination that there *really* wasn't much reason to prefer one over the other.

In the beginning, there was just one property called Cascina Pianpolvere (which dated back to the 1700s). It was divided into three estates at the beginning of the 1900s: Attilio Ghisolfi, Pianpolvere Soprano (owned by the Fenocchio family) and Cascina Pianpolvere (of the Fratelli Adriano). The Pianpolvere Soprano estate was sold in 1998 to the Migliorini family of Rocche dei Manzoni. Today, the estate's top wine is the Barolo Pianpolvere Soprano Riserva (aged between 7-10 years); with the 2016 vintage, a second wine was launched, the Barolo Pianpolvere Soprano Bussia (aged only four years and sold only on the Italian market, such that the first vintage was sold in 2020). Of interest is that many wine loving individuals out there are aware that Pianpolvere Soprano was thought to be the single best vineyard site in all of Barolo by none other than Bruno Giacosa. Giacosa made only four wines labeled Bussia: the 1974, 1975, 1978 and 1979 Riserva Speciale (red label) wines. These wines have a bit of a spotty track record compared to some other Giacosa red labels I have repeatedly tried over the years (certainly, bottles of the 1975 I have had have been hit and miss, but then it was the weakest of those four vintages) but the 1974 and 1978 have been spectacular every time I have tried them. Giacosa told me back in the early-2000s he used to buy the grapes to make these wines from the lower section simply called Pianpolvere (though he never told me from exactly whom he bought the grapes). Ken Vastola of The Fine Wine Geek believes it was from the Pianpolvere estate owned by the Adriano Fratelli, and given the level of expertise on the subject and his passion for Giacosa's wines, that's good enough for me.

The Visette-Arnulfo-Fantini subregion of Bussia can be further broken down in each of its three component parts: there are some very good estates there, the wines of which you can find with relative ease. When it comes to the Visette subregion of Bussia, there are no bigger experts than the folks at the Attilio Ghisolfi estate, a property born from the breakup of the Cascina Pianpolvere. The estate had always made wine but it was a small part of the family business, which revolved mainly around fruit trees (pears, plums, peaches) and selling wine grapes and bulk wine (to the Terre del Barolo cooperative). In 1988, everything changed: the decision to turn to wine production fulltime was taken with young Gianmarco (actually just Marco for everyone) entering into the family workplace. The fruit trees were removed and the land converted to vineyards: estate-bottled wine became the focus (in that fateful 1988, they made a whopping 2000 bottles of Barolo and some Dolcetto d'Alba). Today the estate owns eight hectares (four of Nebbiolo for Barolo production) and makes two Barolos from their Bussia vineyards: the younger vines are used to make the Barolo Bussia, while grapes from the older vines are used for the estate flagship wine, the Barolo Bussia Bricco Visette (the vines at Ghisolfi range in age from five to fifty years old). Skin contact and fermentation run from 15-16 days to a month, fermentation temperatures never exceed thirty degrees Celsius, only natural yeasts are used (he stopped using cultured yeasts in 2000); the Barolo Bussia is aged in 25-45 hectoliter oak barrels for three years in oak (in

Marco's own words, "…we have lots of tannin here so we give them all the time they need to polymerize and smoothen"). To my taste, the Barolos of Visette are amongst the most mineral of all those made in Bussia, plus have a very recognizable almost Serralunga-like steeliness to them, a certain linear rigidity in their delivery of minty (now *that's* very Monforte) sour red cherry and floral aromas and flavors. Nearby, in the Arnulfo subregion of Bussia, the historic Tenuta Arnulfo that had fallen on some hard times was bought in 1988 by the Sartirano brothers who changed the winery's name to Costa di Bussia (they found some documents showing that Arnulfo made his wines on "the coste di Bussia" (the hills of Bussia), and that the property was referred to already in the nineteenth century as "Costa Bussia"). In fact, Arnulfo is a name that has a long and revered history in the area. The estate itself was founded in 1874 by Luigi Arnulfo, a famous figure of Barolo and to whom a museum is dedicated on the ground floor of an ancient farmhouse on the property. Differently from the Arnulfo subregion, the Fantini subregion is narrower, closed, and cooler; its wines are especially fruity versions of Bussia Barolos and despite the mesoclimate are usually broad and generous wines. It is a Bussia subregion that deserves to be better known, because I find its Barolos to be noteworthy. Silvano Bolmida makes an excellent wine from Fantini; and another estate that bottles a good Barolo Bussia Fantini is Cascina Amalia. There, the winery farms 0.6 hectares planted at 450 meters in altitude, with a southwest exposure. The vines were planted only in 2007 on a Diano Sandstone lithology with a high percentage of sand.

Very exciting is the new wine being made by the Terre del Barolo cooperative, included in its high-end Arnaldo Rivera portfolio of single-vineyard district Barolos. Their Barolo Bussia is a blend of three vineyard sites, one in Bussia Soprana's Gabutti and two others in Fantini and Sant'Eligio (the winery considers their Bussia holdings to be two because they view, not unreasonably, Sant'Eligio as being a part of Fantini: see above, *Bussia subregions*). The Nebbiolo vines were planted in Sant'Eligio in 1969 (0.32 hectares), in Gabutti in 2002 (0.39 hectares), and in Fantini in 2003 (0.3 hectares). However, grapes from the Gabutti area have been used only since the 2018 vintage. The Sant'Eligio holding is on the western side of the Monforte hillside ridge, and has a good sandstone presence, a soil highly permeable to water that is blocked when it reaches the marl lower down creating numerous water collections or springs, such as the *fontana di Sant'Eligio* (Sant'Eligio fountain), all of which means that drought is well-tolerated by the vines growing in these areas. The Gabutti vines are located near the Gabutti hamlet of Bussia Soprana; it is the lower-lying (370 meters above sea level) of the three Arnaldo Rivera holdings (compared to Fantini's 390 meters and Sant'Eligio's 440 meters above sea level) and characterized by a warmer mesoclimate, with less of the sandstone and hence slightly more prone to drought. They macerate/ferment for seventeen to nineteen days and age in large five to seven hectoliter French oak casks. This is another uniformly excellent Barolo Bussia wine, year in and year out. The winery personnel thought long and hard whether they should bottle a single Bussia Gabutti wine and another made with the Fantini vines (as mentioned in the *Bussia subregions* section above, I too believe that at least for the time being it is probably best to consider Sant'Eligio as a part of Fantini) but in the end opted to blend higher altitude grapes (those of Fantini-Sant'Eligio) with those of Gabutti so as to make a wine that tries and conveys a general sense of what an ideal Bussia wine might be like. certainly, the Fantini-Sant'Eligio cooler climate fruit confers qualities of freshness and vibrancy to a Barolo of noteworthy colour depth and perfume. We shall see what the future may bring, but for now, the Arnaldo Rivera Barolo is excellent; more importantly, it is recognizably different from the Arnaldo Rivera Barolos made with grapes from, for example, Monvigliero, Cannubi and Villero, as it should be. Gabriele Oderda and his team have a done a stellar job with the Arnaldo Rivera wines: which one you find more to your liking will boil down to individual taste preferences.

Relative to the Pugnane subregion, the talented Marrone sisters (Denise, Serena and Valentina) of the Marrone winery in La Morra have made some truly outstanding Barolos from Bussia over the years (and though a little over-oaking has been a problem at times, some vintages have been unforgettable, witness their magnificent 2013 Barolo Bussia). Their Barolo Bussia made with grapes from Pugnane has an early ripening tannin profile and is quite ripely fruity, despite having Monforte's typical sturdy spine. To my way of thinking, Pugnane is a very underrated part of the 'new' Bussia; by comparison, the soils of the Pugnane subregion in the Bussia are less metal-rich than those of the Pugnane vineyard district (clearly, one segues into the other) but in fact both give rather minerally-tinged Barolos. Marrone's Pugnane vines are 60-65 years old, planted at about 350 meters in altitude, something that further allows for smooth tannins; and the fact it's also a very sunny site also contributes to wines of ripe fleshy charm.

As mentioned previously, for a while Prunotto also made Barolos simply labeled Bussia, and according to winemaker Gianluca Torrengo, they were always wines that were all about elegance; when they tried to change the winemaking so as to make more powerful wines, such as in the 2000 and 2004 vintages, they were less happy with the result than they had expected. This is most likely because Bussia has, at least in some parts, a fertile soil and getting it to harness that exuberance stresses the plant somewhat, so it's maybe not a good idea to try and do so. Today, Prunotto makes a single-vineyard district Bussia wine from the prestigious Colonello vineyard site: the Barolo Bussia Riserva Vigna Colonnello (yes, "that" Colonnello) is most likely Prunotto's best wine today. It is made from one hectare located in that prestigious vineyard area of the Bussia Soprana that was made famous by Aldo Conterno. The wine is aged for at least eighteen months in French oak barrels of various sizes and in stainless steel and bottle prior to being released for sale. It's a beautiful wine in almost all vintages, but needs plenty of cellaring to show its best side.

After such famous names, a small and not yet so well-known winery (yet) producing a Barolo Bussia is the excellent Angelo Germano estate. Their Barolo Bussia is made from south-facing Nebbiolo vines planted in 1963; vinification and maceration (*cappello emerso*) for 12-15 days while aging takes place for two years in 500-liter oak tonneaux (20% new oak or more, depending on the vintage characteristics).

Benchmark wineries/Reference point producers of Barolo Bussia: Aldo Conterno (Bussia Soprana); Arnaldo Rivera (Bussia blend); Attilio Ghisolfi (Bussia Visette), Cascina Amalia (Bussia Fantini), Luigi Arnulfo/Coste di Bussia (Bussia Arnulfo); Giacomo Fenocchio (Barolo Bussia; Bussia Riserva 90 Dì); Marrone (Bussia Pugnane), Poderi Oddero (Bussia Mondoca), Pianpolvere Soprano-Rocche dei Manzoni (Bussia Pianpolvere Soprano), Parusso (Bussia Munie, Bussia Rocche di Monforte); Poderi Colla (Bussia Dardi); Silvano Bolmida (Bussia Fantini).

CAMPASSO

Township	Verduno
Reference Map	See Map of Verduno MGAs (Ch. 10)
Size (ha) (Tot / Barolo MGA)	13.95 / 0,59
Production 2021 (hl)	24.56
Altitude	240 – 340 meters a.s.l. roughly
Exposure	East
N. Claimants MGA	1
Other grape varieties planted:	Barbera; Dolcetto; Pelaverga Piccolo
Land Units	Land Unit of La Morra
Soil (stage):	Tortonian

Producers claiming the MGA

Sobrino Edoardo.

Ian's assessment of the vineyard district, its wines and its potential

Campasso is a Verduno vineyard district, with Monvigliero and Pisapola (also Verduno vineyard districts) to its sides. Though it's almost entirely covered with vines, there are plenty of other varieties grown there besides Nebbiolo. This is because Campasso, given the eastern exposure of most of its vineyards, was, for the longest time, not the ideal site for the king of grapes. That of course may change quickly now given the world of climate change we live in, but to the best of my knowledge there is nobody producing a Barolo Campasso right now. Which is curious, as there have been Barolo Campasso wines made in the past. Cantina Massara owns vineyards in Campasso, but it has varieties other than Nebbiolo planted there, namely Pelaverga Piccolo (also known as Pelaverga Comune), Dolcetto and Barbera too. Their Verduno Pelaverga wine is made almost entirely from vines growing in the Campasso vineyard district, while that which was growing in another Verduno vineyard they own (in the Massara vineyard district) they have uprooted and replaced with Nebbiolo.

Benchmark wineries/Reference point producers of Barolo Campasso: None available.

CANNUBI

Township	Barolo
Reference Map	See Map of Barolo MGAs (Ch. 10)
Size (ha) (Tot / Barolo MGA)	19.53* / 32.83**
Production 2021 (hl)	1,600.82 (of which 101.05 hl of Barolo Riserva *MGA*)
Altitude	230 – 290 meters a.s.l. roughly
Exposure	From east to south; some parcel from northwest to northeast;
N. Claimants MGA	24
Other grape varieties planted:	Barbera; Dolcetto
Land Units	Land Unit of Barolo
Soil (stage):	Tortonian

*   Cannubi Centrale

**   This datum refers to the total number of producers who claim "Cannubi" on their label; it therefore also those whose vineyards are not in the Cannubi Centrale but who by law are now allowed to state "Cannubi" only, if so they wish. For more detailed information about Cannubi producers see Appendix C - Table 3.1: Comparison Cannubi production declarations.

Producers claiming the MGA

Barale; Borgogno; Fratelli Serio & Battista Borgogno; Brezza; Comm GB Burlotto; Camerano; Ceretto; Chiarlo; Damilano; E. Pira E Figli; Elio Altare; Giacomo Fenocchio; Michelina Fontana; Il Gioco dell'Oca di Pittatore; L'Astemia Pentita; Marchesi di Barolo; Poderi Luigi Einaudi; Giuseppe Rinaldi; Aldo Sandrone; Luciano Sandrone; Tenuta Carretta; Tenute del Vino; Viglione Giuseppina.

Wines

Elio Altare - Barolo Cannubi; **Fratelli Barale** - Barolo Cannubi; **Borgogno** - Barolo Cannubi; **Fratelli Serio & Battista Borgogno** - Barolo Cannubi; Barolo Riserva Cannubi; **Brezza** - Barolo Cannubi; **Cascina Adelaide** - Barolo Cannubi; **Chiarlo** - Barolo Cannubi; **Damilano** - Barolo Cannubi; **E. Pira e Figli – Chiara Boschis** - Barolo Cannubi; **Poderi Luigi Einaudi** - Barolo Cannubi; **Paolo Scavino** - Barolo Cannubi (until 2018); **Tenuta Carretta** - Barolo Cannubi; **Arnaldo Rivera** - Barolo Cannubi (from 2019); **Comm. G.B. Burlotto** - Barolo Cannubi; **Giacomo Fenocchio** - Barolo Cannubi; **Marchesi di Barolo** - Barolo Cannubi; **Francesco Rinaldi** - Barolo Cannubi; **L'Astemia Pentita** - Barolo Cannubi; **Reva** – Barolo Cannubi.

What the producers say

Cannubi (or Cannubi Centrale)

Chiara Boschis: "This vineyard has been in the family since 1981. For the new vines, I have selected cuttings with rootstocks that vary according to the type of soil (based on the analysis of the soil and the advice of consultant agronomist from whom I obtain help). I have chosen the most varied mix possible of clones and rootstocks in order to play with diversity. Cannubi has a south exposure on sandy soil and with altitude of 300m and is capable of being perfect maturation to the grapes. In hot years, the vines may suffer from drought, a fact mitigated by the presence of underground water obtained from a well drilled not long ago in the middle of the vineyard. This historical vineyard, which is more or less the central part of the extended Cannubi hillside, has the fame of producing a Barolo of great elegance and finesse. This is a wine of extraordinary harmony that tantalizes the nose with lovely notes of sweet spices and ripe fruit, accompanied by classic balsamic notes of Cannubi (mint and eucalyptus). The imposing structure and decisive tannins leave a long and fantastic finish -- a wine of the highest standard, recognized as such at a national and international level".

Cascina Adelaide: "Our ownership of this vineyard can be traced back to 1999 and the grapes have been always vinified separately. The mineral and spicy characters emerge thanks to the tension that renders famous this *cru*. Cannubi sets itself apart for its typical note of orange peel and for tannins that tighten on the palate".

Enzo Brezza (Brezza): "We own holdings in Cannubi since 1988. From a geological perspective, it's an absolutely unique site: the Saint Agatha marls and the Diano sandstone formations here join and meet, making for very vertical, complex, ageworthy wines".

Stefano Chiarlo (Chiarlo): "We have this vineyard in our portfolio of vineyards since 1987 and we vinify it separately since 1990, but we only make a Barolo Cannubi in great years. We are lucky because our vineyard is in the heart of Cannubi hill, and in 1989 we planted the first terraced vineyard of Barolo. This was done to bring back to life a great site with a slope gradient greater than 50 degrees. Cannubi is a Barolo of intense perfume, almost aristocratic in my view, with an optimal persistence. Blessed with structure but also elegance, it seduces thanks to silky tannins".

Emanuela Bolla (Fratelli Serio e Battista Borgogno): "It has been almost a century since we came into this vineyard. Our three plots are located on the three slopes of the historic part of the Cannubi hill and are vinified separately in order to give our Barolo Cannubi a sense of place. Depending on the climatic conditions of various years, the vineyard with the best exposure and microclimate – from which the grapes derive their best maturation – are used to make the Barolo Cannubi Riserva. The central portion of the Cannubi *cru*, with its exposure, microclimate and composition confers to its wines some unique characteristics, most notably refinement. In hotter years, when drought starts to prevail in the summer, Cannubi's Centrale wines takes on a paler color and lose some power; in rainy vintages, it gives the best results of all, thanks to the water reserved and released during the summer months. In each case, like the old-timers like to say, it's difficult to have a truly bad harvest on the Cannubi Centrale site, because the site is so fantastic that even in difficult years, the quantity of grapes may be lower but the quality is almost always at least good, and more often than not, superlative".

Enrica Scavino (Paolo Scavino): "We began vinifying this cru on its own in 1985 from a rented plot that planted in 1946 and is one of the two vineyards where we have the estate's oldest vines. The Cannubi presents some difficulties in dry years for its soil drains very well; for the exact same reason it works miracles in rainy and cold years. But it is always a Barolo in which the magic of Nebbiolo expresses itself to the fullest: a wine of unique quality, rich and concentrated, with a harmonious and very fine texture".

Ian's assessment of the vineyard district, its wines and its potential

In my lifetime, I have walked Cannubi, or what many believe to be the original Cannubi, more times than I remember. One thing I can tell you immediately (because the memories are always painfully fresh in my mind) is that for a site that gives such elegant and refined wines, climbing up and down its steep slope will have you looking anything but elegant and refined by the time you are done. For the Cannubi Centrale is a con artist: actually very steep, its slope seems manageable when you look at it from below: but when you are actually there, on a hot summer day, even starting at more or less the halfway point of the hill will leave you panting and heaving and trying to pick up your tongue from the floor by the time you reach the top. But have no fear, that's where the con job ends: for in the right hands, this site gives not just one of Barolo's, but one of the world's greatest wines. I can draw on almost forty years of experience with this specific vineyard, so I have plenty to tell you about it. So let me get started: just as soon as I catch my breath from my last walk up and down that slope, that is.

Cannubi is Italy's most famous vineyard, if for no other reason that it is the only one to have been named on a label as early as 1752. I repeat: Cannubi is the first vineyard site to have ever appeared on an Italian wine label: number one, *numero uno*, *le premier*, the first, *shŏuxiān*. Even more pointedly, that wine bottle's label carried, besides the vintage date, only the name of the site, and not the word Nebbiolo or Barolo (at that moment in time, it was "Barolo" that was the least famous name of the three). To have its name placed on a label when that was not at all a common way of doing things, speaks volumes about just how important and relevant Cannubi has been considered throughout history. Lorenzo Fantini (1883), Ferdinando Vignolo Lutati (1920) and Renato Ratti's "*Carta del Barolo*", all cite Cannubi as a top-quality vineyard area (a *sottozona viticola storica di tradizionale vocazione*, or a "recognized historical zone that is traditionally vocated", as written by Ratti). At the same time, it bears noting that Ratti's reference was reserved for a smaller section of Cannubi and not the extended, larger site it is today (vineyard areas that he deemed to be high-quality sites nonetheless, qualifying them as having "particular qualitative characteristics".

The official vineyard district identified as Cannubi is a very long, gently sloping hill encircled by two roads, one lower down that runs at the base of the hill, and one higher up that runs along the summit of the vineyard area. In Cannubi matters, all roads lead not to Rome but to Barolo, and ultimately both those roads take you to the eponymous town. In fact, all the Cannubi vineyards are on the southeast/east-facing flank of this rising, and as mentioned at the beginning of this file, progressively steeper hill (from a low point of about 220 meters above sea level to 320 meters in altitude) that extends from the town of Barolo towards the Val Talloria plain (or vice versa, depending which way you come from). Nowadays, the entire hillside can be called Cannubi, but historically there were many different parts to the hill, each with its own name; so just like for Bussia that is made up of many different subregions that are not officially recognized nowadays as part of the Bussia name (see BUSSIA file), the same is true of the Cannubi vineyard district, that is also made up of many different subregions (See APPENDIX C, *Table 3.3: Barolo vineyard district subregions*). For many but clearly not all producers, the Cannubi hill is made up of an historic Cannubi site (the Cannubi proper or Cannubi Centrale: *centrale* as in 'central', because it more or less sits in the central portion of the extended Cannubi hillside) and four other Cannubi-something vineyard areas. The vineyard owners in other sections have recently been awarded the right to also label their wines 'Cannubi' only (even though the grapes might grow in Cannubi-something sites), but historically these other sites were known by other names as well. Only the Cannubi proper or Cannubi Centrale vineyard area has been always known as Cannubi only. The subregions of the long Cannubi hillside are, moving from the town of Barolo upwards in a northeastern direction: Cannubi Muscatel, then Cannubi Valletta and higher up the hill just above it the Cannubi San Lorenzo, then Cannubi (the Cannubi proper or Cannubi Centrale), and closing out the hill, Cannubi Boschis.

One very interesting and meritorious fact about the extended Cannubi vineyard district is that it has been turned into an organically farmed vineyard area almost in its entirety. It is a bio-district modeled after the one created by the wine producers of the town of Panzano in Chianti Classico, and a lot of the initial work was done with the consulting help of Ruggero Mazzilli, a well-known luminary in Italian organic farming wine circles. The credit for the initiative must go to Chiara Boschis of the E.Pira/Chiara Boschis who was the person who had the idea and then the main proponent of such a move; over the years, she worked hard and interacted closely with her Cannubi colleagues to get them to jump on board. She makes a point of also crediting Enzo Brezza for all the help she gave him, and in also providing his restaurant's terrace, in the marvelously and very conveniently situated Hotel Barolo in the heart of the little town (and where I like to stay any chance I get, but that's probably besides the point) as the meeting venue between all the producers while they discussed and agreed to the project. Rather remarkably, she has succeeded, though at first it was tough going, by her own admission. Today, virtually all the Cannubi producers are farming biologically (all the Cannubi subregions included: only three entities have not joined, one estate and two individuals who sell grapes), so much so that we can speak of a true bio-district, or what has been named the "CannuBio". You will find the list of all the estates that are part of the bio-district at the back of this book (See APPENDIX C, *Table 3.2, Cannubi producers of the bio-district "CannuBio"*).

The historic Cannubi, or Cannubi Centrale: the lay of the land and what sets it apart

The historic portion of Cannubi, which I defined in Decanter magazine as Cannubi Centrale already as early as in a 2012 article, is more or less the central portion of this long and prized tongue of vineyard land. It has the vineyard districts of Cannubi Boschis to its northeast and Cannubi Valletta and Cannubi San Lorenzo to its southwest.

Cannubi Centrale has three different sections and three exposures, though the largest mostly south southeast-facing section dominates and is also reaches highest. In fact, as Cannubi Centrale's altitude figures attest, it is not an especially high vineyard area: the southeasterly exposure ought to ensure Cannubi Centrale is not too hot a habitat, but a series of natural barriers allow its microclimate to be warmer than one would expect (not to mention protected from unfavorable weather). Natural barriers to the elements are the La Morra crest to the west, the Bussia hilltop to the east, and San Giovanni to the south, which ensure good ventilation and relatively warm temperatures especially come summertime. Like almost everywhere else in the Barolo denomination, it is the areas at the bottom of the hillside that are the coolest and most humid, while areas towards the middle of the slope and higher up are marked by relatively dry conditions (and as I mentioned at the beginning of this file, it really *does* get hot there in the summer). That geographical location and its attendant consequences are but just one reason why Cannubi Centrale has always been prized: unlike other sites in the Barolo denomination, it rarely gets hailed upon, for example. Another oft-cited, but mostly inaccurate, reason that Cannubi is considered to be the qualitative cat's meow of all Barolo vineyard sites is that it supposedly sits at the crossroads of Barolo's two main soil types formed during the Tortonian and Serravalian stages of the Miocene epoch. The advantage of such a geologic positioning was long believed to be the reason why Cannubi's

Barolos were wines of such unique balance, complexity and concentration. In fact, this is one of the possible origins and meanings of the vineyard district's name: "*cannubi*" is believed to derive from the word *connubbio* meaning "unity, or marriage", as in the unification of the two soil types (another less likely interpretation refers to the word *canne* or canes, and the fact there used to be lots of them growing there in the past). In fact, the geologic reality of Cannubi is not what it was always thought to be. If for no other reason because we know today that all of Cannubi's different soil lithologies were formed during the Tortonian stage of the Miocene Epoch. Whereas it was once believed that the Diano Sandstones were formed during the Serravalian stage, it now appears that the Diano Sandstones were formed during the Tortonian stage as well, and so it does not appear like Cannubi's soils are a mix of Tortonian and Serravalian origins. Hence, there is really no *connubio* to speak of.

It is true that the soil within the entire Cannubi hillside is marked by a noteworthy presence of sand: but the amount of sand varies greatly within the different Cannubi-something vineyard districts. While the landscape category of the entire Cannubi is categorized as a Land Unit of Barolo, the soil lithology and composition changes throughout, which is but one of the reasons why the various Cannubis should probably not be lumped together under one generic Cannubi heading. Pertinently, while the lithology of the Cannubi hill is generally that of the Saint Agatha Fossil Marls formation formed during the Tortonian stage of the Miocene epoch, it is not that simple. First of all, while Cannubi Centrale, Cannubi Muscatel, Cannubi San Lorenzo, and Cannubi Valletta all share Saint Agatha Fossil Marls formation of the sandy type, Cannubi Boschis is apparently characterized instead by the typical, not sandy, Saint Agatha Fossil Marls formation. Also, Cannubi Centrale is the only one of the Cannubi-somethings to boast not one but three different soil lithologies (Saint Agatha Fossil Marls formation of the sandy type, Saint Agatha Fossil Marls formation of the typical type and the Diano Sandstone). Cannubi Valletta is the only other Cannubi-something vineyard district that is characterized by the presence of two lithologies; all the other-Cannubi-somethings have one only.

And while sand is a way of life in the whole tongue-like extension that is the extended Cannubi hillside, it has always been said that the Cannubi Centrale is where the sand presence is highest. There is a belt-like corridor of layered sand that runs from the lower part of Cannubi Boschis (given its distinct lithology, it is not as sandy as the rest of the extended Cannubi) through the center of the hill right down to the southwestern portion of the hill that is Cannubi Muscatel (also less sandy than the rest of the hill, and richer in clay). So, while the Cannubi Centrale's lithology is of the Saint Agatha Fossil Marls of sandy type like the rest of the extended Cannubi hillside, it boasts even more sand than do other sections of the hillside. It also boasts the presence of the Diano Sandstone formation, that in Cannubi is present only there, save for a small sliver in Cannubi Valletta. It is this sand beltway that makes the extended Cannubi hillside in general, and Cannubi Centrale in particular, so special, given that outside of the beltway there is much more marl than sand, with increased amounts of silt and loam. In fact, there is very little sand to speak of at the lowest altitudes of the extended Cannubi hill, where the marl is heavily prevalent. It is in these lower-lying sections that it is more accurate to speak of a third lithological formation, that of Saint Agatha Fossil Marls of the typical type (therefore, not so sandy, but silty-clay-loamy). Clearly, as Cannubi Boschis is one of the lower-lying portions of the extended Cannubi, it is not so strange that this formation is the dominant one there. Soil sample analysis of the various Cannubi-somethings would seem to bear this out, but it's not so cut and dried. For example, soil sample analysis of the Cannubi Centrale and all the other Cannubi-somethings obtained over the years from the Serio e Battista Borgogno show that the sand content is indeed highest in parts of the Cannubi Centrale, but also that sand percentages vary throughout the hillside and can reach high values in some of the other Cannubi-somethings as well. It is really not so much just a matter of *how much* more sand there is in the Cannubi Centrale's soil, but *where* it is found there. Based on my experience there are sections of Cannubi San Lorenzo that strike me as being even sandier than some sections of the Cannubi Centrale (my data shows that both can average 37% sand soil content, to the best of my knowledge higher than any other Cannubi-something. See CANNUBI SAN LORENZO file). Data from the Brezza estate also shows that the Cannubi Centrale is the Cannubi section mostly loaded with sand; for comparison's sake, I also include the soil composition breakdown of the winery's holdings in other Barolo vineyard districts as well. Interestingly, some of Brezza's vineyards in other vineyard districts of the Barolo commune show even more sand presence in their soil than does their vineyard land in the Cannubi Centrale. These numbers differ slightly from those reported by the Serio e Battista Borgogno estate, as can be seen below:

Cannubi Centrale

Upper and central portions:

Saint Agatha Fossil Marls of the sandy type: 29% Sand, 46% Loam, 25% Clay

Lower portions (to the east):

Saint Agatha Fossil Marls of the typical type: 15% Sand, 60% Loam, 25% Clay

The centrally located beltway:

Diano Sandstone: 15% Sand, 60% Loam, 25% Clay

Cannubi Boschis

Saint Agatha Fossil Marls of the typical type: 15% Sand, 60% Loam, 25% Clay

Cannubi San Lorenzo and Cannubi Muscatel

Saint Agatha Fossil Marls of the sandy type: 29% Sand, 46% Loam, 25% Clay

Cannubi Valletta

Saint Agatha Fossil Marls of the sandy type: 29% Sand, 46% Loam, 25% Clay

Brezza

Vineyard	Loam	Clay	Sand
CANNUBI MUSCATEL	36.8	32.7	30.5
CANNUBI (CENTRALE)	39.5	23.6	36.9
SARMASSA	46.4	30.5	24.2
CASTELLETTO	29.6	31.3	39.1
SAN LORENZO	46.4	29.4	40.5

In summary, the soil of the extended Cannubi hillside is of three main types: at the lowest altitudes, it's mainly silty with some clay and little or no sand; in the central sections, where the Diano Sandstone is present, it is mostly sand, while in the higher reaches it is silt plus a strong presence of sand and a little clay. Though it appears like Cannubi Centrale does not have a monopoly on the sand content of the Cannubi hillside (or of the Barolo commune's territory, for that matter), it certainly has more sand and less clay than other Cannubi-somethings: in this light, the 36.9% sand content of Brezza's Cannubi centrale holding is a great deal higher than any of the other soil samples recorded. And at 23.6% clay content, the Cannubi Centrale is undoubtedly also noteworthy in that light too (for example, compared to the 32.7% clay content of Cannubi Muscatel). That, and the fact that Cannubi Centrale is the only section of the extended Cannubi hillside that boasts three different soil lithologies, showcases that it is geologically distinct from other sections of the Cannubi hillside. For some purists, the heart of the Cannubi hill is located between the Viganò propriety (now owned by Einaudi) and the ex-vineyard of the Canonica family in front of the cemetery. This would effectively eliminate Cannubi Muscatel and Cannubi Boschis from the Cannubi name discussion, vineyards marked only as having "particular qualitative characteristics" (differently from the Cannubi Centrale) in Ratti's original map. But there is no agreement on these matters. In any case, the taste profile and texture of the wines made in the various Cannubi-somethings and the Cannubi Centrale are different too; and the interesting point to make here is that it's really not so much that the wines of one Cannubi-something are better than the others, but, as we shall see, that they are different.

Cannubi Centrale stories: the people and the wines

Cannubi Centrale is about nineteen hectares large, situated on the eastern-facing flank of the Barolo ridge and sandwiched between the vineyard districts of Cannubi Boschis to the northeast and Cannubi Valletta and Cannubi San Lorenzo to the southwest. To the west, but on the other side of a road that runs atop the Barolo ridge separating the eastern flank of the hillside from its western flank, are located, from north to south, the vineyard districts of Crosia, Albarella and San Lorenzo (do not confuse this vineyard district with the similarly-named vineyard district of Cannubi San Lorenzo).

What makes the wines of the Cannubi Centrale so unique is that they are at once magically silky yet powerful: they offer, when well-made, tannins of incomparable silkiness. However, like all Barolo wines, they are no wimps: the Cannubi Centrale's wines still boast an underlying tannic spine that can sometimes turn to grittiness in years of extreme heat and drought if and when the Nebbiolo grapes fail to reach full physiologic ripeness (always a possibility in such years because of the aforementioned high soil sand content of Cannubi Centrale). To my way of thinking, the Barolos of the Cannubi Centrale have a little something in common with those of the true Bussia (the Bussia Soprana), the wines of which are remarkably elegant, almost like those of the Cannubi Centrale but are much more powerful, in the typical way of Monforte's Barolo wines. To put it in other words, Cannubi Centrale is more cheetah, Bussia more leopard: both are spotted big cats of unparalled grace, but one is svelte, the other muscular. And so it is with the wines of those two specific vineyard district subregions.

The fight in the courts of public and private opinion

Clearly, given the importance, fame and history of the Cannubi vineyard site and of its name, it cannot surprise that said name has been the subject of a recent long-winded and acrimonious legal diatribe as to which portion of the vineyard district area really had the right to be identified as 'Cannubi' on bottles. This is not surprising and is a situation that has played out in many other famous vineyard areas of the world (Bernkastel's Doctor vineyard, for example), where an important vineyard becomes an object of desire and everybody and their sister too wants to get a piece of the action.

Though not everybody agrees, some believe that there has always been one historic Cannubi, the Cannubi proper or Cannubi *tout court* if you will. More or less, it corresponds only to the central segment of the hill that is nowadays the extended Cannubi (and that for this reason I also refer to it as Cannubi Centrale). Throughout time, it is the only segment of the hill that has always been known as Cannubi only, the one that has neither had any other name attached to it, nor that has gone by a different name altogether. It is Cannubi, and nothing else. By contrast, all the other segments of the hill also have other names, that were long used and that you can clearly find on the labels of bottles of Barolos from the past. For example, over the decades, the segment of the extended Cannubi hillside known as Valletta has been called Valletta or Cannubi Valletta; then it was Cannubi Valletta; and most recently, Cannubi Valletta or Cannubi. Now put yourselves in the shoes of a Barolo producer: why call a wine by the name of Valletta or Cannubi Valletta when you can just call your wine Cannubi, with all the perceived potential attendant monetary benefits of such an action? After all, if people were allowed to choose between calling their wine Montrachet or Bâtard-Montrachet, what do you think most people would do? The first installment of the "Cannubi-name change sweepstakes" started off in 1994-95 (based on law n°164 of the 10/2/1992, allowing the addition of a geographic mention), when it was proposed that the names of Valletta, Muscatel, San Lorenzo and Boschis might also have the name of 'Cannubi' attached, such that they all could be not just Valletta, but also Cannubi Valletta, and same for Muscatel/Cannubi Muscatel, San Lorenzo/Cannubi San Lorenzo and Boschis/Cannubi Boschis. However, the motion to allow the possibility of a double wording of the site name did not pass. In 2008, the town of Barolo passed the official proposal that the names become officially Cannubi Muscatel, Cannubi Valletta, Cannubi San Lorenzo, Cannubi, and Cannubi Boschis only. This decision was upheld in a subsequent plenary session of the Comitato Nazionale Vini. However, the following year, the Comitato Nazionale Vini was informed of a complaint contesting the decision, which set off the long diatribe and court cases most everyone who follows Italian wine is aware of and that was only recently concluded with the decision to allow all the segments of the hill to be called Cannubi if those who made wine were so inclined. As such, the segments of the extended Cannubi hill, and the Barolos made there, can now all be called Cannubi indistinguishably. Of course, if someone wants to call his or her wine Cannubi Boschis, Cannubi San Lorenzo, Cannubi Muscatel or Cannubi Valletta they are welcome to do so, but not unexpectedly, few choose to do so. The data bears this out: in not even ten years, the number of estates choosing to use a name other than Cannubi has fallen dramatically (see Appendix C. *Table 3.1: Comparison of Cannubi production declarations*). Speaking with producers, it is apparent there is a real push by some in the area to have the vineyard district referred to as Cannubi only. According to some of the locals, the entire hill was always referred to as Cannubi. Others maintain that though it might have been so from time to time, it was a minority point of view and that it is more accurate to refer only to the central section of the hill as 'Cannubi''. Given that each of the Cannubi subregions has specific geological and topographical characteristics (the type of soil, the range of different exposures, the altitude, the numerous small and large undulations in the slope) leading to at times noteworthy differences in expression in wines from the different parts of the extended Cannubi hillside, you can understand why some people feel very strongly that those subdivisions should be the standard manner by which to go about naming Cannubi wines.

When all is said and done, it's not even a matter of one portion of Cannubi being better than another, because all are slightly different from one another, resulting in slightly different wines, and which you prefer amounts to a case of different strokes for different folks. For sure, the whole hill is an exceptionally good place in which to grow Nebbiolo and make Barolo. The subregions do have slightly different soil compositions and orientations, but for the most part are southeast-facing slopes with the sandy-clay marl soils that are typical of the western Tortonian side of the Langhe. The wines of the various Cannubi subregions are certainly different, but all have their merits. Nobody who has a little experience with Barolo's wines will deny that one of Barolo's top ten wines is the Barolo Cannubi Boschis (now called Barolo Aleste) made by Sandrone; the Barolo Cannubi made by G.B. Burlotto (with grapes from Cannubi Valletta) and the Cannubi San Lorenzo made by Ceretto are also standouts. All those wines are just as great as the Barolo Cannubi wines made by Chiara Boschis and Brezza with Cannubi Centrale grapes, so clearly, it is possible to make fantastic Barolo wines from all subregions of the Cannubi hillside. There is beauty in difference.

Cannubi Centrale producers and the wines

Anna Bolla and Federica Boffa of the Serio e Battista Borgogno estate own vineyards in the heart of the Cannubi Centrale. The pair represent the fifth generation and took over when Serio died and now run the estate with their families and four historic team members who have been with the estate for the longest time. The pair began with four hectares (2.7 hectares of which in the Cannubi Centrale) but by 2014 had increased the estate's holdings (either through acquisitions and/or rentals) to ten hectares. Each one of their Cannubi Centrale vineyards has its own name and characteristics; they are vinified separately so has to highlight and study the individual plot characteristics and the personality of the wine each gives. The plots are called: Vigna Gorat (west-facing, it looks towards La Morra and the Castello della Volta, and is characterized by a heavy clay and sandy-loam soil); the Vigna Nuova (east-facing, it looks towards Diano d'Alba and its soil is mostly sandy and loam soil); and the Vigna Battista (that faces south and looks towards Monforte, with a mostly sand and loamy). The Gorat was named in honor of the grandmother of the current owners, nicknamed the *gouretta* (for her charisma and forceful, strong personality that would bend and not break, just like the willow, of which there used to be a row next to the vineyards; historically it was used to tie vines to metal wires in the vineyards). The vineyard was planted in 1982 at 280 meters in altitude, on the heaviest clay-containing soil of the estate (but for all its clay, is still a sandy-loamy clay soil). It is the biggest of the plots of Cannubi vines the estate owns and that accounts for the plot's earlier name, Vigna Grossa (the "big vineyard"); earlier still it was called Vigna Cane, after the family name of a previous owner. The plot called Nuova is a much cooler site (clearly, still sandy-loamy-clay) planted in 1998 at 280 meters above sea level. Last but most certainly not least, given that it's probably the best of the three and the major source of grapes for the estate's Barolo Cannubi Riserva, is the Battista vineyard (so-called because it was Battista's favorite place to hang out), planted in 1992 at 280 meters in altitude like the other two.

An interesting comparison is made possible when tasting the Serio e Battista Borgogno's 2016 Barolo Cannubi and the 2016 Barolo classico made from grapes culled mostly from the Novello commune's Bergera-Pezzolle vineyard district. More nuanced, almost reticent on the nose compared to the more obvious but simpler Barolo classico, the Barolo Cannubi is also silkier, more complex, and broader, with plenty of red berry aromas and flavors complicated by floral and herb nuances. (Interestingly, in this vintage, no grapes from the estate's Vigna Battista were included in the Barolo Cannubi as they were all used to make the Barolo Riserva.) The wine is made in the usual fashion, about forty-five days total maceration, malo done in stainless steel tanks and then is aged for thirty-two months in large Slavonian oak barrels. I also point out that the 2014 Barolo Cannubi is very good here, a clear-cut confirmation of how Cannubi Centrale performs well in bad (meaning rainy) vintages. The 2014 vintage was cold and rainy, but as already mentioned, drainage is never a problem in Cannubi Centrale. Different is the 2013 Barolo Cannubi, where the wine is a blend of the Gorat plot and the Vigna Nuova, though the characteristics of the Cannubi Centrale jump out here too (and it would be strange if it were not so, given that 2013 is a very fine vintage of classic Barolos). It provides an interesting contrast with the estate's 2013 Barolo Cannubi Riserva, in which Nebbiolo grapes from all three of the estate's historic plots are blended together to make the wine and which spent thirty days on the skins and then fifty months in new and old large oak casks. Unlike what the word "Riserva" on the label may lead you to believe, this is actually a gentler, more nuanced, less showy wine than the 2013 Barolo Cannubi, but boasts greater depth and richness. The estate also made a Riserva wine from the Cannubi holdings in 2012, a brave undertaking given the heat of that vintage: it's a blend of grapes from the Gorat and the Battista vineyards, even more surprising given that those two are the estate's warmest sites. Go figure. Go figure too that the wine is actually pretty darn good, despite an obvious, and I dare say unavoidable, grittiness of tannin, the result of the hot growing season and water-related problems.

Chiara Boschis of the E. Pira/Chiara Boschis owns 0.7 hectares in the historic section of Cannubi that she ages twenty-four months in one third new, one third used, and one third twice used oak barrels. She was the first to turn her Cannubi vineyard (in 2014) to organic viticulture and as mentioned earlier in this file has since turned practically everyone else in the vineyard district who owns vines there to the beauty of organic farming. Her Barolo Cannubi is typically characterized, depending on the vintage, by a minty-menthol-eucalyptus-balsamic note (which of the four it will be depends mainly on the degree of heat of the growing season, though I point out that in my experience, the sweeter balsamic note is more characteristic of the Barolos of Cannubi Boschis) that complements the sour red cherry fruit aromas and flavors. The minty-menthol note, which is not oak-related, is found in other Barolos wines from the Cannubi Centrale too (for example, Brezza's) but I find it is usually most discernible in Chiara's wines.

Arnaldo Rivera, the name the Terre del Barolo cooperative has given to its high-end line of wines, has just begun including a Barolo Cannubi in its portfolio of offerings, just one in their large series of wines devoted to Barolo single vineyard district bottlings. The name of Arnaldo Rivera is an apt choice, given that this line of wines is important for the cooperative and that Rivera is an important figure in the history of Barolo wine. This because he was not just the founder of the cooperative itself (in 1958: what began as a small group of local *vignaioli* now boasts 300 members and over 600 hectares under its supervision), but also the Mayor of Castiglione Falletto for a whopping thirty-seven years (a rare politician who was obviously well-liked), not to mention a much-respected local school teacher. All the single-vineyard district bottlings in the Arnaldo Rivera line are vinified in the same manner, so these wines offer a unique opportunity to compare what each of the vineyard districts can deliver. Arnaldo Rivera's Barolo Cannubi is made from a single, southeast-facing vineyard planted at about 300 meters above sea level located at the top of the crest that separates the Cannubi vineyard district from that of Albarella vineyard district. Its lithology is mostly Saint Agatha Fossil Marls of the sandy type (essentially alternating layers of calcium carbonate-rich blue-grey marls and silt, with some sandy layers). The specific vineyard in the Cannubi Centrale is characterized by a shallow soil of sandy-marly nature (so, as stated previously, that means it is located at a medium-high altitude of the Cannubi Centrale hill) where the limestone content is on the high side and that of clay not more than 25% of the total. This means that the Arnaldo Rivera site is blessed with excellent drainage; and though water retention in Saint Agatha Fossil Marls of the sandy type is limited (because of all that sand that makes both evaporation and percolation easy), the percentage of clay, as well as in the more typical variant of Saint Agatha Fossil Marls, allow for water retention and release during the hot summer months. The wine is excellent, very Cannubi-like, refined yet powerful: even better, nobody with even a modicum of Barolo-drinking experience will confuse it for a wine from Serralunga or Monforte, and that's how it should be.

Enrico Scavino and his family has been making a Barolo Cannubi at his Paolo Scavino estate since the 1985 vintage: and thought the grape source has changed slightly over the years, this Barolo is in my experience always one of the top three wines the estate makes every year. It has always struck me how, in blind tastings, it is the Cannubi that is more often than not the estate's most complete, balanced wine, even compared to the Rocche dell'Annunziata Riserva and the Bric del Fiasc (the latter is arguably the Barolo the winery is best known for and in many respects their flagship wine, but I find it is often bested in blind tastings by the other two Barolos, and recently, by Scavino's excellent Barolo Monvigliero too). The estate makes its Barolo Cannubi from 0.55 hectares south/southeast-facing plot planted at about 280 meters above sea level. This exceptionally old vineyard, planted in 1946, is one of the two oldest plots of vines that Scavino oversees. I find that more so than with any other Paolo Scavino Barolo save for their Rocche dell'Annunziata, the truly remarkably good

Barolo Cannubi needs to be cellared for an appropriate amount of time to be enjoyed at its fullest, so *caveat emptor*.

Enzo Brezza is in charge of the Brezza estate located right in the heart of the Barolo village and that makes many outstanding Barolos, amongst which their Barolo Cannubi often shines brightest. A traditionally-minded producer, Brezza farms southeast-facing vines planted in 1994 and 2003 at about 250 meters of altitude in the most historic section of the Cannubi Centrale, right below the weather/meteo station. His Nebbiolo vines therefore grow on that sandy band-like stretch of the Cannubi Centrale mentioned earlier; the soil composition of Brezza's vineyard is: loam 39.5%, sand 36.9%, and clay 23.6%. That very high sand component is immediately obvious after the first sip of Brezza's Barolo Cannubi wine: perfumed but very light on its feet, with a nervous, acid, steely core underlying the bright red berry and sour red cherry nuances the wine is richly imbued with. As mentioned previously, it often exudes a minty-menthol nuance (not balsamic: the sweeter balsamic note is more typical of the wines of Cannubi Boschis) that is also obvious in the wines of Chiara Boschis. And in a marvelous lesson on what terroir is about, it is a completely different wine from Brezza's own Barolo Sarmassa. The two vineyard districts, both located in the Barolo commune's territory, are not be that far removed from each other, but the two wines, made in exactly the same way, are worlds apart.

Benchmark wineries/Reference point producers of Barolo Cannubi: Brezza, Chiara Boschis-E. Pira, Paolo Scavino, Serio e Battista Borgogno.

CANNUBI BOSCHIS (OR CANNUBI)

Township	Barolo
Reference Map	See Map of Barolo MGAs (Ch. 10)
Size (ha) (Tot / Barolo MGA)	12.41 / 5.6 – 5 Owners
Production 2021 (hl)	77.69
Altitude	220 – 260 meters a.s.l. roughly
Exposure	Predominantly from south to southeast; from east to northwest in the remaining parts.
N. Claimants MGA	2
Other grape varieties planted:	Barbera; Dolcetto
Land Units	Land Unit of Barolo
Soil (stage):	Tortonian

Producers claiming the MGA

Il Gioco dell'Oca di Pittatore; Luciano Sandrone.

Wines

Fenocchio Giacomo - Barolo Cannubi; **Il Gioco dell'Oca di Pittatore** – Barolo Cannubi; **L'Astemia Pentita** – Barolo Cannubi (and Riserva); **Luciano Sandrone** - Barolo Aleste; **Virna** - Barolo Cannubi.

What the producers say

Luca Sandrone (Sandrone Luciano): "Cannubi is the sum, because it adds up to the combination of all our other vineyards. It doesn't have the concentration and power of Baudana, the balance of Vignane, the elegance and finesse of Villero nor the almost tropical notes of Merli but it has the same freshness. It's a parcel that is never too hot and the grapes grown here never taste "cooked". Cannubi is the optimal union of all those components that we would like to have in a Barolo"

Virna Borgogno (Virna): "On the hill of Cannubi Boschis one finds two kinds of soils of different origins that can deliver power and elegance. This vineyard became part of our property in 1996 and I have since always vinified it separately. In Cannubi Boschis, one finds noteworthy finesse and elegance in the perfume: intense bouquet of mixed red fruits aromas.

It also has sweet tannins and a pleasant persistence of flavors on the palate. In remarkably dry years, we may notice a certain lack of body and structure".

Ian's assessment of the vineyard district, its wines and its potential

Cannubi Boschis is a name made famous by Luciano Sandrone, one of Barolo's most famous and best producers. Prior to Sandrone christening his 1985 Barolo Cannubi Boschis with that specific vineyard district name (and the brand new, really beautiful, and now iconic blue and white label), the vineyard area was referred to by the specific area's historic name, Monghisolfo. For example, if you can find a bottle, just check out the Barolo Sandrone made in the 1984 vintage: it's the last to carry the old white label that read "Monghisolfo dei Cannubi", written in an elegant freestyle font on a wholly white label. Clearly, changing over to "Cannubi Boschis" had its advantages, given that the new name was a lot easier to pronounce for non-Italians (Boschis was the name of a locally famous family). In fact, with the 2013 vintage, the wine's name changed again, losing the Cannubi Boschis moniker and becoming ALESTE, in honour of his two grandchildren Alessia and Stefano ("Aleste" is the partial acronym of Alessia and Stefano). In an interesting sign of just how important it is to be a recognized, much admired world-class wine producer people trust such as is Sandrone, and of how the winery's name can supersede any name of place Sandrone used to sell his wine as a "lowly" Barolo Cannubi Boschis (instead of a Barolo Cannubi) and now as the Barolo Aleste but neither event hurt sales any.

In fact, Sandrone and the Cannubi Boschis are inextricably linked. Leaving the village of Barolo-and driving along the road at the foot of the Cannubi hillside, the Cannubi Boschis is the last segment of the Cannubi hill you will reach before going into the territory of Castiglione Falletto to the right. (At one point, roughly around the midway point of the Cannubi Boschis extension, there is a road to your right, the via Pugnane, and the Sandrone winery is right there, built across from the Cannubi Boschis itself.) Facing south/southeast like most of, but not all, of the rest of the extended Cannubi hill, the Boschis subregion of the long Cannubi hillside is the most northern and lower-lying. It is also slightly bowl- or amphitheater-shaped and fairly undulating; in fact, almost concave in parts. This particular topographical conformation helps Cannubi Boschis retain early morning warmth, and its Tortonian stage compact marly calcareous-clay with sand and limestone soils account for Barolos that are ripely fruity and smoothly textured, with less of the acid spine of the Barolos from other parts of the extended Cannubi hill. The landscape category Cannubi Boschis belongs to is the Land Unit of Barolo, and the soil lithology is the typical Saint Agatha Fossil Marls; in other words, not of the sandy type that typifies all the other Cannubi-somethings (though not surprisingly, the part of Cannubi Boschis immediately adjacent to the Cannubi Centrale section of the hill is sandier than the rest of the Cannubi Boschis subregion). The combination of this lithology, the lower altitude, and gentler, less steep slope, neatly distinguishes the Cannubi Boschis from all other Cannubi-somethings from a geographic perspective. And to be clear, from the perspective of its wines too.

In general, Cannubi Boschis Barolos are politely-styled and relatively lighter-structured like all the Barolos from the extended Cannubi tend to be, but the wines of Cannubi Boschis are also slightly beefier, more textured wines than those of the Cannubi Centrale and Cannubi San Lorenzo. To confuse the wines of Cannubi Centrale with those of Cannubi Boschis is impossible: just try tasting blind the Barolo Cannubi wines of Brezza and Serio e Battista Borgogno next to those of Sandrone, or of Virna and of Francesco Rinaldi (both made with Cannubi Boschis grapes) and just how different the first two are from the last three will be readily apparent. Furthermore, while the Barolos of both the Cannubi Centrale and the Cannubi Boschis in warmer years will showcase a note of orange peel, floral elements are not exactly a strong suit of Cannubi Boschis (while violet and especially rose petals are very obvious in the wines of the Centrale subregion). Cannubi Boschis wines also have a much stronger balsamic presence than do the wines of the other Cannubi subregions. That much admitted, in my experience the levels of fruitiness and florality of Barolos from the Cannubi Boschis vary greatly with the vintage, more so than with the other Cannubi subregions. And while the extended Cannubi hill is very well protected from bad weather (see CANNUBI CENTRALE file), Cannubi Boschis is a little more exposed and fresher (thanks to the wind currents blowing in from the Tanaro river) such that it is characterized by slightly more adverse climatic effects (for example, in 1995 hail hit Cannubi Boschis more than it did other sections of the extended Cannubi hillside).

There are a number of producers farming Cannubi Boschis, and many of them are real stars. When discussing the wines of Cannubi Boschis, clearly the lion's share of the attention goes to Sandrone and his wine, as well it should. Simply put, this is arguably one of the ten or twelve greatest Barolos in almost every vintage. Like no other producer born during the "modernist Barolo" movement of the 1980s, Sandrone has managed to mesh innovation and tradition together into what ends up tasting like an effortless continuum. Neither traditional nor modern, his are wines that appeal to wine lovers of both inclinations because of their being powerful and fleshy, but lifted and mineral too. Even better, they are never over-oaked. After years working in the cellar at Marchesi di Barolo, he bought his first vineyard in 1973 and made his first wine in the 1978 vintage. The forty years old vines are planted at about 250 meters above sea level and face south and southeast. He harvests his vines there at different times, block by block, and then also tackles them differently in the cellar. The winemaking involves indigenous yeasts, a maceration and alcoholic fermentation in open steel tanks, and malolactic and ageing in French oak 500-liter tonneaux. In 2008, Sandrone launched the *Sibi et Paucis* series of library wines that are released only after appropriate aging in a winery's special cellar: for example, the 2008 Barolo Cannubi Boschis "sibi et paucis" was aged a further six years after the original release date.

Virna Borgogno's Nebbiolo vines in Cannubi Boschis were planted back in 1972, at about 250-260 meters in altitude, facing south/southeast. I'll never forget when Virna, about ten-twelve years ago, served me her 2011 Cannubi Boschis blind (back then the wine was still labeled as a Cannubi Boschis, while since the 2014 vintage, when the estate redesigned its labels, the wine goes by Cannubi only): the balsamic note that greeted my nose was so strong I had no difficulty recognizing the site instantly (admittedly no great shakes, given that the other, also prestigious, Barolo vineyard districts she farms give wines nothing like the Cannubi Boschis). That said, Cannubi Boschis is still a piece of the extended Cannubi hill and a Cannubi subregion, and so, while different from all the other Cannubi wines, they are still wines of wonderful balance that offer relatively soft and approachable tannins ("relative" in that it's still Barolo I'm talking, er writing, about here). You will also find that all Barolos from the Cannubi Boschis are fairly easy to drink already in their youth (deceptively so, in fact), but actually age well.

Francesco Rinaldi makes ageworthy Barolos that are not just extremely well-made (not just from Cannubi but also Brunate: see BRUNATE file), but also well-priced, given the quality in the bottle. Like most everyone else, they choose to label their wine, which is made with about 95% Cannubi Boschis grapes, as a Barolo Cannubi only (the estate does possess a very small section of vines in the Cannubi Centrale). It's a very typical Barolo from Cannubi Boschis: light on its feet but with a beefy core, offering balsamic nuances and plenty of easy-drinking charm, though it is still beautiful twenty years out. Their Barolo Cannubi wine is also remarkably different from the estate's Barolo Brunate, providing wine lovers with a chance to study differences between these two hallowed vineyards thanks to excellent wines made in the same way by the same producer. Francesco Rinaldi is one of the two famous Rinaldi estates of Barolo that was born back in the nineteenth century from the split of the big Barale-Rinaldi firm; not just Francesco Rinaldi and Giuseppe Rinaldi resulted from the division, but the Fratelli Barale estate was so born too.

Claudio Fenocchio of the outstanding Giacomo Fenocchio estate is another producer whose vines are all in Cannubi Boschis but chooses to label his wine as Cannubi only (his website simply states "the historic Cannubi *cru* in the village of Barolo", but Claudio has told me his parents and grand-parents always talked generically about a Cannubi hill, so you understand his point). His southeast-facing vines are roughly thirty years old and cover 0.5 hectares of the Cannubi Boschis vineyard district at 280 meters above sea level. A relatively traditionally-minded estate and an outstanding producer, depending on vintage characteristics Fenocchio uses indigenous yeasts, ferments up to forty days in stainless steel tanks and ages his wine for thirty months in large 20-25 hectoliter Slavonian oak casks and six months in stainless steel tanks. Very elegant and light on its feet, his take on Barolo Cannubi offers plenty of insight into what the Cannubi Boschis wines are about, especially in relation to the other Barolos made by him from other vineyard districts (and he is lucky to farm truly topnotch vineyard district such as Villero and Bussia). Compared to those last two vineyards, Fenocchio's Cannubi bottling is remarkable for its light weight palate presence and graceful texture (neither dense and chewy like his Bussia nor as structured as the Villero, which is also marked by a very different florality. See VILLERO file).

Benchmark wineries/Reference point producers of Barolo Cannubi Boschis: Sandrone (the wine is now labeled as 'ALESTE'). Also good: Francesco Rinaldi (the wine is essentially 95% Cannubi Boschis, the rest is Cannubi Centrale); Giacomo Fenocchio and Virna (100% Cannubi Boschis).

CANNUBI MUSCATEL (OR CANNUBI)

Township	Barolo	
Reference Map	See Map of Barolo MGAs (Ch. 10)	
Size (ha) (Tot / Barolo MGA)	6.24 /4 – 1 Owners	
Production 2021 (hl)		
Altitude	220 – 320 meters a.s.l. roughly	
Exposure	From south to southeast;	
N. Claimants MGA		
Other grape varieties planted:	Barbera; Dolcetto	
Land Units	Land Unit of Barolo	
Soil (stage):	Tortonian	

Wines

Cascina Bruciata - Barolo Cannubi Muscatel

Ian's assessment of the vineyard district, its wines and its potential

Cannubi Muscatel is the piece of the extended Cannubi hill that is closest to the town of Barolo. Like all the other Cannubi-somethings, its landscape category is classified as Land Unit of Barolo. Its soil lithology is the classic Tortonian stage Saint Agatha Fossil Marls of the sandy type that, save for Cannubi Boschis, is the one that characterizes the Cannubi-somethings (see CANNUBI CENTRALE file. See also CANNUBI BOSCHIS). By contrast, its topography and altitude differ from that of the other Cannubi-somethings, in that Cannubi Muscatel's slope is gentler (less steep) and its altitude reaches slightly greater heights (a smidge over Cannubi San Lorenzo). Quite frankly, just looking at the site, and remembering where it is located (proximity to towns usually means a warmer vineyard microclimate), should make one think it *has* to give different wines from those of all the other Cannubi-somethings. Perhaps slightly fruitier, softer, and rounder? Based on the wines I have tasted over the years from this site, I would say that it really is just so.

This Cannubi subregion has the name it does because decades ago it used to be largely planted to Moscato Bianco. This explains the vineyard area's name: *muscatel* from *moscato*. This is actually a feather in Cannubi Muscatel's cap: what people forget nowadays is that once upon a time Moscato Bianco wines were the area's most expensive and sought after, not Nebbiolo's, sales of which were abysmal as recently as the 1960s and 1970s. So just like nowadays it's Nebbiolo that is getting planted just about everywhere (even in sites not particularly suited for it), for most of the nineteenth and twentieth centuries the same was happening with Moscato Bianco. Given its sales potential at the time, it too was getting planted just about anywhere. In other words, the presence of Moscato Bianco in and of itself in a specific site is not so much a comment on that site's suitability (or not) for Nebbiolo, but rather that because it was other grapes and wines that once sold better, it was they that were getting planted everywhere. You only need to think about the plight of Grignolino and Freisa plantings in the Barolo and Barbaresco denominations today to realize just how common such market-driven decisions are still today, and the long-term effects they have. But if people were planting Moscato Bianco in Cannubi Muscatel, and probably a lot of it too given the vineyard area's name, it most likely means that it was probably viewed as a good site by locals and worth investing in. I trust you really don't think that people would have planted a precious, very remunerative grapevine in a truly bad vineyard site, right? Precisely.

That much admitted, some people I have talked to over the years (including famous Barolo producers you all know of) do not believe that Cannubi Muscatel gives Barolos of the same quality level as the rest of the extended Cannubi hill. In fact, those same people say exactly the same thing about Cannubi Boschis and Cannubi Valletta. Reasons cited are varied. For example, that the Cannubi Muscatel's soil has too much clay: besides the fact that the data I have available doesn't really bear that out (at least not throughout the entire Cannubi Muscatel subregion), a little more soil clay doesn't exactly seem to be a problem for Brunate or Sarmassa, for example, the wines of which rank amongst Barolo's best and the soils of which are not exactly shy on clay content. And I can also add that the Barolos I have tasted from Cannubi Muscatel over the years were just outstanding. So I don't think that Cannubi Muscatel cannot give a great Barolo: far from that, actually. Clearly, if clay really is the problem (and I for one don't think so), how successful a wine you might make may might depend on the *degree* and *kind* of clay presence, and admittedly, sometimes even minor shifts in soil composition can be a big deal wine-wise. Just like with all other Barolo vineyard districts as well as in the different Cannubi subregions, it may well be there are areas within Cannubi Muscatel that are better suited than others for growing top quality Nebbiolo. Like it is with every other Barolo vineyard district.

Cannubi Muscatel producers and the wines

This much is evident when you speak with Enzo Brezza of the Brezza estate in Barolo, who is one of the commune's more talented and traditional producers and whose family owns the very comfortable Hotel Barolo and its solid (and underrated) restaurant. Unlike what purely financial considerations might dictate, Brezza used to grow Barbera in Cannubi Muscatel (the seventy-five years old vines were uprooted in 2021 and the family is in the process of deciding what to replant with) and to bottle a Barbera Cannubi Muscatel (it was last made in 2009; from 2010 onwards, those grapes were blended in with Barbera grapes from the Cannubi Centrale to make the estate's Barbera d'Alba Riserva). The Brezza family had chosen to plant Barbera in those plots because they thought they were the right places for that wine grape at that particular point in time. Of course, with the advent of climate change, the thought process may well be a different one today. Very interestingly, besides the Barbera, Brezza's Cannubi Muscatel plots also had some old ungrafted Moscato Bianco vines growing in it, a testimony of what used to be the real lord of the vineyards in Cannubi Muscatel.

The only estate actively producing a Cannubi Muscatel Barolo is Cascina Bruciata, an estate that thanks to passionate owner Carlo Balbo and his very talented team deservedly made a name for itself through a string of extremely impressive wines that I wrote up and scored highly on numerous occasions, such as in Decanter magazine (not just the Barolo Cannubi Muscatel but also an amazing Barbaresco Rio Sordo and a Langhe Freisa that used to be one of Italy's best). In fact, the estate and area were already famous in the nineteenth century, with Lorenzo Fantini mentioning it in his seminal 1879 *Viticoltura e Enologia della Provincia di Cuneo* ('Viticulture and Oenology in the Province of Cuneo). In 2016, Balbo sold the estate to the large Marchesi di Barolo firm, that has long been the single biggest land-owner of vineyard land in this Cannubi subregion (Brezza and Luciano Sandrone also own small parcels in Cannubi Muscatel). Marchesi di Barolo once used to label Barolos with the specific Cannubi subregion name and I remember liking the specific Cannubi Muscatel wines. Currently Cascina Bruciata's website has a detailed description of the Rio Sordo vineyard in Barbaresco, but curiously, not one of the Cannubi Muscatel vineyard, but hopefully that will change.

The Barolo Cannubi Muscatel of Cascina Bruciata has always not just been good, but downright excellent (and beginning with the 2015 vintage, it was certified organically farmed). From an 0.4 hectares plot of fifteen to twenty years old vines planted at 300 to 320 meters above sea level, twenty-four days fermentation in stainless steel tanks and twenty-four months aging in used oak barriques, is born a wine that just bursts with notes of ripe red cherry, balsamic oils, and juniper. Like all wines made from the extended Cannubi hill, it boasts a very smooth texture and pretty floral lift. When I was attending university in Rome, I had occasion to drink the various Barolos made by Marchesi di Barolo back from the days when they were still distinguishing between their Barolos with the longer name of each Cannubi subregion on the wine label. My memory fails me somewhat right now as to the specific wine nuances and I have to search for those old tasting notebooks but what I do remember is that the wines were excellent and in no way better or worse than the other Barolo bottlings from the estate at the time.

Benchmark wineries/Reference point producers of Barolo Cannubi Muscatel: Cascina Bruciata.

CANNUBI SAN LORENZO (OR CANNUBI)

Township	Barolo
Reference Map	See Map of Barolo MGAs (Ch. 10)
Size (ha) (Tot / Barolo MGA)	2,38 / 1,4 – 3 Owners
Production 2021 (hl)	
Altitude	300 – 320 meters a.s.l. roughly
Exposure	From east to southeast;
N. Claimants MGA	1
Other grape varieties planted:	Barbera; Dolcetto
Land Units	Land Unit of Barolo
Soil (stage):	Tortonian

Producers claiming the MGA

Camerano; Ceretto.

Wines

Camerano G. e Figli - Barolo Cannubi San Lorenzo; **Ceretto** - Barolo Cannubi San Lorenzo;

What the producers say

Ceretto Alessandro (Ceretto): "We vinified separately this vineyard since 2003. The main characteristics of Barolos coming from this site are their complexity and their extreme elegance".

Ian's assessment of the vineyard district, its wines and its potential

Rather unfortunately, there are two very similarly named vineyard districts in Barolo: Cannubi San Lorenzo and San Lorenzo. The two are one across from the other, separated only by a small road that runs along the top of the hillside. The eastern-facing flank of the hillside is the one with the extended Cannubi hill draped over it, while San Lorenzo lies on the hillside's other flank. (Size is something the two "San Lorenzos" also have in common, given they are two of the three smallest vineyard districts of the whole Barolo denomination. See SAN LORENZO file. See also Chapter 10, BAROLO MGA VINEYARD DISTRICTS: MAPS AND LAND UNITS) Clearly, it is Cannubi San Lorenzo that is more famous, given that it's part of the extended Cannubi vineyard area.

Lying immediately above the Valletta subregion of Cannubi, Cannubi San Lorenzo's vineyards are situated at the highest average elevation of all the Cannubi-somethings (only Cannubi Muscatel reaches a little farther up, but vineyards in that Cannubi subregion are also planted much lower down than they are in Cannubi San Lorenzo). Besides its elevation, Cannubi San Lorenzo is also characterized by the fact that small as it is, it's a rather homogenous site. Its landscape is categorized as a Land Unit of Barolo, and the lithology is that of the Saint Agatha Fossil Marls of the sandy type, common to most of the extended Cannubi vineyard district and to many vineyard districts nearby. I have been told by numerous locals over the years that along with the Cannubi Centrale, Cannubi San Lorenzo's soil is the sandiest of all the Cannubi-somethings, though once again this reality is dependent on where one does the sampling. In any case, data from the Serio e Battista Borgogno estate would seem to bear this out, as does data from Ceretto's beautiful Cannubi San Lorenzo vineyard from where their outstanding Cannubi San Lorenzo wine is born. The soil composition there is 35% loam (subdivided in 8.6% large-textured loam and 26.5% fine-textured loam); 44.7% sand (subdivided in 11.6% large-textured sand and 33.1% fine-textured sand); and 20.3% clay. Very interestingly, if I average out soil composition data I have relative to the Cannubi Centrale and the Cannubi San Lorenzo, the sand percentage of the two is very similar (37%) and attests to the extreme sandiness of these two specific Cannubi subregions. The Rinaldi sisters at Giuseppe Rinaldi also state their holding in Cannubi San Lorenzo is the sandiest vineyard soil they work with. For sure, the wines from this specific Cannubi subregion are some of the most graceful and magically perfumed of all Barolo wines.

One of Barolo's most famous estates, Ceretto makes a Barolo Cannubi San Lorenzo. Another, Camerano, has made some really marvelous Barolo Cannubi San Lorenzo wines over the years as well; while quality is a little more irregular than at Ceretto, I never pass on the opportunity to see what the estate's wines are like each vintage. Last but not least, Giuseppe Rinaldi blends its grapes from this site along with those of two other vineyard districts to make their Barolo Tre Tine wine.

Ceretto's is a small holding (about 2500 square meters, or 0.25 hectares) in Cannubi San Lorenzo. Their mostly south/southeast (with a little southwest-facing) vines grow at the summit of the district, or at about 320 meters above sea level; the central core of the vineyard (about half of the vineyard extension) was planted ninety (90!) years ago, and the remaining half in 2014. The estate makes about 1800 bottles a year, magnums only, and releases them ten years after the harvest. It is an absolutely spectacular wine.

Camerano is an old estate (its complete name is Camerano 1875, to drive that point home) the headquarters of which are located in the center of Barolo village. I have had some really great wines off and on over the years, and some that were slightly less so, from this estate and have fond memories of my times tasting there given everyone's kindness and willingness to spend time talking and tasting wine. The estate owns vineyards not just in Cannubi San Lorenzo but in Cannubi Centrale too, and is a bastion of traditional winemaking: long skin contacts and fermentations in resin-coated cement and stainless-steel vats, while aging takes place in large 25, 30 and 50 hectoliter Slavonian (but also some French) oak barrels. In my experience, not every vintage is a success here, but when they get it right, their Barolo Cannubi San Lorenzo is outstanding and a great buy. Just make sure you taste before you buy.

Over at the Giuseppe Rinaldi estate you will taste some of the more precise and pure Barolos of all. Giuseppe (Beppe) Rinaldi trained as a veterinarian and loved motorcycles. Above all, he was an astute observer of all things Barolo and a very capable winemaker who believed that great Barolo had to be "angles, not curves" and must be ageworthy too (Rinaldi believed in totally destemming -no winking at Burgundian techniques and whole bunches with him- natural yeasts, skin contact of about 25-30 days, fermentation in large oak vats, and ageing in large Slavonian oak barrels). He took the estate over in 1992/1993 (unfortunately, Beppe passed away at only sixty-nine years of age in September 2018; the estate was then run by his wife Anna -Anna just passed away at the time this book was going into print, my condolences to the family- and the daughters, Marta and Carlotta, who are the sixth Rinaldi generation at the helm). The estate has slowly but surely pole-vaulted to the highest quality echelons of the Barolo denomination (and it also makes one of the five best Freisa wines of Italy: whatever else you do in life, make sure you buy it). Prior to the institution of the official vineyard district names, and partly because of small holdings in each site that limited the volume of wine he could make from each, Rinaldi used to blend the grapes of Cannubi San Lorenzo together with those from his vines in Ravera (and did the same with those of his Brunate and Le Coste vineyard districts). With the official vineyard district names coming into effect, such action was no longer possible; hence the estate's decision to bottle one Barolo Brunate (which is their largest vineyard plot; but even so, the wine will still contain anywhere from 5-15% of Le Coste, depending on the vintage) and a Barolo blend called 'Tre Tine', made with the grapes culled from vineyards they own in the remaining three vineyard districts. This is why we no longer have a Giuseppe Rinaldi Barolo Cannubi San Lorenzo-Ravera wine to speak of (on the plus side, the estate has bought a vineyard in Monforte's famed Bussia vineyard district, a southwest-facing parcel in the section of Bussia that is closest to the Barolo township. See BUSSIA file.) With the Cannubi San Lorenzo, planted with vigorous Nebbiolo clones in 1996, they have reinstituted their grandfather's practice of *tressage*, where the vine's growing tips are tucked back as opposed to being trimmed by hedging (a practice that is now becoming commonplace in many other parts of Italy as well). By avoiding trimming, the growth of lateral shoots is inhibited (Nebbiolo is a very vigorous vine at the best of times, a vigor made worse by the rootstock choices made throughout the denomination in the 1970s and 1980s), thereby increasing the likelihood of making higher quality wine. The Rinaldi sisters believe that the Cannubi San Lorenzo gives perfumed and lighter-styled wines that are more about red fruit than the Brunate.

Benchmark wineries/Reference point producers of Barolo Cannubi San Lorenzo: Ceretto (Camerano is also worth hunting down and trying).

CANNUBI VALLETTA (OR CANNUBI)

Township	Barolo
Reference Map	See Map of Barolo MGAs (Ch. 10)
Size (ha) (Tot / Barolo MGA)	6,2 / 2,84 – 1 Owners
Production 2021 (hl)	0
Altitude	220 – 320 meters a.s.l. roughly
Exposure	From east to south
N. Claimants MGA	0
Other grape varieties planted:	Barbera; Dolcetto
Land Units	Land Unit of Barolo
Soil (stage):	Tortonian

Wines

Comm. G.B. Burlotto - Barolo Cannubi

Ian's assessment of the vineyard district, its wines and its potential

Cannubi Valletta lies just below Cannubi San Lorenzo and in between the Cannubi Centrale and the Cannubi Muscatel. Why is it called so? Most likely, Cannubi Valletta's name derives from its specific topographical conformation, that forms a small valley (a *valletta*, in Italian). In fact, because the long hillside mass on which all the Cannubi-somethings are found on curves more or less at the halfway point of Cannubi Valletta, the latter vineyard's area can be divided into two halves that have different orientations. When standing in front of the slope, you have the half of Cannubi Valletta to the right that is south-facing and the natural westward prolongation of the Cannubi Centrale, while the half on the left (the *valletta*) curves so that the slope is rotated and looks east. For this reason, when I used to ask around already more than twenty years ago about this specific subregion of Cannubi, most of the locals told me that in their opinion not all of Cannubi Valletta was of the same high-quality level. Clearly, in those non-climate change times it was the southern-facing part next to the Cannubi Centrale that was the most coveted half of Valletta. Today, given the not especially high-altitude range at which Cannubi Valletta's vineyards lie, and the generally sandy-rich component of the Cannubi hillside's soil (meaning that water retention is at a premium there), things are not so cut and dried. Not surprisingly, opinions have changed somewhat since I first started posing that question years ago.

Cannubi Valletta producers and the wines

The G.B. Burlotto estate of Verduno is one of the Barolo area's hottest producers these days, and quite rightfully so given they can't seem to make a bad wine even if they tried. Bear with me, but while I'm at it, I wish to mention that the estate makes not just great Barolos, but also one of the country's five or six best Freisa wines, and of course their Verduno Pelaverga (from the Pelaverga Piccolo variety) is the best of the best. So, you only have an embarrassment of riches to choose from at this address. All that being true, the estate is most sought after for its Barolos: while the Barolo Monvigliero is their single most famous wine, their Barolo Cannubi is a gem too. Even better, it showcases the terroir of Cannubi Valletta to brilliant effect. The estate owns 0.7 hectares of vines in Cannubi Valletta (even though the wine's label states Cannubi only), growing at 280 meters above sea level. The soil is the classic Saint Agatha Fossil Marls of the sandy type; a very nutrient-poor soil, when the vineyard was replanted in 1988, a slightly more vigorous rootstock such as the Kober 5BB was chosen. It proved an ideal grape variety-rootstock combination, one that thanks also in no small part to ultra-talented technical director and winemaker Fabio Alessandria guarantees a refined, somewhat steely wine of noteworthy perfume. Currently, the estate that farms the largest part of Cannubi Valletta is Damilano.

Benchmark wineries/Reference point producers of Barolo Cannubi Valletta: G.B. Burlotto.

CANOVA

Township	Grinzane Cavour
Reference Map	See Map of Grinzane Cavour MGAs (Ch. 10)
Size (ha) (Tot / Barolo MGA)	5.75 / 0.0
Production 2021 (hl)	0
Altitude	210 – 250 meters a.s.l. roughly
Exposure	Southwest plus a small part facing east.
N. Claimants MGA	0
Other grape varieties planted:	Dolcetto; white varieties
Land Units	Land Unit of Barolo
Soil (stage):	Tortonian

Ian's assessment of the vineyard district, its wines and its potential

Canova is situated in one of the most northeastern positions of the Barolo denomination, in the commune of Grinzane Cavour. Its only neighboring vineyard district is the very underrated but high quality (trust me) little-known Borzone, of which Canova is essentially the prolongation of. Canova occupies the portion of the hillside slope that does a hard westward turn such that at a glance, Canova's topographical reality is that it ends up looking like the Canadian side of Niagara Falls (in other words, horseshoe shaped).

Canova's landscape category is the Land Unit of Barolo, which among many other things, also tells us that the soil lithology will be most likely that of the Saint Agatha Fossil marls. Which it is, in fact; more precisely, in that formation's typical form (the same as Borzone: it's also the same lithology of other vineyard districts such as Cannubi Boschis). In any case, one glance at the ground when you might find yourself walking there will tell you that Canova's soil is of the poor variety and that grapevines will have a hard time growing too vigorously here (generally speaking, and within reasonable limits this is always a good thing wine-wise).

Canova producers and the wines

Loris Grasso (of the excellent Cascina del Monastero estate in La Morra) has a vineyard in Canova that is fully south-facing, planted to the Nebbiolo 71 clone (a Nebbiolo Michet). Given Michet is in and of itself not very vigorous (see Chapter 1, NEBBIOLO LAMPIA, subchapter: Clones and Biotypes. See also Chapter 2, NEBBIOLO MICHET), Grasso has intelligently matched it with a vigorous rootstock like the Kober BB5. Grasso's vines are still on the young side (planted only in 2016), but he is very happy with the wine, finding it fairly dense and fleshy. He looks to use these grapes to one day make a Barolo del Comune di Grinzane Cavour, as for the moment he's not comfortable yet with exactly what the site can express: understandable enough, given how little time he (or anybody else, for that matter) has worked with Nebbiolo grapevines in Canova. Being a Barolo of Grinzane Cavour it benefits from aging in large, older oak barrels, which makes sense given these are usually Barolos of refinement and a certain austerity, but also a charming lightness of being, and too much new oak or small oak invariably means suffocating their charms by vanillin and other oaky contributions. I should also mention that Grasso believes that Canova is really no different from the nearby vineyard district called Borzone, also of the Grinzane Cavour commune (see BORZONE file), believing it's essentially all the same hill and that it was a mistake to create two different vineyard districts. Once enough single-site Barolos from Canova will be available to taste regularly year after year, we will of course all know more about this site's potential relative to fine Barolo production: but given what I have already told you about Borzone, and that is that it's a little-known vineyard district but that I think very highly of having come away extremely impressed over the years by some microvinifications made with grapes grown there (not to mention Giovanni Canonica's outstanding Barolo del Comune di Grinzane Cavour, partly made with old vine Borzone grapes), then Canova might turn out to be a very good vineyard district indeed. I don't know about you, but my wine glass is ready and waiting.

Benchmark wineries/Reference point producers of Barolo Cannubi Valletta: None available.

CAPALOT (OR CAPALOTTI)

Township	La Morra
Reference Map	See Map of La Morra MGAs (Ch. 10)
Size (ha) (Tot / Barolo MGA)	34.94 / 8.84
Production 2021 (hl)	465.90
Altitude	295 – 440 meters a.s.l. roughly
Exposure	East; southeast in the Gasprina ridge
N. Claimants MGA	10
Other grape varieties planted:	Barbera; Dolcetto
Land Units	Land Unit of La Morra
Soil (stage):	Tortonian

Producers claiming the MGA

Marilena Alessandria; Silvio Alessandria; Alberto Burzi; Crissante Alessandria; Marco Oberto; Poderi Oddero; San Biagio; Giorgio Sandrone; Santamaria; La Roncaglia.

Wines

Silvio Alessandria - Barolo Capalot; **Crissante Alessandria** - Barolo Capalot and Barolo Capalot La Punta; **Alberto Burzi** - Barolo Capalot; **San Biagio** - Barolo Capalot; **Santamaria** - Barolo Capalot; **Cristian Boffa** – Barolo Capalot.

What the producers say

Mariacristina Oddero (Poderi Oddero): "Considering they are from La Morra; these Barolos are a bit less perfumed yet more substantial in size than is the commune's average".

Davide Voerzio (**Roberto Voerzio**): "We have vinified this vineyard since 1996. With a full south exposure, it is one of the first places where the snow melts together with Cerequio. Capalot is appreciated for its remarkable softness of tannic and yet its impressive structure. A profound Barolo, blessed with good complexity showing predominantly spiced notes of cherry. The tannins are not as classic as Brunate but, in my view, nonetheless equally elegant as those of Cerequio".

Roggero Gianluca (San Biagio): "Our acquisition of vineyards in the Pria-Capalot area does not go so far back, and so our first vintage of this wine dates back only to 2004. The east-facing vines are of varying ages and are planted at 350-400 meters above sea level. The soil shows fossils in its midst, confirming its marine sedimentary origin, and is made up of La Morra's classic marly sandy clays ("pria" is an ancient word meaning "stone", also confirming the presence of compacted sands that break into pieces or stones)".

Ian's assessment of the vineyard district, its wines and its potential

To begin with, do not confuse this vineyard district with the very similarly named Cappallotto in the Serralunga commune (just so you remember, the latter is written with two "p's", two "l's" and two "t's", differently from the vineyard district of La Morra we are discussing here. The good news for you is that, given that there aren't too many wines (yet?) made from the somewhat similarly-named Serralunga vineyard district, this shouldn't be hard to do.

Capalot is located in between the towns of La Morra and Santa Maria and is close by other La Morra vineyard districts such as Rocchettevino, Galina, Santa Maria and Bricco Chiesa. Its landscape is that of the Land Unit of La Morra and its lithology the classic Tortonian stage Saint Agatha Fossil Marls (in this case of the laminated type). It is a vineyard that has some fame attached to it, mainly because of iconic producer Roberto Voerzio making a Barolo with Capalot's grapes. However, there are a number of other La Morra estates that own vines in Capalot and use/have used the grapes to make either single- vineyard district designated Barolos or use/used the grapes in their classic Barolo blends. In other words, it's a site that, unlike many other Barolo's vineyard districts, you will get to taste the wines of, or just be made aware of, because producers are quite likely to talk to you about it. Just how truly favored or good a site it is for premium Barolo production is another matter.

All that admitted, beware that understanding the true personality of Capalot's wines, and for that matter the exact potential of the site, is not straightforward. At least not with the information currently at our disposal. This is because back in the early 2000s, a number of very talented producers (Roberto Voerzio, Alberto Burzi, Crissante Alessandria) were making the darkest, most concentrated (bordering on the jammy) wines possible; in fairness, this was a very fashionable style of Barolo in some quarters back then, but all those wines spoke more of the winemaker's signature than they did of the place they came from. Understandably, people were left with the impression that Capalot's wines are very fleshy-ripe, balsamic and downright syrupy. But that was more a stylistic result of viticultural and winemaking choices.

So, what should the Barolos of Capalot taste like? What are the defining traits of Capalot's Barolos? Well, just looking at where the vineyard district is located provides useful insight on the result one can, could, and perhaps should obtain from Capalot (when late harvesting and draconian yield reductions are removed from the equation). Capalot is one of the vineyard districts in the territory of the Santa Maria fraction of the La Morra township: an area characterized by soils boasting a healthy measure of sand (see BRICCO SAN BIAGIO file). At the same time, it is also a very well-ventilated area, making for a cooler mesoclimate and generally more vibrant wines. Furthermore, Capalot's generally mostly eastern exposure (but beware it's not all east-facing, as I shall address below) also contributes to a certain lightness of being of its wines. For sure, many wine producers have told me over the years that Capalot's soil is fertile and pushes vigor: therefore, reducing yields through various methodologies is essential to making a great Barolo with Capalot grapes, so you understand why some producers decided to take the "less is better" route. Green harvests in the last week of July right up into the time of harvest, and a strict selection of bunches and grapes will make it much more likely that the Barolo from Capalot will be a good one. It's just that if you get carried away with the yield reductions so that the grapes end up looking like blueberries, and late harvest them on top of it, well… for some people, that's maybe taking a good thing too far, while for others it's just fine.

Capalot producers and the wines

As mentioned, there are many good wines made from Capalot to choose from, and, you read it here first, more will soon be on the way. One little-known but high-quality estate is that of Silvio Alessandria (or Alessandria Silvio as the old custom in some Italian circles was/is to say the last name before the first). It is run by talented Enzo Alessandria who began making a Barolo Capalot only recently. How recently? Very. The 2018 vintage is his first Barolo from the site (and unfortunately, there's only 2,112 bottles of it). Alessandria owns 0.3 hectares of east/southeast-facing Nebbiolo biotypes Lampia and Michet in Capalot (OK, for the happiness of precision-inclined reading me, it's actually 0.327 hectares) located at about 300 meters in altitude. Most importantly, these are very old vines indeed (40% of which were planted in 1948!). He ages the wine two years in large Slavonian oak barrels after it has spent a few months in glass-lined cement tanks. The wine has good deep ruby-red colour and structure with Capalot-typical floral and dark red cherry aromas and flavors, complicated by a delicate menthol nuance (that personally I believe to be "very Capalot"). The wine is excellent and I for one am happy to see Enzo Alessandria no longer selling it off as a bulk wine, which is exactly what he was doing prior to deciding to bottle it with the 2018 vintage.

While the Silvio Alessandria estate is a Capalot novice, the same cannot be said of the similarly named Crissante Alessandria estate, a name that has gone hand in hand with that of Capalot for a very long time now. In fact, Alberto Alessandria who is in charge now makes not one, but two Barolos from the Capalot. His Nebbiolo vines there face southeast and are planted at 330-340 meters above sea level on limestone and fine sand soil. Part of these Nebbiolo vines are very old indeed: one half was planted in 1951 (I actually had written down during an old interview that part of this old vineyard dated to 1966, but maybe I had tasted too much wine that day); the other half of the vineyard was planted in 2004. I wrote earlier in this file about a certain style of Capalot wine made over the years: well, Crissante Alessandria's Barolo Capalot La Punta Mac Magnum, offered in magnums and first made in 2008 vintage, is made from late harvested grapes (to give you an idea, one month after his other Nebbiolo grapes are picked); the wine ages for at least two years in new 300 liters oak barrels from some of the oldest vines he owns in the vineyard district. The winemaking for the regular Capalot wine is fairly traditional, with fermentations not exceeding twenty-eight degrees Celsius and aging taking place in large oak casks for twenty-four months (while the 2011 Capalot La Punta, a very big ripe but admittedly velvety wine, was aged five years in one new French barrique, differently from the ageing usually taking place in new 300 liters French oak barrels for about two years).

Alberto Burzi is an excellent if little-known La Morra estate that, among other things, farms a very particular piece of the Capalot vineyard district. His Barolo Capalot is made with grapes grown near the collection of houses that is Capallotti, in what is the only fully south-facing portion of the Capalot, and historically known as Gasprina. The vines were planted at 300 meters above sea level back around World War II. Winemaking involves fairly long skin-contact (depending on the vintage, it can last from thirty to sixty days) in temperature-controlled stainless-steel vats with the *cappello sommerso* technique ("submerged cap"). The malolactic transformation and aging a takes place in thirty hectoliter untoasted Austrian oak barrels (not unreasonably, Burzi believes that using non-toasted oak is essential to maintaining full expression of site). Burzi is well-known to die-hard Barolo fans because he was the one renting the Capalot vines to Roberto Voerzio to make Voerzio's much-acclaimed Barolo Riserva Vecchie Vigne dei Capalot e delle Brunate. Beginning with the 2013 vintage, it was Burzi's turn to start making a Barolo Capalot from his own vines; and while the initial vintages were a little jammy and overripe in the style that was prevalent in those days, more recent vintages have shown a welcome easier-to-drink disposition.

Another good Barolo Capalot is made by the little-known, small, producer Cristian Boffa, who deserves your attention; after a lifetime devoted to selling bulk wine, the family-run winery (Cristian with Stefano and mother Marilena) began estate-bottling their wines (their first vintage is the 2015), following in the footsteps of his grandfather Giacomo Alessandria, owner of the Martinat estate (no longer in existence). Similarly, the Santamaria estate, owned by one of the many Viberti-named families of the Langhe and also slightly off the radar of most wine lovers out there, also bottles a Barolo Capalot (from vines that are planted at 330 meters above sea level). I have not had a chance to taste it recently, but certainly look forward to doing so shortly. Poderi Oddero of La Morra is another estate that owns vines in Capalot (they have since 2003; prior to that date, they rented the vineyards in Capalot); their holding is planted with Nebbiolo clones 423 and 415 on SO4 rootstock, a part of which are twenty-two years old and another part recently replanted and so not yet in production. It is Mariacristina Oddero's impression that Capalot's wines are fairly deep in colour, but fresh and vibrant, though perhaps less structured than some other La Morra vineyard districts. Up until now the family has preferred to blend the grapes along with those from other sites to make their Barolo classico because of Capalot's grapes tendency to impart welcome rich color and intense floral and fruity aromas to the final wine. However, as they are very happy with the results they have gotten from Capalot so far, Poderi Oddero looks to add a Barolo Capalot to the estate's portfolio of single-vineyard district Barolos in the next few years. Last but not least, from 2012 until 2017, Gianluca Roggero of the San Biagio estate rented 1.2 hectares of old vines to make a Barolo Capalot: fermentation took place in temperature-controlled stainless-steel tanks, and aging in barriques for about thirty months. He tells me that the wine always reminded him of very ripe red fruit and strong notes of violet and rose; in the mouth menthol and licorice (which I also find routinely in all Capalot wines: see APPENDIX D, *Table 4.5: Ian D'Agata's typical organoleptic descriptors of the Barolos of the vineyard districts*).

From 2012 until 2017, the outstanding Trediberri estate rented 1.2 hectares of Nebbiolo vines within the Capalot, planted at 300 to 350 meters above sea level. The vineyard was situated to the northeast of the La Morra village, spreading out in the direction towards the hamlet of Santa Maria and was planted in 1989 and 1997. Its eastern exposure featured soil containing sandstone rock and sedimentary marl with a noteworthy presence of silt. A point of interest is that because of Capalot's soil, and its cooler east/southeast exposure, many producers have always chosen to blend its grapes with those of the slightly warmer, generally south-facing Berri vineyard district. No surprise then that Trediberri did so too, choosing to make a classic Barolo but also a Langhe Nebbiolo with this blend of grapes. As an aside, not many people out there know that the talented Ciabot Berton estate made their 2002 and 2003 Nebbiolo wine (not a Barolo) entirely from Capalot grapes (they own vineyards in Capalot too); then with the 2004 vintage they blended in some grapes from the Bricco San Biagio.

Benchmark wineries/Reference point producers of Barolo Capalot: Alberto Burzi, Crissante Alessandria (the Barolo Capalot); Silvio Alessandria.

CAPPALLOTTO

Township	Serralunga d'Alba
Reference Map	See Map of Serralunga d'Alba MGAs (Ch. 10)
Size (ha) (Tot / Barolo MGA)	7.52 / 5.76
Production 2021 (hl)	301.38 (of which 101.05 hl of Barolo *MGA* Vigna)
Altitude	220 – 260 meters a.s.l. roughly
Exposure	From west to south
N. Claimants MGA	1
Other grape varieties planted:	
Land Units	Land Unit of Serralunga d'Alba
Soil (stage):	Serravallian

Producers claiming the MGA

Famiglia Lanzavecchia.

Wines

Villadoria – Famiglia Lanzavecchia - Barolo Sorì Paradiso

Ian's assessment of the vineyard district, its wines and its potential

Not to be confused with the La Morra vineyard district that goes by a very similar name, Capalot, the Cappallotto vineyard district is one of the westernmost vineyard districts of Serralunga. To its west there is the territory of the Castiglione Falletto commune and to its east the Baudana vineyard district. Cappallotto is a lower-lying vineyard area located on the western flank of the Serralunga ridge (see chapter 7, BAROLO TERROIR. Subchapter: The Barolo Communes). It's a curious vineyard district that can be divided essentially in two halves that look really like they could have been individually assigned to two separate vineyard districts altogether. For Cappallotto's extension is such that it closes off at the bottom two roughly parallel, short crests jutting out more or less perpendicularly to the main north-south Serralunga ridge. The northern crest, where the Meriame vineyard district is found, slopes down to the Sorì Paradiso: this is one half of Cappallotto. The more or less parallel crest to the south is where the Baudana vineyard district is situated (where the crest juts out from the main Serralunga ridge) and that slopes down towards what becomes the other half of Cappallotto.

Is there a difference between these two parts of Cappallotto [essentially that area beneath Baudana and the area beneath Meriame (the Sorì Paradiso)]? Honestly, I have no idea. All of Cappallotto's landscape is classified as a Land Unit of Serralunga, and the soil lithology there is the very classic (for the commune) Lequio Formation. These compacted sands and marls rich in limestone give Barolo's toughest Barolos when young, and that need plenty of cellaring; but whether there are differences between the two halves of Cappallotto (the exposures certainly vary), at least for the time being, I do not know, but I hope to look into this in the near future. It strikes me the potential is there to likely make what might be at the very least slightly different wines.

Cappallotto producers and the wines

Cappallotto takes its name from the collection of houses, a fraction of a fraction if you will, known as Cappallotto, which in turn took its name from that of a local family. The area is essentially a monopole of the Villadoria estate/Lanzavecchia family that bottle a Barolo called Sorì Paradiso with Nebbiolo from there, with which I honestly have very little experience; it seemed well-made the times I have tried it, but I need to try it on a more regular basis and develop more experience with it so as to gather a better idea of what this particular vineyard district can deliver.

Benchmark wineries/Reference point producers of Barolo Cappallotto: Villadoria.

CARPEGNA

Township	Serralunga d'Alba
Reference Map	See Map of Serralunga d'Alba MGAs (Ch. 10)
Size (ha) (Tot / Barolo MGA)	7,12 / 1.99
Production 2021 (hl)	101.37 (of which 19.04 hl of Barolo Riserva *MGA*)
Altitude	230 – 275 meters a.s.l. roughly
Exposure	From south to southwest plus a small part facing west and northwest.
N. Claimants MGA	3
Other grape varieties planted:	Dolcetto; Favorita; Moscato Bianco; white varieties
Land Units	Land Unit of Barolo
Soil (stage):	Tortonian

Producers claiming the MGA

Teresio Anselmo; Giuseppe Veglio; Vietti.

Wines

Cascina Bruni - Barolo Riserva Rivassotto, Barolo Carpegna, Barolo Marialunga; **Enrico Serafino** – Barolo Carpegna

Ian's assessment of the vineyard district, its wines and its potential

Carpegna is a good example of what has happened to Barolo in the last six to seven years or so. In this instance, I am referring to vineyard land prices that have skyrocketed as a consequence of Barolo's popularity having boomed. Carpegna, though well-thought of, is not one of Barolo's most famous vineyard districts (not by a long shot), and yet a producer recently told me that if he/she had wanted to buy a *giornata* of land there (a *giornata* is an old Piedmontese land measurement unit of about 0.37 hectares, or the amount of land that could be worked with an ox in one day, but do note the unit size changes ever so slightly in different parts of Piedmont) the asking price was 500,000 euros, which means roughly €1,500,000 a hectare. Which for an vineyard district of little fame, is, shall we say, an interesting request? Then again, if you don't ask, you can't get, so it's not like I or anybody else don't understand. Like the man says, nice work if you can get it; you know, prices like these really make one wish he or she had been lucky enough to be born in a family owning hectares and hectares, and more hectares, of Barolo vineyard land.

Carpegna is one of Serralunga's northernmost vineyard districts: it lies next to the Sorano vineyard district on the same slope. To the south and southeast of Carpegna, on another crest jutting out from the main Serralunga ridge, lies another vineyard district, Costabella (Cascina Bruni is an estate that owns vines there too, as well as in Carpegna). Carpegna's landscape unit is classified as a Land Unit of Barolo: not surprisingly, its soil lithology is that of the typical Saint Agatha Fossil Marls, and it is pretty well homogenous throughout the district. Therefore, for the most part, Carpegna's is a calcareous-sandy-loamy soil, with not much sand. This explains the less steely nature of the Barolos made in Carpegna, at least based on my tastings of Cascina Bruni's well-made wines.

Carpegna producers and the wines

Cascina Bruni is the winery most associated with Carpegna. Founded in 1897, it has a long history with this part of Serralunga and in fact the bottom part of the Carpegna slope was once called Bruni (locals still refer to it with that name, rather than Carpegna). While a number of producers own or farm vineyards in this vineyard district [for example, Enrico Serafino (same owner as Vietti) owns 1.93 hectares of south and southwest-facing vines in Carpegna planted in 1987 and 2001; but Terre del Barolo and Luigi Oddero also own vines in Carpegna] at the time of writing, Cascina Bruni is the only producer I know that bottles a Barolo Carpegna. It's a Barolo that is very slow to evolve when young and requires plenty of cellaring to open up and showcase what it has to offer, but those who like chiseled, linear wines will take a shining to its austere elegance.

Cascina Bruni is owned by one of the many Veglio-named families of the Barolo denomination. The ancestors of this Veglio family were originally from Castelletto Uzzone, fought for Napoleon, and bought the

La Favorita estate in Serralunga from the Mirafiori family, later renaming it Cascina Bruni. The estate is run today by Cristiano Maria Veglio, who also follows the vineyards along with Marco Balsimelli. He also makes the wines, and hold on to your hats as this will no doubt be a scoop for many (not all) those reading this book, he does so with the consulting help of none other than Eric Boissenot, the famous French winemaker who oversees winemaking at almost the totality of left bank *cru classés* of note, including the first growths. Previously, Cascina Bruni's consultant was Michel Rolland, so one can't help but think Gene Hackman have been proud (there's a French Connection part 1 and part 2 here). In fact, Veglio adores the wines of Bordeaux and has tasted there extensively over the years; this led him to plant some one thousand Cabernet Sauvignon vines on his property: so besides Barolo, he also makes both a *grand vin* and a *deuxième vin* with these vines. In all honesty, I'm not wild about Cabernet Sauvignon getting planted in Barolo, just as I wouldn't be too thrilled to see it planted in any *cru* of Vosne or Gevrey, but that's just my opinion and preference; and anyways, that's not for me to agree with or not, and it is what it is. Getting back to Nebbiolo, the whole of Cascina Bruni's holdings in Carpegna amount to four hectares and are subdivided into nine plots. The Nebbiolo vines were planted in 1944, 1951, 1958, 1968, 1970, and 1994. Cascina Bruni's link to Carpegna really do go a long way back: and just to keep the Bordeaux connection alive, would you believe me if I told you these plots have been in the family's hands since 1855? Yes, that's right: the year of the famous Bordeaux classification wanted by Emperor Napoleon III. There really is a French flair to this story, isn't there? Who knows, maybe we should just call the place one of Carpégna, Carpègna, or Carpêgna.

Benchmark wineries/Reference point producers of Barolo Carpegna: Cascina Bruni.

CASE NERE

Township	La Morra	
Reference Map	See Map of La Morra MGAs (Ch. 10)	
Size (ha) (Tot / Barolo MGA)	10.21 / 3.91	
Production 2021 (hl)	198.29	
Altitude	300 – 370 meters a.s.l. roughly	
Exposure	From east to south	
N. Claimants MGA	4	
Other grape varieties planted:	Barbera	
Land Units	Land Unit of La Morra	
Soil (stage):	Tortonian	

Producers claiming the MGA
Ca' d' Perulin; Enzo Boglietti; Soc. Agr. Fossati-La Morra-Barolo; Voerzio Roberto.
Wines
Enzo Boglietti - Barolo Case Nere; **Fratelli Casetta** - Barolo Case Nere

What the producers say
Enzo Boglietti: "We acquired this vineyard in 1992 and we have vinified it singly since 1993. It is a Barolo of good structure, with dense tannins of real size and depth".

Davide Voerzio (Roberto Voerzio): "We have vinified separately this cru since 2000. Barolo Case Nere resembles Brunate, but differently from the latter, it shows more of a dark fruit element and then a spicy note of tobacco".

Ian's assessment of the vineyard district, its wines and its potential
     Case Nere takes its name from *canere*, or "the houses that changed colour", because this was an area where furnaces and clay kilns ruled (this is a very good example of why I always want to learn about the history of

particular vineyard: because it is this sort of information that not only helps make wine an even more enjoyable experience than it already is, but also tells you right off the bat quite a bit about the area's soil and wines). In this case, ask yourself now why were there clay kilns here? Exactly.

One of the southernmost vineyard districts of the La Morra commune, Case Nere sits right at the border of the La Morra-Barolo commune territories sloping down from the Fossati and La Serra vineyard districts located just above it. In fact, Fossati, differently from Case Nere is an intercommunal vineyard district shared between the La Morra and Barolo communes, snakes right around Case Nere such that the part of Fossati belonging to the Barolo commune borders Case Nere to the south. Other noteworthy vineyard districts that are close by Case Nere include Sarmassa in Barolo and Cerequio in La Morra, all of which tells you that Case Nere is situated in some pretty prime Nebbiolo/Barolo vineyard territory. This observation is supported by the fact that over 90% of the vineyard district is planted to vineyards and that almost all of that is Nebbiolo. Case Nere's landscape is classified as a Land Unit of La Morra and the soil lithology is that of the Saint Agatha Fossil Marls of the laminated type. It is also true that Case Nere is as good an example as any of just how much the soil varies across Barolo's vineyard districts: for example, even though Case Nere is separated from Fossati by only a small ditch, the two wines could really not be any more different. Part of this is no doubt due to the complexity of Case Nere's limestone-clay-loamy soils, that range in color from white to reddish-yellow, implying very different mineral concentrations and total makeup. For the most part, Case Nere's wines are rounder than those of Fossati, with a mouthfeel that can, in warmer vintages, remind you of Barolos from Sarmassa or Cerequio, though more generally, and especially in cooler years, are rather more nervous and vibrant like the wines of Fossati and La Serra. The Barolos from these vineyard districts really are remarkably different wines: and this despite the vineyards really not being that far removed from each other. It is my experience that, when served similarly-made wines from each one of those these vineyard districts, most people, novices included, have no trouble recognizing the samples as different wines coming from different sites (even better, with a little bit of practice I have seen some of my wine students able to identify which Barolo is from Case Nere, which is from Cerequio and which is from Fossati; for reasons I'm not entirely clear on yet, the hardest to pinpoint and not confuse with the others has always seemed to be the La Serra, which given its tannic framework should really not be the case, but so be it.

Case Nere producers and the wines

Founded in 1986, the Roberto Voerzio estate has quickly surged to the upper echelons of Italian wine fame because of its extremely concentrated, very ripe Barolos that speak as much of blue and black fruit as they do of the Nebbiolo grape's more typical red fruit nuances. The pruning is done so that about 500 grams only of fruit is left on the vine (achieved by reducing the bunches to five per vine and later cutting off the bottom half of the already small bunch), compared to the up to two kilograms typical of some other wineries. Clearly, this leads to very small bunches and berries, as is plainly visible to anyone taking a stroll in Voerzio's vineyards. Beginning with the 2003 vintage, Voerzio blended the grapes of Case Nere with those of Fossati to make his Barolo Riserva Fossati Case Nere 10 Anni (not at all a bad idea, given the two sites give grapes with highly complementary characteristics). The wine was released for sale late, ten years after the vintage (spending twenty-four months in 30% new oak barriques, then seven in glass bottle). It's a big, impressive wine, very dark and brooding, made in the usual Roberto Voerzio style that has many admirers and that I think works especially well with this vineyard (in your humble scribe's opinion, perhaps more so than it does with Cerequio and Brunate). To the best of my knowledge, Voerzio was the first to bottle a Case Nere Barolo; in fact, I believe his Barolo 1999 Riserva was all Case Nere, though the label did not state this at the time. With the 2010, 2011, and 2012 vintages, Voerzio made a Barolo Riserva Case Nere 10 Anni only (no Fossati on the label) but since then he has made a Barolo Fossati (non-Riserva) without Case Nere also named on the label (and no Barolo labeled Case Nere, for that matter). Speaking of labels, the Barolo Case Nere in its various permutations (meaning with and without Fossati tagging along) boasted the completely unmistakable and by now classic Roberto Voerzio estate labels drawn by artist Riccardo Assom featuring stylized people occupied in different vineyard chores.

The Enzo Boglietti estate makes one of the most famous and best Barolo Case Nere wines of all; their vineyard in Case Nere is 1.1 hectares, faces southeast and is planted at an altitude of 350 meters. About 80% of the vines are roughly twenty years old, but 20% are over sixty years old. The soils are mostly silty-clay with still further pockets of clay, planted to Nebbiolo clones CVT 71, CVT141 and CVT CN 142. The estate's wines from this vineyard district are fairly large-shouldered, in my view the most monumental of the Barolos in their lineup, offering hints of ash and tar even at an early age and somewhat darker fruit than most other wines from other La Morra crus you are ever likely to taste. Most pointedly, it's the tannic structure of these wines that really stands out; most likely a result of the high clay content of the soil (the pockets of which help supply freshness). In some ways, Boglietti's Case Nere Barolo has more in common with the wines of the Barolo commune, and aren't very La Morra-like wines at all, but that maybe just be a mistaken impression on my part. No matter, it's a wonderful Barolo. If you wish to try another Barolo Case Nere, Fratelli Casetta make a traditionally-minded one from southwest-facing vines growing between 300 and 400 meters above sea level.

Benchmark wineries/Reference point producers of Barolo Case Nere: Enzo Boglietti. Also good: Roberto Voerzio (look for the 2010, 2011, 2012 vintages).

CASTAGNI

Township	La Morra
Reference Map	See Map of La Morra MGAs (Ch. 10)
Size (ha) (Tot / Barolo MGA)	64.51 / 4.59
Production 2021 (hl)	239.62 (of which 70.93 hl of Barolo Riserva *MGA*)
Altitude	370 – 455 meters a.s.l. roughly
Exposure	East on the slope facing Santa Maria, north and west in the remaining parts
N. Claimants MGA	6
Other grape varieties planted:	Barbera; Dolcetto; Pelaverga Piccolo; white varieties
Land Units	Land Unit of Verduno in the north-west side bordering San Giacomo and Neirane; Land Unit of La Morra in the north-east/east side bordering Rocche dell'Olmo and Roncaglie; Land Unit of Berri in remaining parts (central – south)
Soil (stage):	Messinian

Producers claiming the MGA

Cascina Cappellano; Erbaluna; La Bioca; Diego Morra; Reverdito; Alberto Voerzio.

Wines

Erbaluna - Barolo Castagni; **Reverdito** - Barolo Castagni; **Alberto Voerzio** - Barolo Castagni.

What the producers say

Michele Reverdito (Reverdito): "We own this vineyard since 2003 and immediately started its separate bottling, indicating the cru name on the label. Castagni offers a beautiful nose - fleshy, powerful and multi-faceted – showing notes of violet, herbs like laurel and mint, licorice, ripe cherry and raspberry. In the mouth, it broadens into a savory, juicy Barolo with supple tannins and good persistence."

Ian's assessment of the vineyard district, its wines and its potential

I have had a few Barolo Castagni wines over the years but I am by no means an expert on the vineyard district and what its wines are, or should be like. If for no other reason because there have never been too many wines made exclusively from Nebbiolo grapes grown within this vineyard district. However, things are more complicated than that.

The vineyard district is located in the northeastern reaches of the La Morra commune on the border with the Verduno township. From an aerial perspective and going by the cardinal points of the compass, the Rocche dell'Olmo and Neirane vineyard districts of Verduno border it to the northeast and northwest respectively; to the west there are the vineyard districts of San Giacomo and then Ascheri; to the east, there is the Roncaglie vineyard district (no vineyard districts border Castagni to the south). For sure, this location in the Barolo denomination tells you immediately a little bit about the wines made there because of the likely lithology of the area's soils (it's a specific lithology typical of the northeastern corner of the Barolo denomination that is typical of this part of the La Morra and of the Verduno territories and that is very different from the majority of the Barolo denomination. See chapter 7, BAROLO TERROIR). In fact, Castagni lies on the highest part of a hill that slopes down to the west above the Ascheri and San Giacomo vineyard districts, while to the east its lopes downwards before giving way to the Roncaglie vineyard district. These proximities are also broadcast by Castagni's soil lithology, the Cassano-Spinola Formation of the marly type that is exactly the same as that of Ascheri and San Giacomo (and of the aforementioned Neirane too), but different from that of Roncaglie.

But even with that bit of information, getting to know the wines of the area isn't made any easier because Castagni's geology is especially convoluted, a reality that becomes immediately clear when you realize that Castagni is classified as having not one, not two, but three different Land Unit landscapes (of Verduno, of Berri and of La Morra). And so, Castagni's slope gradients, exposures and altitudes can be quite varied; and its soil too, which while for the most part is of a clay-calcareous nature, also features patches of reddish-coloured clay soils that are very visible to the naked eye. These are mostly found on the slope above San Giacomo and Ascheri and in the wedge-like section of Castagni that is closest to the town of La Morra. Partly because of this, the wines made with grapes from this part of Castagni offer unique hints reminiscent of baked clay and scorched earth, and are the broadest (but not necessarily the most complex) of any of those made in the vineyard district, that generally feature a riper, rounder mouthfeel. By contrast, some of the calcareous-clay zones have veins of chalk running through them, and this may or may not account for just the slightest mineral hint that is apparent in wines made from these sections of Castagni (but in my experience, only in cooler vintages). These are also the Castagni Barolos that are lighter-styled and fresh, and might bring to mind those of Verduno's Neirane (and perhaps Rocche dell'Olmo vineyard districts.

Castagni producers and the wines

A couple of producers I have tried the wines of repeatedly over the years have been making Castagni-designated Barolos of note. Michele Reverdito's wine was first made in the 2004 vintage from vines planted at about 370 meters above sea level and facing west (the estate's website says 270 meters, but that must be a typo, given the altitude at which the vineyard district is located). Erbaluna's Barolo Castagni is made from vines situated around 370-400 meters above sea level and facing east. As the wines are not made in wildly different ways, the differences they convey at each sniff and taste have to do with the site more than anything else. Alberto Voerzio farms grapes in the Castagni vineyard district too (though his most famous holdings are the 1.16 hectares in La Serra and the 0.5 hectares in Fossati). He blends the Castagni grapes into his classic Barolo. By contrast, the Bel Colle estate chooses to plant Pelaverga Piccolo in Castagni with which to make its Verduno Pelaverga wine.

Benchmark wineries/Reference point producers of Barolo Castagni: Reverdito.

CASTELLERO

Township	Barolo
Reference Map	See Map of Barolo MGAs (Ch. 10)
Size (ha) (Tot / Barolo MGA)	13,07 / 5.75
Production 2021 (hl)	301.35
Altitude	220 – 270 meters a.s.l. roughly
Exposure	East on the slope facing Santa Maria; north and west in the remaining parts
N. Claimants MGA	6
Other grape varieties planted:	Barbera; Dolcetto; white varieties
Land Units	Land Unit of Barolo
Soil (stage):	Tortonian

Producers claiming the MGA

Barale Fratelli; Francesco Borgogno; Brezza; Giacomo Fenocchio; Marrone.

Wines

Fratelli Barale - Barolo Castellero; **Brezza** - Barolo Castellero; **Giacomo Fenocchio** - Barolo Castellero

What the producers say

Enzo Brezza: "The typical geologic formation that dominates here is that of the Diano Sandstone. For this reason, this vineyard district's soil is even sandier than that of Cannubi. In my opinion, it gives wines that have good structure but that need time to develop fully, as they usually lack balance when young; for this reason, I suggest to never touch a bottle until seven years after the vintage, especially in the good ones when the wines have even more structure".

Ian's assessment of the vineyard district, its wines and its potential

The vineyard district is located right across from Cannubi Boschis and Cannubi with the Vignane vineyard district immediately to its south and the Bussia vineyard district of Monforte to its east and southeast (this latter, very small, portion is the only part of Bussia that Castellero touches directly). Those are the vineyard districts that surround Castellero based on the four cardinal directions, and while it's good to know what's north and what's south of something, in the case of vineyards and vineyard districts it's good to also have an understanding of the actual topography of the area. Castellero is a vineyard district of the Barolo commune, but is situated right at the border of the Barolo and Monforte communes: it actually lies at the foot of the escarpment that rises upwards and on the two opposing flanks of which are located the Barolo vineyard districts of Vignane and Zuncai on one side and Bussia (or more precisely, the Bussia Sottana subregion) on the other (See BUSSIA file). So, if you were standing right in front of Castellero and looking up at it, Vignane is the vineyard area immediately above and to the right of Castellero (with Zuncai farther away in the background, past Vignane); Bussia Sottana is on the other flank. In fact, immediately to the left of where you are standing there is another ridge that runs more or less parallel to the one where Castellero is located on and that is also part of Bussia (in this case it's the Bussia subregion of Pugnane. See BUSSIA file). Castellero has a variable landscape and soil, but for the most part it is characterized by the Tortonian stage Saint Agatha Fossil Marls in their typical form. This tells us that the wines will have a generous mouthfeel and be readier to drink than wines made from grapes grown in Serralunga and most Monforte vineyards.

I find Castellero's Barolos to be usually quite perfumed and nicely fresh, but with good underlying structure: that's not surprising given what we know about Castellero's soil and its relatively high sand content. The wines don't perhaps stick out for one specific attribute, but are easy to like and drink. This lack of special levels of power, elegance or complexity is the reason why for the most part estates did not really make much single vineyard district wines from Castellero in the past, preferring to use the grapes to make a better, more balanced Barolo classico. Fair enough: the Barolos of Castellero are interesting in that even though the wines never slip into the tier of the best Barolos of any vintage, they are usually quite serviceable Barolos that don't cost an arm and a leg. Or to put it in other terms, these are wines that hit musical notes without ever reaching noteworthy, memorable crescendos, but that doesn't mean you didn't enjoy the sound you were hearing.

Castellero producers and the wines

For my money, the best wines from Castellero are those of Brezza, but those of Fratelli Barale and Giacomo Fenocchio are excellent too. Brezza's vines are roughly fifty years old, as they were planted in 1970 (how time flies: I remember that when I first sat down with Enzo to discuss the Castellero vineyard district at length for what was to later become this book, the vines were less than forty years old!). The south-facing vines are of Nebbiolo Lampia on Kober 5BB rootstock growing at about 300 meters of altitude on mostly sandy-loam/silt soils (to be precise: sand 40%, silt 33%, clay 27%). The wine lacks the structure of Brezza's Barolo from Sarmassa or the perfume of the one from Cannubi (Centrale), but has a gentler tannic texture than both, making for a charming, user-friendly Barolo that's remarkably easy to drink. Brezza's wines are very traditionally made, and so are those of the Fratelli Barale estate, that farms its Castellero vines organically (and use indigenous yeasts selected off the grapes in their own vineyard). The southwest-facing vines were planted in 1978 and 1991.

With his Villero, Claudio Fenocchio at Giacomo Fenocchio makes one of the greatest Barolos of all, but his Barolo Castellero is no slouch either. He first made it in the 2011 vintage (prior to this date, the Castellero grapes were included in the blend of grapes used for the Barolo classico), from a 0.4 hectares plot of roughly forty years old vines planted at 280 meters above sea level. Vinification involves long maceration and fermentation (forty days) and ageing for thirty-six months in large Slavonian oak barrels. Like all of Claudio Fenocchio's wines (Claudio runs the Giacomo Fenocchio estate: by the way, he makes a fantastic Freisa wine as well: don't miss it), his Barolo Castellero is a paragon of balance and thoroughly enjoyable. In ultimate analysis, just about any Barolo Castellero wine you'll buy ought to show well, given these are made by some of the denomination's most talented and dependable producers.

Benchmark wineries/Reference point producers of Barolo Castellero: Barale, Brezza, Giacomo Fenocchio.

CASTELLETTO

Township	Monforte d'Alba
Reference Map	See Map of Monforte d'Alba MGAs (Ch. 10)
Size (ha) (Tot / Barolo MGA)	128.52 / 22.59
Production 2021 (hl)	1,193.62 (of which 44.70 hl of Barolo Riserva *MGA*, 161.01 hl of Barolo *MGA* Vigna)
Altitude	260 – 490 meters a.s.l. roughly
Exposure	From south to southeast in the better exposed parcels, and west, east and north in the remaining parts.
N. Claimants MGA	11
Other grape varieties planted:	Barbera; Dolcetto; white varieties
Land Units	Land Unit of Castiglione in the west side; Land Unit of Serralunga in the north-east side; Land Unit of Barolo in the south-east side;
Soil (stage):	Tortonian and Serravallian

Producers claiming the MGA

Marziano Abbona; Castello di Perno; Conterno Fantino; Comm. G.B Burlotto; Fortemasso; Poderi Gianni Gagliardo; Raineri; Rocche dei Manzoni; Sara Vezza (Saffirio Josetta); Fratelli Seghesio; Mauro Veglio.

Wines

Marziano Abbona - Barolo Pressenda; **Comm. G.B. Burlotto** - Barolo Castelletto; **Castello di Perno** - Barolo Castelletto; **Cascina Chicco** - Barolo Rocche di Castelletto; **Conterno Fantino** - Barolo Castelletto Vigna Pressenda; **Fortemasso** - Barolo Castelletto; **Giovanni Manzone** - Barolo Castelletto; **Poderi Gianni Gagliardo** - Barolo Castelletto;

Raineri - Barolo Castelletto; **Rocche dei Manzoni** - Barolo Riserva 10 Anni Vigna Madonna Assunta La Villa (Castelletto); **Josetta Saffirio** - Barolo, Barolo Persiera (and Riserva), Barolo Riserva Millenovecento48; **Fratelli Seghesio**– Barolo La Villa; **Tenuta Due Corti** - Barolo Castelletto; **Mauro Veglio** - Barolo Castelletto;

What the producers say

Mauro Manzone (Manzone Giovanni): "We bought this back in the '60s and we decided to vinify it separately in 2004. In the glass, Castelletto reminds one of Barolo from Serralunga, because of its wines boast impressive structure and power."

Maurizio Rosso (Gigi Rosso): "Castelletto is characterized by calcareous soil, typical of crus of the Monforte township. It is a powerful and generous Barolo, uniting a voluminous body with notable tannic structure and the ethereal perfumes of preserved fruits, plants and spices. And its potential is better revealed with aging in bottle, developing hints of resin, leather and cocoa beans. Full-bodied, warm and intense, it leaves the palate invigoratingly dry and tannic with a note of tar on the long finish"

Rodolfo Migliorini (Rocche dei Manzoni): "A south to southeast-facing vineyard on clay-limestone soil tinged with bluish-grey marl gives well-structured wines of full body, intense color and fruity bouquet with notes of spices, red fruit and berry fruit. Similar to Santo Stefano, it was in the past a property of the Church – in fact, on the crest of this estate emerges a magnificent little chapel erected in 1500, making the surrounding landscape yet more fascinating and characteristic. Our Barolo Castelletto is made with grapes from the vineyard at Madonna Assunta La Villa in Castelletto, this is the youngest Barolo within our range of production. The first vintage was the 1999, and will be released on the market only in 2009. It is characterized by an extreme aromatic pleasantness and a wide variety of perfumes. The perfume is typical of a wine made with the Nebbiolo grape, spanning from red fruit to underbrush, from tobacco to chocolate, evolving in time. A compact Barolo, of infinite power, meanwhile maintaining a delicate balance. A finely textured and savory wine with the hallmark tannins of Serralunga more so than Monforte".

Mauro Veglio (Mauro Veglio): "We have been working with this vineyard since 1996. The wine is fresh on the nose with notes of ripe fruits (prunes and blueberries), licorice and aromatic herbs like eucalyptus. On the palate, it showcases evident tannin but also harmony confirming this is undeniably as a terroir of Monforte. Castelletto's wines definitely have the most muscle and structure of any of our single-vineyard district Barolos (especially compared to wines made in La Morra's Arborina and Gattera), even if it is somewhat mitigated by our winemaking style. When the wine first enters the market, it is forceful and more closed than the other vineyard districts we make wine from, but after the first year of release you can already appreciate its muscle and balance, and with time the wine exalts a forceful character while remaining fresh."

Ian's assessment of the vineyard district, its wines and its potential

Go figure: for a vineyard district that really doesn't have a lot of hectares planted to it, or even of Nebbiolo with which Barolos are made (for example, Stefano Gagliardo of the Gianni Gagliardo estate estimates that only about 36% of the modern-day Castelletto vineyard district is planted to vines, with 60% of that being Nebbiolo), there's certainly a lot of wines out there bearing the Castelletto vineyard district's name on the label. The fact that such a small portion of the vineyard district's over one hundred hectares are devoted to Nebbiolo for Barolo production would lead you to think that nobody ever thought much of the site's potential as far as great Barolo is concerned. But then you look at that long lineup of names making a Barolo Castelletto see Castelletto table above), and there's obviously many people who like the Barolos they make in Castelletto. Undoubtedly, the landscape and geology of Castelletto is varied enough that, different winemaking techniques employed by the producers aside, Castelletto does have the potential to make a range of Barolos boasting noteworthy diversity in their group.

Castelletto takes its name from an ancient small castle built in the area that no longer stands today. It is one of the last remaining "wild" areas of the Barolo denomination, boasting plenty of forested areas teeming with wildlife: sightings of hawks and wild boar are not rare in this area. Castelletto is located in the easternmost section of the Monforte commune with the vineyard districts of Perno to its north, Ginestra to its south, and Gramolere to its northwest. This position within the Monforte commune's territory tells you right away, broadly, what its wines are going to be like, because we know that, generally speaking, the southeastern portion of the Monforte territory makes some of the boldest, fleshiest, and most structured Barolos of all, and not just of Monforte. For example, to the east, Castelletto looks towards Serralunga and its territory; and for this reason, producers will often tell you Castelletto's wines resemble those of Serralunga. However, it's not so straightforward: Castelletto's landscape is a complex one, boasting (count'em!) not one, not two, but three different Land Units within its boundaries. That wealth of topographies, altitudes (from 260 to 490 meters above sea level), lithologies, exposures, and a whole lot more, also tells you there really are potentially very different styles to Castelletto's Barolos. Therefore, what the Barolos of Castelletto taste like really depends on exactly where within Castelletto's boundaries the Nebbiolo grapes grow. For instance, Giovanni Manzone makes some of the best Castelletto wines of all, but his is hardly a very powerful Barolo Castelletto: he makes what are some of the most elegant wines of the whole vineyard district (and as an important aside, I will also mention that it's a remarkably different wine from the Barolo he makes with his Gramolere grapes, the vines of which are not that distant from those he farms in Castelletto). But while Marziano Abbona's, Conterno Fantino's and Josetta Saffirio's wines are different from those of Manzone (if nothing else, they are more structured and powerful wines).

To better understand the different Barolos of Castelletto, it's good to begin by keeping in mind that the vineyard district is, like all those of Monforte, a large one. There are therefore noteworthy landscape differences within Castelletto's boundaries: its southeastern corner close to Ginestra is classified as a Land Unit of Barolo; the Land Unit of Serralunga characterizes the part of Castelletto towards Perno; and moving westwards in the vineyard district, towards the Bussia and the Novello communes, the landscape turns to the Land Unit of Castiglione. Therefore, the topography, lithology, exposures and altitudes vary greatly within Castelletto (and consequently, so will the wines from each of the various Castelletto subregions).

Castelletto's subregions

Castelletto, like practically all of Monforte's rather large vineyard districts, can be divided into three subregions: Castelletto-proper, Pressenda and La Villa. These are names of historical relevance and importance, and a relatively logical and acceptable case can be made that they should have remained officially in use. However, when the official names of the vineyard districts were drawn up back in 2010, like elsewhere in Monforte it was decided to conglobate them all under one name, in this case "Castelletto". Which is fine enough (after all, it's not as if some wines from Castelletto boast Syrah-like structure and others remind one of Gamay-like lightness: all the Castelletto Barolos share some features in common); but in my humble view, the topographical and geological variations throughout the extended Castelletto vineyard district of today are such that the Barolos made with grapes grown there cannot help but differ from each other. After all, Vosne-Romanée boasts a bevy of *premier crus* such as for example Les Suchots, Les Beaux Monts, Aux (Les) Brulées, and Les Chaumes, all of which are relatively close to one another and each gives a distinct wine, so it cannot surprise that the same might also apply to the Monforte commune's wines. And of Castelletto in particular, given this vineyard district's large size coupled with its topographical and geological diversity.

Of the three Castelletto subregions, Castelletto (or Castelletto-proper) and Pressenda are located in the northern part of the modern-day Castelletto vineyard district, just below Monforte's Perno vineyard district; Pressenda is sandwiched in between two halves of Castelletto-proper. One can therefore make the case that the Castelletto-proper vineyard area should be further subdivided in a western and an eastern Castelletto, with Pressenda in the middle. This might sound like I am getting a little granular but in fact, all these subregions have specific altitudes, geologies and topographies, as hinted at by the three different Land Units that Castelletto is characterized by. Castelletto's third subregion, La Villa, is instead located in the southern part of the official, extended, Castelletto vineyard district, down close by Monforte's Ginestra vineyard district that borders Castelletto immediately to the south.

From a topographical perspective, today's large Castelletto vineyard district slopes down towards the east, such that its highest vineyards are in the center of the vineyard district and to the west, while those lower down are those closer to the border with the Serralunga territory. Lithology-wise, Castelletto once again showcases noteworthy diversity: the Lequio Formation dominates especially up towards Perno, areas of Diano Sandstone are found especially in the vineyard district's higher reaches and also to the west (in the western Castelletto-proper subregion) and the Saint Agatha Fossil Marls in their most typical form prevail down to the south, by Ginestra. It follows that soil texture also differs throughout the Castelletto vineyard district, being looser in Castelletto's southeastern corner closer to Ginestra, while it's a great deal more compact up towards Perno (not at surprising, given that there's mostly a Lequio Formation lithology there), and falls somewhere in between these two extremes westwards in the vineyard district, towards Bussia and the Novello commune. Clearly then, soil-wise, the official Castelletto vineyard district as we know it today is not homogenous. For the most part, I can generalize by saying that Castelletto up to about 360 meters above sea level is essentially characterized by rather pure marl or close to it, while above that altitude and right up to the summit, Castelletto becomes an extremely sandy site. It follows that the Nebbiolo grapes grown at Castelletto's different altitudes will give very different wines based not just on climate factors related to altitude but also to soil composition (all other things being equal).

Pressenda is the most famous subregion of the Castelletto vineyard district: historically, locals have always believed it to be the qualitative heart of the Castelletto vineyard district. Part of the reason for this is the fact it's an area where the transition occurs between the sandier soils (of Diano Sandstone lithology) of the higher reaches and the more compact Lequio Formation and Saint Agatha Fossil marls lower down. This soil transition potentially allows for more complex wines to be made. Pressenda is an also area of Castelletto's where marine fossils are commonly found in the vineyards, something that is not true of the entire, extended, modern-day Castelletto vineyard district.

The western and the eastern sections of Castelletto-proper are not quite as historically famous as those of Pressenda but present geographical features that allow us to infer that the likelihood of making wines that differ not just between each other but also the rest of the extended vineyard district is likely. The western Castelletto-proper is generally characterized by looser-textured soil and Diano Sandstone, while the eastern Castelletto-proper has the more compact soil of the Lequio Formation. The Barolos from these two subregions of Castelletto tend to be some of the biggest and most tannic of the whole vineyard district.

The La Villa subregion is essentially draped over a hillside ridge that runs more or less in an east-west direction: the flank that looks south and towards Ginestra is the one planted mostly to Nebbiolo for Barolo production. Even though it's south-facing, La Villa is characterized by a generally cooler mesoclimate. The subregion takes its name from the hamlet of La Villa, a group of houses located at the center of the subregion. Generally speaking, La Villa is an area with plenty of marl in the soil (the southernmost part of La Villa closer down to Ginestra boasts Saint Agatha Fossil Marls lithology) with loam and clay, but where there is, as usual, an increased presence of sand higher up. It follows that more so than with the wines of the other two northern subregions of Castelletto-proper and Pressenda, the Barolos of La Villa can vary in their textural and organoleptic profiles. Depending of where the Nebbiolo grapes grow in La Villa, Barolos can be either of a paler red colour and endowed with a sharp acid bite and less texture (compared to wines from other sections of La Villa and the other two subregions) or quite tannic and muscular (especially those closest to the Serralunga border and more north, that is farther away from Ginestra).

For the most part, I find Castelletto's Barolos to be very good to excellent Barolos, the majority of which are muscular but also have a vertical profile, thanks to a coolish mesoclimate. Though the Barolo Castelletto is rarely the best Barolo in any producer's lineup of Barolos, the producers who do make Barolo Castelletto wines are amongst the most talented and dependable in the whole denomination. Which in turn means that wine lovers out there have an embarrassment of riches to choose from.

Castelletto producers and the wines

Various Barolo estates own Nebbiolo vineyards in today's Castelletto. Breaking down the producers by whom owns what and where (that is, in which Castelletto subregion), I can summarize holdings more or less so:

Eastern Castelletto-proper: Castello di Perno, Fortemasso, Josetta Saffirio, Marziano Abbona, Terre del Barolo

Western Castelletto-proper: Fortemasso, Giovanni Manzone, Josetta Saffirio, Raineri, Mauro Veglio

Pressenda: Castello di Perno, Conterno Fantino, Fortemasso, Josetta Saffirio, Marziano Abbona, Quinto Chionetti

La Villa: Cascina Chicco, Conterno Fantino, Gianni Gagliardo, Rocche dei Manzoni, Seghesio, Mauro Veglio

One estate that makes a slew of superb Barolos is Conterno Fantino, and it makes a Castelletto Pressenda wine (called Barolo Castelletto Vigna Pressenda). Not unreasonably, they choose to highlight the Pressenda origin of their grapes on the label, given that Pressenda has always been thought of as the area from where the best Castelletto Barolos are made (Conterno Fantino also farms a small vineyard in the La Villa section of

Castelletto). Conterno Fantino's Nebbiolo vines are about 55 to 60 years old: clearly, that venerable vine age might have something (a lot, rather) to do with this Barolo's exceptional suave texture and depth of flavor. Without doubt, it is classic Castelletto in its delivery of broad, ample aromas and flavors, but at the same time - and this is what sets it above most Castelletto Barolos made- it is one of the most elegant versions of Castelletto Barolo out there today. This wine's balance makes one understand why Pressenda is so highly thought of.

The other estate famously associated with the Pressenda portion of Castelletto is Marziano Abbona. The estate first made its Barolo Castelletto in the 1998 vintage. Abbona's Castelletto's holdings are 3.8 hectares large: the east-facing vines are more than forty years old and, are planted between 260 and 370 meters above sea level. They are situated at the interface of the change from Lequio Formation to Diano Sandstone, such that here pure marl is rarer than in the rest of the vineyard district's soils (soil composition analysis there shows 50% sand, 30% loam and 20% clay). However, studying the specific granulometry of the area shows that sand-like particles are not as prevalent as those percentages imply. The wine has an organoleptic profile that is very similar to that of the Barolo Castelletto from Conterno Fantino, boasting very good acid-fruit-tannin balance and Castelletto-typical nuances of red cherry, tobacco and menthol.

A slightly different Barolo Castelletto from those of Conterno Fantino and Marziano Abbona is that made by the Josetta Saffirio estate; this is partly dependent on the fact that more than the other estates mentioned, Saffirio owns vineyards throughout the vineyard district, at different altitudes and on a mix of different soils. Her wines therefore reflect these topographical, altitude and geological realities, and probably more than anybody else's embody what today's Castelletto vineyard district's Barolo is about (but more dark in hue than I am used to in some past vintages). Compared to Pressenda and the portions of Castelletto located at even higher altitudes, in this lower-lying area I have always known the marl content increases while the sandy component decreases, though Sara Vezza, Josetta Saffirio's daughter, has told me in the past that the percentages of loam/silt, sand, and clay are about equal. The wine has undoubtedly a thicker texture and more fruity flesh than the more vertical wines made by Conterno Fantino and Marziano Abbona. All are smashingly good Barolos, so which you will prefer is essentially a matter of individual taste preferences.

Speaking of which, for my taste (and money), the Castelletto Barolo of Giovani Manzone is one of the best, but it's a totally different wine from those made by, for example, Conterno Fantino, Marziano Abbona and Josetta Saffirio. Manzone's Barolo Castelletto is typical of the western sector of Castelletto-proper, and so it's not by chance it is so different from the others. Manzone first made a Castelletto Barolo with the 2004 vintage, when his Nebbiolo vines there were only about four-five years old (the vines had been replanted starting in 1999). His vineyards are located at some of the highest altitudes of the vineyard district (450 meters above sea level), in a sandy-calcareous site with veins of marly-clay and limestone, but where sand dominates (with a Diano Sandstone lithology that is not common in Pressenda and other parts of Castelletto. That much remains true even if you know (well, now you do) that Manzone owns twenty-three different parcels of vines situated on very different soils, some very sandy, some less sandy, and some that have much more clay. It is the vineyard area the Giovanni Manzone family is historically most associated with, vineyards that have been inherited generation after generation from Stefano, the great-grandfather of the current owner. The roughly one hectare of east/southeast-facing vines are planted on a very steep slope give a very austere refined, perfumed and pale coloured Barolo that is absolutely magical in the balanced, refined taste experience it delivers. As an aside, it might interest readers to know that it is in the western portion of the Castelletto vineyard that Manzone planted one plot of vines of his rare vines of Rossese Bianco, a native grape of the Langhe just like Nascetta is (don't confuse this Rossese Bianco grape with that of Liguria: the two wine grapes, though they are both called Rossese Bianco, are not one and the same). A second plot of Rossese Bianco is located in the Gramolere vineyard district and the grapes blended with those of the other single vineyard. The wine is named Rosserto and is just delightful, so I urge you to look for it and to give it a try, for you won't be disappointed (it's a lemony but relatively full-bodied wine, something like what a mix of Sauvignon Blanc and Chardonnay might taste like). Rossese Bianco is a native grape variety that had been completely forgotten until Manzone, rightly in my books, decided that such a state of affairs was a pity.

Estates that make Barolo Castelletto wines that speak of the La Villa subregion include Rocche dei Manzoni and Gianni Gagliardo. Rocche dei Manzoni's Barolo Castelletto is one of the more famous expressions of this vineyard district. A chapel dating back to the 1500s still stands in the area, and for this reason, the Rocche dei Manzoni's Barolo Riserva Castelletto is called Madonna Assunta La Villa. It is released after ten years of aging in a bottle sporting a totally different label from the rest of the estate's wines. The wine was first made with the 1999 vintage from south/southeast-facing vines in an area that has typical Saint Agatha Fossil Marls formation blue-grey marls along with some sand and limestone. It is big, tannic wine but is not devoid of grace and refinement. Gianni Gagliardo's Barolo Castelletto is made from a fully east-facing vineyard site 1.72 hectares large, located at about 260 meters above sea level; it is therefore an example of a Castelletto Barolo born from the lower reaches of the vineyard district, where, as I mentioned earlier, loam and clay tend to dominate. Not surprisingly then, the soil composition of Gagliardo's holding is 55.3% loam, 22.5% clay and 22.2% sand. However, despite its low altitude reality, Gagliardo's steep site is also a rather cool one, and this translates into the wine. The vineyard was planted with Nebbiolo clones 142, 230 and a special selection of old Nebbiolo Michet. The wine shows very good acid-sugar-tannin balance and while big and chunky and closed in its youth opens up with proper cellaring to deliver aromas and flavors of ripe red cherry, menthol and/or eucalyptus (depending on the whether the growing season was relatively cooler or warmer) and a delicately smoky mineral nuance; it offers a good, solid, medium-bodied Barolo drinking experience.

Perhaps many readers who are big fans of the G.B. Burlotto estate in Verduno and its magnificent Monvigliero Barolo are not aware that the estate is now making a Barolo Castelletto (beginning with the 2018 vintage). The G.B. Burlotto Castelletto parcel is 1.07 hectares large, and has east/southeast-facing vines planted between 270 and 300 meters of altitude. It is a vineyard plot that used to belong to the ancient Cascina della Ciornia, planted next to vineyards of the Castello di Perno; in other words, these vines are just immediately outside of the Pressenda subregion in the eastern Castelletto-proper. The soil lithology there is that of the Lequio formation, so highly typical of Serralunga, but before you get carried away and jump immediately to the conclusion that it will be an example of the big and bold style of Castelletto Barolos, keep in mind that winemaker Fabio Alessandria plans, for the moment at least, to make the wine by using only the grapes from the vines planted back in 1973 on the vineyard's uppermost slope (where there is more sand).

Mauro Veglio is another non-Monforte producer making a Barolo Castelletto (the Veglio winery is in La Morra). Not surprisingly, Alessandro Veglio of Mauro Veglio says that the Castelletto Barolo offers the most structure and tannins in the estate's range of Barolo wines, a large single vineyard of four hectares, divided into four different plots. The highest is almost 400 meters in altitude, and as we have been saying all along, he confirms that it is the sandiest of the four and the one that gives the brightest, highest acid Barolos of all those he makes from their plots in Castelletto.

Benchmark wineries/Reference point producers of Barolo Castelletto:

Pressenda: Conterno Fantino, Marziano Abbona; Western Castelletto-proper: Giovanni Manzone; Eastern Castelletto-proper: G.B.Burlotto; Castelletto (blend of subregions): Fortemasso, Josetta Saffirio; La Villa: Gianni Gagliardo, Rocche dei Manzoni.

CASTELLO

Township	Grinzane Cavour
Reference Map	See Map of Grinzane Cavour MGAs (Ch. 10)
Size (ha) (Tot / Barolo MGA)	7.1 / 1.21
Production 2021 (hl)	60.15
Altitude	220 – 260 meters a.s.l. roughly
Exposure	From east to southwest.
N. Claimants MGA	2
Other grape varieties planted:	Barbera; Dolcetto; Pelaverga Piccolo
Land Units	Land Unit of Barolo
Soil (stage):	Tortonian

Producers claiming the MGA

Scuola Enologica Alba; Mario Scavino.

Wines

Arnaldo Rivera - Barolo Castello; **Scuola Enologica Alba** - Barolo Castello;

What the producers say

Stefano Pesci (Arnaldo Rivera -Terre del Barolo): "Castello is in Grinzane Cavour and our vineyard there has the full range of southern exposures, as it looks southeast/south/southwest. We believe it gives rise to a very perfumed, balanced Barolo. The vines were originally planted under the stewardship of Camillo Benso, Count of Cavour, and was recently replanted in 2002. It's a rather dark fruit-endowed Barolo, with plenty of spices and isn't really like any other Barolo we make".

Ian's assessment of the vineyard district, its wines and its potential

I don't know how many of my readers are aware that the Umberto I Enology school of Alba, that forms the local viticulturists and winemakers of the future, is also one of the grower-members of the Terre del Barolo cooperative. Following the creation of the Arnaldo Rivera project in 2013, it was decided to have a Barolo from the Castello vineyard district as one of the single-vineyard district bottlings in the Arnaldo Rivera portfolio along with other very prestigious sites, including Bussia and Cannubi (from where the cooperative also makes single-vineyard district Barolos). The cooperative's Barolo Castello is made from a small 0.5 hectares plot at about 250 meters above sea level on the southwestern-facing slope of the larger vineyard area. Being situated at such a low altitude in a valley-like setting and close to the Talloria stream basin means on the one hand very good diurnal temperature shifts, but on the other that adverse weather events are not uncommon, such as frost episodes. Summers in Castello are hot and humid, but the soil has enough soil water retention capacity for the vineyards not to suffer in years marked by drought.

The Castello vineyard district is located below the castle of Grinzane Cavour and is bordered by only one other vineyard district, Gustava, which is to its east. The soil dates back to 10 million years as it was formed during the Tortonian stage of the Miocene epoch; it's lithology is that of the typical form of Saint Agatha Fossil Marls, that some experts also refer to as Gallo d'Alba Marls (*Marne di Gallo d'Alba*). These are layers of fairly uniform thickness with very little sand present in between the layers but with a strong presence of fossils down deep (hence the word "fossil" in the lithological formation's name). Given that that Castello's slope is not too steep, erosion has never been much of a problem there, hence the colour of the soil that is reddish-brown, due to the presence of iron and manganese oxide and not much limestone, as well as a great deal of loam washed down by the Talloria stream (this ages ago, when the water used to flow at a much higher elevation than it does today). Castello's is one of the more atypical, unique soils of the Barolo denomination: more fertile than others within Barolo's boundaries, the little or no sand present makes for a very compact, packed soil, that helps give a different expression of Nebbiolo.

Castello producers and the wines

Though I know wine lovers often look at cooperative wines with a little suspicion, the Arnaldo Rivera Barolo Castello is excellent (as are in fact all the Barolos in their lineup of single-site vineyard district Barolos). The many Barolos in the Arnaldo Rivera project allow wine lovers to compare similarly-made wines from different vineyard districts, permitting real insight as to what each vineyard district can give and what its wines are all about. The Barolo Castello has a gentler texture than that of Barolos from other communes but that is very typical of the lighter-bodied Barolos of most of the Grinzane Cavour vineyard districts. The aromas and flavors are of ripe red fruit with a hint of sweet spices; while not especially deep or concentrated, they are very precise and boast a very appealing softness and accessibility. It all adds up to a lovely Barolo that will be ready to drink earlier while your other Arnaldo Rivera Barolos from Bussia or Vignarionda age in the cellar.

Benchmark wineries/Reference point producers of Barolo Castello: Arnaldo Rivera (Terre del Barolo).

CEREQUIO

Township	La Morra and Barolo
Reference Map	See Maps of Barolo MGAs and La Morra MGAs (Ch. 10)
Size (ha) (Tot / Barolo MGA)	6.4 (Barolo) + 17.7 (La Morra) / 13.76
Production 2021 (hl)	629.41
Altitude	270 – 400 meters a.s.l. roughly
Exposure	From east to northeast for the parcels facing Brunate, and from south to southeast on the opposite side.
N. Claimants MGA	8
Other grape varieties planted:	Barbera; Dolcetto
Land Units	Land Unit of La Morra
Soil (stage):	Tortonian

Producers claiming the MGA

Batasiolo; Claudio Boglietti; Boroli; Giuseppe Contratto; Damilano; Chiarlo; Flavio Saglietti; Vietti; Voerzio Martini; Roberto Voerzio.

Wines

Batasiolo - Barolo Cerequio; **Boroli** - Barolo Cerequio; **Chiarlo** - Barolo Cerequio; **Damilano** - Barolo Cerequio; **Flavio Saglietti** - Barolo Cerequio; **Vietti** - Barolo Cerequio; **VoerzioMartini** - Barolo Cerequio; **Roberto Voerzio** - Barolo Cerequio; **Gaja** – Barolo Conteisa

What the producers say

Stefano Chiarlo (Michele Chiarlo): "We can trace our association with this vineyard back to 1985: we first made a Barolo solely from it in the 1988 vintage. Our Barolo Cerequio is made only in excellent years: it is a Barolo of generous perfume, rich and poised with a memorable, delicate presence of fine tannins".

Davide Voerzio (Roberto Voerzio): "We vinify this *cru* as a distinct Barolo since 1987. Our Cerequio is an elegant Barolo with fine and round tannins, similar to those of the Pinot Noir wines of Burgundy."

Achille Boroli (Boroli): "Cerequio is an historic cru that was classified already more than a century ago as a first category quality site, as the "best of the best", or *sceltissima*. Our vines are planted at 300 meters above sea level with a south/southeast exposure. Complex and deep there is a strong note of red fruit and licorice in our wine".

Ian's assessment of the vineyard district, its wines and its potential

It is a well-known fact that Cerequio was once thought to be the best vineyard of all Barolo: it was defined as "sceltissimo" in Lorenzo Fantini's 1880 monography on Barolo in which all the best sites were listed only as "scelto". It was also qualified as a top-quality site of absolute prestige in Renato Ratti's *Carta del Barolo)*. That much recognized, whether such a lofty status was mostly consequent to Cerequio having a very warm microclimate (and actually rather hot nowadays) that allowed grapes there to ripen fully in an age when climate change was nowhere in sight, or whether it was due to any other intrinsic merits is not entirely clear. As mentioned previously in this book (see chapter. 7, BAROLO TERROIR) and elsewhere (D'Agata, 2019), historically the best vineyard areas in Barolo were those where the snow melted first, indicating a higher average temperature than that of vineyards where, at the same time of the year, the snow had not yet melted. In this light, Cerequio's nickname of "the riviera of the Langhe" is more than apt: but times change, and in this day and age there are years in which parts of Cerequio are just too hot, at least in terms of its fine winemaking potential (other famous Barolo vineyard areas, such as for example Brunate, are now having the same problem). You might say "how time changes", not just climate change(s). However, it is important to know that there are different slopes and exposures in Cerequio, and so there still exist plenty of exceptional areas within this vineyard district in which to grow Nebbiolo grapes of the highest quality.

Cerequio is located in the La Morra commune but a small part of it spills over into Barolo making it, like Brunate, a rare inter-communal vineyard district. In fact, only a very, very small part is in the Barolo commune's territory, because more than 97% of Cerequio is within the boundaries of La Morra. However, this datum needs to be analyzed and interpreted carefully. While it is true that virtually all of Cerequio falls within the territory of the La Morra commune, the Barolo's commune share of Cerequio vineyards is much higher. This is because roughly one quarter of all the Cerequio area under vine is actually in the territory of the Barolo commune (in other words, of Cerequio's land under vine, roughly 75% falls within La Morra and 25% in Barolo (so you might say that aforementioned 3% carries a lot of weight).

Cerequio is completely surrounded by other vineyard districts (some very famous) in the territories of both La Morra and Barolo. In the La Morra commune, Cerequio is next to the vineyard districts of Brunate to the north; La Serra to the northwest; and Case Nere to the west. In the Barolo commune's territory, the vineyard districts close to it are Sarmassa to the south, Bergeisa to the southeast, and Zonchetta to the east. Cerequio's landscape is that of the Land Unit of La Morra and its soil lithology is mostly Saint Agatha Fossil Marls in their laminated form (mostly blue-grey marls rich in manganese and magnesium of the Tortonian stage). Clearly, the loam and clay dominate in Cerequio (something that is readily apparent when you taste its wines): for example, compared to Cannubi, Cerequio has almost a third less sand based on my soil composition databank (soil sand content range: as low as 17% for Cerequio and as high as 47% for the extended Cannubi vineyard district).

However, it's not all just about the soil, though it certainly characterizes Cerequio's wines. For a vineyard district that is not an especially big one, and is therefore more homogenous in its overall lay of the land and geology than many others, Cerequio boasts quite a bit of topographical and climate diversity nonetheless. Cerequio's vineyard extension can be essentially divided in two flanks. The flank that looks towards Brunate is the cooler of the two, and historically the less favored for Nebbiolo production (it is also somewhat prone to hail, at least it is in this epoch of climate change). The opposite flank, the one looking out towards Case Nere, is mostly south-facing and much warmer (olive trees, a rare sight in the Langhe, can actually grow here, which tells you all you need to know about how warm parts of Cerequio really are).

It is worth knowing that the estates that farm and/or own vineyards in Cerequio are more or less equally divided between the Barolo and the La Morra commune. Roberto Voerzio and Gaja either farm or own the majority of vines in the La Morra section of Cerequio (Damilano and Flavio Saglietti also have small holdings in this section of Cerequio). Chiarlo and Batasiolo have vineyards on both sides of the La Morra-Barolo divide, while Boroli, Giacomo Marengo, Vietti and VoerzioMartini own vineyards on the Barolo side only. In practical terms, what all this means is that when you drink a Barolo Cerequio from Damilano, Gaja, Saglietti and Roberto Voerzio you ought to be tasting the Cerequio of La Morra, when you drink the one by Boroli, Vietti and Giacomo Marengo you are confronted with the Cerequio of Barolo, and when you taste Chiarlo and Batasiolo you are getting a mix of the two. Clear enough.

Producer viticultural and winemaking choices aside, deciding if Cerequio Barolos show differences based on those diverse grape origins is a fun exercise. For the most part, Cerequio's Barolos offer superripe red cherry and red berry notes in spades, and are especially characterized by notes of eucalyptus, which is a defining characteristic of Cerequio's Barolos (eucalyptus: not mint, not menthol, not balsamic oils: while eucalyptus in

Barolos from other vineyard districts is almost always associated to the type of oak used, rather than that specific vineyard district's habitat, it appears to be a real distinguishing trait of Cerequio's wines). Clearly, the eucalyptus presence is at times coupled with notes of mint, an event more common in wines made from grapes sourced in the coolest parts of the Cerequio vineyard area. And though I don't mean to beat this thing to death, but out of the respect and gratitude to the many producers who spent hours of their time explaining this to me over the years, as well as the hours I have put in comparing all the different minty nuances of Barolos from different communes (such as those of Monforte), please note that even the mint descriptor of Cerequio wines is very different from the mint characterizing other vineyard districts such as La Morra's Conca (see Appendix D, *Table 4.5: Ian D'Agata's typical organoleptic descriptors of the Barolos of the vineyard districts*). In any case, I have had enough Barolo Cerequios over the years and across different vintage types to know that the note of eucalyptus is unfailingly present in this vineyard district's wines, and that goes for those made in both communal sections of Cerequio.

Cerequio producers and the wines

Given this vineyard district's small size, there are not many estates bottling a Barolo Cerequio; some of those that own vines there use the grapes to make an estate Barolo rather than bottle a single-vineyard district Barolo. All the wines are very good and some excellent; along with offering that eucalyptus note, all are fairly large-shouldered, tactile and broad, with ripe red fruit aromas and flavors complicated by savory nuances and quite a bit of tannic heft for a wine from la Morra (this is typical of Brunate too, and of all the Barolos from this specific section of the La Morra territory).

The Chiarlo estate is perhaps the one most associated with Cerequio today, both because if its well-known Barolo Cerequio and because of their beautiful Palás Cerequio, a five-star hotel and restaurant nestled among Cerequio's vines. Michele and Stefano Chiarlo farm nine south/southwest-facing hectares in Cerequio planted at about 320 meters above sea level; six hectares were bought in 1988 from an estate that had been farming the site uninterruptedly for over two hundred years. In the best vintages, the grapes from the oldest 0.9 hectares, planted in 1972, are used to make the Barolo Riserva Cerequio. Boroli farms 1.3 hectares in Cerequio of roughly 30 years old vines planted at about 300 meters above sea level. Roberto Voerzio makes a Barolo Cerequio since 1988, and it's one of his most accomplished wines.

Gaja bought his Cerequio holdings in 1995 when he acquired the Marengo e Marenda estate. He released his first Barolo from Cerequio in that vintage, renaming the wine Conteisa Cerequio in the process (and later abbreviated to Conteisa only). The nine and a half hectares face south and are located, according to Gaia Gaja, at an average altitude of 400-430 meters above the sea level. The soil composition there is 49.8% loam, 33.2% clay and 17% sand. Of the nine and a half hectares, four are used to make the single-vineyard district Barolo now called Conteisa, while the other five and a half are used to make the Barolo Dagromis, a blend of Nebbiolo grapes from different site including for example Serralunga's Rivette vineyard district. The oldest vines reach 65 years of age and there is a very high percentage of Nebbiolo Rosé (that is used both for the Conteisa bottling and especially in the Dagromis). Overall, the Conteisa is a Barolo that is not just Cerequio-like, but I would say very La Morra-like too. And excellent, of course. In fact, and I know I digress, but I wish to point out that the old vintages of the Marengo e Marenda estate were excellent, wines that brikliantly showcase just how good traditionally made Barolos could be when made by competent individuals. The winemaker of the estate was Marco Ferrero, and to his credit, he made a series of wonderful Barolos from Cerequio that I remember well and with real joy: the 1971, 1978, 1985 and 1989 were spectacular wines, while the 1990 was a little less thrilling. In fact, Gaja rebottled (with a new, very colorful and modernist-looking label) the wines from previous vintages (starting from 1990, if I remember correctly) that were still left in the cellar at the time of the sale: I remember those wines well because they didn't cost an arm and a leg and gave wine lovers like me a chance to drink relatively older Barolos at a welcomingly inviting price. I bought a slew of those bottles, and not just in Italy, but the U.S.A too and generally really loved drinking them. So keep in mind that for a while there were Barolos from the same vintage (for example 1991 and 1992 for sure, and I think 1990 too) that had been previously released with the original Marengo and Marenda label, so with some luck you can find the same wine bottled with two different labels (the original Marengo e Marenda and Gaja's new one). Any such wine you do find from those years is best drunk up, as they are now on their descending slope of enjoyment: but they're still lovely (only the well-cellared examples, clearly) that offer a nostalgic glimpse back into Barolo as it once used to be. A never nice way to be, I would like to add.

Last but not least, the latest to acquire land in Cerequio has been the Vietti winery. Their plot is one hectare large, planted to 35 years old Nebbiolo vines at about 350 meters above sea level, in the Barolo commune. Vietti's first Barolo Cerequio was made in the 2018 vintage, aged thirty-two months in mix of barriques and larger oak barrels. An inaugural release of only 4925 bottles, Vietti's Cerequio is one of the better 2018 Barolos, showcasing lovely, precise sour red cherry aromas and flavours complicated by menthol, licorice and violet.

Benchmark wineries/Reference point producers of Barolo Cerequio: Boroli, Chiarlo, Gaja (called Conteisa: formerly labeled as Conteisa Cerequio Gromis), Roberto Voerzio.

CERRATI

Township	Serralunga d'Alba
Reference Map	See Map of Serralunga d'Alba MGAs (Ch. 10)
Size (ha) (Tot / Barolo MGA)	12.96 / 2.17
Production 2021 (hl)	46.78 (of which 44.70 hl of Barolo *MGA* Vigna)
Altitude	300 – 390 meters a.s.l. roughly
Exposure	Predominantly south, and from east to southeast in the remaining parts.
N. Claimants MGA	1
Other grape varieties planted:	Dolcetto; white varieties
Land Units	Land Unit of Serralunga d'Alba
Soil (stage):	Serravallian

Producers claiming the MGA

Tenuta Cucco.

Wines

Tenuta Cucco - Barolo Cerrati, Barolo Cerrati Vigna Cucco (Riserva);

What the producers say

Cascina Cucco: "Cerrati is characterized by shallow clay-calcareous soil with marly patches that gives wines of some structure with intense and persistent aromas and flavors. The top wine we make from it is a special selection called Vigna Cucco from the heart and best part of the vineyard area"

Ian's assessment of the vineyard district, its wines and its potential

Cerrati is a Barolo vineyard district that may not be very well-known today, but no less an expert than Renato Ratti thought highly enough of it to qualify its summit, that he identified as Cucco, in his famous Barolo map as a "subzone of particular qualitative characteristics". So not quite at the level of Brunate, Cannubi, Cerequio and the two Rocches, but still.

Cerrati is one of the vineyard districts located on the eastern flank of the Serralunga ridge (which implies a usually cooler mesoclimate), situated between the vineyard districts of Brea (to the north) and Broglio (to the south). Cerrati doesn't touch upon either one saves for a small piece of the latter vineyard district: this is because Cerrati is off on its own hilly crest that juts laterally out from the main north-south ridge that runs more or less the length of the Serralunga township. In effect, much about Cerrati's location tells you a good deal about its wines even before you drink one.

Like Broglio, it is a vineyard district that is very close to the buildings of Serralunga: in many respects, Cerrati's expanse of vineyards lie in the town's northeastern back yard. Proximity to towns and people usually means a slightly warmer mesoclimate (think Pessac in Bordeaux compared to say, Listrac) but whatever potential gain might be had by this location is mitigated, as mentioned previously, by Cerrati's positioning on the eastern side of the Serralunga ridge. The eastern flank is relatively cooler than the western one (see Chapter 8, BAROLO

"CLASSICO" AND BAROLO SINGLE-DISTRICT WINES: THE IMPORTANCE OF SITE); but Cerrati throws you another curve ball, because thanks to its mostly southern and very broad, open, sunlit exposure, it ends up being warmer than might be expected. In fact, only a section of the vineyard district, located lower down the slope, looks southeast: though this limited section of the Cerrati vineyard district is regularly referred to as Posteirone (although locals have told me that historically it was the whole Cerrati area that also went by the name of Posteirone, not just the terminal and lower part of today's vineyard district). The soil lithology is the area's typical Lequio Formation, or compacted reddish-yellowish sandstone and greyish marls, meaning that Barolos from this site are very tannic and structured in their youth and benefit from extended cellaring.

Cerrati producers and the wines

Most of Cerrati's vineyards are owned by the Tenuta Cucco and Schiavenza estates, but the only Barolo Cerrati wines I know are those of Tenuta Cucco. Tenuta Cucco has been making a Barolo Cerrati since 1996, and a Barolo Riserva Vigna Cucco since 1986. This Riserva is made only with grapes from the ancient Cucco area of Cerrati (now called Vigna Cucco) which is the part of Cerrati closest to Serralunga. The Cucco area has always been viewed as the best of this vineyard district, because it is fully south-facing but also because of its altitude (close to 400 meters above sea level, compared to the vineyard district's lower reaches at about 260 meters). The wines, that are now the result of organic agriculture, were once made in a ripely big, mouthcoating style but have gained in finesse in recent years. Schiavenza blends his grapes into the estate's classic Barolo del Comune di Serralunga d'Alba.

Benchmark wineries/Reference point producers of Barolo Cerrati: Tenuta Cucco.

CERRETTA

Township	Serralunga d'Alba
Reference Map	See Map of Serralunga d'Alba MGAs (Ch. 10)
Size (ha) (Tot / Barolo MGA)	39.93 /19.81
Production 2021 (hl)	1052.99 (of which 89.49 hl of Barolo Riserva *MGA*)
Altitude	250 – 395 meters a.s.l. roughly
Exposure	Northwest on the slope facing Fontanafredda; from east to south on the opposite side, and from west to northwest on the parcels facing Baudana.
N. Claimants MGA	14
Other grape varieties planted:	Barbera; Dolcetto; Moscato Bianco and other white varieties
Land Units	Land Unit of Serralunga d'Alba in south-eastern plots; Land Unit of Castiglione in the remaining parts
Soil (stage):	Serravallian

Producers claiming the MGA

Luigi Allaria; Marco Anselma; Flavio Baudana; Giacomo Conterno; Azelia; Bugia Nen; Ca' Rome'; Elio Altare; Garesio; G.D. Vajra; Ettore Germano; Paolo Scavino; Fratelli Revello; Giovanni Rosso; Schiavenza; Sylla.

Wines

Elio Altare - Barolo Cerretta Vigna Bricco; **G.D. Vajra** - **Luigi Baudana** - Barolo Cerretta; **Ca' Romè** - Barolo Vigna Cerretta; Barolo Rapet; **Giacomo Conterno** - Barolo Cerretta; **Garesio** - Barolo Cerretta; **Ettore Germano** - Barolo Cerretta; **Fratelli Revello** - Barolo Cerretta; **Giovanni Rosso** - Barolo Cerretta; **Schiavenza** - Barolo Bricco Cerretta; **Mauro Sebaste** - Barolo Riserva Ghè; **Bugia Nen** (Davide Fragonese) - Barolo Cerretta

What the producers say

Sergio Germano (Ettore Germano): "We own our parcel of vines since 1856, and began vinifying and bottling it separately since 1993. The limestone-based soil of this *cru* is very fine and becomes almost elastic in rainy years. In such conditions, the vines grow well, producing tannic and long-living wines (for this reason, we decide to use small barrels for aging) blessed with deep color and full body that necessitate cellar aging".

Sebaste Mauro: "In 2008 we acquired a vineyard historically named Ghè, of which we are the sole proprietors and have registered and deposited its name. It's a vineyard that is difficult to manage during harvest time. It has a full south exposure and is well ventilated. Since then, it has always been vinified and bottled on its own. It's a delicate Barolo, deep in color, perfumed with notes of rose and violet, and endowed with velvety and elegant tannins".

Aldo Vaira (G.D. Vajra): "We have rented this vineyard since 2009. Looking at the old military maps, we have discovered that historically Cerretta has been distinct from the rest of the zone, a fact that is reflected by the uniqueness of wines coming from this parcel. Cerretta wines have the profundity, intriguing complexity and virility typical of the Serralunga terroir. It can be also defined as austere, with a big structure, very mineral, even if there are it gives impressions of smoothness and sweetness. The finish shows its great aging potential. It has an important tannic texture and a noble acidity, almost hidden behind the richness of the fruit."

Giovanni Rosso: "Partly replanted in 1984 and 2000, the Rosso family owns this set of vines since 1920. There's a calcareous soil and a fairly unique microclimate among the vines given the forest just below it. It tastes very much like a wine from Serralunga".

Ian's assessment of the vineyard district, its wines and its potential

Cerretta is not just the name of an area of vineyards of the Serralunga commune designated as a vineyard district, but it is also that of the hamlet located more or less in the geographic center of it, at its summit. The name "Cerretta" stems (literally, you might say) from the union of the Latin substantive term *cerrus*, meaning a type of oak tree (*cerro*, in Italian), and the suffix *-etum*, meaning a place where a large quantity of said trees grows (*cerretta* or *cerretto*, in Italian). In other words, a *cerretta* (or *cereta* or *cerretto/cereto*) is a forested area of oak trees, much like a *faggeta* is an area loaded with *faggi* (beech trees, in English). Or like an *abetaia*, which is an area full of spruce trees (*abeti*, in Italian). Such forested areas are very common in Italy, such that there are many towns all over the country that boast some variation of these words in their name. *Cereta* is just one such word: for example, and I could give you many others, the towns of Cerretto Langhe (also written as Cerreto Langhe) and Cerreto Castello in Piedmont; Cerreto Guidi (in Tuscany); Cerreto Laziale (appropriately enough, in Lazio); Cerreto Sannita (as you would expect, given the word *sannita* attached to it, it's in Campania); Cerreto d'Esi (in the Marche); and Abbadia Cerreto (in Lombardy). Do not confuse the Italian word "cerreta", that refers to a forested environment made up mostly of oak trees, with the Cerretta Comune, a flower (*Serratula_tinctoria ssp. monticola*) belonging to the *Serratula* genus made up of thistle-like plants (in fact, it belongs to the thistle tribe) and a member of the Eurasian daisy family (for my English-language readers with a green thumb, another common member of this genus is the Serratia plumeless saw-wort, or *Serratula tinctoria*).

Now that we've gotten the always interesting and all-important matters of nomenclature out of the way, I can tell you that like quite a few other Barolo vineyard districts, Cerretta is one of those vineyard areas of the Barolo denomination that has been greatly enlarged with the arrival of the official vineyard district name designations. In fact, and I don't mean to be unkind, perhaps a little too large (at forty hectares, Cerretta is all by itself about two thirds the size of the totality of Chambolle-Musigny's *premier crus*); in fact, it is the third largest of the newly minted (as of 2010) vineyard districts of the Serralunga commune's territory. Normally, this leads to noteworthy heterogeneity of topography (and hence exposures), altitude and soil, but with Cerretta, though differences between wines from different sections certainly exist, in general they do not seem to be as noteworthy as one might have expected

Before the formation of one large vineyard district called simply Cerretta, there were three neighboring but distinct Cerretta areas in the Serralunga commune: Bricco Cerretta, Cerretta (Cerretta proper), and Cerretta Piani. Clearly, sub-dividing vineyard areas to the nth degree undoubtedly complicates the subject for the majority of wine drinkers out there; and so, you can understand that when the time came to officially determine the names and size of the vineyard districts, a little simplification was thought to be a good thing. Clearly, the diversity of nuances in wines made from nearby but different sites contribute to making wine the fascinating beverage that it is; and maybe over time we will be able to characterize the wines from each of the single Cerretta subregions, but presently I think this is still difficult to do, at least in a reliable (repeatable) manner.

The Cerretta vineyard district is located on the eastern flank of the Serralunga ridge, a part of the Serralunga territory that is generally associated with cooler sites than those of its western flank. As it stands today, Cerretta has the Baudana vineyard district to its west (Baudana is located on Serralunga's western flank, just across the road that runs atop the ridge separating the ridge in two flanks creating a neat divide between the vineyard districts of each flank); Teodoro to the east; and Prapò immediately to the south. Looking at it from an aerial perspective, the Cerretta vineyard district of today is very much the shape of a slightly curved three-pronged star (think of the Mercedes symbol some four years old was allowed to happily go wild on). Cerretta Piani is the prong that got the brunt of the four years old glee, starting straight out along the ridge then bending west looking towards the San Rocco and Sorano vineyard districts; Bricco Cerretta is the star's prong that looks towards Baudana; and Cerretta proper is the prong leading out in the other direction, with one of its flanks looking out to the Teodoro vineyard district and the other towards Prapò (this is the flank with the best exposure for Nebbiolo).

When talking Barolo, Cerretta and Prapò are often lumped together, as many argue that Prapò is nothing but the southern prolongation of Cerretta: therefore, it is their view (not mine) that there was no reason to distinguish between the two, given that Prapò is really the same hill as Ceretta. I don't agree at all: and besides, sure, go ahead and make Cerretta even bigger than it already is! At that rate, I might have been able to plant Nebbiolo in front of my apartment in Rome or even here in Shanghai where I live and call it a Barolo Cerretta too. OK, OK, all kidding aside, though I understand why it might be easy to think that Cerretta and Prapò are one of the same (again, they are not), it is a simplistic observation (i.e., based on one being the prolongation of the other) from which an also simplistic inference is drawn that is just plain wrong. Wrong for a number of reasons.

First, as mentioned previously in this book, exposure and altitude are all important (always have been) in determining the type and quality of Barolo that will be made from each vineyard site. And while Prapò is a fully south-looking site, only a very small section of Cerretta boasts fully south-facing vines. That's a pretty big enough difference right there. Second, only small sections of Cerretta and Prapò have soils that are similar ro each other. Third, I have tasted enough wines from these two vineyard districts over the years to know that the Barolos of Cerretta and those of Prapò are very different wines (to wit, just check out how different are the Barolos made from Cerretta and Prapò by the Ettore Germano, or the two made by Schiavenza). Of course, I may also add that, over the last twenty years of tasting away, Prapo's Barolos have always shown much better than those made in Cerretta -anywhere in Cerretta (See PRAPÓ file). And as much as it may displease some to read this, it's actually not even close: Barolos from Prapò have generally silkier tannins, greater aromatic lift and a good deal more refinement [so beware the increasingly high scores being doled out to Cerretta wines like confetti at a marriage: it's a large area (unlike Prapò) where many famous producers have moved into and started making Barolos there, with high scores following hand over fist]. In any case, the two sites *should* have been kept separate, and it is good that they were.

Cerretta's landscape is classified as the Land Unit of Castiglione. Its soil lithology is however not that uniform, with much Diano Sandstone, some Lequio Formation and even Saint Agatha Fossil Marls formation (though the last one is rare). For example, the smaller easternmost part of Cerretta has soil that is more calcareous in nature, while soils in the larger western part of the vineyard district are more clay-rich. This means that the Cerretta Barolos you drink may differ at least in some measure depending on where the Nebbiolo grapes are sourced. However, their differences arise not just from soil diversity, but of climate too. Cerretta is in general one of the fresher vineyard districts of Serralunga, and especially so in Cerretta Piani, mostly because of this subregion's position which makes it subject to stronger wind currents and ventilation. Not by chance, it is my experience tasting Barolos made only with Cerretta Piani grapes that its Barolos are the freshest and most vibrant of the three Cerretta subregions, exuding more often than not notes of aromatic herbs, menthol and orange peel. Compare that to the Barolo Cerretta made by Giacomo Conterno and Ca' Rome', or those of Ettore Germano and Giovanni Rosso that are broader, fleshier and richer (very red fruit-forward, bordering on red cherry nectar and even syrup). I also happen to think that the Barolos born off the portions of Cerretta richer in clay are less interesting, as to my taste at least they are chunky and lacking in nuance. Inevitably, they suffer in comparison with the more refined wines of greater lift made with grapes from the vineyard district's more eastern sections, or the ones with more limestone. And so, while I do think I have a pretty good idea of what the character traits are of the Barolos of the three distinct Cerretta subregions, I also think that I need to build up more of a tasting database with these Barolos. Up until recently there weren't enough wines by which to gain such knowledge.

Though I know locals feel strongly that one Cerretta subregion is better than the others, I'm not sure that I can make a convincing argument one way or the other. Are the wines of Cerretta proper better than those of Bricco Cerretta, or is it vice versa? The same question holds if I were to bring Cerretta Piani into the equation. There are those who uphold the merits of Bricco Cerretta, others the virtues of Cerretta proper, but then where does that leave Cerretta Piani? I ponder the matter because an outstanding example of Barolo Cerretta is the one made by Roberto Conterno of the Giacomo Conterno estate (and I state it is outstanding not because it's Giacomo Conterno we are talking about but because it really is marvelous wine), and his Cerretta holdings are most certainly at least partly in Cerretta Piani. However, his property straddles the "border" with Bricco Cerretta. In other words, an area where the limestone and clay interfaces transition (in fact there is a visible red clay presence forming a sort of boundary in the ground where his vines are, after which there is no more red colour to the soil). And while we are at it, let's also mention that Azelia and G.D. Vajra also make their Barolo Cerretta wines from Cerretta Piani. So clearly, this part of Cerretta Piani obviously can deliver amazing Barolos. Overall, though Cerretta's Barolos may lack the mineral verve and complexity of top Serralunga sites such as Falletto, Francia, and Vignarionda, they are hugely satisfying Barolos that are easy to like.

Cerretta producers and the wines

Over the last ten years or so, the number of Cerretta's producers has swollen noticeably thanks to the influx of many new and often very famous estates joining the ranks of those who already owned vines there and/or who bottled a Barolo Cerretta [in alphabetical order, Altare, Azelia, Ca' Rome', Ettore Germano, Fratelli Revello, Giacomo Conterno, Giovanni Rosso, Mauro Sebaste, Schiavenza, G.D. Vajra (who took over from Luigi Baudana), Vietti and others]. It's getting to the point that that keeping up with all the new Cerretta bottlings is a tall order! It seems likely to me that Cerretta is a vineyard district the wines of which are fatefully destined to be talked about in terms of Cerretta subregions of grape provenance (you read it here first), much as is happening with Bussia, another too large for its own good vineyard district (in the sense that speaking generically of a Bussia Barolo makes very little sense, except to those producers who need to rely on the magic of the Bussia name to help them sell).

At Giacomo Conterno, uber-talented owner Roberto Conterno acquired his Cerretta vineyards in 2008 from the previous Swiss owner (Conterno started working on the vineyard in May, when it promptly hailed that year reducing his yields…how's that for a welcome?). Finally, he first released a Barolo Cerretta with the 2011 vintage. Conterno owns two mostly west-facing large plots of roughly fifteen-twenty years old vines planted fairly high up in the vineyard district, one at about 350 meters and another at 390 meters above sea level. I have tasted the Barolo Cerretta wines from Giacomo Conterno since he started making them directly from barrel and then again once bottled, so I'd say I know them well. The 2018 is very harmonious and long, boasting a lovely acidity extending the flavors in a rather remarkable way; a knockout wine, it is a better wine than the 2018 Francia, a rare event indeed (by contrast, the 2017 Francia is a wildly better wine than the Cerretta of that same vintage). The 2016 Barolo Cerretta is also smashingly good, spicy rich and opulent, complemented by some earthy notes; Roberto likes the 2015 even more, a Barolo of fruitier personality than the more classic 2016. These wines readily showcase not just the red fruit characteristic of Cerretta's Barolos but also their robust frontal tannins that are somewhat less refined than Arione's lateral tannins, to use Roberto's own words. Though his Barolos from Cerretta are never less than excellent, Roberto admits that he's still unsure of the exact quality level of Cerretta vineyard district, a not unreasonable position given he hasn't yet worked with his vineyard holdings much and still needs to build up experience. He does add however that he believes this vineyard district to have noteworthy potential and is curious to see what will happen with a slightly later harvesting approach. And though this is unrelated to Barolo, I just want to point out that the Barbera wines he makes in Cerretta to be just as good as his Barolos: for my money, Giacomo Conterno's Barbera wine from Cerretta is one of three best Barbera d'Alba wines made today (another of the three is his Barbera d'Alba from the Francia vineyard, so don't miss out on either one of them).

Another producer making noteworthy Cerretta wines is Sergio Germano of the Ettore Germano estate, a small, family-run winery that embodies the Serralunga reality very well. Sergio's wines are an excellent way by which to get to know what many vineyard districts can deliver, given that he produces Barolos from a number of great ones, including Cerretta, Prapò, Lazzarito and Vignarionda (he inherited part of the Canale holdings in Vignarionda. See VIGNARIONDA file). To be crystal-clear, Germano owns what are some of the absolutely best vineyard sections of all Cerretta (in the Bricco Cerretta and the best-exposed parts of Cerretta proper). It is the family's home vineyard, and his mother still lives in a house overlooking it. These are mostly south/southwest-facing vines planted in 1949, 1963, and 1995, at about 350-375 meters above sea level. Similarly to Germano, Schiavenza makes wonderful Barolos from both Cerretta and Prapò. When you visit at the Schiavenza winery you feel like you've stepped back in time, engaged in a family-run Barolo world that harkens very much to traditional values. Which means that Schiavenza's wines are not devoid of tannic clout when first released, and need plenty of patience to let that spine soften somewhat; but when it does, the wines are just great. An added bonus is that they are generally very reasonably priced Barolos.

Over in La Morra, Cerretta is the latest single-vineyard district Barolo to have appeared in the portfolio of Barolos made by the Fratelli Revello, the very fine producer of that commune where a bevy of excellent Barolos from many different vineyard districts await (clearly, mostly from La Morra). Remember that the Fratelli Revello split up in 2013, and that the Cerretta holding was assigned in the split to Enzo Revello, who also kept the estate's old and well-known label. Following the split, the Barolo Cerretta and the other Barolos were bottled with separate labels (Revello and Carlo Revello, the names of the two wineries born from the split) but are the same exact wine up until the 2015 vintage included; only with the 2016 vintage are the wines vinified separately in two distinct wineries.

Before the split, Revello's first official vintage of Barolo Cerretta (that is, released for sale) was the 2013, but in fact the first Barolo Cerretta they made was the 2012: given the year however, they opted to blend it into the Barolo Classico save for a few trial bottles kept around for study reasons, and that I am happy to say I got to try and learn from (thanks guys). Their vines are in Cerretta proper, located lower down the slope and on the better-exposed south/southeast facing site looking towards Sinio. The holding is 1.5 hectares of thirty-five years old vines, planted between 250-300 meters above sea level in a soil the composition of which is 44% loam, 27% sand and 29% clay. The estate only uses what they feel is the best part of their holding (about one hectare) to make its Barolo Cerretta. Do take note-of the fact that like at many other Barolo estates, the winemaking at Revello has changed over the years. Back in 2013 and 2014, the wine was aged in small oak barrels for one year and then one more year in fifteen hectoliter barrels; but beginning with the 2015 vintage, it is aged in a fifty-fifty mix of large oak casks and barriques. Revello's Barolo Cerretta tends to be more austere than their Barolos from La Morra (as you'd expect it to be, given the Serralunga provenance - much steeper, cooler, sandier slopes) but boasts very good definition and noteworthy elegance (generally speaking, not exactly a common coin in the world of Cerretta Barolos). Also in La Morra, the Brandini estate first made a Cerretta Barolo wine in 2015, employing temperature-controlled fermentation in stainless steel tanks with four weeks of skin contact and frequent pumping over. The wine is aged in large 20 to 60 hectoliters oak barrels for about thirty months (and then 6-8 months in bottle) and is a solid, well-made Barolo that doesn't disappoint.

Azelia is another non-Serralunga estate that is making a Barolo Cerretta, a wine that they are very proud of because of a personal tie to it. Luigi Scavino, father of Lorenzo, waited thirty years to produce a Barolo Cerretta wine and when he finally did, he dedicated it to the estate's one hundredth anniversary. Their vines are in Cerretta Piani and look towards their vineyards in San Rocco. Like over in some parts of Conterno's vineyards, there is a presence of iron in Azelia's Cerretta soils that possibly adds a spicy component to the fresher elements this Barolo is mostly characterized by. Just in case I had you thinking it seems funny to speak about La Morra and Castiglione Falletto producers when discussing a Serralunga vineyard district, how does Barbaresco grab you? Well, that's where you will have to go if you want to speak with Paola and Giuseppe Marengo of the Ca' Rome'. They farm Cerretta vineyards at 310-370 meters above sea level right next to the Borgata Cerretta, so they are part of the Bricco Cerretta. The wine is traditionally made, big, tannic and textured.

Benchmark wineries/Reference point producers of Barolo Cerretta: Altare (Cerretta proper), Azelia (Cerretta Piani), Ca' Rome' (Bricco Cerretta), Ettore Germano (Bricco Cerretta); Fratelli Revello (Cerretta proper), Giacomo Conterno (Cerretta Piani/Bricco Cerretta), Giovanni Rosso (Cerretta proper), Luigi Baudana (Cerretta Piani).

CERVIANO - MERLI

Township	Novello
Reference Map	See Map of Novello MGAs (Ch. 10)
Size (ha) (Tot / Barolo MGA)	65.2 / 10.07
Production 2021 (hl)	544.48 (of which 47.74 hl of Barolo Riserva *MGA*)
Altitude	350 – 450 meters a.s.l. roughly
Exposure	From east to southeast (Cerviano), from southwest to southeast in the better exposed position of Merli.
N. Claimants MGA	8
Other grape varieties planted:	Barbera; Dolcetto; white varieties
Land Units	Land Unit of Novello
Soil (stage):	Tortonian

Producers claiming the MGA

Marziano Abbona; Serena Anselma; Ca' D' Perulin; Virna (di Borgogno Virna); Tenuta Barac; G.D. Vajra.

Wines

Marziano Abbona - Barolo Cerviano-Merli; **Tenuta Barac** - Barolo Cerviano-Merli

What the producers say

Virna Borgogno (Virna): "We acquired this vineyard in 1999 and vinified it singly for the first time in 2003. Cerviano-Merli is a Barolo of great balance that in hot years like 2004 shows its quality by giving optimal results despite the season's heat"

Luca Sandrone (Sandrone Luciano): "Merli wines set themselves apart with its freshness with a heightened acidity. The aromas are sweet but fresh as well."

Ian's assessment of the vineyard district, its wines and its potential

Soil-wise, this vineyard district is mostly loamy-clay, characterized by the presence of Saint Agatha Fossil Marls in their most typical form of thick blue-greyish marls with very little sand interspersed as thin layers throughout (for example, soil composition in some parts is 57% loam, 28% clay and 15% sand). There are also spots where the Saint Agatha Fossil Marls are of the sandy and of the laminated type. In fact, Cerviano-Merli's lithology is that of the Land Unit of Novello, which means the Saint Agatha Marls are prevalent especially in the middle and higher reaches of the slopes. Though not everyone agrees, I have been told by producers that there are also small areas in the lower reaches of the vineyard district where Lequio Formation lithology is also present (which is in my view wholly consistent with the recognizable steeliness of Cerviano-Merli's Barolos, that do not taste in my opinion as if they were born off *only* Saint Agatha Fossil Marls lithology). In any case, keep in mind that the profile of Cerviano-Merli Barolos will vary with respect also to the altitude at which the grapes are sourced. In general, it's also good to know that despite Cerviano-Merli being situated right next to Ravera, parts of the latter are generally characterized by a much higher soil clay content than parts of the former. I imagine that there are most likely differences between the Cerviano and Merli portions of the vineyard district too, but presently these are not clear to me. At least for the time being, I have not accumulated sufficient tasting data (neither of finished wines nor or microvinifications of single plot or single subregions within this vineyard district) to make definitive statements about the merits of Cerviano relative to Merli. The latter strikes me as being characterized by a sweet south/southeast/southwest exposure, and its wines to have noteworthy finesse and a certain delicate charm, but I don't feel comfortable saying anything more than that for now.

Cerviano-Merli producers and the wines

A number of producers are making Barolos with Cerviano-Merli grapes, and others might in the future. Marziano Abbona farms about 1.5 hectares of 25 years old vines planted in the Cerviano section of the between 400 and 450 meters above sea level. As he first made this wine in the 2001 vintage when Barolos sporting the

Cerviano-Merli name were rare to come by, his has long been the gold standard by which Cerviano-Merli Barolos were judged by.

By contrast to Abbona's wine that has a twenty years history behind it, Tenuta Baràc in San Rocco Seno d'Elvio commune of the Barbaresco denomination has been making an outstanding, organically certified, Barolo Cerviano-Merli since only a few years. Their southeast-facing vines are planted at about 400 meters above sea level and are roughly twenty years old. The wine is tough when young, but smoothens out with appropriate cellaring, and is a very fine example of what this vineyard district can deliver in the right hands.

Mario Giribaldi officially founded his winery in the early 1970s (but in fact it's now three generations and counting producing wine since the early 1900s, as the current owner's grandfather used to make wine for mostly private consumption), that makes very good wines from organic grapes. The estate farms and/or owns nineteen hectares in the townships of Rodello d'Alba, Montelupo Albese, Alba, Barolo, and Novello. Specifically pertaining to Barolo, the estate began renting in 2006 a few vineyards in the Novello vineyard districts of Cerviano-Merli and Ravera. The vines in Cerviano-Merli grow at 345 meters above sea level; one 0.5 hectares plot is 46 years old, while the larger (0.9 hectares) plot was replanted in 2006. In the latter plot grows Nebbiolo Rosé. They bottled the Cerviano-Merli as a Barolo sporting the vineyard's name on the label until the 2016 vintage included, but since then have opted to bottle it as the estate Barolo so as to focus the public's attention on their other single-site Barolo from Ravera that they believe is the deeper and more complex of the two wines.

Luciano Sandrone began vinifying and using Cerviano-Merli grapes with the 2011 vintage of the Barolo Le Vigne, which has always been the estate's more traditional Barolo, made with a blend of grapes from different vineyard sources. These vineyard sources have changed over the years, and beginning with the 2011 vintage, Merli was one of the new vineyard districts that entered the fray, so to speak. The Sandrone vineyard section of Merli is a south-southwest facing amphitheater that catches the afternoon light perfectly. In general, wines made from this specific site are earthy and robust, but with good aromatic complexity and freshness. Virna Borgogno of the Virna estate in Barolo also owns vineyards in this vineyard district that now range between 22-25 years of age. Though she hasn't done so yet, Borgogno has told me that she has been thinking of bottling her Cerviano-Merli Barolo on its own, rather than using the grapes for the classic estate Barolo. If all goes well and she believes her estate can properly showcase the merits of so many different single-site Barolos, she might come out with a Barolo Cerviano-Merli in the next few years. So far, she's happy with the wine and thinks it differs from all the other Barolos she offers in her portfolio.

Benchmark wineries/Reference point producers of Barolo Cerviano-Merli: Mario Giribaldi, Marziano Abbona, Tenuta Baràc.

CIOCCHINI

Township	La Morra
Reference Map	See Map of La Morra MGAs (Ch. 10)
Size (ha) (Tot / Barolo MGA)	11.87
Production 2021 (hl)	
Altitude	210 – 230 meters a.s.l. roughly
Exposure	Predominantly southwest.
N. Claimants MGA	0
Other grape varieties planted:	Barbera; Dolcetto
Land Units	Land Unit of Barolo
Soil (stage):	Tortonian

Ian's assessment of the vineyard district, its wines and its potential

Ciocchini is a vineyard district tucked away in the north-easternmost corner of the La Morra commune, right at the border with the township of Roddi, another of Barolo's eleven communes. It lies immediately east on the prolongation of the same slope where the Roere di Santa Maria vineyard district is also located. Other La Morra vineyard districts not too distant from Ciocchini include Bettolotti, Rive and Santa Maria (not to be confused with the similar sounding vineyard district of Roere di Santa Maria, also in La Morra's territory. See ROERE DI SANTA MARIA file).

It's fair to say that Ciocchini is neither one of the most famous nor most sought-after vineyard districts in the Barolo denomination. For instance, only a paltry one fifth of the area is under vine (and it's not even all Nebbiolo, with the variety representing less than three quarters of the planted wine grapes there). Even some Barolo producers have made, in a lateral way, snide remarks to me about Ciocchini over the years: one such famous quote was "… yes Ian, it really is a pretty good site, it's not Ciocchini, you know". In fairness, many said exactly the same thing about other less well-known vineyard districts as well; and so, as far as having a bullseye for barbs and shots on its back, Ciocchini was actually in very good company. In fact, looking at Ciocchini as a site and analyzing its data hints at a slightly different, better, story. First, Ciocchini's landscape is categorized as a Land Unit of Barolo, same as some ultra-famous vineyard districts such as Fiasco in Castiglione Falletto and Ginestra in Monforte. So that ain't at all bad, as the song goes. Second, its soil lithology of typical Saint Agatha Fossil Marls is the classic one developed during the Tortonian stage and that also characterizes some of the denomination's best vineyard districts, including Conca and Gattera of the La Morra commune, not to mention Cannubi Boschis and Sarmassa of Barolo. Again, that's pretty good vineyard district company for Ciocchini to keep.

However, like Roere di Santa Maria and most of the vineyard districts associated with the Santa Maria fraction of La Morra, Ciocchini's soil is marked by a noteworthy presence of sand (the Saint Agatha Fossil Marls of the sandy type lithology is also present in Ciocchini), and I think this informs, to a degree, local perceptions about Ciocchini being a less qualitative site. However, in asking around and compiling sample soil data over the years, my own research shows that clay is still very much present in Ciocchini (and it would be strange if it were otherwise, given the presence of Tortonian stage marls), and this is especially true of the slope's lower reaches (and I point out how this is also true of other nearby vineyard districts like Santa Maria and Bricco San Biagio).

True, Ciocchini's generally lowish altitude and its sand soil component mean that this is one vineyard area that can theoretically (and in practice too) suffer in hot, droughty years. Just as clearly, its wines are never going to be endowed with massive amounts of flesh and palate weight (always a no-no for those who never met a mouthcoating behemoth they didn't just love, refinement be damned). That Ciocchini's Barolos might be lighter-styled and lacking in oomph is most likely why the site has been underrated by some thus far.

Ciocchini producers and the wines

For these and perhaps other reasons, Barolo Ciocchini wines have never been plentiful, with most estates preferring to blend these Nebbiolo grapes with those from other vineyard districts to make their classic estate Barolos (the denomination's most traditional wines where the sum is often better than their individual parts). A good example of this is provided by the Marrone estate in La Morra, that makes a classic blended Barolo called Pichemej (the estate also makes an outstanding Barolo Bussia. See BUSSIA file). Pichemej is made with grapes from two different vineyard areas featuring very diverse soils: Ciocchini in La Morra and Pugnane in Castiglione Falletto. Unifying the grapes from these two vineyard districts is an excellent example of how making a classic Barolo works (or is intended to work): you blend grapes from different sites such that each contributes something to the finished wine. This is exactly what we have here: Ciocchini is a sandy site of La Morra that gives perfumed but less powerful wines; Pugnane, a part of Bussia in Monforte, has much heavier soil, rich in iron and clay, and its wines are, though not monsters, certainly bigger and more structured than those from Ciocchini. Whereas Ciocchini suffers in droughty years as drainage is almost too good there, the water-retentive capacity of Pugnane's clay ensures that the finished blended wine won't show signs of dry growing seasons. Using the sandy-clay origins to good effect, Pichemej showcases the best of both Barolo worlds.

Benchmark wineries/Reference point producers of Barolo Ciocchini: None currently available.

CIOCCHINI - LOSCHETTO

Township	Novello
Reference Map	See Map of Novello MGAs (Ch. 10)
Size (ha) (Tot / Barolo MGA)	50.10 / 0.56
Production 2021 (hl)	30.47
Altitude	350 – 460 meters a.s.l. roughly
Exposure	Predominantly west.
N. Claimants MGA	1
Other grape varieties planted:	Barbera; Dolcetto; white varieties
Land Units	Land Unit of Vergne
Soil (stage):	Tortonian

Producers claiming the MGA

Stra.

Wines

Stra - Barolo Ciocchini Loschetto.

Ian's assessment of the vineyard district, its wines and its potential

Ciocchini-Loschetto is a large (fifty hectares) Novello vineyard district sandwiched in between the Corini-Pallaretta vineyard area to the south and La Volta in the Barolo commune to the north. It's not an especially well-known source of Barolo and in fact only about half the vineyard district's land is under vine (and of that, only about two thirds is Nebbiolo).

A large part of this vineyard district's extension isn't even planted to vines. The landscape category is that of the Land Unit of Vergne and the soil lithology is, not surprisingly, the same as that of Corini-Pallaretta and of La Volta. Terre del Barolo, Luca Marenco, Mauro Marengo and Stra all own or farm vineyards in this vineyard district. Nevertheless, no Barolos from this area were made until 2014, when the Stra estate made their first Barolo Ciocchini Loschetto (a curious sort of vintage with which to launch a new wine). I don't think I have ever had it, or, if I did, I don't remember it at all. The Mauro Marengo estate in Novello owns vines in Ciocchini-Loschetto, but at the present time chooses not to vinify them, and sells the grapes to other wineries.

Benchmark wineries/Reference point producers of Barolo Ciocchini-Loschetto: Stra.

CODANA

Township	Castiglione Falletto
Reference Map	See Map of Castiglione MGAs (Ch. 10)
Size (ha) (Tot / Barolo MGA)	9.66
Production 2021 (hl)	0
Altitude	240 – 270 meters a.s.l. roughly
Exposure	Southwest on the better exposed slopes, and from north to northeast on the opposite side
N. Claimants MGA	0
Other grape varieties planted:	Barbera; Dolcetto; white varieties
Land Units	Land Unit of Barolo
Soil (stage):	Tortonian

Ian's assessment of the vineyard district, its wines and its potential

Codana is a vineyard district of Castiglione Falletto, situated in between that commune's vineyard districts of Vignolo, Fiasco, Valentino and Monprivato. In fact, Codana is unique among these vineyard districts because it actually extends over two slopes that face each other. One part of Codana's vineyards are located in between those of Monprivato and Vignolo, draping over the southwest-facing slope of one crest; the other Codana grapevines are on another slope (to the south and facing opposite to the previous), such that these vines look north to northeast (this second hillside crest is where you'll find the vineyard districts of Fiasco and Altenasso). For some, the vineyard area takes its name of "Codana" from the Italian *coda* (or tail in English), a reference to the fact that it is the geographic tail end of the Monprivato vineyard.

Codana producers and the wines

I honestly don't know why nobody is making a Barolo Codana currently; admittedly, some of the wineries (but not all) have very small holdings there. But there are some truly super Barolo estates that farm or own vineyards in Codana (Cavallotto, Francesco Rinaldi, Giuseppe Mascarello, Vietti and growers that supply the Terre del Barolo cooperative) so I am quite sure that the resulting wines would be more than just noteworthy. I know this is true because in the past the Giuseppe Mascarello winery did produce a Barolo Codana (from a very small vineyard they bought in 1991) and I absolutely loved it (and not just me: Veronelli was a huge fan of it too). Furthermore, Codana's landscape is that of the Land Unit of Barolo (common to many top-quality vineyard districts like Fiasco and Sarmassa) and its lithology of typical Saint Agatha Fossil Marls is also that of numerous important vineyard districts. And while the northern exposure of one of Codana's two slopes is not ideal for Nebbiolo, the other southwestern-facing one certainly is, so I don't know what to tell you. I just think it's a pity, because Codana is far better than many other vineyard districts that are being aggressively touted nowadays and from where we are witnessing an increasing number of Barolos being made (and hence the need to praise that vineyard area's merits to the high heavens). For now, producers are happy to use Codana's grapes to make estate Barolos in which grapes from different sites are mixed together). For example, Francesco Rinaldi uses its Codana grapes to make their classic Barolo, a blend of grapes from Rocche dell'Annunziata in La Morra, Vignane and Sarmassa in Barolo, as well as Codana in Castiglione Falletto. Giuseppe Mascarello's 0.38 hectares are southwest-facing at about 270 meters in altitude, but are mostly planted to Barbera (only about 25% of their vineyard's holding is devoted to Nebbiolo, so when the estate does make a Barolo Codana, it's in very limited numbers, unfortunately).

Benchmark wineries/Reference point producers of Barolo Codana: None currently available.

COLLARETTO

Township	Serralunga d'Alba
Reference Map	See Map of Serralunga d'Alba MGAs (Ch. 10)
Size (ha) (Tot / Barolo MGA)	14,36 / 0,55
Production 2021 (hl)	23.51
Altitude	350 – 450 meters a.s.l. roughly
Exposure	From west to south on the ridge parallel to Vigna Rionda and from west to northwest in the remaining parts.
N. Claimants MGA	1
Other grape varieties planted:	Barbera; Dolcetto; Moscato Bianco and other white varieties
Land Units	Land Unit of Serralunga d'Alba
Soil (stage):	Serravallian

Producers claiming the MGA

Giacomo Anselma.

Ian's assessment of the vineyard district, its wines and its potential

Collaretto is a small hill of the Serralunga township of the western flank of the ridge that more or less neatly divides the commune's territory in two halves. Driving north, the vineyard district immediately to its south is Briccolina (with which it shares a small part of its border) while the very famous Vignarionda (formerly Vigna Rionda) is to the north on a hillside crest that runs parallel to the one Collaretto is on.

Collaretto's landscape is that of the Land Unit of Serralunga and the soil lithology is the Lequio Formation, the classic compacted sands, limestone and clay soil typical of the area. Not all of this vineyard district's exposures are ideal for Nebbiolo, but those that are seem very suitable to making potentially excellent Barolos.

Collaretto producers and the wines

That said, there aren't too many Barolos made with grapes from this vineyard district only. The only Barolo Collaretto I have tasted multiple vintages over the years is that of Giacomo Anselma (the only other Barolo Collaretto I know is the one of the Gemma estate, but I have not had it too often, something I will try to improve on!). Collaretto's Barolo usually offers aromas and flavors of licorice, raspberry and blueberry, and has the typical steely personality of Serralunga's best wines derived from the high soil limestone content but, at least in Anselma's version, seems to have plenty of flesh too. I have always felt this to be a potentially very good site, so I'm not sure I have an explanation as to why more producers haven't made single-vineyard district Barolos from it. To me, admittedly from the outside looking in, this seems like a missed opportunity.

Benchmark wineries/Reference point producers of Barolo Collaretto: Giacomo Anselma.

COLOMBARO OR COLOMBAIO

Township	Serralunga d'Alba	
Reference Map	See Map of Serralunga d'Alba MGAs (Ch. 10)	
Size (ha) (Tot / Barolo MGA)	3.56	
Production 2021 (hl)		
Altitude	340 – 395 meters a.s.l. roughly	
Exposure	From southeast to northeast.	
N. Claimants MGA	0	
Other grape varieties planted:	Barbera; white varieties	
Land Units	Land Unit of Serralunga d'Alba	
Soil (stage):	Serravallian	

Ian's assessment of the vineyard district, its wines and its potential

One of the many little vineyard districts located on the eastern flank of the Serralunga ridge, Colombaro is sandwiched between the vineyard districts of Broglio to its north and San Bernardo to its south and southwest. Colombaro is not a vineyard district that is especially known for its Barolos and in fact only a little more than half of the vineyard district's land is under vine. And of the total wine grapes planted, only about 25% are Nebbiolo. That said, the soil lithology here is the classic Lequio Formation that can give perfectly fine, steely, powerful Barolos, as it does over in Broglio, another little-known but quality Serralunga vineyard district. What hurts Colombaio most is its northeastern exposures, that are clearly not ideal for Nebbiolo (and to compound the problem, on the already cooler eastern flank of the Serralunga ridge), though climate change may well modify our certainties soon enough.

The historic Pio Cesare estate, the only estate that has its cellars in downtown Alba (and what truly beautiful, magnificent cellars they are) owns vineyards in Colombaro and uses the grapes for their classic Barolo estate wine. They have owned land in Colombaro for 45 years but the southeast-facing vines are very young, having been planted only about five years ago. The estate chose to plant Nebbiolo clones 180 and 141 at 400 meters above sea level on a soil that is roughly 45% loam, 40% clay, and 15% sand. This soil makeup and the relative altitude at which the vines grow explain the freshness of the area's wines. They are also endowed with a good deal of colour and fairly silky tannins. At Pio Cesare, the must spends thirty days on the skins, at a maximum temperature of 28 degrees Celsius, with some *délestages* but no pump overs, and aged in 85% large oak (partly French, partly Eastern European) casks and 15% in French oak barriques.

Another winery that owns vines in Colombaro is Gaja. Their three hectares were planted in 2001 facing south/southwest. It's clay-rich soil and the vineyard district's characteristics means that this is a very late-ripening site, in fact the very last one to be harvested at Gaja each and every year. Gaia Gaja has told me that some local old-timers believe that Colombaro was once considered to be a part of what used to be a larger Vignarionda vineyard area than it is today. I can see why that might be, given that the Colombaro vineyard district area lies on the eastern flank of the Serralunga ridge more or less opposite from Vignarionda on the other side of the road that runs atop the Serralunga ridge. She was interested to know if I had ever heard anything of the sort, and it pains me to have to admit I was, and am, no help to her on this matter. But my curiosity has been stoked now, and perhaps in due course I might be able to shed some light on this issue. Nothing would please me more.

Benchmark wineries/Reference point producers of Barolo Colombaro: None currently available.

CONCA

Township	La Morra	
Reference Map	See Map of La Morra MGAs (Ch. 10)	
Size (ha) (Tot / Barolo MGA)	3 / 1,66	
Production 2021 (hl)	90.13	
Altitude	235 – 255 meters a.s.l. roughly	
Exposure	From southwest to southeast	
N. Claimants MGA	3	
Other grape varieties planted:		
Land Units	For most Land Unit of Barolo (central part); Land Unit of Castiglione on the east side through Bricco Luciani; Land Unit of La Morra on the west side through Giachini;	
Soil (stage):	Tortonian	

Producers claiming the MGA

Mauro Molino; Fratelli Revello; Ratti.

Wines

Mauro Molino - Barolo Conca; **Ratti** - Barolo Conca; **Fratelli Revello** - Barolo Conca

What the producers say

Lorenzo Revello (Fratelli Revello): "The vineyard came into the family in 1997 and we immediately started its separate vinification. In the glass, one can sense that the cru Conca gives structured and warm Barolos".

Matteo Molino (Mauro Mauro): "Il Barolo Conca is our estate's top wine, characterized by a certain austerity and spicy notes that make it long-lived and complex".

Pietro Ratti (Ratti): "Our Conca grapes always give us a structured, flavorful, pleasantly tannic wine".

Ian's assessment of the vineyard district, its wines and its potential

One of the five smallest Barolo vineyard districts, Conca is, as its name implies, a small south-facing amphitheater very open to sunlight but protected from the wind ("conca" in Italian translates to "bowl" in English). Not very steep, it is characterized by a warm, even hot, microclimate that gives rather big, masculine wines (clearly, "big" by La Morra standards).

Conca has long been famous as one of Barolo's most prestigious vineyard sites, thanks to the intrinsic quality of the grapes that grew in the site and the high quality of the wines that could be made with them. In fact, Conca grapes were always much sought for estate blends because many decades ago Nebbiolo had trouble ripening fully in many of today's Barolo vineyard districts, while this was never a problem in the warmer Conca site. And when you realize that 99% of this vineyard district is under vine and that practically all of that is Nebbiolo, then you just know this is a Barolo site of the utmost nobility.

Conca is a vineyard district of the La Morra commune; even more accurately, of the Annunziata fraction of La Morra. It used to be a property of the nearby Abbazia di Marcenasco (abbey of Marcenasco), and was often referred to as the "Conca dell'Abbazia" or "Conca dell'Abbazia di Marcenasco" vineyard (as documented also in Renato Ratti's *carta del Barolo*; certainly, I can vouch that back in the 1980s, I and everybody else who knew Barolo -not that there were many of us even in Italy- used to call Conca with the longer name. Conca benefits from a unique location, surrounded by the vineyard districts of Gattera to the north (and Annunziata too, just a little farther up); Giachini to its west and slightly south; Bricco Rocca to its south; and Bricco Luciani to the east. And not only is Conca situated in a top area of the Barolo denomination, but for such a small site, its soil is remarkably complex too.

While it is natural to assume that Conca ought to be characterized by Saint Agatha Fossil Marls (given it's a La Morra vineyard district), in fact things aren't quite that straightforward. Clearly, the typical Saint Agatha Fossil Marls formation dominates but the diversity of soil within Conca is visible already to the naked eye. For example, the bottom of the slope is much more intensely blue-grey in colour than the rest of the amphitheater: however, Conca's soil where it is closest to Bricco Luciani is of a different lithology, not that of the typical Saint Agatha Fossil Marls but of the Diano Sandstone. Therefore, a Barolo Conca made from this section of the vineyard district can be surprisingly broad-shouldered and structured for a La Morra Barolo (rather more like those of Castiglione Falletto, say). Furthermore, Conca has a warm microclimate, and can get quite hot in summer, further contributing flesh and size. In some ways, the wines of Conca are less La Morra-like than those of the majority of the commune's other sites.

The vineyard district's bowl-like shape and relatively low-lying vines play an important role in helping to fashion relatively round, textured wines that boast ripely fruity aromas and flavors, and noteworthy alcohol clout. The fleshy, sultry and even sexy nature of Conca Barolos is certainly a positive, and quite unlike any other Barolo from La Morra I can think of: as for negatives, about the only thing I can think of is that over the years, as great as the Barolos from Conca are (and they really are great wines) I have always found them to be a hair less complex than the best from Brunate and Rocche dell'Annunziata. But you know, if all you can be in life is a second team all-star rather than a first-team selection, that is still pretty darn outstanding.

Conca producers and the wines

The excellent Mauro Molino estate makes a benchmark Barolo from Conca, from a portion of the vineyard district characterized by the typical Saint Agatha Fossil Marls soil: their 0.38 hectares of vines lie at 250 meters above sea level on calcareous-clay soil (to be precise: 60% loam, 25% clay and 15% sand). Interestingly, Molino has 10% old vines of Nebbiolo Rosé in their Conca vineyard: the presence of this Nebbiolo no doubt contributes to the extremely perfumed, cinnamon spice and floral nose Molino's Barolo Conca exudes in spades. Otherwise, Molino's piece of Conca is all planted to Lampia, which makes sense: Conca is too warm a site and planting it with Nebbiolo Michet would have meant running the risk of making jammy wines. For this same reason, the presence in Conca of Nebbiolo Rosé, a Nebbiolo that resists drought and heat much better than Nebbiolo Lampia, is also a very logical finding (see Chapter 1. NEBBIOLO LAMPIA. See also chapter 3. NEBBIOLO ROSÉ). Musings about the microclimate aside, Conca tends to give wines that are structured, so planting Nebbiolo Michet there is really unnecessary. After all that and telling you that I think Molino's Barolo Conca wine is fantastic, the bad news: unfortunately, less than 3000 bottles a year of this truly excellent Barolo are made by the winery, but do whatever you can to get hold of a bottle.

According to Mauro Molino, back in 2008 there were only three producers making a Barolo Conca, and things haven't changed much since then (to the best of my knowledge there are only five who own/farm, vineyards in Conca: in alphabetical order, Fratelli Ferrero, Fratelli Revello, Mauro Molino, Renato Corino and Renato Ratti). Of Molino's three main vineyard areas (Bricco Luciani, Conca and Gallinotto), he told me that it is Conca that always gives the best-looking grapes and it's the easiest to work. At the same time, Molino also believes that the Barolo Conca is the most interesting of his three Barolos, giving his most structured wines. And even though that's "structured" by the standards of La Morra "structured", the wines are no pansies: in fact, it is my experience from blind tastings that (not so) expert people routinely mistake Barolos from Conca for wines from Serralunga. The structured mouthfeel and tannic spine of the Conca Barolo is there thanks to the soil clay soil content; but at the same time, there is that noteworthy presence of sand that makes for wines that are lively and graceful too.

Piero Ratti of the Renato Ratti estate owns about 6900 square meters in Conca and makes an especially good Barolo Conca that is smooth, broad and perfumed at the same time. It speaks of the Conca soil at the border with Giachini, which gives slightly more politely-styled wines than does the soil the Fratelli Revello work with (see below). Conca is the first Barolo vineyard that Piero's father Renato bought in 1965, and from where he made his initial Barolo Marcenasco wines (labeled at the time with the word "Marcenasco" in big type and the word "Barolo" in much smaller type). Differently from Molino, Ratti didn't think too highly of Conca's somewhat big wines, preferring those from his vineyards in Rocche (now called Rocche dell'Annunziata), an opinion shared by Piero too. Being no fool however, Renato Ratti realized the wines from Conca were well above the general average in Barolo, and that the site had plenty to offer. Therefore, in 1971, Ratti began identifying his wine made with grapes grown in the little holding as from Conca, and not just as a "Marcenasco" Barolo. That much admitted, Conca's wines really are great, but in a different way. For example, compared to Ratti's Rocche dell'Annunziata Barolo, the Conca is always more horizontal and less vertical, with a more luscious and opulent personality (if we accept that wines can be sexy, then I think the Barolos of Conca certainly are). It is also always less complex than Ratti's Barolo of Rocche dell'Annunziata, but at Renato Ratti at least that is more a function of vine age than anything else (the Rocche's vines are about sixty-seventy years old, while those of Conca are about thirty). Degree of complexity notwithstanding, I think Ratti's Conca bottling is practically as good as his Rocche, which tells you much that you need to know about the quality of this site as far as the production of world-class Barolos are concerned.

The Fratelli Revello estate first made a Barolo Conca in 1997 and immediately bought the vineyard. The bottom part of their vineyards used to be planted to Dolcetto, but that was changed over to Nebbiolo in 1992 by the previous owner. The estate split up in 2013, with the Conca vineyard going to Enzo Revello (with his brother Carlo inheriting the Giachini, for example); Enzo also kept the original name of the estate and label. The first vintage of Barolo Conca made by the 'new' Fratelli Revello is therefore the 2016. Their Barolo Conca is aged for 24 months in small oak barriques (of which 30-40% new oak). The vines are planted between 230 and 250 meters above sea level, two thirds of which face full south and one third look east. Planted in 1961, the vineyard holding is 0.8 hectares large but Fratelli Revello only use the best 0.5 portion with which to make their Barolo Conca. The part of Conca where Revello's Nebbiolo grows is characterized by a more compact and sandy soil (60% loam, 15% sand, 25% clay: note that these values are exactly the same as those of Mauro Molino) that tends to give bigger wines than the rest of the vineyard district: it is a lovely wine worth hunting down but it requires a bit more cellaring than Ratti's or Molino's to showcase all it has to offer. Over at Fratelli Ferrero, seeing as if their holding in Conca is very small, they choose to blend its Nebbiolo grapes into their Gattera, so we don't have a Barolo Conca from them to try.

To better understand the eventual differences in the Barolo Conca wines you will taste, drinking the Barolo Conca wines from Molino, Ratti and Fratelli Revello side by side proves a very helpful exercise. In this light, it is useful to know that Molino owns the central portion of the Conca amphitheater, while Ratti's and Revello's portions are located at the opposite extremes of the vineyard district, where, as mentioned previously, there are differences in soil. Clearly, not just soil but the human role here is important too. Back when the Fratelli Revello estate was still one and undivided, they had historically pushed the envelope with Conca grapes. Though aware that the site's very hot microclimate means that the risk of picking overripe grapes is not a small one, they also believed that people like the somewhat surprisingly big, even powerful, and rather "unlike La Morra" wines that can be made there. So, what did they devise? That this is the Barolo holding they harvested last (the first to be harvested was Gattera: there can be as much as three weeks difference in harvest time between the Gattera and the Conca): the extra-ripe, extra-fleshy mouthfeel appealed to their clients. But this late harvesting technique means that Revello's Barolo Conca wines will sometimes boast aromas and flavors of prune, that in my experience are never found in Molino's and Ratti's wines from Conca. In any case, this was as good example as any of the role played by the human factor in wine terroir expression.

For what it's worth, though I love a great Barolo from the Rocche dell'Annunziata (one of my favorite Barolo sites of all), I am also very partial to the charm of Barolos from Conca. I find that while La Morra producers talk about these being massive, muscular Barolos (how funny, no Serralunga producer would ever qualify them as such: sometimes life is really a matter of perspective), Conca Barolos in fact retain noteworthy amounts of gracefulness and are very La Morra-like. Possibly because of its warm, even hot, microclimate, Barolos from Conca are characterized by an intensely juicy and ripe red cherry quality that borders on the opulent, even bodacious, and is not far removed from that of a red fruit nectar complicated by enticing sweet spicy notes. Furthermore, there is always a note of menthol or spearmint: but while Ratti's Barolo Conca is mintier than Molino's, it is less so than Revello's wine, in which the menthol note is so strong the wine takes on notes that resemble those of coffee, even cocoa. I should add that Molino's is also the most floral of all the Barolo Conca wines I have tried over the years, but that has to do with the presence of Nebbiolo Rosé in the midst. Listen now: when all is said and done, just make sure you hunt down Barolos from Conca: it really is, easily, one of Barolo's fifteen, and at no worse twenty, best vineyard districts in the denomination.

Benchmark wineries/Reference point producers of Barolo Conca: Mauro Molino, Renato Ratti. Also good: Fratelli Revello.

CORINI - PALLARETTA

Township	Novello
Reference Map	See Map of Novello MGAs (Ch. 10)
Size (ha) (Tot / Barolo MGA)	105.88 / 1.51
Production 2021 (hl)	80.76
Altitude	380 – 460 meters a.s.l. roughly
Exposure	From west to southwest in the better exposed parcels, and west-northwest in the remaining parts
N. Claimants MGA	2
Other grape varieties planted:	Barbera; Dolcetto; white varieties
Land Units	Land Unit of Vergne
Soil (stage):	Tortonian

Producers claiming the MGA
Cascina Gavetta (Roberto Cogno); Le Strette; Roberto Sarotto.

Wines
Cascina Gavetta - Barolo Corini-Pallaretta; **Le Strette** - Barolo Corini-Pallaretta

What the producers say
Daniele Savio (Le Strette): "We acquired this vineyard in 2005 and started vinifying it on its own since 2011. As far as we managed to understand in the short period of time, we have farmed this area, Barolo from this area is characterized by a good endowment of color, a floral bouquet, freshness and lively but very pleasant tannins".

Ian's assessment of the vineyard district, its wines and its potential

A rather large vineyard district of the Novello commune only about a fifth of which is under vine (three quarters of that is Nebbiolo), Corini-Pallaretta is situated just north of the town of Novello itself and surrounded by three other vineyard districts: Bergera-Pezzole is to its north and northwest, Ciocchini-Loschetto to the northeast (this vineyard district is practically a prolongation of Corini-Pallaretta right up to the border with the Barolo commune and that commune's La Volta vineyard district), and Ravera is to the east.

Corini-Pallaretta's are Barolos mostly brimming with early appeal but with enough underlying structure to age well and improve with time. In short, wines that are easy to like and to understand already when young. A lot of that has to do with the soil, a Tortonian stage Saint Agatha Fossil Marls of the laminated form that is essentially a mix of 45% loam, 30% clay and 25% sand. For sure the greater percentage of clay and loam in this vineyard district's soil (compared for example to its Novello neighbor of Bergera-Pezzolle, which has a larger presence of sandy veins in its soil mix) translates into wines of deeper color and bigger structure, but the clay is fine-particled, allowing for wines of real gracefulness too.

In fact, Corini-Pallaretta's landscape is that of the Vergne Land Unit: not coincidentally, I think, the Barolo vineyard districts of La Volta and Bricco delle Viole are both characterized by this same Land Unit. Knowing readers and Barolo enthusiasts will realize that there are definite textural similarities between the wines of these three vineyard districts (I find this to be especially so between those of La Volta and Corini-Pallaretta). The two vineyard districts share the same lithology: the Saint Agatha Fossil Marls of the laminated form, which no doubt contributes in no small measure to the relatively intense and very pure floral notes that typify the nose of these Barolos (violet, rose, faded field flowers). And also contributes by way of very graceful, silky, light-bodied (for Barolo, so do put that term in context) textures. Corini-Pallaretta's Barolos are also very lively and fresh, and are usually marked by pH values that (at least based on my soil samples analysis values), are lower than those of nearby vineyard districts such as Ravera or Bergera-Pezzolle.

All that being no doubt true, I have to say that it is becoming increasingly clear to me (and not just to me, I might add) that Corini-Pallaretta is not exactly a homogenous site. No surprise, I guess, given how big it is: but that also means that the potential exists to make slightly different Barolos from within its boundaries. The vineyard district's subregions of Corini and Pallaretta [named after the *cascina* Corini and the *cascina* Pallaretta (*cascina* means farmhouse, in Italian)], though they are part of the same officially delimited vineyard district, present noteworthy geological and topographical differences that are inevitably going to have repercussions on the wines made with grapes from each. Clearly, for the moment I don't have enough information (wines too) by which to be able to say more. It is likely that the differences between wines from these two subregions won't be so marked, but there are likely going to be differences nonetheless. For example, Le Strette's Barolo Corini-Pallaretta is made with grapes entirely from the Corini subarea of the vineyard district: but Vajra and La Volta (and to a lesser degree, Bric Cenciurio) own vines in the Pallaretta side of the vineyard district. The Terre del Barolo cooperative owns vines on both sides.

Corini-Pallaretta producers and the wines

Although there are a number of different estates that own Nebbiolo vines in this vineyard district, there aren't that many Corini-Pallaretta Barolos to taste currently with which to form one's palate about. That may not necessarily be due to the perceived quality of this vineyard district's Barolo wines, but rather that it is not yet well-known enough so as to have its name help push sales; at least not in the way that the name "Brunate" or "Vignarionda" might do. For this reason, some wineries prefer to sell off these grapes and concentrate on making Barolos from more famous vineyard districts (for example, the Mauro Marengo winery), or blend them into their classic estate Barolo (Bric Cenciurio). The only Barolo I know of made wholly with grapes from Corini-Pallaretta is the excellent one made by Le Strette: Savio Daniele now has about ten or so vintages of wines under his belt (Le Strette first made this wine in 2011) and so really has to be considered as the single biggest expert on this vineyard district and its wines. At least, I can say that I have tasted every single vintage made by Le Strette upon release, and then again numerous times subsequently, so for what it's worth I have roughly a decade's worth impressions to go on as well. Based on what I have tasted from Le Strette over the years, Corini-Pallaretta's Barolos are characterized by noteworthy freshness and rather silky tannins. Though I'm not sure about their ability to develop mind-boggling levels of complexity, they do boast a recognizable tannin-fruit-acid balance that is very enticing, making for a very enjoyable drink.

Given that Le Strette's Barolo Corini-Pallaretta is both delicious and delightful, and there are in my view a number of factors that help account for this. First, the doubtless talent of owner/winemaker Savio Daniele (an up until recently, before his sad passing away, of his brother Mauro Daniele); and remember that the siblings were winemakers at Ceretto during the time that estate made some of its best wines. Second, the quality of Corini-Pallaretta, which is undoubtedly higher, in my estimation, than that of possibly more than a third of the denomination's other vineyard districts. Third and fourth, the specific soil and relatively old age of the vines that belong to Le Strette. Le Strette's Barolo Corini-Pallaretta is made from roughly one hectare of vines of varying age, but it is not without importance that over half the vines are old. A part (0.6 hectares) of Le Strette's Nebbiolo vines planted in Corini-Pallaretta date back to 1976 and 1981, with only a smaller -0.4 hectares- planting taking place more recently, in 2014. These forty and almost fifty years old vines play no small role in the genesis of wines of impeccable balance. All in all, a very solid Barolo.

Bric Cenciurio's vines in Corini-Pallaretta are located in the southernmost strip of the vineyard district, right at the boundary of the Barolo denomination. Their vineyard is 0.5 hectares large and is a little northwest of Novello, planted in the 1980s on a soil that is marked by a presence of pink clays that the Pittatore family believes contributes to making extremely elegant Barolos; that sense of refinement and lift may also have something to do with the altitude at which these grapes grow (430 meters above sea level).

Benchmark wineries/Reference point producers of Barolo Corini-Pallaretta: Le Strette.

COSTABELLA

Township	Serralunga d'Alba
Reference Map	See Map of Serralunga d'Alba MGAs (Ch. 10)
Size (ha) (Tot / Barolo MGA)	8.29 / 2.81
Production 2021 (hl)	151.82 (of which 33.86 hl of Barolo Riserva *MGA*)
Altitude	220 – 300 meters a.s.l. roughly
Exposure	From west to southwest.
N. Claimants MGA	2
Other grape varieties planted:	Barbera;
Land Units	Land Unit of Barolo mostly; Land Unit of Serralunga on the west and south-west sides
Soil (stage):	Tortonian (and Serravallian)

Producers claiming the MGA
G.D. Vajra; Cascina Bruni (Giuseppe Veglio).
Wines
G.D. Vajra - Barolo Costabella; **Cascina Bruni** - Barolo Costabella (*)

What the producers say
Aldo Vaira: "We acquired this vineyard in 2012; we plan to perhaps release the first bottles from this site in 2016. Costabella is characterized by its power and elegance."

Ian's assessment of the vineyard district, its wines and its potential

Costabella is a relatively little-known vineyard district of Serralunga compared to some other of the commune's much more famous vineyard sites, such as Vignarionda, Lazzarito and Francia. And yet Costabella is not without interest, offering a window through which to look at and analyze the possibilities that a specific terroir may offer relative to wine. Located in the northernmost reaches of Serralunga on its main ridge's western flank, Costabella has the territory of Castiglione Falletto to its west and the San Rocco vineyard district to the east, from which it basically continues on down the slopes. Costabella extends over the south- and west-facing slope of one of the many hillside crests that dart out more or less perpendicularly to the central Serralunga ridge (much like do the spokes of a wheel). The Serralunga vineyard districts of Sorano (in fact partly shared with the commune of Diano d'Alba) and Carpegna are situated on a more northern-facing flank of another crest that runs essentially parallel to the one Costabella is on.

Costabella's landscape will make you think of some areas of the Barolo and Castiglione Falletto communes; in fact, the soil lithology is mostly the typical Saint Agatha Fossil Marls but there are patches of Lequio Formation (the latter is the lithology most typical of Serralunga). Differently from most other Serralunga vineyard districts that are characterized by a very homogenous lithology (all Lequio Formation), Costabella presents noteworthy diversity throughout its boundaries. In this, it is quite different from other nearby vineyard districts such as Carpegna, for example. It also explains how there is the potential to make Barolos that are relatively different from each other without needing to rely too heavily on winemaking alternatives.

There is a lot to learn still about exactly what Costabella can offer but the Vaira family, through the Luigi Baudana estate it took over in 2009, has helped me, and us all, learn about it. Aldo and Milena Vaira got to know Luigi and Fiorina Baudana at a moment in time of the latter couple's existence in which taking a break from it all, retirement in other words, was being contemplated. The friendship that developed between the two families ultimately led to the Vaira's taking over from the Baudana's with the intent to carry the baton and continue broadcasting Luigi Baudana's name and life's work. And so it was that starting with the 2009 vintage, the Vaira family was put in charge of what were then only 4.1 hectares (1.5 hectares of which planted to white varieties from where the winery makes its famous Langhe Bianco Dragone wine, a blend of Riesling, Nascetta, Sauvignon Blanc and Chardonnay).

At Luigi Baudana, Vaira has farmed vineyards in Costabella since 2012. Over the years, the Vaira family has studied their holdings in Costabella closely, including in-depth soil studies performed by no less than the world-famous soil expert French husband and wife duo of Claude and Lydie Bouguignon (more on this shortly).

Baudana's Costabella plots are two, both situated in the upper third of the vineyard district (a relevant point, as I shall mention shortly): the smaller block is situated higher up the slope, while larger plot situated slightly lower down. But even though the differences in altitude between the two plots are really minimal, very early on the family became aware that their Costabella holding was not as homogenous as it had always been thought to be. In this respect, it's the entire Costabella vineyard district that is not homogenous: for example, locals had long been of the opinion that Costabella's lower third, relative to fine wine potential, was less interesting than the middle and upper thirds, believed to have instead noteworthy fine wine potential. This belief was based mostly on the different exposures and degree of luminosity of the three portions of the slope. However, Vaira realized that there were soil differences too present, especially relative to Costabella's upper third: and in general, Baudana's two Costabella blocks have soils the differences of which are visible already to the naked eye. For example, the soil colors of the two blocks are not the same. It only seems logical then to assume that if the two different sections look different, then they probably are: and chances are just as high that the wines made from each would also be different. It follows that Aldo Vaira wished to know more about the terroir of his two Costabella plots. As an in-depth study was required, he hired consultants Lydia and Claude Bourguignon, two of the world's greatest soil experts who have established their Laboratoire Analyze Microbiologique des Sols (LAMS) and a consultancy that has led them to work with some of the world's most famous wine estates. The studies of Costabella performed by the Bourguignon duo demonstrated noteworthy differences between the top and bottom part of the Costabella site; and hinted that such differences could potentially lead to very different wines made from different sections of the Costabella site.

Given that the Vaira family applies the same viticultural and winemaking techniques to the grapes grown in Costabella's two halves, it is fascinating to analyze how differences in exposures, soil chemistry and microbiology, water availability, and other factors can lead to very different wines made from exactly the same grape variety treated in exactly the same way by exactly the same people (so, like, is that enough "exactly" for you? Exactly.) Based on the conclusions drawn from these analyses and the results of tasting evaluations, you won't be surprised to learn then that the Vajra family might even decide to bottle two different Barolos from the Costabella site one day; for all those die-hard Burgundy fans out there, sort of a Costabella-Dessous (the lower block) and a Costabella-Dessus (the upper block), if you will, but that's still up in the (Barolo) clouds. For now, what we know is that Costabella's upper block is planted to Nebbiolo on 1103 Paulsen and 140 Ruggeri rootstocks at an altitude of 298 meters above sea level with a southwest exposure on a 30% hillside slope gradient. The soils there is clay-loam lumps in the top twenty centimeters, yellow-stained clay with good root penetration as far as fifty centimeters lower down, with marls appearing at sixty centimeters of depth where in Bourguignon's own words a "beautiful" root necromass appears in the marl. The soil composition is silt (54%), clay (27%), and sand (13%), with a small but noteworthy change fifteen centimeters deeper down, with the soil's composition changing to silt (58%), clay (31%), and sand (10%). The soil is also well carbonated and shows average activity level of siderobacteria. There's good clay cation exchange concentration (CEC) but slightly low organic matter CEC. Mineral concentrations feature high potassium, calcium, magnesium and nitrogen, with normal phosphorus and sulfur and low to normal sodium levels. By contrast, Vaira's lower block in Costabella is planted to Nebbiolo on the same 1103 Paulsen and 140 Ruggeri rootstocks at a similar altitude (287 meters above sea level), but the vines face west and, at 37%, the hill's slope gradient is a good deal steeper. The physical soil aspects also differ, with a compact loam-rich top soil devoid of porosity; the large roots stay relatively shallow, reaching roughly forty centimeters deep. From 40-80 centimeters, there is rich clay-loam but tellingly, few signs of root penetration. The soil's composition is silt (56%), clay (27%), and sand (16%), is also well carbonated and properly ventilated, with an average activity level of siderobacteria. There is good clay CEC but slightly low organic matter CEC, while the active lime content and soil pH are within normal limits and of mildly alkaline values, respectively. Analysis of the mineral concentrations show high potassium, calcium, magnesium and nitrogen; normal phosphorus and sulfur; low to normal sodium levels.

According to the Bourguignons, the good root penetration of the deeper marly layers in the upper block can potentially lead to wines of mineral personality; by contrast, the compact, packed loamy top soil of the lower block require to be worked. The Upper Block's composition of soil, with clays having inner surfaces of less than 300 m²/g, indicates that resulting wines ought to be more about finesse rather than power; the Lower Block is characterized instead by clays with inner surfaces larger than 300 m²/g, indicating the likelihood of producing broader wines from this site. The good clay CEC but slightly low organic matter CEC in both sites means that increasing humus content of the soils is advisable. The soil pH of the two blocks is alkaline and within norm (typical of the Langhe); the active lime content means that rootstocks such as 420 A, 3309 De Couderc and 161-49 are all suitable for future plantings. The normal mineral concentrations mean there are no micronutrient deficiencies and therefore no supplements or interventions are necessary in this regard.

Costabella producers and the wines

Relative to the Luigi Baudana estate, for the time being the Vaira family chooses to blend its Costabella Nebbiolo grapes into the Luigi Baudana classic estate Barolo, the Barolo del Comune di Serralunga (made nowadays with grapes from the younger Nebbiolo vines grown in the vineyard districts of Baudana and Cerretta and a smaller portion from Costabella). It began adding the grapes from Costabella to the Luigi Baudana estate's classic Barolo with the 2015 vintage (before 2015, the Luigi Baudana estate Barolo was made only from the young vines of Baudana and Cerretta). It's a very good wine that truly delivers a potentially ideal blend of what could be a Serralunga Barolo (from this section of the commune's territory, at least) as it mixes Nebbiolo grapes grown off a Lequio Formation lithology (which characterizes the Luigi Baudana holding in Cerretta), the lithological mix of Lequio Formation and Saint Agatha Fossil Marls of the Baudana vineyard district, and the mostly Saint Agatha Fossil Marls of Costabella. I have been fortunate enough to taste the microvinifications from both plots in Costabella farmed by the Vaira family at the Baudana estate, and all I can say is that the wine is excellent. Slightly lighter-styled and more fruit-forward than Luigi Baudana's Barolo Cerretta and Barolo Baudana wines, but delicious nonetheless.

Cascina Bruni was founded in 1897 and housed in the fifteenth century La Favorita estate (the name of which was changed to the present-day Cascina Bruni); owned by the Veglio family (don't confuse them with the many other Veglio families living and working in the Barolo denomination; see CARPEGNA file) that also farms Costabella. In 2013, they labeled a Barolo Costabella-Matrin (Matrin is one of the subplots Cascina Bruni owns in Costabella), and in 2015 they made a Barolo Costabella, but I haven't yet tasted the 2016. In the past, their Barolo Pilone (check out the 1996, a very good wine) was reportedly all Costabella (Pilone is the name of one of Cascina Bruni's subplots in Costabella). In fact, Cascina Bruni owns five hectares in Costabella, and subdivides it in different plots. The heart of the estate's Costabella holdings were acquired in 1855 (this "heart" is made up of the two plots named Cresta and Pilone); the plots named Giovanninetto and Matrin were bought in 1990; the Belvedere parcel in 2000; and the Matè plot in 2004. There is a reason for these subdivisions, and those reside partly in the differences in soil composition and texture that are present throughout Costabella and that I alluded to at the beginning of this file. Relative to Cascina Bruni's vineyards, Veglio told me that there's a lot more limestone in Costabella than there is in Carpegna (his other important Nebbiolo vineyard holding); and that there are noteworthy differences between the Matrin, Cresta and Pilone plots and the Belvedere and Matè (these two last plots have less limestone and more sand). Not surprisingly, Veglio believes that these two plots give lighter-styled, perfumed wines, compared to those from the older plots, where grapes ripen easily and the resulting wine can clock in with quite the octanes. He also finds that the Matrin plot, especially, gives especially ageworthy wines.

Benchmark wineries/Reference point producers of Barolo Costabella: Cascina Bruni.

COSTE DI ROSE

Township	Barolo
Reference Map	See Map of Barolo MGAs (Ch. 10)
Size (ha) (Tot / Barolo MGA)	16.83 / 6.87
Production 2021 (hl)	373.30 (of which 86.66 hl of Barolo Riserva *MGA*)
Altitude	250 – 310 meters a.s.l. roughly
Exposure	Predominantly east.
N. Claimants MGA	5
Other grape varieties planted:	Barbera; Dolcetto; Riesling and other white varieties
Land Units	Land Unit of Castiglione
Soil (stage):	Tortonian

Producers claiming the MGA

Bric Cenciurio; Silvana Cavallo; G.D. Vajra; Marchesi di Barolo; Pier Giuseppe Pittatore.

Wines

Bric Cenciurio - Barolo Costa di Rose (Riserva); **G.D. Vajra** - Barolo Coste di Rose; **Marchesi di Barolo** - Barolo Coste di Rose;

What the producers say

Alessandro Pittatore (Bric Cenciurio): "We became the owner of this vineyard at the beginning of the 1900s and we have started to do its separate vinification in 1999. What makes Barolo Coste di Rose so unique is its freshness and longevity; in more difficult years, it can have edgier tannin".

Ernesto Abbona (Marchesi di Barolo): "Coste di Rose is a prestigious hill facing full east in the territory of Barolo township. The fact that it's directly facing Bussia of Monforte and characterized by slope of more than 40 degrees contribute to the maturation of grapes, which is especially important for Nebbiolo, a grape that needs sun and heat. The Nebbiolo really finds itself on soils particularly rich in quartz, sand and fine silt with a dash of clay, instilling in this Barolo intensely fine perfumes, reminiscent of wild mint. Of delicate color and structure, it's a Barolo that gives immediate drinking pleasure, balance and harmony".

Ian's assessment of the vineyard district, its wines and its potential

Coste di Rose is one of those vineyard areas that throws you into a quandary, given that it easily upsets all you know (or think you know) about Barolo, its soils and the wines you'd expect to be made there. For example, as Coste di Rose is a vineyard district located in the Barolo denomination, its Barolos ought to be of the softer, fleshier kind when young, right? Wrong. And as it's in the Barolo commune, it's soils ought to be mostly Saint

Agatha Fossil Marls of one kind or another, correct? With all your certainties thrown into the wind like this, it's almost enough to make you want to hang out the "gone fishing" sign and do something else in life.

All kidding aside, no, not really, I will not go off fishing just yet (though I'd like to): because even though it's a confusing little number, Coste di Rose happens to be the source of some really very, very good Barolos indeed. Generally underrated, in fact. Yes, Coste di Rose is a vineyard district situated in the Barolo commune, that much is true. It's completely sandwiched between the vineyard districts of Preda to the north and northwest and Boschetti to the west, both of which are in the Barolo commune; but to the south it has San Giovanni; and to the east and northeast, Monrobiolo di Bussia and Bussia, all three of which are vineyard districts of the Monforte territory.

This proximity to the territory of Monforte d'Alba makes it easier to understand and appreciate how it is that Coste di Rose's soil, despite it being a vineyard district of the Barolo commune and formed during the Tortonian stage has a lithology that is mostly not that of Saint Agatha Marls, but of Diano Sandstone (there is in Coste di Rose a small presence of Saint Agatha's Marls of the sandy type too). What this means is that there will be slightly different Barolos made with Coste di Rose grapes, all other things being more or less equal, depending on where the Nebbiolo grows within the vineyard (that is either on mostly Saint Agatha Fossil Marls soil or Diano Sandstone: to make this easy, remember that the former soil lithology characterizes the wines of La Morra and Barolo, while the latter lithology is more typical of the Barolos made in Castiglione Falletto and Monforte d'Alba: so you can well imagine what to expect from the Barolos from each pair of lithological sources). There are plenty of fossils peppered throughout Coste di Rose (the area was formed during a time of marine sedimentary deposit uprisings) and based on what I just told you, you won't be surprised to know it's a rather sandy site (something that is easily discernible with the naked eye), with very fine loam and a low clay content. It is also a very steep vineyard area (40% slope gradient), and given how steep its slope is, the risk of erosion with Coste di Rose is a constant, a risk that is made even worse because of the soil's high sand content. To be precise, individual soil sample analyses data clearly shows that it's the higher portions of Coste di Rose that are sandier, whereas marl dominates lower down, but I understand the risk posed by such a steep slope, because no matter how you slice it, Coste di Rose *is* sandy. However, there are also advantages to the steep gradient: thanks to it and a mostly east-facing exposure, Nebbiolo growing there receives enough sunlight despite Coste di Rose being a hidden, narrow vineyard tract of land that was always a very cool place. Clearly, that Nebbiolo has no longer any trouble ripening there is mostly a consequence of these climate change-challenged times we live in, but the fact remains that because of Coste di Rose's combination of topographical conformation, it's sandy soil, steep slope and exposure, and the phase of global warming we are in now, the Coste di Rose vineyard district has entered a sweet spot for Nebbiolo maturation that is in many respects ideal, making it nowadays an ideal Nebbiolo terroir for very fine Barolo production. Whereas very famous Barolo vineyards such as Cerequio and Brunate are having a much tougher time of late because of climate change (they have suddenly gone from being warmer sites that were intensely desired to sites that are almost too warm in more years than not now), Coste di Rose finds itself in a fortuitous moment in time where just about everything you'd want to come together in one Nebbiolo-growing spot has come about.

In fact, Coste di Rose has always been looked upon kindly as a vineyard area, and it was more famous once than it is today; over the years, locals have told me as much time and again, and that Coste di Rose grapes were highly sought for their acidity and perfume. However, the absence of famous producers making wine from it meant the vineyard district never gained the visibility and notoriety that it might have otherwise had. This is unlike what happened to, for example, Capalot in La Morra once it started getting farmed by Roberto Voerzio, or more recently to Serralunga's Cerretta now that it seems like everybody and their brothers and sisters are also making wines from it. But in the long run, Coste di Rose lost its winemaking appeal, and not only because it was too cold a spot to have Nebbiolo ripen properly in more years than not. If truth be told, part of the unwillingness of many to go and farm vines in Coste di Rose was most likely due not just to the relatively cool site it once used to be but because of it being an extremely steep, hard to work site that was and is difficult to reach (still today, access to Coste di Rose is only by way of a small, tight, pothole- and rock-loaded dirt road). No doubt, judgement of the site's perceived value back in the 1970s, 1980s and 1990s (when people did not see climate change coming and when big dark fleshy wines were right up there amongst the more important things in life including yoyos, fanny packs, disposable razors and pre-sliced bread), was probably also clouded by the type of Barolo you make with Coste di Rose grapes. In my experience, Coste di Rose gives usually steely wines of noteworthy freshness and refinement, and that are almost always marked by a strong note of barely ripe raspberry and wild spearmint (spearmint, not peppermint or menthol). They are also Barolos that lack mind-boggling gobs of sweet fleshy ultra-ripe fruit: to put it in a different if not truly correct way, Coste di Rose Barolos are for those who prefer Serralunga to La Morra. In fact, an analysis of Coste di Rose's clay particles show that they are of a fairly simple type, especially in their inner layers (clay particles are layered leaflets of wildly varying interactivity, charge and complexity); this datum, coupled with the high soil manganese, magnesium and iron concentrations, and a basic but not so alkaline soil pH (lower than that of other vineyard districts and of many other parts of the Langhe), makes for highly perfumed, lifted wines (clearly, I refer to a year of normal weather, not a 2003 or 2007). But perfumed, light on their feet and steely wines were not what people wanted back in the 1990s, and the fact that in colder years the wines could be tinged by obvious green streaks made Coste di Rose fall off most wine radars. Today, with climate change upon us, things are different, and Coste di Rose is most likely one of Barolo's ten or fifteen up and coming sites. When made by truly competent producers, the wines are certainly potentially wonderful: witness the Barolo Coste di Rose made by G.D. Vajra, that is nowadays often the best Barolo in that estate's portfolio.

Coste di Rose producers and the wines

Over the years, I have had occasion to taste numerous vintages of Barolo from Coste di Rose. As mentioned, the G.D. Vajra estate's version is especially impressive, and I was really blown away by how good their first ever wine from there was (the 2015 vintage). Talk about hitting the ground running: the excellent vintage no doubt had a say, but still, that Barolo is in many ways a truly revelatory opus (while providing further confirmation of the Vaira family's talent, though there was never any doubt there). In fact, Giuseppe Vaira (Vaira is how you spell the family name, but the estate name is spelled Vajra) has repeatedly told me that when it came to Coste di Rose, they grappled long and hard in the family with the decision of whether to make it or not: the question being, should they go solo vineyard district wine with it or keep the grapes as useful blenders for the classic estate Barolo? The dilemma was mostly because their Coste di Rose vines are planted very low down on the vineyard district's slope: in the end, they chose the former option, and good for them because their Barolo Coste di Rose is simply splendid.

Over the years, the underrated Bric Cenciurio estate has made some really lovely wines from this vineyard district. Bric Cenciurio was founded by Franco Pittatore in the early 1990s and owns about thirteen hectares of vineyards (ten in Roero and three in Barolo, most of which is in the Coste di Rose vineyard district plus a little piece in Monrobiolo di Bussia vineyard district). They made their first Barolo from Coste di Rose in the 1999 vintage. The estate owns two plots there for a total of about 1.8 hectares: significantly (see below), these holdings are located at the most southern extreme of the vineyard district, right at the border with Monforte's San Giovanni vineyard district. One plot is higher up at 320 meters above sea level, faces east/southeast and was planted in the 1950s (it's one hectare large); the second plot is 0.8 hectares and located lower down. Unfortunately, it was destroyed by the famous hail episode of 1986 and had to be replanted (they went with Nebbiolo clones CN36, CN111, CN142, CN230 Rauscedo 1, and CN230 Rauscedo 2). Very interestingly, the soil in Bric Cenciurio's holdings is characterized by the rarer Saint Agatha Fossil marls of the sandy type lithology: in fact, exactly the same soil lithology of the San Giovanni vineyard district in Monforte that borders Coste di Rose immediately to its south, so it is all pretty logical. Why this is important is that Bric Cenciurio's Barolo Coste di Rose is born off a really different soil than that of other estates making Barolo from Coste di Rose, something worth knowing when you taste the various wines. Even more interestingly, this is an estate that has Nebbiolo Rosé growing in its vineyards. The latter Nebbiolo makes up about 10% of the grapes in Bric Cenciurio's Coste di Rose plots, both in the older plot and in the younger one that was replanted with nursery clones: among these, there was also Nebbiolo CN111, which was log thought to be Nebbiolo Rosé but that in recent revisionist Langhe history is being said by some to be a Nebbiolo Lampia biotype that looks and behaves like Nebbiolo Rosé (See chapter 3, NEBBIOLO ROSÉ). Sure, whatever makes them happy. What all this means is that Bric Cenciurio's Barolo Coste di Rose is far less steely and structured than those made by estates where the Nebbiolo sits on the Diano Sandstone lithology. Bric Cenciurio's version of Barolo from Coste di Rose is really beautiful, but can be tricky: in cooler years, the tannins can be angular (remember: climate change or no climate change, it's still a site that is on the cooler side), in hot years the tannins can be gritty (remember: there's plenty of sand there, though it's mostly found in the site's higher reaches), but in warmer, balanced, truly great years such as 2015 and 2016 (in other words not 1992, 1997, 2003 or 2007) the site does remarkably well and the wine can be unforgettable. Bric Cenciurio's wines are some of the most under the radar of the entire denomination, which means they are knockout buys available more or less for a song. By the way, for the "believe it or not" moments gifted by this book, the Pittatore family planted six rows of Riesling in the Coste di Rose, and they make in fact a Langhe Riesling wine with these grapes (as well as from other Riesling vines planted in the Roero). Last but not least, Marchesi di Barolo also makes a very good Barolo Coste di Rose. In fact, I often find it to be by and large their best wine in most vintages, showcasing much better balance, perfume and gracefulness than their Cannubi bottling.

Benchmark wineries/Reference point producers of Barolo Coste di Rose: Bric Cenciurio, Marchesi di Barolo, G.D. Vajra.

COSTE DI VERGNE

Township	Barolo
Reference Map	See Map of Barolo MGAs (Ch. 10)
Size (ha) (Tot / Barolo MGA)	10,52 / 0.17
Production 2021 (hl)	9.19
Altitude	420 – 480 meters a.s.l. roughly
Exposure	South-southwest
N. Claimants MGA	1
Other grape varieties planted:	Dolcetto
Land Units	Land Unit of Vergne in the south side; Land Unit of Berri in the remaining parts
Soil (stage):	Tortonian

Producers claiming the MGA

Camparo.

Ian's assessment of the vineyard district, its wines and its potential

From the aerial perspective I am employing in this book to help you understand where the vineyards are, Coste di Vergne is to the west of the vineyard districts of Bricco delle Viole (of which it can be considered to be, more or less, a prolongation), to the south of Serradenari and just north of the San Ponzio vineyard district, from which it is separated by the collection of houses that make up the hamlet of Vergne.

Coste di Vergne is an extremely high in altitude vineyard district, and that is most likely why it has never much been associated with Nebbiolo and Barolo production. This even more so in the past, when climate change hadn't arrived in full force yet and so there was no hoping of getting the Nebbiolo grape to ripen fully there in something like seven years out of ten (if that). In fact, the site is south-facing and has a fairly rich, complex soil, so nowadays the vineyard is neither quite as late-ripening nor as devoid of "Nebbiolo for Barolo" interest as it might have been in the past.

Coste di Vergne producers and the wines

At least for now, because of its eagle's nest position, most producers have chosen to plant this site with grapes such as Barbera (Viberti) and Dolcetto (G.D. Vajra). The next time you drive to Vergne to have lunch at the excellent Buon Padre trattoria or to visit one of the Barolo estates there, stop along the way, lift your head up, and you can see Coste di Vergne's grapevines hover at the top of the hill that slopes down with Bricco delle Viole below to its left and Fossati to the right (the three vineyard districts share the same hill).

Having never tasted a Barolo from Coste di Vergne, and not even a series of microvinifications over the years (as yet) I cannot say anything about any organoleptic descriptors of Barolos that might be made there, or anything regarding the site's potential Barolo-making quality.

CROSIA

Township	Barolo
Reference Map	See Map of Barolo MGAs (Ch. 10)
Size (ha) (Tot / Barolo MGA)	9.62
Production 2021 (hl)	
Altitude	220 – 250 meters a.s.l. roughly
Exposure	Northwest
N. Claimants MGA	0
Other grape varieties planted:	Barbera; Dolcetto; white varieties
Land Units	Land Unit of Barolo
Soil (stage):	Tortonian

Ian's assessment of the vineyard district, its wines and its potential

Crosia is a vineyard district in the Barolo commune situated next to the Albarella vineyard district on a west to northwest-facing flank of a hill. On the other, east-facing flank of the same hill you find other vineyard districts such as Cannubi San Lorenzo and Cannubi Centrale. In other words, if you were to stand at the top of the hill on the side of the road (careful now, they drive fast there) that runs the length of the top of the ridge, with the town of Barolo slightly to the right of your back, you would have Cannubi Boschis sloping down your right and Crosia down to the left. Honestly now, it never ceases to amaze me how two vineyards sharing the same hill and with more or less only different exposures can have such different histories. The Cannubi Centrale and Cannubi Boschis are two of Italy's most famous vineyard sites, while Crosia… well, Crosia is not. Which tells you what you need to know about the historical importance of climate in the making of world-class Barolos. After all, only about one third of the Crosia surface area is under vine, and of that, only one third is Nebbiolo. For this reason, there have never been too many Barolo wines sporting the name of "Crosia" on the label. In the early 1900s, Giacomo Viberti settled at the foot of the Barolo commune, making wine for home use and to sell to his friends. In the early 1970s, his son Enzo and his wife planted vines there and founded the wine estate named Viberti Giacomo & Figli in 1975. Enzo's son Paolo then joined the fray, and the estate is now Viberti Giacomo (di Paolo Viberti) [don't confuse this Viberti, based in Barolo, with the other innumerable Viberti families and estates (such as Osvaldo Viberti, Viberti, Eraldo Viberti, Roccheviberti, still others) located in Vergne, La Morra and elsewhere also making Barolo wines in the denomination]. The estate makes a Barolo named "La Crosia", but I really have not had much experience with it and don't know that much about it (so I don't know whether the grapes come from the Crosia vineyard district or not), though I look forward to get to know it better in the near future.

Benchmark wineries/Reference point producers of Barolo Crosia: Not available.

DAMIANO

Township	Serralunga d'Alba
Reference Map	See Map of Serralunga d'Alba MGAs (Ch. 10)
Size (ha) (Tot / Barolo MGA)	15.98 /
Production 2021 (hl)	
Altitude	240 – 385 meters a.s.l. roughly
Exposure	Predominantly from north to northwest.
N. Claimants MGA	0
Other grape varieties planted:	Barbera; Dolcetto; white varieties
Land Units	Land Unit of Serralunga d'Alba
Soil (stage):	Serravallian

Ian's assessment of the vineyard district, its wines and its potential

"Location, location, location" is not everything it's always cracked up to be; but sometimes, it sure as heck is. Damiano is a Serralunga vineyard district that literally hugs the world-famous Vignarionda along its southern border (it's the other slope of the same hillside crest); and yet, while Vignarionda's Barolos are every sommelier's and collector's wet dream, Damiano nobody's ever heard of (never mind the wines). How unlucky is that? Of course, not that much Barolo could be made in Damiano anyways, given that only about 25% of the vineyard district's surface area under vine is planted to Nebbiolo.

Damiano is one of the many Serralunga vineyard districts that is found on the western side of the hillside ridge that runs roughly north-south and more or less through the middle of the commune's territory. While it has Vignarionda to the south, the three vineyard districts directly north of it are no slouches in the fine wine department either: moving from the top of the slope down, these are Rivette, Marenca and Margheria. So, the only vineyard district of that quintet that is not associated with at the very least well-known wines is poor Damiano. Needless to say, I have never tasted any Barolo from this site, and no microvinifications either. Given its location, its landscape classified as a Land Unit of Serralunga, and its Lequio Formation soil lithology, if it wasn't for its north to northwestern exposure, Damiano might actually be a good place to try and make Barolo in. However, until climate change becomes even stronger than it already is (not that is something we should wish for), it's not likely that Damiano will ever be anything but Barolo-challenged. Though as things stand today, climate-wise, Nebbiolo might actually ripen enough in Damiano to be used in estate Barolo blends, clearly, I'm sure nobody is wishing for climate change to become any more impactful than it already such that world-class Barolos can be made from Damiano as well.

Benchmark wineries/Reference point producers of Barolo Damiano: None currently available.

DRUCÀ

Township	Barolo
Reference Map	See Map of Barolo MGAs (Ch. 10)
Size (ha) (Tot / Barolo MGA)	5.03
Production 2021 (hl)	
Altitude	320 – 370 meters a.s.l. roughly
Exposure	From east to northeast.
N. Claimants MGA	0
Other grape varieties planted:	
Land Units	Land Unit of La Morra
Soil (stage):	Tortonian

Ian's assessment of the vineyard district, its wines and its potential

Drucà is a vineyard district situated to the northeast of the town of Barolo, sandwiched in between the vineyard districts of La Volta, Paiagallo and Ruè, to the northwest of the town of Barolo. Though I know of one estate that farms Nebbiolo there and includes the grapes in their classic Barolo estate blends, there has never been, to the best of my knowledge, anyone making a single- vineyard district or site-specific Barolo wine from Drucà.

Benchmark wineries/Reference point producers of Barolo Drucà: None currently available.

FALLETTO

Township	Serralunga d'Alba
Reference Map	See Map of Serralunga d'Alba MGAs (Ch. 10)
Size (ha) (Tot / Barolo MGA)	8.90 / 5.50
Production 2021 (hl)	265.20 (of which 115.60 hl of Barolo Riserva *MGA* Vigna)
Altitude	330 – 425 meters a.s.l. roughly
Exposure	South in the central part, west and southwest in the remaining parts.
N. Claimants MGA	1
Other grape varieties planted:	Barbera
Land Units	Land Unit of Serralunga d'Alba
Soil (stage):	Serravallian

Producers claiming the MGA

Bruno Giacosa.

Wines

Bruno Giacosa - Barolo Falletto; Barolo Falletto Vigna Le Rocche (Riserva)

What the producers say

Bruno Giacosa (Bruno Giacosa): "We have owned these vines since the beginning of the 1980s. Since 1982, we have been vinifying and bottling-this wine separately as Barolo Falletto. In 1997 we produced a Barolo Le Rocche del Falletto (and since 2011, with the official vineyard district name, as Barolo Falletto Vigna Le Rocche). The Falletto site gives structured and tannic Barolos but that are at the same time very elegant and complex. In very hot years, the south-facing vineyard fares worse in that while the technological maturation is fast attained, the phenolic maturation lags behind".

Ian's assessment of the vineyard district, its wines and its potential

Falletto is a Serralunga vineyard district that is a *monopole* of the world-famous Bruno Giacosa estate and is located in the southern half of the Serralunga commune. More specifically, on the western-facing flank of the Serralunga ridge that divides the commune more or less in two in a north-south direction. Falletto is one of the easiest vineyard districts to admire from the road: in fact, in this specific part of the Serralunga territory, the long north-south ridge circles in a convex fashion to the east, so Falletto is an amphitheater that occupies the bowl of the 'C' shaped curve formed as the hillside curves. Given its location, Falletto is surrounded by numerous vineyard districts: Manocino is to its northeast, Lirano to the north, Ornato to its west, Boscareto to the south (essentially the one vineyard district that Falletto's slope looks out towards) and a very small piece of Badarina to the southeast.

As die-hard Barolo lovers know, for the longest time Giacosa had always made wine only from bought grapes; this until 1982, when he finally became a vineyard owner in his own right, purchasing the Falletto site from Luigi Brigante. Giacosa made his name by producing one great Barolo (and Barbaresco) after another from grapes he bought in various communes of the denomination that he more or less knew like the contents of his own pockets (however, he very clearly preferred sites characterized by soils formed during the Serravalian stage, and actually he told me so on numerous occasions). So he knew the vineyards of both Barolo and Barbaresco extremely well, and always thought highly of Falletto. Though Giacosa never released a Barolo wine labeled with the Falletto name prior to his purchase of it (as is commonly done by everyone else too: after all, there is no sense in hiking up the value, and hence the price, of a vineyard before you are in the position to buy it), he had bought grapes from there since at least 1958 (for those of you into scoops, this is, to the best of my knowledge, a never before published datum). Brigante, who used to sell his wine off in bulk except in great years, also made a few Falletto-labeled wines from a number of top vintages including 1971 and if memory serves me well, 1978 too (I confess to being unable to read parts of my own handwriting in old notebook of the time).

Falletto producers and the wines (monopole)

With the beginning of the twenty-first century, practically all Giacosa's estate-bottled Barolos (but not all) were produced with Falletto grapes; to this effect, he subdivided the hill in different sections so as to make more than one Barolo from it. Over the years, Giacosa sold a Barolo Falletto and a Barolo Le Rocche del Falletto (with the official naming of the vineyard districts, the latter's name was changed to Barolo Vigna Le Rocche). In the best vintages, he made a Riserva Barolo from the Le Rocche. As always, Giacosa's non-Riserva and Riserva wines all had exactly the same label: the only thing that changed was the label's colour (white label for the *normale*/non-riserva, and a more or less red label for the *riserva*). The Barolo Riserva Le Rocche bottling (once again: as of the 2011 vintage, Barolo Riserva Vigna Le Rocche) was first made only with the 1997 vintage. Prior to this date, the grapes were used to make the Falletto Riserva wines. Which you'll admit, is something worth knowing when you are out buying, given that fake bottles are always a possibility.

Beware now of a couple of routinely made mistakes. The Barolo Falletto was not always just a white label wine, as has been reported (and as you can still read today on some websites): that's just plain wrong (for example, Giacosa made a Riserva, red label, Barolo Falletto in the 1986, 1990, and 1996 vintages). Furthermore, while it is commonly said, still today, that the Le Rocche del Falletto Barolo is made with grapes from the three or four parcels facing due south more or less at the top of the hill, that is not completely true either. Nowadays, in especially hot years, some of the grapes from the lower lying plots (that bathe in a cooler microclimate) can find their way into the Le Rocche del Falletto wine as well. The quality of the Falletto site is attested to by the fact that, as if the outstanding wines made there by Bruno Giacosa first and his daughter Bruna afterwards were not enough, some time ago one of the world's twenty most famous wine producers looked into the possibility of buying the Falletto site and the whole Bruno Giacosa estate (there is nobody reading these pages, and I mean nobody, who would not recognize the name). Clearly, one of the world's greatest wineries such as is the Bruno Giacosa estate, that has made some of Italy's most memorable wines, will always be coveted by those with the financial means to buy it and the interest in wine to do so. It's only normal that it be so.

Falletto has a Serralunga Land Unit lithology, and the wines born from it are austere, powerful, and steely, but with the flesh and ripeness typical of the southern portion of the Serralunga commune (traits that are greatly heightened in those wines made from grapes grown in vineyard sites of its western flank). Clearly, this is just the case with Falletto. The wines boast, at the white label (non-Riserva) level too, an incredibly penetratingly perfumed, vibrant aroma profile and a level of balance to the tannin-acid-fruit elements that only a small number of the world's "great" wines offer. The nuances of red cherry, cinnamon, oriental wood, rose and violet are at once piercing and suave, voluptuous and multifaceted, deep and precise. In all honesty, it's not just Falletto that is a standout vineyard area for Nebbiolo: the Bruno Giacosa estate has made an unbelievable number of great Barolos (and Barbarescos) over the years from many other different sites, including Villero, Rocche di Castiglione (then just called Rocche) and especially Vignarionda (then spelled Vigna Rionda). Bruno and Bruna formed a super-talented duo, and surrounded themselves with other very talented people over the years, but a lot of the Bruno Giacosa estate magic resides in the unbelievable quality of grapes Bruno was able to identify and source from specific vineyard districts. To my taste, Giacosa's best wines of all time were actually his Barbarescos, though the Barolos from the Vignarionda (Vigna Rionda, when Giacosa used to make them) were practically as spectacular and the Le Rocche del Falletto site and wines are at that level too. But in ultimate analysis it's really all just a case of different strokes for different folks: you like Monet, I like Renoir; you like the Stones, I like the Beatles; you like Welles and I like Hitchcock, and so forth. In the end it becomes impossible to choose between the many great wines Giacosa has made over the years. For example, I hold out hope for the 2001 Falletto Riserva Le Rocche to join the ranks of one of Italy's all-time top 10 or 15 greatest wines, but I know other very knowledgeable wine lovers whose palate I trust that are pinning their hopes on some other of the estate's wines. By the way, the 2014 Le Rocche del Falletto made by daughter Bruna (whose exact, important, role and talent have gone slightly unrecognized over the years) in what was, weather-wise, a hellacious year for Barolo is nothing short of exceptional, and further proof of just how great a vineyard site Falletto is for Nebbiolo.

Benchmark wineries/Reference point producers of Barolo Falletto: Bruno Giacosa (*monopole*).

FIASCO

Township	Castiglione Falletto
Reference Map	See Map of Castiglione MGAs (Ch. 10)
Size (ha) (Tot / Barolo MGA)	8.3 / 5.38
Production 2021 (hl)	267.86 (of which 5.79 of Barolo Riserva *MGA*)
Altitude	225 – 275 meters a.s.l. roughly
Exposure	From south to southwest in the better exposed parcels; from west to north in the remaining parts
N. Claimants MGA	4
Other grape varieties planted:	Barbera; Dolcetto
Land Units	Land Unit of Barolo
Soil (stage):	Tortonian

Producers claiming the MGA

Azelia; Cavalier Bartolomeo; Poderi Oddero; Paolo Scavino.

Wines

Azelia - Barolo Bricco Fiasco; **Cavalier Bartolomeo** – Barolo Riserva Fiasco; **Paolo Scavino** - Barolo Bric del Fiasc (and Riserva)

What the producers say

Enrica Scavino (Paolo Scavino): "This vineyard belongs to our family since 1921. We started vinifying it separately since 1978 when my father Enrico convinced my grandfather Paolo to do so to gauge the site's potential. Bric del Fiasc always shows a purity and the grand structure typical of Castiglione Falletto's Barolos. In the vineyard, both Tortonian and Serravalian soils can be found, leading to wines that offer a combination of great freshness and power. In the glass, Bric del Fiasc expresses both the classic and elegant side of Barolo but requires time to develop its complexity – there is a classic imprint of earth on the aromas, which also speak of dense fruits, vibrant and refined tannins. A complex Barolo, mineral, balsamic with a good acidity that support the weighty structure of this cru".

Mariacristina Oddero (Poderi Oddero): "In my opinion, the soil of this site is very similar to that of Villero. Which also means it's heterogenous, such that there are zones with a significant presence of silt and clay that are water-retaining, and others soils that are not at all blessed with that trait. The site always gives a Barolo with broad shoulders, intense notes of fruits and spices (a hallmark characteristic of Barolos coming from Castglione Falletto). We opt for traditional vinification and maceration and fermentation for 25 to 30 days or more. We use Austrian and Slavonian oak barrels, ranging from 20 hectoliters to 105 hectoliters in capacity".

Luigi Scavino (Azelia): "The wine we called Bricco Fiasco has always been our estate's top wine. The vines were planted in the '40s by my father Lorenzo. Today those vines are something like seventy years old and they give very small bunches and grapes, so the wine is very concentrated. Our first vintage as a single-vineyard area wine was the 1978. We macerate roughly for 22 days, and age the wine about two years in barriques. We believe it's a very balanced wine, rich in red fruit flavors and flowers".

Ian's assessment of the vineyard district, its wines and its potential

One of Castiglione Falletto's most famous vineyard districts, Fiasco borders others that are also well-known if not downright famous: Altenasso to its north and mostly northwest, Codana is to its east (Codana is located on another hillside crest running more or less parallel to the one Fiasco is on), Brunella to its southeast (and one could make the case that the lower reaches of Fiasco are nothing but a prolongation of the lower slope of Brunella) and Villero is to its southwest (on another crest running more or less parallel to its own). In fact, part of today's Fiasco occupies the slope just above the Altenasso vineyard district, and in fact it would be more correct to view this part of the Fiasco as the upper slope of the Altenasso (just look at the hill). For sure, given that Altenasso is less famous than Fiasco, those who had always called their holdings Fiasco would have been none too happy to have to switch to Altenasso. Not by a long shot, in fact. And the rest, as they say, is history, given that when the official vineyard districts were drawn up the upper part of Altenasso became officially a part of Fiasco too [in fact, Altenasso is an excellent site (see ALTENASSO file)].

Fiasco has at least a forty years long history of great wines to its credit, but a debate lingers over the origin and meaning of its name. There are two major hypotheses. The first holds that the name Fiasco derives from the shape of the vineyard area, which is sort of broader and round at the base supposedly giving it a (wine?) flask-looking shape. That may well be, but I've been there a ton of times over the last thirty or so years, have looked at Fiasco from every which way but loose, and all I can say in conclusion is that it certainly does look like a flask from above: in fact, you'll no doubt find it to be so as well, especially after you've had a lot, and I mean a lot, of Barolo Fiasco wines to drink that day. The other option, which actually seems like the more likely one to me, is that it is called 'fiasco' in reference to the habit that local vineyard workers had of bringing a water bottle, or *fiasco* (flask, in English) into the vineyard with them so they'd have something to keep cool and hydrated with while picking grapes or working the vineyard. For the Fiasco district is shaped like an amphitheater and is therefore a hot site (hence its fame as a very good place for Nebbiolo, especially in decades past when climate change was nowhere to be seen, er, felt yet).

What makes Fiasco special is its unique combination of soil and climate characteristics (not to mention the overall very high talent level of the producers making wine from its grapes). It's a relatively low-lying vineyard district, not reaching even 300 meters in altitude, and this contributes to the warm microclimate the vines are immersed in. Exposure also plays a role, of course: for example, in comparison to other famous Castiglione Falletto vineyard districts, Fiasco is mostly south to southwest-facing, while nearby Rocche di Castiglione (a much cooler site on average) is southeast-facing; and Villero, also nearby, is south and southwest-facing (and can get very hot).

Relative to Fiasco's terroir, not just exposure and altitude are important in determining the profile of this vineyard district's wines. In fact, Fiasco's soil is very complex. The dominant lithology is the typical Saint Agatha Fossil Marls (with some of the sandy type mixed in as well), formed during the Tortonian stage of the Miocene epoch. Hence, the generally blueish-grey tint of the soil, thanks to high concentrations of manganese and magnesium, among other minerals. However, according to some producers I have spoken with over the years, what is not usually mentioned is that there are pockets of soil in this district that are of Serravalian origin, lighter in color (yellowish-beige-reddish) and rich in compacted sands and limestone. Whereas the former type of soil gives juicier, fleshier, rounder wines, the latter type is known for steely tannic wines, and it is the combined presence of the two that help make Fiasco's wines more complex than the average. Just consider that it was the presence of the same mix that has long been held to be the trump card of Cannubi (that has since been proven to be an erroneous belief. See CANNUBI CENTRALE file). In fact, a short walk in any Fiasco vineyard will clearly show you how the earth beneath your feet changes at almost every step. For example, at the Brovia estate, the ground changes three times; one area has obviously whitish soil in color (rich in limestone); another section is visibly clay-rich; and yet another shows clear-cut elements of both limestone and clay present in copious amounts.

Fiasco producers and the wines

Oddero also owns a large vineyard holding in Fiasco, 2.5 hectares entirely planted to Nebbiolo at 280 meters in altitude. The vine age is variable in this holding, with some grapevines planted by the Vignolo Family over fifty years ago, others planted at the end of the 1980s and a small piece replanted in March 2021 (a massal selection of the best Nebbiolo vines from Poderi Oddero's vineyards in Vignarionda, Monvigliero and Villero). The vines have mostly south to southwest to western orientations. Poderi Oddero chooses not to bottle a single-vineyard district wine from this site (one can argue that they have more than enough single-district bottlings as it is), but since 1985 it is used in the blend of the Barolo classico, together with grapes from Bricco Chiesa and Capalot. According to Maria Cristina Oddero, the soil here is very similar to the soil of their vineyard in Villero.

The first wine carrying the Fiasco moniker on the label that I remember seeing was Paolo Scavino's iconic 1978 Barolo Bric del Fiasc, a wine I have been fortunate enough to have numerous times over the years, at different stages of its development. For sure, it has always been an utterly wonderful Barolo, one that showcased clearly, from the get-go, the immense potential for high quality Barolos that the Fiasco site could deliver. Reportedly, it is the first Barolo ever made to carry that specific vineyard designation on the label, though the Scavino family of the Azelia winery also produced their Barolo Fiasco for the first time in 1978 (unfortunately, I don't believe I have ever had that wine, and if I have, memory fails me now). No matter which of those two estates you choose to buy the wines of (the owners of which have the same last name, Scavino: for Enrico Scavino of Paolo Scavino and Luigi Scavino of Azelia are cousins), you will never be disappointed: I can't remember ever tasting a wine that was ever less than very good from either the Paolo Scavino or Azelia wine estates. Sure, there were stages in which an estate might have gotten carried away with toasty new oak and being overly-enamored with rotomacerators (meaning too short if intense macero/fermentation times), but these two wineries are as good as any in Barolo. Their Barolos are excellent: the ones from Fiasco especially have always shown a fleshy, ripe red cherry personality, even of red cherry nectar, and sweet spices that is really quite enchanting.

Azelia owns 1.5 hectares in Fiasco, planted in 1939 by Lorenzo Scavino (grandfather of another Lorenzo, the new generation at the helm) between 250 meters up to 285 meters above sea level. Not surprisingly, the grape bunches are very small, boasting thick-skinned grapes that have highly concentrated juice. The highest portion of the Fiasco vineyard is narrower (this is why some say it reminds of the bottle or flask neck): this is the section of the vineyard district from where they used to make the wine they called Barolo Bricco Fiasco (words like "Bricco" are no longer allowed for estate wines in association with the official vineyard district name, unless of course it is part of the official name, such as with Bricco Rocche or Bricco Chiesa). As an interesting aside, at the top of Azelia's plot in Fiasco, there is a 200 years old vine that is canopy-trained and that acts as a giant umbrella providing shade and respite for those standing in the vineyard (even the oxen that work or worked there too); there is also a water well, allowing the workers to get water right there and then (and fill up their flasks with it: as already mentioned, therein is another origin of the vineyard district's name), a good thing because the Fiasco vineyard is steep and carrying water up the hill is a sweat-inducing chore in what is, as previously mentioned, a relatively fairly hot vineyard district.

Benchmark wineries/Reference point producers of Barolo Falletto: Azelia, Paolo Scavino.

FONTANAFREDDA

Township	Serralunga d'Alba
Reference Map	See Map of Serralunga d'Alba MGAs (Ch. 10)
Size (ha) (Tot / Barolo MGA)	58.42 / 12.31
Production 2021 (hl)	644.82 (of which 130.56 of Barolo *MGA* Vigna)
Altitude	220 – 315 meters a.s.l. roughly
Exposure	Predominantly southwest, south, west and northwest in the remaining parts
N. Claimants MGA	2
Other grape varieties planted:	Barbera; Dolcetto; Freisa; white varieties
Land Units	Land Unit of Barolo mostly; Land Unit of Castiglione in the higher parcels bordering Sorano
Soil (stage):	Tortonian

Producers claiming the MGA

Fontanafredda -Casa E. di Mirafiore.

Wines

Fontanafredda - Casa E. di Mirafiore - Barolo Fontanafredda, Barolo Fontanafredda Vigna La Rosa.

Ian's assessment of the vineyard district, its wines and its potential

The only wine I know of and have any experience with from this site is that of the Fontanafredda estate (that's right, estate and vine district have the same name). Currently, the Fontanafredda estate bottles a single vineyard wine from this vineyard district called Barolo Fontanafredda Vigna La Rosa, but in fact it has a long history of bottling a number of different Barolos from specific portions of the whole vineyard district.

One of the most memorable moments I have had in wine (memorable as in revelatory) was at the beginning of my wine writing career, when I was in my early 20s and a university student in Rome. One fateful evening, I attended a wine dinner held in a swanky via Veneto hotel organized by the Rome chapter of the International Wine&Food Society (founded by André Simon, *it was a* truly wonderful world-wide organization with chapters in cities all over, and to the events of which sybarites flocked to: needless to say, I was a proud, if very young, card-carrying member). The occasion was the presentation of Fontanafredda's brand new 1982 Barolos (in 1985, if memory doesn't fail me), that for the first time in a while featured the release of the winery's many different single-vineyard Barolos all at once (though many had been made off and on in previous years, as Barolo Riserva and Riserva Speciale wines too, for example in 1971, 1974 and 1978, but even as early as 1961: I still have bottles in one of my cellars).

It was a fantastic evening full of friendship, great wine and food and to this day I maintain that the Fontanafredda winery has never made better wines than those 1982s (for example, they were quite a bit superior to the estate's still good 1985 wines: the latter was also an excellent vintage, but for some reason, the winery just aced the 1982 vintage). Those wines were the: Barolo Vigna San Pietro, Barolo Vigna Gattinera, Barolo Vigna Bianca, Barolo Vigna La Rosa, Barolo Vigna Gallaretto, Barolo Vigna La Villa, Barolo Vigna La Delizia, and Barolo Vigna Lazzarito. The names of those single vineyards are relevant, because a few were wines made from individual portions of what is today the rather large Fontanafredda vineyard district. In fact, they are still the names of the subregions one could divide this large vineyard district into, if he or she was so inclined. And of course, I am.

Today the extended Fontanafredda vineyard district can be divided into three main segments: the most northern is known as Gallaretto (do not confuse this first segment of the Fontanafredda vineyard district with the vineyard district of Diano d'Alba that has exactly the same name). The Gallaretto segment can actually be further sub-divided into two portions, the San Pietro and the Gallaretto proper (today the winery refers to this whole first segment as the Vigna San Pietro, probably in order to avoid confusion with the aforementioned Diano d'Alba vineyard district also called Gallaretto where they also own vineyards).

This first segment is the lowest-lying section of the Fontanafredda vineyard district and is characterized by typical Saint Agatha Fossil Marls and gives the most forward Barolos of the bunch, wines that boast relatively easy accessibility and early appeal. I well remember that the 1982 Barolo Vigna San Pietro I mentioned previously was the readiest to drink already in 1985 (and we were told it would be so) but also that it was an amazing wine, not the deepest or most concentrated of the bunch but the best balanced and very sexy in its luscious red fruity flesh (in fact, my second favorite wine that evening, right after the marvelous 1982 Barolo Vigna Lazzarito). That much said, this is still Barolo we are talking about, and of Serralunga no less (though the soil in this vineyard district is of Tortonian stage in origin, and therefore has more in common with that of the communes of La Morra and Barolo, rather than of Serralunga). So, the wine even from this first segment of the Fontanafredda vineyard district is no wimp: in fact, they must have thought so at Fontanafredda too, given that in the past they made Barolo San Pietro Riserva and even Riserva Speciale wines (for example in the 1978 vintage: clearly, the wine would never have held up to that lengthy oak aging if it didn't have real structure and backbone to support it).

The second segment of the Fontanafredda vineyard district follows from the Gallaretto segment and reaches the winery buildings or just slightly past the halfway point of the vineyard district's length. Originally known as Gattinera, just like the first segment, it can also be subdivided in two portions: Bianca (Vigna Bianca) and Gattinera proper. The wines are sturdier than those of the first segment and require more time, both in your glass and in your cellar, to open up and show all they have to offer. While I always liked any Barolos from Bianca I may have tried over the years, I was usually less impressed by those of Gattinera (proper or otherwise), finding them to be a little monolithic.

The third and last segment of the vineyard district is known as Vigna La Rosa: it reaches the border with the Sorano vineyard district. Actually, there is one more segment to the Fontanafredda vineyard district, and it is called Garil, that continues on after La Rosa curving back up into the direction of the winery buildings in the middle of the vineyard district. This is the only section of the vineyard district with which I really have no experience and have never tasted the wines of: for example, they made a 1971 Barolo Garil, but I have no memory whatsoever of it, though I am sure I have tried it at one time or another.

Fontanafredda producers and the wines

Today, the only single vineyard/site wine made from within the ranks of the Fontanafredda vineyard district by the eponymous winery is the Barolo Vigna La Rosa. The grapes with which the wine is made are sourced from a vineyard holding that is a little more than two hectares large, planted at 250-310 meters above sea level with a south to southwest exposure. The vineyard is named after '*la bela Rosin*', the nickname of the lady who was initially the lover and then the morganatic wife of Italy's King Vittorio Emanuele II, the owner of the Fontanafredda estate. The lady's full name was actually Rosa Maria Chiara Teresa Aloisia Vercellana (now that's a mouthful) who by all accounts was quite beautiful, hence the characterization of *bela*, or *bella*. The vineyard has a complex marly clay and compacted sand soil. The wine does remind you of roses, as the name of the vineyard recalls (though the rose descriptor is very typical of good Barolos and Nebbiolo wines from most sites and the vineyard's name, as mentioned, is reportedly unrelated to the flower). Fontanafredda is a big producer and the wines are competently made, and this one is relatively ageworthy too. As mentioned previously, their Barolo Vigna La Rosa is the only one bearing the Fontanafredda vineyard district's name, so if you want to see what this vineyard district can deliver from at least one of its specific segments, this is pretty well it, short of finding some of the older vintages of other single-site bottlings I mentioned earlier in this file.

Benchmark wineries/Reference point producers of Barolo Fontanafredda: Fontanafredda.

FOSSATI

Township	Barolo and La Morra
Reference Map	See Maps of Barolo MGAs and of La Morra MGAs (Ch. 10)
Size (ha) (Tot / Barolo MGA)	23.2 (Barolo) + 10.6 (La Morra) / 13.91
Production 2021 (hl)	714.69 (Of which 291.56 of Barolo Riserva *MGA*)
Altitude	340 – 480 meters a.s.l. roughly
Exposure	Predominantly east.
N. Claimants MGA	12
Other grape varieties planted:	Barbera; Dolcetto; Freisa; white varieties
Land Units	Land Unit of La Morra
Soil (stage):	Tortonian

Producers claiming the MGA

460 Casina Bric; Enzo Boglietti; Borgogno; Cesare Bussolo; Collina San Ponzio; Dosio; Fossati-La Morra-Barolo-Soc.; G.D. Vajra; Icardi; Egidio Oberto; Poderi Gianni Gagliardo; Francesco Vaira; Roberto Voerzio.

Wines

460 Casina Bric - Barolo Fossati; **Enzo Boglietti** - Barolo Fossati; **Borgogno** - Barolo Fossati; **Cesare Bussolo** - Barolo Fossati; **Cascina Adelaide** - Barolo Fossati; **Collina San Ponzio** - Barolo Fossati and Barolo Riserva; **Dosio** - Barolo Fossati and Barolo Riserva Fossati; **Icardi** - Barolo Fossati; **Egidio Oberto** - Barolo Fossati; **Poderi Gianni Gagliardo** - Barolo Fossati; **G.D. Vajra** - Barolo Fossati (*)

What the producers say

Enzo Boglietti (Boglietti): "We have owned this land for three generations and started to vinify the vineyard on its own in 1996. For us, the highlights of this Barolo are its elegance and balance on the palate. A small defect –though it may be seen as a quality in certain years – is that it has a fresher exposure, resulting in problems of maturation in less ideal vintages".

Cascina Adelaide: "We started its own vinification in 2004 and find it has always a darker color than our other Barolos. This wine possesses the power of Barolo and all the perfume and elegance of the soil of La Morra. It's a powerful and austere Barolo, scented with notes of cassis and black fruits and distinguished for its vigorous almost chewy tannins."

Aldo Vaira (G.D. Vajra): "In our family for generations, we began this site's vinification on its own and bottling in 1985, and are now doing reconstructive work in the vineyard. Fossati is characterized for its lovely drinkability".

Davide Voerzio (Roberto Voerzio): "We have been vinifying separately this *cru* since 2000. The Barolo of Fossati is more similar to that of La Serra than that of Cerequio, as it has powerful and classic tannins. In respect to La Serra, one finds a darker fruit here and a notable note of spices. We like to make a Riserva from this site that is ahead ten years."

Ian's assessment of the vineyard district, its wines and its potential

Is Fossati a somewhat underappreciated site, even by Barolo producers? I think it might be, though with 74% of the vineyard district planted to vines of which 85% is Nebbiolo, somebody obviously likes it enough. It's just that you rarely if ever hear anybody talk about Barolos from Fossati. Francia? Sure? Bussia? Even more sure. And Brunate too, and Vignarionda and… but rarely do you hear someone mention Fossati in the same breath. But I think Fossati probably deserves better, and climate change will probably help this vineyard district gain some of the spotlight that is currently shunning it.

It's an inter-communal vineyard district, shared by the communes of La Morra and Barolo. You can see it easily while you drive from La Morra to Barolo along a secondary road. It is bordered by many other vineyard districts: in the La Morra territory there is La Serra to its north and Case Nere to the east; in the Barolo territory, it's Sarmassa to the east, Liste to the southeast, San Pietro to the south and Bricco delle Viole to the southwest. It's an interesting site in that many producers you talk to will tell you (just read the comments of some of them above) that Fossati gives powerful, structured Barolos, but in my experience that has frankly never been the case. Wines of a clear-cut tannic undercurrent, yes; powerful *à la* Monforte or Serralunga, no. Furthermore, its mainly eastern exposure, high altitude and La Morra Land Unit landscape all point to wines that ought to be fresh, lively and not so massive and powerful. What I do think is typical of Fossati's Barolos is a neatly recognizable balsamic minty note (not quite as dry as that of menthol but not quite as sweet as that of traditional balsamic vinegar) that is consistent with the site's altitude and generally cooler climate reality. To put it into more objective and perhaps simpler terms, this is a site characterized by a lot of sand and that sees the cold morning sun: not exactly a recipe by which to make powerful, fleshy wines, right? Which is exactly what you'll find too, when you taste enough wines over the years. It may also be that because of its exposure, climate and geology, Fossati Barolos made in cold years have tannins that fail to reach complete physiological maturation and so the wines can taste gritty, but with climate change, the Barolos from Fossati are more often than not perfumed and smoothly tannic.

Fossati producers and the wines

Giovanni Montanaro, born in 1900, owned both the Fossati farmhouse and a portion of the Fossati vineyard; he was the father of the wife of current Boglietti owner Enzo Boglietti (the estate's other vineyard holdings, such as in Brunate and Boiolo come by way of his own grandfather, Matteo Boglietti). Today the winery owns 1.8 hectares of vines in Fossati (a small piece of which spills over into Barolo: in fact, Boglietti is, to the best of my knowledge, the only winery that owns Fossati vineyard plots in both communes), planted between 370-420 meters above sea level. They opted for Nebbiolo clones CVT 36, CN111, CVT 230 and CVT CN 142; in fact, as of 1998, the plantings were about 60% 230 and 40% CN111. It is not without interest that they have Nebbiolo Rosé in their vineyard (clone CN111, now believed to be a Nebbiolo Lampia clone that looks and behaves like Nebbiolo Rosé (thought the majority of those I have talked to do not agree with this proposed new reinterpretation of reality). See NEBBIOLO ROSÉ file), because this has a huge bearing on the way the finished wine smells and tastes (the Boglietti Fossati Barolo is very floral, perfumed, light on its feet, with a spicy, savory quality, all of which are hallmarks of Nebbiolo Rosé). About 30% of the vines are over 60 years of age, another 70% are less than twenty years old; they face mostly east to southeast. The wine is aged for about thirty months in used barriques and *foudres*.

Gianni Gagliardo owns a very small plot of vines in Fossati, only 0.19 hectares large, planted facing northeast (it was overgrafted in 2013) at 380 meters in altitude with a special "Gagliardo" massal selection of Nebbiolo Michet. There are only 899 plants in the vineyard and less than 1100 bottles made in the winery a year, so this Barolo Fossati is available for sale only in a special "Experience Box" that contains one bottle each of Gianni Gagliardo's individual vineyard district bottlings (Castelletto, Fossati, Lazzarito Vigna Preve, Monvigliero). Gagliardo's holding is close by a forest and is characterized by a relatively cool microclimate, so much so that this is usually their last Nebbiolo vineyard to be harvested each year. It is a lovely wine, vertical in the way that Barolos from Fossati tend to be, but boasting a surprising mix of warmer weather notes of red cherry syrup and cooler weather ones (eucalyptus, gentian). It is usually one of my favourite Barolos from Gagliardo in every vintage.

Dosio farms about 1.2 hectares in Fossati of forty-five years old vines they bought in 1982. Their piece is on the lower-lying part of the slope that is in the Barolo territory. Made only in the best years (in fact, it was the first ever Barolo bearing a vineyard site name the estate ever made, back in 1986), beginning with the 2008 vintage a Barolo Fossati Riserva has been made too. Talented Marco Dotta, formerly of the outstanding De Gresy estate in Barbaresco, made wines there for some time, and though he has since moved on to new projects, he got to know Fossati well during his time at Dosio. He told me he believes the wines to have generally excellent balance and to develop notes of chocolate and hay in time, even some leathery nuances.

Cascina Adelaide owns vineyards at about 400 meters above sea level, and their soils seem to have more red clay than in other vineyards I have walked in Fossati. Maybe that accounts in part for a certain large-shouldered personality to this estate's excellent Fossati Barolo wines, at least compared to some others made from this vineyard district. It is the most recent addition to the winery's large portfolio of Barolo wines and sites. Borgogno owns 3.2 hectares of southeast-facing vines there, planted between 290 and 350 meters above sea level. They use the grapes for their Barolo estate wine. As elsewhere, there is a good percentage of sand in their vineyard's soil. Viberti's classic Barolo 'Buon Padre' is made with grapes from Fossati, as well as from San

Pietro, San Ponzio, La Volta, Albarella, Terlo, Ravera, Perno, Monvigliero. Brezza owns vines in Fossati, but since it is a north-facing plot, he planted Dolcetto there instead. G.D. Vajra has also planted Dolcetto in Fossati, thanks to which the winery makes his outstanding Dolcetto d'Alba Coste&Fossati, but also uses his Fossati Nebbiolo grapes in the Barolo Albe. For those who like Roberto Voerzio's wines, a cheaper but similar alternative is represented by the wines of Cesare Bussolo (who trained under and worked with Voerzio). The recipe is a familiar one to those who know Roberto Voerzio: bunches reduced to very small sizes (if not quite the 500 grams of Voerzio, still less than a kilogram per vine) and very thick wines that border on the jammy. The wines are very well made, and for those who like the style, hard to beat. By contrast, those who prefer lift and freshness look elsewhere.

Benchmark wineries/Reference point producers of Barolo Fontanafredda: Boglietti, Cascina Adelaide, Cesare Bussolo, Gianni Gagliardo.

FRANCIA

Township	Serralunga d'Alba
Reference Map	See Map of Serralunga d'Alba MGAs (Ch. 10)
Size (ha) (Tot / Barolo MGA)	15,80 / 7.82
Production 2021 (hl)	418.20 (of which 418.20 of Barolo Riserva *MGA*)
Altitude	360 – 445 meters a.s.l. roughly
Exposure	From west to southwest, except for a small part facing east-southeast
N. Claimants MGA	1
Other grape varieties planted:	Barbera
Land Units	Land Unit of Serralunga d'Alba
Soil (stage):	Serravallian

Producers claiming the MGA

Giacomo Conterno.

Wines

Giacomo Conterno - Barolo Francia

Ian's assessment of the vineyard district, its wines and its potential

Francia is one of the most southernmost vineyard districts of the Serralunga commune: only Arione is farther south. In fact, Francia is almost entirely surrounded by the Boscareto vineyard district: from above, it is obvious how the latter encircles Francia, seemingly swallowing it in the trough of its C-shaped extension of vineyard land. Therefore, Boscareto lies to the south, southwest, west and north of Francia: a small piece of Badarina snuggles up to Francia to the northeast, while Arione, as mentioned, lies immediately south and mostly to the southeast of Francia. Francia is situated almost completely on the western flank of the Serralunga ridge that divides the commune's territory more or less in two halves; its vines have a mostly west- and south to southwest facing exposure, save for that little piece of the hill that looks to Badarina, which face east/southeast. This last piece is where Conterno has planted most of the Barbera vines he uses to make his outstanding Barbera d'Alba Francia (for my money of the two best such wines of the entre denomination).

Francia's landscape is that of the Land Unit of Serralunga, and its soil lithology is the classic Lequio Formation that gives Barolo's steeliest, most powerful, but also very lifted, wines. A monopole of the Giacomo Conterno estate, much like Falletto and Bricco Rocche are monopoles of the Bruno Giacosa and Ceretto wineries respectively, it is not exaggerated to define it as one of Italy's ten or twelve single greatest vineyard areas.

Francia producers and the wines (monopole)

Let's face it: very few places in Italy can boast not just one, but two wines of the level of the famous Giacomo Conterno Barolo Francia (formerly Cascina Francia: as with other now official vineyard district names, the site's name changed over to "Francia" with the official 2011 naming of Barolo's vineyard districts) and Barolo Riserva Monfortino. The latter is for many of the world's most knowledgeable wine experts Italy's greatest wine (or tied with Sassicaia), and I would have to say it's near impossible to argue the point. I'll go one step further, and add that while up to the 2001 vintage I would choose another red wine as my top wine of Italy, ever since then my choice falls upon Monfortino more often than not. All of which should not make one forget about the Barolo Francia, which is one of the top Barolos of the denomination (just check out how truly amazingly great was the 1994, a poor vintage, but the Barolo Francia is an unforgettably great, great, great wine).

In fact, much like it was for Château Trotanoy in the days when it was shown together with Petrus at the *En Primeurs* tastings in the JP Moueix tasting room, Giacomo Conterno's Barolo Cascina Francia main problem in life is that it lives with Monfortino as its stablemate. So much like Trotanoy always ended up being an (almost) also-ran because Petrus casts a shadow it is simply impossible to step out of, so Monfortino obfuscates the amazingly bright light that the Francia vineyard shines on any of the Barolos made from it. Continuing on with the Bordeaux analogy, but stepping for a moment onto the left bank, it is important to be aware of the fact that Francia has the uncanny ability, Château Latour-like, to deliver great Barolos even in vintages marred by poor weather. For example, as I mentioned just above, the 1994 Barolo Cascina Francia was likely the best Barolo of that sorry vintage. And as also mentioned previously, Francia's greatness as a truly outstanding vineyard site is confirmed by the fact it is so not just for Nebbiolo, but for other varieties as well: for example, the aforementioned Barbera d'Alba wine. But what readers probably do not know is that Giacomo Conterno also made one of Italy's two or three best Freisa wines with Francia grapes too. All of which speaks to what an amazing site the Francia vineyard district really is.

That much admitted, for those who don't know, I will point out that Monfortino was not always made with grapes from Francia: this is only logical, given that the winery bought Francia in 1974 (and so the first Monfortino made entirely with grapes from Francia is the 1978). Back in the first part of the twentieth century Monfortino was made with grapes from Monforte (why did you think it's called "Monfortino"?). The wine has now come (almost) full circle, because beginning with the 2015 vintage a small amount of grapes from other vineyard districts (but not from Monforte) in which the Giacomo Conterno estate has recently bought vineyards (namely Arione: see ARIONE file) are now blended into the Monfortino Barolo.

If there is only one infinitesimally small observation I can make about Francia (which I admit is like trying to find fault with the beauty of the Venus de Milo or of Leonardo's Mona Lisa) is that its wines are less exciting in especially hot vintages (I would venture that it's probably not by accident that Monfortino is rarely made in such vintages, with exceptions, while it is made without much problem in years of horribly cold/wet weather, such as 2002). However, it is not that in hot years Francia performs less than admirably: quite the contrary. Just imagine that even in 2003, one of the hottest years on record, Roberto Conterno still harvested in the second week of October. The cooling effect of the Francia soil limestone, and the citrussy acidity that it infuses the wines with, made for a Barolo Cascina Francia that year that was, yes, 14.8% in alcohol, but endowed with plenty of freshness and lively acidity.

In ultimate analysis, Francia, with its strongly calcareous soil and sunny, warm mesoclimate, gives Barolos characterized by a delicate spiciness and truly beautiful minerality (if we accept that minerality can be beautiful) not to mention a ferrous quality, combined with a red cherry nectar presence of almost syrup-like concentration. It is my experience that the single most important descriptor of Francia Barolos is licorice, an organoleptic feature that becomes especially prominent in time; and not just in the Barolos, but in the Barbera wines too. By contrast, the notes of eucalyptus that some associate with the wines of Francia are in my opinion not due to the site itself, but are partly a result of winemaking and Conternos' penchant for a certain degree of well-measured extraction and long macerations, not to mention pushing the later harvest envelope as far as it will reasonably go. No matter: with or without notes of licorice and/or eucalyptus, after all is said and done, when it comes to Francia, it all adds up to a simply unforgettable series of wines..

Benchmark wineries/Reference point producers of Barolo Francia: Giacomo Conterno (monopole).

GABUTTI

Township	Serralunga d'Alba
Reference Map	See Map of Serralunga d'Alba MGAs (Ch. 10)
Size (ha) (Tot / Barolo MGA)	14.24 / 7.7
Production 2021 (hl)	419.36
Altitude	250 – 350 meters a.s.l. roughly
Exposure	From west to southeast passing through south
N. Claimants MGA	2
Other grape varieties planted:	Barbera; Dolcetto
Land Units	Land Unit of Serralunga d'Alba
Soil (stage):	Serravallian

Producers claiming the MGA

Franco Boasso; Maria Rosa Pozzetti; Sordo (Giovanni Sordo).

Wines

Cappellano - Barolo Otin Fiorin Piè Franco, Barolo Otin Fiorin Piè Rupestris; **Franco Boasso (Gabutti)** –- Barolo Gabutti; **Sordo** - Barolo Gabutti, Barolo Gabutti Riserva

What the producers say

Boasso: "Fermentation lasts 12 to 15 days, while the wine is aged in new 25 hectoliter oak barrels for about three years. For us, wines from this site express notes of tar, licorice, smoke and ash, with fainter nuances of violet and rose".

Sordo: "Renato Ratti qualified this area as an important one in his famous map: "*a first-quality site, in one of the more interesting and prestigious subzones of Serralunga*". The wines are fairly savory with notes of resin, peach leaf and licorice".

Ian's assessment of the vineyard district, its wines and its potential

Gabutti, one of the many vineyard districts found on the Serralunga ridge's western flank, is really but the lower-lying extension of another vineyard district, the Parafada. And while halfway through its extension the hillside crest over which this vineyard district is draped over veers sharply north and away from Parafada towards the Prabon vineyard district, the vines in the best part of Gabutti maintain a full range of southern exposures, running from southeast to the south and southwest. Therefore, from an aerial perspective, Parafada lies immediately east of Gabutti, and Serralunga's Prabon is due north (from this point of view much like Gabutti is the continuation of Parafada, a case can be made that Prabon is itself the northern prolongation of Gabutti).

Gabutti is one of the vineyard districts of the northern half of the Serralunga commune (which can be taken to be all those vineyard districts located northwards of the town). Generally speaking, the wines of Serralunga's northern half present noteworthy differences when compared to those of its southern half, mostly in relation to microclimates and soil compositions. However, because of its steep slope, relatively low altitude and mostly south-facing vines (in its best section), Gabutti is a generally warmer site than many of the ones up in the north and gives bold, textured wines that are quite a mouthful. This is especially true of the portions of the site that are farthest from Parafada: in my experience, and I may well be wrong, wines made with grapes grown closer to Parafada are somewhat gentler and tend to have paler red colors thanks to the looser, sandier soils there. Soils that nonetheless contribute to the tannic mouthful typical of Gabutti wine: not surprising, given its Lequio Formation lithology.

Gabutti producers and the wines

Various estates produce a Barolo from Gabutti. Boasso owns 0.5 hectares on a fairly calcareous southeast-facing site that benefits from great luminosity (not always the case with Gabutti). Only the best grapes from the vineyard are used to make their Barolo Gabutti, and the wine is very well-made and enjoyable. Sordo and of course Cappellano do as well. Chiara Boschis of Barolo's famous E. Pira/Chiara Boschis winery also farms vines in Gabutti: she began renting there in 2010 and uses those grapes for her Barolo Via Nuova (made since then with the grapes not just from Gabutti but Terlo and Ravera too). She tells me she is generally happy with the site and the grapes it gives, but for now is not considering making a Barolo Gabutti.

Clearly, the most famous Barolo Gabutti is that of Cappellano, but the Franco Boasso-Gabutti and Sordo Barolo Gabutti are also good wines. All are however slightly different in style. Based on the Gabutti wines I have tried many times and over many vintages, I'd say the wines from Cappellano and Boasso are usually very mouthcoating and textured, with more or less very generous doses of alcohol-derived warmth showing depending on the vintage, while Sordo's are a little more floral and fresher, but also somewhat lighter in texture (as much as any Serralunga Barolo can be defined as "lighter" in style). Which you prefer really depends on the degree of mouthcoatingness you prefer, because once you get past all the hype, I, and not just I, find there is only so much Gabutti Barolos have to offer. For me many of its wines are just too ripe and high in alcohol, but that's probably on me, and others will no doubt like Gabutti's wines more. Still, I have to draw a line somewhere, and the fact is that in twenty plus years of serious wine tasting, no Barolo Gabutti I have memory of, though clearly good wines, ever left me with an eye-opening, jaw-dropping taste experience. Then again, Renato Ratti seemed to think highly of the site (according to his *Carta del Barolo* map), and so it may all boil down to different strokes for different folks. And therein lies part of the beauty of wine.

In fact, my favorite Barolo Gabutti of all actually never even carried the name Gabutti at all. Have you ever heard of Grignorè? Yes, no? Well, here goes. The Barolo Grignorè was a small-batch Barolo made by Ceretto in exclusivity for the Guido restaurant of Costigliole d'Asti, Michelin starred and one of Italy's best dining spots for decades. The wine was born out of the friendship between Marcello Ceretto and Guido Alciati, the restaurant's owner. From 1980 to 1990, Ceretto vinified the grapes from the Grignorè subregion of Gabutti. Guido's son, Piero, continued this collaboration even after the restaurant moved from Costigliole d'Asti to Pollenzo and its Agenzia; clearly, when the restaurant and agency were bought by the owner of Fontanafredda and Borgogno, the partnership ended (a loss for everyone involved, restaurant clients included). Therefore, 1999 is the last vintage of that wine produced for Guido. It was a lovely, at times fantastic, traditional Barolo *(cappello sommerso* maceration and aging three years in large fifty-five hectoliter Slavonian oak barrels) that spoke of cherries macerated in alcohol, forest floor, nutmeg and peppery roasted coffee beans and tobacco. Don't pass on it if you see it on some restaurant wine list.

Benchmark wineries/Reference point producers of Barolo Gabutti: Boasso-Gabutti, Cappellano, Sordo.

GALINA

Township	La Morra
Reference Map	See Map of La Morra MGAs (Ch. 10)
Size (ha) (Tot / Barolo MGA)	8.74 / 2.13
Production 2021 (hl)	101.61
Altitude	260 – 310 meters a.s.l. roughly
Exposure	From southeast to east-northeast
N. Claimants MGA	3
Other grape varieties planted:	Barbera; Dolcetto; Pelaverga Piccolo
Land Units	Land Unit of Barolo in the east side bordering Bricco Chiesa; Land Unit of La Morra for the remaining parts
Soil (stage):	Tortonian

Producers claiming the MGA

Crissante Alessandria; Poderi Oddero; San Biagio.

Wines

Crissante Alessandria - Barolo Galina

Ian's assessment of the vineyard district, its wines and its potential

Galina is located in the La Morra commune just below the road from Capalot up above and next to the Bricco Chiesa and Santa Maria vineyard districts. To date and to the best of my knowledge, there is only one producer selling a Barolo carrying the Galina vineyard site on the label (but at least it's a good one).

The soil of Galina was formed during the Tortonian stage of the Miocene epoch, and therefore the soil lithology is that of the Saint Agatha Marls Formation, mostly of the laminated type. However, it is my experience that Galina soil composition varies between the two extremes of the vineyard district's extension, and is mostly of two types: closer to Bricco Chiesa, the soil is richer in clay while the soil in the rest of the vineyard district and especially of the areas closer to Capalot have a slightly higher percentage of sand and a good deal of limestone too.

The whitish color of most of Galina's soils and the rush of citrussy acidity when you taste its wines speak of that limestone presence. From what I have been able to discern over the years, the wine tastes of small red berries and licorice. However, the number of Barolo Galina wines I have tried over the years has been forcibly limited by the paucity of estates bottling one, what I did taste never struck me as the biggest or most complex Barolo I had ever tasted. But what I have tasted boasted very good balance.

Galina producers and the wines

The Crissante Alessandria estate produces a Barolo Galina from about 0.8 hectares of vines planted at 270-290 meters in altitude. Alberto Alessandria, the current generation at the helm, told me that one fifth of the vineyard was planted to Nebbiolo back in 1999, but the rest of the site was replanted in 2014 (prior to that year, the vineyard boasted some very old, even ungrafted, Nebbiolo vines dating back to 1922 and 1940; unfortunately, they produced very little grapes and so had to be uprooted). Recent vintages have been aged in tonneaux rather than barriques (non-new barriques were chosen because of the small extension of vines in Galina and hence the low volume of grapes produced each year such that filling a larger barrel would have been impossible). In typical Galina fashion, Crissante Alessandria's wine from this vineyard district is marked by relatively high citrussy acidity that provides noteworthy lift and a steely, edgy (but optimally ripe) quality that is very refreshing. Put it this way: if Alessandria's Capalot Barolo is more like a baroque church dome (independently of whether the grapes are late harvested or air-dried, the Capalot tends to give joyful wines of irresistible violetty, fruity charm), the Galina is more of a gothic steeple, taut and laser-like. There is however sneaky size and concentration to the wine, most likely because Alessandria's holdings are closer to the Bricco Chiesa side of Galina, and the soil there has sand limestone on the upper parts of the slope but a lot more clay and marl lower-down.

Benchmark wineries/Reference point producers of Barolo Galina: Crissante Alessandria.

GALLARETTO

Township	Diano d'Alba
Reference Map	See Map of Diano d'Alba MGAs (Ch. 10)
Size (ha) (Tot / Barolo MGA)	15.36
Production 2021 (hl)	
Altitude	220 – 305 meters a.s.l. roughly
Exposure	Predominantly northeast
N. Claimants MGA	
Other grape varieties planted:	Barbera; Dolcetto; white varieties
Land Units	Land Unit of Barolo
Soil (stage):	Tortonian

Ian's assessment of the vineyard district, its wines and its potential

Gallaretto is only one of three vineyard districts in the commune of Diano d'Alba (and one of the three, Sorano, is shared with Serralunga). It is by far the longest of the three, a long narrow strip of vines running roughly in a southwest to northeast direction. Do not confuse this vineyard district with a segment of the Fontanafredda vineyard district that goes by the same name (see FONTANAFREDDA file). Although about 90% of Gallaretto is planted to vines, only a third of the total is Nebbiolo. Simply put, the exposures and rigid climate of this vineyard district is such that Nebbiolo does not find itself quite at home, at least up until now.

Gallaretto producers and the wines

The only two estates I know of with land in Gallaretto are Fontanafredda (the winery) and La Contrada di Sorano. The latter owns 0.4 hectares of east-facing vines there planted at 300 meters in altitude back in 1970 right below the town of Diano d'Alba (though the geology of their vineyard soil is more typical of Serralunga). Their inaugural vintage was the 2015 and both that wine and their 2016 Barolo were made only with grapes from this plot of vines (the estate also owns 1.2 hectares in the Sorano vineyard district and vineyards in the San Rocco vineyard district too). Their Barolo is truly remarkable: its high quality aside, it is a rare Barolo that is 100% Nebbiolo Rosé, something that the wine's refined perfume and translucently pristine mouthfeel give away immediately, at first sip. Owner Paolo Baudana grew up in the hamlet of Sorano, his parents owned vines and made wine for home use selling the rest in bulk. Paolo and his wife Cristina have kicked things up a notch, farm organically and founded the estate in 2013. The wines are fermented for about forty-five days on the skins (submerged cap) in stainless steel and aged in barriques and tonneaux (there's limited space in their tiny garage-like cellar). I think it's a perfectly fine Barolo of early appeal and easy accessibility, broadcasting well its typical Tortonian age Saint Agatha Fossil Marls soils (and therefore somewhat reminiscent in style of some of the Barolos of the La Morra and Barolo communes.

Benchmark wineries/Reference point producers of Barolo Gallaretto: La Contrada di Sorano.

GARRETTI

Township	Grinzane Cavour
Reference Map	See Map of Grinzane Cavour MGAs (Ch. 10)
Size (ha) (Tot / Barolo MGA)	9.00 / 5.95
Production 2021 (hl)	321.16
Altitude	220 – 265 meters a.s.l. roughly
Exposure	From south to southwest
N. Claimants MGA	2
Other grape varieties planted:	Barbera; Dolcetto
Land Units	Land Unit of Barolo
Soil (stage):	Tortonian

Producers claiming the MGA
La Spinetta; Pio Cesare.

Wines
La Spinetta - Barolo Campè; Barolo Vigneto Garretti

What the producers say
Giorgio Rivetti (La Spinetta): "Campè is a well-balanced Barolo, fruity, round with supple tannins. On the nose, an expressive bouquet reveals itself with notes of rose, violet, blueberry and chocolate; on the palate it is potent and complex with polished tannins and a long finish".

Ian's assessment of the vineyard district, its wines and its potential

If Garretti isn't the easternmost vineyard district of the Barolo denomination, then it comes really close to running away with that title. Located in the territory of the commune of Grinzane Cavour, it is only one of eight vineyard districts there and shares borders with one only, Gustava. Garretti's landscape is characterized as a Barolo Land Unit, meaning that its lithology is that of Saint-Agatha Fossil Marls, here in their most typical form. To a degree, this bit of knowledge tells you what to expect from the wines made there. The sample soil analyses I have studied over the years show that the mix is approximately 45% loam, 35% clay and 20% sand.

Garretti producers and the wines

If wine lovers know anything about Garretti or have had a chance to taste wines from the vineyard district it is undoubtedly thanks to the La Spinetta estate, where Giorgio Rivetti was the first producer to make a single-vineyard district wine from this site. In fact, other estates own vines there (Cantina del Conte, Pio Cesare), but the Cantina del Conte is the only other estate that bottles a Barolo solely from Garretti grapes, while Pio Cesare, for example, prefers to blend its grapes from other vineyard districts into their classic estate Barolos, as the house has always tended to do.

La Spinetta's owns roughly eight hectares in Garretti, planted facing south from 240 to 270 meters above sea level. The vines are divided into roughly three sections: a lower one where the vines are on average about thirty years old, and a central and upper portion where vines are as much as 65-70 years old (not by chance this is thought to be the best part of the estate's Garretti holdings). Rivetti was able to buy this vineyard, called Campè, in 2000: the first Barolo Campè Riserva from Garretti was the 2000, while the first Barolo Campè dates back to the 2001 vintage.

Much younger vines in Garretti are those of the famous Pio Cesare winery: the Boffa family owns land in Garretti since 1985 and planted Nebbiolo clone 142 in 2000. However, since the beginning, the Boffa family has vinified these vines separately (as it does with all its many vineyards scattered throughout the Barolo denomination). The Nebbiolo is planted at 300 meters above sea level and faces southwest. Winemaking is classic (maximum fermentation temperatures of 28 degrees Celsius and in stainless steel) such that it doesn't mark the wines too much, given an aging process that involves 85% large oak barrels and 15% barriques (part French, part Eastern European oak). I find it very interesting, relative to what it tells us about the site, that Pio Cesare's best wines from Garretti thus far have been the 2008, 2013 and 2016, all very classic, even cool, years (vintages that, especially the 2008 and 2013, harkened back to the weather of the 1980s). This leads me to think Garretti performs best in years that are not extremely hot (I caution readers who do not know me and haven't followed my tasting notes over the years by way of the International Wine Cellar, Vinous, Decanter and now the TerroirSense Wine Review that I consider a wine to be outstanding and successful when it's balanced, rather than just massive and mouthcoating with little or no grace). Somewhat surprisingly given what I just told you, Pio Cesare's 2007 from Garretti was also one of the best ever wines they made from the site (right up there with the other three); but before you start thinking this throws a monkey wrench into our line of reasoning (because 2007, differently from '08,'13 and '16 was an extremely hot year), I should mention that 2007 was a year in which all the wines of Grinzane Cavour showed extremely well (for example, 2007 was a vintage in which La Spinetta also made some of its best wines ever). Last but not least, as mentioned previously, the Cantina del Conte in Grinzane Cavour also makes a Barolo and Barolo Riserva with Garretti grapes. This family run cellar works very traditionally and is owned by the Pellissero family (do not confuse it with the Pellissero family of Treiso or with Pasquale Pellissero of Neive, two well-known producers of the Barbaresco denomination).

Due to the paucity of wineries owning vines and making wines from this vineyard district, nobody has never been much aware of Garetti and what its wines might be really like, or for that matter what the vineyard district's defining wine characteristics might be. Rivetti is an excellent winemaker and La Spinetta a model estate, but there can be no doubt that his wines reflect his own signature style more than they do the habitat in which the grapes grow.

Benchmark wineries/Reference point producers of Barolo Garretti: Cantina del Conte, La Spinetta.

GATTERA

Township	La Morra
Reference Map	See Map of La Morra MGAs (Ch. 10)
Size (ha) (Tot / Barolo MGA)	30.02 / 6.15
Production 2021 (hl)	333.77
Altitude	220 – 290 meters a.s.l. roughly
Exposure	From southeast to southwest in the better exposed parcels; east and from north to northeast in the remaining parts
N. Claimants MGA	6
Other grape varieties planted:	Barbera; Dolcetto; white varieties
Land Units	Land Unit of Castiglione for the most; Land Unit of Barolo for the lower parcels bordering Bricco Manzoni e Bricco Luciani
Soil (stage):	Tortonian

Producers claiming the MGA

Gianfranco Bovio; F.lli. Ferrero; Monfalletto; F.lli. Revello; Angelo Veglio; Mauro Veglio.

Wines

Gianfranco Bovio - Barolo Gattera, Barolo Riserva Gattera; **Monfalletto (Cordero di Montezemolo)** - Barolo Gattera and Riserva Gorette**; Fratelli Ferrero** - Barolo Gattera; **Fratelli Revello** - Barolo Gattera; **Angelo Veglio** - Barolo Gattera; **Mauro Veglio** - Barolo Gattera.

What the producers say

Alberto Cordero di Montezemolo (Monfalletto): "Our family has been the proprietor of the Monfalletto vineyard since always (1340) and we have vinified it apart for more than a century (Bricco Gattera only since 1997). The clay soil that has calcareous soil mixed in confer to Monfalletto elegance and complexity. Our best plot, the Bricco Gattera, is situated at the foot of a centenary Lebanon cedar tree, on the highest southwest-facing slope of the Gattera cru. These are very old vines at about 300 meters above sea level in rich and clay soil provide an ideal maturation for an austere and complex Barolo".

Revello Lorenzo (Flli. Revello): "We acquired this property in 1970 and started its separate vinification in 1999. Gat The Gattera *cru* gives elegant and tannic Barolo".

Veglio Mauro (Veglio Mauro): "Among our Barolos, the Gattera is noted for being the most similar to the classic Barolo. It's accessible early, and has soft tannins possibly because of the warm microclimate and its south to southwest exposure".

Ian's assessment of the vineyard district, its wines and its potential

Gattera, named after a farmhouse, built on the site, is a relatively large vineyard area (nearby the Annunziata fraction of La Morra) that can be divided into many different subregions. Unlike though with vineyard districts like Bussia, Ginestra and Mosconi where such an undertaking would be not just useful but highly logical too, with Gattera it is less important to proceed so. Not because there aren't differences between wines made from the different subregions (there are: see below) but because these differences do not jump out at you quite as much and so, in the interests of simplifying the denomination and its wines for everyone, one can grasp why leaving Gattera as is makes a modicum of sense. In any case, it is my opinion that if one wanted to, the Gattera vineyard could be subdivided in: the Monfalletto hill (that gives its name to the famous Monfalletto winery owned by the Cordero di Montezemolo family), Gorette (see below) and Turnalonga (of which there are different spellings, including Turna Langa and Turna d' l'Orient), which was historically the name of what is today considered to be the lower part of the Gattera vineyard district.

In some ways, Gattera is a complex *cru*. Situated in La Morra's territory, for the most part its wines are typical of that commune, but there's an undeniable underlying power and texture to them that is quite unlike those of the rest of the Annunziata fraction of La Morra (where Gattera is located) and absolutely nothing like those of La Morra's Santa Maria fraction. In fact, Gattera boasts soils of different lithologies, with the change occurring especially between lower and upper portions of the slope. Lower down, the typical Saint Agatha Fossil Marls (but with varying proportions of the laminated and sandy forms as well) dominates, while the upper reaches have at least some presence of Diano Sandstone. Clearly, the wines born off the Saint Agatha Marls give wines of the ilk you'd associate mostly with La Morra and/or Barolo (these are the sections of Gattera closest to Bricco Luciani and Bricco Manzoni), while the Diano Sandstone gives wines that have more in common with those of Castiglione Falletto and parts of Monforte. As a general indication (but keep in mind that, as mentioned, the soil varies within the vineyard district), you can think of Gattera as being a mostly loamy site: 60-65% loam, 18-25% clay and 15-20% sand). Again, while Gattera's wines have an undeniable creaminess to them and are accessible early on in life (as wines from La Morra tend to be), their textural richness has an underlying tannic backbone that is more pronounced than that of many other Barolos from La Morra. A little experience in tasting these wines will go a long way in allowing you to recognize this even if you are neither aware of the overriding lithology of the vineyard district nor of from exactly where within the vineyard district the grapes used to make the Barolo you are drinking were grown. You know, when all is said and done, this shouldn't surprise much: after all, Gattera is positioned very close to the territory of Castiglione Falletto [from which it is separated by the diagonal line of La Morra's three Bricco-something vineyard districts (Bricco Manescotto, Bricco Manzoni and Bricco Luciani) that run northeast to southwest along the border with the Castiglione Falletto commune]. Therefore, that proximity to Castiglione Falletto commune is well exemplified in Gattera' preponderant lithology, which is not the one mostly typical of the La Morra commune.

In some ways, you might say that Gattera is a lucky vineyard district in that there is a plethora of extremely talented producers making wine from grapes grown within its boundaries (of course, this means that we as wine lovers are lucky too). The situation is such that the likelihood of your choosing an excellent Barolo from Gattera is very likely indeed, even though you may not be acquainted with the estate you are about to try the wine of. Off the top of my head, I cannot think of ten other Barolo vineyard districts where the likelihood of picking up a so-so wine are as low as they are with a wine from Gattera: which is another way of saying that Gattera is one of the top ten top value sites in all of the Barolo denomination. To put it as bluntly as possible just so what I am trying to say is completely clear, Gattera is one of the ten Barolo vineyard districts that is least likely to leave you feeling like you got shafted. Poetic, I know.

In my experience, Barolos made from Gattera grapes offer, for the most part, obvious notes of camphor and dried herbs, with building white and especially black truffle notes present already when the wines are young but that build with time in a very recognizable manner. By contrast, should you find an obvious note of pomegranate in the older vintages of the Barolo Gattera wines of the Fratelli Revello estate, you should know that this is a descriptor almost unique to their Gattera Barolo. Why? Well, because there was once a decent presence of Nebbiolo Rosé in their vineyard: look for the wines from 1999 and the early 2000s and you will be pleasantly surprised. I know I scour the wine lists of restaurants all over Italy looking just for it, not just because it is unique in its aroma profile, but because it is truly delicious too. So, you see, a little knowledge (or a lot, depends on your point of view) really does go a long way in increasing the quantum of solace you can derive from our favorite pastime (i.e., drinking wine).

Gattera producers and the wines

Given the Cordero di Montezemolo family's and estate's historic association with the Monfalletto hill, it would be unfair to begin any discussion of Gattera and its wines anywhere else. The Cordero di Montezemolo family has ties to wine since the 1340s; in the 1830-1840s, what had been initially a mostly local endeavor, became a business with sales taking place over extended distances. Today, the estate (certified organic) is run by Alberto and Elena, who inherited the estate in 1941 through their grandfather Paolo. The estate is famous not just for its many excellent wines, but also for the Lebanon cedar tree that lives atop the Monfalletto hill. The tree is well over one hundred years old, and to refer to it as simply 'majestic' is probably doing it a disservice: it really is quite the sight (and in fact, it's so large and tall that if you just look up from time to time when in the Barolo denomination, even at some distance from La Morra, chances are good you *will* see it). The tree was planted in 1856, on the day when Costanzo Falletti di Rodello and Eulalia Della Chiesa di Cervignasco, ancestors of the current Cordero di Montezemolo sibling duo, tied the knot and decided to plant the cedar as a sign of their forever love and as a symbol of the devotion of the area's people to their land.

Appropriately enough, the estate's historic wine, in some respects their flagship, is undoubtedly their Barolo Monfalletto, that was one of the first truly modern Barolos made in Italy. Up until the 1987 vintage, it was entirely made with grapes from Gattera; afterwards, depending on the vintage, the Barolo Monfalletto has been blended partly with grapes from the Bricco Manescotto (note that about 5% of the vines are of Nebbiolo Rosé). Besides the Barolo Monfalletto, the estate makes two other La Morra Barolos wholly with Gattera grapes, the Barolo Gattera and the Barolo Riserva Gorette bottlings (the estate also makes one other estate Barolo, called Enrico VI, with grapes from the estate's holdings in the Villero vineyard district of Castiglione Falletto. See the VILLERO file). So, when it comes to Gattera, there really is no bigger expert than the Cordero di Montezemolo estate.

The Barolo Gattera and the Barolo Riserva Gorette were born from the observation that Cordero di Montezemolo's Gattera plots and vines on the Monfaletto hill presented many different exposures, undulations, altitudes, biotypes, age, and other factors. Logically, the family decided to subdivide their Gattera vineyard extension: in the end, it was eight different plots of vines that they harvest and vinify separately. In three of these parcels, there are some fifty years old vines that give a slightly richer, deeper Barolo than the Monfalletto. With these they make their vineyard district-labeled Barolo, the Barolo Gattera. It was in 1997 that Giovanni Cordero di Montezemolo decided to launch this "super-Gattera" bottling (in fact back then it was made only from one plot on the southwestern area of the hill below the big cedar tree), that in the words of Alberto Cordero di Montezemolo (Giovanni's son) is "an extreme Monfalletto, a bigger, deeper expression of site since it comes from richer soil". In fact, the original plot had been hampered by somewhat sickly vines, and so it was replanted in 1987 with fifteen different Nebbiolo clones (80% Michet biotype) from Rauscedo. This is why the wine is made from three different plots nowadays, but the total volume is the same, one fifty hectoliter fermenting bin. Beware that this wine has had different names over the years. For example, the labels of the 1998, 1999 and 2000 read "Barolo Vigna Bricco Gattera"; beginning in 2001, it read "Barolo Bricco Gattera"; and finally, with the arrival of the official vineyard district names, the wine became Barolo Gattera. Beware, because you will read in wine articles and websites everywhere of a Barolo Bricco Gattera wine in reference to the wines of 2013, 2015 and 2016 vintages, and that's just wrong. Clearly, the estate could have decided to call the wine Barolo Gattera Vigna Bricco to keep the connection with the previous incarnation of "Bricco Gattera" but as the estate's and family names are already long, they opted to go with Gattera only. In any case, what is most impressive about this "vineyard within the vineyard" is that its wines, at least in my opinion, have improved not just by leaps and bounds, but rather by gigantic ones, in a very short time. The 2004 was the first truly grand wine made from these specific Gattera plots. There have been many standouts after that, but in the early years the wine was clearly held back by what were at the time still relatively young vines (just think for a moment that the vines from which the grapes are sourced to make this wine reached twenty years of age only in 2008) as well as by the 100% oaking with barriques that took place at the time; something that made, in my view at least, for some tough and chunky wines in the early going. Clearly, not so anymore.

The Barolo Riserva Gorette is made from the Gorette subplot within Gattera, a few rows planted with seventy different Nebbiolo clones roughly 35-40 years of age (plants less than seven years old are used only to make the estate's Langhe Nebbiolo) located at the foot of the cedar tree and that face southeast at about 250-310 meters above sea level, like practically all of the estate's vines. The wine is sold only after a lengthy aging process of roughly two to two and a half years in barrel, then six to seven more in bottle. It is bottled in magnums only (anywhere from 500 to 1000 bottles/year and only in specific vintages, such as 2013, 2015 and 2018) and is only sold to visitors directly at the winery like Alberto's grandfather, Paolo, used to do. Suffice it to say that all the vintage of the Riserva Gorette are classics.

The outstanding Fratelli Revello winery in La Morra bottles many different Barolos bearing single-vineyard district names. Historically, their most important vineyard site has always been the Giachini (see GIACHINI file), and they only made their first Barolo Gattera with the 1999 vintage (initially called Vigna Gattera, this too changed with the launch of the official names of the vineyard districts). At first, the Revello siblings were not quite sure about Gattera's potential, in that this was the estate's only site where the Nebbiolo vines were not fully south-facing (the Revello holdings in Gattera are divided in two parts, an upper southeast-facing plot close to the winery, and a lower piece that faces full south). In the end, they decided to go ahead because of the site's intensely white, calcareous-rich soils of their vineyard. Very interestingly, they opted to age their Barolo from Gattera in large barrels at first, and not in barriques like all their other Barolos, though the vinification was the same for all them. If you just knew how all-pervasive the barrique dogma was in the 1990s in Italy, you realize the intestinal fortitude it took for the Revello clan to do the right thing by Gattera (given the impeccable logic behind such a decision, I'd venture to say for all wine- and especially Barolo-lovers too). In fact, the bottom part of Revello's vineyard in Gattera was initially planted to Dolcetto (back in 1988): this is because in the past, before climate change, the Nebbiolo did not ripen well enough in this area. Finally, the Dolcetto was changed over to Nebbiolo in 1992, but even then, those grapes were never used initially for the Barolo Gattera bottling: a less steep portion of the site, its grapes were better suited for making classic Barolo (those grapes help produce a Barolo of early appeal and easier accessibility). By contrast, the upper portion of Revello's Gattera vines were planted in 1954. They have a mostly southeast exposure, with a small tongue jutting out that looks full south, and the fresher microclimate the vines there means Revello's Barolo Gattera is a pretty good bet even in hot years (for example, their 2003 was one of the better La Morra Barolos in that sorry vintage). As discussed previously (see ANNUNZIATA file; see also CONCA file) the Revello brothers split in 2013 and the Gattera vineyards all went to Enzo, who also kept the estate name and label. His holding there has a soil composition of 53% loam, 22% sand and 25% clay. The one hectare of vines are planted at 230-260 meters above sea level: interestingly, one third of the site looks full south and is located in the *turna lunga* portion of the vineyard district while the remaining two thirds, planted right by the winery building, are east-facing. In this last part the Fratelli Revello actually have some vines of Nebbiolo Rosé.

One of my favorite Barolos from Gattera is the one by the Bovio winery: maybe not Barolo's sexiest name nowadays, but truth be told, this winery's wines rarely disappoint and are very fairly priced. It's also one of the many wines that had to change name with the institution of the official vineyard district names: once labeled Vigna Gattera (for example as early as in 2000), it then became Gattera only, like all the other Barolos from this vineyard district. Today the estate is run by Gian Bovio's daughter Alessandra and her husband Marco who took over from Alessandra's father (sadly, he passed away a few years ago) and who had made the wines at the estate since the 1970s. Always more famous as an exceptional maitre'd and owner of the Belvedere restaurant in La Morra (for many years either the best restaurant, or at no worse, one of the two best of the Barolo denomination), Gianfranco Bovio also made excellent Barolos. Bovio made Barolos from different sites over the years, but to my taste, the Barolo Gattera was always his best wine (I still have bottles of the 1982 I bought in Rome as a young university student: to think I paid only 14,500 lire for each bottle, the equivalent of today's eight U.S. dollars!). Bovio's vines in Gattera are literally in the Monfalletto's winery back yard and are surrounded by those of the Monfalletto estate. I well remember that day, now many years ago, when I was standing atop of the Monfalletto hill with Alberto Cordero di Montezemolo and we had Bovio's vines right in front of us. Alberto told me that they had talked numerous times with Bovio about buying his vines, or perhaps exchanging them with some of theirs from another, similarly prestigious site, but that Bovio would have none of it. Trust me: you cannot help but love Barolo, and wine, when you see Alberto, while standing there shaking his head in disbelief while telling me all that they had tried doing to get Bovio to budge. It's hard not to smile in admiration at Gian Bovio's visceral attachment to his vines, he who was such a restaurant man. It's the way in Barolo.

The Mauro Veglio winery also makes an excellent Barolo Gattera, a site it began to farm already in the 1960s when Angelo Veglio (father of Mauro Veglio, who currently runs the estate) bought some of his first vineyards there. The wine was originally called Barolo Vigneto Gattera, and then became simply Gattera with the arrival of the official names of the Barolo vineyard districts. In fact, at Veglio they had proceeded to change the wine's name before then: as you can check rather easily, while the 2007 was still labeled as Vigneto Gattera, the 2009 was already Gattera only. Today, the estate's Gattera holdings are larger, thanks to a merger that took place in 2017 between members of the Veglio family leading to the unification of their vineyard land. Mauro's nephew, Alessandro, added his vineyards to those of his uncle such that the estate now farms 3.5 hectares of southeast to southwest-facing Nebbiolo vines planted at roughly 250 meters above sea level. Some of the vines are very old indeed, dating back to the early 1950s. In terms of the Barolo Gattera, it will only benefit from this merger: while Mauro's vines, planted in the 1950s face southwest (and therefore bask in a warmer and more luminous microclimate), Alessandro's face southeast (their habitat is therefore fresher, both because of greater wind activity and lower average temperatures). According to the Veglios, "…Among our Barolos, the Gattera is noted for being the most similar to the classic Barolo. It's accessible early, and has soft tannins, possibly because of the warm microclimate and its south to southwest exposure".

Another estate that has long been associated with the Gattera site is Fratelli Ferrero. Today the estate makes a Barolo Pinin, the classic estate blend (70% grapes from the Bricco Luciani and another 30% bought grapes from other sites), a Barolo Bricco Luciani and a Barolo Gattera. Once in a while the estate also bottled a Barolo labeled 'Gattera e Luciani', but clearly that is no longer possible. It's either one or the other, unless the percentage of grapes from one of the two sites is 15% or less; but even then, you still have to identify the wine with the name of the site that supplies 85% of the grapes. Fratelli Ferrero first made a Barolo Gattera wine in 1990. Their vines in Gattera lie between 245 to 270 meters above sea level and were planted in 1960. The estate isn't as famous as some others in the area, but the wines are excellent

Benchmark wineries/Reference point producers of Barolo Gattera: Bovio, Fratelli Ferrero, Fratelli Revello, Monfaletto.

GIACHINI

Township	La Morra
Reference Map	See Map of La Morra MGAs (Ch. 10)
Size (ha) (Tot / Barolo MGA)	14.87 / 2.64
Production 2021 (hl)	143.53
Altitude	220 – 255 meters a.s.l. roughly
Exposure	From south to southwest in the better exposed parcels; prevalently east in the remaining parts
N. Claimants MGA	4
Other grape varieties planted:	Barbera; Dolcetto
Land Units	Land Unit of La Morra for the most; Land Unit of Barolo for the lower parcels bordering Bricco Rocca;
Soil (stage):	Tortonian

Producers claiming the MGA

Carlo Revello; Giovanni Corino; Silvio Grasso; F.lli Revello.

Wines

Giovanni Corino - Barolo Giachini, Barolo Vecchie Vigne; **Silvio Grasso** - Barolo Giachini; **Fratelli Revello** - Barolo Giachini

What the producers say

Lorenzo Revello (Flli. Revello): "We bought these vineyards in 1954 and first made it as a site-specific Barolo in 1994. In our estimation, Giachini gives Barolos that are elegant, almost gentle in nature".

Federico Grasso (Silvio Grasso): "Giachini boasts a calcareous-clay soil and gives a more ready-to-drink Barolo than some other vineyard districts in the area."

Ian's assessment of the vineyard district, its wines and its potential

Giachini is situated in the territory of the Annunziata fraction of the La Morra commune, bridging that fraction's two most famous vineyard sites, Rocche dell'Annunziata to its west and Conca to its northeast. Immediately north of Giachini is the large Annunziata-vineyard district, and immediately south is Bricco Rocca. It's a fairly low-lying vineyard district, and yet its southwest section (the one around the Cascina Gallinotto: but do not confuse this Gallinotto with the specific section with exactly the same name but that is part of the Berri vineyard district) is much more broadly open and sunny, differentiating it neatly from the lower reaches of both Rocche dell'Annunziata and Conca, the two vineyard districts at its sides (while the marl and limestone soils are fairly similar). In fact, Giachini can be ideally thought of as the prolongation of Rocche dell'Annunziata, but at a lower altitude, and the two vineyard districts have similar sandy-rich, marl and limestone soils, but different exposures (Rocche dell'Annunziata's vines look towards La Morra, while Giachini's look out towards Castiglione Falletto).

Clearly, Giachini's fairly noteworthy soil sand component places this vineyard at a disadvantage in hot, droughty years, though compared to those of Rocche dell'Annunziata its wines hold the advantage of being ready to drink sooner. In my experience, compared to the Barolos of other famous La Morra vineyard districts, Giachini's wines have a softer texture than for example Rocche dell'Annunziata's and Gattera's: this is not all that surprising, given that the lithology is only that of the Saint Agatha Marls (there is no presence of Diano Sandstone such as there is in Gattera, for example. See GATTERA file). Very interestingly, in Renato Ratti's famous map and vineyard classification, he included the Giachini area within the boundaries of Rocche dell'Annunziata; and in fact, Ratti actively bought grapes from what is now called Giachini for his own Rocche wine, as it was then called (and today the Renato Ratti estate owns vines in Giachini). And while there are some similarities between Giachini's Barolos and those of Rocche dell'Annunziata, Giachini's Barolos are very different from those of Conca, even though the two vineyard areas are literally next to each other.

The telltale descriptor you will find time and again in similarly-made Giachini Barolos is of medicinal herbs, with menthol (drier tasting) and balsamic oils (sweeter tasting) not too far in the background. In this light, it's amazing just how different the Barolos from Giachini are compared to those of Conca, considering that Conca is really only a hop, skip and jump away (see CONCA file). Even though Giachini's wines are broad and generous like those of Conca (but in the mouth only: on the nose, Giachini wines are typically always a little reticent at first, and especially so if compared to Conca's, which are almost flamboyantly exotic in their olfactory profile). With a little tasting experience, the minty profile of Conca is also recognizably different from Giachini's (see CONCA file). In fact, while the Barolos of both vineyard districts showcase a minty nuance, these two "mint" notes are very different. Conca Barolos are characterized by a strong note of pennyroyal (which is a mint-like herb of the Lamiacee family, *mentha pulegium,* native to Europe, North Africa and the Middle East characterized by a gentler minty nuance, and has a sweeter aroma and flavor that is more akin to that of spearmint as compared to peppermint), while Giachini's minty tones are more reminiscent of a sharper, drier menthol, (possibly veering towards balsamic nuances in warmer years) and even peppermint.

Giachini producers and the wines

For my money, the two estates that make the two best Barolo Giachini wines are Giovanni Corino (one of the largest landowners in Giachini) and Fratelli Revello. Interestingly, both these estates have their vineyards in the northeastern section of the vineyard district, which is characterized by a cooler microclimate compared to the Giachini vineyards locates in the southwestern section around the Cascina Gallinotto. Corino is a very underrated Barolo estate that for my money really belongs amongst the top twenty of the entire denomination. Owner Giuliano Corino is a man blessed with exceptional talent, and his are Barolos of a purity and translucency that can be really remarkable. Giachini was the first single-site Barolo that the Corino estate chose to bottle separately in 1987 as a single vineyard site wine, from vines planted at about 235-250 meters above sea level on a clay-calcareous soil that has good water retentive capacity. Rotofermenters are of used for macerations for four-five days, malo is carried out in stainless steel, and the wine is aged in French oak barriques (30-35% new) for twenty-four months.

The Fratelli Revello estate was formally divided between the brothers Enzo and Carlo in 2013. Enzo kept the name of the estate and the label, while Carlo has gone off and created his own brand. The first vintage each brother produced entirely on his own was the 2016, while the 2013, 2014, 2015, still unbottled, were divided up between the two (shades of the Renato and Giuliano Corino split of the Giovanni Corino estate that occurred before that of the Revello's). Historically, Giachini had always been the most important Barolo bottled by the Fratelli Revello. Their plot was planted with Nebbiolo Lampia vines way back in 1954 and replanted in 1995, between 235 to 250 meters in altitude, facing mostly south to southeast. At the time when the estate first made its Barolo Giachini, it was also adding all of its Rocche dell'Annunziata grapes (but as of the 1996 vintage they have used those grapes to make a separate Barolo Rocche dell'Annunziata). This was logical enough to do, given that they only owned only 0.2 hectares of vines in the Rocche dell'Annunziata, and that at the time Barolo had not yet known the boom in popularity it is enjoying now; so there seemed to be little point in going to the expense and extra work of making a separate wine from the site (see ROCCHE DELL'ANNUNZIATA file).

I have always found Revello's Barolo Giachini to be more open than the other Barolos they made (especially fifteen years ago when the Giachini vines were still relatively young, or at least, younger than those of their other vineyard sites). It was characterized by a different elegance than say Rocche dell'Annunziata or Gattera. For example, while the Barolo Gattera is very fine in its texture and savory in organoleptic profile, their Barolo Giachini was more floral, less savory but richer and deeper on the palate. It is a wine that has a "brings you in" quality and one sip makes one wish for another almost right away. It was arguably the best expression of Barolo from the La Morra township of all the Revello wines and I am sure Carlo Revello, who inherited most of it from the sibling split (save for a small 0.5 hectare portion), will continue to do a great job. I am certainly very curious to see how the new wines that will result from the family split will turn out, and how they will age, which was never the strongest suit of that estate's wines. Currently, the Fratelli Revello estate's holding in Giachini is located at 220 ai 250 meters in altitude and the soil composition is 20% sand, 55% loam and 25% clay. The vines face eastwards and were planted in 1988. Among the various owners of Giachini, the excellent Silvio Grasso also owns one full south-facing hectare in Giachini, planted at 200 meters above sea level. The vines are about forty years old.

Benchmark wineries/Reference point producers of Barolo Giachini: Giovanni Corino, Fratelli Revello. Also good: Silvio Grasso.

GIANETTO

Township	Serralunga d'Alba
Reference Map	See Map of Serralunga d'Alba MGAs (Ch. 10)
Size (ha) (Tot / Barolo MGA)	22.40 / 9.42
Production 2021 (hl)	511.72
Altitude	280 – 360 meters a.s.l. roughly
Exposure	West in the better exposed parcels; from northwest to east in the remaining parts
N. Claimants MGA	4
Other grape varieties planted:	Dolcetto
Land Units	Land Unit of Serralunga d'Alba
Soil (stage):	Serravallian

Producers claiming the MGA

Brovia; Famiglia Anselma; Garesio; Guido Porro.

Wines

Famiglia Anselma - Barolo Gianetto (*); **Garesio** - Barolo Gianetto; **Guido Porro** - Barolo Gianetto;

Ian's assessment of the vineyard district, its wines and its potential

Gianetto is one of the two easternmost vineyard districts of the Serralunga commune, located in the northern half of Serralunga's territory and on the eastern flank of its ridge. It develops over two slopes. One slope looks out towards Lazzarito and Bricco Voghera vineyard districts (it is essentially the prolongation of the latter to the north and west); on the other slope Gianetto follows right after Brea. Its lithology is the classic Serralunga Lequio Formation, which gives bold, age-worthy Barolos but that in Gianetto, possibly because Barolos are made only from the very best exposed sites and because the vineyard district's soils boasts a bit more sand than other nearby vineyard districts, surprisingly tends to give wines that are more forward and approachable in their youth than expected, given their Serralunga origin.

Gianetto producers and the wines

The only producer I know making wines with grapes wholly sourced from Gianetto is the outstanding if perhaps little-known Guido Porro estate. This winery has been making wine for roughly four generations but only started estate bottling in the 1980s, and today son Fabio is the next generation up to bat working alongside and following in the footsteps of father Guido. In 1996, when Guido (the fourth generation) took over from his father Giovanni, the estate also began to bottle wines by specific vineyard sites. In the process, it has built up quite a reputation for its Barolos, especially those expressing different aspects/subzones of the famous Lazzarito vineyard district. Porro's Barolos are some of the most graceful of the entire denomination, wines of truly uncommon refinement and grace. Of recent vintages, both his 2015 and 2016 Barolo Gianettos were outstanding. Porro bought his one hectare in Gianetto back in 2007: the Nebbiolo was planted in 1998 around 280 meters above sea level with a southwest exposure (but I have also been told it is south/southwest and even southeast). Gianetto is the second last Barolo vineyard holding to have come into the Porro family fold: the last vineyard arrival into said fold was in 2010 by way of inheritance, when Porro was one of the lucky three (along with colleagues Davide Rosso of Giovanni Rosso and Sergio Germano of Ettore Germano) to gain a piece of the ultra-famous Vignarionda vineyard district. See VIGNARIONDA file). All of Guido Porro's wines are characterized by an exceptional elegance and silky tannins: all have a mouthfeel quite unlike the majority of Barolos you will taste, and the Gianetto is no different. Part of the secret of these traditionally made wines (15-

25 days of fermentation, aging in large 25 Hl Slavonian oak barrels) is grapes picked at optimal physiologic ripeness and a partial extraction of pips during fermentation to remove any potentially green tannins. Whatever Porro's "secret" recipe is, it works. And then some.

Benchmark wineries/Reference point producers of Barolo Gianetto: Guido Porro.

GINESTRA

Township	Monforte d'Alba
Reference Map	See Map of Monforte d'Alba MGAs (Ch. 10)
Size (ha) (Tot / Barolo MGA)	114.36 / 30.03
Production 2021 (hl)	1,528.78 (of which 234.06 hl of Barolo Riserva *MGA*, and 232.66 hl of Barolo *MGA* Vigna)
Altitude	290 – 540 meters a.s.l. roughly
Exposure	From southeast to southeast in the better exposed parcels; east, west and north in the remaining parts
N. Claimants MGA	11
Other grape varieties planted:	Barbera; Dolcetto; white varieties
Land Units	Land Unit of Barolo mostly; Land Unit of Castiglione for the highest and western parcels
Soil (stage):	Tortonian and Serravallian

Producers claiming the MGA

Cascina Chicco; Marisa Conterno; Conterno Fantino; Domenico Clerico; Gemma; Elio Grasso; Immobiliare Agricola Piemontese; Renzo Seghesio; Rocche Dei Manzoni; Paolo Conterno; Diego Conterno.

Wines

Cascina Chicco - Barolo Riserva Ginestra; **Domenico Clerico** - Barolo Ciabot Mentin and Barolo Pajana; **Diego Conterno** - Barolo Ginestra; **Conterno Fantino** - Barolo Ginestra Vigna Sorì Ginestra, Barolo Ginestra Vigna del Gris; **Paolo Conterno** - Barolo Ginestra (and Riserva), Barolo Riva del Bric; **Gemma** - Barolo Riserva Giblin; **Elio Grasso** - Barolo Ginestra Casa Matè, Barolo Gavarini Chiniera, Barolo Riserva Runcot; **Renzo Seghesio (Cascina Pajana)** - Barolo Ginestra, Barolo Vigna Pajana

What the producers say

Renzo Seghesio (Seghesio Cascina Pajana): "We own these vineyards since 1996 and have been vinifying the various plots separately since 2012. We use the name Vigna Pajana for the wine made from one plot of vines, and the other we label Ginestra. The Vigna Pajana wine is darker in color, and generally is the bigger, more tannic wine. The Ginestra is fresher, fruitier and balanced, more open than the tougher Pajana, that requires more time in the bottle to be ready to drink".

Diego Conterno: "It's the historic vineyard of the family, that gives very balanced wines, to my taste that are spicy and balsamic at once".

Paolo Conterno: "We were lucky to inherit about ten hectares in this famous site that gives ripe wines of the utmost elegance, and yet powerful too. We also make a wine called Riva del Bric from this site, because we feel it conveys a different expression of Ginestra in the glass".

Ian's assessment of the vineyard district, its wines and its potential

There is no doubt that Ginestra is one of the denomination's ten greatest Barolo vineyard areas. That laudatory comment still applies, even though the Ginestra vineyard district of today is much bigger than the original; but fortunately, most of the vineyard land added on to the Ginestra proper is of very high quality as well. Of such high viticultural and winemaking quality in fact that you can make the case most of them should have been named their own vineyard districts.

Ginestra is one of the southeasternmost areas of the Monforte commune's territory, just south of Castelletto and north of Mosconi, both Monforte vineyard districts. This is an area of the Barolo denomination where some of the biggest and fleshiest Barolos are made, wines boasting a noteworthy degree of ripeness while remaining lifted (Mosconi's, more than Ginestra's, are immediately recognizable because of this. See MOSCONI file). These Barolos could not be any more different from those of other parts of Monforte, such as Bussia Soprana (see BUSSIA file), farther up in the Monforte territory to the northeast, or of Serralunga, the wines of which are often described as big and tannic, but that are far steelier and more lifted than those of Monforte (or anywhere else in the Barolo denomination, for that matter). But any way you slice it, Ginestra is a blessed piece of Nebbiolo vineyard land from where some of the greatest Barolos are and have been made over the years; in this respect, it is only fair to recognize that Ginestra's fame as a top-quality site has been helped in no small measure by the bevy of extremely talented producers who own vineyards there.

At almost 115 hectares, Ginestra is however a very large vineyard district (this is exactly why the officially delimited MGA-named vineyard districts cannot be viewed as "crus", or even truly site-specific vineyard areas but rather are large vineyard districts, areas that have numerous subregions within (see chapter 8, BAROLO "CLASSICO" AND BAROLO SINGLE-DISTRICT WINES: THE IMPORTANCE OF SITE. See also BUSSIA file). The extended Ginestra vineyard district of today can be divided into four subregions (as it was before the official launching of the names), the most important one of which is Ginestra proper; the other three are Gavarini, Grassi and Pajana. These last three were not famous as recently as the 1970s, but clearly, perceptions changed once competent producers began making estate-bottled, site-specific wines there and exporting them all over the world. It is not so much a matter of one Ginestra subregion being better than another, but rather of each site giving gorgeous but different wines, much like the wines of Griotte(s)-Chambertin, Mazis-Chambertin and Charmes-Chambertin differ too, and yet all make outstanding if different wines and all are part of the Gevrey-Chambertin commune's territory. Ultimately, which site and which wines you prefer will depend mostly on where your individual tastes run.

Ginestra proper is a long ridge covered in vines: its geological and altitude realities have a definite bearing on the wines made from each of the ridge's different sections. It can be broken down roughly into three sections, ranging roughly from 300 to 450 meters above sea level, each of which is the source of at least one very famous Barolo Ginestra wine. But be aware that these three sections give very different wines, a consequence of the geographical and topographical reality of Ginestra proper. To give you a practical example, on March 4, 2004, while I was visiting the area, a southern-facing portion of the slope before me had no snow, while a more eastern-facing part was full of snow: and this always at the same altitude of 360 meters above sea level! From a geological perspective, things change quite a bit too: at about 300 meters above sea level (essentially where Conterno Fantino's Vigna del Gris is located) up to about 360 meters in altitude Ginestra is practically all or mostly marl, while the portion up to 500 meters in height is, for practical wine-purposes, more or less all sand. Even so, there are variations of this soil reality throughout the vineyard district. Moving from up top down the slope, there is Clerico in the uppermost reaches (from where the estate makes its Barolo Ginestra Ciabot Mentin, previously called Ciabot Mentin Ginestra); then in the middle section there are Elio Grasso (from where they make their Barolo Ginestra Casa Matè: note that Casa Matè is written with the French accent *grave*, not *aigu*, on the final 'e', as in 'è') and Conterno-Fantino (this is where the Barolo Sorì Ginestra is made from). Lower down, there are the large vineyard holdings of Paolo Conterno and again Conterno-Fantino (these are the vines from where he makes his Barolo Ginestra Vigna del Gris). To use a real estate analogy, that stretch of vineyards is about as close in value and in importance to those of a section of Bond Street in London or Fifth Avenue in New York City as you'll find anywhere in Barolo.

Pajana is a short hillside crest that results from a split that occurs at the tail-end of the crest on which Ginestra-proper is located; lower in altitude than Ginestra-proper, Pajana runs roughly parallel and just north of it. Pajana is characterized by soils that make for what are some of Monforte's most pleasantly massive wines when young (generally speaking, it has a bit more clay than the Ginestra-proper) and that never fail to impress in blind tastings but that also have an undercurrent of steely acidity, no doubt in relation to its Lequio Formation lithology. Historically, the Pajana Barolos of Clerico and Renzo Seghesio were the most famous wines made from Pajana, but as good as they are (and they really are), I have never felt Pajana's wines to have either the refinement or the complexity of the best from Ginestra-proper. But I'm splitting hairs here: these Monforte sites are some of the best in all Barolo, and the wines mostly exceptional.

Further north is another separate hillside crest that runs parallel to those of Ginestra proper and Pajana. This is where the Ginestra subregions of Gavarini and Grassi are found. Gavarini's vineyard area is practically a monopole of the Elio Grasso estate. From grapes sourced within its confines, Elio Grasso makes two famous Barolos: the Gavarini Chiniera and the Riserva Rüncot (for precision's sake, note that "Rüncot" is written with the umlaut on the 'u'). The Rüncot is made from vines replanted in 1989 and 1990 just below those of the Chiniera which is the higher section of the two (note that as it is a Riserva, the Barolo Riserva Rüncot is not made every year).

Moving eastwards, in the direction of Serralunga, from Gavarini you arrive at Ginestra's fourth subregion, Grassi, essentially the prolongation of Gavarini on the same hillside crest. Grassi is characterized by slightly more clay in the soil than Gavarini and Ginestra-proper, and this is why its wines can resemble those of Pajana somewhat (but not quite as massive and tactile). Grassi's central portion is its sweet spot, from where its best Barolos are made.

Ginestra producers and the wines

As already mentioned, when it comes to the extended Ginestra vineyard district, wine lovers are spoiled: there are many competent producers making great wines in this vineyard district, so there's an embarrassment of riches to choose from. Conterno Fantino makes two different Barolos from the Ginestra proper site, both of which are arguably amongst the twenty or thirty best wines of the entire denomination: Barolo Ginestra Vigna del Gris and the Barolo Ginestra Vigna Sorì (previously known as Barolo Sorì Ginestra). The Vigna del Gris, so-called because of its very fine, greyish-looking marly and sand soil (*gris* is a local dialect for *grigio* in Italian, which is "grey" in English), is lower down and looks southeast, while the Sorì Ginestra vines grow at a higher altitude and look south. The Vigna del Gris has a bit more sand than the Vigna Sorì Ginestra site, plus it's lower-lying, and so it gets harvested on average one to two days earlier, depending on the vintage. The Vigna del Gris is remarkable also for its presence of old vine Nebbiolo Rosé (absent in the Vigna Sorì, and you can tell after just one sip of both wines): the combination of higher soil content and Nebbiolo Rosé really mark the Vigna del Gris, and help explain why it is such a steelier, more rigid and far more perfumed wine than the richer, fleshier, more tactile Vigna Sorì. As it always is in such cases when two excellent versions of something are being considered, which of the two wines you prefer ultimately says more about you than it does about the two similarly outstanding wines.

Some of Clerico's vines in his Ciabot Mentin area were 40 years old already in 2008 when I was taking one of my many vineyard walks around there with Domenico. The estate typically divides its Ginestra holdings into the Pajana and Ciabot Mentin sections. The Pajana vines are situated at 330-340 meters above sea level and face east to/through southeast. It is an extremely interesting piece of todays' extended Ginestra vineyard district: about 1.1 hectares large (one plot was acquired in 1990), the vines here are planted on Lequio Formation lithology. According to Oscar Arrivabene, who manages the Clerico winery, the soil is 53.4% loam, 23.5% sand and 23.1% clay, but with a high percentage of limestone (not at all surprising given its Lequio Formation lithology). The Barolo from Pajana is generally broad and large, not to mention bordering on the massive, but with a steely spine, and expresses marvelous aromas and flavors of ripe red cherry and blood orange. By contrast, the Nebbiolo vines of Clerico's Ciabot Mentin portion of the Ginestra (a much larger parcel than the Pajana: three hectares made up of two vineyard plots bought in 1981 and 1992) are planted higher up between 390 and 420 meters above sea level and look south (the plot called Gepe) and southeast (the plot called Sottocasa). Furthermore, the soil lithology is completely different than that of Pajana, being that of the Saint Agatha Fossil Marls of the sandy type. Here the soil breakdown is 46.1% loam, 32.5% sand and 21.4% clay. Those percentages are clearly different from those I mentioned earlier for Pajana, and give you a wealth of information regarding what could/might/should be expected of the wines made with grapes from each site. Clerico's Nebbiolo biotypes between the Ciabot Mentin and Pajana portions are different too: both areas are mostly planted with Nebbiolo Lampia, though some older vines of Nebbiolo Michet exist and perhaps a few stragglers of Nebbiolo Rosé too can be found in the Gepe portion of the Ciabot Mentin. Adding that bit of knowledge to all the other information you now have about the two sites (meaning Nebbiolo biotypes planted in each, exposure, altitude and more), allows you to realize immediately now why and how much Clerico's Barolo Pajana is such a different wine from the winery's Barolo Ciabot Mentin; in fact, based on what we know, it would be very strange if the two wines were NOT very different. The Ciabot Mentin tends to give Barolos marked by extremely pure and dark fruit notes but also boasts a certain rigidity to the underlying tannic backbone (depending on the vintage and how much fleshy fruit the wine comes endowed with), with notes of mint and menthol dominating (with some people picking up hints of anise as well).

Elio Grasso's Gavarini Chiniera was first made with the 1978 vintage. The roughly thirty-five years old vines grow between 350 to 400 meters in altitude and face south. After years of using heavily toasted barriques, the estate now ages this wine in 25 hectoliter Slavonian oak barrels, and I am among those who believe this allows for much better transparency of site in your glass. Elio Grasso's wines have always been amongst the better wines made anywhere in the denomination, but nowadays seem to shine with more translucency than ever before. The Barolo Ginestra Casa Matè is made from roughly forty years old vines grown in an amphitheater-like section that is fully south-facing at an altitude of 300 to 350 meters above sea level. This wine too was first made in the 1978 vintage and is aged like the Gavarini Chiniera. The Barolo Rüncot is made from the best grapes grown a little lower down from those sourced to make the Chiniera: differently from the other two Barolos, it is aged in French oak barriques.

Diego Conterno is an upcoming Barolo producer whose wines are getting more and more attention. His family is related to that of Conterno-Fantino (in 2000, Diego sold his interest in Conterno-Fantino, took his Ginestra holdings and set up shop elsewhere), but the Ginestra sites the two estates farm, and the wines they make, differ. The new estate, organic certified since 2014, is now run by Diego and son Stefano, and first made a Barolo in 2003 (to the best of my knowledge it was all Ginestra fruit, but not so labeled), but I'd say their first truly great Barolo was the 2005, a very underrated Barolo vintage. In Ginestra, the Diego Conterno estate owns two hectares, one portion of which, planted in 1982, faces full south and is considered to be the heart of their vineyard holdings; it is their version of Sorì Ginestra, located just above the plot owned by Conterno-Fantino. Their first Barolo labeled as a Ginestra wine dates back to the 2010 vintage. Of note, Diego Conterno's 2015 Barolo was the first to be made with grapes not just from Ginestra proper, but Pajana too (as well as from Bricco San Pietro and San Giovanni), while their 2016 Barolo del Comune di Monforte d'Alba had 60% of the grapes coming from Pajana and 40% from the Gris section of Ginestra proper. Their Barolo Ginestra wines are also excellent, and I especially liked their 2013, made essentially from those two hectares I wrote about previously facing full south and at the heart of their Ginestra holdings.

Paolo Conterno owns a very large portion of Ginestra, and his Barolos Ginestra wines are relatively easy to find in the marketplace. His vines grow slightly lower down than those of other producers such as Conterno Fantino, at about 300 to 350 meters in altitude on a very steep (up to 38%) slope gradient, and face mostly south and southeast. He makes a Nebbiolo wine called Bric Ginestra from his youngest (roughly 25 years old) southeast-facing vines also planted in Ginestra. His are bigger, fleshier Barolo Ginestra wines that speak very much of Monforte. More interestingly, for those who might not know, Conterno actually has long grown Barbera in Ginestra too. The wine has always been quite famous but had to be renamed; it is now called "La Ginestra" given that the official MGA names of Barolo's vineyard districts (and of Barbaresco) cannot be used for any wine other than Barolo and Barbaresco (hence Paolo Conterno's Barbera d'Alba Ginestra wine has now become the Barbera d'Alba "La Ginestra"). Paolo Conterno has always had a real knack with Barbera, and his bottling from Ginestra is historically both an important and a very good Barbera wine: so, if you like big fleshy mouthcoating Barberas with more than enough lift, then this is the wine for you. Last but not least, it will interest the biggest Barolo fans among my readers to know that apparently Prunotto was making a Ginestra already back in 1964, but that I have never had that wine. For sure, it would be great to try a bottle.

Benchmark wineries/Reference point producers of Barolo Ginestra: Clerico, Conterno Fantino, Elio Grasso, Paolo Conterno. Also good: Diego Conterno, Renzo Seghesio.

GRAMOLERE

Township	Monforte d'Alba
Reference Map	See Map of Monforte d'Alba MGAs (Ch. 10)
Size (ha) (Tot / Barolo MGA)	41.40 / 8.85
Production 2021 (hl)	459.83 (of which 176.66 hl of Barolo Riserva *MGA*)
Altitude	370 – 470 meters a.s.l. roughly
Exposure	Predominantly southwest; west and north in the remaining parts
N. Claimants MGA	4
Other grape varieties planted:	Barbera; Dolcetto; white varieties
Land Units	Land Unit of Castiglione
Soil (stage):	Tortonian

Producers claiming the MGA

Fratelli Alessandria; Famiglia Anselma; Claudio Pressenda (Cascina Gramolere); Giovanni Manzone.

Wines

Fratelli Alessandria - Barolo Gramolere; **Cascina Gramolere** - Barolo; **Giovanni Manzone** - Barolo Bricat, Barolo Gramolere (and Riserva)

What the producers say

Mauro Manzone (Giovanni Manzone): "Our ownership of this vineyard can be traced back to the '60s; we started doing separate vinifications for Gramolere in 1979 and for the Barolo Bricat in 1994".

Alessandria Fratelli: "We believe wines made from this particular ridge express delicate notes of aromatic herbs, balsamic vinegar and mint, mixed in with classic nuances of leather and licorice".

Ian's assessment of the vineyard district, its wines and its potential

Gramolere is an underrated Barolo vineyard district of which I like not just to drink the wines of, but to also talk and write about, because I think it deserves to be better known and appreciated for its exact worth. It helps that at least two extremely talented producers make excellent Barolos from there: Fratelli Alessandria, whose winery is in Verduno and farms/owns most of its vineyards in that commune; and Giovanni Manzone, based in Monforte d'Alba. Interestingly, as Fratelli Alessandria's wines are all similarly made, their Barolo portfolio provides easy insight into terroir diversity, and the general differences between the Barolos of the Verduno and Monforte communes. At the same time, the many different Barolos from the Monforte commune made by Giovanni Manzone offer insight into the differences between Monforte vineyard districts, but even more specifically to Gramolere, as he makes more than one Barolo from this vineyard district (including, when the year's weather cooperates, a Riserva). By the way, here is a real scoop for you: most people don't know that Fratelli Alessandria's vineyard in Gramolere was actually planted by Giovanni Manzone and his father (because an Alessandria married the sister of Giovanni Manzone). In fact, that was the first Gramolere vineyard ever planted by Manzone. Funny how life works, don't you think? The estate that is most associated today with this specific vineyard district started out by planting somebody else's vineyard there first.

The Gramolere vineyard district is straight up north of the town of Monforte d'Alba, situated in the center, the heart even, of the Monforte commune's territory. Size-wise, it is one of that commune's smallest vineyard districts (see chapter 10, BAROLO VINEYARD DISTRICTS: MAPS AND LAND UNITS). You realize this is a noteworthy feature in and of itself, given that Monforte is the one Barolo denomination commune that, in some ways rather admirably, managed to elevate the making of extremely large official vineyard districts into something of an art form. What I mean by that is that, unlike other Monforte vineyard districts such as Bussia and Ginestra where if you don't know the subregions of each -and the traits of the very different wines made within each of those subregions- you have little or no hope of distinguishing, understanding even, the wines thereof, the same is not true with the smaller, slightly more homogenous Gramolere. Before you get too excited,

Gramolere requires you to do a little bit of homework too (hey, it's still Monforte and Italy we are talking about). But as far as homework goes, it's fun. A lot of fun, even.

Gramolere is bordered by the vineyard districts of Perno to the northeast and east; to the northwest and west by Bussia; and to the southeast and east by the Castelletto. In fact, the Gramolere vineyard district is draped over the slopes of a short hilly crest that is nothing more than the continuation of the one the Castelletto vineyard district is also on. Gramolere's landscape is classified as a Land Unit of Castiglione and therefore its main soil lithology is, not surprisingly, that of the Diano Sandstone. Speaking broadly, Gramolere is characterized by a clay-calcareous soil rich in sand, stones, and fossils. This explains the area's name of 'gramolere", which derives from *gramun* and *pere* (no, fruit is not part of the equation here: in English, those two dialect words translate to "weeds" and "stones", because in days now long gone by not much more than that was found there).

Gramolere is actually an historic name, always used in the past to refer to the land located between what are today's Bussia and Castelletto vineyard districts. Save for weeds, the arid, water-challenged soil of Gramolere (thanks to the sand and stones ensuring almost too good drainage) didn't allow much else to grow. Much like the original Bussia that locals historically subdivided into an upper Bussia Soprana and a lower-lying Bussia Sottana, the same is true of Gramolere. There is a Gramolere Soprana portion, that has better exposure and from where the vineyard district's best Barolos are made: it faces south/southwest, while slightly lower down there is the Gramolere Sottana portion that faces instead northwest and the soil of which is much richer in clay than Gramolere Soprana's (for a quick recap and look at the many subregions of the Monforte commune's designated vineyard districts, see Appendix C, *Table 3.3 Barolo vineyard district subregions*). In the past, Nebbiolo never fully ripened in Gramolere Sottana (part of it extends outside of what is the modern-day Barolo denomination's territory). For all these reasons, the Giovanni Manzone estate planted Barbera in this part of the Gramolere vineyard district, as well as one of its two vineyards of the ultra-rare Rossese Bianco (a local native white grape of which there are only about three producers making wines from nowadays- a crying shame in my opinion, because this little native cultivar really offers plenty and deserves to be better known. See CASTELLETTO file).

In my experience, I have found that the Barolos of Gramolere are some of the gentler ones made in the Monforte commune: clearly, I use the world "gentler" in relation to Monforte's wines, which are, across the board, some of the most powerful and the fleshiest wines of all Barolo (remember that I consider the Barolos of Serralunga just as powerful as those of Monforte, but more steely than fleshy (see chapter 7, BAROLO TERROIR, The Barolo Communes sub-chapter). So, even though Monforte's Barolos are powerful by definition, it is undoubtedly true that the wines of Gramolere fall in the middle of the "degree of power spectrum", meaning somewhere in between the rather suave Barolos of the Bussia Soprana subregion and the almost massive wines of the southeastern corner of the Monforte territory, most notably made with the Nebbiolo grapes from Mosconi and parts of Ginestra. OK, OK: if you really pinned my back to the wall, then I'd tell you that the wines of Gramolere, with their paler color and more polished tannins, are in fact much closer in style to those of Bussia.

Gramolere producers and the wines

When discussing the wines of Gramolere, it would be unjust to start with anybody but the Giovanni Manzone estate, the winery that has done the most over the years to bring Gramolere's potential and the quality of its wines into the limelight. The Giovanni Manzone estate, run by Mauro Manzone, owns 3.5 hectares in this vineyard district that he farms organically; clearly, he uses low sulfur doses in his winemaking. His two Gramolere plots range in altitude from 330-470 meters above sea level, and he has vines both in the Soprana portion (therefore that face south/southwest) and in the Sottana portion (that face northwest).

Mauro makes three different Gramolere Barolos: the Barolo Gramolere, the Barolo Gramolere Riserva and the Barolo Bricat, each showcasing a different aspect of Gramolere and the wines this vineyard district can give. Beware that these wines have changed names over the years, and this is clearly verifiable on the labels of the bottles you buy. Remember that when buying old vintages of any wines, it's always good to know the history of the estate making said wines, as well as of each bottle such that you know what to expect and what to look for. Make note then of the fact that the Giovanni Manzone Barolos were initially labeled as "Le Gramolere" (I remember a wonderful Giovanni Manzone 1990 Barolo Le Gramolere, a wine that really opened my eyes to the noteworthy quality level of this estate's wines). Therefore, up until the 2004 vintage included, the Giovanni Manzone bottle labels show "Le Gramolere" and not "Gramolere", as it is today; beginning with the 2005 vintage, the wording was changed to "Gramolere" only. This is true not just of the Barolo Gramolere and the Barolo Gramolere Riserva, but also of the Barolo Bricat: initially labeled as Barolo Le Gramolere Bricat, it then became Barolo Bricat only, and this even though the Bricat is a single vineyard within the larger Gramolere vineyard district. So, in theory, the winery could very well label this vine as Barolo Gramolere Vigna Bricat instead of Barolo Bricat (as it stands today); but clearly, the shorter version of the name is probably much more user-friendly (both communication- and sales-wise).

The 1971 vintage was the Giovanni Manzone winery's first Barolo Gramolere; today, this wine is made from roughly thirty-five years old vines planted facing south/southwest on a steep slope on the typical limestone-clay soil with sand, rich in fossils and rocks. By contrast, Manzone's Barolo Gramolere Riserva is made from the estate's oldest vines in the vineyard district (over fifty-year-old vines) and is released about seven years after the harvest (after a prolonged aging in oak and bottle). Last but not least, there is the Barolo Bricat, actually my favorite of Giovanni Manzone's three Barolos from Gramolere. And if you know me at all, then you'd know it could not have been otherwise, given that this is the vineyard in which Manzone grows some Nebbiolo Rosé. This cultivar's presence, however small, characterizes this Barolo greatly; together with the Bricat's plot specific soil and exposure. And so, it is easy to understand why Manzone's Barolo Bricat, despite being made with Gramolere grapes, is really different from his other two Gramolere Barolos. Differently from Manzone's Barolo Gramolere and the Barolo Gramolere Riserva, the Barolo Bricat is paler in color, gentler in texture, more floral and piercing in perfume with a sweetly spicy flavor nuance (the latter I think quite possibly a contribution of the Nebbiolo Rosé). The Bricat is a one-hectare plot (it's worth knowing that the Barolo Bricat is a single vineyard wine: once again, the Bricat vineyard is located within the much larger Gramolere vineyard district) lying at 350 meters in altitude (from 320 to 390 meters, to be exact) planted with south/southwest facing fifty years old Nebbiolo Lampia and Nebbiolo Rosé vines. The plot takes its name from the previous owner, Luigi Cortellesi, who was nicknamed "Bricat" because of his temper (in Piedmontese, a *bricat* is a matchstick, making it an ideal nickname for people that are quick to flare up). Amidst his vines, Cortellesi had built a tool shed or *ciabot* (that consequently came to be known as the Ciabot Bricat) and loved to spend as much time as possible there alone (maybe a good thing, in view of his inflammable personality). In fact, "bricat" is also a dialectal derivation of the Italian word *bricchetto* (a small *bricco*, or hill), and therefore *bricat* could also be a reference to the hillock portion of the area where Cortellesi built his *ciabot*. Anyways, Giovanni Manzone bought the vineyard in 1989, and made his first vintage of Barolo Bricat in 1994: not exactly a memorable year, but the wine was a real eye-opener, speaking volumes about the site's potential. I remember that '94 very well, having tasted it upon release at Manzone and many times after that: it was truly excellent, and especially so if and when compared to most of the Barolos made in that so-so year. That fact in itself tells you quite a bit worth knowing about not just Manzone's considerable talent level but also the intrinsic high quality of the Bricat vineyard site.

Bricat lies at the foot of the Gramolere Soprana very close to a large forested area (there aren't so many of those left in the Barolo denomination) and so its vines live in a very different microclimate from that of the rest of Gramolere. Furthermore, while the Bricat's soil is the clay-limestone rich in sand that characterizes the rest of Gramolere too, it is atypical in that it has a noteworthy red clay presence beneath the topsoil. Its presence contributes a measure of structure and spiciness but at the same time memorable elegance and lightness of being too (though as I have already mentioned I think that a large part of that sweet spiciness and refinement are due to the Nebbiolo Rosé growing there). For sure, the Barolo Bricat has much greater levity and translucency on the palate than do Manzone's Barolo Gramolere and Gramolere Riserva, boasting more refined tannins than the at times rustic ones of those two bottlings. It follows that the Barolo Bricat, drinkable in fine form at a relatively younger age, needs less time in the cellar to round into form than do Manzone's two Barolo Gramolere wines (but the Barolo Bricat is still a Monforte Barolo, so in a good vintage I still wouldn't recommend touching a bottle before fifteen years of age in order to enjoy it at its fullest).

I mentioned at the beginning of this file that Manzone is intimately associated with the Gramolere vineyard district: this is not due just to the excellent wines he makes there. Over the years the family has invested heavily in this vineyard district and has worked to upkeep its legacy and history. Commendably, the family not only bought the Ciabot Bricat, but also the Casa della Marchesa, a building located in the hamlet of Gramolere and owned by the Marchesa (Marquise, in English) Scarampi del Cairo who housed some of her sharecroppers there, as well as the Crutin delle Gramolere, a farmhouse and cavity turned water well that in times past, when there were no public waterworks, was all-important as a source of spring water.

The other estate that most lovers of Barolo associate with Gramolere is Verduno's Fratelli Alessandria, a family involved with wine since at least the eighteenth century. Their vines in Gramolere are roughly fifty years old and planted at an average of 400 meters above sea level, facing mostly west/southwest. Like most of this estate's Barolos, their Gramolere is fermented for 22 to 30 days in stainless steel at maximum temperatures of 28-30 degrees Celsius and is aged for three years in 20-40 hectoliters Slavonian and French oak casks. They first made a Barolo Gramolere in the 2001 vintage (a great way to start given how great that year was for Barolo's wines). It's an excellent Barolo and a great way by which to get to know the magic that is Gramolere. I never pass up a chance to drink any of the Fratelli Alessandria Barolos (so not just their Barolo Gramolere), and neither should you, because they really are excellent wines.

Benchmark wineries/Reference point producers of Barolo Gramolere: Giovanni Manzone. Also good: Fratelli Alessandria.

GUSTAVA

Township	Grinzane Cavour
Reference Map	See Map of Grinzane Cavour MGAs (Ch. 10)
Size (ha) (Tot / Barolo MGA)	8.31 / 3.23
Production 2021 (hl)	166.54
Altitude	220 – 270 meters a.s.l. roughly
Exposure	From east to south through southwest, plus a small part facing north
N. Claimants MGA	3
Other grape varieties planted:	Barbera; Dolcetto; Freisa
Land Units	Land Unit of Barolo
Soil (stage):	Tortonian

Producers claiming the MGA

Scuola Enologica Alba; Fondazione Cassa di Risparmio di Cuneo; Pio Cesare.

Ian's assessment of the vineyard district, its wines and its potential

Gustava is one of the many little-known vineyard districts of Barolo of little if any repute. There have never been too many Barolos Gustava made, and so that tells us plenty right there. A recent land sale saw a hectare of Gustava go for about Euro 500,000, which is certainly noteworthy, but still something like four to six times below the price (and that's a conservative estimate) that one of Barolo's better vineyard areas would fetch if and when they become available for sale, and so that tells us even more. Still, that a quality estate such as Pio Cesare have long owned vines in Gustava and blends its grapes into their Barolo classico is cause for hope. For my money, if highly knowledgeable wine people like Pio Boffa (who sadly passed away in 2021 in relation to Covid-19) and his nephew Cesare Pio like the wine from Gustava, then that's good enough for me.

Gustava is an official vineyard district of the Grinzane Cavour commune, the middle of three vineyard districts occupying the southern-facing flank of the hillside crest that runs east-west, positioned just below the town of Grinzane Cavour. To Gustava's west lies the vineyard district of Castello while to its east is the vineyard district Garretti. The landscape is the Land Unit of Barolo and the lithology is the typical Saint Agatha Fossil Marls, meaning this area was formed during the Tortonian stage of the Miocene Epoch and that its wines ought to remind one more of the wines of La Morra and Barolo, rather than those of Monforte and Serralunga. The vineyard area's clay-marly soil with high concentrations of manganese and magnesium (data of soil sample analyses show average soil composition values in percentages to be more or less 45% loam, 35% clay and 20% sand) is in fact of the type usually associated with softer and generally earlier-maturing Barolos.

Pio Cesare has been blending its Gustava grapes into its Barolo classico since 1985. Their southeast-facing Nebbiolo vines were planted in 1965 and in 2012 at about 300 meters above sea level. Of note, while the 1965 plantings are of a massal selection, the 2012 vines are of Nebbiolo clones 185, 71, 141, 415, and 308 (see chapter 1, NEBBIOLO LAMPIA, Biotypes and clones sub-chapter; see also Appendix A: *Table 1.3: List of Nebbiolo clones recognized officially by the Ministry of Agriculture Registry of Grape varieties and Clones*; see also *Table 1.4: Abridged characteristics of the most important Nebbiolo clones*). Microvinifications from this site show that the best wines were those made in essentially classic years such as 2008, 2013 and 2016, and that tells us something about Gustava's terroir. Recently, in 2020, the greater part of Gustava was bought by the Cassa di Risparmio di Cuneo, an Italian bank, securing the vineyard for the Alba School of Oenology. Reportedly, part of the wine made will be auctioned off each year, the proceeds of which will benefit various charities. Admittedly a meritorious project, quality of the wine aside.

Benchmark wineries/Reference point producers of Barolo Gustava: None of any note currently available/recommended.

LA CORTE

Township	Grinzane Cavour
Reference Map	See Map of Grinzane Cavour MGAs (Ch. 10)
Size (ha) (Tot / Barolo MGA)	7.87
Production 2021 (hl)	0
Altitude	210 – 290 meters a.s.l. roughly
Exposure	Predominantly southwest;
N. Claimants MGA	0
Other grape varieties planted:	Barbera; Dolcetto; Grignolino; white varieties
Land Units	Land Unit of Barolo for the most; Land Unit of Gallo d'Alba for the lower parcel in the north-west side
Soil (stage):	Tortonian

Ian's assessment of the vineyard district, its wines and its potential

La Corte is yet another of the Barolo vineyard districts that not many have ever heard of, if for no other reason because there are no (as yet) Barolo La Corte wines to taste. The vineyard district juts out northward and that will be to your right as you drive from Grinzane Cavour (the commune to which the La Corte vineyard district belongs to) towards the industrial part of Gallo d'Alba. Otherwise, it's easy to see on your left as you drive towards Diano d'Alba on the road that separates it from the Gustava vineyard district.

La Corte's landscape is complex, but its soil lithology is essentially that of the typical Saint Agatha Fossil Marls that characterize most of the Grinzane Cavour commune. To the best of my recollection and to my ability to read through scribbled notebooks going back thirty years ago when computers were not exactly a thing, I believe that I have neither tasted a Barolo from La Corte, nor any micro-vinifications from it before such wines were to be assembled in an eventual estate Barolo blend. I might have tasted La Corte wine if its wine was perhaps included in some Langhe Nebbiolo or Nebbiolo d'Alba blend, but honestly, I don't know. And it really wouldn't make much of a difference because I had neither a clue as to what I was tasting nor as to what I should be looking for in order to identify La Corte's presence in the blend. That being so, inferring that La Corte must have a measure of potential is easy enough to do, given that about 80% of its extension is under vine and most of that is Nebbiolo. You would hardly think anybody would plant so many vines there, and Nebbiolo at that (not the easiest variety to grow) if people didn't see something they liked in La Corte and its wines. So maybe in the future some competent producer will start making single-vineyard district Barolos from this site and I for one cannot wait to happily look, sniff and taste away, and in the process learn more about this site and its wines. Honestly, the *terroiriste* can only be happy at that thought. And so, until then it is.

Benchmark wineries/Reference point producers of Barolo La Corte: None currently available.

LA SERRA

Township	La Morra
Reference Map	See Map of La Morra MGAs (Ch. 10)
Size (ha) (Tot / Barolo MGA)	17.79 / 10.78
Production 2021 (hl)	515.96
Altitude	370 – 450 meters a.s.l. roughly
Exposure	From east to southeast; northeast in the part bordering Boiolo
N. Claimants MGA	13
Other grape varieties planted:	Barbera; Dolcetto
Land Units	Land Unit of La Morra
Soil (stage):	Tortonian

Producers claiming the MGA

Renata Marilena Bianco; Sergio Bianco; Agostino Bosco; Alberto Burzi; Cesare Bussolo; Ca' d' Perulin; Marcarini; Reverdito; Sabina Reverdito; Sordo (Giovanni Sordo); Alberto Voerzio; VoerzioMartini; Roberto Voerzio.

Wines

Agostino Bosco - Barolo La Serra; **Marcarini** - Barolo La Serra; **Mauro Molino** - Barolo La Serra; **Alberto Voerzio** - Barolo La Serra; **VoerzioMartini** - Barolo La Serra; **Roberto Voerzio** - Barolo La Serra; **Reverdito** - Barolo La Serra.

What the producers say

Agostino Bosco: "This vineyard has been a part of our family since 1930 but it was only in 2007 that we started to let it play solo in the vinification process. The soil is tufaceous (limestone) and calcareous clay: the exposure and soil composition endow this wine with both structure and tannins suitable for a long cellar life. The bouquet presents complex aromas of berry marmalade and brandied cherries, with notable spicey notes".

Davide Voerzio (Roberto Voerzio): "We began vinifying this wine on its own at the end of the '80s. Our wine has a decisive tannic structure (it's the most tannic wine among our cru wines) and offers a prevalent note of dark fruit on the nose, while finishing with good softness on the finish".

Mauro Molino: "La Serra distinguishes itself for its fresh, refined aromas and flavors".

Marcarini: "La Serra is an historic wine of our estate. We have always made it like our Barolo Brunate, but it gives a very different, fresher, more perfumed but just as structured wine".

Ian's assessment of the vineyard district, its wines and its potential

La Serra is a famous vineyard of the La Morra commune, if for no other reason because of the great wines (easily recognizable because of their iconic gold-colored label), made at the Marcarini estate by Elvio Cogno there from the 1960s until 1990. La Serra is located in that section of the La Morra territory that is closest to the Barolo township: for the most part, this is where La Morra's biggest wines are made ("biggest" being relative to La Morra, which gives some of the Barolo denomination's more graceful, perfumed wines). As much as I firmly believe that, producer alchemy aside, it is geology (and soil type) that most determines the characteristics of whichever Barolo you might be drinking (see chapter 7. BAROLO TERROIR), La Serra provides a shining example of just how important exposure and altitude are in shaping a Barolo's profile. Why do I think it might be so? Easy.

La Serra is situated above (as in higher up) the vineyard districts of Cerequio, Case Nere and Brunate that are to its southwest, south, and southeast, respectively. To La Serra's west there is Fossati, and to its east there is Boiolo, where the hillside on which La Serra is draped curves and turns somewhat, meaning that here the vines can face even northeast, instead of the vineyard district's mostly east/southeast exposure. However, despite its proximity to Cerequio and Brunate, La Serra's wines are fresher and lighter (as in having less palate-weight and inherent creaminess) in style than the Barolos of those other two famous vineyard districts. This is mostly due to different altitudes and exposures because the soil lithologies are essentially similar between the three. Brunate, Cerequio and La Serra are all mostly characterized by the laminated form of the Saint Agathe Fossil Marls, meaning the classic La Morra blue-grey clay-marls rich in manganese and magnesium, plus or minus sand and limestone. However, La Serra is characterized more by an obviously white, nutrient-poor clay-calcareous soil containing plenty of stones; speaking broadly, it is more calcareous than Brunate and Barolos. Even more importantly, La Serra's Nebbiolo vines grow on average at much higher altitudes than those of the vineyard districts below it (vineyards start at 350 meters above sea level and climb upwards, while in Brunate and Cerequio they start below 300 meters in altitude). Furthermore, La Serra's prevalent exposure is east/southeast, which is very different from Brunate's and Cerequio's most important Barolo slopes that face south/southwest. In other words, La Serra is a much cooler vineyard district, less sunny and more ventilated (certainly compared to one part of Cerequio and to Brunate, that are two of La Morra's -and of the entire Barolo's denomination- warmer sites).

It follows that La Serra Barolos seem more vibrant, crisper even, than most of those made in the section of La Morra closest to the town of Barolo. At the same time, it also means that La Serra Barolos are also less fleshy and marked by a much more obvious tannic bite (but clearly, when the grapes are optimally ripe the tannins are neither gritty nor harsh), which isn't always everybody's cup of tea, er, of Barolo. Frankly, I don't mind the tannic framework of La Serra's wines, or its only nuanced degree of fleshiness; furthermore, it may well be that the encroaching climate change (actually, already encroached) may have something to say in regards to this vineyard district's wines in the future.

If truth be told, and as hard as it may be for some locals to accept, but already now in hot vintages such as 1997 and 2007, the Barolos from La Serra can turn out to be more interesting if not better than those of more famous, warmer, sites such as Cerequio and Brunate. Clearly, that statement is true only if and when comparing wines made with Nebbiolo grapes that are similarly grown and the wines similarly made by similarly competent producers.

La Serra producers and the wines

The most famous La Serra Barolos of all have historically been those of the Marcarini estate, and more recently, those of Roberto Voerzio. The two estates could not be more different in their approach to viticulture and winemaking; consequently, the Barolo La Serra wines of each were so different that they really weren't in any way comparable. And that makes it harder to understand both the wines of any given vineyard site ought to be about.

Marcarini's vines lie at about 380 meters above sea level facing south/southwest and were replanted in 1992 and 2002. However, any Barolo lover worthy of his spittoon has at one time or another tasted older vintages of Marcarini's Barolo La Serra (for example, the 1964 and 1971 were truly memorable wines: and still are, if cellared in good conditions). By contrast, Roberto Voerzio completed his first harvest in the La Serra area in 1987. A believer in extremely low yields, he green harvests to a fault and goes one step further by cutting the bottom part of the bunch when the right time comes so as to further concentrate the juice in his grapes (the grape bunches can weigh as little as 500 grams or less). In the end, this means that like with his other Barolo vineyards, he culls a truly small amount of grapes. It all makes for very concentrated, very dark-colored wines of great purity that find favor with a certain set of wine lovers.

There are other very fine wine estates that farm this vineyard district. Mauro Molino estate owns 0.4 hectares in La Serra, and I find their wines to be very fine, easy to drink and lovely: they really exhibit La Serra's characteristic acid spine, making for wines of noteworthy tension and tannic bite. VoerzioMartini is a relatively new estate that bought the property of Gianni Voerzio, the "other" Voerzio in La Morra but whose wines were very different from those of his more famous brother Roberto, though also quite good. Gianni Voerzio made a Barolo La Serra wine that was famous in its heyday (actually, the estate also made an even more amazing Freisa wine from vineyards planted on highly sandy soils right under the bastions of La Morra). It is also worth knowing that Gianni Voerzio's Barolo La Serra specified on the back label that it was made with 100% Nebbiolo Michet (just check any old bottle, for example the 1982 vintage) and the Voerzio Martini estate specifies the same about its wine. The southwest-facing vines in La Serra were planted at roughly 430 meters above sea level back in 1971. A relatively new estate on the Barolo scene, VoerzioMartini's wine is very traditional and well-made, a good Barolo to search out for as it won't cost you an arm and a leg. But wait, La Serra and its many Voerzios do not stop there! That's because in 2006, Alberto Voerzio, cousin of Gianni and Roberto, decided to jump into the wine battlefield too. He owns about four hectares of vines, one of which is in La Serra (he bought his first vines in 2002 thanks to the help and advice of his cousin Roberto, who told him to do so quickly, because otherwise he would buy the vineyards himself). Alberto Voerzio's wines, besides being noteworthy for a pretty and colorful label, are nicely silky and easygoing. In a perfect world, just what you'd expect of a La Morra Barolo.

Benchmark wineries/Reference point producers of Barolo La Serra: Marcarini, Roberto Voerzio. Also good: Alberto Voerzio, VoerzioMartini.

LA VIGNA

Township	Diano d'Alba
Reference Map	Figure – Diano
Size (ha) (Tot / Barolo MGA)	4.48
Production 2021 (hl)	0
Altitude	260 – 280 meters a.s.l. roughly
Exposure	South to southeast.
N. Claimants MGA	0
Other grape varieties planted:	Barbera; Dolcetto; Freisa; white varieties
Land Units	For the most Land Unit of Barolo (eastern slopes);
Soil (stage):	Tortonian and Serravalian

Ian's assessment of the vineyard district, its wines and its potential

One of only three vineyard districts of the Diano d'Alba commune, I have never had a single Barolo from this site, or even know of any Langhe Nebbiolo or Nebbiolo d'Alba wines that might have been made with grapes from it. However, while Diano d'Alba is famous for its outstanding Dolcetto di Diano d'Alba wines (mark my words: the most balanced and in many cases the best, though not the most famous, Dolcetto wines of all) the same cannot yet be said for its Barolos. My belief is that the Diano d'Alba territory can in fact give very good to excellent Barolos, and vineyard districts like Gallaretto and Sorano (the part of the vineyard district of the latter that is included in the Diano d'Alba township's territory too) with which I have a bit more experience do make, or can make, very good and even excellent Barolos. In a day and age when elegant wines are finally back in fashion, I don't see any reason why La Vigna cannot do so as well. And in this light, the fact that over 90% of the La Vigna vineyard district is under vine, and that over 90% of that is Nebbiolo tells me that there are plenty of others who think so too.

Benchmark wineries/Reference point producers of Barolo La Vigna: None currently available.

LA VOLTA

Township	Barolo
Reference Map	See Map of Barolo MGAs (Ch. 10)
Size (ha) (Tot / Barolo MGA)	46.3 / 13.3
Production 2021 (hl)	712.99 (of which 263.56 hl of Barolo Riserva *MGA*)
Altitude	380 – 420 meters a.s.l. roughly
Exposure	Predominantly west, plus a small east-facing part which overlooks the town of Barolo
N. Claimants MGA	6
Other grape varieties planted:	Barbera; Dolcetto; white varieties
Land Units	Land Unit of Vergne
Soil (stage):	Tortonian

Producers claiming the MGA

Viberti; Famiglia Anselma; Luca Marenco; Sordo (Giovanni Sordo); Stra; G.D. Vajra.

Wines

Cabutto - Tenuta La Volta - Barolo La Volta; **Stra** - Barolo La Volta; **Viberti** - Barolo Riserva La Volta

What the producers say

Claudio Viberti (Viberti): "La Volta's wines are generally fresh but soft and ready to drink fairly soon. Our vines are mostly south/southeast, between 380 and 400 meters above sea level. The soils are typically clay with veins of limestone tufa. The vineyards are right next to the Castello de La Volta, built in the first part of the 1200s".

Ian's assessment of the vineyard district, its wines and its potential

I love the Barolos of La Volta. Unfortunately, it's one of those vineyard districts of Barolo that the vast majority of all those reading these words have hardly ever heard of, which is a pity. Trust me: La Volta's Barolos, though neither blockbusters nor superripe and fleshy, can be really spectacular. A case in point being the Barolos of the Cabutto-Tenuta Castello La Volta estate that I have been fortunate enough to taste numerous times over the years, each time coming away nothing less than impressed. I remember first tasting them a tasting organized in Rome in the early 2000s and jotting down the estate name, for I had not yet visited the winery and was curious to know more. Needless to say, I have since made up for my ignorance at the time of the Rome tasting. And I'm glad I have.

Clearly, to appreciate the Barolos of La Volta at the fullest, you have to like wines that are more floral than fruity, perfumed, and lighter in style as opposed to tannic, mouthcoating behemoths. But if Chambolle-Musigny is your thing rather than Nuit-Saint-Georges, or if you pine for Margaux instead of Pauillac (but clearly, while greatly enjoying and appreciating the wines from all four: I'm talking preferences and tastes here, not individual merits of those Appellations), then read on, my kindred spirit.

La Volta is a vineyard district of the Barolo commune: it's named after the castle that sits at the summit of the hillside on which vineyards are draped from both north to south and east to west. The same hillside is where you will also find Bricco delle Viole. You can see the La Volta vineyard area very easily when you drive down the winding road that from the town of La Morra takes you to the town of Barolo (it seems straightforward said like that, but in fact I should include the word "eventually", given the road will take you to Barolo after quite a few left and right turns, some of them sharp). You will find yourself at one point driving through the middle of the Bricco delle Viole and as you keep moving lower down, you'll drive through a small piece of San Pietro and then do the same through La Volta. A much larger section of La Volta will be on your right, and a smaller one to your left (the beautiful Castello della Volta will be visible in its full if slightly dilapidated glory on your right). It's actually a pretty drive I must have done something like a million times (OK, OK, maybe a little less, but still a lot!) and I never tire of it: the scenery is beautiful.

The La Volta vineyard district is completely surrounded by a bunch of other vineyard districts, some famous, others less so. To its west, there is Bricco delle Viole; to its southwest, San Ponzio; to the south, it's the Barolo-Novello commune border, and over in the territory of the Novello commune, the Ciocchini-Loschetto vineyard district; to the east, and lower down the hill, Paiagallo and Terlo; to the northeast, Drucà; to the north, a small piece of Rué; and finally, to its northwest, San Pietro. Its soil's lithology is the Saint Agatha Fossil Marls of the laminated type, and the wines are appropriately suave, lifted and perfumed as is typical of the Barolos born off Tortonian age soils. My analysis shows La Volta's soil composition to be more or less 58% loam, 27% sand and only 15% clay. This tells us that that La Volta, or at least the sections of the vineyard district that were sampled, has a low plasticity index; or to put it in simpler terms, that La Volta is not characterized by especially good water-retention capacity. It follows that it is a site that can suffer in hot droughty years. I find Barolos from La Volta to have an intense note of both fresh and dried rose petal and rosehips, violet, and currants (both red and black), blackberry jam, cinnamon, and nutmeg. Definitely not blockbusters, but when well-made, these are some of the most pristine and pure Barolos you'll taste, wines of a beautiful translucency of fruit, paragons of balance and suave disposition: one sip, and it's very much like silk draping over your taste buds. Poetic, I know: but trust me, so can be the wines of this little-known vineyard district.

La Volta producers and the wines

For my money, the best estate at showcasing everything the La Volta vineyard district has to offer is the Cabutto-Tenuta della Volta estate. It is little-known by most wine lovers today, mostly because it's a small family-run winery (in the words of Michael Palij MW: "…a cellar devoid of fashion but that has authenticity in its DNA") that makes wines of perfume rather than size and gets very little press as a result. But to be clear, the fault here does not lie with the estate. Moving right along, the Cabutto-Tenuta della Volta is actually an historic Barolo estate that was founded in 1920 when Domenico Cabutto bought the farmstead of Volta from the Marquis Gastone di Mirafiori (cadet nephew of Vittorio Emanuele II, then the King of Italy). Today the winery is run by Osvaldo and Bruno Cabutto, brothers who produce very traditional wines that are true-to-type to both the site and the grape variety and who do so by following eco-friendly agriculture practices. Again, according to Michael Palij MW, who in my view knows Barolo and Italian wine much better than most people I have met in my close to forty or so years in wine "… Cabutto-Tenuta della Volta must count as the most exciting viticultural discovery since Pompei". A little exaggerated, maybe? Well, a little hyperbole never hurt anybody, and besides, I for one actually don't think he's that far off the mark. And when Palij talks, I am amongst those who listen. You should too.

The Viberti estate also owns two vineyards in the La Volta vineyard district, one of which has been in the family since forever and another more recently acquired. The grapes from the south-facing side of their holding of 1.5 hectares planted at 370-400 meters above sea level, are blended with those of many other vineyard districts to make their estate's classic Barolo Buon Padre. In exceptional years, a Barolo Riserva La Volta is also made (this Riserva is aged in conical vats for a period of forty-six months, followed by a brief period of three months in steel and a further twelve months of aging in bottle). The grapes for the Barolo Riserva are sourced from the highest 0.45 hectares portion of the vineyard Viberti owns in La Volta. In those years in which the Riserva is made, only the grapes from the lower-lying 1.1 hectares of the La Volta holding are used to make the Barolo Buon Padre. Even more so than the classic Barolo Buon Padre, the Barolo La Volta Riserva always reminds me, and everyone else with a functioning nose, of a strong aroma of rose petals and of rosehips.

The very fine but little-known Mauro Marengo estate (also a fine producer of Nascetta del Comune di Novello, the delicious aromatic white wine original of the Novello commune) farms about one hectare of vines in La Volta planted in 1973 and 2019 between 410 and 420 meters above sea level. The wine is exceptionally good and very La Volta: high acidity, noteworthy but generally polished tannic bite (that the acidity brings to the fore) and very perfumed, pretty notes of both red and dark berries. Call me a believer.

Benchmark wineries/Reference point producers of Barolo La Volta: Cabutto-La Volta. Also good: Viberti, Mauro Marengo.

LAZZARITO

Township	Serralunga d'Alba
Reference Map	See Map of Serralunga d'Alba MGAs (Ch. 10)
Size (ha) (Tot / Barolo MGA)	30.00 / 15.58
Production 2021 (hl)	791.31 (of which 44.54 hl of Barolo *MGA* Vigna)
Altitude	260 – 390 meters a.s.l. roughly
Exposure	From south to west-northwest; east on the slope facing Gianetto
N. Claimants MGA	10
Other grape varieties planted:	Barbera; Dolcetto; white varieties
Land Units	Land Unit of Serralunga d'Alba
Soil (stage):	Serravalian

Producers claiming the MGA

Famiglia Anselma; Franco Boasso; Casa E. di Mirafiore; Frama; Ettore Germano; Poderi Gianni Gagliardo; Guido Porro; Alessandro Rivetto; Vietti.; Villadoria (Daniele Lanzavecchia).

Wines

Famiglia Anselma - Barolo Lazzarito; **Casa E. di Mirafiore** - Barolo Lazzarito; **Ettore Germano** - Barolo Riserva Lazzarito; **Poderi Gianni Gagliardo** - Barolo Lazzarito Vigna Preve; **Guido Porro** - Barolo Vigna Lazzairasco, Barolo Vigna S. Caterina; **Reva** - Barolo Lazzarito; **Alessandro Rivetto** - Barolo Lazzarito; **Vietti** - Barolo Lazzarito; **Villadoria** - Barolo Lazzarito.

What the producers say

Sergio Germano (Ettore Germano): "We own this plot since 2002 and have started its separate vinification and bottling since 2003. We have old vines that give a sense of origin to the wine, uniting elegance and power".

Luca Currado (Vietti): "We own this plot since always, and recently we have made further acquisitions. Lazzarito produces wine that are intense, extremely polished with a robust structure and velvety texture. Elegant notes of figs, prunes and spices, marked by a good tannic structure and a sense of minerality, all of which are prolonged by a lasting finish"

Ian's assessment of the vineyard district, its wines and its potential

I'm often asked what the typical Serralunga Barolo tastes like, and my answer is always the same: like those made in Lazzarito. I have always believed Lazzarito to provide the archetype of Serralunga Barolo: steely, but also powerful, tannic, lifted, vibrant, and in need of time to mature fully. Clearly, there are noteworthy differences among the Barolos made within Serralunga's borders, such as those between wines made with grapes grown either the northern or southern halves of the commune's territory (the southern half of the Serralunga territory extends immediately below the town of Serralunga itself). For example, the wines from the northern part of the territory are cooler and more rigid, those from the southern half are in my view best thought of as an ideal mix of the Barolos of Serralunga and of Monforte, rather than Serralunga proper. But for the most part, the wines of Lazzarito showcase very well what the Barolos of Serralunga have to offer. I also believe Lazzarito to be one of the greatest vineyard districts of all Barolo, and clearly I'm not the only one who thinks it's just a swell place in which to grow grapes. You can infer as much, like I do, from the data that shows 85% of Lazzarito's extension to be under vine, of which 88% is Nebbiolo. The fact Lazzarito is not as famous as it probably should be is most likely because (but not just) hampered by the lack of famous producers such as Bruno Giacosa and Giacomo Conterno making wine there (and this despite having at least three standout estates making Barolo Lazzaritos: Ettore Germano, Guido Porro and Vietti). The steely, somewhat unyielding nature of Lazzarito Barolos when young has no doubt also contributed to the site failing to jump out and grab headlines; but with appropriate cellaring, Lazzarito Barolos can potentially rank with the denomination's very best. In this light, the fact that the Barolo Lazzarito is almost always the best wine in the portfolio of any producer lucky enough to own vines there tells you just about everything you need to know about this vineyard district's exact winemaking potential and overall "cru" quality level.

Given Lazzarito its due, what characterizes this vineyard district and its wines? First off, its name, that has an altogether rare origin for Barolo (and for that matter, the rest of Italy too). Most likely, the name "Lazzarito" derives from the Italian word of *lazzaretto*, the medieval hospitals where those taken ill by the plague were treated (apparently, there was once just such a hospital in this area). "Lazzarito" is also another name of the Cascina (farmhouse) Santa Giulia located more or less in the historic center of the vineyard district. Worth knowing too is that Lazzarito is an historically famous name, reported in official municipal documents dating back to 1610 (though not necessarily in association with the quality of wines made there).

The vineyard district itself is located in the northern half of the commune's territory, but on the western flank of the Serralunga ridge, just above Serralunga itself. The vineyard district of Parafada is immediately to the west (indeed, it takes over from Lazzarito on the same slope and the two share the well-known La Delizia single vineyard area: see below) while the vineyard districts of Gianetto and Bricco Voghera are to the east. This location ensures that Lazzarito has a relatively cooler microclimate (given its placement in the northern half of the territory) but one that is made warmer by its position on the western flank, as well as by its altitude. The highest part of the slope, around 380-390 meters above sea level, is also greatly influenced by the wind known as 'Marin" which heats up the immediate area, a good thing at this altitude. In fact, Lazzarito is the rare Serralunga vineyard district that is sliced through by the road that runs atop the Serralunga ridge (and that goes through town as well). Consequently, Lazzarito is divided in a larger portion situated on the prized warmer western flank, and a smaller one on the cooler eastern flank (clearly, it's the latter half that is the least important of the two).

As with other Barolo vineyard districts that are all too often just too large, it is my opinion that the larger western-facing part of Lazzarito can be, and should be, sub-divided into its four historical subregions. The Lazzarito proper is an amphitheater that is more or less situated between 330 and 390 meters above sea level (it is that section of the vineyard district that is located right at and below the aforementioned Cascina Santa Giulia). Moving north towards Parafada, the second subregion, known as La Delizia, straddles the boundary between Lazzarito and the Parafada vineyard district, with the latter gaining the lion's share of it. The southernmost portion of Lazzarito, not far removed from the houses of Serralunga d'Alba, is known as the Santa Caterina subregion. Last but not least, lower down on Lazzarito's slope, say from about 260 to 320 meters above sea level, grow the vines of the fourth subregion known as Lazzaraisco. Santa Caterina and Lazzaraisco were once considered separate from Lazzarito and were ultimately included within Lazzarito's boundaries only in the 1990s: they are two very high-quality Barolo production areas that historically have been most associated with the outstanding wines of the Guido Porro estate.

Lazzarito's landscape is the classic Land Unit of Serralunga, and it has the just as Serralunga-classic Lequio Formation lithology. Therefore, Lazzarito's rather loose soil is very rich in compacted sands and much limestone; but according to my soil sample analyses, in some sections especially it also has more sand than many other Serralunga vineyard districts (save for parts of Arione). It is a very different reality from that of other Serralunga vineyard districts such as Prapò and Cerretta that are richer in clay and dominated by sandstone (and characterized by the Castiglione Land Unit) or Riva (the part that falls within Serralunga's boundaries, characterized by the Barolo Land Unit). And though it's hard to generalize with Lazzarito, because as we have seen there are many different subregions within this vineyard district, it is mostly a slow-ripening site, one of the last to be harvested in the denomination despite being one of the first in which budburst occurs (in some parts of Lazzarito, at least). Portions of the vineyard district also show surprising vigor, considering the amount of limestone in the soil. In ultimate analysis, Lazzarito's soil is the perfect complement to its mesoclimate, with climate and geology combining to give Barolo wines marked by the utmost steeliness, tension, and purity.

Lazzarito producers and the wines

The Guido Porro estate can be viewed as a "Lazzarito-expert" of sorts. This because it makes not just one Barolo Lazzarito, but two others from different Lazzarito subregions: the Barolo Vigna Santa Caterina and the Barolo Lazzaraisco. Of the two, the Santa Caterina vineyard area is the smaller (about one hectare), is situated higher up the slope (at 350 to 390 meters above sea level) and has the younger vines (roughly 35 years old). It is also characterized by a soil richer in clay, giving it an advantage in droughty years, but not all of it is ideal for Nebbiolo (only its southwestern-facing portion is used to make Barolo; otherwise, Barbera is also planted).

By contrast, the Lazzaraisco section is immediately south of Lazzarito-proper, separated from it by a small road winding out of the collection of buildings called I Vei. Less than two hectares large and situated between 300 and 350 meters above sea level, its fifty years old vines face south/southwest; it is very well-protected from the natural elements, so much so that it can get fairly hot there in some years. No doubt, this is precisely why the specific Lazzaraisco area has always been held in high esteem by older locals, who lived in a time when "climate change" were words nobody had ever heard of and Nebbiolo didn't ripen fully in more years than not. Today, this may no longer be the case, though there is no denying that the Barolo from Lazzaraisco is noticeably different from that of Lazzarito-proper: softer and rounder, but just as complex, if perhaps less piercing and mineral. I really like the wines from this estate and find Guido Porro to be another producer who flies under the radar (see GIANETTO file). However, his fortunes will probably see an uptick now that he too has inherited part of the Canale vineyards in Vignarionda (from where Bruno Giacosa made some of his, and Italy's, greatest wines ever). Porro makes exceptionally good wines of truly noteworthy delicacy and lightness of being (to give you an idea just *how* light on their feet, his wines are less weighty than many made from La Morra vineyards) that deserve to be better known.

Sergio Germano, of the Ettore Germano estate, also makes a very good Barolo Lazzarito. He too is a somewhat underrated producer: terroir-lovers ought to take note that his Barolos always convey noteworthy somewhereness. So much is obvious when tasting his many Barolos from different vineyard districts side by side, as the wines he makes from Lazzarito, Prapò and Cerretta really do speak of each single district area's characteristics. Given a certain "monastic" mouthfeel to Germano's wines, all of which are never especially memorable for generous gobs of fleshy fruit (in part due to his winemaking style), Ettore Germano wines are routinely underrated in blind tastings or by those who are easily impressed by round wines of noteworthy mouthfeel. I don't know: perhaps Germano's notoriety will also be kicked up a notch after his having stuck gold a few years ago when named one of the three heirs of Tommaso Canale. This meant inheriting a part of Canale's prized vineyards in the Vignarionda. This windfall notwithstanding, Germano is also lucky in that he owns 0.8 hectares in Lazzarito too, planted in 1931 at 320-360 meters above sea level. It might interest you to know that his are the oldest vines in all of Lazzarito. His vineyard site is a warm one (for Lazzarito, that is) and the south/southwest-facing vines have no trouble ripening grapes there every year. Germano's vineyards are also characterized by a strong presence of soil iron that seems to make for even tougher tannins than Lazzarito usually gives; for this reason, Germano releases his Barolo Lazzarito as a Riserva. Not unreasonably, he is of the idea that the wine needs more time in oak (so three years in barrel) to polish off the tannic clout it is endowed with.

Perhaps the best-known estate making a Barolo with Lazzarito grapes is Vietti: it owns roughly 1.7 hectares of southwest-facing forty years old vines there. With Vietti, the analysis of Lazzarito's exact standing in the pantheon of "greatest Barolo vineyard sites" becomes slightly complex. At least in my opinion, Vietti's Barolo Lazzarito has never been quite up to the level of the estate's magnificent Barolos from the Rocche di Castiglione and Villero. Why this is I have no idea, given that Luca Currado is one of the most talented and knowledgeable people in all of Barolo; clearly, my impression could just be a matter of personal preferences or that I could well be wrong. In the past, Vietti's Barolo Lazzarito was often the estate's most rigid and most oaky wine, one in which the signature of site was honestly hard to come by. In fairness, Vietti's Lazzarito Barolo (like all the estate Barolos in fact) improves greatly with age and at fifteen to twenty years from the vintage is usually spectacular. So it is a really good wine that like all Lazzarito wines requires ample cellaring; and in this specific wine's case, maybe even more than others.

Gianni Gagliardo has long made a Barolo Lazzarito that was simply identified with the name of Preve. Today, with the official names of the vineyard districts in effect, the wine is called Barolo Lazzarito Vigna Preve. The vines are planted with Nebbiolo clones 230, 142, 71, 423 and a special Gagliardo massal selection (Nebbiolo Michet) at 390 meters in altitude on a soil of 56.4 % loam, 22.7% clay and 20.9% sand. The Preve location of Lazzarito is on a ridge that runs towards the area's castle and is highly exposed to both sunlight and wind, something that I think is apparent when tasting Gagliardo's wine, which always strikes me as being more forward and readier to drink than any other Barolo from Lazzarito I have come and come across.

Clearly, the winery everyone gets to taste the Barolo Lazzarito of is Fontanafredda, the large estate that used to be owned by the King of Italy and since then many different owners. The estate has a long tradition of easy drinking commercial but well-made Barolos and that is still true today; some of the older vintages are especially good (1971, for example) and even more so are the 1982 Barolos. In fact, the 1982 Fontanafredda Barolo Lazzarito is a non-walking poster of the importance of site: it was heads and shoulders above the rest of the lineup of Fontanafredda's Barolos of that vintage. I still have an amazingly vivid recollection of the tastings I conducted on all those wines back in the mid-1980s when I was living in Rome (see FONTANAFREDDA file). Wow, the 1980s: that's a lot of Barolo under the bridge. By the way, the Fontanafredda estate has often bottled a Barolo La Delizia over the years (also as a Riserva) but it did not always write the name "Lazzarito" on the label. Therefore, beware all the websites that report or mention Lazzarito on every single La Delizia bottling made: that is just not so. As an example, take the 1982 Barolo Lazzarito La Delizia: as such, that wine doesn't exist though the source of the grapes was Lazzarito.

Benchmark wineries/Reference point producers of Barolo Lazzarito: Ettore Germano, Guido Porro. Also good: Gianni Gagliardo, Reva, Vietti. Famiglia Anselma, Fontanafredda and E.Mirafiore make solid wines that are easier to find than many.

LE COSTE

Township	Barolo
Reference Map	See Map of Barolo MGAs (Ch. 10)
Size (ha) (Tot / Barolo MGA)	6.01/ 1.73
Production 2021 (hl)	86.50
Altitude	290 – 320 meters a.s.l. roughly
Exposure	South-southeast in the central part, east on the lateral parts
N. Claimants MGA	4
Other grape varieties planted:	Dolcetto
Land Units	Land Unit of Barolo for the most; Land Unit of La Morra in the southern parcels bordering Rivassi
Soil (stage):	Tortonian

Producers claiming the MGA

Diego Pressenda; Giacomo Grimaldi; Luciano Sandrone; Silvano Bolmida.

Wines

Giacomo Grimaldi - Barolo Le Coste

Ian's assessment of the vineyard district, its wines and its potential

An historically relevant vineyard district, named in documents already centuries ago, don't confuse this Le Coste vineyard of the Barolo commune with the very similarly named Le Coste di Monforte. The latter, as its name readily implies, belongs to the Monforte commune. Le Coste we are talking about here is a small vineyard area immediately south of the town of Barolo, one that is situated between the vineyard areas of Terlo, Rivassi (the lion's share of Le Coste is nearest to this vineyard district) and Boschetti. Officially categorized as a vineyard district with Tortonian stage soil and a lithology of Saint Agatha Fossil Marls of the sandy type, Le Coste is best thought of as a loamy-clay site that is also very sandy. The sand component and its average altitude means that the wines from Le Coste are nicely suave and fruity, but the loam and clay elements are such that they also boast a good tannic spine while having just enough lift.

For sure, Le Coste is a vineyard area everyone I have ever talked to seems to be very high on. And so perhaps it is not by accident that a number of very well-known, famous even, Barolo producers either own vines in Le Coste and/or make Barolo with its grapes (though mostly destined to blends). Le Coste is where the Giuseppe Rinaldi estate long made one of its two Barolos that clearly identified the site by name on its label (the Barolo Brunate-Le Coste that many readers no doubt remember). Up until 2010, it was easy to find bottles of

Giuseppe Rinaldi Barolo Brunate-Le Coste but using two MGA names on the same label is no longer allowed. The Rinaldis were left wondering what to do (they had the same problem with their other outstanding Barolo that had been labeled until then as Cannubi San Lorenzo-Ravera). The estate opted to make a Barolo Brunate only and a second Barolo called Tre Tine: it is in the latter that they blend the grapes from their three other historic vineyard district holdings of Le Coste, Ravera and Cannubi San Lorenzo. In fact, some of their Le Coste grapes still go into their Barolo wine identified just as Brunate (a Barolo made mostly with Brunate grapes: the law says that this is legal as long as no more than 15% of the total grapes used come from the second vineyard, in this case Le Coste).

The sandy nature of Le Coste is brought to the fore here: of all the various Rinaldi-owned Barolo vineyards, it is the holding in Le Coste that is their sandiest (which may come as a surprise to some readers, given that the estate owns a piece of Cannubi San Lorenzo, a site not exactly known for its gargantuan levels of clay). The plot in Le Coste was replanted in 1986 by Beppe's father, because that's the year one of the worst hail episodes in the history of Barolo hit the area (in May 1986). The hail was so bad that it leveled entire vineyards, all of which needed to be replanted, despite many (commendably) tried to save the old vines. Have you ever found yourself wondering why so many Barolo estates (of Barolo and La Morra especially) have vines planted in 1986? Well, now you know why. You might also be asking yourself why Rinaldi blended his Le Coste grapes with Brunate, and why he did not choose to just make two different single-site Barolos. Fact is that Rinaldi's piece of Le Coste is not especially big (0.6 hectares) and so blending these grapes with those of Brunate was a logical and convenient step to take. Also, Le Coste gives a totally different wine than that of Brunate (thanks to totally different soils); hence, the blending of the grapes from these two sites was also a means by which to achieve a more balanced wine, not to mention a Barolo in line with those made by the area's historical habit of assembling grapes from different vineyard sources).

Le Coste producers and the wines

The high-quality Novello estate of Giacomo Grimaldi makes an excellent Barolo Le Coste (and as things stand currently, it is the only one to do so). It has owned its southwest-facing vines in this area since the 1930s; at 0.8 hectares, the estate's holding is a small one. This estate's wines always offer a fruity, creamy mouthful of Barolo that is really hard not to be smitten with. Granted, we only have this one to go by, but based on it and how it has performed over more than a decade of vintages, the Barolos of Le Coste appear like they might be lovely wines with plenty to offer, and I wish more estates were bottling a wine from there. Masnaghetti, who has studied and mapped the Barolo vineyard districts extensively, believes Barolos from Le Coste harken back to those of Cannubi. I'm always happy to study this matter some more and see. For sure, it just forces me to have to drink more Barolos from Le Coste, hardly a chore or a bad thing, to tell you the truth.

Recently, world-famous Barolo producer Luciano Sandrone's name has become associated with Le Coste. Sandrone used to rent a vineyard in this area and during his frequent vineyard forays came upon a section of old Nebbiolo vines (in 1987) that were different-looking from all the others. One grapevine in particular stood out: this particular Nebbiolo grapevine was characterized by very loosely-packed and much smaller than usual bunches and grapes, not to mention leaves that had noteworthy indentations and hairy lower pages (the leaf's lower page is its underside: in the Nebbiolo vines Sandrone came across in his vineyard, the leaf's lower page is hairy and not smooth like it is in "normal" Nebbiolo). As curiosity drives an inquisitive man like Sandrone, took it upon himself to study it going as far as replanting selected vines from the vineyard in 1990 and having genetic analysis done. It turns out that the vine really is Nebbiolo (the genetic tests confirmed as much in 2017), albeit a strange-looking one (but as we have seen, there are countless Nebbiolo clones and biotypes: see chapter 1, NEBBIOLO LAMPIA, Clones and biotypes subchapter). Once the grapevine was identified as being really of Nebbiolo, Sandrone started making a Barolo with it, that he ages for three years in large oak barrels (first in tonneaux and then in large oak casks). The first vintage of this Barolo was bottled in 2017 and released for sale in 2019. It is a bigger, broader, richer Barolo than all the others he makes, and one that thanks to its great underlying structure develops slowly. The wine is called Vite Talin (from the Italian words "vite" meaning 'grapevine', and "talin", which is a local nickname for 'Natale', the name of the previous owner of the vineyard plot in Le Coste where Sandrone discovered this new biotype of Nebbiolo).

Benchmark wineries/Reference point producers of Barolo Le Coste: Giacomo Grimaldi. Also good: though it's more an expression of Nebbiolo biotype than it is of site, don't miss out on Sandrone's Barolo Vite Talin, a rarity that offers a chance to taste a Barolo made with a newly discovered Nebbiolo biotype, different from Lampia, Michet, Rosé and all the others mentioned earlier in this book (see chapter 1, NEBBIOLO LAMPIA).

LE COSTE DI MONFORTE

Township	Monforte d'Alba
Reference Map	See Map of Monforte d'Alba MGAs (Ch. 10)
Size (ha) (Tot / Barolo MGA)	50.34 / 10.27
Production 2021 (hl)	529.73 (of which 66.84 hl of Barolo *MGA* Riserva)
Altitude	370 – 500 meters a.s.l. roughly
Exposure	Predominantly from east to south. Southwest and north in the remaining parts.
N. Claimants MGA	7
Other grape varieties planted:	Barbera; Dolcetto
Land Units	Land Unit of Castiglione in the western parcels bordering Mosconi and Ginestra; Land Unit of Barolo in the remaining parts
Soil (stage):	Tortonian

Producers claiming the MGA

Piero Benevelli; Cascina Amalia; Famiglia Anselma; Walter Gagliasso; Lalu'; Pecchenino; Luciano Sandrone.

Wines

Famiglia Anselma - Barolo Le Coste di Monforte; **Piero Benevelli** - Barolo Le Coste di Monforte; **Silvano Bolmida**– Barolo Le Coste di Monforte; **Cascina Amalia** - Barolo Le Coste di Monforte; **Lalù** - Barolo Le Coste di Monforte; **Pecchenino** - Barolo Le Coste di Monforte and Barolo San Giuseppe; **Diego Pressenda** - Barolo Le Coste di Monforte

What the producers say

Silvano Bolmida: "Our family owns this vineyard since 2002, and we started vinifying it on its own in 2009. Its heavier soil is compensated by a good slope gradient and a southwest exposure so that even in very sunny years, the grapes are safe from sunburn".

Marco Parusso: "We are owners here since 1999. Between 2003 and 2009, we blended it with our grapes from Mosconi (that are now used as part of our Barolo Classico); but from 2010, Le Coste di Monforte is vinified on its own. Our Barolo Le Coste presents a more masculine character with hints of earth, underbrush, truffle, tobacco, and wet leaves. It is a Barolo of breed, characterized by much structure, with abundant tannins and aromas".

Orlando Pecchenino "Since 2004, we are proprietors of this vineyard. In the glass, Barolo Le Coste is elegant, and infused with aromas of small fruits, licorice, spices, tobacco and even nuances of truffle".

Ian's assessment of the vineyard district, its wines and its potential

In many respects, Le Coste di Monforte represent an interesting conundrum. On one hand, Barolo loving insiders are well aware that this is one of the vineyard districts where Giacomo Conterno used to buy grapes for his Barolo Monfortino (when the family did not yet own the Francia *monopole*). This implies the Nebbiolo growing in Le Coste di Monforte ought to be of pretty darn good quality. On the other, only about half of Le Coste di Monforte is under vine, and it's not even all Nebbiolo (Nebbiolo represents just about two thirds of the grapevines planted there). This implies that the vineyard district, at least as it has been officially delimited today, isn't such great shakes as far as Nebbiolo and Barolo are concerned. Figuring out where the truth lies is but one of the things that makes wine, and in this case Barolo, so fascinating.

What helps shed light on the matter is the realization that Le Coste di Monforte is a fairly complex vineyard district that thanks to myriad combinations of exposure, altitude and soil (without even mentioning the human element, that obviously plays a role), gives rather different wines depending on exactly where within its boundaries the grapes are grown. There are undoubtedly some vineyard districts about which speaking in terms of a Barolo somewhereness can be attempted without getting laughed out of the room (because as we have seen many are far too large to do so effectively), but doing so with Le Coste di Monforte really *is* hard to do unless you really do your homework first. In that case, arriving at a reasonable guess at what the Le Coste di Monforte Barolo you are drinking should be like is not impossible.

First off, the landscape of Le Coste di Monforte can be divided in two: it's the Land Unit of Castiglione in the vineyard district's western sector close to Ginestra and Mosconi, while it's the Land Unit of Barolo in the rest of the vineyard district. This implies that there are different topographies, lithologies and altitudes, among other things, throughout this entire vineyard district, and so it is, in fact. For example, soil lithology-wise, Le Coste di Monforte is characterized by the presence of both the Saint Agatha Fossil Marls of the sandy type and of the Diano Sandstone (the former is more abundant than the latter). The Diano Sandstone dominates mostly in parts of the western sector of Le Coste di Monforte (though it isn't much talked about, there's even some Lequio Formation there). However, it's not just the lithology that changes within Le Coste di Monforte: for example, while most of the vines are planted at relatively high altitude and often with eastern exposures, these aspects also change throughout the vineyard district.

Historically, it is those vineyard areas of Le Coste di Monforte that look full south that have always been considered to be the vineyard district's best, while the higher-altitude sections that look east were always been considered as less favorable (not surprisingly, given that in times devoid of climate change the Nebbiolo ripens late there and is subject to the vagaries of bad weather). Over the years, I have been told by some locals that it was from the south-facing, lower-lying areas in the western section of today's Le Coste di Monforte (where the landscape is that of the Castiglione Land Unit) that Giacomo Conterno estate sourced grapes with which to make the prized Monfortino. Others I have spoken about this subject have instead mentioned another area called Castlé, over in the eastern sector of Le Coste di Monforte, so I'm not sure what to think. It might well be that Conterno bought in more than one area.

Le Coste di Monforte producers and the wines

A number of different estates have farmed over the years, and still farm or own vineyards, in Le Coste di Monforte, including for example Anselma, Bersano, Diego Conterno, Orlando Pecchenino, Piero Benevelli, Sandrone, and Scarpa. Pecchenino has long been a strong proponent and advocate of Le Coste di Monforte's Barolo. He is especially happy with one south-facing vineyard of his of thirty plus years of age planted at 440 meters above sea level. He told me that the Nebbiolo grapes there are always perfect, always seemingly able to adapt to whatever the weather conditions might be. Luciano Sandrone had been following Le Coste di Monforte's grapes since 2000, when a friend and the owner of a small vineyard plot in the vineyard district asked him to vinify his grapes for him. Both Luca and Luciano Sandrone have told me that they were left flabbergasted when they realized the extremely high quality of the grapes involved. So much so that they never lost sight of the vineyard plot in question, and when it came up for sale in 2021, they bought it. In fact, the grapes from this 1.92 hectares, planted at 410 meters above sea level, have been used to make the Sandrone Barolo Le Vigne bottling since 2019 (along with grapes from Vignane, Baudana, Cerviano-Merli and Villero). I cannot say any more than I already have, but suffice it so say this is an especially historic, prestigious and outstanding section of the Le Coste di Monforte vineyard that Sandrone was fortunate enough to buy.

Diego Conterno began renting vineyard land in Le Coste di Monforte in 2018. Related to the family running Conterno-Fantino (he founded that estate in 1982 along with his cousin Claudio Conterno and Guido Fantino), Diego Conterno set off on his own in 2000, making his first Barolo in the 2003 vintage (all 1300 bottles of it, from the Ginestra vineyard district). Having trained and worked with Beppe Colla at Prunotto, his penchant is for making traditional Barolos. His estate's Barolo Le Coste di Monforte comes from high altitude vines and a rather cool site that gives a perfumed Barolo redolent of floral and minty nuances. At Piero Benevelli, they have been farming this area for something like six generations. It's Massimo running the show today and his wines are amongst the best of the vineyard district. They work 2.5 hectares of vineyards in Le Coste di Monforte, and the vines are about 25 years old. The wine is larger-scaled and broader than some other Barolos from this vineyard district (rather than floral, this one is unabashedly fruity, with reminders of prunes and dark cherry, plus pepper and camphor); it's aged one year in used 225 liter barriques, then another in 40 hL Slavonian oak barrels. Lara Rocchetti and Luisa Sala of the Lalù estate, founded only in 2019, farm 0.3 southeast-facing hectares in Le Coste di Monforte (as well as 0.5 hectares La Morra's Roncaglie, and 1.5 hectares in Monforte's Bussia Brovi, opposite to Bussia Corsini), but make a Barolo only from their holding in Le Coste di Monforte, which already tells you quite about the perceived value of this vineyard district. Amalia (Cascina in Langa) owns one hectare in Le Coste di Monforte, planted in 1982 at about 400 meters above sea level. The 2010 was their first vintage (a nice way by which to kick things off). Silvano Bolmida began producing a Barolo Le Coste di Monforte with the 2013 vintage, the last Barolo to have been added to his portfolio. Ferdinando Principiano uses his Le Coste di Monforte grapes to make a Nebbiolo Langhe: it's a lovely wine, and if you told me that you thought this lovely wine was very much like lighter styled declassified Barolo, let's just say I wouldn't say you were wrong. Gastaldi used to own vines in this vineyard district but sold his property to Massolino of Serralunga. Last but not least, Barolo lovers and collectors will be thrilled to know that in the 2017 vintage Roagna made 2000 bottles of a Le Coste di Monforte Barolo.

Benchmark wineries/Reference point producers of Barolo Le Coste di Monforte: Diego Conterno, Pecchennino, Piero Benevelli, Silvano Bolmida.

LE TURNE

Township	Serralunga d'Alba
Reference Map	See Map of Serralunga d'Alba MGAs (Ch. 10)
Size (ha) (Tot / Barolo MGA)	7.40
Production 2021 (hl)	0
Altitude	250 – 335 meters a.s.l. roughly
Exposure	From west to west-northwest
N. Claimants MGA	0
Other grape varieties planted:	Barbera; Dolcetto; white varieties
Land Units	Land Unit of Serralunga d'Alba
Soil (stage):	Serravallian

Ian's assessment of the vineyard district, its wines and its potential

I have never tasted a wine made with Nebbiolo from this vineyard district. At least, not knowingly. Le Turne is a little-known vineyard district of Serralunga that is essentially the western prolongation of the Margheria vineyard district. The two drapes over the tip of a short hillside crest that juts out from the main Serralunga ridge: other better-known vineyard districts located on the same crest are Rivette and Marenca. But while Rivette, Marenca and Margheria (in order of decreasing proximity to the main Serralunga ridge that cuts through the commune's territory in a north-south direction) are all fairly famous vineyard districts of Serralunga, it's safe to say nobody has ever heard of Le Turne.

Given the latter's landscape of the Land Unit of Serralunga, and Lequio Formation soil lithology, both very classic of Serralunga (and that Le Turne shares with the three more famous districts of Rivette, Marenca and Margheria), you'd have to think Le Turne ought to give, at the very least, decent Barolos. In fact, Le Turne provides another shining example of just how important the vineyard exposure is in the making of great Barolos: this because while Le Turne's soil isn't that different from the best vineyards in the commune, and its altitude is not so high at all, the part of the slope where Le Turne curves west/northwest, leads to there being a much cooler, if not cold, microclimate. Still, that almost 100% of Le Turne is under vine is telling: though it might not be warm enough for Nebbiolo to ripen fully there, other grape varieties apparently do very well.

Benchmark wineries/Reference point producers of Barolo Le Turne: None currently available.

LIRANO

Township	Serralunga d'Alba
Reference Map	See Map of Serralunga d'Alba MGAs (Ch. 10)
Size (ha) (Tot / Barolo MGA)	12.77 / 0.35
Production 2021 (hl)	18.63
Altitude	320 – 390 meters a.s.l. roughly
Exposure	Northwest
N. Claimants MGA	1
Other grape varieties planted:	Barbera; Dolcetto
Land Units	Land Unit of Serralunga d'Alba
Soil (stage):	Serravallian

Producers claiming the MGA

Pio Cesare.

Ian's assessment of the vineyard district, its wines and its potential

Careful: there is Lirano, and then there is Lirano. The Lirano vineyard district of Serralunga (on the cooler eastern-facing flank, between the Manocino and Serra vineyard districts) is where you can make Barolo, but there is also a Lirano in the Roddi commune, more or less a few stones throws away, that is outside of the Barolo denomination (therefore any Nebbiolo grown there cannot be used to make Barolo). Which is an interesting situation, given that it's a perfectly fine Barolo vineyard area (if we don't allow that one, then we should not allow a good chunk of the denomination, but that's a discussion for another time). Lirano's soil lithology is the classic Lequio Formation that gives tannic, ageworthy wines. However, the vineyard district's Achille's heel is its northwest exposure, which makes bringing Nebbiolo in at full, optimal ripeness a real chore, and more often than not, downright impossible. Not by chance only a little more than half of Lirano is under vine, and of that less than half is planted to Nebbiolo. The site is undoubtedly a cool one, but as we shall see below, there are signs that quality Nebbiolo grapes for Barolo production can be grown there.

Lirano producers and the wines

Pio Cesare has owned land in Lirano since 1999; the vineyards are roughly forty-five years old, face west and are planted at about 380 meters above sea level. The soil composition is 50% clay, 40% loam and 10% sand (in an interesting differentiation of vineyards sites based on soil composition, note that the soil composition in the area also called Lirano but outside the Barolo denomination is characterized by as much as 50% sand). Pio Cesare uses the Nebbiolo grapes from Lirano to make their Barolo estate vineyard blend. Cesare Pio has followed microvinifications of Lirano Barolos and has told me over the years that the wine is always best in hot years such as 2007, 2011 and 2017. Who knows? Perhaps if climate change continues on unabated (clearly, we all hope not) Lirano might yet produce world-class Barolos one day that will bear the vineyard district's name on the label.

Benchmark wineries/Reference point producers of Barolo Lirano: None currently available.

LISTE

Township	Barolo
Reference Map	See Map of Barolo MGAs (Ch. 10)
Size (ha) (Tot / Barolo MGA)	12.45 / 4.94
Production 2021 (hl)	268.01 (of which 187.54 hl of Barolo Riserva *MGA*)
Altitude	290 – 370 meters a.s.l. roughly
Exposure	From east to southeast in the better exposed parcels, and northeast in the remaining parts
N. Claimants MGA	2
Other grape varieties planted:	Barbera; Dolcetto
Land Units	Land Unit of La Morra
Soil (stage):	Tortonian

Producers claiming the MGA

Borgogno; Francesco Boschis; Damilano.

Wines

Borgogno - Barolo Liste; **Francesco Boschis** – Barolo (*); **Damilano** - Barolo Liste.

What the producers say

Damilano: "These vineyards are easy to see while driving down hill on the Strada Provinciale Alba-Narzole, moving past the Castello della Volta. Liste gives a fairly atypical wine characterized by plenty of pigments and tannins".

Borgogno: "Liste's soil differs from that of the immediately surrounding vineyard areas. It's also a site that is characterized by many different exposures, from south to southeast and even north, at varying altitudes. So many different Barolos may be born there".

Ian's assessment of the vineyard district, its wines and its potential

If you were to look at Liste from above, say from a drone, a glider or a low-flying airplane, and you imagined it to be a clock, then it would have the vineyard districts of Fossati at roughly twelve o'clock, San Pietro at nine o'clock, Ruè at six o'clock and Sarmassa at three o'clock. In fact, it drapes over both flanks of the middle section of a small crest that has San Pietro up top and a section of Sarmassa lower down.

At a little less than thirteen hectares, Liste is a rather small vineyard district, usually a good thing in that that normally small vineyard district size implies a relative homogeneity of site, but in Liste's case things are not quite so cut and dried. Topographically, it is shaped like a donkey's back (a hump), thereby offering a large diversity of exposures. The lithology is essentially Saint Agatha Fossil Marls (mostly of the laminated type, but also of the more typical form), and so the soil certainly isn't going to be behind dark-colored, very tannic Barolos. In such cases, it's more than likely that it is the winemaking that accounts for the wine's personality, as opposed to the site's physical parameters. Barolos made from Liste decades ago, such as those of the Borgogno estate (when it was still owned by the Boschis family) were never especially dark or tannic (just a little lean, but that's another matter).

In my experience, Liste can gives wines of some interest, but it really only does so in truly outstanding vintages: in such years the wines have a bit more weight, but still fall very much within the range of the Barolo commune's typically early maturing, easygoing Barolo blueprint, if with a little greater palate presence and structure. Giuseppe Boschis, when he still owned Borgogno, didn't even bottle a Borgogno Barolo Liste from the excellent 1999 vintage because he didn't think it offered anything more than his regular Barolo, which is a statement in and of itself.

Liste producers and the wines

Today's noteworthy producers of Barolos from Liste are Damilano and Borgogno. In both cases, I think the Barolo Liste is by far the best wine of the winery. The former's wines tend to be darker and more balsamic, the latter's lighter and vibrant, though both show good amounts of density and concentration, often with nuances of eucalyptus oil and resin.

Benchmark wineries/Reference point producers of Barolo Liste: Borgogno, Damilano.

MANOCINO

Township	Serralunga d'Alba
Reference Map	See Map of Serralunga d'Alba MGAs (Ch. 10)
Size (ha) (Tot / Barolo MGA)	5.55
Production 2021 (hl)	
Altitude	340 – 430 meters a.s.l. roughly
Exposure	Northwest
N. Claimants MGA	0
Other grape varieties planted:	Barbera
Land Units	Land Unit of Serralunga d'Alba
Soil (stage):	Serravallian

Ian's assessment of the vineyard district, its wines and its potential

I have never tasted a Barolo made with grapes only from this vineyard district, though a number of producers own vineyards there and blend the grapes into their classic estate Barolo. I have yet to taste a series of microvinifications over a number of vintages, but that's on me for I had numerous opportunities to do so over the last five years or so and for one reason or another (Covid being a big part of that), I have been unable to follow-through on this project.

Manocino producers and the wines

Today, one producer who farms Manocino and uses it grapes in his Barolo is the talented Enrico Rivetto of the Rivetto estate in Serralunga. Over the years, during winery visits and vineyard walks, he told me that his vines are up at about 420 meters above sea level, and the cool microclimate of his vineyard means these are his Nebbiolo grapes he almost always picks last. Not surprisingly he has also told me over the years that Manocino gives the freshest of his Barolos, with tapering acidity, noteworthy minerality, and good aging potential. In fact, even though there is nobody making a Barolo from Manocino as such, just the fact that over 80% of the land under vine in this vineyard district is in fact planted to Nebbiolo makes one think (well, me at least) that there might be more there than presently meets the eye. Time will tell.

Benchmark wineries/Reference point producers of Barolo Manocino: None currently available.

MANTOETTO

Township	Cherasco
Reference Map	Figure - Cherasco
Size (ha) (Tot / Barolo MGA)	2.76 / 2,28
Production 2021 (hl)	123.91
Altitude	345 – 360 meters a.s.l. roughly
Exposure	From west to southwest, plus a small part facing northwest
N. Claimants MGA	1
Other grape varieties planted:	Dolcetto
Land Units	Land Unit of Verduno
Soil (stage):	Pliocene

Producers claiming the MGA

Umberto Fracassi.

Wines

Umberto Fracassi - Barolo Mantoetto

Ian's assessment of the vineyard district, its wines and its potential

Over the years I have heard many people take pot shots at both Cherasco as a Barolo commune ("it didn't deserve to be included in the group of eleven" is the most common snide remark) and at Mantoetto as a vineyard district ("that area is not worthy of being a *cru*"). Not so, and I don't think those are fair assessments. I have had enough of these wines over the years to find them not just perfectly acceptable, but fine Barolos, wines of a delicate balance and very pretty. In fact, the wine from Mantoetto is an historic wine, made already in the 1880 vintage. That there was real pride of place in the Mantoetto hill (located in the territory of the San Michele fraction of Cherasco at the border with today's La Morra commune), is well demonstrated by the wine's label of the late 1800's: 'Barolo del Mantoetto'. Clearly, almost one hundred and fifty years ago, the Marquis of Torre Rossano (the noble title of the Fracassi Ratti Mentone family) were proud of their terroir, and clearly indicated as much with their wine labels. I think they should have been, and should be.

For the Barolo Mantoetto really does speak of its specific area's soil and lithology. It is commonly said that Mantoetto and the Cherasco commune's territory are characterized by a lithology consistent with that of the gypsiferous-sulfurous formation of the Messinian stage, a lightish soil that gives politely-styled Barolos. It is the same soil type of La Morra's Bricco Cogni and Verduno's Neirane, both of which are vineyard districts that give Barolos of a profile similar to those of Mantoetto. Another recent view states that Mantoetto, and a portion of the Cherasco commune's territory, are characterized not by the gypsiferous-sulfurous formation of the Messinian stage but rather marls that were formed in an earlier time, the Pliocene (the Pliocene is the epoch that immediately precedes the Miocene), though consensus on the matter appears to be lacking and the debate remains open. Unfortunately, geological studies on this specific portion of the Barolo denomination are apparently insufficient presently, or at the very least not up to date, as mentioned earlier in this book (See chapter 7, BAROLO TERROIR, Barolo Geology sub-chapter). In any case, no matter to which geologic time the soils belong to and were formed in, we can all certainly agree that they are lighter-textured soils that give just as lightly-textured and politely styled Barolos like are all those born off either the gypsiferous-sulfurous formation or soils dating back to the Pliocene. It follows that it is neither logical to expect, nor fair to demand, a wine from such soil to deliver power and size. In other words, a Barolo from Mantoetto cannot be, and should not be, the second coming of something made in Monforte or Serralunga. Rather, Barolos from such a soil as Mantoetto's should play the cards of elegance, lightness of being, and perfume. Well-made Mantoetto Barolos have an element of that and a sneaky amount of creaminess, though clearly, they are no blockbusters, and that is perhaps a part of their infinite charm. Speaking frankly, if people tasting wines from this vineyard district are left disappointed because the wines aren't big, strapping, and tannic, oozing oodles of flesh and power, the problem isn't really the wine or the vineyard district.

Mantoetto producers and the wines

This vineyard district is in many respects a real *numero uno*, as in number one. By that I mean that Mantoetto is the only one vineyard district in the Cherasco commune; that there is only one producer of Barolo Mantoetto, Fracassi (but the full name is actually Umberto Fracassi Ratti Mentone); and that there is only one Barolo Mantoetto currently made. You'll admit, that's a whole lot of *uno*s, or "ones". Jesting aside, this is a somewhat under the radar wine that deserves better. It deserves better beginning with people's perception of the vineyard area's value. Fracassi Mentone's Barolo Mantoetto is an under the radar gem offering grace and refinement, traits not to be automatically taken for, or confused with, dilution. If you know, you know.

Benchmark wineries/Reference point producers of Barolo Mantoetto: Umberto Fracassi Ratti Mentone.

MARENCA

Township	Serralunga d'Alba	
Reference Map	See Map of Serralunga d'Alba MGAs (Ch. 10)	
Size (ha) (Tot / Barolo MGA)	7.46 / 1.47	
Production 2021 (hl)		
Altitude	275 – 355 meters a.s.l. roughly	
Exposure	From west to south.	
N. Claimants MGA	1	
Other grape varieties planted:	Barbera	
Land Units	Land Unit of Serralunga d'Alba	
Soil (stage):	Serravallian	

Producers claiming the MGA
Luigi Pira.
Wines
Luigi Pira - Barolo Marenca

What the producers say
Pira Luigi: "We replanted our vineyard in 1990, but even with relatively young vines, the wine has always been a typical Serralunga Barolo, powerful, tannic and ageworthy".

Ian's assessment of the vineyard district, its wines and its potential

Marenca is situated immediately to the west of the town of Serralunga, on a short crest that juts out perpendicularly from the western flank of the Serralunga ridge. It's a small amphitheater that has the vineyard districts of Margheria to its west (out at the end of the crest); Damiano to its south; and Rivette to its east, essentially separating it from Serralunga's houses. It is an historically famous vineyard site of the commune, possibly because its amphitheater-like contour allows for its fully south-facing sections to maximally capture the sun's rays and the protection afforded it by the Rionda hill keeps the cold northerly winds at bay. The ensuing slightly warmer meso-climate helped the Nebbiolo grapes ripen in a day and age when that was not always the case, year in and year out, which must have made some sections of Marenca highly prized. For sure, it has long had the reputation of being one of the more outstanding Barolo vineyards, so much so that Renato Ratti included it in his top sites in his *Carta del Barolo* ("first category"). Between the relatively average altitude, the Serralunga Land Unit soils characterized by Lequio Formation lithology and the general warmer mesoclimate, the potential to make powerful Barolos typical of Serralunga is certainly all there.

There are only two owners in Marenca: Gaja and Luigi Pira, with each estate owning about half of Marenca's vineyard area. Gaja's famous Barolo Sperss is actually a blend of grapes from the Marenca and the nearby Rivette vineyard district: while Gaja's total vineyard extension in these two vineyard districts amounts to 7.5 hectares, 5.7 of those are in Marenca. The soil composition of Gaja's holding in Marenca is 46% loam, 42% clay and only 12% sand, but those are average numbers, for as I shall explain the soil in Marenca changes considerably from area to area within the vineyard district. The vines were planted between 300-350 meters in altitude with varied exposures (the vineyard starts out facing southwest, then full south, then west) and in successive stages (in 1964, 1966, 1977, and 1978). It's a climatically favored site: just imagine that in thirty years of owning vines there, Gaja has never once experienced hail there (differently from its holding in Cerequio, another super-famous vineyard district of Barolo). Marenca's wine is more varied in its olfactory and taste profile as well as in its mouthfeel than those made with grapes from Rivette: depending on how the soil changes, so do Marenca's Nebbiolo grapes and consequently so do the Barolos. Off more compact, limestone and clay-rich sections of the vineyard, Marenca's Nebbiolo grapes will have thick skins and give brooding, more powerful wines; grapes born off slightly more marly soils tend to give richly fruity wines; and those grapes born off the rare sandier parts of the vineyard district (but in a nod to what I wrote earlier, and that is the great diversity of soils within Marenca, keep in mind that some sections of Marenca can have as much as 19% soil sand) will have thinner skins and the wines be notable for floral perfume. In Gaja's Barolo Sperss, the Marenca component contributes notes of dark cherry, peat, grilled beef, and especially a note of common mugwort or wormwood (an aromatic flower/shrub of the *Artemisia* genus, that actually grows in the Marenca vineyard; in Italy grow many different species of Artemisia (long associated with medicinal purposes and with witchcraft in medieval times), but the most common is *Artemisia vulgaris*, and it has the plant's characteristic aroma: by contrast, *Artemisia campestris,* also common at these latitudes and especially so on sandier soils, is neither aromatic nor is it used for medicinal purposes. Closer to the Alps, it would be more likely that the Artemisia species growing is the *Artemisia glacialis*, where the shrub is used to make the famous Genepy *amaro* digestive drink).

That much said, to date, Luigi Pira is the only one bottling a Barolo sporting Marenca's name on the bottle's label. Pira's two hectares (some were replanted in 1990) lie at about 350 meters above sea level and face west mostly (you will read and hear the vines face south/southwest) and from those Pira makes a truly powerful wine that is typical of the commune, but even more specifically, of Marenca: what sets Marenca apart from the majority of Serralunga's vineyard districts is that its wines are not just about power, but noteworthy fleshiness of fruit too. Pira's wine is a case in point: broad, large, mouthcoating and fleshy, but never devoid of noteworthy amounts of elegance, it offers a very good example of what Marenca can deliver. Pira's Marenca from the recent 2015 and 2016 vintages are excellent: should you decide to see for yourself, keep in mind both are wines that require an hour's worth (at least) of decanting ahead, but you can get away with less with the 2015. Not surprisingly much more approachable than the classic 2016, it's Marenca-typical notes of ripe red cherry, mugwort, iron shavings, even of tobacco leaf and crushed rocks, are obvious. I have had complete verticals of Pira's Barolo Marenca in Italy and almost complete ones in the USA, and have always found it to be a big thick wine that is always outstanding. It's also a very good food wine. For all intents and purposes, Marenca has to be viewed as one of Barolo's best vineyard districts.

Benchmark wineries/Reference point producers of Barolo Marenca: Luigi Pira

MARGHERIA

Township	Serralunga d'Alba
Reference Map	See Map of Serralunga d'Alba MGAs (Ch. 10)
Size (ha) (Tot / Barolo MGA)	8.10 / 4.57
Production 2021 (hl)	248.34
Altitude	240 – 335 meters a.s.l. roughly
Exposure	From west to south.
N. Claimants MGA	4
Other grape varieties planted:	Barbera; white varieties
Land Units	Land Unit of Serralunga d'Alba
Soil (stage):	Serravallian

Producers claiming the MGA

Azelia; Franco Boasso; Luigi Pira; Massolino.

Wines

Azelia - Barolo Margheria; **Franco Boasso (Gabutti)** - Barolo Margheria; **Luigi Pira** - Barolo Margheria; **Massolino – Vigna Rionda** - Barolo Margheria.

What the producers say

Franco Massolino (Massolino-Vigna Rionda): "This vineyard was acquired in the end of the '70s. Its single-vineyard bottling started in 1985. In the cellar, the wine is macerated up to 18-21 days and is aged in 25 to 100 hectoliter oak casks. Margheria, thanks to slightly higher percentage of sand, has in our view, a unique spiciness and elegance - especially when young with respect to our other *crus* - and despite that, will reward the patient winelovers".

Scavino Luigi (Azelia): "The Marghera is a vineyard of rare beauty. Fully south facing. The clayey and calcareous soil of Serralunga d'Alba manifests itself in all its complexity. Tufaceous marls give richness in extracts and power to the wine. Minerality and flavor: the Margheria openly expresses the strong and austere character of the Serralunga Barolos. Complex aromas, black fruits, licorice, and spices in the typical Serralunga style. An energetic Barolo, in which the tannins give density and depth to the wine. Mineral, earthy, savory".

Ian's assessment of the vineyard district, its wines and its potential

Margheria is situated on the terminal part of a hillside crest that juts out perpendicularly to the main Serralunga ridge running north-south down the middle of the commune's territory. Curiously, the Cascina (farmhouse) Marenca, built at the top of the hillside crest where both Marenca and Margheria are located, probably is situated closer to Margheria than it is Marenca. Go figure. In any case, Margheria is sandwiched in between the vineyard districts of Marenca and Le Turne; Margheria follows Marenca on the slope of the same hillside crest, but then turns slightly westwards as the crest finishes with a broad, rounded tip. Its vineyards are therefore not found just on the flank of the crest, but also drape over its rounded tip where they give way to those of Le Turne, which as mentioned previously is the vineyard district that follows Margheria on the same crest. However, unlike Le Turne, Margheria's vines do not ever look north, explaining why it is the much more famous vineyard district of the two.

Differently from all the vineyard districts immediately around it (Marenca, Le Turne, and Damiano to its south, on another parallel hillside crest and the slope of which looks out to Margheria) there are numerous producers selling Barolo Margheria wines. Another difference is that Margheria's wines are some of the lighter, seemingly rounder ones of the Serralunga commune (clearly, 'lighter' and 'rounder' in the context of Serralunga, because Margheria's are still powerful and delicately austere Barolos), that are certainly very different from the bigger, more-structured wines of nearby Marenca, for example. The biggest reason, apart slightly lower-lying vines (and possibly a warmer mesoclimate in the middle and higher sections of Margheria), is the amount of sand in the soil. Despite its Lequio Formation lithology being exactly the same as Marenca's, Margheria has a higher soil sand content and so that explains, at least in part, the less massively-styled and more floral wines that

I generally associate with this vineyard district. That however is not the case with wines made from Margheria's south-facing vines, which tend to give bigger, more tactile wines closer in the style to Marenca's, though nowhere near as big as those Barolos can be. In other words, you have to know who has vines where to understand why the Barolo Margheria you are drinking tastes the way it does. In any case, all Margheria Barolos age exceptionally well.

Margheria producers and the wines

The Luigi Pira estate (named after Luigi, who gave way to son Gianpaolo, later joined by Romolo and Claudio) makes a Barolo Margheria and drinking it side by side with their Barolo Marenca is an enlightening affair, offering plenty of insight on the two different sites and their wines. The Pira estate is also lucky in that its west-facing 1.5 hectares in Margheria are extremely old vines, well over fifty years old, and that depth shows through in the wines. Another set of west-facing vines are those of Franco Boasso, who first made a Barolo Margheria in 2003 and who's vines occupy the lower sector of the tip of the crest, close to where Margheria's vines give way to those Le Turne. Massolino also owns 1.5 hectares of old vines (forty years old), planted with a southwest exposure at about 280 meters in altitude. Azelia owns 1.9 hectares of sixty years old vines planted high up on the hill, between 250-330 meters above sea level (the estate's website states up to 360 meters, but that's impossible, given that Margheria only goes up as far as 335 meters), and make about 6000 bottles/year. The estate's vineyards are however some of the highest of all if not the highest in the vineyard district, as they are situated right beneath the Cascina Marenca: also high up are Gaja's Margheria vines, four hectares in the subzone known as Feia (which is, perhaps, a reference to sheep, that once grazed happily in the area), and next to those of Azelia in the direction of Marenca. This is an area where soil water is abundant and the vines tend to be characterized by very green luxurious canopies. You know, when all is said and done, I would have a hard time telling which Barolo Margheria wines to pick; they really are all excellent Barolos and for the most part do a very good job of conveying what Margheria is about.

Benchmark wineries/Reference point producers of Barolo Margheria: Azelia, Franco Boasso, Luigi Pira, Massolino.

MARIONDINO O MERIONDINO

Township	Castiglione Falletto
Reference Map	Figure Castiglione
Size (ha) (Tot / Barolo MGA)	13.11 / 5.26
Production 2021 (hl)	285.55
Altitude	270 – 350 meters a.s.l. roughly
Exposure	From west to northwest
N. Claimants MGA	4
Other grape varieties planted:	Barbera; white varieties
Land Units	Land Unit of Castiglione and Land Unit of Barolo in the northernmost plots.
Soil (stage):	Tortonian

Producers claiming the MGA

Vincenzo Asteggiano; Armando Parusso; Paolo Scavino; Luigina Schellino.

Wines

Armando Parusso - Barolo Mariondino

What the producers say

Marco Parusso (Armando Parusso): "We have owned vines here since 1901 and have vinified it separately since 1986. In terms of topography, Mariondino has a western exposure, one that is defined by the Langhe people the "Sori d'la Seira" for it enjoys the last bit of sunlight before sunset".

If nothing else, this vineyard district is in the running for the title of "MGA vineyard district with the largest number of different yet similar permutations of its name". Take your pick: Mariondino, Meriondino, Monriondino and even Rocche Moriondino, plus a few more I cannot remember at time of writing. In this book I will use the name Mariondino, as I always do, because that's the name used by Marco Parusso of the excellent Armando Parusso estate who has been making a wine from this site for as long as I can remember, a wine that has accompanied me for most of my wine writing days. Happily, the different spelling of its name is not all we need to remember Mariondino for, because it is actually a pretty good vineyard district for Barolo production. That much becomes immediately apparent when you realize the three vineyard districts Mariondino is located between.

Mariondino is the southernmost vineyard district of the Castiglione Falletto commune (save for a small piece of Rocche di Castiglione that juts into the territory of Monforte. See ROCCHE DI CASTIGLIONE file). It is sandwiched in between Villero to the north and Bussia (in Monforte) to the south/southwest; to its east, on the other side of the little road that runs north-south in the Castiglione Falletto commune, lies Rocche di Castiglione. This geographical location explains clearly why some prefer the name of Rocche Moriondino to Mariondino: as Maurizio Rosso of the Gigi Rosso estate told me, using the name of Rocche Moriondino (he believes to be the only producer currently doing so) makes it clearer to everyone that this vineyard district is part of the same hill as the ultra-famous Rocche di Castiglione (for many experts, perhaps the single greatest Barolo vineyard district of all). While Rocche di Castiglione is draped over the eastern flank of the hill, Rocche Moriondino is on the other side of the hill, that looks west.

The current Mariondino is made up of three subregions: Serra, which is the section higher up closest to Villero that was once its own vineyard district but that was partitioned between Mariondino, Villero and Bricco Rocche once the official MGA names of the vineyard districts came into being in 2010; Mariondino proper that goes from Villero to more or less the halfway point of the slope; and Valletti that reaches out towards Bussia.

Not that large but with a varied topography such that there are many different exposures within (even northwest), the best parts of Mariondino are those that faces west/southwest. Historically, though it was also planted with Nebbiolo, those parts of the large Valletti section of Mariondino that are northwest-facing were once just too cold for Nebbiolo to ripen fully there, and the Barolos had tannins that were as tough as nails when young (producers were better off planting Barbera and Dolcetto, and some did just that). Marco Parusso once told me (2002? 2004? I don't remember and can't quite make out my writing in an old notebook where I recorded a specific interview with the date) that while he believed the best part of Mariondino to be of *grand cru* quality level, he also believed that the northwestern-facing sections were worthy of a hypothetical premier cru status at most. Clearly, such assessments may well have changed now, twenty years or so after those words were first spoken; in fact, one might make the case that Valletti is, in some ways, better off in this day and age.

In reality, it's not just the exposure that made Valletti's wines seem tough and tannic when young, but its soil too. Mariondino's mostly marly-clay soil has copious sandstone and sand presence: the lithology is that of Saint Agatha Fossil Marls of the sandy type and this contributes to giving not just powerful wines but very perfumed ones too (they bear some resemblance to those of Villero, that has the same soil lithology as Mariondino). I find that it is not without interest that as Mariondino is the last vineyard district of the Castiglione Falletto commune's territory moving south, it is very close to the territory of Monforte. This proximity shows in the Valletti area wines of Mariondino, that are generally more structured than those made with grapes from the other sections of Mariondino (and of other Castiglione Falletto vineyard districts, for that matter).

Mariondino producers and the wines

Parusso owns west-facing vines planted not far from the winery, at about 290 meters above sea level and that are 20-40 years old. I find his Mariondino wine to come across as a ripe, seemingly soft Barolo, with an almost sexy, sultry quality, but with a sneaky tannic undercurrent that is not immediately apparent because of this wine's forward personality. But it's there all-right. Claudio Viberti of the Roccheviberti estate farms vines in Mariondino but chooses to use them to make a Langhe Nebbiolo wine (he blends the grapes with those of younger vines from his other vineyard district sources, including Bricco Boschis and Rocche di Castiglione).

Benchmark wineries/Reference point producers of Barolo Mariondino: Parusso.

MASSARA

Township	Verduno
Reference Map	See Map of Verduno MGAs (Ch. 10)
Size (ha) (Tot / Barolo MGA)	50.31 / 2.19
Production 2021 (hl)	116.27
Altitude	230 – 370 meters a.s.l. roughly
Exposure	Predominantly southwest, plus some parcels facing south and northwest.
N. Claimants MGA	2
Other grape varieties planted:	Barbera; Dolcetto; Pelaverga Piccolo; white varieties
Land Units	Land Unit of La Morra in the western and north-western parcels bordering Riva Rocca and Pisapola; Land Unit of Barolo in the remaining parts
Soil (stage):	Tortonian

Producers claiming the MGA

Vincenzo Asteggiano; Armando Parusso; Paolo Scavino; Luigina Schellino.

Wines

Cantina Massara - Barolo Massara (*); **Castello di Verduno** - Barolo Massara

What the producers say

Marcella Bianco (Castello di Verduno): "Our Massara vineyard was acquired in 1910 through Cavalier G.B. Burlotto directly from Italy's Royal Savoia family. The vines are located in one of the higher viticultural zones of Verduno, at an altitude of 265 meters above sea level, 1.22 hectares entirely planted to Nebbiolo. The soil is whitish in color with a dominant clay-limestone composition. The favorable east to southeast exposure and scrupulous selection of grapes contribute to the elegant and perfumed personality of the wine, destined for greater power and a long cellar life. This is a Barolo that takes time to open up and develop. Aromatically, it is generous with an elegant blend of fruits and spices: black pepper, fruit jam, maraschino cherry, thyme, geranium and violet. Fresh on the palate, the wine finishes long on a good structure and fine tannins".

Gian Carlo Burlotto (Cantina Massara): "This vineyard district is the productive heart of our estate, that we and others consider to be one of the Barolo denomination's best vineyard areas. Massara gives a rich, big-boned Barolo that shows what Verduno can give".

Ian's assessment of the vineyard district, its wines and its potential

Massara is a vineyard district in the township of Verduno: over the years, I have found that locals have a high opinion of it and its wines. I am not entirely sure that lofty reputation is justified, unless we speak of a very specific part of the vineyard district's vineyard extension; after all, only about a third of Massara is under vine, and of that, not even two thirds is planted to Nebbiolo. Clearly, I'm not the only one who wonders.

As all Barolo-lovers know, Verduno is one of the eleven townships (or communes) of the Barolo denomination; and it is known for giving among the lighter-styled, most perfumed Barolos of all, wines that for the most part are graceful and refined. This is in relation to a number of Verduno-specific factors (see chapter 7, BAROLO TERROIR, The Barolo Communes sub-chapter) but they are not at work throughout the entire Massara vineyard district's extension, a good chunk of which presents very different features from the rest of that commune's territory. And so, it follows that Massara's Barolos *would* be (*should* be) different from the majority of Verduno's. Not that a Barolo from Massara will ever be mistaken for one from Monforte or Serralunga by most wine lovers, because it's still a Verduno vineyard area we are talking about. However, there is no doubt that some of Massara's wines are at one extreme of the Verduno commune's Barolo-style spectrum. Massara is one of the largest of Verduno's eleven vineyard districts, and so there is a large range of topographies, altitudes, soil types and microclimates within it. To make a blanket statement relative to Massara's Barolos being amongst the biggest or the most textured from Verduno is somewhat perilous; but that statement does hold some water, and that much is fairly obvious when tasting many similarly-made Barolos from this vineyard district over numerous vintages. Fact is: the type of Barolo Massara you will drink depends on where within the Massara vineyard district the Nebbiolo grapes used to make it were sourced.

Massara is located in the center of the Verduno territory, immediately to the east of the town itself. This location informs the wines, but also informs you about them (See chapter 7, BAROLO TERROIR, The Barolo Communes sub-chapter). Massara is surrounded by the following vineyard districts: Campasso to its north; Pisapola to its northwest; Riva Rocca to the west; Boscatto to the southwest; Breri to its northeast and east; and Roere di Santa Maria of the La Morra commune to its south and southeast. But the western part of Massara that is closest to the town of Verduno (and therefore to the vineyard districts of Pisapola and Riva Rocche) is characterized by a lighter clay-calcareous soil than that of the vineyard district's eastern section that slopes towards the La Morra commune. Though both halves of Massara have soils of Saint Agatha Fossil Marl lithology (of the laminated form), there is more clay in the soil of Massara towards La Morra. These soils have something in common with the Diano Sandstone formation (known to give bigger, more textured wines) but some experts view them as a separate formation called La Morra Conglomerates due to a more fluvial than marine origin (see chapter 7, BAROLO'S TERROIR, Barolo's geology sub-chapter). In any case, there is no doubt the vineyard district's soil closer to the La Morra border differs from that found closer to Verduno and that around the Cascina Massara, a farmhouse bearing the same name as the vineyard district situated in the northernmost reaches of the Massara vineyard district. Furthermore, altitudes in the Cascina Massara area are generally higher too, allowing for wines of slightly higher acidity that makes the tannins in the wines seem livelier and more piercing.

Massara producers and the wines

Castello di Verduno is an historic Italian wine estate (the pretty old labels of this estate's wines carried the wording of "Cantina del Castello di Re Carlo Alberto" or "Cellar of the Castle of King Alberto") that has long been associated with an excellent Barolo Massara. It is an example of the Massara Barolos made off lighter soils. Their Massara vines were planted mostly facing east (and some southeast) back in 1988 and 1992 at about 300 meters above sea level in a well-protected spot close to the Verduno town's main lookout point (*belvedere*). The soil is fairly heavy (55% clay), but with also plenty of sand (30%), and noteworthy amounts of limestone as hinted at by the soil's white color. Their Barolo Massara is a lovely wine redolent of flowers and herbs; it's maybe not the most complex Barolo you'll ever taste (the estate's Barolo Monvigliero is a good deal more complex) but it delivers a suave, relatively thick mouthful at every sip and offers plenty of easygoing drinking charm. Interestingly, the estate's 2015 Barolo Massara is lighter and fresher than the 2016, when it should really be the other way around (2015 was the warmer of the two vintages, though it was characterized by cool nights making it an also superlative Barolo vintage).

Depending on the vintage, Castello di Verduno also uses some of its Massara grapes to make its classic estate Barolo, along with Nebbiolo sourced in a number of different vineyard districts, including Castagni and Neirane. The wine is usually mostly Castagni (up to 70% of the total grapes used can come from this specific vineyard district) but there's usually varying percentages of Massara's grapes in the blend too (for example, 10% in 2015; 50% in 2014; none in 2013). Remembering what I just wrote relative to the 2015 Barolo Massara, that 2015 was a very successful vintage at Castello di Verduno is demonstrated by just how good the classic 2015 Barolo is too, independently of how much Massara vineyard district grapes were included in the final blend.

Clearly, no winery is more closely attached to the Massara vineyard district than that of Gian Carlo Burlotto (yet another Verduno Barolo producer whose last name is Burlotto, a common family name in the area), given that the estate's name, Cantina Massara, is also that of the vineyard district. The estate, founded in the 1910s, was originally known as Andrea Burlotto, and run by Angelo and his sons, from whom Gian Carlo bought the estate in 2013 and renamed it Cantina Massara (a name with the family had long been associated with). The forty-five years old vines are planted facing southeast (lower down) through southwest (those located slighter up the slope). The Barolos are very fine.

Benchmark wineries/Reference point producers of Barolo Massara: Castello di Verduno, Gian Carlo Burlotto-Cascina Massara.

MERIAME

Township	Serralunga d'Alba
Reference Map	See Map of Serralunga d'Alba MGAs (Ch. 10)
Size (ha) (Tot / Barolo MGA)	17.14 / 7.11
Production 2021 (hl)	335.96
Altitude	230 – 360 meters a.s.l. roughly
Exposure	From west to southwest plus a small part facing west-northwest
N. Claimants MGA	8
Other grape varieties planted:	Barbera; Dolcetto; white varieties
Land Units	Land Unit of Castiglione in the north-eastern parcels bordering Cerretta; Land Unit of Serralunga d'Alba in the remaining parts
Soil (stage):	Serravallian

Producers claiming the MGA

Marilena Alessandria; Brandini; Casa E. di Mirafiore; Daniele Lanzavecchia; Gian Paolo Manzone; Riikka Maria Sukula; Osvaldo Viberti; Vietti.

Wines

Brandini - Barolo Meriame (Barolo del Comune di Serralunga); **Gian Paolo Manzone (Cascina Meriame)** - Barolo Meriame (and Riserva); **Enrico Serafino** – Barolo Meriame (*); **Osvaldo Viberti** - Barolo Serralunga (Meriame) (*); **Sukula** – Barolo Meriame

What the producers say

Gian Paolo Manzone: "Bought in 1999, the quality of the site was such that we started its separate vinification immediately. The maceration process lasts from 15-20 days based on the vintage conditions. The younger vines (now 25 years old) are always aged in big oak casks while the older vines (now 65 years of age) are aged in 350-liter tonneaux. In our view, the mixed clayish and calcareous soil structure, its amphitheater-like shape and the optimal exposure play a key role in the extraordinary quality of the Nebbiolo grapes we pick there."

Riikka Sukula: "We have vinified this vineyard on its own since 2006, the year we bought it. Meriame is notable for its intense ruby color, offering on the nose intense and elegant perfumes of small berry fruits, cherry and spices and finishing long with elegant yet lively tannins".

Ian's assessment of the vineyard district, its wines and its potential

Meriame is located in the northern half of the Serralunga territory, with the vineyard districts of Cappallotto to the northwest, Baudana to the northeast, Cerretta to the northeast and east, Lazzarito to its southeast and Parafada to the south, with which it shares a very small part of its border. It's an essentially bowl-shaped vineyard area, with vines facing from southeast through southwest and that looks out across the valley to Castiglione Falletto. Though Meriame's soil is characterized by a Lequio Formation lithology, its composition changes somewhat within its boundaries, such that wines from Meriame's section closest to Cerretta tend to be fleshier and softer compared to those made almost anywhere else in the vineyard district, that tend to be more steely and rigid, especially in their youth.

Meriame producers and the wines

Though others are now producing Barolo from Meriame and sticking its name on the label, it's only fair to recognize that this vineyard district was essentially made famous by Gian Paolo Manzone of the Cascina Meriame (for the longest time the only one making a single-vineyard district wine from Meriame). Speaking generally, and based mostly on tasting Manzone's wines over the years, it is a vineyard district that is a source of very good, solid Barolos that age well; though they have never struck me as wines of mind-bending complexity, I like their balance and personality. A personality of slightly readier to drink, earthier, savory Barolos than are most from this commune. Meriame is in a very pretty part of Serralunga, one where the bucolic care-free setting is just what the doctor ordered for all those with frayed nerves from long work weeks, and the estate is very much worth a visit.

Benchmark wineries/Reference point producers of Barolo Meriame: Gian Paolo Manzone.

MONPRIVATO

Township	Castiglione Falletto
Reference Map	See Map of Castiglione MGAs (Ch. 10)
Size (ha) (Tot / Barolo MGA)	7.12 / 6.60
Production 2021 (hl)	218.03 (of which 46.92 hl of Barolo *MGA* Riserva)
Altitude	240 – 320 meters a.s.l. roughly
Exposure	From west to south.
N. Claimants MGA	2
Other grape varieties planted:	
Land Units	Land Unit of Castiglione in the south-eastern side bordering the Castiglione village; Land Unit of Barolo in the remaining parts
Soil (stage):	Tortonian

Producers claiming the MGA

Giuseppe Mascarello e Figlio; Sordo (Giovanni Sordo).

Wines

Giuseppe Mascarello e Figlio - Barolo Monprivato, Barolo Monprivato Riserva Cà d' Morissio; **Sordo** - Barolo Monprivato

What the producers say

Giuseppe Mascarello e Figlio: "This vineyard has been in the family since 1904. The vines are about 280 meters above sea level, planted on marly-clay-loam soil with a good presence of limestone".

Ian's assessment of the vineyard district, its wines and its potential

A truly historic Barolo vineyard district (it was first mentioned in official documents in 1666), Monprivato has also always more or less been ranked among Barolo's top ten-twelve vineyards. No less an expert than Renato Ratti listed it as one of the eleven "first category" (i.e., the best) vineyards of all Barolo in his *Carta del Barolo*, but the list of credible experts who have gone on record saying the same thing over the years is a long one. I have no problems admitting to being in their company.

Undoubtedly, the vineyard's fame was made by the Giuseppe Mascarello estate that over the years has produced a long series of unforgettable wines. The Mascarello family bought the Monprivato vineyard in 1904, but first launched the Monprivato name on its Barolo's label only in 1970 [apparently, from 1904 to 1920 Maurizio Mascarello (grandfather of current owner Mauro) did make his Barolo with grapes only from Monprivato, though the wine was simply labeled "Barolo" as was customary at the time]. Over the years, the estate enlarged its Monprivato holdings (most notably in 1985, with the acquisition of the outstanding vineyards owned by Violante Sobrero: I remember being a university student in Rome at the time and the news of that sale hit hard, as it always does when a famous estate ceases to exist, though everybody in the know agreed the vineyards could not have gone to a better winery). As the only Barolo Monprivato for the longest time was that made by Giuseppe Mascarello estate, many believed the site to be a Giuseppe Mascarello monopole (much like Falletto is of Bruno Giacosa and Francia of Giacomo Conterno) but another producer, Sordo, is also making a

Barolo Monprivato nowadays. Independently of how good the Sordo wine maybe, it is only fair to recognize that the benchmark Barolo from Monprivato is the one being made by Mauro Mascarello and his children.

Monprivato is located northwest of Castiglione Falletto, below a road on the other side of which is Bricco Boschis (in the distance, to Monprivato's north and northeast); the vineyard districts of Codana are to its northwest and west, while Valentino is to its southwest and south. The soil is rich in limestone: importantly, it is richer in Diano Sandstone close to the town of Castiglione Falletto and in Saint Agatha Fossil Marls of the sandy type in the more western sections of the vineyard district. The vines have a mostly southwest orientation throughout, ensuring that good grape maturity is reached in almost all vintages and that wines of noteworthy elegance, citrussy acid lift and underlying power are made.

Monprivato producers and the wines

Monprivato's name is intrinsically linked to that of Giuseppe Mascarello estate. Over the years, much has been made of the estate being planted largely with the Michet Nebbiolo biotype (it's not a clone: see Chapter 1, NEBBIOLO LAMPIA. Biotypes and clones sub-chapter), and this is understandable, given the close association of the Giuseppe Mascarello estate with this particular biotype of Nebbiolo. And though I totally understand the family's attachment to Nebbiolo Michet, I do think that removing vines of Nebbiolo Rosé to make way for even more Nebbiolo Michet (which is exactly what happened when the estate decided to make its super luxury Barolo Riserva Ca'd'Morissio) was a mistake (the Barolo Riserva Ca'd'Morissio, the first vintage of which was the 1993 vintage was made from Michet vines planted in 1988 and was launched in the market on 1999: it's a Monprivato supercru, if you will). I don't think either the Barolo Monprivato or the Barolo Riserva showcase the refinement and perfume that were highly typical of previous, older vintages of the Monprivato Barolo (a grace, perfume and refinement that were most likely amplified by the presence of the Nebbiolo Rosé, when it was still there). Nevertheless, Giuseppe Mascarello's Barolo Monprivato is still one of the better and most famous Barolos of all (especially some of the older vintages are among the best Barolos ever made, by anyone); if you love Barolo, then this is one wine you should most definitely try.

As mentioned earlier, Sordo now also makes a Barolo Monprivato. It shares some of the elements that typify the Monprivato Barolo made by Mascarello: a panoply of red berries, citrus peel, rose petals, violet and minerals greet the nose and the palate. There is a magical translucency to this wine, a mix of perfume and steely power that are really fairly unique in the panorama of Barolo. The greatness of Monprivato is well exemplified by the fact Sordo's version is easily one of the best, and to my way of thinking most likely the best, Barolo in Sordo's large portfolio of single-vineyard district bottlings.

Benchmark wineries/Reference point producers of Barolo Monprivato: Giuseppe Mascarello. Also good: Sordo.

MONROBIOLO DI BUSSIA

Township	Barolo
Reference Map	See Map of Barolo MGAs (Ch. 10)
Size (ha) (Tot / Barolo MGA)	4.23 / 1.16
Production 2021 (hl)	62.34
Altitude	240 – 270 meters a.s.l. roughly
Exposure	From west to northwest.
N. Claimants MGA	4
Other grape varieties planted:	Barbera; Dolcetto; Freisa; white varieties
Land Units	Land Unit of Barolo
Soil (stage):	Tortonian

Producers claiming the MGA

Diego Barale; Fratelli Barale; Bric Cenciurio; Lodovico Cabutto.

Bric Cenciurio - Barolo Monrobiolo di Bussia

What the producers say

Bric Cenciurio: "This vineyard has been part of our land-holdings since 1900 and it was in 1999 that we started its own vinification".

Ian's assessment of the vineyard district, its wines and its potential

Strange how famous Bussia is and instead how little-talked about is this vineyard district, one that also boasts the magic word "Bussia" in its name and essentially prolongs the Bussia vineyard district to the west. Another strange thing about Monrobiolo di Bussia is that it's a district physically divided into two separate pieces by another: in fact, a thin strip of the Bussia vineyard district's land that snakes through divides Monrobiolo di Bussia into a larger northern and a smaller southern segment. The northern segment is bordered by the Barolo commune's vineyard districts of Zuncai to the north, Preda to the northwest, and Coste di Rose to the west; for the rest it is surrounded by Monforte's much larger Bussia vineyard district. The smaller southern piece of Monrobiolo di Bussia is surrounded by Bussia to the north, east (the Bussia Soprana subregion of Bussia lies eastwards, just above Monrobiolo di Bussia), and south; Coste di Rose is to its west. Overall, Monrobiolo di Bussia can be viewed as being a low-lying vineyard district, essentially the lowest part of the Bussia that opens up and looks towards the Barolo valley.

Monrobiolo di Bussia producers and the wines

Bric Cenciurio is a relatively young winery born in the early 90s that grew further when owner Franco Pittatore decided to add vineyards to those he already owned in the Roero. Despite owning vines in Monrobiolo di Bussia and elsewhere since the early 1900s, their estate only made its first Barolos much, much later, at the end of the 1990s. The first Barolo Monrobiolo di Bussia dates to the 1999 vintage, made from the about 0.6 hectares of (in 1999, the family also made its first Barolo Coste di Rose, where it owns about two hectares, See COSTE DI ROSE file).

Bric Cenciurio's Monrobiolo di Bussia holding has vines that are as much as forty-five to fifty years old: importantly, there's 5-10% Nebbiolo Rosé among them, but for the most part, the vineyard is planted to Nebbiolo clones CN36, CN111, CN142, CN230 Rauscedo 1, and CN230 Rauscedo 2. Though it is generally believed that Monrobiolo di Bussia is characterized by a mostly typical Saint Agatha Fossil Marls lithology, Pittatore told me during a winery visit that Monrobiolo di Bussia is characterized by the Diano Sandstone formation as well (his vineyard area in the vineyard district, at least). In effect, it is the latter lithology that is more typical of the Monforte commune (though less so along the border with the Barolo commune). Furthermore, he told me that compared to his Coste di Rose holdings over in the Barolo commune, Monrobiolo di Bussia is characterized by less limestone and more loam and sand (for the scientifically inclined, the sand/loam+clay ratio is 0.84/1).

Unfortunately, given the limited amount of vines they own in Monrobiolo di Bussia, only about 1000-1100 bottles/year of Barolo from this vineyard district are made (clearly, they are able to make a little more Barolo Coste di Rose, about 3500 bottles/year). The Barolos are traditionally made: macero/fermentations of 35-40 days (in stainless steel, and if weather allows, they go with natural ferments; aging takes place in 25-35 hectoliter casks (the Coste di Rose) and 500 liters tonneaux (Monrobiolo di Bussia) for two years). I have tasted every vintage ever made of the Bric Cenciurio Barolo Monrobiolo di Bussia: no doubt, living in Italy (at the time) is a big advantage for a wine writer writing about Italian wines. Especially so with a wine such as Bric Cenciurio's Monrobiolo di Bussia Barolo which is made in smaller than what would already be Lilliputian volumes. I'll just cut to the chase and tell you that I think it's an excellent Barolo, leading me to think it's a real pity that there are not more producers bottling single-site wines from this vineyard district. Though the wine has clear-cut Monforte power, with a strong tannic spine at its core (though part of that is also due Bric Cenciurio's viticulture and winemaking), its winning hand is that it has a noteworthy glycerol richness and generally smooth tannins. Over the years, I have always found it to present notes of black cherry and cocoa, even woodsy nuances. According to Pittatore, the Barolos of this vineyard district practically always exude an unmistakable note of balsamic vinegar, and I agree with that, often finding myself using a similar descriptor of this district's wines (the cocoa and woodsy notes that I also get in the wines may very well be described as having a balsamic edge as well).

Other loose ends about this vineyard district that will prove of interest to Barolo lovers is that siblings Diego and Damiano Barale, of the famous winery in Barolo, will be producing their 2018 estate, classic, Barolo with a blend of grapes from Monrobiolo di Bussia and San Giovanni. In due course, we will therefore have an opportunity to know more about this vineyard district through their work and accumulated vineyard and cellar experiences. Last but not least, since 2015 Maria Teresa Mascarello of the legendary Bartolo Mascarello estate (also in Barolo) has been renting in Monrobiolo di Bussia, not too far from where the estate already has their Dolcetto and Freisa vines.

Benchmark wineries/Reference point producers of Barolo Monrobiolo di Bussia: Bric Cenciurio.

MONTANELLO

Township	Castiglione Falletto
Reference Map	See Map of Castiglione MGAs (Ch. 10)
Size (ha) (Tot / Barolo MGA)	23.48 / 5.41
Production 2021 (hl)	216.92
Altitude	220 – 313 meters a.s.l. roughly
Exposure	From west to south.
N. Claimants MGA	2
Other grape varieties planted:	Barbera; Dolcetto
Land Units	Land Unit of Castiglione in the south-eastern side, next to Bricco Boschis; Land Unit of Barolo in the remaining parts
Soil (stage):	Tortonian

Producers claiming the MGA
Fratelli Monchiero; Tenuta Montanello.
Wines
Fratelli Monchiero – Barolo Montanello (and Riserva); **Tenuta Montanello** - Barolo Montanello

What the producers say
Tenuta Montanello: "Bartolomeo Racca bought Tenuta Montanello in 1864 from Patrizio Filippo di Scagnello, Count of Castiglione Falletto. For a long time, it was the site of the Langhe's first wine cooperative, the Cantina Sociale di Castiglione Falletto (thirty-six members by the end of the 1800s). Today, Tenuta Montanello is still owned by the Racca family: the fifth generation is now manning the helm."

Ian's assessment of the vineyard district, its wines and its potential

Montanello is one of the northernmost Barolo vineyard areas of the Castiglione Falletto commune, stretching out in a band-like fashion for almost the entire length of the western section of the commune, looking out towards the territory of La Morra. However, only a small southeastern piece of Montanello actually borders another vineyard district of the commune: the Bricco Boschis, of which it represents a continuation. Interestingly, it is there where Montanello's bigger and most structured wines are made (the soil in this part of Montanello is dominated by a Diano Sandstone lithology rather than the typical Saint Agatha Fossil Marls that characterize the majority of this vineyard district). It follows that wines made at this edge of Montanello actually have more in common with some of the wines of Monforte, or with the biggest ones made in Castiglione Falletto (clearly, it's hard to say so unless you are tasting a Barolo made with Nebbiolo grapes only from this portion of the vineyard district: but just so you know, Fratelli Monchiero own vines only in this section). For the most part, Montanello's soil is characterized by a high percentage of sand mixed in with clay (for accuracy's sake, sample lab analysis show 43% loam, 38% sand and 19% clay), so that the resulting wines boast a very good balance between brute force and grace. That level of sand, by the way, is really quite high. What that means is that while there's undoubtedly an element of truth in the generalization that Montanello Barolos can be on the relatively tannic and rigid side when young, and need plenty of time in a good cellar to develop fully, that reality depends where in the vineyard district the Nebbiolo grapes used to make the Barolo you are drinking come from. In fact, I have always believed Montanello to be a vineyard district that deserves to be better known than it is; in my experience at least, Montanello's Barolos, though not likely to ever be the most complex Barolos you will taste in your lifetime, are usually very satisfying, offering good levels of both perfume and power and noteworthy acid-tannin-fruit balance.

To my taste, Montanello Barolos are often characterized by notes of ripe red cherry and red plum with a delicate but obvious sweet spicy note (more nutmeg and star anise than cinnamon). For wines with such a tannic undercurrent (especially those made in the western half of the district, towards Castiglione Falletto), I always come away impressed by how much sweet, ripe, easily accessible red fruit the vineyard district seems to pack into the wines (especially from wines made where the Saint Agatha Fossil Marls dominate, but not just).

Montanello producers and the wines

The Monchiero Fratelli estate makes a very good Barolo Montanello from vines located in the eastern section of the, a vineyard holding they bought in the 1990s. In truth, Vittorio Monchiero believes that Montanello delivers wines of real tannic power, and I'm not about to disagree with him (especially given the part of Montanello his vines grow in). After all, it is for that reason that at Monchiero Fratelli they choose to release their Barolo Montanello almost always as a Riserva, such that the extra oak aging can further soften the noteworthy tannic framework the wine is endowed with. Tenuta Montanello, the winery that owns the lion's share of the vines in the vineyard district, also makes a good Barolo Montanello that's worth looking for. Over the years I have had many older wines from this property, some of which have held up quite well (the 1978, for sure; the 1968, a weak year for all Barolo, somewhat less), but it's the wines being made nowadays that I find more interesting. If you stop to consider that about 40% of the estate's Nebbiolo was planted in 1943 and the remaining Nebbiolo in 1992, you realize that you are dealing with a real *vecchie viti/vieilles vignes* Barolo, because even the estate's younger vines are now thirty years old. Never underestimate the importance of old vines.

Benchmark wineries/Reference point producers of Barolo Montanello: Fratelli Monchiero, Tenuta Montanello.

MONVIGLIERO

Township	Verduno
Reference Map	See Map of Verduno MGAs (Ch. 10)
Size (ha) (Tot / Barolo MGA)	25,5 / 17.67
Production 2021 (hl)	917.40 (of which 67.40 hl of Barolo *MGA* Riserva)
Altitude	220 – 310 meters a.s.l. roughly
Exposure	From southeast to southwest passing through south, plus a small part facing north and northeast.
N. Claimants MGA	25
Other grape varieties planted:	Barbera; Dolcetto; Pelaverga Piccolo; white varieties
Land Units	Land Unit of La Morra
Soil (stage):	Tortonian

Fratelli Alessandria; Comm GB Burlotto; Cadia; Castello di Verduno; Maria Eleonora Gallesio; Gianluigi Giachino; Silvano Giachino; Livio Grasso; Sabino Grasso; I Bre'; Antonio Morra; Diego Morra; Eugene Piccolo; Poderi Luigi Einaudi; Poderi Gianni Gagliardo; Poderi Oddero; Poderi Roset; Domenico Priola; Gianni Ramello; Giorgio Sandrone; Scarpa; Edoardo Sobrino; Paolo Scavino; Sordo (Giovanni Sordo); Vietti; Voerzio Martini.

Wines

Fratelli Alessandria - Barolo Monvigliero; **Arnaldo Rivera** - Barolo Monvigliero; **Bel Colle** - Barolo Monvigliero (and Riserva); **Brangero** - Barolo and Barolo Monvigliero; **Comm. G.B. Burlotto** - Barolo Monvigliero; **Cadia** - Barolo Monvigliero; **Cantina Massara (Burlotto)** - Barolo Monvigliero; **Castello di Verduno** - Barolo Monvigliero (and Riserva); **I Brè** – Barolo Monvigliero; **Diego Morra** - Barolo Monvigliero; **Poderi Luigi Einaudi** – Barolo Monvigliero; **Poderi Gianni Gagliardo** – Barolo Monvigliero; **Poderi Oddero** – Barolo Monvigliero; **Poderi Roset** - Barolo Monvigliero; **Pietro Rinaldi** – Barolo Monvigliero; **Paolo Scavino** - Barolo Monvigliero; **Edoardo Sobrino** - Barolo Monvigliero; **Sordo** (Giovanni Sordo) - Barolo Monvigliero (and Riserva); **Vietti** - Barolo Monvigliero; **Viberti** – Barolo Monvigliero.

What the producers say

Enrica Scavino (Paolo Scavino): "This vine was vinified for the first time separately in 2000, but we still blended it with grapes from other vineyard sites to make our Barolo classico. We started its single bottling in 2007 when our family was able to acquire this land in a vineyard district that everyone considers the grand cru of Verduno. The idiosyncrasy of Monvigliero is the powerful combination of mineral sensation and elegance on the palate, with very present but silky tannins. It's a Barolo of great finesse and aromatic complexity".

Marcella Bianco (Castello di Verduno): "The hill of Monvigliero at 280 a.s.l. is fully south-facing and has a fine white marly soil. Our holding is 0.3 hectares in surface area, replanted in 1969 and with its grapes we make a Barolo Riserva that is distinguished for a delicate finesse of aromas and for its elegant aromas and flavors ranging from red fruit to spices (especially cinnamon), completed by balsamic and minty notes. A soft tannin and a fine balance between structure and acidity render Monvigliero even more approachable and easy to understand by those who are just starting to drink Barolo".

Stefano Pesci (Arnaldo Rivera): "Monvigliero has a long tradition of excellence. Our vines were planted in 1948 and again in 1968, 1976, 1992 and 2002. We find spicy notes of white pepper and a dose of minerality".

Sordo: "Fully south-facing, the wine we make in Monvigliero always reminds us of faded rose petals, underbrush and sweet pipe tobacco, but also coffee and cocoa".

Fratelli Alessandria: "Our vineyard is over thirty-five years old, planted at about 320 meters above sea level. It's always a very floral and refined Barolo".

Bel Colle: "Always thought of as one of the best vineyard sites of the entire Barolo denomination, not just Monvigliero, our Barolo Monvigliero is floral, refined and fresh".

Ian's assessment of the vineyard district, its wines and its potential

Drinking a number of Monvigliero Barolos all in the same session will have you grasp fairly quickly that you are in the presence of an entirely different Barolo-animal. And a truly great one. This is exactly what I found happening to me back in the early- to mid-2000s, when I began tasting Barolos from this site made by different producers. Clearly, most everyone became first acquainted with Monvigliero after drinking the outstanding Barolo made there by G.B. Burlotto estate, and it was no different for me. But as often happens anytime a vineyard area is off most people's radar and there's but one wine garnering headlines, everyone was of the impression that G.B. Burlotto's wine was so distinctive because of the talent and winemaking ability of G.B. Burlotto's technical director Fabio Alessandria, rather than any specific merit of Monvigliero.

This viewpoint was tough to shake for many years, if for no other reason that Fabio Alessandria really *is* that talented. Even after other excellent Barolo Monvigliero wines began cropping up, professionals and wine lovers alike still resisted the notion that Monvigliero could rank with the best: the *status quo* is a hard thing to change, and it takes time. I well remember one of Barolo's most famous producers of all (if you are taking the time to read this book, then you know of him/her) who told me flat out that there wasn't anything special to Monvigliero but rather the success one specific wine was explainable by the Burgundian techniques employed to make it (i.e., whole bunches). I thought he/she was completely wrong already then in his/her assessment then and I still do now. In the same light, another ultra-famous producer (yes, you know this one too) told me that even though they had been making wine from Monvigliero for years, they preferred to blend it into their classic Barolo, because they didn't find anything special about it. This he/she was telling me while I was sitting there in his/her tasting room and thinking that the sample of Barolo Monvigliero they had just served me was wildly better than any of the other Barolos (save for one) in the winery's lineup of Barolos I had tasted up until then that afternoon (including those bearing much more famous vineyard names on the label). But visiting Barolo estate after estate, year after year, confirmed that Monvigliero was indeed special and that there must have been something more to the G.B. Burlotto Barolo Monvigliero magic than just one man's undeniable talent level. It seemed to me that producers were missing out on not looking to bottle a Barolo Monvigliero. That was then. How times change.

In fact, that Monvigliero could be the source of great Barolos really shouldn't have been much of a surprise. Its vineyard area has long enjoyed a reputation as one the best and most famous Barolo vineyard districts (at one point in time considered to be on a par with that of Cannubi). But like many other Barolo vineyard areas, it had fallen out of the limelight during Barolo wine's tough times. Remember that for most of the latter part of the twentieth century, Barolo's fortunes were nothing like they are today: its wines garnered very little interest (more than one producer will tell you that as recently as thirty years ago they were glad to throw in a case of Barolo when people bought their Dolcetto and Barbera wines). And I can vouch for the fact that really not so long ago, say mid-1980s Italy (I should know, I was there, and I lived the moment), nobody spoke of the Barolos from Monvigliero (or of Verduno, for that matter). In the very limited Italian wine circles of the time (remember that practically nobody was doing/holding guided wine tastings in Italy prior to 1980), the only Barolos vineyard names anybody mentioned were Cannubi, Villero, Brunate, the two Rocches, and Vigna Rionda (the names and spellings in use back then: today, the "two Rocches" are Rocche dell'Annunziata and Rocche di Castiglione; Vignarionda was spelled Vigna Rionda). It was even worse abroad. Clearly, much Barolo has flowed under the bridge since then; and Monvigliero has since, quite rightly, gained back its place in the sun as one of Barolo's ten-twelve top vineyard sites. Just looking at some vineyard data helps drive home the point of just how popular Monvigliero has become today: according to Gianni Gagliardo, 84% of the vineyard district is under vine, and 87% of that is Nebbiolo. Putting those numbers in another way, let's just say there's not much land left there that hasn't yet been planted to Nebbiolo.

The reasons why Monvigliero produces memorable and unique Barolos are many. A bucket list of these includes its location in the denomination, with the Tanaro river nearby; soil type; exposure; altitude; and slope gradient. All these factors combine to make Monvigliero's Barolos some of the most unique of the whole denomination.

Location-wise, from an aerial perspective, Monvigliero is bordered by the Verduno vineyard districts of Rodasca to the north and northwest; Campasso to the west and southwest; and Breri and San Lorenzo di Verduno to the south and southeast. But down on the ground, from both geographic and topographic viewpoints, there is a lot more to know than just that. Monvigliero is situated in the northern half of the Verduno commune: it's the second northernmost vineyard area of the Barolo denomination (only Rodasca, also in the Verduno commune, extends further north). The vineyard districts of Rodasca (differently from all the others I am mentioning here, a mostly north-facing site), Pisapola, Campasso, and Monvigliero are draped over the flank of the Verduno ridge that looks west, out to the Tanaro river (a ridge that divides the northern sector of the Verduno commune in two flanks (one that looks west, which is where Monvigliero is situated, and the other that looks east). The ridge moves in a southwestern direction towards the town of Verduno, where it veers sharply, and due south). And though this location is by no means the only factor that contributes to the uniqueness of Monvigliero's wines (see below), the relative proximity to the river (say compared to other Verduno vineyard districts such as Massara, Breri and San Lorenzo di Verduno located on the opposite flank (the eastern-facing one) of the ridge, helps to differentiate between the Barolos (as well as from those of other Verduno vineyard districts). Monvigliero's specific climate reality influences the physiological behaviour of its Nebbiolo: for example, it's one of Barolo's vineyard districts in which budburst occurs earliest in the year; likewise, the harvest also usually takes place earlier than in many other Barolo vineyard districts. However, an important, defining festure of Monvigliero is that its Nebbiolo's vegetative cycle, in normal years, is a long one. Clearly, the combination of the Tanaro river's thermoregulating effect (gentler temperatures, greater diurnal temperature shifts) on the micro- and mesoclimates of Monvigliero and the other vineyard district's nearby on the same flank of the ridge, soils and exposures play an all-important role too in determining the uniqueness of wines from this area.

In fact, there are other factors besides proximity to the river and its role at play. For example, the soil lithology differs greatly within the Verduno commune. Monvigliero's soil was formed during the Tortonian stage of the Miocene epoch, but unlike the classic or typical Saint Agatha Fossil Marls lithology that characterize much of the soils that originated during that time, Monvigliero's Saint Agatha Fossil Marls are of the laminated type. Both kinds of Saint Agatha Marls are of marine origin, but differently from the typical form of Saint Agatha Fossil Marls, the laminated form is typified by very thin layers of clay-silt marls, plenty of limestone and very little sand. Most importantly, while the typical Saint Agatha Fossils Marls formation has low fertility, the laminated form does not, providing more nutrients to the rooting systems. The laminated form also retains water better, an advantageous situation in droughty and hot conditions. The presence of high concentrations of sand places Monvigliero at a risk for drought-related problems, but having Saint Agatha Fossil Marls lithology of the laminated type, which are less sandy than those of the typical and sandy forms, is undoubtedly an advantage (at least in hot, dry years it is).

Monvigliero's low altitude is another important factor in explaining its wines: not only does it help generate bigger temperature variance between winter and summer, but the relatively low-lying hilltops between the Tanaro river plain and the Barolo valley are protective against the strong wind currents that affect other, higher-lying sites of Verduno. Furthermore, the absence of said wind currents allows for the warm, humid air arising from the Tanaro river and blowing towards and onto the Verduno ridge to linger, thereby providing a warmer microclimate for the vines growing there. Monvigliero's gentle slope (15%) further allows the hot air to hover in the immediate vineyard area.

Last but not least, Monvigliero's mostly full south exposure guarantees better and fuller ripening of its Nebbiolo grapes. In ultimate analysis, it is the combination of soil, proximity to the river and vineyard exposure that determines the specific character traits of the Barolos not just of Monvigliero but of the Barolos coming from its side (western-facing) of the Verduno ridge: deeper color, riper red and even blue fruit, thicker textures. Compare these to the lighter hues, the sour red fruit and much more floral aromas and flavors of Barolos made on the other side of the ridge, as showcased for example by the wines from Rocche dell'Olmo and Breri (that much clarified, let me make clear that Verduno's Barolos, and therefore Monvigliero's too) are always marked by trademark refinement and lightness of being and generally relatively pale red colors).

Monvigliero producers and the wines

Without doubt, the most famous Barolo Monvigliero is that of the G.B. Burlotto estate. The winery farms three plots in the vineyard district. The fully south-facing vines extend over two hectares (2.02 hectares, for precision's sake), planted between 250-300 meters above sea level. Vine age varies among the vineyards, with the oldest having been planted in 1958, and others in 1987 and 2015. Its wine is the gold standard by which all others in Monvigliero are judged by.

The Viberti estate is one of the many now making a Barolo Monvigliero; their first vintage from this site is the 2017, made with grapes sourced from a plot slightly less than one hectare (0.8 hectares) large, planted in 1982 at 240 meters in altitude, owned by a family friend. While a part of the grapes are used to make the estate's classic Barolo called Buon Padre (made by blending together the grapes of very many vineyard districts Viberti owns or rents vineyards in), the majority of the Monvigliero grapes were used for the new single bottling of Barolo Monvigliero (made with 25-50% whole bunches: Claudio Viberti told me directly that he plans on "treating Monvigliero's Nebbiolo like it was a Pinot Noir"). Interestingly, and a sign that Monvigliero's charms rest on it being able to give wines of amazing perfume and penetrating but light-bodied personality, Viberti has opted against making this wine as a Barolo Riserva (besides, the estate already makes three different Barolo Riservas from the Bricco delle Viole, La Volta and San Pietro). Gian Carlo Burlotto and Gianluca Burlotto also make a Barolo Monvigliero at their Cantina Massara estate (the first vintage of which was the 2015) from a 0.25 hectare rented south-facing plot situated in the heart of the vineyard site. Arguably the Verduno commune's most famous estate along with G.B. Burlotto, the fifth generation Fratelli Alessandria have been making some of the denomination's finest wines for many years now and their Barolo Monvigliero is no exception to the rule. Their forty-five years old vines on average lie between 300-320 meters above sea level and are south-facing.

Since 2014, Gianni Gagliardo owns 0.25 hectares in Monvigliero (for the more precise among us, I am told it is actually 0.2556 hectares) at 290 meters in altitude on soil the composition of which is 46.3% loam, 31.1% clay, and 22.6% sand. The vineyard area faces south and was planted in 1973 with 1250 grapevines of a special massal selection of Nebbiolo Michet. First made in the classic and thoroughly outstanding 2016 vintage, theirs is an interesting rendition of Barolo from the Monvigliero, as it's less floral than many other Barolo Monvigliero wines, but at the same time it's also more intensely mineral than most. Nuances of white moss, even lichen, violet and lavender ensure that the floral/delicately herbal nature of Monvigliero's wines (that I don't believe results only from a copious use of whole bunches) is upheld in Gagliardo's version too, but this wine's mineral edge is not typically found in other wines from this site. No matter, it's an excellent Barolo, and appropriately enough, very politely-styled like every self-respecting Barolo Monvigliero ought to be.

The traditionally-minded, very well-respected Poderi Oddero estate of La Morra bought 0.80 hectares in Monvigliero in 2018. The vines are planted at an altitude of 280 meters above sea level and the winery will release their first Barolo Monvigliero with the 2020 vintage. Meanwhile, the wine they made from this site in the 2018 and 2019 vintages was blended into their Barolo classico. Over in Castiglione Falletto, the Paolo Scavino winery owns 0.84 hectares of southeast-facing vines planted at 310 meters above sea level. They bought and made their first Barolo Monvigliero in 2007. The vines were planted in 1965 and 2005: I have no problems saying this wine literally left me open-jawed when I tasted it for the first time, directly at the winery even before it had been officially released. Already then Scavino's Barolo Monvigliero was as good as their Barolo Cannubi and Rocche dell'Annunziata Riserva, and most definitely better than any other Barolo in their lineup. Given that the estate's most famous wine has always been the Barolo Bric del Fiasc, you understand why I was so thunderstruck: the underdog knocking out the champion, so to speak, and those are the sort of things I commit to memory and then go looking into, year after year. And as it was once again one of the two or three best Barolos Scavino made in the subsequent vintages too, that pretty well sealed the deal for me relative to Monvigliero being a grade AAA+ site. Still today it is one either Scavino's best Barolo or at no worst one of their two/three best in almost every vintage.

Benchmark wineries/Reference point producers of Barolo Monvigliero: G.B. Burlotto. Also good: Castello di Verduno, Fratelli Alessandria, Gianni Gagliardo, Paolo Scavino, Viberti.

MOSCONI

Township	Monforte d'Alba
Reference Map	See Map of Monforte d'Alba MGAs (Ch. 10)
Size (ha) (Tot / Barolo MGA)	75.95 / 13.19
Production 2021 (hl)	703.53 (of which 98.63 hl of Barolo Riserva *MGA*, and 45.97 hl of Barolo *MGA* Vigna)
Altitude	310 – 530 meters a.s.l. roughly
Exposure	From east to south in the better exposed parcels; from west to north in the remaining parts.
N. Claimants MGA	13
Other grape varieties planted:	Barbera; Dolcetto; white varieties
Land Units	Land Unit of Castiglione in the western side for the highest parcels; Land Unit of Barolo for the central and eastern side;
Soil (stage):	Tortonian

Producers claiming the MGA

Famiglia Anselma; Piero Benevelli; Bera; Bussia Soprana; Ca' Sul Bric; Cascina Chicco; Domenico Clerico; Conterno Fantino; E. Pira E Figli (Chiara Boschis); Armando Parusso; Pio Cesare; Poderi Gianni Gagliardo; Giovanni Rocca.

Wines

Famiglia Anselma - Barolo Mosconi (*); **Piero Benevelli** - Barolo Mosconi; **Bussia Soprana** - Barolo Mosconi (and Riserva); **Domenico Clerico** - Barolo Percristina; **Conterno Fantino** - Barolo Mosconi Vigna Ped; **Armando Parusso** - Barolo Mosconi; **E. Pira e Figli – Chiara Boschis** - Barolo Mosconi; **Poderi Gianni Gagliardo** – Barolo Mosconi; **Pio Cesare** – Barolo Mosconi; **Giovanni Rocca** - Barolo Mosconi; **Rocche dei Manzoni** - Barolo Big d' Big

What the producers say

Chiara Boschis (E. Pira e Figli-Chiara Boschis): "We started vinifying Mosconi in 2009, and find its Barolo to have power, color and structure thanks to a clay-limestone soil that retains water, releasing slowly, like a sponge, in dry seasons".

Rodolfo Migliorini (Rocche dei Manzoni): "Our vineyard in Mosconi has a full south exposure; the soil is calcareous and sandy, but our Barolo is distinguished by offering early drinking pleasure thanks to generally velvety tannins".

Ian's assessment of the vineyard district, its wines and its potential

Mosconi is situated in the southernmost portion of the Monforte commune, close to three other vineyard districts: to the north and west there is Ginestra; to the west and south lies Le Coste di Monforte; and to the southeast there is Ravera di Monforte. Mosconi is no doubt a very well-situated vineyard district in a part of the Monforte commune's territory associated with some excellent wines: but it behooves me to point out that Mosconi's rocket-like trajectory to fame is only a little more than ten-fifteen years old. Just like Ravera in Novello and Cerretta, it is a vineyard district you hear a lot about nowadays mostly because many very famous, talented (and very likable too, which never hurts) producers have moved in and started making Barolos Mosconi wines. But nobody ever talked about Mosconi as a Barolo site of interest as recently as the 1980s. Then one winery starts making a good wine there and almost all of a sudden everybody jumps on the bandwagon, and the site becomes the greatest thing since pre-sliced bread. But the fact remains that, still today, less than 40% of Mosconi is under vine: furthermore, less than 50% of that is planted to Nebbiolo. Does that tell you something? It should.

In fairness, the Nebbiolo grapes of some parts of Mosconi were always highly thought of, regularly sought, and sourced by *negozianti* who made large volumes of estate Barolos. It also speaks to the quality of Mosconi that it appears that Giovanni Conterno of Giacomo Conterno used to buy grapes in this area with which to make his Monfortino (but the same is said of Le Coste di Monforte: it may well be that he bought grapes from both areas). And while Mosconi is a very large vineyard districts, I find its Barolos to be much more homogenous in style than those of other large vineyard districts such as Novello's Ravera and Serralunga's Cerretta. Even better, these are Barolos that more often than not express a recognizable Mosconi-somewhereness. However, given Mosconi's large size, its noteworthy range in altitude and in soil diversity, much like Bussia, Ginestra, and other vineyard districts, it's yet another vineyard district of the Monforte commune that can be broken down into smaller subregions, each of which with the potential to give distinctive wines (see Appendix C, *Table 3.3: Barolo vineyard district subregions*. See also: BUSSIA file, GINESTRA file, SAN PIETRO file and CERRETTA file).

For sure, I believe that the Barolos from Mosconi are some of Monforte 's most uniquely powerful and dark wines (I mean dark ruby-red, never anywhere near "dark" as in purple or inky: if that's the case, then it's not Barolo you're drinking, but something else). That's saying quite something, given that Monforte's Barolos are by definition not exactly pushovers. But whether we talk of more powerful or just plain powerful wines, it is true that there exists the potential for an array of different Barolos from Mosconi, depending on where within the vineyard district the grapes are sourced.

It is my opinion that Mosconi can and should be subdivided into three distinct subregions. The subregion of Mosconi Palazzo, named so because it is where the Cascina Palazzo is located, corresponds essentially to the western half of the extended Mosconi vineyard district of today. The eastern half of today's Mosconi can in turn be subdivided into two subregions: a northern section, which is Mosconi-proper and a southern subregion of more or less equal size that is the area historically known as Conterni. A collection of houses and buildings known as a *borgata* (plural: *borgate*) sits in highest part of each of these two subregions. The Borgata Mosconi is atop Mosconi-proper, while the Borgata Conterni in is found at the summit of the Conterni subregion. I subdivide Mosconi in these three subregions based on noteworthy topographical, altitude and geological differences. And yes, they do all add up to very different Barolos. Without wanting to beat this thing to death,

I can make a pretty good case that as things stand today, there is no such thing as a Barolo Mosconi *tout court*. It's the problem you have when vineyard districts are drawn up too large.

Speaking broadly, Mosconi Palazzo ranges from about 400-490 meters above sea level and it is the Mosconi subregion that reaches the highest altitudes. It also has a different landscape and soil than that of the eastern half of the Mosconi vineyard district and its two subregions: in the western half of Mosconi, where Mosconi Palazzo is situated, the landscape category is that of the Castiglione Land Unit and the soil lithology is essentially that of the Diano Sandstone (with patches of Lequio Formation). By contrast, the landscape of the eastern half of the present-day Mosconi, where you find Mosconi-proper and Mosconi Conterni, is categorized as a Land Unit of Barolo, and the soil lithology is the Saint Agatha Fossil Marls of the sandy type. The latter soil lithology is especially typical of the Conterni subregion, with that of Mosconi-proper falling somewhere in between that of Mosconi Conterni and Mosconi Palazzo (but is closer to the latter's). It follows that the Barolos of Mosconi Palazzo are those with the deepest darkest colors; rich fleshy black and dark red cherry fruit; and strong balsamic notes, not to mention mouth-coating texture. Next in line for depth of color, flesh and size are those of Mosconi-proper. The Conterni subregion's wines are the most perfumed and lifted of all Mosconi's wines, reflecting the larger presence of soil sand and limestone (and less clay), reflective of the difference in lithology (from a Diano Sandstone dominated section of Mosconi to one that is more marked by the Saint Agatha Fossil Marls Formation). That said, Mosconi Conterni's Barolos, while noticeably lighter on their feet and less chunky than those of the other two Mosconi subregions, are still pretty powerful Barolos. In ultimate analysis, it is not that one area of Mosconi is better than the other: but the wines really are different. Mosconi Palazzo and Mosconi-proper Barolos are full-frontal wines that make an immediate impact upon the first sip, while Conterni's are more refined and graceful. All can be memorable, and I find that Mosconi Barolos are so impactful in their full-frontal delivery of their charms that people *do* remember them.

It should be apparent by now that relative to the wines, there is a night and day difference between the Barolos of Mosconi Palazzo and Mosconi-proper, and those of Conterni: the three subregions should have been kept as separate vineyard districts. And especially so Conterni. Therefore, while it is broadly true that Mosconi's Barolos have more size, flesh, and power of many of other Monforte Barolos (and are almost instantly recognizable in blind tastings because of this), that statement is in fact mostly true if you are referring to the wines of Mosconi Palazzo and Mosconi proper. This is because Conterni's reality is such that its wines, though by no means easy to confuse with those of say Monvigliero or Cannubi Centrale, are less powerful not just of other Mosconi wines, but of many other Monforte vineyard districts, such as for example those of Ginestra (at least, the marlier sections of Ginestra: see GINESTRA file)

As mentioned earlier in this file, many different producers are now making Barolos from Mosconi. The good news for wine lovers is that some of the denomination's brightest stars have bought land and vineyards there, which means that if it's a Barolo Mosconi you want, well, you really do have an embarrassment of riches to choose from. In the historic part of Mosconi, or Mosconi-proper, there are Domenico Clerico, Conterno Fantino, Silvano Casiraghi of Bussia Soprana, Pio Cesare (that made its first vintage of Barolo Mosconi with the 2015 vintage, despite the winery owning vineyards in Mosconi since practically forever) and a few others. Over in Conterni, there are, among others, Gianni Gagliardo (who owns vines next to those of Chiara Boschis and first made a Barolo Mosconi in the 2015 vintage from vines at about 350 meters in altitude). Piero Benevelli and Famiglia Anselma own vines in the Mosconi Palazzo (see complete recap below).

Mosconi producers and the wines

Arguably (maybe not so arguably) the most famous Barolo Mosconi of all is Clerico's Barolo Percristina (named after his daughter who sadly passed away at a very young age). Clerico's first vintage was the 1995 (the year Clerico bought the vineyard plot). The wine is made from south-facing vines planted in 1968 between 390-410 meters above sea level. The soil lithology is the classic Saint Agatha Fossil marls but to be frank they don't seem to be of the sandy type, given a soil composition of 60.5% loam, 25.9% clay and only 13.6% sand. There is also plenty of active lime in the soil.

Another noteworthy Barolo Mosconi is the one made by Conterno Fantino, called Vigna Ped. This estate began farming very old vines in 2000 and made its first Barolo from Mosconi in the 2004 vintage (a nice way to start things off, given the very good, even excellent, if slightly overrated quality of the vintage). The winery's Mosconi vines are close to those they own in Ginestra (the two vineyard districts vines run along two parallel bands both with full south exposure). Claudio Conterno has told me repeatedly over the years that he believes his Mosconi Vigna Ped to be a very elegant wine, always silky and readier to drink than his wines from Ginestra, for example, even with the same fermentation regimens, but frankly I am not so sure. I mean, I agree with almost everything he tells me, but on this count I remain unconvinced. Perhaps it has to with different oaking regimens, but I do not find his Barolo Mosconi to be especially nuanced or graceful, quite the contrary. To me, it always speaks of toasty and coconutty oak, not to mention vanilla and dark chocolate, and to be a much thicker wine than his more lifted Barolos from Ginestra. Actually, I find his to be a textbook Barolo Mosconi (not made with Mosconi Conterni grapes, that is), with tannins that grab your taste buds and won't let go, and a tannic clout and fleshy chocolaty mouthfeel that is similar to those made by Clerico and Bussia Soprana. Which is exactly why most people like the wines, so who am I to argue? As all three are made from grapes grown in the Mosconi-proper section of the vineyard district, any differences that you might find in the wines reflect mostly winemaking decisions and choices made in the vineyard and cellar. For example, Clerico's Percristina ages thirty-six months in barriques and then another two years or so in fifty hectoliter barrels. Then again, Mosconi Barolos are so fleshy and massive wines that they can take that sort of oaking.

In 2008, Chiara Boschis bought her vineyards in Mosconi: hers are however in the Conterni subregion. She was so impressed by the grapes she picked and vinified that she found herself wanting to make a single site wine from Mosconi, rather than blend its grapes into a traditional estate Barolo (as had been her initial intention). And when in 2010 she began renting in Gabutti of Serralunga, she turned her Barolo Via Nuova into a blend of grapes from Gabutti, Ravera and Terlo, keeping the Mosconi grapes separate and making a Barolo solely from that specific Barolo vineyard district. I understand why she was so impressed with her grapes from Mosconi. I was too, when I tasted her wine for the first time from barrel, about a year before it was to go into bottle, and then again multiple times after that. Her Barolo Mosconi really struck me not just for its unique mix of palate weight and flesh, but also for its extremely elegant mouthfeel. It had the recognizable Mosconi nuances (actually not so nuanced, with all Mosconi wines, even those of Conterni) of cocoa and balsamic oils, but what most impressed me was how its noteworthy underlying power was brilliantly buffered by truly remarkable elegance (now *that* is Conterni-typical). My opinion of the wine hasn't really changed with subsequent vintages. Do make sure you go out and try this wine as it's an absolute beauty.

The Gianni Gagliardo estate also owns vineyards in the Conterni subregion: 1.26 hectares of Nebbiolo clones 142 and 230 facing east and south, planted at 350 meters above sea level. Soil sample analysis data from this site tells us that the Mosconi Conterni soil there is about 53% loam, 15.7% clay and, not surprisingly given what we know about the Mosconi Conterni's wine profile, 31.3% sand. There are however noteworthy differences between the winery's two vineyard blocks: the one facing south has a warmer microclimate and more limestone, while the east-facing block has a more vigor-inducing soil richer in organic matter. As the latter is close to a forested area, it tends to have a cooler microclimate than the south-facing block not just by virtue of its eastern exposure. It all translates to the grapes in the two blocks getting picked as much as seven to eight days apart in most vintages. The wine is very impressive (just like the one also made with Mosconi Conterni grapes by Chiara Boschis), so I see why Conterni's Nebbiolo grapes have long had a very good reputation. Gagliardo's wine is one of his better single-vineyard district bottlings, teeming with nuances of ripe red cherry, pomegranate, violet, lavender, green tea and a hint of cocoa. For what it's worth, that last descriptor is one I almost always associate with Mosconi's wines no matter the subregion the grapes are sourced from. Unfortunately, not much of this pretty wine is made, given the Lilliputian size of the vineyard holding: only 566 bottles and thirty magnums were made in the 2018 vintage.

Benchmark wineries/Reference point producers of Barolo Mosconi: a) Mosconi Conterni: E. Pira/Chiara Boschis, Gianni Gagliardo; b) Mosconi proper: Clerico, Conterno Fantino, Pio Cesare; c) Mosconi Palazzo: Famiglia Anselma, Piero Benevelli.

NEIRANE

Township	Verduno
Reference Map	See Map of Verduno MGAs (Ch. 10)
Size (ha) (Tot / Barolo MGA)	37.59 / 1.97
Production 2021 (hl)	102.97
Altitude	330 – 400 meters a.s.l. roughly
Exposure	West
N. Claimants MGA	2
Other grape varieties planted:	Barbera; Dolcetto; Freisa; Pelaverga Piccolo; white varieties
Land Units	Land Unit of Verduno
Soil (stage):	Messinian

Producers claiming the MGA

Comm. GB Burlotto; Agostino Bosco; Villa Lanata

Wines

Agostino Bosco - Barolo Neirane

What the producers say

Agostino Bosco: "My family acquired this vineyard in 1998 but it was only in 2007 that we vinified it and bottled it separately for the first time. The soil is predominately loose sand that leaves the wine scented with violet and red fruits. Barolo Neirane are usually elegant wines that offer tremendous great drinking pleasure. Facing southwest, the vineyard needs extra care in order to save the grapes from being scorched in the summer. The fermentation time varies from 20-25 days and barrel aging takes place in 18-25 oak casks".

Ian's assessment of the vineyard district, its wines and its potential

Triangular in shape (from above its shape looks something like that of India), Neirane is one of the southernmost vineyard districts of Verduno; south and southwest there are the La Morra vineyard districts of San Giacomo and Castagni; to the east and southeast lie the Verduno vineyard districts of Boscatto and Rocche dell'Olmo.

In order to understand what Neirane's Barolos are (ought to be) like, knowing a few simple facts will prove helpful. First off, I did not make a point of underscoring Neirane's southern position within the Verduno commune's territory for a lack of something better to do: that location is actually very relevant as far as determining the type of Barolo you will get. Verduno's geology is fairly complex (see Chapter 7, BAROLO TERROIR, Barolo Communes subchapter): for example, the southern half (more or less) of the Verduno territory is characterized by a different lithology than the northern sector. The Saint Agatha Fossil Marls Formation (mostly of the laminated type) formed during the Tortonian stage of the Miocene epoch typifies the northern reaches of the Verduno territory; but in the southern half it is the Cassano-Spinola Formation of the marly type (which is Neirane's) that dominates (together with the Gypsiferous-Sulfurous formation formed during the Messinian stage). Veins of sand characterized the latter formation, and these can actually be found in Neirane's soil too, but this is not the norm; and where they do appear, it is usually very deep down, at twenty meters or more below the surface. Interestingly, at the G.B. Burlotto estate they have dug pits as part of ongoing soil studies and they have shown that the Nebbiolo roots in Neirane do not dig that far down, and so the presence or absence of sand there is not so relevant after all. As for the Cassano-Spinola Formation of the marly type, it is in fact the more typical lithology of that sector of the La Morra commune that is closest by the Verduno border: La Morra's vineyard districts of Ascheri, Castagni (and farther away, Bricco Cogni) are all characterized by it, as is the Boscatto vineyard district of the Verduno township. In any case, it is a formation that though marly and laminated like that of the northern area is much younger (by about one million years, so much so that Neirane has different fossils in the soil than other Verduno vineyard districts, such as for example Monvigliero), and is characterized by less limestone. In other words, Neirane's soil and subsoil complex is a mostly loamy-clay mix with a little sand and not as much limestone as you will find further north in the commune. This is actually too easy to see with the naked eye too, because the soil color in the southern part of the Verduno territory is darker than that of Monvigliero and the northern part of Verduno [a hazelnut color in the south in contrast to the whiter shade up north: the difference is a consequence of the former's slightly greater clay content (but also a different, more evolved clay) and of less limestone].

I have found Barolos from Neirane to be perfumed, marked by vibrant freshness and a certain peachy-citrussy quality; they are deceptively light-bodied wines ("light-bodied" by Barolo standards, because there is actually quite a bit of tannic structure, and Neirane Barolos have more than those of Monvigliero and the northern part of Verduno) with flavors of small red berries, sour red cherry, citrus fruit, white peach, and flowers (violet but also red rose), not the riper, darker cherry fruit of Monvigliero and other northern Verduno vineyard districts. However, with age, Neirane's Barolos tend to put on volume and gain notes of darker fruit and herbs that are nowhere to be seen in younger vintages.

Neirane producers and the wines

My observations relative to Neirane's Barolos derive mostly from having tasted the G.B. Burlotto Barolo Neirane over the years. G.B. Burlotto owns 1.1 hectares in Neirane, planted facing west at about 360 meters above sea level (more or less the same altitude as their plots in Rocche dell'Olmo and Boscatto). This area was once referred to as that of the Madonnina ("little Madonna") because of its proximity to a small church there. As mentioned, I have vivid recollections of the 1993, 1995 and the 1996 Barolo Neirane, for instance. Interestingly, I find that G.B. Burlotto's Neirane Barolo shows a little darker red fruit and an overall riper quality than that I associate with other Barolos from Neirane, possibly because G.B. Burlotto's vineyards are in the very first section of the Neirane vineyard district which starts immediately outside of the town of Verduno. There the mesoclimate is warmer than in the rest of the vineyard district. Unfortunately, the winery no longer makes a Barolo Neirane, but blends its grapes along with those of Rocche dell'Olmo and Boscatto, plus a dollop from Monvigliero, to produce the estate's Barolo Acclivi, specifically constructed to represent a Barolo that best exemplifies the Verduno terroir (or in other words, what a Barolo from Verduno should "ideally" taste like).

Agostino Bosco is a small family-run estate in La Morra, that besides making a Barolo from that town's vineyard district of La Serra, also makes a Barolo Neirane from vines planted facing southwest, at about 350 meters above sea level. Winemaking is traditional, with aging in large Slavonian oak casks. Its Barolo Neirane represents an interesting contrast with the one that G.B. Burlotto used to make, because its vineyards are on the border with the San Giacomo vineyard district, which means they are located at the opposite extremes of the vineyard district. In the same area of Neirane as Bosco's are the vineyards of another Burlotto, Gian Carlo, of the Cantina Massara. He produces a Barolo classico with grapes from the vineyard districts of Neirane, Castagni and Massara. The 2015 was 20% Neirane; the 2014 might have been even a little more, while the 2013 almost certainly did, given that it was blend of only Castagni and Neirane.

Benchmark wineries/Reference point producers of Barolo Neirane: Agostino Bosco.

ORNATO

Township	Serralunga d'Alba
Reference Map	See Map of Serralunga d'Alba MGAs (Ch. 10)
Size (ha) (Tot / Barolo MGA)	6.70 / 5.77
Production 2021 (hl)	307.35
Altitude	300 – 395 meters a.s.l. roughly
Exposure	From south to southwest, plus a small part facing east and north
N. Claimants MGA	2
Other grape varieties planted:	Only Nebbiolo
Land Units	Land Unit of Serralunga
Soil (stage):	Serravallian

Producers claiming the MGA

Pio Cesare; S. Caterina.

Wines

Palladino - Barolo Ornato; **Pio Cesare** - Barolo Ornato

What the producers say

Palladino "Our ownership of this vineyard started in 2009. Ornato has a southern exposure, producing a Barolo that is savory with balsamic and earthy notes, full-bodied and with a particularly solid structure good for long aging".

Ian's assessment of the vineyard district, its wines and its potential

Ornato is one of Serralunga's southern vineyard districts, that part of the commune's territory that extends below the town and that is associated with the broadest, larger-scaled Barolos of the commune. Wines that still have that steely core for which Serralunga's Barolos are famous, but here the skeleton has more flesh on it, making some of the wines not too distant in style from those of parts of Monforte. And this is exactly the case with Ornato's wines.

From an aerial vantage point, Ornato is situated in between the Serralunga vineyard districts of Briccolina to the west, Boscareto to the south, Falletto to the southeast, Serra and Lirano to the east. In fact, a small piece of Ornato snakes along the top, in the *bricco* position, of the slope where Briccolina is located. Though it's not an especially large vineyard district (actually, it is one of the Barolo denomination's smallest), it is very long, an amphitheater running east-west; but not surprisingly, not all the areas within it have the same fine wine potential. The landscape is that of the Land Unit of Serralunga, and the soil lithology is the just as classic Lequio Formation. Therefore, Ornato is characterized mostly by limestone, compacted sands, and clay, with a minor presence of sandstone.

Ornato producers and the wines

The estate historically associated with Ornato is clearly Pio Cesare, for the longest time the only estate making wine from it; the Boffa family bought their share of the vineyard site in 1971-1972 from Vittorino Gancia. At 6.59 hectares, it is the almost totality of the vineyard district (Ornato is only 6.7 hectares large), making Ornato very close to being a Pio Cesare *monopole*. Recently, the very fine Palladino winery has also begun making a Barolo Ornato from two very small plots. So though not quite a monopole, nobody knows Ornato better than Pio Cesare's family and staff.

Given the length of the vineyard district, Ornato, a fairly steep site, presents a diversity in exposures (mostly south, southwest and southeast, but not just) and so at Pio Cesare they use the grapes from only three fully south-facing Ornato vineyard plots planted at about 360 meters above sea level to make their Barolo Ornato, which is the winery's top wine. (Clearly, this may vary occasionally, depending on the vintage's characteristics.) Pio Cesare first made their Barolo Ornato in the excellent 1985 vintage (talk about hitting the ground running) and you realize right away that Ornato must be truly special for then owner Pio Boffa to go ahead with a single-site bottling, given that he was the staunchest defender of traditional Barolo around [Barolo made by blending grapes from different sites: in fact, Pio never failed to correct everybody and anybody within earshot (both his and of others) when someone spoke of "entry-level" Barolo: a very fair, insightful and acceptable position that I embrace wholeheartedly still today]. Recently, with a new generation now at the helm, the estate has relented somewhat and is bottling a second single-site Barolo from Mosconi as well.

Pio Cesare's Barolo Ornato is made in a fairly traditional manner, with stainless steel fermentation and aging almost entirely in large Slavonian oak barrels (but a small percentage of wine does age in barriques in the first twelve months). The Barolo Ornato has garnered essentially nothing but awards, high praise, and accolades over the decades for Pio Cesare. But for all the immense respect I have for the Pio Cesare estate and its remarkably nice family, people I actually like to sit down with at dinner or in front of a glass of wine and talk about other stuff too, I have never liked their Barolo Ornato. Again, I stress mine was a minority opinion, and I may have well been mistaken in my lack of appreciation. But there's no accounting for tastes, and in the 1990s and early 2000s, the wine was, for my taste at least, simply too toasty and chocolaty, a wine that most likely held appeal for international palates and markets that clamored for dark, vanilla-cocoa bombs loaded with oak and toasty-coffee notes and little acidity to speak of. But in the end, it doesn't matter, for fashions change and winemaking also change with the times. I find the Ornato Barolos made in recent vintages to be nothing short of exceptional: for example, don't miss Pio Cesare's 2015 and 2016 Barolo Ornatos, that are about as good as any Barolos made in those two superlative vintages.

Palladino is one of my favorite under-the-radar Barolo wineries (though it's not really under the radar with Italy's Barolo lovers) and I have always liked their wines: certainly not the fleshiest or roundest Barolos you'll ever taste (in fact they're rather tough when young) but with an elegant austerity that speak nicely of Nebbiolo and Serralunga. They bottle a Barolo Ornato from a roughly one-hectare extension of vines (two plots) planted at 350-395 meters above sea level. Their Barolo Ornato is not very different from Pio Cesare's recent bottlings of Ornato, and that tells you this small site is able to give very homogenous, recognizably site-specific wines. Ornato Barolos are always endowed with impressive structure, but the tannic backbone in Palladino's beautiful wine is not devoid of fruity flesh and it's easy to appreciate the refinement this wine is imbued with at every sip.

Benchmark wineries/Reference point producers of Barolo Ornato: Palladino. Also good: Pio Cesare.

PAIAGALLO

Township	Barolo
Reference Map	See Map of Barolo MGAs (Ch. 10)
Size (ha) (Tot / Barolo MGA)	12.35 / 5.82
Production 2021 (hl)	288.54 (of which 81.60 hl of Barolo Riserva *MGA*, and 45.97 hl of Barolo *MGA* Vigna)
Altitude	310 – 380 meters a.s.l. roughly
Exposure	From east to south.
N. Claimants MGA	4
Other grape varieties planted:	Barbera; Dolcetto
Land Units	Land Unit of La Morra
Soil (stage):	Tortonian

Producers claiming the MGA

Broccardo, Giovanni Canonica; Casa E. di Mirafiore; Mauro Veglio.

Wines

Giovanni Canonica - Barolo Paiagallo; **Casa E. di Mirafiore** - Barolo Paiagallo; **Broccardo** - Barolo Paiagallo; **Mauro Veglio** - Barolo Paiagallo

What the producers say

Gianni Canonica (Canonica Giovanni): "This vineyard has always been part of the family estate. For us, the typical descriptors of Barolos from Paiagallo are red fruit and licorice."

Ian's assessment of the vineyard district, its wines and its potential

Paiagallo is a small, not especially high vineyard district that overlooks the houses of Barolo to its east (also to its east, north of the town, is Cannubi Muscatel); Drucà lies to the north and mostly northwest; La Volta to its west; and Terlo is directly south. Paiagallo's proximity to Cannubi Muscatel is especially relevant: Paiagallo and Cannubi Muscatel are part of the same hill, with the former higher up and the latter lower down, if on different flanks. This is why, in its lower-lying reaches, Paiagallo, which is characterized by a Tortonian stage soil that is mostly loamy-clay in nature with only a little sand (the lithology is Saint Agatha Fossil Marls of the laminated type), has a larger percentage of sand close to Cannubi Muscatel (which like all Cannubis, has its fair share of sand).

Paiagallo's soil of Tortonian origin goes a long way in explaining the showy, fruity, ready-to-drink sooner personality of its Barolos; but it's not the only factor that helps understand this vineyard district's wines. In this respect, Paiagallo's lay of the land also plays a noteworthy role. Though it's a relatively low-altitude site (and close to a town, which usually also means a warmer mesoclimate) Paiagallo is actually situated on the colder than expected flank (explaining the historical dearth of Barolos from there). It is close by a very open valley where cold winds blow strongly, slowing grape growth in the early part of the year, but then accelerating it during fairly warm summers, so much so that the potential for sunburned grapes is high. For the most part, any time you taste a Barolo from Paiagallo, you will notice that they are almost always unabashedly fruity wines, independently of the producer you are tasting the wine of (when it comes to Paiagallo's Barolos what I find changes most from producer to producer is not the amount of fruit but the polish of the tannins). I also find that the Barolos of Paiagallo always remind me quite a bit of the Barolos from Terlo, another Barolo commune MGA vineyard district that, perhaps not surprisingly, is located right next to it.

Paiagallo producers and the wines

The best producer of Paiagallo Barolos is without question Giovanni Canonica (the estate's name: the Canonica running the show now is Gianni, Giovanni's son), a producer of a talent level comparable to names such as Aldo Conterno, Bartolo Mascarello, Bruno Giacosa and Giacomo Conterno. The Canonica family owned two hectares in Paiagallo (it's now three as the estate inherited another hectare from Gianni's wife side of the family) under the Castello della Volta. The holding was once planted to Barbera, but it was uprooted in favor of Nebbiolo because the Barbera had esca disease. The original choice fell on Barbera because the site was too cool for Nebbiolo to ripen fully there, but today the Nebbiolo ripens (and then some): actually, its fresher microclimate makes it so it's actually a good spot for Nebbiolo nowadays. The vines are 20-30 years old presently. His Barolo Paiagallo is extremely impressive, made from organically-farmed grapes treated very traditionally (grapes pressed by foot; very long fermentations in wood with native yeasts and without temperature control; aging in large used wood barrels and with very low doses of sulphur used). The wine is rich and fleshy yet light on its feet enough not to come across as heavy or chunky (though alcohol levels can creep up, Canonica's wines are so balanced you don't really end up noticing their octane levels). Canonica's Barolo Paiagallo exudes notes of ripe dark plum, dark forest berries, menthol, sweet pipe tobacco, and an intense note of candied (not fresh) violet. I find there's an unabashedly in your face plum and dark berry compote fruity exuberance to this wine in almost vintages. It makes a fascinating contrast with Canonica's other stellar (and for my money and palate, even greater) Barolo, the Barolo del Comune di Grinzane Cavour (see BORZONE file). To be clear, I think Canonica is one of Barolo's ten best producers, right up there with Giacomo Conterno, Bruno Giacosa, Bartolo Mascarello, Aldo Conterno and very few others, so do whatever you can to get your hands on his (very limited in number) wines.

Other wineries also own vines in Paiagallo. Veglio has south/southeast facing vines planted in the mid-1980s. The estate made its first Barolo Paiagallo, a very good wine indeed, in the outstanding 2016 vintage. E. Pira/Chiara Boschis, E. Mirafiore and Scarzello all own vines in Paiagallo; Fontanafredda's is made from a specific section of Paiagallo called La Villa. The E. Mirafiore winery, owned by Fontanafredda, also makes a Barolo from this vineyard district, but labels it only as Barolo Paiagallo.

Benchmark wineries/Reference point producers of Barolo Paiagallo: Giovanni Canonica. Also good: Veglio.

PANEROLE

Township	Novello	
Reference Map	See Map of Novello MGAs (Ch. 10)	
Size (ha) (Tot / Barolo MGA)	41.52 / 3.53	
Production 2021 (hl)	191.94	
Altitude	320 – 390 meters a.s.l. roughly	
Exposure	From east to west passing through south.	
N. Claimants MGA	4	
Other grape varieties planted:	Barbera; Dolcetto; white varieties	
Land Units	Land Unit of La Morra in the north-eastern parcels bordering San Giovanni; Land Unit of Novello for the remaining parts;	
Soil (stage):	Tortonian	

Producers claiming the MGA
Giorgio Blangino; Cascina Ballarin; Franco Conterno (Cascina Sciulun); Vietto.

Wines
Cascina Ballarin - Barolo Panerole; **Franco Conterno** - Barolo Panerole; **Vietto** - Barolo Panerole.

What the producers say
Davide Vietto (Vietto): "Since 2001, we have vinified and bottled our grapes from this vineyard district as a Barolo Panerole. In terms of personality, Panerole Barolo has an imposing presence and great aging potential with aggressive tannins when still young – thus it cannot be easily appreciated in youth. The wine expresses generous notes of violet, licorice, cinnamon and sweet tobacco, and finishes on a pleasantly spicy note".

Ian's assessment of the vineyard district, its wines and its potential

Panerole is a vineyard district located in the southeastern tip of Novello's territory, next to the border with the Monforte commune. Therefore, it is surrounded by the Novello vineyard districts of Ravera to the northwest and west and by Cerviano-Merli to the west; the Monforte vineyard districts of Bricco San Pietro and San Giovanni are respectively to its south, southeast, and east; and to the east.

For terroir-lovers, Panerole provides an excellent case-study material on the subject. For while we don't know that much about Panerole's terroir and fine Barolo potential, what we do know is more than enough to allow us insight into its wines. Panerole's landscape varies throughout the vineyard district, but the dominant soil lithology is the laminated form of the Saint Agatha Fossil Marls of the Tortonian stage (the sandy type is also present but is less abundant). However, it's not just the soil that changes throughout Panerole: exposures and altitudes vary quite a bit too. This suggests that different Barolos from Panerole might also be common.

Panerole producers and the wines

In effect, this hypothesis can be evaluated to a degree by the two Barolo Panerole wines I know well and have tasted enough different vintages repeatedly of over the years. Vietto (the largest vineyard land owner in Panerole) has almost all their vines up in the northern half of the Panerole vineyard district, while those of Franco Conterno are at the opposite extreme of the, down south close to the border with the Bricco San Pietro vineyard district. Why is this relevant? Simple. The soil at the northern end of the vineyard district is richer in sand than that at the lower end, and if you taste the wines of these two producers that aspect becomes immediately apparent (especially if you are into geo-sensorial tasting at all: for more on the subject see: Rigaux, Zhu, D'Agata 2022, in press). This greater presence of sand is easily discernible upon examining the wines. Vietto's are the more perfumed of the two, and also the finer-grained and lighter-bodied. Conterno's are certainly more tactile, slightly tougher wines especially when young, and that require some cellaring to show best. But both are very fine Barolos.

Benchmark wineries/Reference point producers of Barolo Panerole: Franco Conterno, Vietto.

PARAFADA

Township	Serralunga d'Alba
Reference Map	See Map of Serralunga d'Alba MGAs (Ch. 10)
Size (ha) (Tot / Barolo MGA)	7.92 / 3.05
Production 2021 (hl)	157.00 (of which 5.53 hl of Barolo *MGA* Vigna)
Altitude	260 – 370 meters a.s.l. roughly
Exposure	From southeast to southwest.
N. Claimants MGA	3
Other grape varieties planted:	Barbera; white varieties
Land Units	Land Unit of Serralunga d'Alba
Soil (stage):	Serravallian

Producers claiming the MGA

Casa E. di Mirafiore; Massolino – Vigna Rionda; Poderi Sorì; Pierangela Salvano.

Wines

Massolino – Vigna Rionda - Barolo Parafada; **Palladino** - Barolo Parafada; **Poderi Sorì** - Barolo Parafada

What the producers say

Franco Massolino (Massolino-Vigna Rionda): "This vineyard was bought at the end of the '70s and we started bottling it on its own in 1990. It is the old vines that really make our Parafada wine. In the vineyard, the soil is compact, very calcareous: the slope is steep with a full southern exposure. This is classic Serralunga: powerful and complex."

Palladino: "This vineyard has been part of our estate since 2005. In the glass, Parafada expresses more fruity notes, reminiscent of raspberry and cherry with vanilla as the backdrop. It's a Barolo that is elegant and spicy, austere and concentrated, balanced with its acidity and tannins."

Ian's assessment of the vineyard district, its wines and its potential

In the northern half of the Serralunga territory but on the western flank of the Serralunga ridge, Parafada is a relatively small vineyard district that has Lazzarito to its east and south, Gabutti to its west, and a small strip of Meriame to the north. The best part of Parafada faces full south, and though southeast and southwest exposures are also present, for the most part the exposure is more uniform here than in many other vineyard districts of the northern Serralunga area. The landscape is a Land Unit of Serralunga, and the soil lithology is the classic Lequio Formation of much of the Serralunga commune.

In general terms, Parafada's wines are more elegant and have more refined tannins than those of Gabutti but are just as textured; and while they lack the innate refinement and complexity of the best wines from Lazzarito, Parafada's Barolos approximate their power. In short, there's a lot to like about Parafada's Barolos: their mix of strength and fruity exuberance is very appealing (a fruity exuberance that is not always present in the wines of its neighboring vineyard districts). However, not everyone is impressed by this vineyard district's wines. Over the years a number of normally soft-spoken Barolo producers have all have more or less pointed out that if Parafada was never much famous for its Barolos, there was likely a reason (nudge nudge, wink wink) with one going as far as mentioning that Renato Ratti, in his now-famous map, omitted this site altogether. I was honestly surprised by the number of them all saying the same thing: normally when you ask producers about other vineyard areas it is rare to hear them spend many negative words in general, and even rarer always on the same place. Go figure. Especially because those Parafada Barolos available everywhere, such as those by Massolino-Vigna Rionda and Palladino are most often excellent wines and a real treat to taste and drink.

Parafada producers and the wines

Thanks to the excellent wines of the Massolino-Vigna Rionda estate, even though Parafada is small and there's not that many other Barolos made from it, it's a vineyard area that many wine lovers are aware of. Massolino briefly aged this wine in barriques, anathema to traditional-loving diehards but they stopped doing so in 2006. Theirs is 1.2 hectares holding of roughly sixty years old vines planted at 320 meters above sea level and fully south-facing. Massolino's Parafada Barolo is always marked by fresh red fruit aromas with bright floral top-notes, with lively acidity lifting the fresh crisp flavors on the long, suave finish. This sensation of brightness has been further heightened with the introduction of longer and slower fermentations carried out at lower temperatures in old used oak casks (as opposed to cement) allowing for the fruit and floral nuances to lose some of its rigidity and extend and fill out. Palladino is another estate that makes excellent Barolo Parafada wines. Their one hectare is planted between 260 and 3790 meters above sea level and is fully south-facing.

Benchmark wineries/Reference point producers of Barolo Parafada: Palladino, Massolino-Vigna Rionda.

PARUSSI

Township	Castiglione Falletto
Reference Map	See Map of Castiglione MGAs (Ch. 10)
Size (ha) (Tot / Barolo MGA)	13.41 / 7.98
Production 2021 (hl)	318.66
Altitude	220 – 290 meters a.s.l. roughly
Exposure	From west to southwest in the better exposed parcels, and from east to northwest in the remaining parts,
N. Claimants MGA	6
Other grape varieties planted:	Barbera; Dolcetto
Land Units	Land Unit of Barolo
Soil (stage):	Tortonian

Producers claiming the MGA

Massolino - Vigna Rionda; Pierangelo Bolla; Claudio Boschiazzo; Chionetti; Rosoretto; Sordo (Giovanni Sordo).

Wines

Gianfranco Bovio - Barolo Parussi; **Chionetti** - Barolo Parussi; **Deltetto** - Barolo Parussi; **Massolino – Vigna Rionda** - Barolo Parussi; **Rosoretto** - Barolo Parussi (and Riserva); **Sordo** - Barolo Parussi.

What the producers say

Franco Massolino (Massolino–Vigna Rionda): "We acquired this vineyard in the winter of 2006, and so our first vintage being only the 2007, Parussi for us still an ongoing "discovery" – in fact, our first try in making wines from grapes that are grown outside of the Serralunga territory. So far, we have uncovered a very "masculine" character supported by powerful and at times astringent tannins, a balsamic bouquet and certainly a long cellaring potential".

Sordo Giovanni (Sordo): "An amphitheater situated on the gentle slope that from Castiglione Falletto moves down the road that leads to Alba. Parussi's Barolos remind me of mint, sage, and sweet spices. The tannins are obvious but not usually harsh"

Ian's assessment of the vineyard district, its wines and its potential

Parussi is the northernmost vineyard district of the Castiglione Falletto territory, situated north of Montanello and to the west of Piantà. The latter is the vineyard district immediately on the other, eastern, side of the ridge that divides the northern Castiglione Falletto territory in two. Not all of Parussi is equally suited to high-quality Barolo production (and in fact only about half of it is planted to Nebbiolo with which to make Barolo) as some sections of it face east and even northwest. But the location on the western flank means that the better-situated Parussi vineyards bask in a potentially sunny and warmer microclimate. This, coupled with the soil lithology of typical Saint Agatha Marls Formation that dominates here, makes it so that Parussi's wines are adequately ripe and fruity and Tortonian stage in style, while exhibiting the tannic frame of the Castiglione Falletto commune. In fact, Parussi's are some of the fleshier and bigger Barolos made in this commune. Generally speaking, I find Parussi's wines to seem somewhat monastic at first sniff and taste, in that they are not blessed with gobs of fresh fruit but rather deliver their aromas and flavors of red fruits, sweet spices, licorice and herbs in a linear manner, with good purity and precision but also sneaky depth and concentration. Medium-to full-bodied, with red fruit and herb aromas and flavors, they are Barolos that are usually ready to drink sooner than those of Villero or Monprivato, two other Castiglione Falletto communes, but always seem to age well.

Parussi producers and the wines

A number of producers have made excellent Barolos from Parussi over the years. The best Barolo Parussi to my mind has always been the one by Gianfranco Bovio, a solid but slightly underrated producer of very well-made wines that don't usually cost an arm and a leg. The winery usually made their Barolo Parussi as a Riserva, so you just know Bovio thought highly of the site. Bovio's vines in Parussi are planted at about 230 meters above sea level and have a full south exposure. In fact, Bovio's Parussi is full-bodied and fleshy, with impressive underlying structure provided by usually noble tannins that nicely support the flavors of red cherry, camphor, licorice and sweet spices. At once velvety and powerful, this is a Barolo, like many of the better ones from the Castiglione Falletto commune, that is deceptively easy and ready to drink at a young age, but that will also age twenty or so years effortlessly. Like I wrote earlier, I have always had a soft spot for this estate's wines, finding them to be both drinkable and ageworthy, and very food-friendly. For this reason, I am very happy to report that while the estate had stopped making this wine in 2004, it has started up production once again, coming back with a spectacular 2016 (with slightly less than 2000 bottles made, I guess the only bad bit of news is the paltry volumes it was made in).

Massolino-Vigna Rionda has made a Barolo Parussi since the 2007 vintage from a 1.65-hectare patch of roughly forty years old southeast to southwest-facing vines planted at about 290 meters above sea level. The wine is aged for thirty months in large oak casks and is characterized by notes of ripe red fruits, sweet spices, tar and licorice, with hints of menthol: very Castiglione Falletto, in fact. It is an excellent wine as all the Barolos from this winery tend to be. Massolino's Barolo Parussi is an especially interesting wine in that it showcases what the family can accomplish with Nebbiolo from Castiglione Falletto, given that all their other single vineyard district wines are from Serralunga. Allowing for some variation depending on the vintage, Massolino's Parussi is much more richly fruity and spicy than their Serralunga Barolos from Parafada, Margheria and Vignarionda, especially so in the mid-palate and on the finish. In some years, especially the warmer ones like 2015, the wine can turn out rather powerful for a Barolo from Castiglione Falletto, but that shouldn't surprise as this is a hallmark of the Barolos of Parussi, which tends to give some of that commune's bigger-boned wines. Some fruit from Parussi goes into Massolino's classic Barolo too, also made with Nebbiolo grapes from the vineyard districts of Briccolina, Broglio, Collaretto, and Le Turne.

Another truly outstanding Barolo Parussi was the one made by Conterno Fantino: the winery rented vines in the vineyard district and was last able to make it in the 2001 vintage, just before the rental contract was not renewed. The 2001 is certainly a good wine, but this is one very rare instance in which aa winery actually made a really good 1997 Barolo (that wine was most likely the best Barolo Parussi Conterno Fantino ever made). Quinto Chionetti is one of the best, if not the best, producers of Dolcetto di Dogliani but the estate also makes a Barolo Parussi from lower-lying vines situated around 200 meters above sea level. Sordo makes an excellent Barolo Parussi. If it's not the best Barolo in his portfolio, it's at the very least in the top three or four.

Benchmark wineries/Reference point producers of Barolo Parussi: Bovio, Chionetti, Massolino-Vignarionda, Sordo.

PERNANNO

Township	Castiglione Falletto	
Reference Map	See Map of Castiglione MGAs (Ch. 10)	
Size (ha) (Tot / Barolo MGA)	15.98 / 4.37	
Production 2021 (hl)	234.96 (of which 5.53 hl of Barolo Riserva *MGA*)	
Altitude	240 – 320 meters a.s.l. roughly	
Exposure	From east to southeast.	
N. Claimants MGA	3	
Other grape varieties planted:	Barbera; Dolcetto	
Land Units	Land Unit of Barolo	
Soil (stage):	Tortonian	

Producers claiming the MGA

Bongiovanni; Fratelli Monchiero; Federica Sobrero.

Wines

Cascina Adelaide - Barolo Pernanno; **Cascina Bongiovanni** - Barolo Pernanno; **Fratelli Monchiero** - Barolo Pernanno (*); **Sobrero** - Barolo Riserva Pernanno

What the producers say

Cascina Adelaide: "We have vinified this vineyard separately since 2007. White tufa, shining in the sun, allows these Nebbiolo vines to express delicacy, austerity and transparence in the overall structure. Qualities that can only arise from this part of the Barolo hill. It lends itself to early drinking, to ready drinking pleasure. Notes of mint, medicinal herbs all point to its origin and the sweet tannins always fine and elegant.".

Enrica Scavino (Paolo Scavino): "Particularly sunny during the morning, this *cru* offers favorable conditions for the cultivation of Nebbiolo. The morning dew evaporates, the grapes do not overheat excessively as summer temperatures remain pretty mild in the afternoon. The ripening of the grapes is gradual and the wines from this cru are aromatic and elegant".

Ian's assessment of the vineyard district, its wines and its potential

Pernanno is an interesting site that probably hasn't gotten as much attention as it deserves. It's essentially the larger half of a hillside that is divided in two by a fissure: the section of the hill that falls to the left of the road that leads into the town of Castiglione Falletto is the one that has historically been known as Pernanno. It has soils of Saint Agatha Marls Formation (mostly of the typical form, but also of the sandy form, and even some Diano Sandstone), hence mostly loamy-clay in nature but with a higher than usual proportion of sand in pockets, contributing to wines of both flesh and power. I find there is an underlying linearity to Pernanno's Barolos wines, but they also have plenty of perfume (no doubt contributed to by the sand effect and a cooler mesoclimate in most of the district). Historically, while most of Pernanno has been planted to vines (80% of the district is under vine and of that more than 90% is Nebbiolo), it is the central segment that has always been considered to be the most favorable for the production of high-quality Barolos. Some producers also swear by Cerroni, the segment at the end of Pernanno that segues into Piantà, another vineyard district of Castiglione Falletto, but I do not have that much experience (yet) with Nebbiolo wines from there.

Pernanno producers and the wines

Cascina Bongiovanni makes a very fine Barolo Pernanno from two hectares of 40-60 years old vines facing southeast and planted on mostly clay-loamy soils. Interestingly, the wine is aged in barriques, making it a throwback to the nineties. Francesco Sobrero first made his Barolo Pernanno in 1993, from one hectare of very old vines planted in 1946 at about 350 meters above sea level. Then, in 1998, he began making it as a Riserva, which tells you that the winery believes Pernanno gives wines of a structure that may withstand, and actually benefit, from extended oak-aging. That is interesting on number of levels, not the least of which is that Sobrero's Pernanno Barolo counts 20% Nebbiolo Rosé in its mix (it's roughly 70% Nebbiolo Michet, 20% Nebbiolo Rosé and only 10% Nebbiolo Lampia; in other words, a real rarity nowadays). At Paolo Scavino, an estate that boasts one of the most impressive collections of high-quality vineyards in many different top sites of the denomination, they farm 1.5 hectares of east/southeast-facing Pernanno vines planted back in 1976 and 2001 at about 76 and 2001 at about 300 meters above sea level.

I think Pernanno is a good source of high-quality Barolos: what they lack in complexity (in comparison to Barolos from the denomination's greatest vineyard districts) they make up for in steely, juicy, spicy charm.

Benchmark wineries/Reference point producers of Barolo Pernanno: Cascina Adelaide, Cascina Bongiovanni.

PERNO

Township	Monforte d'Alba
Reference Map	See Map of Monforte d'Alba MGAs (Ch. 10)
Size (ha) (Tot / Barolo MGA)	190.96 / 30.91
Production 2021 (hl)	1567.97 (of which 324.92 hl of Barolo Riserva *MGA*,
	100.45 hl of Barolo *MGA* Vigna, 51.68 hl of Barolo Riserva *MGA* Vigna)
Altitude	220 – 450 meters a.s.l. roughly
Exposure	From west to southwest in the better exposed parcels facing Bussia, from east to southeast on the opposite side.
N. Claimants MGA	22
Other grape varieties planted:	Barbera; Dolcetto; white varieties
Land Units	Land Unit of Serralunga d'Alba in the eastern slopes; Land Unit of Castiglione in the remaining parts
Soil (stage):	Tortonian and Serravallian

Producers claiming the MGA

Marziano Abbona; Franco Adriano; Cascina Corte Di Barosi; Cascina Del Monastero; Cascina Tiole; Castello Di Perno; Roberto Cogno; Diego Conterno; Fortemasso; Giuseppe Galvagno; Paolo Giordano; Giuseppe Mascarello E Figlio; La Fusina; Stefano Oreste; Giorgio Pira; Bruno Pressenda; Raineri; Rocche Dei Manzoni; Elio Sandri; Sara Vezza; Schiavenza; Sordo (Giovanni Sordo).

Wines

Cascina del Monastero - Barolo Perno; **Cascina Tiole** (Grasso Massimo) - Barolo and Barolo S. Stefano; ; **Feyles Sorelle De Nicola** - Barolo Riserva Perno Vigna della Serra; **Paolo Giordano** – Barolo Perno; **La Fusina** - Barolo; **Giuseppe Mascarello e Figlio** - Barolo S. Stefano di Perno (*); **Stefano Oreste** - Barolo Perno; **Giorgio Pira** - Barolo Perno Laut, and Barolo Riserva Perno Terre del Mago; **Raineri** - Barolo Perno; **Rocche dei Manzoni** - Barolo Perno Vigna Cappella di S. Stefano; **Elio Sandri** - Barolo Perno (and Riserva) (*); **Sordo** - Barolo Perno (and Riserva); **Paola Sordo** – Barolo Perno

What the producers say

Rodolfo Migliorini (Rocche dei Manzoni): "The vineyard is dominated by an ancient Romanic chapel dating back to the XII century, dedicated to St. Steven, Santo Stefano in Italian. It gives a Barolo that is distinguished for its great elegance, shown by its rich and persistent bouquet of ample and refined notes of violet and marasca cherry, and a palate that gives a sense of completeness and harmony".

Luciano Racca (Raineri): "We introduced our separate vinification of Perno (and of S. Stefano di Perno) in 2006. Perno exudes an elegance similar to that of Bussia, distinct from Ginestra and Mosconi that give more structured and powerful Barolos with more decisive tannins. Noted for aromas of violet, dried rose, ripe fruit and a hint of tobacco, mushroom and balsamic note, the wine is intense and persistent on the finish, of perfect harmony and balance".

I Brè: "Perno has the highest concentration of land use for cultivation in the region. It's a soil, composed of Mesozoic marine limestone, marls, and shales and is perfectly suited to growing Dolcetto, Nebbiolo and Pelaverga. The wines produced from these vineyards are particularly noted for their magnificent color and intense sensory expression".

Sordo: "A powerful Barolo with plenty of extract and structure, with notes of ripe fruit, and even cocoa, mint and vanilla that are in my view unrelated to the oak used".

Ian's assessment of the vineyard district, its wines and its potential

At 190 hectares large, Perno is one of the three biggest vineyard districts in all of Barolo (see chapter 10, Barolo vineyard districts: Maps and Land Units). Furthermore, about half the vineyard district isn't even under vine and less than three quarters of that is planted to Nebbiolo. Based on that, if you are a negative person, you would think, why bother? In fact, Perno boasts well-recognized, site-specific Nebbiolo areas within its vast expanse of land that give highly interesting and diverse Barolos that clearly speak (can speak/could speak) of a finite somewhereness. And that happens to be true even if you aren't a happy go-lucky positive person like I am.

Perno is a vineyard district occupying the northeastern corner of the Monforte commune. In fact, it wasn't even part Monforte once: the area of Perno (and Castelletto too) were annexed to the Monforte territory only in 1922 (some locals have told me a year later). Imagine that back then it was only six hectares large. Perno the vineyard district takes its name from Perno the village, a sparse collection of houses located more or less in the middle of the vineyard district itself. The Pira and Rocche di Castiglione vineyard districts of the Castiglione Falletto commune are situated just north of Perno, while to the east, Perno looks across the valley towards Serralunga vineyard districts, such as Gabutti. To the south and southeast lie Monforte's Castelletto and Gramolere, respectively. To the east there is the vast expanse that is Bussia.

Like just about every other Monforte vineyard district, Perno is much too large: this means that relative to site-specific Barolos, there is no point in talking of Perno as a whole. Simply put, there is no such thing as a "Perno-somewhereness", and don't let people who have a vested interest lead you to believe otherwise. There are definite subregions within Perno: Perno Disa, Perno Cerretta (or Ceretta) and Perno Santo Stefano. Do not confuse the Perno Cerretta (that locals often call Cerretta di Perno), with the better-known Cerretta vineyard district of Serralunga; as I pointed out earlier in this book, the name of Cerretta is actually a very common one in all of Italy, not just Barolo (See CERRETTA file). That much aside, the first two subregions, Cerretta and Disa, are located in the western half of Perno, while the latter, Perno Santo Stefano, is included within the vineyard district's eastern half.

As a general rule, the sections of Perno closest to Serralunga tend to give wines that, perhaps not surprisingly, are more similar to that commune's Barolos rather than those of Monforte. There are a number of different factors that contribute as much, summarized by the two different landscape categories to which the eastern and western halves of the Perno vineyard district belong to (Land Unit of Serralunga for the western half closest to the Serralunga commune; Land Unit of Castiglione dominating in the rest of the vineyard district, most notably its eastern half). Therefore, there can be a very large difference in the altitudes the vineyards grow at in Perno, and slope gradients will vary quite a bit too. For example, parts of Perno Cerretta are characterized by being very steep and difficult to farm; that, plus its remoteness, led to it not having that many takers in the past, at least as far as following Nebbiolo vineyards there was concerned. As a result, for the longest time, Perno and Cerretta di Perno were largely abandoned.

The soil composition of Perno changes throughout (which is to be expected, considering how big it is); but for the most part, its lithology is that of the Diano Sandstone formation. However, there are also pockets of Lequio Formation and even of the typical Saint Agatha Fossil Marls. To be more precise, because it can help relative to the wines made in this vineyard district, the soil lithology of the western half of Perno closest to the Serralunga border shows pockets of Lequio Formation (the clay-limestone and compacted sands typifying most of Serralunga's vineyard sites), while the more central and especially eastern reaches of Perno are dominated by the Diano Sandstone (with some of the typical Saint Agatha Fossil Marls too).

To put all of that in the simplest and most practical terms possible, the wines of the westernmost reaches of Perno tend to resemble those of the northern reaches of Serralunga while those from the rest of the denomination resemble more those typically associated with Monforte. Therefore, you would expect the Barolos of Perno Disa and Perno Cerretta to be bigger and tougher than those of Perno Santo Stefano, which should have a gentler mouthfeel. In fact, slope gradient and altitude also play a large role: those wines made with Perno Cerretta grapes sourced at higher altitude steep slopes are usually marked not just by power and Serralunga-like tannic-structure, but also by freshness and sharper acidities. Clearly, individual viticultural and winemaking decisions will greatly impact what the finished wines taste like, but those baseline observations remain true. After all, it's true that you can make your Chambertin any which way you like, but getting it to be like if it were from Latricières or Griottes would take a truly huge effort and a noteworthy lack of vision.

Perno producers and the wines

I especially like the Perno subregion of Santo Stefano and its wines: my personal view is that it should have been named a distinct vineyard district. Perno Santo Stefano, or Santo Stefano di Perno as it used to be called, is located right below the town of Perno and gives full-bodied, powerful Barolos like you'd expect from the

Monforte commune but with noteworthy amounts of flesh, sweetness, and complexity. Producers love to use Nebbiolo from this Perno subregion to give more vertical classic estate Barolos more oomph. The Giuseppe Mascarello estate has made great Perno wines in the past, and owns vines facing west that look towards Bussia. Another famous estate farming this part of Monforte is the Rocche dei Manzoni estate. Valentino Migliorini and his family began producing a Barolo from the Santo Stefano area in 1993, the Barolo Perno Cappella di S. Stefano (once called *vigna* Cappella di S. Stefano) and it almost always has been, in every vintage, my favorite wine of theirs. The vines a range of exposures (southeast through south to southwest. The 2000 was especially good, in what was an overrated year for Barolo. Gianmatteo Raineri has a small holding in Santo Stefano di Perno that is planted with southwest-facing, forty years old vines at about 350 meters above sea level. This is a small and not yet well-known Barolo producer, but its wines are excellent.

Cascina del Monastero, run by the talented Grasso family (careful now, don't confuse your Grassos: there are many talented Grasso families making Barolo, and Barbaresco too, for that matter) also has vines in the Santo Stefano subregion. Their oldest vineyard there dates back to the 1950s and is located right below the chapel, while their larger vineyard (replanted in 2000) is not far away. Of note, these two plots were once farmed and taken care of by Don Conterno, the "parroco di Perno" (the Perno parish priest, in English). Loris Grasso describes his winemaking as fairly traditional, consisting in skin contact and fermentation taking place in stainless steel containers and lasting for 25-40 days, malolactic and aging occur in large oak barrels for anywhere from thirty-six to as much as sixty months depending on the vintage and the wine. The wines are bottled unfined and unfiltered. For sure, theirs is a more tannic wine than that of Giuseppe Mascarello, but remarkably perfumed in the manner of the Santo Stefano Barolos.

A very good example of what the Barolos of the Perno Cerretta subregion are like is given by that by Sordo. Made from 25-40 years old vines, it's a slightly bigger Perno Barolo, but with enough complexity and lift so that it doesn't seem overly chunky. The best example of Perno Disa Barolo is that made by the excellent Elio Sandri estate, a very traditional, full-bodied, deep Barolo that greatly rewards aging. Luciano Sandrone has been farming Nebbiolo grapes in Perno Cerretta and blends them with those of four other vineyard districts to make his world-famous Barolo Le Vigne.

Benchmark wineries/Reference point producers of Barolo Perno: a) Perno Cerretta: Giorgio Pira; b) Perno Disa: Elio Sandri; c) Perno Santo Stefano: Raineri, Giuseppe Mascarello, Rocche dei Manzoni.

PIANTÀ

Township	Castiglione Falletto
Reference Map	See Map of Castiglione MGAs (Ch. 10)
Size (ha) (Tot / Barolo MGA)	6.27 / 0.46
Production 2021 (hl)	25.23
Altitude	220 – 275 meters a.s.l. roughly
Exposure	East
N. Claimants MGA	1
Other grape varieties planted:	Barbera; Dolcetto; white varieties
Land Units	Land Unit of Barolo
Soil (stage):	Tortonian

Producers claiming the MGA

Casavecchia.

Wines

Casavecchia - Barolo Piantà

Piantà is one of those vineyard districts that nobody has yet heard much of, Italians included, and yet, the one Barolo you can taste from there is pretty good. That shouldn't be so surprising given that though little-known, over 80% of the district is planted to vines, and close to 80% of that is Nebbiolo. So clearly somebody sees something there. Piantà is the northernmost vineyard district of Castiglione Falletto, situated right above Pernanno on the western flank of the Castiglione Falletto commune's territory. Rather low-lying but at the same time relatively cool, facing east, the wines are nicely vibrant and have good tannic backbone with enough sweet fruity flesh to make them interesting and easily accessible.

Piantà producers and the wines

Marco Casavecchia of the Cantina Casavecchia (actually a family-run operation with brothers Marco, Luca and Carlo all involved in the running of the winery, along with other members of the family) located in Diano d'Alba is the only producer I know of making a Barolo Piantà, and if not, his is certainly the only one that I have tried over a number of vintages. He owns 0.66 hectares of southeast-facing Nebbiolo vines planted at 250 meters above sea level. The wine is uncomplicated and easy to like.

Benchmark wineries/Reference point producers of Barolo Piantà: Casavecchia.

PIRA

Township	Castiglione Falletto	
Reference Map	See Map of Castiglione MGAs (Ch. 10)	
Size (ha) (Tot / Barolo MGA)	6.66 / 5.32	
Production 2021 (hl)	274.43	
Altitude	250 – 300 meters a.s.l. roughly	
Exposure	Southeast	
N. Claimants MGA	1	
Other grape varieties planted:	Barbera; white varieties	
Land Units	Land Unit of Barolo	
Soil (stage):	Tortonian	

Producers claiming the MGA

Roagna (I Paglieri).

Wines

Roagna - Barolo Pira; Barolo Pira Vecchie Viti and Barolo Riserva Pira

Ian's assessment of the vineyard district, its wines and its potential

There is only one producer making wines from Pira, the remarkably talented Luca Roagna: this is because Pira is a Roagna *monopole*, just like Francia is a Giacomo Conterno monopole and Falletto is a Bruno Giacosa monopole. And even though I think that Luca's best wines are his Barbarescos (some of Italy's and the world's greatest red wines, especially in their Vecchie Viti versions), there is no doubt that his Barolo Pira is a doozy. And Roagna's Vecchie Viti Pira is exceptional.

Pira is one of the southernmost vineyard districts of Castiglione Falletto, close by Rocche di Castiglione to the west and to the north; Scarrone is to the north and the east; while to the south it's all Perno, in the territory of Monforte. It might be interesting for you to know that the local Cascina Pira was originally known as Cascina della Rocca: its name was changed to Pira in the 1700s, when the farmhouse (*cascina*, in Italian) was given the family name of the then owners. In fact, in land registry documents dating back to those times, both of those names are recorded, one of the reasons Luca Roagna decided to call one of his wines La Rocca e La Pira. Clearly, with the arrival of the official MGA names of the vineyard districts, he was no longer able to use the "La Rocca e La" part and now his Barolo just goes by the name of Pira (from where the grapes are sourced). The Roagna family was originally from Barbaresco where their estate was founded at the end of the1800s by Luca's great-great-grandfather, who was already making wine at the time (and actually won a gold medal at the Expo in Chicago). His last name was Rocca, but when Maria Candida Rocca married Giovanni Roagna in 1929 the estate became known as Roagna. The family bought Pira in 1989: today the vineyard district is planted to seven hectares of vines, 4.88 of which are of Nebbiolo (the rest is Barbera and Chardonnay). Roagna makes three different Barolos from Pira: the Barolo Pira, the Barolo Pira Vecchie Viti and the Barolo Pira Riserva. The Vecchie Viti bottling is made in extremely limited numbers from the oldest vines on the estate (the *youngest* of which were planted back in 1937); the Barolo Riserva is also made from very old vines, but even the Barolo Pira is made from 25-50 years old vines.

The vineyard district's Land Unit is that of Barolo, and the lithology is by Saint Agatha Fossil Marls (in Pira's case of the sandy type). A taste of the wines will tell you that too: Pira's are very typical Barolos of Castiglione Falletto, but born off a sandier site, where forward ripe fruit of Tortonian stage soils makes the wines resemble those of La Morra and Barolo, yet with an underlying tannic spine that is very reminiscent of Monforte's wines, and everything is tied together by Castiglione Falletto's hallmark balance. From a viticultural standpoint, Pira is blessed with an ideal habitat and mesoclimate: its vines are protected by adverse weather effects thanks to the Rocche di Castiglione higher up, and lower down the slope by a small stream that runs down from Monforte's Bussia. Furthermore, Pira's soil is very complex, in turn allowing to make complex wines: the Roagna family has studied its vineyard soils extensively and can break down Pira into six smaller subzones. These are characterized by different vine age (mostly massal selections from old Pira vines) and soil type, ranging from very Tortonian-like blue-grey marls to positively Serravalian compacted sands and limestone.

Pira producers and the wines (monopole)

Speaking generally, Pira's soil sand component means the site has very good drainage. More specifically, Pira's southeast-facing slope that looks towards Perno is characterized by soils boasting a wealth of very calcareous-rich (white in color) rocky and sandy loam with very little clay, while the soils of those sections that look to La Morra have more clay. The flank of Pira that looks to Monforte was formed by the disgregation of the soils of the Rocche di Castiglione, and so that tells you plenty about the potential quality of this part of Pira. Which means that the latter section of Pira gives very refined wines, compared to the more clay-rich areas the wines of which are bigger and darker, but also just a tad less elegant. No matter: there are fewer wines better than the Barolo Pira Vecchie Viti; and the Barolo Pira itself is accessible and easy to like, a beautifully translucent, pale red colored wine of grace and refinement (and in which a partial presence of whole bunches contributes to the organoleptic and textural profile).

Benchmark wineries/Reference point producers of Barolo Pira: Roagna (monopole).

PISAPOLA

Township	Verduno
Reference Map	See Map of Verduno MGAs (Ch. 10)
Size (ha) (Tot / Barolo MGA)	9.73 / 1.98
Production 2021 (hl)	101.69
Altitude	280 – 350 meters a.s.l. roughly
Exposure	Southeast
N. Claimants MGA	2
Other grape varieties planted:	Barbera
Land Units	Land Unit of La Morra
Soil (stage):	Messinian

Producers claiming the MGA

Ascheri; Edoardo Sobrino.

Wines

Ascheri - Barolo Pisapola.

Ian's assessment of the vineyard district, its wines and its potential

Pisapola is a Verduno vineyard district located immediately outside of the town, in the northern section of the commune's territory. Like Campasso and Monvigliero, Pisapola is draped over the western flank of the ridge that divides the Verduno territory into two flanks. Opposite to Pisapola, across the road that runs atop the ridge, and on the eastern flank, lies Massara.

Independently of the human element, these two flanks have very different terroirs and Pisapola's is certainly more like that of Campasso, and to a lesser extent, Monvigliero than it is to any other vineyard district of the commune. Because of its proximity to the river, Pisapola's vines are blessed with a slightly warmer microclimate, but a largely southeastern exposure ensures freshness. The soils are of the Messinian stage gypsiferous-sulfur formation, though there are also some of the Saint Agatha Fossil Marls of the laminated type that so characterize Monvigliero.

Pisapola producers and the wines

To the best of my knowledge the only producers bottling a Barolo Pisapola today are Ascheri and Edoardo Sobrino, but others include grapes from this vineyard district into their classic estate Barolos. Ascheri began releasing his single vineyard Barolos from 1999, but only does so in exceptional vintages such as the 2013, 2015 and 2016 (fair enough). In Pisapola, Ascheri owns 1.6 hectares of southeast-facing vineyards planted at about 340 meters above sea level on soils of the Saint Agatha Marls Formation that is not especially sandy. The wine is all Verduno delicacy, with pretty nuances of red fruit and flowers, hints of orange peel and violet. Pisapola's wines have elements in common with those of Monvigliero but as Fabio Alessandria of the famous G.B. Burlotto estate tells me, they are usually darker in color than those he makes in Monvigliero. To my taste they also have less palate weight too but are nicely accessible at an early age and perfumed. Frankly, I don't mind a good Barolo Pisapola. Not at all, actually.

Benchmark wineries/Reference point producers of Barolo Pisapola: Ascheri, Edoardo Sobrino.

PRABON

Township	Serralunga d'Alba
Reference Map	See Map of Serralunga d'Alba MGAs (Ch. 10) d'Alba
Size (ha) (Tot / Barolo MGA)	3.84 /
Production 2021 (hl)	0
Altitude	240 – 310 meters a.s.l. roughly
Exposure	West
N. Claimants MGA	0
Other grape varieties planted:	Dolcetto; white varieties
Land Units	Land Unit of Serralunga d'Alba
Soil (stage):	Serravallian

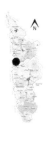

Ian's assessment of the vineyard district, its wines and its potential

One of the smallest vineyard districts of all, Prabon is located in the Serralunga commune's territory. It is the natural prolongation of Gabutti and is characterized by a similar lithology of Lequio Formation. I honestly cannot recall if I have ever had a Barolo from Prabon, or if I have tried estate Barolos made with Prabon grapes. Until then, judgement reserved.

Benchmark wineries/Reference point producers of Barolo Prabon: None currently available.

PRAPÒ

Township	Serralunga d'Alba
Reference Map	See Map of Serralunga d'Alba MGAs (Ch. 10)
Size (ha) (Tot / Barolo MGA)	8.33 / 5.52
Production 2021 (hl)	296.73
Altitude	270 – 380 meters a.s.l. roughly
Exposure	From south to southeast
N. Claimants MGA	6
Other grape varieties planted:	Only Nebbiolo
Land Units	Land Unit of Castiglione in the western side (the highest plots); Land Unit of Serralunga d'Alba in the remaining parts (the lowest)
Soil (stage):	Serravallian

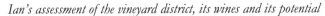

Producers claiming the MGA

Ceretto; Ettore Germano; Davide Fregonese (Bugia Nen); Paolo Scavino; Schiavenza; Luigi Vico.

Wines

Ceretto - Barolo Prapò; **Ettore Germano** - Barolo Prapò; **Davide Fregonese (Bugia Nen)** - Barolo Prapò; **Paolo Scavino** - Barolo Prapò; **Schiavenza** - Barolo Prapò (and Riserva); **Luigi Vico** - Barolo Prapò.

What the producers say

Alessandro Ceretto (Ceretto): "From 1982 we vinify Prapò separately because we believe that it's a Barolo that that reflects all the virtuosity and aristocracy this wine is capable of. Equipped with a solid structure and body, thanks to its optimal acidity and tannic structure, it is suitable for long-term cellar aging".

Sergio Germano (Ettore Germano): "We acquired this vineyard in 1964 and we started bottling it on its own in 1995. The soil of this *cru* –with respect to Cerretta – is very fine strata of sandstones and sands (with the presence of iron turning the soil brownish-red in color) but with a slightly looser structure because of its high content in limestone. Compared to Ceretta, Prapo's wines have less color but are certainly finer and more elegant".

Mauro Sebaste: "In 1994 we bought this parcel and ever since it has been vinified and bottled separately from the others. Prapò is a powerful Barolo in terms of its tannic character and its aromas are slow to open, especially when young".

Ian's assessment of the vineyard district, its wines and its potential

Do you like Batman? I do, always have, ever since I was a little kid and used to read the comic and to look at the cheesy television show full of "pow", "bang" and "wham" (and having Julie Newmar as the Catwoman didn't exactly hurt either). Anyways, as the Ceretto family knows very well, I have been a huge fan of their Prapò Barolo since day one. I am a huge believer in the quality that Prapò can deliver, in the right hands. For a variety of reasons pertaining to Prapò's soil, exposure, altitude, location, and topography, I believe it to be one of the Barolo denomination's fifteen-twenty best vineyard districts. What does any of that have to do with Batman? Well, because from an aerial perspective, Prapò looks something like Batman's logo, or more simply, the vineyard district has the shape of a stylized bat. And like the steely muscles and brooding personality of the Caped Crusader, Prapò's Barolos are also steely and brooding.

Prapò is one of the Serralunga vineyard districts located on the eastern flank of the ridge that cuts through the Serralunga denomination in a north-south direction; but importantly, its rather steep slope rotates so that the vines have a southeastern/south exposure (one tract of Prapò however looks out to the Alta Langa). It's easy to see Prapò's vineyards on your left when driving down the road that passes through the Cerretta and Meriame vineyard districts on the way to Serralunga. Prapò is located on the lower-lying, mostly south-facing prolongation of the Cerretta hill; therefore, Cerretta surrounds Prapò to the north, east and west. Prapò has a fresh, windy mesoclimate which also ensures long hang times for the Nebbiolo. In other words, Prapò's wines boast not just typical Serralunga power, but also noteworthy complexity and elegance, and are rarely if ever jammy and/or superripe. Furthermore, in the words of Marcello Ceretto, the relatively cool site "provides us with an advantage in rainy years and an opportunity in hot ones".

Just like its wines, Prapò's soil is complex, in that it is dominated by the Diano Sandstone Formation in its upper portions and especially in its western reaches, while its all Lequio Formation lower down and throughout most of the vineyard district (dominating in its central and eastern sections). It follows Prapò's is a small vineyard district, its Barolos can express a specific Prapò-somewhereness depending on where the Nebbiolo grapes grow. Prapò's wines are generally characterized by a deep red color (the clay); penetrating perfume [thanks in part to its *sorì del mattino* (east-facing) aspect) and limestone-rich soils] of dark red fruit and sweet spices (the sandstone); and an austere, very refined and vibrant mouthfeel that hints at a noteworthy mineral presence and citrussy acidity (the limestone again) with obvious, absolutely Prapò-typical, balsamic undertones. Possibly in relation to its southern/southeastern exposure (an important feature to look for when analyzing vineyard districts on the eastern flank of the Serralunga ridge: exposure-wise, Prapò is much better off than most of Cerretta) Prapò's wines are always complex and lifted, ripe and suave. One last, important, thing about Prapò: producer competence allowing, it is remarkably adept at giving remarkably great wines even in average and off years (not by chance it is the only single-site Barolo that Ceretto made in the difficult 2014 vintage). That Château Latour-like quality is not something many other sites in the Barolo denomination can brag about.

Prapò producers and the wines

A bunch of wineries either farm or make wine from Prapò. Clearly, the most important Barolo Prapò is the one made by Ceretto, a wine that rarely disappoints: more often than not, it turns out to be the best Ceretto Barolo of the vintage. Ceretto owns 2.3 hectares in Prapò that they bought back in 1972. The vines were planted facing south in 1973 (they are the Ceretto estate's oldest Nebbiolo vines) and again in 1987, between 310 and 370 meters above sea level. The soil composition is the classic mix of clay (53%), loam (28%) and sand (19%), with the area's typical alkaline soil pH (8,05), plus a noteworthy presence of iron. There's no other way I can say it, except that the wine is exceptionally good.

The talented Sergio Germano of the Ettore Germano estate farms 1.5 hectares of Nebbiolo planted in 1969, 1999 and 2012 (the average age of Germano's Prapò vines is about 45 years), at an altitude ranging from 330 to 370 meters above sea level. Long skin contact and aging in large oak casks makes for very traditional wines. His wines boast a noteworthy steeliness that is a bit of a Germano-signature, but his Barolo Prapò always seems to be the richest, fleshiest, and purest of all his Barolos (at least until the Barolo Vignarionda came along). The wine is a gem.

The Paolo Scavino estate, that over the years has quietly built up one of the most impressive line-up of vineyards in an extremely large number of vineyard districts (to the best of my knowledge, one of the three largest number of vineyard districts wines I can think of) farms 0.78 hectares of Nebbiolo planted in 2010 at about 370 meters above sea level facing south/southeast. He does not (yet?) bottle it as a single-site wine though. The Mauro Sebaste estate of La Morra has also been making a Prapò wine for a long time now it ages in 400 and 1600 liters oak barrels for thirty-six months. At once austere and refined, but not devoid of flesh, I think it is the best wine in the estate portfolio.

Benchmark wineries/Reference point producers of Barolo Prapò: Ceretto. Also good: Ettore Germano, Mauro Sebaste.

PREDA

Township	Barolo
Reference Map	See Map of Barolo MGAs (Ch. 10)
Size (ha) (Tot / Barolo MGA)	20.68 / 3.80
Production 2021 (hl)	197.65
Altitude	230 – 300 meters a.s.l. roughly
Exposure	From south to southeast
N. Claimants MGA	3
Other grape varieties planted:	Barbera; Dolcetto; white varieties
Land Units	Land Unit of Barolo
Soil (stage):	Tortonian

Producers claiming the MGA

D'Arcy; Philine Isabelle; Virna.

Wines

Cascina Adelaide - Barolo Preda; **Philine Isabelle** - Barolo Preda (from 2020).

What the producers say

Cascina Adelaide: "The separate vinification of this vineyard was initiated in 1999. In general, this Barolo is particularly expressive, marked by aromas of prune and blackberry, with an iodine and minty quality".

Ian's assessment of the vineyard district, its wines and its potential

Preda is one of the last outposts of the Barolo commune; in fact, its eastern flank looks out across the plain towards Bussia. It is located close by numerous vineyard districts such as Vignane, Zuncai, Monrobiolo di Bussia, Coste di Rose and Boschetti all of which are vineyard districts of the Barolo commune save for Monrobiolo di Bussia (as in fact the "Bussia" in that name suggests).

Not all of Preda has an exposure and mesoclimate that are ideal for Nebbiolo (or grapevines in general: only about half the district is under vine). The Land Unit is that of Barolo, meaning essentially a lithology of Saint Agatha Fossil Marls (mostly of the sandy type), but with lots of clay about a meter down, so parts of Preda are characterized by good water-retention capacity making it a good site from where to source grapes in hot, droughty years.

Locals believe that Preda's Barolos are usually fruit-forward but structured: their early appeal and easy accessibility belie a serious tannic spine. Notes of red fruit and menthol dominate, while underbrush and herbs are pretty rare in wines from Preda. I have had only two wines repeatedly over the years that are either wholly made with Preda grapes (Cascina Adelaide) or almost (Virna Borgogno). Cascina Adelaide has fourteen years old vines planted at 270-300 meters above sea level. Their wine usually benefits from six or seven years of cellaring prior to popping a cork. Virna Borgogno farms Preda too and includes about 85% of those grapes in her classic estate Barolo (the other 15% comes from her vines in Sarmassa). She has told me over the years that in her mind Preda is a very good vineyard district, and that in fact she really should make a Barolo Preda too. However, as for now she has enough single-site Barolos in her portfolio, and so she is holding off for the time being.

Benchmark wineries/Reference point producers of Barolo Preda: Cascina Adelaide.

PUGNANE

Township	Castiglione Falletto
Reference Map	See Map of Castiglione MGAs (Ch. 10)
Size (ha) (Tot / Barolo MGA)	4.97 / 2.36
Production 2021 (hl)	106.13
Altitude	240 – 270 meters a.s.l. roughly
Exposure	East
N. Claimants MGA	2
Other grape varieties planted:	Barbera; Dolcetto
Land Units	Land Unit of Barolo
Soil (stage):	Tortonian

Producers claiming the MGA

Giancarlo Boasso; Cascina Pugnane (Fratelli Ghisolfi).

Wines

Giancarlo Boasso - Barolo Pugnane; **Cascina Pugnane (Fratelli Ghisolfi)** - Barolo Pugnane.

Ian's assessment of the vineyard district, its wines and its potential

At a superficial glance, and without knowing the history of the Barolo zone and of its wines, it might seem that Pugnane is a vineyard district of Castiglione Falletto located all on its own (it is not surrounded by any other vineyard district) in the southwestern corner of the commune.

In reality, Pugnane once extended into the territory of Monforte d'Alba too, making it an inter-communal vineyard area (see BUSSIA file). However, with the creation of the official names of the vineyard district names in 2010, the name Pugnane was limited to the part of that vineyard extension that fell within the Castiglione Falletto commune only, while the Monforte portion was included in the Bussia vineyard district. Pugnane was always one of my favorite sources for high-quality, very textural yet refined Barolos, and many great ones have been in fact made there over the years (Bruno Giacosa and Giuseppe Mascarello, for instance). Luigi Veronelli, the father of modern Italian wine writing, also believed that Barolos from Pugnane were top notch.

Pugnane's soil is mostly characterized by the typical Saint Agatha Marls formation, with plenty of clay-loam rich in iron and only small amounts of sand, but with a good level of limestone, explaining both the broad, tactile but vibrant mouthfeel of Pugnane's wines. However, the wines are always blessed with more than enough freshness, so that they are fairly lifted for wines of their size. In general, it is the Castiglione Falletto portion of the original Pugnane that is characterized by the fresher of the two mesoclimates. The Pugnane Barolos made with grapes from the Bussia subregion also have very good amounts of lift, but are more tactile, mouthfilling, rich and ripe than the Barolos from Castiglione Falletto's section of Pugnane. I think that Pugnane's Barolos benefit from extended cellaring, as in my experience they usually start to come into their own after eight years from the vintage, but I also think most end up being drunk well before their due-date, given the copious amounts of charm they are imbued with already at a young age.

Pugnane producers and the wines

Estates that farm the Pugnane of Castiglione Falletto, and therefore can label their Barolo with the Pugnane vineyard district name, include Mario Marengo (from La Morra), Cascina Pugnane/Fratelli Ghisolfi and Giancarlo Boasso. Just for some excitement, beware that there exists another estate (besides that of the Fratelli Ghisolfi) that is making Barolo that also has the word Pugnane in its name, but that has nothing to do with the Pugnane vineyard district: the Azienda Agricola Pugnane. In spite of its name, it does not bottle a Barolo Pugnane, but rather a Barolo Villero (yes, I know: never a dull moment, with Barolo). By contrast, the Fratelli Ghisolfi winery, also known as Cascina Pugnane, does bottle a Barolo Pugnane. The latter winery owns six hectares in Pugnane, of which 4.5 hectares are under vine. The winery, run by siblings Ivan and Enzo Ghisolfi, produces only a very limited number of Barolo Pugnane a year, as well as of a Barolo Bussia. At time of writing, I have had only a few vintages of these wines over the years and have not analyzed them as well or as deeply as I have most of the Barolos from the entire denomination, so I hesitate to dig deeper into what their benchmark characteristics and descriptors might be. Though to be clear, I quite like the Barolos of Pugnane.

Benchmark wineries/Reference point producers of Barolo Pugnane: Cascina Pugnane, Giancarlo Boasso.

RAVERA

Township	Novello (and 4% in Barolo)
Reference Map	See Maps of Barolo MGAs (Ch. 10) and See Map of Novello MGAs (Ch. 10)
Size (ha) (Tot / Barolo MGA)	124.95 / 38.47
Production 2021 (hl)	2,002.75 (of which 305.36 hl of Barolo Riserva *MGA* and 50.37 hl of Barolo *MGA* Vigna)
Altitude	300 – 480 meters a.s.l. roughly
Exposure	Predominantly east in the higher parts, from south to southeast on the better exposed parcels of Cascina Nuova, and between south and southwest in the parcels between Cascina Parusso and Bricco Pernice
N. Claimants MGA	30
Other grape varieties planted:	Barbera; Dolcetto; white varieties
Land Units	Land Unit of Novello for the southern plots bordering Cerviano-Merli and Panerole; Land Unit of La Morra for the remaining parts
Soil (stage):	Tortonian

Producers claiming the MGA

Marziano Abbona; Fratelli Abrigo; Giovanni Abrigo; Marinella Silvana Adriano; Broccardo; Giovanni Alessandria; Cagliero; Elvio Cogno; Luca Cogno; Roberto Cogno; Ambrogio Dogliani; Famiglia Anselma; G.D. Vajra; Gianni Germano; Mario Giribaldi; Giacomo Grimaldi; Marco Intelisano; La Bioca; Maria Marenco; Mauro Marengo; Vergilio Moscone; Domenico Musso; Paolo Scavino; Pio Cesare; Re'va; Sara Vezza; Sordo (Giovanni Sordo); Vietto; Villa Lanata; Vietti;

Wines

Marziano Abbona - Barolo Ravera; **Fratelli Abrigo** - Barolo Ravera; **Giovanni Abrigo** - Barolo Ravera; **Broccardo** - Barolo Ravera; **Cagliero** - Barolo Ravera; **Elvio Cogno** - Barolo Cascina Nuova, Barolo Ravera, Barolo Riserva Vigna Elena, Barolo Bricco Pernice; **G.D. Vajra** - Barolo Ravera; **Mario Giribaldi** - Barolo Ravera Riserva (*); **Giacomo**

Grimaldi - Barolo Ravera; **La Bioca** - Barolo Ravera; **Lo Zoccolaio** - Barolo Ravera (and Riserva); **Mauro Marengo** - Barolo Ravera; **Rèva** - Barolo Ravera; **Arnaldo Rivera** - Barolo Ravera; **Paolo Scavino** - Barolo Ravera; **Sordo** - Barolo Ravera; **Paola Sordo** - Barolo Ravera; **Vietti** - Barolo Ravera; **Vietto** - Barolo Ravera.

What the producers say

Cagliero: "This vineyard was added to our list of properties in 1938 and it has been vinified separately since always, bearing the name of the cru on the label".

Valter Fissore (Elvio Cogno): "The first production of our Ravera *cru* dates back to 1990. The Ravera *cru* has been always considered as a site of prestige and merit of Novello for its diversity of soil and for its topography that give unique wines of strong and distinct personalities. But the biggest quality of Ravera Barolos is their elegance, a result of the perfect interaction between clones and soil, splendid exposure of the vineyard and geographical layout (altitude, ventilated microclimate that gives natural protection again excessive humidity during harvest). The soil is mainly calcareous, which gives a pronounced mineral edge to the wine and guarantees an incredible longevity".

Aldo Vaira (Vajra): "It was in 2001 that we began renting this vineyard and we made our first Barolo labeled Ravera in 2010. Ravera is characterized for being a Barolo of extreme elegance".

Luca Currado (Vietti): "The acquisition of this vineyard dates back to 1995. Our plot in Ravera has a favorable southwestern exposure, blessed with a clay-limestone soil. Our Ravera has changed significantly since the first release. At the beginning, it was our modern interpretation and we realized that we needed to make some modifications accordingly. Today, ten years after the first experiment, we have changed to a more traditional style; our Ravera today is a very classic and traditional Barolo, robust in its tannic structure. It is noteworthy for its fresh and floral nose, which will evolve into spices and mint when time is given. Its elegant and savory, with decisive and fine tannins captured in its impressive structure and concentration"

Sordo: "Our vineyard in Ravera looks full south. We are very happy to have the opportunity to make a wine from this, the most famous vineyard site of Novello, that gives big wines of elegance"

Ian's assessment of the vineyard district, its wines and its potential

Ravera is an extremely large vineyard district of the Novello commune that is similarly named to a Ravera vineyard district of Monforte: in an effort to avoid confusion, the latter has been dubbed Ravera di Monforte. In fact, the Ravera vineyard district of Novello is not entirely "of Novello": about 4% of the vineyard district's territory actually spills over into the Barolo commune (and believe it or not, the two sections present noteworthy differences). So, by definition, Ravera ought to be considered as an intercommunal vineyard district (that is divided between two communes). In fact, it's good to know that some producers, such as Claudio Viberti of the Viberti estate in Vergne, go as far as speaking of a "Ravera di Barolo", but for all intents and purposes, given the extremely small size of the part of Ravera that is within the Barolo commune's territory, Ravera is generally viewed as a vineyard district of Novello.

From an aerial perspective, Ravera is surrounded to the north by the Barolo vineyard districts of Terlo and Rivassi; to the east by Barolo's Boschetti and Zoccolaio, as well as Monforte's San Giovanni; to the southeast by Panerole and to the south by Cerviano-Merli (both Novello vineyard districts); last but not least, to the west by Ciocchini-Loschetto and Corini-Pallaretta (also vineyard districts of Novello).

At close to 150 hectares, Ravera is a very large vineyard districts [for sake of comparison, remember that Burgundy's Valmur (in Chablis) and Griottes-Chambertin (in Côte de Nuits) are 13 hectares and 2.63 hectares large, respectively; and that even a relatively large Grand Cru such as Alsace's Schoenenbourg is still only 53.4 hectares]. What that really means is that Ravera cannot help but be characterized by a large diversity of soils, exposures, altitudes and topographies. Therefore, it follows that there can be noteworthy differences between Barolos carrying the Ravera name on the label (even when viticulture and winemaking are more or less the same). Clearly, not all Ravera's vast expanse of land will be ideally suited to growing Nebbiolo of the finest quality: at 124.95 hectares large, that would be just wishful thinking. In fact, less than half of the vineyard district's extension is even planted to Nebbiolo for Barolo production, and that does mean something. And so, knowing the exact boundaries of the vineyard district; recognizing a few landmarks within it; and being aware of where the location of the Nebbiolo vines of the estate's making a Barolo Ravera wine, will help you better understand the wine you are tasting.

For the most part, the Ravera area was formed during the Tortonian stage of the Miocene epoch, and its soil lithology is mostly Saint Agatha Fossil Marls of the laminated type; however, there are areas characterized also by Saint Agatha Marls Formation of the sandy type (which is the lithology that characterizes the small piece of Ravera that falls within the territory of the Barolo commune) and by the Diano Sandstone formation. As the latter gives much bigger, tougher wines than those born off Saint Agatha Marls Formation soils, and the two different types of Saint Agatha Marls lithology also give wines that are different, you understand that where the Nebbiolo vines grow in Ravera makes one heck of a difference. And that therefore, no, the vineyard is not all the same; and no, the wines are not all the same; and no, they are not all of the same quality. Just sayin'.

It follows that, as the lithology changes within Ravera's boundaries (and in truth, it does so throughout the whole Novello territory), some Ravera (and Novello) wines resemble those of La Morra, while many others have more in common with those of Monforte. As you move up Ravera's slope, there is an increase in the presence of Saint Agatha Marls of the sandy type and of Diano Sandstone. In other words, Ravera's soil is sandier higher up and richer in clay lower down, which means that the lower reaches are those with the better plasticity index (they hold on to water better). Which should also mean that, give or take, Ravera's wines are usually more perfumed and more lifted when made with grapes picked up high while they are usually darker-coloured and more structured when made with Nebbiolo grapes grown on the bottom sections of the vineyard district. Of course, it's never quite that cut and dried.

There are also other terroir factors at work in Ravera that have a bearing on what the Barolo Ravera you drink will taste like. For one, the western portion of the Ravera vineyard district is also relatively close to the Tanaro River valley (of Monchiero) while the eastern section is not; proximity to the Tanaro in this part of the commune's territory (and of the entire denomination) accounts for a gentler mesoclimate compared to other sections of Ravera as well as the rest of the Novello commune. Unfortunately, it also has a hand in the hail-related episodes Ravera is often subjected to. You might say what one hand gives, the other does take away.

Other important terroir-influencing factors to consider are altitude and exposure. The altitude at which the Nebbiolo vines are planted in Ravera ranges in general between 300 to 470 meters above sea level, and that is quite a climb; in the Barolo denomination, that difference in height has a huge influence on what finished wines will taste like. Furthermore, there are almost infinite nooks, crannies, and hillocks along that climb, and so vines in Ravera can face in almost every direction. And while most of the Nebbiolo in Ravera is southeast-facing, there are vines that face full south, southwest and west too. To give you a concrete example, Paolo Scavino's Nebbiolo in Ravera is planted at 430 meters above sea level facing east, while the Nebbiolo Cogno uses to make his Barolo Ravera is planted at 370 meters above sea level and faces south/southeast. Given those realities and some differing winemaking tweaks, the two wines cannot help but be different. It would be extremely strange if they weren't. Because independently of mildly different winemaking choices those two very fine estates might make, the differences in altitude and topography inevitably factor in the way their wines look, smell and taste.

After all that, you would not be wrong in saying that there are many different "Raveras" within Ravera. Breaking down this large vineyard district into different subregions is not just possible but, as always, a very good idea too, because the vineyard district's different sections will give different wines. And as you might have already read in other sections of this book, I believe this to be the best approach by which to understand the wines of each specific vineyard district (for example, see BUSSIA file; see also MOSCONI file). Clearly, knowing the lay of the land and geology of each specific subregion of the Ravera vineyard area will only be of help if you also know who grows his or her grapes where. That much recognized, Ravera is fairly complicated and for the most part, I still find it difficult to pinpoint the origin of the grapes within Ravera that are used to make the specific wines I am tasting blind. On this subject, in his excellent MGA books, Masnaghetti subdivides Ravera into four sectors, but honestly I have not yet grasped fully all the nuances of the district's topography, altitude and other terroir-related factors and how they might translate into the wines. In my view, there are two subregions of in Ravera that are most important and from where the best wines are made are: the amphitheater immediately below the Cascina Nuova (where the Cogno estate is located) that looks out towards the Cascina Pratorotondo; and the second is another amphitheater, facing south/southwest and that opens up just below the road that connects the Cascina Parusso to the Cascina Ravera. Importantly, the latter amphitheater is located in the area of Ravera that was historically known as Bricco Pernice, a name resurrected by Valter Fissore of Cogno when he launched his flagship Barolo Ravera wine called, appropriately enough, Bricco Pernice too. In my estimation, the other Ravera subregions worth considering, as far as I see them given that I find their Barolos to be different from those made in the other Ravera subregions, are the Terlo prolongation/Cascina Serra subregion and the Ravera di Barolo section (that part of ravera whoch falls within the territory of the Barolo commune). Clearly, there are also the Barolo Ravera wines made with grapes from the entire Ravera vineyard district: for example, Terre del Barolo farms vineyards that are found in more than one Ravera subregion.

Ravera producers and the wines

Cogno has long been the estate most identified with the Ravera vineyard district, if for no other reason that it was Elvio Cogno who brought it to everybody's attention. The family first bought the area around the Cascina Nuova, and later that of the Bricco Pernice, by most accounts the two best patches of vineyard land in all Ravera (and I think it's fair to say most everybody would add "… and of Novello too"). Importantly, the estate has chosen to highlight the different possibilities that the Ravera vineyard district offers by using a Burgundian approach to their Barolo Ravera wines. They have done so by subdividing their Ravera holdings so as to make three very different wines. These three wines are called Barolo Ravera, Barolo Ravera Bricco Pernice, and Barolo Ravera Riserva Vigna Elena. The Barolo Ravera is made with grapes from 60 and 70 years old Nebbiolo Lampia and 40 years old Nebbiolo Michet vines; the Barolo Bricco Pernice, first made in 2005, is 100% Lampia (with its smaller and thicker-skinned berries, it gives the estate's most tannic wines; which is curious, given it's Michet that usually has smaller berries and thicker skins); and last but not certainly not least given that for my money (and not just mine) it is the estate's best wine, the Barolo Ravera Riserva Vigna Elena, a 100% Nebbiolo Rosé first made in the 1997 vintage (the Nebbiolo Rosé clone CN 111 was planted in 1991: for the longest time, the Barolo Ravera Riserva Vigna Elena was the only Barolo made with 100% Nebbiolo Rosé). Fissore remembers that their goal was to make a Barolo with equal percentages of what were then mistakenly thought to be three Nebbiolo "clones" -Lampia, Michet, and Rosé- but the Nebbiolo Rosé delivered such a great wine all by itself that they decided to make a wine with it only (see chapter 3, NEBBIOLO ROSÉ). "The wine was so good it made it easy for us to decide what to do" smiles Fissore at the memories.

Of the three Cogno Barolos from Ravera, the Barolo Ravera is the most linear and straightforward: a generous mouthful of wine with lively tannins and good size. The Barolo Ravera Bricco Pernice is a masterpiece, a wine that meshes together a uniquely luscious mouthfeel (uniquely because it is also remarkably vibrant) and gobs of creamy fruit but with a solid backbone of polished tannins guaranteeing years of evolution. The Barolo Ravera Riserva Vigna Elena is the lone Riserva of the trio (that in itself tells you a little something about its extremely high-quality level but also about its intrinsic tannic structure) and is marked by the exceptional purity and translucency of the Nebbiolo Rosé cultivar offering its panoply of small red berries, sultry-sexy red cherries, and sweet spice notes, not to mention exceptional floral inner-mouth perfume. It's an amazing Barolo of which I recently wrote up the first ever exclusive vertical of (D'Agata, 2022) for the *TerroirSense Wine Review*; however, in many respects, the wine actually strikes me as an atypical expression of the Nebbiolo Rosé grape variety (see chapter. 3, NEBBIOLO ROSÉ). It is important to know all that, but it is just as important to know that while Cogno's Bricco Pernice Barolo is an example of a Ravera Barolo from the second subregion I mentioned previously (the one associated with the Cascina Parusso and the Cascina Ravera), the Barolo Riserva Vigna Elena is instead an example of a Ravera Barolo born in first subregion (the amphitheater below the Cascina Nuova; you can admire the Vigna Elena vineyard from one of the Cogno winery's balconies). Unfortunately, given that these two Barolos are made with slightly different Nebbiolo grapevines, inferring much about the Ravera subregions by comparing the two is impossible.

After reading the discussion about Cogno's three different Ravera Barolos, you might find yourself asking: but is there a Barolo that embodies or broadcasts what this vineyard district's characteristics are, as opposed to those of just one subregion? Yes, there is. I think that the Barolo Ravera of the Terre del Barolo cooperative is just such a wine: specifically, that of their Arnaldo Rivera lineup. The Arnaldo Rivera project by the Terre del Barolo cooperative boasts an impressive portfolio of Barolo vineyard district wines (Arnaldo Rivera is one of the more beloved figures in Barolo history, a longtime schoolteacher and mayor of Castiglione Falletto that everybody respected). The coop's Ravera holdings are about 3.8 hectares large and are dislocated throughout the vineyard district, in all four subregions of Ravera. These vines are roughly forty years old, planted in a relatively cool mesoclimate, on lighter-coloured, slightly siltier (with very little sand), thinner-layered Saint Agatha Fossil marls (almost 60% loam and around 28-30% clay). Though this soil type has low organic content and limits vigor, the clay-silt presence allows the vines to weather drought well by holding on to water and to release it back to the grapevine roots at opportune times, making these good Barolos to bet on in hotter, water-challenged vintages. Rivera's Ravera vines (no pun intended) lie on a 15% gradient and are south-facing, planted at 400 meters above sea level. The wine is an excellent example of the broad, youthfully chunky and tactile wine that typifies most Barolos from Ravera when young, but that invariably develop nuance and a refined quality with age.

You might already be aware that Abrigo is a very common last name in Barolo and Barbaresco, and so it won't surprise you then to know that there is an Abrigo making wine in Ravera too. Founded in 1968, the Giovanni Abrigo estate is located in Diano d'Alba (one of the eleven communes of the Barolo denomination) and has produced many excellent wines not just with Nebbiolo, but with Dolcetto and Barbera too. They began farming and making Barolo only as of 2013, when they took over a two hectares parcel of vines in Ravera previously tended to by Marziano Abbona (who made a Barolo there until the 2012 vintage). You know, I wasn't kidding before when I mentioned that Abrigo is a very common family name in the Barolo denomination: just so you know, and don't get (too) confused, another two hectares of Ravera vines located right next to those of Giovanni Abrigo are farmed by a very similarly named estate, Fratelli Abrigo (who, wouldn't you know it, also bottle their own Barolo Ravera wine, with which I have however very little experience). Apparently, the Fratelli Abrigo vines were rented out to them by the same owner that also rents out vines to Giovanni Abrigo (she did so after her husband passed away).

Giovanni Abrigo's Ravera Nebbiolo vines are located in the small subregion of Ravera that is essentially a prolongation of the Barolo commune's Terlo vineyard district. This is the subregion where the Mario Giribaldi and Mauro Marengo wineries also have their wines. What I can tell you is that this really is a different Ravera from the rest of the vineyard district. For example, it is an area marked by strong ventilation with very noteworthy diurnal temperature shifts. The area can be somewhat more prone to hail episodes (given its proximity to storm currents flowing in from the Tanaro River valley area) but at Giovanni Abrigo, they tell me that they have only suffered through one such episode over nine vintages, which is admittedly a pretty encouraging track record. But mostly, it's the soil in this section of Ravera that is different: mostly of Tortonian origin and mostly of Saint Agatha Marl of the laminated type lithology, its clay-rich soil has a bit more sand than in other parts of Ravera – to be precise, 45% loam, 30% clay and 25% sand- and so though it's a soil that still has good water retention capacity, it offers better drainage than that of other sections of Ravera. The higher proportion of sand, the higher altitude vines, and strong diurnal temperature shifts helps account for the general freshness and elegance of the Giovanni Abrigo Barolo Ravera wine compared to the Barolo Ravera wines made by other wineries.

If you like, you can reach Abrigo's vines by taking the Ravera Road that leads out from the cemetery in Novello (in the direction of Monforte) past the houses of Barolo; after the first two houses on the right there is a dirt road that leads to Abrigo's 1.98 hectares of Ravera subdivided in five different plots. Three of the plots are 35 years old vines and two are 25 years old, mostly southeast-facing, and all at more or less 400 meters above sea level (in other words, there is little geographical difference between the plots). The style of Abrigo's Barolo Ravera has changed slightly over the years, mostly the result of different oaking regimens employed. The first few vintages (2013 and 2014) were more heavily marked by notes of new oak (Garbellotto Slavonian oak 1000 liters barrels, plus 500 and 600 liters French oak tonneaux) because the winery's cellar at the time was quite small and did not allow for larger oak containers. That changed with the 2017 vintage when the estate enlarged its cellar facility by uniting adjoining buildings, and again in 2019 when they built an underground facility; this allowed the use of much larger 30 e 40 hectoliter Taransaud French oak barrels as well. The wines are fairly traditionally made, with grapes that are picked as late as possible to ensure full polyphenolic ripeness, and the use of *cappello sommerso*.

Mauro Marengo is another quality estate that farms Ravera; and at 2.5 hectares, a sizeable amount, in fact. The Nebbiolo was planted in 1997 and 2008 between 380 and 430 meters above sea level. Interestingly while the lithology in the higher portions is that of the Saint Agatha Fossil Marls of the sandy type, these give way to those of the laminated type lower down. Marengo's wines from this part of the Ravera are typically balsamic and fruity with very fine tannins, but I find have more weight on the palate than the majority of the wines of the communes of Barolo and La Morra (save for that section of La Morra close to Barolo -where Brunate and Cerequio are located- and that is characterized by a warmer mesoclimate). Another little-known but high-quality winery making good Barolo from Ravera is Mario Giribaldi, from two vineyard blocks (0.8 hectares of forty-seven years old vines and 0.5 hectares replanted in 2015) situated at about 360 meters in altitude. These two plots are right by their holdings in Novello's Cerviano-Merli vineyard district, separated from each other by a small road. The estate's winemaker, Matteo Giribaldi, told me that the soil composition in their part of Ravera is 52% loam, 21% clay and 27% sand. The Barolo is an especially pretty one, offering notes of red berries, nutmeg and grilled white pepper, with usually silky tannins providing support to the fresh fruit.

Many other famous estates are now farming Ravera and making Barolos bearing the vineyard district's name. Paolo Scavino farms 2.7 hectares of rather young vines planted between 1999 and 2012 situated at 430 meters above sea level and facing east; the wine is fresh yet very powerful, a combination (freshness and power) that is very much what you'd expect to find in most Barolos from Ravera. G.D. Vajra and Vietti are but two more of the big Barolo names that have bought vineyard land in Ravera. The former's vines are in the area below the Cascina Nuova (though their exposure is different than that of Cogno's); the latter's vines are in the Bricco Pernice area.

Last but not least, should you want to try a Barolo Ravera from the Barolo commune, go with the one made by Cagliero or Viberti. Viberti's vineyards are planted on a clay-rich soil that has a lithology of laminated Saint Agatha Fossil Marls. The wines are balanced and nicely textured. Claudio Viberti, who began sourcing grapes from a vineyard owned by the Cravero family in 2013, liked the grapes and wine so much he even made a Barolo Ravera Riserva, though he also used a part of the Ravera grapes for his classic blend Barolo Buon Padre. Unfortunately, the Giuseppe Rinaldi winery that also grows its Ravera Nebbiolo in the Barolo commune's territory, blends its grapes into their Tre Tine Barolo, made with grapes from three different vineyard districts. As good as the Tre Tine Barolo is, and it is very good, it does not allow us much insight into what differences there might be in Barolo Ravera wines made with Nebbiolo grown in the Barolo commune's portion of the Ravera vineyard district.

Benchmark wineries/Reference point producers of Barolo Ravera: a) <u>Ravera</u>: Arnaldo Rivera; b. <u>Ravera (Terlo prolongation subregion to Cascina Serra)</u>: Giovanni Abrigo, Mario Giribaldi, Mauro Marengo; c. <u>Ravera (Cascina Parusso to Cascina Ravera subregion)</u>: Cogno (Bricco Pernice), Vietti; d. <u>Ravera (Cascina Nuova to Cascina Pratorotondo subregion)</u>: Cascina del Monastero, (Cogno Riserva Vigna Elena: more so than a wine of Ravera, this Barolo is more about what Nebbiolo Rosé expresses from this subregion of Ravera); e. <u>Ravera (Barolo commune subregion)</u>: Cagliero, Viberti.

RAVERA DI MONFORTE

Township	Monforte d'Alba
Reference Map	See Map of Monforte d'Alba MGAs (Ch. 10)
Size (ha) (Tot / Barolo MGA)	36.63 / 6.35
Production 2021 (hl)	339.21 (of which 75.00 hl of Barolo Riserva *MGA*)
Altitude	330 – 430 meters a.s.l. roughly
Exposure	From east to south in the better exposed parcels, from northeast to northwest in the remaining parts
N. Claimants MGA	8
Other grape varieties planted:	Barbera; Dolcetto; white varieties
Land Units	Land Unit of Barolo
Soil (stage):	Tortonian and Serravallian

Producers claiming the MGA

Piero Benevelli; Cascina Chicco; Famiglia Anselma; Davide Marengo; Ferdinando Principiano; Giuseppe Principiano; Giovanni Rocca; Flavio Roddolo.

Wines

Piero Benevelli - Barolo Ravera di Monforte; **Ferdinando Principiano** - Barolo Ravera di Monforte; **Giovanni Rocca** - Barolo Ravera di Monforte; **Flavio Roddolo** - Barolo Ravera di Monforte

Ian's assessment of the vineyard district, its wines and its potential

Ravera di Monforte, so named to distinguish it from the now more famous Ravera of Novello, is in the southeastern corner of the Monforte commune. To the east, lies the territory of Serralunga; to its north and northwest lies Mosconi, while to the south and southwest there is the Le Coste di Monforte vineyard district. In fact, Ravera di Monforte is the continuation of the eastern half or arm of the Le Coste di Monforte vineyard district (a very complex vineyard area shaped like a "Y": see LE COSTE DI MONFORTE file) with which it shares a similar soil lithology, but is generally steeper. But like many other Barolo vineyard districts and especially so the very large ones of Monforte (Bussia, Mosconi, Castelletto...just take your pick), there are clearly identifiable subregions within Ravera di Monforte that have a basis in history, not to mention that each gives just as clearly identifiable wines.

The two subregions of Ravera di Monforte are the Ravera di Monforte-proper and Pilone (or, Ravera di Monforte-Pilone). To help you situate the two, just remember that both subregions drape over the two flanks of the ridge on which there is also one of the two "arms" of the Le Coste di Monforte vineyard district: Ravera di Monforte-proper follows right after Le Coste di Monforte and is more or less fully south-facing; in turn, Ravera di Monforte-Pilone follows Ravera di Monforte-proper, spreading out to the end of the ridge, is lower lying, and east to southeast facing.

Speaking generally, one could limit him or herself to saying that overall Ravera di Monforte is a vineyard district that gives gentler, softer Barolos than is the normal in the Monforte commune: and in fact Ravera di Monforte's soil (sample composition: loam (47%), sand (28%) and clay (25%) is similar to that of large swaths of the Barolo and La Morra communes (essentially, Saint Agatha Fossil Marls of the sandy type) but its altitude (on average, Ravera di Monforte has some of the highest-situated vines of all the Monforte territory) and orography are very different from those of the majority of Barolo's and La Morra's vineyard areas, such that the wines of the three are ultimately different too. In fact, differences in altitude and exposure are all important with the wines of Ravera di Monforte.

Historically, it was always felt that the best sections of this vineyard area are those looking full south, which are mostly those of the Ravera di Monforte-proper: in these cases, the Barolos have very good color, a real vertical personality with noteworthy acid spines, with lively but quite elegant tannins. Not unexpectedly, for the most part grapes sourced in this vineyard district's higher reaches give more mineral, lifted Barolos, while those from wines growing lower down are richer and rounder.

Ravera di Monforte producers and the wines

Numerous excellent wineries are making Barolos from Ravera di Monforte. As a guideline, those wineries that farm vines in the Ravera di Monforte proper are Giuseppe and Francesco Principiano, Ferdinando Principiano, Flavio Roddolo, Francone, and Vietti. By contrast those that own/farm only in Ravera di Monforte-Pilone are Cascina Chicco and Piero Benevelli. Giovanni Rocca owns almost all his vineyards in this subregion, but also has a small patch of vines in the Ravera di Monforte proper. Pecchennino has vines in both, situated at the extreme opposites of the vineyard district's extension.

The Giovanni Rocca estate makes a good Barolo Ravera di Monforte from vines planted in 1974 at 335 meters above sea level and facing southeast. Another dandy is the Ferdinando Principiano Barolo Ravera di Monforte, made from 1.4 hectares (of which 0.6 hectares were planted in 1934) situated at about 400 meters above sea level. His view is that the sandier soils present here make for more graceful, forward, open-knit Barolos than those one typically associates with the Monforte commune. Importantly, this is the vineyard where Principiano began his foray into natural viticulture (back in 2002) now part of the *Falci Prometheus* project in which vineyard are cropped between rows by hand with the use of a scythe (*falci*) in order to lessen biodiversity damage (besides clearly reducing pollution of all kinds). Massimo Benevelli, of the Piero Benevelli estate, fashions another knockout Barolo Ravera di Monforte from two hectares planted in 1960. The outstanding Francone winery from Neive in the Barbaresco area also owns vines in this vineyard district, in the Ravera di Monforte-proper area just before the start of the Pilone subregion, planted between 400-430 meters above sea level. Given their small extension of vines, they blend these grapes with those from their Bricco Chiesa holding in the La Morra commune. This is reasonable given that by so doing, he unites the roundness and softness of the Bricco Chiesa wine with the verticality and tighter tannic grain of the one from Ravera di Monforte, such that in the end, the sum is probably more than the individual parts.

When all is said and done, there's actually a lot to like in this vineyard district, perhaps also in relation to encroaching (read: already encroached) climate change. Frankly, Ravera di Monforte is one Barolo vineyard district worth getting to know, and that I think more will be heard from in the years to come.

Benchmark wineries/Reference point producers of Barolo Ravera di Monforte: a. Ravera di Monforte (whole area): Giovanni Rocca, Pecchennino; b. Ravera di Monforte-proper: Giuseppe and Francesco Principiano, Ferdinando Principiano, Flavio Roddolo, Vietti; c. Ravera di Monforte-Pilone: Cascina Chicco, Piero Benevelli.

RAVIOLE

Township	Grinzane Cavour
Reference Map	See Map of Grinzane Cavour MGAs (Ch. 10)
Size (ha) (Tot / Barolo MGA)	11.39 / 1.45
Production 2021 (hl)	78.68 (of which 24.28 hl of Barolo Riserva *MGA*)
Altitude	220 – 265 meters a.s.l. roughly
Exposure	Southeast and southwest in the better exposed parcels, and west in the remaining parts
N. Claimants MGA	3
Other grape varieties planted:	Barbera; Dolcetto
Land Units	Land Unit of Barolo
Soil (stage):	Tortonian

Producers claiming the MGA

Cascina Cappellano; Damilano; Eredi di Mario Scavino; La Carlina.

Wines

Cascina Cappellano - Barolo Raviole (and Riserva); **Damilano** - Barolo Raviole; **La Carlina** - Barolo Raviole.

Ian's assessment of the vineyard district, its wines and its potential

No, we are not talking about a plate of pasta (which, if anything, would be "raviolo" or "ravioli"). Raviole is a vineyard district of the commune of Grinzane Cavour: call me food-fixated or what, but from an aerial perspective, Raviole actually has the shape of a stylized *raviolo* too. This is because its half-moon-*raviolo* shaped vineyard extension can be divided in two sections, a smaller one that looks to Grinzane Cavour and a larger one that faces west and looks towards Gallo d'Alba. Both are planted to vineyards.

Like most everyone else finding Barolo Raviole wines has been hard to come by, so I am not a huge expert of Barolos from this vineyard district (while I can hold my own talking about and eating my way through plenty of *ravioli*!). Over the last forty or so years I have not tasted enough wines or microvinifications to say anything definitive relative to what Raviole's Barolos ought to be, or are, like. That much admitted, there are clues we can follow that might help us arrive at a possible conclusion relative to our noble pursuit of learning what the Raviole terroir and its wines might be/are all about. Listening to what the locals might have to say on the subject is also always a good idea, though unfortunately in this day and age dominated by financial considerations that has to be done attentively.

To get our sleuthing off on the right foot, we can start by saying that Raviole's landscape is that of the Land Unit of Barolo, which as you should all be aware by now, gives us an amazing amount of information. Second, Raviole is a vineyard district of Grinzane Cavour, and that too gives us a boatload of information given that the Barolos of this commune have many points in common. Third, we know that about 75% of Raviole is under vine and that about 90% of what is planted there is Nebbiolo. Clearly, locals think Raviole is a good site for grape-growing (otherwise nobody in his or her right mind would have proceeded to do so); furthermore, that Raviole allows Nebbiolo to grow well and make good wines with the grape. Perhaps not at the level of Barolo, but the fact it is used to bottle Langhe Nebbiolo is already a good sign (remember that sometimes producers choose to bottle a Langhe Nebbiolo instead of a Barolo not because the site is unable to deliver wine of real depth and complexity but just because the vines might be still too young to be used to make Barolo. Of course, they might also choose to do so because the site *really* cannot give Nebbiolo wines of any special quality or depth). Last but not least, exposures in most of the vineyard district are actually quite good, ranging from full south to southwest in what is essentially a cooler-climate area of the Barolo denomination, a reality compensated to a degree also by the lower-lying heights at which the vineyards are planted. So, there you go: I think there's plenty there by which to make an educated guess at what a Barolo from Raviole should look, smell and taste like. Clearly, if after all that and you end up being disappointed when tasting your Barolo Raviole because it's not ultra-dark, thick and mouthcoating, well, that's another story.

Raviole producers and the wines

The only Barolo Raviole wines with which I have had any experience with are those of Cascina Cappellano and Damilano, and found that both were very competently made. I've also had the 2016 Barolo Raviole from Veglio Luigi e Massimo, who farms organically, but at the present time, I really have not had enough of the Barolos from this vineyard district and these producers to say anything meaningful.

I will only add that the outstanding if very underrated Bruna Grimaldi estate includes grapes from this vineyard district in their classic estate Barolo di Grinzane Cavour (the commune where the winery is located, not to mention the birthplace of Bruna's father Giovanni). This lovely Barolo is a blend of grapes from their holdings in Raviole (0.84 hectares planted in 2000 at 280 meters above sea level in the larger and warmer section of the vineyard district that looks out to Gallo d'Alba) and Borzone. Clearly, this Barolo does not boast a vineyard district's name on its label; rather, it's called Camilla which is the historic name of the vineyard in Raviole but is also the name of one of the four farmhouses in the immediate area that used to belong to the Castello di Grinzane Cavour. It is a lovely Barolo, approachable and smooth, and showcases very good balance in most vintages. All that being so, I have no problem suggesting you look for it, for you won't be disappointed.

Benchmark wineries/Reference point producers of Barolo Raviole: Cascina Cappellano, Damilano.

RIVA ROCCA

Township	Verduno
Reference Map	See Map of Verduno MGAs (Ch. 10)
Size (ha) (Tot / Barolo MGA)	13.55 / 0.86
Production 2021 (hl)	46.53
Altitude	270 – 340 meters a.s.l. roughly
Exposure	From south to southeast, plus a small parcel facing northeast
N. Claimants MGA	2
Other grape varieties planted:	Barbera; Dolcetto; Pelaverga Piccolo
Land Units	Land Unit of La Morra
Soil (stage):	Messinian

Producers claiming the MGA

Claudio Alario, Villa Lanata.

Wines

Claudio Alario - Barolo Riva Rocca; **Reverdito** - Barolo Riva Rocca (*)

What the producers say

Claudio Alario: "Barolo Riva Rocca is a more feminine Barolo, which matures earlier in comparison to Sorano. We had the pleasure of acquiring this vineyard in 1995".

Michele Reverdito (Reverdito): "This vineyard was purchased in 2006. Riva Rocca is a *cru* that rewards us with harmonious wines, elegant and particularly perfumed, which is more known for its early-drinking nature than for its big structure".

Ian's assessment of the vineyard district, its wines and its potential

Riva Rocca is a vineyard district that lies on the immediate outskirts of the town of Verduno, where the hilly crest that divides the northern arm of the commune's territory into two sections turns towards south. It is one of Verduno's vineyard districts lying on the eastern flank of this crest, sandwiched in between the Boscatto and Massara vineyard districts. Its soil lithology is quite complex, with elements of the gypsiferous-sulfur formation of the Messinian stage intermixed with Saint Agatha Fossil Marls of the laminated type and even some marly type Cassano Spinola Formation. Perhaps thanks to this complexity and a generally sunnier and warmer exposure, especially in the portions of the vineyard district closer to the town of Verduno some Riva Rocca Barolos can be surprisingly textured. For the most part however, they strike me as being the lighter-styled, perfumed wines not unlike those of Boscatto but different from those of Monvigliero on the other flank of the same ridge and of the more southern Verduno vineyard districts like Neirane (especially in the latter's sections closest the La Morra commune. See NEIRANE file; and MONVIGLIERO file).

Riva Rocche producers and the wines

A number of quality-oriented producers are now making a Barolo Riva Rocca. Claudio Alario has been making it since the 1995 vintage from southeast-facing vines that are roughly thirty years old now. His winemaking style is such that the wine is balsamic and mouthcoating; I think it's an excellent wine but also that it showcases the winery's signature more so than that of the site. The just as excellent Barolo Riva Rocca from Michele Reverdito is also on the thicker side for what one normally expects from a Verduno Barolo. He made his Barolo Riva Rocca for the first time in 2010 (a very good but overrated Barolo vintage, it was still good way to launch things off) from east-facing vines planted at 270 meters above sea level. Yet another excellent wine, but not made entirely with Riva Rocca grapes is the estate Barolo made by the outstanding Fratelli Alessandria winery. For this they blend grapes from Riva Rocca with those of four other Verduno vineyard districts (Boscatto, Campasso, Pisapola and Rocche dell'Olmo are the other four).

Benchmark wineries/Reference point producers of Barolo Riva Rocca: Alario, Reverdito.

RIVASSI

Township	Barolo
Reference Map	See Map of Barolo MGAs (Ch. 10)
Size (ha) (Tot / Barolo MGA)	6.72 / 0.23
Production 2021 (hl)	12.51
Altitude	290 – 320 meters a.s.l. roughly
Exposure	From east to north east
N. Claimants MGA	1
Other grape varieties planted:	Barbera; Dolcetto; Ruchè
Land Units	Land Unit of La Morra
Soil (stage):	Tortonian

Producers claiming the MGA

Francesco Boschis.

Ian's assessment of the vineyard district, its wines and its potential

Located in the Barolo commune, due south of the town and the Le Coste vineyard district, Rivassi is sandwiched between Terlo (to its west), Ravera (to its south) and Boschetti (which lies to its east). In fact, a large chunk of Rivassi can be viewed as more or less a continuation of Le Coste, something that is especially evident when you look at Sandrone's vineyards there.

More than one producer has told me over the years that while they believe Rivassi to give potentially a very good Barolo, the main advantage it offers is that its grapes seem to improve blends to which they are added. This mostly by way of the highly perfumed and finely tannic wine that they say is typical of Rivassi's Barolo. In this light, the soil lithology of Saint Agatha Fossil Marls of the sandy type undoubtedly contributes. I really wouldn't know as I do not believe I have ever tasted a microvinification of Nebbiolo wine that was only from Rivassi, but memory fails me now. I might have in some cellar, but in a day and age when laptops did not exist yet, and therefore I cannot find any such record. For sure, there is nobody bottling a Barolo Rivassi at date of this writing.

Rivassi producers and the wines

If I have ever tried a Barolo Rivassi it was a very long time ago, and I have no recollection of it: for sure, I haven't tasted any in the last fifteen years or so. Sandrone chooses to grow Dolcetto in this vineyard district (keep in mind that, unlike it is with many other Barolo producers, the Dolcetto d'Alba is a very important wine for Sandrone, as he makes, and successfully sells, around 30,000 bottles a year of it. Scarzello owns vines in Rivassi and he blend those grapes with those from Sarmassa to make his Barolo del Comune di Barolo. Last but not least, I am hopeful that Loris Grasso of Cascina del Monastero will decide to bottle a Barolo Rivassi wine sometime in the near future. He is currently studying what the vineyard district can deliver (he has only been farming the site since 2021, so the jury's still out), but tells me he has been very impressed by his potential Barolo wine from there. I will be visiting Loris soon so as to be able to do the same. For, given his level of insight and skill, if he reputes Rivassi highly, well, that's good enough for me.

Benchmark wineries/Reference point producers of Barolo Rivassi: None currently available.

RIVE

Township	La Morra
Reference Map	See Map of La Morra MGAs (Ch. 10)
Size (ha) (Tot / Barolo MGA)	38.16 / 5.36
Production 2021 (hl)	287.35 (of which 36.23 hl of Barolo *MGA* Vigna)
Altitude	210 – 270 meters a.s.l. roughly
Exposure	South in the central parts, and southeast on the lateral parts.
N. Claimants MGA	2
Other grape varieties planted:	Barbera; Dolcetto
Land Units	Land Unit of Barolo for the most (the highest plots); Land Unit of Gallo d'Alba for the remaining parts (the lowest)
Soil (stage):	Tortonian

Producers claiming the MGA
Negretti; Luigi Oddero e Figli.
Wines
Negretti - Barolo Mirau; **Luigi Oddero e Figli** - Barolo Specola

Ian's assessment of the vineyard district, its wines and its potential

Rive is a vineyard district located in the Santa Maria fraction of La Morra, on the other side from Bettolotti and next to Bricco Chiesa. However, the soil of Rive is similar to that of the other two vineyard districts only in the higher reaches, otherwise it differs completely.

The landscape of Rive changes too, with the upper sections classified as a Land Unit of Barolo and the lower ones belonging to the Gallo Land Unit. The soil lithology in each section is also different, with the former characterized by the typical Saint Agatha Fossil Marls lithology, meaning more marl and less sand. By contrast, the middle part of the slope and lower reaches of the long Rive hill is essentially characterized by alluvial debris. In fact, while people, even those in the know, tend to think of the Santa Maria fraction of La Morra as having a mostly sandy soil, this is only partly true: the lower-lying sections (all those that slope down towards the plain) are actually very rich in marl, with round stones.

Beware that just the soil changes throughout Rive, its exposure does too: it is not only full south, as I have been told on more than one occasion by locals who should know. Rather, while the central part of the vineyard area is fully south-facing, the parts off to the sides look to the southeast. Producers growing grapes in Rive include Luigi Oddero, Negretti, Ciabot Berton, Eraldo Viberti and Osvaldo Viberti.

Rive producers and the wines

Luigi Oddero's classic estate Barolo is roughly 30% Rive, depending on the vintage (with other vineyard districts contributing including Castiglione Falletto's Scarrone (the part that as known as Rocche dei Rivera), Baudana and Broglio). As a note of interest, Rive is where you'll find the Specola tower, built by Luigi Parà: it is depicted on the Luigi Oddero estate's wine labels. In fact, the estate also makes a Barolo called Specola, from their Nebbiolo vineyard in Rive planted at about 230 meters above sea level and facing southeast (beware that the estate's website states the altitude of the vineyard to be 230 meters above sea level in one place of the website and 260 meters in another). The wine is apparently made entirely with Rive grapes but the estate has chosen not to bottle it with the vineyard district's name.

Ciabot Berton's classic estate Barolo is a blend of grapes from Rive, Roggeri and Bricco San Biagio. The founder of the estate, Giovenale, only owned vines in Bricco San Biagio; but then, after marrying Maria Beatrice Roggero he also ended up with vineyards in Roggeri and Rive as well. Just about any wine made by Ciabot Berton is always worthy of recommendation, so my advice is to go right ahead!

Benchmark wineries/Reference point producers of Barolo Rive: Luigi Oddero e Figli (Barolo Specola).

RIVETTE

Township	Serralunga d'Alba
Reference Map	See Map of Serralunga d'Alba MGAs (Ch. 10)
Size (ha) (Tot / Barolo MGA)	10.00
Production 2021 (hl)	0
Altitude	320 – 385 meters a.s.l. roughly
Exposure	Southwest, plus a small part facing west and northwest
N. Claimants MGA	0
Other grape varieties planted:	White varieties
Land Units	Land Unit of Serralunga d'Alba
Soil (stage):	Serravallian

Ian's assessment of the vineyard district, its wines and its potential

Rivette was once a very highly-regarded vineyard site of Serralunga, but you'd never know it as nobody is making Barolo from it today. And yet it is located favorably, immediately outside the western edge of town, just above the Marenca and next to the Damiano vineyard districts of Serralunga.

Rivette producers and the wines

A few estates have vines in Rivette: the best-known owner in Rivette is Gaja, but Massolino and Pira also own plots there. If you didn't know this was one of the Barolo sites owned by Gaja, I am sure you would realize it was just so the second your gaze were to fall on the slope: all the vines are planted in Gaja's trademark direction, that is vertical to the slope (*ritto chino* in Italian, and not *ritocchino* as is often written/reported), and not transversely across the slope as is usually done.

In masterclasses and wine courses all over the world, wine lovers and sommeliers have often asked me the reason why Gaja decided to plant white varieties there (in fact, less than 10% of all of Rivette is planted to Nebbiolo; Gaja owns 1.56 hectares there of Nebbiolo, planted in 1966). So why the white grapes? For one, Rivette is a generally high altitude and cool site, and white grapes do well there. Secondly, Gaja owned enough Nebbiolo vines at the time he bought the property, and was then looking for a spot to plant white grapes instead (at a time when Chardonnay and Sauvignon Blanc were real novelties in Italy and their wines all the rage: though it might seem strange today given the Burgundy-crazed world we live in, you need to know that only thirty-forty years ago people in Italy used to leave Puligny-Montrachet bottles on store shelves and hoard Gaja white wines instead). Therefore, his decision not to plant more Nebbiolo in Rivette was not necessarily a judgement on Rivette's potential quality as a source of Barolo wine. However, Gaja does have Nebbiolo in Rivette, and it would be surprising if it were otherwise given the exceptional quality of the site (Rivette was listed already at the time of Renato Ratti's *Carta del Barolo* as a first category quality site: in other words, one of the eleven that were reputed by him to be the best of the best). The soil composition is a mostly loam-clay mix with some sand. The clay is very reddish in colour and rich in minerals. Gaja's Nebbiolo vines are planted between 330-350 meters above sea level facing southwest. The combination of specific soil, altitude and old vines means that Gaja's Rivette grapes are characterized by thick-skins the grapes are usually the last of Gaja's Nebbiolo to be harvested. The Barolo wine from Rivette is not just powerful but elegant. For those who have never had the opportunity to verify it on their own, let me tell you that listening to Gaia Gaja talk about her vineyards and the Barolos (and Barbarescos) that are made with the grapes of each is an absolute joy. There lies a wealth of knowledge she is endowed with on the matter.

Benchmark wineries/Reference point producers of Barolo Rivette: None currently available.

ROCCHE DELL'ANNUNZIATA

Township	La Morra
Reference Map	See Map of La Morra MGAs (Ch. 10)
Size (ha) (Tot / Barolo MGA)	29.92 / 20.63
Production 2021 (hl)	1,043.40 (of which 93.00 hl of Barolo Riserva *MGA* and 15.50 hl of Barolo *MGA* Vigna)
Altitude	240 – 385 meters a.s.l. roughly
Exposure	Southeast in the highest part, and from south to southwest in the remaining part
N. Claimants MGA	18
Other grape varieties planted:	Barbera
Land Units	Land Unit of La Morra
Soil (stage):	Tortonian

Producers claiming the MGA

Lorenzo Accomasso; Cascina Rocca; Renato Corino; Erbaluna; Mario Gagliasso; Renato Molino; Andrea Oberto; Fabio Oberto; Carlo Revello; Francesco Rinaldi; Rocche Costamagna; Ratti; Paolo Scavino; Aurelio Settimo; Renato Tontine; Trediberri; Mauro Veglio; Roberto Voerzio.

Wines

Lorenzo Accomasso - Barolo Rocche (and Riserva), Barolo Rocchette (and Riserva), Barolo Le Mie Vigne (Elena); **Franco Molino (Cascina Rocca)** - Barolo Rocche dell'Annunziata (and Riserva); **Renato Corino** - Barolo Rocche dell'Annunziata (and Riserva); **Erbaluna** - Barolo Rocche dell'Annunziata; **Mario Gagliasso** - Barolo Rocche dell'Annunziata; **Renato Molino** - Barolo Rocche dell'Annunziata; **Andrea Oberto** - Barolo Rocche dell'Annunziata (Vigneto Rocche); **Fabio Oberto** - Barolo Rocche dell'Annunziata; **Ratti** - Barolo Rocche dell'Annunziata; **Fratelli Revello** - Barolo Rocche dell'Annunziata; **Rocche Costamagna** - Barolo Rocche dell'Annunziata; Barolo Bricco Francesco (Riserva); **Francesco Rinaldi** – Barolo Rocche dell'Annunziata; **Paolo Scavino** - Barolo Riserva Rocche dell'Annunziata; **Aurelio Settimo** - Barolo Rocche dell'Annunziata (and Riserva); **Trediberri** - Barolo Rocche dell'Annunziata; **Mauro Veglio** - Barolo Rocche dell'Annunziata; **Roberto Voerzio** - Barolo Rocche dell'Annunziata; **Arnaldo Rivera** - Barolo Rocche dell'Annunziata;

What the producers say

Renato Corino: "Our Rocche dell'Annunziata parcel is cultivated and vinified separately since 1990 and since 1995 also bottled on its own. Rocche dell'Annunziata is without a doubt a *cru* where the combination of a full south exposure with 50 years old vines (or older), gives a Barolo full complexity and power".

Enrica Scavino (Paolo Scavino): "We bought this parcel in 1990 and have since vinified it as Barolo Riserva Rocche dell'Annunziata. On the nose, it is a Barolo of remarkable elegance; whereas on the palate, it shows harmonious complexity – intense but extremely elegant too".

Nicola Oberto (Trediberri): "We have owned our plots in this vineyard since forever but only in 2010 we were able to vinify and bottle this *cru* on its own. Rocche dell'Annunziata is a Barolo characterized by a clean note of rose especially, and great complexity. It fares worse in hot years because the water-retaining capacity of its sandy soil is not exceptional".

Tiziana Settimo (Aurelio Settimo): "We have vinified this parcel since 1962 when our estate was founded. Rocche dell'Annunziata gives a Barolo ripe fruits and supple tannins, its elegance and balance. The major difficulty that we encounter with this wine is that sometimes we have to explain its pale color, which is instead very typical of the Nebbiolo grape, and especially so when cultivated on this *cru*".

Lorenzo Revello (Flli. Revello): "We bought this vineyard plot in 1995 and we began vinifying it on its own in 1996. This cru gives birth to elegant Barolo with a good structure".

Davide Voerzio (Voerzio Roberto): "This is the most elegant among our *cru* bottlings and 2000 was its first vintage. It doesn't have the power of Brunate and of the La Serra, but is blessed with a profound sweetness of fruit with fine and round tannins. It gives immediate pleasure with its drinkability. Rocche is characterized more by floral and fruity notes than by spicy ones – hints of red and citrus fruit".

Renato Ratti (Ratti): "The vineyard of Rocche dell'Annunziata is historically considered one of the most important of the Barolo area. The typical blue marl soil with some layers of sand gives an incredible elegance and deep and persistent bouquet of roses and licorice. It offers delicate and persistent aromas of licorice, rose and tobacco. Full flavored, warm and moderately tannic".

Alessandro Locatelli (Rocche Costamagna): "Our parcel slopes down from 347 m a.s.l. to 320 m a.s.l. with a southwest aspect and it's a single plot of 5.2 hectares cultivated with Nebbiolo which gives Barolo Rocche dell'Annunziata and only in great years and in small quantity, we make the Barolo Bricco Francesco. Its name celebrates Francesco Costamagna, the revered forefather of the current owners".

Ian's assessment of the vineyard district, its wines and its potential

I think Rocche dell'Annunziata is one of Barolo's best vineyard areas, a true *grand cru* if there ever was one. Where it might fall exactly in a hypothetical classification I don't know, so let's just say 'Top 10', and be done with it. I'm in good company too: among the locals, it has always been one of the most talked-about and sought-after pieces of vineyard land in all Barolo, right up there with say Cannubi Centrale and Rocche di Castiglione. That's not just hearsay or individual opinions, but a fact also borne out from the prices people are willing to pay to buy any amount of land there. Historically too, Rocche dell'Annunziata was all-important. It was once part of the vaster expanse of *Marcenascum*, a holding of the Benedictine abbey of S. Martino, the existence of which was documented back in 1194. Later, a venue that could well be today's Rocche dell'Annunziata and identified as "Rocha" was reportedly mentioned in a 1477 medieval local land registry document (I say "reportedly" because I haven't yet had the time to go see the document, but I will). What matters most to us wine lovers is how good Rocche dell'Annunziata's wines are: over the years, some of the greatest Barolos I have tasted have come from this vineyard.

Rocche dell'Annunziata is situated between the town of La Morra and its fraction Annunziata, surrounded by the vineyard districts of Rocchettevino, Boiolo, Torriglione, and Giachini. Blessed by a very favorable mesoclimate, with plenty of sunlight and protected from the wind, Rocche is one of the first places in La Morra where the winter snow melts first, always an important feature for those locals looking to buy grapes and wines. As we know, where the snow melts first has long been considered a distinguishing feature of Barolo's best and most famous vineyards; through its combination of exposure, topography, climate and soil Rocche dell'Annunziata gives some of Barolo's most complex wines. However, the Rocche dell'Annunziata of today is not all one and the same: despite some locals saying differently, it is not a homogenous site in terms of exposure, soil, or mesoclimate.

The Rocche dell'Annunziata vineyard district of today can be divided into at least two subregions. One part is lower down on the slope and faces southwest: this is the 'real' Rocche dell'Annunziata, or the Rocche dell'Annunziata-proper. The other part is higher up on the slope and stretches out towards La Morra; it has a variable but mostly southeast exposure. It was added on to the original expanse of vineyards at a later time so today's official MGA vineyard district is larger than the original Rocche was [Rocche dell'Annunziata was once simply called Rocche; then with the advent of the official MGA name designations it was reasonably lengthened so as to avoid confusion with Castiglione Falletto's own famous Rocche vineyard (and now called Rocche di Castiglione. See ROCCHE DI CASTIGLIONE file)]. These two sections of Rocche dell'Annunziata are neatly separated by the little street that forks off from the main La Morra-Annunziata road and takes you in the direction of the Torriglione hamlet. As you drive along on this road in the direction of Torriglione, the lower-lying section on your left is the real Rocche dell'Annunziata, while to your right is the upper part that spreads out towards La Morra and Boiolo and that was added on later. Over the years, Pietro Ratti, Tiziana Settimo, Renato Corino, Lorenzo Accomasso and many others have lamented to me in no uncertain terms that these are two very different parts to the Rocche dell'Annunziata of today. In the words of one famous producer "…Unfortunately, they have increased its size down towards the town (La Morra) but mercifully, only partially so; still though, it's a different site. It fails to express Rocche's magical perfume and has an east-south exposure while the true Rocche is southwest, with much redder soils".

In fact, the area above the road was once known not as Rocche dell'Annunziata but as Rocchette (in fact, it is so indicated in Renato Ratti's *Carta del Barolo*); and while perhaps not held to be as prized a vineyard land as the original Rocche dell'Annunziata, it was still very highly thought of and famous, boasting a very long history too. In fact, the area was viewed as distinct from Rocche dell'Annunziata already in the 1200s, when it was called La Rocchetta nelle Rocche. So, a "Rocchette" as such never really existed, or at least it didn't "officially" with that name; if anything, the area should have been referred to as "La Rocchetta". The reason why the name of "Rocchette" became increasingly used is that it was most likely an everyday way to reference it among locals and because Lorenzo Accomasso, one of La Morra's (and all of Barolo's) most respected and talented traditional winemakers liked to use the name "Rocchette" for his Barolo, and so labeled his wine. Where this becomes all very confusing, and somewhat surprising, is that by Accomasso's own admission his plots of vines were never a part of the real Rocchetta area but are actually in the Rocche dell'Annunziata-proper. He told me it was just that he liked the sound of the name "Rocchette" and chose to use that name to label his wine. And because of Accomasso's fame and his wine's renown, the habit of referring to a specific, small section of the Rocche dell'Annunziata-proper as "Rocchette" (essentially where Accomasso's plots of vines are) slowly took hold. So for example, when I visited at Renato Corino's winery, another very talented La Morra producer, and spoke with him about La Morra's terroir and its history, I remember he would also refer to the "Rocchette" as the qualitative heart of the "real" Rocche vineyard, meaning by that the "Rocchette" area that had so been renamed by Accomasso (Renato Corino's vines in Rocche dell'Annunziata are right next to Accomasso's). Accomasso's outstanding Barolo is justly famous and much sought by collectors and those in the know, but the historical Rocchette, or actually the Rocchetta area, was another one.

Not just the exposure and the altitude change within this vineyard district's boundaries: the soil changes too. The Rocche dell'Annunziata vineyard district is characterized by a soil that dates back to the Tortonian stage and it has a lithology of mostly Saint Agatha's Fossil Marls of the laminated type, transitioning in places to the sandy type. There also exist patches here and there of Diano Sandstone Formation, especially in the lower reaches of the vineyard district. To put it in somewhat simpler terms, Lorenzo Accomasso himself explained to me that in his views there are three different soils in the Rocche dell'Annunziata: a type that is very poor in nutrients; a type that has more clay; and a type with a higher sand content. One day while walking the vineyard with him, he actually showed me how easy it was to recognize which one of these soil-types we were standing on just by looking at the leaves of the vines in front of us. Clearly, in those areas where the soil is richer in clay there is generally better water retention, and so the leaves are rarely yellow or withered even in water-challenged summers; and for the most part, water retention is good in Rocche dell'Annunziata (this is one of the reasons locals believe this is one vineyard district the wines of which are especially worth looking for in hot, droughty vintages). However, it is not so cut and dried: while it is true that the historic parts of Rocche dell'Annunziata are characterized by good water retention, in areas within the vineyard district that have an increased soil sand presence water runoff can be a problem in hotter years. Much of these sandier areas aren't rich just in sand, but in stones too: in fact, it is because of the copious presence of stones in parts of the vineyard district that some locals strongly believe this is why the vineyard district was called Rocche in the first place (*rocche* as in "rocks"), though not everyone agrees. In any case, most Barolo producers will tell you that drought never poses much of a headache in Rocche.

Fact is, soil composition varies greatly throughout Rocche dell'Annunziata: as mentioned, the sections at higher altitudes have more loam, while silt and sand increase lower down. For example, Rocche dell'Annunziata soil samples from higher altitudes show a composition of loam (52%), sand (27%) and clay (21%); but moving towards the lower parts of the slope there is a noteworthy increase in silt and especially sand (with that percentage climbing up to 36%). In fact, some producers and locals in the know believe that those really low-lying portions of the vineyard district where the sand is much more abundant should not be a part of Rocche dell'Annunziata at all. Interestingly, during one of my interviews about twelve years ago, one very well-known producer summed up this view very neatly and succinctly "...that sandier section is a different area altogether, it should not be called Rocche dell'Annunziata because normally Rocche has no problems with drought, unlike Cannubi, for example". This recollection always brings a smile to my face: that "unlike Cannubi" thrown in there is a very La Morra-esque producer comment, and I could tell there was some measure of glee in uttering it.

You know, in ultimate analysis, all of the above wouldn't really matter and would be of little interest outside of soil and terroir geek communities if it weren't for the fact that Rocche dell'Annunziata's wines are just so darn good. It really is a unique terroir, one that gives very complete wines. The best wines from Rocche dell'Annunziata have a unique perfume, one of the most intensely floral of all Barolo, where the red rose notes really shine. According to Carlo Revello, it is what sets the wines of Rocche dell'Annunziata apart from those of all the other vineyard districts (not just of La Morra), and I'd say you'd be hard pressed to find a producer who disagrees with that view. But perfume isn't Rocche dell'Annunziata's only trump card: its wines also showcase a rich, textured, and complex mouthfeel with a very pure, precise and intense note of red fruit and licorice that are both beguiling and memorable. Revello goes one step further and readily admits that compared to other very high quality La Morra vineyard districts like for example Giachini and Conca, Rocche dell'Annunziata's wines are more powerful than the former and more elegant than the latter. He should know, given he farmed/s all three. Most people you'll talk to will also say that Rocche dell'Annunziata's wines are some of the most refined wines of all Barolo.

Below is a list of Barolo estates that farm/own vines in the Rocche dell'Annunziata vineyard district of today and where their vines are located within the vineyard district. As you can see, there are producers who tend to vines only in the upper part, those who make wine from grapes grown only in the lower (original) sections of the district, and those who have vines in both sections.

a. <u>Producers with plots in the lower (original) Rocche dell'Annunziata, or Rocche dell'Annunziata-proper</u>: Aurelio Settimo, Francesco Rinaldi, Franco Molino, Fratelli Revello, Gagliasso, Renato Corino, Renato Ratti, Roberto Voerzio, Trediberri.

b. <u>Producers with plots in the upper Rocche dell'Annunziata</u>: Andrea Oberto, Bartolo Mascarello (1.2 hectares), Erbaluna, Paolo Scavino, Rocche Costamagna, Terre del Barolo (Arnaldo Rivera), Veglio.

c. <u>Producers with plots in both the upper and lower Rocche dell'Annunziata</u>: Accomasso (whose lower section plots are in the specific subregion of Rocchette), Gagliasso, Roberto Voerzio.

Rocche dell'Annunziata producers and the wines

Clearly, the individual who has the most to say about Rocche dell'Annunziata is Piero Ratti, given that his estate has always been the one most associated with the site and his father Renato was one of the great old sages of Barolo (such as for example Aldo Conterno, Alfredo Currado, Bartolo Mascarello, Bruno Giacosa, Elvio Cogno, and Violante Sobrero) and also the first to really study the denomination's terroirs in modern times (see Chapter 8, BAROLO "CLASSICO" AND BAROLO SINGLE-DISTRICT WINES: THE IMPORTANCE OF SITE). According to Piero Ratti, a little bit of sand present throughout the whole of Rocche dell'Annunziata is what confers elegance to its wines, and Renato Corino agrees. For him, the sand accounts for the site's absolutely typical floral notes (in his opinion, iris even more so than rose), but also for the fact its wines are never too deeply coloured. The exceptionally fine tannins the Rocche dell'Annunziata Barolos are also known for maybe partly a consequence of both sand and silt, an analysis that many producers (Accomasso, Corino, Oberto, Revello, Settimo, others) I have talked to over the years agree with. Interestingly (interesting because he should know), Ratti also states that Rocche dell'Annunziata is a difficult "cru" but that "…when you finally understand it, you fall in love and you never let it go". Renato Corino says Rocche dell'Annunziata's wines are always quite closed when young and that they need time; Lorenzo Accomasso says the same thing ("…you need to give them at least ten years). Corino, and Ratti are blessed to be farming very old vines (Corino's plot was originally planted in 1954, Ratti was farming fifty to sixty years old vines already in 2008, but clearly, replantings due to necessary replacement of old and diseased vines and rental leases expiring take a toll on such numbers).

Another estate that is lucky to farm very old vines in the Rocche dell'Annunziata is Trediberri. Young Nicola Oberto is one of the brightest lights in all of Barolo, and I am proud to say that I was the first to bring him and his great wines to the attention of the English-language wine world when I was writing my *D'Agata&Comparini guide to Italy's Best Wines* in the first decade of the 2000s. He and his family are in fact the owners of three old vine parcels in the Rocche the grapes of which were long part of the blend of Renato and Piero Ratti's world-famous Barolo Rocche. Nicola Oberto's father was for years the cellarmaster at Renato Ratti: when young Nicola was ready to start concretely working in wine production, the desire to create their own estate and make their own wines led to the family reappropriating itself of the vines they owned in the Rocche dell'Annunziata. Normally, a famous and talented estate such as Ratti losing old vines is never good news for those who love wine, but Trediberri is an exceptionally talented outfit that makes remarkably good wines and so this return into the fold of the Oberto family vines was ultimately a good thing. Readers should be aware that, as not all three plots came back into the fold at the same time, the oaking regimen employed at Trediberri for their Barolo Rocche dell'Annunziata differed over the years. Simply put, up to 2013 the only small volumes of wine they could make (as the rest of their Rocche vines were still rented out to Ratti) required using smaller oak barrels (up until 2013, Trediberri vinified only 777 liters of Rocche dell'Annunziata wine). After 2013, the

Obertos were able to expand production volumes and moved to using large 20 to 25 hectoliter Slavonian oak barrels. Trediberri's three different plots are 1.3 hectares large and close to the winery stretching out from the road at the bottom of the valley leading toward Barolo at 242 meters above sea level to the road leading to Torriglione up at 270 meters. Some of the vines, planted in 1951 and 1961, are very old indeed; other more recent plantings took place in 1989 and 1999.

Another estate that has long been identified with the Rocche dell'Annunziata is the traditionally-minded Aurelio Settimo. Their first vineyards in the Rocche were planted in 1946, next to the Cascina San Martino, but the oldest vines today date back to 1961 (that's still pretty old, folks); their Rocche dell'Annunziata holdings are subdivided in eight plots averaging about 35 years of age (15-60 years of age). Settimo's wines are neither jammy nor needlessly powerful; very traditional, every sip takes you back to another place in time. A nice trip, I may add. Tiziana Settimo, who runs the winery now, famously even made a Barolo Rocche dell'Annunziata in the rain-plagued 2002 vintage (a little light perhaps, and it would have been very strange had it been otherwise; but not a bad wine at all, I may add). I remember other producers asking me when visiting them at their wineries to taste wines if the rumors of her making a '02 Rocche were true (in fact, many asked me the very same thing about Roberto Conterno when rumours were rampant he would make a 2002 Monfortino, and nobody could believe that either). Tiziana' s answer to as to "why?" she made a Rocche that year was disarmingly natural: "… because it comes from there: so why not call it by its name?" Settimo is lucky that she farms not just very old vines but that are planted on the original Rocche dell'Annunziata (just a bit lower down from Ratti's and Roberto Voerzio's plots). Last but not least, from the 1960s to 2006 Aurelio Settimo's wine label showed only the words "Barolo Rocche" (as was common at the time: Ratti's and everyone else's wines were also just called Rocche). Then in 2007, the name was changed over to "Rocche dell'Annunziata".

Mario Gagliasso is a high quality but little-known producer (little-known outside of immediate local circles, that is) also lucky to be farming the original Rocche dell'Annunziata site. I first interviewed Mario and his son Luca (now the winemaker) back in 2005, and again in 2007 and 2008: the estate owned vineyard plots in future vineyard districts of Novello, Monforte, and La Morra, but at the time were producing wine only from Torriglione and Rocche dell'Annunziata. Back then they also devoted a great deal of their time and energy to their excellent country bed and breakfast and restaurant. The Gagliasso estate started out as bottlers; in 1931 it was known as Michele Gagliasso e Figli, but since 1987 it was Mario Gagliasso. Today Luca Gagliasso watches over 0.9 hectares in Torriglione and 1.8 hectares in Rocche; they made their first Barolo Rocche dell'Annunziata in 1994. It's an estate that always believed in green harvesting a lot (leaving only rumors, 1-1.2 kilos per plant) which combined with Nebbiolo clones such as 142 and 71 (see chapter 1, NEBBIOLO LAMPIA, Clones And Biotypes subchapter), as well as newer clones derived from those two (all of which give amongst the beefier Barolos you will ever try) made for at times some overly big, top-heavy wines (this especially in the Barolos made from Torriglione, while for the most part the Rocche dell'Annunziata was more graceful). In any case, that tendency has been happily reined in and the wines worth seeking.

Fratelli Revello is another very fine wine estate the wines of which offer real insight into terroir: their large portfolio of single vineyard district-bottlings is a great way to understand La Morra's Annunziata subregion. Historically, their most important vineyard area was the Giachini (which they first released to the market in 1994): back then, their Rocche dell'Annunziata grapes all went into that bottling. This is not surprising given that the Giachini was always considered their most important wine and that they only had 0.2 hectares in Rocche to begin with. It was in 1996 that they released a Rocche bottling (Revello's Rocche holding was originally planted in 1954). Today the Revello brothers have split up (see GIACHINI file; see also ANNUNZIATA file). In the division, the Rocche dell'Annunziata site went to Carlo Revello; the Fratelli Revello estate rented a smaller parcel for a while, but as that rental agreement was not renewed, they no longer produce wine from this vineyard district. Speaking about very small vineyard plot ownerships, the outstanding Francesco Rinaldi of La Morra has owned its plots in the original Rocche dell'Annunziata since 1969, located at about 280 meters above sea level and planted with Nebbiolo from 1970 to 1983. Up until now and for the time being, they blend the grapes into their classic estate Barolo. Given how famous the Rocche dell'Annunziata vineyard district is, a much better businessman or simply someone less idealistic than I, might suggest to go ahead and bottle the wine on its own, even if in lilliputian volumes, and charge a fortune for it. As it turns out, the estate decided to go ahead and launch their own Barolo Rocche dell'Annunziata for the first time ever with the 2018 vintage. Commendably, they aren't charging a fortune for it

When it comes to Barolo and La Morra in particular, it is impossible not to speak of Accomasso. His Barolos were never, and are not, wines that those who unfailingly like and score highest the more chocolaty, richer and riper Barolos can like, the same people who often found flaws with Accomasso's wines where no flaws existed. For those who have never heard of him, or tasted his wines, I will just say that Accomasso's wines are cut of the same cloth as those of Bruno Giacosa, Renato Ratti, Elvio Cogno, Aldo and Giacomo Conterno, and Bartolo Mascarello. Deciding whether they are as good or not as the wines of all those gentlemen is not my point here: it's to highlight that his wines are bastions of traditionally made Barolos that speak of La Morra and the Rocche dell'Annunziata like few others do. And to think that Accomasso, not inclined to speaking in public and hardly a master of marketing and public relations, might have remained under the radar for who knows how long. A small producer who originally made wine just to serve in the family's La Morra restaurant, he was "discovered" internationally when importer Robert Chadderon began importing his wines into the USA. As mentioned previously, the largest part of his Nebbiolo Rocche holdings is in the subregion he called Rocchette but actually located in the original portion of Rocche or the Rocche dell'Annunziata-proper. Accomasso chose to use a different name by which to label his wine not just because he liked the sound of it, but also because he believes Rocche and Rocchette give different wines. In his view, the two areas are distinct and should be kept separate; for example, he points out that wines of Rocche are generally bigger and more textured than those of his Rocchette. Certainly, his wines are remarkably lifted and perfumed, very light on their feet, speak of flowers and high acid red fruit, lemon and orange peel and are about as far removed from thick mouthcoating brooding Barolo as you can imagine. How much of the differences that distinguish his Barolo Rocche dell'Annunziata from other Barolos also made with Rocche dell'Annunziata grapes are due to veritable differences in the various terroirs of the vineyard district and how much are due to different viticultural decisions and winemaking techniques is open to question. But for sure, it has always been my view that Accomasso's wines are masterpieces.

Benchmark wineries/Reference point producers of Barolo Rocche dell'Annunziata: <u>a. Rocche dell'Annunziata-proper</u>: Aurelio Settimo, Fratelli Revello, Renato Corino, Renato Ratti, Trediberri; b. <u>Rocche dell'Annunziata-above the road (Rocchette)</u>: Andrea Oberto, Paolo Scavino, Terre del Barolo (Arnaldo Rivera); c. <u>Rocche dell'Annunziata</u> (made with grapes from both sections of the district): Accomasso, Gagliasso, Roberto Voerzio.

ROCCHE DELL'OLMO

Township	Verduno
Reference Map	See Map of Verduno MGAs (Ch. 10)
Size (ha) (Tot / Barolo MGA)	36.88 / 3.29
Production 2021 (hl)	173.67
Altitude	310 – 405 meters a.s.l. roughly
Exposure	Prevalently east
N. Claimants MGA	3
Other grape varieties planted:	Barbera; Dolcetto; Pelaverga
Land Units	Land Unit of La Morra
Soil (stage):	Messinian

Producers claiming the MGA

Comm. GB Burlotto; Marchesi di Barolo; Villa Lanata.

Ian's assessment of the vineyard district, its wines and its potential

Rocche dell'Olmo is located in the far south-eastern corner of the Verduno township, on the border with the territory of La Morra. It is sandwiched between the Verduno vineyard districts of Boscatto (to its north and northeast) and Neirane (to its east), and La Morra's Castagni (which is directly south) and Silio (to its east).

Rocche dell'Olmo is a vineyard district characterized by mostly a Cassano Spinola Formation lithology (a sandy soil that is less rich in limestone than the Saint Agatha Fossil Marls of the laminated type that characterizes northern Verduno vineyard districts such as Monvigliero but that is also present in Rocche dell'Olmo). There are also pockets of the gypsiferous-sulfur formation that was formed in the Messinian stage. Those type of soils, plus the mostly eastern exposure and altitude (300-400 meters above sea level) contribute to the Barolos of Rocche dell'Olmo being amongst the freshest of the commune, boasting good energy and focus, with a very lively floral lift. Do not confuse Rocche dell'Olmo, the vineyard site with an inexpensive generic Barolo labeled "Rosa dell'Olmo" and sold in the past at Trader Joe's.

Rocche dell'Olmo producers and the wines

I don't know of anybody now making a Barolo with Nebbiolo wholly from this vineyard district, but many wineries (for example, G.B. Burlotto, I Brè, and Fratelli Alessandria) own vines there and use the grapes to make their classic estate Barolos. Interestingly, Fabio Alessandria of G.B. Burlotto has told me (and many other people too) that in the winery they refer to their wine from Rocche dell'Olmo as their "crazy horse", in reference to the fact it can perform unpredictably from year to year. G.B. Burlotto 's holdings of 1.25 hectares are very high up (360-70 meters above sea level) and classically east-facing. Even more interesting is that, in hot years like 2007, 2015, and 2017, winemaker Fabio Alessandria always invariably increases the percentage of Rocche dell'Olmo in the estate's Barolo Acclivi blend (which is the G.B. Burlotto Barolo meant to showcase what the "ideal" Barolo of the Monvigliero township is all about). In effect, just anybody you'll talk to who vinifies Nebbiolo grapes in this vineyard district will tell you that the wines are especially easy to like because of their lightness of being and freshness.

Benchmark wineries/Reference point producers of Barolo Rocche dell'Olmo: None currently available.

ROCCHE DI CASTIGLIONE

Township	Castiglione Falletto (and Monforte d'Alba)
Reference Map	See Map of Castiglione MGAs (Ch. 10)
Size (ha) (Tot / Barolo MGA)	14.36 + 1.97 / 7.67
Production 2021 (hl)	368.23
Altitude	300 - 350 meters a.s.l. roughly
Exposure	Prevalently southeast, east and south in the remaining parts
N. Claimants MGA	10
Other grape varieties planted:	Barbera; Dolcetto
Land Units	Land Unit of Castiglione
Soil (stage):	Tortonian

Producers claiming the MGA

Brovia; Cantina Terre Del Barolo; Ceretto; La Briacca (Vincenzo Asteggiano); Fratelli Monchiero; Poderi Oddero; Roagna (I Paglieri); Roccheviberti; Paolo Scavino; Giovanni Sordo; Vietti.

Wines

Brovia - Barolo Rocche di Castiglione; **Ceretto** - Barolo Rocche di Castiglione; **La Briacca** - Barolo Rocche di Castiglione; **Fratelli Monchiero** - Barolo Rocche (and Riserva); **Poderi Oddero** - Barolo Rocche di Castiglione; **Roccheviberti** - Barolo Rocche di Castiglione; **Roagna (I Paglieri)** - Barolo Rocche di Castiglione; **Sordo** - Barolo Rocche di Castiglione; **Paola Sordo** - Barolo Rocche di Castiglione; **Arnaldo Rivera** - Barolo Rocche di Castiglione; **Vietti** - Barolo Rocche di Castiglione; **Ca' Barun** – Barolo (*).

What the producers say

Mariacristina Oddero (Poderi Oddero): "Our family has been the proprietor of this vineyard since 1967. This vineyard has a southeastern exposure, often running into risks of summer rainstorms and hails. The soil is loose with shallow mother rock: nutrients-poor, we need to fertilize with organic matter every two years. The lack of water retention also creates potential water stress for the vines in hot years".

Alex Sanchez (Brovia): "Brovia family owns this vineyard since 1968. Rocche di Castiglione's Barolo is extremely refined and elegant, with intense but balanced aromas, expressing notes of violet, strawberry, cherry, dry prune, minty and licorice, with balsamic nuances. On the palate, the wine opens up gently, filling up the space with elegantly balanced flavor, finishing with a persistent length".

Claudio Viberti (Roccheviberti): "The land has been part of the family since 1958 but its wine wasn't introduced as a single-site bottling until 2003. The vinification (plus maceration) process can take 20 to 25 days. Then the wine is aged not only in 300-liter barrels but also 25 to 30 hectoliter oak casks – mostly French oak and to a lesser extent Slavonian oak. Exuberant perfume is what makes Rocche di Castiglione, which is also elegant, and balanced. In my experience, alcohol levels are never too high in this wine".

Luca Currado (Vietti): "It's part of the family estates since always. About three to five weeks of maceration is the norm and for aging, we use 225-liter barriques and 25, 33 and 44 hectoliter Austrian oak casks for thirty-one months. Rocche is finely textured, voluptuous and complete with intense aromas of dry rose, licorice, spices and truffles, which can evolve into leather and dry fruits. Assertive yet balanced tannins guarantee great aging potential".

Ian's assessment of the vineyard district, its wines and its potential

Rocche di Castiglione dukes it out with Monprivato and Villero as the best vineyard area of the Castiglione Falletto commune, but most locals and real experts I know would ultimately pick Rocche as the top dog in that fight. In fact, Rocche di Castiglione is unanimously held to be one of the top four or five Nebbiolo vineyard sites in all of Barolo, and many consider it the best one of all, period (See Appendix D, Tables 4.3 and 4.4 to see which Barolo vineyard districts producers like best). For sure, its grapes have been historically prized by the *negozianti*, who were willing to pay top dollar, er *lire*, for its grapes: and this despite the fact that the Rocche's grapes (for back then the area was simply known as Rocche: "Rocche di Castiglione" came into being only with the official launching of the MGA-names of the vineyard districts) were never the most packed with colour and sugar. In other words, despite the fact that Barolos made with the Rocche's grapes were neither the most deeply coloured nor particularly endowed with alcohol (both a major no-no for the *negozianti*, who paid by grape bunch weight and by potential alcohol level and used intensity of grape colour as a measure of grape ripeness), whatever Rocche grapes were available for sale usually got gobbled up immediately.

To give you another example of the high esteem that Rocche di Castiglione has always been held in, all you need to know is that while Beppe Colla is usually credited for having been the first person in Barolo-land to bottle a wine with a *cru*'s name on the label (he chose, not unreasonably, to do so with Bussia), it is generally accepted that the next person to do so in time (or at the same time) was Alfredo Currado of Vietti with his Barolo Rocche. That Currado chose Rocche for his *primera ves* is telling.

Rocche di Castiglione used to be called simply Rocche: but with the launching of the officially delimited and named vineyard districts of Barolo in 2010, the site's name was changed, and lengthened, in order to avoid confusion with La Morra's similarly famous and qualitative Rocche dell'Annunziata vineyard district. The Rocche di Castiglione vineyard district is a narrow piece of land that begins at the town of Castiglione Falletto, runs for about 1.5 kilometers along the border with Monforte's territory and ends up in Bussia (because two hectares of Rocche di Castiglione's 16.4 total hectares actually fall within the territory of Monforte, much like most of Brunate is in La Morra's territory but a small section of it is in the Barolo zone).

Today, the Castiglione Falletto vineyard districts of Scarrone and Pira are situated to the east of Rocche di Castiglione (and further east still there is Perno, in Monforte) while the Castiglione Falletto vineyard districts of Valentino, Bricco Rocche, Villero and Mariondino are located to the west of Rocche di Castiglione. In fact, just like it happened with Bussia, Cannubi, Rocche dell'Annunziata and all the more prestigious vineyard sites of Barolo (plus just about any site in Monforte), Rocche di Castiglione has been enlarged too, such that today's vineyard district does not correspond to Rocche di Castiglione's historical boundaries. For example, this vineyard district has been extended to the north and east, such that Rocche di Castiglione now touches the Pira and Scarrone vineyard districts, but that was never the case once. Rather, Rocche di Castiglione extended from a small section within Monforte (but stricter cartographers would insist from the border with Monforte only, and not from within it, no matter how small an area) up to where the road going from the town of Monforte to

Castiglione Falletto does a hairpin turn. Where the turn starts, that was no longer considered to be the "real" Rocche dell'Annunziata. In the tract of land in between the original Rocche di Castiglione, Pira to the east and Scarrone to the northeast, there was a small circular patch of vines known as Lipulot, the wines of which resemble those of Scarrone much more than those of Rocche di Castiglione (in fact, in the past what is Scarrone today never existed as such either: the whole southern half of what is called Scarrone today used to be known as Rocche Rivera, and you'll find many old vintages of Barolos bearing that name. See SCARRONE file. For more on Lipulot, see below).

I am not making these observations for the sake of making them or to show you how erudite I am in all matters of Barolo. There are reasons why such precision is not just justified but necessary. You see, old names and boundaries had a logic to them: in the case of Rocche di Castiglione, the reduced extension was in relation to the area's topography and its soil characteristics. More or less where the road does that hairpin turn, there is an evident change in the area's soil, because that is where the marl-dominated tract of Rocche di Castiglione ends: therefore, it made sense not to call the part lying beyond that point "Rocche" too. In fact, the area once known as Lipulot has not just a different soil but exposure too (compared to the "real" Rocche di Castiglione, the soil is a more compact brownish-yellowish Diano Sandstone Formation and the exposure is south, not southeast like Rocche di Castiglione's). Therefore, a logic existed behind the state of things as they used to be: then again, I also totally understand should anyone say that there is also plenty of logic in stretching boundaries every which way you can so as to cash in on a prestigious site's name in today's commercially-driven world, but we won't go there. Or maybe we already have.

It follows that to fully understand Rocche di Castiglione's wines it is also important to know this vineyard district's topographical reality. And that is that Rocche di Castiglione falls off, literally cliff-like, from the eastern flank of the crest that runs south from the town of Castiglione Falletto (by contrast, most of this commune's vineyard districts are located on the western side of this ridge). This explains the site's name of Rocche, which translates to "cliffs" in English; or, for the more literary-minded amongst my readers, a very Tennyson-like 'crags' (last I checked, no eagles though).

Hence, Rocche di Castiglione is characterized by a very, very steep slope that is still today one of the wilder parts of the Barolo denomination, with the forest dominating down low. The extremely steep slope ("the vines seem to be hanging on almost miraculously" says Marcello Ceretto) and mostly southeast orientation means plenty of sunlight and heat (this is one of the first sites in all Castiglione Falletto where budburst occurs in the spring), but it's mostly the gentler morning sun (*sorì del mattino*) allowing for more even, less extreme ripening conditions. The combination of Rocche di Castiglione's steep slope and its very loosely-packed soil and subsoil [thin topsoil with a mostly Diano Sandstone Formation lithology (large limestone rocks within a marl-loam sandstone base)] also offer excellent drainage. There is a high soil phosphorus content which ensures very good but slow ripening.

The thing that strikes you immediately about Rocche di Castiglione is just how light, fine-grained and white the soil is, especially in its central, and by most accounts, the best part. This soil has made Rocche di Castiglione famous, but in fact not all Rocche di Castiglione is characterized by it. The percentages of loam/clay/sand vary greatly within Rocche di Castiglione from north to south: generally speaking, sand dominates in the southernmost parts of the vineyard district as far down as right into the Monforte territory, while marl starts to become prevalent a bit to the north, more or less at the height where the border between Rocche di Castiglione and Villero begins.

Such changes in soil colour and texture are visible already to the naked eye; but if you're a numbers person, my data of the soil composition up and down the length of the vineyard district bear out this noteworthy variability of soil. For example, the loam/clay/sand percentages in the area where Ceretto is located (in the heart of the Rocche di Castiglione vineyard district) it's 20.5% loam, 59% clay and 20.5% sand; but at Poderi Oddero, whose parcel of Rocche di Castiglione vines is actually located deep in the Monforte territory, the percentages are 50% loam, 15% clay and 37.6% sand. Clearly, while Rocche is characterized by a white fine soil, its soil reality is very different from north to south so it is hard to generalize with just one soil description that's good for all of Rocche. Nevertheless, the site's fame is such that, like flies are attracted to honey, so are wine producers to Rocche di Castiglione: everybody and their sister would like to make wine there (whether they can afford any land there nowadays is another kettle of fish, er, bunch of grapes). Still, there are plenty of estates making a Barolo Rocche di Castiglione and so wine lovers are happily confronted with an embarrassment of riches.

The Monchiero estate (or more precisely, Monchiero Fratelli: here, once again, beware that Monchiero is an extremely common family name in the Barolo area, and that there are very many wine producers that go by that handle) is located in Monforte and owns south-facing Nebbiolo vines in both the central and more northern portion of the Rocche di Castiglione vineyard district in Lipulot. Vittorio Monchiero, not unreasonably, believes that this vineyard district delivers wines characterized by a remarkable tannic finesse, and it's impossible to argue with that assessment. In fact, Barolos from Rocche di Castiglione are generally deceptively easy to drink already when young, and despite being from the Castiglione Falletto territory (that, relative to tannic power and texture, gives wines that fall somewhere in between those of Barolo and those of Monforte), they can be enjoyed soon after release while also having the capacity to age, in good years, thirty years and more. Monchiero Barolo Rocche wines often have a stronger note of ripe plum and even prune that I find less evident in Barolo Rocche wines from other producers (perhaps brought forth by the Lipulot grapes), but they are very fine Barolos indeed.

On the same note, the Barolo Rocche di Castiglione of Roccheviberti (the estate farms forty years old vines growing at 300-350 meters above sea level) is often very dark in colour, an anomaly given what I know of the site and my experience drinking the wines. I guess every specific vineyard throws its hat into the ring in its own specific and unique way.

Rocche di Castiglione producers and the wines

Of course, one of the greatest of all Barolo Rocche di Castiglione wines is the one made by Vietti (beware that at Vietti they bottle not just a Barolo Rocche di Castiglione, made with grapes from this specific vineyard district, but also a similarly-named Barolo estate wine called Castiglione that is made with a blend of grapes from Novello, Barolo, Castiglione Falletto and Barolo communes, and not with grapes only from Castiglione Falletto and the Rocche di Castiglione). Vietti's vines in Rocche di Castiglione are some of the oldest ones around, planted in in the 1940s, 1950s, and 1960s. Of note, while most people believe that Vietti's best and most important Barolo is the Villero (they do so mostly on the basis that it is always released as a Riserva), Luca Currado is quick to point out that his Rocche is just as good and to his way of thinking, possibly the better of the two wines.

An exciting newcomer to the Rocche di Castiglione sweepstakes is the venerable house of Ceretto. The family owns 0.41 hectares at 300-350 meters above sea level, southeast facing of course, that were planted in 1991, right in the best, central part of the vineyard district. It was Gianluigi Marengo, who after having begun his training under the stewardship of Marcello Ceretto in 1987, was tasked with overseeing the planting of the 0.41 hectares (4,147 square meters, to be exact) of Rocche di Castiglione plot. Historically, they had always blended this plot's grapes into their classic estate Barolo, but recently decided to bottle it as a solo effort. As usual it is an exciting effort, as Ceretto is one of Italy's best wineries.

Back on the subject of Rocche di Castiglione's extended boundaries, two wines labeled Rocche di Castiglione and that you can easily taste today reflect different sections of this vineyard district. Poderi Oddero is a very famous Barolo estate of La Morra now brilliantly run by Mariacristina Oddero and her family. In 1967, they bought 0.63 hectares of vines planted at 325 meters above sea level in Rocche di Castiglione. It was Mariacristina's grandmother who encouraged her two sons, Giacomo (Mariacristina's dad) and his brother Luigi to go and buy the plot in Rocche di Castiglione: her father remembers vividly still today how she pushed them to "look outside of their friendly confines in order to grow". In fact, being the family's first ever acquisition outside the communal boundaries of La Morra is not the only "first" that Rocche di Castiglione boasts: curiously, for a family and an estate so intimately linked to La Morra, Rocche di Castiglione was also, with the 1982 vintage, the very first Barolo they bottled under a vineyard site name (which is a clearcut example of just how famous and reputed this vineyard district's wines were, and are). The most interesting thing about Poderi Oddero's parcel of Rocche di Castiglione vines is that they are located in that small sliver of the vineyard district that is located within Monforte, but soil-wise it is certainly very much like the best part of Rocche. The heart of the vineyard is very old, with most vines being easily about seventy years old; the vines face east, all the vineyard work is done by hand (the vines were planted at a time when the rows were spaced tightly together so machinery is not usable, and the estate avoids topping anyways).

The Roagna estate needs no introduction, as it is one of Barbaresco (and Barolo's) most famous. Now guided by the brilliant and extremely talented Luca Roagna, the winery has made a plethora of remarkable wines over the last decade (those made by Luca's father were also amongst the best too) and like the energizer bunny, the estate just keeps on going and going. The latest great wine to come out of the winery is the new Barolo Rocche di Castiglione. Made for the first time in the 2016 vintage, it is in fact made with 100% Lipulot grapes, the only such Barolo made today. Roagna owns 0.49 hectares of fifty years old vines there that face full south (typical of Lipulot: as mentioned above, though included in the Rocche di Castiglione vineyard district, this specific vineyard area has a completely different exposure and soil type compared to the historical extension of Rocche di Castiglione). The wine is gorgeous, light and layered, but with more of a Scarrone-like quality to it than a Rocche di Castiglione-somewhereness (by that I mean it lacks the almost aerial levity of Rocche wines from the sandier portions of the site but rather showcases the richer, more compellingly sweet and suave personality of the better Scarrone wines). Released for the first time in 2016, this wine may well become a Vecchie Viti bottling one day.

Last but certainly not least, a wine that is no longer made but that is on the one hand absolutely excellent (if you can find old bottles lying around) and on the other hand also very important in my personal growth as a wine expert, is the Barolo Rocche di Castiglione Falletto made for a while by Bruno Giacosa. To the best of my knowledge, Giacosa only made this wine in the 1970s and early 1980s. It was an excellent wine ("born balanced", I remember thinking when drinking it) with an admirable depth of luscious red fruit, a hint of tobacco in the background and a good deal of complexity (always the hallmark of a true *grand cru*, which Rocche di Castiglione undoubtedly is) beneath its deceptively easy to drink charm. Giacosa didn't own any grapevines at the time but just sourced the fruit he liked best and made wine accordingly. From exactly whom he bought the grapes with which he made his Barolo Rocche di Castiglione Falletto (that's what he called the wine) is not known. I do know some of his Castiglione Falletto grape sources, as Giacosa also made classic estate Barolo, there is no way of knowing if the grapes from where I know he did buy in the commune ended up in the Rocche di Castiglione Falletto bottling or rather in the estate Barolo blend. Thus, despite there being some hypotheses flying about that you will hear of when visiting the area, I am afraid that this is one secret the *Maestro* has taken with him. Interestingly, as good as Bruno Giacosa's Barolo Rocche di Castiglione Falletto wines were, and believe me, they really were (and still are) immensely good, the *Maestro* himself must not have been as convinced, because he never used his (various?) source/sources of Rocche grapes to make a Barolo Riserva, or red label wine. That Giacosa practically never did so tells us clearly he did not think the wines had either the stuffing (the pedigree, really) to hold up to prolonged oak aging or the complexity and depth to merit his coveted red label. Whatever the reason was, he mostly made white label wines there: would he have made red label wines had he sourced his grapes from somewhere else in the Rocche? I don't know. But even though the question lingers, I point out the white label Giacosa Rocche di Castiglione Barolos were, and are, just amazing wines. I only wish I had more bottles of them in my cellar.

In ultimate analysis, it's objectively very hard to find a "bad" Rocche di Castiglione Barolo: most are exceptionally good wines. The best are Barolos of a balance unlike that of any other, wines that combine an enchanting levity, an elegant gracefulness, and sneaky levels of concentration and power. It's a combination that makes these wines really stand out amongst all other Barolos, and once you have tasted enough you begin to recognize them in blind tastings fairly easily (admittedly, it's easier to do with older vintages). Add that these are very perfumed Barolos of utmost precision, and that they are remarkably forward and ready to drink early on (completely different from the Barolos of Villero, for example, that can be almost brutally powerful and that require much more time to be optimally drinkable) and you understand why the Barolos of Rocche are and were so highly thought of.

At this point of our Rocche di Castiglione story, it seems only fitting I leave you with a more personal "Rocche" story. I remember very well how during my university days in Rome I regularly sought out Barolo Rocche wines because I knew they'd always be a sure bet. Tellingly, I did not do so for other Barolo vineyard sites, such as Brunate and Cannubi, and that in and of itself does tell me something. Remember that at the time I was a student, which essentially translates to "someone with (more or less) limited financial resources". But Rocche's wines appealed to me for their compelling sweetness, power, early accessibility and refinement. At least compared to other Barolos that though good and at times very good, lacked that amazingly suave personality. It helped that one of my favorite Rome wine shops still had, in the 1980s, quite a few bottles of the

Bruno Giacosa 1978 Barolo Rocche di Castiglione Falletto. Those wines were my companions when I was moving my first steps in the wine field, and thanks to that lovely *enoteca* (that I still frequent every time I get back to the Eternal City), I was able to hone my palate on this and other wines from the *maestro* for many years at exceptionally reasonable prices. But the funny part of this story is that back then nobody in Italy was really buying much Barolo; it had been relegated to mostly a Christmas gift or wine for drinking only in special occasions. And even fewer people knew anything about Barolo vineyard site quality. I think I ended up buying every bottle of that Giacosa Rocche wine the store had. Finally, one day, upon my arriving at the cash register with yet another one of those bottles in tow and ready to pay, the *enoteca*'s owner, curious that a teenager (I was nineteen or twenty years old at the time, a period that in pediatric medical terms corresponds to the "third or late teenager" stage) was always coming in not just to drink wine but also always getting the same exact wine, asked me why it was that I kept buying that same wine (and vintage) and wasn't trying something else. He asked me what was so special about it. My erudite and highly qualified answer was "…because I like it". Clearly, that medical student-caterpillar of yesterday had not yet turned into the wine writer-butterfly of today.

Benchmark wineries/Reference point producers of Barolo Rocche di Castiglione: a. Rocche di Castiglione: Brovia, Paolo Scavino, Vietti; b. Rocche di Castiglione-Lipulot: Roagna; c. Rocche di Castiglione-Monforte: Poderi Oddero.

ROCCHETTEVINO

Township	La Morra
Reference Map	See Map of La Morra MGAs (Ch. 10)
Size (ha) (Tot / Barolo MGA)	34.98 / 3.18
Production 2021 (hl)	173.01 (of which 99.99 hl of Barolo Riserva *MGA*)
Altitude	280 - 440 meters a.s.l. roughly
Exposure	Prevalently east, and northeast in the lowest section
N. Claimants MGA	5
Other grape varieties planted:	Barbera; Dolcetto
Land Units	Land Unit of La Morra
Soil (stage):	Tortonian

Producers claiming the MGA

Gianfranco Bovio; Giancarlo Marengo; Marco Oberto; Gianni Ramello; San Biagio.

Wines

Gianfranco Bovio - Barolo Rocchettevino; **Ciabot Berton (Marco Oberto)** - Barolo Rocchettevino; **Gianni Ramello** - Barolo Rocchettevino; **San Biagio** - Barolo Rocchettevino; **Eraldo Viberti** - Barolo Rocchettevino

What the producers say

Giovanni Ramello (Gianni Ramello): "Our family acquired this vineyard in 1960 plus another parcel in 2006. For a long time, we were the only proprietor of this *cru*, and we have always bottled it separately. This Barolo is characterized mainly by notes of dog rose and vanilla in the first few years that tend to evolve into spices, leather and licorice with age".

Marco Oberto (Ciabot Berton): "Rocchettevino has been part of the family estate since the middle of the '90s and it has been vinified and bottled separately since 2008. The Rocchettevino gives a Barolo scented with spices and flowers, accompanied by soft fruity notes. The palate is clean and complex with a balanced body and acidity in perfect harmony with the classic tannins of Nebbiolo".

Ian's assessment of the vineyard district, its wines and its potential

　　Rocchettevino may seem like a strange name at first (given that there already existed unrelated Rocchette and Rocchetta areas in the La Morra area) but in fact the name of Rocchettevino is both a long established one and one of considerable prestige. Already in 1477, the vineyards of "Ronchetovinum" were listed in local land registry documents as belonging to one of the top production areas of the La Morra zone. You will find Rocchettevino in the Annunziata area of La Morra, where it is surrounded by many different La Morra vineyard districts: Capalot, Santa Maria, and Roggeri are to its north, while Boiolo and Rocche dell'Annunziata are south of it. The smaller Arborina vineyard district is to the east.

Rocchettevino is a very easy vineyard district to see: while driving on the road that takes you from La Morra to Annunziata (in the direction of Castiglione Falletto and Barolo lower down), it's the vineyard area to your left (clearly indicated by many winery signs stating that specific part of the vineyard belongs to them), though where the road does a quick series of some really tight hairpin turns you have Rocchettevino to your right too. The first section of Rocchettevino, the one that you first encounter on the road leaving La Morra on the way to Annunziata on your left, is referred to by same locals as La Pria (but La Pria is more correctly viewed as the southern prolongation of the Capalot vineyard district; the first section of Rocchettevino is the mere prolongation of La Pria southwards). In effect, just like with for example Cannubi, Rocche dell'Annunziata and Rocche di Castiglione, Rocchettevino also has an historic area that we can call Rocchettevino, and it is that section of the vineyard district that begins right after, or if you prefer below, the road that veers left off the main La Morra-Annunziata Road in the direction of the fraction of Santa Maria. But while differentiating between the various parts of the Rocche dell'Annunziata and Rocche di Castiglione is a good idea for the wines from each could not be any more different, I'm not sure the same is true of Rocchettevino. Maybe it's just me, but I don't find noteworthy differences in the Barolo Rocchettevino wines from the two portions of this vineyard district. For example, if I compare Bovio's version to that of Ciabot Berton in the same vintage (and I have done so numerous, and I mean really numerous times over the years in an effort to see if I could identify similarities and differences both in blinded and non-blinded fashion) I really don't come away with any definitive impression one way or another. I think the Rocchettevino Barolos from the two segments are really quite similar; and while the altitude range is noteworthy, lithology and exposure differences aren't. By the way, this vineyard district has always been especially famous not just for Nebbiolo and Barolo, but for its Dolcetto. For example, Lorenzo Accomasso as always made a very good Dolcetto from Rocchettevino.

Comparing Rocchettevino to one of its neighboring vineyard districts such as Roggeri offers a really good lesson in terroir. Roggeri is very clay-rich and its Barolos are some of the darkest wines of the entire denomination (see ROGGERI file). By contrast, the Barolo of Rocchettevino is more classic, pale red in color (a very pretty crimson ruby-red, I may add), notably more floral and spicier, and generally characterized by tougher tannins that need longer oak aging to refine and smoothen.

On a side but important note, one thing you also really need to know is that the Rocchettevino is not far away from the outstanding Bovio restaurant, where you owe it to yourself to stop and have lunch (or many lunches, if you really know how to live). Bovio is himself an outstanding producer of Barolo Rocchettevino (see below).

Rocchettevino producers and the wines

Barolo experts and insiders are very aware that the Barolos of Rocchettevino are examples of good-buy wines that punch well above their weight class. You too need to know about them. Neither the site nor the wineries are the sexiest around and so both fly under the radar, but good wine isn't about being hip or looking hip for the sake of others. One of the very best, I dare say emblematic, producers of Barolo from Rocchettevino is Ciabot Berton, run by the sibling team of Marco and Paolo Oberto. They first made a Barolo Rocchettevino with the 2018 vintage; prior to their making a Barolo from there, the site was planted to Arneis (which they used to sell to Cordero di Montezemolo) but they uprooted it in the 2000s. It follows that the Nebbiolo vines are now slightly more than fifteen years old, planted at 350-450 meters above sea level. Clearly, Ciabot Berton's vines are in the highest section of Rocchettevino where Nebbiolo did not ripen well before the arrival of climate change (and that's why -partly- the area was famous for its Dolcetto, which wants relatively cool climates to deliver its almost magical perfume). It should interest you to know that Marco Oberto wrote his wine school/oenology degree thesis on the three Nebbiolo clones he planted there and the wines each gave.

Eraldo Viberti makes a little less than 3000 bottles of an excellent Barolo Rocchettevino from 0.8 hectares of by now almost twenty years old vines planted at about 350 meters above sea level, with what looks to me a mostly southeast exposure (though I am told the vines also face south: what can I tell you). Gianni Ramello first made his Barolo Rocchettevino in 2000: another small-batch wine, it's certainly worth looking for. A slightly larger-scaled Barolo Rocchettevino is that by the San Biagio winery, made from vines planted in 1997 slightly lower down in the vineyard district, at 300 meters above sea level. Gianfranco Bovio made a wonderful wine from this vineyard district, that, for sheer value, was hard to beat: fresh, savory and marked by a vibrant note of violet. His legacy is being continued both at the restaurant and in the winery by his daughter Alessandra and her husband Marco. Their Barolo Rocchettevino is never a behemoth, but rather graceful and accessible already in its youth, while delivering sneaky levels of concentration and complexity. It really is an excellent restaurant wine, where often you only have young vintages to choose from. Allow me to say that the Bovio Barolo Rocchettevino offers plenty of immediate appeal and refinement, just like Gianfranco did.

The famous Vietti winery also owns vineyards in Rocchettevino, and blends grapes from this vineyard district with those from Le Coste di Monforte, Mosconi, Ravera, Scarrone, Teodoro and Fiasco to make the classic estate Barolo Castiglione. Rocchettevino's contribution to the blend is mostly a nice perfumed lift.

Benchmark wineries/Reference point producers of Barolo Rocchettevino: Bovio, Ciabot Berton, Eraldo Viberti.

RODASCA

Township	Verduno	
Reference Map	See Map of Verduno MGAs (Ch. 10)	
Size (ha) (Tot / Barolo MGA)	6.41	
Production 2021 (hl)		
Altitude	200 - 270 meters a.s.l. roughly	
Exposure	From north to northwest	
N. Claimants MGA	0	
Other grape varieties planted:	Barbera; Dolcetto; Pelaverga Piccolo	
Land Units	Land Unit of La Morra	
Soil (stage):	Tortonian	

Wines

Antonio Brero - Barolo Rodasca.

Ian's assessment of the vineyard district, its wines and its potential

Rodasca is the northernmost vineyard district of the Verduno township, making it one of the (if not the) Barolo's denominations vineyard districts situated farthest north. My insistence on the word "north" is not by accident, given that there's a lot of "north" about Rodasca: in fact, this vineyard area's exposure is also mostly north. The only producer I know currently vinifying Rodasca Nebbiolo grapes is Antonio Brero, but as he only makes about 100 bottles a year it's not exactly the easiest wine for you to find and try (do not confuse this *Signor* Brero with another, Corrado Brero of the I Brè winery).

Benchmark wineries/Reference point producers of Barolo Rodasca: Antonio Brero.

ROERE DI SANTA MARIA

Township	La Morra
Reference Map	See Map of La Morra MGAs (Ch. 10)
Size (ha) (Tot / Barolo MGA)	35.41 / 0.64
Production 2021 (hl)	34.82
Altitude	205 - 270 meters a.s.l. roughly
Exposure	From south to southeast
N. Claimants MGA	1
Other grape varieties planted:	Barbera; Dolcetto
Land Units	Land Unit of Barolo
Soil (stage):	Tortonian

Producers claiming the MGA

Fratelli Monchiero.

Wines

Fratelli Monchiero - Barolo Roere di Santa Maria

What the producers say

Fratelli Monchiero: "From vineyards in La Morra, a very balanced but surprisingly powerful Barolo, thanks to soils that are reminiscent of those we farm in Castiglione Falletto".

Ian's assessment of the vineyard district, its wines and its potential

Santa Maria is a small fraction of La Morra characterized by a very unique type of Barolo quite unlike that made anywhere else in the commune (or the denomination, for that matter). Even better, it's an area the somewhereness of which is recognizable across wines made by different producers. It is situated in the northernmost section of the La Morra township, in between the Silio and Ciocchini vineyard districts of La Morra that close it off at the sides and across from the Verduno vineyard districts of Breri, Massara and Boscatto. Its soil is made up of the Saint Agatha Fossil Marls Formation of the laminated type which, along with a relatively low-lying altitude and mostly south/southwest exposure gives wines than on the one hand offer early appeal and relatively softer tannins, on the other are bigger in structure than one might expect from this neck of the La Morra woods.

Roere di Santa Maria producers and the wines

The only Barolo I know that is made wholly from this vineyard district is Fratelli Monchiero's Barolo Roere di Santa Maria. The Monchiero siblings, Remo and Maggiorino, began producing wines under their own label in the 1950s from their winery in Castiglione Falletto, but they also owned vines in La Morra because that's where the family was originally from. Maggiorino's son Vittorio has brought the estate into the modern age, now helped since 2017 by his elder son Luca and soon younger son Stefano too. Fratelli Monchiero owns southwest-facing vines in Roere (their web site says south, but I don't think it's so). Confusingly, the vines grow in the locality of Ciocchini, which is also the name of the vineyard district right next to Roere di Santa Maria. The vines are close to thirty years old and this is the historic vineyard of the family, where the current owner's grandfather was born. The Barolo is a very typical one of this vineyard area, with aromas and flavors of fresh red berries and violet, characterized by an easygoing personality and lightly tannic structure that makes them ready to drink already at a relatively young age.

There are other producers that also farm grapevines here, though they choose to use the grapes in estate Barolo blends. The Bruna Grimaldi winery of Serralunga makes a Barolo estate blend called Camilla, in honour of a vineyard that was always known as "La Camila" and its farmhouse that was one of the four that belonged to the Castello di Grinzane Cavour. Grapes from different vineyards are used to make this Barolo, and one of them is planted with a south-facing vines at about 240 meters above sea level in Roere di Santa Maria. These vines were planted back in 1972. Osvaldo Viberti, a talented Barolo producer best known for his Barolo Serra dei Turchi makes his classic estate Barolo with grapes from three different La Morra vineyards, one of them in Roere di Santa Maria. Like all his wines, and like all those from this specific vineyard district, it isn't exactly the last word in complexity, but drinks wonderfully well already young, delivering a gentle fruitiness but with a good Nebbiolo acid and tannic backbone, and food-friendliness.

Benchmark wineries/Reference point producers of Barolo Roere di Santa Maria: Fratelli Monchiero.

ROGGERI

Township	La Morra
Reference Map	See Map of La Morra MGAs (Ch. 10)
Size (ha) (Tot / Barolo MGA)	21.31 / 2.39
Production 2021 (hl)	130.00
Altitude	240 - 340 meters a.s.l. roughly
Exposure	From east to southeast in the better exposed parcels, and northeast in the remaining parts
N. Claimants MGA	2
Other grape varieties planted:	Barbera; Dolcetto; white varieties
Land Units	Land Unit of La Morra
Soil (stage):	Tortonian

Producers claiming the MGA

Crissante Alessandria; Ciabot Berton (Oberto Marco).

Wines

Crissante Alessandria - Barolo Roggeri; **Ciabot Berton (Oberto Marco)** - Barolo Roggeri (and Riserva)

What the producers say

Marco Oberto (Ciabot Berton): "The Roggeri vineyard has been owned by the maternal side of my family since the beginning of the 20th century and was farmed by the Oberto clan in the 1970s. Its separate vinification and bottling as a single-site Barolo was introduced in 1993. Thanks to a deep and fresh soil that gives excellent results even in particularly hot years, Roggeri's wines are usually rich in polyphenols and acidity. It requires, nonetheless severe leaf thinning in cooler years".

Ian's assessment of the vineyard district, its wines and its potential

Roggeri is a vineyard district of La Morra close to the houses that make up the fraction of Santa Maria, and is surrounded by the vineyard districts of Santa Maria, Capalot, Rocchettevino, and Bricco San Biagio. It extends about 100 meters upwards (from 240-340 meters above sea level) and is a rather typical vineyard area characterized by soils of Saint Agatha Fossil Marls Formation (of the laminated type) lithology especially rich in clay and that therefore hold on to water well. It follows that in hot years (such as 1997, 2003, 2007, 2011 and 2017) it might be worth looking for Barolo Roggeri wines. Clearly, the flip side of this is that in years of normal weather Roggeri's vines, are usually harvested as much as ten days later than those of a vineyard district very close by such as Bricco San Biagio. As I have already written in the ROCCHETTEVINO file, comparing Rocchettevino and Roggeri offers noteworthy insight into the intricacies of terroir. I choose Rocchettevino as a measuring stick for Roggeri because the Ciabot Berton estate farms both and makes wines from each, so the comparison of the sites and their wines is a little bit more level.

The differences in altitude and soil between these two vineyard areas is remarkable (and those differences translate into the wines): compared to Rocchettevino, Roggeri is very clay-rich (average soil composition of 46%

loam, 26% sand and 28% clay) and always one of the last vineyards to be harvested because it holds on to water (and so the vegetative cycle there is longer). Not only, but its Barolos have more polyphenols, something that is visible already from the color: Roggeri's Barolos are some of the darkest Barolos of the entire denomination, and I repeat that this deep shade of color is typical of all the Barolos from Roggeri I have tried over the years, independently of the producer making the wine. By contrast, the Barolo of Rocchettevino is very classic and lighter in color (a very pretty crimson ruby-red, I may add), notably more floral and spicier, and generally characterized by tougher tannins that need longer oak aging to refine and smoothen.

Roggeri producers and the wines

Numerous estates make good Barolos from Roggeri. Ciabot Berton first made it in 1993, but (happily) changed its winemaking approach to Roggeri's grapes over the years to reach a less "in your face" style of wine. Their Barolo Roggeri was at first aged all in new barriques, then in 50% used barriques and 50% large barrels (beginning with the 2003 vintage). Their classic estate Barolo also contains some Roggeri grapes, as it is a blend of grapes picked in Roggeri, Bricco San Biagio and Rive.

At Crissante Alessandria, Angelo Alessandria told me they own about 2.2 hectares in Roggeri, the oldest of which were planted back in 1957, then some more in other following years (the youngest in 2019). The vines face southeast (some face south) at different altitudes ranging from 240 to 280 meters above sea level. The wine is aged for two years in large oak barrels. The large Poderi Oddero estate in la Morra also owns vines in Roggeri, though historically it planted Barbera (and a little Dolcetto), not Nebbiolo, there. Their one-hectare vineyard is located at 320 meters above sea level in the Le Rù zone of Roggeri, where the vines are still very young (four years old) and therefore the grapes are currently still being used to make a Langhe Nebbiolo; but clearly, the goal is to use these Nebbiolo grapes in the estate's classic Barolo blend.

Roggeri is not one of my favorite vineyard districts of Barolo. The wines always seem to me to be chunky and thick, with very little grace and refinement, though I accept that this may be on me and related to the kind of wines I think Nebbiolo does best (hence, the Barolos I prefer to drink). Those who prefer richer, tactile, bigger wines will undoubtedly love the wines of Roggeri: and for example, there is no denying that Ciabot Berton's Barolo Roggeri is an excellent wine. Personally, I prefer their other Barolos, but there's no accounting for tastes: you like Picasso, I like Monet, you like mustard, and I like ketchup, and so forth. It also didn't help any that in the beginning, probably because of Roggeri's rich clay soil giving bigger, tannic wines, most producers felt compelled to oak (to death) their Roggeri Barolos, many of which tasted more like a Merlot-wannabe than what my idea of Barolo is.

Benchmark wineries/Reference point producers of Barolo Roggeri: Ciabot Berton, Crissante Alessandria.

RONCAGLIE

Township	La Morra	
Reference Map	See Map of La Morra MGAs (Ch. 10)	
Size (ha) (Tot / Barolo MGA)	36.42 / 2.73	
Production 2021 (hl)	147.03	
Altitude	250 - 440 meters a.s.l. roughly	
Exposure	From east to southeast	
N. Claimants MGA	4	
Other grape varieties planted:	Barbera; Dolcetto	
Land Units	Land Unit of La Morra	
Soil (stage):	Tortonian	

Producers claiming the MGA

Chionetti; Pio Cesare; Bruna Silvio; Eraldo Viberti.

Wines

Chionetti - Barolo Roncaglie; **Renato Corino (Stefano Corino)** - Barolo Roncaglie; **Eraldo Viberti** - Barolo Roncaglie.

Ian's assessment of the vineyard district, its wines and its potential

First off, don't confuse this Roncaglie, a vineyard district of La Morra and located up near the border with Verduno and that commune's Rocche dell'Olmo vineyard district, with the Roncaglie vineyard district of the Barbaresco denomination (the wines of which have been made famous by the Poderi Colla estate).

The Roncaglie of Barolo is sandwiched between the La Morra vineyard districts of Castagni and Silio and overlooks Capalot and Bricco Chiesa, as well as the fraction of Santa Maria. Like other vineyard districts, it can be divided into an upper and lower segment, Roncaglie Soprana (or Soprano) and Roncaglie Sottana (or Sottano). The main differences between these two subregions of Roncaglie relate to altitude and topography, given that the former is higher up (300/350-440 meters above sea level) and has more or less the same exposure throughout; while the latter is lower down (250-300/350 meters above sea level) with varying exposures.

Soil composition-wise (the values I have average out at about 60% silt/loam, 30% clay and 10% sand), but with plenty of limestone, but I do not have enough data (yet?) to make an accurate statement about differences in soil component percentages between the Soprana and the Sottana parts. Be aware that while the Soprana/Sottana subdivisions are unofficial, they have been in place for centuries in the Langhe, and were always based on geographic and observational data. Which means the wines made in each portion were usually different, not just in style and quality. Whether that also applies to Roncaglie's two segments we really have no way of knowing, for the simple reason that there just aren't enough Barolos made by enough producers from this vineyard district.

Roncaglie producers and the wines

The only Barolo made in Roncaglie has been for the longest time the one of Eraldo Viberti, whose wines are really good. Today we also have the new Barolo made by the Renato Corino, named after his son Stefano, to also go on and learn from, but I need to get more experience with it over many more vintages.

The previous reference to Renato Corino and Roncaglie is an interesting one, and an example of how life works out in funny ways sometimes. Back in the mid-2000s, maybe around 2006 or 2007, during a long interview and tasting session at his house, Renato Corino told me flat out that Roncaglie "è una zona bellissima" (in English, a very beautiful area) that he described as being much more calcareous than marly, and that he believed could give really great wines. He also rather acutely added that it must have meant something that Gaja decided to buy vineyard land near there too. At another time, during a 2007 visit to his brother Giuliano's winery (the Corino estate, or in full, the Corino di Corino Giovanni estate) to taste wines and interview away there as well (all the useful, interesting and hopefully pertinent stuff that resulted from such visits you are reading now in this book, by the way), agreed, telling me that Roncaglie was likely the best of Santa Maria's vineyard areas (the Corino siblings used to own vineyards there but had to sell in a moment of economic difficulty). And so, there is a measure of irony in the fact that the Barolo Roncaglie Stefano Corino is now the new, latest wine to be released by the Renato Corino estate. It is made from 0.46 hectares of Nebbiolo vines first planted in 1997, at 295-320 meters above sea level. The wine is aged in a mix of once and twice used tonneaux and barriques (30%). Carlo Revello of the outstanding Fratelli Revello estate has also told me over the years that in his view Roncaglie is one of the two best areas of the Santa Maria subregion of La Morra. At one point in time (back around 2010-2012 or so, memory fails me now) the Luigi Oddero estate was also looking to buy in Roncaglie, and that has to mean something too.

An extremely important estate associated with Barolo (and Barbaresco) is Scarpa (sommelier and wine lovers alert: Scarpa makes some of the best Barbera d'Asti and especially Freisa wines around), located in Castel Rocchero, outside the Barolo in the Asti area. The wines were made by one of the great winemakers of his time, Carlo Castino, who was Scarpa's longtime enologist (since 1962) and the nephew of Mario Pesce, and who passed the winemaking baton to current ultra-competent winemaker Silvio Trinchero in 2007. Gleaning knowledge over the years from the combination of Pesce, Carlo Castino, and Silvio Trinchero has made for an unbelievable learning opportunity Barolo (and Barbaresco) any wine lover would have greatly appreciated and cherished. The winery owns 0.9 hectares in Roncaglie, planted at about 380 meters in altitude with vines that are now from forty to fifty-two years old. The soil there is 50% loam with more or less equal percentages of sand and clay. The vineyard is in front of the Church of S.Maria above the road that runs from Silio to La Morra (and hence is the Roncaglie Soprana), close to where Scarpa used to source grapes to make their famous Barolo Tettimorra. The winery made its first Roncaglie Barolo in the 2019 vintage but decided not to claim the vineyard district designation for it; but they tell me that will likely change in the future as they study the vineyard and become more comfortable with it and its wine.

Benchmark wineries/Reference point producers of Barolo Roncaglie: Eraldo Viberti, Renato Corino/Stefano Corino, Scarpa.

RUÈ

Township	Barolo
Reference Map	See Map of Barolo MGAs (Ch. 10)
Size (ha) (Tot / Barolo MGA)	8.49 / 0.64
Production 2021 (hl)	35.00
Altitude	280 - 320 meters a.s.l. roughly
Exposure	From east to northeast
N. Claimants MGA	1
Other grape varieties planted:	Barbera; Dolcetto
Land Units	Land Unit of La Morra
Soil (stage):	Tortonian

Producers claiming the MGA
Angelo Germano.
Wines
Producers/Wines
Angelo Germano - Barolo Ruè

Ian's assessment of the vineyard district, its wines and its potential

Ruè is a vineyard district of the commune of Barolo located across and up the slope from the lower-lying Cannubi Muscatel and the town of Barolo, surrounded by the vineyard districts of Sarmassa, Liste, San Pietro, La Volta and Drucà (Ruè is essentially a prolongation of the latter). Its soil is Tortonian in origin and hence is mostly of the typical Saint Agatha Fossil Marls Formation lithology, with patches of the laminated type too.

Though small and not very famous, this vineyard district is important to wine lovers because it is one of the sources of Nebbiolo grapes for Bartolo Mascarello's iconic Barolo, a benchmark wine in many more ways than one (the estate owns 5000 square meters of Nebbiolo there and another 2500 square meters of Dolcetto). However, the Bartolo Mascarello estate believes in the value of the traditional Barolo made by blending grapes from different sites, and so does not bottle a Barolo Ruè as such.

Ruè producers and the wines

The only Barolo Ruè made today I know of is the excellent one by the Angelo Germano estate, very well run by Davide Germano. The estate first made a Barolo from the Ruè way back in 1903: today's vines, if not quite that old, are still almost septuagenarian (some of them at least), given that the current vines were planted between 1955 and 1985. The vines lie at 300 meters above sea level and face east; Davide Germano tells me that this is the vineyard he loves the most because it never gives him any problems and he loves its wines. His winemaking involves 12-15 days of maceration (*a cappello emerso*) and aging for two years in classic 500-liter tonneaux (20% new oak, the remainder is decided based on the characteristics of the year and the wine). I only have Germano's Barolo to go on by which to express an opinion on Ruè, but I like the light on its feet and very pristine aromas and flavors of red rose petals, of candied violet, minerals and at times even of truffle. Based on what I have tasted from this winery I think the site is a truly excellent one and Angelo Germano's wines most certainly worth looking for and cellaring.

Benchmark wineries/Reference point producers of Barolo Ruè: Angelo Germano.

SAN BERNARDO

Township	Serralunga d'Alba
Reference Map	See Map of Serralunga d'Alba MGAs (Ch. 10)
Size (ha) (Tot / Barolo MGA)	4.44 / 1.76
Production 2021 (hl)	95.74 (of which 95.74 hl of Barolo Riserva *MGA*)
Altitude	335 - 385 meters a.s.l. roughly
Exposure	From east to southeast
N. Claimants MGA	2
Other grape varieties planted:	Only Nebbiolo
Land Units	Land Unit of Serralunga d'Alba
Soil (stage):	Serravallian

Producers claiming the MGA

Palladino.

Wines

Palladino - Barolo Riserva San Bernardo

What the producers say

Palladino: "Since 1978, we vinify San Bernardo's grapes with the maceration lasting for 30 days and we age in big French and Slavonian oak casks (37 hectoliter) for the first two years and then one more year in small barriques (50% new and 50% of second use)".

Enrica Scavino (Paolo Scavino): "We own small plots on the top of the hillside in Serralunga d'Alba village where our old vines produce small, sparse clusters of Nebbiolo. The acidity at maturity stays high levels though the wine is always well balanced".

Ian's assessment of the vineyard district, its wines and its potential

San Bernardo is a Serralunga vineyard district, located to the eastern flank of the Serralunga ridge in between the vineyard districts of Serra and Colombaro, just below the town. Its soil lithology is classic Serralunga, in other words the Lequio Formation with a soil composition averaging 57% loam, 23% sand and 20% clay. In terms of topography, San Bernardo enjoys a southeastern exposure (more east than south), which is obviously a favorable one now that climate change is with us.

San Bernardo producers and the wines

The only Barolo San Bernardo I know of and have tasted repeatedly over the years is the one by Palladino, whose vines cover about two hectares facing southeast between 330-390 meters above sea level (350 meters above sea level on average). San Bernardo also provides more than half the grapes for the estate Barolo. Palladino's wines are powerful, minerally Barolos and the San Bernardo in particular, which he chooses to bottle as a Riserva, seems to be less fruity and more mineral than some other wines I have tasted from this winery over the years. Palladino's wines, that I personally quite like, will never be mistaken by anyone as fruit bombs and so their San Bernardo Barolo too is pleasantly austere on the long, floral finish. No baby fat, just a mouthful of very serious Barolo that ages well. It's a beautiful, traditionally made wine. I'm sure you'll agree, there's a lot worse in life.

Benchmark wineries/Reference point producers of Barolo San Bernardo: Palladino.

SAN GIACOMO

Township	La Morra
Reference Map	See Map of La Morra MGAs (Ch. 10)
Size (ha) (Tot / Barolo MGA)	69.24 / 0.42
Production 2021 (hl)	22.68
Altitude	240 - 370 meters a.s.l. roughly
Exposure	Predominantly west
N. Claimants MGA	1
Other grape varieties planted:	Barbera; Dolcetto; white varieties
Land Units	Land Unit of Verduno
Soil (stage):	Messinian

Producers claiming the MGA

Cantina Stroppiana.

Wines

Cantina Stroppiana - Barolo San Giacomo

What the producers say

Michele Reverdito (Reverdito): "We have this vineyard since 2003. San Giacomo bestows a good tannic structure and a harmonious nature to wines, which are fruity, fresh and structured. We only produce the Riserva level and it is only made in the best vintages".

Ian's assessment of the vineyard district, its wines and its potential

San Giacomo is located in the northwestern corner of the La Morra commune (in fact it's vineyard district that reaches farthest out west) right below the Bricco Cogni vineyard district. It is a long strip of land that runs from the northwest down to the southeast, sandwiched in between Verduno's Neirane vineyard district to the north and Ascheri to the south. It is sealed off to the east by La Morra's Castagni vineyard district. The soil lithology is of the Cassano Spinola formation of the marly type with a high presence of clay, and the wines in my opinion reflect this (relatively politely styled Barolos with some heft, but perhaps not the last word in complexity).

What might seem a little demeaning for San Giacomo, at least at first glance, is that it has one of the lowest surface areas under vine of all the vineyard districts of Barolo: less than 10% of its total extension is under vine. And of that, not even a fifth is Nebbiolo. So clearly, in people's minds the district must not be especially suited to giving Nebbiolo wines of noteworthy depth and structure. And even though climate change has made previously difficult sites to farm somewhat more manageable (at least in terms relative to the wine grapes growing there reaching optimal maturity, if nothing else), those numbers are hard to argue. And yet, there a couple of outstanding Barolo estates farming the site and making excellent Nebbiolo wines and Barolos from it. .

The fact remains that what Barolos you will drink from San Giacomo are really pretty good. In fact, Michele Reverdito chose to bottle a Barolo Riserva from the site, so clearly his vineyards can give wines of enough depth and structure to be able to stand up to the extra oak aging that a Riserva Barolo requires. In more recent times Reverdito has decided to use the grapes from his roughly twenty years old vines in San Giacomo to make his Langhe Nebbiolo wine called Simane, which is essentially a declassified Barolo San Giacomo. Reverdito believes there to be too much clay in San Giacomo to make a nuanced, multifaceted Barolo wine, but this Nebbiolo is about as good as the Barolos of many of his colleagues. Cantina Stroppiana's Barolo San Giacomo is also a lovely, earthy/truffle/red cherry/violet/orange peel/star anise/camphor-laced Barolo that will prove drinkable soon after release but age better than you might expect. A product of very old vines planted in 1962 at 400 meters above sea level, it is one of the many excellent wines made in the Barolo territory that fly under the radar while everyone clamors for the wines of more famous and expensive names. The winery was founded by Giuseppe, passed on to Oreste, and is now run by Oreste's son Dario and his family. They also make a good Barolo Bussia (a Riserva too) from the Bussia Soprana subregion (see BUSSIA file).

Benchmark wineries/Reference point producers of Barolo San Giacomo: Cantina Stroppiana.

SAN GIOVANNI

Township	Monforte d'Alba
Reference Map	See Map of Monforte d'Alba MGAs (Ch. 10)
Size (ha) (Tot / Barolo MGA)	68.48 / 7.77
Production 2021 (hl)	419.56 (of which 112.57 hl of Barolo Riserva *MGA*)
Altitude	260 - 440 meters a.s.l. roughly
Exposure	East on the slope facing Bussia, west on the opposite side
N. Claimants MGA	6
Other grape varieties planted:	Barbera; Dolcetto; white varieties
Land Units	Land Unit of Castiglione for the highest plots (bordering Bricco San Giovanni and Boschetti towards Barolo and Bricco San Pietro towards Monforte); Land Unit of La Morra for the remaining parts;
Soil (stage):	Tortonian

Producers claiming the MGA

Gianfranco Alessandria; Diego Barale; Broccardo; Famiglia Anselma; Villa Lanata.

Wines

Gianfranco Alessandria - Barolo and Barolo San Giovanni; **Broccardo** - Barolo San Giovanni

Ian's assessment of the vineyard district, its wines and its potential

First things first: don't confuse Monforte's San Giovanni vineyard district with Barolo's similarly named Bricco San Giovanni vineyard district. In fact, this San Giovanni takes its name from that of the collection of homes that make up the San Giovanni fraction located in between Barolo and Monforte. Therefore, it won't surprise to know that Monforte's San Giovanni vineyard district lies right at the border with the Barolo commune and is in fact next to the Barolo commune's vineyard districts of Coste di Rose (immediately north of San Giovanni); Boschetti, Bricco San Giovanni and Zoccolaio to the northwest; Ravera in the Novello commune to the west; Panerole to the southwest; Bricco San Pietro to the south; and a piece of Bussia to its east. What you really need to know about this vineyard district, besides the fact that the Gianfranco Alessandria has long made very good wines from it, is that it is a *schiena d'asino* (a donkey's back). This is in reference to its shape, like that animal's back, and so a summit that slopes off to the two sides. Clearly, one slope looks towards Ravera in Novello and the other towards Monforte's Bussia (this is where Alessandria's vines are).

San Giovanni producers and the wines

Overall, San Giovanni strikes me as a fairly steep site that can reach noteworthy elevations. I've walked it, and though a beautiful place, it's a pain to do so, especially on hot summer days. San Giovanni is characterized by a mostly Saint Agatha Fossil Marls lithology of the sandy type but there is also the presence of Diano Sandstone (in fact the more typical soil lithology of the Monforte commune) and this mix accounts to a degree for the powerful, steely and yet lifted Barolos that I typically associate with San Giovanni.

Gianfranco Alessandria is the name to watch and think of when discussing Barolo San Giovanni. Alessandria took over running the winery in 1986 when he inherited the family's 5.5 hectares (today the estate is about seven hectares large thanks to new rentals) and by the end of the 80s he had decided to estate bottle a small part of his wines rather than to continue selling the grapes like his father had done (he was spurred on in this decision by Mauro Veglio, his cousin). He ages his Barolo in used neutral oak barrels save for the San Giovanni that sees a bit of new oak. Virna Borgogno, of the winery Virna, also owns vines in San Giovanni but she chooses to make a Barbera d'Alba from this site, though she also grows Nebbiolo there. Diego Conterno also owns vines in San Giovanni: the winery's estate Barolo is made with a blend of grapes from San Giovanni, Bricco San Pietro and Ginestra (the 2015 also included some grapes from the Pajana section of Ginestra, besides the ones he normally sources from the Vigna del Gris area made famous by Conterno Fantino).

Benchmark wineries/Reference point producers of Barolo San Giovanni: Gianfranco Alessandria.

SAN LORENZO

Township	Barolo	
Reference Map	See Map of Barolo MGAs (Ch. 10)	
Size (ha) (Tot / Barolo MGA)	2.13 / 0.84	
Production 2021 (hl)	39.94 (of which 9.83 hl of Barolo Riserva *MGA*)	
Altitude	300 - 310 meters a.s.l. roughly	
Exposure	From west to northwest	
N. Claimants MGA	2	
Other grape varieties planted:	Barbera; Dolcetto	
Land Units	Land Unit of Barolo	
Soil (stage):	Tortonian	

Producers claiming the MGA

Brezza; Cavalier Bartolomeo.

Wines

Cavalier Bartolomeo - Barolo San Lorenzo

Ian's assessment of the vineyard district, its wines and its potential

Here is another vineyard district the name of which can cause confusion, because as far as Saints go, there are a lot of San Lorenzo-named sites in the Langhe (and in the rest of Italy, for that matter). The two best-known of our many San Lorenzo-somethings are actually Cannubi San Lorenzo and San Lorenzo in Verduno. The San Lorenzo discussed in this space is another 'San Lorenzo'-named vineyard district of the commune of Barolo; in fact, it's a small vineyard expanse that lies on the other side from the just as small but more famous Cannubi San Lorenzo. Differently from the latter, San Lorenzo has a mostly west to northwest exposure (I use the word "mostly" because while true for the most part, it is still a generalization: for example, Enzo Brezza's

Dolcetto vines in San Lorenzo face southwest. San Lorenzo's soil is of Tortonian origin and its lithology is mostly typical Saint Agatha Fossil Marls.

Despite its lack of size and volume of wines bearing the vineyard district's name, San Lorenzo's name is actually well-known to Barolo lovers all over the world because it is one of Bartolo Mascarello's historic vineyard sites from where he sourced grapes by which to make his legendary Barolo. Until recently, the estate used to include grapes from San Lorenzo in its very traditional Barolo made with a blend of grapes from different vineyard sites. Mascarello owns about 0.9 hectares in San Lorenzo: 0.6 hectares are planted to Barbera, and another 0.3 hectares were of Nebbiolo. However, in 2015 the decision was finally made to uproot the Nebbiolo vines for too many had died out due to old age (the estate in the meantime has supplemented the missing San Lorenzo grapes with those coming from the recently rented vineyards in Monrobiolo di Bussia. See MONROBIOLO DI BUSSIA file).

San Lorenzo producers and the wines

The only estate currently bottling a Barolo San Lorenzo is the little-known but frankly underrated Cavalier Bartolomeo estate, run by father and son team of Dario and Alex. It was founded back in 1924 by Bartolomeo Borgogno in the Garbelletto area of Castiglione Falletto, which is actually very close to the town of Barolo. The estate makes a number of very good wines (see ALTENASSO file) including this Barolo, that prior to the arrival of the official vineyard district names and boundary limits was at times bottled as a Cannubi San Lorenzo (for example, the 2009 vintage) but is "just" a San Lorenzo today, as it should be. No matter: it's a lovely wine, fresh and suave, but with more ripeness, very good depth and size that one might expect from a Barolo of the Barolo township. It does all that, but without losing the trademark elegance of this commune's Barolos. So, for my money, I'd say congratulations on a job well done.

Benchmark wineries/Reference point producers of Barolo San Lorenzo: Cavalier Bartolomeo.

SAN LORENZO DI VERDUNO

Township	Verduno
Reference Map	See Map of Verduno MGAs (Ch. 10)
Size (ha) (Tot / Barolo MGA)	32.46 / 4.21 (of which 53.72 hl of Barolo Riserva *MGA*)
Production 2021 (hl)	228.32
Altitude	210 – 260 meters a.s.l. roughly
Exposure	From south to southwest in the better exposed parcels, northeast in the remaining part.
N. Claimants MGA	5
Other grape varieties planted:	Barbera; Dolcetto; Pelaverga Piccolo; white varieties
Land Units	Land Unit of Barolo
Soil (stage):	Tortonian

Producers claiming the MGA

Fratelli Alessandria; Cascina San Lorenzo; Silvano Giachino; Diego Morra; Daniele Pelassa.

Wines

Fratelli Alessandria - Barolo San Lorenzo di Verduno; **Daniele Pelassa** - Barolo San Lorenzo di Verduno

Ian's assessment of the vineyard district, its wines and its potential

Thanks to the excellent Fratelli Alessandria estate and their outstanding Barolo San Lorenzo di Verduno, this vineyard district has had the spotlight shone on it throughout the years. San Lorenzo di Verduno is the northeasternmost vineyard district of the Verduno commune, on the same eastern-facing flank of the ridge as the Breri vineyard district, which lies immediately to its west. The famous Monvigliero vineyard district is located on the opposite flank of the same ridge San Lorenzo di Verduno is on (while the former is on the western-facing flank, the latter is on the side that looks east). San Lorenzo di Verduno is a relatively low-lying site, has a soil lithology of the Saint Agatha Fossil marls of the laminated type (that is typical of this part of the Verduno commune's territory: exactly the same as that of the nearby Monvigliero and Breri vineyard districts). Given those topographical and geological realties, it follows that a very specific kind of Barolo will be made from here. It is not strange that I believe the Barolos of San Lorenzo di Verduno to fall somewhere in between those of Breri and those of Monvigliero: just as perfumed but a little deeper and denser than those of Breri, but perhaps not quite as complex and dense as those of Monvigliero. Still, they are remarkably good.

San Lorenzo di Verduno producers and the wines

Fratelli Alessandria is a family-run outfit that traces its winemaking roots back to the eighteenth century. Their Barolo San Lorenzo di Verduno has to be considered the benchmark for this vineyard district, the wine all others have to be judged by. The winery has been making it since the 1997 vintage, jumping the 2014 vintage because in that sorry rain-plagued vintage yields were so low they decided to blend what juice they had into their classic estate Barolo. Their vines in San Lorenzo di Verduno average twenty-five years of age, face south, and grow at about 250 meters above sea level. The fermentation and maceration are carried out in temperature-controlled stainless-steel tanks for twelve to fifteen days. The wine spends the first six to ten months in 500 liters barrels and the next two years in 20-30 hectoliter French and/or Slavonian oak casks and is put on sale after another six months in bottle. Another estate that owns vines in San Lorenzo di Verduno is Corrado Breri's I Brè estate. Five of the winery's hectares are located in this vineyard district, and the grapes are used to make the classic estate Barolo blend. Daniele Pelassa and Diego Morra also own vineyards in the vineyard district; of the two, it is the former, an estate founded in 1960 by Mario Pelassa, that bottles a Barolo San Lorenzo di Verduno worth looking for, but I really need to hunt some more bottles down.

Benchmark wineries/Reference point producers of Barolo San Lorenzo di Verduno: Fratelli Alessandria.

SAN PIETRO

Township	Barolo
Reference Map	See Map of Barolo MGAs (Ch. 10)
Size (ha) (Tot / Barolo MGA)	17.36 / 0.85
Production 2021 (hl)	46.32
Altitude	350 - 410 meters a.s.l. roughly
Exposure	From east to northeast
N. Claimants MGA	1
Other grape varieties planted:	Barbera
Land Units	Land Unit of La Morra
Soil (stage):	Tortonian

Producers claiming the MGA

Viberti.

Wines

Viberti - Barolo Riserva San Pietro

What the producers say

Claudio Viberti (Viberti): "The name of the wine comes from the chapel of Saint Peter, or San Pietro in Italian, that is clearly visible on the hill that overlooks the town of Barolo. Differently from the Bricco delle Viole, which we are also thankful and honored to farm, and some other vineyard districts, it is one of the smaller vineyard districts of the commune. Its wines are complex and with noteworthy aging potential".

Ian's assessment of the vineyard district, its wines and its potential

San Pietro lies to the northeast of the town of Barolo surrounded by the commune's vineyard districts of Fossati, Liste, Bricco delle Viole and La Volta. Shaped like an amphitheater, its vineyards face mostly east through to the northeast, with a few sections that look to the south. This viticultural reality, combined with the site's relatively high altitude and generally cooler clay-rich calcareous soil (despite it being of Tortonian origin and its Saint Agatha Fossil Marls of the laminated type lithology that usually gives more approachable, easygoing Barolos of generally early appeal), brings to the fore some of the more austere traits the higher-altitude, cooler-climate Barolos of this commune can sometimes deliver in spades. The only wine we have to go by to test that hypothesis is Viberti's Barolo San Pietro, as he is the only producer currently bottling a Barolo from this vineyard district. In exceptionally good years, is made as a Barolo San Pietro Riserva (Viberti does the same with his holdings in La Volta and Bricco delle Viole). Viberti (don't get your Vibertis confused, as there are many families with the same last name making Barolo: this is the Viberti Giovanni estate that is now run by Claudio and that owns the excellent restaurants of Buon Padre in Vergne and the Locanda La Gemella in Barolo).

San Pietro producers and the wines

Did I mention austere traits in Barolos made with San Pietro grapes? Then enter Viberti's Barolo San Pietro Riserva, and the thing immediately throws you a curve ball: despite it being from San Pietro, and a Riserva no less, Viberti's wine is a lot more approachable now than I, you, or anyone else might expect. Claudio Viberti sources grapes in San Pietro from vineyards planted in a section of the vineyard district very close to Fossati. Viberti owns three plots right below and next to Fossati (you can get a good idea of this from the producer's excellent website 'Vineyards' section, in which his vineyard holdings have been clearly drawn out in pastel colors and are very easy to see and understand) but uses only one plot to make his Barolo, situated at about 390 meters above sea level (this information is not available on the website and is why you need to visit the wineries and actually talk to people in order to really learn). There, the lay of the land forms a depression, a concave bowl of sorts, and so despite the vines looking westwards and the grapes catching the sun all day long, the cooler microclimate is noteworthy. In fact, San Pietro in general is an area that was once always too cold for Nebbiolo grapes to ripen easily and fully each year, but all that changed beginning with the 2003 vintage and the onset of climate change in full force. Of note, the soil has a higher proportion of sand than is common with vineyard districts of Saint Agatha Fossil Marls of the laminated type lithology. The grapes are fermented in vertical hatched steel tanks; fermentation times vary from sixteen to twenty-four days, depending on the year's weather. The wine undergoes temperature-controlled alcohol fermentation and malo in stainless steel tanks, and is aged in non-toasted casks for twenty-four months (regular Barolo) and up to forty-six months for the Riserva, depending on the vintage. All the Barolo San Pietro bottlings I have tasted from this site and producer, be they the regular or the Riserva, have been marked by a strong note of underbrush (forest floor) and savory spices, not to mention a very classic ferrous/raw meat/tar nuance, and a pleasant verticality that results from the slightly cooler-climate bowl shaped topography. Viberti's Barolo San Pietro becomes especially interesting with age, so this is a Barolo I really recommend you cellar eight to ten years after the vintage date. It is also worth knowing that the wine has especially blossomed after the 2003 vintage, possibly as a result of increased vine age but especially because of the advent of climate change.

Benchmark wineries/Reference point producers of Barolo San Pietro: Viberti.

SAN PONZIO

Township	Barolo
Reference Map	See Map of Barolo MGAs (Ch. 10)
Size (ha) (Tot / Barolo MGA)	17.54 / 1.86
Production 2021 (hl)	101.19
Altitude	380 – 410 meters a.s.l. roughly
Exposure	From northeast lo northwest passing through south.
N. Claimants MGA	2
Other grape varieties planted:	Barbera; Dolcetto; white varieties
Land Units	Land Unit of Vergne
Soil (stage):	Tortonian

Producers claiming the MGA

Luca Marenco; Roberto Sarotto.

Ian's assessment of the vineyard district, its wines and its potential

The San Ponzio vineyard district is located in the most southwestern corner of the Barolo commune, sandwiched between Bricco delle Viole in Barolo to the north and Bergera-Pezzole in Novello to the south. San Ponzio takes its name from a group of houses named after the patron Saint Ponzio, protector of the small village of Vergne, itself a fraction of the town of Barolo.

The landscape here (Land Unit of Vergne) is of a relatively high-altitude vineyard district with mostly north-looking exposures. The soil lithology is the Saint Agatha Fossil Marls of the laminated type formed during the Tortonian stage of the Miocene epoch which ought to give elegant Barolos of some depth and in this light the extremely fine sandy soils are a logical finding. But the soil is quite compact, such that despite the site's sandiness, San Ponzio has very good water retention, making it an interesting site even in droughty years. Also, even though sandy soils are thought of as "warm", the fact that San Ponzio looks towards the Tanaro River, means Nebbiolo always had a tough time ripening. In fact, less than half of San Ponzio is planted to vineyards and of those less than a third are of Nebbiolo. It doesn't surprise then that no Barolo San Ponzio is commercially available at present. But in fact, it's not all doom and gloom for us Barolo lovers.

From what locals have told me over the years, San Ponzio's Barolos are not especially loaded with huge amounts of depth or complexity but offer easy drinkability and early appeal, not to mention lovely perfume. For this reason, a producer such as Viberti uses his grapes from this vineyard district to make his classic estate Barolo blend called Buon Padre. It was first made with the 1923 vintage and at that time only with grapes from the San Pietro and La Volta vineyard districts. It was always meant for sale only at the family restaurant (the excellent Trattoria Buon Padre in Vergne). Today the source of grapes for this wine have changed quite a bit, and the Barolo Buon Padre features grapes from many different vineyards in San Pietro, San Ponzio, La Volta, Fossati, Albarella, Terlo, Ravera, Perno, and Monvigliero. While San Ponzio's exposure runs the gamut from northwest to northeast with peeks north and south, Viberti's vineyards look to the west. In this case, the warmer western exposure is probably a good thing as it adds just a little more body to what are wines of finesse and grace. What I find interesting about this site is that, despite its northernly exposure, its altitude and its lack of historical pedigree, very little of it is planted to white grape varieties (less than five percent of the area under vine). Maybe people in Barolo either really like red wines or don't like white wines much! All kidding aside, what that information might be *really* telling us is that San Ponzio is probably better for viticulture and red wines than we suspect, and presently are aware of. Time will tell.

Benchmark wineries/Reference point producers of Barolo San Ponzio: None currently available.

SAN ROCCO

Township	Serralunga d'Alba
Reference Map	See Map of Serralunga d'Alba MGAs (Ch. 10)
Size (ha) (Tot / Barolo MGA)	6.43 / 1.91
Production 2021 (hl)	103.70
Altitude	280 – 320 meters a.s.l. roughly
Exposure	West and East
N. Claimants MGA	2
Other grape varieties planted:	Dolcetto
Land Units	Land Unit of Castiglione
Soil (stage):	Tortonian

Producers claiming the MGA

Azelia; San Biagio.

Wines

Azelia - Barolo San Rocco.

What the producers say

Luigi Scavino (Azelia): "This is the first vineyard our family bought in Serralunga d'Alba, named after the chapel on the hill that looks right at the vineyard. In the 1600s, it was customary to bring those suffering from disease (most often the plague) to the chapel looking for a blessing from San Rocco, patron saint but also protector from the plague. It's a very clay-rich site, and so our Barolo San Rocco is quite rich and meaty, and that benefits from prolonged aging".

Ian's assessment of the vineyard district, its wines and its potential

At the northern end of the Serralunga commune's territory, in between the vineyard districts of Costabella to its west, Sorano to its north and Baudana just south of it, San Rocco is a vineyard district made famous by the Scavino family of Castiglione Falletto's excellent Azelia estate. It is a small site that straddles the top of the Serralunga ridge, hence with its vines growing on both the western and eastern flanks of the ridge.

Even though San Rocco is a vineyard district of Serralunga, its soil lithology is not the classic Lequio Formation (that in my mind characterizes the most typical, purest Barolo forms of Serralunga), but rather the typical Saint Agatha Fossil Marls with Diano Sandstone Formation. The former is more commonly associated with the territories of Barolo and La Morra; and the latter is more commonly associated with the communes of Monforte and Castiglione Falletto. Coupled with an altitude that is not especially noteworthy (and, in the case of Azelia's wine, their winemaking style too), it cannot really surprise then that the Barolo of San Rocco is characterized by a fleshier mouthfeel, a sense of ripeness and roundness and less of the laser-like citrus acidity and mineral sheen of the wines from some other Serralunga vineyard districts. In my experience, San Rocco's Barolos are real crowd pleasers, offering at once heft and ripe sweet fruity flesh.

San Rocco producers and the wines

The Azelia winery's first vintage of their Barolo San Rocco was the 1995, but the vineyards were planted in 1953. The Nebbiolo vines lie on both sides of the road that runs atop the Serralunga ridge and cuts the San Rocco vineyard district's expanse of vineyards in two halves. In total, Azelia owns about 2.1 hectares in San Rocco planted at 320 meters above sea level. Lorenzo Scavino will tell you it's a vineyard district that has special meaning for the family, given that it was the first important vineyard holding they bought outside of their own commune (a rare event back in the early 90s). But Luigi Scavino always liked the Barolos of Serralunga and so he was happy to buy himself a vineyard there. San Rocco's soil is especially rich in clay, and the resulting wine is very structured and powerful, with a mineral, earthy and almost saline bent (the clay) and boasting descriptors that are, somewhat surprisingly, about black fruit (blackberry, blackcurrant) than Nebbiolo's more typical red fruit. Last but not least, for those who like to take photos I point out that the view from San Rocco is incredible:

you can see the whole Castiglione Falletto hill with the easy to recognize castle at its summit (easy to recognize in that it is the only one of Barolo's many castles that has a circular tower). It's a place that offers a picture-perfect view, or if you prefer, a living postcard. La Contrada di Sorano is a small, high-quality winery that owns a small plot in San Rocco planted in 2009 to Nebbiolo Lampia, and with the 2019 vintage began making with the Nebbiolo from their three vineyard districts (Collaretto, San Rocco and Sorano) a classic Barolo of Serralunga. Good things really do come in small packages.

Benchmark wineries/Reference point producers of Barolo San Rocco: Azelia.

SANT'ANNA

Township	La Morra
Reference Map	See Map of La Morra MGAs (Ch. 10)
Size (ha) (Tot / Barolo MGA)	73.30 / 6.16
Production 2021 (hl)	300.17
Altitude	310 - 400 meters a.s.l. roughly
Exposure	From west to southwest in the better exposed parcels, and from northeast to northwest in the remaining parts
N. Claimants MGA	1
Other grape varieties planted:	Barbera; Dolcetto; white varieties
Land Units	Land Unit of Verduno
Soil (stage):	Messinian

Producers claiming the MGA

Tenuta L'Illuminata.

Wines

Tenuta L'Illuminata - Barolo Sant'Anna (and Riserva).

What the producers say

Guido Folonari (Tenuta L'Illuminata): "This vineyard has been part of the estate for 20 years now and it didn't take us long before introducing a single bottling of S. Anna. This vineyard brings freshness to the aromas -often floral- and elegance to the tannins and gives savory and pleasurable Barolo. In the cellar, the duration of fermentation can vary from 25 to 40 days depending on the vintage, and aging takes place in a mix of 225l barriques and 25hectoliter France oak casks".

Ian's assessment of the vineyard district, its wines and its potential

Sant'Anna is one of La Morra's westernmost vineyard districts situated just south of Ascheri and north of Brandini, right on the border with the Cherasco commune. I know of only one Barolo (two actually: a classico and a riserva) made wholly with grapes from this one site, but I have not had enough experience with them to be able to state with the utmost confidence what a Sant'Anna 'somewhereness' in the glass might be all about. The altitude is fairly uniform, with a range spanning only about ninety meters; by contrast, the exposure varies greatly throughout the vineyard district.

In the past, it was commonplace to speak of a Sant'Anna Soprana (Soprano) and a Sant'Anna Sottana (Sottano), taking the names after those of two local farmhouses (or *cascine*). The *Soprano/Sottano* differentiation was always a very popular one in the Barolo area (the Bussia Soprana and Bussia Sottana are perhaps the most famous example of this) and not unlike the *-du Haut* and the *-du Bas* of French fame (or if you prefer, the *-dessus* and the *-dessous*). Just like in Burgundy, Soprano and Sottano were a local manner by which to subdivide and identify agricultural extensions, but I have never been told by anyone that, exposure aside, there was much of a change present (in the soil, for example: the lithology is mostly Cassano-Spinola Formation of the marly type and some gypsiferous-sulfur soils) between these two areas of Sant'Anna. Clearly, the fact there was the habit of specifically referring to one area as a Soprana and another as a Sottana, though it might just have been a simple tool by which to identify the areas, might also imply that there was a difference in the fruits and vegetables produced in each subarea. Relative to Nebbiolo and Barolo, we have no way of knowing.

Sant'Anna producers and the wines

For now, the two Barolos made from Tenuta l'Illuminata are perfectly acceptable in their linearity and freshness, always a good thing when looking for food-friendly wines, perhaps without much palate weight (clearly, the Riserva has more) but with good balance.

Benchmark wineries/Reference point producers of Barolo Sant'Anna: Tenuta L'Illuminata.

SANTA MARIA

Township	La Morra
Reference Map	See Map of La Morra MGAs (Ch. 10)
Size (ha) (Tot / Barolo MGA)	71.00
Production 2021 (hl)	
Altitude	210 - 330 meters a.s.l. roughly
Exposure	Predominantly northwest, west in the better exposed parcels
N. Claimants MGA	0
Other grape varieties planted:	Barbera; Dolcetto; white varieties
Land Units	Land Unit of La Morra
Soil (stage):	Tortonian

Ian's assessment of the vineyard district, its wines and its potential

"You know Ian, it wasn't so long ago that locals were ashamed to have to tell people that they owned vines in Santa Maria" was the honest and surprising admission made to me in a 2007 interview by one of the area's most famous, best-known and talented producers (if you like Barolo, you all know this person, or at least have heard of him/her). Clearly, that sentiment was in reference to a time long gone by, and it really no longer applied already at the time of my interview. In fact, the producer's intent was only to make a point, and not to denigrate the Santa Maria vineyard district as such: his point being that whereas fifty years earlier Santa Maria was not much considered in terms of its capacity to allow production of great wines, already by the end of the first decade of the twenty-first century opinions had begun to change..

Clearly, Santa Maria is a bit of a catch-all vineyard district that encompasses the vineyard areas outside of better-known, historically more relevant specific vineyard areas, but that does not mean the area is without interest. In fact, its exposures and soils change within its boundaries, such that some areas are potentially interesting for Barolo production (or to a greater degree than others).

As its name implies, the Santa Maria vineyard district is located in the Santa Maria subzone of the La Morra commune. It runs in a northeast to southwest direction, more or less parallel and in between the Rive and Serra dei Turchi vineyard districts. A piece of Santa Maria extends further southwest insinuating itself between Galina to its north, Roggeri to its south and reaching so far southwest to get close to Capalot. Though Santa Maria is believed to be an essentially sandy site giving lighter Barolos of not much depth or complexity (at least that's what everybody tells you when you ask), in fact the area of the Santa Maria vineyard district that sits between La Morra and the houses of Santa Maria is actually characterized by a good amount of soil clay, even more clay than you will find for example in parts of Roggeri (and that's saying something) and Rocchettevino. In fact, Santa Maria's soil lithology is that of the Tortonian stage typical Saint Agatha Fossils Marls formation, with smaller amounts of the laminated and sandy forms, such that clay and loam really do dominate the soil composition there. In other words, some parts of this vineyard district undoubtedly have the potential to give slightly bigger wines than most expect; clearly, no behemoths, but somewhat more mouthcoating than what we might expect.

Benchmark wineries/Reference point producers of Barolo Santa Maria: None currently available.

SARMASSA

Township	Barolo
Reference Map	See Map of Barolo MGAs (Ch. 10)
Size (ha) (Tot / Barolo MGA)	33.74 / 8.66
Production 2021 (hl)	419.03 (of which 51.35 hl of Barolo Riserva *MGA*,
	75.48 hl of Barolo *MGA* Vigna and 22.36 hl of Barolo Riserva *MGA* Vigna)
Altitude	240 - 300 meters a.s.l. roughly
Exposure	From south lo southwest for the slope of the Merenda estate, and from northeast to southeast in the central part of the cru. From northwest to southwest on the San Lorenzo side
N. Claimants MGA	7
Other grape varieties planted:	Barbera; Dolcetto; white varieties
Land Units	Land Unit of Barolo in the south-eastern plots bordering San Lorenzo; Land Unit of La Morra for the remaining parts
Soil (stage):	Tortonian

Producers claiming the MGA

Cav. Enrico Bergadano; Brezza; Marchesi Di Barolo; Scarzello; Cabutto - Tenuta La Volta; Virna; Roberto Voerzio.

Wines

Cav. Enrico Bergadano - Barolo Sarmassa (and Riserva); **Brezza** - Barolo Sarmassa and Barolo Riserva Sarmassa Vigna Bricco; **Cabutto - Tenuta La Volta** - Barolo Riserva del Fondatore; **Marchesi di Barolo** - Barolo Sarmassa; **Scarzello** - Barolo Sarmassa Vigna Merenda; **Virna** - Barolo Sarmassa; **Roberto Voerzio** - Barolo Sarmassa

What the producers say

Ernesto Abbona (Marchesi di Barolo): "The vineyards of Sarmassa have been a part of the patrimony of the Abbona family since the second half of nineteenth century. But it wasn't until the beginning of the '70s that we began producing single-site bottlings from it. The soil of Sarmassa is predominantly clay-limestone, very compact with a notable presence of stones. It ranks among the most late-ripening vineyard areas of the commune and is generally the last to be harvested – in most vintages, climate change allowing, close to the end of October. The result is a structured, intensely colored, tannic and long-lasting Barolo".

Federico Scarzello (Scarzello): "I cannot say with certainty how long this vineyard has been in the family because as far as I know my family had it for a long time, so long that it was nicknamed "di Merenda". All the parcels are vinified separately and are blended in together at the end. In particular, the best parcels of Sarmassa, in the best years, are bottled separately with the vineyard name of "Vigna Merenda", the first vintage of which being the 1978. In the cellar, the maceration time varies from 35 to 65 days based the characteristics of the harvest. For aging, we use 25 hectoliter French and Slavonian casks and some 500 liters tonneaux. The wine, has substantial structure but extremely fine and elegant tannins".

Virna Borgogno (Virna): "Our ownership of this vineyard dates back to 1960 when the winery was founded and its separate vinification was launched in 2010. The maceration lasts for 10 to 15 days depending on the vintage, after which the wine is aged in 300 and 500 liters French oak barrels and 30 and 60 hectoliter oak casks for two years. Powerful and austere, Sarmassa is a quintessential Barolo though in years of drought, the ratio of alcohol and structure may be such that it upset the wine's overall balance".

Enzo Brezza (Brezza): "Our family has owned vines in this vineyard since forever, some of which are more than seventy years old, and have been making a Barolo Sarmassa since 1979. Then from 2011, as a special Vigna Bricco bottling too. In my view, its wines are best in hot and dry years, for the soil's water retentive capacity is such that the capacity vines rarely suffer from water stress. Though our vinification really does not change from Barolo to Barolo, we do tend to macerate the Sarmassa longer, as we find its skins usually have softer tannins and so there is no risk in prolonging skin contact".

Ian's assessment of the vineyard district, its wines and its potential

I won't beat around the bush and come right out and say it: Sarmassa is one of Barolo's greatest vineyard areas of all, easily in the denomination's top 20. That's just how good, no, great, it is. And now that we have gotten that out of the way, we can talk a little more about its specifics.

In many ways, Sarmassa is a curious vineyard area: everyone agrees it's one of Barolo's greatest vineyard areas, which is fair, but then there's also much confusion, even amongst producers. You visit one, and he/she tells you the soils were formed during the Serravalian; you visit the next estate on your list, and they tell you the soils are Tortonian. Then you go to the third vineyard visit and winery tasting you scheduled for the day, where you hear Sarmassa's wines are better in years of drought, because the clay-rich soil can hold on to water better; next in line, the day's fourth fellow/gal looks at you straight in the eye and tells you that in hot and droughty years the wines can sometimes be excessively high in alcohol and be marred by somewhat grainy tannins. Last but not least, the fifth and last visit of the day is where you learn, as you're reaching for your aspirins, that long macerations are no problem because the skin tannins of Sarmassa grapes are just fine. And don't get me even started about a "bricco" area in Sarmassa that is nowhere near the highest part of the slope (the word *bricco* is usually reserved for the top, sunniest part of a hill).

You think I just made all of that up? Not at all. Trust me: been there, done that. And you want to talk exposures? One person will tell you Sarmassa's vines face mostly southeast, another full south, yet another west… In truth, they are probably all correct in their assessments: Sarmassa, though not especially huge (at thirty-three hectares and change it is a small vineyard district by MGA-named dimension standards) is spread out over many different slopes and directions. With Sarmassa, things are very much in the eyes of the beholder; or more precisely, given the complexity of Sarmassa's topography and geology, on where that beholder and his/her eyes happen to be standing.

It is my view that Sarmassa's vineyard extension can be divided in not one, not two, not three but four (4!) sections, all which are confined within a relatively small area. Generally speaking, Sarmassa is a low-lying vineyard district located at the bottom of where four hilly crests converge, with its vineyards extending upwards up the slopes. If you like analogies, think of Sarmassa like a vineyard area that is shaped like a wide bowl (which it is) or a tulip-like flower the walls (of the bowl) or the petals (of the flower) climb upwards in four directions. And so, Sarmassa's vineyards cover the bases (or lowest portions) of these four crests and climb upwards, to a greater or lesser degree, on each. This is why I think it is reasonable to break down Sarmassa into four sections, that I have named in the following manner, basing myself on historic reference points and or topographical realities: Sarmassa Bricco (first section); Sarmassa Sotto Ruè (second section); Sarmassa Sotto Liste (third section), Sarmassa Merenda (lower down fourth section) and Sarmassa Mandorla (higher up fourth section). The first section is Sarmassa Bricco and it lies on the side of the hill the other flank of which is occupied by the famous extended Cannubi hill; the second section (the smallest of the four), Sarmassa Sotto Ruè, lies at the foot of the hilly crest where Ruè is; the third section, Sarmassa Sotto Liste, is just below Liste; and the fourth section that climbs up towards Cerequio can be further subdivided in a lower fourth section, Sarmassa Merenda, and one higher up, Sarmassa Mandorla. In fact, and not to make all this more complicated than it already is, there could be yet another historical area of Sarmassa worth adding to the fray: that which is around yet another farmhouse, Cascina Sarmassa, above which are the few vineyard plots that make up the second, very small, section of today's Sarmassa. Everyone seems to forget about this section now, but I fail to see why. Just sayin'.

Got that? What all that means is that different parts of what is today's Sarmassa vineyard district can potentially give different wines (just how different though is debatable: see below). For sure, locals historically referred to specific wines from specific areas of Sarmassa. Wines thought to be, if not markedly different, specific enough to warrant distinguishing between them. Three areas and their wines were, and still are, most famous: the Mandorla area (Vigna della), an area that takes its name from the farmhouse (*cascina*) on the slope of the Sarmassa section that leads to Cerequio; the Merenda area (Vigna), where there is also a *cascina* of almost the same name (Cascina Marenda or Merenda), below the Mandorla at more or less just above the halfway point on the same slope; and last but not least, the Vigna Bricco, which became a "vigna" only after the onslaught of the official MGA names (that wiped out the historical use of the word 'bricco', as in the 'Bricco Sarmassa' that was previously in use), an area located on the section of Sarmassa that lies on the other flank of the same hill where the extended Cannubi hill is found. It follows that the landscape units of Sarmassa vary greatly depending on which of its sections you are in (see the introductory facts and figures table above at the start of this Sarmassa file).

Sarmassa's Barolos are generally considered to be the most massive of the Barolo commune, and I'd say rightly so; but there are exceptions, and it all depends on where the grapes are sourced within Sarmassa. Sarmassa's soils are, despite what apparently some producers believe, classic Tortonian stage soils but of slightly different lithologies in various sections of the vineyard district. For example, the section of Sarmassa closest to the town of Barolo and the San Lorenzo vineyard district has typical Saint Agatha Fossil Marls, while the rest of Sarmassa's soils is more of the laminated type with many areas more or less rich in sand (more typical of the sandy type of Saint Agatha Fossil Marls). The Barolos from these areas will lack the flesh and size that characterize the Sarmassa Barolos made closer to the Barolo township but generally have an element of grace and austerity to them (the wines of the Marenda and especially the Mandorla area, for example). The Barolos from these two historical areas (the fourth section of Sarmassa I alluded to earlier) are easy to recognize in a lineup of Sarmassa Barolos because of their lighter red colour compared to the rest (their pretty red colour is very elegant in my books and is the ideal complement to the greater grace of the wines).

All this is further complicated because of the steep gradient of Sarmassa's slope, that has led over time to a noteworthy washout of the topsoil leaving a very compact calcareous-clay that does in fact resemble soils and subsoils of the Serravalian stage (so this is probably why some producers think their soils are of Serravalian origin rather than Tortonian). Sarmassa's soil reality is enhanced by its large presence of stones, that together with the clay, limit Nebbiolo's vigor (always a good thing with Nebbiolo, a vigorous grape variety). The generally strong presence of clay and large stones (that also serve to retain and reflect heat) means that Sarmassa can be a rather warm site and that the combination of this microclimate and soil can make for the most powerful Barolos of the entire Barolo township's territory. But this is not true of every portion of the Sarmassa vineyard district, that as we have seen is an extremely complex topographical, geological and climate reality. And so it is that the section of the vineyard district that is especially warm is the part of Sarmassa's slope that climbs up towards Cerequio (the one with the Merenda and Mandorla areas). By contrast, those portions of Sarmassa that climb up towards Liste or up on the flank of the long hilly crest that has the Cannubi site on the other flank are both cooler.

As mentioned earlier in this admittedly long dissertation on Sarmassa, from each of these subzones specific Barolos used to be made, or are still being made today, by a number of producers. That much admitted, it is important to know that in my experience Sarmassa's Barolos do present more similarities than not. In ultimate analysis, what makes Sarmassa a site of *grand cru* quality is not just the power (for example, Sarmassa's wines from the Cerequio slope) or precision (for example, Sarmassa wines from the Bricco, the slope on the flank opposite to the Cannubis) of its Barolos, but the fact they are also very complex, deep wines.

Sarmassa producers and the wines

Without doubt, Brezza is the one winery most famously associated with Sarmassa, from where it has made more than one bottling over the years. For the most part, the estate is blessed with very old vines: already during interviews I conducted there back in the late 2000s (2005-06-08-09), their Sarmassa vines were over 70 years old (planted in 1941), others younger but still thirty-five years of age (this in 2009) and the youngest of all had been planted in 1989. Brezza's Nebbiolo vines grow in the Sarmassa Bricco and Sarmassa Sotto Ruè subregions: the former holding is much larger than the latter: in fact, Brezza is by far the largest vineyard owner of the Sarmassa Bricco subregion.

Brezza used to make not just a Barolo Sarmassa but also a Bricco Sarmassa (the names "Bricco-something" are no longer allowed, unless they are the recognized, official, name of the vineyard district such as is the case with for example Bricco Rocche and Bricco Chiesa); now Enzo makes a Barolo Riserva from there instead. Use of the world 'bricco' was because locally, the part of the Sarmassa to the south (on the flank that climbs up towards Cannubi San Lorenzo) was always known as the "bricco": in other words, it was an historic name, not a flight of fancy. The curious thing is that it's not really a *bricco* at all. In fact, it's lower-lying than the upper part of Sarmassa's slope that goes towards Cerequio, so it is not the actual highest part of the vineyard district, as any self-respecting *bricco* ought to be and imply. But as there are undulations throughout the gradient with a slight mounding up and reaching out to the top of the slope, I guess it can be looked at as a *bricco* of sorts. When it comes to winemaking, Enzo is a traditionalist: with a family connection to Bartolo Mascarello (who was Enzo's uncle), it probably couldn't be otherwise. He owns vines in some of the very best Barolo vineyards of all, such as the Barolo commune's Cannubi Centrale and Cannubi Muscatel, Castellero, and Sarmassa. And though he loves all his Barolos, I know Enzo has a fondness for the chewiness of Sarmassa's wines as opposed to Cannubi's verticality, for example. Brezza also makes an excellent, forward and inexpensive Barolo classico from partly sourced grapes coming in from Novello and from Monforte d'Alba, and a really delicious Freisa wine, so don't miss it! The Brezza estate is really an excellent source of high quality, traditional Barolo.

The Cabutto-Tenuta La Volta estate makes a Barolo Sarmassa from its holdings in the third Sarmassa subregion, Sarmassa Sotto Liste. They own very old vines here and use these grapes to make the estate's Riserva Barolo, which they call Barolo Riserva del Fondatore.

Federico and Federica Scarzello are the owners of the Scarzello estate (ex-Giorgio Scarzello), who make the benchmark example of Barolo from Sarmassa's Merenda subregion. In fact, the name of their Barolo Sarmassa is Barolo Sarmassa Vigna Merenda. Along with Brezza, Scarzello is the largest vineyard owner in Sarmassa and the estate has made some great wines from there over the years [especially a truly amazing Barbera d'Alba, labeled Sarmassa for as long as it was possible to do so (Scarzello grows Barbera in the lower reaches of his Sarmassa holdings, because there Nebbiolo fares slightly less well). Their Nebbiolo vines are fifteen and twenty-five years old and are planted between 250-300 meters above sea level on a mostly clay-rich soil, similar to that of the area closest to the Barolo township and the San Lorenzo vineyard district. They are very good examples of Barolos that are fleshy and round, with the power one usually associates with Sarmassa's Barolo.

Estates that have made or are making wine from the Mandorla area of Sarmassa have included or still include Bergadano and Virna. Bergadano is one of the two wineries (the other is Franco Molino) that belong under the umbrella name of the Cascina Rocca estate (since 1999, the name of the family's bed and breakfast). The two wineries were united by marriage, given that the Franco Molino winery was born in the 1940s, while the Bergadano estate was founded in 1974 by Enrico Bergadano. Today the winery is run by Piercarlo Bergadano, who is the husband of Silvana Molino: while Bergadano makes the wines and follows the vineyards along with his technical team, Silvana is in charge of the marketing, communication and sales of the estate wines. The winery's Barolo Sarmassa is made under the banner of Bergadano: 1.4 hectares in Sarmassa planted in 1950 and 1997 at about 250 meters in altitude facing south are the source of the Bergadano Barolo Sarmassa. As is typical of the Mandorla area there is virtually no sand in the soil there and the Barolo Sarmassa born there is more on the austere and linear side, without the mouthcoating flesh and size of the Barolos of the Sarmassa Bricco area, for example. There are also extremely old vines of Barbera in Sarmassa planted back in 1960, and so a Barbera d'Alba from Sarmassa plots is also made, but under the Franco Molino label.

Virna Borgogno, Italy's first woman to earn a degree in oenology and viticulture (congratulations again) runs (along with her sister) the namesake Virna estate. Sarmassa is an important part of the winery's Barolo offer. Virna's vines are in a very exposed site in Sarmassa, a section that is very warm (because it is naturally protected from the wind: so warm in fact that her grandfather used to refer to it as "Africa"). To give you an idea, her vines are in the area of the Mandorla, above Scarzello and Bergadano, and just below those of Roberto Voerzio. Importantly, her Nebbiolo vines in Sarmassa (and not just there in fact) are actually not all just of Nebbiolo but of Nebbiolo Rosé too (about 10% of the total); clearly, given the way this poor grape was treated in the '80s and '90s, it managed to survive there only because it was very old Nebbiolo Rosé and the old vines were spared (see chapter 3, NEBBIOLO ROSÉ). At 10%, it makes its presence felt, with the resulting Barolo having a more filigreed mouthfeel and more perfume than you'd normally expect in a wine from other parts of Sarmassa. Virna, very understandably, considers herself lucky to have it, because as she very acutely points out "besides the fact that it's a very interesting grape that handles heat and drought well, there's not much of it left and whatever vines there are usually quite old, so the wines we can make with Nebbiolo Rosé in the blend are going to be even better because of old vines".

SCARRONE

Township	Castiglione Falletto
Reference Map	See Map of Castiglione MGAs (Ch. 10)
Size (ha) (Tot / Barolo MGA)	20.55 / 10.53
Production 2021 (hl)	558.72 (of which 119.50 hl of Barolo *MGA* Vigna)
Altitude	220 - 330 meters a.s.l. roughly
Exposure	From southeast to southwest in the better exposed parcels, and from east to north in the remaining parts
N. Claimants MGA	4
Other grape varieties planted:	Barbera
Land Units	Land Unit of Barolo
Soil (stage):	Tortonian

Producers claiming the MGA

Bava; Fratelli Giacosa (Canavere); Giovanni Sordo; Luigi Oddero e Figli.

Wines

Bava - Barolo Scarrone; **Fratelli Giacosa** - Barolo Scarrone Vigna Mandorlo (and Riserva); **Luigi Oddero e Figli** - Barolo Rocche Rivera.

What the producers say

Maurizio Giacosa (Fratelli Giacosa): "We own vines in Scarrone since 1994 and vinified it separately immediately. The maceration time varies from 20 to 50 days depending on the vintage and the aging takes place – for all the wines – in 30 to 60 hectoliter oak casks. Scarrone is a warm site, which means on one hand, optimal maturation for the grapes, and on the other, difficulties linked to the possible overwhelming heat. The heart of this vineyard enjoys the highest altitude - known as Vigna Mandorlo - giving wines rich in polyphenols, concentrated and profound. In the glass, the wine is intense and profound ruby in color, endowed with an imposing structure that combines a sense of austerity and pleasure."

Alberto Zaccarelli (Luigi Oddero e Figli): "In the township of Castiglione Falletto, under the castle wall, one finds a plot perched on the hilltop, the only one planted in *ritto chino* fashion (i.e., vertically to the slope). The wine offers distinct perfume of truffle, licorice and faded flowers, at times even spices."

Giulio Bava (Bava): "We own vines in Scarrone since 1989, and try to make a traditionally-minded Barolo. We think it's a very typical wine of Castiglione Falletto, powerful but gentle at the same time. Still this Barolo will benefit from extended cellaring, especially in the very best years".

Ian's assessment of the vineyard district, its wines and its potential

As it is officially drawn up today, Scarrone is the farthest east-reaching vineyard district of the Castiglione Falletto commune. It snakes around the town of Castiglione Falletto and looks to Serralunga's territory in its eastern section, while to the southwest and west it borders the Castiglione Falletto vineyard districts of Rocche di Castiglione and Pira. It's that last part that can, and perhaps should be, questioned. You see, in the "modern age" (i.e., post-2010 and the arrival of the official MGA names of the vineyard districts) Scarrone is laid out as a vineyard district that covers a whole lot more ground than it once did. Scarrone as a site historically never "saw" Pira and the Rocche di Castiglione: unless of course someone was standing there with a telescope, that is. For it once used to be that Scarrone constituted a far smaller extension of vineyards than it does today: the lower half of what is Scarrone today was actually known as Rivera (or Rocche Rivera) and this was the part that reached Pira (and that's all: it never reached Rocche di Castiglione at all, separated from it by plenty of fallow land and a patch of vines known as Lipulot, now included within the enlarged Rocche di Castiglione vineyard district pulling on the vineyard district so it basically reaches the 'new' Scarrone). By the way, Rocche Rivera's name derives from the unification of the words *rocche* (castles or cliffs, in Italian) and Rivera, the family name of Arnaldo Rivera, longtime mayor of Castiglione Falletto and wine producer. In the end, does all this matter? Maybe, maybe not. For sure, it is interesting to note that the best Scarrone Barolos have historically come from the Rivera part of today's Scarrone. At the same time, Bava's very fine Barolo Scarrone comes from Scarrone's more northern reaches, so it's not so cut and dried.

In more or less in the central portion of the vineyard district and also its highest point there is the Vigna Mandorlo, from where the Fratelli Giacosa make an excellent wine. Lower down, the Luigi Oddero e Figli estate produces a delicious Barolo Rocche Rivera (I'm guessing I don't need to tell you why the wine is called so). Due to the fact the vineyard district is now characterized by a gradual contoured shape, vineyards within have different exposures; and while the soils throughout Scarrone are relatively homogenous, there are sections that present noteworthy differences. In lithological terms, Scarrone is made up mostly by typical Saint Agatha Fossil Marls, but there are areas of Diano Sandstone too: if you just stop to think for a moment about that simple fact, then you realize immediately just how different the Barolos of Scarrone can potentially be. To make it a little easier, as a general rule it is worth knowing that the highest sections of the vineyard district are richer in sand, with less clay and loam than the lower ones: and this *does* have a bearing on the finished wines. Clearly, to be able to pick up that geological reality with greater ease when you will be tasting or enjoying a Scarrone Barolo at dinner, you need to know is where in this vineyard district the producer whose wine you are drinking owns his/her vines.

Scarrone producers and the wines

The Luigi Oddero e Figli estate boasts one of the best technical teams in all of Barolo (for one, er two, the consultant winemakers Dante Scaglione and Francesco Versio, who long worked together at Bruno Giacosa) and makes its Barolo Rocche Rivera from three hectares planted between 220-380 meters. The technical team has worked long and hard on this site and over time has been able to identify and subdivide its Scarrone holding in three sections. The highest piece, fully south-facing, is the one characterized by vines planted perpendicularly to the hill (the *ritto chino* system mentioned in "What the producers say" section above) as well as by a greater soil sand content amidst the clay and loam. It is from this section of their Scarrone holdings that Luigi Oddero makes the Barolo Rocche Rivera. Lower down, the soil clay and loam increase, and the grapes are used to make a Langhe Nebbiolo. Though these last grapes give perfectly likeable juicy and fruity Nebbiolo, it is the grapes from the highest section that give the more complex deeper wine, and hence are used to make the Barolo. In my experience, these grapes do not just deliver more structure to the finished wine, but also noteworthy saline and spicy elements.

I point out that Scarrone never gives Barolo-behemoths: in this it is very much a Barolo of Castiglione Falletto, wines that are more about balance than sheer volume and power. Only in the warmest years does Luigi Oddero's wine have really noteworthy structure. Last but not least, relative to this Luigi Oddero Barolo: remember I told you earlier that Scarrone now reaches Rocche di Castiglione? Well, about 5% of the Luigi Oddero Scarrone vineyard actually falls within the Rocche di Castiglione vineyard district: but since the grapes there, once transformed into wine, would end up amounting to only about two barriques or one tonnneaux of wine, the estate just goes ahead and bottles all the wine as a Barolo Scarrone Rocche Rivera (remember that an MGA-labeled Barolo only needs to have 85% of its grapes coming from the MGA vineyard district named on the label). In fact, about 30% of the classic estate Luigi Oddero Barolo (depending on the vintage) is made with Scarrone grapes too.

The Fratelli Giacosa's Scarrone Barolo is excellent too: it's called Vigna Mandorlo (Barolo Scarrone Vigna Mandorlo: don't confuse this with the Mandorla subregion of the Sarmassa vineyard district. See SARMASSA file) in honour of the *mandorlo*, or almond tree, which requires a temperate climate to be able to grow and survive. The fact that the almond tree can grow in this area attests to the warmer microclimate of this section of Scarrone. The Fratelli Giacosa vines are subdivided in many different plots beginning at the foot of the castle on a roughly 25-35% slope gradient between 300-380 meters above sea level.

Benchmark wineries/Reference point producers of Barolo Scarrone: Fratelli Giacosa, Luigi Oddero e Figli, Bava.

SERRA

Township	Serralunga d'Alba
Reference Map	See Map of Serralunga d'Alba MGAs (Ch. 10)
Size (ha) (Tot / Barolo MGA)	10.28 / 4.71
Production 2021 (hl)	274.49
Altitude	350 - 390 meters a.s.l. roughly
Exposure	From east to northeast on the eastern side and from west to southwest on the opposite side.
N. Claimants MGA	7
Other grape varieties planted:	Barbera; Dolcetto
Land Units	Land of Serralunga d'Alba
Soil (stage):	Serravallian

Producers claiming the MGA

Sergio Giudice; Icardi; Silvana Mauro; Pio Cesare; Prunotto; Giovanni Rosso; Rosanna Vivaldo.

Wines

Icardi - Barolo Serra (and Riserva); **Giovanni Rosso** - Barolo Serra

Ian's assessment of the vineyard district, its wines and its potential

Serra is located in the southern half of the Serralunga territory just below the town of Serralunga itself, straddling the ridge with its two halves lying over the two flanks that drop off from the top of the ridge. It has therefore the vineyard districts of San Bernardo to the northeast; Collaretto to the northwest; Ornato to the west and southwest; and Lirano to the east and southeast. Broadly speaking, one might say that geologically and exposure-wise it does not differ much from the San Bernardo vineyard district (at least one producer I've talked to over the years feels strongly about this and didn't even see the need for two different vineyard districts), but things are a little more complex than that.

Serra's exposure is very different depending which flank you are on: vines face east to northeast on the eastern flank of the ridge and west to southwest on the opposite, western side. And although the lithology is all Lequio Formation (very typical of the Serralunga commune) the soil also changes considerably. In samples analysis data I have from southeastern-facing sites (at about 300-340 meters above sea level), it is 57% loam, 23% sand and 20% clay; but from the other flank it is 40% loam, 20% sand and 40% clay.

Serra producers and the wines

Giovanni Rosso makes the only Barolo Serra I know, and like practically all his wines, it's excellent. He owns about one hectare facing southeast at 378 meters above sea level; the vines were planted in 1984, 1996 and 2003, the first vintage was 2004. He owns east-southwest facing plots that are both higher up and lower down the slope: the higher ones need not be deleafed, while the lower ones need both thinning and deleafing. The wine is rich, dense, creamy and full of reminders of licorice, menthol and a dark red cherry nectar quality (almost of black cherry). It's not the most refined Barolo you'll ever drink, but it's hard to argue with its sexy, sultry immensely easy to like charms. Pio Cesare owns vines since 1998; his east-facing vines of Nebbiolo clones 141 and 185 are planted at 400 meters above sea level. The wine is blended into the estate's classic Barolo.

Benchmark wineries/Reference point producers of Barolo Serra: Giovanni Rosso.

SERRA DEI TURCHI

Township	La Morra
Reference Map	See Map of La Morra MGAs (Ch. 10)
Size (ha) (Tot / Barolo MGA)	22.03 / 5.10
Production 2021 (hl)	270.18
Altitude	200 - 260 meters a.s.l. roughly
Exposure	From south to southeast, plus an east and northwest facing parts.
N. Claimants MGA	5
Other grape varieties planted:	Barbera; Dolcetto; white varieties
Land Units	Land Unit of Castiglione for the highest plots bordering Borgata Serra dei Turchi; Land Unit of Barolo for the remaining plots descendants to Gallo d'Alba
Soil (stage):	Tortonian

Producers claiming the MGA

Poderi Grimaldi; Poderi Gianni Gagliardo; Pugnane (Fratelli Sordo); Tenute Stefano Farina; Osvaldo Viberti.

Wines

Poderi Gianni Gagliardo - Barolo Serra dei Turchi; **Osvaldo Viberti** - Barolo Serra dei Turchi; **San Silvestro** - Barolo Serra dei Turchi.

What the producers' say

Viberti Osvaldo: "This site gives very broad Barolos that have rich aromas and flavors of fruit macerated in alcohol, even cocoa and licorice".

Ian's assessment of the vineyard district, its wines and its potential

Serra dei Turchi, or the "mountain area of the Turks" is a name that traces its historical roots to the presence of a military camp of Saracens that had been set up where the vineyard district is located today. Despite that historical root, Serra dei Turchi, a little Rodney Dangerfield-like, has long gotten no respect. At the very least, it is one of those vineyard areas of Barolo that few people seem to ever talk or write about. While other Barolo vineyard districts have recently jumped into the limelight, often for no other discernible reason other than some big-name producers having invested there, Serra dei Turchi is among those that remain in the background. But I for one think its Barolos are delicious, easygoing and approachable at an early age, and can be really excellent. Others obviously think so too: while only about 68% of the vineyard district is planted to vines, 86% of that is Nebbiolo for Barolo production, and so…

Perhaps the "lightness thing" is due to where the vineyard district lies: in the La Morra commune, just below Santa Maria and next to Bricco San Biagio, not exactly two vineyard area names that roll off the tongue of the hipper, hotshot wine lovers out there. And even less so of those people for whom size in wine matters. And yet, people who know the Barolo area well (many producers included) are very aware of what Serra dei Turchi can deliver and believe it doesn't get the love it deserves. I'm certainly not the only one who thinks Serra dei Turchi is heavily underrated. For example, no less an expert than Pietro Ratti has told me clearly over the years that "Serra dei Turchi is much better than people think: it's a tongue of soil that is very different from Ciocchini and other areas around it. Serra dei Turchi boasts a different soil and its vineyards lie generally higher up". And a large number of my readers would be really surprised to know where some well-known, bigger, Barolo houses go buy ready-made Barolo from producers there in difficult years (like in the rain-plagued 2002 vintage) when their own productions had been forcibly and greatly reduced.

Clearly, Serra dei Turchi is not a high-lying vineyard area, and its low altitude (only 200-260 meters above sea level) can pose problems in hot droughty years, with wines that boast tannins they shouldn't be exactly boasting about, given their grittiness. But it is blessed with very interesting soils, that in parts of the vineyard district are of the Tortonian stage (mostly typical Saint Agatha Fossil Marls but also a little of the sandy type); and though I know not everyone believes so, I have been repeatedly told that's some parts of Serra dei Turchi have pockets of Diano Sandstone lithology. Therefore, complexity in the finished wines should not be hard to come by, depending on where the estate's vineyards lie. For sure, an increasing number of producers have looked to buy or rent in Serra dei Turchi, and now more and more estates are farming and making wine from there. An example is Gaja, who bought 2.2 hectares in 2016 that were planted with east (one third) and southeast facing (about two thirds of the total) in 1996. Gaia Gaja has characterized the soil to me as being extremely sandy, and I'm not at all surprised. And speaking of sand, its presence is brought to the fore in the vineyards farmed by the Gianni Gagliardo estate, where soils composition is loam (46.3%), sand (28.2%), and clay (25.5%). The estate actually has two adjacent plots located at about 210 meters above sea level: one is a convex-shaped hillock, what in Italy and France are described as having the shape of donkey's back (*schiena d'asino* or *dos d'ane*), and the other a concave bowl-shaped vineyard area. The estate's Nebbiolo vines are of clones 142 and 230, two that give very typical wines, for the most part very graceful and not excessively thick, which makes them perfectly suited to the geological and lithological reality of Serra dei Turchi. That too is terroir: even better, that too is interpreting and broadcasting terroir intelligently.

Serra dei Turchi producers and their wines

I have less experience with San Silvestro's bottling of Serra dei Turchi Barolo, but I can vouch for the quality in every Osvaldo Viberti bottle of Barolo Serra dei Turchi I have ever tried (clearly some vintages having been more successful than others, as is the case with everybody's wines). I have had practically every vintage of Barolo Serra dei Turchi made by Osvaldo Viberti over the last fifteen years to know that the wines are better than average. It is always nicely broad, with rich ripe and generally suave red cherry and sweet spice aromas and flavors, complicated by hints of milk chocolate and lightly roasted Arabica (not Robusta) coffee beans being the norm. If I have one caveat, be aware perhaps of droughty years, when the sandy nature of the soil can sometimes lead to tough or gritty tannins. But for the most part, given that the wine doesn't cost a pretty (or even ugly) penny, wine lovers would do well to reach out and see for themselves: I doubt anyone will be left disappointed by having done so. In this respect, all the good things I can say about Serra dei Turchi as a source of approachable, delicious and fun Barolo is the wine made by the Gianni Gagliardo estate. Always blessed with a generous mouthfeel, the wine is only apparently subtle but actually packs a lot more texture and depth than it seems at first. Here too there is a generous red ripe cherry presence, not to mention a noteworthy salinity that speaks for all the sand in the site's soil.

Benchmark wineries/Reference point producers of Barolo Serra dei Turchi: Osvaldo Viberti. Also good: Gianni Gagliardo.

SERRADENARI

Township	La Morra
Reference Map	See Map of La Morra MGAs (Ch. 10)
Size (ha) (Tot / Barolo MGA)	101.19 /14.24
Production 2021 (hl)	773.39
Altitude	450 - 540 meters a.s.l. roughly
Exposure	From south to southwest for the vineyards overlooking the town of Barolo and Cascina Sorella, west and from south to southwest in the remaining parts.
N. Claimants MGA	6
Other grape varieties planted:	Barbera; Dolcetto; white varieties
Land Units	Land Unit of Berri
Soil (stage):	Messinian

Producers claiming the MGA

460 Casina Bric; Dosio; Malvirà; Ratti; Giulia Negri (Serradenari); Cabutto - Tenuta La Volta

Wines

460 Casina Bric - Barolo Serradenari; **Dosio** - Barolo Serradenari; **Giulia Negri** - Barolo Serradenari, Barolo Marassio.

Marco Dotta (past consultant winemaker to numerous estates including Dosio): "Dosio's vineyard in Serradenari was planted in 2001 and very soon it was appreciated the site was worthy of its own bottling. When I was there, the fermentation process lasted for eighteen to twenty days and for aging we used the 25 hectoliter Slavonian oak cask. In my opinion, as a wine, Serradenari is characterized by a fruit-driven nose reminiscent of red cherry, rose and violet. Based on my experience, it's a site that gives Barolo blessed with optimal balance between acidity and the tannic structure".

Giulia Negri (Serradenari): "Serradenari is the highest vineyard area of Barolo, sort of a small balcony overlooking Piedmont, at the foot of the Langhe, in front of the Ligurian Alps right to the Cervino, with the gorgeous Monviso that dominates down the middle. I think of my wine as soft and feminine, rich in nuances of violet, ginger, licorice and vanilla".

Ian's assessment of the vineyard district, its wines and its potential

Serradenari is a very interesting, potentially excellent Barolo site. Its name is interesting. Its wines are interesting. Its estates have interesting histories. And it's an interesting vineyard district in that it's a sign of the times. In the end, it all amounts to making the time you'll spend with Serradenari, its producers, and wines a rather interesting time. How interesting is all of that?

Serradenari's name derives from an unhappier time: in medieval times, during not infrequent outbreaks of the plague, poor families would literally take to the hills in an effort to escape it (literally, running for their lives). In so doing, they would take all their belongings and few savings along with them. Hence, ever since about the 1450s, the area has been known as "Sara D'nè", or Serradenari, meaning "to hold one's money in his or her own hands". The word *serra* means to "hold on tightly to"), while *denari* means "money". Given the Covid-19 infested times we live in nowadays, that story is very of the times. And while the etymology (as in the chronological account of the birth and development of a particular word or element of a word) of this vineyard area's name is interesting already as is, there is more to it. This because *serra* is also the Italian word for cliffs or more exactly, a "mountainous chain that proceeds in a linear manner". And Serradenari is the highest vineyard area of La Morra and all Barolo. And given that, in another sign of the times we live in, numerous estates (for example Renato Ratti and Boroli, neither one of which farmed or owned land in Serradenari until only recently) have recently bought vineyards in this vineyard district attracted by its high altitude and cooler mesoclimate, you might say there is not just a *serra* here, but also plenty of *denari* moving around too (as in money -*denari*- related to land sales).

Until very recently, Serradenari and its wines were never talked about much, but that does not appear to have been the case centuries ago. An old municipal map drawn by Filippo Ravenale (a land surveyor in La Morra) dating back to the thirtieth of September 1880 declares Serradenari as the highest of all Barolo vineyards, where "*ove trovansi circa cinque giornate di barolo e barbera*", or in English, "where you find five *giornate* of Barolo and Barbera". A *giornata* is an old Italian measuring unit that was once used all over the country, but that in a deliciously Italian way meant, and still means, different sizes to different people (depending on which commune and which region you were from). In Piedmont, a *giornata* was equivalent more or less to 0.38 hectares, or the amount of vineyard land that in theory one could work on in one day all by himself.

Serradenari producers and the wines

For my good fortune, I am very well acquainted with the Barolos of Serradenari having been the first international wine writer to visit the area and taste the wines from barrel. For example, I well remember the time at the Serradenari estate when they hadn't even finished building the winery yet: I literally tasted with the winemaker while he lied belly-down on top of the tightly bunched up barrels -I'm not kidding- using the "thief" to pull wine from different barrels by just moving his arm around from barrel to barrel). Happy memories of a Barolo, and a time, that, somewhat sadly, no longer exist.

In 2001, Toni Negri, whose family had owned the Serradenari estate for something like one hundred and fifty years, looked to reorganize things and began planting vines in 2002 (for example, with Nebbiolo clone 71). He had to plant anew because his father Francesco had actually uprooted all the grapevines in order to plant a forest where he could go hunting for white truffles (still very much an activity at the Serradenari estate, for visitors and clients too). According to Negri, when he began planting there were no other vineyards in the immediate area; and I can vouch that in late 2004 when I first visited, my gaze fell upon a really beautiful panorama (still is, in fact) that was however pretty well devoid of vineyards. As he was just starting out, Negri's 2004 Barolo was made for him by another well-regarded local producer, then in 2005 he went solo. In the meantime, he had called upon well-known and much travelled consultant winemaker Roberto Cipresso to make his wines. Cipresso wanted to plant Chardonnay and Pinot Noir there (though we can shake our heads at this now, keep in mind it common to do so in those times). The estate planted Chardonnay and Pinot Nero selecting Burgundy clones from the excellent Tutzer nursery in Alto Adige, to go along with the Nebbiolo (Cipresso stopped consulting in 2009, though I have had contrasting dates given to me over the years: it might have been 2007 instead).

In the meantime, Negri's daughter Giulia had graduated with a Master's degree from a prestigious Italian business school in Management and Innovation Technology. For a certain time, the family's thought had been to sell the estate once it was up and running, but Giulia found herself spending more and more time at Serradenari and in the vineyards instead of in Milan. Until the happy day in 2012 when she decided to make wine her life and moved permanently to the Langhe. At the time, she didn't care too much for the Serradenari wines: having spent time in Burgundy where she has friends, she wanted to make different wines than those being made at Serradenari. And so, Giulia created her own line and brand, 'Giulia Negri', that in her father's and her own words "… were very different wines from Serradenari's". In any case, her father left her to (wo)man the show as of 2014: she started out with one Pinot Noir, one Chardonnay, and one Nebbiolo vineyard. In 2017, she took over formally the (whole) kit and caboodle: the estate was briefly referred to as Serradenari by Giulia Negri but quickly became today's Giulia Negri-Serradenari. At the time, Giulia could count on six and a half hectares of vineyards (and twelve hectares more of woods) that were so divided: one hectare of Pinot Nero (Pinot Noir), 0.5 hectares of Chardonnay and rest of Nebbiolo, but a number of things were destined to change.

In 2015, after having commissioned geologic studies of her holdings, she decided she was going to make three Barolos, from three distinct vineyards that differ slightly for altitude and exposure, but that most importantly have three different soils. These three Barolos are: La Tartufaia (mostly clay-loam but with a very strong presence of sand; the vines are planted at 460 meters above sea level and face west); Serradenari (mostly clay-loam with calcareous marl; the vines are planted at 520 meters above sea level and face southwest); and Marassio (mostly clay-loam with limestone; the vines are planted at 536 meters above sea level and face west). The grand total of annual Barolo production was only of about 20,000 bottles. Of the three, there's slightly more of the La Tartufaia. Her vinification consisted in 40-45 days maceration-fermentation in truncated conical wooden vats (with temperatures never allowed to creep up above 30-31°C); aging took place in 25 hectoliter used barrels (about 24 months long for the La Tartufaia, thirty for the other two).

Giulia's wines are elegant and lively, and speak of her relatively high-altitude vineyards: lots of acid nerve and perfumed violet and floral aromas, with flavors of fresh red berries and menthol. The Barolo La Tartufaia strikes me as a more essential, more linear wine, in which the presence of the soil sand is very obvious. Not especially fleshy, it's very pure and perfumed, an essence of Nebbiolo. The Serradenari and Marassio are richer and deeper, with the Serradenari having more lift and complexity, not to mention citrussy acid lift. But no matter how you slice them, er, drink them, the wines are excellent.

The other estate that has had a long association with Serradenari is Dosio. In 2010, the Dosio estate bought two hectares planted in 1974 at 450-480 meters above sea level and began making a Barolo. It chose, not unreasonably, to age it in large oak barrels (currently for eighteen months or more, depending on the vintage).

Bruno Giacosa also made a Barolo from Serradenari, though it was never labeled as such. Giacosa called his Barolo 'Croera di La Morra', because the Nebbiolo grapes were sourced from the Croera fraction of Serradenari where he had bought a plot at the beginning of the 2000s. Croera itself is an area of Serradenari that takes its name from a small collection of houses located just east of, and right at the border with, the Berri vineyard district; it's also just above the La Serra vineyard district and underneath the Bricco del Dente mountaintop. In terms of Barolo landscape, it's an extreme area that has been described to me by one very acute producer as a Star Trek-like "Barolo's last frontier". Giacosa only made a Barolo (a white label non-Riserva) from there in one vintage, the 2004. Although Giacosa was left unimpressed by his 2004 Barolo Croera, never making it again (in fact, it is the only La Morra Barolo the *maestro* ever made) and sold the vineyard in 2012, I point out that it wasn't a bad wine at all, quite the contrary. And he wasn't the only famous name in Barolo buying grapes from Croera: Renato Ratti did too, so Croera must have had something going for it.

And wouldn't you know it, but Pietro Ratti, son of Renato Ratti, certainly thinks it does. It just so happens that the Renato Ratti winery bought the Cascina Sorello in Serradenari and 4.5 hectares of vineyards previously owned by Boroli, making its first ever Barolo Serradenari in the 2019 vintage (the wine will be released in 2023). The 20 to 40 years old vines are planted at almost 500 meters above sea level, and just like it is over at Giulia Negri, the grapes are still being harvested in October (despite climate change) as was commonplace twenty years ago all over Barolo but is rare nowadays. The wine is aged partly in barriques and partly in 25 hectoliter casks for two years.

Benchmark wineries/Reference point producers of Barolo Serradenari: Giulia Negri. Also good: Renato Ratti.

SILIO

Township	La Morra
Reference Map	See Map of La Morra MGAs (Ch. 10)
Size (ha) (Tot / Barolo MGA)	41.56 / 0.72
Production 2021 (hl)	24.29
Altitude	230-350 meters a.s.l. roughly
Exposure	Prevalently east-northeast, plus a small part facing southeast
N. Claimants MGA	1
Other grape varieties planted:	Barbera; Dolcetto
Land Units	Land Unit of La Morra in the southern plots bordering Roncaglie; Land Unit of Barolo for the remaining parts;
Soil (stage):	Tortonian

Producers claiming the MGA

Rizieri.

Ian's assessment of the vineyard district, its wines and its potential

Well, I don't know about you, but I've never had a Barolo Silio before, and that tells me something. And if I have, I don't remember it, and that tells me something too. In fact, Silio is not a grapevine wasteland, as numerous producers grow Nebbiolo there: it's just they choose to use it to make either Langhe Nebbiolo or Nebbiolo d'Alba wines or to blend the grapes in with others to make a classic Barolo.

Silio is a vineyard district located in the northernmost reaches of the La Morra territory, sandwiched in between the vineyard districts of Roere di Santa Maria and Roncaglie. Rocche dell'Olmo and Boscatto in the Verduno commune are across from it to its west and northwest, respectively. The vineyard district's soil is the typical one of the northern part of the Verduno commune too, the Tortonian origin Saint Agatha Fossil Marls of the laminated type (which is the same soil lithology of Monvigliero, for example). By contrast, while soil is more less homogenous throughout Silio, exposures are varied, as is the altitude. Gaia Gaja tells me that the soil is somewhat reminiscent of that of Serralunga, even though the vineyard district is in La Morra. Unfortunately, as no Barolos are made with Silio grapes only, and I have never had any microvinifications from this site alone, there's really very little I can say about past or future Barolos made from Silio. Perhaps in time the site will be proven to be a very good one (given how many people grow Nebbiolo there it's likely a good one, and maybe climate change will help it give even more interesting Nebbiolo wines in the future), but until we have a sufficient body of wines made from there, and over sufficient vintages, jury's out.

Benchmark wineries/Reference point producers of Barolo Silio: None currently available.

SOLANOTTO

Township	Castiglione Falletto
Reference Map	See Map of Castiglione MGAs (Ch. 10)
Size (ha) (Tot / Barolo MGA)	2.86
Production 2021 (hl)	0
Altitude	220 - 270 meters a.s.l. roughly
Exposure	From west to southwest.
N. Claimants MGA	0
Other grape varieties planted:	Barbera; Dolcetto
Land Units	Land Unit of Barolo
Soil (stage):	Tortonian

Ian's assessment of the vineyard district, its wines and its potential

Solanotto is a vineyard district of Castiglione Falletto that follows on the same slope the better-known Vignolo district, but in fact both are on the same hilly crest that also harbors the ultra-famous Monprivato (at the other end of the same crest) and Codana. Solanotto's vineyard area is draped over the terminal part of the crest, and most of it has a fair amount of sunlight exposure (as Solanotto's name implies: perhaps a reference to *sole* or sun, but not every local I have talked to agrees with this interpretation).

It has always struck me as somewhat curious, strange even, that a local producer had never tried bottling a single-site Barolo from it. I mean, we are talking about a hillside that boasts one of Barolo's ten or twelve most famous and best vineyards of all (Monprivato), plus two others that are, at the very least, above average premier crus (Codana and Vignolo). So how uninteresting can a Solanotto Barolo really be? Clearly, I am well aware that even a few hundred meters in one direction or another will make a huge difference in the quality of Barolo produced, but it seems to me that Solanotto is a bit of a missed opportunity. After all, it cannot be by accident that the list of those who have owned/rented/rent or own vineyards in Solanotto reads like a "who's who" of Castiglione Falletto Barolo producers, including Azelia, Cavallotto, Paolo Scavino, and Vietti.

When I look and think about this hilly crest, it has always struck me as being not unlike the hillside range that characterizes the Alsace towns of Kaysersberg and Kientzheim. Standing on the road stretching from Kaysersberg towards Kientzheim (with your back to Domaine Weinbach, one of the world's thirty or so best wine domains), you have before you an impressive land mass that boasts not one not two not three but four *grand crus* one right after another: left to right, these are the Schlossberg, the Furstentum, the Mambourg and the Markrain. The analogy holds in that the Schlossberg, the most famous of those four (Riesling-wise, at least, because the Mambourg has long been one of Alsace's most important sites for Gewurztraminer), lies at one end of the range while the Markrain, way at the other end, is the least famous of the bunch and its wines understandably less sought after. But even the Markrain's wines are, by all measures, still pretty impressive and I can't help but think that the story with Solanotto, also located at one extreme of a hilly crest, could very be the same.

Clearly, because of its conformation at the tip of the crest, exposures vary in Solanotto, and so not just Nebbiolo, but many other typical native grapes of Piedmont are planted there too. By contrast, the soil is rather homogenous, mostly the Tortonian stage typical Saint Agatha Fossil Marls, the lithology that most characterizes the Barolos of the La Morra and Barolo communes. Clearly, the combination of the more convex, sun-exposed areas, relatively low altitude, and with mostly west to southwest exposures should all combine to give round, pleasantly accessible Barolos full of fruit and charm.

Solanotto producers and the wines

The Cavalier Bartolomeo estate made for many years what was one of my 'Top-Ten Barolo Best Buys', their Barolo Altenasso-Solanotto. So, you understand why I think that Solanotto could potentially have quite a bit to say in terms of fine wine (in fact, I think highly of Altenasso as a Barolo-producing site too). It helps that winemaker Dario Borgogno, who has been making wine from Solanotto for years, has great vines to work with: the 0.38 hectares are planted with fifty-five years old Nebbiolo at about 360 meters above sea level.

Today the estate labels the wine as a Barolo Altenasso only. They don't have much Solanotto to work with and make wine from (at least not enough that they could make a Barolo Solanotto on its own), and so the Solanotto grapes still find their way in the Altenasso bottling. According to Dario Borgogno, Solanotto's Barolo is very different from Altenasso's, which is the more tannic and rustic when young of the two and in need of at least three years or so from the vintage to smoothen out (see ALTENASSO file). By contrast, Solanotto's Barolo is characterized by very ripe but fresh red fruit aromas and flavors, and a truly noteworthy amount of alcohol: the grapes ripen well and have no trouble packing in sugar, and this translates to a wine that is not at all shy on octanes and endowed with a lovely creaminess of fruit and compelling sweetness. In any case, it is an aromatically, perfumed wine that nicely complements the tougher, more structured Barolo from Altenasso: the two work very well together.

Benchmark wineries/Reference point producers of Barolo Solanotto: None currently available.

SORANO

Township	Serralunga d'Alba and Diano d'Alba
Reference Map	See Map of Serralunga d'Alba MGAs (Ch. 10) and Figure – Dian…
Size (ha) (Tot / Barolo MGA)	9.94 (Serralunga d'Alba) + 4.76 (Diano) / 6.39
Production 2021 (hl)	347.66
Altitude	250 – 320 meters a.s.l. roughly
Exposure	South to southeast on the slope of Diano d'Alba, from south to northwest on the slope facing Castiglione Falletto
N. Claimants MGA	7
Other grape varieties planted:	Barbera; Dolcetto; Freisa
Land Units	For the most Land Unit of Barolo (eastern slopes); Land Unit of Castiglione in the western slopes bordering Carpegna and San Rocco;
Soil (stage):	Tortonian

Producers claiming the MGA

Claudio Alario; Ascheri; Cortino; Fratelli Gerlotto; Groppone; Le Cecche; Mura Mura.

Wines

Alario Claudio - Barolo Sorano; **Ascheri** - Barolo Sorano; **Fratelli Gerlotto** - Barolo Sorano; **Le Cecche** - Barolo Sorano; **San Biagio** - Barolo Sorano; **Grimaldi** - Barolo Sorano.

What the producers say

Claudio Alario (Alario): "We came to acquire this vineyard in 2004. Sorano is the exact opposite of another of our vineyard sites, Riva Rocca: late-ripening, Sorano's wine has a more masculine and powerful character".

Gianluca Roggero (San Biagio): "Il Barolo Sorano was made by us for the first time in 2005. Texture-wise it's a very typical wine of Serralunga d'Alba."

Ian's assessment of the vineyard district, its wines and its potential

Sorano is one of those rare inter-communal vineyard districts, in this case divided up between the communes of Serralunga d'Alba and Diano D'Alba. It extends around the hamlet of Sorano (Borgata Sorano), a collection of houses located more or less in the middle of the vineyard district, but entirely within the larger Serralunga side. The smaller of the two sections of Sorano is the one that falls in the Diano d'Alba commune, running for its entire length in a manner more or less parallel to another Diano d'Alba vineyard district located to its south, La Vigna. The larger part of Sorano is in the Serralunga side, close by the vineyard districts of San Rocco to the south and Carpegna to the west and northwest. Like a few other Serralunga vineyard districts, Sorano's vineyards extend over both flanks of the Serralunga ridge that runs north-south through the entire denomination. However, beware that the road that runs atop the ridge and that normally serves as your guide to where the western-facing and eastern-flanks are (and therefore the respective portions of the vineyard districts) throws you a curve ball this time around. This is because while the road normally splits the vineyard district in two, such that when you are driving say going northwards, the two parts of the vineyard district drop off to your sides (clearly, to the left you have the western-facing flank; while off to your right is the eastern-facing flank), things are not so in the case of Sorano. Here, the entire Serralunga portion of the vineyard district is off to your right side. And so, as you drive from San Rocco up to the Borgata Sorano, the first segment of the Serralunga portion of Sorano is on the eastern-facing flank of the ridge; then the road turns sharply to the west and south away from the ridge (more or less at the Borgata), and so the next segment of Serralunga's Sorano (that basically starts at the Borgata Sorano and reaches the Carpegna vineyard district) is still to your right, but that's now the western-facing flank of the ridge. By contrast, the section of Sorano of the Diano d'Alba commune is draped over one long, slightly curvilinear eastern facing hillside flank.

What all that should make obvious is that there will inevitably be noteworthy differences in Sorano's vineyard areas in relation to exposure and meso- and micro-climates, but also of soil; in fact, such diversity is not just limited to the Diano d'Alba and Serralunga sections. To begin with, the two communal segments of Sorano are very different exposure-wise. As we have seen, the Serralunga segment has a more complicated, tortuous geography (reflected especially in its topography, while its altitude range and gradient are more or less the same as that of the Diano d'Alba side). Because of this, vines of the Serralunga segment can face in all possible directions, including south and north; by contrast the vast majority of the vineyards on the Diano d'Alba side face south/southwest. Soil-wise, the Serralunga side of Sorano is characterized by the presence of the Diano Sandstone, as well as a little of the typical Saint Agatha Fossils Marls formation. The Diano d'Alba side's lithology is instead almost all of the typical Saint Agatha Fossils Marls formation, with very little or any of the Diano Sandstone. Remembering just how different the Diano Sandstone and the typical Saint Agatha Fossils Marls formation lithologies are, that gives you quite a bit of information as to what the wines of each side of the Sorano vineyard district might be like.

Most of the wineries that own or rent vines in the Sorano vineyard district will tell you theirs are on the Serralunga side, which is fine, but estates that have theirs on the Diano d'Alba side are not worse off. Taking into account the range in exposures and soil lithology, it follows that the Barolos made within the Sorano vineyard district are potentially quite different one from the other. Given that Barolo's wine estates mostly have vineyards in just one of the two communes, that allows the interested Barolo enthusiast to distinguish fairly easily between the Barolo Sorano wines of Serralunga and those of Diano d'Alba. Which he or she prefers will be due mostly to individual taste preferences: both communes are associated with very good Barolos. Of course, ask anyone and they will immediately say, in that charmingly oblivious kneejerk sort of way, that the Serralunga side's Barolos are just so much the better ones (well, did you really expect otherwise?). Maybe so, but not necessarily. Rather than a world of blacks and whites, competently made wines have a way of fitting into a realm dominated by different shades of greys (fifty or otherwise), and so it is once again here. For example, the Diano d'Alba part of Sorano being characterized by soils that have more in common with those of La Morra and Barolo will give you a type of wine that is very different from that of the Serralunga section. So which Sorano Barolo you like best might also be in relation to which Barolo wine profile you prefer

Sorano producers and the wines

The most famous producer that has long been associated with Sorano is Claudio Alario; for many years, his was in fact the only Barolo Sorano that easy to find. Still today, most people consider his wine to be the benchmark by which all other Barolo Sorano ought to be judged by. An excellent wine, it is. Made from a one-hectare vineyard facing south. It is aged for twenty-four months in barriques, then another year in large oak casks. Alario tends to make rich, fleshy, often balsamic-tinged wines in which the oak can sometimes be too assertive: no matter how distinctive they are and how much they reflect the winemaker's signature, few people who try Alario's wines end up not liking them. He's just a very talented producer. I would add that his is also the gold-standard by which to judge the Barolo Sorano wines made in the Serralunga commune's territory.

Le Cecche is another estate making a Barolo Sorano (the estate takes its name from an eighteenth-century hamlet initially made up of three small farms only) from vines it bought there in 2010. While the winery is in the Diano d'Alba commune, their south-facing vines, planted at 280-300 meters above sea level and on clay-gravel soils, are in the Serralunga portion of the vineyard district. The wine is aged for about twenty-four months in French oak barriques and tonneaux (30% new). Since 1999, Ascheri also produces a Barolo Sorano, that like his other top site wines are only released in very good years like 2013 and 2016. His Sorano vines bask in a relatively cooler microclimate, not just because they lie at about 300 meters above sea level but because they face even northwest. I think the Sorano is Ascheri's best Barolo, one that impresses less for its size and flesh but rather for very good perfume and balance. It doesn't tire the palate and its magical perfume speaks of the Nebbiolo Rosé present in the mix (as much as 20%). Last but not least, San Biagio makes a Barolo Sorano from the two plots situated relatively high up the slope in the Serralunga portion of the vineyard district, a wine that reminds you of small red and blue fruits and of tobacco with hints of menthol.

Over on the Diano d'Alba side, Luigino Grimaldi farms Nebbiolo planted in 1979 that faces south/southeast at a relatively high altitude, ranging from 320 to 370 meters above sea level. Fratelli Gerlotto is another very good producer of Barolo Sorano (and also of hazelnuts, don't miss them: Piedmont's hazelnuts are the world's best, and Fratelli Gerlotto has them vacuum packed offerings are delicious). Both these wines are fairly traditionally made Barolos, and while they lack the power of some of those made on the Serralunga side, they showcase lovely balance and precision, not to mention a light on their feet quality that will keep them dancing on your taste buds long after you'll have finished the bottle. The small but high-quality producer La Contrada di Sorano owns a small parcel of vines in this vineyard district that though belonging to the Diano d'Alba territory has a lithology and soil more typical of Serralunga. The Nebbiolo vines are of Nebbiolo Lampia and were planted in 2009. The winery blends them with their Nebbiolo grapes from the Collaretto and San Rocco vineyard districts to make classic estate Barolo (see COLLARETTO file. See also SAN ROCCO file).

Benchmark wineries/Reference point producers of Barolo Sorano: a) <u>Sorano (Serralunga commune)</u>: Alario, Ascheri, La Contrada di Sorano, Le Cecche; b) <u>Sorano (Diano d'Alba commune)</u>: Fratelli Gerlotto, Luigino Grimaldi.

SOTTOCASTELLO DI NOVELLO

Township	Novello
Reference Map	See Map of Novello MGAs (Ch. 10)
Size (ha) (Tot / Barolo MGA)	59.73 / 15.52
Production 2021 (hl)	837.39
Altitude	340 - 420 meters a.s.l. roughly
Exposure	From south to southeast
N. Claimants MGA	6
Other grape varieties planted:	Barbera; Dolcetto; white varieties
Land Units	Land Unit of Novello
Soil (stage):	Tortonian

Producers claiming the MGA

Ca' Viola; Natalina Cappa; Giacomo Grimaldi; Le Ginestre; Massimiliano Passone; Comm. Armando Piazzo.

Wines

Ca' Viola - Barolo Sottocastello di Novello (and Riserva); **Giacomo Grimaldi** - Barolo Sottocastello di Novello; **Le Ginestre** - Barolo Sottocastello (and Riserva); **Armando Piazzo** - Barolo Riserva Sottocastello di Novello (and Riserva).

What the producers say

Beppe Caviola (Ca' Viola): "The parcel was acquired at the turn of the last century and we have vinified it separately under the Barolo Sottocastello di Novello denomination since 2006. Geographically, the vineyard district is located at the meeting point of the two main soil origins that create the Langhe region, Tortonian and Serravalian, the combination of which impart an optimal balance between elegance and complexity to the wine".

Ian's assessment of the vineyard district, its wines and its potential

Sottocastello di Novello is a vineyard district located in the southernmost portion of the Novello commune, right below the town itself, that is literally surrounded, cradled even, in the concavity of Sottocastello di Novello's wine glass bowl-like (why not?) shape. Therefore, the Novello vineyard district of Cerviano-Merli is to the north while Bricco San Pietro (of the Monforte commune) is to the east.

Sottocastello di Novello is blessed with a mesoclimate characterized by mild temperatures, continued breezes and optimal sun exposure, though hail can be a problem at times. The soil lithology is moistly Saint Agatha Fossil marls of the laminated type, but as elsewhere in Novello there are patches of the same lithological formation but of the sandy type, as well as of Diano Sandstone.

Sottocastello di Novello producers and their wines

Sottocastello di Novello is one of the better-known Novello vineyard districts, mostly on the strength of the excellent wines made by the Giacomo Grimaldi estate. Their interpretation of the vineyard district's Barolos strike me as having very good flesh and richness, usually dark fruit (darker than in most other Barolos that are almost always about red fruit), camphor and balsamic oils, with good underlying tannic structure, a sweet fleshy mix that is close to the wines of the Barolo and La Morra communes. Giacomo Grimaldi has owned/farmed land in this historic vineyard district of Novello since 1930. Their vines are planted on clay-calcareous soils face southwest. The Le Ginestre estate's vines in Sottocastello di Novello face south/southeast and are planted at an average of 400 meters above sea level. Both Barolos showcase good sweet fruit and flesh, while having more vertical personalities and greater lift than many Barolos from Ravera, which is the other truly famous vineyard district of Novello.

Benchmark wineries/Reference point producers of Barolo Sottocastello di Novello: Giacomo Grimaldi.

TEODORO

Township	Serralunga d'Alba
Reference Map	See Map of Serralunga d'Alba MGAs (Ch. 10)
Size (ha) (Tot / Barolo MGA)	23.58 / 1.27
Production 2021 (hl)	58.97
Altitude	230- 340 meters a.s.l. roughly
Exposure	From east to northeast
N. Claimants MGA	2
Other grape varieties planted:	Barbera; Dolcetto; Freisa; white varieties
Land Units	For the most Land Unit of Serralunga (eastern slopes); Land Unit of Castiglione for the plots bordering Cerretta.
Soil (stage):	Serravallian

Producers claiming the MGA

Giovanni Veglio e Figli; Vietti.

Wines

Cascina Luisin – Barolo del Comune di Serralunga; **Piergiorgio Savigliano** - Barolo Teodoro (*).

One of Serralunga's vineyard districts located far to the east in the commune's territory, Teodoro is in many respects an eastwards prolongation of the better-known Cerretta vineyard district. Teodoro presents a range of exposures and of soils, so there is the potential for different expressions of Barolo to be made; unfortunately, only a few Barolo Teodoro wines are made and they are not amongst the easiest to find.

Teodoro's soil lithology is not one but variable: in some sections of the vineyard district, it can be similar to parts of Castiglione Falletto and to parts of Monforte (Diano Sandstone), while in and others it is more typical of Serralunga (Lequio Formation). For the most part, there is a considerable presence of gravel in the calcareous-clay soil type. Teodoro's mesoclimate is also fairly strongly influenced by the nearby Talloria stream that helps make it a cooler site as opposed to Baudana or Vignarionda, two better-known and warmer vineyard district s of Serralunga.

In all honesty, I have had too few wines from this vineyard district to have formed over time any real impression about them, but I find it noteworthy that about three quarters of the vineyard district is under vine and most of that is Nebbiolo (clearly, somebody thinks you can make good wine in Teodoro, and so it probably is). The wines I have tried from barrel or as microvinifications prior to being blended in with those of other vineyard districts have always struck me for their perfumed lift and vibrancy: rose, pomegranate and candied orange peel are the descriptors that over the years I have, time and again, most often jotted down besides the name of Barolos from Teodoro.

Teodoro producers and their wines

The one really good wine I have had from here over the years, time and again, and that therefore makes me think Teodoro deserves to better known is the Barolo del Comune di Serralunga d'Alba Léon by the outstanding and somewhat underrated Cascina Luisin (an estate of Barbaresco, not Barolo). Their one hectare (just about) of southeast-facing, roughly forty years old vines, planted at about 300 meters above sea level, looks towards Sinio and is separated from Cerretta just by a little road. The Minuto family (owners of Cascina Luisin) likes to ferment in cement tanks for about fifty days (depending on the vintage: so, it was fifty in 2015, for example) and then age the wine in 30 hectoliter casks for three years. In fact, this wine is not all Teodoro, as some grapes from their holding in Cerretta are also blended in. The wine's name, Léon, is in honour of Leone, the vineyard's original owner. It was first released for sale in the 2001 vintage (they had made a couple of barriques in 2000 as a trial, they liked what they had, and so went for it). In a Barolo world where it's always the same names getting talked about and written up, I cannot recommend you this lovely, well-balanced, very precise Barolo strongly enough.

The new Fratelli Revello state (that resulted from a family split up in 2013) led by Enzo Revello has held onto its piece of Teodoro. The undertaking was not an easy one. The Teodoro holdings came into the family thanks to Luciana, Enzo's wife. Up until 2018, the vineyards (3.5 hectares in Cerretta and 1.5 hectares in Teodoro) were handled by the two brothers, then in 2019 the Fratelli Revello rented out the entire holding and bought it outright in 2020 (given that Luciana had seven brothers you realize it was quite the expense). Anyhow, the Teodoro parcel is planted at 260-330 meters above sea level very close to the Cerretta holdings of the Ettore Germano winery and to those they own in Cerretta (the lower-lying ones). As the hill curves, these vines face east (not south like their Cerretta vines), and is a rather sandy calcareous site. Mario Oliviero owns vines in Teodoro: his Teodoro plots are at 280 meters in altitude and were planted in 1995. He used to blend them with those of the Bricco Rocca to make the estate's Barolo Vigne Unite bottling, but starting in 2018, this Barolo will become the estate's Barolo del Comune di La Morra bottling, in which the grapes from Bricco Rocca will be blended with those of two new holdings he has long-term leases on in the La Morra commune's territory (one in Annunziata, planted in 1968; and the other in Boiolo, with Nebbiolo that was planted in 1999). According to Oliviero, the Barolo from Teodoro is especially dark in colour, richly fruity and spicy and characterized by a very strong tannic backbone, and that's good enough for me. Last but not least, the famous Vietti winery owns vineyards in Teodoro and blends its fruit with that of the Rocchettevino, Ravera, Scarrone, Le Coste di Monforte, Mosconi, and Fiasco vineyard districts to make their classic Barolo Castiglione estate blend. Luca Currado believes that Teodoro's relatively cool climate and highly sandy soil makes it ideal for whole bunch vinification, and so he vinifies his Teodoro grapes with about 60% whole bunches (in other words, with stems).

No doubt, the inclusion of Teodoro grapes to the Castiglione blend has undoubtedly increased the latter's perfume and lift.

Benchmark wineries/Reference point producers of Barolo Teodoro: Cascina Luisin.

TERLO

Township	Barolo	
Reference Map	See Map of Barolo MGAs (Ch. 10)	
Size (ha) (Tot / Barolo MGA)	22.03 / 8.36	
Production 2021 (hl)	439.02 (of which 89.42 hl of Barolo *MGA* Vigna)	
Altitude	320 - 400 meters a.s.l. roughly	
Exposure	Prevalently east	
N. Claimants MGA	6	
Other grape varieties planted:	Barbera; Dolcetto; white varieties	
Land Units	Land Unit of La Morra	
Soil (stage):	Tortonian	

Producers claiming the MGA

Cagliero; Vittorio Camerano; Cantine Prandi; Mauro Marengo; Poderi Luigi Einaudi; Tenute Del Vino.

Wines

Camerano - Barolo Terlo; **Poderi Luigi Einaudi** - Barolo Terlo and Barolo Terlo Vigna Costa Grimaldi; **L'Astemia Pentita** - Barolo Terlo (and Riserva).

What the producers say

Enrica Scavino (Paolo Scavino): "Our vineyard area is surrounded by woods, on a gentle slope, a rather fresh area. It is always one of the last vineyards we harvest, the vines are very old and have low yields".

Ian's assessment of the vineyard district, its wines and its potential

To the southwest of the town of Barolo, the Terlo vineyard district has the Novello commune's Ravera to the south and to the west; Le Coste and Rivassi also to the west; Paiagallo directly to the north and La Volta to the east. It has been somewhat enlarged with the advent of the official vineyard district names (in the past, its extension did not reach quite as high up as Paiagallo), but for the most part the vineyard district is true to what it used to be.

Characterized by a mostly Saint Agatha Fossil Marls lithology of various types (sandy and laminated, mostly), but there are sections of Terlo that boast more sand and others more sandstone and other still that are very rich in clay, a relatively high altitude and an eastern exposure, Terlo's wines can sometimes be surprisingly tannic and rigid, especially in their youth, but when they are firing on all cylinders, are just great wines. Terlo's are Barolos that develop slowly and while great on their own (but more so than with other Barolos form the Barolo commune, they require a bit of cellaring to show their best) and are therefore also perfect for Barolo estate blends because they provide a framework for fruit from other vineyard districts less known for their tannic power

Terlo producers and their wines

A number of excellent producers make really outstanding Barolos from Terlo: the estate that makes exceptionally good Barolos from Terlo is Luigi Einaudi (their 2017 Barolo Terlo Vigna Costa Grimaldi Barolo is a major knockout in a hot vintage where many even famous estates had trouble). Einaudi owns about 1.6 hectares of vines in Terlo that face southeast and planted back in 1977 between 300-320 meters in altitude. It is an exceptionally good Barolo, layered and thick yet vibrant and perfumed, I urge you to try and get a hold of any time you can. The Mauro Marengo estate farms about two hectares of Nebbiolo in Terlo that was planted in 1966 and 2020 between 380 and 400 meters above sea level. The soils are of the Saint Agatha Fossil Marls lithology of the sandy type higher up and shift to the laminated type lower down. The Barolo is exceptionally fresh and vibrant, nervous even, and expresses more floral (violet and rose) than fruity aromas and flavors, but he chooses to blend it with grapes from other vineyard districts (La Volta and Ravera) so as to make a classic estate Barolo. In my experience, it is a Barolo that ages very well. A little bit of Terlo grapes are included in the blend of Viberti's classic estate Barolo Buon Padre (along with those of many other vineyard districts: see SAN PIETRO file) and Chiara Boschis of the E. Pira/Chiara Boschis estate uses Terlo grapes in her famous Barolo Via Nuova blend.

Benchmark wineries/Reference point producers of Barolo Terlo: Luigi Einaudi.

TORRIGLIONE

Township	La Morra
Reference Map	See Map of La Morra MGAs (Ch. 10)
Size (ha) (Tot / Barolo MGA)	7.62 / 1.12
Production 2021 (hl)	55.41
Altitude	250 - 285 meters a.s.l. roughly
Exposure	From east to southeast in the better exposed parcels, northeast in the remaining parts
N. Claimants MGA	3
Other grape varieties planted:	Barbera; Sauvignon Blanc and other white varieties
Land Units	Land Unit of La Morra
Soil (stage):	Tortonian

Producers claiming the MGA

Gagliasso; Trediberri; Roberto Voerzio.

Wines

Mario Gagliasso - Barolo Torriglione; **Roberto Voerzio** - Barolo Torriglione

What the producers say

Davide Voerzio (Roberto Voerzio): "The single vinification of this cru can be traced back to 1996. In our opinion, this is a cru similar to Brunate and La Serra because of its warm microclimate. Powerful and substantial Barolos are typical of Torriglione, also characterized by spicy and dark fruit notes and more pronounced tannins than those of Brunate".

Ian's assessment of the vineyard district, its wines and its potential

Torriglione is a La Morra vineyard district situated between Rocche dell'Annunziata to the north and Boiolo to the south; Brunate is farther away. Torriglione forms the hill located at the foot of the hamlet that give it its name (and also to a small stream that flowed nearby the Rio del Torriglione, but every time I've been there recently it looked rather dry to me.

Torriglione's lithology is mostly the typical Saint Agatha Marls formation with areas that are slightly sandier (a typical Torriglione soil sample analysis shows 40% loam, 35% clay and only 25% sand) but for the most part, Torriglione is a clay-rich site. Its clay component (a heavy, compact clay) is very obvious when tasting the wines, that are almost always unfailingly big, chunky, chewy and large-scaled wines (with little of the grace of those of Cannubi, for example). In fact, the clay of Torriglione is so tough and compact that Nicola Oberto of Trediberri told me that the houses in the area are built directly onto the marl, without foundations. Torriglione's mesoclimate is a rather humid site, so wines from rainy years are less successful than those made in droughty ones.

Torriglione producers and the wines

Locals have long held Torriglione's Barolos in high esteem. Without doubt, the estate most associated with Torriglione is Gagliasso, and the family really loves the site and its wines. At least, Luca Gagliasso loves the chewy texture of Torriglione's Barolo. The estate is a relatively new one (in 2008 they only had two hectares of vineyards in production; see ROCCHE DELL'ANNUNZIATA file) but they also owned other vineyard land in Novello, La Morra and Monforte. In Torriglione they own 0.9 hectares, fully south-facing. Their Barolo Torriglione is really the poster-like advertisement of what Torriglione Barolos are all about: big, muscular, fleshy, fruit-forward, almost Castiglione Falletto- and Monforte-like (if without quite the same tannic backbone). Maybe not the most nuanced Barolos you will ever taste, but also more than likely to leave you impressed.

Trediberri owns a very steep plot in Torriglione right below the winery and in front of Rocche dell'Annunziata that is between 250-270 meters above sea level. The vines were planted in 1955, 1985, 1992, 1995 and have different exposures because of a curve in the hill's topography, ranging from east- to fully south-facing [but in the larger one hectare east-facing part the estate grows mostly Barbera (and some Sauvignon Blanc!), while it's the south-facing 0.5-hectare section that is planted to Nebbiolo]. As a curiosity, Bartolo Mascarello, the grand old master of Barolo, used to refer to his plots in Rocche dell'Annunziata as being of Torriglione (it's easy enough to verify: just check any label of his Barolo from the 1980s, for example). They were never in Torriglione, and even Maria Teresa Mascarello was never able to give me a reason as to why her dad would have thought so. No matter, considering how great Bartolo's Barolo was and is, had the old man wanted to call his parcel Rome or Turin, well, you know what? Fine by me.

Benchmark wineries/Reference point producers of Barolo Torriglione: Gagliasso.

VALENTINO

Township	Castiglione Falletto
Reference Map	See Map of Castiglione MGAs (Ch. 10)
Size (ha) (Tot / Barolo MGA)	11.68 / 0.28
Production 2021 (hl)	14.96
Altitude	240 - 320 meters a.s.l. roughly
Exposure	East in the better exposed parcels, and from northwest lo northeast in the remaining parts
N. Claimants MGA	1
Other grape varieties planted:	Barbera; Dolcetto,
Land Units	Land Unit of Castiglione in the highest plots bordering Castiglione village; Land Unit of Barolo in the remaining parts.
Soil (stage):	Tortonian

Producers claiming the MGA

Lorenzo Cordero.

Ian's assessment of the vineyard district, its wines and its potential

Valentino is to the east of the town of Castiglione Falletto, sandwiched in between the vineyard districts of Monprivato, Brunella, Fiasco and Codana. It can be very easily seen when you stand on the hilltop of the Boroli estate in Brunella, a monopole of theirs (if you look from one side of the winery building; if you circle round the building and look from the other side of the winery, then you can see Villero). Exposures and soil lithology vary in Valentino, but there is a noteworthy presence in sand throughout.

I have never tasted a Barolo Valentino, so I admit to being no help whatsoever here. Then again, I'm not sure that a Barolo from Valentino has ever been made. But with a name like that, at the very least any wine has some ready-made built-in marketing potential.

Benchmark wineries/Reference point producers of Barolo Valentino: None currently available.

VIGNANE

Township	Barolo	
Reference Map	See Map of Barolo MGAs (Ch. 10)	
Size (ha) (Tot / Barolo MGA)	11.56 / 3.46	
Production 2021 (hl)	179.06	
Altitude	230 - 290 meters a.s.l. roughly	
Exposure	West	
N. Claimants MGA	4	
Other grape varieties planted:	Barbera; Dolcetto; white varieties	
Land Units	Land Unit of Barolo	
Soil (stage):	Tortonian	

Producers claiming the MGA

Eraldo Borgogno; Aldo Bianco; Paolo Scavino; Luciano Sandrone.

Wines

Eraldo Borgogno – Barolo Vignane; **Gillardi** – Barolo Vignane

Ian's assessment of the vineyard district, its wines and its potential

An official vineyard district of the Barolo commune, Vignane is located to the northeast of the town and surrounded by the vineyard districts of Castellero to the north, Bussia (in Monforte) to the east, Zuncai to the south, and Preda to the west. Its soil is of mostly of a typical Saint Agatha Fossils Marls lithology; its altitude is really not that high (but higher up than Castellero, of which it is really the prolongation up the same slope); and its vines face mostly west. All of which combines to give softer, more user-friendly, perfumed, suave wines that are accessible early, at least in my experience.

The Barolos of Vignane have the perfume and lift of the Barolos of La Morra but also the size and texture of those from Castiglione Falletto (well, almost), so that when all is said and done, they really do remind you of a Barolo from the commune of Barolo. Maybe for this reason, Vignane Barolo performs well in blends. Apparently, adding a little Vignane to the Barolos made from sites known for their elegantly austere but ultimately more rigid wines and all of a sudden, the sum is much better than its individual parts. To put it in other words, every time I have tasted micro-vinifications of young Nebbiolo wines from Vignane destined to become Barolo after the required minimum aging period, I always came away impressed by their balance. So much so in fact that if I had to point out just one descriptor for Vignane's Barolo, it would not be a fruit or floral or spice descriptor, but rather equilibrium. These are wines that seem like they were born suave. In fact, Barolos that are very commune of Barolo-like.

Luca Sandrone of Sandrone believes that "... As strange as it may seem, Vignane Barolos have aromas that are similar to some Barolos of Serralunga: but compared to Serralunga's wines they are always lighter-styled, fruitier, and fresher. It's certainly a less tannic Barolo than Baudana's, for example". By contrast, his brother Luciano sticks closer to home, saying that Vignane's Barolo is more like that of Cannubi Boschis (the grapes of which they use to make their Barolo Aleste), but without quite the aromatic complexity of that famous site's best wines. The siblings agree that Vignane delivers wines of real elegance. Certainly, they are not the only producers whom you ask for an opinion about Vignane and all seem to have nothing but good things to say (always probably best to ask those who have no ties to Vignane whatsoever). From an historical perspective too, it appears like Vignane was always very highly thought: after all, it has always been planted mostly to Nebbiolo, and this even in past times when Barbera was a much more remunerative grape. That much appears true because most of Vignane is under vine and most of what is planted is Nebbiolo. So obviously more than one person out there likes what Vignane delivers Barolo-wise. And yet it has always struck me as curious that there aren't any singles-site bottlings made from Vignane. You want Brunate? Or Rocche di Castiglione? Or Monvigliero? Take your pick. But Vignane…nyet, at least up until recently.

Vignane producers and their wines

Bric Cenciurio is but one of many estates that use Vignane grapes in a blend with those from other vineyard districts. For example, their Barolo del Comune di Barolo (called so only beginning with the 2018 vintage: previously, it was called Barolo Pittatore) is a blend of Nebbiolo grapes from Vignane and Zuncai. Their Vignane holdings are 0.8 hectares large, with vines planted in the 1970s and that face slightly west. Given Vignane's proximity to Monforte, it does not surprise that Bric Cenciurio's vineyards are characterized by a preponderant Diano Sandstone lithology, making for potentially slightly bigger wines than is the norm from this site. Giacolino Gillardi, who has long been a key member of the Ceretto family is now the only one making a Barolo Vignane that I know of. It's excellent.

I don't have much experience with the Barolo Vignane from Eraldo Borgogno, but I can be excused, given that it hadn't been made for forty or so years. That's because the Borgogno family ran a restaurant in Barolo for something like five generations, but stopped in the 1980s. The Barolo they made from their vineyards was used for the restaurant patrons, a house wine if you will. But when they hung up their pots and pans, they also sold their vineyards, save for those in Vignane that they rented out. When that rental agreement needed to be renewed, Eraldo Borgogno decided to take the vines back and at a happy and healthy seventy years of age started making his wine again, thanks to the help of his cousin Federico Scarzello (one of the nicest people and wine producers of all Barolo, I would like to add). Listen, I don't know about you, but a story like this one just makes me want to go out and get to know the guy, not just his wine. I am certainly looking forward to trying Eraldo Borgogno's wines over numerous vintages.

Benchmark wineries/Reference point producers of Barolo Vignane: Gillardi.

VIGNARIONDA

Township	Serralunga d'Alba
Reference Map	See Map of Serralunga d'Alba MGAs (Ch. 10)
Size (ha) (Tot / Barolo MGA)	10.24 / 8.20
Production 2021 (hl)	433.17 (of which 217.47 hl of Barolo Riserva *MGA*)
Altitude	260- 360 meters a.s.l. roughly
Exposure	From south to southwest in the central nucleus, and west in the final part which turns towards Monforte d'Alba
N. Claimants MGA	10
Other grape varieties planted:	Barbera; Dolcetto
Land Units	Land Unit of Serralunga d'Alba
Soil (stage):	Serravallian

Producers claiming the MGA

Giacomo Anselma; Pierangelo Ferretti; Ettore Germano; Massolino (Vigna Rionda); Luigi Pira; Guido Porro (Cascina S. Caterina); Luigi Oddero e Figli; Poderi Oddero; Regis; Giovanni Rosso.

Wines

Giacomo Anselma - Barolo Riserva Vignarionda; **Ettore Germano** - Barolo Vignarionda; **Massolino – Vigna Rionda** - Barolo Vigna Rionda; **Poderi Oddero** - Barolo Riserva Vignarionda; **Luigi Pira** - Barolo Vignarionda; **Guido Porro** - Barolo Vigna Rionda; **Regis** - Barolo Vigna Rionda; **Giovanni Rosso** - Barolo Vigna Rionda Ester Canale Rosso; **Arnaldo Rivera** - Barolo Vignarionda; **Luigi Oddero e Figli** - Barolo Vigna Rionda

What the producers say

Franco Massolino (Massolino-Vigna Rionda): "Our first vineyard in this site was acquired in the '30s. We bottled it as a single-site wine for the first time in 1982 and then, since 1995, only as a Riserva. For us, Vignarionda is the essence of Barolo, uniting power and complexity with elegance like practically no other vineyard district of Barolo".

Mariacristina Oddero (Poderi Oddero): "We acquired our holdings in this site back in the early 1980s. Vigna Rionda has an excellent microclimate for ensuring full grape ripeness, loose soil, which however cannot hold onto water as much as we'd like; unless we are very careful with our viticulture, in the hotter years the vineyard (our vineyard, at least) suffers from some drought-related stress and problems related to sunburn. However, the soil is rich in active limestone (the highest of the entire Barolo area) and micronutrients, and the resulting wine is of a complexity like none other in the immediate area. It's also the longest-aging Barolo we at Poderi Oddero know of, so much so that it's not the easiest wine to like and appreciate when young, it takes time to evolve and resolve what are often hard and angular tannins. A structured Barolo, perhaps less fruity and floral than others, but with a complex and very exciting taste".

Stefano Pesci (Arnaldo Rivera): "Our vines were planted in 2003. A very powerful yet elegant Barolo".

Luigi Pira: "The Vignarionda is actually our youngest single-site Barolo bottling, having begun its course as such only in 1997. The west-facing vineyard was planted in 1994. Forest berries and sweet tobacco are common notes in our wine, as are licorice and forest floor".

Alberto Zaccarelli (Luigi Oddero & Figli): "A beautiful amphitheater, fully south-facing at 350 meters above sea level in the case of our 0.8 hectares of vines. Possibly also because of that prolonged aging in bottle, our version strikes me as being a little readier than some other Vignarionda Barolos; as strange as it may seem, at the same moment in time, it seems to us to be less tannic and unevolved than our wine from Scarrone. And we love the minty herb and licorice nuances this wine has in spades".

Ian's assessment of the vineyard district, its wines and its potential

Is Vignarionda Barolo's single most important or best vineyard site of all? Those who pine for Rocche di Castiglione, the Cannubi Centrale, or Brunate might object, but the fact remains that few Barolos out there get tastebuds salivating and checkbooks opened in quite the same way that the wines made from this magical vineyard district do. Clearly, a good deal of that stems from Bruno Giacosa's fantastic red label reserve Barolos of the 70s' and 80s; but no matter which estate you visit or drink all the wines of, it is the Barolo of Vignarionda that always stands head and shoulders above all the other Barolos in any winery's lineup. And not by a small margin, usually.

Vignarionda's name is the new spelling of Vigna Rionda, which was changed with the 2010 launch of the official MGA vineyard district names (in order to leave the world "vigna" for real single-vineyard wines made within a MGA- designated vineyard). In the Vigna Rionda spelling, it is easier to see how the name might derive from *rotonda*, or round, supposedly in reference to the site's more or less rounded topographical conformation. In other words, *vigna rionda* from *arionda*, or *rotonda*; *riunda* is another spelling form that has been mentioned in the past, though I've never seen it on any labels, and I think have seen them all, or very close to it. However, as some producers did not, and do not, wish to lose the association with the original Vigna Rionda name (you can hardly blame them), some took to writing the name as VignaRionda, instead of Vignarionda. But what is it about the Vignarionda that gets everybody so excited about it? Why is Vignarionda such a fabulous source of great Barolo? Is it really the site or is it more a matter of just one man (or a few very talented men) making magic happen with grapes from there? Well, there are many facets to the potential wine greatness that can be achieved from Vignarionda.

Vignarionda is located in the southern half of the Serralunga commune and on the western-facing flank of the Serralunga ridge that runs north-south and divides the commune more or less in two. The entirety of

Vignarionda's border to the north is close by the Damiano vineyard district, while to the south lies the Collaretto vineyard district, but at a distance away on a separate, parallel, ridge to the one where Vignarionda is.

One reason explaining the greatness of Vignarionda as a Barolo-producing site is that it is a very sheltered vineyard district down in a lower-lying position off Serralunga's western ridge, protected from cold winds blowing in from the northwest by both the Castelletto (especially) and Perno hills. For the same reason, Vignarionda practically never gets hailed upon, and storms in its immediate area are rare. The heart of Vignarionda, its most classic section if you will, is fully south- and southwest-facing (a smaller piece of Vignarionda rounds out westwards as the hilly crest it drapes over curves to the west and north), and this sunlit exposure further aids in creating an ideal microclimate for the vines. It is the center of the hill that is generally recognized to be its best section [the section from where Bruno Giacosa used to source grapes from Aldo Canale (vineyards since inherited by Giovanni Rosso, Guido Porro, Ettore Germano: see below), as well as Luigi Oddero, Poderi Oddero, Giacomo Anselma and the Terre del Barolo coop]. However, all of the Vignarionda is a blessed site for Nebbiolo, and the lowest-lying plots and those where the hill turns west are also highly coveted by all those I have talked to over the years.

Vignarionda belongs to the landscape Land Unit of Serralunga and its soil is the typical Serralunga Lequio Formation lithology. Or in other words, compacted sands and marls with plenty of limestone: depending on the soil samples you analyze, the limestone content can vary anywhere from 14-30%, which to help you gain perspective, is the highest average concentration of soil limestone of the entire Serralunga commune). Combining the data obtained over the years from sample soil analysis, the typical soil composition of Vignarionda ranges between 58-68% loam, 17-30% sand and 12-18% clay. For sure, Vignarionda's soil is not viewed as being particularly fertile (because of its generally lowish clay content), but is very rich in elements including potassium, phosphorus, manganese, magnesium, boron, and iron. Locals believe that it is thanks to that wealth of limestone and of mineral elements that Vignarionda's Barolos are not just complex, but marked by slightly higher acidity than is common. That acidity, coupled with the inherent structure wines from this vineyard district inevitably have in spades, means a more prolonged aging requirement compared to Barolos from other sites. This is one of the reasons why many estates choose to release their Barolo Vignarionda only as a Riserva wine (and as a Riserva Speciale decades ago when that term was still allowed and in use). Vignarionda's Barolo is at once concentrated and refined, fruity and spicy, herbal and floral, though I would say the fruity and floral components are less obvious than they are in Barolos from other sites, such as say Rocche di Castiglione, Monprivato or Cannubi Centrale. Most interestingly, you will find after having tasted enough Vignariondas Barolos in your life, that this vineyard district's Barolos are unique also in the way the tannin help support the fruit in lighter-styled vintages. Usually, with other great vineyards, it's usually the acidity that helps out. This is not a throwaway observation but is linked to the particular polyphenol profile of Vignarionda wines in which the tannins are all important. Granted, Barolos are tannic wines by definition, but with Vignarionda's wines they play an even more important role than usual in the way that finished wines will taste. This is partly because Vignarionda is a relatively hot site (all the phenological phases such as budburst and flowering occur earlier in the year here than in most other Serralunga vineyards) and its high content in sand further contributes to the potential for stress (related to water, heat and nutrient deficiency, that as I have pointed out are all characteristics of the Vignarionda). It follows that to make great wines from this vineyard is not easy, but if the producer can manage his or her vines in such a way that the water deprivation (rather than water stress, given that there is no form of stress that is truly good for anyone or anything) the vines encounter is just in the right amount, then that' when the Barolos of Vignarionda know really no rivals.

Vignarionda producers and the wines

Clearly, the most famous Vignarionda Barolo of all was the one made by Bruno Giacosa (well, to be precise, his were actually Barolo Collina Rionda wines most of the time; but not always: see below). Now, it might strike the accidental reader as a little ungenerous to begin writing about Vignarionda in terms of a wine that no longer exists (except for old vintages); but in fact, with Vignarionda you really need to know the past in order to understand the present. To learn about the history of this vineyard district's wines is the best way to go about understanding the hows, whos and whys of some of the newer wines being made from Vignarionda today. At Bruno Giacosa, the reserve (*riserva*) Barolos and Barbarescos are labeled with a red label, while the non-reserve wines have a white label. To be clear, if and when you find a bottle of Giacosa's red label reserve wine from Vigna Rionda that was properly cellared (which is actually very hard to do with old Italian wines), it will most likely turn out to be the most profound Italian wine you will have tasted up to that point in your life. Only a handful of Italian and world wines from anywhere can stand up to them. These reserve wines are of a level of concentration, depth, complexity, and refinement that is beyond description. For sure, very Barolo, and very Serralunga Barolo at that: but also way beyond that.

Bruno Giacosa made a Barolo from the Vigna Rionda in Serralunga d'Alba from 1967 to 1993 included. Giacosa hit the ground running with the 1967 vintage, one of the three best Barolo vintages of the 1960s. Not surprisingly then, he made both a Barolo and a Barolo Riserva Speciale that year; please note, not a Barolo Riserva, as is commonly and mistakenly reported. Giacosa red label Barolo Vigna Rionda wines were all Riserva Speciale wines right up until the 1978 vintage included; only in 1982 did they become "just" Riserva wines, mostly on account of the change in the labeling laws (changes that amounted to more than just a change in name only, because different oaking and aging regimens were introduced for Italian wine). The change from "Riserva Speciale" to "Riserva' can be easily verified just by looking at the bottles of older Giacosa vintages: beginning with the 1982 vintage (and 1985 for the Barbarescos), Giacosa switched from his previous habit of placing the vintage and wine status (Riserva Speciale) on the neck label of his Barolos and Barbarescos. After these dates, he placed the vintage in a clearly visible position directly on the front label (more or less in the middle), placing the word "riserva" (again, no longer 'Riserva Speciale') in a diagonal band up in the top left-hand corner of the label. When the wine bottles still had neck labels but the wines were of the non-Riserva category (and hence bottled with white labels), the neck label would carry the vintage without anything else written there (for example, check out the 1970 Barolo Vigna Rionda di Serralunga d'Alba white label wine).

As Giacosa used the red label to identify his reserve wines, anytime he bottled a wine that was good enough for a specific vineyard site on the name but maybe not quite with the depth and structure of his reserve wines (that stayed much longer in oak), he would bottle them with a white label. And so, given that from 1968 to 1970 the vintages weren't of the most memorable kind (though I would argue, strongly, that 1970 is a far better vintage in Barolo than it is generally credited to be) Giacosa only bottled white label Barolos from Vigna Rionda. For some reason I can't explain, while Giacosa started out calling the white label wines as Vigna Rionda, from the 1971 vintage onwards he used the term of Collina Rionda for both the white labels and red label reserve wines, perhaps because the grapes were coming from different sections of the hillside and not just one vineyard. In fact, it's more complicated than that. Make note of the fact that Giacosa labeled his 1967, 1968 and 1969 white label Barolo Vigna Rionda as "Barolo Cru Vigna Rionda di Serralunga d'Alba". Obviously, the *maestro* must have felt like the wine's name was not long enough already, and so, just for good measure, decided to throw add the word "cru" there too. However, I have seen the 1970 white label carrying the "Vigna Rionda di Serralunga d'Alba" name only, without the addition of the word 'cru'; and then the 1971 white label wine becomes called "Collina Rionda di Serralunga d'Alba". I tell you all of this not because I have nothing better to do with my time than to look at single words on neck and front bottle labels, but in an effort to caution you from buying fakes. For example, I was recently asked to authenticate a bottle of "1971 Bruno Giacosa Barolo Cru Vigna Rionda di Serralunga d'Alba" bought at auction by a wealthy Asian collector (like I don't have enough to do, but this investigative work is actually a part of my job that I enjoy greatly: and besides, I really don't like wine-loving people getting taken for a ride) that was almost certainly bogus. The bottle was a white label wine but to the best of my knowledge, the word "cru" does not appear on the labels after the 1969 vintage. Furthermore, the neck label had been clearly reglued (poorly) back on to the bottle: most likely, this was originally a bottle of the '68 or '69 white label wine that had been made to look like it was of the far better, and more expensive, 1971 vintage (it is unreasonable to think it might have been of the 1967 vintage that was another outstanding vintage in Barolo, while the '68 and '69 vintages were nothing to write home about, making them likely candidates).

For those who don't know, Giacosa didn't own any vines in what is today's Vignarionda but rather bought grapes from trusted sources he usually had long working relationships with (in fact, Giacosa never owned any vineyards until he bought the Falletto property. See FALLETTO file). As many wine lovers and collectors know, Giacosa bought Vignarionda grapes from Aldo Canale (who used his grapes from the Vigna Rionda to also bottle a Barolo Vigna Rionda under his own label and name: maybe you can find -with some luck- bottles of this wine around, that from what I have tasted to date, are still holding up well). Some locals say Giacosa also bought must and/or finished wine from Canale as well, but I don't know for sure; and I cannot find any mention of this in my winery visits notebooks going back to the 1980s. Anyhow, the last year Giacosa bought grapes from Canale was with the 1993 vintage (he made a white label Barolo Collina Rionda di Serralunga that year). From 1998 to 2010, it was Tommaso Canale (Aldo's son) who took over the winery and made wine, while still selling some grapes and wines to other producers. And so, it was that, from 2003 to 2006 included, Roagna also produced a Barolo Vigna Rionda with Canale's grapes. In this case, it is sure that Canale also sold fermented juice and not grapes, but Luca Roagna has told me repeatedly that he worked closely with Canale in following the winemaking process. If you have the cash and a little luck, you can still find bottles of the Roagna Barolo Vigna Rionda from these four vintages. Independently of vintage variation, they are marvelous wines that showcase both the pedigree of the vineyard and Luca's noteworthy talent. The only other individual I know of who bottled a wine in the past with grapes bought from Canale's Vigna Rionda holdings was Giuseppe Mascarello (Mauro's father). He did so in 1979, when Giacosa passed on the grapes because he felt the price had been unjustifiably raised to an amount he deemed excessive. Mascarello did not buy the grapes again while Giacosa continued to do so after that one missed vintage, in effect essentially cementing his legacy as a result.

Tommaso Canale died without heirs in 2010, and the research began to identify to who the estate would fall to. Three winemaking families of Serralunga were determined to be the heirs: and so it is that Canale's holdings were divided up amongst the estates of Ettore Germano, Guido Porro and Giovanni Rosso. Roughly 1.2 hectares of Canale's property (more than half of the holdings, of which 0.85 hectares of Vignarionda) went to the family of Davide Rosso of the Giovanni Rosso estate (he is the son Ester Canale Rosso, Aldo's niece: her father Amelio was Aldo Canale's brother). The rest of the estate was divided amongst Guido Porro (of the estate of the same name) and Sergio Germano (of the Ettore Germano estate), who were received 0.41 hectares each. What's unfortunate is that, viticulturally speaking, Canale's vineyards had fallen onto hard times, many had died, and others were diseased. Porro and Germano both decided to uproot their holdings and start afresh by replanting new Nebbiolo vines. The intellectual in me honestly shudders at such actions firmly believing that old biotypes can always (and should always) be salvaged for once uprooted they are forever lost; but sometimes this just can't be done, given the state of things. Fortunately, Davide Rosso was a little luckier and was able to hold on to a small patch (0.4 hectares) of the original Canale vines (planted in 1946) from where he made his first wine in 2011 and sold it as a Futures. The wine's bottle has a label harkening back to that of Aldo Canale's wines and even more similar to that of Tommaso Canale, renaming the wine "Ester Canale Rosso" in the process. The full name of the wine is Barolo Ester Canale Rosso, subtitled "Poderi dell'Antica VignaRionda"; in fact, the subtitle was originally spelled differently, as in "Poderi dell'Antica Vigna Rionda", with a separation between the words *vigna* and *rionda,* (just check out the labels of the 2011 and 2012, for example). You can imagine how well that flew with Italy's bureaucrats. In any case, it is now one of Barolo's three or four most expensive wines. Rosso ages it in 16 hectoliter Slavonian oak barrels for anywhere from sixteen to thirty-two months depending on the vintage (for example, in 2018, a year of lighter-styled wines, the aging was down to twenty-two months). The other vines he inherited he also uprooted, and like Porro and Germano, proceeded to replant in 2011. Porro made his first Barolo from Vignarionda in 2014, while Germano made a Langhe Nebbiolo (a thoroughly fantastic wine, I may add); Germano made his first Barolo from Vignarionda in 2015 and it too is spectacular.

The two Oddero estates of La Morra also make excellent Vigna Rionda Barolos. In 2006, the two Oddero brothers, Luigi and Giacomo, split with the former and created his own label and estate, that counts many prized vineyard sites. Including those of the famous Vignarionda. With Luigi's passing in 2010, his wife Lena took over managing the estate: to her credit, she surrounded herself with arguably the most talented staff in all Barolo, or close to it. The consultant winemaker is none other than Dante Scaglione, who worked for years with Bruno Giacosa; he promptly called upon his *protégé* there, Francesco Versio, one of, if not the, brightest young minds in all Barbaresco and Barolo. But also, Luciano Botto (viticulture), Alberto Zaccarelli (in sales) and many other lucid minds are on the team. After all that, what about the wine? Luigi Oddero's Barolo Vignarionda is very Serralunga in its youthful rigidity, thought the Giacosa-esque ability to coax sweet tannins and luscious fruit is evident even in the wine's first few years of life. Over at Poderi Oddero, another wonderful Barolo Vignarionda awaits. Mariacristina and her team farm 0.77 hectares of Vignarionda planted at 340 meters above sea level. The vine age is variable, given that the oldest part right in the middle of their plot was planted in 1972, while the highest section of their vineyard (240 vines) dates to 1983. The youngest vines were planted in 2007 and are in the lowest part of the vineyard. Very importantly, the high part of the vineyard has vines of Nebbiolo Rosé, a variety that Mariacristina is quick (and honest) to admit had always left her wondering in the past because of the pale color of its wines. She has since come around on her views, saying Nebbiolo Rosé is "… a very interesting variety, given that it is much more drought-resistant than Nebbiolo and very hardy. Plus, its wine is actually very recognizable, and it has grown on me" (See chapter 3, NEBBIOLO ROSÉ). Poderi Oddero first made a Barolo Vignarionda in the 1985 vintage (I have tasted every single vintage of this wine ever made numerous times and recently written what is to the best of my knowledge the most in-depth and complete vertical of this wine for the *TerroirSense Wine Review* of which I am the Editor-in-Chief, and you can read it at: terroirsense.com/en/). Beginning with the 2016 vintage, it becomes a Barolo Riserva. While I am at it, I would like to point out something about this wine, because it speaks volumes about Mariacristina and the Poderi Oddero estate. You know how estates tell you they only make a specific wine in the best vintages and then you see it on sale almost every vintage? Well, not so at Poderi Oddero, a class act where in miserable years they *really don't* make the Barolo Vignarionda. For example, none was made in 1992, 1994, and 2002; and only 1200 bottles were made in the less than memorable, hotter than hell 2003 vintage. A very traditional estate, Poderi Oddero's is yet another Barolo Vignarionda that really needs, in good years, at least fifteen years in the cellar, or you will miss out on everything this amazing site and wine have to offer. I also want to point out, because it is both important and relevant, that the two Oddero families own some of the best situated parcels of vines in all of Vignarionda, right in the heart of the site (which is by everyone's account, not just mine, the best part of the vineyard area). By the way, next to the plots owned by Poderi Oddero and Luigi Oddero are those owned/farmed by Giovanni (Davide) Rosso, Ettore Germano, Guido Porro, Giacomo Anselma, and the Terre del Barolo coop. Just sayin'.

Franco and Roberto Massolino are the fourth generation working at the Massolino winery, founded in 1896 by Giovanni Massolino. This is the winery that is the biggest owner of the Vignarionda vineyard district: they own roughly a third of it (about three hectares of the total ten) and make one of this vineyard district's most famous and best-known wines. The family is so linked with the site that they actually attached the name of the vineyard to that of the winery (as in "Massolino Vigna Rionda"). Their vines are about forty years old and planted at about 340 meters above sea level. Theirs has always been looked upon as one of the best examples of Barolo Vignarionda, and the family has tinkered with the wine recently in an effort to further create a unique identity for what is the estate's flagship Barolo. And so it is that, beginning with the 2016 vintage (not by chance a great one), they launched another Vignarionda wine, with a black label. The Vignarionda Riserva Black Label is bottled only in the best vintages, while those not designated as such will continue to be released as Barolo Riserva Vignarionda wines with the usual cream-colored label. The black label Vignarionda is fermented using natural ambient yeasts in large conical oak casks and is aged between 30 and 42 months, depending on the vintage (so for example, the Black Label 2016 was aged thirty-six months). In general, Massolino' version of Vignarionda Barolo, like all their wines, is characterized by greater creaminess and fleshiness than some of the other wines you'll taste from this site. Another high-quality estate that owns a large part of Vignarionda is Luigi Pira (don't confuse it with the Barolo commune's also outstanding E.Pira/Chiara Boschis winery). His wine is an excellent example of why even the portion of this vineyard district that faces west/southwest is just a fantastic site for Nebbiolo, in that his Barolo Vignarionda is just as good as everybody else's. The vines are still relatively young, planted in 1994 at about 350 meters above sea level, but the wine, first made in the 1997 vintage, has always been nothing short of excellent. Giacomo Anselma also makes a Barolo Riserva Vignarionda worth looking for, as does the Terre del Barolo cooperative with their excellent lineup of single-site Barolos that are part of the Arnaldo Rivera project.

Benchmark wineries/Reference point producers of Barolo Vignarionda: Ettore Germano, Giacomo Anselma, Giovanni Rosso, Guido Porro, Luigi Oddero e Figli, Luigi Pira, Massolino, Poderi Oddero.

VIGNOLO

Township	Castiglione Falletto
Reference Map	See Map of Castiglione MGAs (Ch. 10)
Size (ha) (Tot / Barolo MGA)	3.57 / 2.55
Production 2021 (hl)	91.43 (of which 80 hl of Barolo Riserva *MGA*)
Altitude	220 – 260 meters a.s.l. roughly
Exposure	Southwest
N. Claimants MGA	2
Other grape varieties planted:	Dolcetto
Land Units	Land Unit of Barolo
Soil (stage):	Tortonian

Producers claiming the MGA

Cavallotto Bricco Boschis; Luigina Schellino.

Wines

Cavallotto Bricco Boschis - Barolo Riserva Vignolo

What the producers say

Alfio Cavallotto (Cavallotto - Bricco Boschis): "We have been making this as a Barolo Riserva Vignolo since 1989. It's a very classic Barolo born from Tortonian soil, fairly structured and powerful. It's rich clay content make it really excellent in droughty years, though we find the wine is not usually as complex as our Vigna San Giuseppe, also a Riserva".

Enrica Scavino (Paolo Scavino): "The Vignolo cru was named in honor of Ferdinando Vignolo Lutati, an aristocrat and great connoisseur not just of Barolo but of its soils: he was the first in 1927 to define in an organized way the Barolo zone and its best vineyard sites and wines".

Ian's assessment of the vineyard district, its wines and its potential

Named after Ferdinando Vignolo-Lutati (1878-1966), one of Castiglione Falletto's most famous citizens, Vignolo is a vineyard district of Castiglione Falletto that gives what are for my money the commune's most structured wines (and the toughest, when young). It is situated in that prime piece of Castiglione Falletto vineyard real estate that: the same ridge also boasts the vineyard districts of Monprivato, Codana and at its end, Solanotto (with Vignolo situated between Codana and Solanotto).

Landscape-wise, Vignolo is characterized by the Barolo Land Unit, which means a lithology of mostly typical Saint Agatha Fossil Marls. Of note, in Vignolo these are much less sandy than those of the nearby Bricco Boschis, for example. A typical Vignolo soil sample shows a composition of 50% loam, 20% sand and 30% clay; but in fact, I think this is one strange vineyard district in that its wines taste like they were made on soils that are practically equal percentages of clay and sand (like I said, tough, steely wines with not much in the way of flesh). Vignolo's Barolos are excellent but being so powerfully structured, even a little foursquare in their youth, you need to age them accordingly. I find that you can actually smell the clay in the Barolos of Vignolo, but also lots of white pepper and deep red cherry, with a hint of menthol. To my way of thinking and tasting, they really are Barolos that are almost Monforte-like (or of parts of Monforte, at least).

Vignolo producers and the wines

There are very few owners of Vignolo. The best-known producer of wines from the site are the Cavallotto brothers of Bricco Boschis. To date, theirs is the only Barolo Vignolo produced. Cavallotto bought their holdings in 1989 (three plots for a total of 2.13 hectares planted in 1945, 1970 and 1996) that had been previously farmed by Paolo Scavino, and they choose to only make a Riserva wine (very understandably I might add, given the forementioned tannic frame of Vignolo's Barolos). Cavallotto laughs when he recalls the sale: "*Nomen Omen*, you know? We bought it from a guy also called Cavallotto! But what's even funnier is that when we bought our vineyard there, we actually thought we were buying a lighter soil that would give us lighter-styled Barolos, and instead we got the opposite".

Benchmark wineries/Reference point producers of Barolo Vignolo: Cavallotto/Bricco Boschis.

VILLERO

Township	Castiglione Falletto
Reference Map	See Map of Castiglione MGAs (Ch. 10)
Size (ha) (Tot / Barolo MGA)	22.07 / 15.47
Production 2021 (hl)	695.79 (of which 67.59 hl of Barolo Riserva *MGA*)
Altitude	230 – 350 meters a.s.l. roughly
Exposure	Southwest in the central part of the *cru*, and west-southwest in the remaining parts
N. Claimants MGA	16
Other grape varieties planted:	Barbera; Dolcetto; white varieties
Land Units	Land Unit of Barolo; Land Unit of Castiglione in the eastern / south-eastern sidebordering Brunella and Rocche di Castiglione
Soil (stage):	Tortonian

Producers claiming the MGA

Brovia; Boroli; Cascina Rocca; Ettore Fontana; Angelo Germano; Giuseppe Mascarello E Figlio; Renato Molino; Monfalletto (Cordero Di Montezemolo); Poderi Oddero; Pugnane (Fratelli Sordo); Luciano Sandrone; Federica Sobrero; Vietti; Marco Vietti; Nicoletta Vietti; Zocca Rita.

Wines

Boroli - Barolo Villero (and Riserva); **Brovia** - Barolo Villero; **Giacomo Fenocchio** - Barolo Villero; **Livia Fontana** - Barolo Villero; **Angelo Germano** - Barolo Villero; **Giuseppe Mascarello e Figlio** - Barolo Villero; **Monfalletto - Cordero di Montezemolo** - Barolo Enrico VI; **Poderi Oddero** - Barolo Villero; **Pugnane Fratelli Sordo** - Barolo Vigna Villero; **Arnaldo Rivera** - Barolo Villero; **Sordo** - Barolo Villero; **Vietti** - Barolo Riserva Villero; **Franco Molino (Cascina Rocca)** - Barolo Riserva Villero.

What the producers say

Alberto Cordero di Montezemolo (Monfalletto): "Our family owns a Villero vineyard parcel since 1959 and in 1971 chose to vinify it separately, calling it Enrico VI. The maceration lasts for six to nine days plus another ten days to complete the alcohol fermentation. The wine ages in different types of barrels, from smallest to the biggest, French and of Slavonian oak for a period of 18 to 24 months. Villero is distinctive for its very compact calcareous soil rich in micronutrients. Our old vines, together with a south exposure and the altitude of 300 meters. contribute to the power and complexity of this site's wines".

Mariacristina Oddero (Poderi Oddero): "Our family acquired this vineyard (together with Fiasco) in 1970 from none other than Ferdinando Vignolo Lutati, born in Castiglione Falletto. Our traditional vinification means maceration with fermentation for 25 to 30 or more days, and Austrian and Slavonian oak barrels of different sizes, ranging from 20 to 105 hectoliters. Villero is the expression of a soil that is rich in clay and limestone, compared to for example Rocche di Castiglione from the same township. It produces a Barolo of power and roundness".

Alex Sanchez (Brovia): "The Brovia family acquired this vineyard in 1991. During the vinification the wine macerates for three weeks in cement tanks, followed by aging in French and Slavonian oak in 30-42hectoliter oak casks. Villero is a classic Barolo, big in structure and body: it's one of the most historical vineyards in Castiglione Falletto".

Luca Currado (Vietti): "This vineyard has been part of the family since always and recently we have made a few more acquisitions in the area. For Villero, we opt for long macerations that last for three to five weeks. Our intention is to produce the Barolo Villero Riserva only in years when the characteristics of terroir and the aging potential are, based on our experience, above average".

Luca Sandrone (Luciano Sandrone): "Villero exemplifies elegance and finesse: moderately tannic with a slightly deeper color than most".

Ian's assessment of the vineyard district, its wines and its potential

Truly one of Barolo's greatest vineyard areas, it can be argued that Villero should be included in any list of top five or at no worse top ten Barolo vineyards. Given how difficult it is to agree upon this sort of things, let's just go with the latter and say then that it is one of Barolo's best vineyard sites. List it any lower down than "top-10" in your personal classification of Barolos' best at your own risk and peril.

Villero is an historically famous vineyard site that today is a vineyard district of Castiglione Falletto. It is one of the many southwest-facing slopes that branch off horizontally from the main ridge that runs from Monforte to Castiglione Falletto. There are numerous famous vineyard districts all around it: Fiasco, Brunella, Bricco Rocche, Rocche di Castiglione and Mariondino. It is especially interesting to compare the wines of Villero with those of Rocche di Castiglione and Monprivato, arguably the other two great sites of the Castiglione Falletto commune. While they all share a Castiglione Falletto somewhereness, the three Barolos are really quite different, a difference resulting from slightly different soils, altitudes, and exposures throughout their individual boundaries.

Villero's landscape is characterized by the Barolo Land Unit, which should translate to Saint Agatha Fossil Marls (mostly of the typical and sandy forms). However, locals maintain Villero lies at a transition area for lithologies, where the Saint Agatha Marls meet the Diano Sandstone formation. Certainly, Villero's exact soil composition varies throughout the vineyard area's extension. Generally speaking, the sandstone diminishes at the lower altitudes, areas that are also less prone to erosion and even landslides. For example, soil sample analysis shows that just below the Brunella district, Villero's soil is very compact and characterized by a high clay and limestone content, with only about 5-15% sand (there's about 60% loam and 25-35% clay too); it is an area the wines of which are undoubtedly 'very-Villero', meaning very mineral and very powerful. It's that low content in sand that is really what distinguishes Villero and its wines from the Rocche di Castiglione district (parts of it, at least: see ROCCHE DI CASTIGLIONE file) and its wines. For the most part, Villero's soil is also fairly deep and fertile too.

But there's more than just soil to Villero's greatness. Exposure and hence microclimate too contribute to the fleshiness and size of Villero's wines. The warmer southwest exposure (only the final portion of Villero's slope and its upper reaches tend to look full west) and the high degree of luminosity and wind protection afforded not only by the main north-south ridge but also by the Mariondino set of hills just to the south as well as the higher Brunella hillsides just to its north, all contribute to create wines of power and heft. The sections of Villero that are not southwest-facing (in fact, the site is almost all southwest-facing as it's fairly homogenous from a topographical point of view) have always been believed to be less favorable to the making of premium-level Nebbiolo wines. Clearly, with the advent of climate-change such opinions may not last.

Given their broad nature and noteworthy power and heft, it is not unreasonable to categorize Villero's Barolos as rather horizontal wines (compared to say Rocche di Castiglione's more vertical wines); but what sets this vineyard district and its wines apart from most other sites in the Barolo denomination that also can give highly structured, even massive wines, is that Villero Barolos are also unfailingly remarkably lifted and refined. It is a fairly unique combination of power and grace, one that is really not all that common in Barolo. Or at least not to the extent that it is in Villero's wines. You will find that Villero's Barolos boast real acid lift and noteworthy tannic spine but a spine that is buffered by the typical Castiglione Falletto suave and luscious fruit-loaded midpalate. They really are wines that lift Castiglione Falletto's trademark balance to the nth degree.

Villero producers and the wines

Given how famous Villero is, it's not surprising that there are plenty of estates making a Barolo Villero. The Poderi Oddero estate owns 0,80 hectares in Villero, part of which were replanted in 2008 with Nebbiolo clone 71 on 420A rootstock). The remaining section was once owned by Vignolo Lutati (Poderi Oddero bought the plot from Vignolo Lutati's heirs), one of Barolo's most important historic figures (see chapter 5, THE HISTORY OF BAROLO). The vines in this plot, that are well over sixty years of age, are still standing and reasonably productive. Poderi Oddero released its first Barolo Villero in the 2004 vintage, while prior to that date they included its grapes into their classic estate Barolo blend. Villero, which Mariacristina Oddero tells me was used to be called "Villario" once, is her one vineyard district with which she feels a special bond. It's the vineyard that her father Giacomo Oddero (another famous man of the Barolo denomination that greatly contributed to setting up the original Barolo DOC guidelines back in 1967) likes to spend as much time as possible in and for which he has a soft spot.

Villero is such a well-known and highly-regarded site of Barolo that La Morra's famous Cordero di Montezemolo-owned Monfalletto estate chose it for their first venture outside the friendly confines of La Morra, where the estate has always been based. It is from Villero they make their outstanding Barolo Enrico VI: perhaps less fashionable today than other 'latest flavors of the month-Barolos' that are all the rage right now with some people, but the Barolo Enrico VI has long enjoyed one of the greatest reputations in Italy and is still today one of the denomination's best wines. For those interested in the nuances of terroir, there is nothing better to do than tasting, side by side, Monfaletto's Barolo of same name (from La Morra) or their Barolo Gattera (also of La Morra) and the Enrico VI (from Castiglione Falletto): the Enrico VI is a much deeper, richer wine than the Monfalletto, marked by darker fruit aromas and flavors, along with notes of eucalyptus, licorice. Of note, the larger amount of soil limestone in the Villero vineyard makes for a very different acid and tannic structure. But Enrico VI's microclimate too, that tends to be cooler and less ventilated, also contributes to the sense of size and sturdiness of this wine compared to the more floral personality of those from La Morra. (In my experience, this difference between the two origins is immediately obvious upon tasting even to novices.) Cordero di Montezemolo's holding is about two hectares large, planted at an altitude of 300 meters above sea level in iron-rich soil and the southwest-facing Nebbiolo vines are over fifty years old. By the way: the name "Enrico VI" was coined in early 1970s by Paolo Cordero di Montezemolo to commemorate the birth of his sixth child (1959) named Enrico along with the purchase of this prestigious Barolo vineyard in 1965.

The excellent Brovia estate has owned a piece of Villero since 1961: their Barolo Villero is also an austere classic wine. Historically, Brovia's plot was viewed by locals as being hampered by a slightly less favorable exposure, but (and this is an example of why I personally believe that soil is always the single most important factor in determining the quality of Barolo you will make and drink) it never seemed to hurt Brovia's wine any, which has always been nothing but remarkably delicious. According to Alex Sanchez, the southwest exposure is less good in warm years but then the wine just needs more time to show all it has to offer: this is precisely why in years past they used to release it one year later than their other Barolo.

Boroli's vines in Villero face south/southwest and are planted at about 280-300 meters in altitude. He ages his Barolo Villero in a mix of oak barrels of different sizes for twenty-four months and then in bottle for another twenty-four prior to releasing it for sale. The wine is excellent, probably the best in his lineup, but it *does* need lots of cellaring: don't even think of touching a bottle before it has been ten to twelve years after the vintage. Luciano Sandrone is yet another famous name that now farms in Villero, where he established a long-term lease in early 2011. The 1.5 hectares vineyard boasts vines that are fifteen to more than forty-five years old. Sandrone uses the Villero grapes for his Le Vigne bottling (as of the 2011 vintage). Much less famous than Sandrone but a very good Barolo producer in his own right, Angelo Germano makes a good Barolo Villero from Nebbiolo vines planted at 350 meters above sea level, aging it for two years in 500-liter tonneaux (about 20% new oak depending on the vintage). Sordo also owns a small vineyard in Villero (about 0.5 hectares) that gives a brooding wine redolent of tobacco and leather nuances. Last but not least, one of the best Barolo Villero wines of all is that made by Giacomo Fenocchio: it is in Villero that owner Claudio Fenocchio boasts his oldest vineyards, a that are further enriched by the presence of some Nebbiolo Rosé (anywhere from 5-10% of the vines, but it used to be even more about fifteen years ago): the end result is one of the more powerful but yet elegant wines in all Barolo-land and always much superior to Fenocchio's more famous Bussia Barolo (more famous only because it is usually labeled as a Riserva wine, and so everyone falls for it hook, line and sinker: but don't be a label-drinker and choose his Villero, for there is no comparison between the two). By complete contrast, over at Vietti it is their Barolo Villero that is always labeled as a Riserva, and it is the estate's most sought after and expensive wine. That said, Luca Currado's Barolo Rocche di Castiglione is practically as good, at least in my opinion. But with wines of this ilk, it really becomes a matter of what you like best in wine, for they are both exceptional Barolos.

Clearly, one of the most famous Barolo Villero wines of all was that made by the *maestro* himself, Bruno Giacosa. Giacosa only made the wine (as a white label mostly, save for the great 1978 vintage when he also made a red label Riserva Speciale) from 1978 to 1996. He sourced grapes from vines facing south/southwest right in the middle of the Villero hill. Giacosa told me he stopped making this Barolo after a while because the farmer he used to buy grapes from insisted on keeping his yields too high, so in the end Giacosa just gave up and moved on. You will hear other stories, but this is what Giacosa told me directly, face to face, and I had a good relationship with him. That much said, I have to say, Giacosa's white label Villero wines are amazingly good; even better, they are really drinking marvelously well presently. Any chance you get to taste one, go for it!

Benchmark wineries/Reference point producers of Barolo Villero: Boroli; Brovia; Giacomo Fenocchio; Poderi Oddero.

ZOCCOLAIO

Township	Barolo
Reference Map	See Map of Barolo MGAs (Ch. 10)
Size (ha) (Tot / Barolo MGA)	5.95 / 3.44
Production 2021 (hl)	187.00
Altitude	315- 360 meters a.s.l. roughly
Exposure	From west to southwest
N. Claimants MGA	1
Other grape varieties planted:	Barbera; Dolcetto
Land Units	Land Unit of La Morra
Soil (stage):	Tortonian

Producers claiming the MGA

Villa Lanata.

Ian's assessment of the vineyard district, its wines and its potential

The southernmost vineyard district of the Barolo commune, Zoccolaio has Boschetti to its north, San Giovanni to the south and Bricco San Giovanni to the east. It is in effect the prolongation of the western-facing slope of Boschetti that continues on as the slope where the San Giovanni vineyard district is.

Zoccolaio producers and their wines

There used to be only one estate making a Barolo Zoccolaio, and that was the estate of the same name, but now the wine is a blend of grapes coming from the communes of Barolo, Monforte d'Alba and Verduno. Zoccolaio has never been an especially famous site, even though the not so low altitudes, the southwest/west exposures and fairly complex soil lithology of Saint Agatha Fossil Marls and Diano Sandstone ought to be the ingredients by which to make solid Barolos. Such as for example was the Barolos of the Lo Zoccolaio estate that I have visited and found to be good. Perhaps not the last word in complexity, but the south-vines of the Lo Zoccolaio estate made for some very easygoing, delicious Barolos that was easy to like. Oh well.

Benchmark wineries/Reference point producers of Barolo Zoccolaio: none currently available.

ZONCHETTA

Township	Barolo
Reference Map	See Map of Barolo MGAs (Ch. 10)
Size (ha) (Tot / Barolo MGA)	12.28
Production 2021 (hl)	
Altitude	230 - 280 meters a.s.l. roughly
Exposure	Prevalently east-northeast
N. Claimants MGA	0
Other grape varieties planted:	Barbera; Dolcetto; white varieties
Land Units	Land Unit of Barolo
Soil (stage):	Tortonian

Ian's assessment of the vineyard district, its wines and its potential

Located between Brunate, Cerequio, Bergeisa, Albarella, Crosia, and well north of Barolo, Zonchetta is a little-known vineyard district of the Barolo commune. Currently only about half of Zonchetta is under vine, and of that, less than a quarter is planted to Nebbiolo. Clearly, there are no Barolo Zonchetta wines being produced currently. Don't confuse this wine with the Barolo Zonchera made many years by Ceretto as a vineyard blend Barolo, and excellent wine, but that they stopped making in 2010 and had nothing to do with this vineyard district.

Benchmark wineries/Reference point producers of Barolo Zonchetta: None currently available.

ZUNCAI

Township	Barolo
Reference Map	See Map of Barolo MGAs (Ch. 10)
Size (ha) (Tot / Barolo MGA)	7.81
Production 2021 (hl)	
Altitude	240 - 300 meters a.s.l. roughly
Exposure	From west to southwest.
N. Claimants MGA	0
Other grape varieties planted:	Barbera; Dolcetto; white varieties
Land Units	Land Unit of Barolo
Soil (stage):	Tortonian

Ian's assessment of the vineyard district, its wines and its potential

Right below Vignane and surrounded by Monforte's Bussia, Zuncai is a little-known vineyard district of the Barolo commune that ought to give very good wines. Its soil is the classic Tortonian stage typical Saint Agatha Fossil Marls (with some of the sandy form also present), a good altitude range and southwest to west exposures. In effect almost the entire district is planted to grapevines, of which three quarters is Nebbiolo, so you just know people like the site.

Bric Cenciurio owns vines in Zuncai has always blended the grapes with those of other vineyard districts to make their Barolo Pittatore (that beginning with the 2018 vintage changed its name to Barolo del Comune di Barolo). They have 0.8 hectares with a mostly Diano Sandstone formation and a western-facing aspect.

Benchmark wineries/Reference point producers of Barolo Zuncai: none currently available.

Chapter 10

BAROLO VINEYARD DISTRICTS: MAPS AND LAND UNITS

Michele Longo

THE BAROLO COMMUNES AND THE LAND UNITS

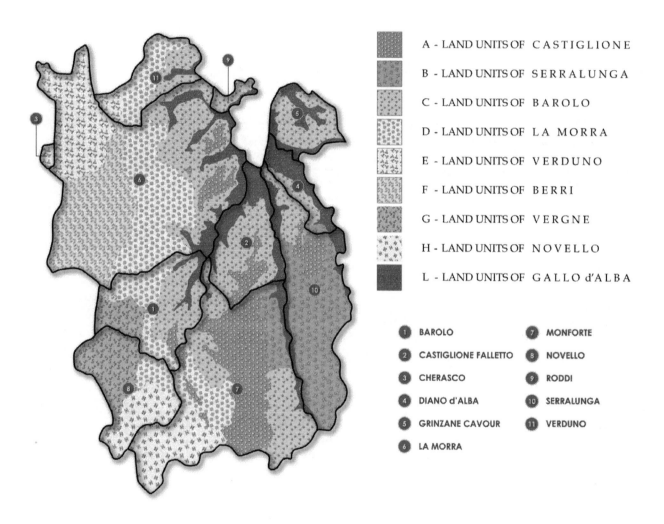

A - LAND UNITS OF CASTIGLIONE

B - LAND UNITS OF SERRALUNGA

C - LAND UNITS OF BAROLO

D - LAND UNITS OF LA MORRA

E - LAND UNITS OF VERDUNO

F - LAND UNITS OF BERRI

G - LAND UNITS OF VERGNE

H - LAND UNITS OF NOVELLO

L - LAND UNITS OF GALLO d'ALBA

1 BAROLO

2 CASTIGLIONE FALLETTO

3 CHERASCO

4 DIANO d'ALBA

5 GRINZANE CAVOUR

6 LA MORRA

7 MONFORTE

8 NOVELLO

9 RODDI

10 SERRALUNGA

11 VERDUNO

The maps of each Commune MGA vs Land Units in the following subchapters have been developed by our friend Raffaele Grillone by overlapping the official map of the MGAs (by the "*Consorzio di tutela Barolo Barbaresco Alba Langhe and Dogliani*") and Land Units Map (by Soster and Cellino, 2000); clearly, this entails a small degree of approximation in the attribution of the Land Units of each MGA, but minimally so.

THE BAROLO MGAS BY SIZE

MGA	Commune	Size (ha)
Bricco San Pietro	Monforte d'Alba	380,09
Bussia (Total)	Monforte - Barolo	298,89
Bussia	Monforte d'Alba	292,31
Perno	Monforte d'Alba	190,96
Ravera (Total)	Novello - Barolo	130,41
Castelletto	Monforte d'Alba	128,52
Ravera	Novello	124,95
Ginestra	Monforte d'Alba	114,36
Annunziata	La Morra	109,42
Corini-Pallaretta	Novello	105,88
Serradenari	La Morra	101,19
Berri	La Morra	87,89
Boiolo	La Morra	87,79
Brandini	La Morra	87,14
Ascheri	La Morra	83,96
Mosconi	Monforte d'Alba	75,95
Sant'Anna	La Morra	73,30
Santa Maria	La Morra	71,00
San Giacomo	La Morra	69,24
San Giovanni	Monforte d'Alba	68,48
Cerviano-Merli	Novello	65,17
Castagni	La Morra	64,51
Sottocastello di Novello	Novello	59,73
Bettolotti	La Morra	58,76
Fontanafredda	Serralunga d'Alba	58,42
Breri	Verduno	53,94
Boscareto	Serralunga d'Alba	53,15
Le Coste di Monforte	Monforte d'Alba	50,34
Massara	Verduno	50,31
Ciocchini-Loschetto	Novello	50,10
Bergera-Pezzole	Novello	48,69
Bricco Ambrogio	Roddi	48,24
La Volta	Barolo	46,34
Bricco delle Viole	Barolo	45,74
Bricco Cogni	La Morra	43,91
Silio	La Morra	41,56
Panerole	Novello	41,52
Gramolere	Monforte d'Alba	41,40
Cerretta	Serralunga d'Alba	39,93
Rive	La Morra	38,16
Neirane	Verduno	37,59
Rocche dell'Olmo	Verduno	36,88
Ravera di Monforte	Monforte d'Alba	36,63
Roncaglie	La Morra	36,42
Roere di Santa Maria	La Morra	35,41
Rocchettevino	La Morra	34,98
Capalot	La Morra	34,94
Fossati (Total)	Barolo - La Morra	33,79
Sarmassa	Barolo	33,74
San Lorenzo di Verduno	Verduno	32,46
Gattera	La Morra	30,02
Lazzarito	Serralunga d'Alba	30,00

MGA	Commune	Size (ha)
Rocche dell'Annunziata	La Morra	29,92
Bricco San Biagio	La Morra	28,84
Brunate (Total)	La Morra - Barolo	28,34
Boscatto	Verduno	27,96
Bricco Manescotto	La Morra	27,01
Monvigliero	Verduno	25,51
Cerequio (Total)	La Morra - Barolo	24,12
Boschetti	Barolo	23,87
Teodoro	Serralunga d'Alba	23,58
Montanello	Castiglione Falletto	23,48
Fossati	Barolo	23,19
Gianetto	Serralunga d'Alba	22,40
Villero	Castiglione Falletto	22,07
Serra dei Turchi	La Morra	22,03
Terlo	Barolo	22,03
Roggeri	La Morra	21,31
Badarina	Serralunga d'Alba	21,02
Preda	Barolo	20,68
Scarrone	Castiglione Falletto	20,55
Cannubi	Barolo	19,53
Brunate	La Morra	19,19
Baudana	Serralunga d'Alba	19,00
Briccolina	Serralunga d'Alba	17,93
La Serra	La Morra	17,79
Cerequio	La Morra	17,68
Bricco Boschis	Castiglione Falletto	17,65
San Ponzio	Barolo	17,54
San Pietro	Barolo	17,36
Meriame	Serralunga d'Alba	17,14
Coste di Rose	Barolo	16,83
Rocche di Castiglione (Tot.)	Castiglione - Monforte	16,33
Bricco Luciani	La Morra	16,09
Pernanno	Castiglione Falletto	15,98
Damiano	Serralunga d'Alba	15,98
Francia	Serralunga d'Alba	15,80
Gallaretto	Diano d'Alba	15,36
Giachini	La Morra	14,87
Collaretto	Serralunga d'Alba	14,36
Rocche di Castiglione	Castiglione Falletto	14,36
Gabutti	Serralunga d'Alba	14,24
Bricco Chiesa	La Morra	14,00
Campasso	Verduno	13,95
Riva Rocca	Verduno	13,55
Parussi	Castiglione Falletto	13,41
Mariondino	Castiglione Falletto	13,11
Castellero	Barolo	13,07
Cerrati	Serralunga d'Alba	12,96
Lirano	Serralunga d'Alba	12,77
Liste	Barolo	12,45
Cannubi Boschis o Cannubi	Barolo	12,41
Paiagallo	Barolo	12,35
Zonchetta	Barolo	12,28

MGA	Commune	Size (ha)	MGA	Commune	Size (ha)
Broglio	Serralunga d'Alba	12,15	Castello	Grinzane Cavour	7,10
Bricco Manzoni	La Morra	11,98	Borzone	Grinzane Cavour	7,08
Ciocchini	La Morra	11,87	Bergeisa	Barolo	7,00
Valentino	Castiglione Falletto	11,68	Rivassi	Barolo	6,72
Vignane	Barolo	11,56	Ornato	Serralunga d'Alba	6,70
Raviole	Grinzane Cavour	11,39	Pira	Castiglione Falletto	6,66
Brea	Serralunga d'Alba	10,99	Bussia	Barolo	6,58
Bricco Rocca	La Morra	10,94	Cerequio	Barolo	6,43
Arborina	La Morra	10,81	San Rocco	Serralunga d'Alba	6,43
Fossati	La Morra	10,60	Rodasca	Verduno	6,41
Coste di Vergne	Barolo	10,52	Pianta'	Castiglione Falletto	6,27
Serra	Serralunga d'Alba	10,28	Cannubi Muscatel	Barolo	6,24
Vignarionda	Serralunga d'Alba	10,24	Cannubi Valletta	Barolo	6,24
Case Nere	La Morra	10,21	Le Coste	Barolo	6,01
Rivette	Serralunga d'Alba	10,00	Zoccolaio	Barolo	5,95
Albarella	Barolo	9,96	Canova	Grinzane Cavour	5,75
Sorano	Serralunga d'Alba	9,94	Arione	Serralunga d'Alba	5,72
Pisapola	Verduno	9,73	Manocino	Serralunga d'Alba	5,55
Codana	Castiglione Falletto	9,66	Ravera	Barolo	5,46
Crosia	Barolo	9,62	Druca'	Barolo	5,03
Brunate	Barolo	9,16	Brunella	Castiglione Falletto	5,01
Garretti	Grinzane Cavour	9,00	Pugnane	Castiglione Falletto	4,97
Falletto	Serralunga d'Alba	8,90	Sorano	Diano d'Alba	4,76
Galina	La Morra	8,74	La Vigna	Diano d'Alba	4,48
Rue'	Barolo	8,49	San Bernardo	Serralunga d'Alba	4,44
Prapo'	Serralunga d'Alba	8,33	Altenasso	Castiglione Falletto	4,27
Gustava	Grinzane Cavour	8,31	Monrobiolo di Bussia	Barolo	4,23
Fiasco	Castiglione Falletto	8,30	Bablino	Grinzane Cavour	4,00
Costabella	Serralunga d'Alba	8,29	Bricco San Giovanni	Barolo	3,84
Margheria	Serralunga d'Alba	8,10	Prabon	Serralunga d'Alba	3,84
Parafada	Serralunga d'Alba	7,92	Vignolo	Castiglione Falletto	3,57
La Corte	Grinzane Cavour	7,87	Colombaro	Serralunga d'Alba	3,56
Zuncai	Barolo	7,81	Conca	La Morra	3,00
Torriglione	La Morra	7,62	Solanotto	Castiglione Falletto	2,86
Cappallotto	Serralunga d'Alba	7,52	Mantoetto	Cherasco	2,76
Marenca	Serralunga d'Alba	7,46	Cannubi San Lorenzo	Barolo	2,38
Le Turne	Serralunga d'Alba	7,40	San Lorenzo	Barolo	2,13
Bricco Voghera	Serralunga d'Alba	7,15	Rocche di Castiglione	Monforte d'Alba	1,97
Carpegna	Serralunga d'Alba	7,12	Bricco Rocche	Castiglione Falletto	1,46
Monprivato	Castiglione Falletto	7,12			

MAP OF BAROLO MGAS

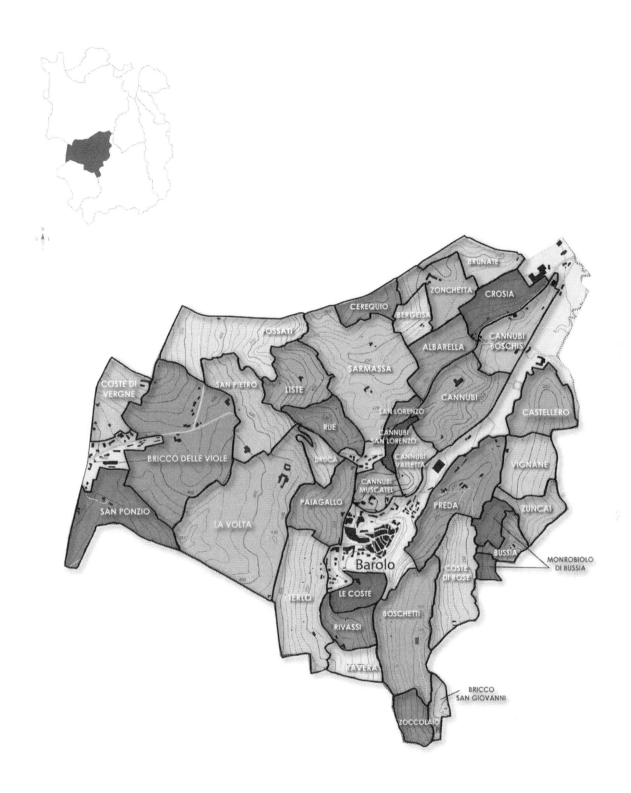

BAROLO MGAS VS LAND UNITS

1 ALBARELLA
2 BERGEISA
3 BOSCHETTI
4 BRICCO DELLE VIOLE
5 BRICCO SAN GIOVANNI
6 BRUNATE
7 BUSSIA
8 CANNUBI
9 CANNUBI BOSCHIS
10 CANNUBI MUSCATEL
11 CANNUBI SAN LORENZO
12 CANNUBI VALLETTA
13 CASTELLERO
14 CEREQUIO
15 COSTE DI ROSE
16 COSTE DI VERGNE
17 CROSIA
18 DRUCÀ
19 FOSSATI

20 LA VOLTA
21 LE COSTE
22 LISTE
23 MONROBIOLO DI BUSSIA
24 PAIAGALLO
25 PREDA
26 RAVERA
27 RIVASSI
28 RUÉ
29 SAN LORENZO
30 SAN PIETRO
31 SAN PONZIO
32 SARMASSA
33 TERLO
34 VIGNANE
35 ZOCCOLAIO
36 ZONCHETTA
37 ZUNCAI

A - LAND UNITS OF CASTIGLIONE
B - LAND UNITS OF SERRALUNGA
C - LAND UNITS OF BAROLO
D - LAND UNITS OF LA MORRA
E - LAND UNITS OF VERDUNO
F - LAND UNITS OF BERRI
G - LAND UNITS OF VERGNE
H - LAND UNITS OF NOVELLO
L - LAND UNITS OF GALLO d'ALBA

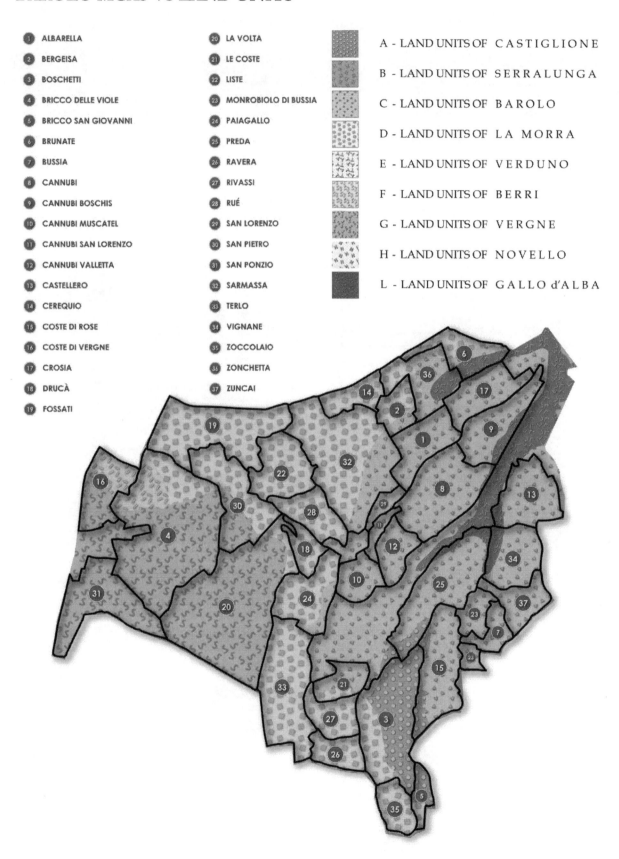

MGA	Size (ha)	Land Units
La Volta	46.34	Land Unit of Vergne
Bricco delle Viole	45.74	Land Unit of Vergne; Land Unit of La Morra; Land Unit of Berri
Sarmassa	33.74	Land Unit of Barolo in the south-eastern plots bordering San Lorenzo; Land Unit of La Morra for the remaining parts
Boschetti	23.87	Land Unit of La Morra
Fossati	23.19	Land Unit of La Morra
Terlo	22.03	Land Unit of La Morra
Preda	20.68	Land Unit of Barolo
Cannubi	19.53	Land Unit of Barolo
San Ponzio	17.54	Land Unit of Vergne
San Pietro	17.36	Land Unit of La Morra
Coste di Rose	16.83	Land Unit of Castiglione
Castellero	13.07	Land Unit of Barolo
Liste	12.45	Land Unit of La Morra
Cannubi Boschis	12.41	Land Unit of Barolo
Paiagallo	12.35	Land Unit of La Morra
Zonchetta	12.28	Land Unit of Barolo
Vignane	11.56	Land Unit of Barolo
Coste di Vergne	10.52	Land Unit of Vergne in the south side; Land Unit of Berri in the remaining parts
Albarella	9.96	Land Unit of Barolo
Crosia	9.62	Land Unit of Barolo
Brunate	9.16	In the lower parcels of Brunate, Land Unit of La Morra is combined with Land Unit of Barolo.
Rue'	8.49	Land Unit of La Morra
Zuncai	7.81	Land Unit of Barolo
Bergeisa	7.00	Land Unit of La Morra
Rivassi	6.72	Land Unit of La Morra
Bussia	6.58	Land Unit of Barolo
Cerequio	6.43	Land Unit of La Morra
Cannubi Muscatel	6.24	Land Unit of Barolo
Cannubi Valletta	6.24	Land Unit of Barolo
Le Coste	6.01	Land Unit of Barolo for the most; Land Unit of La Morra in the southern parcels bordering Rivassi
Zoccolaio	5.95	Land Unit of La Morra
Ravera	5.46	Land Unit of La Morra
Drucà	5.03	Land Unit of La Morra
Monrobiolo di Bussia	4.23	Land Unit of Barolo
Bricco San Giovanni	3.84	Land Unit of Castiglione
Cannubi San Lorenzo	2.38	Land Unit of Barolo
San Lorenzo	2.13	Land Unit of Barolo

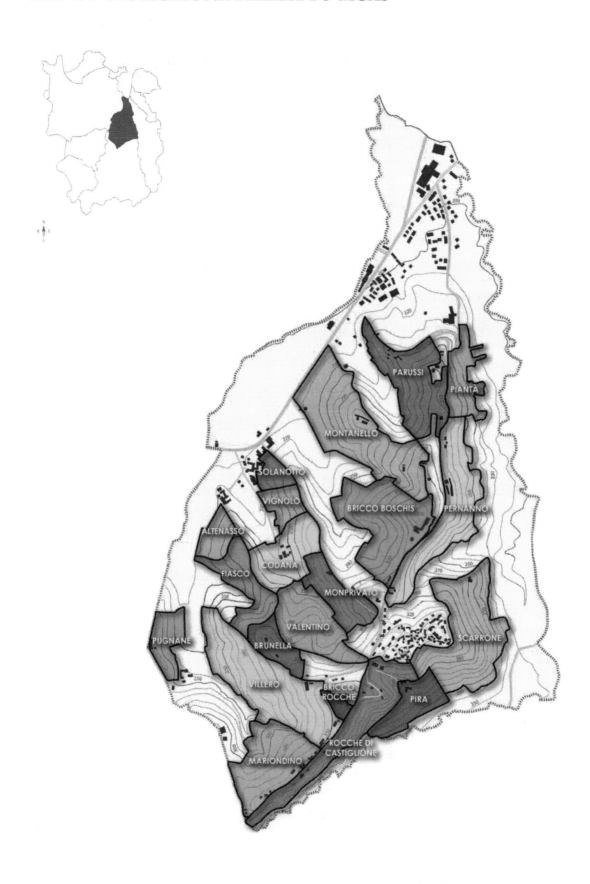

CASTIGLIONE MGAS VS LAND UNITS

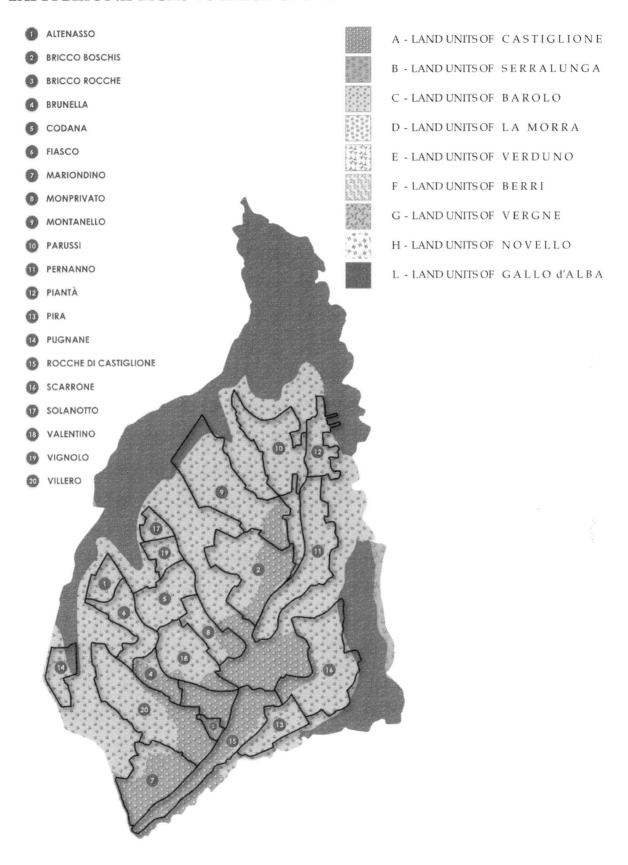

1 ALTENASSO
2 BRICCO BOSCHIS
3 BRICCO ROCCHE
4 BRUNELLA
5 CODANA
6 FIASCO
7 MARIONDINO
8 MONPRIVATO
9 MONTANELLO
10 PARUSSI
11 PERNANNO
12 PIANTÀ
13 PIRA
14 PUGNANE
15 ROCCHE DI CASTIGLIONE
16 SCARRONE
17 SOLANOTTO
18 VALENTINO
19 VIGNOLO
20 VILLERO

A - LAND UNITS OF CASTIGLIONE
B - LAND UNITS OF SERRALUNGA
C - LAND UNITS OF BAROLO
D - LAND UNITS OF LA MORRA
E - LAND UNITS OF VERDUNO
F - LAND UNITS OF BERRI
G - LAND UNITS OF VERGNE
H - LAND UNITS OF NOVELLO
L - LAND UNITS OF GALLO d'ALBA

MGA	Size (ha)	Land Units
Montanello	23.48	Land Unit of Castiglione in the south-eastern sidebordering Bricco Boschis; Land Unit of Barolo in the remaining parts
Villero	22.07	Land Unit of Barolo Land Unit of Castiglione in the eastern / south-eastern sidebordering Brunella and Rocche di Castiglione
Scarrone	20.55	Land Unit of Barolo.
Bricco Boschis	17.65	Land Unit of Barolo in the west side; Land Unit of Castiglione in the east side.
Pernanno	15.98	Land Unit of Barolo.
Rocche di Castiglione	14.36	Land Unit of Castiglione
Parussi	13.41	Land Unit of Barolo
Mariondino o Monriondino o Rocche Moriondino	13.11	Land Unit of Castiglione and Land Unit of Barolo in the northernmost plots.
Valentino	11.68	Land Unit of Castiglione in the highest plots bordering Castiglione village; Land Unit of Barolo in the remaining parts.
Codana	9.66	Land Unit of Barolo
Fiasco	8.30	Land Unit of Barolo
Monprivato	7.12	Land Unit of Castiglione in the south-eastern sidebordering Castiglione village; Land Unit of Barolo in the remaining parts
Pira	6.66	Land Unit of Barolo
Pianta'	6.27	Land Unit of Barolo
Brunella	5.01	Land Unit of Barolo in the north-east side bordering Fiasco; Land Unit of Castiglione in the remaining parts
Pugnane	4.97	Land Unit of Barolo
Altenasso o Garblet Sue' o Garbelletto Superiore	4.27	Land Unit of Barolo
Vignolo	3.57	Land Unit of Barolo
Solanotto	2.86	Land Unit of Barolo
Bricco Rocche	1.46	Land Unit of Castiglione

MAP OF CHERASCO MGA AND LAND UNITS

A - LAND UNITS OF CASTIGLIONE

B - LAND UNITS OF SERRALUNGA

C - LAND UNITS OF BAROLO

D - LAND UNITS OF LA MORRA

E - LAND UNITS OF VERDUNO

F - LAND UNITS OF BERRI

G - LAND UNITS OF VERGNE

H - LAND UNITS OF NOVELLO

L - LAND UNITS OF GALLO d'ALBA

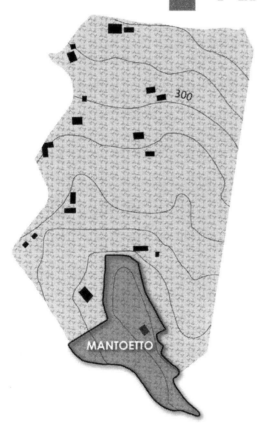

MGA	Size (ha)	Land Units
Mantoetto	2.76	Land Unit of Verduno

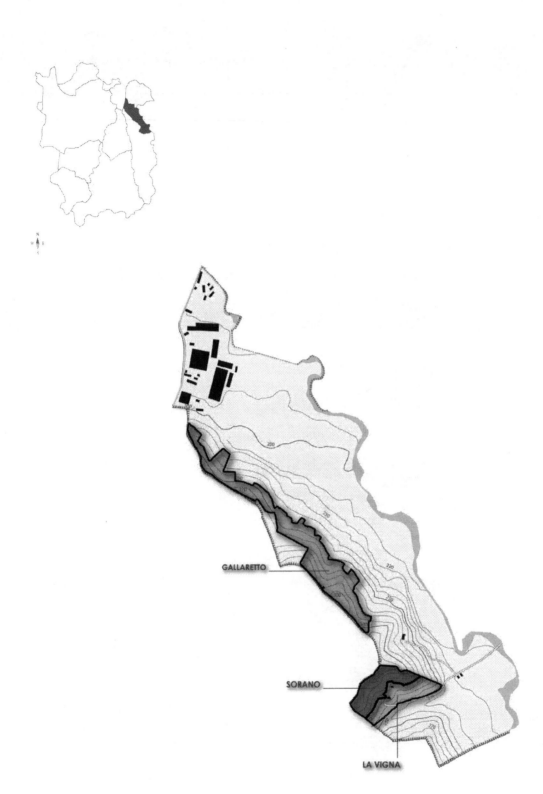

DIANO D'ALBA MGAS VS LAND UNITS

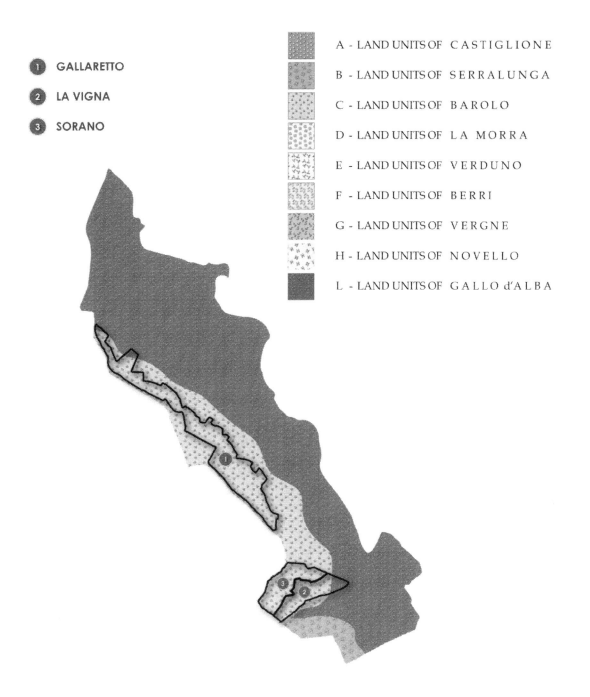

MGA	Size (ha)	Land Units
Gallaretto	15.36	Land Unit of Barolo
Sorano	4.76	For the most Land Unit of Barolo (eastern slopes); Land Unit of Castiglione in the western slopes bordering Carpegna and San Rocco;
La Vigna	4.48	For the most Land Unit of Barolo (eastern slopes);

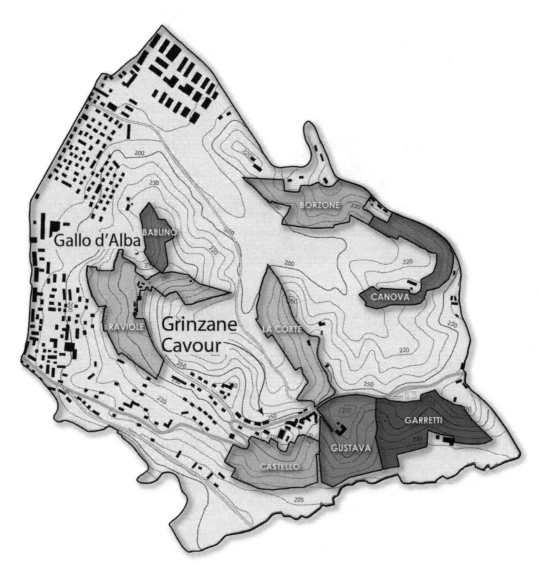

GRINZANE CAVOUR MGAS VS LAND UNITS

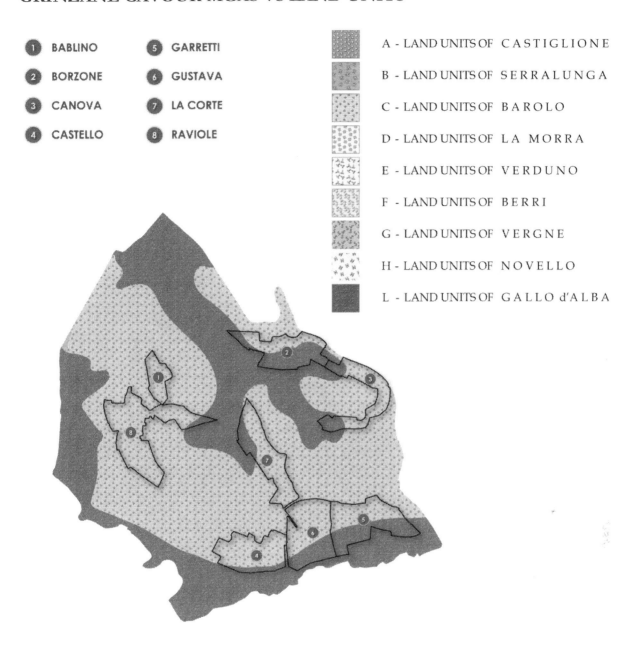

1 BABLINO **5** GARRETTI

2 BORZONE **6** GUSTAVA

3 CANOVA **7** LA CORTE

4 CASTELLO **8** RAVIOLE

A - LAND UNITS OF CASTIGLIONE

B - LAND UNITS OF SERRALUNGA

C - LAND UNITS OF BAROLO

D - LAND UNITS OF LA MORRA

E - LAND UNITS OF VERDUNO

F - LAND UNITS OF BERRI

G - LAND UNITS OF VERGNE

H - LAND UNITS OF NOVELLO

L - LAND UNITS OF GALLO d'ALBA

MGA	Size (ha)	Land Units
Raviole	11.39	Land Unit of Barolo
Garretti	9.00	Land Unit of Barolo
Gustava	8.31	Land Unit of Barolo
La Corte	7.87	Land Unit of Barolo
Castello	7.10	Land Unit of Barolo
Borzone	7.08	Land Unit of Barolo
Canova	5.75	Land Unit of Barolo
Bablino	4.00	Land Unit of Barolo

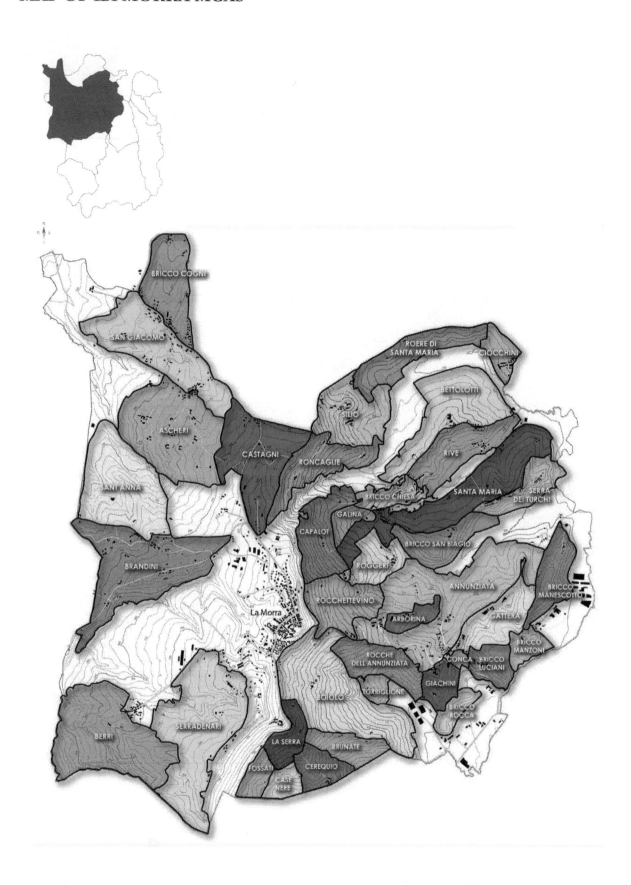

LA MORRA MGAS VS LAND UNITS

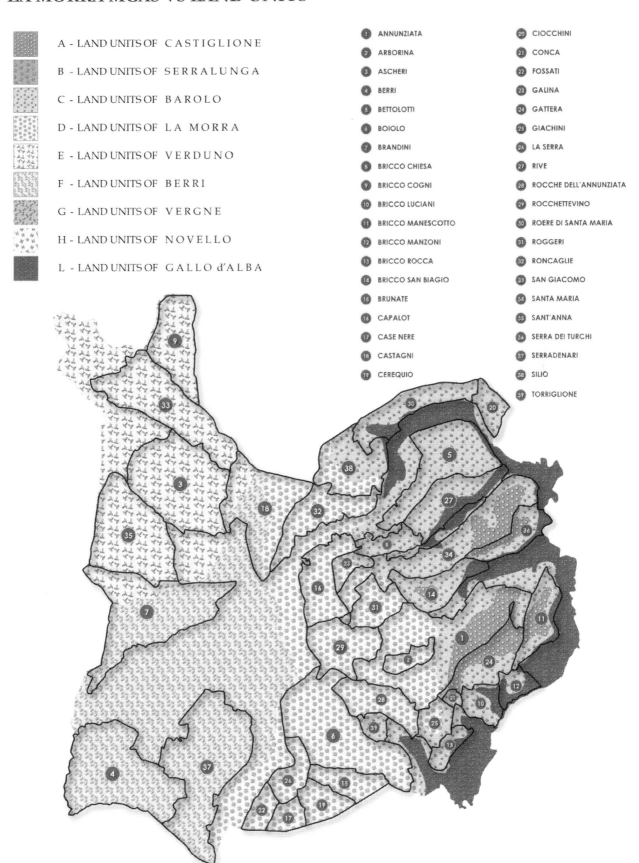

A - LAND UNITS OF CASTIGLIONE

B - LAND UNITS OF SERRALUNGA

C - LAND UNITS OF BAROLO

D - LAND UNITS OF LA MORRA

E - LAND UNITS OF VERDUNO

F - LAND UNITS OF BERRI

G - LAND UNITS OF VERGNE

H - LAND UNITS OF NOVELLO

L - LAND UNITS OF GALLO d'ALBA

1 ANNUNZIATA
2 ARBORINA
3 ASCHERI
4 BERRI
5 BETTOLOTTI
6 BOIOLO
7 BRANDINI
8 BRICCO CHIESA
9 BRICCO COGNI
10 BRICCO LUCIANI
11 BRICCO MANESCOTTO
12 BRICCO MANZONI
13 BRICCO ROCCA
14 BRICCO SAN BIAGIO
15 BRUNATE
16 CAPALOT
17 CASE NERE
18 CASTAGNI
19 CEREQUIO

20 CIOCCHINI
21 CONCA
22 FOSSATI
23 GALINA
24 GATTERA
25 GIACHINI
26 LA SERRA
27 RIVE
28 ROCCHE DELL'ANNUNZIATA
29 ROCCHETTEVINO
30 ROERE DI SANTA MARIA
31 ROGGERI
32 RONCAGLIE
33 SAN GIACOMO
34 SANTA MARIA
35 SANT'ANNA
36 SERRA DEI TURCHI
37 SERRADENARI
38 SILIO
39 TORRIGLIONE

MGA	Size (ha)	Land Units
Annunziata	109.42	Land Unit of Barolo - Land Unit of La Morra - Land Unit of Castiglione
Serradenari	101.19	Land Unit of Berri
Berri	87.89	Land Unit of Berri
Boiolo	87.79	Land Unit of La Morra
Brandini	87.14	Land Unit of Berri for the most; Land Unit of Verduno for the parcels bordering Sant' Anna
Ascheri	83.96	Land Unit of Berri
Sant'Anna	73.30	Land Unit of Verduno
Santa Maria	71.00	Land Unit of La Morra
San Giacomo	69.24	Land Unit of Verduno
Castagni	64.51	Land Unit of Verduno in the north-west side bordering San Giacomo and Neirane; Land Unit of La Morra in the north-east/east side bordering Rocche dell'Olmo and Roncaglie; Land Unit of Berri in remaining parts (central – south)
Bettolotti	58.76	Land Unit of Barolo
Bricco Cogni	43.91	Land Unit of Verduno
Silio	41.56	Land Unit of La Morra in the southern plots bordering Roncaglie; Land Unit of Barolo for the remaining parts;
Rive	38.16	Land Unit of Barolo for the most (the highest plots); Land Unit of Gallo d'Alba for the remaining parts (the lowest)
Roncaglie	36.42	Land Unit of La Morra
Roere di Santa Maria	35.41	Land Unit of Barolo
Rocchettevino	34.98	Land Unit of La Morra
Capalot	34.94	Land Unit of La Morra
Gattera	30.02	Land Unit of Castiglione for the most; Land Unit of Barolo for the lower parcels bordering Bricco Manzoni e Bricco Luciani;
Rocche dell'Annunziata	29.92	Land Unit of La Morra
Bricco San Biagio	28.84	Land Unit of Barolo for the most, Land Unit of Castiglione in the central and higher parts
Bricco Manescotto	27.01	Land Unit of Barolo and Land Unit of Castiglione in the central part
Serra dei Turchi	22.03	Land Unit of Castiglione for the highest plots bordering Borgata Serra dei Turchi; Land Unit of Barolo for the remaining plots descendants to Gallo d'Alba
Roggeri	21.31	Land Unit of La Morra
Brunate	19.19	Land Unit of La Morra
La Serra	17.79	Land Unit of La Morra
Cerequio	17.68	Land Unit of La Morra
Bricco Luciani	16.09	Land Unit of Barolo
Giachini	14.87	Land Unit of La Morra for the most; Land Unit of Barolo for the lower parcels bordering Bricco Rocca;
Bricco Chiesa	14.00	Land Unit of Barolo
Bricco Manzoni	11.98	Land Unit of Barolo
Ciocchini	11.87	Land Unit of Barolo
Bricco Rocca	10.94	Land Unit of Barolo
Arborina	10.81	Land Unit of La Morra
Fossati	10.60	Land Unit of La Morra
Case Nere	10.21	Land Unit of La Morra
Galina	8.74	Land Unit of Barolo in the east side bordering Bricco Chiesa; Land Unit of La Morra for the remaining parts
Torriglione	7.62	Land Unit of Barolo
Conca	3.00	For most Land Unit of Barol (Central Part); Land Unit of Castiglione on the east side through Bricco Luciani; Land Unit of La Morra on the west side through Giachini;

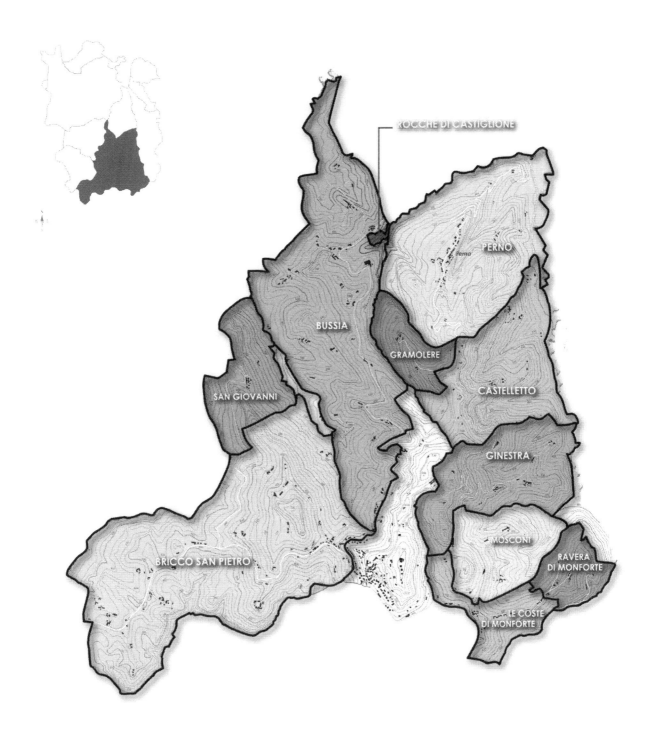

MONFORTE D'ALBA MGAS VS LAND UNITS

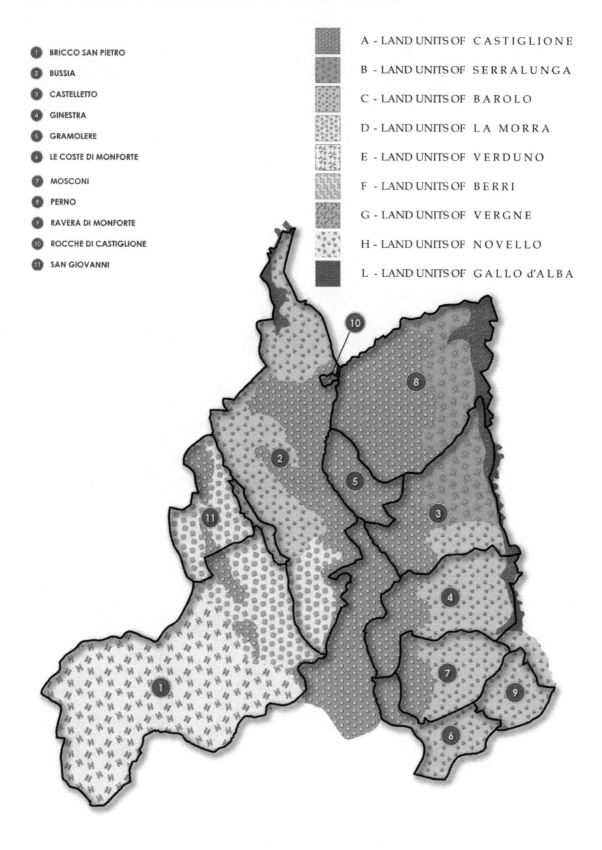

1. BRICCO SAN PIETRO
2. BUSSIA
3. CASTELLETTO
4. GINESTRA
5. GRAMOLERE
6. LE COSTE DI MONFORTE
7. MOSCONI
8. PERNO
9. RAVERA DI MONFORTE
10. ROCCHE DI CASTIGLIONE
11. SAN GIOVANNI

A - LAND UNITS OF CASTIGLIONE
B - LAND UNITS OF SERRALUNGA
C - LAND UNITS OF BAROLO
D - LAND UNITS OF LA MORRA
E - LAND UNITS OF VERDUNO
F - LAND UNITS OF BERRI
G - LAND UNITS OF VERGNE
H - LAND UNITS OF NOVELLO
L - LAND UNITS OF GALLO d'ALBA

MGA	Size (ha)	Land Units
Bricco San Pietro	380.09	Land Unit of La Morra and Land Unit of Castiglione in the north/north-east side; Land Unit of Novello in remaining parts
Bussia	292.31	Land Unit of La Morra near Monforte (Bussia Corsini); Land Unit of Castiglione for the higher parcels; Land Unit of Barolo for the remaining parts.
Perno	190.96	Land Unit of Serralunga d'Alba in the eastern slopes; Land Unit of Castiglione in the remaining parts
Castelletto	128.52	Land Unit of Castiglione in the west side; Land Unit of Serralunga in the north-east side; Land Unit of Barolo in the south-east side.
Ginestra	114.36	Land Unit of Barolo for the most; Land Unit of Castiglione for the highest and western parcels.
Mosconi	75.95	Land Unit of Castiglione in the western side for the highest parcels; Land Unit of Barolo for the central and eastern side.
San Giovanni	68.48	Land Unit of Castiglione for the highest plots (bordering Bricco San Giovanni and Boschetti towards Barolo and Bricco San Pietro towards Monforte); Land Unit of La Morra for the remaining parts.
Le Coste di Monforte	50.34	Land Unit of Castiglione in the western parcels bordering Mosconi and Ginestra; Land Unit of Barolo in the remaining parts
Gramolere	41.40	Land Unit of Castiglione.
Ravera di Monforte	36.63	Land Unit of Barolo.
Rocche di Castiglione	1.97	Land Unit of Castiglione.

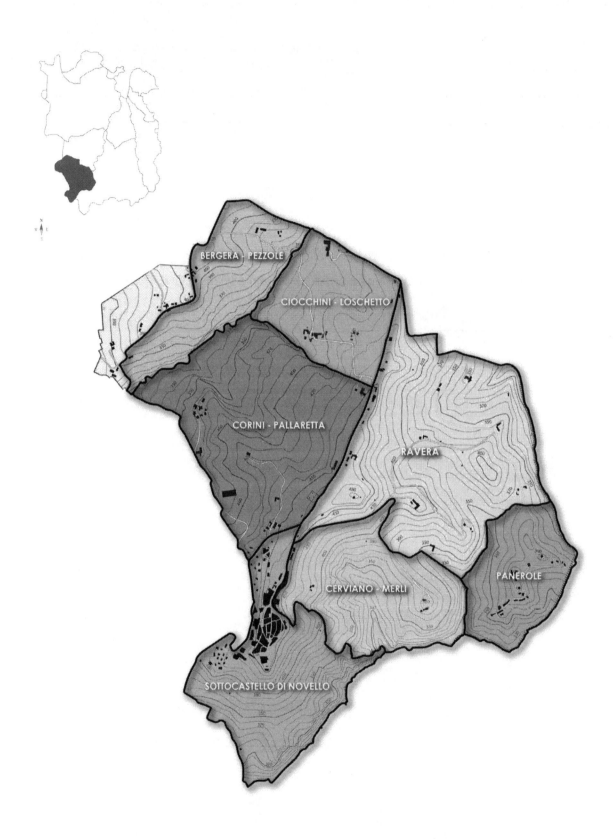

NOVELLO MGAS VS LAND UNITS

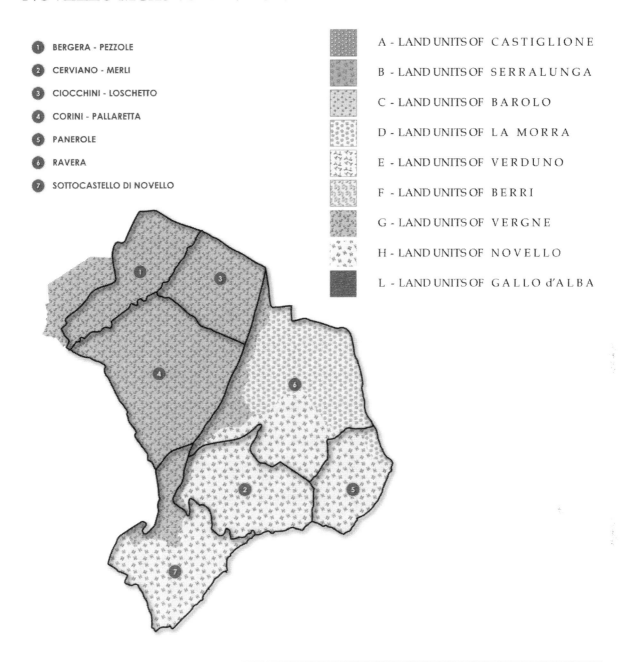

Legend (MGAs):
1. BERGERA - PEZZOLE
2. CERVIANO - MERLI
3. CIOCCHINI - LOSCHETTO
4. CORINI - PALLARETTA
5. PANEROLE
6. RAVERA
7. SOTTOCASTELLO DI NOVELLO

Legend (Land Units):
A - LAND UNITS OF CASTIGLIONE
B - LAND UNITS OF SERRALUNGA
C - LAND UNITS OF BAROLO
D - LAND UNITS OF LA MORRA
E - LAND UNITS OF VERDUNO
F - LAND UNITS OF BERRI
G - LAND UNITS OF VERGNE
H - LAND UNITS OF NOVELLO
L - LAND UNITS OF GALLO d'ALBA

MGA	Size (ha)	Land Units
Ravera	124.95	Land Unit of Novello for the southern plots bordering Cerviano-Merli and Panerole; Land Unit of La Morra for the remaining parts
Corini-Pallaretta	105.88	Land Unit of Vergne.
Cerviano-Merli	65.17	Land Unit of Novello
Sottocastello di Novello	59.73	Land Unit of Vergne in the northern side; Land Unit of Novello for the remaining parts.
Ciocchini-Loschetto	50.10	Land Unit of Vergne.
Bergera-Pezzole	48.69	Land Unit of Vergne.
Panerole	41.52	Land Unit of La Morra in the north-eastern parcels bordering San Giovanni; Land Unit of Novello for the remaining parts;

MAP OF RODDI MGA AND LAND UNITS

▦	A - LAND UNITS OF CASTIGLIONE
▦	B - LAND UNITS OF SERRALUNGA
▦	C - LAND UNITS OF BAROLO
▦	D - LAND UNITS OF LA MORRA
▦	E - LAND UNITS OF VERDUNO
▦	F - LAND UNITS OF BERRI
▦	G - LAND UNITS OF VERGNE
▦	H - LAND UNITS OF NOVELLO
▦	L - LAND UNITS OF GALLO d'ALBA

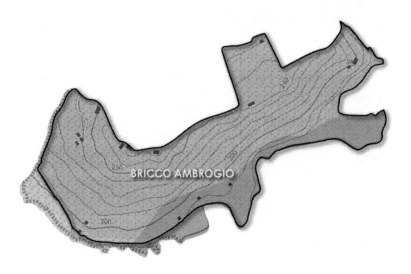

BRICCO AMBROGIO

MGA	Size (ha)	Land Units
Bricco Ambrogio	48.24	Land Unit of Barolo for the most

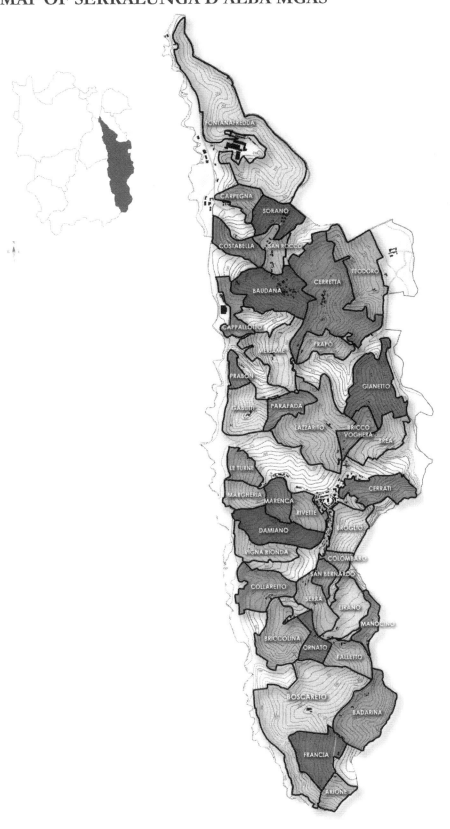

SERRALUNGA D'ALBA MGAS VS LAND UNITS

1 ARIONE
2 BADARINA
3 BAUDANA
4 BOSCARETO
5 BREA
6 BRICCOLINA
7 BRICCO VOGHERA
8 BROGLIO
9 CAPPALLOTTO
10 CARPEGNA
11 CERRATI
12 CERRETTA
13 COLLARETTO
14 COLOMBARO
15 COSTABELLA
16 DAMIANO
17 FALLETTO
18 FONTANAFREDDA
19 FRANCIA

20 GABUTTI
21 GIANETTO
22 LAZZARITO
23 LE TURNE
24 LIRANO
25 MANOCINO
26 MARENCA
27 MARGHERIA
28 MERIAME
29 ORNATO
30 PARAFADA
31 PRABON
32 PRAPÒ
33 RIVETTE
34 SAN BERNARDO
35 SAN ROCCO
36 SERRA
37 SORANO
38 TEODORO
39 VIGNA RIONDA

A - LAND UNITS OF CASTIGLIONE

B - LAND UNITS OF SERRALUNGA

C - LAND UNITS OF BAROLO

D - LAND UNITS OF LA MORRA

E - LAND UNITS OF VERDUNO

F - LAND UNITS OF BERRI

G - LAND UNITS OF VERGNE

H - LAND UNITS OF NOVELLO

L - LAND UNITS OF GALLO d'ALBA

MGA	Size (ha)	Land Units
Fontanafredda	58.42	Land Unit of Barolo for the most; Land Unit of Castiglione in the higher parcels bordering Sorano;
Boscareto	53.15	Land Unit of Serralunga d'Alba
Cerretta	39.93	Land Unit of Serralunga d'Alba in south-eastern plots; Land Unit of Castiglione in the remaining parts
Lazzarito	30.00	Land Unit of Serralunga d'Alba
Teodoro	23.58	For the most Land Unit of Serralunga (eastern slopes); Land Unit of Castiglione for the highest plots bordering Cerretta.
Gianetto	22.40	Land Unit of Serralunga d'Alba
Badarina	21.02	Land Unit of Serralunga d'Alba
Baudana	19.00	Land Unit of Castiglione in the higher parcels; Land Unit of Serralunga d'Alba in the remaining parts
Briccolina	17.93	Land Unit of Serralunga d'Alba
Meriame	17.14	Land Unit of Castiglione in the north-eastern parcels bordering Cerretta; Land Unit of Serralunga d'Alba in the remaining parts
Damiano	15.98	Land Unit of Serralunga d'Alba
Francia	15.80	Land Unit of Serralunga d'Alba
Collaretto	14.36	Land Unit of Serralunga d'Alba
Gabutti	14.24	Land Unit of Serralunga d'Alba
Cerrati	12.96	Land Unit of Serralunga d'Alba
Lirano	12.77	Land Unit of Serralunga d'Alba
Broglio	12.15	Land Unit of Serralunga d'Alba
Brea	10.99	Land Unit of Serralunga d'Alba
Serra	10.28	Land Unit of Serralunga d'Alba
Vignarionda	10.24	Land Unit of Serralunga d'Alba
Rivette	10.00	Land Unit of Serralunga d'Alba
Sorano	9.94	For the most Land Unit of Barolo (eastern slopes); Land Unit of Castiglione in the western slopes bordering Carpegna and San Rocco;
Falletto	8.90	Land Unit of Serralunga d'Alba
Prapo'	8.33	Land Unit of Castiglione in the western side (the highest plots); Land Unit of Serralunga d'Alba in the remaining parts (the lowest)
Costabella	8.29	Land Unit of Barolo
Margheria	8.10	Land Unit of Serralunga d'Alba
Parafada	7.92	Land Unit of Serralunga d'Alba
Cappallotto	7.52	Land Unit of Serralunga d'Alba
Marenca	7.46	Land Unit of Serralunga d'Alba
Le Turne	7.40	Land Unit of Serralunga d'Alba
Bricco Voghera	7.15	Land Unit of Serralunga d'Alba
Carpegna	7.12	Land Unit of Barolo
Ornato	6.70	Land Unit of Serralunga d'Alba
San Rocco	6.43	Land Unit of Castiglione
Arione	5.72	Land Unit of Serralunga d'Alba
Manocino	5.55	Land Unit of Serralunga d'Alba
San Bernardo	4.44	Land Unit of Serralunga d'Alba
Prabon	3.84	Land Unit of Serralunga d'Alba
Colombaro	3.56	Land Unit of Serralunga d'Alba

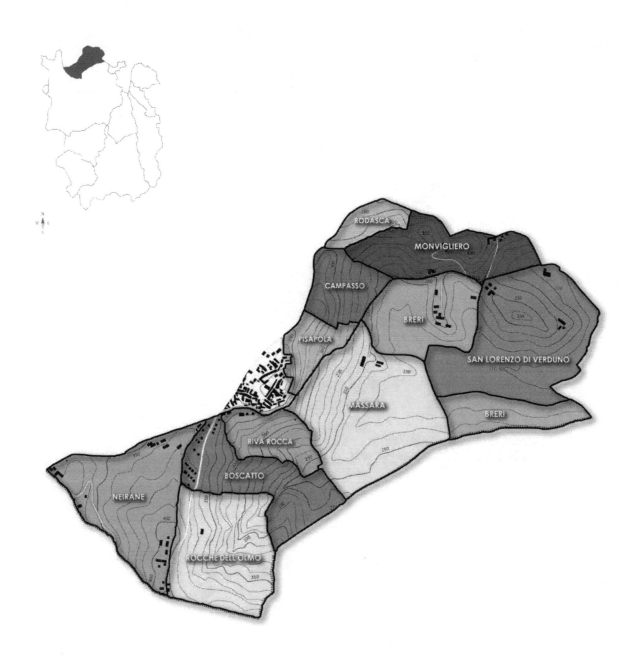

VERDUNO MGAS VS LAND UNITS

1. BOSCATTO
2. BRERI
3. CAMPASSO
4. MASSARA
5. MONVIGLIERO
6. NEIRANE
7. PISAPOLA
8. RIVA ROCCA
9. ROCCHE DELL'OLMO
10. RODASCA
11. SAN LORENZO DI VERDUNO

A - LAND UNITS OF CASTIGLIONE
B - LAND UNITS OF SERRALUNGA
C - LAND UNITS OF BAROLO
D - LAND UNITS OF LA MORRA
E - LAND UNITS OF VERDUNO
F - LAND UNITS OF BERRI
G - LAND UNITS OF VERGNE
H - LAND UNITS OF NOVELLO
L - LAND UNITS OF GALLO d'ALBA

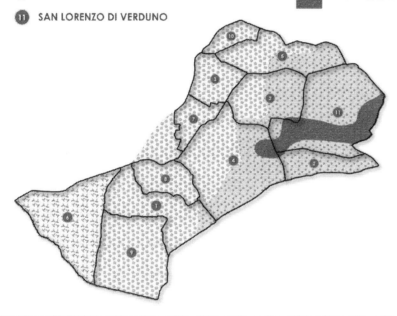

MGA	Size (ha)	Land Units
Breri	53.94	Land Unit of La Morra, Land Unit of Barolo
Massara	50.31	Land Unit of La Morra in the western and north-western parcels bordering Riva Rocca and Pisapola; Land Unit of Barolo in the remaining parts
Neirane	37.59	Land Unit of Verduno
Rocche dell'Olmo	36.88	Land Unit of La Morra
San Lorenzo di Verduno	32.46	Land Unit of Barolo
Boscatto	27.96	Land Unit of La Morra.
Monvigliero	25.51	Land Unit of La Morra, Land Unit of Barolo.
Campasso	13.95	Land Unit of La Morra
Riva Rocca	13.55	Land Unit of La Morra
Pisapola	9.73	Land Unit of La Morra
Rodasca	6.41	Land Unit of La Morra

APPENDICES

Table 1.1: List of names Nebbiolo has historically been known by

Name	Area
Brunenta, Prunenta and/or Prünent	Typical in Piedmont's Val d'Ossola -or Ossola Valley, in English- situated in the Verbano-Cusio-Ossola province
Chiavennasca	In Lombardy's Valtellina area, in the Sondrio province
Melasca, Melaschetto and Melascone Nero	Near the city of Biella, in Alto Piemonte
Martesana	Near Como in Lombardy
Nibieul Burghiri	On the left bank of the Tanaro river, around the commune of S. Stefano Roero
Picotener, Picoutener or Picotendro	In Valle d'Aosta and the Canavesano area of northern Piedmont, especially in the Carema denomination
Spanna	In northeastern Piedmont

Nebbiolo names recalling places of origin

Nebbiolo Canavesano	Nebbiolo d'Asti	Nebbiolo di Barbaresco	Nebbiolo di Barolo
Nebbiolo di Bricherasio	Nebbiolo di Carema	Nebbiolo d'Ivrea	Nebbiolo di Lorenzi
Nebbiolo di Masio	Nebbiolo di Moncrivello	Nebbiolo di Monsordo	N. di Nizza della Paglia
Nebbiolo di Piemonte	Nebbiolo di Sciolze		

Nebbiolo names referring to the grape's specific characteristics and sensory attributes (sight, smell or taste) and viticultural/enological traits

COLOR	Nebbiolin Nero and Nebbiolo Rosato Nebbiolo Cobianco (or Còbianc or Cobianco) Nebbiolo Corosso (or just Còruss or Corosso) Nebbiolo Femmina (or Nebieul Fumela)	Nebbieul Maschio, Nebbiolin, Nebbiolin Comune
SIZE	Nebbiolin Canavesano ("the small Nebbiolo of the Canavese area") Nebbiolin Lungo	Pignolo and Pugnent Spana Grossa Spana Piccolo

Table 1.2: List of erroneous Nebbiolo attributions

Barbesino	Barolo	Nebbiolo Bianco	Nebbiolo d'Antoni or Uva d'Antoni
Nebbiolo di Beltram	Nebbiolo di Dronero	Nebbiolo-Dolcetto	Nebbiolo Pajrolé and Nebbiolo Pirulé
Nebbiolo di Stroppo	Nebbiolo Occellino	Nebbiolo Pignolato	Nebbiolo Polastro
Nebbiolo Rosato	Spanna-Nebbiolo or Spannibio	Spannina	Spanni

Table 1.3: List of Nebbiolo clones recognized officially by the Ministry of Agriculture Registry of Grape varieties and Clones

(*)	Clone name	Date allowed	(*)	Clone name	Date allowed
1	I - RAUSCEDO 3 (Michet)	24/12/1969	25	I - UNIMI-VITIS NEB VV10	2009
2	I - RAUSCEDO 6 (Chiavennasca)	24/12/1969	26	I - UNIMI-VITIS NEB VV11	2009
3	I - RAUSCEDO 1 (Lampia)	24/12/1969	27	I - VCR 270 (Chiavennasca)	2009
4	I - CN 36	01/10/1980	28	I - VCR 275 (Chiavennasca)	2009
5	I - CN 111	01/10/1980	29	I - VCR 130	2009
6	I - CVT CN 142	23/01/1990	30	I - VCR 135	2009
7	I - CVT CN 230	1990-	31	I - VCR 139	2009
10	I - CVT 63 (Michet)	2001	32	I - VCR 172	2009
11	I - CVT 66 (Michet)	2001	33	I - VCR 178	2009
12	I - CVT 71 (Michet)	2001	34	I - VCR 278	2011
13	I - CVT 308 (Picotener)	2001	35	I - VCR 284	2011
14	I - CVT 415 (Picotener)	2001	36	I - VCR 372	2011
15	I - CVT 423 (Picotener)	2001	37	I - VCR 373	2011
16	I - 12 (Chiavennasca)	2002	38	I - CVT C2	2012
17	I - 21 (Chiavennasca)	2002	39	I - VCR 169	2013
18	I - 34 (Chiavennasca)	2002	40	I - VCR 186	2013
19	I - CVT 141	2004	41	I - CVT E6	2014
20	I - CVT 180	2004	42	I - CVT F6	2014
21	I - CVT 185	2004	43	I - CVT G9	2015
22	I - CVT 4	2005	44	I - CVT B 10	2016
23	I - VCR 430	2007	45	I - CVT C 15	2016
24	I - UNIMI-VITIS NEB VV1	2009	46	I - CVT F5	2016

(*) Clones in order of appearance

Table 1.4: Abridged characteristics of the most important Nebbiolo clones

CLONE	ORIGIN	REG.	BIOTYPE	VIGOUR	PRODUCTIVITY	WINE QUALITY*
CN 36	Barolo	1980	Lfit	++/+++	+++irreg	++//+++
CN 111	La Morra	1980	NR	+++	++/+++	+++
CVT CN 142	Neive	1990	Lfic	++	+/++	+++ //++
CVT CN 230	Neive	1990	Lfit	++	+++	++// ++
CVT 63	La Morra	2001	M	++/+++	+/++	+++//+++
CVT 66	La Morra	2001	M	++/+++	+/+++	+++//+++
CVT 71	La Morra	2001	M	++/+++	+/++	+++/+++
CVT 308	Carema	2001	P	+	+/++	++//+++
CVT 415	Donnas (VdA)	2001	P	+	+	+++//+ Langhe;++ (VdA)
CVT 423	Pont St. Martin (VdA)	2001	P	+/++	+/++	+++//+ (Langhe);+++ (VdA)
CVT 141	Neive	2003	L	++	++	++//+/++
CVT 180	Neive	2003	L	+++	+/++	++//+/++
CVT 185	Neive	2003	L	++/+++	+/++	+++//++
CVT 4	Serralunga	2004	L	++/+++	+/++	+++//+/++
CVT C2	Ghemme	2012	Scb	++/+++	++/+++	+++
CVT E6	Canale (Roero)	2014	L	+++	++	++/+++// -
CVT F6	Vezza d'Alba (Roero)	2014	L	++/+++	++	++/+++// - -
CVT G9	Monteu Roero (Roero)	2014	L	++	+/++	++/+++// - -
CVT B10	Gattinara	2016	S	++	++	+++?u.ex.
CVT C15	Gattinara	2016	S	+/+++	+/++irreg	+++? u.ex.
CVT F5	Gattinara	2016	S	++	++irreg	++?u.ex.

Legend

Biotype	
Lfit	Lampia a Foglia Intera
Lfic	Lampia a Foglia Incisa
NR	Lampia
M	Nebbiolo Rosé
P	Picotener
Scb	Spanna Cobianco
S	Spanna

Vigour/Productivity/Wine Quality	
+	poor
+/++	poor to intermediate
++	intermediate
++/+++	intermediate to excellent
+++	excellent
- -	refers to the fact I do not have enough experience with the clone's wines
?u.ex	under exam;
	means the clone has not been in production long enough to allow a fair assessment of its winemaking potential. The ? is referred to the current, hypothetical, tentative wine quality assessment

*: *Wine quality refers to the evaluations given by the nurseries based on their microvinifications results and their tasting panel opinions. In my experience, I have routinely found that all such tasting panels, including those of major wine competitions where large numbers of wines are tasted daily and the experience of the individual tasters is extremely variable, darker, bigger wines almost always receive the highest scores/ the most preferences. This is why nursery quality evaluations referred to the wines made with each almost always penalize those clones that give paler color, more fragrant and less structured wines. In an effort to provide more useful, pragmatic and accurate tasting evaluations of each clone's potential, I have included a column of my own evaluations in relation to wines made with each clone. These evaluations, though admittedly personal and subjective, reflect thirty years of tasting Nebbiolo wines and a palate much more in tune with what many people want out of a wine they're going to eat with.*

: *In a sign of how times change, I point out that the assessments of the quality of Nebbiolo Rosé wines made back in the 1990s was uniformly poor (I have tables where the wine quality is rated with one + or one * only; but wouldn't you know it, in the 21st century, most tables and assessments award CN 111 wines ++ or **. As for me, there's never been a doubt in my mind: the quality of wines made with CN 111 is, and always has been, of +++ or * level.*

Table 1.5: Viticultural and winemaking characteristics of Nebbiolo's most common clones

CN 36:

One of the five oldest clones of Nebbiolo to have been developed, and added to Italy's national registry of clones in 1980, the CN 36 is a Lampia a Foglia Intera characterized by medium-high vigor, high fertility and good but irregular productivity. Phenological aspects: CN 36 budbreaks early and ripens late, while flowering and *véraison* occur at the same times of the year as other clones. It has high and average sensitivity to oidium (powdery mildew) and grey rot, respectively. Its bunch is medium-large (it weighs about 300 grams), conical in shape, medium-long, and medium-tightly packed, with one to two well-developed wings.

The grapes are medium-small in size (average weight: 1.7 grams/single grape or berry) and slightly oval in shape. In my experience, CN 36 gives lovely wines that are characterized more by fragrance and refinement than they are by sheer power; they also have above average acidity, similar to that of all Nebbiolo clones developed until 2001 (included). But as it was always the case in the very misguided 90s when all everyone wanted to do was drink jam rather than wine (and very dark and sweet jam at that), the fact this clone isn't able to give muscular wines means that a number of shall we say fashion-sensitive producers largely phased it out in many vineyards, a real shame (although, in fairness, its irregular productivity was no walk in the park and that undoubtedly contributed to CN 36 falling out of favor).

That said, many Barolos made from older vineyards still have a good amount of CN 36 in them. With a little practice, it's easy to recognize Barolos that are just so: the aromas of violet are purer and more intense than in most other wines made with a preponderance of other clones.

CN 111:

One of the five oldest (1980) clones, and make no mistake, one of the best "Nebbiolo" clones ever developed: I wrote the name Nebbiolo in quotation marks because recently it has been postulated that the outstanding CN 111, always thought to be a clone of Nebbiolo Rosé (the only official clone of Nebbiolo Rosé, in fact), might be instead a clone of Nebbiolo Lampia clone that more than any other, looks and behaves like a Nebbiolo Rosé. (But hardly any producer I have talked to and who has worked with this clone over the years thinks/believes CN 111 to be a Lampia at all.).

The CN 111's vigor, fertility and productivity are all very high: Like CN 36, CN 111 is an early-budding and generally late ripening clone (but even more so than with other clones of the various Nebbiolo biotypes, this behavior is highly dependent on the terroir CN 111 grows in), while flowering and véraison occur at the same times of the year as other clones. And again, like CN 36, it has high and average sensitivity to oidium and grey rot, respectively. Its leaf is extremely large, and characterized by having only three lobes (Nebbiolo Lampia's leaf can also have three lobes, but almost always has five; in my experience, leaves of the Michet biotype never have anything but five lobes). CN 111's bunch varies in size, but is most often medium-small to medium in size (the average weight is 280 grams), conical or cylindrical in shape, generally long, and tightly packed, and is often but not necessarily winged.

The grapes are medium-small in size (the average weight is less than 1.8 grams/berry) and slightly oval, not round, in shape. The grapes are characterized by higher total acidities than any other clone of the various Nebbiolo biotypes (malic acid concentrations are especially high). Because CN 111 is perceived to give wines strong on perfume but light on colour and structure, it has always been planted parsimoniously in Langhe vineyards, but was always present to some degree (nowadays you find it mostly in the Langhe's oldest vineyards). In my experience, CN 111 wines are characterized (but not always) by a truly mesmerizing perfume of wild red roses, rosehip tea, candied rose petals, red cherries and redcurrants, but of red cherry and raspberry extract/nectar too; notes of nutmeg, cumin and cinnamon are always evident even in young wines, and the brown spice note, along with a hint of herbaceous tobacco increase as the wines age.

There is always a mineral presence too. Wines can also more powerful than people believe, though they are for the most part steely and lifted. However, when planted in clay-rich soils, the clone tends to give somewhat bigger, more structured wines. Some Nebbiolo CN 111 clones give darker and bigger than expected wines even in sandy soils, so I believe there is a spectrum of different grapevines within members of the CN 111 group, that have resulted over time by adapting to their specific habitats (see chapter 3, NEBBIOLO ROSÉ).

Depending on the mutations they have accumulated over time, some behave more like Nebbiolo Rosé and others behave more like Nebbiolo Lampia. Last but not least, there are specific Nebbiolo CN 111 and original Nebbiolo Rosé grapevines in the field that have been hit by the fan leaf-virus and that are for all intents and purposes examples of Nebbiolo Rosé-Michet, because just like the Nebbiolo Lampia hit by fanleaf and known as Nebbiolo Michet, the same has happened to plants of Nebbiolo Rosé, with all the consequences the virus entails (see chapter 4, NEBBIOLO ROSÉ). However, that statement needs to be viewed in the context of current scientific knowledge, because there appear to be plants of Nebbiolo Michet in the field that have no virus whatsoever (see chapter 2, NEBBIOLO MICHET) so it may not necessarily be that all wild Michet populations are virus-affected.

CVT CN 142:

Registered in 1990, this clone is derived from the Lampia a Foglia Incisa biotype (unlike clone CVT CV 230, added to the national registry of clones in the same year and that is instead a Lampia a Foglia Intera biotype). Clone CVT CN 142 is characterized by medium vigor, medium fertility and low to only medium productivity; in fact, though opinions diverge (don't they always, in Italy) it is apparently the least productive of all the CVT Nebbiolo clones.

CVT CN 142 budbreaks medium-early and ripens late, while flowering and *véraison* occur at the same times of the year as other clones. It has high and average sensitivity to oidium and grey rot, respectively. Its leaf is medium-small, with five lobes, indented (which is not surprising, given it's a Lampia a Foglia Incisa biotype), and with a downier inferior page (underside) than it is in other Nebbiolo clones. The bunch is conical in shape, medium-large to large (weight: 310 grams on average), long, and medium-tightly packed, with two to three well-developed wings. The grapes are medium-small in size (average weight 1.9 grams/grape), very short, slightly oval in shape and very dark blue in color (CVT CN 142 is one of the darker-berried Lampia clones; despite this observation, its wines are neither as dark nor as tannic as those made with CVT CN 230).

In my experience, CVT CN 142 gives wines characterized by good but harmonious acidity and deep colour, with average to slightly above average tannic clout. I also find wines made with this clone to have a spicy nose and higher than average alcohol by volume (compared to wines made with other Nebbiolo clones). My personal opinion is that it is a good "jack of all trades" Nebbiolo clone that hits no special highs, but no lows either.

CVT CN 230:

Another of the earliest Nebbiolo clones to have been developed, this Lampia a Foglia Intera was sourced in Neive and included in Italy's national registry of clones in 1990 along with its stablemate CVT CN 185. Unlike that clone which is a Nebbiolo Lampia a Foglia Incisa, the CVT CN 230 is a Lampia a Foglia Intera.

It is characterized by medium vigor, high fertility and high productivity: CN 230 budbreaks medium-early but ripens late, while flowering and véraison occur at the same times of the year as most other Nebbiolo clones. It has high and average sensitivity to oidium and grey rot, respectively. Its leaf is large and with three lobes; its bunch is pyramidal in shape, quite large (average weight: 340 grams), tightly packed, with at least two if not three well-developed wings. The grapes are fairly dark in color, medium-small in size (average weight: 1.9 grams) and slightly oval in shape, with on average even more bloom than is common with this variety (remember that, most likely, it is the noteworthy bloom that gives Nebbiolo its name).

In my experience, CVT CN 230 gives powerful Barolos of medium acidity, with the typical Nebbiolo floral aromas (rose, violet) strongly marked by spicy nuances (more so than with wines made with other Nebbiolo clones). The wines also strike me as darker than those of many other clones (the numbers would seem to bear this out: for example, total anthocyanin concentrations of experimental micro-vinifications boast 20% and 25% more total anthocyanins than do CN 36 and CN 111, respectively).

CVT 63:

This clone, derived from a Nebbiolo Michet biotype growing in La Morra, is characterized by medium-high vigor, moderate fertility and productivity: CVT 63 budbreaks early but ripens late, while flowering and *véraison* occur at the same times of the year as most other Nebbiolo clones. It has better than average resistance to grey rot but is quite susceptible to oidium, like practically all Nebbiolo grapevines. The leaf is jagged and with five lobes, as is almost always the case with the Michet biotypes; its bunch is pyramidal in shape, quite small (it weighs only about 200 grams, or close to 100 grams less than most other Nebbiolo clones not derived from Michet) and short, tightly packed, with short wings. The grapes are small in size and slightly oval in shape, with plenty of bloom (more so then in other clones).

CVT 63 gives powerful Barolos of medium to low acidity, with the typical Nebbiolo floral aromas (rose, violet) strongly marked by spices and tobacco. A very typical Michet wine, with plenty of structure and color; this clone sports some of the highest total anthocyanin and polyphenol concentrations of any Nebbiolo clone. But then, just looking at its small compact bunch and the small berries (hence high skin to pulp ratio) you would expect the wine to be just so. CVT 63's trump card is that its wines are not over the top, boring, behemoths, but retain Nebbiolo's typical grace and charm despite all their power.

CVT 66:

Another Michet clone registered in 2001, CVT 66 is characterized by medium-high vigor, moderate fertility and productivity. CVT 66's phenology differs considerably from other Nebbiolo clones. It budbreaks and changes color (*véraison*) early; and while flowering occurs at the same times of the year as most other Nebbiolo clones, it ripens earlier than most. It has better than average resistance to grey rot and, like all Nebbiolos, is fairly sensitive to oidium.

This is a rare Michet with leaves that have for the most part only three lobes, and that are less heavily indented than other members of the Michet group. Its bunch is usually cylindrical in shape (at times somewhat conical), small (average weight of 210 grams which is similar to other Michet-derived clones) and loosely-packed, with small if any wings. The grapes are medium-small in size and slightly oval in shape, with a good if not especially noteworthy amount of bloom.

In my experience, CVT 66 gives some of the most dark and powerful Barolos of all, and not especially shy on total acidity. It is one of the Nebbiolo clones the wines of which I find most associated with licorice nuances, tobacco and varied notes of spice (Bourbon vanilla, mint, anise). Analytically, this clone has anthocyanin and polyphenol concentrations that are at, or close to, the top, of the Nebbiolo clone heap. I like this clone's wines, save for the fact that they can be rather high in alcohol (mainly because CVT 66 grapes have no trouble packing in the sugars).

CVT 71:

It's fair to say that CVT 71 is one of the all-time most successful Nebbiolo clones. It has been planted massively by producers everywhere in the Langhe, mostly because it delivers color and structure without being over the top, such as clone 58. A Michet from la Morra that was first registered in 2001, it is characterized by medium-high vigor and below average fertility and productivity levels. CVT 71's phenology differs slightly from most other Nebbiolo clones, with a relatively early budbreak and average time of flowering, but *véraison* occurs slightly earlier than other nebbiolo clones and it also ripens slightly sooner too (so in other words, medium-early *véraison* and medium-late harvest).

It has high and average resistance to grey rot and oidium, respectively. Its leaf is medium-small, heavily indented, and with five lobes; its bunch is small in size (average weight: 195 grams), short and cylindrical in shape, rarely if ever winged, and tends to be loosely-packed. The grapes are medium-small in size, slightly oval in shape, and with a good amount of bloom. CVT 71 has the lowest acidity levels of all the Michet clones of its generation (indeed, some of the lowest total acidity, tartaric acid and malic acid levels of any Nebbiolo clone) but just like them, the highest total anthocyanin and polyphenol concentrations of any Nebbiolo clone developed to date.

Like all the Michet clones it can give notes of superripe fruit, even of fruit that has been macerated in alcohol, and noteworthy alcohol levels, but part of the reason for its remarkable success not just with producers and wine lovers alike is that CVT 71 wines are rarely over the top, nicely combining power and grace. Its wines are chunkier and more closed down initially than those made with CVT 66, which in my view often have a minty, slightly more fragrant note that those made with CVT 71 do not (though much of that impression will depends on the commune in which the grapes are planted in: for some reason, I find all the Michets to perform better in Monforte than they do in La Morra, for example, though I may be wrong).

CVT 308:

One of my favorite Nebbiolo clones of all, the CVT 308 is a Picotener original of Carema in northern Piedmont. It was registered in 2001. It is characterized by slightly below average vigor, fertility and below average to average productivity levels. CVT 308's phenology is similar to most other Nebbiolo clones, with relatively early budbreak, average flowering and *véraison*, and a late harvest.

It has high and average resistance to grey rot and oidium, respectively. Its leaf is large and usually has five lobes (though examples of trilobed leaves with CVT 308 are not rare), with an especially downy underside; the bunch is usually cylindrical in shape, with very small wings, and medium-small in size (average weight: 250 grams); though not especially loosely-packed, it's not that compact either. The grapes vary greatly in size, ranging from medium-small to medium-large in size (average weight: 1.9-2 grams) and are slightly oval in shape, with good amounts of bloom.

The CVT 308 wines never strike me as being especially dark, and are often marked by elegant notes of herbs and sweet spices (nutmeg and white pepper, especially, but also sandalwood, cinnamon, and potpourri. Notes of menthol and camphor are also recognizable. In my experience, CVT 308 gives some of the most balanced and perfumed Barolos of all, if not the most powerful (and this despite boasting relatively high anthocyanin and polyphenol levels).

And though it is also characterized by some of the lowest total acidity and malic acid concentrations of all Nebbiolo clones, its wines never strike me as being acid-deficient. Again, the CVT 308 clone weaves its specific brand of magic thanks to wines of masterful balance and grace.

CVT 415:

Another Picotener clone registered in 2001, CVT 415 is characterized by slightly below average vigor, fertility and productivity. CVT 415's phenology differs considerably from other Nebbiolo clones, with medium-early budbreak, véraison and flowering; it also ripens slightly earlier than most other Nebbiolo clones.

It has average and good resistance to oidium and grey rot, respectively. Its leaves are characterized by five and even seven lobes and are more jagged than Picotener CVT 308; the medium-small bunch (average weight: 230 grams) is short and pyramidal-shaped, not especially tightly-packed, and rarely has any wings. The grapes are medium-small in size and slightly oval in shape, with a good amount of bloom. In my experience, CVT 415 gives dark and powerful Barolos characterized by not especially high levels of acidity, and is another of the Nebbiolo clones the wines of which I find to be quite spicy (not peppery) with notes of brown spices, tobacco and vanilla dominating.

One aspect of CVT 415 wines is their generally highish alcohol levels (it's one of the Nebbiolo clones that packs in sugar the best) but also the tendency to have aromas and flavors that easily veer towards the ultra-ripe fruit, even cooked fruit, and compotes (prunes, cherries macerated in alcohol), especially in warm years.

CVT 141:

CVT 141 was sourced in Neive and registered in 2004. It is simply labeled as a Nebbiolo of the Lampia biotype, without specifying if it belongs to the Lampia a Foglia Intera or to the Lampia a Foglia Incisa subgroup, but in my opinion, it belongs to the "a Foglia Incisa" subgroup and should be so classified. This Nebbiolo clone is characterized by medium vigor and below average to medium fertility and productivity levels. CVT 141's phenology is similar to that of most other Nebbiolo clones, with a relatively early budbreak and average time of flowering and véraison and a relatively late harvest time. It has average and good resistance to oidium and grey rot, respectively.

Its leaf has five lobes, is medium-small and heavily indented; its bunch is medium-small in size (average weight: 250 grams), pyramidal and slightly elongated in shape, winged, it's neither loosely-packed nor tightly packed. The grapes are medium-small in size (average weight: 1.9 grams), slightly oval in shape, and with a good amount of bloom. CVT 141's analytical parameters confirm all you already knew about the infatuation of the late twentieth and early twenty-first centuries with big, dark, fleshy, low pH and tannic wines.

In fact, this clone has the lowest acidity levels (total, tartaric and malic acid) of any Nebbiolo clone developed until this point in time, but also boasts the highest total polyphenol and second highest total anthocyanin concentrations of any Nebbiolo clone developed before it. As you would expect, the wines made with CVT 141 are powerful and spicy. As you would not expect, the wine's color is lighter and less ruby-purple hued than that of wines made with the Michet clones (all of which share similar total anthocyanin numbers as CVT 141, but remember that color is a function not just of how much anthocyanins there are, but by how easily they are released). In fairness many producers feel that this clone is less extreme than some other newer generation clones like for example 58. In Alfio Cavallotto's estimation, one should never use more than 3-5 of the latter clones, while up to 25% of this one is fine.

CVT 180:

Registered in 2004, it is another Nebbiolo clone simply labeled as deriving from the Lampia biotype, without specifying if it belongs to the Lampia a Foglia Intera or to the Lampia a Foglia Incisa subgroup. Another point of contention with this clone is its exact place of origin: while it has been reported in the literature as being from Barbaresco, it appears that the original vineyards were actually in Neive. I have observed rows of this grapevine numerous times and I'll admit it's not easy to decide to which subgroup the clone belongs to (while I think it's much easier to take an educated guess with clone CVT 141, for example); it may well just be an intermediate form between the two biotypes.

The clone is characterized by high vigor and below average to medium fertility and productivity levels. CVT 180's phenology differs slightly from other Nebbiolo clones, with a relatively early budbreak and early to average time of flowering and *véraison*; it also ripens slightly earlier in the fall. It has average and good resistance to oidium and grey rot, respectively. Its leaf is only medium-sized, with five lobes usually; its bunch is medium-small in size, among the smallest of the non-Michet Nebbiolos (average weight: 230 grams), short and pyramidal in shape, with one small wing, and average tightness.

The grapes are also small in size (average weight: 1.8 grams), slightly oval in shape, with a good amount of bloom and really quite dark (blue-black, almost). CVT 180 is yet another clone released for sale in the early twenty-first century and it clearly reflects both what producers as well as wine critics wanted, and nurseries were trying to deliver, at that time: big, low pH wines. And so, CVT 180's acidity parameters are the lowest of any Nebbiolo clone developed previously (and very similar to those CVT 141) and clocks in with by far the highest total anthocyanin and polyphenol concentrations of any Nebbiolo clone developed to date (although in my experience, CVT 180's wine color is usually not as dark as you would expect it to be by looking at the numbers). This has never been a favorite Nebbiolo clone of mine; and though I realize that size matters for some people, I have always ascribed, and still do, to the notion that less is usually more.

CVT 4:

Strange as it may seem given the quality of the wines associated with Serralunga, the CVT 4 was the first Nebbiolo clone ever to be sourced from that commune (so relatively late in the clone game). Registered in 2005, it is another Nebbiolo Lampia clone simply labeled as such, without specifying if it belongs to the Lampia a Foglia Intera or to the Lampia a Foglia Incisa subgroup.

The clone is characterized by high vigor and below average to medium fertility and productivity levels. CVT 4's phenology is similar to the majority of all other Nebbiolo clones, with a relatively early budbreak, with flowering and véraison occurring at the same time as most other Nebbiolos, and just like them, it is also a late ripener. It has average and high resistance to oidium and grey rot, respectively. Its leaf is medium-small and indented, with five lobes. Its bunch is medium-small in size (average weight: 240 grams), short and cylindrical in shape, rarely winged, and boasts average tightness.

The grapes are medium in size (2 grams average weight) and more oval in shape than those of other Nebbiolos, quite dark blue-black in color. Developed along the lines of other Nebbiolo clones of its era (meaning the goal with it was to deliver wines that were dark, low in acidity and tannic) CVT 4 is characterized by the lowest acidity levels of any Nebbiolo clone developed previously (for comparison's sake, it has a third less total acidity and about half the malic acid concentrations of clones CVT 63 and 66, and three times less total and malic acidity levels of Nebbiolo CN 111). That said, it does not boast especially high anthocyanin and polyphenol concentrations. In my view this clone is a good example of the sum being better than its parts, as the wines made with it, though usually not the most vibrant are well-balanced and structured enough to please.

CVT C2:

Validated by the Italian national registry in 2012, this is a fairly unique Nebbiolo clone in that it was selected from old plants of the now-rare Nebbiolo Cobianco biotype (còbianc, in local dialect), grown mostly in Alto Piemonte (Boca, Gattinara, Ghemme). Differently from the Corosso biotype, which cannot as yet be the object of clonal selection and propagation (all the Corosso grapevines examined so far are affected by viruses, and it is illegal to propagate virused plants).

The Nebbiolo Cobianco mother plant from which the C2 clone was developed was selected in an old vineyard of Ghemme in the 1980s, and then propagated in two experimental vineyards in Gattinara; the grapevines were followed for three years, with morphologic, enologic and health status parameters monitored. The results were analyzed and compared to CVT 185 and CN 230, two other high quality Nebbiolo clones planted in the same vineyards. In general, it is characterized by medium-high vigor and good fertility. It has average and good resistance to oidium and grey rot, respectively. The leaves are large, with five lobes, moderately indented to highly indented; and the inferior page is downy. The bunches are medium-sized (weight: 200-300 grams) and mostly cylindrical in shape; there is usually one wing; grapes are medium-small (weight 1.7-1.9 grams) and round.

Experimental C2 wines I've tasted tend to be darker colored than those made with most other Nebbiolo clones (certainly more so than those produced with the CN 230), slightly higher in total acidity (but low malic acid concentrations appear to be a C2 hallmark) and with higher alcohol by volume (unfortunately, in my view).

Table 1.6. Viticultural and enological aspects of Nebbiolo clones developed outside of Piedmont

R1:

One of three oldest Nebbiolo clones, it is a Nebbiolo Lampia (though no further specifications are given to whether it is a Lampia a Foglia Intera or a Foglia Incisa, but at the time those doing the looking probably weren't even aware of their existence), sourced in the countryside of Alba and added to the national registry of clones in 1969. The R1 is characterized by above average vigor and slightly above average productivity. CN 36 budbreaks early and ripens late, while flowering and *véraison* occur at the same times of the year as other clones. It has high and average sensitivity to oidium and grey rot, respectively. It has medium-large bunch and berries. Like all the older generations of Nebbiolo clones, the R1 gives perfumed, fresh medium-bodied wines that are more about grace than power.

R3:

One of three oldest Nebbiolo clones, it is a Michet, sourced in the countryside of La Morra and added to the national registry of clones in 1969. It is characterized by average vigor and slightly above average productivity. CN 36 budbreaks early and ripens late, while flowering and véraison occur at the same times of the year as other clones. It has high and average sensitivity to oidium and grey rot, respectively. It has medium-small bunches and berries.

R6:

One of three oldest Nebbiolo clones, it is a Nebbiolo Chiavennasca, sourced in the Valtellina countryside in and added to the national registry of clones in 1969. It is characterized by above average vigor and productivity. CN 36 budbreaks early and ripens late, while flowering and véraison occur at the same times of the year as other clones. It has high and average sensitivity to oidium and grey rot, respectively. It has medium-large bunches and berries. Its wines are some of the most delicate Nebbiolos of all, downright graceful, and very typical of the Nebbiolo wines you drink in Lombardy and Valle d'Aosta.

VCR 430:

A Nebbiolo Lampia (whether it is a Lampia a Foglia Intera or a Foglia Incisa is not specified) sourced in the countryside of La Morra and added to the registry in 2007. It is another miserly clone, characterized by below average vigor and productivity. CN 36 budbreaks early and ripens late, while flowering and *véraison* occur at the same times of the year as other clones. It has high and average sensitivity to oidium and grey rot, respectively. It has medium-small bunches and fairly small to medium-small berries. Not surprisingly given its morphological aspect, its wines are structured and tannic.

VCR 130:

A Nebbiolo Lampia (whether it is a Lampia a Foglia Intera or a Foglia Incisa is not specified) sourced in the countryside of La Morra and added to the registry in 2009. It is characterized by average vigor and slightly above average productivity. CN 36 budbreaks early and ripens late, while flowering and véraison occur at the same times of the year as other clones. It has high and average sensitivity to oidium and grey rot, respectively. It has medium-small bunches and berries. Its wines are fairly structured and tannic.

VCR 135:

A Nebbiolo Lampia (whether it is a Lampia a Foglia Intera or a Foglia Incisa is not specified) sourced in the countryside of La Morra and added to the registry in 2009. It is one of the more miserly clones, characterized by below average vigor and productivity. CN 36 budbreaks early and ripens late, while flowering and *véraison* occur at the same times of the year as other clones. It has high and average sensitivity to oidium and grey rot, respectively. It has medium-small bunches and fairly small to medium-small berries. Its wines are graceful and perfumed.

VCR 178:

A Nebbiolo Lampia (whether it is a Lampia a Foglia Intera or a Foglia Incisa is not specified) sourced in the countryside of Treiso and added to the registry in 2007. It is another of the more miserly clones, characterized by below average vigor and productivity. CN 36 budbreaks early and ripens late, while flowering and véraison occur at the same times of the year as other clones. It has high and average sensitivity to oidium and grey rot, respectively. It has medium-small bunches and fairly small to medium-small berries. Its wines are extremely well-balanced, offer a nice spicy nuance, and age well.

VCR 270:

This is a Nebbiolo Chiavennasca, sourced in the countryside in Tirano (Valtellina) and added to the national registry of clones in 2009. It is characterized by very slightly average vigor and average productivity. CN 36 budbreaks early and ripens late, while flowering and *véraison* occur at the same times of the year as other clones. It has high and average sensitivity to oidium and grey rot, respectively. It has medium-sized bunches and berries, with highish levels of skin anthocyanins. Its wines exude noteworthy spiciness, have good tannic backbones and tend to age very well.

VCR 275:

This is a Nebbiolo Chiavennasca, sourced in the countryside in Ponte in Valtellina and added to the national registry of clones in 2009. It is characterized by average vigor and slightly above average productivity. CN 36 budbreaks early and ripens late, while flowering and *véraison* occur at the same times of the year as other clones. It has high and average sensitivity to oidium and grey rot, respectively. It has medium-sized bunches that are more loosely packed than most and medium to medium-small berries. Its wines are fairly powerful and unlike the VCR 270 wines that are characterized by spices, this clone's wines are more about floral and red fruit aromas and flavors.

Table 1.7. Documented presence/absence of Nebbiolo Michet (various clones and massal selections) holdings of Barolo wineries

Aldo Clerico	Yes
Aurelio Settimo	No
Boglietti	No
Borgogno Fratelli	Yes; from a massal selection
Brezza	No
Bric Cenciurio	Yes
Brovia	Yes. CVT 71 and CVT 66
Bruno Giacosa	Yes. CVT 71
Ca' Viola	Yes. CVT 71 and CVT 63
Cagliero	No
Cascina Adelaide	Yes. CVT 71 and from massal selection.
Cascina del Monastero	Yes, CVT 71
Cavallotto	Yes. 33-35% of these are of the "real" Nebbiolo Michet, because it derives from an old massal selection. The new clones, dating back from late 80's (new in the sense they have been more or less recently developed, but are in fact not really quite so new, are CVT 71.
Ceretto	No
Chiara Boschis - E. Pira & Figli	Yes. 30-40%. A mix of all Michet clones.
Ciabot Berton	Yes. CVT 71
Claudio Alario	No
Comm. GB Burlotto	Yes. Hard to say. CVT 71 and Rauscedo R3
Conterno Fantino	Yes
Cordero di Montezemolo	Yes
Dezzani	Yes
Domenico Clerico	Probably in the "Percristina" vineyards and in the "Gepe Alto" vineyard (used in the Ginestra Ciabot Mentin)
Dosio	Yes. CVT 71
Elvio Cogno	Yes. 40%. Rauscedo R3 and a massal selection (from vines 70 years old)
Ettore Germano	No
Francesco Rinaldi	Very few.
Franco Conterno	Yes
Gaja	Yes
GD Vajra	Yes
Gianni Gagliardo	Yes
Gianni Ramello	Yes; from a massal selection
Gigi Rosso	No
Giovanni Canonica	Yes; from a massal selection
Giovanni Manzone	Yes
Giuseppe Mascarello	Yes
Giuseppe Rinaldi	No
La Contrada di Sorano	Yes
Le Strette	Yes. CVT 71
Marchesi di Barolo	Yes
Mario Marengo	Yes; from a massal selection

Massolino	No
Mauro Molino	Yes
Mauro Sebaste	Yes. CVT 71
Michele Chiarlo	Yes
Nadia Curto	Yes
Poderi Oddero	No
Palladino	Yes; from a massal selection
Paolo Manzone	Yes; from a massal selection
Paolo Scavino	Yes. CVT 71
Parusso	Yes; from a massal selection
Pecchenino	Yes; from a massal selection
Pianpolvere Soprano	Yes
Poderi Aldo Conterno	Yes; in very small percentages, patchy in all our vineyards
Poderi Colla	Yes; from a massal selection
Raineri	No
Renato Corino	Yes
Renzo Seghesio	Yes. CVT63
Revello Fratelli	Yes
Reverdito	Yes; from a massal selection
Rivetto	Yes: CVT 71 (29%); CVT 4 (3%)
Rivetto	Yes; from a massal selection
Rocche dei Manzoni	Yes
Roccheviberti	Yes
Scaletta	Yes. CVT71, CVT63, CVT 4
Scarzello	Yes
Silvano Bolmida	Yes; from a massal selection
Silvio Alessandria	Yes
Silvio Grasso	Yes
Sukula	Yes. CVT71, CVT63
Trediberri	No
Vietti	Yes; less than 10%. CVT 4 e CVT 71 in some of the new vineyard and a massal selection in a small vineyard
Vietto	No
Virna Borgogno	Yes; from a massal selection

Table 1.8. Documented presence/absence of Nebbiolo Rosé /clone CN 111 holdings of Barolo wineries

Accomasso	Yes, it's present in all the old vineyards, in small percentages; it is an historic part of the denomination and it is historically inaccurate to say otherwise
Agostino Bosco	No
Aldo Conterno	No
Angelo Negro	No
Arnaldo Rivera (Terre del Barolo)	Of course, it's present in all the old vineyards, it's unrealistic to state otherwise
Ascheri	Yes, Sorano
Attilio Ghisolfi	Yes, but only four rows
Aurelio Settimo	No
Bartolo Mascarello	Yes, in small percentages it is present in all the old vineyards of Barolo
Boglietti	Yes, in Arione
Bolmida	No
Bric Cenciurio	5-10% in Monrobiolo di Bussia
Brovia	Rocche di Castiglione.
Bruno Giacosa	There are very old vines that look and behave as if they are Nebbiolo Rosé/CN 111 but we have never had them studied
Ca' Viola	No
Cagliero	No
Canonica	Yes, in Borzone (makes the Barolo del Comune di Grinzane Cavour)
Cascina Adelaide	No
Cavallotto	15% in the Vigna Punta Marcello of the Bricco Boschis (its highest and southeast facing portion), but there are plants in the Vigna San Giuseppe too
Ceretto	No
Chiara Boschis – E. Pira e Figli	Yes, in Liste (used to make the Barolo Via Nuova as well as the Langhe Nebbiolo)
Ciabot Berton	No
Claudio Alario	No
Conterno Fantino	Yes, in Ginestra
Contrada di Sorano	Yes
Cordero di Montezemolo	Yes, very old vines in the Monfalletto
Corino	No
Cortese	No
Curto	Not that we are aware of, but some old vines look like it might be
Dezzani	Yes
Dosio	No
Ettore Germano	No
Francesco Sobrero	Yes, Pernanno
Fratelli Borgogno	Yes, clone CN111
Fratelli Giacosa	No
Gaja	Yes
GD Vajra	All the old massal selections are CN111 or Nebbiolo Rosé (30 %). Especially in the Bricco delle Viole, but it is one of Barolo's three historic Nebbiolo varieties and it is planted everywhere in the denomination, everybody has more or less some, it just goes unrecognized because Nebbiolo's grapes themselves tend to become pinker with age.
Giacomo Conterno	Yes, there are bound to be in the old vineyards, it was always planted in the vineyards historically in small percentages
Gianni Abrigo	Yes, small percentages
Gianni Ramello	No
Gigi Rosso	We only have fifteen rows we use for experimental study purposes
Giovanni Manzone	Yes, Gramolere Bricat:

Giovanni Viberti	Yes, it's present in small percentages in all the old vineyards. I also make a Nebbiolo Rosato wine with 100% CN 111/Nebbiolo Rosé
Giuseppe Rinaldi	Yes, but less than 2%
La Contrada di Sorano	Yes
La Spinetta	No
Le Strette	No
Marchesi di Barolo	Yes, old massal selections are present in all our vineyards
Mario Giribaldi	Yes, Cerviano-Merli
Mario Marengo	No
Massolino	No
Mauro Molino	Yes, Conca
Mauro Sebaste	No
Michele Chiarlo	No
Poderi Oddero	Yes, old vines are present in all the MGAs
Palladino	No
Paolo Manzone	No
Paolo Scavino	No
Parusso	No
Pecchenino	It's very hard to say without proper studies but our old vines for sure have CN 111
Pian Polvere	No
Poderi Colla	No
Raineri	Yes, for Langhe Nebbiolo.
Renato Corino	No
Renzo Seghesio	No
Revello Fratelli	Yes, Gattera
Reverdito	No
Rivetto	No
Rizzi	No
Rocche dei Manzoni	No
Roccheviberti	No
Scaletta	Yes, we use it for our Langhe Nebbiolo
Scarzello	Yes, for sure, it is part of Barolo's heritage and history and so all the old vineyards have it in small portions
Silvio Grasso	No
Sukula	No
Sylla Sebaste	
Tenuta L'Illuminata	No
Tenuta Rocca	No
Trediberri	No
Vietti	Yes, Lazzarito
Vietto	No.
Virna Borgogno	Yes, in Sarmassa and Cannubi.

Table 2.1: Hectares under vine in Barolo, Roero and other Langhe denomination

DENOMINATION	Hectares (2021)	Production 2021 (hl)
ALTA LANGA SPUMANTE	340.44	20,976.53
BARBARESCO	755.14	39,504.75
BARBERA D'ALBA	1,487.34	90,277.19
BAROLO	2,213.73	111,872.97
DOGLIANI	587.72	24,768.61
DOLCETTO D'ALBA	804.37	42,566.06
DOLCETTO DI DIANO D'ALBA	140.61	6,461.01
LANGHE NEBBIOLO	939.52	65,766.74
NEBBIOLO D'ALBA	1,135.48	71,535.11
ROERO	149.36	7,343.51
ROERO ARNEIS	786.98	52,020.82
VERDUNO PELAVERGA	25.80	1,568.61

Table 2.2: Hectares under vine in Barolo of Nebbiolo and other grape varieties

BAROLO		CASTIGLIONE FALLETTO	
Grapes varieties	Hectares (2021)	Grapes varieties	Hectares (2021)
Nebbiolo N.	307.78	Nebbiolo N.	181.83
Barbera N.	22.12	Barbera N.	20.20
Dolcetto N.	11.74	Dolcetto N.	12.40
Chardonnay B.	4.62	Chardonnay B.	7.72
Sauvignon B.	2.08	Pinot Nero N.	1.79
Freisa N.	1.95	Freisa N.	1.51
Cabernet Sauvignon N.	1.04	Viognier B.	1.29
Merlot N.	1.02	Merlot N.	1.20
Albarossa N.	0.93	Sauvignon B.	0.77
Riesling Renano B.	0.91	Cabernet Sauvignon N.	0.64
Pinot Nero N.	0.34	Syrah N.	0.12
Nascetta B.	0.19	Grignolino N.	0.12
Arneis B.	0.17		
Ruche' N.	0.14		
Favorita B.	0.04		

CHERASCO

Grapes varieties	Hectares (2021)
Barbera N.	14.82
Nebbiolo N.	12.99
Favorita B.	1.73
Dolcetto N.	1.62
Arneis B.	0.89
Chardonnay B.	0.78
Nascetta B.	0.70
Merlot N.	0.68

GRINZANE CAVOUR

Grapes varieties	Hectares (2021)
Nebbiolo N.	77.83
Barbera N.	9.54
Dolcetto N.	7.94
Arneis B.	1.20
Chardonnay B.	1.07
Favorita B.	0.74
Merlot N.	0.24

DIANO D'ALBA

Grapes varieties	Hectares (2021)
Dolcetto N.	216.79
Nebbiolo N.	158.31
Barbera N.	75.43
Chardonnay B.	25.48
Arneis B.	13.23
Favorita B.	9.44
Merlot N.	8.30
Pinot Nero N.	5.62
Sauvignon B.	4.11
Cabernet Sauvignon N.	2.20
Nascetta B.	2.10
Freisa N.	1.48
Riesling Renano B.	1.25
Viognier B.	0.90
Syrah N.	0.76
Traminer Aromatico Rs.	0.46
Bonarda N.	0.18
Cabernet Franc N.	0.15
Grignolino N.	0.13
Moscato Bianco B.	0.04
Riesling Italico B.	0.02

LA MORRA

Grapes varieties	Hectares (2021)
Nebbiolo N.	684.69
Barbera N.	87.97
Dolcetto N.	60.80
Chardonnay B.	20.19
Nascetta B.	4.07
Merlot N.	3.87
Viognier B.	2.72
Pinot Nero N.	2.33
Cabernet Sauvignon N.	2.02
Sauvignon B.	1.60
Pelaverga Piccolo N.	1.56
Freisa N.	1.45
Riesling Renano B.	1.41
Arneis B.	1.09
Riesling Italico B.	0.35
Petit Verdot N.	0.27
Cabernet Franc N.	0.20
Moscato Bianco B.	0.15
Albarossa N.	0.12
Manzoni Bianco B.	0.09
Syrah N.	0.09
Neretta Cuneese N.	0.03
Pelaverga N.	0.02

MONFORTE D'ALBA	
Grapes varieties	**Hectares (2021)**
Nebbiolo N.	683.14
Barbera N.	169.42
Dolcetto N.	167.55
Chardonnay B.	38.56
Pinot Nero N.	15.03
Sauvignon B.	7.95
Nascetta B.	7.16
Merlot N.	5.95
Cabernet Sauvignon N.	3.45
Freisa N.	3.41
Riesling Renano B.	3.05
Manzoni Bianco B.	3.03
Rossese Bianco B.	2.86
Viognier B.	2.32
Syrah N.	1.60
Favorita B.	1.09
Erbaluce B.	0.93
Arneis B.	0.92
Albarossa N.	0.87
Timorasso B.	0.43
Baratuciat B.	0.36
Pinot Grigio G.	0.33
Grignolino N.	0.21
Cabernet Franc N.	0.11
Moscato Bianco B.	0.04

NOVELLO	
Grapes varieties	**Hectares (2021)**
Nebbiolo N.	274.19
Barbera N.	32.23
Dolcetto N.	27.36
Nascetta B.	16.23
Chardonnay B.	2.33
Sauvignon B.	1.90
Merlot N.	1.39
Freisa N.	1.19
Pinot Nero N.	1.18
Erbaluce B.	0.52
Pinot Grigio G.	0.47
Viognier B.	0.44
Pinot Bianco B.	0.23
Arneis B.	0.20
Syrah N.	0.11
Favorita B.	0.04

RODDI	
Grapes varieties	**Hectares (2021)**
Nebbiolo N.	62.80
Barbera N.	37.24
Dolcetto N.	12.23
Pelaverga Piccolo N.	3.49
Arneis B.	2.54
Chardonnay B.	1.46
Freisa N.	1.20
Merlot N.	1.20
Favorita B.	1.03
Neretta Cuneese N.	0.40
Cabernet Sauvignon N.	0.39
Sauvignon B.	0.36
Petit Verdot N.	0.15
Manzoni Bianco B.	0.14

VERDUNO	
Grapes varieties	**Hectares (2021)**
Nebbiolo N.	135.58
Pelaverga Piccolo N.	22.20
Barbera N.	20.12
Dolcetto N.	13.50
Chardonnay B.	2.94
Sauvignon B.	1.68
Pelaverga N.	1.40
Pinot Nero N.	0.90
Favorita B.	0.77
Freisa N.	0.53
Nascetta B.	0.43
Merlot N.	0.41
Grignolino N.	0.27
Arneis B.	0.10

SERRALUNGA D'ALBA	
Grapes varieties	**Hectares (2021)**
Nebbiolo N.	401.6114
Moscato Bianco B.	27.3191
Barbera N.	24.4665
Dolcetto N.	20.183
Chardonnay B.	15.0521
Merlot N.	8.6857
Pinot Nero N.	7.7212
Sauvignon B.	2.3868
Cabernet Sauvignon N.	1.6362
Nascetta B.	1.2685
Pinot Bianco B.	1.1804
Petit Verdot N.	1.0785
Riesling Renano B.	1.0355
Viognier B.	0.495
Freisa N.	0.472
Manzoni Bianco B.	0.25
Favorita B.	0.2291
Rossese Bianco B.	0.143
Brachetto N.	0.0309

Table 2.3: Hectares of Nebbiolo planted in the Barolo denomination by commune

COMMUNE	Denomination	Hectares under vine 2021
BAROLO	Barolo	271.58
	Langhe Nebbiolo	35.41
CASTIGLIONE FALLETTO	Barolo	152.81
	Langhe Nebbiolo	28.86
CHERASCO	Barolo	2.73
	Langhe Nebbiolo	10.23
DIANO D'ALBA	Barolo	19.54
	Langhe Nebbiolo	9.32
GRINZANE CAVOUR	Barolo	63.16
	Langhe Nebbiolo	11.39
LA MORRA	Barolo	553.41
	Langhe Nebbiolo	129.43
MONFORTE D'ALBA	Barolo	471.26
	Langhe Nebbiolo	131.73
NOVELLO	Barolo	192.43
	Langhe Nebbiolo	45.56
RODDI	Barolo	25.10
	Langhe Nebbiolo	4.68
SERRALUNGA D'ALBA	Barolo	351.78
	Langhe Nebbiolo	48.80
VERDUNO	Barolo	109.93
	Langhe Nebbiolo	21.54

Table 2.4: Number of organically farmed hectares in Barolo

Harvest 2021	Hectares under vine	Organic Farming (ha)	Organic Farming (%)
BAROLO	271.58	57.90	21.3%
CASTIGLIONE FALLETTO	152.81	45.02	29.5%
CHERASCO	2.73		0.0%
DIANO D'ALBA	19.54	2.35	12.0%
GRINZANE CAVOUR	63.16	15.82	25.1%
LA MORRA	553.41	73.96	13.4%
MONFORTE D'ALBA	471.26	90.69	19.2%
NOVELLO	192.43	20.40	10.6%
RODDI	25.10	1.25	5.0%
SERRALUNGA D'ALBA	351.78	86.40	24.6%
VERDUNO	109.93	3.60	3.3%
TOTAL	**2,213.72**	**397.40**	**18.0%**

Table 3.1: Comparison Cannubi production declarations

	Size (ha)	2013			2021		
		Size Claimed (ha)	N. Claimants MGA	Production (hl)	Size Claimed (ha)	N. Claimants MGA	Production (hl)
Cannubi	19.53	25.48	19	136,464.44	32.83	25	160,082.20
Cannubi Boschis	12.41	5.55	5	29,757.48	1.47	2	7,769.00
Cannubi Muscatel	6.24	0.21	1	1,129.48			
Cannubi San Lorenzo	2.38	1.43	3	7,369.16	1.00	1	5,418.24
Cannubi Valletta	6.24	2.85	1	15,436.00			
TOTALE	**46.79**	**35.51**	**29**	**190,156.56**	**35.30**	**28**	**173,269.44**

Comparison of data provided by "Department of Agriculture of the Region Piemonte" [Size Claimed (ha), Number of Claimants and Production Claimed (hl)] on the basis of the producer claims for each MGA in 2013 and 2021

	Size (ha)	2014 (*)		2018 (**)	
		N. owners/ tenants	Name	N. owners/ tenants	Name
Cannubi (or Cannubi Centrale)	19.53	19	Barale, Serio &Battista Borgogno, Brezza, Cagnasso, Camerano, Cascina Adelaide, Chiarlo, Damilano, Fontana M, Marchesi di Barolo, B. Mascarello, E. Pira, Rinaldi F., Poderi Einaudi, L. Sandrone, P. Scarzello, Giulia Sebaste, Tenuta Carretta	16	E. Altare, Barale, Borgogno, Serio &Battista Borgogno, Brezza, Camerano, Cascina Adelaide, Chiarlo, Damilano, Marchesi di Barolo, B. Mascarello, E. Pira, Poderi Einaudi, L.Sandrone, P. Scavino, Tenuta Carretta
Cannubi Boschis	12.41	9	Alessandria, G. Fenocchio, A.Pittatore, M.Pittatore, L. Prandi, F. Rinaldi, L. Sandrone, A&R Sandrone, Vezza	7	Alessandria, G. Fenocchio, F. Rinaldi, L. Sandrone, Virna, Pittatore, Vezza
Cannubi Muscatel	6.24	5	Brezza, Cascina Bruciata, Marchesi di Barolo, L. Sandrone, Comune di Barolo	5	Brezza, Cascina Bruciata, Marchesi di Barolo, L. Sandrone, Comune di Barolo
Cannubi San Lorenzo	2.38	4	Borgogno, Camerano, Ceretto, G. Rinaldi	4	Borgogno, Camerano, Ceretto, G. Rinaldi
Cannubi Valletta	6.24	3	Comm. GB Burlotto, Damilano, P. Scarzello	2	Comm. GB Burlotto, Damilano

(*): From the presentation: "La disfida dei Cannubi, come stravolgere una verità storica"

(**): From: "BAROLO MGA VOL. I - The Barolo Great Vineyards Enciclopedia" - Second Edition (2018) - Alessandro Masnaghetti Editore - ENOGEA

Table 3.2: Cannubi producers of the bio-district "CannuBio"

Barale Fratelli	Damilano	Giuseppe Rinaldi
Brezza	Elio Altare	Michele Chiarlo
Cascina Adelaide	Francesco Rinaldi	Poderi Einaudi
Ceretto	G.B. Burlotto	Serio e Battista Borgogno
Chiara Boschis – E. Pira & Figli	Giacomo Fenocchio	Astemia Pentita

Table 3.3: Barolo vineyard districts subregions

MGA /BAROLO VINEYARD DISTRICT	SUBREGIONS
BUSSIA	1. Pugnane 2. Bussia Sottana 3. Munie 4. Rocche di Monforte 5. Bussia Soprana 6. Mondoca 7. Dardi 8. Pianpolvere and Pianpolvere Soprano 9. Visette, Arnulfo and Fantini 10. Corsini
CANNUBI	1. Cannubi (Cannubi Centrale) 2. Cannubi Boschis 3. Cannubi Muscatel 4. Cannubi San Lorenzo 5. Cannubi Valletta
CASTELLETTO	1. Castelletto-proper or Castelletto (Eastern Castelletto-proper and Western Castelleto-proper) 2. Pressenda 3. La Villa
CERRETTA	1. Cerretta or Cerretta proper 2. Bricco Cerretta 3. Cerreta Piani
GINESTRA	1. Ginestra or Ginestra proper 2. Pajana 3. Grassi 4. Gavarini
GRAMOLERE	1. Gramolere Soprana 2. Gramolere Sottana
MOSCONI	1. Mosconi Palazzo 2. Mosconi or Mosconi proper 3. Conterni or Mosconi Conterni
PERNO	1. Perno Disa 2. Perno Cerretta 3. Perno Santo Stefano
RAVERA	1. Cascina Nuova 2. Bricco Pernice 3. Ravera di Barolo 4. Ravera di Terlo
RAVERA DI MONFORTE	1. Ravera di Monforte proper 2. Ravera-Pilone
ROCCHE DELL'ANNUNZIATA	1. Rocche dell'Annunziata di Sopra or Rocchette 2. Rocche dell'Annunziata di Sotto or Rocche dell'Annunziata proper
RONCAGLIE	1. Roncaglie Soprana 2. Roncaglie Sottana

SARMASSA	First section: Sarmassa Bricco
	Second section: Sarmassa Sotto Ruè
	Third section: Sarmassa Sotto Liste
	Fourth section:
	    Upper: Sarmassa Mandorla
	    Lower: Sarmassa Merenda

Table 3.4: Soil Component percentages of the Brezza winery's vineyards in Barolo

Vineyard	Loam	Clay	Sand
CANNUBI MUSCATEL	36.8	32.7	30.5
CANNUBI	39.5	23.6	36.9
SARMASSA	46.4	30.5	24.2
CASTELLETTO	29.6	31.3	39.1
SAN LORENZO	46.4	29.4	40.5

Table 4.1: Ian D'Agata & Michele Longo Top Barolo vineyard districts

Ian	Michele
Bricco Rocche	Bricco Rocche
Brunate	Brunate
Bussia	Bussia (Romirasco, Dardi, Mondoca)
Cannubi centrale	Cannubi Centrale
Falletto	Cerequio
Francia	Falletto
Ginestra	Francia
Lazzarito	Ginestra
Monprivato	Lazzarito
Monvigliero	Monvigliero
Rocche dell'Annunziata	Pira
Rocche di Castiglione	Rocche dell'Annunziata
Romirasco	Rocche di Castiglione
Vignarionda	Vignarionda
Villero	Villero

Table 4.2: Most underrated Barolo vineyard districts

Bettolotti
Borzone
Boscatto
Broglio
Cannubi Muscatel
Conca
Coste di Rose
Pugnane
Rocchettevino
Sorano

Table 4.3: Top 15 Barolo vineyard districts according to Barolo's producers

MGA	Score % (*)
Cannubi	63%
Brunate	55%
Vigna Rionda	48%
Bussia	38%
Rocche di Castiglione	29%
Cerequio	27%
Ginestra	25%
Rocche dell'Annunziata	21%
Francia	14%
Monvigliero	13%
Prapò	13%
Villero	13%
Falletto	9%
Monprivato	9%
Mosconi	9%

(*) Score % indicates the percentage, of the total of producers interviewed, indicating that MGA as a "Top 5" MGA

Table 4.4: Top 10 Barolo vineyard districts Barolo's producers would love to own/be gifted

MGA	Score % (*)
Cannubi	20%
Brunate	14%
Bussia	12%
Vigna Rionda	12%
Cerequio	10%
Ginestra	6%
Monvigliero	6%
Boscareto	4%
Francia	4%
Mosconi	4%

(*) Score % indicates the percentage, of the total of producers interviewed, indicating that they would love to own/be gifted that MGA

Table 4.5: Ian D'Agata's typical organoleptic descriptors of the Barolos of the vineyard districts

Albarella: violet, red cherry

Altenasso: ripe red cherry, raspberry nectar, sweet spices

Annunziata: redcurrant, violet, rose, orange peel

Arborina: violet, strawberry, sour red cherry, (Arborina di testa: south- and eastern-facing section); red cherry, plum (southeastern-facing and central portions); brown spices, orange peel (central areas with red clay inclusions).

Arione: sour red cherry, tobacco, minerals

Ascheri: earth, leather, graphite, red fruit compote

Bablino: not enough tasting data available

Badarina: musk, balsamic oils

Baudana: prunes, fruit jam (red cherry)

Bergeisa: red cherry, cinnamon, licorice

Bergera-Pezzole: sweet spices, red fruit

Berri: spearmint (Gallinotto); cool red berries, herbs

Bettolotti: botanicals, including mint, incense and bay leaf; dry spices, even curry

Boiolo: tea, balsamic oils (juniper), earth tones.

Borzone: red cherry, tobacco

Boscareto: dried flowers, anise, leather

Boscatto: red fruit, licorice, blue flowers such as violet (to help, think of Boscatto as offering aromas and flavours that are an ideal cross between the characteristic descriptors of the Barolos of Neirane and Rocche dell'Olmo)

Boschetti: licorice (and light balsamic nuances)

Brandini: red cherry, peach

Brea: both crisp and ripe red cherry, chlorophyll and underbrush

Breri: pure rose (very intensely floral); at times peony with spicy overtones, strawberry, citrus fruit

Bricco Ambrogio: floral (violet, rose, peony), red cherry, peach, passion fruit, sandalwood, pine needles, dried lilac

Bricco Boschis: red cherry, aromatic herbs, tobacco

Bricco Chiesa: violet, redcurrant, sour red cherry, violet, orange peel

Bricco Cogni: licorice, violet, sour red cherry

Bricco delle Viole: wild violet, sour red cherry, minerals

Bricco Luciani: violet, ripe red fruit, licorice, sweet spices, minerals

Bricco Manescotto: dark red fruit (black cherry as opposed to sour red cherry, for example), dark plum, menthol nuances (rather than sweeter balsamic ones), licorice, forest floor, licorice, blackberry

Bricco Manzoni: red cherry, balsamic oils, ferrous note/steeliness/minerals.

Bricco Rocca: violet, rose, ripe dark red cherry

Bricco Rocche: ripe red cherry, raspberry nectar, sweet pipe tobacco, cinnamon, marzipan, sandalwood

Bricco San Biagio: wild rose, strawberry jelly, iris, orange peel, menthol, violet

Bricco San Giovanni: not enough tasting data available

Bricco San Pietro: red cherry, licorice, balsamic oils, anise, violet, tar, cloves

Bricco Voghera: more black fruit (black cherry, blackberry, plums, even prunes) than red

Briccolina: sour red cherry, minty herbs, blood orange

Broglio: generally very delicate fruity nuances of sour red cherry, apricot, red berries

Brunate: brown spices (nutmeg more so than cinnamon), flowers (violet, rose, iris, peony), fresh citrus (in cooler years), red cherry

Brunella: ripe red cherry, tobacco, botanicals

Bussia

- a. Bussia Soprana (Cicala): leather, balsamic oils, earth
- b. Bussia Soprana (Colonello): rose and violet, strawberry, orange peel
- c. Bussia Soprana (Romirasco): sweet spices, raspberry, quinine, and herbs
- d. Corsini: orange peel, violet, tobacco
- e. Dardi: eucalyptus, earth, dark red cherry
- f. Munie: peach, red cherry, strawberry nectar, sweet spices
- g. Pianpolvere/Pianpolvere Soprano: red cherry, cinnamon, marzipan
- h. Pugnane: tobacco, ripe red cherry, porcini, mint
- i. Visette: minerals, sour red cherry, violet, rose

Campasso: not enough tasting data available

Cannubi Centrale: redcurrant, sour red cherry, orange peel, minerals, violet (with eucalyptus and spearmint very present in cooler years)

Cannubi Boschis: balsamic oils (menthol in warmer years), darker cherry than the rest of the Cannubi hill, fresh and dried roses, orange peel, minerals

Cannubi Muscatel: red fruit, minerals

Cannubi San Lorenzo: sour red cherry, violet, rose

Cannubi Valletta: balsamic oils, mint, rose

Canova: not enough tasting data available

Capalot: menthol, very ripe dark red (almost blue) fruit, violet pastille, licorice

Cappallotto: not enough tasting data available

Carpegna: not enough tasting data available

Case Nere: tobacco, ash, red-almost blue fruit (darker than most)

Castagni: baked clay, scorched earth, faded rose petal (near the town of La Morra); gently mineral, sour red cherry, orange peel to the northeast (closer to the Rocche dell'Olmo MGA of Verduno)

Castellero: red cherry, tobacco, flowers

Castelletto: flowers (violet, rose), pomegranate, rosemary, thyme and pennyroyal (not mint) on the sandier portions at higher elevations (essentially, those areas above 360 meters above sea level); resin (eucalyptus), cocoa, tobacco in the sections at lower altitudes on marly soils.

Castello: gentle spices; some describe black fruit (black cherry, plum) but I have personally always found red fruit reminders (red cherry, crystallized cranberry) in Castello's wines, plus gentle notes of rosemary and thyme

Cerequio: eucalyptus, wintermint, *ramassin* (small wild plums typical of the area), dark black cherry, lemon peel

Cerrati: not enough tasting data available

Cerretta: flowers more so than fruit, fresh citrus, forest floor (Cerretta proper); ripe red fruit; in general, a vertical wine.

Cerviano-Merli: fresh tropical fruit, peach (Merli portion); dark tobacco, licorice, botanical herbs (Cerviano section).

Ciocchini: not enough tasting data available

Ciocchini-Loschetto: not enough tasting data available

Codana: not enough tasting data available relative to current vintages; in the past, Codana Barolo bottlings I have tried struck me as being amongst the lightest and best-balanced of the commune, with very fruit-forward sour red cherry and red berry notes, plus hints of rose petals, tobacco and orange peel.

Collaretto: licorice, raspberry and blueberry

Colombaro: not enough tasting data available

Conca: ripe red cherry, strawberry (even of jam or of syrup), *burnìe* (the smell and taste of fruits conserved in jars, typically peach/apricot in syrup), pennyroyal (not mint), balsamic oils, sweet spices.

Corini-Pallaretta: floral, sour red cherry

Costabella: red cherry, botanical herbs, plums, forst floor

Coste di Rose: wild raspberry, wild spearmint

Coste di Vergne: not enough tasting data available

Crosia: not enough tasting data available

Damiano: not enough tasting data available

Drucà: not enough tasting data available

Falletto: ripe cherry, raspberry, sandalwood, nutmeg, rose, herbs

Fiasco: ripe red cherry, earth, balsamic oils

Fontanafredda: San Pietro: soft ripe red cherry, red berries; Bianca/Gattinera: darker red cherry, botanicals; La Rosa: floral

Fossati: balsamic mint, blueberry, cyclamen (perennial flowering plants of the primrose family), gentian. Occasionaly: spices, chocolate, dried herbs/hay

Francia: licorice; orange peel, ferrous quality/mineral.

Gabutti: dried flowers, redcurrant (in the area closer to Parafada); balsamic oils, potpourri, tar (in the other sections)

Galina: redcurrant, violet, graphite, licorice

Gallaretto: violet, rose, sour red cherry, mandarin, kirsch, salinity.

Garretti: spicy, floral

Gattera: sour red cherry (pomegranate in older wines such as those by Fratelli Revello that are made with a little Nebbiolo Rosé in the blend), dark cherry, peach, camphor, dried herbs, balsamic oils or mint (in my experience, the last two are noticeable especially in retro-nasal olfaction)

Giachini: medicinal herbs, menthol, balsamic oils; ripe red fruit (riper/sweeter than that of Gattera, for example), white pepper, rosemary (the last one especially by retro-nasal olfaction).

Gianetto: violet, rose.

Ginestra: Ginestra proper: floral (rose, violet and sild strawberry/raspberry and blood orange are very typical descriptors of the wines of the lower Ginestra proper such as in the Vigna del Gris; peppermint and balsamic oils (some might say anise) in the higher portions of Ginestra proper such as Vigna Sorì and Vigna Ciabot Mentin).

Gramolere: spearmint, licorice, aromatic herbs

Gustava: red fruit, violet, pepper, garden herbs, delicate minerality in the background

La Corte: not enough tasting data available

La Serra: licorice, spices (non-sweet), red cherry, plum, violet, forest floor

La Vigna: not enough tasting data available

La Volta: violet, minerals, licorice

Lazzarito: Balsamic oils, violet, lavender, poppyseeds, sour red cherry (peach and figs in riper years)

Le Coste: ripe plum, strawberry (of almost crushed, overripe berries), balsamic oils,

Le Coste di Monforte: earth, licorice, tobacco, blood orange, forest floor (western sector of the MGA vineyard district); coffee and torrerefaction (higher, east-facing sections of the vineyard district)

Le Turne: not enough tasting data available

Lirano: not enough tasting data available

Liste: balsamic nuances

Manocino: not enough tasting data available

Mantoetto: red cherry, strawberry, herbs, coffee

Marenca: common mugwort (or wormwood), iron, peat, grilled meat, ripe red cherry

Margheria: red rose, violet, rose (more floral than fruity save for those Margheria Barolos made with only south-faciong vines and therefore riper fruit flavours are more common)

Mariondino: rose, sour red cherry (Serra subregion); forest floor, iron, camphor (Valletti subregion); ripe red cherry, peach, apricot, tobacco (Mariondino proper)

Massara: violet, red cherry, herbs

Meriame: red cherry, tobacco, minerals

Monprivato: sour red cherry, minerals

Monrobiolo di Bussia: black cherry, balsamic vinegar, woodsy, cocoa

Montanello: ripe red cherry, red plum, delicate sweet spices (more nutmeg and star anise than cinnamon), prune

Monvigliero: sour red cherry, redcurrant, rose, violet, lavender, white moss, eucalyptus

Mosconi: fruit macerated in alcohol, cocoa, tar, balsamic oils, green tea, dried orange peel: almost a note of cotton candy (there is an intrinsic sweet note to the wines of Mosconi)

Neirane: ripe red cherry (in the part of the MGA vineyard district closest to Verduno); red berries, violet, rose, white peach

Ornato: balsamic oils, minerals, tar, pepper

Paiagallo: dark red (almost blue) fruit (plums, black cherry and blueberries), menthol, sweet pipe tobacco, and an intense note of candied (not fresh) violet

Panerole: licorice, red cherry

Parafada: ripe red cherry, raspberry, dried figs, anise

Parussi: sweet spices, mint, tobacco

Pernanno: mineral, licorice, aromatic herbs, red cherry, spices

Perno: ripe dark red cherry, dried rose, licorice, tobacco

Piantà: not enough tasting data available

Pira: red cherry, tobacco

Pisapola: violet, rose, orange peel, sour red berries

Prapò: balsamic resin, dark red fruits, sweet spices

Preda: iodine, violet, menthol, red cherry

Pugnane: ripe red cherry, tobacco

Ravera: more perfumed (flowers) and higher acidity (higher altitudes), chunkier and tough (lower plots); wild rose, violet, iodine, ash, tobacco, white peach, red cherry and even balsamic elements (but never to the extent that these can be found in Bricco delle Viole's wines).

Ravera di Monforte: potpourri, red cherry (Ravera di Monforte proper); red plum, tobacco and at times darker fruit including black cherry, plum, blackberry (lower-lying parts, Pilone amphitheatre).

Raviole: not enough tasting data available

Riva Rocche: dried rose petal, mint

Rivassi: not enough tasting data available

Rive: sweet sices, licorice, citrus fruits/ (tangerine, blood orange; and peach)

Rivette: not enough tasting data available

Rocche dell'Annunziata: wild red rose, pomegranate, tamarind, citrus fruits, peach (raspberry, kirsch, licorice in riper versions: whether riper in style or because of the vintage, no matter)

Rocche dell'Olmo: licorice, violet

Rocche di Castiglione: licorice, balsamic nuances (not resins or oils, that are stronger), red fruit cocktail. Truffle and leather in older wines.

Rocchettevino: dark plums, violet, balsamic nuances (only in wines made with grapes from the site's highest elevations), truffle.

Rodasca: not enough tasting data available

Roere di Santa Maria: fresh red berries, violet

Roggeri: macerated black cherry,

Roncaglie: black tea, redcurrants, balsamic nuances

Ruè: red cherry, red rose, minerals, violet

San Bernardo: rose, violet

San Giacomo: red cherry, tobacco, underbrush

San Giovanni: dark berries, ginger, orange peel

San Lorenzo: softe red fruit (cherry, plums); hints of tobacco

San Lorenzo di Verduno: Mostly flowers (rose, iris, violet, peony)

San Pietro: tar, underbrush, savoury spices

San Ponzio: very floral (violet, rose)

San Rocco: Black cherry, blackberry, redcurrant, tobacco, savoury spices (in general, a Barolo vineyard district that is amost as mucg about black fruit as it is of red fruit)

Sant'Anna: violet, redcurrants

Santa Maria: redcurrants, violet

Sarmassa: ripe red and dark cherry, blackberry, underbrush, licorice

Scarrone: red cherry, strawberry, tobacco, vanilla and sweet spices (unrelated to oak)

Serra: red cherry, black cherry nectar, licorice, sandalwood

Serra dei Turchi: broad spicy red cherry, strawberry, rose and violet.

Serradenari: violet, balsamic nuances.

Silio: not enough tasting data available

Solanotto: not enough tasting data available

Sorano: dark cherry, balsamic resins, coffee beans, plum, violet

Sottocastello di Novello: dark red plum, blueberry, violet, sweet spices

Teodoro: violet, very fruity and spicy (pepper, cinnamon). Also slightly darker coloured wines than is the norm with Barolo, but clearly nowhere near inky or purple (it's still Nebbiolo, after all).

Terlo: Fresh aromas that are more floral (violet, rose, iris, lavender) than fruity (red cherry), and with plenty of acid lift so as to make the tannins stick out.

Torriglione: toasty (not oak-derived, but an intrinsic descriptive quality of the vineyard site), ripe black cherry, ripe plum.

Valentino: not enough tasting data available.

Vignane: violet, sour red cherry (very balanced and elegant aromas and flavours)

Vignarionda: truffle, raspberry nectare, red cherry, watermelon, smoked rubber, licorice, wet earth

Vignolo: white pepper, menthol, red cherry, earth

Villero: violet, dark red (almost blue) fruit, minerals, eucalyptus, spices (nutmeg), cocoa and licorice

Zoccolaio: not enough tasting data available (in the past, fresh red fruit, herbs and balsamic nuances).

Zonchetta: not enough tasting data available.

Zuncai: not enough tasting data available.

BIBLIOGRAPHY

Antonioli, S. 2015. Primi risultati del recupero e valorizzazione degli antichi vitigni valtellinesi. *Tesi di laurea in Valorizzazione e Tutela dell'Ambiente e del Territorio Montano.* Edolo: Unimont.

Berta, P., G. Mainardi. 1997. *Piemonte - storia regionale della vite e del vino.* Milano: Ediz. U.I.V.

Bigliazzi J., M. Scali, E. Paolucci, M. Cresti, and R. Vignani. 2012. DNA Extracted with Optimized Protocols Can Be Genotyped to Reconstruct the Varietal Composition of Monovarietal Wines. *American Journal of Enology and Viticulture* 63: 4 568-573.

Boccacci, P., W. Chitarra, A. Schneider, L. Rolle, and G. Gambino. 2019. Molecular approaches to study genetic traceability and physiological responses of grapevines affected by viruses and/or phytoplasmas. *Food Chemistry* 312:126100.

Boehm, R., S. Bednarz. 1994. Geography for Life. *National Geographic Standards.* Washington: National Geographic Society.

Bongiolatti, N. 1993. "Breve storia dei vitigni valtellinesi". *Rezia Agricola e Zootecnica,* gennaio-febbraio.

Bors, W., W. Heller, C. Michel, and M. Saran. Flavonoids as antioxidants: determination of radical-scavenging efficiencies. *Methods Enzymol.* 1990; 186:343–355.

Botta, R., A. Schneider, A. Akkak, N. S. Scott, and M. R. Thomas. 2000. Within cultivar grapevine variability studied by morphometrical and molecular marker-based techniques. *Acta Hortorticulturae* 528: 91–96.

Cabezas, J. A., J. Ibáñez, D. Lijavetzky, D. Vélez, G. Bravo, V. Rodríguez, I. Carreño, A. M. Jermakow, J. Carreño, L. Ruiz-García, M. R. Thomas, and J.M. Martinez-Zapater. 2011. A 48 SNP set for grapevine cultivar identification. *BMC Plant Biol.* 11, 153.

Calorio, M., M. Giardino, F. Lozar, L. Perotti, and R. Vign. 2017. "Earth Science knowledge and Geodiversity awareness in the Langhe area" *Geophysical Reasearch Abstracts* Vol. 19, EGU2017-10150-1.

Carbonell-Bejerano, P., C. Royo, R. Torres-Pérez, J. Grimplet, L. Fernandez, J. Franco-Zorrilla, D. Lijavetzky, E. Baroja, J. Martínez, E. García-Escudero, J. Ibáñez and J. M. Martínez-Zapater. 2017. Catastrophic Unbalanced Genome Rearrangements Cause Somatic Loss of Berry Color in Grapevine. *Plant Physiol* 175(2): 786–801.

Castañeda-Ovando, A., M. de Lourdes Pacheco-Hernández, and E. Páez-Hernández. 2009. Chemical studies of anthocyanins: A review. *Food Chemistry* 113(4): 859-871.

Cho, M.J., L.R. Howard, R. L. Prior and J. R. Clark. 2004. Flavonoid glycosides and antioxidant capacity of various blackberry, blueberry and red grape genotypes determined by high-performance liquid chromatography/mass spectrometry. *J Sci Food and Agr* 84(13):1771–1782.

D'Agata, I. 2022. Vertical tasting report: Cogno Barolo Ravera Riserva Vigna Elena 1997-2016. *TerroirSense Wine Review,* Vertical Reports: September 9, 2022.

D'Agata, I. 2022. Vertical tasting report: Oddero Barolo Vignarionda & Barolo Viognarionda Riserva 1989-2015. *TerroirSense Wine Review,* Vertical Reports: June 17, 2022.

D'Agata, I. 2019. Italy's Native Wine Grape Terroirs. Berkeley: Univeristy of California Press.

D'Agata, I. 2014. Native Wine Grapes of Italy. Berkeley: Univeristy of California Press.

D'Agata, I. 2012. Know your Cannubis. *Decanter,* Italy issue, January.

D'Agata, I., M. Longo. 2021. The grapes and wines of Italy: the definitive compendium region by region. Amazon Press.

Desbons, P. *Le comte Odart, ampélographe tourangeau, Mémoires de l'Académie des Sciences, arts et Belles-Lettres de Touraine*, vol.XXVI. In Les scientifiques tourangeau», 2013, p. 287-301 Mémoires de l'Académie des Sciences, Arts et Belles-Lettres de Touraine, tome 26, 2013, p. 1-15

Emanuelli, F., S. Lorenzi, L. Grzekowiak, L., and V. Catalano. 2013. Genetic diversity and population structure assessed by SSR and SNP markers in a large germplasm collection of grape. *BMC Plant Biol.* 13, 39.

Escribano-Bailón, M.T., M. T. Guerra MT, J. C. Rivas-Gonzalo, and C. Santos-Buelga. 1995. Proanthocyanidins in skins from different grape varieties. *Zeitschrift für Lebensmittel-Untersuchung und Forschung* 200: 221–224.

Fantini, L. 1885. *Monografia sulla viticoltura ed enologia in provincia di Cuneo*. Reprint, 1973. Alba: Cavalieri dell'Ordine dei Vini e del Tartufo di Alba.

Filippetti, I., C. Intrieri, M. Centinari, B. Bucchetti, C. Pastore. 2005. *Vitis* 44 (4), 167–172.

Fossen, T., L. Cabrita, O.M. Andersen.1998. Colour and stability of pure anthocyanins influendec by pH including the alkaline region. *Agris* 63(4): 435-440.

Gallesio, G. 1995. *I Giornali di Viaggio* (Baldini, E.). Firenze: Accademia dei Georgofili.

Gambino, G., A. Dal Molin, P. Boccacci, A. Minio, W. Chitarra, C.G. Avanzato, P. Tononi, I. Perrone, S. Raimondi, A. Schneider, M. Pezzotti, F. Mannini, G. Gribaudo, and M. Delledonne. 2017. Whole-genome sequencing and SNV genotyping of 'Nebbiolo' (*Vitis vinifera* L.) clones. *Scientific Reports* 7: 17294.

Garner, M., P. Merritt. 2000. *Barolo Tar and Roses. A study of the wines of Alba*. London: Century.

Gelati, R. 1968. Stratigrafia de l'Oligo-Miocene delle Langhe tra le valli dei fiumi Tanaro e Bormida di Spigno. *Riv. It. Pal. Strat.* 74, 865-967, 34 ff.

Gerini C. 1884. *Prospetto statistico dei comuni della provincia di Sondrio, classificati a seconda delle varietà dei vitigni nei medesimi coltivati*. in Bollettino ampelografico, fascicolo XVII. Roma: Eredi Botta.

Golicz, A.A., P.E. Bayer, G.C. Barker, P.P. Edger, H. Kim, P. A. Martinez, C.K. Kenneth Chan, A. Severn-Ellis, W.R. McCombie, I.A.P. Parkin, A.H.Paterson, J.C.Pires , A.G Sharpe, H. Tang, G.R. Teakle, C.D. Town, J. Batley, and D.Edwards. 2016. The pangenome of an agronomically important crop plant Brassica oleracea. *Nat Commun* 7(1):13390.

Gonzàles-Techera, A., S. Jubany, I. Ponce, I. Ponce de Leon, E. Boido, E. Dellacassa, F. Carrau, P.Hinrichsen. 2004. Molecular diversity within clones of cv Tannat (*Vitis vinifera*). *Vitis* 43, 179–185.

Gregory, Kenneth J. 2000. *The Changing Nature of Physical Geography*. 2d ed. London: Arnold.

Guidoni, S., P. Allara, and A. Schubert. 2002. Effect of Cluster Thinning on Berry Skin Anthocyanin Composition of *Vitis vinifera* cv. Nebbiolo. Am J Enol Vitic 53: 224-226.

Guidoni, S.A., Ferrandino, A., and Novello, V. 2008. Effects of Seasonal and Agronomical Practices on Skin Anthocyanin Profile of Nebbiolo Grapes. *American Journal of Enology and Viticulture,* 59, 22-29.

Haines-Young, R. and J.Petch. 1986. *Physical Geography: Its Nature and Methods*. London: Harper and Row.

Hübner S, N. Bercovich, M. Todesco, J.R. Mandel, J. Odenheimer, E. Ziegler, J.S. Lee, G.J. Baute, G.L. Owens, C.J. Grassa, D.P. Ebert, K.L. Ostevik, B.T. Moyers, S. Yakimowski, R. R. Masalia, L, Gao, I. Ćalić, J.E. Bowers, N.C Kane, D. Z H Swanevelder, T. Kubach, S. Muños, N.B. Langlade, J.M. Burke, and L. H. Rieseberg. 2019. Sunflower pan-genome analysis shows that hybridization altered gene content and disease resistance. *Nat Plants* 5(1):54–62.

International Commission on Stratigraphy (ICS); Subcommission on Neogene Stratigraphy: (https://stratigraphy.org/subcommissions#neogene

Ligari, P. 1988 (1752). *Ragionamenti d'Agricoltura*. Sondrio: Banca Popolare di Sondrio.

Kosugi, S., Y. Momozawa, X. Liu, C. Terao, M. Kubo, Y. Kamatani. 2019. Comprehensive evaluation of structural variation detection algorithms for whole genome sequencing. *Genome Biol* 20(1):117.

Maestri, S., G. Gambino, G. Lopatriello, A. Minio, I. Perrone, E. Cosentino, B. Giovannone, L. Marcolungo, M. Alfano, S. Rombauts, D. Cantu, M. Rossato, M. Delledone, and L. Calderón. 2022. 'Nebbiolo' genome assembly allows surveying the occurrence and functional implications of genomic structural variations in grapevines (*Vitis vinifera* L.). *BMC Genomics* 23, 159.

Maino, M., A. Decarlis, F. Felletti, and S. Seno. 2013. Tectono-sedimentary evolution of the Tertiary Piedmont Basin (NW Italy) within the Oligo–Miocene central Mediterranean geodynamics. *Tectonics* Volume 32, Issue 3 June Pages 593-619

Manescalchi, A. and G. Dalmasso. 1939. *Storia della Vite e del Vino in Italia*. Milano: Gualdoni Editore.

Mannini F. 1995. *Grapevine Clonal Selection in Piedmont (Northwest Italy): Focus on Nebbiolo and Barbera*. Proc. Int. Symposium on 'Clonal selection', Portland, Oregon, USA, 20-32.

Mannini, F., A. Mollo, D. Santini, E. Marchese, and R. Tragni. 2013. Nebbiolo, un nuovo clone. *Millevigne* 2:6-9.

Mannini F., D. Santini, A. Mollo, G. Mazza, P. Cascio and D. Marchi. 2015. Influenza della componente ambientale sui composti aromatici dell'uva e del vino della cv Nebbiolo. *L'Enologo* 5, 79-85.

Mannini, F., D. Santini, A. Mollo, D. Cuozzo, and R. Tragni. 2016. Studio sulla stabilità ambientale di quattro cloni di Nebbioloin diverse realtà colturali del Piemonte. *L'Enologo* 3: 85-92.

Mannini, F. 2015. Il Nebbiolo e il suo patrimonio clonale: stato dell'arte. *Mille Vigne* 3: 8-9.

Margaria, P., A. Ferrandino, P. Caciagli, O. Kedrina, A. Schubert, and S. Palmano. 2014. Metabolic and transcript analysis of the flavonoid pathway in diseased and recovered Nebbiolo and Barbera grapevines (Vitis vinifera L.) following infection by Flavescence dorée phytoplasma. *Plant Cell Environ* 37: 2183-2200.

Masnaghetti, A. 2018. *Barolo MGA Vol. I. The Barolo Great Vineyards Enciclopedia*. Monza: Alessandro Masnaghetti Editore.

Massè, D. 1932. *Il paese di Barolo*. Reprinted, 1992, Barolo: Marchesi di Barolo.

Massonnet, M., N. Cochetel, A. Minio, A. M. Vondras, J. Lin, A. Muyle, J. F. Garcia, Y. Zhou, M. Delledonne, S. Riaz, R. Figueroa-Balderas, B. S. Gaut and D. Cantu. 2020. The genetic basis of sex determination in grapes. *Nat Commun* 11, 2902 (2020). https://doi.org/10.1038/s41467-020-16700-z

Moncada, X., F. Pelsy, D. Merdinoglu, and P. Hinrichsen. 2006. Genetic diversity and geographical dispersal in grapevine clones revealed by microsatellite markers. *Genome* 49, 1459–1472.

Morgante, M., E. De Paoli, and S. Radovic. 2007. Transposable elements and the plant pan-genomes. *Curr Opin Plant Biol* 10(2):149–55.

Mutti, E., L. Papiani, D. DiBiase, G. Davoli, S. Mora, S. Segadelli, and R. Tinterri. 1995. *Il Bacino Terziario Epimesoalpino e le sue implicazioni sui rapporti tra Alpi e Appennino*. Estratto da Memorie di Scienze Geologiche vol 47.

Mutti, E., D. Di Biase, N. Mavilla, and M. Sgavetti. *The Tertiary Piedmont Basin*. 64th EAGE Conference and Exhibition. At: Florence, May 2002.

Barolo Terroir: Grapes, Crus, People, Places.

Myles, S., A.R. Boyko, C.L. Owens, and E.S. Buckler. 2011. Genetic structure anmd domestication history of the grape. *Proc Natl Acad Sci* 108, 3457-3458.

Nakamura S., K. Haraguchi, N. Mitani, and K. Ohtsubo. 2007. Novel Preparation Method of Template DNAs from Wine for PCR to Differentiate Grape (Vitis vinifera L.) Cultivar. *Journal of Agricultural and Food Chemistry* 55 (25):10388–10395.

Nesteroff, W. 1973a. The sedimentary history of the Mediterranean during the Neogene, in: *Init. Rep. Deep Sea Drilling Project*, Ryan, DWF et al, eds. v XIII, Washington, D.C.: U.S. Govt. Printing Office, p. 1257-1261.

Nesteroff, W. 1973b. *La crise de salinité messinienne dans la Méditerranée: enseignemnets des forages Joides et du bassin de Sicile,* 23rd CIESM Congr., Athens (1972), *Bull. Geol. Soc. Greece*, vol. X, p. 154-155.

Nuvolone, G. 1798 (2002). *Sulla coltivazione delle viti e sul metodo migliore di fare e conservare i vini. Istruzione: Calendario georgico compilato e pubblicato dalla Società Agraria di Torino per l'anno VII e VIII.* Torino. Ristampa Enoteca del Piemonte, Sorì Edizioni.
Viticulture, 2012, vol. 63, no. 4, pp. 568–573

Oganesyants L.A., R.R. Vafin, A.G. Galstyan, V.K. Semipyatny, S.A. Khurshudyan, and A.E. Ryabova. 2018. *Foods and Raw Materials* 6 (2): 438–448.

Ohguro, H., I. Ohguro, M. Katai, S. Tanaka. 2012. Two-year randomized, placebo-controlled study of black currant anthocyanins on visual field in glaucoma. *Ophthalmol* 228(1):26–35.

Orlandi, M.G. 2011. Barolo: A love story. World of Fine Wine (33). http://www.worldoffinewine.com/news/barolo-a-love-story-4923447/; https://www.intravino.com/vino/barolo-una-storia-damore/).

Pereira L., H. Guedes-Pinto, and P. Martins-Lopes. 2011. An Enhanced Method for Vitis vinifera L. DNA Extraction from Wines. *American Journal of Enology and Viticulture* 62 (4): 547–552.

Pojer, E., F. Mattivi, D. Johnson, and C.S. Stockley. 2013. The case for anthocyanin consumption to promote human health: a review. *Compr Rev Food Sci Food Saf* 12(5):483–508.

Ponza, M. 2012. *Vocabolario Piemontese-Italiano e Italiano-Piemontese del Sacerdote Michele Ponza.* Ulan Publishers.

Raimondi, S., G. Tumino, P. Ruffa, P. Boccacci, G. Gambino, and A. Schneider. 2020. DNA-based genealogy reconstruction of Nebbiolo, Barbera and other ancient grapevine cultivars from northwestern Italy. *Sci Rep* 10: 15782

Riaz, S., K.E. Garrison, G.S. Dangl, J.M. Boursiquot, and C.P. Meredith. 2002. Genetic divergence and chimerism within ancient asexually propagated grapevine cultivars. *Journal of the American Society for Horticultural Science* 127 (4): 508-14.

Riccardi Candiani, A. 2012. *Louis Oudart e I vini nobili del Piemonte. Storia di un enologo francese.* Brà: Slow Food Editore.

Roach, M.J., D.L. Johnson, J. Bohlmann, H.J.J. van Vuuren, S.J.M. Jones, I.S. Pretorius, S.A. Schmidt, A.R. Borneman. 2018. Population sequencing reveals clonal diversity and ancestral inbreeding in the grapevine cultivar Chardonnay. *PLoS Genet* 14(11): e1007807.

Roggia, C., 2014. Flavescence dorée phytoplasma titre in field-infected Barbera and Nebbiolo grapevines. *Plant Pathology* 63: 31-41.

Rolle, L., F. Torchio, A. Ferrandino, S. Guidoni. 2012. Influence of Wine-Grape Skin Hardness on the Kinetics of Anthocyanin Extraction. *International Journal of Food Properties* 15:2; 249-261.

Rosenberg, Matt. "Geography Definition." ThoughtCo, Aug. 27, 2020, thoughtco.com/definitions-of-geography-1435594.

Santini D., A. Mollo, P. Cascio, and F. Mannini. 2012. *Differences in field and cellar performances of two clones of 'Nebbiolo' (Vitis vinifera L.) due to different areas of production in Piedmont (north-west Italy):* 2, 64-67. IXE Congres Des Terroirs Vitivinicoles-Actes, Dijon-Reims 25-29 June 2012.

Schneider A., F. Mannini, G. Culasso G. 1991. Contributo allo studio dell'eterogeneità del 'Nebbiolo': tradizione e attualità. *Quad Vitic Enol Univ Torino* 15: 31-43.

Schneider, A., P. Boccacci, and R. Botta. 2003. Genetic relationships among grape cultivars from North-Western Italy. *Acta Hort* 603: 229-233.

Schneider, A., P. Boccacci, D.R. Torello Marinoni, R. Botta, A. Akkak, and J. Vouillamoz. 2004. "The genetic variability and unexpected parentage of Nebbiolo." *Proc. 1st Int. Conference on Nebbiolo grapes on CD* (http:www.nebbiolograpes.org). At: Sondrio, Valtellina, Italy, 23–25 June 2004.

Silvestroni O., D. Di Pietro, C. Intrieri, R. Vignani, I. Filippetti, C. Del Casino, M. Scali, and M. Cresti. 1997. Detection of genetic diversity among clones of cv: Fortana (Vitis vinfera L.) by microsatellite DNA polymorphism analysis. Vitis 36:147-150.

Soster, M. and A. Cellino. 1998. Caratterizzazione delle aree vitivinicole del Barolo: un'esperienza pluriennale. *Quaderni Regione Piemonte Agricoltura* 13: 10.

Soster, M. 2000. "Barolo. Studio per la caratterizzazione del territorio, delle uve e dei vini dell'area di produzione". Torino: Regione Piemonte.

Soster, M., and A. Cellino. 2002. *La zonazione del Barolo.* Regione Piemonte.

Tablino, L. 2015. Alle Radici del Barolo #1, 1751-1865. http://tablino.it/969/radici-barolo/?lang=it

Tablino, L. 2015. Alle Radici del Barolo #2: Cavour e i Falletti di Barolo. http://tablino.it/970/radici-barolo-cavour-falletti-barolo/?lang=it

Tamura, H. and A. Yamagam. 1994. Antioxidative activity of monoacylated anthocyanins isolated from Muscat Bailey A grape. *J Agric Food Chem* 42 (8): 1612–1615.

This, P., T. Lacombe, T. MR. 2006. Historical origins and genetic diversity of wine grapes. *Trends Genet* 22(9):511–9.

Unstead, J.F. The Meaning of Geography. In: *The Geographical Teacher*. Vol. 4, No. 1 (Spring, 1907): 19-28.

Vignolo-Lutati, F. 1929a. "Sulla delimitazione delle zone a vini tipici". *Annali di Agricoltura della R. Accademia di agricoltura di Torino.*

Vignolo-Lutati, F. 1929b. *Le Langhe e la loro vegetazione: con carte: geologica ed oro-idrografica e profili.* Torino: Luigi Cecchini.

Wang H, G. Cao, and R.L. 1997. Oxygen radical absorbing capacity of anthocyanins. *J Agric Food Chem* 45(2):304–309.

Wegscheider, E., A. Benjak, A. and A. Forneck. Clonal Variation in Pinot Noir Revealed by S-SAP Involving Universal Retrotransposon-Based Sequences. *Am J Enol Vitic* 60: 104–109, 2009.

Zoia, D. 2004. *Vite e Vino in Valtellina e Valchiavenna.* Sondrio: L'Officina del libro.

INDEX, BAROLO VINEYARD DISTRICTS

INDEX, PRODUCERS AND WINES

Barolo Ravera
Barolo San Giovanni

Brovia

Barolo Brea - Ca' Mia
Barolo Capezzana Garblet Suè
Barolo Rocche di Castiglione
Barolo Villero

Bruna Grimaldi

Barolo Badarina; Barolo Badarina Riserva (Vigna Regnola)
Barolo Bricco Ambrogio

Bruno Giacosa

Barolo Falletto; Barolo Falletto Vigna Le Rocche (Riserva)

Bugia Nen (Davide Fragonese)

Barolo Cerretta

Bussia Soprana

Barolo Bussia, Barolo Vigna Colonnello and Barolo Riserva Gabutti della Bussia
Barolo Mosconi (and Riserva)

Ca' Brusà

Barolo Bricco San Pietro Vigna d'Vaj (and Riserva 10 years)

Ca' Viola

Barolo Sottocastello di Novello (and Riserva)

Ca' Barun

Barolo (*).

Ca' Romè

Barolo Vigna Cerretta; Barolo Rapet

Cabutto - Tenuta La Volta

Barolo La Volta
Barolo Riserva del Fondatore

Cadia

Barolo Monvigliero

Cagliero

Barolo Ravera

Camerano

Barolo Terlo

Camerano G. e Figli

Barolo Cannubi San Lorenzo

Camparo

Barolo Boiolo

Cantina Massara

Barolo Monvigliero

Cantina Massara

Barolo Massara (*)

Cantina Stroppiana

Barolo San Giacomo

Cantina Tre Pile

Barolo Bussia

Cappellano

Barolo Otin Fiorin Piè Franco, Barolo Otin Fiorin Piè Rupestris

Casa E. di Mirafiore

Barolo Lazzarito
Barolo Paiagallo

Casavecchia

Barolo Piantà

Cascina Adelaide

Barolo Baudana

Cascina Adelaide

Barolo Cannubi
Barolo Fossati
Barolo Pernanno
Barolo Preda

Cascina Amalia

Barolo Bussia
Barolo Le Coste di Monforte

Cascina Ballarin

Barolo Bricco Rocca and Barolo Riserva Bricco Rocca Tistot
Barolo Bussia
Barolo Panerole

Cascina Bongiovanni

Barolo Pernanno

Cascina Bruciata

Barolo Cannubi Muscatel

Cascina Bruni

Barolo Costabella (*)
Barolo Riserva Rivassotto, Barolo Carpegna, Barolo Marialunga

Cascina Cappellano

Barolo Raviole (and Riserva)

Cascina Chicco

Barolo Riserva Ginestra
Barolo Rocche di Castelletto

Cascina del Monastero

Barolo Annunziata (Bricco Riund)
Barolo Bricco Luciani
Barolo Perno
Barolo Riserva Bricco Rocca Riund

Cascina Gavetta

Barolo Corini-Pallaretta

Cascina Gramolere

Barolo

Cascina Luisin

Barolo del Comune di Serralunga

Cascina Pugnane

Barolo Bussia

Cascina Pugnane (Fratelli Ghisolfi)

Barolo Pugnane

Cascina Sot

Barolo Bricco San Pietro (and Riserva)

Cascina Tiole

Barolo and Barolo S. Stefano

Castello di Perno

Barolo Castelletto

Castello di Verduno

Barolo Massara
Barolo Monvigliero (and Riserva)

Cav. Enrico Bergadano

Barolo Sarmassa (and Riserva)

Cavalier Bartolomeo

Barolo Altenasso
Barolo Riserva Fiasco
Barolo San Lorenzo

Cavallotto Tenuta Bricco Boschis

Barolo Bricco Boschis, Barolo Riserva Bricco Boschis Vigna San Giuseppe

Barolo Riserva Vignolo

Ceretto

Barolo Bricco Rocche

Barolo Brunate

Barolo Bussia

Barolo Cannubi San Lorenzo

Barolo Prapò

Barolo Rocche di Castiglione

Cesare Bussolo

Barolo Fossati

Chiarlo

Barolo Cannubi

Barolo Cerequio

Chionetti

Barolo Parussi

Barolo Primo and Barolo Bussia Vigna Pian Polvere

Barolo Roncaglie

Ciabot Berton

Barolo Rocchettevino

Barolo Roggeri (and Riserva)

Claudio Alario

Barolo Riva Rocca

Claudio Boggione

Barolo Brunate

Collina San Ponzio

Barolo Fossati and Barolo Riserva

Comm. G.B. Burlotto

Barolo Cannubi

Barolo Castelletto

Barolo Monvigliero

Conterno Fantino

Barolo Ginestra Vigna Sorì Ginestra, Barolo Ginestra Vigna del Gris

Conterno Fantino

Barolo Castelletto Vigna Pressenda

Barolo Mosconi Vigna Ped

Costa di Bussia – Tenuta Arnulfo

Barolo Bussia; Barolo Bussia Vigna Campo dei Buoi; Barolo Bussia Luigi Arnulfo and Barolo Bussia Riserva

Crissante Alessandria

Barolo Capalot and Barolo Capalot La Punta

Barolo Galina

Barolo Roggeri

Cristian Boffa

Barolo Capalot

Damilano

Barolo Brunate (*)

Barolo Cannubi

Barolo Cerequio

Barolo Liste

Barolo Raviole

Daniele Pelassa

Barolo San Lorenzo di Verduno

Dario Stroppiana

Barolo Bussia and Bussia Riserva

Davide Fregonese (Bugia Nen)

Barolo Prapò

Deltetto

Barolo Parussi

Diego Conterno

Barolo Ginestra

Diego Morra

Barolo Monvigliero

Diego Pressenda

Barolo Bricco San Pietro

Domenico Clerico

Barolo Aeroplanservaj

Barolo Ciabot Mentin and Barolo Pajana

Barolo Percristina

Dosio

Barolo Fossati and Barolo Riserva Fossati

Barolo Serradenari

E. Molino

Barolo Bricco Rocca and Barolo Riserva del Fico

E. Pira e Figli – Chiara Boschis

Barolo Cannubi

Barolo Mosconi

Edoardo Sobrino

Barolo Monvigliero

Egidio Oberto

Barolo Fossati

Elio Altare

Barolo Arborina

Elio Altare

Barolo Cannubi

Barolo Cerretta Vigna Bricco

Elio Grasso

Barolo Ginestra Casa Matè, Barolo Gavarini Chiniera, Barolo Riserva Runcot

Elio Sandri

Barolo Perno (and Riserva) (*)

Ellena (Giuseppe Ellena)

Barolo Ascheri

Elvio Cogno

Barolo Cascina Nuova, Barolo Ravera, Barolo Riserva Vigna Elena, Barolo Bricco Pernice

Enrico Serafino

Barolo Carpegna

Barolo Meriame (*);

Barolo Riserva Briccolina

Enzo Boglietti

Barolo Arione

Barolo Boiolo

Barolo Brunate

Barolo Case Nere

Barolo Fossati

Eraldo Borgogno

Barolo Vignane

Eraldo Viberti

Barolo Rocchettevino

Barolo Roncaglie

Erbaluna

Barolo Castagni
Barolo Rocche dell'Annunziata

Eredi Lodali
Barolo Bric Sant'Ambrogio e Barolo Lorens

Ettore Germano
Barolo Cerretta
Barolo Prapò
Barolo Riserva Lazzarito
Barolo Vignarionda

F.lli Manzone
Barolo Bricco San Pietro Fraschin

Fabio Oberto
Barolo Brunate (*)
Barolo Rocche dell'Annunziata

Famiglia Anselma
Barolo Bussia and Barolo Bussia Vigna Pian Polvere
Barolo Gianetto
Barolo Lazzarito
Barolo Le Coste di Monforte
Barolo Mosconi (*)

Ferdinando Principiano
Barolo Boscareto and Barolo del Comune di Serralunga
Barolo Ravera di Monforte

Feyles Sorelle De Nicola
Barolo Riserva Perno Vigna della Serra

Flavio Roddolo
Barolo Ravera di Monforte

Flavio Saglietti
Barolo Brunate
Barolo Cerequio

Fontanafredda - Casa E. di Mirafiore
Barolo Fontanafredda, Barolo Fontanafredda Vigna La Rosa

Fortemasso
Barolo Castelletto

Francesco Borgogno
Barolo Vigneti Brunate

Francesco Boschis
Barolo (*)

Francesco e Giuseppe Principiano
Barolo Boscareto

Francesco Rinaldi
Barolo Cannubi
Barolo Brunate
Barolo Rocche dell'Annunziata

Franco Boasso (Gabutti)
Barolo Gabutti
Barolo Margheria

Franco Conterno
Barolo Bussia Riserva
Barolo Panerole

Franco Molino (Cascina Rocca)
Barolo Riserva Villero
Barolo Rocche dell'Annunziata (and Riserva)

Fratelli Abrigo
Barolo Ravera

Fratelli Adriano
Barolo Tenuta Pian Polvere

Fratelli Alessandria
Barolo Gramolere
Barolo Monvigliero
Barolo San Lorenzo di Verduno

Fratelli Barale
Barolo Bussia, Bussia Riserva
Barolo Cannubi
Barolo Castellero

Fratelli Casetta
Barolo Case Nere

Fratelli Ferrero
Barolo Bricco Manzoni
Barolo Gattera

Fratelli Gerlotto
Barolo Sorano

Fratelli Giacosa
Barolo Bussia
Barolo Scarrone Vigna Mandorlo (and Riserva)

Fratelli Massucco
Barolo

Fratelli Monchiero
Barolo Montanello (and Riserva)
Barolo Pernanno (*)
Barolo Rocche (and Riserva)
Barolo Roere di Santa Maria

Fratelli Moscone
Barolo Bussia

Fratelli Revello
Barolo Cerretta
Barolo Conca
Barolo Gattera
Barolo Giachini
Barolo Rocche dell'Annunziata

Fratelli Savigliano
Barolo Boiolo (*)

Fratelli Seghesio
Barolo La Villa

Fratelli Serio & Battista Borgogno
Barolo Cannubi; Barolo Riserva Cannubi

G.D. Vajra
Barolo Bricco delle Viole
Barolo Costabella
Barolo Coste di Rose
Barolo Fossati (*)
Barolo Ravera

G.D. Vajra - Luigi Baudana
Barolo Baudana
Barolo Cerretta

Gaja
Barolo Conteisa

Garesio
Barolo Gianetto

Garesio
Barolo Cerretta

Gemma
Barolo Riserva Giblin

Giacomo Anselma
Barolo Collaretto

Barolo Riserva Vignarionda

Giacomo Conterno

Barolo Arione

Barolo Cerretta

Barolo Francia

Giacomo Fenocchio

Barolo Bussia; Bussia Riserva; Barolo Bussia 90 Dì;

Barolo Cannubi

Barolo Castellero

Barolo Villero

Giacomo Grimaldi

Barolo Le Coste

Barolo Ravera

Barolo Sottocastello di Novello

Gian Paolo Manzone

Barolo Meriame (and Riserva)

Giancarlo Boasso

Barolo Pugnane

Gianfranco Alessandria

Barolo and Barolo San Giovanni

Gianfranco Bovio

Barolo Arborina

Barolo Gattera, Barolo Riserva Gattera

Barolo Parussi

Barolo Rocchettevino

Gianni Ramello

Barolo Rocchettevino

Gillardi

Barolo Boiolo (*)

Gillardi

Barolo Vignane

Giorgio Pira

Barolo Perno Laut, and Barolo Riserva Perno Terre del Mago

Giovanni Abrigo

Barolo Ravera

Giovanni Canonica

Barolo Paiagallo

Giovanni Corino

Barolo Arborina

Barolo Bricco Manescotto

Barolo Giachini, Barolo Vecchie Vigne

Giovanni Manzone

Barolo Bricat, Barolo Gramolere (and Riserva)

Barolo Castelletto

Giovanni Rocca

Barolo Mosconi

Barolo Ravera di Monforte

Giovanni Rosso

Barolo Cerretta

Barolo Serra

Barolo Vigna Rionda Ester Canale Rosso

Giulia Negri

Barolo Serradenari, Barolo Marassio

Giuseppe Mascarello e Figlio

Barolo Monprivato, Barolo Monprivato Riserva Cà d' Morissio

Barolo S. Stefano di Perno

Barolo Villero

Giuseppe Rinaldi

Barolo Brunate

Barolo Bussia (from 2019)

Gomba

Barolo Boschetti Sernìe, Barolo Boschetti (Riserva as well)

Grimaldi

Barolo Sorano

Guido Porro

Barolo Gianetto

Barolo Vigna Lazzairasco, Barolo Vigna S. Caterina

Barolo Vigna Rionda

I Brè

Barolo Monvigliero

I Brè

Barolo Corona Teresina

Icardi

Barolo Fossati

Barolo Serra (and Riserva)

Il Gioco dell'Oca di Pittatore

Barolo Cannubi

Josetta Saffirio

Barolo, Barolo Persiera (and Riserva), Barolo Riserva Millenovecento48

L'Astemia Pentita

Barolo Terlo (and Riserva)

L'Astemia Pentita

Barolo Cannubi

La Bioca

Barolo Bussia

Barolo Ravera

La Briacca

Barolo Rocche di Castiglione

La Briccolina

Barolo Briccolina

La Carlina

Barolo Raviole

La Fusina

Barolo Perno

La Spinetta

Barolo Campè; Barolo Vigneto Garretti

La Spinona

Barolo Bergera

Lalù

Barolo Le Coste di Monforte

Le Cecche

Barolo Borzone

Barolo Bricco San Pietro

Barolo Sorano

Le Ginestre

Barolo Sottocastello di Novello (and Riserva)

Le Strette

Barolo Bergeisa

Barolo Bergera Pezzole

Barolo Corini-Pallaretta

Livia Fontana

Barolo Villero
Barolo Bussia Riserva

Lo Zoccolaio

Barolo Ravera (and Riserva)

Lodovico Cabutto

Barolo

Lorenzo Accomasso

Barolo Annunziata
Barolo Rocche (and Riserva), Barolo Rocchette (and Riserva), Barolo Le Mie Vigne (Elena)

Luciano Sandrone

Barolo Aleste

Luigi Oddero e Figli

Barolo Rocche Rivera
Barolo Specola
Barolo Vigna Rionda

Luigi Pira

Barolo Marenca
Barolo Margheria
Barolo Vignarionda

Luigi Vico

Barolo Prapò

Malvirà

Barolo Boiolo

Marcarini

Barolo Brunate
Barolo La Serra

Marchesi di Barolo

Barolo Cannubi
Barolo Coste di Rose
Barolo Sarmassa

Marco Curto

Barolo Arborina; Barolo La Foia

Mario Gagliasso

Barolo Rocche dell'Annunziata
Barolo Torriglione

Mario Giribaldi

Barolo Ravera Riserva (*)

Mario Marengo

Barolo Bricco delle Viole
Barolo Brunate and Riserva

Mario Olivero

Barolo Bricco Ambrogio

Marrone

Barolo Bussia

Marziano Abbona

Barolo Cerviano-Merli
Barolo Pressenda
Barolo Ravera

Massolino – Vigna Rionda

Barolo Margheria

Massolino – Vigna Rionda

Barolo Parafada
Barolo Parussi
Barolo Vigna Rionda

Mauro Marengo

Barolo Ravera

Mauro Molino

Barolo Bricco Luciani
Barolo Conca
Barolo Gallinotto
Barolo La Serra

Mauro Sebaste

Barolo Riserva Ghè

Mauro Veglio

Barolo Paiagallo

Mauro Veglio

Barolo Arborina
Barolo Castelletto
Barolo Gattera
Barolo Rocche dell'Annunziata

Monfalletto - Cordero di Montezemolo

Barolo Enrico VI

Monfalletto (Cordero di Montezemolo)

Barolo Gattera and Riserva Gorette

Monti

Barolo Bricco San Pietro
Barolo Bussia; Bussia Riserva

Negretti

Barolo Bricco Ambrogio
Barolo Mirau

Osvaldo Viberti

Barolo Serra dei Turchi
Barolo Serralunga (Meriame) (*)

Palladino

Barolo Ornato

Palladino

Barolo Parafada
Barolo Riserva San Bernardo

Paola Sordo

Barolo Perno
Barolo Ravera
Barolo Rocche di Castiglione

Paolo Conterno

Barolo Ginestra (and Riserva), Barolo Riva del Bric

Paolo Giordano

Barolo Perno

Paolo Scavino

Barolo Bric del Fiasc (and Riserva)
Barolo Bricco Ambrogio
Barolo Cannubi (until 2018)
Barolo Monvigliero
Barolo Prapò
Barolo Ravera
Barolo Riserva Rocche dell'Annunziata

Pecchenino

Barolo Le Coste di Monforte and Barolo San Giuseppe

Pecchenino

Barolo Bussia

Philine Isabelle

Barolo Preda (from 2020).

Pianpolvere Soprano

Barolo Riserva Bussia Pianpolvere Soprano

Pierangelo Bosco

Barolo Boiolo

Piergiorgio Savigliano

Barolo Teodoro (*)

Piero Benevelli

Barolo Le Coste di Monforte

Barolo Mosconi

Barolo Ravera di Monforte

Pietro Rinaldi

Barolo Monvigliero

Pio Cesare

Barolo Mosconi

Barolo Ornato

Podere Ruggeri Corsini

Barolo Bricco San Pietro

Barolo Bussia Corsini

Poderi Aldo Conterno

Barolo Bussia, Barolo Riserva Granbussia, Barolo Bussia Cicala, Barolo Bussia Colonnello, Barolo Bussia Romirasco

Poderi Colla

Barolo Dardi Le Rose Bussia

Poderi Fogliati

Barolo Bussia

Poderi Gianni Gagliardo

Barolo Castelletto

Barolo Fossati

Barolo Lazzarito Vigna Preve

Barolo Monvigliero

Barolo Mosconi

Barolo Serra dei Turchi

Poderi Luigi Einaudi

Barolo Cannubi

Poderi Luigi Einaudi

Barolo Bussia (from 2016)

Barolo Monvigliero

Barolo Terlo and Barolo Terlo Vigna Costa Grimaldi

Poderi Oddero

Barolo Bricco Chiesa (*)

Barolo Brunate and Riserva

Barolo Bussia Vigna Mondoca

Barolo Monvigliero

Barolo Riserva Vignarionda

Barolo Rocche di Castiglione

Barolo Villero

Poderi Roset

Barolo Monvigliero

Poderi Sorì

Barolo Baudana

Barolo Parafada

Prunotto

Barolo Bussia and Barolo Riserva Bussia Vigna Colonnello

Pugnane Fratelli Sordo

Barolo Vigna Villero

Raineri

Barolo Castelletto

Barolo Perno

Ratti

Barolo Conca

Barolo Rocche dell'Annunziata

Regis

Barolo Boscareto (*);

Barolo Vigna Rionda

Renato Corino

Barolo Arborina

Barolo Rocche dell'Annunziata (and Riserva)

Renato Corino (Stefano Corino)

Barolo Roncaglie

Renato Molino

Barolo Rocche dell'Annunziata

Renzo Seghesio (Cascina Pajana)

Barolo Ginestra, Barolo Vigna Pajana

Reva

Barolo Cannubi

Barolo Lazzarito

Rèva

Barolo Ravera

Reverdito

Barolo La Serra

Reverdito

Barolo Ascheri

Barolo Badarina

Barolo Bricco Cogni

Barolo Bricco San Pietro (from 2016)

Barolo Castagni

Barolo Riva Rocca (*)

Ribote

Barolo Bussia

Rivetto

Barolo Briccolina

Roagna

Barolo Pira; Barolo Pira Vecchie Viti and Barolo Riserva Pira

Barolo Rocche di Castiglione

Roberto Sarotto

Barolo Bricco Bergera and Riserva Audace

Roberto Voerzio

Barolo Brunate

Barolo Cerequio

Barolo La Serra

Barolo Rocche dell'Annunziata

Barolo Sarmassa

Barolo Torriglione

Rocche Costamagna

Barolo Rocche dell'Annunziata; Barolo Bricco Francesco (Riserva)

Rocche dei Manzoni

Barolo Perno Vigna Cappella di S. Stefano

Rocche dei Manzoni

Barolo Big d' Big

Barolo Riserva 10 Anni Vigna Madonna Assunta La Villa (Castelletto)

Barolo Vigna - Bricco San Pietro (Barolo d'La Roul)

Roccheviberti

Barolo Bricco Boschis

Barolo Rocche di Castiglione

Rosoretto

Barolo Parussi (and Riserva)

San Biagio

Barolo Bricco San Biagio

Barolo Capalot

Barolo Rocchettevino

Barolo Sorano

San Silvestro

Barolo Serra dei Turchi

Scarzello

Barolo Boschetti

Barolo Sarmassa Vigna Merenda

Schiavenza

Barolo Broglio and Barolo Riserva Broglio

Barolo Cerretta

Barolo Prapò

Scuola Enologica Alba

Barolo Castello

Silvano Bolmida

Barolo Le Coste di Monforte

Silvano Bolmida

Barolo Bussia, Bussia Riserva and Barolo Vigne dei Fantini

Silvio Alessandria

Barolo Bettolotti

Barolo Bricco Chiesa

Barolo Capalot

Silvio Grasso

Barolo Annunziata Vigna Plicotti

Barolo Bricco Luciani

Barolo Bricco Manzoni (Barolo Ciabot Manzoni)

Barolo Giachini

Simone Scaletta

Barolo Bricco San Pietro and Riserva (Barolo Chirlet)

Sobrero

Barolo Riserva Pernanno

Sordo

Barolo Monprivato

Barolo Gabutti, Barolo Gabutti Riserva

Barolo Monvigliero (and Riserva)

Barolo Parussi

Barolo Perno (and Riserva)

Barolo Ravera

Barolo Rocche di Castiglione

Barolo Villero

Stefano Oreste

Barolo Perno

Stra

Barolo Ciocchini Loschetto

Barolo La Volta

Sukula

Barolo Meriame

Sylla Sebaste

Barolo Bussia

Sylla Sebaste

Barolo Bricco delle Viole

Tenuta Barac

Barolo Cerviano-Merli

Tenuta Carretta

Barolo Cannubi

Tenuta Cucco

Barolo Cerrati, Barolo Cerrati Vigna Cucco (Riserva)

Barolo Riserva Bricco Voghera

Tenuta Due Corti

Barolo Castelletto

Tenuta L'Illuminata

Barolo Sant'Anna (and Riserva)

Tenuta Montanello

Barolo Montanello

Tenuta Rocca

Barolo Bussia

Barolo del Comune di Serralunga d'Alba

Trediberri

Barolo Rocche dell'Annunziata

Barolo Trediberri

Umberto Fracassi

Barolo Mantoetto

Viberti

Barolo Ravera

Barolo Riserva Bricco delle Viole

Barolo Riserva La Volta

Barolo Riserva San Pietro

Vietti

Barolo Brunate

Barolo Cerequio

Barolo Lazzarito

Barolo Monvigliero

Barolo Ravera

Barolo Riserva Villero

Barolo Rocche di Castiglione

Vietto

Barolo Panerole

Barolo Ravera

Vietto

Barolo Bricco San Pietro

Villadoria

Barolo Lazzarito

Vinory

Barolo Bricco San Pietro (from 2019).

Barolo Bussia Vigna Fantini (from 2018)

Virna

Barolo Cannubi

Barolo Sarmassa

VoerzioMartini

Barolo Cerequio

Barolo La Serra

Made in the USA
Monee, IL
18 January 2024

9e0bec5a-d582-4077-a4b8-80dc581d48e6R01